CORNERSTONE
BIBLICAL
COMMENTARY

CORNERSTONE
BIBLICAL
COMMENTARY

The Gospel of Luke
Allison A. Trites

Acts
William J. Larkin

GENERAL EDITOR
Philip W. Comfort

with the entire text of the
NEW LIVING TRANSLATION

TYNDALE HOUSE PUBLISHERS, INC. CAROL STREAM, ILLINOIS

Cornerstone Biblical Commentary, Volume 12

Visit Tyndale's exciting Web site at www.tyndale.com

Library of Congress Cataloging-in-Publication Data

Cornerstone biblical commentary.
    p. cm.
  Includes bibliographical references and index.
  ISBN-13: 978-0-8423-3438-9 (hc : alk. paper)
  ISBN-10: 0-8423-3438-6 (hc : alk. paper)
  1. Biblical—Commentaries. I. Trites, Allison A. II. Larkin, William J.
  BS491.3.C67 2006
  220.7′7 dc22   2005026928

Printed in Malaysia

12 11 10 09 08 07 06
  9   8   7   6   5   4   3   2   1

C O N T E N T S

CONTRIBUTORS TO **VOLUME 12**

Luke: Allison A. Trites
BA, University of New Brunswick;
BD, Eastern Baptist Theological Seminary;
ThM, Princeton Theological Seminary;
D. Phil., Oxford University;
Retired Payzant Distinguished Professor of Biblical Studies, Acadia Divinity College.

Acts: William J. Larkin
BA, Wheaton College;
BD, Princeton Theological Seminary;
PhD, University of Durham;
Professor of New Testament and Greek, Columbia Biblical Seminary and School of Missions.

GENERAL EDITOR'S PREFACE

The *Cornerstone Biblical Commentary* is based on the second edition of the New Living Translation (2004). Nearly 100 scholars from various church backgrounds and from several countries (United States, Canada, England, and Australia) participated in the creation of the NLT. Many of these same scholars are contributors to this commentary series. All the commentators, whether participants in the NLT or not, believe that the Bible is God's inspired word and have a desire to make God's word clear and accessible to his people.

This Bible commentary is the natural extension of our vision for the New Living Translation, which we believe is both exegetically accurate and idiomatically powerful. The NLT attempts to communicate God's inspired word in a lucid English translation of the original languages so that English readers can understand and appreciate the thought of the original writers. In the same way, the *Cornerstone Biblical Commentary* aims at helping teachers, pastors, students, and lay people understand every thought contained in the Bible. As such, the commentary focuses first on the words of Scripture, then on the theological truths of Scripture—inasmuch as the words express the truths.

The commentary itself has been structured in such a way as to help readers get at the meaning of Scripture, passage by passage, through the entire Bible. Each Bible book is prefaced by a substantial book introduction that gives general historical background important for understanding. Then the reader is taken through the Bible text, passage by passage, starting with the New Living Translation text printed in full. This is followed by a section called "Notes," wherein the commentator helps the reader understand the Hebrew or Greek behind the English of the NLT, interacts with other scholars on important interpretive issues, and points the reader to significant textual and contextual matters. The "Notes" are followed by the "Commentary," wherein each scholar presents a lucid interpretation of the passage, giving special attention to context and major theological themes.

The commentators represent a wide spectrum of theological positions within the evangelical community. We believe this is good because it reflects the rich variety in Christ's church. All the commentators uphold the authority of God's word and believe it is essential to heed the old adage: "Wholly apply yourself to the Scriptures and apply them wholly to you." May this commentary help you know the truths of Scripture, and may this knowledge help you "grow in your knowledge of God and Jesus our Lord" (2 Pet 1:2, NLT).

PHILIP W. COMFORT
GENERAL EDITOR

ABBREVIATIONS

GENERAL ABBREVIATIONS

b.	Babylonian Gemara	Heb.	Hebrew	NT	New Testament
bar.	baraita	ibid.	*ibidem,* in the same place	OL	Old Latin
c.	*circa,* around, approximately	i.e.	*id est,* the same	OS	Old Syriac
cf.	*confer,* compare	in loc.	*in loco,* in the place cited	OT	Old Testament
ch, chs	chapter, chapters	lit.	literally	p., pp.	page, pages
contra	in contrast to	LXX	Septuagint	pl.	plural
DSS	Dead Sea Scrolls	𝔐	Majority Text	Q	Quelle ("Sayings" as Gospel source)
ed.	edition, editor	*m.*	Mishnah	rev.	revision
e.g.	*exempli gratia,* for example	masc.	masculine	sg.	singular
et al.	*et alli,* and others	mg	margin	*t.*	Tosefta
fem.	feminine	ms	manuscript	TR	Textus Receptus
ff	following (verses, pages)	mss	manuscripts	v., vv.	verse, verses
fl.	flourished	MT	Masoretic Text	vid.	*videur,* it seems
Gr.	Greek	n.d.	no date	viz.	*videlicet,* namely
		neut.	neuter	vol.	volume
		no.	number	*y.*	Jerusalem Gemara

ABBREVIATIONS FOR BIBLE TRANSLATIONS

ASV	American Standard Version	NCV	New Century Version	NKJV	New King James Version
CEV	Contemporary English Version	NEB	New English Bible	NRSV	New Revised Standard Version
ESV	English Standard Version	NIV	New International Version	NLT	New Living Translation
GW	God's Word	NIrV	New International Reader's Version	REB	Revised English Bible
HCSB	Holman Christian Standard Bible	NJB	New Jerusalem Bible	RSV	Revised Standard Version
JB	Jerusalem Bible	NJPS	The New Jewish Publication Society Translation (*Tanakh*)	TEV	Today's English Version
KJV	King James Version			TLB	The Living Bible
NAB	New American Bible				
NASB	New American Standard Bible				

ABBREVIATIONS FOR DICTIONARIES, LEXICONS, COLLECTIONS OF TEXTS, ORIGINAL LANGUAGE EDITIONS

ABD *Anchor Bible Dictionary* (6 vols., Freedman) [1992]

ANEP *The Ancient Near East in Pictures* (Pritchard) [1965]

ANET *Ancient Near Eastern Texts Relating to the Old Testament* (Pritchard) [1969]

BAGD *Greek-English Lexicon of the New Testament and Other Early Christian Literature,* 2nd ed. (Bauer, Arndt, Gingrich, Danker) [1979]

BDAG *Greek-English Lexicon of the New Testament and Other Early Christian Literature,* 3rd ed. (Bauer, Danker, Arndt, Gingrich) [2000]

BDB *A Hebrew and English Lexicon of the Old Testament* (Brown, Driver, Briggs) [1907]

BDF *A Greek Grammar of the New Testament and Other Early Christian Literature* (Blass, Debrunner, Funk) [1961]

BHS *Biblia Hebraica Stuttgartensia* (Elliger and Rudolph) [1983]

CAD *Assyrian Dictionary of the Oriental Institute of the University of Chicago* [1956]

COS *The Context of Scripture* (3 vols., Hallo and Younger) [1997–2002]

DBI *Dictionary of Biblical Imagery* (Ryken, Wilhoit, Longman) [1998]

DBT *Dictionary of Biblical Theology* (2nd ed., Leon-Dufour) [1972]

DCH *Dictionary of Classical Hebrew* (5 vols., D. Clines) [2000]

DJD *Discoveries in the Judean Desert* [1955–]

DJG *Dictionary of Jesus and the Gospels* (Green, McKnight, Marshall) [1992]

DOTP *Dictionary of the Old Testament: Pentateuch.* (T. Alexander, D.W. Baker) [2003]

DPL *Dictionary of Paul and His Letters* (Hawthorne, Martin, Reid) [1993]

EDNT *Exegetical Dictionary of the New Testament* (3 vols., H. Balz, G. Schneider. ET) [1990–1993]

HALOT *The Hebrew and Aramaic Lexicon of the Old Testament* (L. Koehler, W. Baumgartner, J. Stamm; trans. M. Richardson) [1994–1999]

IBD *Illustrated Bible Dictionary* (3 vols., Douglas, Wiseman) [1980]

IDB *The Interpreter's Dictionary of the Bible* (4 vols., Buttrick) [1962]

ISBE *International Standard Bible Encyclopedia* (4 vols., Bromiley) [1979–1988]

KBL *Lexicon in Veteris Testamenti libros* (Koehler, Baumgartner) [1958]

LCL Loeb Classical Library

L&N *Greek-English Lexicon of the New Testament: Based on Semantic Domains* (Louw and Nida) [1989]

LSJ *A Greek-English Lexicon* (9th ed., Liddell, Scott, Jones) [1996]

MM *The Vocabulary of the Greek New Testament* (Moulton and Milligan) [1930; 1997]

NA^{26} *Novum Testamentum Graece* (26th ed., Nestle-Aland) [1979]

NA^{27} *Novum Testamentum Graece* (27th ed., Nestle-Aland) [1993]

NBD *New Bible Dictionary* (2nd ed., Douglas, Hillyer) [1982]

NIDB *New International Dictionary of the Bible* (Douglas, Tenney) [1987]

NIDBA *New International Dictionary of Biblical Archaeology* (Blaiklock and Harrison) [1983]

NIDNTT *New International Dictionary of New Testament Theology* (4 vols., C. Brown) [1975–1985]

NIDOTTE *New International Dictionary of Old Testament Theology and Exegesis* (5 vols., W. A. VanGemeren) [1997]

PGM *Papyri graecae magicae: Die griechischen Zauberpapyri.* (Preisendanz) [1928]

PG *Patrologia Graecae* (J. P. Migne) [1857–1886]

TBD *Tyndale Bible Dictionary* (Elwell, Comfort) [2001]

TDNT *Theological Dictionary of the New Testament* (10 vols., Kittel, Friedrich; trans. Bromiley) [1964–1976]

TDOT *Theological Dictionary of the Old Testament* (8 vols., Botterweck, Ringgren; trans. Willis, Bromiley, Green) [1974–]

TLNT *Theological Lexicon of the New Testament* (3 vols., C. Spicq) [1994]

TLOT *Theological Lexicon of the Old Testament* (3 vols., E. Jenni) [1997]

TWOT *Theological Wordbook of the Old Testament* (2 vols., Harris, Archer) [1980]

UBS^3 *United Bible Societies' Greek New Testament* (3rd ed., Metzger et al.) [1975]

UBS^4 *United Bible Societies' Greek New Testament* (4th corrected ed., Metzger et al.) [1993]

WH *The New Testament in the Original Greek* (Westcott and Hort) [1882]

ABBREVIATIONS FOR BOOKS OF THE BIBLE

Old Testament

Gen	Genesis	1 Sam	1 Samuel	Esth	Esther
Exod	Exodus	2 Sam	2 Samuel	Ps, Pss	Psalm, Psalms
Lev	Leviticus	1 Kgs	1 Kings	Prov	Proverbs
Num	Numbers	2 Kgs	2 Kings	Eccl	Ecclesiastes
Deut	Deuteronomy	1 Chr	1 Chronicles	Song	Song of Songs
Josh	Joshua	2 Chr	2 Chronicles	Isa	Isaiah
Judg	Judges	Ezra	Ezra	Jer	Jeremiah
Ruth	Ruth	Neh	Nehemiah	Lam	Lamentations

Ezek	Ezekiel	Obad	Obadiah	Zeph	Zephaniah
Dan	Daniel	Jonah	Jonah	Hag	Haggai
Hos	Hosea	Mic	Micah	Zech	Zechariah
Joel	Joel	Nah	Nahum	Mal	Malachi
Amos	Amos	Hab	Habakkuk		

New Testament

Matt	Matthew	Eph	Ephesians	Heb	Hebrews
Mark	Mark	Phil	Philippians	Jas	James
Luke	Luke	Col	Colossians	1 Pet	1 Peter
John	John	1 Thess	1 Thessalonians	2 Pet	2 Peter
Acts	Acts	2 Thess	2 Thessalonians	1 John	1 John
Rom	Romans	1 Tim	1 Timothy	2 John	2 John
1 Cor	1 Corinthians	2 Tim	2 Timothy	3 John	3 John
2 Cor	2 Corinthians	Titus	Titus	Jude	Jude
Gal	Galatians	Phlm	Philemon	Rev	Revelation

Deuterocanonical

Bar	Baruch	1–2 Esdr	1–2 Esdras	Pr Man	Prayer of Manasseh
Add Dan	Additions to Daniel	Add Esth	Additions to Esther	Ps 151	Psalm 151
Pr Azar	Prayer of Azariah	Ep Jer	Epistle of Jeremiah	Sir	Sirach
Bel	Bel and the Dragon	Jdt	Judith	Tob	Tobit
Sg Three	Song of the Three	1–2 Macc	1–2 Maccabees	Wis	Wisdom of Solomon
	Children	3–4 Macc	3–4 Maccabees		
Sus	Susanna				

MANUSCRIPTS AND LITERATURE FROM QUMRAN

Initial numerals followed by "Q" indicate particular caves at Qumran. For example, the notation 4Q267 indicates text 267 from cave 4 at Qumran. Further, 1QS 4:9-10 indicates column 4, lines 9-10 of the *Rule of the Community;* and 4Q166 1 ii 2 indicates fragment 1, column ii, line 2 of text 166 from cave 4. More examples of common abbreviations are listed below.

CD	Cairo Geniza copy of the *Damascus Document*	1QIsa[b]	Isaiah copy [b]	4QLam[a]	Lamentations
		1QM	*War Scroll*	11QPs[a]	Psalms
		1QpHab	*Pesher Habakkuk*	11QTemple[a,b]	*Temple Scroll*
1QH	*Thanksgiving Hymns*	1QS	*Rule of the Community*	11QtgJob	*Targum of Job*
1QIsa[a]	Isaiah copy [a]				

IMPORTANT NEW TESTAMENT MANUSCRIPTS

(all dates given are AD; ordinal numbers refer to centuries)

Significant Papyri (𝔓 = Papyrus)

𝔓1 Matt 1; early 3rd
𝔓4+𝔓64+𝔓67 Matt 3, 5, 26; Luke 1-6; late 2nd
𝔓5 John 1, 16, 20; early 3rd
𝔓13 Heb 2-5, 10-12; early 3rd
𝔓15+𝔓16 (probably part of same codex) 1 Cor 7-8, Phil 3-4; late 3rd

𝔓20 James 2-3; 3rd
𝔓22 John 15-16; mid 3rd
𝔓23 James 1; c. 200
𝔓27 Rom 8-9; 3rd
𝔓30 1 Thess 4-5; 2 Thess 1; early 3rd
𝔓32 Titus 1-2; late 2nd
𝔓37 Matt 26; late 3rd

𝔓39 John 8; first half of 3rd
𝔓40 Rom 1-4, 6, 9; 3rd
𝔓45 Gospels and Acts; early 3rd
𝔓46 Paul's Major Epistles (less Pastorals); late 2nd
𝔓47 Rev 9-17; 3rd

𝔓49+𝔓65 Eph 4-5; 1 Thess
1-2; 3rd
𝔓52 John 18; c. 125
𝔓53 Matt 26, Acts 9-10;
middle 3rd
𝔓66 John; late 2nd
𝔓70 Matt 2-3, 11-12, 24; 3rd
𝔓72 1-2 Peter, Jude; c. 300

𝔓74 Acts, General Epistles; 7th
𝔓75 Luke and John; c. 200
𝔓77+𝔓103 (probably part of
same codex) Matt 13-14,
23; late 2nd
𝔓87 Phlm; late 2nd
𝔓90 John 18-19; late 2nd
𝔓91 Acts 2-3; 3rd

𝔓92 Eph 1, 2 Thess 1; c. 300
𝔓98 Rev 1:13-20; late 2nd
𝔓100 James 3-5; c. 300
𝔓101 Matt 3-4; 3rd
𝔓104 Matt 21; 2nd
𝔓106 John 1; 3rd
𝔓115 Rev 2-3, 5-6, 8-15; 3rd

Significant Uncials

ℵ (Sinaiticus) most of NT; 4th
A (Alexandrinus) most of NT;
5th
B (Vaticanus) most of NT; 4th
C (Ephraemi Rescriptus) most
of NT with many lacunae;
5th
D (Bezae) Gospels, Acts; 5th
D (Claromontanus), Paul's
Epistles; 6th (different MS
than Bezae)
E (Laudianus 35) Acts; 6th
F (Augensis) Paul's Epistles; 9th
G (Boernerianus) Paul's
Epistles; 9th

H (Coislinianus) Paul's
Epistles; 6th
I (Freerianus or Washington)
Paul's Epistles; 5th
L (Regius) Gospels; 8th
Q (Guelferbytanus B) Luke,
John; 5th
P (Porphyrianus) Acts—
Revelation; 9th
T (Borgianus) Luke, John; 5th
W (Washingtonianus or the
Freer Gospels) Gospels; 5th
Z (Dublinensis) Matthew; 6th
037 (Δ; Sangallensis) Gospels;
9th

038 (Θ; Koridethi) Gospels;
9th
040 (Ξ; Zacynthius) Luke; 6th
043 (Φ; Beratinus) Matt,
Mark; 6th
044 (Ψ; Athous Laurae)
Gospels, Acts, Paul's
Epistles; 9th
048 Acts, Paul's Epistles,
General Epistles; 5th
0171 Matt 10, Luke 22;
c. 300
0189 Acts 5; c. 200

Significant Minuscules

1 Gospels, Acts, Paul's
Epistles; 12th
33 All NT except Rev; 9th
81 Acts, Paul's Epistles,
General Epistles; 1044
565 Gospels; 9th
700 Gospels; 11th

1424 (or Family 1424—a
group of 29 manuscripts
sharing nearly the same
text) most of NT; 9th-10th
1739 Acts, Paul's Epistles; 10th
2053 Rev; 13th
2344 Rev; 11th

f¹ (a family of manuscripts
including 1, 118, 131, 209)
Gospels; 12th-14th
f¹³ (a family of manuscripts
including 13, 69, 124, 174,
230, 346, 543, 788, 826,
828, 983, 1689, 1709—
known as the Ferrar group)
Gospels; 11th-15th

Significant Ancient Versions

SYRIAC (SYR)
syrᶜ (Syriac Curetonian)
Gospels; 5th
syrˢ (Syriac Sinaiticus)
Gospels; 4th
syrʰ (Syriac Harklensis) Entire
NT; 616

OLD LATIN (IT)
itᵃ (Vercellenis) Gospels; 4th
itᵇ (Veronensis) Gospels; 5th
itᵈ (Cantabrigiensis—the Latin
text of Bezae) Gospels, Acts,
3 John; 5th
itᵉ (Palantinus) Gospels; 5th
itᵏ (Bobiensis) Matthew, Mark;
c. 400

COPTIC (COP)
copᵇᵒ (Boharic—north Egypt)
copᶠᵃʸ (Fayyumic—central Egypt)
copˢᵃ (Sahidic—southern Egypt)

OTHER VERSIONS
arm (Armenian)
eth (Ethiopic)
geo (Georgian)

TRANSLITERATION AND NUMBERING SYSTEM

Note: For words and roots from non-biblical languages (e.g., Arabic, Ugaritic), only approximate transliterations are given.

HEBREW/ARAMAIC

Consonants

א	aleph	= '		מ, ם	mem	= m
בּ, ב	beth	= b		נ, ן	nun	= n
גּ, ג	gimel	= g		ס	samekh	= s
דּ, ד	daleth	= d		ע	ayin	= '
ה	he	= h		פּ, פ, ף	pe	= p
ו	waw	= w		צ, ץ	tsadhe	= ts
ז	zayin	= z		ק	qoph	= q
ח	heth	= kh		ר	resh	= r
ט	teth	= t		שׁ	shin	= sh
י	yodh	= y		שׂ	sin	= s
כּ, כ, ך	kaph	= k		תּ, ת	taw	= t, th
ל	lamedh	= l				(spirant)

Vowels

ַ	patakh	= a		ָ	qamets khatuf	= o
ַה	furtive patakh	= a		ֹ	holem	= o
ָ	qamets	= a		וֹ	full holem	= o
ָה	final qamets he	= ah		ֻ	short qibbuts	= u
ֶ	segol	= e		ֻ	long qibbuts	= u
ֵ	tsere	= e		וּ	shureq	= u
ֵי	tsere yod	= e		ֲ	khatef patakh	= a
ִ	short hireq	= i		ֳ	khatef qamets	= o
ִ	long hireq	= i		ְ	vocalic shewa	= e
ִי	hireq yod	= i		ַי	patakh yodh	= a

Greek

α	alpha	= a		ε	epsilon	= e
β	beta	= b		ζ	zeta	= z
γ	gamma	= g, n (before γ, κ, ξ, χ)		η	eta	= ē
δ	delta	= d		θ	theta	= th
				ι	iota	= i

κ	*kappa*	= *k*		τ	*tau*	= *t*
λ	*lamda*	= *l*		υ	*upsilon*	= *u*
μ	*mu*	= *m*		φ	*phi*	= *ph*
ν	*nu*	= *n*		χ	*chi*	= *ch*
ξ	*ksi*	= *x*		ψ	*psi*	= *ps*
ο	*omicron*	= *o*		ω	*omega*	= *ō*
π	*pi*	= *p*		'	*rough*	= *h (with*
ρ	*rho*	= *r (ṗ = rh)*			*breathing*	*vowel or*
σ, ς	*sigma*	= *s*			*mark*	*diphthong)*

THE TYNDALE-STRONG'S NUMBERING SYSTEM

The Cornerstone Biblical Commentary series uses a word-study numbering system to give both newer and more advanced Bible students alike quicker, more convenient access to helpful original-language tools (e.g., concordances, lexicons, and theological dictionaries). Those who are unfamiliar with the ancient Hebrew, Aramaic, and Greek alphabets can quickly find information on a given word by looking up the appropriate index number. Advanced students will find the system helpful because it allows them to quickly find the lexical form of obscure conjugations and inflections.

There are two main numbering systems used for biblical words today. The one familiar to most people is the Strong's numbering system (made popular by the *Strong's Exhaustive Concordance to the Bible*). Although the original Strong's system is still quite useful, the most up-to-date research has shed new light on the biblical languages and allows for more precision than is found in the original Strong's system. The Cornerstone Biblical Commentary series, therefore, features a newly revised version of the Strong's system, the Tyndale-Strong's numbering system. The Tyndale-Strong's system brings together the familiarity of the Strong's system and the best of modern scholarship. In most cases, the original Strong's numbers are preserved. In places where new research dictates, new or related numbers have been added.[1]

The second major numbering system today is the Goodrick-Kohlenberger system used in a number of study tools published by Zondervan. In order to give students broad access to a number of helpful tools, the Commentary provides index numbers for the Zondervan system as well.

The different index systems are designated as follows:

TG	Tyndale-Strong's Greek number	ZH	Zondervan Hebrew number
ZG	Zondervan Greek number	TA	Tyndale-Strong's Aramaic number
TH	Tyndale-Strong's Hebrew number	ZA	Zondervan Aramaic number

So in the example, "love" *agapē* [TG26, ZG27], the first number is the one to use with Greek tools keyed to the Tyndale-Strong's system, and the second applies to tools that use the Zondervan system.

1. Generally, one may simply use the original four-digit Strong's number to identify words in tools using Strong's system. If a Tyndale-Strong's number is followed by a capital letter (e.g., TG1692A), it generally indicates an added subdivision of meaning for the given term. Whenever a Tyndale-Strong's number has a number following a decimal point (e.g., TG2013.1), it reflects an instance where new research has yielded a separate, new classification of use for a biblical word. Forthcoming tools from Tyndale House Publishers will include these entries, which were not part of the original Strong's system.

The Gospel of
Luke

ALLISON A. TRITES

INTRODUCTION TO
Luke

THE GOSPEL OF LUKE, which has been described as "the most beautiful book in the world,"[1] is the first part of a two-volume work devoted to the life of Jesus and the opening years of the Christian church. In Luke's Gospel, we are introduced to "everything Jesus began to do and teach" prior to his ascension (described in 24: 50-51; Acts 1:6-11). In the second volume, the book of Acts, Luke picks up the story of the years following the Ascension, showing the growth of the Christian movement and noting the stages of its expansion from Jerusalem to Rome.[2] These two books, when taken together, constitute about 27% of the New Testament. Thus, Luke's perspective on the life of Jesus and the early Christian movement is vitally important if one is to gain a good grasp of the overall message of the New Testament. Our attention will be devoted primarily to Luke's Gospel, although similarities and points of contact with the book of Acts will be noted where appropriate.

AUTHOR

Though Luke's Gospel doesn't name its author, most scholars today acknowledge Luke as the author of both the third Gospel and the book of Acts. Luke was certainly not the most prominent person in the early church, so it is difficult to believe that his name would be attached to the Gospel unless he were actually the author. There is a strong and persistent tradition in the early church that Luke wrote the third Gospel and the book of Acts. This view receives support from the Muratorian Fragment (which reflects the view of the church in Rome c. AD 170–190); from Irenaeus, bishop of Lyons (c. 185); and later, from the influential church leaders Eusebius (d. 339) and Jerome (d. 420). This traditional view was the general consensus until the rise of modern critical biblical scholarship in the last two hundred years and indeed has continued to be widely held to the present day. Most scholars still attribute both the Gospel of Luke and the book of Acts to Luke, the beloved physician and traveling companion of the apostle Paul (Harrington 1968:13).

The "Gospel according to Luke" is the title given at the close of this Gospel in 𝔓75, the oldest surviving Greek manuscript that contains nearly all of Luke (dated about AD 175–225), but this tradition is not certain and has been attacked in modern times. However, two features from the internal evidence of Luke–Acts must be carefully noted. First, the author does not present himself as an eyewitness of most of the events in the two-volume work, particularly those related to the life and ministry of Jesus (1:1-2), relying instead on his own study of the traditions taken from eyewitnesses and ministers of the word (1:2-4). Second, he appears to view himself as a companion of Paul in the "we" sections of Acts (Acts 16:10-17; 20:5-15; 21:1-18; 27:1–28:16). This latter feature reduces the search for possible authors.

Some critics view the "we" sections simply as a literary device designed to create the effect or impression of an eyewitness (Haenchen, Pervo). The picture of Paul in Acts is also contrasted with the self-portrait drawn in the Pauline epistles, both in terms of its historical accuracy and its theological characteristics. Such arguments have led a few writers to deny that the author of the third Gospel was a companion of Paul (Vielhauer, Robbins). However, the connection of Luke as a traveling companion of Paul has been ably defended by Fitzmyer, who has argued that a creative literary device does not offer an adequate explanation of the appearance and disappearance of the "we" sections in such a capricious manner (Fitzmyer 1989:16-22). In addition, some "sailing" references lack the "we" terminology, though they would be suitable insertions if the aim were just to increase the impression of vividness (e.g., Acts 13:4, 13; 14:26; 17:14; 18:18, 21).

In fact, a strong case has been made that the portrait of Paul in his epistles should be seen as compatible with that presented in Acts (Bruce 1962:24-27). According to the internal evidence of Luke–Acts, it is reasonable to conclude that the author was personally acquainted with Paul as a traveling companion and was most probably a second-generation Christian. He was committed to the task of communicating the Good News in an accurate and responsible manner.

His prologue is unique among the Gospels and displays an elevated literary style that is clearly reminiscent of the classical historians of the ancient world like Thucydides, Polybius, and Herodotus (Talbert 1989:7-11; Winter and Clarke 1993:1-29). However, the most illuminating parallels to the prologue are probably the prefaces of Josephus in his two-volume work *Against Apion*, discussed in the notes on 1:1-4. To sum up, Luke stacks up well against his contemporaries as a responsible historian of Christian origins.

For the modern reader of Luke's Gospel, it is interesting and significant that there are three helpful references to Luke in the New Testament. He is mentioned in Philemon when Paul sends greetings to Philemon from Epaphras, a fellow prisoner, and then adds similar greetings from Mark, Aristarchus, Demas, and Luke, who are described appreciatively as "co-workers" (Phlm 1:24). The second reference is found in Colossians, where greetings are given from a group including Epaphras, Luke, and Demas (Col 4:10-14). There, Luke is explicitly described as "the beloved physician" (Col 4:14, KJV) and is listed with Christian colleagues who were Gentiles (the Jewish believers are listed in Col 4:11), making it probable that he, too, was a Gentile. The third reference to Luke appears in 2 Timothy, where once more Paul is in prison and notes rather plaintively, "Only Luke is with me" (2 Tim 4:11).[3] Evidently, Paul valued the help and support of Luke as a trusted confidant and aide.

In addition to these direct references to Luke, there are several "we" passages in

Acts that support Luke's authorship. They suggest that the author was a participant in the action and a traveling companion of the apostle Paul (Acts 16:10-18; 20:5-15; 21:1-18; 27:1-28:16). They show no marked differences in style or vocabulary from the rest of Acts, so the whole book appears to be the product of one author. The style and vocabulary of Acts also seem to harmonize well with the Gospel of Luke, pointing strongly to a single writer as the author of both books. In addition, the theological perspective of Luke's Gospel and that of Acts seem to be consistent. Both books stress the historical matrix of redemptive events, the role of the Holy Spirit, the place of angels, the importance of prayer, the fulfillment of Old Testament promises in the life of Christ and in the developing work of the Christian church, and the realization of God's purpose in holy history. This conclusion is confirmed by the fact that both volumes are dedicated to Theophilus (1:3; Acts 1:1) and that the second volume specifically refers to the first one (Acts 1:1), thus linking Acts directly with Luke's Gospel.

Another element that has been used to support Luke's authorship has been the medical language of Luke–Acts, and comparisons have been made between Luke and other ancient doctors like Hippocrates (fourth–fifth century BC) and Galen (second century AD).[4] Much less stress has been placed upon this element in recent years in view of studies that have shown that medical language was used in ancient times by educated people who were not physicians.[5] However, this recent argument has probably been pressed too far, so that while vocabulary and style do not decisively prove that Luke was a physician, the evidence of Luke–Acts reveals an author who was deeply concerned about human pain and suffering (see 4:38; 13:10-17; 14:1-4; Acts 9:32-42; 28:8-9).

Vincent Taylor, one of the great authorities on Luke's Gospel in the twentieth century, made a perceptive comment:

> The objections to Lukan authorship turn mainly upon the historical problems that meet us in Acts, especially the difficulty of reconciling the account of the Apostolic Council in Acts 15 with Paul's personal narrative in Galatians 2:1-10 and the problem raised in Acts 15:23-29. These problems belong mainly to the study of the Acts and all that can be said here is that the difficulties have been exaggerated, especially if it is remembered that the aims and circumstances of Luke and Paul were different.[6]

Accepting Luke as the author of both the third Gospel and the Acts of the Apostles, we can begin to paint a portrait of the remarkable person who stands behind these writings. E. P. Blair describes Luke as follows:

> He was broad in his sympathies, compassionate toward the poor and outcasts in society, genuinely pious, self-effacing, radiantly joyful, charmingly urbane, and deeply loyal. He remained with Paul to the end, doubtlessly serving him in medical and other ways, and earned the great apostle's gratitude and admiration.[7]

Little is known about Luke's personal life, though the Anti-Marcionite Prologue to Luke claims that he never married and died at the ripe old age of 84 in Boeotia (Greece; though some place his death in Bithynia [Turkey] or Ephesus), being "full of the Holy Spirit."[8] There are a variety of traditions regarding his activities in his later years and the place and manner of his death. Some writers have connected him with Antioch in Syria (as does the Anti-Marcionite Prologue) and have noted the detailed references in Acts to that city (Acts 6:5; 11:19-27; 13:1; 14:26; 15:22-35). Others, drawing attention to the "we" passages of Acts, have suggested that Luke had a special link with Philippi. They argue that Luke was the "man from Macedonia" who appeared in a vision to Paul at Troas, worked with Paul in evangelizing his native land, remained in Philippi, and later resumed contact with Paul and the missionary team when they returned to Philippi (Acts 16:8-17; 20:5-6). Certainly, there are detailed references in Acts to both Antioch (Acts 6:5; 11:19-27; 13:1; 14:26; 15:22-35) and Philippi (Acts 16:8-17; 20:5-6), but any conclusions drawn from these references remain speculative.

Despite the limitations of our knowledge, much can be learned about the author's interests and concerns from the study of Luke's Gospel and the book of Acts, where many of the same themes frequently appear (e.g., concern for the poor, interest in the stories of women, the importance of prayer), each of which is discussed below.

Before closing this section on authorship, it must be said that J. W. Wenham (1991) has proposed that the author of the third Gospel and Acts is Lucius, a prophet and teacher who came from Cyrene and served as a leader in the church at Antioch in Syria (Acts 13:1). A man by the same name is noted elsewhere in the New Testament as an associate of Paul (Rom 16:21). However, there is no clear evidence that either of these two people is the same as the reputed author of the Gospel of Luke and Acts (Achtemeier 1985:582), despite the creative attempt of Wenham to connect Lucius with the better-known Luke.

DATE AND OCCASION OF WRITING

Luke's Gospel has been dated as early as AD 59–63 and as late as the latter part of the second century. The question of dating is a complex one and involves the book of Acts as an integral part of Luke–Acts. Paul's ministry certainly dominates the second half of Acts, and the last quarter of the text is occupied with Paul's trip to Rome as a prisoner awaiting trial. However, Acts ends without telling us the outcome of Paul's trial, leading some to argue that it had not taken place by the time Acts was complete. In this view, Acts, and possibly Luke–Acts, is dated in the early 60s AD.

Many scholars have opposed this view (cf. Fitzmyer 1981:54-56; Nolland 1989:xxxix; C. A. Evans 1990:2). They note that Luke himself called attention to the fact that other Gospel accounts had preceded his (1:1), and Mark's Gospel was almost certainly one of his sources. Thus, acknowledging that Luke used Mark in the composition of his Gospel, most scholars opt for a date for Luke–Acts after the destruction of Jerusalem in AD 70, positing a date between AD 70 and 90.

However, a strong case can be made for an early date. William Larkin, in his work on Acts in this volume, argues for a date for Luke–Acts in the early 60s, and this view has also been defended by such notable scholars as F. F. Bruce (1962:21-24) and Richard Longenecker (1981:235-238). Similarly, Carson, Moo, and Morris would place Luke in the early 60s (a possible date for Acts) and Mark in the late 50s or early 60s (1992:116-117). They draw attention to the lack of mention of the Neronian persecution, the destruction of Jerusalem, and the deaths of Paul and James (AD 62). In addition, they remark that Luke would likely have noted Paul's release from prison or execution if it had taken place before he wrote. They further observe that Paul's epistles were highly valued in the early church but are ignored in Acts—a difficult feature to account for in a later dating. In addition, they find it unlikely that Luke would present as friendly a view of Rome as we find in Luke–Acts *after* the Neronian persecution of the mid-60s. Moreover, on the contents of Acts, Bruce notes how well they fit the premise of an early date: "Prominence is given in Acts to subjects which were of urgent importance in the church before AD 70, but which were of less moment after that date. Such were the terms of Gentile admission to church fellowship, the coexistence of Jews and Gentiles to the church, the food requirements of the apostolic decree [ch. 15]" (Bruce 1990:14, 17). We conclude that such cumulative evidence points to a date for Luke–Acts in the early 60s.

It is only fair to note that a few scholars have opted for a second-century date. John Knox and J. C. O'Neill, based on comparisons with writers like Josephus, Justin Martyr, and Marcion, have advanced a date of the early- or mid-second century. However, the peaceful situation between the Christian church and Rome depicted in the book of Acts seems to be different from the climate described by Christian writers of even the late first and early second centuries, such as Clement of Rome (c. AD 96) and Ignatius (AD 117). Luke presents a relatively friendly outlook on the Roman authorities, a position that would have been much more difficult to maintain after imperial persecution became more widespread in the second century (note, for instance, the correspondence about persecuting Christians between Pliny, the governor of Bithynia, and the Emperor Trajan).[9] A second-century date, then, seems to be ruled out as quite improbable. Despite widespread disagreement on the issue, a first-century date of about AD 62 seems the most reasonable option for Luke–Acts.

The place of writing was probably Rome, though other places have been suggested, including Asia Minor and Greece. "The Monarchian Prologue to Luke promotes the latter option, but its reliability is suspect. It was at Rome that Luke could have used the time profitably to put the finishing touches" on his work.[10] Its destination would depend on Theophilus's place of residence, and that is unknown. However, the minute descriptions of places in Palestine seem to point to readers who were not familiar with that region but were more knowledgeable about other areas under Roman jurisdiction. Antioch, Ephesus, and Achaia are all possible destinations, but the matter must be left open in the absence of further evidence.

AUDIENCE

We have already noted that the Gospel was specifically addressed to Theophilus (1:3), a name that means "lover of God." While the book is profitable to anyone who loves God, it is probable that it was directed to a specific individual who bore that name. The description of the person as "most honorable" (Gr., *kratistos* [TG2903, ZG3196]) seems to point to a Roman official or at least a man of high social position and wealth, as elsewhere in Luke–Acts the name is only associated with Roman governors (Acts 23:26; 24:2[3]; 26:25). It is quite possible that this man served as a patron or benefactor of Luke, facilitating the copying and distribution of his work.[11] Such a dedication to a publisher was a common practice at the time. Some writers have suggested that there were those in the imperial circle who were friendly to the Christian message, and the fact that Luke's writings were addressed to a person in the higher echelons of Roman society might cause these elites to consider the Christian proclamation with greater seriousness. This idea is drawn from what is observed in similar ancient dedicatory prefaces (e.g., *Letter of Aristeas* 1:1-12; Talbert [1989:7-11] also discusses other examples; cf. C. A. Evans 1990:19).

Generally in such prefaces there is a definite attempt on the part of such writers to reach those who would appreciate a "characteristic love of learning." Thus, it is quite likely that an appeal to similar readers might have been a part of Luke's intentional strategy for the acceptance of the gospel message. The fact that Luke's preface is presented in the most stylistic and literary Greek in the New Testament is significant. Luke apparently intended to reach out to open-minded, well-educated readers who would find such a carefully balanced, sophisticated statement of purpose to be meaningful. The impact of a cultured, well-organized approach to the presentation of his case by Luke could have possibly had this effect, even if it was not the intended result of his dedication to Theophilus. At the same time, the actual contents of his two-volume work are plainly concerned with a wider, more universal audience, including the poor, the disadvantaged, the marginalized, and women. It is a gospel that shows the breadth of God's mercy, which reaches out to all branches of the human family.

In addition, Luke's precise description of his historical method helps the modern person to identify with the original audience by showing the reader what to expect from Luke's work. He took his historical task seriously, and the text gives every evidence of fulfilling his stated historical aims. It is therefore necessary to pay close attention to his preface, which serves as an explanation of his methodology in both books (1:1-4). Here Luke, following the conventions of Greek-speaking historians like Thucydides and Josephus, carefully spells out his historical method so that his readers might know the principles by which he worked. First, he notes that other writers had attempted to explain the historical foundation of Christian origins before him. Second, he observes the special role of "the eyewitnesses and ministers of the word" (1:2, RSV), who could attest everything from the beginning and made careful use of their evidence. Third, he intended to provide "a careful account" of the Christian movement. Fourth, he claims that he had made a thorough investigation of the facts of the case. Fifth, he names Theophilus as the intended recipient of his work in his dedication (cf. Acts 1:1); and sixth, he presents the historical evidence so that his readers (Theophilus and other interested persons) might know the solid historical basis of the things they had been taught. Thus, the message was intended for Theophilus's instruction (1:4), but it was clearly designed also for all those readers among whom the work was circulated and those who would hear the message orally (note the warning given in 8:18: "So pay attention to how you hear").

CANONICITY AND TEXTUAL HISTORY

Irenaeus (mid-second century AD) was among the first to recognize the four Gospels (Matthew, Mark, Luke, and John) as being the exclusively canonized Gospels (*Against Heresies* 3.11.11). The Muratorian Canon (c. AD 200) also affirmed Luke's Gospel as part of the canon, as did Eusebius (*Ecclesiastical History* 6.14.7) in about 325 and Athanasius in 367 (presenting the canon of the Western church in his festal letter).

There are several early manuscripts of the Gospel of Luke. Manuscripts of the second and third century include 𝔓4, 𝔓45, 𝔓69, 𝔓75, 𝔓111, and 0171. There are also more than fifteen uncial manuscripts from the fourth to tenth centuries that contain complete or nearly complete texts of Luke; among them are the following: א and B (fourth century); C, D, and W (fifth century); P and 040 (sixth century); L (eighth century); K, M, U, and V (ninth century); and S (tenth century). Two other important manuscripts for Luke are Q and T of the fifth century, although each contains less than half of Luke.

Of all these manuscripts, 𝔓75 is the most accurate copy of Luke. The manuscript, produced by a very careful scribe, manifests a type of text that was followed by another careful scribe—the one who produced the fourth-century manuscript known as codex Vaticanus (see Porter 1962:363-376). 𝔓75 and B (Vaticanus) provide the best textual witness to the original wording of Luke's Gospel. Though its extant portion is much smaller than what is in 𝔓75 and B, the second-century papyrus 𝔓4 is also an excellent witness. In fact, 𝔓4 exhibits 95% agreement with 𝔓75 in the 440 verses where 𝔓4 and 𝔓75 overlap. It should also be added that 𝔓75 further affirms א and B in including several portions of Luke 22–24 that were excluded by codex Beza (D) and erroneously considered "Western non-interpolations" by Westcott and Hort. (For further discussion on this, see Comfort 2007).

LITERARY STYLE

Luke had great gifts as a writer, and these are evident in the artistic quality of his work (see Cadbury 1919–1920). The third Gospel truly offers an artist's portrait of Jesus, who is seen as embodying the Greek ideals of the good, the true, and the beautiful. Luke had a fine command of the Greek language, a rich and extensive vocabulary, and a wide-ranging style that could employ classical elegance (as in the preface, 1:1-4) or express Semitic idiom reflecting the language of the Greek Old

Testament (1:5–2:52).[12] His style shows remarkable cultural and geographical sensitivity, a point clearly revealed in the speeches of Luke–Acts. Thus, to take but one example, the speech of Paul in Aramaic in Acts 22 has a Jewish ambience, while his speeches given to Greek audiences have a greater Hellenistic flavor.[13] There is a winsome graciousness about the language of Luke–Acts that greatly strengthens its appeal.

Luke was a master of vivid description, as is demonstrated in his account of the shipwreck in Acts 27. Certainly, we see this same skill in his Gospel in the colorful portraits of such figures as Mary, Elizabeth, Zechariah, Anna, Simeon, John the Baptist, Herod Antipas, the weeping women at Jerusalem, and the Roman centurion at the cross, to name but a few. Similarly, in Acts there are striking accounts of Peter and John, Ananias and Sapphira, Philip, Stephen, Sergius Paulus, Simon Magus, Lydia, the Philippian jailer, Elymas, Eutychus, and, above all, Paul, the apostle to the Gentiles. Luke's characters come alive in both Luke and Acts.

This artistic quality is also apparent in the stories Jesus told. Many of the most treasured parables of the Master have come down to us from Luke's pen. One need only think of such moving parables as the rich fool (12:16-21), the barren fig tree (13:6-9), the great banquet (14:16-24), the shrewd manager (16:1-9), and the unworthy servants (17:7-10). Probably the two most loved parables found in Luke are those of the good Samaritan and the prodigal son (10:25-37; 15:11-32).

The hymns of the third Gospel that are placed so beautifully among the Nativity stories are another indication of Luke's artistry. The Song of Mary (the *Magnificat,* 1:46-55), the Song of Zechariah (the *Benedictus,* 1:68-79), the Song of Simeon (the *Nunc Dimittis,* 2:29-32), and the Song of the Angels (the *Gloria in Excelsis,* 2:14) have been rich resources for Christian worship and praise through the ages. They are still widely used and appreciated today.

The attractiveness of Luke's writing has been increasingly recognized in recent years. Richard Pervo, for example, has written an interesting book highlighting the entertaining elements in the book of Acts.[14] In his *Profit with Delight,* Pervo has drawn attention to the thrilling adventures, hair-raising escapes, and miraculous works that mark the advance of the Christian mission and make exciting reading. Clearly, Luke knew how to hold his readers' attention. He used a wide range of materials, including the evidence of eyewitnesses, oral tradition, parables, letters, historical documents, and early Christian teaching and preaching, to present his message about Christ and the developing Christian community. He balanced a deep concern for responsible historical method with an equal concern for a winsome, artistic presentation of the Christian cause he loved and served.

STRUCTURE

Many outlines of Luke's Gospel have been suggested, dividing the text into two (Gooding 1987:9), three (Hull 1967; Ellis 1981:32-36), four (Ringe 1995:v-xi; Talbert 1989:vii-viii), five (Summers 1972:15-18), six (Marshall 1978:Contents), or more sections, sometimes treating the last chapter as a conclusion on "The Consummation of the Ministry of Jesus" (Hull 1967:432). Fred Craddock (1990) arrives at seven parts, breaking down the Passion story into "The Ministry of Jerusalem" (19:29–21:38), "The Passion Narrative" (22:1–23:56), and "The Resurrection Narrative" (24:1-53). To be candid, any outline of the Gospel of Luke is somewhat arbitrary, highlighting certain features (e.g., the ministry of John the Baptist [3:1-20] is listed as a separate section in Morris [1974:61]) at the expense of others (Summers, for instance, stresses Jesus as "the universal Savior" in his outline [1972:15-18]). It should be noted that there are clear division markers at 1:5; 3:1; and 9:51, but it is less clear where the central section ends (is it at 19:10, 27, or 44?). In any case, as the central section ends, Jesus is approaching or arriving at the holy city, where he is destined to offer himself as the universal deliverer: "For the Son of Man came to seek and save those who are lost" (19:10). Perhaps the essential eight-part outline, presented by Joseph Fitzmyer (1981:134-142), employed by Craig A. Evans (1990:15), and utilized by Robert Stein, is as useful an outline as any. With slight alterations, we follow Stein's eight sections (1992:31-35) here, counting the introduction or prologue as a section:

I. The Historical Prologue (1:1–4)
II. The Infancy Narratives of John the Baptist and Jesus (1:5–2:52)
III. The Preparation for Jesus' Ministry (3:1–4:13)
IV. Jesus' Ministry in Galilee (4:14–9:50)
V. Jesus' Journey to Jerusalem (9:51–19:27)
VI. Jesus' Ministry in Jerusalem (19:28–21:38)
VII. Jesus' Passion (22:1–23:56)
VIII. Jesus' Resurrection and Ascension (24:1-53)

In any case, we must not forget that Luke himself has given us a broad two-part outline by breaking his overall material into a Gospel and a book of Acts, thus connecting the story of Jesus and the story of the early church. Luke presents in a historical, yet artistic, manner the undeniable links between the life and work of Jesus on the one hand and the ongoing life of the church on the other. In the first volume, he talks "about everything Jesus began to do and teach until the day he was taken up to heaven" at the Ascension (Acts 1:1-2). The Ascension is described in greater detail in Acts, and the unfolding tale of the early church is unfolded in the following narrative. The strong sense of the fulfillment of God's promises in the coming of Jesus and the providential direction of the church in its worldwide mission are clearly evident in both volumes.

MAJOR FEATURES AND THEMES

Historical Character. Luke's Gospel, as I have already noted regarding the preface, highlights the historical character of the Christian movement (Marshall 1970:53-76). His prologue is unique among the Gospels, and indeed in the whole New Testament, and displays an elevated literary style that is clearly reminiscent of the classical historians of the ancient world, like Thucydides, Polybius, and Herodotus (Talbert 1989). However, the most illuminating parallels to the prologue are probably the prefaces of Josephus in his two-volume work *Against Apion*, discussed in detail in the notes on Luke 1:1-4.

The central events on which the Christian church was founded "were not done in a corner," as Paul reminded King Agrippa (Acts 26:26). They were well known and could be located in space and time and placed in an imperial context. Thus, Luke took care to date the birth of Jesus in the reign of Augustus Caesar (2:1) and gave an elaborate sevenfold dating for the ministry of John the Baptist, noting as contemporaries one Roman emperor, four local rulers, and two Jewish high priests (3:1-2, 19-20; Acts 4:5-6). It was important to Luke to show that the Christian faith had a solid historical foundation. He was deeply concerned to give a reliable account of both the life of Christ and the first stages in the growth and expansion of the Christian church from a small sect in Jerusalem to a movement that had reached as far as the imperial capital, Rome.

Scholars have debated Luke's qualifications as a historian. Some have viewed him as treating his sources with considerable freedom, for sociological (Esler) or theological reasons (Conzelmann, Dibelius, Golder, Haenchen). Items critically examined include the Roman census associated with Quirinius, the correct historical placement of the rebellion under Theudas (Acts 5:36), Luke's accounts of the trials of Jesus, the details of the resurrection, the genuineness of the speeches in Acts, the historicity of the Jerusalem council, and Luke's portrait of Paul. These issues must be studied one by one, and assessments not surprisingly will vary. This is due both to the complex character of the evidence and the differing philosophical worldviews of the interpreters. Still, when Luke's sources can be identified and examined, he appears to be trustworthy (Marshall 1970). In his presentation of customs, locales, and settings, he shows a remarkable concern for accuracy (Hemer, Hengel; see note on 1:3).

This historical concern is amply attested in Acts (note, for instance, Acts 4:5-6; 5:37; 11:28; 18:2). Luke displays a historical interest in the titles of local officials (e.g., the "city council," or *politarchēs* [TG4173, ZG4485] in Thessalonica, Acts 17:6-8), Roman provinces (e.g., Asia, Bithynia, Macedonia, and Achaia), important cities such as Antioch on the Orontes River in Syria (where the disciples were first called Christians, Acts 11:26), and the major places visited by Paul on his missionary trips (e.g., Antioch in Pisidia, Iconium, Lystra, and Derbe). In fact, "Luke can be properly appreciated as a theologian only when it is recognized that he is also an historian" (Marshall 1970:18). To sum up, Luke stacks up well against his contemporaries as a responsible historian of Christian origins.

Universal Gospel. Luke's Gospel and its companion volume, Acts, present the gospel tidings as intended for the whole world. At the beginning of the gospel story, the prophecy of Simeon mentions that Jesus is to be "a light to reveal God to the nations" as well as "the glory of your people Israel" (2:32; cf. Acts 13:47-48; 15:14-17). Similarly, at the close of the story, the message from the risen Lord notes that "this message would be proclaimed in the authority of his name to all the nations, beginning in Jerusalem: 'There is forgiveness of sins for all who repent'" (24:47). Similarly, Acts opens with the statement that, after the coming of the Spirit, the disciples were to "[tell] people about me everywhere—in Jerusalem, throughout Judea, in Samaria, and to the ends of the earth" (Acts 1:8). Evidently, Luke saw a wideness in God's mercy that reached out to all people, Jew and Gentile alike.

This universal note is revealed in many ways in Luke–Acts. For example, it is clearly sounded in the Lukan genealogy, where the ancestry of Jesus is traced back to the beginning of the whole human family—not just as far as Abraham, as in Matthew's Gospel (3:23-38; Matt 1:1-17). Similarly, when Luke quotes Isaiah 40:3-5 in his description of John the Baptist's ministry, he alone of the Evangelists includes the words "all people will see the salvation sent from God" (3:6). In the next chapter, Jesus' programmatic statement of his mission in Nazareth significantly mentions the prophetic ministry of Elijah and Elisha to outsiders, namely, the widow of Zarephath and Naaman the Syrian (4:25-27). Other manifestations of this idea follow: Jesus' astounding commendation of the faith of a Gentile centurion (7:9); a rebuke given to two of the apostles for mean-spirited bigotry (9:50); the record of the now-famous parable in which a despised Samaritan shows true neighborliness to a man attacked by thieves after a Jewish priest and Levite had "passed by on the other side" (10:30-37); and a thankful Samaritan when nine Jews failed to offer thanks (17:16-17). Plainly, in Luke's view, the Kingdom of God was to include people "from all over the world"—those who would make the appropriate response of repentance and faith, while unbelieving and impenitent Jews would "be thrown out" (13:28-30; cf. 13:1-5).

This concern for the entire world is also evident throughout Acts, as is clear from the missionary journeys of the apostles and other Christian workers. The Spirit-filled witnesses were instructed by the risen Christ to communicate the message throughout the world, moving from Jerusalem "to the ends of the earth" (Acts 1:8). While the message of salvation was always offered to Jews first, it was then extended to the Gentiles (Acts 13:46; cf. Rom 1:16), and this extension was perceived to be in harmony with Scripture. Thus, Luke cites Paul quoting Isaiah 49:6 as biblical justification for bringing God's salvation "to the Gentiles" (Acts 13:47). Paul was a divinely "chosen instrument" to take the gospel message "to the Gentiles and to kings, as well as to the people of Israel" (Acts 9:15; 22:21; 26:16-18). God was commanding "everyone everywhere to repent of their sins and turn to him" (Acts 17:30). Luke's global perspective is beautifully summarized in Peter's comment to the household of Cornelius: "In every nation [God] accepts those who fear him and do what is right" (Acts 10:35). Luke–Acts truly presents a message for people from every walk of life. No sincere seeker is turned away.

Emphasis on the Holy Spirit. A third feature of Luke–Acts is the pronounced interest in the role of the Holy Spirit. Luke presents the Spirit as the point of continuity between the life of Jesus and the life of the church, being featured in both Luke 24 and Acts 1-2. The Spirit's activity is evident from the early chapters of Luke. In the first chapter, the angel Gabriel prophesies that John the Baptist will be "filled with the Holy Spirit" (1:15). Later, the same angel tells Mary that the Holy Spirit will come upon her and that she will be the mother of the Son of God (1:35). Zechariah is "filled with the Holy Spirit" and given the gift of prophecy (1:67-79), and Simeon, in the Temple, is filled with the Holy Spirit and praising God as he holds the Christ child in his arms (2:25-32).

The Holy Spirit was, of course, also active in the ministry of Jesus, who is described as "full of the Holy Spirit" (4:1; cf. 3:22, the Spirit coming upon him at his baptism). The Spirit led Jesus into the wilderness for a time of testing, and afterward, Jesus returned to Galilee "filled with the Holy Spirit's power" (4:14). When Jesus spoke in Nazareth about his mission, he quoted Isaiah 61:1, "The Spirit of the LORD is upon me," declaring, "The Scripture you've just heard has been fulfilled this very day!" (4:18-21). Later in his ministry, Jesus was "filled with the joy of the Holy Spirit" as he uttered a remarkable prayer of thanksgiving (10:21).

In Luke's view, one of God's finest gifts to his people comes when the heavenly Father gives the Holy Spirit "to those who ask him" (11:13). The Spirit is promised to help disciples in speaking for Christ when they are brought to trial (12:11-12). There is no forgiveness for those who blaspheme the Holy Spirit (12:10). In view of the Spirit's power, it is not surprising that the disciples were told to remain in Jerusalem until after the Holy Spirit had come and filled them with "power from heaven" (24:49).

The role of the Holy Spirit is even more significant in Acts, where there are some 56 references to the Spirit. Once again, Jesus told the disciples to wait for the Spirit (Acts 1:4), and the Holy Spirit came upon them in power on the day of Pentecost (Acts 2:1-4). Subsequently, the disciples were filled with the Spirit and empowered by the Spirit. It would take us too far afield from the purposes of this commentary to trace in detail all the references to the Spirit in Acts. Suffice it to say that Luke saw the Spirit of God leading the church, guiding its decisions, advancing its mission, and empowering its messengers (Acts 4:8; 6:3, 5; 8:29; 9:17; 11:15; 13:2, 4, 9; 15:28; 16:6-7; 20:28). It is through the power of the Spirit that "signs and wonders" are performed, giving the Christian message credibility (Acts 4:29-31; 8:13; 14:3). Some have described the book as "the Acts of the Holy Spirit," in this way recognizing the dominant role of the Spirit in the development of the Christian mission.

Luke's Christology. Luke's thinking is very God-centered (cf. J. B. Green 1995:22-49), and his Gospel stresses the theme "God's Way Triumphs" (Stanton 1990:81-101). In this triumph, God is seen preeminently at work to fulfill his purposes in salvation history in Jesus. Thus, the Christology of Luke, both in the Gospel and Acts, is rich and many sided, as a brief review of his titles for Jesus indicates (for other features, see J. B. Green 1995:50-121). Luke is particularly fond of the title "Son of Man," which he uses some 25 times (e.g., 6:5; 9:26; 11:30). This term allows him to address Jesus' humanity (5:24; 7:34; 9:58); his suffering, death, and resurrection (9:22, 44; 18:31-33); and his future coming in glory at the time of consummation and judgment (17:24, 26, 30; 21:27; 22:69). He also speaks of Jesus as "Son of God" (1:35; cf. 1:32), "Christ" or "Messiah" (2:11, 26; 9:20; 23:39; Acts 2:36; 9:22), "Prophet" (7:16; 13:33; 24:19; Acts 3:22; cf. Luke 4:24; 9:8, 19), "Lord"

(7:19; 9:54; 19:31; Acts 2:36; 10:36; 16:31), "Master" (5:5; 8:24, 45; 9:33, 49; 17:13) or "Teacher" (the term *didaskalos* [TG1320, ZG1437] is used some 14 times, generally of Jesus; e.g., 6:40; 7:40; 8:49; 9:38; 10:25; 20:21; 22:11), "Savior" (2:11; Acts 5:31; 13:23), "King" (19:38; 23:2-3, 37-38), "son of David" (20:41-44), and "servant" (Acts 3:13, 26; 4:27, 30). The fact that Jesus suffered, died, and is raised "on the third day" as predicted (9:22; 13:31-33; 18:33; 24:46) means humanity has been granted a deliverer, for God has kept his promises (24:6-7, 25-27, 44; Acts 2:16-21, 23-36; 13:16-43). This news evokes a summons to repentance and faith "so that your sins may be wiped away" (Acts 3:19; cf. Luke 13:3, 5; 15:7, 10; Acts 2:38; 8:22; 17:30; 26:20). Luke affirms this unique divine offer in the apostolic preaching he shares with his readers: "There is salvation in no one else! God has given no other name under heaven by which we must be saved" (Acts 4:12; cf. Acts 16:30-31). The apostles energetically announce that "there is peace with God through Jesus Christ, who is Lord of all" (Acts 10:36). The unfolding narrative of Acts demonstrates emphatically that this is a message for the whole world (Acts 1:8; 9:15; 26:16-18).

Message of Joy. More than any other Evangelist, Luke highlights the joy that comes with the Christian message. An angel announced the birth of John the Baptist, the forerunner of Jesus, to John's father, Zechariah, as a joyous event (1:14; cf. 1:44, 58). The angels announced the birth of Jesus to the shepherds as "good news that will bring great joy to all people" (2:10); the reason for this jubilation is that the "Savior—yes, the Messiah, the Lord—has been born" (2:11). Similarly, the hymns of praise of Mary, Zechariah, and Simeon exude the joy that God gives his people in the fulfillment of his promises (1:46-55, 68-79; 2:29-32). When the seventy-two disciples returned from their preaching mission, they "joyfully" reported to Jesus that even the demons were subject to them when they invoked his name (10:17); in the same hour, Jesus "was filled with the joy of the Holy Spirit" and uttered a prayer of thanksgiving (10:21-22). Several parables speak of people rejoicing in recovering something that had been lost (15:3-10). Here, there is a striking feature—Luke cites the words of Jesus that there will be joy in heaven over even one sinner who repents (15:7, 10). The loving father welcomed the prodigal son back with a feast and joyful celebration (15:23-24), and the penitent Zacchaeus welcomed Jesus into his home "in great excitement and joy" (19:6). The third Gospel closes on an exuberant note, mentioning the "joy and wonder" of the disciples in the presence of the risen Lord (24:41) and their return to Jerusalem with "great joy" after the ascension of Christ to heaven (24:52).

The same joyous note continues in Acts. When Philip preached the Good News of Christ in Samaria, the message was received enthusiastically, and Luke added, "So there was great joy in that city" (Acts 8:8). Similarly, when Paul proclaimed Christ in Antioch of Pisidia, the Gentiles "were very glad and thanked the Lord for his message" (Acts 13:48). The Ethiopian eunuch accepted the Christian message and "went on his way rejoicing" (Acts 8:39), and the believers in Antioch "were filled with joy and with the Holy Spirit" (Acts 13:52). Similarly, there was real joy when Paul and Barnabas passed through Phoenicia and Samaria and related in detail the conversion of the Gentiles on their way to the church council in Jerusalem (Acts 15:3). The Philippian jailor and his entire household also rejoiced in their newfound faith (Acts 16:34). In Luke's view, the message that "there is peace with God through Jesus Christ, who is Lord of all" (Acts 10:36) is one that brings joy to the world.

The joy that Jesus brings is also accompanied by appropriate praise. This theme is also found in Luke. Over and over again, Luke stresses the practice and value of praise on the lips of God's people (cf. *aineō* [TG134, ZG140] in 2:13, 20; 19:37; 24:53; Acts 2:47; 3:8-9). Glorifying God is given special attention in Luke–Acts as well (cf. *doxazō* [TG1392, ZG1519] in 2:20; 5:25-26; 7:16; 13:13; 17:15; 18:43; 23:47; Acts 4:21; 11:18; 13:48; 21:20).

Focus on Prayer.   Another major theme in Luke–Acts is prayer. Sometimes, Luke has been described as "the Evangelist of prayer," and there is plenty of evidence to support that claim in both Luke and Acts. To begin with, Jesus is clearly seen as a man of prayer (5:16; 9:29; 10:21-22; 11:1). Luke alone presents Jesus praying at his baptism, before the calling of the twelve apostles, and just before Peter's great confession of faith (3:21; 6:12-13; 9:18). Only Luke tells us explicitly that Jesus on several occasions went to a mountain for the express purpose of prayer (6:12; 9:28). Only Luke has parables that highlight the importance of persevering in prayer (11:5-8; 18:1-8) and underscore the need for humility in the presence of God (18:9-14).

There is also instruction in prayer for Christian disciples (11:2-4, 9-13; cf. Matt 6:5-15). The prayer of Jesus for Peter is found only in Luke (22:31-32), and the prayer on the Mount of Olives, in the Lukan version, significantly both begins and ends with an exhortation for Christians to pray so that they might gain similar victories over their temptations (22:39, 46). Jesus prayed earnestly to his Father as he approached his death (22:42) and again at the hour of death (23:46; cf. Ps 31:5). Further, the third Gospel begins with Zechariah and the people in prayer in the Temple and ends with the followers of Jesus praising God in the Temple (1:5-22; 24:53).

The prayer theme continues abundantly in Acts. The first disciples gathered together continually for prayer (Acts 1:14). They prayed earnestly for an apostolic replacement for Judas (Acts 1:24-25) and for their leaders when they were in prison (Acts 4:24-31). When they needed help in taking care of the Greek-speaking widows, they sought divine guidance, and in due course the apostles prayed and laid hands on the seven men chosen to meet the need (Acts 6:6). It is particularly noteworthy here that Luke recognized the duty of the apostles to devote themselves to prayer as well as to teaching and preaching (Acts 6:4).

Many other indications of prayer appear in Acts. Peter and John prayed that a group of Samaritans would receive the Holy Spirit (Acts 8:15). Simon the magician was counseled by Peter to pray for forgiveness, and Simon himself requested intercession (Acts 8:22, 24). Saul of Tarsus prayed before Ananias came to help him (Acts 9:11). Peter prayed for Tabitha, and God restored her life (Acts 9:40). Cornelius prayed, and Peter came to meet his spiritual need when directed to do so by God in a time of prayer (Acts 10:2, 9-20, 30-33; 11:5). The early Christians at Antioch fasted and prayed before sending out Barnabas and Saul (Paul) as their missionaries (Acts 13:3), and they appointed leaders in the churches after they had fasted and prayed (Acts 14:23). Paul and Silas prayed and sang hymns at midnight in jail in Philippi (Acts 16:25), and the Ephesian elders knelt to pray with Paul as they bade him farewell at Miletus (Acts 20:36). There was a similar time of prayer when Paul and his party were bid good-bye by the Christians in Tyre (Acts 21:5-6). Paul also prayed for and healed people on Malta (Acts 28:8-9).

Thus, prayer is a focal element in Luke–Acts and an important element in the life of the church. By it, both Jesus and his followers are sustained in doing the will of God, resisting temptations, and fulfilling the divine purpose. Prayer has a vital place in holy history, and God uses it in advancing his plan for the world. Luke stressed the transfer value of all these examples of prayer for Christian disciples "to show that they should always pray and never give up" (18:1).

The Graciousness of God. Luke and Acts both draw attention to the graciousness of God expressed through Jesus Christ. There is a remarkable sympathy and tenderness expressed toward those who are in any kind of pain or distress (e.g., Luke literally speaks of those who are "troubled" with evil spirits, using the word *enochleomai* [TG1776A, ZG1943], 6:18; cf. Acts 5:16, where the related word *ochleō* [TG3791, ZG4061] is similarly used). Jesus is viewed as concerned about the plight of lepers (5:12-14; 7:22; 17:11-19), widows (7:11-16; 21:1-4), the sick (5:17-26; 13:10-13), and little children (18:15-17). In Luke's Gospel, Jesus is presented in a way that highlights his concern for the sinful, the sorrowing, and the suffering.

A few specific examples will make this clear. Note, for instance, the five miracles of healing that are not mentioned in the other Gospels. In the first one, Jesus restored a boy from Nain, who is touchingly described as "a widow's only son" (7:11-17). Here, Luke tells us Jesus' heart "overflowed with compassion" (7:13; note similar references to the "compassion" of the Good Samaritan and the "love and compassion" of the father for the prodigal son in 10:33 and 15:20). In the second case, Christ healed a pitiful woman who "had been bent double for eighteen years and was unable to stand up straight" (13:10-17). In the third instance, he healed a man suffering from dropsy, "whose arms and legs were swollen" (14:1-5). In the fourth example, ten lepers were cured of leprosy after crying out in anguish to Jesus for mercy (17:11-19). In the final case, we have the healing of the wounded ear of Malchus; while the severing of the ear is noted in both Matthew and Mark, only Luke mentions the touch of Jesus and the resulting healing (22:50-51; cf. Matt 26:51; Mark 14:47; and note John 18:10, which both mentions the man's name and observes, as Luke does, that it was his "right" ear). In each of these cases, there is a delicate description and an expression of real concern for the suffering person.

Other cases point in the same direction. The sufferer whom Jesus met in one of the villages he visited is said to have had "an advanced case of leprosy" (5:12). The mother-in-law of Peter is described as suffering from a "high fever" (4:38), and the beggar Lazarus is said to be plagued with "open sores" (16:21). Similarly, the terrible suffering of the demon-possessed boy, the only son of his father, is movingly described (9:37-43). The description in each case suggests that the writer was sensitive to human suffering.

The book of Acts also reveals this note of tenderness and compassion. One senses the exhilaration felt at the healing of the cripple in the Temple as all the people saw him "walking, leaping, and praising God" (Acts 3:8-9). There is also the moving account of the healing of Aeneas, who "had been paralyzed and bedridden for eight years" (Acts 9:33), and of Tabitha, whose life had made a deep impact on others (Acts 9:39).

Concern for the Poor. Luke gave special attention to the needs of the poor (4:18; 6:20; 7:22; 12:33; 14:13; 18:22; 19:8), a point often noted in commentaries on Luke. Significantly, Luke did not record the saying of Jesus at his anointing in Bethany: "You will always have the poor among you, and you can help them whenever you want to" (Mark 14:7; cf. Matt 26:11; Luke omits this whole incident and has a different story in 7:36-50, where Jesus is anointed by a sinful woman, whose forgiveness he proclaims; cf. France 1987:362). However, Jesus was born in poverty and placed in a manger (2:7, 12, 16). His birth was proclaimed to the poor, announced to shepherds in the fields (2:8-20). When Jesus was presented in the Temple, his parents brought the offering prescribed for the poor (2:24; cf. Lev 12:8). Navone has noted other details documenting Luke's concern for the poor (1970:103-105).

Luke also gives frequent warnings about the dangers of riches and the need for compassion on those less fortunate. Luke stresses the serious danger of covetousness. This is clear in the parable of the rich fool (12:13-21) and in the story of the rich man's indifference to the pitiable condition of Lazarus (16:19-31). The pressing needs of the poor are recognized in Zacchaeus's repentance, where he decided to give half of his wealth to the poor (19:1-10). Luke alone records Jesus' counsel to "sell your possessions and give to those in need" (12:33) as well as his encouragement to invite the poor to dinner (14:12-13). Note also 16:1-13, where the "shrewd" saint is characterized as helping the poor and laying up treasures in heaven. All of this emphasis is an outgrowth of God's regard for the poor in the gift of his Son, about whose coming Mary sang, "He has filled the hungry with good things and sent the rich away with empty hands" (1:53; cf. Miller 1959:12).

In summary, Luke passionately attacked the evils of materialism and saw this as a major emphasis in his Lord's teaching. He was aware that wealth could be idolatrous (cf. Col 3:5), and he saw that "the love of money is the root of all kinds of evil," leading some people, who crave it, to wander from the Christian faith that they have professed (1 Tim 6:10). In addition, concern for the poor is frequently featured in Acts—the early church following its Lord in this respect (Acts 4:34-35; 9:36; 10:4, 31; 20:35; 24:17).

Sensitivity toward Women. Perhaps one of the most obvious ways Luke's graciousness is displayed is in his sensitive treatment of women, a subject that is so impor-

tant that it deserves to be looked at in its own right.[15] Only Luke tells us of the
women who followed Jesus and provided for him and the apostles by "contributing
their own resources" (8:1-3). A sinful woman anointed Christ with a beautiful jar of
expensive perfume, and the Master told her that her many sins had been forgiven
and that her loving act was appreciated (7:36-50). Jesus, unlike the contemporary
rabbis, instructed women (10:38-42). He also used a woman as the leading character in the parables of the lost coin and of the persistent widow (15:8-10; 18:1-8),
and a poor widow was given honorable mention for the sacrificial character of her
Temple gift (21:1-4). Jesus addressed special words to the "daughters of Jerusalem"
as he faced his impending death (23:28-31). Later, the women from Galilee went to
see where he was buried, and they returned on Easter Sunday, bringing the spices
they had prepared (23:55–24:7).

Women are also prominent in Acts. They were present when some 120 believers
gathered for prayer in the upper room (Acts 1:14-15). Women, like men, were certainly "brought to the Lord" (Acts 5:14). They, too, shared the hard knocks of persecution and imprisonment for their faith (Acts 8:3; 9:2; 22:4), and they also followed
their Lord in the waters of baptism (Acts 8:12). Timothy's mother is mentioned as a
believer (Acts 16:1). Women came together for religious purposes in Philippi (Acts
16:13), and a conspicuous convert in that city was Lydia, a merchant who sold
"expensive purple cloth" and offered hospitality to the visiting preachers (Acts
16:14-15). When Paul preached in Thessalonica, "quite a few prominent women"
of the city were converted (Acts 17:4); a similar thing happened in Berea (Acts
17:12), and in Athens, a notable woman named Damaris became a believer (Acts
17:34). A particularly striking Jewish convert was Priscilla, who with her husband,
Aquila, worked with Paul in Corinth and offered helpful counsel to Apollos, explaining "the way of God even more accurately" (Acts 18:26).

Women, then, have an important and prominent place in Luke–Acts, and God's
grace was certainly extended to them. Indeed, Peter declared on the day of Pentecost
that the ancient prophecy of Joel was coming true: " 'In the last days,' God says,
'I will pour out my Spirit upon all people. Your sons and daughters will prophesy.
. . . In those days I will pour out my Spirit even on my servants—men and women
alike—and they will prophesy' " (Acts 2:17-18; cf. Joel 2:28-29). A striking fulfillment of this prophecy comes in the case of the four unmarried daughters of Philip
the evangelist, all of whom had the gift of prophecy (Acts 21:9).

Interest in Angels. Perhaps one of the more unexpected features of Luke–Acts is
Luke's deep interest in angels. There are more than a dozen references to angels in
the third Gospel and about the same number in Acts. At first sight, it might seem
surprising to modern thinkers that a man who was so deeply interested in history
would include accounts of the supernatural, but Luke, like Josephus and other historians of his time, found no difficulty in recording accounts of angelic activities as
historical fact.

Angels are prominent at the outset of Luke's Gospel: the angel Gabriel appeared
to Zechariah and Mary (1:11-20, 26-38); an angel of the Lord appeared to the

shepherds in the fields and an angelic host was seen praising God and singing, "Glory to God in highest heaven" (2:9-15); and Jesus was given his name by the angel Gabriel "even before he was conceived" (2:21). Even Satan referred to angels in the temptation account, quoting Psalm 91:11-12 (4:10-11).

Later, Jesus warned his audience that those who are ashamed of him on earth will be put to shame when the Son of Man returns in his glory "and in the glory of the Father and the holy angels" (9:26). In like manner, Jesus spoke of acknowledging or denying him on earth and of a comparable acknowledgment or denial by the Son of Man before the angels of God (12:8-9). Jesus also commented, "There is joy in the presence of God's angels when even one sinner repents" (15:10). Jesus spoke of angels carrying Lazarus "to be with Abraham" (16:22), and he made a comparison between those who are raised from the dead (in the coming age) and angels (20:36). Finally, two angels appeared to the women at the empty tomb, and reference is later made to the angelic encounter of these women (24:4, 23).

In the book of Acts, two angels appeared after Christ's ascension (Acts 1:10-11), an angel released Peter and John from prison (Acts 5:19), and Stephen's face was compared to an angel's (Acts 6:15). There are also frequent references to angels in Stephen's speech itself (Acts 7:30, 35, 38, 53). An angel guided Philip to the Ethiopian eunuch (Acts 8:26), and an angel directed Cornelius to Peter (Acts 10:3-8, 22, 30; 11:13). Later, an angel freed Peter from prison, and believers mistook Peter for his angel (Acts 12:7-15). An angel executed divine judgment on Herod Agrippa, striking him dead (Acts 12:20-23). While Sadducees rejected belief in angels, Pharisees wondered if an angel had spoken to Paul (Acts 23:8-9). Near the end of Acts, an angel assured Paul of God's protection in the midst of a storm (Acts 27:23-24).

Thus, angels are very much in evidence throughout Luke–Acts. They are active in helping to carry out the divine plan of salvation, and they participate in key events of holy history such as the birth of Jesus, the resurrection of Christ, and the final judgment. While the prominence of angels might be an enigma to some moderns, it is part and parcel of Luke's understanding of redemptive history. God's "secret agents" have an important role in Luke's thinking; indeed, he would agree with the writer of Hebrews that angels are "spirits sent to care for people who will inherit salvation" (Heb 1:14).

Fondness for Meal Scenes.   Scholars have noted Luke's special interest in table etiquette, households in which meals were shared, and the important place given to table fellowship (DJG 796-800). There are more meals in Luke's Gospel than in any other. In fact, of the ten banquet scenes in the third Gospel, seven of them are found exclusively in Luke's account. The first meal mentioned is a dinner party that Levi gave for Jesus. While there are parallels to it in Matthew and Mark, only Luke describes it as a great feast or "banquet" (5:29-35; cf. Matt 9:9-13; Mark 2:13-17). The two other accounts shared with the other Gospels are the feeding of the five thousand (9:10-17; cf. Matt 14:13-21; Mark 6:30-44; John 6:1-13) and the covenant meal that Jesus shared with the disciples, often called "the Last Supper" or "the Eucharist" (22:14-30; cf. Matt 26:20-25; Mark 14:17-21).

Of special interest to us are the seven meals that are recorded only in Luke's Gospel. The first of these is a meal at a Pharisee's house, made memorable by the woman who anointed Christ's feet (7:36-50). The second is the well-known meal Jesus ate at the home of Mary and Martha, his close friends (10:38-42). The third and fourth are once again eaten in the company of Pharisees (11:37-54; 14:1-24); the latter case was marked by the healing of a man "whose arms and legs were swollen" (14:1-6). The fifth case is the meal with Zacchaeus, who showed the reality of his life-changing encounter with Jesus by making a remarkable restitution (19:1-10). The last two meals are postresurrection ones: the risen Christ breaks bread with Cleopas and his companion and later shares a meal including broiled fish with his disciples (24:18, 29-35, 41-43).

There are also seven parables of Jesus that Luke has placed in the context of table fellowship, or that feature meal imagery, or both. These are the two debtors (7:41-50), the friend at midnight (11:5-8), the rich fool (12:13-21), the choice places at the table (14:7-11), the banquet invitations (14:12-14), the great supper (14:15-24; cf. Matt 22:1-10), and the unprofitable servants (17:7-10).

Luke, then, draws special attention to the banqueting theme. This ties in with his theme of joy, for the coming of Jesus brings good news of great joy. The Kingdom of God involves happiness and celebration. It is something to be enjoyed and shared with others. Also, table talk provides an opportunity for teaching, discussion, and healthy interaction. All of this was characteristic of Jesus' fellowship with sinners, and Luke saw fit to highlight it in his account of the life of Christ. A consensus has developed among scholars who have studied Luke's interest in table fellowship. Luke's presentation of Jesus as a teacher in the context of meals highlights an element that was important in the ancient world, and Luke was clearly influenced by his knowledge of the symposium tradition that was well established in Greco-Roman literature (D. E. Smith 1987).

Forgiveness. Luke was certainly aware of the problem of human sinfulness. This led him to take seriously the real need that people have for divine forgiveness (1:77; 3:3; 7:47-49; 11:4; 24:47). A striking instance of Jesus dealing with the issue is found in the case of the paralytic, where Jesus declared, "Young man, your sins are forgiven" (5:20). His enemies were thinking to themselves: "Who does he think he is? That's blasphemy! Only God can forgive sins!" (5:21; cf. 7:49). Nevertheless, Jesus claimed that he, as the Son of Man, had "authority on earth to forgive sins" (5:24). Similarly, on another occasion, Jesus, anointed by a sinful woman in the house of Simon the leper, forgave her sins (7:47-49).

Jesus taught his disciples how to pray, and his model prayer clearly requests that sins be forgiven "as we forgive those who sin against us" (11:4). Forgiveness was commanded in the Christian community: "If another believer sins, rebuke that person; then if there is repentance, forgive" (17:3). This kind of attitude was to be extended on repeated occasions, on the condition of a sincere request by a penitent person (17:4). The Lord himself had demonstrated the perfect spirit of forgiveness on the cross, showing no bitterness toward those who put him to death (23:34

[though this verse is not found in many ancient mss]; cf. Acts 7:60). After the resurrection of Jesus, it became clear that the work of Jesus had been vital in making true forgiveness possible. Indeed, at the core of the Christian message was the fact that repentance and forgiveness of sins were to be preached in Jesus' name to all nations, beginning at Jerusalem (24:47; cf. 5:32; Acts 20:21).

The book of Acts also stresses the importance of forgiveness. The exaltation of Jesus to the Father's right hand as "Prince and Savior" was to give the people of Israel an opportunity to repent and receive forgiveness (Acts 5:31). On the day of Pentecost, Peter told the inquiring crowd what to do: "Each of you must repent of your sins, turn to God, and be baptized in the name of Jesus Christ to show that you have received forgiveness for your sins. Then you will receive the gift of the Holy Spirit" (Acts 2:38). Thus, the apostolic preaching stressed the availability of forgiveness through the work of Christ: "We are here to proclaim that through this man Jesus there is forgiveness for your sins" (Acts 13:38; cf. Eph 1:7). The offer of forgiveness was in full agreement with the Scriptures, for the Hebrew prophets taught that "everyone who believes in him will have their sins forgiven through his name" (Acts 10:43). This message was not limited to the Jews but was extended to the Gentiles as well, as Paul was told by the risen Lord: "They will receive forgiveness for their sins and be given a place among God's people, who are set apart by faith in me" (Acts 26:18). The importance of forgiveness of sins is underscored throughout Luke–Acts.

Emphasis on Salvation. Before leaving the themes of Luke, something must be said about the importance of salvation, a theme that is given great prominence in Luke–Acts. Luke used two Greek words for "salvation": *sōtēria* [TG4991, ZG5401] (1:69, 71, 77; 19:9; Acts 4:12; 7:25; 13:26, 47; 16:17; 27:34) and *sōtērion* [TG4992A, ZG5402] (2:30; 3:6; Acts 28:28). He called both God (1:47) and Jesus "Savior" (*sōtēr* [TG4990, ZG5400]; cf. 2:11; Acts 5:31; 13:23). In addition, he was fond of using the verb *sōzō* [TG4982, ZG5392] (save) in a spiritual sense (cf. 7:50; 8:12; 13:23; 19:10; Acts 2:21, 47; 4:12; 11:14; 15:11; 16:30-31).

Jesus was acclaimed from the beginning as the promised deliverer: "The Savior—yes, the Messiah, the Lord—has been born today in Bethlehem, the city of David!" (2:11). Similarly, the prophet Anna acknowledged the infant Christ in the Temple as the child of promise, talking "about the child to everyone who had been waiting expectantly for God to rescue Jerusalem" (2:38). This salvation was not limited to the Jews, for it was intended for all humanity (3:6).

Jesus, like John the Baptist before him, called on the Jewish people to repent and turn to God, warning them that failure to do so would inevitably bring judgment upon them (13:1-5; cf. 3:3-14; Matt 3:7; 12:34; 23:33). God's offer of grace was not to be spurned with impunity, for all those who refused it would find themselves rejected and "thrown out" (13:28). By contrast, those who responded positively could be assured of a warm reception (cf. 15:7, 10, 20-32). A classic illustration of a true response is found in Zacchaeus, who was told that "salvation has come to this home today. . . . For the Son of Man came to seek and save those who are lost"

(19:9-10). The third Gospel closes with a beautiful summary of the great salvation that has been made available through Christ (24:46-47).

Acts reiterates this message, repeating it again and again in the great sermons that outline the apostolic preaching (see chs 2, 3, 7, 10, 13, 17, 22, 26). Christ is presented as the central figure in God's plan of salvation. Thus, Peter declared on the day of Pentecost, "So let everyone in Israel know for certain that God has made this Jesus, whom you crucified, to be both Lord and Messiah!" (Acts 2:36). In fact, the apostles spoke plainly before the Jewish religious leaders, boldly stating the unique place of Christ: "There is salvation in no one else! God has given no other name under heaven by which we must be saved" (Acts 4:12).

The apostles and their fellow workers fearlessly proclaimed this gospel message. They wasted no time in spreading the news that "there is peace with God through Jesus Christ, who is Lord of all" (Acts 10:36). In this way, the Good News was presented on ever-broadening horizons to "the ends of the earth" (Acts 1:8; cf. Acts 13:46-47), and people were brought "from darkness to light and from the power of Satan to God" (Acts 26:18). Salvation was offered to the Gentiles as well as the Jews (e.g., Acts 15:14; 28:28), and Acts notes that many repented and believed (Acts 2:41, 47; 6:1; 11:18, 21; 14:1, 21; 16:14, 34; 17:4, 34; 21:20). The book of Luke, like Acts, highlights the message of salvation, a message that is for all people throughout the world.

The Sovereignty of God. One final element in Luke's two-volume work must be noted. It is the sovereignty of God—a theme that runs clearly through both books. Believing that God is in charge of history, Luke makes no apology for adopting a God-centered perspective. In both the Gospel and Acts, there runs this tremendous sense of divine necessity (note the frequent use of the impersonal Gr. word *dei* [TG1163, ZG1256] to indicate this feature). Certain things were "necessary" because an almighty, sovereign God had decided that the given event or action was to happen to fulfill the divine plan and to accomplish a previously ordained divine purpose. In other words, God, having determined the course of all history, was working out a definite purpose. A few instances in both works make this God-centered pattern obvious.

In Luke's Gospel, this feature is evidenced in the words of the boy Jesus, who reminded his parents, "Didn't you know that I must be in my Father's house?" (2:49). It surfaces again in Jesus' public ministry, where he spoke of the divine mandate for his itinerant ministry: "I must preach the Good News of the Kingdom of God in other towns, too, because that is why I was sent" (4:43). It is plainly indicated in the passion predictions: "The Son of Man must suffer many terrible things" (9:22; cf. 17:25; 18:31-34; 24:7). Jesus, in Luke's Gospel, is presented as governed by an overriding sense of divine destiny that is particularly evident as he faced his impending death: "For the time has come for this prophecy about me to be fulfilled: 'He was counted among the rebels' [Isa 53:12]. Yes, everything written about me by the prophets will come true" (22:37). One of the most moving instances of God's direction in holy history is given in the Emmaus story as the risen Christ reproved his companions: "You foolish people! You find it so hard to believe all that the prophets wrote in the Scriptures. Wasn't it clearly predicted that the Messiah would have to suffer all these things before entering his glory?" (24:25-26). The divine plan had been unmistakably mapped out: "Yes, it was written long ago that the Messiah would suffer and die and rise from the dead on the third day"; this message of repentance and faith in Christ was to be shared among the nations, beginning in Jerusalem (24:46-47).

The same strong emphasis on God's sovereign plan for history is found in Acts (e.g., Acts 2:23; 4:28; 20:22-24). Once again, it is presented in such a way as to highlight the central place of Christ in God's plan (Acts 3:20-21; 17:3; 26:15-18). Luke saw Jesus as the Messiah appointed beforehand by God. Similarly, the apostles were declared to be those whom "God had chosen in advance" to be his witnesses (Acts 10:41). Energized by the Holy Spirit, the disciples were to take the message concerning Christ throughout the world and share it with all people (Acts 1:8). Paul, for instance, felt impelled by the Spirit to go to Macedonia and Achaia with the gospel and then to take it to Rome (Acts 19:21). The whole perspective of Luke and Acts stresses that a sovereign God was working his purpose out in history, and his plan would be fulfilled! Lonsdale Ragg's glowing tribute to Luke may serve as a fitting conclusion to this introduction:

> *What St. Luke was as a man is reflected in his writings. Wide and deep sympathy, love of souls, interest in simple things, in manhood and womanhood, in childhood and domesticity, in the joy of life, in prayer, worship, praise, and thanksgiving; historical sense, keen observation, loyalty to fact; gift of narrative, dramatic, and artistic sense, and a certain genial humor; deep enthusiasm for the Saviour, the Divine-Human Christ, and for the first missionary heroes of the Ascended Lord— all these are there, and much more. No wonder his Gospel is described by Renan as "the most beautiful book ever written" (1922:ix).*

OUTLINE
  I. Preface (1:1-4)
  II. The Nativity Stories (1:5-2:52)
    A. The Birth of John the Baptist Foretold (1:5-25)
      1. Zechariah's background (1:5-7)
      2. Zechariah's Temple service (1:8-10)
      3. The angel Gabriel visits Zechariah (1:11-17)
      4. Zechariah's response (1:18-22)
      5. The conception of John the Baptist (1:23-25)
    B. The Birth of Jesus Foretold (1:26-38)
    C. Mary Visits Elizabeth (1:39-45)
    D. The Magnificat: Mary's Song of Praise (1:46-56)
    E. The Birth of John the Baptist (1:57-66)

J. The Sign of Jonah (11:29-32; cf. Matt 12:38-42)

K. Receiving the Light (11:33-36; cf. Matt 6:22-23)

L. Jesus Criticizes the Religious Leaders (11:37-54; cf. Matt 23)

M. A Warning against Hypocrisy (12:1-12; cf. Matt 10:26-33)

N. Parable of the Rich Fool (12:13-21)

O. Teaching about Money and Possessions (12:22-34)

P. Be Ready for the Lord's Coming (12:35-48; cf. Matt 24:43-51)

Q. Jesus Causes Division (12:49-59; cf. Matt 10:34-36)

R. A Call to Repentance (13:1-5)

S. Illustration of the Barren Fig Tree (13:6-9)

T. Jesus Heals on the Sabbath (13:10-17)

U. Parables of the Mustard Seed and the Yeast (13:18-21;
cf. Matt 13:31-33; Mark 4:30-32)

V. The Narrow Door (13:22-30; cf. Matt 7:22)

W. Jesus Grieves over Jerusalem (13:31-35; cf. Matt 23:37-39)

X. Jesus Heals on the Sabbath (14:1-6)

Y. Jesus Teaches about Humility (14:7-14)

Z. Parable of the Great Feast (14:15-24; cf. Matt 22:1-10)

AA. The Cost of Being a Disciple (14:25-35)

BB. Parable of the Lost Sheep (15:1-7)

CC. Parable of the Lost Coin (15:8-10)

DD. Parable of the Lost Sons (15:11-32)

EE. Parable of the Shrewd Manager (16:1-18)

FF. Parable of the Rich Man and Lazarus (16:19-31)

GG. Teachings about Forgiveness and Faith (17:1-10; cf. Matt 18:6-7, 15;
Mark 9:42)

HH. Ten Healed of Leprosy (17:11-19)

II. The Coming of the Kingdom (17:20-37; cf. Matt 24:37-39;
Mark 13:21)

JJ. Parable of the Persistent Widow (18:1-8)

KK. Parable of the Pharisee and Tax Collector (18:9-14)

LL. Jesus Blesses the Children (18:15-17; cf. Matt 19:13-15;
Mark 10:13-16)

MM. The Rich Man (18:18-30; cf. Matt 19:16-30; Mark 10:17-31)

NN. Jesus Again Predicts His Death (18:31-34; cf. Matt 20:17-19;
Mark 10:32-34)

OO. Jesus Heals a Blind Beggar (18:35-43; cf. Matt 20:29-34;
Mark 10:46-52)

PP. Jesus and Zacchaeus (19:1-10)

QQ. Parable of the Ten Servants (19:11-27; cf. Matt 25:14-30)

RR. The Triumphal Entry (19:28-40; cf. Matt 21:1-9; Mark 11:1-10)

SS. Jesus Weeps over Jerusalem (19:41-44)

VI. The Passion Story (19:45–24:53)
   A. Jesus Clears the Temple (19:45-48; cf. Matt 21:12-13; Mark 11:15-19; John 2:13-17)
   B. The Authority of Jesus Challenged (20:1-8; cf. Matt 21:23-27; Mark 11:27-33)
   C. Parable of the Evil Farmers (20:9-19; cf. Matt 21:33-46; Mark 12:1-12)
   D. Taxes for Caesar (20:20-26; cf. Matt 22:15-22; Mark 12:13-17)
   E. Discussion about Resurrection (20:27-40; cf. Matt 22:23-33; Mark 12:18-27)
   F. Whose Son Is the Messiah? (20:41-47; cf. Matt 22:41-46; Mark 12:35-37a)
   G. The Widow's Offering (21:1-4; cf. Mark 12:41-44)
   H. Jesus Foretells the Future (21:5-38; cf. Matt 24:4-36; Mark 13:5-37)
   I. Judas Agrees to Betray Jesus (22:1-6; cf. Matt 26:1-5, 14-16; Mark 14:1-2, 17-21)
   J. The Last Supper (22:7-30; cf. Matt 26:17-19, 26-29; Mark 14:12-16, 22-25)
   K. Jesus Predicts Peter's Denial (22:31-38; cf. Matt 26:30-35; Mark 14:26-31; John 13:36-38)
   L. Jesus Prays on the Mount of Olives (22:39-46; cf. Matt 26:36-46; Mark 14:32-42)
   M. Jesus Is Betrayed and Arrested (22:47-53; cf. Matt 26:47-56; Mark 14:43-52; John 18:2-11)
   N. Peter Denies Jesus (22:54-65; cf. Matt 26:57-75; Mark 14:53-72)
   O. Jesus before the Council (22:66-71; cf. Matt 26:57-68; Mark 14:53-65)
   P. The Trials of Jesus before Pilate and Herod (23:1-25; cf. Matt 27:1-2, 11-14; Mark 15:1-5; John 18:33-38)
   Q. The Crucifixion of Jesus (23:26-43; cf. Matt 27:32-44; Mark 15:21-32; John 19:16-27)
   R. The Death of Jesus (23:44-49; cf. Matt 27:45-56; Mark 15:33-41; John 19:28-37)
   S. The Burial of Jesus (23:50-56; cf. Matt 27:57-61; Mark 15:42-47; John 19:38-42)
   T. The Resurrection of Jesus (24:1-12; cf. Matt 28:1-10; Mark 16:1-8; John 20:1-10)
   U. The Walk to Emmaus (24:13-34)
   V. Jesus Appears to the Disciples (24:35-49)
   W. The Ascension of Jesus (24:50-53; cf. Acts 1:6-11)

ENDNOTES

1. Ernest Renan, *The Life of Jesus*, cited by Cadbury (1961:337). Renan also calls Luke "a divine artist. In the perusal of his gospel there is the greatest charm; for to the incomparable beauty of the foundation (provided in the canonical Gospels), common to them all, he adds a degree of skill in composition which singularly augments the effects of his portrait, without seriously injuring its truthfulness." Compare this statement with a more recent assessment by Graham Stanton, who, in noting that many readers find this Gospel the most attractive, observes that Luke's Gospel "seems to lack the harsh severity of some parts of Matthew, the terseness and the enigmatic features of Mark, and the 'other-worldliness' of John" (Stanton 1990:81).

2. See Stagg 1955; Marshall 1992; Talbert 1984a.

3. For classic discussions of the problem of the authorship of the Pastoral Epistles, see P. N. Harrison, *The Problem of the Pastoral Epistles* (London: Oxford University Press, 1921) and D. Guthrie, *The Pastoral Epistles and the Mind of Paul* (London: Tyndale Press, 1956). For useful reviews of the evidence, see Lee M. McDonald and Stanley E. Porter, *Early Christianity and its Sacred Literature* (Peabody, MA: Hendrickson, 2000), 488-497; D. A. Carson, D. J. Moo, and L. Morris, *An Introduction to the New Testament* (Grand Rapids: Zondervan, 1992), 359-385; E. Ellis, "Pastoral Letters," in DPL, 658-666.

4. See W. K. Hobart, *The Medical Language of St. Luke* (London: Longmans, Green, 1882) and Adolf von Harnack, *Luke the Physician: The Author of the Third Gospel and the Acts of the Apostles*, trans., J. R. Wilkinson, New Testament Studies 1 (New York: Putnam, 1907).

5. H. J. Cadbury (1919–1920:1.39-72). Note the wise words of R. E. O. White (1987:9), who affirms that for all the cautious remarks that scholars make to say that the evidence does not "prove" that Luke was a physician, "some evidence of a medical man's outlook may be found in the Gospel—accurate observation for example. Luke describes miracles, diseases, and symptoms very precisely; he specifies a 'high' fever, 'full' of leprosy, and avoids calling hemorrhage a 'disease' as Mark does. And though Luke tells that story of the woman who had suffered long from hemorrhage, he omits Mark's statement that she 'had suffered much under many physicians, and had spent all that she had, and was no better but rather grew worse.'"

6. Vincent Taylor (1962:2.181). For a recent treatment of this issue, see Parsons and Pervo (1993), who consider the dimensions of generic unity, narrative unity, and theological unity.

7. See E. P. Blair 1987:247; see also Trites 1995.

8. For the text of the Anti-Marcionite Prologue to Luke (dated c. AD 160–180), see Harrington 1968:13.

9. In AD 112, Pliny had to decide whether the confession of being a Christian was a crime, that is, "whether punishment attaches to the mere name apart from secret crimes, or the secret crimes connected with the name. Meanwhile this is the course I have taken with those who were accused before me as Christians. I asked them whether they were Christians, and if they confessed, I asked them a second time with threats of punishment. If they kept to it, I ordered them for execution" (quoted from Stevenson 1963:13). The emperor Trajan confirmed this policy.

10. Morris A. Inch (1988:1362). Note the cautious remarks of John Nolland (1989:xxxix): "The considerable discussion about the place of composition is, in my judgment, quite indecisive. Luke is certainly a man of cosmopolitan outlook, but further than that I hesitate to go."

11. E. J. Goodspeed, 50 years ago, argued that Theophilus may have been Luke's literary patron or publisher. See his article "Some Greek Notes: Was Theophilus Luke's Publisher?" *Journal of Biblical Literature* 73 (1954): 84-96. Ellis makes the same point (1981:66). Fitzmyer cites as possible parallels for patrons in the Greco-Roman world of the time Maecenas and Horace *Odes* 1:1; Atticus and Cicero (Fitzmyer 1981:299).

12. For examples of Luke's use of the Gr. text of the OT (the LXX), see C. F. D. Moule, *An Idiom Book of the Greek New Testament* (Cambridge: Cambridge University Press, 1968).

13. On the use of speeches in Acts, see Soards 1994.
14. See Pervo 1987. For a comprehensive study of Luke–Acts emphasizing the use of literary criticism, see Brawley 1991 and Kurz 1993.
15. For an excellent article and bibliography on this subject, see D. M. Scholer, "Women," in DJG, 880-887. For recent feminist studies on Luke, see Amy-Jill Levine 2002.

COMMENTARY ON

Luke

◆ **I. Preface (1:1-4)**

Many people have set out to write accounts about the events that have been
fulfilled among us. ²They used the eyewitness reports circulating among us
from the early disciples.* ³Having carefully

investigated everything from the beginning, I also have decided to write a careful
account for you, most honorable Theophilus, ⁴so you can be certain of the truth of
everything you were taught.

1:2 Greek *from those who from the beginning were servants of the word.*

NOTES

1:2 *They used the eyewitness reports.* Eyewitness testimony, often overlooked and under-
recognized by form critics (such as Schmidt, Bultmann, and Dibelius), is a basic factor to
be reckoned with in understanding the historical basis of the Gospels. If the date of the
Gospel is early, the eyewitnesses mentioned here would still be available for interview and
consultation in large measure. As time went on, their numbers would naturally decrease.
Paul recognized this fact when he wrote to the Corinthians. He noted that the risen Lord
"was seen by more than 500 of his followers at one time, most of whom are still alive,
though some have died" (1 Cor 15:6).

Eyewitnesses were crucial in establishing the truth of details, and this point is accepted
by Luke in establishing and explaining his historical method. In OT times, eyewitnesses
were required, for example, in establishing a verdict in criminal cases (Deut 17:6; 19:15).
This principle of multiple witnesses was generally accepted and utilized in NT times as
well (Matt 18:16; John 8:17; 2 Cor 13:1; Heb 10:28; 1 John 5:7-9). The central events
both of the life and ministry of Jesus and of the early church were anchored in eyewitness testimony (cf. 1 John 1:1-4) that was carefully investigated by Luke (Trites
1977:55, 139, 198).

"In particular the prominence accorded to Peter as eyewitness informant behind Mark (e.g.,
Mark 8:29, 32ff; 9:2, 5; 11:21; 14:29, 33, 37, 54, 66-72; 16:7; cf. Luke 22:54-62) . . . helps to
secure a strong line of continuity between the Gospel . . . as 'story' and Jesus of Nazareth as
'history'" (Head 2001:293). The relationship between Mark and Peter is also strongly supported by external evidence (e.g., Papias, the Anti-Marcionite Prologue, Irenaeus). Similarly,
eyewitness testimony is preserved in the Q material, the roughly 230 verses preserved in
Matthew and Luke (e.g., the Temptation, recorded in both Matt 4:1-11 and Luke 4:1-13).
For further discussion, see Head 2001.

1:3 *a careful account.* Luke was concerned about unfolding the events of Jesus' life "carefully" or "accurately" (*akribōs* [TG199, ZG209]). He thus described his historical procedure and
also noted his interest in providing "certainty" or "truth" (*asphaleia* [TG803, ZG854]; 1:4). For
further comment on Luke's preface, see "Audience" in the Introduction. On the different
approaches taken in Germany and Britain to evaluate Luke's historical work, see van

Ommwern 1991. On the use of ancient prefaces to historical works, see Earl (1990), who points out that most ancient historical prefaces do not directly address the one to whom the work was dedicated. This is an unusual feature of the Lukan preface that is worthy of note. For a discussion of Luke's prologue in appreciation of Luke-Acts as a whole, see Dillon 1981; Alexander 1993; Brawley 1991:86-106.

COMMENTARY

As noted in the Introduction, Luke used a preface to spell out his historical method so that his readers might know the principles on which he worked. First, he noted that other writers had attempted to explain the historical foundation of Christian origins before him. Second, he observed the special role of "the eyewitness reports circulating among us from the early disciples," who could attest everything "from the beginning," and made careful use of their evidence. Third, he intended to provide "a careful account" of the Christian movement. Fourth, he claimed that he had made a thorough investigation of the facts of the case. Fifth, he named Theophilus as the intended recipient of his work in his dedication (cf. Acts 1:1); and sixth, he presented the historical evidence so that his readers (Theophilus and other interested persons) might know the solid historical basis of the things they had been taught.

Luke's preface emulates the formal practice of the Greek-speaking historians of the time. The way Josephus introduced his famous book *Against Apion* is particularly instructive, for it is a work composed of two parts, with an introduction or preface to the entire work at the beginning of Book 1 and a brief summary and review at the beginning of Book 2:

> In my history of our *Antiquities,* my excellent Epaphroditus, I have, I think, made sufficiently clear the extreme antiquity of our Jewish race. Since, however, I observe that a considerable number of persons discredit the statements of my history concerning our antiquity, I consider it my duty to devote a brief treatise to all these points in order at once to convict our detractors of malignity and deliberate falsehood, to correct the ignorance of others, and to instruct all who desire to know the truth concerning the antiquity of our race. As witnesses to my statements I propose to call the writers who, in the estimation of the Greeks, are the most trustworthy authorities on antiquity as a whole. (*Against Apion* 1.1-4)
>
> In the first volume of this work, my esteemed Epaphroditus, I demonstrated the antiquity of our race, I shall now proceed to refute the rest of the authors who have attacked us. (*Against Apion* 2.1)

These two statements of Josephus shed considerable light on Luke's introduction, which really serves as a historical preface to his two-volume work. There are a number of remarkable similarities between the comments of Josephus and Luke's preface. In each case, two volumes are closely connected and linked together by the same author, and the same person is addressed in both volumes; in the case of Luke–Acts, it is Theophilus, who is mentioned in 1:3 and Acts 1:1. Furthermore, Josephus directed his book to "my excellent Epaphroditus," and Luke used the same honorific language to address Theophilus (*kratiste;* 1:3). Both writers were concerned to teach and instruct their readers, and both were committed to the use of responsible historical methods to arrive at the truth. Both also utilized "the most trustworthy authorities"; in Luke's case, these included those who were "eyewitnesses" of the events of the life of Christ and of the early disciples. Finally, both were concerned to demonstrate their historical credibility by offering convincing evidence or "proof" (the word *tekmērion* [TG5039, ZG5447] being used by both Josephus [*Against Apion* 1.2] and Luke [Acts 1:3, lit. "with many proofs"]).

There is, however, one significant difference in approach between Luke and Josephus. Josephus was rather critical of some of his historical predecessors who, in his opinion, had done less than justice to the Jewish people. Luke, on the other hand, did not attack or disparage those who had written before him. All the same, he believed that he had something distinctive to contribute and set out to produce "a careful account" of Christian origins, building constructively on those who had gone before him. He wanted to give Theophilus and all his readers or auditors (those who hear the text orally) solid grounds to reassure them of the truth they had been taught (1:4). Luke undertook his historical work with the utmost seriousness—the task of studying the sources, interrogating the witnesses, evaluating the evidence, and arranging the matter in a logical way. For him, responsible critical investigation of sources and evidence was absolutely necessary to the historiographical task he had set for himself. His aim was to provide a narrative or "account" (*diēgēsis* [TG1335, ZG1456], 1:1) that would offer solid information about Christ and the early church. Luke's "order" (*kathexēs* [TG2517, ZG2759], 1:3) is not precisely defined and should be interpreted as synonymous with "systematic," as Stein has argued (1983). For instance, the journey of Jesus to Jerusalem is an excellent example of Luke's principle of order, though incidents in this section are not always presented in chronological sequence (9:51–19:27; so Stagg 1967:499-512). "The 'main point' of the Prologue [and the "order" it claims] is that 'Christianity is true and is capable of confirmation by appeal to what has happened'" (Morris 1974:67, quoting Stonehouse 1951:44).

◆ **II. The Nativity Stories (1:5–2:52)**
  ## A. The Birth of John the Baptist Foretold (1:5–25)
    ### 1. Zechariah's background (1:5-7)

⁵When Herod was king of Judea, there was a Jewish priest named Zechariah. He was a member of the priestly order of Abijah, and his wife, Elizabeth, was also from the priestly line of Aaron. ⁶Zechariah and Elizabeth were righteous in God's eyes, careful to obey all of the Lord's commandments and regulations. ⁷They had no children because Elizabeth was unable to conceive, and they were both very old.

NOTES
1:5 *Herod was king of Judea.* This was Herod the Great, who ruled from 37 to 4 BC over Judea, Galilee, Samaria, and a large part of Perea and Syria. On the life of Herod the Great, see Grant 1971.

COMMENTARY

This is the first substantial part of the third Gospel. In the preface (1:1-4), Luke outlined the historical method that he would use in both the Gospel and Acts. He now begins his account by telling of two miraculous births (1:5–2:52) before presenting the preparation for the ministry of Jesus—outlining the ministry of John the Baptist and describing the baptism, genealogy, and temptation of Jesus (3:1–4:13). These accounts set the stage for Luke's major presentations of the ministry of Jesus in Galilee (4:14–9:50), the ministry of Jesus on the journey to Jerusalem (9:51–19:44), the final ministry of Jesus in Jerusalem (19:45–23:56), and the concluding accounts of Jesus' resurrection and ascension (24:1-53).

Luke took pains to locate the family background of Jesus and his forerunner, John the Baptist (see also 3:1-2). There is a deliberate contrast presented between John the great prophet and Jesus the greater prophet. This is exemplified in the account of the two annunciations: note the contrast between Zechariah's doubts (1:18-20) and Mary's humble reception of the news (1:38). Luke made it clear that Zechariah was a Jewish priest who lived "when Herod was king of Judea" (1:5). The reference here is to Herod the Great, who ruled from 37 to 4 BC (see note on 1:5). He was a brilliant but ruthless man who put his wife Mariamne and two of his own sons to death because of his fearful paranoia. He was the ruler who cruelly slaughtered the innocents (all children two years of age and under) in Bethlehem and its vicinity, a tragedy noted in Matthew's Gospel (Matt 2:13-18).

Luke placed Zechariah in one of the twenty-four groups that offered priestly service in the Temple, namely, "the priestly order of Abijah" (1:5). The details of these priestly courses are spelled out in 1 Chronicles 24:1-18. These arrangements had been in place since King David's time, and Abijah was one of the heads of the priestly families (1 Chr 24:10; Neh 12:17). Zechariah had an honorable place in the religious establishment at Jerusalem and each year served on rotation for two weeks in the Temple in addition to his service on the Jewish high holy days.

Zechariah and his wife, Elizabeth, who was also a descendant "from the priestly line of Aaron," are presented as devout Jewish people who were "righteous in God's eyes" (1:5-6). They made it their constant aim to please God, and they were meticulous in their religious practices, "careful to obey all of the Lord's commandments and regulations" (1:6; cf. Deut 30:15-20). They were earnest and sincere in their profession of faith. But their one great disappointment as a couple was the absence of children. This was a very serious thing for devout Jews, because children were considered a sign of God's blessing upon the marriage. For example, Psalm 128, speaking of the happiness of those who "fear the LORD," waxes eloquent on the theme of family bliss: "How joyful and prosperous you will be! Your wife will be like a fruitful grapevine, flourishing within your home. Your children will be like vigorous young olive trees as they sit around your table. That is the LORD's blessing for those who fear him" (Ps 128:2-4). In the absence of children, there was a sense of falling away from God's approval. Women particularly struggled with the stigma of barrenness and were often subject to social reproach—something frequently noted in the Old Testament, as in the cases of Sarai, Rebekah, Rachel, and Hannah (Gen 16:1-3; 25:21; 30:23; 1 Sam 1:1-18). Zechariah and Elizabeth had lived for many years with this perplexing situation; no relief seemed in sight, for "they were both very old" (1:7).

◆ 2. Zechariah's Temple service (1:8-10)

⁸One day Zechariah was serving God in the Temple, for his order was on duty that week. ⁹As was the custom of the priests, he was chosen by lot to enter the sanctuary of the Lord and burn incense. ¹⁰While the incense was being burned, a great crowd stood outside, praying.

NOTES

1:9 *he was chosen by lot*. The lot was an oracular device used in making a selection from a number of choices. In the OT, the casting of lots was employed in the determination of God's will (Num 27:21), the division of land (Josh 18:11; 19:1, 10, 17, 24, 32, 40), the allocation of military duties (Judg 20:9), the appointment of persons to settle in Jerusalem during its restoration (Neh 11:1), and the assignment of tasks to priests and Levites (1 Chr 24:5-18; 25:8; 26:13). The guilty verdicts pronounced on Achan and Jonathan were probably determined by lot, though the word is not used in the Heb. text (Josh 7:14-18; 1 Sam 14:41-42). The casting of lots was used to settle disputes (Prov 18:18; Jonah 1:7). In the NT, Jesus' executioners cast lots for his garments (23:34; Matt 27:35; Mark 15:24; John 19:24), and lots were cast to select Matthias as a replacement for Judas (Acts 1:26). After the coming of the Holy Spirit (Acts 2:1-4), lots became unnecessary. The Holy Spirit was available to lead Christians into spiritual truth. In fact, Jesus had promised this special help from the Holy Spirit: "He will teach you everything and will remind you of everything I have told you" (John 14:26; 16:13). The book of Acts is full of examples where the Spirit of God guided believers in their actions and decisions (see Acts 10:19; 11:12; 13:2; 15:28; 16:6-7).

1:10 *a great crowd stood outside, praying*. As the people were waiting in devout expectation that God would answer their prayers while the incense rose, it appears that God guided the lots so that the angel of the Lord appeared to Zechariah at the most sacred moment of his life.

COMMENTARY

The Jewish Temple in New Testament times was an impressive establishment that had been subjected to massive reconstruction under Herod the Great, a process that began in 20 BC and was not completed until AD 64. As in the case of the earlier Temples of Solomon and Zerubbabel, there were several outer courts, each one being higher and more sacred than the preceding one. First, there was the Court of the Gentiles, then, the Court of the Women, and finally, the Court of the Israelites, which was only open to ritually clean Jewish men. Beyond that, only the priests could proceed to enter the Temple building itself. Here was located the sanctuary (*naos* [TG3485, ZG3724], called in Heb. the *hekal* [TH1964, ZH2121]) and beyond it the Holy of Holies, where the high priest entered only once a year on the Day of Atonement.

The Holy Place, where Zechariah was called to serve on this momentous occasion, was a remarkable structure. It contained the table on which were kept the special Bread of the Presence, the altar of incense, and the seven-branched lampstand, all of which were constructed of gold. Gold panels overlaid the entire interior of the structure. This was the resplendent, sacred setting in the heart of the Temple in which Zechariah, the old priest, was accosted by the angel.

It was one of the duties of the priest to provide the incense for the altar of incense, located just in front of the Most Holy Place. He brought fresh incense each day before the morning sacrifice and again after the evening sacrifice (Exod 30: 6-8). A priest would be fortunate to offer incense here once in a lifetime; since lots were cast for the duty assignments, some priests would never have such a privilege. The incense was a symbol of the prayers of the people ascending to God (Ps 141:2; Rev 5:8; 8:3-4; cf. Lev 16:12-13; 2 Chr 2:4; 13:10-11; Mal 1:11), and thus, it was not surprising that the worshipers were praying outside of the Holy Place while the burning of incense was occurring. If ever there was an appropriate occasion for a divine message, this was it! Like Moses before him, Zechariah had a divine encounter in the course of fulfilling his duty (cf. Exod 3:1-2). He was in the sanctuary, carrying out the work he had been assigned, when "an angel of the Lord appeared" (1:11).

◆   ## 3. The angel Gabriel visits Zechariah (1:11-17)

[11]While Zechariah was in the sanctuary, an angel of the Lord appeared to him, standing to the right of the incense altar. [12]Zechariah was shaken and overwhelmed with fear when he saw him. [13]But the angel said, "Don't be afraid, Zechariah! God has heard your prayer. Your wife, Elizabeth, will give you a son, and you are to name him John. [14]You will have great joy and gladness, and many will rejoice at his birth, [15]for he will be great in the eyes of the Lord. He must never touch wine or other alcoholic drinks. He will be filled with the Holy Spirit, even before his birth.* [16]And he will turn many Israelites to the Lord their God. [17]He will be a man with the spirit and power of Elijah. He will prepare the people for the coming of the Lord. He will turn the hearts of the fathers to their children,* and he will cause those who are rebellious to accept the wisdom of the godly."

1:15 Or *even from birth.*   1:17 See Mal 4:5-6.

NOTES

1:11 *an angel of the Lord.* On the place of angels in Jewish thought, see D. S. Russell (1964:235-249). On the general use of angels in the Bible, see Gardner (1995:44-49).

1:13 *God has heard your prayer.* Luke highlights the importance of prayer for Jesus (5:16; 6:12; 9:18, 29; 11:1) and for his disciples (11:2-4, 9-13; 22:40, 46). He notes prayers of adoration and thanksgiving (10:21) and intercession (22:31-32). In fact, Luke, uniquely among the four Gospels, employs prayer parables to stress the importance of persevering in prayer (11:5-8; 18:1-8) and to urge the need for humility in the presence of God (18:9-14). In addition, praising God is an important dimension of prayer (2:20; 19:37; 24:53; Acts 2:47; 3:9). Luke continues to stress the vital place of prayer in Acts (1:14; 2:42, 47; 4:24-31; 6:4, 6; 10:9; 13:3; 14:23; 16:25; 20:36; 28:8). Prayer also plays an essential role in advancing the Kingdom of God (e.g., 6:12-13; 11:2; Acts 1:14; 4:24-31; 12:12; 13:2-3; 21:5). For more on the place of prayer in Lukan thought, see Trites 1978. For prayer in Jesus' life, see Spencer 1990. For nontechnical, general studies of prayer in the NT, see Coggan 1970 and Fisher 1964.

1:14 You will have great joy. Luke's vocabulary of joy is quite rich. "Joy" (*chara* [TG5479, ZG5915]) is often mentioned (1:14; 2:10; 8:13; 10:17; 15:7, 10; 24:41, 52; Acts 8:8; 12:14; 13:52; 15:3), and "rejoicing" (*agalliasis* [TG20, ZG21]) is noted in 1:14, 44. The verb *agalliaō* [TG21½1A, ZG22] is used (1:47; 10:21; Acts 2:26; 16:34), as is the verb *chairō* [TG5463/5463A, ZG5897] (1:14; 6:23; 10:20; 13:17; 15:5, 32; 19:6, 37; Acts 5:41; 8:39; 11:23; 13:48; 15:31). People also "rejoice together" (*sungchairō* [TG4796/4796A, ZG5176], 1:58; 15:6, 9). See also NIDNTT 2:352-354; Morrice 1985.

COMMENTARY

As noted in the Introduction, Luke was deeply interested in the role of angels. This is the first of many appearances of angels in Luke–Acts, and it is a notable one. The angel's name is Gabriel (1:19), one of only two angels specifically identified in the Bible (see Dan 8:16; 9:21; Michael is the other angel mentioned in Scripture; see Dan 10:13, 21; Jude 1:9; Rev 12:7). While some noncanonical Jewish books have extensive treatments of angels (e.g., *1 Enoch* 37–71), the biblical writings are remarkably restrained in their teaching on the place of angels. One of the angels' main functions is to communicate messages from God and offer reassurance of divine favor, as is the case with Zechariah. In the process of communication, however, the angel had to allay the fear that overwhelmed Zechariah and reassure him of God's favor: "Don't be afraid, Zechariah! God has heard your prayer. Your wife, Elizabeth, will give you a son" (1:13).

A number of features shared with other biblical appearances of angels may be noted here. First, fear is a common human reaction to an angelic message in the Bible (cf. 1:30; Judg 6:22-23; 13:22; Matt 1:20). Second, the angel's message was an answer to prayer (cf. Dan 10:12). The repeated petitions of this godly man and his wife were at last to be answered. This theme of a prayer-hearing and prayer-answering God will be repeated in Luke: "I tell you, keep on asking, and you will receive what you ask for. Keep on seeking, and you will find. Keep on knocking, and the door will be opened to you" (11:9). Remarkable answers to prayer are also found in Acts; to take but one instance, the earnest, united prayer of believers for courage was answered by God's filling them with the Holy Spirit and enabling them to speak for Christ with great boldness (Acts 4:24-31). Additionally, the angel, who was located significantly on the right side of the altar (1:11), in the place of power, was charged with the task of reassuring a mortal, a feature also found in the Old Testament (Gen 21:17; cf. 1:30; 2:10). The angel revealed the name of the child, a feature that is repeated later in the annunciation to Mary (1:31).

It is noteworthy that John's name means "the Lord is gracious," so the name here as elsewhere in the Bible is a pointer to the significance of the person in holy history (cf. Hos 1:6, 9; Matt 1:21). John's place in salvation history is wonderfully described—the angel declares that he "will be great in the eyes of the Lord" (1:15). In the angel's message, the note of joy that is so characteristic of Luke's writings is sounded. The reproach of childlessness would be taken away, and the old priest was encouraged by the news that "many will rejoice at his birth" (1:14). But that is not all. A number of other remarkable features of John's career are outlined in Gabriel's message. For example, John was to take a Nazirite vow of total abstinence from alcoholic drinks (1:15; cf. Num 6:1-21). In his case, this was to be a lifelong commitment, like that of Samson and Samuel (Judg 13:4-7; 1 Sam 1:11), each of whom had functioned as a powerful leader of the people of God in testing times. For his special ministry, John was to be endued with the Holy Spirit, "even before his birth" (1:15; cf. Jer 1:5). He was to exercise an important prophetic role in leading a national back-to-God movement, and large numbers of people would respond to his call.

Luke will discuss John's itinerant ministry in some detail later (3:1-19). His ministry summoned people to make a clear-cut confession of sin, repent of all known evil, and turn to God. The genuineness of one's response was to be indicated by submission to baptism at John's hands. Thus, John's task was to prepare the way for the Lord's coming (1:17), a role that Luke saw foreshadowed in Elijah's life and predicted in the prophets (3:4-6; cf. Isa 40:3-5). The ministry of Elijah is particularly helpful in describing the character of the prophetic ministry of John. It was Elijah who had issued a dramatic challenge to the people of God in the face of a militant paganism (1 Kgs 18:21-40). John the Baptizer was to fulfill a similar prophetic role in calling God's people back to their covenant with God. John was not Elijah revived from the dead, but his ministry was to be characterized by a similar prophetic earnestness, a passion for reformation, and a forthright denunciation of ungodliness. His ministry was to be, in reality, a fulfillment of Malachi's prophecy: "Look, I am sending you the prophet Elijah before the great and dreadful day of the LORD arrives. His preaching will turn the hearts of fathers to their children, and the hearts of children to their fathers" (Mal 4:5-6). The angel predicted John's effectiveness: "He will turn many Israelites to the Lord their God. . . . He will turn the hearts of the fathers to their children [see Mal 4:5-6], and he will cause those who are rebellious to accept the wisdom of the godly" (1:16-17). The whole angelic declaration underscores the unique and irreplaceable part John was to have in the plan of God as the forerunner of the Messiah (1:13-17).

◆ 4. Zechariah's response (1:18-22)

[18]Zechariah said to the angel, "How can I be sure this will happen? I'm an old man now, and my wife is also well along in years."

[19]Then the angel said, "I am Gabriel! I stand in the very presence of God. It was he who sent me to bring you this good news! [20]But now, since you didn't believe what I said, you will be silent and unable to speak until the child is born. For my words will certainly be fulfilled at the proper time."

[21]Meanwhile, the people were waiting for Zechariah to come out of the sanctuary, wondering why he was taking so long. [22]When he finally did come out, he couldn't speak to them. Then they realized from his gestures and his silence that he must have seen a vision in the sanctuary.

NOTES

1:19 *this good news.* For further background, see R. E. Brown 1986.

1:20 *my words will certainly be fulfilled.* The angel's "good news" (1:19) would be fulfilled, for God keeps his promises and honors his commitments, an important theme in Luke–Acts. Note the use of the verb "fulfill" (*plēroō* [TG4137, ZG4444]) in 1:20; 4:21; 21:22; 22:16; 24:44; Acts 1:16; 3:18.

1:22 *they realized.* The verb *epiginōskō* [TG1921, ZG2105], used here, involves clear recognition and true knowledge (cf. 5:22; 23:7; 24:16, 31).

his gestures. The verb *dianeuō* [TG1269, ZG1377] (nod), which appears only here in the NT, is used twice in the LXX, both times in reference to winking (Ps 34[35]:19; Sir 27:22). How Zechariah nodded or beckoned to the people is not stated, but the fact that he was rendered "mute" (*kōphos* [TG2974, ZG3273]) is emphatically declared.

a vision. Zechariah had seen a "vision" (*optasia* [TG3701, ZG3965]), a word often applied to a supernatural encounter in the NT and LXX. Abraham (Gen 15:1), Moses (Exod 3:2-3), Samuel (1 Sam 3:2-15), Daniel (Dan 9:23; 10:1, 7-8, 16), Peter (Acts 10:9-12), Paul (Acts 26:19; 2 Cor 12:1), and the women at the empty tomb after the Resurrection (24:23) are all reported as having experienced visions.

COMMENTARY

The consternation and bewilderment of the old priest are understandable and certainly have biblical parallels. Zechariah, like Abraham, Gideon, and Hezekiah, asked God for a sign (Gen 15:8; Judg 6:17; 2 Kgs 20:8; cf. 1 Cor 1:22). However, in Zechariah's case, he was subjected to divine discipline because of his unbelief (1:20). Abraham's wife Sarah had similarly doubted God's promise in patriarchal times: "Can an old woman like me have a baby?" (Gen 18:13). She, too, was rebuked in a forceful way by means of a rhetorical question: "Is anything too hard for the Lord?" (Gen 18:14). The divine promise of a son to Sarah was fulfilled, and in due course Elizabeth, too, would conceive and bear the promised son. The angel's "good news" to Zechariah would also be fulfilled (1:20). Gabriel, who is the bearer of the message, had privileged knowledge of the divine intentions, for he stood "in the very presence of God" (1:19). Incredulity must be duly punished, and therefore Zechariah was struck with muteness until the promised child was born. God's words, communicated by this authoritative heavenly messenger, would be fulfilled "at the proper time" (1:20). God's purposes were destined to triumph despite the faltering faith of an old man!

Zechariah's protracted delay was perplexing to the people who had been praying outside the Holy Place. As he tarried, they kept on "wondering" (imperfect tense in 1:21). The Talmud remarks that the priests were accustomed to returning soon to prevent anxiety on the part of the people. It was believed that a priest might incur divine judgment in such a sacred environment and possibly die (Lev 16:13). When Zechariah finally appeared, his inability to speak made it impossible for him to pronounce the traditional Aaronic blessing (Num 6:24-26), for which the people had been waiting. His agitated manner and enforced silence suggested that something unusual had happened. His repeated gestures convinced them that he had "seen a vision in the sanctuary" (1:22).

Such divine visions were not unknown in Israel's history—note, for instance, the visions of Abraham (Gen 15:1-17), Amos (Amos 7:1-9; 8:1-3), and Daniel (Dan 7). One of the most famous of them was Isaiah's, when he "saw the Lord" in the Temple and experienced God's cleansing and a call to service (Isa 6:1-8). Ezekiel was another prophet who "saw visions of God" (Ezek 1:1; 10:1-7; 37:1-14), and he, too, was called and commissioned (Ezek 2:1–3:27). Now, once again, God was speaking to his servant and disclosing his will for a coming great prophet who was to herald the advent of the Messiah.

◆   5. The conception of John the Baptist (1:23-25)

23When Zechariah's week of service in the Temple was over, he returned home. 24Soon afterward his wife, Elizabeth, became pregnant and went into seclusion for five months. 25"How kind the Lord is!" she exclaimed. "He has taken away my disgrace of having no children."

NOTES

1:23 *service in the Temple.* The word *leitourgia* [TG3009, ZG3311], used here, was often employed in classical Gr. to describe public service rendered at the expense of the citizen. In biblical Gr., as Alfred Plummer has noted (1896:18), it is used, as in this instance, "of priestly service in the worship of God" (see Num 8:22; 16:9; 18:4; 2 Chr 31:2) and "also of service to the needy" (2 Cor 9:12; Phil 2:30). Paul also used this word in urging Christians to present their lives as living sacrifices to God, which is their priestly service (Rom 12:1). For a helpful treatment, see EDNT 2.347-349.

COMMENTARY

Priests were on duty for one week every six months. Zechariah completed his week's service at the Temple as part of the division of Abijah (1:5) and returned home. While it was common for many priests to live on Ophel, Jerusalem's hill just south of the Temple mount, Zechariah's home was located in an unspecified town in the hill country of Judea (1:39-40). Tradition has associated Zechariah with the town Ein Karem, a suburb on the southern outskirts of Jerusalem. It was at this time that Elizabeth conceived her son in accordance with the divine promise given by Gabriel. At the beginning of her pregnancy, she "went into seclusion for five months" (1:24), not wishing to hear any more reproaches for her supposed condition; after that, it would be clear to all that the Lord had taken away her barrenness. As she pondered God's dealings with her, Elizabeth reflected on his gracious intervention and praised him for his kindness. The living God had removed the stigma of childlessness, and her heart was full of joy, thanksgiving, and gratitude for the goodness of God.

◆   B. The Birth of Jesus Foretold (1:26-38)

26In the sixth month of Elizabeth's pregnancy, God sent the angel Gabriel to Nazareth, a village in Galilee, 27to a virgin named Mary. She was engaged to be married to a man named Joseph, a descendant of King David. 28Gabriel appeared to her and said, "Greetings, favored woman! The Lord is with you!"

²⁹Confused and disturbed, Mary tried to think what the angel could mean. ³⁰"Don't be afraid, Mary," the angel told her, "for you have found favor with God! ³¹You will conceive and give birth to a son, and you will name him Jesus. ³²He will be very great and will be called the Son of the Most High. The Lord God will give him the throne of his ancestor David. ³³And he will reign over Israel* forever; his Kingdom will never end!"

³⁴Mary asked the angel, "But how can this happen? I am a virgin."

³⁵The angel replied, "The Holy Spirit will come upon you, and the power of the Most High will overshadow you. So the baby to be born will be holy, and he will be called the Son of God. ³⁶What's more, your relative Elizabeth has become pregnant in her old age! People used to say she was barren, but she's now in her sixth month. ³⁷For nothing is impossible with God.*"

³⁸Mary responded, "I am the Lord's servant. May everything you have said about me come true." And then the angel left her.

1:28 Some manuscripts add *Blessed are you among women.* **1:33** Greek *over the house of Jacob.* **1:37** Some manuscripts read *For the word of God will never fail.*

NOTES

1:26 *God sent the angel Gabriel.* Gabriel, according to Jewish tradition, served as one of the three angels who made known to Abraham the birth of Isaac (Gen 18:1-15). Gabriel is mentioned in Dan 8:16; 9:21 and gave Daniel "insight and understanding" about the coming of the Messiah (Dan 9:20-27). In the intertestamental period, he was pictured as one of the archangels or "angels of the presence" who were depicted as standing before God to offer service and present "the prayers of the saints" (Tob 12:15; *Jubilees* 2:2; 1QH 6:13).

1:28 *Greetings, favored woman!* The Vulgate, the ancient translation of the Scriptures into Latin, rendered the angel's words of address to Mary as *Ave, Maria,* meaning "Hail, Mary." Since the Vulgate was the Western church's principal version of the Bible for a thousand years, this translation has been widely influential in fostering the practice of addressing prayers to Mary as the one who bestows grace upon the faithful. However, the Gr. words simply greet Mary in the traditional way, "Greetings!" (*chaire* [TG5463, ZG5897]; cf. Acts 15:23), and acknowledge that she is the *recipient,* not the *dispenser,* of grace. This is clear from the use of the perfect passive participle *kecharitōmenē* [TG5487, ZG5923]. Note the perceptive comment of Fitzmyer (1989:74): "Mary has been shown favor, being chosen to be this Son's mother. Yet she is not only 'the mother of [the] Lord' (1:43), but the one first depicted as a 'believer,' with all the doubts and anguish that that relationship to him will always entail." On the broader subject, see R. E. Brown (1977) for a complete discussion of the infancy narratives in Matthew and Luke.

1:32 *Son of the Most High.* "Most High" is a commonly used title of God in both the OT and the NT (1:32, 35, 76; 6:35; 8:28; Gen 14:18-20; 2 Sam 22:14; Pss 46:4; 91:1; Dan 3:26; Acts 7:48; 16:17; Heb 7:1). The title "Son of the Most High" can mean two things, one pointing to the divine Son of God and the other referring to the Messiah born in time. Luke 1:32-33 clearly highlights the messianic role of the promised Deliverer. Jesus is challenged as the "Son of God" in Luke's temptation account (4:3, 9), and the demons recognize him as "the Son of God" before they are silenced (4:41). Jesus was acclaimed by the heavenly voice at the Transfiguration as "my Son, my Chosen One" (9:35). When asked about this point-blank by the Jewish council, he accepted the claim as true (22:70), though his perceived claim to be "God's Messiah, the Chosen One," is challenged by the leaders and the crowd at his crucifixion (23:35). In Acts, Paul preaches in the synagogues that Jesus is "the Son of God" (Acts 9:20). See also EDNT 3.409-410, which provides a concise summary of the NT use of "most high": "the 13 occurrences of *hupsistos* [TG5310/A/B, ZG5736] refer to God (9 times) and to the heavens (4 times). Outside of Mark 5:7 and Heb 7:1, *hupsistos* as a designation for God is limited to the Lukan dual work."

1:33 *his Kingdom will never end!* See note on 4:43.

1:35 *the baby to be born.* On the birth narrative, see R. E. Brown 1977 and the literature cited in DJG (74). On the Virgin Birth, see Machen 1930; Boslooper 1962; R. E. Brown 1973; Cranfield 1988.

1:36 *your relative Elizabeth.* The question of whether Elizabeth was Mary's aunt, cousin, or other relative cannot be determined with certainty. However, Luke did not employ here the Gr. word that is used elsewhere to describe John Mark's relation to Barnabas as his "cousin" (*anepsios* [TG431, ZG463]; Col 4:10). Here, the unusual noun *sungenis* [TG4773.1, ZG5151] (found only here in the NT) is a word simply meaning "relative." Since the exact relation is unspecified, the translation "relative" (NLT, CEV, TEV, NIV) or "kinswoman" (JB, RSV, REB) is quite adequate.

1:37 *nothing is impossible with God.* The angel Gabriel stated a great theological truth that is often mentioned in the Bible (Gen 18:14; Isa 40:26-29; Jer 32:17, 27; Matt 19:26; Mark 14:36). God is sovereign, the Creator of "heaven and earth, the sea, and everything in them" (Acts 14:15), and he is in charge of the world and everything in it (Pss 24:1-2; 89:11; Acts 4:24). God is able to make the barren woman conceive (Gen 18:14; 1 Sam 1:19-20).

COMMENTARY

The next angelic visit took place in Galilee rather than Jerusalem. Gabriel was sent to Nazareth, a rather unpretentious village in Galilee (cf. the skeptical remark of Nathanael about Nazareth in John 1:46). The angel came to visit Mary, who is twice described as a virgin (*parthenos* [TG3933, ZG4221]). Mary was engaged to Joseph, "a descendant of King David" (1:27), and thus connected with the royal family, from which the Messiah was to come (cf. 2 Sam 7:8-16). In those days, betrothal was a more serious commitment than it is today, and the tie could only be broken by a formal decree of divorce. One can understand the reluctance of Joseph, being an honorable man, to go through with the intended marriage when he learned that Mary was expecting a child—a point mentioned in Matthew 1:19-25. This angelic visitation is often termed "the Annunciation," for it was a tremendous announcement.

Not surprisingly, Mary, like Zechariah, was afraid, confused, and distressed by the angel's message (see the commentary on 1:11-17). This same heavenly figure who had comforted and instructed Zechariah now informed Mary that she was to be uniquely blessed: "You will conceive and give birth to a son, and you will name him Jesus" (1:31, the name meaning "Savior"; cf. Matt 1:21). Like his predecessor, John the Baptist, Jesus would be a truly great person in holy history; in fact, he would be called both "Son of the Most High" and "Son of God," titles that would be meaningful to Luke's readers and that indicate a definite and special relationship to God (1:32, 35). His destiny was to receive from God "the throne of his ancestor David" (1:32); as Messiah, his rule over Israel would be an everlasting one (1:33; cf. 1 Cor 15:24-28; Rev 11:15).

Quite naturally, Mary queried the method God would use to accomplish this grandiose plan. She had not been married, so it was very difficult for her to understand how she could become pregnant under these circumstances and serve as the mother of the long-promised Messiah. She was not unwilling to be an instrument of the divine purpose (1:38), but she was honestly perplexed about the manner of its accomplishment.

The angel offered the frightened girl much-needed reassurance. She was comforted by the words "the Lord is with you!" (1:28). Note similar words given by an angel to Gideon (Judg 6:12) and comparable divine messages given to Joshua and David (Josh 1:5; 1 Sam 10:7; cf. 24:4-8; Matt 28:5). In fact, the angel insisted that Mary had "found favor with God!" (1:30). The promise of the Virgin Birth is related with a sense of reverence and mystery: "The Holy Spirit will come upon you, and the power of the Most High will overshadow you. So the baby to be born will be holy" (1:35). The instrumentality of the Holy Spirit is prominent here, and the holiness of the Christ child is asserted. The Word was indeed becoming flesh (John 1:1-5, 14).

Reviewing the annunciations to Zechariah and Mary, it is evident that they share many common features. The same angel (Gabriel) addressed both Zechariah and Mary. Zechariah and Mary were both addressed personally by name. Both were frightened by the angel's appearance before them. Both received reassurance of God's favor toward them, and both were promised a son. In the message each received, each was told that the promised son would be great in the eyes of the Lord, and each was informed as to what the promised child's name would be. Interestingly, both were given a sign (muteness for Zechariah, word of Elizabeth's pregnancy for Mary). Clearly, in both cases, the child's conception involved the special intervention of God, and the activity of the Holy Spirit is prominently noted. In both cases, the angel made an appropriate statement before departing. In each instance, there was an expectation that the revelation was true and would be fulfilled.

The first annunciation, however, was really a stepping-stone for the second. As Luke's Gospel makes unmistakably clear, John's role was subservient to that of Jesus. John was the forerunner, while Jesus was the long-expected Messiah. The one annunciation was the preparation for the other, and the interweaving of the destinies of the two men was signaled before either was born by the interaction of the two expectant mothers (1:39-45). Elizabeth acknowledged the superior honor that had been given to Mary and acclaimed her as "the mother of my Lord" (1:43). As Zechariah's prophecy makes clear, John's task was to "prepare the way for the Lord" (1:76). He would clear the path for the greater one—the Messiah (3:16).

◆ C. Mary Visits Elizabeth (1:39-45)

³⁹A few days later Mary hurried to the hill country of Judea, to the town ⁴⁰where Zechariah lived. She entered the house and greeted Elizabeth. ⁴¹At the sound of Mary's greeting, Elizabeth's child leaped within her, and Elizabeth was filled with the Holy Spirit.

⁴²Elizabeth gave a glad cry and exclaimed to Mary, "God has blessed you above all women, and your child is blessed. ⁴³Why am I so honored, that the mother of my Lord should visit me? ⁴⁴When I heard your greeting, the baby in my womb jumped for joy. ⁴⁵You are blessed because you believed that the Lord would do what he said."

NOTES

1:39 *Mary hurried.* Whether Mary traveled alone and whether it was safe for Mary to travel alone or not, we do not know, for the text is silent about these matters. However, it is evident that "Mary lost no time in paying a visit to her kinswoman. Gabriel visited her in Elizabeth's sixth month (v. 36), and she returned home after a visit of about three months (v. 56), apparently before the birth of John. She must have therefore set out almost immediately after the angel's visit" (Morris 1974:74).

1:41 *Elizabeth's child leaped within her.* Luke is the only NT author to use the verb *skirtaō* [TG4640, ZG5015]; it speaks of "leaping" or "springing about" as a sign of joy, just as lambs skip about gaily (cf. Mal 4:2 [3:20], LXX). It occurs three times: John the Baptist is twice said to "leap" in the womb of his mother with joy at the coming of the Messiah (1:41, 44), and in Luke's record of the Beatitudes, Christians who have experienced hatred, exclusion, mocking, and cursing for their faith are told to "be happy!" and "leap for joy!" (6:23). Regarding the relationship between Mary and Elizabeth, see note on 1:36.

1:42 *Elizabeth gave a glad cry.* The verb *anaphōneō* [TG400, ZG430] is used only here in the NT; it is sometimes used in the LXX in contexts of worship and praise (1 Chr 15:28; 16:4-5, 42; 2 Chr 5:13). The theme of joy is certainly prominent in these nativity stories.

God has blessed you above all women, and your child is blessed. The language of blessing often appears in Luke's writing (*eulogeō* [TG2127, ZG2328], "praise, bless"). Zechariah and Simeon "bless" God (1:64; 2:28). Jesus "blesses" the loaves and fish and, later, the bread at Emmaus (9:16; 24:30). Christians are instructed to "bless" those who curse them (6:28). The Messiah is hailed as "blessed" in his entry into Jerusalem (19:38). The Gospel closes with Jesus lifting up his hands to bless his followers as he is taken up into heaven (24:50-51). On their return to Jerusalem, the disciples stay continually at the Temple, blessing or praising God (24:53). In the book of Acts, Peter recalls God's promise to Abraham that through his offspring all families on earth would be blessed and then notes that God, having raised his servant (Jesus), sent him to Israel first to "bless you by turning each of you back from your sinful ways" (Acts 3:25-26). In Luke's eyes, the Christian message is clearly associated with blessing. For more detail, see EDNT 2.79-80.

1:45 *blessed because you believed.* Faith is an important issue in Luke's Gospel. He references it often, showing positive and negative examples of people struggling with faith and implicitly inviting the reader to believe and be blessed (1:20; 1:45; 8:12; 8:50; 22:67; 24:25). The same recognition of the place of faith is found in Acts (Acts 4:4, 32; 5:14; 8:12; 9:42; 10:43; 11:17; 16:31, 34). Faith is an essential element in the correct response to God (Heb 11:6).

COMMENTARY

In this little vignette, we have a wonderful glimpse of Luke the artist, who succeeded in painting an unforgettable picture of the encounter of two women whose sons were to have vital roles in bringing God's salvation into history. This charming story serves to historically connect the two special births that the angel Gabriel announced to Zechariah and Mary. The mothers of John and Jesus met at Mary's initiative and shared their joy (a Lukan theme). Mary would have traveled three or four days to get from Nazareth to the hill country of Judea. She must have regarded the visit as a matter of urgency and importance, since verse 39 makes note of her haste (see note on 1:39).

Elizabeth, for her part, welcomed Mary's visit and expressed her sense of privilege at the coming of Mary, "the mother of my Lord" (1:43). Like her husband,

Zechariah (1:67), Elizabeth was filled with the Holy Spirit and was enabled to prophesy, exclaiming to Mary, "God has blessed you above all women, and your child is blessed" (1:41-42, echoing the angel's words to Mary in 1:28). The gift of prophecy is also mentioned in 2:36 in reference to Anna, and there are similar references to women prophesying in Acts, where it is noted as having been predicted in Scripture and practiced in the early church (Acts 2:17-18; 21:9).

Elizabeth served as a witness to the greatness of Jesus and to his superiority to John. An interesting feature of the story is the prenatal joy of the unborn John, who "jumped for joy" at the arrival of Mary, the mother of Jesus (1:44; cf. 1:41). Elizabeth also recognized Mary's faith that "the Lord would do what he said" (1:45). By contrast, Elizabeth's husband had been punished with muteness because he hadn't believed the angel's words (1:20).

Elizabeth openly recognized that Mary had been signally "blessed" by God (1:42). Elizabeth herself is presented in an admirable light as a devout person who was sensitive to God's plan, full of joy at the kindness of God in answering prayer, and generous in her recognition of the special place given to Mary, her relative (see note on 1:36). Elizabeth acknowledged Mary's more exalted role in salvation history and expressed joy at Mary's arrival (1:43). Elizabeth was subsequently to give birth to John the Baptist, Jesus' forerunner, who gave prenatal recognition to Jesus, the promised Messiah (1:44). Later, in his public ministry, John would recognize and proclaim the superiority of Jesus (3:16; Matt 3:11; Mark 1:7; John 1:26-27; Acts 13:25).

◆ D. The Magnificat: Mary's Song of Praise (1:46-56)

46Mary responded,

"Oh, how my soul praises the Lord.
47   How my spirit rejoices in God my
            Savior!
48 For he took notice of his lowly servant
            girl,
      and from now on all generations
            will call me blessed.
49 For the Mighty One is holy,
      and he has done great things for me.
50 He shows mercy from generation to
            generation
      to all who fear him.
51 His mighty arm has done tremendous
            things!
      He has scattered the proud and
            haughty ones.

52 He has brought down princes from
            their thrones
      and exalted the humble.
53 He has filled the hungry with good
            things
      and sent the rich away with empty
            hands.
54 He has helped his servant Israel
      and remembered to be merciful.
55 For he made this promise to our
            ancestors,
      to Abraham and his children
            forever."

56Mary stayed with Elizabeth about three months and then went back to her own home.

NOTES

1:46 *how my soul praises the Lord.* On Mary's song of praise, see DJG 525-526; Farris 1985; Keck and Martyn 1966:111-130. The verb *megalunō* [TG3170, ZG3486] (make large) is used here metaphorically to mean "exalt, praise, glorify" (cf. Acts 10:46).

1:47 my spirit rejoices in God my Savior! The verb *agalliaō* [TG21, ZG22] is employed in Mary's song to indicate that her spirit "exults" or "rejoices" in God (the cognate noun *agalliasis* [TG20, ZG21] is used in 1:44 to describe John's prenatal "joy"); it is also used of Jesus' rejoicing when the disciples returned and reported on their mission (10:21). Mary's reference to God as "Savior" is a familiar biblical designation (2 Sam 22:3, 47; Ps 24:5; Isa 45:21; Mic 7:7; 1 Tim 2:3; Titus 2:10; 3:4). Jesus is also described in many places in the NT as "Savior" (2:11; John 4:42; Acts 5:31; Titus 1:4; 2 Pet 1:1, 11; 1 John 4:14).

1:50 He shows mercy. "Mercy" (*eleos* [TG1656, ZG1799]) is often mentioned in Luke's Gospel, and there are several notable examples in the near context. Divine mercy extends to those who "fear" or reverence God (1:50). Elizabeth's neighbors and relatives were aware that the Lord had shown her great mercy (1:58). Zechariah's prophecy celebrated the fact that God, in the past, had provided mercy for his ancestors and was about to display that tender mercy again (1:72, 78). Several times later in the Gospel, people ask for mercy (16:24; 17:11-13; 18:38-39), and the Good Samaritan also exemplifies this trait, being the one who showed mercy to the wounded man (10:37). Luke saw mercy as commendable in people and as indispensable to the character of God (EDNT 2:429-431).

1:51 His mighty arm. The arm (*brachiōn* [TG1023, ZG1098]) of God is a symbol of his divine power.

COMMENTARY

Mary's song of praise is the first of four hymns that Luke includes in the nativity stories. The first hymn, called the Magnificat, derives its name from the first word of Mary's song in the Latin Vulgate and means "glorifies." This magnificent hymn is a wonderful example of Jewish piety and poetry and highlights God's power, holiness, and mercy. For centuries, it has had a significant place in Christian worship. It is used, for example, in the Anglican tradition in the service of evening prayer and is often sung with a choir in a beautiful musical rendition. Mary's song is a winsome, moving expression of trust and devotion.

In the opening words, Mary offers praise and "rejoices in God" her "Savior," the one who intervenes to deliver and rescue his people (1:47). She exults in God's gracious condescension to use her, however weak and lowly, as the privileged instrument of the divine purpose. She was conscious of her unique role in holy history (1:48). She knew that God had acted powerfully in her life and acknowledged that "he has done great things for me" (1:49). These blessings were received with thankfulness and humility, for God is "the Mighty One," while she was only "his lowly servant" (1:48-49).

Mary expressed complete confidence in God's mercy—the divine, undeserved kindness offered to those who respect and reverence God and live in accordance with his will (1:50). Mary's assertions in verses 51-53 have special importance because they introduce the themes of social concern and reversal of roles in Luke's Gospel (Fitzmyer 1989:67). She believed that her almighty and sovereign God was able to topple the powerful and exalt the humble (1:52). Her statement "He has helped his servant Israel and remembered to be merciful" (1:54) echoes Micah 7:20, where the prophet declares, "You will show us your faithfulness and unfailing love as you promised to our ancestors Abraham and Jacob long ago." Mary had clearly placed her entire trust in God's loyalty to the covenant; she believed in his wonderful divine faithfulness to the people of God.

The hymn of Mary has much in common with Hannah's prayer in 1 Samuel 2:1-10. Hannah, too, had been barren until God intervened and gave her a child. As a jubilant mother, she rejoiced, offered personal thanksgiving for the blessing of a child, and affirmed God's control over human life and history and divine victory over enemies. God is the God of surprises and reversals. Both hymns exalt a God who vindicates the poor and takes care of the hungry. Hannah spoke of the poor being raised up to sit with the rulers, while Mary spoke of the rulers being toppled from their thrones. Mary's hymn celebrates God's providential activity and intervention in the affairs of the world, the life of Israel, and Mary's own life. God is the one who acts to fulfill sacred promises to the people of God (1:55). God is clearly powerful, for God's "mighty arm has done tremendous things!" (1:51). God is concerned for those who are hungry, both physically and spiritually (1:53), and divine intervention is able to bring down the rich, the proud, and the haughty (1:51-53). God is the God of the upside-down kingdom, who stands everything on its head! Thus, it is not surprising that the Magnificat has spoken so powerfully to people in parts of the world where suffering and oppression are most grievous, as R. M. Brown has pointed out (1984:74-82). Here, the hope of God's promised liberation has been richly nurtured!

This beautiful hymn gives expression to many themes that will reappear in Luke–Acts: (1) the note of joy and praise; (2) divine compassion and concern for the poor and the lowly; (3) the danger of wealth, riches, power, and arrogance; (4) the place of women in the plan of God; (5) confidence in God's willingness and power to keep promises; and (6) the sense that God has a purpose that is in the process of being worked out in history and will ultimately be fulfilled in God's own time and way.

The passage closes with a mention of the length of Mary's visit. She spent three months with Elizabeth (1:56). A comparison of 1:56-57 with 1:26 suggests that Mary remained there until just before the birth of John the Baptist.

◆   E. The Birth of John the Baptist (1:57-66)

57When it was time for Elizabeth's baby to be born, she gave birth to a son. 58And when her neighbors and relatives heard that the Lord had been very merciful to her, everyone rejoiced with her.

59When the baby was eight days old, they all came for the circumcision ceremony. They wanted to name him Zechariah, after his father. 60But Elizabeth said, "No! His name is John!"

61"What?" they exclaimed. "There is no one in all your family by that name." 62So they used gestures to ask the baby's father what he wanted to name him. 63He motioned for a writing tablet, and to everyone's surprise he wrote, "His name is John." 64Instantly Zechariah could speak again, and he began praising God.

65Awe fell upon the whole neighborhood, and the news of what had happened spread throughout the Judean hills. 66Everyone who heard about it reflected on these events and asked, "What will this child turn out to be?" For the hand of the Lord was surely upon him in a special way.

NOTES

1:59 *they all came for the circumcision ceremony.* Circumcision was an ancient Jewish rite that involved cutting off the foreskin of a male's penis. While it was practiced by other nations (Jer 9:25-26), it had a special meaning for the Jewish people. It served as the sign of the covenant that God made with Abraham (Gen 17:9-14). It was a pointer to God's claim upon the chosen people (Ezek 44:6-7). Normally, the rite was performed on the eighth day after birth, as is the case with John here (Gen 17:12; 21:4; Acts 7:8). It is note-worthy that baptism, the rite that came to mark initiation into the Christian community, was intended for women as well as men, while the old Jewish rite had been restricted to the male sex (Acts 8:12; Gal 3:27-28). For further information, see Bevere (2000:256); Thielman (1994:119-144); Cohen (1989).

1:66 *the hand of the Lord was surely upon him in a special way.* For a similar emphasis on the gracious hand of God in the OT, see Ezra 7:6, 9, 28; 8:18, 31; Neh 2:8.

COMMENTARY

The promised child was born to Elizabeth and Zechariah amid great rejoicing. The baby boy was welcomed as an answer to prayer and the fulfillment of the promise made by the angel Gabriel. Elizabeth's friends and relatives shared her joy, and there was a general recognition by her neighbors and relatives of the gracious hand of God in the whole process.

In due course, the baby was circumcised in keeping with the Jewish law (Gen 17; Exod 12:48; Lev 12:3). In spite of attempts by well-meaning folk to have him called Zechariah after his father, Elizabeth refused, declaring bluntly, "No! His name is John!" (1:60). While John was not a traditional family name, both parents vigor-ously insisted on it. In those days, it was common to name a son after his father. The speechless Zechariah was assumed to be deaf, so the folk applying the pressure for the use of his name tried to communicate with him by making "gestures" (1:62). After calling for the use of a writing tablet that was probably a wooden board with a recess that held wax in which marks could be made and erased (NBD 1266), Zecha-riah wrote plainly, "His name is John" (1:63). At that moment, his dumbness ended, and the old priest "began praising God" (1:64), a theme often observed in Luke (2:13-14; 17:15; 24:53).

The marked impression that John's birth made upon "the whole neighborhood" was noted by Luke (1:65). The news spread rapidly throughout the Judean hills, causing people to ponder these events and ask what they meant. The level of spiri-tual expectation was definitely raised (cf. 3:15), and the stage was being set for the forerunner's future work in preparing the way for the Messiah (cf. 3:4-6).

Once again, a number of Lukan themes may be noted: (1) the note of joy, here in the context of the birth of a promised child; (2) the fulfillment of God's promises to his servants; (3) the emphasis on praise (1:64; 2:13, 20; 18:43; 19:37; 24:53; Acts 2:47; 3:8-9); (4) the presence of multiple witnesses to God's mighty acts—a theme particu-larly important in Acts in attesting the death and resurrection of Jesus (24:48; Acts 2:32; 3:15; 5:32; 10:39-41; 13:31; 22:15; 26:16); and (5) the stress on the "hand of the Lord" in this event (1:66; Acts 4:30; 7:50; 11:21; 13:11; all of these passages speak liter-ally of "the hand of the Lord" active in accomplishing his divine purpose in history).

◆ F. Zechariah's Prophecy (1:67-80)

⁶⁷Then his father, Zechariah, was filled with the Holy Spirit and gave this prophecy:

⁶⁸"Praise the Lord, the God of Israel,
because he has visited and
redeemed his people.
⁶⁹He has sent us a mighty Savior*
from the royal line of his servant
David,
⁷⁰just as he promised
through his holy prophets long
ago.
⁷¹Now we will be saved from our
enemies
and from all who hate us.
⁷²He has been merciful to our ancestors
by remembering his sacred
covenant—
⁷³the covenant he swore with an oath
to our ancestor Abraham.
⁷⁴We have been rescued from our
enemies
so we can serve God without fear,

⁷⁵in holiness and righteousness
for as long as we live.

⁷⁶"And you, my little son,
will be called the prophet of the
Most High,
because you will prepare the way
for the Lord.
⁷⁷You will tell his people how to find
salvation
through forgiveness of their
sins.
⁷⁸Because of God's tender mercy,
the morning light from heaven is
about to break upon us,*
⁷⁹to give light to those who sit in
darkness and in the shadow
of death,
and to guide us to the path
of peace."
⁸⁰John grew up and became strong in
spirit. And he lived in the wilderness until
he began his public ministry to Israel.

1:69 Greek *has raised up a horn of salvation for us.* 1:78 Or *the Morning Light from Heaven is about to visit us.*

NOTES

1:67 *filled with the Holy Spirit.* Elizabeth is similarly described earlier in the chapter as "filled with the Holy Spirit" (1:41), and the angel told Zechariah that his son (John the Baptist) would be "filled with the Holy Spirit, even before his birth" (1:15). Similarly, in the book of Acts, several church leaders are said to be "full of the Holy Spirit" (Acts 6:5; 7:55; 11:24). On Zechariah's prophecy, see Farris (1985:127-142).

1:68 *he has visited and redeemed his people.* In Luke's view, the coming of Christ is a divine "visit" intended to bring blessing and salvation to those who receive it with repentance and faith. Twice in Zechariah's song, the verb *episkeptomai* [TG1980, ZG2170] (visit) is used (1:68 and 1:78, where the light from heaven is about to "break upon us"). In 7:16, the crowd also uses the word after Jesus raises a widow's son from the dead: "God has visited his people today." Similarly, in Acts, reference is made to the "time God first visited the Gentiles to take from them a people for himself" (Acts 15:14). God is thus seen in Luke–Acts as active in visiting the world in the work of Christ and his church. Later, it is said that Israel did not recognize the time of its "visitation" (cf. 19:44, where the cognate noun *episkopē* [TG1984, ZG2175] is used). Israel rejected the opportunity God offered the covenant people in Jesus, with disastrous consequences.

1:73 *he swore with an oath.* God's use of an oath as a vow is noted here, once in Acts (Acts 2:30), and in Heb 3:11, 18; 4:3; 6:13, 16; 7:20-22. On the use of oaths in the Bible, see Trites (1977:28-32).

1:80 *John grew up and became strong in spirit.* On the general use of *auxanō* [TG837, ZG889] (grow, increase) in the NT, see EDNT 1.178-179. The Gr. verb *krataioomai/krateoō* [TG2901A, ᶻᴳ3194] (become strong), found only four times in the NT (e.g., 1 Cor 16:13; Eph 3:16), is used to describe both John the Baptist and Jesus (1:80; 2:40). See also the notes on 2:40 and 2:52.

ministry. Lit. "manifestation" (*anadeixis* [ᵀᴳ323, ᶻᴳ345]); the word is found only here in the NT.

COMMENTARY

Once again, Luke presents a beautiful hymn announcing some of the great themes of salvation. As in the case of the hymns of Mary, Simeon, and the angels, there is a strong note of worship and praise. While Mary's song resembles a psalm, Zechariah's is more like a prophecy. Zechariah, like his wife Elizabeth, is described as "filled with the Holy Spirit" (1:67; cf. 1:41). In both cases, the Spirit's presence is indicated by joyful praise and prophecy.

The *Benedictus*, to use the Latin name for Zechariah's song (meaning "blessed," taken from the first word of the song in the Vulgate version), is very God centered in its orientation. Zechariah praised the God of Israel, who entered human history in a purposeful way and came to redeem his people. This deliverance involved a divine act of intervention, namely, the sending of a redeemer, literally, a "horn of salvation" (1:69). This "horn" points to the strength of the redeemer ("a deliverer of victorious power," NEB) and is a frequently used image in the Old Testament (Deut 33:17; Ps 22:21; Mic 4:13). The deliverer is said to come from David's line (cf. Matt 1:1 and the acclamation of Jesus as "Son of David" in 18:38-39), and the divine rescue operation is seen as the fulfillment of God's promises made through "his holy prophets" in earlier times (1:70; cf. 24:27; Acts 3:18-24; 10:43). God is said to be "remembering his sacred covenant" (1:72; cf. Gen 6:18; 9:15; Ps 105:8-9; 106:45) and thus keeping faith with the people of God. The covenantal commitments are being honored (cf. Gen 22:16-18), and this salvation will bring the deliverance of God's people from their enemies and empower them to serve aright in holiness and righteousness forever (1:74-75, lit. "for all our days").

Zechariah and Mary were looking for a Savior-Rescuer to deliver them from their political enemies (most notably, Rome and its minions), who would then establish a Davidic kingdom on earth (2 Sam 7:12-16; Ps 89:4, 26-37). The Jews had endured the struggles of the Maccabean years a century-and-a-half before, during which time the forces of Syria, under the tyrannical leadership of Antiochus Epiphanes, had martyred a considerable number of their patriots. (The story of the heroic resistance of the family of Mattathias to this enforced Hellenization is graphically told in the book of 1 Maccabees.)

After the Roman general Pompey entered Jerusalem with his legions and captured the city in 63 BC, the Romans were in charge. They tried to act more leniently toward their Jewish subjects, but the very privileges they extended to the Jews heightened anti-Semitism. With the exception of the aristocratic Sadducees, who collaborated with the Romans in the interest of maintaining their own political power, the Jews responded to the Romans with what has been described as "sullen contempt." Caird (1955:32) reports that in Palestine, the common people treated Rome as a scapegoat on which to load all their economic and political grievances. The grievances were real enough, for Palestine was over-populated, the Jews lived under a double system of taxation, civil and religious, and although Roman taxes were collected by reliable officials, the collection of customs was still farmed out by auction to the *publicani*, who were hated alike for their exactions and for taking service under Rome.

For Zechariah and Mary, and most of their Jewish contemporaries, then, redemption meant liberation from Rome. They were expecting a Messiah who would come "to rescue Israel" from its foreign oppressors (24:21). They did not realize what kind of Savior Jesus had become until after his death and resurrection, when Jesus explained to his disciples the intent of the Old Testament prophets that "the Messiah would have to suffer all these things before entering his glory" (24:25-27; cf. 24:44-46; Matt 26:24; 1 Pet 1:10-11). It is this concern for political emancipation that comes to expression again at the Ascension, when the apostles earnestly inquire of Jesus, "Lord, has the time come for you to free Israel and restore our kingdom?" (Acts 1:6). Though Jesus gave repeated predictions of his passion and subsequent resurrection (9:22, 44-45; 18:32-33; Matt 16:21; Mark 8:31; 9:31; 10:33-34), the disciples were very slow to grasp the import of his teaching until after his death and resurrection.

Thus, in Zechariah's prophecy, he proclaimed deliverance from the tyranny and oppression of Israel's enemies (1:71, 74), but it would not be restricted to national security and liberation. It would also include a moral and spiritual emancipation and would result in the forgiveness of their sins (1:75).

Zechariah exulted in the fact that God was going to use his son in a special capacity as "the prophet of the Most High" (contrast this designation with the superior one given to Jesus, who is called "the Son of the Most High" in 1:32). John's work is described as that of a true forerunner, who would "prepare the way for the Lord" (*kurios* [TG2962, ZG3261], here used as a title for Jesus; cf. 1:17; 3:1-6). Thus, John's task was a significant one in holy history: showing the Jewish people their need for salvation and directing the lost to the forgiveness of sins. All of this divine activity was ultimately attributable to "God's tender mercy" (1:78), and the climax was to be the advent of the rising sun, "the light from heaven," a beautiful figure of the coming Messiah (cf. similar images of a star, light, or sun in the OT: Num 24:17; Isa 9:2; 60:1; Mal 4:2). John's role was to give light to those whose lives were morally darkened and to point them to "the path of peace" (1:79; cf. 2:14; Isa 9:2). Zechariah was full of thanksgiving for the goodness and kindness of God. Not one word of the divine promise had failed!

In reviewing Zechariah's prophecy, many key notes of Lukan theology are sounded: the focus on the praise of God; the importance of the Christ event (God "has sent us a mighty Savior from the royal line of his servant David," 1:69); the fulfillment of God's promises given through the holy prophets, thus realizing the covenant made with Abraham; deliverance from enemies by the gracious intervention of God; the special role of John the Baptist in announcing the coming of the

Messiah; and the new opportunity to serve God forever, without fear, in holiness and righteousness.

The first chapter of Luke ends with a summary statement about John that will later be matched by a summary statement about Jesus (1:80; cf. 2:52). Significantly, John's early life is placed in the wilderness "until he began his public ministry to Israel." In view of the fact that John's parents were old when he was born, it is likely that they died before he was an adult; he apparently grew up in the Wilderness of Judea (cf. Matt 3:1), located between the Dead Sea and Jerusalem, probably in the general vicinity of the discovery of the Dead Sea Scrolls in 1947. Whether or not he was a member of the Qumran community is a matter of speculation and debate. In any case, John eventually launched his public ministry and appeared openly to Israel.

◆   ## G. The Birth of Jesus (2:1-7; cf. Matt 1:18-25)

At that time the Roman emperor, Augustus, decreed that a census should be taken throughout the Roman Empire. ²(This was the first census taken when Quirinius was governor of Syria.) ³All returned to their own ancestral towns to register for this census. ⁴And because Joseph was a descendant of King David, he had to go to Bethlehem in Judea, David's ancient home. He traveled there from the village of Nazareth in Galilee. ⁵He took with him Mary, his fiancée, who was now obviously pregnant.

⁶And while they were there, the time came for her baby to be born. ⁷She gave birth to her first child, a son. She wrapped him snugly in strips of cloth and laid him in a manger, because there was no lodging available for them.

NOTES

2:1 the Roman Empire. Several times, Luke used the word *oikoumenē* [TG3625, ZG3876] (from which we get our modern word *ecumenical*) to refer to "the inhabited earth, the world" (e.g., 4:5; 21:26; Acts 24:5). Sometimes, he used it to refer to the world's inhabitants, that is, humankind (Acts 17:31). Sometimes, it has specific reference to the Roman world, as here (cf. Acts 11:28; 17:6). Emperor Augustus was the nephew and adopted son of Julius Caesar.

2:2 This was the first census taken when Quirinius was governor of Syria. Publius Sulpicius Quirinius was appointed consul of Rome in 12 BC. Later, he was given the privilege of acting as tutor to Gaius Caesar (adopted son of Augustus Caesar) and accompanying him on his travels eastward. In AD 6, he was appointed legate of Syria, a position he held for a number of years. As governor of Syria, Quirinius enacted a census in AD 6 (Josephus *Antiquities* 18.26; Acts 5:37). Since Jesus was born between 6 and 4 BC, per the history of Matthew (see commentary on Matt 2:1), Luke's dating does not align with this census. In short, there must have been a previous census some 10–12 years earlier. If so, Quirinius must have also served in the governorship of Syria at that time and made a previous census.

According to F. F. Bruce, an ancient inscription describes the career of an officer whose name is not preserved but whose duties seem to describe Quirinius. This inscription says that when that man became imperial legate of Syria, he entered upon that office for a "second time." Though the wording is ambiguous, it could mean that he served in that capacity twice in Syria. If so, he could have easily instituted a census at that time (see NBD 1004).

For a careful assessment of the difficult problems posed by the mention of Quirinius and the census noted by Luke (2:1-2), see Hoehner (1977:11-27) and DJG (67-68), which says that "the upshot of all this is that Luke's reference to the census does not suggest a different date for Jesus' birth than does the Matthean evidence."

2:4 Joseph was a descendant of King David. Luke's nativity narrative stresses Joseph's genealogical connection with the Davidic monarchy, while Matthew's account highlights the conflict between King Herod and the child heralded by the magi as "the newborn king of the Jews" (Matt 2:1-12). Matthew's Gospel emphasizes the theme that Jesus is "King of the Jews" (Matt 27:11, 29, 37; note also his fondness for the "Son of David" language in Matt 9:27; 12:23; 15:22; 20:30-31; 21:9, 15; 22:42), though the use of the title is also found in the other Gospels, particularly in the passion accounts (23:3, 37-38; Mark 15:2, 9, 12, 18, 26; John 18:33, 39; 19:3, 19, 21). For a full treatment of Herod as a Jewish king, see Grant 1971.

2:7 her first child, a son. This is the sole use that Luke makes of the word "firstborn" (*prōtotokos* [TG4416, ZG4758]; Matt 1:25 refers to the infant simply as a "son"). The term is used elsewhere in the NT in several important passages that stress the unique and preeminent place of Christ in the plan and purpose of God (Rom 8:29; Col 1:15, 18; Heb 1:6; Rev 1:5). Here, the word "firstborn" signifies "nothing about Mary's subsequent childbearing; the word is more a technical term in reference to the child upon which God laid full claim (Num 3:11-13)" (Coogan 2001: NT 99).

She wrapped him snugly in strips of cloth and laid him in a manger, because there was no lodging available for them. The swaddling clothes were simply "long strips which could wrap the child round and round. That Mary wrapped the child herself points to a lonely birth" (Morris 1974:83). The accommodation facilities of little Bethlehem were stretched to the limit by the demands imposed by the Roman census (2:1-5). Traditionally, the story has told us "there was no room in the *inn*" (KJV, NKJV, NIV, NASB). However, there is another possibility, for the rare word used here (*kataluma* [TG2646, ZG2906]) might not mean an "inn" but rather a "guest room" in a house, as in 22:11 (and Mark 14:14), where it is used to describe the room where the Last Supper was held. It is thus possible that the room had been planned for Joseph and Mary but was occupied by others by the time they showed up.

COMMENTARY

The story of the birth of Jesus is told simply but powerfully. Luke places it in a large, worldwide frame; the Evangelist was interested in setting the nativity in a global context. The imperial setting was during the reign of the first emperor, Augustus Caesar (31 BC-AD 14), who was one of the most remarkable leaders Rome ever produced. Augustus (meaning "exalted," a title bestowed on him by the Roman senate in 27 BC) had replaced the republican form of government with an imperial administration embracing the entire Mediterranean world, had established the Roman peace (the famous *Pax Romana*), and had brought in a golden age in Roman architecture and literature.

Luke tells us that Quirinius was governor of Syria when the census was taken. Although there has been much debate concerning the date of this census (see note on 2:2), Brindle (1994) thinks Luke was referring to a census that occurred late in Herod the Great's reign and that preceded the well-known census of Quirinius (c. AD 6). In Brindle's view, Quirinius held office on two occasions, first from 6 to 4 BC and then from AD 6 to 9, with a census being associated with each term. The reference in the nativity account is to the first one, while Acts 5:37 speaks of the second census. This allows Luke's dating of Jesus' birth to align with the historical facts in Matthew, who places the birth of Jesus during the reign of Herod the Great, who died in 4 BC.

The census was used by Rome for both military and revenue purposes and was therefore mandatory: "All returned to their own ancestral towns to register for this census" (2:3). Though the Jews were exempt from military service, they were still required to register for purposes of taxation. In the case of the holy family, this procedure involved a three- or four-day journey from Nazareth in Galilee to Bethlehem, the ancestral home of Joseph (2:4; cf. 1:27), located about five miles south of Jerusalem in Judea. The fact that Mary was in the last stages of pregnancy would make this trip particularly arduous and uncomfortable for her.

Matthew, in his account of the nativity, saw the birth of Jesus in Bethlehem as the fulfillment of the prophecy given seven centuries earlier by the prophet Micah: "And you, O Bethlehem in the land of Judah, are not least among the ruling cities of Judah, for a ruler will come from you who will be the shepherd for my people Israel" (Matt 2:6, quoting Mic 5:2; cf. 2 Sam 5:2). The fact that the leading priests and teachers of religious law could supply this answer to the inquiring magi from the east indicates messianic expectation was well known, at least by some members of the religious establishment. The promised Messiah was to be linked with David's family and to come from David's town, Bethlehem (cf. 1 Sam 17:12, 58; 20:6). On this point both Matthew and Luke agree, though they present the nativity of Jesus quite differently in their respective accounts.

Some commentators have wondered why Mary would have accompanied Joseph, for it is questionable whether she was required to be registered. "In view of her pregnancy's full term, however, and in view of the criticism which might have been directed against her for being pregnant before her marriage, it is not surprising that she accompanied Joseph" (C. A. Evans 1990:35).

Wrapping the newborn baby in "strips of cloth" was not unusual, for this was the normal practice in infant care at the time. It is interesting that there are several references in the Lukan nativity story to a manger (2:7, 12, 16). This has "traditionally been taken to mean that Jesus was born in a stable. He might have been. But it is also possible that the birth took place in a very poor home where the animals shared the same roof as the family. A tradition going back to Justin says it occurred in a cave (*Dialogue with Trypho* 78) and this could be right. Some have thought that the birth took place in the open air (possibly the courtyard of the inn), that being where a manger would most likely be. We do not know" (Morris 1974:84). In any case, the circumstances point to Jesus' birth as taking place in poverty, obscurity, and possibly rebuff and rejection (cf. John 1:11). Thus, the lowly Son of Man entered this world in a most unpretentious way. The presence of the shepherds in Luke's nativity account is noteworthy (2:8, 15). They were considered dishonest (*b. Sanhedrin* 25b) and were viewed as "unclean according to the standards of the law. They represent the outcasts and sinners for whom Jesus came [Luke 19:10]. Such outcasts were the first recipients of the good news" (Stein 1992:108).

Tolbert sees this as theologically appropriate: "All the poor, insignificant, forgotten people of the world can gather around the manger and dare to believe that the Babe who lies there really belongs to them" (1970:29). This would fit in nicely with Luke's presentation of a Savior for all people everywhere.

◆ H. The Shepherds and Angels (2:8-20)

⁸That night there were shepherds staying in the fields nearby, guarding their flocks of sheep. ⁹Suddenly, an angel of the Lord appeared among them, and the radiance of the Lord's glory surrounded them. They were terrified, ¹⁰but the angel reassured them. "Don't be afraid!" he said. "I bring you good news that will bring great joy to all people. ¹¹The Savior—yes, the Messiah, the Lord—has been born today in Bethlehem, the city of David! ¹²And you will recognize him by this sign: You will find a baby wrapped snugly in strips of cloth, lying in a manger."

¹³Suddenly, the angel was joined by a vast host of others—the armies of heaven—praising God and saying,

¹⁴"Glory to God in highest heaven,
   and peace on earth to those with
      whom God is pleased."

¹⁵When the angels had returned to heaven, the shepherds said to each other, "Let's go to Bethlehem! Let's see this thing that has happened, which the Lord has told us about."

¹⁶They hurried to the village and found Mary and Joseph. And there was the baby, lying in the manger. ¹⁷After seeing him, the shepherds told everyone what had happened and what the angel had said to them about this child. ¹⁸All who heard the shepherds' story were astonished, ¹⁹but Mary kept all these things in her heart and thought about them often. ²⁰The shepherds went back to their flocks, glorifying and praising God for all they had heard and seen. It was just as the angel had told them.

NOTES

2:9 *an angel of the Lord appeared among them.* On the role of angels, see NIDNTT 1.13-16, 101-103; Gardner 1995:44-49; and commentary on 1:11-17.

2:11 *the Lord.* This is an important title Luke used and applied to Jesus. In the LXX, the term "Lord" (*kurios* [TG2962, ZG3261]) was consistently used to designate the sacred tetragrammaton (Heb. *yhwh* [TH3068, ZH3378]), the personal name for God. For a helpful article on the nuances of Jesus as Savior and Lord in Luke–Acts, see Bock 1986. Bock argues that the early church (including Luke) understood "Jesus as Lord" to mean that Jesus is "the divine Mediator and Dispenser of Salvation" (1986:146; cf. Luke 9:20; Acts 4:12; 16:30-31). However, this confession of Jesus' lordship is only a part of saving faith, for it also demands a life lived in submission and obedience to Jesus.

2:13 *a vast host . . . praising God.* Luke made good use of the language of praise. The verb *aineō* [TG134, ZG140] is used three times for this theme in Luke and three times in Acts, though Luke only uses the noun "praise" in 18:43. "The praise indicated by these words is consistently directed toward God" (EDNT 1.39-40). The angels and shepherds praised God at the birth of Christ, and the pilgrim crowds did so at Christ's triumphal entry into Jerusalem (2:13, 20; 19:37). The Gospel closes with the disciples blessing God in the Temple (24:53). The new Christian community praised God, and the man healed in the Temple offered praise (Acts 2:47; 3:3-9).

2:14 *peace on earth to those with whom God is pleased.* The NLT's translation is to be preferred to the KJV's familiar "good will toward men," which is based on later and inferior manuscripts. The NLT reading is supported by excellent textual evidence (ℵ* A B* D W). Moreover, in the DSS there are striking parallels found in the Qumran Hymns, noted by Fitzmyer (1981:411-412), that speak of "the sons of his [God's] good pleasure" (1QH 12[4]:32-33; 19[11]:9) and "men of his [God's] good pleasure". For a detailed evaluation of the textual evidence, see Metzger (1971:133).

COMMENTARY

While Matthew described the visit of the impressive delegation from the east, Luke drew attention to the humble shepherds from the fields adjacent to Bethlehem. The Christ event brought good news to poor, despised, local people like the shepherds. For the most part, shepherds were written off by the Jewish religious establishment for their failure to keep the Sabbath and all the minute regulations imposed by the ruling Jewish hierarchy. But these shepherds had spiritual longings and hungers, and the Christian message was for them as well as for those more favorably placed on the social and economic scale.

Luke, advocate of the poor, the disadvantaged, and the sick, highlighted the visit of the angel to these shepherds. Their life was often lonely, cold, and rugged; on occasion, their work could demand that they "live in the out-of-doors" (the literal meaning of the verb *agrauleō* [TG63, ZG64], used only in 2:8) to ensure the safety and health of their sheep. It was a marginal, uncomfortable life at best, made more painful by the derision they experienced from those who observed the Jewish way of life more scrupulously.

The angel's epiphany frightened the shepherds. According to the biblical accounts, most people were afraid when they encountered an angel (1:30; Judg 6:22-23; 13:22; Acts 10:4; cf. Rev 1:17). The shepherds were "terrified" (2:9), but they were reassured by the angel, even as Zechariah and Mary had been previously reassured (see 1:12-13, 30). The message was not meant to strike panic in the hearts of those who received it but rather to offer them something exciting and thrilling: "I bring you good news that will bring great joy to all people. The Savior . . . has been born today in Bethlehem!" (2:10-11). The shepherds responded promptly and obediently to the angelic initiative by going to Bethlehem to see the Savior.

Luke's nativity story is rich in Old Testament associations, spiritual symbolism, and worship elements. Following is a list of noteworthy features: First, as in the cases of Moses, Gideon, and Zechariah, God spoke to people who were busy carrying out their daily work (1:11-20; Exod 3:1-10; Judg 6:11-24). Second, the advent of Christ was marked by a display of the divine glory that highlighted the supernatural nature of the event (2:9). Also, the positive and universal character of the angelic message would "bring great joy to all people" (2:10). That message is anchored in Christ, who is the promised deliverer or Savior. Further, the interpreting angel was joined by a host of other angels who praised God and invoked his peace upon all those pleasing God (2:14). This note of worship and praise is often sounded in Luke's work (2:13, 20; 5:25; 7:16; 13:13; 17:15; 18:43; 19:37; Acts 2:47; 3:8-9). In addition, the enthusiasm of the shepherds to investigate the nativity for themselves is clearly spelled out (2:15-16), and their role in broadcasting news of the Savior's birth is carefully recorded (2:17-18). Also, the devotional spirit of Mary is recognized and honored—she "kept all these things in her heart and thought about them often" (2:19; cf. 2:51). She wondered what it all meant, even as the patriarch Jacob had done at the disclosure of Joseph's remarkable dreams (Gen 37:11). The shepherds eventually returned to their work as before, but as changed men. There was a new note of gratitude and praise to God for the privileges that they had been granted in hearing the angel's encouraging message and in viewing the Christ child for themselves. Finally, Luke closes the passage with a typical reminder that God keeps his promises. In this case, it is a reminder that the shepherds followed the angel's instructions and found the Messiah "just as the angel had told them" (2:20).

◆   I. Jesus Is Presented in the Temple (2:21-24)

²¹Eight days later, when the baby was circumcised, he was named Jesus, the name given him by the angel even before he was conceived.

²²Then it was time for their purification offering, as required by the law of Moses after the birth of a child; so his parents took him to Jerusalem to present him to the Lord. ²³The law of the Lord says, "If a woman's first child is a boy, he must be dedicated to the LORD."* ²⁴So they offered the sacrifice required in the law of the Lord—"either a pair of turtledoves or two young pigeons."*

2:23 Exod 13:2.   2:24 Lev 12:8.

NOTES

2:21 *Eight days later, when the baby was circumcised.* In the ancient Near East, the practice of circumcision was well known (Gen 21:4; 34:14-22). Male circumcision signified the covenantal relationship that God had established with the people of Israel (Gen 17:9-14; Josh 5:2-3). It was traditionally carried out on the eighth day, and it involved cutting off the foreskin of the penis (Gen 17:12; Exod 12:48; Lev 12:3). See note on 1:59.

COMMENTARY

The circumcision of Jesus took place at the traditional time, the eighth day (2:21; cf. Gen 17:12; 21:4; Lev 12:3; Phil 3:5), as did that of John the Baptist (1:59). Mary and Joseph were evidently determined to be scrupulous in carrying out the proper procedures, being "careful to obey all of the Lord's commandments and regulations," as Zechariah and Elizabeth had been (1:6). Thus, Jesus and John were both named at the time of their circumcision, and both were named according to the divine revelation communicated by Gabriel (1:11-13, 26-31).

The provision of a purification offering is another indication of the law-abiding character of Joseph and Mary (2:22). Leviticus 12 describes the process of purification required after childbirth. For a boy, a forty-day period had to elapse before the mother could present the prescribed offerings in the Temple for her purification. It normally involved presenting "a one-year-old lamb for a burnt offering and a young pigeon or turtledove for a purification offering" (Lev 12:6). The offerings were given to the priest, who presented them to the Lord. Then, the woman would be considered ritually clean again after her bleeding at childbirth. However, in the case of poor folk, two turtledoves or two young pigeons were acceptable substitutes (Lev 12:8). The fact that mention is made of the less-expensive substitutes suggests that Joseph and Mary had limited financial resources.

According to the law of Moses, every firstborn male, whether animal or human, was to be dedicated, or consecrated, to the Lord (Exod 13:2, 12). The animals were normally sacrificed, but the firstborn sons were to serve God faithfully for the rest of their lives. In practice, the Levites were called in as substitutes to fulfill this role in place of all the firstborn sons of Israel (Num 3:11-13; 8:17-18).

The presentation of Jesus in the Temple reminds one of Hannah, who presented her young son Samuel to the Lord (1 Sam 1:22-28). Samuel became a leader of God's people, a prophet, and a true spokesman for God (see 1 Sam 12:1-2). Now an even greater one was to be presented by his parents; this one was to rule over Israel forever (1:32-33). So Joseph and Mary made the five-mile journey from Bethlehem to Jerusalem to present the infant Jesus in the Temple (which was then undergoing a complete reconstruction work by Herod the Great). It was a momentous day in holy history.

◆　J. The Prophecy of Simeon (2:25-35)

25At that time there was a man in Jerusalem named Simeon. He was righteous and devout and was eagerly waiting for the Messiah to come and rescue Israel. The Holy Spirit was upon him 26and had revealed to him that he would not die until he had seen the Lord's Messiah. 27That day the Spirit led him to the Temple. So when Mary and Joseph came to present the baby Jesus to the Lord as the law required, 28Simeon was there. He took the child in his arms and praised God, saying,

29"Sovereign Lord, now let your servant
　　die in peace,
　　as you have promised.
30I have seen your salvation,
31　which you have prepared for
　　all people.
32He is a light to reveal God to the
　　nations,
　　and he is the glory of your people
　　Israel!"

33Jesus' parents were amazed at what was being said about him. 34Then Simeon blessed them, and he said to Mary, the baby's mother, "This child is destined to cause many in Israel to fall, but he will be a joy to many others. He has been sent as a sign from God, but many will oppose him. 35As a result, the deepest thoughts of many hearts will be revealed. And a sword will pierce your very soul."

NOTES

2:29 *Sovereign Lord*. This is the interesting term *despotēs* [TG1203, ZG1305] (master, lord), used occasionally of God or Christ in the NT (2 Pet 2:1; Jude 1:4; Rev 6:10). It is the root of the English word "despot," though it should not be equated to it; the ancient term did not summon today's negative connotations. Luke uses this striking title twice (2:29; Acts 4:24), both times highlighting the fact that God is in charge of history. With the birth of Jesus, God's salvation entered history (2:30), and later, believers cried out to their sovereign God in prayer at a time of crisis (Acts 4:24-31).

now let your servant die in peace. For a detailed discussion of Simeon's song and the other hymns of Luke 1-2, see R. E. Brown (1977, 1986) and Farris (1985:143-160).

2:32 *a light to reveal God to the nations.* By describing Jesus as "a light to the Gentiles," Simeon was identifying Jesus as the Isaianic Servant-Messiah (cf. Isa 42:6; 49:6). For the use of the Isaianic Servant theme here and in other places in Luke, see T. S. Moore (1997).

2:33 *Jesus' parents were amazed.* The element of amazement sounded here is frequently mentioned in Luke (who used the verb *thaumazō* [TG2296, ZG2513], "wonder, be amazed," often). Earlier, the people "wondered" at Zechariah's long delay in offering the incense in the Temple sanctuary (1:21). Here, Joseph and Mary are "amazed at what was being said" about Jesus (2:33). Later in Luke, the residents of Nazareth were "amazed by the gracious words" of Jesus (4:22). Jesus was "amazed" by the faith of a Roman officer (7:9). Amazement gripped those who saw Jesus still the storm and later heal the demon possessed (8:25; 9:43; 11:14). A number of other situations resulted in amazement, or "wonder," as well (cf. 11:38; 20:26; 24:12, 41).

C O M M E N T A R Y

Simeon was presented by Luke as a man who shared with others the fervent hope and expectation that God would fulfill his promises, send the Messiah, and thereby bring comfort and consolation to his oppressed people (2:25-26; cf. 2:38; 23:51; 24:21). Simeon's words come as the joyful climax of a long and faithful life in the service of God. His prophecy is the last of the four beautiful hymns found among Luke's birth stories. The Song of Simeon, like the Song of Zechariah, the Song of Mary, and the Song of the Heavenly Host, celebrates God's glorious intervention in the affairs of his people for the achievement of his holy purposes.

A number of interesting details appear in Luke's description of Simeon. He was a man who lived close to the center of Jewish life in Jerusalem. In lifestyle, he was a godly man, "righteous and devout" (2:25), and he was filled with the Holy Spirit (like Zechariah, Elizabeth, and Mary). Full of messianic expectations, Simeon was the recipient of a special divine revelation concerning the Messiah's coming. Under the Spirit's direction, he entered the Temple and was thus in the right place at the right time to see the promised Messiah. With joy he cradled the Christ child lovingly in his arms and offered a blessing for the parents (even as Eli had done in earlier times, 1 Sam 2:20). In his speech, he directed a special word of counsel to Mary, mother of the Messiah, and also noted the central significance of Christ for human destiny. In view of the wonderful messianic revelation he had been so graciously given, Simeon responded appropriately with words of praise.

The thoughtful words of Simeon, often called the *Nunc Dimittis* (taken from the Latin Vulgate, meaning "[You] now dismiss"), contain rich elements of poetry and prophecy. They both celebrate God's deliverance in sending the promised Messiah and prophesy the mixed reaction that his coming would provoke. There is a striking universalism here that is reminiscent of certain passages in Isaiah (see Isa 42:6; 49:6; 52:10; 60:1-3). In addition, there is a strong element of future hope, a feature that is also present in Anna's prophecy. While Simeon is said to be "eagerly waiting for the Messiah to come and rescue Israel" (2:25; cf. 23:51; Isa 40:1-2; 49:13), Anna is described as specifically looking forward to God's "rescue" of Jerusalem (2:38; cf. 24:21). In each case, hope was pinned entirely on the faithfulness of God (the

Gr. verb *prosdechomai* [TG4327, ZG4657] being used to describe the waiting in both 2:25 and 2:38).

We should take notice of a number of features of Simeon's prophecy, many of which are echoed elsewhere in Luke. Simeon begins by recognizing God's sovereignty, a theme in Luke (see the Introduction). He gratefully acknowledges that God has kept his promise to him, so that he is now quite happy to die (2:29). Among other things, he recognized Christ as the Savior, a Lukan theme shared with other New Testament writers (1:69, 77; 2:11; Acts 4:12; cf. Matt 1:21; John 4:42; Phil 3:20; Titus 2:13; Heb 5:9; 2 Pet 1:11; 1 John 4:14), and he saw the universal scope of salvation offered in Christ "for all people" (2:31). Luke noted that Simeon perceived the dual significance of Christ both as a "light to reveal God to the nations" (2:32a; cf. Isa 42:6; 49:6) and as "the glory of [God's] people Israel" (2:32b; cf. Isa 46:13; 60:1-2). Simeon also predicted the tragic rejection of Christ by "many in Israel" (2:34; cf. 19:44) and foresaw its grievous consequences (2:34-35; cf. 20:17-19; 23:28-31). In particular, he anticipated the pain of both Mary and Jesus (cf. 2:34-35, 48; John 19:25-27), providing the first hint of Christ's sufferings in Luke's Gospel. These words astonished Joseph and Mary (2:33).

◆   ## K. The Prophecy of Anna (2:36-40)

36Anna, a prophet, was also there in the Temple. She was the daughter of Phanuel from the tribe of Asher, and she was very old. Her husband died when they had been married only seven years. 37Then she lived as a widow to the age of eighty-four.* She never left the Temple but stayed there day and night, worshiping God with fasting and prayer. 38She came along just as Simeon was talking with Mary and Joseph, and she began praising God. She talked about the child to everyone who had been waiting expectantly for God to rescue Jerusalem.

39When Jesus' parents had fulfilled all the requirements of the law of the Lord, they returned home to Nazareth in Galilee. 40There the child grew up healthy and strong. He was filled with wisdom, and God's favor was on him.

2:37 Or *She had been a widow for eighty-four years.*

NOTES

2:36 *prophet.* Lit., "prophetess" (*prophētis* [TG4398, ZG4739]), a rare word used only twice in the NT, here in reference to Anna and in Rev 2:20 in reference to the disreputable Jezebel.

2:37 *she lived as a widow to the age of eighty-four.* The Gr. text here can be understood in one of two ways: either that Anna was eighty-four years old or that she had lived on *after* the death of her husband of seven years for eighty-four more years. The NLT and most translations support the former view, but Williams's translation (2000) opts for the latter. The wording can be translated literally "she was advanced in many days, having lived with a husband seven years from her virginity, and herself a widow for eighty-four years" (Plummer 1896:72). The possibility of the longer age cannot be ruled out categorically. Judith, for example, reportedly lived to 105 years and was an exemplary model that was highly esteemed (Jdt 16:21-23).

2:40 *There the child grew up healthy and strong.* See the notes on 1:80 and 2:52. There is a close parallel drawn by Luke between John the Baptist's development and that of Jesus, and both accounts seem to be partly modeled on the account of the maturation of Samuel: "Samuel grew up in the presence of the LORD" (1 Sam 2:21). The same two verbs are used in both cases and in the same tenses: "he grew up and became strong" or "he grew up healthy and strong" (*ēuxanen* [TG837, ZG889] and *ekrataiouto* [TG2901A, ZG3194]; 1:80; 2:40). However, there is no statement about John the Baptist that is parallel to 2:52. While John "lived in the wilderness" until the commencement of his public ministry, Jesus grew up in Nazareth and shared in normal social life there. On the growth theme in Luke–Acts, see Trites (1996).

COMMENTARY

Anna is another devout, elderly person like Zechariah, Elizabeth, and Simeon. She is introduced as a widow, an octogenarian, and a person of remarkable devotion to God (2:36-37). Her piety expressed itself in her constant attendance at the Temple and in a life of worship that included both prayer and fasting (cf. 5:33-39 and comments). She is described as a "prophetess" (see note on 2:36). Luke depicts Anna's devotional spirit in glowing terms. Anna, like Elizabeth and Mary, "is one of the three pious women who witness to the importance of Jesus in the redemption of God's people" (DJG 32).

Several features of Anna's religious life are similar to those we have observed in Simeon. To begin with, she was a person who plainly knew and loved God. She had developed her spiritual life over many years and was faithful in her devotional life, communing regularly with God in both public and private worship. She was sensitive to the direction of God and lived in expectation of the promised messianic deliverance. Like Simeon, she knew how to praise God and was able to share her faith openly with others, speaking in the Temple to "all who were looking forward to the redemption of Jerusalem" (2:38, NIV; cf. 21:28, where reference is made to "redemption" again). She perceived that the answer to her prayers would be fulfilled in Jesus.

The presentation of Jesus in the Temple was, as we have seen, in strict accordance with "all the requirements of the law of the Lord" (2:39). Joseph and Mary exhibited a humble spirit of obedience to God, and the Temple visit was marked by their unforgettable encounters with Simeon and Anna, two of God's chosen servants who had challenged, encouraged, and blessed them.

When Joseph and Mary left Judea, they traveled northward to their home in Nazareth. There, in beautiful Galilee, Jesus "grew up healthy and strong" (2:40). Luke makes mention of the wisdom of Jesus and notes that "God's favor was on him" (2:40). With these simple words, Luke summarizes the early childhood years of Jesus. There is nothing here of the fanciful accounts that later arose in the apocryphal gospels that try to fill in the hidden years of Jesus' life (see note on 2:52). His growth and development were wholesome and normal, and Luke notes the favorable hand of God upon the whole process.

◆   L. The Childhood of Jesus (2:41-52)

⁴¹Every year Jesus' parents went to Jerusalem for the Passover festival. ⁴²When Jesus was twelve years old, they attended the festival as usual. ⁴³After the celebration

was over, they started home to Nazareth, but Jesus stayed behind in Jerusalem. His parents didn't miss him at first, ⁴⁴because they assumed he was among the other travelers. But when he didn't show up that evening, they started looking for him among their relatives and friends.

⁴⁵When they couldn't find him, they went back to Jerusalem to search for him there. ⁴⁶Three days later they finally discovered him in the Temple, sitting among the religious teachers, listening to them and asking questions. ⁴⁷All who heard him were amazed at his understanding and his answers.

⁴⁸His parents didn't know what to think. "Son," his mother said to him, "why have you done this to us? Your father and I have been frantic, searching for you everywhere."

⁴⁹"But why did you need to search?" he asked. "Didn't you know that I must be in my Father's house?"* ⁵⁰But they didn't understand what he meant.

⁵¹Then he returned to Nazareth with them and was obedient to them. And his mother stored all these things in her heart.

⁵²Jesus grew in wisdom and in stature and in favor with God and all the people.

2:49 Or *"Didn't you realize that I should be involved with my Father's affairs?"*

NOTES

2:42 *When Jesus was twelve years old.* This was the time when young Jewish males began to be prepared for admission to the moral and religious responsibilities of adult life (*m. Avot* 5:21). "From regulations set down in the later tractate *m. Niddah* 5:6 it was deduced that a Jewish boy became obligated to observe the Torah at the age of thirteen. (Of much later origin is the modern expression, bar mitzvah, 'son of the commandment,' as well as the ceremony related to it.) There is reason to think that some of the late Mishnaic regulations were somewhat applicable to the time of Jesus—at least in this case. From the age of thirteen on, he would have been obliged to take part in the pilgrimage to Jerusalem" (Fitzmyer 1981:440; cf. Bock 1994:264). Jesus' age here coincides with the Jewish tradition that Samuel commenced his prophetic ministry at the age of twelve (Josephus *Antiquities* 5.348). This seems likely in view of the deliberate and repeated allusions to Samuel's birth and upbringing (note that 2:40 clearly echoes 1 Sam 2:21, 26, and the Magnificat [1:46-55] is carefully framed in terms that recall Hannah's prayer of praise in 1 Sam 2:1-10).

2:47 *All who heard him were amazed.* Luke notes the element of astonishment by the verb *existēmi* [TH1839/1839A, ZH2014] on a number of occasions, the first of which appears here. Cf. 8:56; 24:22; Acts 2:7, 12; 8:9, 11, 13; 9:21; 10:45; 12:16. Cf. also note at 2:33 on Luke's use of *thaumazō*.

2:48 *His parents didn't know what to think.* Joseph and Mary were "astonished" (*exeplagēsan* [TG1605, ZG1742]) at finding Jesus in the precincts of the Temple. Cf. the use of this word in 4:32; 9:43; Acts 13:12.

2:52 *Jesus grew.* An unusual verb is used here to describe Jesus' growth. The verb speaks of advancing against obstacles (*prokoptō* [TG4298, ZG4621]). In the Gr. imperfect active tense here, it has the force of "he kept cutting his way forward as through a forest or jungle as pioneers did" (Robertson 1930:2.35). See also the notes on growth in 1:80 and 2:40.

Regarding the later, noncanonical accounts of the hidden years of Jesus' life before "he began his public ministry" (3:23), see James 1924, a book that is often available in second-hand bookshops, or, for a newer edition, see Hennecke, Schneemelcher, and Wilson 1963. For a good review of the material, see DJG 286-291.

COMMENTARY

The one incident from the childhood of Jesus that Luke records is the memorable trip to Jerusalem with his parents when he was twelve years old. Jewish boys at this age began to get ready for their responsibilities as adult members of the community, so this was a time of preparation and transition. All Jewish males were required by the law to visit the Temple each year to attend the three great feasts of Passover, Pentecost, and Shelters (Exod 23:14-17; Deut 16:16). Distance made it difficult for many to attend all three, but most Jews tried to be present at Passover, the great feast that celebrated their national deliverance from Egypt (Exod 12:14-20). Generally, families accompanied the men to the holy city, so it was not surprising that children could be temporarily lost while visiting with their relatives and friends (2:44).

The three-day search for Jesus was an agonizing time for Joseph and Mary (2:48), as any parent of a lost child can testify. Eventually, they found Jesus in the courts of the Temple, "sitting among the religious teachers, listening to them and asking questions" (2:46). In replying to his worried parents, Jesus intimated that they should have known that he would be in his Father's house (2:49). This suggests a filial consciousness on the part of Jesus (cf. 10:21-22). He knew he had a special relationship with his heavenly Father, and this led him quite naturally to be discussing the things of God in his "Father's house." His parents, however, "didn't understand what he meant" (2:50), so there was a different perception of the situation and a resulting misunderstanding.

This beautiful cameo from the childhood of Jesus closes with the return of the holy family to Nazareth. Contrary to the fantastic pictures found in the apocryphal gospels (e.g., the *Infancy Gospel of Thomas*, where the boy Jesus at five years of age takes soft clay and fashions it into twelve sparrows that fly away [Hennecke et al. 1963:393]), there is no indication here of a wonder boy—Jesus did no miracles in his early years, as evidenced by passages like Mark 6:3a and Matthew 13:55. Despite his precocity, Jesus was submissive and obedient to his parents (2:51). It is not surprising that his mother stored up all these memories in her heart (Luke's second reference to Mary's spiritual sensitivity about her son's life and ministry, 2:51; note the comment on Mary's devotional spirit in 2:19). The last glimpse we have of the boy Jesus in Nazareth is a winsome one, as Luke speaks well of the wholesome, full-orbed development of Jesus physically, mentally, spiritually, and socially: "Jesus grew in wisdom and in stature and in favor with God and all the people" (2:52).

This memorable incident clearly functions as a transitional marker between Jesus' infancy and adulthood. As C. A. Evans (1990:42) has correctly noted, "It also illustrates Jesus' growth and wisdom (2:40). The opening verse not only sets the stage for the episode itself, but once again underscores the faithfulness and piety of Joseph and Mary. Seen against the Passover celebration, Jesus' teaching in the Temple might very well anticipate his final teaching in the Temple at Passover time during Passion Week" (see 21:37). The lively discussion Jesus carried on with the

Jewish rabbis in the Temple highlights Jesus' strong sense of mission at an early age and his serious preparation for it—a point evident in his response to his relieved parents: "Why did you need to search? . . . Didn't you know that I must be in my Father's house" (2:49). His heavenly "Father's affairs" (see NLT mg) had to take precedence over the concern of his earthly "father" (2:48). Jesus plainly signaled in this intense encounter with the religious leaders and teachers that he was totally absorbed in his Father's affairs. Later in his ministry, he would commend the same attitude on the part of his followers (12:31; Matt 6:33).

◆ **III. The Preparation for Jesus' Ministry (3:1–4:13)**
    A. John the Baptist Prepares the Way (3:1-20)
       1. John the Baptist (3:1-6; cf. Matt 3:1-6; Mark 1:2-6; John 1:19-23)

It was now the fifteenth year of the reign of Tiberius, the Roman emperor. Pontius Pilate was governor over Judea; Herod Antipas was ruler* over Galilee; his brother Philip was ruler* over Iturea and Traconitis; Lysanias was ruler over Abilene. ²Annas and Caiaphas were the high priests. At this time a message from God came to John son of Zechariah, who was living in the wilderness. ³Then John went from place to place on both sides of the Jordan River, preaching that people should be baptized to show that they had repented of their sins and turned to God to be forgiven. ⁴Isaiah had spoken of John when he said,

"He is a voice shouting in the
   wilderness,
'Prepare the way for the LORD's
   coming!
   Clear the road for him!
⁵The valleys will be filled,
   and the mountains and hills
   made level.
The curves will be straightened,
   and the rough places made
   smooth.
⁶And then all people will see
   the salvation sent from
   God.'"*

3:1a Greek *Herod was tetrarch.* Herod Antipas was a son of King Herod.   3:1b Greek *tetrarch;* also in 3:1c.
3:4-6 Isa 40:3-5 (Greek version).

NOTES
3:1-2a Special note should be taken of Luke's interest here in cultural, geographical, and chronological markers (cf. 1:5; 2:1), a point well noted by J. B. Green (1995:3-4): "These geo-political markers, occurring in the early chapters of the Gospel, are some of the most obvious, but there are many others. Some are quite subtle. For example, the preface of Luke (1:1-4) situates the author socially as one capable of writing learned Greek, who might have trafficked in technical professional writing, and who generally had an appreciation for the labours of those who work with their hands. Luke's *narrative*, then, presents a *theological program* deeply embedded in the cultural currents of the first-century Mediterranean world." By this elaborate sevenfold dating, Luke situates the ministry of John the Baptizer in the religious, political, and cultural context of the time.

3:2 *At this time a message from God came to John son of Zechariah.* On the special role of John in redemptive history, see Fitzmyer (1989:86-116).

3:3 *John went from place to place on both sides of the Jordan.* On the ministry of John the Baptist, see McKnight 1991, Scobie 1964:60-86, Wink 1968, and Witherington 1990.

3:4 *a voice shouting in the wilderness.* The onomatopoeic word *boaō* [TG0994, ZG1066] means "shout, call aloud, cry out," and the sound clearly points to the sense. It certainly implies that the speaker intends to be heard, as in the case of John the Baptist (see EDNT 1.223).

Prepare the way for the LORD's coming! This quotation from Isa 40:3 is of striking significance, not only for John the Baptizer's message of repentance but also for the proclamation of the early church. It served as a source of the church's first self-designation. Repeatedly, believers are described in Acts as followers of "the Way," an early name for Christianity (Acts 9:2; 19:9, 23; 22:4; 24:14, 22; cf. John 14:6—"I am the way"). On "The Lucan Picture of John the Baptist as Precursor of the Lord," see Fitzmyer 1989:86-116.

3:6 *then all people will see the salvation sent from God.* Luke's use of Isa 40:3-5 is considerably more extensive than that of the other Gospels, which use only Isa 40:3. This has the effect of highlighting the radical moral and spiritual preparations that the forerunner would introduce in setting the stage for the Messiah's coming. Luke's account also stresses the fact that the divine deliverance would be made known to the whole human family, a theme of major importance in Luke-Acts (2:31-32; 13:29; 24:46-47; Acts 4:12; 9:15; 10:43; 13:47; 26:23).

COMMENTARY

Comparing the three Synoptic accounts, it is obvious that Luke alone highlights the historical setting of John's ministry. He specifically dated John's work to the reign of Tiberius Caesar. The "fifteenth year" (3:1) probably points to a date around AD 26. The other rulers listed offer further detail about the chronological period. When Herod the Great died in 4 BC, his kingdom was divided among his sons Archelaus, Herod Antipas, and Herod Philip. Archelaus was not an effective ruler, so he was deposed in AD 6, and Roman prefects took over Judea. Thus, in John the Baptist's day, the Roman prefect was Pontius Pilate, who ruled Judea, Samaria, and Idumea (AD 26–36). Herod Antipas was appointed ruler of Galilee and Perea, with the title "tetrarch," and ruled from 4 BC to AD 39. Herod Philip, from 4 BC to his death in AD 33, ruled as tetrarch of Iturea and Traconitis, territories located north and east of the Sea of Galilee (which Josephus notes as including Auranitis, Gaulanitis, and Batanaea), though the precise limits of his tetrarchy cannot be identified today. Similarly, Lysanias, who is only mentioned here in the New Testament, served as tetrarch of Abilene, and the accuracy of Luke's reference to him has been shown by "an inscription from ancient Abilene dating from AD 15–30" that contains a reference to "Lysanias the tetrarch" (C. A. Evans 1990:51). Lysanias also appears to be mentioned by Josephus (*Antiquities* 19.5.1; 20.7.1).

Luke also gives the names of the high priests at the time. Under Roman rule, the high priesthood had become a political appointment. Annas was appointed high priest by Quirinius, the legate (governor) of Syria in AD 6. He held office until Valerius, the Roman procurator of Judea, deposed him in AD 15. Six members of his family succeeded him, but the Jews continued to recognize his authority (John 18:13). The dominance of Annas "during these years is underscored in Luke 3:2 and Acts 4:6, where Annas is listed together with Caiaphas as high priest, as in John 18:13, where Jesus' trial begins with an appearance before Annas" (Mills 1990:32). John's ministry, then, is to be dated about AD 26–29. To sum up, Luke provides a datable setting for the life and ministry of John the Baptist. Moreover, he prepared the way for the reception of the Christian message in the book of Acts, where he would show that message reaching ever-wider sections of society. "In its expansion from Jerusalem to Rome, the gospel will encounter not only the poor, lame, halt, and blind but also high priests, synagogue rulers, city officials, leading women, ship captains, imperial guards, governors, and kings, finally appealing to the emperor himself. Luke's universality is not only geographical, but also social, political, and economic" (Craddock 1990:47).

Matthew located the ministry of John in the wilderness of Judea (Matt 3:1). Luke's Gospel agrees that John the Baptizer, at the commencement of his public ministry, was "living in the wilderness" (3:2; cf. 1:80). Luke noted that in John's itinerant ministry, "John went from place to place on both sides of the Jordan River, preaching that people should be baptized to show that they had repented of their sins and turned to God to be forgiven" (3:3). Luke, like his fellow Gospel writers, underscored the earnestness of John's preaching, his national summons to repentance, and the strong ethical dimensions of his proclamations. The seriousness of his call to repentance was to be met by a willingness on the part of Jews to submit to the public act of baptism. It was a strong message that demanded a clear moral response and radical change. John's baptism was closely connected with repentance "and therefore was not a proselyte baptism which seems to have been practiced by some synagogues when receiving non-Jews. The Qumran sect also practiced baptism [in the form of ritual lustration], but it was a repeated act of cleansing. John's baptism was within his total ministry of preparing the way of the Lord, making hearts ready for the one soon to come 'who is mightier than I'" (Craddock 1990:47).

All three synoptic Gospel writers cite the famous passage in Isaiah about "a voice shouting in the wilderness" (Isa 40:3), and all three relate it to the ministry of John the Baptist. All three Evangelists also record his words: "Prepare the way for the LORD's coming!" (3:4; Matt 3:3; Mark 1:3). The fact that the Greek words are identical in Matthew, Mark, and Luke suggests that these concepts were burned indelibly into early Christian tradition. John, who belted out his message in a bold, forthright fashion, called people to understand that God Almighty had something to say to the covenant people about the coming of the Messiah! This is made clear in Mark by his words of introduction to the Isaiah passage, which cite Malachi 3:1 as the divinely planned method of introducing the Messiah: "Look! I am sending my messenger ahead of you, and he will prepare your way" (Mark 1:2).

◆   ## 2. John's preaching of repentance (3:7-9; cf. Matt 3:7-10)

7When the crowds came to John for baptism, he said, "You brood of snakes! Who warned you to flee God's coming wrath? 8Prove by the way you live that you have repented of your sins and turned to God. Don't just say to each other, 'We're safe, for we are descendants of Abraham.' That means nothing, for I tell you, God can create children of Abraham from these very stones. 9Even now the ax of God's judgment is poised, ready to sever the roots of the trees. Yes, every tree that does not produce good fruit will be chopped down and thrown into the fire."

NOTES

3:7 You brood of snakes! John's stern words address the people as a "brood of snakes." This striking phrase was also used by Jesus (see Matt 12:34; 23:33). The metaphor refers to poisonous vipers that are both dangerous and deadly (cf. Acts 28:3, where the same Greek word, *echidna* [TG2191, ZG2399], is used of a literal snake that attacked Paul).

3:8 Prove by the way you live that you have repented of your sins. Repentance is clearly "an important theme in Luke's Gospel, where it is connected with the preaching of Jonah (11:32), John the Baptist (3:3, 8; cf. 3:10-14) and Jesus (10:13; 13:3-5; 17:3-4). Repentance is presented as a central element in the preaching of Jesus (5:32; cf. 15:7, 10), and is included in the Lukan version of the Great Commission (24:47)" (Trites 1977:130).

COMMENTARY

Both Matthew and Luke gave us a sample of John's uncompromising preaching. Matthew's account notes the fact that John's ministry got the attention of the Pharisees and Sadducees, who came out in considerable numbers to hear him preach (Matt 3:7). Luke's account stresses the large "crowds" that came out to hear this bold preacher (*ochlos* [TG3793, ZG4063], 3:7). The people who attended John's ministry were met with words of rebuke and a stark challenge.

John the Baptist was obviously not catering to those with "itching ears," merely teaching what people would like to hear (cf. 2 Tim 4:3). Instead, he was earnestly calling for a radical reorientation of life to God: "Prove by the way you live that you have repented of your sins and turned to God" (3:8; cf. Matt 3:8). Pious words or professions of faith were not enough. Simply claiming to be descendants of Abraham proved nothing. God was the God of miracles; he could change stones into children of Abraham. In view of the imminent threat of divine judgment, a thorough "change of mind" (that is, repentance: *metanoia* [TG3341, ZG3567]) was called for, and there was not a moment to spare (3:3, 8; cf. 5:32). Repentance was a costly thing to be thoughtfully considered, and it was an essential feature of the preaching of John, Jesus, and the early church (5:32; 10:13; 24:47; Acts 5:31; 11:18; 13:24; 20:21; 26:20). Failure to repent invited catastrophe: "Every tree that does not produce good fruit will be chopped down and thrown into the fire" (3:9; cf. Matt 3:9). The privilege of Jewish heritage was plainly not enough. The prophet demanded a strong sense of social responsibility to avert the possibility of a terrible judgment that would "sever" their roots (3:9). John's message was drastic and clearly offensive to many Jewish traditionalists who thought they were good enough—just as many churchgoers do today!

◆   3. John's ethical teaching (3:10-14)

¹⁰The crowds asked, "What should we do?"

¹¹John replied, "If you have two shirts, give one to the poor. If you have food, share it with those who are hungry."

¹²Even corrupt tax collectors came to be baptized and asked, "Teacher, what should we do?"

¹³He replied, "Collect no more taxes than the government requires."

¹⁴"What should we do?" asked some soldiers.

John replied, "Don't extort money or make false accusations. And be content with your pay."

NOTES

3:10 *The crowds asked, "What should we do?"* In Acts, the same question was asked in the same words by those who heard Peter's moving speech on the day of Pentecost: "What should we do?" (*ti poiēsōmen* [TG4160, ZG4472]; Acts 2:37).

3:11 *If you have two shirts, give one to the poor.* The garment mentioned here was a "tunic" or "shirt" (*chitōn*), worn next to the skin and used by both sexes as a basic element of clothing. John's ethical demands put teeth in the repentance called for. "For John repentance had the same basic meaning as for all Jews, namely, that of turning from sin in contrition and confession, and of turning to the will of God. Only in two particulars can we say that John modified the conception, namely, first in the urgency that he attached to it, and second in the way in which he associated it with baptism" (Kraeling 1951:71). As DJG has noted (387), "both Mark and Luke call John's rite of baptism a 'baptism of repentance,' which presumably means a baptism that expresses a willingness to repent and live a life that bears fruit corresponding to repentance (cf. Matt 3:8; Luke 3:8, 10-14)."

3:12 *tax collectors.* Luke often mentions Jesus' concern for tax collectors (see 5:29; 7:29; 15:1; 19:2). They were treated as scum by the Jews. This attitude is understandable given the fact that the Jews were subject to both civil and religious taxation. The Romans doled out the collection of customs revenues to "publicans," who were hated both for the money they extracted from the people and for their collaboration with the foreign power occupying their country, namely, Rome.

COMMENTARY

Only Luke gives us further details about the nature of John's call to repentance. He spelled out what this meant in terms of specific groups—namely, the crowd, the tax collectors, and the soldiers. Each group asked for clear guidance in making an ethical response to John's demanding preaching. Thus, the question was sharply posed by each group: "What should we do?" (3:10-14). John was asked for counsel because he was recognized as a "teacher" who had been divinely authorized to carry out his mission (3:12).

John told the crowds to share their food and surplus clothes with the poor, who are often an object of concern in Luke–Acts (4:18; 6:20; 7:22; 12:33; 14:13; 19:8; Acts 4:34-35; 9:36; 10:4, 31; 24:17). There was to be real help given to those who were lacking proper food and clothing, the basic necessities of life. The tax collectors were not to exploit people to fill their own pockets but simply to collect the taxes required by the Roman authorities (3:13). The need for such counsel is indicated in 19:1-10, where Zacchaeus, a formerly corrupt tax collector, makes full restitution for wrongly acquired tax gains. The soldiers, for their part, were instructed not to use bullying, false accusation, or extortion in the execution of their duties. In addition, they were told to "be content" with their pay (3:14). Thus, John sought to prepare people in practical ways for the coming of Jesus. Repentance was a serious matter and required a significant change in lifestyle. The crooked things had to be made straight if a highway was to be prepared for the Lord's coming (3:4-5).

◆   ## 4. John's preaching about the Messiah (3:15-18; cf. Matt 3:11-12; Mark 1:7-8)

¹⁵Everyone was expecting the Messiah to come soon, and they were eager to know whether John might be the Messiah. ¹⁶John answered their questions by saying, "I baptize you with* water; but someone is coming soon who is greater than I am—so much greater that I'm not even worthy to be his slave and untie the straps of his sandals. He will baptize you with the Holy Spirit and with fire.* ¹⁷He is ready to separate the chaff from the wheat with his winnowing fork. Then he will clean up the threshing area, gathering the wheat into his barn but burning the chaff with never-ending fire." ¹⁸John used many such warnings as he announced the Good News to the people.

3:16a Or *in.*   3:16b Or *in the Holy Spirit and in fire.*

NOTES

3:16 *I baptize you with water; but someone is coming soon who is greater than I am.* For close literary parallels to this passage on John's messianic preaching, see Matt 3:11-12 and Mark 1:7-8. All three Synoptic accounts underscore the unworthiness of John to go before Jesus, the fact that Jesus was mightier than John, and the inferiority of John's baptism in water in relation to the cleansing action Jesus would introduce in baptizing with the Holy Spirit. Luke and Matthew are particularly graphic, using images of clearing, gathering, and burning to describe the radical nature of the Spirit's work to be unleashed in the coming of the Messiah.

3:17 *He is ready to separate the chaff from the wheat with his winnowing fork.* The *ptuon* [^{TG}4425, ^{ZG}4768] (fan; cf. KJV), mentioned in 3:17 and its parallel, Matt 3:12, is a "simple wooden pitchfork" (Souter 1953:224), so the modern translation "winnowing fork" is accurate and helpful (cf. Isa 30:24). As such, it presents a vivid image of divine judgment by sifting. The separation of the grain from the chaff involved a cleanup operation in which the grain would be preserved but the chaff utterly destroyed.

never-ending fire. This is a powerful image intended to warn John's Jewish contemporaries of the seriousness of sin and the certainty of God's dealing with it in inescapable judgment. The preaching was designed to lead people to repentance and practical righteousness in preparation for the promised Messiah, whose coming was imminent.

COMMENTARY

John's words about the Messiah are faithfully presented in all three synoptic Gospels, but the fullest account is provided by Luke (3:15-18; cf. Matt 3:11-12; Mark 1:7-8). Luke stressed the high level of messianic excitement that John's ministry aroused and the possibility that the Jewish people were considering whether or not John himself might be the promised Messiah. All three accounts make it perfectly clear that John, for his part, made no claims to messiahship but regarded himself as unworthy of performing even the most menial service for the Messiah, "the coming one."

Luke underscores a number of features in John's ministry. First, he notes the expectancy that John's fervent preaching evoked. The Jewish people were wondering about John's role in the divine plan (3:15). Luke's Gospel reveals John's complete disavowal of messianic claims (as also in John 1:20-23). Luke points out John's open recognition of "the coming one" as infinitely superior to himself. Indeed, the third Evangelist indicates that John was acutely conscious of his own unworthiness vis-à-vis the Messiah. John the Baptist, in Luke's view, contrasted his preliminary, preparatory baptism with that of "the coming one," whose radical baptism would be "with the Holy Spirit and with fire" (3:16; the fire is not mentioned in Mark's account). In sum, John envisaged a radical cleansing and judgment of Israel. In Luke, John's solemn warnings are depicted as a necessary preparation for the Good News. After this colorful description of John, Luke closes out John's prophetic ministry by noting his imprisonment.

Finally, this passage deserves to be compared with the fourth Gospel, where some of the same themes are mentioned. John's preparatory role is noted (John 1:6-7), and the fourth Evangelist insists, "John himself was not the light; he was simply a witness to tell about the light" (John 1:8). John pointed out Christ to people, insisted on the Messiah's superiority to himself, and acknowledged Christ's preexistence (John 1:15). He "preached the truth" so that people could be saved (John 5:33-35). He declared plainly that he was not the Messiah but only a forerunner sent to prepare the way; he was the best man, as it were, sent to bring Jesus and his bride together (John 3:28-30). The fourth Evangelist was intent on showing the complete subordination of John to Jesus, probably because of a situation where some claims were still being made for John as a rival leader (cf. Acts 19:1-7).

◆　　 ## 5. John's imprisonment (3:19-20; cf. Matt 14:6-11; Mark 6:17-28)

19John also publicly criticized Herod Antipas, the ruler of Galilee,* for marrying Herodias, his brother's wife, and for many other wrongs he had done. 20So Herod put John in prison, adding this sin to his many others.

3:19 Greek *Herod the tetrarch.*

NOTES

3:19 *John also publicly criticized Herod Antipas.* This is the only place in Luke–Acts where the verb *elenchō* [TG1651, ZG1794] (rebuke) appears. On the general use of this verb in the NT, see EDNT (1.427-428). For a detailed study of Herod Antipas, see Hoehner (1972:110-171).

for marrying Herodias, his brother's wife. This was a clear-cut case of immorality (Lev 18:16; 20:21), where Herod Antipas had left his first wife, the daughter of Aretas IV (the King of Nabatea), and married Herodias, who had been previously married to his half brother, Herod Philip.

COMMENTARY

Mark and Matthew also speak of John's incarceration, but they defer their discussion until they record John's death at the hands of Herod Antipas (Matt 14:1-12; Mark 6:14-29). Luke includes John's clash with Herod here because it is historically appropriate to finish his treatment of John before discussing the ministry of Jesus. He presents John as an uncompromising preacher of righteousness. John's rectitude is clearly indicated in his blunt, public attack on Herod for marrying Herodias, his brother Philip's wife, and for other sins. John had offended some religious leaders, and now he had also attacked a powerful political figure who could arrest and imprison him when provoked into action by his vengeful wife. Herod Antipas put John in prison for this public criticism of his actions. Josephus tells us that the location of the prison was Machaerus, the remote fortress located east of the Dead Sea (*Antiquities* 18.5.2). The role of Herodias in engineering John's death is stressed in both Mark and Matthew (Matt 14:6-11; Mark 6:17-28). Luke viewed Herod's action as another revealing indication of the man's sinfulness. Later, Luke notes the fact that Herod suffered from a sense of guilt from beheading John, wondering if John had been raised from the dead (9:7-9).

In Luke's account, John's imprisonment is recorded prior to the account of the baptism of Jesus to show the transience of John's role before the preeminent significance of Jesus is presented (cf. John the Baptist's statement: "He must become greater and greater, and I must become less and less," John 3:30). Luke, therefore, does not mention John at Jesus' baptism, possibly as part of a subtle warning against a Baptist sect that may have developed from disciples of John who never converted to following Jesus (see Erickson 1993).

◆   ## B. The Baptism of Jesus (3:21-22; cf. Matt 3:13-17; Mark 1:9-11)

²¹One day when the crowds were being baptized, Jesus himself was baptized. As he was praying, the heavens opened, ²²and the Holy Spirit, in bodily form, descended on him like a dove. And a voice from heaven said, "You are my dearly loved Son, and you bring me great joy.*"

3:22 Some manuscripts read *my Son, and today I have become your Father.*

NOTES
3:21 As he was praying. Jesus prayed fervently at many critical points in his life, such as at his baptism (3:21), before times of conflict (5:16), before choosing the twelve disciples (6:12-13), in facing his impending suffering (22:39-46), for his friends (such as Peter, 22:31-32), and in the face of death (23:46). He also taught prayer parables to his disciples (11:5-8; 18:1-8) and prayed so powerfully that the disciples requested instruction from him in the art of prayer (11:1). His prayer brought blessing to him and spiritual power (9:29, 43). He urged his disciples to address their requests to a God who answers prayer (11:9-13; cf. Matt 7:7-11). For further discussion on the importance of prayer in Luke's presentation of Jesus and the ministry of the early church, see Trites 1978.

the heavens opened. This is apocalyptic language and imagery and is also used in the parallel accounts of the baptism of Jesus (Matt 3:13-17; Mark 1:9-11). The "splitting apart" of the heavens (Mark 1:10) indicates a transcendent communication from God breaking into the human sphere and dramatically revealing the divine will. For more on the baptism of Jesus, see Averbeck 1980; Beasley-Murray 1962; Campbell 1996; DJG 55-58; NIDNTT 1.143-161; TDNT 1.529-546.

3:22 and the Holy Spirit, in bodily form, descended on him like a dove. Using pictorial language, Luke describes the Holy Spirit as descending like a dove, in this way pointing to the breaking of the divine into the human plane, authorizing and empowering Jesus to carry out the mission entrusted to him by the Father. Observe also the careful appropriation of Ps 2:7: "The LORD said to me, 'You are my son.'" This Scripture was used as a messianic psalm that was applied to Jesus and later given great importance in the early church (e.g., Acts 13:33; Heb 1:5; 5:5). Furthermore, note the echo of Isa 42, where the language of the Lord's chosen servant is mentioned: the one "who pleases me" (Isa 42:1). Jesus is divinely hailed by the heavenly voice (the *bath qol*, lit., "daughter of the voice") as the Father's chosen instrument to accomplish God's will: "You are my dearly loved Son, and you bring me great joy" (3:22). In his baptism, Jesus was plainly endorsed and equipped to execute the task he had been given by the Father.

a voice from heaven said. The heavenly voice is also mentioned in the other Synoptic accounts (Matt 3:17; Mark 1:11). The heavenly voice is mentioned in the Gospels on two other occasions: (1) on the Mount of Transfiguration (9:35; cf. Matt 17:5; Mark 9:7) and (2) in the Temple during the final week of Jesus' public ministry (John 12:28). For a recent study of the former incident, see Trites (1994); on the latter, see Barrett (1978:425), who notes that "whereas in the rabbinic literature these voices are looked upon as a sort of inferior substitute for prophecy the New Testament commonly represents them as the directly heard voice of God."

COMMENTARY

Having written about John's life and work, Luke turned to the ministry of Jesus. The first event in his public ministry was his baptism, whereby he was divinely acknowledged as the Son of God and equipped for the task of accomplishing the divine will (cf. Acts 10:38: "You know that God anointed Jesus of Nazareth with the Holy Spirit and with power"). Luke's baptismal account is the shortest of the three Synoptic accounts. It makes no mention of John as the agent of the baptism, for Luke had already described John's imprisonment. It does not describe the location, which is identified as the Jordan River in Matthew and Mark, nor does it give details about the trip from Galilee to the site of the baptism, as Matthew and Mark do (cf. Matt 3:13; Mark 1:9).

Luke's account places the event in a corporate setting where many other Israelites were being baptized as part of a national movement. The verb "baptize" suggests that the mode was immersion, for the Greek verb *baptizō* [TG907, ZG966] means "dip, plunge, submerge." Jesus' baptism was connected with prayer, and this is significant, for, in Luke's view, prayer changes things (cf. 6:12; 9:18, 28-29; 11:1; 22:32, 41-42; 23:46). Another noticeable feature in Luke is the incident's close connection with the descent of the Holy Spirit to empower Jesus for his ensuing ministry (cf. 4:18).

Significantly, Luke notes that the descent of the Spirit was accompanied by the heavenly voice acclaiming Jesus as the beloved Son (cf. Matt 3:17; Mark 1:11; see also Ps 2:7; Isa 42:1; 44:2; Heb 1:5). It is clear that Jesus enjoyed the full approval of his Father as he began his public ministry.

In Luke's concise account of the baptism, the reader is shown how Jesus voluntarily joined the national back-to-God movement led by John the Baptist and accepted baptism at his hands. Matthew records the reluctance of the Baptist to baptize Jesus but appends the significant words of explanation offered by Jesus: "It should be done, for we must carry out all that God requires" (Matt 3:15). Jesus accepted baptism, conscious of the fact that he dwelled in the midst of an unclean people who needed to seek God, and he had to be clearly linked with them in this movement back to God. "If he was to lead them into God's kingdom, he himself must enter it by the only door open to them. He must be their representative before he could be their king; he must be 'counted among the rebels' before he could see all that would be accomplished by his anguish (Isa 53:11-12). The words from heaven were more than a divine appointment; they were the divine approval of the course to which Jesus committed himself in accepting baptism" (Caird 1963:77).

◆   C. The Record of Jesus' Ancestors (3:23-38; cf. Matt 1:2-16)

[23]Jesus was about thirty years old when he began his public ministry.
Jesus was known as the son of Joseph.
Joseph was the son of Heli.
[24]Heli was the son of Matthat.
Matthat was the son of Levi.
Levi was the son of Melki.
Melki was the son of Jannai.
Jannai was the son of Joseph.
[25]Joseph was the son of Mattathias.
Mattathias was the son of Amos.
Amos was the son of Nahum.
Nahum was the son of Esli.
Esli was the son of Naggai.
[26]Naggai was the son of Maath.
Maath was the son of Mattathias.
Mattathias was the son of Semein.
Semein was the son of Josech.
Josech was the son of Joda.
[27]Joda was the son of Joanan.
Joanan was the son of Rhesa.
Rhesa was the son of Zerubbabel.
Zerubbabel was the son of Shealtiel.
Shealtiel was the son of Neri.
[28]Neri was the son of Melki.
Melki was the son of Addi.
Addi was the son of Cosam.
Cosam was the son of Elmadam.
Elmadam was the son of Er.
[29]Er was the son of Joshua.
Joshua was the son of Eliezer.
Eliezer was the son of Jorim.
Jorim was the son of Matthat.
Matthat was the son of Levi.
[30]Levi was the son of Simeon.
Simeon was the son of Judah.

Judah was the son of Joseph.
Joseph was the son of Jonam.
Jonam was the son of Eliakim.
[31]Eliakim was the son of Melea.
Melea was the son of Menna.
Menna was the son of Mattatha.
Mattatha was the son of Nathan.
Nathan was the son of David.
[32]David was the son of Jesse.
Jesse was the son of Obed.
Obed was the son of Boaz.
Boaz was the son of Salmon.*
Salmon was the son of Nahshon.
[33]Nahshon was the son of Amminadab.
Amminadab was the son of Admin.
Admin was the son of Arni.*
Arni was the son of Hezron.
Hezron was the son of Perez.
Perez was the son of Judah.
[34]Judah was the son of Jacob.
Jacob was the son of Isaac.
Isaac was the son of Abraham.
Abraham was the son of Terah.
Terah was the son of Nahor.
[35]Nahor was the son of Serug.
Serug was the son of Reu.
Reu was the son of Peleg.
Peleg was the son of Eber.
Eber was the son of Shelah.
[36]Shelah was the son of Cainan.
Cainan was the son of Arphaxad.
Arphaxad was the son of Shem.
Shem was the son of Noah.
Noah was the son of Lamech.
[37]Lamech was the son of Methuselah.

Methuselah was the son of Enoch.   38 Kenan was the son of Enosh.*
Enoch was the son of Jared.   Enosh was the son of Seth.
Jared was the son of Mahalalel.   Seth was the son of Adam.
Mahalalel was the son of Kenan.   Adam was the son of God.

3:32 Greek *Sala*, a variant spelling of Salmon; also in 3:32b. See Ruth 4:22.   3:33 Some manuscripts read
Amminadab was the son of Aram. Arni and *Aram* are alternate spellings of Ram. See 1 Chr 2:9-10.   3:38 Greek
Enos, a variant spelling of Enosh; also in 3:38b. See Gen 5:6.

NOTES
3:23 *Jesus was known as the son of Joseph. Joseph was the son of Heli.* There is a marked
difference between the record of Jesus' ancestors here and that recorded in Matt 1:1-17,
particularly in the list from David's descendants to Jesus. Four reasons for the difference
have been proposed: (1) Julius Africanus (AD 170–245) argued that both lists present Jesus'
legal descent through Joseph, Matthew giving Joseph's natural lineage and Luke giving
Joseph's legal lineage; (2) Annius of Viterbo (c. AD 1490), Martin Luther, and many today
think Matthew provides Joseph's ancestry and Luke provides Mary's; (3) Tertullian (c. AD
160–230), followed by a few modern scholars, suggested that Matthew provides Mary's
lineage and Luke provides Joseph's; and (4) an approach that is favored by several modern
scholars suggests that Matthew is giving Jesus' legal lineage and Luke is giving Joseph's
natural lineage (cf. DJG 258).

The second view mentioned above seems most reasonable: "Joseph is called the 'son of
Heli' in Luke apparently in order to conform with Jewish legal custom; this can only mean
that he was the son of Heli in the sense that he was the husband of Heli's daughter. Luke
carefully specifies that Jesus was not *really* Joseph's son. For Luke, a Greek, to trace Mary's
genealogy is not inappropriate, for Luke always shows a special interest in the women who
followed Jesus" (Lindsell 1965:1536).

The subject of biblical genealogies is a complex one. On the synoptic genealogies, see Abel
1973:203-210; Hood 1961; Overstreet 1981. Note especially M. D. Johnson 1969 and,
more generally, R. R. Wilson 1977. On the general theme of the ethnicity of Jesus, see
Charlesworth 1991.

COMMENTARY
Luke's placement of the genealogy of Jesus between the accounts of the baptism and
the Temptation is, at first sight, very puzzling. However, the incisive comment of
Craddock here puts the matter in perspective by noting that the genealogy provides
a fitting closing for the first three chapters:

> First, we are told Jesus was approximately thirty when he began his ministry.
> This is one of only two Gospel references to Jesus' age as an adult (John
> 8:57). Second, the genealogy links Jesus to God through Adam. Finally, the
> genealogy dramatizes a point continually made by Luke: Jesus is in continu-
> ity with his heritage, a true child of Israel. The family line is traced through
> Joseph, the legal, but not the biological father of Jesus. (Craddock 1990:53)

Accordingly, Luke "substantiates Jesus' messianic claims by adducing evidence of
his Davidic descent (cf. Rom 1:3; Mark 10:48; Acts 2:30)" (Caird 1963:77).

In addition, there is a strong connection that binds the baptism, genealogy, and
temptation together in the sense that he who was equipped at his baptism to do the
work of the Son of God was born the Son of God, and he had to be put to the test as
the Son of God (see 1:35; 3:22, 38; 4:3, 9). In Luke's mind, the relation of Jesus to

the Father was important for all the other sons and daughters of Adam. The prefacing of the temptation narrative with the universal genealogical account reminds us that the victory Jesus achieved over temptation has implications for all the descendants of Adam.

Luke's genealogy of Jesus works backward from Joseph to Adam, while Matthew's Jewish-focused account operates the other way round, running from Abraham to David, then to the exile in Babylon, and finally on to Christ (Matt 1:2-17). Among the more significant names is Zerubbabel, "the son of Shealtiel" (3:27; cf. Ezra 3:2, 8; Hag 1:1), first governor of Judah after the exile, who, together with the priest Jeshua, led the rebuilding of the Temple in Jerusalem. "Reference to Zerubbabel in the lineage of Jesus in both Matt 1:12-13 and Luke 3:27 is significant in fulfilling the typology of Hag 2:23, in which Zerubbabel serves as a prototype of Jesus, the 'chosen signet' of the Lord" (Gardner 1995:682). David, "son of Jesse" (3:32), is prominent in both Luke (13 times) and Acts (11 times) as a major player in salvation history, and here as an important royal ancestor of Jesus. Abraham is another key figure in Luke's genealogy, a person who is frequently cited in Luke–Acts (15 times in Luke, 8 times in Acts), where his cardinal role in Jewish history is recognized (e.g., 1:55, 73; 3:8; 13:16, 28; 19:9; Acts 3:13, 25; 7:2, 32; 13:26). Some antediluvian figures are also named, including Noah (Gen 6:9–9:28; cf. 17:26-27), Methuselah (renowned for his remarkable longevity—969 years, Gen 5:21-27; cf. 1 Chr 1:3), Enoch (who enjoyed "close fellowship with God" throughout his life, Gen 5:21-24), Seth (Gen 4:25-26), and Adam, "the son of God" (i.e., the first man, 3:38; cf. Gen 2:19–3:24; Rom 5:12-19). It was important to Luke to show the relationship of Jesus to the whole human family.

Jesus was not a mythological figure but a genuine historical person with a real family tree. Luke's stated concern is that "all people will see the salvation sent from God" (3:6, quoting Isa 40:5). Jesus is related to all people as "the son of Adam, . . . the son of God" (3:38), and this has the profoundest significance for the whole human family. "By calling Adam son of God he makes a link between the baptism and God's purposes in creation. Man was designed for that close filial relationship to God which was exemplified in Jesus, and which Jesus was to share with those who became his disciples" (Caird 1963:77-78). A new creation was taking shape, for Christ was destined to be the "firstborn among many brothers and sisters" (Rom 8:29; cf. 2 Cor 5:17).

Another feature that must be addressed is the marked difference between the record of Jesus' ancestors in Matthew and Luke. When the two accounts are compared, a number of observations can be made. While Matthew related Jesus to the family of King David and to Abraham, the father of the Jewish people, Luke traced the genealogy of Jesus back to the beginning of the whole human family. Matthew's list consists of 42 names; Luke's involves 79. While Matthew's account moves from Abraham forward to Jesus, Luke's account proceeds from Jesus backward to Adam. While Matthew's account is somewhat stylized, schematic, and selective, Luke's is more complete and universal in outlook. In addition, while Matthew's account might employ a numerological device (the number 14 possibly pointing to the importance of David, being the numerical value of the Heb. consonants in his name—namely, five plus four plus five), Luke does not appear to use this device. In spite of the fact that the accounts are practically identical from Abraham to David, they clearly diverge from David on; this probably means that the two accounts are based upon independent traditions.

Various suggestions have been made to account for these differences (see note on 3:23). Some commentators have argued that Matthew was restricting his list to the heirs of the throne of David, while Luke was attempting to provide a more exhaustive account of the lineage of Joseph to David. A more likely explanation, however, suggests that while Matthew traced the official line of Joseph, who was the legal father of Jesus, Luke concentrated on the line of Mary, Jesus' actual blood mother. Luke does not mention Mary, because it was customary to stress the male role in genealogies (see Gen 11:10-29; Exod 6:14-20; Ruth 4:18-22; 1 Chr 1:1-44). Nonetheless, Luke's preface to the genealogy introduces a significant reminder of the virginal conception, telling the reader that Jesus was "the son, so it was thought, of Joseph" (3:23, NIV). This phrase (translated as "Jesus was known as the son of Joseph" in the NLT) is intended as a clear signal to the reader to recall the angelic message of Gabriel, who told Mary that she, a virgin, would give birth to the Son of God, the one who would occupy the throne of his ancestor David and reign forever (1:30-35).

Luke in no way wanted to undermine the significance or importance of the Virgin Birth. Yet, he wanted to place Jesus carefully in a broad historical context to show his firm roots in history and his vital connection with the whole of humankind—a connection that foreshadowed the scope of the salvation Jesus would bring. Luke used his material carefully and responsibly (cf. 1 Chr 1:1-4, 24-27; 2:1-15; Ruth 4:18-22), and the end product clearly is in harmony with the purposes stated in his preface (1:1-4).

◆   D. The Temptation of Jesus (4:1-13; cf. Matt 4:1-11; Mark 1:12-13)

Then Jesus, full of the Holy Spirit, returned from the Jordan River. He was led by the Spirit in the wilderness,* ²where he was tempted by the devil for forty days. Jesus ate nothing all that time and became very hungry.

³Then the devil said to him, "If you are the Son of God, tell this stone to become a loaf of bread."

⁴But Jesus told him, "No! The Scriptures say, 'People do not live by bread alone.'*"

⁵Then the devil took him up and revealed to him all the kingdoms of the world in a moment of time. ⁶"I will give you the glory of these kingdoms and authority over them," the devil said, "because they are mine to give to anyone I please. ⁷I will give it all to you if you will worship me."

⁸Jesus replied, "The Scriptures say,

'You must worship the LORD your God
    and serve only him.'*"

⁹Then the devil took him to Jerusalem, to the highest point of the Temple, and said, "If you are the Son of God, jump off! ¹⁰For the Scriptures say,

'He will order his angels to protect
    and guard you.
¹¹And they will hold you up with their
    hands
    so you won't even hurt your foot
    on a stone.'*"

¹²Jesus responded, "The Scriptures also say, 'You must not test the LORD your God.'*"

¹³When the devil had finished tempting Jesus, he left him until the next opportunity came.

4:1 Some manuscripts read *into the wilderness.* 4:4 Deut 8:3. 4:8 Deut 6:13. 4:10-11 Ps 91:11-12.

NOTES

4:2 *he was tempted by the devil.* The verb *peirazō* [TG3985, ZG4279] (test, tempt) can be used in a good sense or a bad sense. In the former use, God or Christ can "put someone to the test" so that true character is proved and revealed (e.g., John 6:6; Heb 11:17). In a bad sense, the verb can mean "entice to evil, tempt" (e.g., Gal 6:1; Jas 1:13-14). The devil tempts people in this way (1 Cor 7:5; 1 Thess 3:5; Rev 2:10) and so boldly attacked Christ (Matt 4:1; Mark 1:13; cf. Heb 2:18; 4:15). Matthew specifically calls him "the tempter" (*ho peirazōn* [TG3985, ZG4279]; Matt 4:3; cf. 1 Thess 3:5) and notes Jesus' strong resistance to and dismissal of him: "Get out of here, Satan" (Matt 4:10). The cognate verb *ekpeirazō* [TG1598, ZG1733] (put to the test, tempt) is used in both 4:12 and Matt 4:7 as a quotation from Deut 6:16. In these passages, it has the strongly negative sense of putting God to the test—something that Jesus absolutely refused to do. For more on this, see Pokorny 1973–1974 and DJG 821-827.

for forty days. The reference to forty days recalls Moses' fast after the golden calf incident (Deut 9:18, 25; cf. 1 Kgs 19:8; Matt 4:2). A context involving idolatry or temptation to idolatry is found there as well as in 1 Kgs 19 and here (4:7).

4:3 *Son of God.* On the significance of the "Son of God" theme in the narrative structure of Luke, see Wren (1984).

4:4 *The Scriptures say.* The context of each quotation Jesus cites from Deuteronomy shows that Israel failed in the same temptation. Jesus, in effect, is saying, "I know what you are doing. It worked with Israel; it won't work with me."

4:6 *I will give you the glory of these kingdoms and authority over them.* The word for "authority" is used in the temptation account, where the devil promises Jesus authority (*exousia* [TG1849, ZG2026], also used in 4:32, 36; 5:24; cf. NIDNTT 2.606-611) over all the kingdoms of the world. Jesus refused the devil's offer. Luke presented Jesus as exercising true authority in his ministry, working and speaking in the power of the Holy Spirit (4:1, 14, 18; 9:1). Similarly, Matthew closes his Gospel with Jesus declaring that he had been given "all authority in heaven and on earth" and then issuing the great commission (Matt 28:18-20).

4:10 *He will order his angels to protect and guard you.* The Scripture cited is Ps 91:11. One textual tradition sees this promise fulfilled in Gethsemane: "Then an angel from heaven appeared and strengthened him" (22:43). On the role of angels, see the comments on 1:11-17.

4:13 *he [the devil] left him until the next opportunity came.* Luke uses the word *kairos* [TG2540, ZG2789] here for "opportunity." He also uses the related term *eukairia* [TG2120, ZG2321] (favorable opportunity) of Judas's attempt to betray Christ (22:6; see EDNT 2.232-235).

COMMENTARY

Luke concludes his account of the preparation for Jesus' ministry by giving a detailed record of the temptation of Jesus. This is closely paralleled by a similar account in Matthew's Gospel (Matt 4:1-11) and by a much briefer one in Mark (Mark 1:12-13). Matthew and Luke derived their material from a common source, though they reversed the order of the last two temptations and put their own personal stamp on the material in accordance with their different aims and purposes.

All three accounts acknowledge the following: (1) the Holy Spirit directed Jesus into this experience; (2) the Temptation occurred in the wilderness; (3) the devil was the one who attempted to entice Jesus into evil; and (4) the testing lasted forty days. Only Mark connects the Temptation directly to the baptism by the word "immediately" (*euthus* [TG2117, ZG2317]; Mark 1:12). While Mark's fondness for this word must be noted (he used it over 40 times), it seems likely that the one event followed hard on the heels of the other. Another unique feature in Mark's account is the enigmatic reference to the wild animals (Mark 1:13). In Jewish tradition, wild animals were subject to the righteous man and preeminently to the Messiah (e.g., Hos 2:18: "On that day I will make a covenant with all the wild animals and the birds of the sky and the animals that scurry along the ground so they will not harm you"; cf. Isa 11:6-9; 35:9; 65:20-25). Note a similar thought in the *Testament of Levi* 5:2: "If you do well, even the unclean spirits will flee from you; and the beasts will dread you."

There are many features in the temptation narrative that Luke shares with Matthew and not Mark. To begin with, both note the absence of food. Luke observes that Jesus "ate nothing all that time" (4:2); Matthew speaks of fasting (Matt 4:2). Presumably, Jesus drank water during this prolonged period, for there is no mention of thirst. Another common feature is that both Matthew and Luke detail three temptations, and they are the same ones in both accounts. Moreover, both see Jesus' hunger as the springboard for the first temptation. In addition, both view the temptations as directed toward Jesus as the "Son of God" (4:3, 9; Matt 4:3, 6). Jesus was wrestling with the nature of his unique vocation. The Father had acclaimed him in his baptism as "my dearly loved Son" (3:22; Matt 3:17; see also Mark 1:11), but in what way would he fulfill that calling? Would he be primarily a miracle worker, turning stones into bread or performing spectacular feats that would dazzle the adoring crowds as he invoked angelic intervention? Would he seize, by military might, all the kingdoms of the world and reign in power over his enemies? Or would he find another route to conquer human hearts and realize the Father's purpose? Jesus' temptation experience entailed a careful probing of alternative routes to the Kingdom of God.

Another common point in Matthew and Luke is the obvious fact that both accounts stress the importance of the Scriptures to Jesus in meeting temptations (4:4, 8, 12; Matt 4:4, 7, 10). The book of Deuteronomy was particularly significant in the thinking of Christ at this time, for he quoted it three times to fend off the devil's temptations (Deut 8:3; 6:13, 16). Jesus truly wielded "the sword of the Spirit, which is the word of God" (Eph 6:17), thereby leaving his followers an excellent model for using the Scriptures responsibly and effectively in coping with their own temptations. It should also be noted that Matthew and Luke alike show a clear recognition of the fact that even the devil can quote Scripture and misuse it to subvert the purposes of God (4:9-11; Matt 4:5-7).

Both Evangelists speak of the seductive glory and splendor of the kingdoms of the world offered by the devil to Jesus (4:5-7; Matt 4:8-9). The Temptation presented an easy way to achieve world conquest without taking the costly way of self-renunciation and self-sacrifice that eventually led to the Crucifixion. The price exacted, however, was to worship Satan, and Jesus refused.

Luke, like Matthew, underlined Jesus' insistence in the encounter that worship belongs to God alone (4:8; Matt 4:10). Both accounts also demonstrate the central role of the Temple in Jewish thinking. This was certainly the place where one could attract attention by a flamboyant display of power. Jesus (unlike the Simon mentioned in Acts 8:9-13) refused to use his great power to dazzle people and thereby win superficial allegiance. Matthew and Luke alike insist that God is not to be put to the test in a presumptuous way (4:12; Matt 4:7). The coming of the Kingdom of God could only be achieved by employing ethical means to realize ethical ends. There was no place for shortcuts or cheap substitutes. In both accounts, the devil's defeat in the encounter is carefully noted (4:13; Matt 4:10-11). Also, Matthew and Luke are quite candid in assessing future conflicts in that both acknowledge that there would be other times of testing and temptation (e.g., 22:28, 40-46; Matt 26:36-46).

There are a number of special features in Luke's temptation narrative worthy of notice. First of all, Luke stressed the central place of the Spirit in the incident. Jesus entered the Temptation "full of the Holy Spirit" (4:1), and he returned to Galilee "filled with the Holy Spirit's power" (4:14). Thus, Luke connected the Temptation with the baptism of Jesus, where "the Holy Spirit . . . descended on him like a dove" (3:22). The geographical reference to the Jordan River is also a reminder of the link between these two events (4:1; cf. 3:3).

It should also be noted that Luke pointed to the visionary character of the experience, for the devil showed Jesus all the kingdoms of the world "in a moment of time" (4:5). In addition, Luke made the Temple challenge the climax of the whole event (4:9-12). The Temple occupied a tremendous place in Jewish thought and religious culture, and its importance is certainly highlighted in Luke–Acts. In Acts, Stephen recognizes that God "doesn't live in temples made by human hands" (Acts 7:48). Stephen instead pointed beyond the Temple to Christ as the true place of salvation (Acts 7:44-56; cf. John 4:21-26; Acts 4:12; 16:31).

In his presentation, Luke is conscious of an element of timing in the Temptation (4:13). Elsewhere, he notes Jesus speaking of the time of testing (8:13). Sensitivity to divine timing calls for constant vigilance in the face of temptation (11:4; 21:36; 22:40, 46). Mark and Matthew also stress the need for careful vigilance in their respective Gospels (Matt 24:42-44; 25:13; Mark 13:32-37; 14:34-38).

In summary, the temptation experience was a vital element in the preparation of Jesus for his public ministry. He was led by the Spirit but tempted by the devil. Two supernatural powers were struggling to control him. How would he exercise his messianic vocation? Would he simply be an economic wonder worker, filling people's stomachs and satisfying their physical needs? No, human beings needed more than that! Would he succumb to the enticing prospect of complete political control? The answer was an absolute "no" if the means was anything other than obedience to the Father. A similar point is made in John's account of the feeding of the five thousand, where Jesus deliberately escaped from those who "were ready to force him to be their king" (John 6:15). Only the living God is worthy of absolute love and worship. Would Jesus be a spellbinder, dazzling people with fantastic displays of power? No, for the Scriptures plainly teach that one must not test the Lord in such a provocative way. The path to bring many to glory would not allow such measures. The Son of Man would have to walk the hard road of obedience and suffering that would take him to crucifixion.

◆ IV. Jesus' Ministry in Galilee (4:14-9:50)
A. Jesus Rejected at Nazareth (4:14-30)

[14]Then Jesus returned to Galilee, filled with the Holy Spirit's power. Reports about him spread quickly through the whole region. [15]He taught regularly in their synagogues and was praised by everyone.

[16]When he came to the village of Nazareth, his boyhood home, he went as usual to the synagogue on the Sabbath and stood up to read the Scriptures. [17]The scroll of Isaiah the prophet was handed to him. He unrolled the scroll and found the place where this was written:

[18]"The Spirit of the LORD is upon me,
     for he has anointed me to bring
     Good News to the poor.
He has sent me to proclaim that
     captives will be released,
     that the blind will see,
that the oppressed will be set free,
[19]   and that the time of the LORD's
     favor has come.*"

[20]He rolled up the scroll, handed it back to the attendant, and sat down. All eyes in the synagogue looked at him intently. [21]Then he began to speak to them. "The Scripture you've just heard has been fulfilled this very day!"

[22]Everyone spoke well of him and was amazed by the gracious words that came from his lips. "How can this be?" they asked. "Isn't this Joseph's son?"

[23]Then he said, "You will undoubtedly quote me this proverb: 'Physician, heal yourself'—meaning, 'Do miracles here in your hometown like those you did in Capernaum.' [24]But I tell you the truth, no prophet is accepted in his own hometown.

[25]"Certainly there were many needy widows in Israel in Elijah's time, when the heavens were closed for three and a half years, and a severe famine devastated the land. [26]Yet Elijah was not sent to any of them. He was sent instead to a foreigner—a widow of Zarephath in the land of Sidon. [27]And there were many lepers in Israel in the time of the prophet Elisha, but the only one healed was Naaman, a Syrian."

[28]When they heard this, the people in the synagogue were furious. [29]Jumping up, they mobbed him and forced him to the edge of the hill on which the town was built. They intended to push him over the cliff, [30]but he passed right through the crowd and went on his way.

4:18-19 Or *and to proclaim the acceptable year of the LORD.* Isa 61:1-2 (Greek version); 58:6

NOTES

4:16 *he went . . . to the synagogue . . . and stood up to read.* Synagogue worship practices allowed any person whom the local authorities invited to read a Scripture lesson to do so. Also, if there was a suitable teacher present, this person could be given an opportunity to speak. This practice is seen in Acts 13:15 in Antioch of Pisidia: "After the usual readings from the books of Moses and the prophets, those in charge of the [synagogue] service sent [Paul and Barnabas] this message: 'Brothers, if you have any word of encouragement for the people, come and give it.'"

4:18 *The Spirit of the LORD is upon me.* The passage Jesus read from was Isa 61:1-2. Jesus read the Scripture in a striking way that day, boldly declaring, "The Scripture you've just heard has been fulfilled this very day!" (4:21). Jesus read the Heb. version, which Luke translated into Gr. following the LXX. On the use of the OT text here, see the detailed work of Koet (1989).

He has sent me to proclaim. On the importance of proclamation in the NT, see Stott 1961, DJG 625-630, and the note on 8:1. Almost half of the 54 occurrences of "proclaim" (*euangelizomai*) in the NT are found in Luke–Acts.

he has anointed me to bring Good News to the poor. For the importance of this passage for Christology, see Irudhayasamy (2003). On the literary importance of the passage for Luke's missiology, see Siker (1992). Luke often shows Jesus' concern for the poor (cf. 6:20; 7:22; 12:33; 14:13; 18:22).

captives will be released. Talbert (1989:55-56) has clarified the meaning of *aphesis* [TG859, ZG912] in Luke 4:18: "The word *aphesis* in normal Christian use means 'forgiveness,' and the evangelist elsewhere certainly employs the term in this way (1:77; 3:3; 24:47; Acts 2:38; 5:31; 10:43; 13:38; 26:18). It is therefore possible for the reader to hear this undertone in the word. The term is also used to mean 'release from captivity.' This is certainly its meaning in the context of Isaiah 61 and 58 and seems to be the dominant intent of Luke 4:18. Luke's view of Jesus' mission, as set forth in 4:18-19, [seems] to include preaching, physical healing, and exorcism."

4:21 *The Scripture you've just heard has been fulfilled this very day!* The recovery of prophecy was considered a prominent feature of the coming messianic age; this is quite evident in the NT (Kaiser 1982:15; cf. 4:18; Isa 11:1-5; 61:1; Joel 2:28; John 3:34; Acts 2:16-18).

4:25 *many needy widows in Israel.* On widows, see notes on 2:36-40; 7:11-17; 18:1-8; 20:41-47.

4:27 *many lepers in Israel.* On lepers, see notes on 5:12-16; 7:21; 17:11-19.

COMMENTARY

Luke sets this proclamation at Nazareth in the context of Jesus' Galilean ministry (4:14-15; cf. Matt 4:12-17; Mark 1:14-15). Once again, the author highlights Jesus' spiritual power. He who had received the Spirit's power at his baptism and had endured the testing in the wilderness now returned unscathed by the demonic attacks to commence his ministry in Galilee "filled with the Holy Spirit's power" (4:14). Luke describes this tour as a teaching mission based in the Galilean synagogues and generally evoking a favorable response. Thus, Jesus' fame spread throughout the surrounding country, and he "was praised by everyone" (4:15).

Mark's account specifically informs the reader that the Galilean preaching tour did not commence until after John the Baptist had been arrested (Mark 1:14). Matthew notes that Jesus had heard of John's arrest and took it as a signal to leave Judea and return to Galilee (Matt 4:12). In addition, Matthew locates Capernaum as the central point for Jesus' Galilean ministry and viewed this setting, in close proximity to the Gentiles, as the fulfillment of Isaiah's prophecy (Matt 4:13-16; cf. Isa 9:1-2). Luke places this incident at the beginning of his record of the Galilean ministry even though he was aware of previous miracles that Jesus had performed earlier in Capernaum (4:23). It seems to serve as a kind of frontispiece to the record of Jesus' public minstry, outlining, as a kind of emancipation proclamation, the program of Jesus and the subsequent mission of the early church that flowed from it. In addition, Luke reminds the reader that Nazareth was the boyhood home of Jesus (4:16), the place where he was known best by his kinsfolk and acquaintances.

Luke notes the faithfulness of Jesus' attendance at the synagogue on the Sabbath day (4:16), thus setting a good example of regular public worship for his followers (cf. Acts 2:42; Heb 10:25). Luke also notes the practice of allowing a visiting teacher to read a passage of Scripture and explain it to the congregation (4:17-27; cf. Acts 13:15). In addition, Luke mentions the attendant in the synagogue (the *hupēretēs* [TG5257, ZG5677] or *khazzan*; 4:20).

Special notice is taken of the text that Jesus read on this occasion (Isa 61:1-2a). In the services held in the Jewish synagogue, the first lesson was taken from one of the first five books of the Old Testament (the Torah), broken down into 155 units designed to complete the reading of the whole Pentateuch in a three-year cycle. Malcolm Tolbert (1970:45) has well described how the oral reading took place in the synagogues:

> In Palestine and Babylon the reading of each verse of the Hebrew text was followed by a translation into Aramaic, the lingua franca of the Middle East. The reading from the prophets followed the lection from the Torah . . . [it is not clear if the selection of this passage came from the head of the synagogue]. Perhaps the choice was left to the reader's discretion. Any person could be invited to read the scripture lesson, which was followed by a sermon when a competent teacher was present. Commonly, scripture was read while standing, but the sermon was delivered while seated (see Luke 4:16, 20).

The words Jesus read speak powerfully of the Messiah's ministry of preaching, healing, and liberating the poor, blind, and oppressed (4:18-19). In order to meet human needs of every kind, the Messiah was to be "anointed" with the Holy Spirit and thereby empowered to carry out his divinely appointed role (4:18; a point also made in Acts 4:27; 10:38). Through his reading, Jesus was announcing the coming of the messianic age, "the time of the LORD's favor" (4:19), alluding to the Year of Jubilee (Lev 25:8-55), which occurred every fifty years and required that debts be canceled, all Hebrew slaves be freed, and ancestral property be returned to the family that originally owned it (NBD 1043). Isaiah's prediction primarily regarded the liberation of Israel from Babylonian captivity, but Jesus proclaimed liberation from sin and its enslaving consequences.

Luke's account emphasizes that Jesus saw himself as the fulfillment of this remarkable prophecy (4:21). The members of the synagogue "looked at him intently" (4:20). Both the remarkable text used and Jesus' declaration of its fulfillment justified their rapt attention. However, there were ambivalent reactions toward Jesus. On the one hand, "everyone spoke well of him" (4:22a), and yet, there was puzzled astonishment at the gracious words that Jesus spoke: 'How can this be?' they asked. 'Isn't this Joseph's son?'" (4:22b; see note on 2:47).

Luke presents Jesus as giving expression to the perceived questions of the Nazareth townspeople (4:23) and highlights his insistence upon the basic truth contained in the proverbial maxim that "no prophet is accepted in his own hometown" (4:24; cf. Matt 13:57; Mark 6:4; John 4:44). Jesus then indicated that others, even Gentiles, would be open to his ministry by recounting the merciful ministry of Elijah and Elisha to the widow of Zarephath and Naaman the Syrian, respectively (1 Kgs 17:8-24; 2 Kgs 5:1-19). This triggered the open hostility of the people (4:28). We know from Josephus (*Antiquities* 14.9.2) that the Syrians and the Galileans were mortal enemies. "It was therefore most offensive to them that Jesus should instance how two Syrians had been preferred to all Israel" (Schonfield 1958:150). As a result, a mob attempted to murder Jesus by pushing him over a cliff on the outskirts of Nazareth (4:29), but Jesus escaped through the crowd. (Some commentators have seen this escape as miraculous, but Luke does not use any of the usual terms for miracles to describe Jesus' exit from this threatening scene.)

This was a sad occasion for Jesus. He came to his own kinsfolk and acquaintances and met scorn and rejection (cf. John 1:11). He was dismissed as too well known to be special, and, as Mark's Gospel sadly observes, the Nazareth locals "were deeply offended and refused to believe in him" (Mark 6:3; cf. John 7:5). Luke's account goes even further in exposing the murderous intention of the citizens, thereby revealing the tragic nature of the encounter. They did not perceive that God in Christ was visiting them, a charge that Jesus later made against the people of Jerusalem (19:44; cf. 1:68; 7:16). Therefore, they missed their golden opportunity.

Viewing the subsequent course of Jesus' ministry, we can see numerous examples that fulfill the programmatic pattern here set forth: Jesus released a leper from his disease (5:12-15), freed a paralytic (5:17-26), healed a man with a withered hand (6:6-11), delivered a centurion's servant (7:2-10), raised a man from the dead (7:11-17), and offered forgiveness to a woman who was a flagrant sinner (7:37-50).

◆ B. Jesus Casts Out an Evil Spirit (4:31-37; cf. Mark 1:23-28)

³¹Then Jesus went to Capernaum, a town in Galilee, and taught there in the synagogue every Sabbath day. ³²There, too, the people were amazed at his teaching, for he spoke with authority.

³³Once when he was in the synagogue, a man possessed by a demon—an evil* spirit—began shouting at Jesus, ³⁴"Go away! Why are you interfering with us, Jesus of Nazareth? Have you come to destroy us? I know who you are—the Holy One sent from God!"

³⁵Jesus cut him short. "Be quiet! Come out of the man," he ordered. At that, the demon threw the man to the floor as the crowd watched; then it came out of him without hurting him further.

³⁶Amazed, the people exclaimed, "What authority and power this man's words possess! Even evil spirits obey him, and they flee at his command!" ³⁷The news about Jesus spread through every village in the entire region.

4:33 Greek *unclean;* also in 4:36.

NOTES

4:32 *he spoke with authority.* See note on 4:6.

4:33 *a man possessed by a demon.* Like Satan, the demons were once numbered among the good angels but sinned and consequently had been sentenced to eternal judgment (cf. Isa 14:12-17; Ezek 28:12-19; Matt 25:41; 2 Pet 2:4; Jude 1:6). They are malevolent agents who actively oppose the purpose of God. Belief in the existence and activities of demons is offensive and disturbing to many people today. Some would view accounts of demon possession in the NT entirely as examples of mental illness. On the other hand, many take the activities of spirits seriously but might make the mistake of dismissing mental illnesses completely. While there may be cases where exorcisms are difficult to distinguish from healing (e.g., 11:14-23; Matt 12:22), the distinction in principle is important. "To be 'possessed' by a spirit from 'outside' is quite different from nervous or mental disorder, and has different symptoms. . . . possession is just as real as psychological disorder, and it troubles many today, as it did in NT times" (Keeley 1982:209).

This spiritual battle with demonic forces is recognized in Eph 6:12. The NT teaches that through his death and resurrection, Jesus defeated the power of death and Satan (1 Cor 15:54-57; Col 2:13-15). The apostles healed the sick and cast out demons in Jesus' name, for there is no name greater than the name of Jesus (Phil 2:9-11). On the general subject of demons and exorcism, see DJG 163-172, Fitzmyer 1989:146-174, and Twelftree 1985.

4:34 *Go away! Why are you interfering with us?* "This is an attempt of the demon to gain control over Jesus" (Gundry 1993:174-176).

4:35 *Be quiet!* The verb used for silencing the evil spirit is an interesting one, seldom found in the Gospels and only here in Luke (*phimoō* [TG5392/A, ZG5821], "muzzle, silence"; cf. Matt 22:12, 34; Mark 1:25; 4:39). It is a strong word, here issuing the authoritative command "Be muzzled!"

COMMENTARY

The next incident recorded in Luke is set in Capernaum, which Luke clearly identifies, like Nazareth (1:26), as "a town in Galilee" (4:31). This was presumably for readers who were not familiar with that area and is also a link with 4:14-15. It is also important as the location of Luke's first report of Jesus' working as an exorcist.

The reader here enters into an area of cultural difference, and the immense distance between biblical times and our own time becomes patently clear. To cite one commentator, "the Bible says little about demon possession before or after the incarnation, but much during Jesus' ministry. In scripture, this phenomenon is part of the conflict between Jesus, who came to destroy the works of the devil (1 John 3:8), and evil" (Morris 1974:119). Modern medicine has offered alternative ways of explaining these illnesses, but "this does not mean that demon possession can be dismissed as outmoded science" (Caird 1963:88), as Rudolf Bultmann attempts to do in his book *Jesus Christ and Mythology* (1958).

Caird's comment is insightful. He gives this explanation of how exorcism relates to the subject of the Kingdom of God, which was the major concern of the ministry of Jesus:

> Ancient opinion ascribed to demon possession any disease which involved loss of control—epilepsy, delirium, convulsions, nervous disorders, mental convulsions, mental derangement—and which therefore suggested the pres-

ence of an invading power. It was primarily not a medical but a religious diagnosis. [It asserted that this illness was] an evil thing from which men could be rescued only by the superior power of God. The exorcisms of Jesus were thus the preliminary skirmishes in the campaign to be waged by him on behalf of the kingdom of God against the kingdom of satan. (1963:88-89)

This exorcism was set in the midst of Jesus' teaching ministry in Galilee, where the works and words of the Messiah are clearly being presented together. Luke's account of the exorcism stresses the great power and authority of Jesus, who was mighty in deeds as well as in words (4:31-37). The incident is a striking example of the emancipation that the Messiah brought to disordered persons. It took place on the Sabbath, an interesting detail in view of the strong attacks against Jesus for supposed violations of the Sabbath day (Luke mentions five healings on the Sabbath, a subject in which he was evidently interested; cf. 4:31-41; 6:6-11; 13:10-17; 14:1-6).

Jesus was recognized by the demons as "the Holy One sent from God," an unusual expression pointing to the divine origin of Jesus (used only in 4:34; Mark 1:24; John 6:69; cf. Acts 2:27). However, Jesus bluntly silenced the unclean spirit. Here and in 4:41 and 5:14, we observe what is known as the messianic secret. The messiahship of Jesus could easily be misunderstood, so it was important for Jesus to disclose it at the right time in order to avoid giving a false impression of his message and ministry. This theme is particularly developed in Mark's Gospel (see Mark 1:25, 44; 5:43; 7:36; 8:30; 9:9) and is present in Matthew as well (Matt 8:4; 9:30). (On the messianic secret, see Blevins 1981 and Tuckett 1982.)

Though the demons had accurate knowledge about Jesus' identity (cf. Matt 8:29; Mark 1:24), they were forbidden to share it. In view of the adversarial character of the demons (a point brought out strongly in 4:34), their confession of Jesus' messianic identity was both inappropriate and untimely. It is clear from the great commission and similar passages that Jesus intended witness to be given to him by disciples, not demons (24:46-49; Matt 28:18-20; John 15:27; Acts 1:8; 9:15; 26:16-18).

Jesus cast out the demon, not by a magical formula (cf. the technique of the sons of Sceva who are mentioned in Acts 19:13-16), but by his powerful word. The evil spirit came out without injuring the man (4:35), though here and in other cases there was evidently a struggle (cf. 8:28-33; 9:42), because the Kingdom of God was attacking and overcoming the kingdom of evil. The story of the exorcism served to spread the popularity of Jesus far and wide throughout the region (4:37; cf. 4:14).

The incident is beautifully symmetrical, for Luke placed equal emphasis on Jesus' authority in his teaching and in his casting out the evil spirit (4:32, 36). The story is part of a larger unit that shows how Jesus became well known throughout the Galilean countryside (4:14-41).

◆ C. Jesus Heals Many People (4:38-41)

38After leaving the synagogue that day, Jesus went to Simon's home, where he found Simon's mother-in-law very sick with a high fever. "Please heal her," everyone begged. 39Standing at her bedside, he rebuked the fever, and it left her.

And she got up at once and prepared a meal for them.

⁴⁰As the sun went down that evening, people throughout the village brought sick family members to Jesus. No matter what their diseases were, the touch of his hand healed every one. ⁴¹Many were possessed by demons; and the demons came out at his command, shouting, "You are the Son of God!" But because they knew he was the Messiah, he rebuked them and refused to let them speak.

NOTES

4:39 *she got up at once and prepared a meal for them.* Luke's account of the healing of Peter's mother-in-law stresses the instantaneous nature of the healing and its completeness. It also highlights the woman's keenness to serve: she acted "at once" (*parachrēma* [ᵀᴳ3916, ᶻᴳ4202]). NIDNTT 3.36 states, "This adverb occurs 18 times in the NT, with 10 occurrences in Luke and 6 in Acts and in Matt 21:19-20. In 15 instances *parachrēma* is used in the miracle stories (healings—Luke 1:64; 4:39; 5:25; 8:44, 47, 55; 13:13; 18:43; Acts 3:7; miracles of punishment—Matt 21:19; Acts 5:10; 12:23; 13:11; a miracle of opening doors—Acts 16:26) of the immediate or instantaneous occurrences of the miracle."

4:40 *No matter what their diseases were, the touch of his hand healed every one.* Luke's Gospel gives attention to the reality of pain and suffering (e.g., 5:12; 14:2) and the compassion of Jesus to meet human need (cf. 5:12-15, 17-26; 6:6-11; 8:43-48; 14:1-6). Faith is prominent in many Lukan healing passages (5:12; 7:9; 8:50; 17:19; 18:42). There are also examples of exorcisms (4:31-37; 8:26-39; 9:37-43) and two cases where Jesus restores people to life (7:11-15; 8:40-42, 49-56). Jesus' reply to the messengers from John the Baptist (7:22; cf. Matt 11:5) serves as a summary of his healings: "The blind see, the lame walk, the lepers are cured, the deaf hear, the dead are raised to life." Healings continued in the early church in the name of Jesus (Acts 3:1-11; 4:10; 8:7; 16:18; 19:11-12). For useful studies on the miracles recorded in the Gospels, see H. C. Kee 1983; Theissen 1983; van der Loos 1965; Wenham and Blomberg 1986. For a more thorough work toward a medical explanation of the NT data, see Howard 2001.

COMMENTARY

Jesus' departure from the synagogue was followed by a visit to the home of Simon Peter, whose mother-in-law was sick (cf. 1 Cor 9:5 on Peter's marital status). Matthew, Mark, and Luke all record this healing (cf. Matt 8:14-15; Mark 1:29-31), but only Luke, "the beloved doctor" (Col 4:14), describes the fever as a "high" fever (4:38).

Mark observes that this was the home of Andrew as well as Simon (Mark 1:29). This is because the two men were brothers (Matt 4:18; Mark 1:16; John 1:40). Mark also mentions the fact that James and John, two other prominent apostles, accompanied Jesus on this occasion (Mark 1:29). They would be able to speak of this event as eyewitnesses (cf. 1:2; 1 John 1:1-4). In addition to describing the woman's illness, Luke speaks of Christ's "standing at her bedside" (4:39). This detail underscores his deep concern for a person who was experiencing great suffering. All three synoptic writers stress the woman's grateful response to her healing and her eagerness to be of service (4:39; cf. Mark 1:31; Matt 8:15).

One of the most interesting features of Luke's account is the reference to Jesus' rebuking the fever, just as he is said to have rebuked (*epitimaō* [ᵀᴳ2008, ᶻᴳ2203]) the evil spirit in 4:35. This suggests that the illness in question was contrary to the divine purpose and therefore to be opposed. This healing, like the rebuke of the evil spirit and, later, of the wind and waves (8:24), reveals the lordship of Jesus.

The reference to the sun going down (4:40) is significant, for it meant that the Sabbath was over. According to the tradition of the elders, a Jew could not carry a burden on that day or walk more than a Sabbath day's journey—about two-thirds of a mile. The fact that people commenced carrying sick family members to Jesus as the Sabbath was ending indicated their eagerness to contact Jesus and their confidence in his power. Their trust in the healing power of Jesus was abundantly rewarded: "No matter what their diseases were, the touch of his hand healed every one" (4:40). The remarkable, transforming touch of Jesus brought wholeness, not only to those physically ill, but also to those who suffered from demonic oppression. As was noted above, the demons had supernatural knowledge of Jesus' identity, but they were expressly forbidden to testify concerning it. Since they were enemies of the Lord, their testimony was unacceptable.

In reviewing this phase of the Galilean ministry, it is clear that Jesus was particularly effective in Capernaum, where his preaching, teaching, and healing ministry met with a remarkable response from the people of the community and the surrounding area. A line from one of the speeches in Acts could serve as a summary of the import of the Capernaum ministry: "Jesus went around doing good and healing all who were oppressed by the devil, for God was with him" (Acts 10:38).

◆ D. Jesus Continues to Preach (4:42-44)

[42]Early the next morning Jesus went out to an isolated place. The crowds searched everywhere for him, and when they finally found him, they begged him not to leave them. [43]But he replied, "I must preach the Good News of the Kingdom of God in other towns, too, because that is why I was sent." [44]So he continued to travel around, preaching in synagogues throughout Judea.*

4:44 Some manuscripts read *Galilee.*

NOTES

4:43 *I must preach the Good News of the Kingdom of God.* This is the first mention of the phrase "the Kingdom of God" in Luke–Acts. Luke uses it over 30 times in his Gospel and occasionally in Acts (e.g., Acts 1:3; 14:22; 28:23, 31). In Acts, the Christ-centered emphasis comes to the fore as the early church preaches "that there is peace with God through Jesus Christ, who is Lord of all" (Acts 10:36). In the Gospel, Luke acknowledges the eternal kingship of Christ (1:33) and shows the central place of the Kingdom of God in the life and work of Jesus (8:1; 10:9-11; 12:31-32; 16:16; 22:29-30). Luke highlights the special place of Christ the King in bringing in the Kingdom of God (4:43; 8:10; 9:2, 11; 11:20; 17:21); the need for receiving the Kingdom with humility, sincerity, and self-sacrifice (9:60-62; 18:16-17, 24, 29-30); the importance of proclaiming the message of the Kingdom (8:1; 9:2, 60; 10:9; 16:16); and the future climax of the Kingdom (13:28-29; 14:15; 17:20; 19:11; 21:31; 22:16-18). Certainly, Luke is faithful in representing the Kingdom of God as the grand overall theme of the ministry of Jesus.

4:44 *preaching in synagogues.* This is Jesus' first mission trip, not the one in ch 9. He took several trips (9:1-6; 10:1-12; see Schnabel 2004). Matthew, like Luke, highlights Jesus' public ministry: "Jesus traveled throughout the region of Galilee, teaching in the synagogues and announcing the Good News about the Kingdom" (Matt 4:23). Jesus later commissioned the apostles and others to continue this ministry of preaching and teaching (10:1-24; Matt 10:1-15; Mark 6:7-13). For useful summaries on early Christian preaching, see Dodd 1936 and Mounce 1960.

Judea. This reading has the excellent support of 𝔓75 ℵ B C L Q R. Other manuscripts (A D 33 𝔐) change it to "Galilee" and still others (W 1424) to "of the Jews." The reference to Judea in 4:44 is at first glance surprising, for Luke had been describing a Galilean ministry, hence the change in later manuscripts. The comment of John Nolland (1990:216) is perceptive and helpful: "The Galilean ministry, exemplified by the incidents in Nazareth and Capernaum, is not restricted to Galilee but repeated on equal terms in the cities of the whole of Judea (used in the wide sense for the whole of Jewish Palestine as at 1:5; 6:17; 7:17; 23:5; and in Acts)."

COMMENTARY

At this point, Luke, following Mark, notes the departure of Christ from Capernaum: "Early the next morning Jesus went out to an isolated place" (4:42). The purpose of this withdrawal is given in Mark: "Jesus got up and went out to an isolated place to pray" (Mark 1:35). There must be private time for quietness and reflection in the presence of God for the time in public to be fruitful and useful to God's purposes. Even so, the constant pressure of the crowds was there, and they searched for him until they found him (4:42). Quite naturally, they pressed him to remain in Capernaum, because they appreciated the mighty acts of healing and exorcism that he had done in their midst. However, Christ refused in order to fulfill a more comprehensive mandate from God: "I must preach the Good News of the Kingdom of God in other towns, too, because that is why I was sent" (4:43). This statement underscores Jesus' strong sense of vocation. He knew that he had been "sent" by God to faithfully carry out a mission. The great underlying theme of that mission was the Kingdom of God, and that kingly sovereignty was taking shape in Jesus' ministry of preaching, teaching, healing, and casting out demons. The "I must" dimension points out the imperative nature of the task. The scope of that mission would take Jesus to "other towns"—a theme that is developed in the journey motif in Luke's Gospel (9:51–19:44) and then carried forward into a worldwide ministry in the early church through the extensive travels of Paul and others (cf. Acts 1:8; 9:15; 22:15, 21). The importance of Jesus' preaching and his use of the synagogue to do so are noted; both elements also feature prominently in the work of the apostles as described in Acts.

◆   E. The First Disciples (5:1-11; cf. Matt 4:18-22; Mark 1:16-20)

One day as Jesus was preaching on the shore of the Sea of Galilee,* great crowds pressed in on him to listen to the word of God. ²He noticed two empty boats at the water's edge, for the fishermen had left them and were washing their nets. ³Stepping into one of the boats, Jesus asked Simon,* its owner, to push it out into the water. So he sat in the boat and taught the crowds from there.

⁴When he had finished speaking, he said to Simon, "Now go out where it is deeper, and let down your nets to catch some fish."

⁵"Master," Simon replied, "we worked hard all last night and didn't catch a thing. But if you say so, I'll let the nets down again." ⁶And this time their nets were so full of fish they began to tear! ⁷A shout for help brought their partners in the other boat, and soon both boats were filled with fish and on the verge of sinking.

⁸When Simon Peter realized what had happened, he fell to his knees before Jesus and said, "Oh, Lord, please leave me—I'm too much of a sinner to be around you." ⁹For he was awestruck by the number of fish they had caught, as were the others with him. ¹⁰His partners, James and John, the sons of Zebedee, were also amazed.

Jesus replied to Simon, "Don't be afraid! From now on you'll be fishing for people!" ¹¹And as soon as they landed, they left everything and followed Jesus.

5:1 Greek *Lake Gennesaret*, another name for the Sea of Galilee.   5:3 *Simon* is called "Peter" in 6:14 and thereafter.

NOTES

5:1 *Sea of Galilee*. The Gr. text reads "Lake Gennesaret" (cf. NLT mg). Though he uses the word "sea" (17:2, 6; 21:25), Luke prefers to call this body of water a "lake" (*limnē* [TG3041, ZG3349]; cf. 8:22-23, 33), possibly to contrast it with the Mediterranean, which he describes as a "sea" (*thalassa* [TG2281, ZG2498]; Acts 27:40; 28:4).

5:4 *Now go out where it is deeper, and let down your nets to catch some fish.* In spite of Jesus' lack of experience as a fisherman, the instructions he gave on this occasion were quite definite and authoritative. Peter and his companions, on the other hand, were seasoned fishermen, knowing the lake and the best places to lower their dragnets for a good catch, so it was illogical for them to heed the injunction to go out deeper. Experience had taught them the places where the fish gathered, and those places had been explored "all last night" (5:5). This situation called for real faith in Jesus that ran contrary to their own thoughts. Though perhaps doubtful, their response was one of submission and obedience to the Master. The result was astounding (5:6).

5:5 *Master.* The Gr. word *epistatēs* [TG1988, ZG2181] (teacher, master) is used six times in Luke's Gospel when people address Jesus. The frightened disciples addressed him this way in the midst of the storm on the lake (8:24), and Peter spoke to Jesus this way here (5:5), when the crowds pressed upon Jesus (8:45), and on the Mount of Transfiguration (9:33). John did so once in consulting Jesus about a rival exorcist (9:49). The final use is the urgent appeal of ten men with leprosy who cried out, "Jesus, Master, have mercy on us!" (17:13). The more common word for "teacher" is *didaskalos* [TG1320, ZG1437], a term Luke uses 17 times (e.g., 9:38; 10:25; 11:45; 12:13; 18:18). Elsewhere in the Gospels, "Rabbi," the Heb. word for "(my) Teacher," is used frequently when Jesus was addressed (Matt 23:7-8; 26:25, 49; Mark 9:5; 10:51; John 1:38, 49; 3:2, 26; 6:25; cf. John 20:16, "Rabboni"). Luke never uses the term "Rabbi," probably for the purpose of better communicating with Gentile readers.

5:8 *Oh, Lord, please leave me—I'm too much of a sinner to be around you.* Peter dropped to his knees at this point and addressed Jesus as "Lord." Here, Peter emulates a theme of contrition also exhibited by Isaiah, Jeremiah, and Ezekiel (Isa 6:5; Jer 24:7; 31:31-34; Ezek 11:19). On the Christological issues, see Marshall 1967:77-93; Marshall 1976; and Moule 1977. Evidently, the presence of such a holy person made him aware of his own sinfulness and brought him to the point that he called Jesus "Lord," a change from 5:5, where he called him "Master." The Gospel of Luke is rich in names and titles given to Jesus. He is described as "Jesus" (2:52; 4:1, 14; 9:1; 18:38), "Jesus of Nazareth" (4:34; 18:37; 24:19; cf. Acts 2:22; 3:6; 4:10; 10:38; 22:8), "the Son of God" (1:35; 4:3, 9, 41; 22:70), "the Son of

Man" (Jesus' favorite title for himself; e.g., 5:24; 6:5; 9:22, 44, 58; 12:8, 10; 18:8; 19:10; 22:22; 24:7), "the Savior" (2:11; cf. 19:10; John 4:42; 1 John 4:14), "the Messiah" or "Christ" (2:11; 3:15; 4:41; 9:20; 20:41; 22:67), "the son of David" (18:38-39; 20:41), the "Son" (9:35; 10:22), "my Chosen One" (9:35), "my dearly loved Son" (3:22), "Master" (5:5; 8:24, 45; 9:33, 49; 17:13), "the King" (19:38), "the King of the Jews" (23:38-39), "Son of the Most High God" (8:28; cf. Mark 1:23-24), and here as "Lord" (clearly Luke's favorite title for Jesus—2:11; 5:8, 12; 6:46; 7:6, 13, 19; 9:54, 59; 10:1; 11:1; 18:6). For a helpful treatment of the titles "Savior," "Christ," and "Lord," see C. A. Evans 1990:36-37. On "Son of Man," see note on 5:24.

5:10 *From now on you'll be fishing for people!* Luke uses a vivid word for "catch" here (*zōgreō* [TG2221, ZG2436]) that means "capture alive" or "capture for life." It is a profound thought that Christian discipleship really involves Jesus Christ capturing someone for life. His disciples were called to have a vital part in this challenging enterprise.

COMMENTARY

This calling of the first disciples is found in Matthew, Mark, and Luke. Matthew appears to follow Mark very closely. While all three stories have a fishing setting, Luke explicitly places the calling of the first four disciples against the background of a miraculous draft of fish, and in some ways his account resembles a post-resurrection miraculous catch on the Sea of Tiberias, one of John's names for the Sea of Galilee (John 21:1-14; cf. John 6:1), though the differences between the two incidents outweigh the similarities.

All three synoptic Gospels agree on the location as being by the Sea of Galilee, though Luke preferred to describe it as "the Lake of Gennesaret" (5:1, NLT mg; cf. 5:2; 8:22-23, 33). Likewise, all three place the incident in the context of the Galilean ministry. Luke notes the large crowds pressing in upon Jesus "to listen to the word of God" (5:1). Jesus was obviously gaining a popular following and used the lakeside setting to address the throngs.

Matthew and Mark add a few details of interest. They note that Peter's partner in the boat was his brother Andrew (Matt 4:18; Mark 1:16). They cite Christ's specific invitation to discipleship and evangelism: "Come, follow me, and I will show you how to fish for people!" (Matt 4:19; Mark 1:17). Mark remarked that James and John left "their father, Zebedee, in the boat with the hired men" and went with Jesus (Mark 1:20). The old fishing business would continue, but a new fishing enterprise was about to begin.

Luke offers a graphic account of the calling of two sets of fishermen who worked together as "partners" in a common business (5:7). According to Luke's narrative, Jesus noticed two boats at the water's edge that were unoccupied. Luke told his readers that the reason the boats were empty was that "the fishermen had left them and were washing their nets" (5:2; in Mark's account, the fishermen are described as "repairing" their nets [Mark 1:19], which would involve cleaning, mending, and folding the nets for future use). Then, Jesus entered one of the boats and gave instructions to Peter, its owner (5:3). The boat provided both an opportunity to escape the press of the people and a suitable place to speak: "So he sat in the boat and taught the crowds from there" (5:3).

Luke states quite directly the command Christ gave to Peter: "Now go out where it is deeper, and let down your nets to catch some fish" (5:4). Although Peter was hesitant to obey, he also showed deep respect for Jesus, addressing him as "Master" (5:5). The overwhelming success of the catch follows (cf. the similar event in John 21:6), such that Luke notes, "Their nets were so full of fish they began to tear!" (5:6). Other details fill out the picture. The fishermen signalled to their partners in the other boat for help and filled both boats completely with fish, to the point that they were in danger of "sinking" (the verb *buthizō* [TG1036/A, ZG1112], "cause to sink," is used only here in the NT). Then, Peter uttered a confession of his sinfulness and unworthiness in the light of the marvelous intervention of the Master.

The fishermen were amazed at the magnitude of the catch (5:9; cf. note on 2:33). Jesus response to Simon was instructive for them all: "Don't be afraid! From now on you'll be fishing for people!" (5:10). Luke closes the scene with a brief reference to the radical commitment of these keen disciples: "As soon as they landed, they left everything and followed Jesus" (5:11).

Luke's account applies to disciples in any era, for it highlights the importance of obedience to Jesus, an openness to his leading, a willingness to put one's resources at his disposal, and a sense of personal unworthiness in his presence. Commitment to Jesus is a radical thing, and discipleship is demanding!

◆ F. Jesus Heals a Man with Leprosy (5:12-16; cf. Matt 8:1-4; Mark 1:40-45)

¹²In one of the villages, Jesus met a man with an advanced case of leprosy. When the man saw Jesus, he bowed with his face to the ground, begging to be healed. "Lord," he said, "if you are willing, you can heal me and make me clean."

¹³Jesus reached out and touched him. "I am willing," he said. "Be healed!" And instantly the leprosy disappeared. ¹⁴Then Jesus instructed him not to tell anyone what had happened. He said, "Go to the priest and let him examine you. Take along the offering required in the law of Moses for those who have been healed of leprosy.* This will be a public testimony that you have been cleansed."

¹⁵But despite Jesus' instructions, the report of his power spread even faster, and vast crowds came to hear him preach and to be healed of their diseases. ¹⁶But Jesus often withdrew to the wilderness for prayer.

5:14 See Lev 14:2-32.

NOTES

5:12 *leprosy.* For brief studies on "leprosy," see the articles in Achtemeier 1985:555-556 and Freedman 2000:801. "The biblical term for leprosy seems to be broadly generic, covering skin diseases of many types. Whatever its precise nature, leprosy was a dreaded plague, bringing horror and despair, and provoking anguished and desperate supplications" (Mills 1990:508-509). Barclay (1975:32-33) speaks of three kinds of leprosy: The first is *nodular leprosy*, in which the flesh becomes ulcerated and eventually the person dies. The second is *anaesthetic leprosy*, in which all sensation is lost, so that through injury and ulceration the person gradually falls apart. This form of leprosy takes two or three times as long to kill a person as nodular leprosy. The third kind is the most common, in which the two diseases occur at once. These as well as other skin disorders were classified as leprosy. According to Jewish law, all of these were treated only by isolation (Lev 13–14). Cf. note on 17:12.

5:16 *Jesus often withdrew to the wilderness for prayer.* On the prayer emphasis in the Lukan writings, see Trites 1978. On the general place of prayer in Jesus' life, see Spencer and Spencer 1990. For a study of the oscillating pattern of times of engagement and times of withdrawal in the ministry of Jesus, see Trites 1997.

COMMENTARY

Leprosy was a general term covering a wide variety of skin diseases. Because it was contagious and usually incurable, it required careful regulation in biblical times (cf. 2 Kgs 15:5). The laws for the diagnosis and treatment of leprosy are given in Leviticus 13, and the laws of purification that permitted readmission to society are described in Leviticus 14. Lepers were ceremonially unclean (Lev 13:8, 11, 20, 22, 44), cut off from the house of God (2 Chr 26:21), forbidden to mingle with others (Num 5:2; 12:14-15), and forced to cry, "Unclean! Unclean!" in the presence of others (Lev 13:45). Several leprosy stories are given in the Old Testament (e.g., Num 12:1-15; 2 Kgs 7:1-20), and one of them records the remarkable healing of Naaman, the commander of the Syrian army (2 Kgs 5:1-27). The healing of lepers was a prominent feature of the ministry of Jesus (7:22; 17:12-19; cf. Matt 10:8).

Following Jesus' calling of the first disciples is the compassionate cleansing of a leper (5:12-16). Though the name of the village is not given, the location was probably in Galilee (cf. 5:1; Mark 1:39-40). The incident is mentioned in Matthew, Mark, and Luke. Mark's account is the fullest. He mentions several features that are unique to his presentation, including the reference to the compassion that Jesus showed the man (Mark 1:41) and the fact that the healing made it impossible for Jesus to enter any town openly (Mark 1:45). Matthew makes no mention of Jesus' increasing popularity or his difficulty in entering towns publicly. Luke, like Mark, notes that the healed man was solemnly charged not to tell anyone (5:14; cf. Mark 1:43) and that, despite this, word got out (Luke, unlike Mark, is silent about how the word spread). As a result, large crowds sought Jesus for instruction and healing (5:15; cf. Mark 1:45).

The man in question had "an advanced case of leprosy," so the poignancy of his plight is highlighted by Luke (5:12). In desperate earnestness, the man fell down and prostrated himself before Jesus, imploring his help. Jesus indicated a willingness to heal him, pronounced the decisive words of healing, and "instantly the leprosy disappeared" (5:13).

In all three Gospel accounts, there is an attitude of intense respect for the power and authority of Jesus: "Lord, . . . if you are willing, you can heal me and make me clean" (5:12; cf. Mark 1:40; Matt 8:2). All three versions show the willingness of Jesus to heal, and all three cite the same healing command. All three accounts note the man's prostrating himself before Jesus, and all three report that the healing took place instantly. In both Matthew and Luke, the leper humbly addresses Jesus as "Lord" (5:12; Matt 8:2). In addition, all three accounts carefully state the instructions that Jesus issued about priestly certification of the cure (cf. Lev 13:49; 14:2-3) and the command for silence (5:14; cf. Mark 1:43-44; Matt 8:4).

The injunction for silence may have been prompted by several factors, including the likelihood that if Jesus' miracles were too highly publicized, his teaching ministry might be overshadowed or ignored, and his high profile might hasten his death, decreasing the time of his earthly ministry. Such commands for silence are also seen elsewhere (8:56; Matt 9:30; 12:16; Mark 1:44; 5:43; 7:36). In spite of the command for silence, the news about Jesus "spread even faster, and vast crowds came to hear him preach and to be healed of their diseases" (5:15). Instead of letting this popularity overmaster him, Jesus "often withdrew to the wilderness for prayer" (5:16), a feature noted only by Luke. These were times of fellowship with the Father that often marked the life of Jesus and were characteristic of his ministry (3:21; 5:16; 6:12; 11:1; 22:31-32, 39-46; 23:46). Luke, sometimes called "the Evangelist of prayer," mentions these times of prayer as the hidden source of divine strength behind Jesus' public ministry. Mark's Gospel also notes Jesus' times of withdrawal in order to rejuvenate himself (e.g., Mark 1:35; 3:13; 6:32). The journey outward was energized by the journey inward.

◆ G. Jesus Heals a Paralyzed Man (5:17-26; cf. Matt 9:2-8; Mark 2:3-12)

¹⁷One day while Jesus was teaching, some Pharisees and teachers of religious law were sitting nearby. (It seemed that these men showed up from every village in all Galilee and Judea, as well as from Jerusalem.) And the Lord's healing power was strongly with Jesus.

¹⁸Some men came carrying a paralyzed man on a sleeping mat. They tried to take him inside to Jesus, ¹⁹but they couldn't reach him because of the crowd. So they went up to the roof and took off some tiles. Then they lowered the sick man on his mat down into the crowd, right in front of Jesus. ²⁰Seeing their faith, Jesus said to the man, "Young man, your sins are forgiven."

²¹But the Pharisees and teachers of religious law said to themselves, "Who does he think he is? That's blasphemy! Only God can forgive sins!"

²²Jesus knew what they were thinking, so he asked them, "Why do you question this in your hearts? ²³Is it easier to say 'Your sins are forgiven,' or 'Stand up and walk'? ²⁴So I will prove to you that the Son of Man* has the authority on earth to forgive sins." Then Jesus turned to the paralyzed man and said, "Stand up, pick up your mat, and go home!"

²⁵And immediately, as everyone watched, the man jumped up, picked up his mat, and went home praising God. ²⁶Everyone was gripped with great wonder and awe, and they praised God, exclaiming, "We have seen amazing things today!"

5:24"Son of Man" is a title Jesus used for himself.

NOTES

5:17-26 This incident in Luke's Gospel is important in terms of the outworking of God's purpose in Jesus' life and identity. "This episode is strategic since it shows the beginning of the opposition that will eventually lead to Jesus' arrest, trial, and execution" (C. A. Evans 1990:88).

5:21 *That's blasphemy!* This is the only use of the noun "blasphemy" (*blasphēmia* [^{TG}988, ^{ZG}1060]) in Luke–Acts, though the adjective *blasphēmos* [^{TG}989, ^{ZG}1061] is used of speaking against God in Acts 6:11. Blasphemy is slanderous speech against someone (e.g., Matt 12:31; 15:19; Mark 3:28; 7:22). It is particularly used of impious speech against God (cf. Matt 26:65; Mark 14:64; John 10:33). Similarly, the verb "blaspheme" (*blasphēmeō* [TG987, ZG1059]) denotes reviling or slandering a person (22:65; Mark 15:29; Acts 13:45; 18:6; 1 Pet 4:4). It is often employed in speech directed against God (see Matt 9:3; 26:65; Mark 2:7; John 10:36), and Jesus solemnly warned that "anyone who blasphemes the Holy Spirit will not be forgiven" (12:10; see Abbott-Smith 1923:82). "In this case Jesus' claim to 'forgive sins' provoked the charge of blasphemy, since it was thought to be something only God could do. Since all sin is against God, only God, it was reasoned, could forgive sin" (C. A. Evans 1990:92). For helpful general treatment of blasphemy in the Gospels, see DJG 75-77; Bromiley 1985:107-108.

5:24 *the Son of Man.* This is the first of 25 instances in Luke where the title "Son of Man" appears. This title is drawn from OT usage that imbues it with rich meaning. On the one hand, God addressed the human prophet Ezekiel by this title frequently (e.g., Ezek 2:1; 3:1; 4:1; 5:1; 6:1), commissioning him to condemn false prophets and make the people of God aware of their sins (Ezek 13:1-23; 16:1-58). Yet, in Daniel, a glorified dimension is stressed in the idea of "someone like a son of man coming with the clouds of heaven" (Dan 7:13). Here, the Son of Man is given divine "authority, honor, and sovereignty" and rules an eternal and indestructible worldwide kingdom (Dan 7:14).

There seem to be three main ways in which this phrase is employed. First, it is used to describe the earthly life of Jesus, the Son of Man: he ate and drank with tax collectors and sinners (7:34); he was homeless (9:58); and his followers would suffer persecution (6:22). While a word spoken against the earthly Son of Man could be forgiven, he claimed "authority on earth to forgive sins" and lordship over the Sabbath. His very presence on earth constituted a "sign" to those around him (11:30). The ministry of the Son of Man was redemptive, for he came "to seek and save" those who were lost (19:10).

The second group of "Son of Man" sayings speaks of the Lord's suffering, death, and vindication. A typical example is 9:22, the first of the Passion predictions: "The Son of Man must suffer many terrible things. . . . He will be rejected by the elders, the leading priests, and the teachers of religious law. He will be killed, but on the third day he will be raised from the dead." Other intimations of the Son of Man's sufferings follow (9:44; 17:24-25; 18:31-33; cf. 24:7). The suffering of Jesus is accepted as necessary for the fulfillment of the divine purpose: "For it has been determined that the Son of Man must die" (22:22). Tragically, it was Judas who betrayed the Son of Man with a kiss (22:48).

The third group of "Son of Man" sayings looks to the future glory of Jesus and thereby speaks of "the day when the Son of Man returns" (17:22). There are many references to the return of the Son of Man (17:24, 26, 30; 18:8), an event associated "with power and great glory" and calling for alertness and preparation (12:40; 21:27). The triumphant Son of Man, completely vindicated, will serve as the great judge on the last day, and, therefore, disciples are to be prepared to "stand before the Son of Man" (21:36). Jesus told the Jewish council that the time was soon coming when he, as the mighty Son of Man, would be "seated in the place of power at God's right hand" (22:69). This was an amazing statement of his future victory and ultimate triumph.

It is interesting that the title "Son of Man" is found mainly in the Gospels, and there it appears on the lips of Jesus as the principal designation for himself. The authenticity of some of the Son of Man sayings has been challenged by Rudolf Bultmann and others (see Bultmann 1963), but on questionable grounds. There seems to be no compelling reason why Jesus could not have taken this term and used it to describe the varied aspects of his ministry. Its relative opaqueness would make it difficult for his enemies to attack him, and yet, his disciples could be instructed about the most crucial elements of his life, work, and ministry. For a balanced treatment of the Son of Man theme, see Higgins 1980; S. Kim 1983; Lindars 1983; Cargounis 1986; and Marshall 1975:63-82. Moule (1977:22) concludes, "'the Son of Man', so far from being a title . . . put by [the early church] onto the lips of Jesus, is among the most important symbols used by Jesus himself to describe his vocation."

5:26 they praised God. Praise is frequently mentioned in Luke–Acts (2:13, 20; 5:25-26; 7:16; 13:13; 17:15; 18:43; 23:47; Acts 4:21; 10:46; 11:18; 13:48; 21:20).

amazing things. Here, Luke uses the rare word *paradoxa* [TG3861/A, ZG4141] to describe Jesus' astonishing miracles.

COMMENTARY

This healing story is also found in Matthew and Mark. Luke and Mark both give a more detailed account of the event, with Mark describing graphically the tearing up of the roof to gain access to Jesus (Mark 2:4). Only Luke mentions the presence of the Pharisees and teachers of the Jewish law "from every village in all Galilee and Judea, as well as from Jerusalem" (5:17). This detail indicates the increasing fame of Jesus and the emerging antagonism. Opposition to Jesus' work was rising from these leaders, and they were apparently there to check him out. Their hostile attitudes emerge in verse 21, where we are told that the Pharisees and teachers of religious law protest: "That's blasphemy! Only God can forgive sins!" Blasphemy was condemned in the Torah (Lev 24:10-11, 14-16, 23). In these protests, we see "the first intimation of the charge for which the Jews will crucify Jesus (Mark 14:64)" (Ellis 1981:104).

The controversial nature of the occasion is carefully described. On the one hand, there was Jesus in the midst of an active, popular ministry. On the other hand, there were the religious critics who were offended by the claims of Jesus and were prepared to attack him. In this tense situation, "the Lord's healing power was strongly with Jesus" (5:17). Another element in this volatile setting was a small group of men who truly cared for a needy paralytic.

The determined friends of the paralyzed man were not to be discouraged by the crowds that were thronging Jesus. When they couldn't obtain access, they went up to the roof of the house where he was teaching and made an opening in the roof to lower the sick man into Jesus' presence (5:19). Their persistence paid off, for Jesus graciously addressed the case, first forgiving the paralytic's sins and then healing him. Luke emphasizes the immediate restoration as the healed man "jumped up, picked up his mat, and went home praising God" (5:25). The amazement of the eyewitnesses is noted in 5:26 as the man's joy was shared by the bystanders, and "they praised God, exclaiming, 'We have seen amazing things today!'"

There are several important things to observe in this healing. First, Jesus noted the faith of the men who had taken such innovative action to bring the paralyzed man to the source of help (5:20). Second, Jesus gave attention to the man's spiritual condition before turning to his physical condition, thereby suggesting the paramount importance of one's experiencing the forgiveness of sins. Forgiveness is a central note in the apostolic preaching that is frequently underscored in Luke–Acts

(5:20-24; 7:47-49; 11:4; 12:10; 17:3-4; Acts 5:31; 13:38; 26:18). Third, Jesus, acting as the "Son of Man," gave tangible evidence of his power to forgive sin by healing the paralyzed man, who was instantly restored to complete mobility. A similar demonstration of power is recorded in Acts, where Peter, acting "in the name of Jesus Christ the Nazarene," heals a crippled beggar in the Temple. Instantly, the man is restored and enabled to walk, jump, and praise God (Acts 3:6-9). Such healings were strong evidence that the messianic signs mentioned in Isaiah were demonstrated in the ministry of Jesus of Nazareth (cf. Isa 35:5-6; 42:7; 61:1-2). As such, they served as part of the early church's argument that Jesus is the Christ, the Savior and Lord (Acts 3:6-10; 4:8-17; cf. John 20:30-31).

◆ ## H. Jesus Calls Levi (Matthew) (5:27-32; cf. Matt 9:9-13; Mark 2:13-17)

27Later, as Jesus left the town, he saw a tax collector named Levi sitting at his tax collector's booth. "Follow me and be my disciple," Jesus said to him. 28So Levi got up, left everything, and followed him.

29Later, Levi held a banquet in his home with Jesus as the guest of honor. Many of Levi's fellow tax collectors and other guests also ate with them. 30But the Phar-isees and their teachers of religious law complained bitterly to Jesus' disciples, "Why do you eat and drink with such scum?*"

31Jesus answered them, "Healthy people don't need a doctor—sick people do. 32I have come to call not those who think they are righteous, but those who know they are sinners and need to repent."

5:30 Greek *with tax collectors and sinners?*

NOTES

5:29 *Levi held a banquet in his home with Jesus as the guest of honor.* This is the first of Luke's many banqueting scenes, and only he describes it as a "banquet" (*dochē* [TG1403, ZG1531]), a word sometimes used in the LXX (Gen 21:8; Esth 1:3) and also in 14:12[13]. There are ten of these feasting scenes in Luke's Gospel, and seven of them are unique to Luke (7:36-50; 10:38-42; 11:37-54; 14:1-24; 19:1-10; 24:29-35, 41-43). In commenting on Luke's fondness for banquets, Fred Craddock has remarked, "It was common in the Hellenistic world for banquets to be the setting for philosophers and teachers to offer their wisdom. (Note, for example, Plato's *Symposium*, where Socrates engages in vigorous discussion in the setting of a banquet.) But for Luke the image of Jesus at table was that of one who accepted and received all kinds of people, the proof of which was in the breaking of bread" (1990:1032).

Many of Levi's fellow tax collectors and other guests also ate with them. Isaiah pictures an eschatological banquet in which the Lord of Heaven's Armies "will spread a wonderful feast for all the people of the world" (Isa 25:6; cf. Jer 31:12-14). This was viewed as a day of blessing, when rich food and wine, symbols of abundant spiritual blessings, would be enjoyed freely (Isa 55:1; cf. 2 Baruch 29:5-7). Jesus, in like fashion, invited people to drink of the water of life, and the Bible closes with a similar invitation to "drink" of "the water of life" (John 4:10, 14; 7:37; Rev 22:17). On the importance of table fellowship in the ancient world and in the ministry of Jesus, see DJG 296-300; Neyrey 1991:361-387; D. E. Smith 1987, 1989. On taxes and tax collectors, see notes on 18:10; 19:2; 20:22.

COMMENTARY

Following the healing of the paralytic, Luke turns his attention to Jesus' calling of Levi. Levi is identified with Matthew (a name meaning "gift of God") in Matthew's Gospel and as "Levi son of Alphaeus" in Mark's Gospel (Matt 9:9-13; Mark 2:13-17). Just as God had called Moses while he was tending his flock (Exod 3:1), so Jesus called Levi while he was at his regular occupation, "sitting at his tax collector's booth" (5:27). (The same may be said of Jesus' earlier calling of the fishermen in ch 5.) Mark identifies the setting as the Galilean lakeshore where Jesus was teaching the crowds (Mark 2:13), and the place was probably Capernaum, since it was a customs post for Herod Antipas on the road that ran from Damascus through Capernaum to the Mediterranean Sea and then down into Egypt (the same road is mentioned in Isa 9:1). The call to follow Jesus was personal and direct: "Follow me and be my disciple." It required a personal response, and Levi gave it: "So Levi got up, left everything, and followed him" (5:28).

His new commitment to follow Jesus was made known to others when "Levi held a banquet in his home with Jesus as the guest of honor" (5:29). This occasion gave Jesus a chance to mingle with the guests and meet many of Levi's former colleagues and friends. It was an ideal opportunity to share the message of the Kingdom of God with a wider circle of people, including those who collected taxes and thus collaborated with the Romans. These people were derisively termed "sinners" along with other questionable people, such as adulterers, thieves, and notoriously evil folk (cf. 7:34; Matt 9:10-11; 21:31-32; Mark 2:15-16). Tax collectors were loathed, because they were notoriously dishonest and were viewed as traitors working for either Rome (which ruled Judea directly) or Herod (who ruled Galilee directly). In 5:30, as well as 7:34 and 15:1, tax collectors and sinners are considered virtually synonymous (C. A. Evans 1990:53).

The fact that Jesus fraternized with such people made him a strong target of criticism (Matt 11:19). The Pharisees and the teachers of religious law, whom Luke had already mentioned as critical of Jesus (5:17, 21), openly complained to Jesus' disciples (5:30). The established religious leaders deliberately sought to separate themselves from such disreputable people.

Jesus' answer is remarkable, for it points to the moral necessity of responding to need. Just as one goes to a physician when conscious of a physical problem, so one should seek spiritual help from a spiritual source when the problem is spiritual. Without a real sense of need, no help can be given to "those who think they are righteous" (5:32). A radical "change of mind" (*metanoia* [TG3341, ZG3567]) is demanded.

◆   I. Discussion about Fasting (5:33-39; cf. Matt 9:14-17;
        Mark 2:18-22)

33One day some people said to Jesus, "John the Baptist's disciples fast and pray regularly, and so do the disciples of the Pharisees. Why are your disciples always eating and drinking?" 34Jesus responded, "Do wedding guests fast while celebrating with the groom? Of course not. 35But someday the groom will be taken away from them, and then they will fast."

³⁶Then Jesus gave them this illustration: "No one tears a piece of cloth from a new garment and uses it to patch an old garment. For then the new garment would be ruined, and the new patch wouldn't even match the old garment.

³⁷"And no one puts new wine into old wineskins. For the new wine would burst the wineskins, spilling the wine and ruining the skins. ³⁸New wine must be stored in new wineskins. ³⁹But no one who drinks the old wine seems to want the new wine. 'The old is just fine,' they say."

NOTES

5:33 One day some people said. The Gr. here simply says, "And they said." Luke sets this episode in the context of the banquet at Levi's house recorded in the preceding verses.

John the Baptist's disciples fast and pray regularly. Similarly, the Pharisees practiced fasting regularly, and some prided themselves in observing the custom twice a week on Mondays and Thursdays (18:12). John Wesley fasted once a week on Wednesdays. On the practice of fasting, see A. Kee 1969. On the prayer theme, see the notes on 5:16; 6:12; 11:1-13; 18:1.

5:34 Do wedding guests fast while celebrating with the groom? Here, the form of the question in Gr. makes it clear that the answer expected is "No, you can't make the wedding guests fast" (see Zerwick 1988:192).

5:36 illustration. Lit., "parable" (parabolē [TG3850, ZG4130]). Luke uses the word 17 times and features some of Jesus' most memorable parables, or "illustrations," such as the barren fig tree (13:6-9), the prodigal son (15:11-32), the shrewd manager (16:1-9), the persistent widow (18:1-8), and the Pharisee and the tax collector (18:9-14). Parables were the principal teaching device Jesus used to communicate his message of the in-breaking Kingdom of God to mixed audiences, which often included people who were hostile as well as disciples and casual hearers. Each parable was really "a comparison drawn from nature or daily life and designed to illuminate some spiritual truth, on the assumption that what is valid in one sphere is valid also in the other" (Hunter 1960:8). For more discussion on the general subject, see Hunter 1971, Jeremias 1975, and Stein 1981. On Luke's parables particularly, see Bailey 1976.

5:39 But no one who drinks the old wine seems to want the new wine. 'The old is just fine,' they say. This unusual remark, found only in Luke, "is difficult to interpret. It may be ironic, indicating that contentment with the old prevents openness to the new" (Coogan 2001:106).

COMMENTARY

Fasting is a well-known practice among Jews, Christians, and Muslims. It was prominent in biblical times—Moses, David, Ezra, Nehemiah, the Jews in Esther's day, Jesus, Saul (Paul), and the Christian prophets and teachers at Antioch all fasted at times of special urgency (Exod 34:28; 2 Sam 12:21-23; Ezra 8:21-28; Neh 1:4; Esth 4:3, 16; Matt 4:2; Acts 9:9; 13:2-3). There is ample evidence of the practice on occasions of unusual need or national crisis. It was usually associated with the confession of sin and penitence (Neh 9:1-37; Ps 69:10; Isa 58:5). It was generally connected with earnest intercession for God's help (Judg 20:26; cf. 2 Chr 7:14; 2 Macc 13:12), sometimes for personal reasons (2 Sam 12:16; Ps 35:13), and often in the face of national calamities (2 Sam 1:12; Ezra 8:21-23; Esth 4:16; Joel 2:12-15). The only day that the practice of fasting was mandatory for all Jews liturgically was on the Day of Atonement (Lev 16:29-34), though fasting was often recognized as meritorious in Jewish circles (2:37; 5:33; 18:12; Tob 12:8). On the practice in New Testament times, note the fasting of Paul and Barnabas in the appointment of elders for the churches (Acts 14:23) and several references to Paul's going hungry and thirsty in the discharge of his apostolic labors (2 Cor 6:5; 11:27).

This issue, as we see here in Luke 5, was a point of contention with the critics of Jesus (cf. Matt 9:14-15; Mark 2:18-20). John the Baptist's followers are said to "fast and pray regularly" (5:33). John the Baptist's instruction in prayer is later mentioned when Luke introduces Jesus' teaching on prayer (11:1). By Luke's account, it was apparently at the banquet that this particular dispute arose. The religious leaders objected that Jesus' disciples were feasting instead of fasting (5:33), thereby contrasting Jesus' ministry with John's. John was most likely subject to a Nazirite vow, which involved abstinence from alcoholic drinks (1:15; cf. Num 6:1-4). John had grown up in the wilderness and developed an ascetic lifestyle with an austere diet consisting of locusts and wild honey (Matt 3:4; Mark 1:6). By contrast, Jesus attended banquets, and his disciples enjoyed a freedom not found in circles associated with John the Baptist or the Pharisees. While Jesus sometimes fasted in private and recognized the spiritual value of fasting as a voluntary matter in a time of special need (4:2; cf. Matt 4:2; 6:16-18), he strongly opposed fasting as a legalistic practice or a showy form of piety. There was a proper time for feasting and for fasting. Now was the time for celebration, when the bridegroom (Jesus) was with them and the Kingdom of God was bringing joy to those who welcomed it. After Jesus was taken away from them, there would be ample time for fasting.

The two illustrations Jesus gave were intended to clarify the relationship between the old order and the new one he was introducing. An old outer garment (*himation* [TG2440, ZG2668]) is not patched with a piece of new, unshrunk cloth, because the new patch shrinks and pulls away from the old cloth, leaving an even bigger hole than before (5:36). Similarly, no one pours new wine into old wineskins, for fear of losing the wine and ruining the skins (5:37). The problem presented by the wineskins can be quite simply explained: "Skins of small animals were sewn up for wine containers (Josh 9:4, 13). When new, they could expand with the pressure created by the fermenting wine, whereas an old skin would split" (Nolland 1989:249).

Jesus recognized the fact that this teaching was unacceptable to his conservative critics, who were governed by the "old is better" philosophy (5:39). In these circumstances, a parable was the ideal way of putting a challenge to them and making them think (5:36). The Kingdom of God presented a radical call to a new way of life that demanded repentance and change. They must decide for themselves, but, in doing so, they were accountable for their decisions and the ensuing results.

◆   J. Discussion about the Sabbath (6:1-5; cf. Matt 12:1-8; Mark 2:23-28)

One Sabbath day as Jesus was walking through some grainfields, his disciples broke off heads of grain, rubbed off the husks in their hands, and ate the grain.

²But some Pharisees said, "Why are you breaking the law by harvesting grain on the Sabbath?"

³Jesus replied, "Haven't you read in the Scriptures what David did when he and his companions were hungry? ⁴He went into the house of God and broke the law by eating the sacred loaves of bread that only the priests can eat. He also gave some to his companions." ⁵And Jesus added, "The Son of Man* is Lord, even over the Sabbath."

6:5"Son of Man" is a title Jesus used for himself.

NOTES

6:1 *Sabbath day*. On the Sabbath, see Evans and Porter 2000:1031-1035 and the full bibliography cited there; see also Carson 1982.

***his disciples . . . rubbed off the husks in their hands*.** The word *psōchō* [TG5597, ZG6041] is used only here in the NT. It means "rub so as to thresh." In other words, the action of the disciples was interpreted as threshing, which was seen as a violation of the accepted rabbinic rules for keeping the Sabbath (Rice 1982). "The Lukan version of the story of plucking the ears of grain on the Sabbath goes beyond Mark 2:23 par. Matt 12:1 (plucking and eating) in saying (6:1) that the disciples *rubbed* the ears of grain in their hands. For Luke this rubbing of the ears is important as a prerequisite for eating" (EDNT 3.504). See the Jewish tractate *Shabbat* in the Mishnah.

6:5 *The Son of Man is Lord, even over the Sabbath*. On the use of "Son of Man," see note on 5:24 and DJG 775-781.

COMMENTARY

Luke's account of the plucking of grain on the Sabbath is the briefest of the three Synoptic accounts and parallels Mark's text quite closely. All three Synoptics reveal a hostile setting, where Jesus' critics were watching for something they could attack. They are glad to seize upon the action of his disciples as a means of finding fault with Jesus. According to the traditional 613 rules and regulations laid down by Jewish traditionalists for keeping the law, the disciples were guilty on several counts of Sabbath-breaking, for they had been plucking the grain, rubbing it in their hands, and then consuming it.

Jesus was not content to let the casuistry of the Pharisees go unchallenged. He reproached his critics by asking them, "Haven't you read?" (6:3); he then reminded them of a very important biblical precedent, the case of Israel's great monarch, David (1 Sam 21:1-6). Leaving the royal court, David had fled from King Saul, who had clearly announced his opposition to David and his plans to kill him (1 Sam 20:31-33). David went into hiding as a fugitive, taking a few men with him. In the wilderness, David and his companions became hungry, but the new king had to be wary of those who were tracking him down to put him to death. In this critical situation, David went into the house of God, ate the special bread reserved for the priests alone, and then gave some to his companions (6:4; cf. Exod 25:30; Lev 24:5-9). Similarly, the disciples of Jesus were hungry and had acted in a forbidden manner. In both cases, godly men technically broke the law, though they were acting within the spirit of the law. Jesus would later point out that it is "lawful" to do good and to save life on the Sabbath (6:9; cf. 13:10-17; 14:1-6; Isa 58:6-7).

From the incident involving David, Jesus drew a significant deduction, namely, that human need was more important than a cultic regulation. Moreover, he asserted his own divinely given authority as Son of Man, boldly declaring to his opponents, "The Son of Man is Lord, even over the Sabbath" (6:5). In saying this, Jesus was really asserting a claim of equality with God, who had established the Sabbath day in the first place (Exod 20:8-11; Deut 5:12-15). He was suggesting that the work of God is unending and that it was appropriate for him to participate and continue that work. This parallels John 5:17, where Jesus answered the Jewish leaders who had accused him of breaking the Sabbath rules, "My Father is always working, and so am I." To the hostile Jews who were challenging him, this was tantamount to blasphemy, a crime that was punishable under Jewish law by death (Lev 24:16; Matt 26:66; cf. Acts 6:11 and the note on Luke 5:21). The Gospels show repeatedly that Jesus was accused of this crime: "You, a mere man, claim to be God" (John 10:33; cf. Luke 22:66-71; Matt 26:65).

In Matthew's account, he highlights the superiority of Christ to the Temple (Matt 12:6) and the principle of compassion: "I want you to show mercy" (Matt 12:7; cf. Hos 6:6). He also stresses the wrongfulness of the critics in condemning those who weren't guilty (Matt 12:7). Luke, following Mark and writing mainly for Gentile readers, was content to cite one biblical precedent and focus on the authority of Jesus as the Son of Man. In the next Sabbath incident, Luke will show the compassion of Jesus expressed in a stirring rhetorical question (6:9), and in the Sermon on the Plain, he will cite the teaching of Jesus: "You must be compassionate, just as your Father is compassionate" (6:36).

◆   K. Jesus Heals on the Sabbath (6:6-11; cf. Matt 12:9-14; Mark 3:1-6)

⁶On another Sabbath day, a man with a deformed right hand was in the synagogue while Jesus was teaching. ⁷The teachers of religious law and the Pharisees watched Jesus closely. If he healed the man's hand, they planned to accuse him of working on the Sabbath.

⁸But Jesus knew their thoughts. He said to the man with the deformed hand, "Come and stand in front of everyone." So the man came forward. ⁹Then Jesus said to his critics, "I have a question for you. Does the law permit good deeds on the Sabbath, or is it a day for doing evil? Is this a day to save life or to destroy it?"

¹⁰He looked around at them one by one and then said to the man, "Hold out your hand." So the man held out his hand, and it was restored! ¹¹At this, the enemies of Jesus were wild with rage and began to discuss what to do with him.

NOTES

6:6 *On another Sabbath day.* See note on 6:1.

6:7 *The teachers of religious law and the Pharisees watched Jesus closely.* Observe the use of *paratēreō* [TG3906, ZG4190] (keep one's eye on, watch carefully). Jesus was a marked man! Luke uses this same word in two other passages where people are watching Jesus with hostile intent (14:1; 20:20; see also Acts 9:24, where Paul's enemies keep close watch on the city gates in order to kill him). On the general use of this verb in the NT, see EDNT 3.35.

6:11 *what to do with him.* Note Mark and Matthew's statement that they plotted Jesus' death (Mark 3:6; Matt 12:14).

COMMENTARY

The next occasion of controversy took place on another Sabbath day. It is interesting to observe Luke's manner of presentation. As Schweizer has remarked, "He carefully organizes the controversies of Mark into a fundamental disagreement between Jesus and the pharisaic scribes (5:17, 21, 30, 33; 6:2, 7)" (1984:109). In the present case, their hostile intention is once again ostensible—"they planned to accuse him of working on the Sabbath" (6:7).

Luke's account of the healing is graphic. The healing took place in a Jewish synagogue, where Jesus was engaged in a teaching ministry (6:6). Luke specifies that it was the man's right hand that required healing (cf. 22:50, where he specifies the right ear); he was interested in matters of detail and had "carefully investigated" the background of the life of Christ (1:3). Jesus faced the religious leaders directly, for he "knew their thoughts" (6:8). He invited the man with the deformed hand to step forward where he could be seen. After challenging his critics with a searching question about the constructive use of the Sabbath to save human life rather than destroy it (6:9), Jesus proceeded to heal the man's hand, and though the man's hand was restored to normal use, Jesus' opponents became furious with him for his flagrant disregard of their Sabbath regulations. They began to discuss with one another what they might do to Jesus (6:11). In their eyes, he was a dangerous enemy who must be put out of action, a point made even more strongly in the other Gospels (Matt 12:14; Mark 3:6).

This healing occurred amid a growing sense of antagonism and enmity. Instead of being pleased at the man's evident restoration, the enemies of Jesus became more determined to plot against him. Mark notes that Jesus was "deeply saddened by their hard hearts" (Mark 3:5); he was angry because they had no concern or pity for this man's plight. Their only interest was to watch Jesus like a hawk so that they could nab him for Sabbath infractions (6:7).

◆   **L. Jesus Chooses the Twelve Apostles (6:12-16; cf. Matt 10:1-4; Mark 3:13-19)**

[12]One day soon afterward Jesus went up on a mountain to pray, and he prayed to God all night. [13]At daybreak he called together all of his disciples and chose twelve of them to be apostles. Here are their names:

[14]Simon (whom he named Peter), Andrew (Peter's brother), James, John,

Philip, Bartholomew, [15]Matthew, Thomas, James (son of Alphaeus), Simon (who was called the zealot), [16]Judas (son of James), Judas Iscariot (who later betrayed him).

NOTES

6:12 *a mountain.* The Gr. *to oros* [TG3735, ZG4001] "may refer to mountainous terrain rather than to a particular mountain" (Gundry 1993:166).

he prayed to God all night. On the importance of prayer in Luke, see Conn 1972 and
L. O. Harris 1967. On the prayer emphasis in Luke–Acts, see Trites 1978.

Some have noted a significant three-part pattern here: Jesus practiced solitude, communing
alone with the Father (6:12); he gathered the disciples as a community for instruction,
fellowship, and support (6:13; cf. Mark 3:14); and he led them out to minister to those in
need (6:17-19). This set of spiritual disciplines (solitude, community, and ministry) has
undoubted transfer value for modern disciples of Jesus.

6:13 *he called together all of his disciples and chose twelve of them to be apostles.* The
word "apostle" (*apostolos* [TG652, ZG693]) has been frequently studied. See Agnew 1986;
Herron 1983; Gardner 1995:52-56. On the dual role of the apostles as eyewitnesses and
advocates of Christ, see Trites 1977:114-116.

6:14 *Bartholomew.* The identity of Bartholomew is unclear. He is noted only in the lists of
the apostles (6:13-16; Matt 10:1-4; Mark 3:13-19; Acts 1:13). While the synoptic Gospels
and Acts all give the name Bartholomew, John presents Nathanael (John 1:45). Packer, et
al. (1982:137) summarize, "Some scholars believe that Bartholomew was the surname of
Nathanael. The Aramaic word *bar* [TA1247/10120, ZA10120] means 'son,' so *Bartholomew* literally meant 'son of Talmai.' (The Bible does not identify Talmai for us, but he might have
been named after the King Talmai of Geshur (2 Sam 3:3). Assuming that Bartholomew is
the same person as Nathanael, we learn a bit more about his personality from the Gospel
of John. Jesus called Nathanael 'an Israelite . . . in whom is no guile' (John 1:47)."

COMMENTARY

At the beginning of his public ministry, Jesus elicited a response from his hearers,
and some responded by becoming his followers. In Mark's Gospel, one can trace
several stages in Jesus' work with his disciples. First, there was the initial call to follow him, which probably took place in the vicinity of Capernaum. That call
included two sets of brothers from the area, namely, the fishermen Simon Peter and
Andrew, and James and John (Mark 1:16-20; cf. 5:1-11). The only other person's
call that is described in detail is that of Levi or Matthew (meaning "gift of God;"
Mark 2:14; cf. 5:27-32; Matt 9:9). These calls were probably typical of Jesus' calling
of the other disciples, whose specific stories are not recorded. The call was a summons: "Follow me" with the promise attached: "I will show you how to fish for
people!" (Mark 1:17; cf. 5:10). The apparent suddenness of the call does not imply
that the disciples had no prior knowledge of Jesus (see John 1:35-42).

The second stage was Jesus' deliberate choice of twelve men from the larger band of
followers: "Then he appointed twelve of them and called them his apostles" (Mark
3:14). The Twelve were granted the privilege of being with Jesus more often and more
closely and were taught the nature and character of the Kingdom of God, which was
breaking into history in Jesus' person and work (Mark 1:14-15; cf. Matt 4:17).

The third stage was that of apostleship—the actual sending forth of this special
group into mission as Jesus' authorized representatives (9:1-6; Matt 10:1-16; Mark
3:13-18 cf. 10:1-2). Indeed, the word *apostolos* [TG652, ZG693] meant "one sent out," a
person commissioned by another to act as his agent and emissary—in this case,
a person dispatched by Jesus Christ as his personal representative to announce the
Good News of the Kingdom of God. The Jewish principle of agency (*shaliach;*
cf. TDNT 1.414-420) applied here: "The one who goes is as him who sent him"

(*m. Berakhot* 5:5). Jesus states this principle directly in the fourth Gospel: "As the Father has sent me, so I am sending you" (John 20:21; cf. 13:20). Matthew communicates this in connection with Jesus sending out of the Twelve: "Anyone who receives you receives me, and anyone who receives me receives the Father who sent me" (Matt 10:40; cf. Matt 18:5). Luke, too, highlighted the importance of the principle in the sending out of the seventy-two other disciples who were to participate in the larger mission: "Anyone who accepts your message is also accepting me. And anyone who rejects you is rejecting me. And anyone who rejects me is rejecting God, who sent me" (10:16; cf. John 17:18).

Luke 6 is our first introduction to the concept of apostleship in this Gospel. The call of the twelve apostles came after careful thought and deliberation by Jesus. All three synoptic Gospels record the event as initiated by Jesus. Luke draws attention to the prayerfulness of Jesus in choosing the Twelve (6:12). (As we have seen, this is a frequent theme in Luke–Acts; e.g., 3:21; 5:16; 9:18, 28-29; 11:1; 22:32, 41; Acts 1:14; 4:24-31; 9:11; 10:2, 9.) The choice was preceded by an all-night prayer vigil, after which he "called together all of his disciples and chose twelve of them to be apostles" (6:13). In this way, Luke made it clear that there was a larger number of followers of Jesus. This verse also helps explain the fact that Jesus later chose "seventy-two other disciples and sent them out" in addition to the twelve apostles (10:1, 17; cf. 9:1-6). Still later, Luke will note the 120 followers of Christ who assembled in an upstairs room after the Resurrection to pray and appoint Matthias as an apostolic replacement for Judas (Acts 1:12-26).

The apostles are carefully listed in all three Gospels and in Acts 1:13, though the details vary. While the lists vary, the selection of the Twelve shows that Jesus was intent on creating a new Israel modeled after the twelve tribes but owning him as Master and Lord. Peter is mentioned first in all the accounts, suggesting his leadership role. He, indeed, was the first to confess Jesus as the Messiah, and after Judas's suicide, he spoke to the 120 about filling the leadership vacuum. He had a preeminent role on the day of Pentecost, and he explained the gospel to the Gentile household of Cornelius (cf. 9:20; Acts 1:15-22; 2:14; 10:9–11:18). Judas Iscariot was always named last, and in each Gospel, the fact of his shameful betrayal is noted (6:16; Matt 10:4; Mark 3:19; John 13:2; 18:2-3). Following Peter, Luke notes his brother Andrew and then James and John, who are identified as brothers in both Matthew and Mark and nicknamed by Jesus "Sons of Thunder" (Mark 3:17; cf. Matt 10:2).

Though the identity of Bartholomew is somewhat unclear, it is likely he is to be identified with Nathanael (John 1:45; see note on 6:14). In John's Gospel, Nathanael is linked with Philip; Luke's list places the two in succession. Next, we read of Matthew, whose other name was Levi (Mark 2:14), the man who gave a feast for Jesus (5:27-32; cf. Matt 9:9-13; Mark 2:14-17). James the son of Alphaeus is probably to be identified with James the younger (Mark 15:40). John's Gospel speaks of a "Judas (not Judas Iscariot)" (John 14:22), evidently to distinguish this man from the perfidious Judas Iscariot. "Judas son of James is mentioned in Luke 6:16 and Acts 1:13 as one of the Twelve whom Jesus selected to be apostles. In the place where this name falls in the Lucan lists, Matt 10:3 and Mark 3:18 have Thaddaeus. It may be another name for the man to keep him from being confused with Judas, the betrayer of Jesus" (Gardner 1995:390). The name Thaddaeus may be an alternate form of Theudas, taken from the Aramaic *tada* (Jastrow, 1647), which means "breast." So Thaddaeus might have been a nickname that meant "one close to the breast" or "beloved" (Packer et al. 1982:138).

The fellowship of these men was vitally important to Jesus, and he later paid the eleven a tribute by acknowledging, "You have stayed with me in my time of trial" (22:28). Their sacrifice was to be amply repaid, and they were promised, in due course, the opportunity of eating and drinking with the Messiah in his Kingdom, sitting "on thrones, judging the twelve tribes of Israel" (22:30).

◆   M. Crowds Follow Jesus (6:17-19; cf. Mark 3:7-12)

[17]When they came down from the mountain, the disciples stood with Jesus on a large, level area, surrounded by many of his followers and by the crowds. There were people from all over Judea and from Jerusalem and from as far north as the seacoasts of Tyre and Sidon. [18]They had come to hear him and to be healed of their diseases; and those troubled by evil* spirits were healed. [19]Everyone tried to touch him, because healing power went out from him, and he healed everyone.

6:18 Greek *unclean.*

NOTES

6:17 *When they came down from the mountain, the disciples stood with Jesus on a large, level area.* While the Sermon on the Plain (6:17-49) has many similarities with Matthew's Sermon on the Mount (Matt 5–7), Matthew includes a number of sayings in his version that Luke introduces at other points in his narrative of Jesus' ministry (e.g., 12:22-32 = Matt 6:25-34). It seems likely that Matthew has assembled many of the sayings of Jesus that were originally spoken on different occasions into a single discourse. For instructional purposes, he presents a clear, cohesive account of the nature, character, demands, and blessings of discipleship (Trites 1992:179-180). Luke, for his part, prefers to introduce these memorable sayings as they were used at various points in the unfolding story of Jesus' ministry. For studies comparing the Sermon on the Mount in Matthew with the Sermon on the Plain in Luke, see Carson 1978; Cox 1992; W. D. Davies 1964; Guelich 1982; Gundry 1994:65-137.

6:19 *healing power went out from him, and he healed everyone.* Luke–Acts is keenly interested in the concept of "power" (*dunamis* [TG1411, ZG1539]), a term used about 15 times in Luke and 10 times in Acts and employed here by Luke to refer to the effectiveness of Jesus' healing work. The power of God is most evident in the ministry of Jesus. He returned from his temptation in the "power" of the Spirit (4:14). He carried out his preaching and healing ministry with "power," and even evil spirits obeyed him and fled at his command (4:36). The "Lord's healing power was strongly with Jesus" as he healed a paralyzed man and a woman with a hemorrhage (5:17; 8:46). Similarly, Jesus first gave his apostles, and subsequently the seventy-two disciples, "power" and authority to cast out demons and heal (9:1; 10:19). When Jesus entered Jerusalem, the crowds praised God for the expressions of divine "power" they had witnessed (19:37). Ultimately, the Son of Man would appear "with power and great glory," and he would sit "in the place of power at God's right hand" (21:26-27; 22:69). (For further details on "power," see EDNT 1.55-58.)

COMMENTARY

After choosing the twelve apostles, Jesus descended from the slopes of the mountain and was "surrounded by many of his followers and by the crowds" (6:17). This provides the setting in which Luke presented the "Sermon on the Plain" (6:17-49). Jesus' teaching and great power attracted crowds from a wide cross section of the land, including people "from all over Judea and from Jerusalem and from as far north as the seacoasts of Tyre and Sidon" (6:17). There are similar accounts of Jesus' popularity in the other Gospels (Matt 4:25; 5:1; 12:15; Mark 3:7-8; John 6:2). The dual purpose of the crowds is plainly stated: they came "to hear him and to be healed" (6:18). A notable part of Christ's ministry was the deliverance of those who were troubled by evil spirits (6:18). He was so effective as a healer and exorcist that "everyone tried to touch him" (6:19). Luke notes that, in the presence of a demanding public, "healing power went out from him, and he healed everyone" (6:19). This statement is essentially repeated in the book of Acts, where Peter declares to the household of Cornelius that "Jesus went around doing good and healing all who were oppressed by the devil, for God was with him" (Acts 10:38).

Jesus' power was passed on to his apostles, as is evident in Acts. The disciples were promised power from the Holy Spirit that would enable them to bear witness for Christ in ever-widening spheres (Acts 1:8). The apostles continued to perform miracles but claimed no "power" for themselves (Acts 3:12). When they were questioned about the source of their evident power, they attributed it to Jesus (Acts 4:10). They "testified powerfully to the resurrection of the Lord Jesus" (Acts 4:33). Similarly, Stephen, full of the Spirit (Acts 6:5), exhibited power in performing "amazing miracles and signs among the people" (Acts 6:8), and the same was true of Philip and Paul (Acts 8:13; 19:11). There was a case of fraudulent power presented by Simon the sorcerer, who called himself "the Power of God" (Acts 8:10), but he was sternly rebuked by Peter and told to repent (Acts 8:18-24).

◆   N. The Beatitudes (6:20-23; cf. Matt 5:2-12)

²⁰Then Jesus turned to his disciples and said,

"God blesses you who are poor,
     for the Kingdom of God is yours.
²¹God blesses you who are hungry now,
     for you will be satisfied.
God blesses you who weep now,
     for in due time you will laugh.

²²What blessings await you when people hate you and exclude you and mock you and curse you as evil because you follow the Son of Man. ²³When that happens, be happy! Yes, leap for joy! For a great reward awaits you in heaven. And remember, their ancestors treated the ancient prophets that same way.

NOTES

6:20 There is an A-B-A pattern to each blessing here, with the promise of blessing followed by the ethical responsibility and then the spelling out of just what the promised blessing would be—great reward in heaven. Each beatitude is introduced by the word "blessed" (*makarioi* [ᵀᴳ3107, ᶻᴳ3421]). It is a statement of happiness, in Gr. not needing a verb to complete the thought; e.g., "O, the blessedness of the poor!" For useful studies of the Beatitudes, see Muto 1984; Hieke 2001.

God blesses you who are poor. There is a stark contrast drawn in 6:20-23 between the difficult present "now" (6:21) and the glorious future "in heaven" (6:23). Social and economic issues are faced but presented from a theocentric, eschatological perspective: "For a great reward awaits you in heaven" (6:23). On the issues of poverty and riches, see TDNT 4.885-915; Chilton and McDonald 1987; Davids 1980:40-58; Donahue 1989; Hoppe 2004; Pilgrim 1981; Seccombe 1982; Verhey 1984.

COMMENTARY

The Lukan Sermon on the Plain (6:17-49) is much shorter than Matthew's famous Sermon on the Mount, containing only 34 verses instead of the 111 in Matthew's version (Matt 5:1–7:29). It seems that Luke was more concerned than Matthew to present his material in a historical sequence. As White has remarked: "Matthew has gathered into one 'discourse,' sayings of the Master first spoken on various occasions, adding them to what was said on *this* occasion, and so presenting a clear, connected summary of the Master's teaching on discipleship. Luke preferred to record these sayings as they were spoken at different points in the story" (1979:20). As I have noted elsewhere (Trites 1992:179), "many of the sayings in Matthew's Sermon are not found in Luke's Sermon, but reappear elsewhere (e.g., Matt 6:22-23 [cf. Luke 11:34-36]; Matt 6:24 [cf. Luke 16:13]; Matt 6:25-34 [cf. Luke 12:22-32]; Matt 7:7-11 [cf. Luke 11:9-13]; Matt 7:13-14 [cf. Luke 13:23-24])." Luke preferred a chronological arrangement, while Matthew favored a topical presentation. Both are equally valuable and clearly serve different purposes. When we take into account the different approaches of Matthew and Luke, it is not surprising that Luke's Sermon on the Plain is roughly one-third the length of Matthew's Sermon on the Mount.

The first part of each sermon is similar, for it contains the "Beatitudes," or blessings (6:20-23; cf. Matt 5:1-12), and yet, even here, there are significant differences. The Lukan Beatitudes present only four blessings, and these are set in sharp contrast with four corresponding woes (6:20-23, 24-26). They are arranged in a striking antithetical parallelism. Matthew's list is quite different, containing nine beatitudes. The first eight of these are arranged in a common fashion and make clear use of the kind of parallelism that is characteristic of Hebrew poetry. In contrast, the last beatitude in Matthew is presented in the second person, while all the others are found in the third person. While some have speculated that there were only eight original beatitudes in Matthew, there is no textual evidence to support this view. The stylistic change is probably due simply to a different source. For our purposes, the change is interesting in that the use of the second person makes the connection between the ninth beatitude in Matthew and the fourth beatitude in Luke clear: "God blesses *you* when people mock you and persecute you and lie about you and say all sorts of evil things against you because you are my followers. Be happy about it! Be very glad! For a great reward awaits you in heaven. And remember, the ancient prophets were persecuted in the same way" (Matt 5:11-12; cf. 6:22-23). There are some differences in the two accounts. For example, only Luke says the suffering and defamation take place on account of the Son of Man, but the common elements are undeniable. The road of Christian discipleship is clearly marked by the prospect of suffering, but divine rewards in the Kingdom are the prospect held out for the faithful.

Turning to study Luke's version of the Beatitudes, we see that God's blessing is pronounced on the poor (not qualified by the phrase "in spirit" as in Matthew's version), the hungry, the sorrowful, and the persecuted. The unusual nature of these affirmations must be candidly acknowledged: "Jesus here, paradoxically, calls those happy whom the world commonly pities: the discouraged, sorrowful, lowly, spiritually depressed, merciful, the inwardly pure, the peacefully inclined, and the persecuted. This is the exact opposite of the world's standards. But in each case the blessing is not in the unfortunate condition itself, but in the glorious rewards of the future" (Halley 1952:384). It is a summons for the Kingdom person to live in the light of eternity, believing that the ultimate reckoning is in the hands of a loving, gracious, faithful God.

They are promised that the hungry will be satisfied; the weeping will give place to laughter and joy; and those hated, mocked, cursed, and excluded on account of their identification with the Son of Man will be rewarded. God is not unfair to his conscientious servants. Their faithfulness will be amply rewarded, and they are charged to remember that the ancient prophets had suffered similar indignities from their own people. The encouraging charge given to similarly hard-pressed disciples in the book of Revelation might be mentioned here: "Remain faithful even when facing death, [and] I will give you the crown of life" (Rev 2:10).

◆   O. Sorrows Foretold (6:24-26)

24 "What sorrow awaits you who
      are rich,
   for you have your only happiness
      now.
25 What sorrow awaits you who are fat
      and prosperous now,
   for a time of awful hunger awaits
      you.

What sorrow awaits you who
      laugh now,
   for your laughing will turn to
      mourning and sorrow.
26 What sorrow awaits you who are
      praised by the crowds,
   for their ancestors also praised
      false prophets.

NOTES

6:24 *What sorrow awaits you who are rich.* James contains similar warnings to the rich in his letter, and the theme is common in the NT (Jas 1:9-11; 2:1-7; 5:1-6; cf. Matt 6:19-21; 13:22; Mark 4:19; 1 Tim 6:17; Rev 3:17). On "poverty and possessions" in Luke–Acts, see Donahue 1989; Navone 1970:103-117; Tuckett 1997:94-110.

6:25 *a time of awful hunger awaits you.* Luke's Gospel, like the book of Acts (Acts 4:32-35; 11:28-30), shows a real interest in those who are physically hungry. For example, Mary's song praises God as the one who "has filled the hungry with good things" (1:53). Luke's beatitude, unlike Matthew's, is not spiritualized into a hunger for justice or righteousness but is stated quite concretely: "God blesses you who are hungry now, for you will be satisfied" (6:21; cf. Matt 5:6). Furthermore, Luke was interested in speaking about food;

he used the verb "eat" (*esthiō* [TG2068, ZG2266]) 33 times in his Gospel. This goes hand in hand with Luke's fondness for banquet scenes (see Introduction). This, of course, does not deny the importance of spiritual needs, for Jesus affirmed quite unmistakably the OT principle, "People do not live by bread alone" (4:4 [Deut 8:3]).

COMMENTARY

Only Luke's Sermon contains the four woes, though Matthew elsewhere notes the seven woes pronounced by Christ against his opponents (Matt 23:1-36). The blessings and woes are placed in striking contrast by Luke, and the statements are short and pithy. The order of the woes parallels that of the blessings in 6:20-22. The background of the woes can be traced to the prophetic oracles of the Old Testament that pronounced divine judgment on those who opposed the purposes of God, including the rich who exploited the poor (e.g., Isa 30:1; Jer 23:1-4; Ezek 34:2; Amos 5:18; Hab 2:6; Zech 11:17). Jesus' demands are clear and categorical. There are real choices to be made, and they have serious, eternal consequences. Jesus castigated those who are presently rich, smugly prosperous, self-satisfied, and careless. God, the great Judge, will turn their laughter into "mourning and sorrow," and all their present delight will vanish on the day of reckoning. By contrast, Jesus is the champion of the poor, the hungry, the despised, and the persecuted (cf. 4:18; 7:22; 12:33; 14:13; 16:19-31; 18:22).

Luke highlights Jesus' concern for the poor in both his synagogue sermon in Nazareth (4:18) and here in his Sermon on the Plain (6:20), where the plight of the poor is contrasted with that of the rich (6:24). Jesus gave special prominence to the needs of the poor (7:22; 12:33; 14:13; 18:22; 19:8). He clearly attacked the evils of materialism and directed people to the Kingdom of God, acting as its lowly Servant-King. Note the helpful comment on poverty by John Navone (1970:103-105), who has devoted a whole chapter to this topic:

> Poverty is a fundamental mark of blessedness in the thought of Luke (6:20). The joy of the kingdom belongs to the poor. Mary exclaims: "My soul proclaims the greatness of the Lord and my spirit *rejoices* in God my savior; because he has regarded the poverty (*tapeinōsin*) of his servant" (1:46-48). . . . Jesus, the servant of the Lord (Acts 3:13, 26; 4:27, 30; cf. Luke 22:27), is born in poverty and laid in a manger (2:7, 12, 16). His birth is announced to the poor, to the shepherds in the fields. When Jesus was presented in the Temple, his parents made the offering of the poor (2:24; cf. Lev 12:8).

Only Luke's Gospel mentions Jesus' instruction to "sell your possessions and give to those in need" (12:33), and it notes Jesus' encouragement to "invite the poor" to a meal (14:13).

In Luke's Gospel, the rich seem to be those whose desires have already been satisfied by wealth, pleasure, and honor. Of the rich, Jesus said, "How hard it is for the rich to enter the Kingdom of God! In fact, it is easier for a camel to go through the eye of a needle than for a rich person to enter the Kingdom of God!" (18:24-25). Navone (1970:105-106) states, "Wealth almost precludes genuine discipleship. Zacchaeus (19:1-10) was 'very rich'; it is only after he has given half his possessions to the poor that he is told salvation has come to his house." When all of Jesus' teachings on poverty and wealth are assessed, it is clear that a Christian should use his possessions in the interest of the poor and needy inside and outside the community (K. Kim 1998:286-287). Following Jesus' teachings, the early church was concerned with meeting the needs of the poor (Acts 2:45; 4:34-35; Rom 15:25-28; 1 Cor 16:1-4; 2 Cor 8-9). Acts records both good and bad models of sharing and contrasts the fine example of Barnabas with the unworthy one of Ananias and Sapphira (Acts 4:36-5:11).

◆ **P. Love for Enemies (6:27-36; cf. Matt 5:38-47)**

27"But to you who are willing to listen, I say, love your enemies! Do good to those who hate you. 28Bless those who curse you. Pray for those who hurt you. 29If someone slaps you on one cheek, offer the other cheek also. If someone demands your coat, offer your shirt also. 30Give to anyone who asks; and when things are taken away from you, don't try to get them back. 31Do to others as you would like them to do to you.

32"If you love only those who love you, why should you get credit for that? Even sinners love those who love them! 33And if you do good only to those who do good to you, why should you get credit? Even sinners do that much! 34And if you lend money only to those who can repay you, why should you get credit? Even sinners will lend to other sinners for a full return.

35"Love your enemies! Do good to them. Lend to them without expecting to be repaid. Then your reward from heaven will be very great, and you will truly be acting as children of the Most High, for he is kind to those who are unthankful and wicked. 36You must be compassionate, just as your Father is compassionate.

NOTES

6:27 *I say, love your enemies!* Luke makes many references to those who hate believers and persecute them because of their faith (6:22; 12:11; 21:12-19; Acts 4:18-21, 29; 6:12-14; 7:54-59; 14:19; 16:19-24). Christians, like their Master, would certainly face "enemies" (*antikeimenoi* [TG480, ZG512]; 21:15; cf. 13:17), but with God's help, they could demonstrate a "faith expressing itself in love" (Gal 5:6). Their enemies were in danger of finding themselves "fighting against God" (*theomachoi* [TG2314, ZG2534]; Acts 5:39), as Gamaliel reminded the Jewish council when it considered how to handle the irrepressible apostles who were spreading the claims of Christ throughout Jerusalem. On the treatment of enemies, see TDNT 2.811-816; Seitz 1969; Bauer 1981:1.351-355.

6:29 *If someone slaps you on one cheek, offer the other cheek also.* The Jewish people at the time of Jesus were subject to the control of Rome, so the force of Roman military occupation was keenly felt on the personal level. On the use of Roman force, see Horsley 1993; Herzog 2000:111-143.

6:35 *the Most High.* On this title, see note on 1:32.

COMMENTARY

At the very heart of Jesus' teaching, in both the Sermon on the Mount and the Sermon on the Plain, is the emphasis on the love of one's enemies (6:27-36; Matt 5:39-42, 44-48). Here, Jesus spells out his famous teaching on nonviolence: "If someone slaps you on one cheek, offer the other cheek also" (6:29). The policy of compliance is explained more fully in Matthew's version: "If you are sued in court and your shirt is taken from you, give your coat, too. If a soldier demands that you carry his gear for a mile, carry it two miles" (Matt 5:39-41). There is a spirit of kindness and generosity suggested here that goes beyond a legal obligation imposed by an external authority, an expression of unselfish caring for which the Christian name is *agapē* [TG26, ZG27]. Jesus summed it up perfectly in the Golden Rule: "Do to others as you would like them to do to you" (6:31; cf. Matt 7:12).

This maxim is sometimes found in negative form outside of the Bible. For example, the famous Jewish rabbi Hillel was called upon to summarize the law while standing on one leg, and he replied, "What is hateful to you, do not to your fellow. That is the whole law and all the rest is commentary" (cited by Caird 1963:104). But, as George Caird has wisely observed, "an ethical programme which consists in not-doing, especially when it has to be expounded in a vast commentary of rules and ceremonies, can hardly be compared with one which calls for positive and unlimited benevolence" (1963:104). And this ethical plan of action finds its perfect positive embodiment in the life, ministry, and death of Jesus, the servant *par excellence*, who declared, "I am among you as one who serves" (22:27).

The ethic commended by Jesus in this passage is one of unstinting mercy and generosity: "Give to anyone who asks" (6:30; cf. Matt 5:42). It is not based on a crude system of calculation, a *quid pro quo* kind of exchange where something is given in return for a favor bestowed. Acts of goodness directed towards one's friends are nothing special, for even people with no religious profession of faith perform them. True followers of Christ are called to go beyond such common and expected acts of goodness: "If you do good only to those who do good to you, why should you get credit? Even sinners do that much! And if you lend money only to those who can repay you, why should you get credit? Even sinners will lend to other sinners for a full return" (6:33-34; cf. 14:12-14). A more openhanded, unselfish policy is expected of Kingdom people, who are to be motivated by more than prudential considerations and enlightened self-interest. Their concern should be to reach beyond their kith and kin, close friends, business associates, and colleagues to embrace even those who are actively hostile and working against Christian disciples: "Love your enemies! Do good to them. Lend to them without expecting to be repaid" (6:35). There is to be a willing surrender of goods and services if it is called for, leaving the results in the hands of God with the conviction that the judge of all the earth will do right: "Then your reward from heaven will be very great, and you will truly be acting as children of the Most High, for he is kind to those who are unthankful and wicked" (6:35b). The whole foundation for the disciples' approach to others was to be based upon the character of the God they served: "You must be compassionate, just as your Father is compassionate" (6:36; cf. Matt 5:7; 18:32-35; Jas 2:13).

This was clearly the attitude that Jesus himself displayed toward his enemies. He healed the slashed ear of the servant of the high priest who had come with others to arrest him on the Mount of Olives (22:50-51). He forgave the sins of a paralyzed man and a sinful woman, had compassion on the women of Jerusalem, and assured the penitent thief on the cross that he would be with him in paradise (5:20-26; 7:47-49; 23:28-31, 43). This was also the attitude of the early Christians, who accepted persecution without hatred toward their persecutors, "rejoicing that God had counted them worthy to suffer disgrace for the name of Jesus" (Acts 5:41). In like manner, Paul and Silas sang hymns and prayed after being severely beaten and flogged, and Paul shouted out in concern to save the life of the Philippian jailor, who was on the point of committing suicide (Acts 16:25-28). Perhaps the most remarkable expression of forgiveness comes from the lips of the dying Stephen, who prayed for his enemies: "Lord, don't charge them with this sin!" (Acts 7:60).

◆   **Q. Don't Condemn Others (6:37-42; cf. Matt 7:1-5)**

37"Do not judge others, and you will not be judged. Do not condemn others, or it will all come back against you. Forgive others, and you will be forgiven. 38Give, and you will receive. Your gift will return to you in full—pressed down, shaken together to make room for more, running over, and poured into your lap. The amount you give will determine the amount you get back.*"

39Then Jesus gave the following illustration: "Can one blind person lead another? Won't they both fall into a ditch?

40Students* are not greater than their teacher. But the student who is fully trained will become like the teacher.

41"And why worry about a speck in your friend's eye* when you have a log in your own? 42How can you think of saying, 'Friend,* let me help you get rid of that speck in your eye,' when you can't see past the log in your own eye? Hypocrite! First get rid of the log in your own eye; then you will see well enough to deal with the speck in your friend's eye.

6:38 Or *The measure you give will be the measure you get back.* 6:40 Or *Disciples.* 6:41 Greek *your brother's eye;* also in 6:42. 6:42 Greek *Brother.*

NOTES

6:37 *Do not judge.* This prohibition of supercilious, condemnatory judgments does not rule out the command to discern and admonish, which Paul presents as a Christian duty, provided it is done in a spirit of gentleness by one who has received the Holy Spirit (Gal 6:1; cf. Heb 3:13).

6:42 *Hypocrite!* A hypocrite is "one who outwardly plays the part of a religious man to perfection, but is inwardly alien to the spirit of true religion" (Souter 1953:270). Luke's first use of "hypocrite" is paralleled in Matthew's Sermon on the Mount (Matt 7:5). Jesus rebuked the attitude that turns a blind eye to one's own faults while at the same time arrogantly criticizing others. Jesus called some of his contemporaries "hypocrites" for discerning the weather but failing to discern the spiritual signs of the time (12:56; cf. Matt 16:2-3). He also used the term "hypocrite" of the synagogue leaders who opposed the healing of a crippled woman on the Sabbath (13:15-17). On the use of *hupokritēs* [TG5273, ZG5695], see EDNT 3.403-404. All occurrences of this word are found in the Gospels. Most of them are found in Matthew (Matt 6:2, 5, 16; 7:5; 22:18; 23:13-15; 24:51), with one use in Mark (Mark 7:6) and three occurrences in Luke (6:42; 12:56; 13:15).

COMMENTARY

The teaching of Jesus forbade the exercise of unfair or hypocritical judgment of others (6:37; cf. Matt 7:1). He would not tolerate people treating others with an attitude of superiority or condescension—especially when the one doing this was morally impure. Jesus' admonition was directed against a censorious spirit that was hypercritical of others and blind to its own faults and failings (6:41-42). It called for disciples to clean up their own acts first, and then they would possess the moral authority to deal with the faults of others. At this point, Jesus resorted to the use of hyperbole, making the figurative statement, "Hypocrite! First get rid of the log in your own eye; then you will see well enough to deal with the speck in your friend's eye" (6:41-42). Caird tells us that "the parable of the log and the speck is an example of the humorous hyperbole with which Jesus so often administered gentle reproof (cf. 18:25; Matt 23:24). This is a parable about personal relationships. Pseudo-religion, which Jesus calls hypocrisy, is forever trying to make people [look] better; and the cure for it is in the mirror" (1963:106). In other words, a certain honesty, humility, and self-scrutiny were called for in dealing with the sins of others. Paul urges this attitude in writing to the Galatians about correcting a fellow believer (Gal 6:1).

Jesus recognized the natural tendency of people to be blind to their own faults while having a great awareness of the sins and shortcomings of others. This is the point of his challenge regarding blindness: "Can one blind person lead another? Won't they both fall into a ditch?" (6:39). The illustration makes it crystal clear that one must seriously examine oneself before attempting to correct what might be really only a minor fault in someone else. The yardstick of divine judgment must never be forgotten: "The standard you use in judging is the standard by which you will be judged" (Matt 7:2).

Luke contains several features that are not present in the parallel passage in Matthew. Significantly, he mentions the need for forgiveness, a theme to which he frequently returns in Luke–Acts (e.g., 1:77; 3:3; 5:20-24; 12:10; 24:47; Acts 2:38; 10:43; 13:38; 26:18): "Forgive others, and you will be forgiven" (6:37). In addition, Luke stresses the need for overflowing generosity: "Give, and you will receive. Your gift will return to you in full—pressed down, shaken together to make room for more, running over" (6:38). Once again, Luke captures a vital note in the teaching of Jesus, who gave himself freely to others and encouraged his followers to act in the same way. In the book of Acts, Luke mentions that in the early days of the church in Jerusalem, the believers, in keeping with this teaching, shared everything they had (Acts 2:44).

Luke's Gospel shares with Matthew the saying of Jesus that "students are not greater than their teacher" (6:40; Matt 10:24-25); similar sentiments are found in other passages (John 13:16; 15:20). Luke also has the unique comment that "the student who is fully trained will become like the teacher." In our culture, it is often asserted that a leader's personal life should be considered completely separate from his or her professional life, but this separation, Fred Craddock (1990:92) has noted, was not the case in Luke's time:

In Luke's culture, modeling behavior, especially for a teacher, was a primary responsibility, and imitation of one's teacher was the basic mode of learning. Many New Testament texts support this understanding of the teacher-disciple relationship (Acts 20:17-35; 1 Cor 4:15-17; 11:1; Phil 3:17; Titus 2:7). . . . Luke is not saying that imperfections disqualify a leader. On the contrary, Luke's point [in verses 39-40] is that the disqualifying factor is not flaws but blindness to one's flaws, an unwillingness to be self-critical and honest with oneself.

◆   ## R. The Tree and Its Fruit (6:43-45; cf. Matt 7:16-20)

[43]"A good tree can't produce bad fruit, and a bad tree can't produce good fruit. [44]A tree is identified by its fruit. Figs are never gathered from thornbushes, and grapes are not picked from bramble bushes. [45]A good person produces good things from the treasury of a good heart, and an evil person produces evil things from the treasury of an evil heart. What you say flows from what is in your heart.

N O T E S

6:43-45 The parallel passage to 6:43-45 on the sources of good and evil is Matt 7:16-20. The passage in Matthew is introduced by a warning against false prophets, who appear genuine on the outside ("harmless sheep") but are really vicious wolves (Matt 7:15). Note the perceptive comment of Guelich (1982:393-394): "Using two related metaphors whose original *Sitz im Leben* may well have been in Jesus' ministry among the 'righteous,' Matthew inverted them (7:16, par. Luke 6:44; 7:18, par. Luke 6:43) and expanded them by first developing a positive counterpart to the negatively formulated saying regarding good and bad trees then by adding the judgment saying from the Baptist's preaching and finally by concluding with a repetition of 7:16a in 7:20 that forms an inclusion and makes application of 7:16-19 to the false prophets of 7:15." The image of the good and bad fruit might possibly be taken from Isaiah's parable of the vineyard (Isa 5:1-7) or Jeremiah's two baskets of figs, one fresh and the other spoiled (Jer 24:1-10).

6:45 *A good person produces good things from the treasury of a good heart, and an evil person produces evil things from the treasury of an evil heart.* There is also a version of this saying in the *Gospel of Thomas*, logion 45: "A good man brings forth good out of his treasure, an evil man brings forth evil things out of his evil treasure, which is in his heart, and speaks evil things."

C O M M E N T A R Y

Jesus stressed the need for practical goodness to be demonstrated in the lives of his followers. This clearly recalled John the Baptist's ethical preaching, where repentance was a major note, calling for concrete acts of service that showed others the reality of the change their relationship with God had produced (3:10-14). It was imperative to live responsibly in the light of God's impending judgment on sinners. John had underscored the reality of coming divine judgment in the ears of his audience: "Even now the ax of God's judgment is poised, ready to sever the roots of the trees. Yes, every tree that does not produce good fruit will be chopped down and thrown into the fire" (3:9; cf. Matt 3:10).

The stark moral choice placed before the original hearers was also placed by the Evangelist before his readers: "A tree is identified by its fruit. Figs are never gathered from thornbushes, and grapes are not picked from bramble bushes" (6:44). This decisive choice has to be faced, a point also developed a second time in Matthew's Gospel as Jesus rebukes the Pharisees in strong terms reminiscent of John the Baptist ("you brood of snakes!" Matt 12:33-35). Jesus insisted that "good fruit" outwardly identified a believer's good character (that is, incontrovertible evidence of a new life is made clear in commendable outward actions). The letter of James makes a similar point: "How can you show me your faith if you don't have good deeds? I will show you my faith by my good deeds" (Jas 2:18).

Jesus was concerned about the moral influence that would be exercised by those who chose to follow him. He knew that their real authority and magnetism would depend on the kind of people they were. Accordingly, he insisted that character was foundational to ethical performance and needed to be duly tested (cf. 1 John 4:1-3). The analogy he uses in 6:44 is simple, gripping, and memorable. Professions of faith had to be marked by appropriate action.

A basic principle operates here, one that applies in the spiritual world as well as in the agricultural realm: "A good tree can't produce bad fruit, and a bad tree can't produce good fruit" (6:43). Only God can make a person thoroughly good, and only such a person can produce the kind of lifestyle required. Jesus was concerned that Kingdom people be truly good persons, not hypocrites (cf. 6:42). He knew that it is the thought life that defiles a person: "For from within, out of a person's heart, come evil thoughts, sexual immorality, theft, murder, adultery, greed, wickedness, deceit, lustful desires, envy, slander, pride, and foolishness. All these vile things come from within; they are what defile you" (Mark 7:21-23). Jesus proclaimed a profound truth: "What you say flows from what is in your heart" (6:45). Here was a deep-seated challenge that called for a radical commitment to God to enable one to live as God intends.

◆   ## S. Building on a Solid Foundation (6:46-49; cf. Matt 7:24-27)

46"So why do you keep calling me 'Lord, Lord!' when you don't do what I say? 47I will show you what it's like when someone comes to me, listens to my teaching, and then follows it. 48It is like a person building a house who digs deep and lays the foundation on solid rock. When the floodwaters rise and break against that house, it stands firm because it is well built. 49But anyone who hears and doesn't obey is like a person who builds a house without a foundation. When the floods sweep down against that house, it will collapse into a heap of ruins."

N O T E S

6:46 *So why do you keep calling me 'Lord, Lord!' when you don't do what I say?* On the essential importance of obedience for true discipleship, see M. Green (1989:92), who stresses its indispensable character: "Obedience that transforms our characters ([Matt] 5:11-12), that affects our influence (5:13-16), that shows itself in practical righteousness (5:17-48), that touches our devotional life (6:1-18), that radically alters our ambitions (6:19-34), that transforms our relationships (7:1-12) and that marks us out as totally wholehearted servants of the King (7:13-27). That is what Jesus is looking for."

6:49 anyone who hears and doesn't obey is like a person who builds a house without a foundation. The connection between hearing and obeying, often noted in the OT (Exod 24:7; Deut 4:1; 7:12; 28:1-2; Jer 7:23; 9:13; 11:4, 7), is also mentioned in James and Romans (Rom 2:13; Jas 1:22-25).

COMMENTARY

Jesus taught that a casual profession of faith is not enough. To be a true disciple, one must actually submit oneself to his lordship. Discipleship was not simply a matter of using pious cliches, but of genuine obedience. This includes a willingness to put into practice the things that Jesus taught. Actions speak louder than words!

The parable of the two houses presents another marked contrast. Matthew's version is plainly set in Palestine (Matt 7:24-27), where one builder constructs a house on rock and the other builds on an apparently attractive piece of sandy ground, not noticing that it is a dry river bed or "wadi," which, in winter, will become a raging torrent. "Luke has adapted the parable to Gentile geography and climate. In his version the sensible man digs down through the soil to the underlying rock; the short-sighted one builds on the surface, and the damage to the house is done by the flooding river. But the meaning is the same in each case. The man who hears and does is safe against every crisis, while the man who only hears is inviting disaster" (Caird 1963:107).

Stott has commented on the parallel passage in Matt 7:21-27: "The truth on which Jesus is insisting is that neither an intellectual knowledge of him nor a verbal profession, though both are essential in themselves, can ever be a substitute for obedience. The question is not whether we *say* nice, polite words, orthodox, enthusiastic things to or about Jesus; nor whether we *hear* his words, listening, studying, pondering and memorizing until our minds are stuffed with his teaching; but whether we *do* what we say and *do* what we know, in other words, whether the lordship of Jesus which we profess is one of our life's major realities" (1978:209).

◆   ## T. Faith of the Roman Officer (7:1-10; cf. Matt 8:5-13; John 4:46-53)

When Jesus had finished saying all this to the people, he returned to Capernaum. ²At that time the highly valued slave of a Roman officer* was sick and near death. ³When the officer heard about Jesus, he sent some respected Jewish elders to ask him to come and heal his slave. ⁴So they earnestly begged Jesus to help the man. "If anyone deserves your help, he does," they said, ⁵"for he loves the Jewish people and even built a synagogue for us."

⁶So Jesus went with them. But just before they arrived at the house, the officer sent some friends to say, "Lord, don't trouble yourself by coming to my home, for I am not worthy of such an honor. ⁷I am not even worthy to come and meet you. Just say the word from where you are, and my servant will be healed. ⁸I know this because I am under the authority of my superior officers, and I have authority over my soldiers. I only need to say, 'Go,' and they go, or 'Come,' and they come. And if I say to my slaves, 'Do this,' they do it."

⁹When Jesus heard this, he was amazed. Turning to the crowd that was following

him, he said, "I tell you, I haven't seen faith like this in all Israel!" ¹⁰And when

the officer's friends returned to his house, they found the slave completely healed.

7:2 Greek *a centurion;* similarly in 7:6.

NOTES

7:2 Roman officer. Lit., "centurion," a term used to denote a Roman military leader who commanded a hundred men. On the role of centurions in the NT, see Gardner 1995:97-98.

7:8 I am under the authority of my superior officers, and I have authority over my soldiers. This is similar to "words used by the Roman legate Petronius to the Jews gathered at Tiberias in Galilee in trying to persuade them to accept the erection of Caligula's statue in the Temple. Josephus quotes him as saying, 'For I am subject to authority as well as you are' (*War* 2.10.4)" (Schonfield 1958:155).

7:9 I haven't seen faith like this in all Israel! Faith is of tremendous importance in Luke–Acts. In Luke's Gospel, Jesus commends the faith of many persons, including: the men who carried a paralyzed man to Jesus (5:20), a Roman officer (7:9), a sinful woman (7:50), a hemorrhaging woman (8:48), a Samaritan leper (17:19), and a blind beggar (18:42). Jesus rebuked the disciples for lack of faith during the midst of a storm (8:25) and raised a searching question about whether the Son of Man would find faith on the earth when he returned (18:8). Later, the disciples themselves requested, "Show us how to increase our faith" (17:5). Out of genuine concern for Peter, Jesus pleaded in prayer for him that his faith should not fail (22:32). True faith is powerful and effective (17:6).

Similarly, faith plays a vital role in Acts (3:16; 4:4; 10:43; 11:21; 13:48; 14:1; 19:18). Stephen is "full of faith" (Acts 6:5); Barnabas is "strong in faith" (Acts 11:24). Numerous Gentiles exercise faith (e.g., Acts 14:9; 16:31-34). Young converts are "strengthened in their faith" (Acts 16:5). To sum up, Paul's central message was "the necessity of repenting from sin and turning to God, and of having faith in our Lord Jesus" (20:21). See also note on 1:45.

COMMENTARY

The healing of the Roman officer's servant is told with real skill and warmth. After Jesus had returned to Capernaum, he was met by a delegation of Jewish leaders. They begged him to rescue a centurion's servant who was at the point of death (7:2). The centurion was a Roman officer normally in charge of a hundred men. The Jewish residents in the area respected the man, for he loved the Jewish people and had built a synagogue for them. Jesus accompanied them, but just before they reached the house, the officer sent some friends to plead his unworthiness and to ask directly for help. The man clearly acknowledged the authority of Jesus and believed he could intervene even in this crisis situation: "Just say the word from where you are, and my servant will be healed" (7:7). Jesus commended the centurion for his faith, declaring that it outstripped anything he had seen in the land of Israel (7:9). This is one of only two places in the Gospels where Jesus is said to be amazed—here in Capernaum by faith and in Nazareth by unbelief (7:9; Mark 6:6).

The primary interest of the incident is in the positive response of the centurion that evoked such words of praise from Jesus. Jesus had been summoning his Jewish contemporaries to follow him, and the response had been mixed. Some people were offended by his remarks in the Nazareth synagogue that had suggested God's compassion extended even to the hated Syrians (4:25-29). Some, including John the Baptist and members of his circle, were puzzled by the different manner in which Jesus was exercising his messianic vocation (7:20-23). And some were antagonized by the astounding nature of his claims (e.g., to be the "true bread that came down from heaven," John 6:58-66). But here, in a Gentile outsider, Jesus found a man who had confidence that God was vitally at work in his ministry. The centurion's military experience in the forces controlled by Herod Antipas served as a stepping-stone to faith and taught him about the chain of command. He reasoned that, just as he gave orders to those under his command, so Jesus could exercise authority in the spiritual sphere to the forces under his command. Just as the military man acknowledged that he was subject to his commanding officer, so he perceived that Jesus, in truth, was acting in true submission to his commander (that is, God) and could exercise his commission accordingly. The Gentile officer perceived that God was at work in Jesus, bringing in his divine Kingdom and exercising powerful works of healing and benevolence. No wonder Jesus commended him!

In addition to the man's remarkable faith, there are several other features worth noting. First, the man was a Gentile, and that was important to Luke who was writing principally for Gentiles. Second, the poignancy of the request is stressed—the servant was "highly valued" (7:2) by his master, and the master himself was highly esteemed by the local Jewish community, who sent some of their respected leaders to intercede urgently for the needed healing (cf. Acts 10:2-3, where another centurion is highly respected). Third, the source of the healing took place at some distance from the bedside, thus underlining the power of Jesus to heal without being present on the spot. Fourth, the officer's faith was based not only on his military experience but also on his strong confidence in the power of Jesus to intervene and bring healing. Fifth, this faith was totally vindicated when the friends returned and found his servant "completely healed" (7:10).

There is a parallel account in Matthew's Gospel that adds several details (Matt 8:5-13). In Matthew, we learn that the servant was confined to bed, paralyzed, and in terrible suffering (Matt 8:6). Matthew reports the positive offer of Christ to help: "I will come and heal him" (Matt 8:7). Jesus, in commending the officer's faith, predicted the coming of people from all points of the compass to participate in the great banquet with Abraham, Isaac, and Jacob "in the Kingdom of Heaven," but he added a solemn note of judgment that many Israelites "will be thrown into outer darkness, where there will be weeping and gnashing of teeth" (Matt 8:11-12).

There is a similar (but not the same) healing account in John regarding a government official from Capernaum who approached Jesus in Cana of Galilee on behalf of his son who was very sick with a fever (John 4:46-53). The official pleaded directly for his little boy, but Jesus sent him home with the promise that his son would live. The official's servants met him on his way home and reported that the boy had been healed at the very hour Jesus had spoken to him. The upshot of this incident was that the officer and his whole household believed in Jesus. John notes that this was "the second miraculous sign Jesus did in Galilee after coming from Judea" (John 4:54).

◆ U. Jesus Raises a Widow's Son (7:11-17)

¹¹Soon afterward Jesus went with his disciples to the village of Nain, and a large crowd followed him. ¹²A funeral procession was coming out as he approached the village gate. The young man who had died was a widow's only son, and a large crowd from the village was with her. ¹³When the Lord saw her, his heart overflowed with compassion. "Don't cry!" he said. ¹⁴Then he walked over to the coffin and touched it, and the bearers stopped. "Young man," he said, "I tell you, get up." ¹⁵Then the dead boy sat up and began to talk! And Jesus gave him back to his mother.

¹⁶Great fear swept the crowd, and they praised God, saying, "A mighty prophet has risen among us," and "God has visited his people today." ¹⁷And the news about Jesus spread throughout Judea and the surrounding countryside.

NOTES

7:12 *The young man who had died was a widow's only son.* Only three times does Luke use the word *monogenēs* [TG3439, ZG3666] (only-born, only). In each case, there is a touching poignancy in the situation and a hint of compassion on the part of Jesus for a very needy case. The "only" son in 7:12 is the sole hope of support for a widow who would naturally expect her son to provide for her. The daughter of Jairus was his "only" daughter, so her loss would be particularly painful (8:42). The suffering epileptic boy was the "only" child of his father, who begged Jesus for help in a tragic situation (9:38). Luke paints Jesus as a warm person who addressed striking cases of human need with loving sympathy and compassion. On the NT use of *monogenēs*, see Moody 1953; IDB 3.604; EDNT 2.439-440. The NT repeatedly underscores the sad economic plight of widows (7:13; 21:1-4; Mark 12:41-44; 1 Tim 5:3-16; Jas 1:27). For biblical references to widows, see NIDNTT 3.1073-1078 and notes on 2:37; 18:3; 20:47; 21:1-4.

7:16 *Great fear swept the crowd.* On the "great fear" mentioned here, observe the common OT statement: "Fear of the LORD is the foundation of true knowledge" (Prov 1:7; cf. Job 28:28; Ps 111:10; Prov. 9:10; Eccl 12:13). The first followers of Jesus were discovering this truth and growing in their faith, recognizing that "a mighty prophet" had arisen among them and that God had "visited his people" (7:16; cf. Acts 2:43, "a deep sense of awe," and Acts 19:17, "a solemn *fear*," all three passages translating the same Gr. word, *phobos* [TG5401, ZG5832], "fear"). The themes of awe, prophecy, and God's visitation of his people have already been introduced in Luke's opening chapter (1:65, 67, 78), and God's visitation of his people appears again in Luke–Acts (19:44; Acts 15:14), as does Jesus' role as prophet (cf. 7:39; 13:33-34; 24:19; Acts 3:22-23; 7:37).

COMMENTARY

There are more references to widows in Luke–Acts than anywhere else in the New Testament. The devout Anna, a widow, was present to recognize and praise God at the coming of the infant Christ (2:36-38). Widows from the time of Elijah are mentioned (4:25-26; cf. 1 Kgs 17:8-24). A persistent widow is the subject of one of Jesus' parables on prayer (18:1-8), and some widows are mentioned as the victims of shameless exploitation (20:47). Jesus gives one widow's sacrificial offering special recognition (21:1-4). In Acts, the needs of the Hellenistic widows are attended to, and the presence of the weeping widows at the raising of Tabitha is noted (Acts 6:1-7; 9:39-41). Luke was clearly aware of the concerns of widows, and that awareness finds expression in this case, where a widow's needs were acknowledged and met by Jesus.

This remarkable incident, found only in Luke's Gospel, is placed just after the healing of the centurion's servant. The crowd mentioned in 7:9 was still following Jesus, and the "disciples" (7:11) were present, probably meaning the twelve apostles. The group was approaching Nain, a village in southern Galilee, located about 25 miles southwest of Capernaum. They met a large funeral procession coming out of the community and men bearing the corpse of a young man, the only son of a widow.

Luke describes the scene simply but effectively. Jesus' heart "overflowed with compassion" (7:13) for the grieving mother. After urging her to stop crying, he walked over to the bier, touched the body, and commanded the young man to get up. "Then the dead boy sat up and began to talk! And Jesus gave him back to his mother" (7:15).

Some commentators have seen a close link between this story and a similar one in the Old Testament where a non-Israelite widow at Zarephath had her son restored to life by the prophet Elijah (1 Kgs. 17:8-24; see Brodie 1986). At the end of that account, the widow told Elijah: "Now I know for sure that you are a man of God, and that the LORD truly speaks through you" (1 Kgs 17:24). The successful prophetic intervention had convinced her of the prophet's authenticity. Similarly, in the Gospel story, the people declared, "A mighty prophet has risen among us" (7:16).

The Nain incident is one of three instances recorded in the Gospels where Jesus raises the dead. Two of these incidents are included in Luke, and the other one is the raising of Lazarus, recorded only in John 11. The two cases in Luke both involve young people—a young man here and a young woman in the next chapter, the twelve-year-old daughter of Jairus (a leader of the local Jewish synagogue; 8:41-42, 49-56). Taken together, they serve as convincing evidence that "the dead are raised to life" (7:22). This message was duly conveyed to John the Baptist's disciples, who came asking about Jesus' credentials (7:18-23).

This striking exhibition of divine power did not go unnoticed. It resulted in a heartfelt expression of praise to God, and the people exclaimed, "God has visited his people today" (7:16). The miracle raised the level of spiritual expectancy among the people. God was evidently at work in their midst, and they "were all filled with awe" (7:16, NIV). The outcome of this mighty demonstration of power was the spreading of Jesus' fame "throughout Judea and the surrounding countryside" (7:17). The power of God was at work in the land, and the news of the one in whom God was acting was being widely broadcast. The messianic program announced by Jesus (4:18-19) was truly in the process of being fulfilled.

◆   ## V. Jesus and John the Baptist (7:18-35; cf. Matt 11:2-6)

[18]The disciples of John the Baptist told John about everything Jesus was doing. So John called for two of his disciples, [19]and he sent them to the Lord to ask him, "Are you the Messiah we've been expect-ing,* or should we keep looking for someone else?"

[20]John's two disciples found Jesus and said to him, "John the Baptist sent us to ask, 'Are you the Messiah we've been

expecting, or should we keep looking for someone else?' "

²¹At that very time, Jesus cured many people of their diseases, illnesses, and evil spirits, and he restored sight to many who were blind. ²²Then he told John's disciples, "Go back to John and tell him what you have seen and heard—the blind see, the lame walk, the lepers are cured, the deaf hear, the dead are raised to life, and the Good News is being preached to the poor. ²³And tell him, 'God blesses those who do not turn away because of me.*'"

²⁴After John's disciples left, Jesus began talking about him to the crowds. "What kind of man did you go into the wilderness to see? Was he a weak reed, swayed by every breath of wind? ²⁵Or were you expecting to see a man dressed in expensive clothes? No, people who wear beautiful clothes and live in luxury are found in palaces. ²⁶Were you looking for a prophet? Yes, and he is more than a prophet. ²⁷John is the man to whom the Scriptures refer when they say,

'Look, I am sending my messenger
ahead of you,
and he will prepare your way
before you.'*

²⁸I tell you, of all who have ever lived, none is greater than John. Yet even the least person in the Kingdom of God is greater than he is!"

²⁹When they heard this, all the people— even the tax collectors—agreed that God's way was right,* for they had been baptized by John. ³⁰But the Pharisees and experts in religious law rejected God's plan for them, for they had refused John's baptism.

³¹"To what can I compare the people of this generation?" Jesus asked. "How can I describe them? ³²They are like children playing a game in the public square. They complain to their friends,

'We played wedding songs,
and you didn't dance,
so we played funeral songs,
and you didn't weep.'

³³For John the Baptist didn't spend his time eating bread or drinking wine, and you say, 'He's possessed by a demon.' ³⁴The Son of Man,* on the other hand, feasts and drinks, and you say, 'He's a glutton and a drunkard, and a friend of tax collectors and other sinners!' ³⁵But wisdom is shown to be right by the lives of those who follow it.*'"

7:19 Greek *Are you the one who is coming?* Also in 7:20. 7:23 Or *who are not offended by me.* 7:27 Mal 3:1. 7:29 Or *praised God for his justice.* 7:34"Son of Man" is a title Jesus used for himself. 7:35 Or *But wisdom is justified by all her children.*

NOTES

7:18 *John the Baptist.* For an excellent bibliography on John the Baptist, see DJG 383-391; see note on 3:3.

7:21 *Jesus cured many people of their diseases.* On the illnesses and diseases noted in the Bible, see Pousma 1975. See also the notes on leprosy at 5:12; 17:12.

7:27 *Look, I am sending my messenger ahead of you, and he will prepare your way before you.* The passage is taken from Mal 3:1, and, on the lips of Jesus, it clearly highlights the special role of John the Baptizer in redemptive history. According to the divine plan, he was to function as the forerunner for the Messiah, going ahead of the Lord to prepare the way for him morally and spiritually. This role is described earlier in the third Gospel when the angel speaks to reassure Zechariah: "He will turn many Israelites to the Lord their God. . . . He will prepare the people for the coming of the Lord" (1:16-17). Jesus thus testified to John's special place in holy history (7:28) yet pointed out the surpassing privileges of even the humblest disciples in the Kingdom of God that was taking shape in his person and work.

7:34 *The Son of Man.* See note on 5:24.

COMMENTARY

Luke has already shown his readers the startling, uncompromising nature of John's preaching: "You brood of snakes! Who warned you to flee God's coming wrath?" (3:7). John's ministry had been carried on in "the wilderness," not in the luxury of a royal palace (7:24-25), and his forthright rebuke of Herod Antipas for marrying Herodias (and for other wrongs he had committed) had been offensive enough to land him in prison (3:19-20). Jesus, on the other hand, did attend banquets and made time to share meals with many, including friends, Pharisees, tax collectors, notorious sinners, and disciples (7:36-50; 10:38-42; 11:37-54; 14:1-24; 19:1-10; 24:29-35, 41-43). Both John and Jesus suffered criticisms that were distorted, malicious interpretations of their respective ministries. John had been the stalwart forerunner of Jesus, nobly calling Israel to repentance and instructing people about concrete ways in which they could honor God, but he was now in jail.

According to Josephus, Herod Antipas had imprisoned John in Machaerus, the remote mountain fortress located on the east side of the Dead Sea, about 15 miles from the mouth of the Jordan River (*Antiquities* 18.5.2). In that solitary location, John had time to reflect about the mission and work of Jesus, and there were apparently some unresolved issues that were bothering him. In this troubled frame of mind, he sent two of his disciples to ask the burning question of Jesus: "Are you the Messiah we've been expecting, or should we keep looking for someone else?" (7:19). Jesus' response to John's searching question was given at the very time he was engaged in an extensive healing ministry; the Evangelist reports, "Jesus cured many people of their diseases, illnesses, and evil spirits, and he restored sight to many who were blind" (7:21). Jesus' answer, therefore, was simple: "Go back to John and tell him what you have seen and heard—the blind see, the lame walk, the lepers are cured, the deaf hear, the dead are raised to life, and the Good News is being preached to the poor" (7:22). The items are presented in an ascending scale, reaching a climax in the raising of the dead and the proclamation of the gospel to the poor. Jesus' answer made a close connection between his healing ministry and the OT predictions that declared that these things would happen in the time of the Messiah (cf. Isa 29:18-19; 35:5-6; 42:7; 61:1-2; cf. 4:18-21); for John, it would be an implicit affirmation that Jesus was the Messiah.

John's understandable doubt and disappointment could be safely put aside, for the telltale messianic signs were plainly in evidence. Jesus did not want John to give in to doubt and despair. The messengers were to tell him, "God blesses those who do not turn away because of me" (7:23). After the departure of John's disciples, Jesus was able to speak to the crowds about the significance of John's ministry. John was no weak, mealymouthed person, swayed by every passing whim and catering to the current trends and fashions. He was no courtly figure, living in the lap of luxury and fraternizing with the rich and famous. No, he was a true prophet sent from God (7:26; cf. John 1:6-8). By repeated use of a rhetorical question ("What did you go out [into the desert] to see?" 7:24, 26, NIV), Jesus challenged his hearers to face the serious moral and ethical issues posed by John as an authentic spokesman for God. He then went on to pay John a well-deserved tribute. He acknowledged that John was indeed a genuine prophet and proceeded to recognize John's unique place in holy history as the divinely chosen forerunner of the Messiah. This role had been carefully outlined in the Scriptures: "Look, I am sending my messenger ahead of you, and he will prepare your way before you" (7:27, citing Mal 3:1; cf. Exod 23:20; Matt 11:10; Mark 1:2).

The final accolade Jesus gave to John is memorable and enigmatic: "I tell you, of all who have ever lived, none is greater than John. Yet even the least person in the Kingdom of God is greater than he is!" (7:28). Jesus thus both affirmed the special role of John in the purpose of God and yet placed him squarely in the old covenant, which was a preparation for the new age. Now that the messianic age had come and the humblest believer had access to blessings in the Kingdom of God, of which John had only prophesied and foretold, "the least NT saint had a higher privilege in Christ as part of his bride (the church, Eph 5:25-27, 32) than John the Baptist, who was only a friend of the bridegroom (John 3:29)" (Barker 1985:1458).

Luke's account goes on to present a clear contrast between the response of two groups in Jesus' audience. The great majority, including even the tax collectors, acknowledged that "God's way was right, for they had been baptized by John" (7:29), thus admitting that they were sinners who needed God's forgiveness and cleansing. They were clearly opposed by the Pharisees and the experts in the Jewish law, who tragically had "rejected God's plan for them, for they had refused John's baptism" (7:30). These religious diehards apparently had no deep consciousness of personal sinfulness and were unprepared to humble themselves in the face of John's imperious summons to clean up their act. Luke perceived the nature of this rejection, and, in a later chapter, he records the lament of Jesus over those who were not willing to repent (13:34-35).

Jesus used a parable to depict the stubborn refusal of many of his contemporaries to respond positively either to his message or to John's. They were like petulant children playing games in the public square, complaining to their friends: "We played wedding songs, and you didn't dance, so we played funeral songs, and you didn't weep" (7:32). They were childish in the extreme and critical of both the Messiah and his herald. Criticizing and complaining were the only things they were good at! They opposed John's message on the grounds that it was too rigorous and ascetic, so he was accused of being demon possessed. In an equally evil way, they opposed the message of Jesus, criticizing him as one who ate and drank too much and as one who was a companion of the most disreputable sinners. Nothing suited them.

Nonetheless, both John and Jesus had their distinctive places in holy history. The two men had different roles in the divine economy, and, therefore, different things were required of them. John rightly called people to repentance, and hence it was appropriate that he should have an ascetic lifestyle and a stern, uncompromising way of life, reminding Israel of its sinfulness. Jesus, friend of tax collectors and sinners, showed the joy of the new life that men and women could enjoy in the Kingdom of God, and, therefore, it was fitting that he should have a place for feasting and celebrating life in that Kingdom.

◆ W. Jesus Anointed by a Sinful Woman (7:36-50)

36One of the Pharisees asked Jesus to have dinner with him, so Jesus went to his home and sat down to eat.* 37When a certain immoral woman from that city heard he was eating there, she brought a beautiful alabaster jar filled with expensive perfume. 38Then she knelt behind him at his feet, weeping. Her tears fell on his feet, and she wiped them off with her hair. Then she kept kissing his feet and putting perfume on them.

39When the Pharisee who had invited him saw this, he said to himself, "If this man were a prophet, he would know what kind of woman is touching him. She's a sinner!"

40Then Jesus answered his thoughts. "Simon," he said to the Pharisee, "I have something to say to you."

"Go ahead, Teacher," Simon replied.

41Then Jesus told him this story: "A man loaned money to two people—500 pieces of silver* to one and 50 pieces to the other. 42But neither of them could repay him, so he kindly forgave them both, canceling their debts. Who do you suppose loved him more after that?"

43Simon answered, "I suppose the one for whom he canceled the larger debt."

"That's right," Jesus said. 44Then he turned to the woman and said to Simon, "Look at this woman kneeling here. When I entered your home, you didn't offer me water to wash the dust from my feet, but she has washed them with her tears and wiped them with her hair. 45You didn't greet me with a kiss, but from the time I first came in, she has not stopped kissing my feet. 46You neglected the courtesy of olive oil to anoint my head, but she has anointed my feet with rare perfume.

47"I tell you, her sins—and they are many—have been forgiven, so she has shown me much love. But a person who is forgiven little shows only little love." 48Then Jesus said to the woman, "Your sins are forgiven."

49The men at the table said among themselves, "Who is this man, that he goes around forgiving sins?"

50And Jesus said to the woman, "Your faith has saved you; go in peace."

7:36 Or *and reclined.* 7:41 Greek *500 denarii.* A denarius was equivalent to a laborer's full day's wage.

NOTES

7:36 *One of the Pharisees asked Jesus to have dinner with him.* On Luke's interest in dining and banqueting scenes, see "Major Features and Themes" in the Introduction.

7:38 *her hair.* In Jewish society at that time, it was scandalous and indecent for a woman to let down her hair in public. It seems probable that she was a prostitute or perhaps an adulteress (7:37), so perhaps she was callous to the cultural norm, but it is more likely she was overcome with repentance and thankfulness (cf. 2 Sam 6:16-23). Accordingly, Jesus passed over the scandal and emphasized to her and to those around him the forgiveness and salvation available to all who repent and believe (7:48, 50). Christian women were later instructed to dress modestly and decently (1 Tim 2:9).

putting perfume on them. Lit., "anointing them." Anointing was of three kinds: (1) ordinary—after bathing, as a mark of respect (7:46), and for burial (Mark 14:8; 16:1); (2) sacred—both things and people, such as prophets (1 Kgs 19:16), priests (Exod 28:41; Num 3:3), and kings (1 Sam 9:16; 1 Kgs 1:39); and (3) medical—for the sick and wounded (10:34; Isa 1:6; Mark 6:13; Jas 5:14).

COMMENTARY

Luke's Gospel shows the loving, compassionate interest of Jesus in sinners, and the encounter of Jesus with the sinful woman here is a striking instance of it. Jesus insisted that sinners were the proper objects of his concern: "I have come to call not those who think they are righteous, but those who know they are sinners and need to repent" (5:32).

This incident appears to be unique to Luke, though there are other stories in the other Gospels of a woman's anointing Jesus. In John's Gospel, there is an anointing of Jesus that takes place in Bethany at a dinner given in Jesus' honor, where Martha served and Lazarus was also a guest (John 12:1-8). In John's Gospel, the woman who anointed Jesus' feet is identified as Mary, and the objection comes from Judas, whose own pilfering from the apostolic purse is noted (John 12:3-6). Jesus defended Mary's action as preparation for his burial (John 12:7). John's account seems to refer to the same incident recorded in Matthew and Mark (Matt 26:6-13; Mark 14:3-9). Luke's account appears to describe a different incident from the others: "In the one case the woman is unnamed [Luke]; in the other she is identified as Mary, the sister of Martha and Lazarus (John 12:1-3); the host in Galilee was Simon the Pharisee (7:36, 40); in Bethany the host was Simon the leper (Matt 26:6; Mark 14:3); the concluding remarks of Jesus are quite dissimilar in the two incidents. Furthermore, there is no New Testament evidence for identifying the anonymous 'sinner' of [Luke] 7:37 with Mary Magdalene" (Lindsell 1965:1545; cf. Caird 1963:115; France 1987:362). A. T. Robertson's judgment given many years ago still makes sense: "The anointing in Galilee (mentioned by Luke) must be distinct from the anointing at Bethany, near Jerusalem, more than a year later" (1922:60). The only common features between Luke and the other accounts are the fact of a woman anointing Jesus' feet and the name Simon.

In Luke's account, the anointing is set in the house of a Pharisee who invited Jesus to share a meal in his home. An immoral woman discovered Jesus was present and brought an alabaster jar—probably a long-necked bottle filled with expensive perfume—to anoint Jesus. Evidently, she was conscious of her sinfulness and came in penitence to Jesus, seeking forgiveness and cleansing. She expressed her contrition in her tears that fell on his feet and in her humble attitude of service as she wiped the Master's feet with her hair. There was a strong expression of gratitude, for she "kept kissing his feet and putting perfume on them" (7:38). Jesus acknowledged her heartfelt expression of love and declared, "So I tell you, her great love proves that her many sins have been forgiven" (7:47, REB).

The Pharisee who had invited Jesus to dine was inwardly critical of the sinful woman's action. He thought the action was inappropriate, and it led him seriously to question the legitimacy of Jesus' place in the divine plan: "If this man were a prophet, he would know what kind of woman is touching him. She's a sinner!" (7:39). The thoughts of the Pharisee were perceived by Jesus, who responded with a thought-provoking parable: Of two debtors, one owed only fifty pieces of silver, and the other owed five hundred. Jesus asked which one might be expected to show the greater gratitude. Simon conceded that the man who was forgiven ten times as much as the other debtor would be more grateful. This response led Jesus to draw a striking contrast between Simon and the woman of whom he had been so critical.

The Pharisee had shown no gratitude and indeed had not performed the customary acts of hospitality characteristic of an oriental host. Jesus pointedly reminded him, "A person who is forgiven little shows only little love" (7:47). By contrast, the woman had never ceased expressing her love and gratitude, so that the Lord had received her graciously and forgiven her many sins. She was saved by her faith (7:50), and her humble service was an expression of her gratitude and thanksgiving. The Lord had delivered her, and now she was gently told, "Go in peace" (7:50b).

This incident underscores the power of Jesus to forgive sins, which we have already seen (7:48; cf. 5:24). Tragically, this very power to forgive sin caused people to question the person and work of Christ: The other guests ask, "Who is this who even forgives sins?" (7:49 NIV). The claim to forgive sin is at the very heart of the apostolic preaching, and it is certainly central in Luke's own understanding of the gospel. To use the words of Paul's sermon in Pisidian Antioch: "We are here to proclaim that through this man Jesus there is forgiveness for your sins" (Acts 13:38).

◆ ## X. Women Who Followed Jesus (8:1-3)

Soon afterward Jesus began a tour of the nearby towns and villages, preaching and announcing the Good News about the Kingdom of God. He took his twelve disciples with him, ²along with some women who had been cured of evil spirits and diseases. Among them were Mary Magdalene, from whom he had cast out seven demons; ³Joanna, the wife of Chuza, Herod's business manager; Susanna; and many others who were contributing their own resources to support Jesus and his disciples.

NOTES

8:1 *began a tour.* Luke uses the interesting verb *diodeuō* [TG1353, ZG1476] (journey about) to convey "the idea of a continuing wandering ministry (imperfect tense), rather than a journey from one point to another" (Marshall 1978:316).

preaching and announcing the Good News about the Kingdom of God. Here, Luke uses two characteristic words for "preaching and announcing" the Good News about the Kingdom of God. These words are *kērussō* [TG2784, ZG3062] (preach, herald, proclaim; cf. 4:44; 9:2; 23:47; Acts 8:5; 9:20) and *euangelizomai* [TG2097/A, ZG2294] (bring the Good News, announce the Good News; cf. 4:18; 7:22; 9:6; Acts 5:42; 8:4, 12). The use of the two verbs "alongside each other gives a hendiadys: 'preaching the good news of'" (Marshall 1978:318) and corresponds to Mark's phrase "preached . . . Good News" (Mark 1:14).

8:2 *along with some women.* This reference is crucial for Luke's understanding of the place of women in the thinking of Jesus in what was, at that time, a predominantly patriarchal world. On the countercultural role of women in the Gospels, Bilezikian's (1985:96-97) comments are perceptive: "This overt participation of women in the latter part of the ministry of Jesus established an audacious precedent in the Palestinian world at that time (confirmed in Mark 15:41). The disciples' amazement at the fact that Jesus had dared to speak to women in a public place at an earlier stage of His ministry gives a measure of the prejudices that had to be overcome (John 4:27). The bold initiative of involving women in His ministry was doubtless carried out with sufficient tact and precautions as not to create a scandal among the very people whom Jesus wanted to reach. Yet, by its very existence, it made a cogent statement about the nature of female roles within the emerging new community of which the Twelve and other followers of Jesus constituted the predictive microcosm." Similarly, see M. J. Evans 1983:46; Craddock 1990:106-107; and more generally, Stagg and Stagg 1978; Grenz 1995; DJG 880-887; Witherington 1984.

8:3 *many others who were contributing their own resources to support Jesus and his disciples.* Luke clearly draws attention here to these women as patrons of the apostolic band. They used their resources to further the mission of Jesus and the apostles (cf. Phoebe, who is mentioned as a patron of the church in Cenchrea, the eastern port of Corinth [Rom 16:1-2]). For recent feminist approaches to Luke, see Levine (2002), who includes a fine study on this passage by Witherington (2002).

COMMENTARY

Much of Jesus' public ministry in Galilee had been centered in Capernaum. From there, he had gone into the surrounding area on his first mission tour, when he had preached in the synagogues (4:43-44). Then he took to the road again, moving from one town and village to another in an itinerant ministry, "preaching and announcing the Good News about the Kingdom of God" (8:1). He had the companionship of the Twelve on the journey, and this would be an opportunity to train them for their future work. Others were there as well, as Luke notes the presence of some women who had been cured by Jesus of evil spirits and diseases (8:2). This was unusual, for rabbis generally did not teach women or include them in their circle of disciples.

These women included Mary Magdalene, the deeply disturbed person whom Christ had delivered from demonic forces. She came from Magdala, the Galilean town located on the northwestern corner of the Sea of Galilee, roughly halfway between Tiberias and Capernaum. This Mary is not to be confused with the sinful woman of Luke 7 or with Mary of Bethany, who is mentioned in John 12. Mary Magdalene became a devoted follower of Christ, and John's Gospel records a special resurrection appearance Jesus made to her (John 20:11-18). We know nothing more about Susanna, who is only mentioned here. Joanna was "the wife of Chuza, Herod's business manager" (8:3). She belonged to a privileged segment of society that was connected with Herod Antipas, the ruler of Galilee who was seeking to kill Jesus (13:31-32). These were just a few of the women who helped the apostolic band, "contributing their own resources to support Jesus and his disciples" (8:3). "The courage of the women is to be admired as much as Jesus' initiative in establishing this ministry. Joanna [for instance] and her husband, Chuza, had probably decided that if Simon Peter could leave his wife and household to obey Jesus' call to discipleship, so could she" (Bilezikian 1985:96). Note the similar remark of Craddock: "Given the seductions and traps of money and power, it is not only commendable but remarkable that they found ways to put both money and power in submission to the gospel. No doubt there were social and political costs in their commitment. Even more remarkable is the fact that the risks associated with discipleship are compounded for them as women" (1990:107). These female disciples showed their loyalty to Christ by following him to the very end, being present at the Crucifixion, at the entombment, and on the morning of the Resurrection (23:49, 55-56; 24:1; cf. Acts 1:14).

The inclusion of women in the larger company of those who followed Jesus is significant. Women had traditionally been largely confined to the home in the Jewish world, and Jesus was enlarging their place in the new order. While only Jewish men could receive the covenantal sign of circumcision, women, as well as men, were baptized into the Christian community (Acts 8:12) and took their share of persecution and suffering along with the men (Acts 8:3; 9:2; 22:4). They prayed with the men after Jesus' ascension (Acts 1:14), and they, too, experienced the outpouring of the Spirit on the day of Pentecost (Acts 2:1-4, 16-21). While women continued to serve in traditional ways (e.g., Tabitha, Acts 9:36-39), women such as Lydia and Priscilla were becoming more and more prominent as the gospel reached out into the Hellenistic world (Acts 16:14-15; 18:1-3, 26). Another example of this trend would be the four unmarried daughters of Philip the evangelist, who were prophetesses (Acts 21:9; cf. 2:17; 1 Cor 11:5).

◆ Y. Parable of the Farmer Scattering Seed (8:4-15; cf. Matt 13:1-23; Mark 4:1-20)

⁴One day Jesus told a story in the form of a parable to a large crowd that had gathered from many towns to hear him: ⁵"A farmer went out to plant his seed. As he scattered it across his field, some seed fell on a footpath, where it was stepped on, and the birds ate it. ⁶Other seed fell among rocks. It began to grow, but the plant soon wilted and died for lack of moisture. ⁷Other seed fell among thorns that grew up with it and choked out the tender plants. ⁸Still other seed fell on fertile soil. This seed grew and produced a crop that was a hundred times as much as had been planted!" When he had said this, he called out, "Anyone with ears to hear should listen and understand."

⁹His disciples asked him what this parable meant. ¹⁰He replied, "You are permitted to understand the secrets* of the Kingdom of God. But I use parables to teach the others so that the Scriptures might be fulfilled:

'When they look, they won't really see. When they hear, they won't understand.'*

¹¹"This is the meaning of the parable: The seed is God's word. ¹²The seeds that fell on the footpath represent those who hear the message, only to have the devil come and take it away from their hearts and prevent them from believing and being saved. ¹³The seeds on the rocky soil represent those who hear the message and receive it with joy. But since they don't have deep roots, they believe for a while, then they fall away when they face temptation. ¹⁴The seeds that fell among the thorns represent those who hear the message, but all too quickly the message is crowded out by the cares and riches and pleasures of this life. And so they never grow into maturity. ¹⁵And the seeds that fell on the good soil represent honest, good-hearted people who hear God's word, cling to it, and patiently produce a huge harvest.

8:10a Greek *mysteries.*   8:10b Isa 6:9 (Greek version)

NOTES

8:10 Jesus' statement might sound like anti-evangelism, but it is really a sober assessment of the spiritual issues in his teaching on the Kingdom of God. God did not force truth on any person but gave people an opportunity to be introduced to the Kingdom that was taking shape in the life, death, and resurrection of Jesus.

8:11 *This is the meaning of the parable.* It has been fashionable for the last hundred years, since the days of Adolf Jülicher's *The Parables of Jesus* (1888–1889), to dismiss all allegorical elements in the parables, attributing these features to the Evangelist or to the early church. However, there seems to be no insuperable reason here why Jesus himself should not have provided the explanation to this parable when the disciples expressly asked for help and clarification as to its meaning. On the whole subject, see Blomberg (1990) and the bibliography cited in the notes on 5:33-39; 7:36-50. On the combination of tradition and theology in this parable, see Marshall 1969.

8:12 *have the devil . . . take it away . . . and prevent them from believing and being saved.* A similar link between believing and being saved is found in Acts 16:31. The role of the devil in taking the message away from people is also pointed out by Paul in 2 Cor 4:4 and Acts 26:18.

8:15 *people who hear God's word, cling to it, and patiently produce a huge harvest.* Only Luke's account notes that the ideal people who hear God's message bring forth fruit "patiently" (lit., "with patient endurance"). See the notes on the parables at 5:33-39; 10:30-37; 16:1-18, 19-31. For helpful general treatments, see DJG 591-601; Jeremias 1966; Kistemaker 1980; Stein 1981.

COMMENTARY

All three synoptic Gospels contain the parable of the sower, more accurately called the "parable of the soils." Luke's account is the briefest of the three, showing remarkable skill in condensing the Marcan material without losing anything vital. Luke placed the teaching in the context of the growing popularity of Jesus, for people "were now gathering in large numbers" and were making "their way to him from one town after another" (8:4, REB). Jesus seized this occasion as a teaching opportunity to challenge the crowd that gathered to hear his word. For such a mixed audience, the parable was an ideal means of communicating truth. It could challenge some hearers, while holding the attention of all. There was also the possibility that some of the unforgettable parables that Jesus told would remain in the minds of his hearers and later become more meaningful after the Cross, the Resurrection, the Ascension, and the coming of the Spirit on the day of Pentecost. The parable thus served Jesus as an important vehicle of religious truth, and it is given a prominent place in each of the synoptic Gospels.

Mark's version of this parable seems to be the earliest one. Mark depicted a large crowd present at the lakeside (Mark 4:1), and he stressed Jesus' didactic activity in teaching them in the form of parables (Mark 4:2). As in the parallel accounts, Mark notes the different kinds of soil, the different kinds of response, and the different results. He also notes different levels of fruitfulness on the fertile soil and the absence of fruit on the choked soil (Mark 4:7-8).

Matthew basically gives a slightly condensed version of Mark's account, placing it in a whole chapter devoted to parables (Matt 13:1-52). He tells us that Jesus left the house and sat by the lake, perhaps indicating that this was public teaching, not a private communication Jesus had with his disciples when they were alone (Matt 13:1; cf. Mark 7:17; 9:28). Matthew altered Mark by eliminating the direct references to "teach" and "teaching," for the didactic element is clear from the context.

In addition, like Luke, Matthew omitted the reference to the absence of fruit from the seed that was choked (8:7; Matt 13:7). Matthew reversed the order in which he described the productivity of the good soil (Matt 13:8).

Luke's presentation focuses on this particular parable alone (8:4) rather than presenting it as a sample. He alone observes that the seed along the footpath was "stepped on" (8:5). In the case of the seed that fell on rocky ground, no mention is made of the sun scorching the plants; he simply observes that the seed "began to grow, but the plant soon wilted and died for lack of moisture" (8:6). In an abbreviated version, Luke tells us that the seed in the fertile soil multiplied a hundred times. Then, Jesus called for response and appropriate action: "Anyone with ears to hear should listen and understand" (8:8; cf. Matt 13:9; Mark 4:9).

When the disciples requested an explanation of the parable (8:9), Jesus drew attention to the privileged position of his disciples, for God had given them an opportunity to "understand the secrets of the Kingdom of God" (8:10). This was not the case with outsiders, who also heard the parables. These parables, while revealing spiritual truth to the sensitive and openhearted, also served to veil or conceal truth from others. This strange, paradoxical situation had been anticipated in the Scriptures, and the words of the prophecy of Isaiah were truly illuminating: "When they look, they won't really see. When they hear, they won't understand" (8:10, quoting Isa 6:9; cf. Matt 13:13; Mark 4:12). The parables, while offering insight and enlightenment to genuine inquirers, often served to confirm many people in their spiritual blindness.

The parable's meaning is carefully explained in all three accounts. Luke's unpacking of the spiritual significance of the parable is very straightforward, recognizing the destructive activity of the evil one, who comes and takes the message away "from their hearts," thus preventing them "from believing and being saved" (8:12). Luke's account also acknowledges the transient reception of the Christian message that brings joy when the gospel is welcomed; the tragedy is that people with shallow roots only "believe for a while, then they fall away when they face temptation" (8:13). The seeds that fell among thorns "represent those who hear the message, but all too quickly the message is crowded out by the cares and riches and pleasures of this life. And so they never grow into maturity" (8:14; cf. Matt 13:22; Mark 4:19). This tragic suffocation of the word makes the seed unproductive. In contrast, the seed that fell on the good soil was very fruitful, producing a hundred times what was sown. This buoyant touch of optimism is the encouraging note on which the parable ends (8:15).

◆   **Z. Illustration of the Lamp (8:16-18; cf. Matt 13:12; Mark 4:21-25)**

16"No one lights a lamp and then covers it with a bowl or hides it under a bed. A lamp is placed on a stand, where its light can be seen by all who enter the house. 17For all that is secret will eventually be brought into the open, and everything that is concealed will be brought to light and made known to all.

18"So pay attention to how you hear. To those who listen to my teaching, more understanding will be given. But for those who are not listening, even what they think they understand will be taken away from them."

NOTES

8:16 *No one lights a lamp and then covers it with a bowl.* On the use of lamps in Palestine, see the articles of R. H. Smith (1964a, 1964b, 1966). Some writers take vv. 16-17 as a reference to the final judgment rather than as a reference to the proclamation of Jesus, as I do below. Incontestably, Paul notes the coming of a final day of judgment "when God . . . will judge" the secrets of human hearts (Rom 2:16) and urges people to be ready for that day (2 Cor 5:10; cf. 2 Tim 1:12).

8:18 *So pay attention to how you hear.* Jesus stressed the importance of his disciples' attentiveness to and responsibility for using his teaching well (6:47-49; 19:26; Matt 7:24-27; 13:12; 25:29; Mark 4:25).

COMMENTARY

Luke, following Mark, adds a section on the right use of parables (8:16-18; cf. Mark 4:21-25). He knew that Jesus intended his teaching to be disseminated widely, for it is the very nature of truth that it should be known and shared: "For all that is secret will eventually be brought into the open, and everything that is concealed will be brought to light and made known to all" (8:17). While much of Jesus' teaching was in the form of parables (cf. Matt 13:34; Mark 4:33), there was a real concern to communicate truth and make it available to honest seekers. Just as a lamp was intended to give light, so Jesus' instruction was intended to bring illumination. For this to happen, the message could not be hidden away but rather had to be presented in a public place, where it could be observed and its influence felt (8:16). This open presentation of the truth laid a solemn obligation upon those who received it: "So pay attention to how you hear," Jesus urged (8:18). His hearers were accountable! The apostle Paul was aware of the seriousness of personal accountability and tried to act accordingly: "We reject all shameful deeds and underhanded methods. We don't try to trick anyone or distort the word of God. We tell the truth before God, and all who are honest know this" (2 Cor 4:2).

Jesus promised future opportunities for growth and development to those who responded appropriately: "To those who listen to my teaching, more understanding will be given" (8:18b). But the sobering converse was also true, even though it was difficult to accept: "But for those who are not listening, even what they think they understand will be taken away from them." (8:18c). The serious correlative responsibility of listening and doing is also a theme developed in the book of James (1:19-22).

◆ AA. The True Family of Jesus (8:19-21; cf. Matt 12:46-50; Mark 3:31-35)

19Then Jesus' mother and brothers came to see him, but they couldn't get to him because of the crowd. 20Someone told Jesus, "Your mother and your brothers are outside, and they want to see you." 21Jesus replied, "My mother and my brothers are all those who hear God's word and obey it."

NOTES

8:19 *they couldn't get to him because of the crowd.* At least four general groups of people in the crowds addressed by Jesus have been identified by scholars: disciples, disciples' crowd, hard-core opponents, the opponents' crowd, and various combinations of the above categories. The identification of the audience is generally given in most Gospel stories of Jesus, and this information is helpful in learning who was addressed in the teaching that was given (cf. J. A. Baird 1969).

COMMENTARY

Is Jesus rejecting his earthly family here or asserting Kingdom priorities? John's account of the Crucifixion includes Jesus' tender concern for his mother (John 19:26-27), so the former possibility seems highly unlikely (but note 12:51-53, where the Kingdom in some cases brings family divisions; cf. Matt 10:34-39). Jesus was not neglecting family relationships or duties but rather stressing the primacy of the Kingdom for his disciples. All three synoptic Gospels record this incident, in which members of Jesus' family arrived on the scene and sought a conference with him, probably because they thought he was becoming mentally unbalanced and wanted to take charge of him (cf. Mark 3:31). There is no reference to Joseph, so it is probable that he was dead by this time. In any case, only his mother and brothers showed up.

There has been a long-standing debate through the centuries as to the identification of the "brothers" of Jesus. Three major views circulated in the ancient church. The first theory, suggested by Epiphanius, argued that the brothers were sons of Joseph by a previous marriage. The second explanation, attributed to Jerome and advocated in modern times by many Roman Catholics, interpreted the reference more broadly, not to "Mary's children but near relations, cousins perhaps, which both Hebrew and Aramaic style 'brothers,' (cf. Gen 13:8; 14:16; 29:15; Lev 10:4; 1 Chr 23:22)" (Wansbrough 1990:1631). The most likely view, however, which can be traced to Helvidius, is the strict literal one, which understands the brothers as the four persons mentioned as Mary's sons in Mark 6:3, namely, James, Joseph, Judas, and Simon. In this view, they were the younger half brothers of Jesus, the offspring of Joseph and Mary. This interpretation makes good sense in the context and is in harmony with Matthew 1:25, which seems to assume a normal conjugal relationship between Joseph and Mary after the birth of Jesus.

According to Mark's account of this incident, the family members remained outside and sent someone in to call Jesus (Mark 3:31). He was busy at the time with a crowd of people who were evidently receptive to his teaching and open to the will of God. At that point, he "looked at those around him and said, 'Look, these are my mother and brothers'" (Mark 3:34). He was acutely aware of those who were truly interested in learning about life in the Kingdom of God!

Matthew's account faithfully follows Mark in a slightly condensed fashion. Jesus specifically pointed to his disciples and declared, "Look, these are my mother and brothers. Anyone who does the will of my Father in heaven is my brother and sister and mother!" (Matt 12:49-50). Luke's version is even more concise, and it connects this passage with the teaching on parables that precedes it: "My mother and my brothers are all those who hear God's word and obey it" (8:21). This theme of hearing and obeying the word of God or the words of Jesus was important to Luke (6:47; 8:21; 11:28), as it was to other biblical writers (Matt 7:21, 26; John 14:21; Jas 1:22; 1 John 2:5; 2 John 1:6).

◆   **BB. Jesus Calms the Storm (8:22-25; cf. Matt 8:18, 23-27; Mark 4:35-41)**

22One day Jesus said to his disciples, "Let's cross to the other side of the lake." So they got into a boat and started out. 23As they sailed across, Jesus settled down for a nap. But soon a fierce storm came down on the lake. The boat was filling with water, and they were in real danger.

24The disciples went and woke him up, shouting, "Master, Master, we're going to drown!"

When Jesus woke up, he rebuked the wind and the raging waves. Suddenly the storm stopped and all was calm. 25Then he asked them, "Where is your faith?"

The disciples were terrified and amazed. "Who is this man?" they asked each other. "When he gives a command, even the wind and waves obey him!"

NOTES

8:24 *When Jesus woke up, he rebuked the wind.* On Luke's use of the verb "rebuke," see EDNT 2.42-44 and the commentary on 4:38-41. In Luke's Gospel, Jesus rebukes a fever (4:39), evil spirits (4:35, 41; 9:42), wind and waves (8:24), aggressive or insensitive disciples (9:55; 18:15-16), and some of the critics of his followers (19:39-40).

COMMENTARY

The stilling of the tempest on the Sea of Galilee (called by Luke a "lake," 8:22-23; see note on 5:1) was such a memorable event that it found a place in each of the synoptic Gospels. Though the time reference is vague ("one day," 8:22), the details of that day on the lake etched themselves indelibly on the minds of the disciples.

Mark mentions a couple of points of interest: Jesus was "sleeping at the back of the boat with his head on a cushion" (Mark 4:38), and, in their desperate fear and panic, the disciples frantically "woke him up, shouting, 'Teacher, don't you care that we're going to drown?'" (Mark 4:38). They were troubled at his apparent lack of concern for their critical situation. Matthew also notes that Jesus was sleeping, despite the fact that the storm had overtaken them on the lake with "waves breaking into the boat" (Matt 8:24). Matthew, like Mark and Luke, includes the desperate call for help addressed to Jesus (Matt 8:25), and then he adds the challenging words of reproof directed to the scared disciples: "Why are you afraid? You have so little faith!" (Matt 8:26). Luke also writes about the Master drifting off to sleep during the storm (using the word *aphupnoō* [TG879, ZG934], "fall asleep," found only in 8:23 in the NT). Then, Luke adds a graphic account of the boat filling up with water, thereby putting the disciples in danger (8:23).

In all three accounts, the powerful intervention of the Lord is dominant. He exercised mastery over all the elements, and so the wind and the waves quietly accepted his rebuke. This display of power evoked a sense of wonder that the disciples were "terrified and amazed" in the presence of this numinous and transcendent one (8:25; cf. Matt 8:27; Mark 4:41).

In the Old Testament, it was Yahweh, the great God of the covenant, who was seen to be in charge of the elements. Speaking of God's power, the psalmist could confidently declare, "He calmed the storm to a whisper and stilled the waves" (Ps 107:29; cf. Pss 65:7; 89:9; 93:3-4). It was to this powerful God that the people of God cried for help, and they were glad when God brought them safely to their desired haven (Ps 107:28, 30). Significantly, the disciples cried to Jesus in their hour of crisis. He was their "Master" (to use one of Luke's favorite terms of address), from whom they received the needed deliverance.

The fact that Jesus had exercised such powers, which were attributed only to God in the Old Testament, evoked in the disciples the crucial question of his identity: "Who is this man? . . . When he gives a command, even the wind and waves obey him!" (8:25). They had to give serious thought to the person and work of Christ and come to some decision about his place in the plan and purpose of God. In time, they would realize Jesus' divinity.

◆   ## CC. Jesus Heals a Disturbed Man (8:26-39; cf. Matt 8:28-34; Mark 5:1-20)

26So they arrived in the region of the Gerasenes,* across the lake from Galilee. 27As Jesus was climbing out of the boat, a man who was possessed by demons came out to meet him. For a long time he had been homeless and naked, living in a cemetery outside the town.

28As soon as he saw Jesus, he shrieked and fell down in front of him. Then he screamed, "Why are you interfering with me, Jesus, Son of the Most High God? Please, I beg you, don't torture me!" 29For Jesus had already commanded the evil* spirit to come out of him. This spirit had often taken control of the man. Even when he was placed under guard and put in chains and shackles, he simply broke them and rushed out into the wilderness, completely under the demon's power.

30Jesus demanded, "What is your name?"

"Legion," he replied, for he was filled with many demons. 31The demons kept begging Jesus not to send them into the bottomless pit.*

32There happened to be a large herd of pigs feeding on the hillside nearby, and the demons begged him to let them enter into the pigs.

So Jesus gave them permission. 33Then the demons came out of the man and entered the pigs, and the entire herd plunged down the steep hillside into the lake and drowned.

34When the herdsmen saw it, they fled to the nearby town and the surrounding countryside, spreading the news as they ran. 35People rushed out to see what had happened. A crowd soon gathered around Jesus, and they saw the man who had been freed from the demons. He was sitting at Jesus' feet, fully clothed and perfectly sane, and they were all afraid. 36Then those who had seen what happened told the others how the demon-possessed man had been healed. 37And all the people in the region of the Gerasenes begged Jesus to go away and leave them alone, for a great wave of fear swept over them.

So Jesus returned to the boat and left, crossing back to the other side of the lake. ³⁸The man who had been freed from the demons begged to go with him. But Jesus sent him home, saying, ³⁹"No, go back to your family, and tell them everything God has done for you." So he went all through the town proclaiming the great things Jesus had done for him.

8:26 Other manuscripts read *Gadarenes;* still others read *Gergesenes;* also in 8:37. See Matt 8:28; Mark 5:1. 8:29 Greek *unclean.* 8:31 Or *the abyss,* or *the underworld.*

NOTES

8:26 *Gerasenes.* This has the support of 𝔓75 B D. Other mss (ℵ L 038 040) read "Gergesenes"; others (A W 044 𝔐) read "Gadarenes." The best-supported reading points to Gerasa, which probably is to be identified with Khersa (Kursi), a small village on the eastern side of the Sea of Galilee that fits the topography. This site is not to be confused with Gerasa in Perea, a town 40 miles to the south. Also, one has to note the name Gadara, which referred to a whole region southeast of the Sea of Galilee (Matt 8:28). It seems that the alternate readings here are scribal efforts to improve the geographical reference. The scribes knew of Gerasa located in Perea and the district of Gadara but were not familiar with Khersa, a site that archaeologists have excavated in the twentieth century. Thus, the NLT rightly speaks of "the region of the Gerasenes" in 8:26. On the architectural and religious features of this place, see Richardson (2002), who examines five cities in the Near East in the Roman and early Byzantine periods: Palmyra, Petra, Gerasa (of Perea), Caesarea Maritima, and Jerusalem.

8:28 *Why are you interfering with me?* See note on 4:34.

8:29 *Jesus had already commanded the evil spirit to come out of him.* On the subject of exorcism, see Garrett 1989, Twelftree 1985, and commentary on 4:31-37.

8:31 *the bottomless pit.* This is the only reference in the Gospels to the abyss (*abussos* [TG12, ZG12]), the place of confinement for spirits, including the dead (Rom 10:7; cf. Deut 30:13) and the demons or evil spirits. In the book of Revelation, this place is described as "the bottomless pit" (Rev 9:1-2, 11; 20:1). It is the abode of the beast, of the antichrist (Rev 11:7; 17:8), of Abaddon, (the angel of the underworld, Rev 9:11), and of the devil (Rev 20:3).

8:32 *There happened to be a large herd of pigs feeding on the hillside nearby.* Pigs were viewed as unclean, and Jewish law strictly prohibited eating pork (Deut 14:8; cf. Isa 65:4). However, "pigs were raised for the large Gentile population that lived in sections of Palestine" (Coogan 2001:112).

COMMENTARY

This is the only account of Jesus traveling into Gentile territory in Luke. "Otherwise, Jesus carries out no Gentile mission even though he also heals a Samaritan leper whom he calls a foreigner (17:18)" (Brawley 1991:90). The man plainly lived in Gentile territory, situated across the lake from Galilee (8:26). Jesus' movement into the Gentile world was an important indicator of the future outreach of the message about Jesus, which was to be taken by Spirit-empowered disciples, who would tell "people about me everywhere—in Jerusalem, throughout Judea, in Samaria, and to the ends of the earth" (Acts 1:8). The book of Acts shows the ever-widening impact of the Christian message on the Gentile world, far outstripping its original Jewish base in Palestine. It was a whole gospel for the whole world.

When Jesus climbed out of the boat and stepped foot in this pagan area, this pitiful, tortured man met him. Homeless and naked, he had lived in a cemetery for a long time (8:27). He had been alienated from his community and was completely incapable of normal social contact with others. Despite the fact that he had often been shackled and chained, he would simply break the fetters that bound his hands and feet and rush out into the wilderness, completely out of control. Luke noted that the man had often been subject to demonic power (8:29). Of the Gerasene it is fair to say that "all the symptoms described have the note of authenticity: the morbid preoccupation with graves, the abnormal strength, the insensitivity to pain, the refusal to wear clothes, and the multiple and fluctuating self. The man conceived himself to be possessed by a whole regiment of demons; like the country he lived in, he was enemy-occupied territory, and it may well be that his condition arose out of a traumatic experience associated with the Roman occupation" (Caird 1963:121).

The encounter of Jesus with this disturbed man has a number of hostile features. The man saw Jesus as an enemy, shrieked, and fell to the ground before him, screaming, "Why are you interfering with me, Jesus, Son of the Most High God?" (8:28a). The reference to "the Most High God" emphasizes that this was a Gentile person, for this divine title was commonly used by Gentiles (Gen 14:19; Acts 16:17). The tormented man then supplicated for mercy: "Please, I beg you, don't torture me!" (8:28b). The incident shows a preternatural recognition of Jesus by the evil spirit, and it highlights the fact that a titanic spiritual struggle was taking place in which Jesus was encountering demonic forces.

The account is reminiscent of the earlier exorcism that had taken place in Capernaum (4:31-37), where Jesus had encountered similar vigorous opposition when the man with the evil spirit cried out at the top of his voice, "Go away! Why are you interfering with us, Jesus of Nazareth? Have you come to destroy us?" (4:34). There, too, the evil spirit claimed special knowledge of Jesus' true identity as "the Holy One sent from God" (4:34). Though these evil spirits protested, Jesus' authority granted the afflicted person restored health and vitality.

Why Jesus gave the demons permission to enter into the swine instead of sending them directly to the abyss is not entirely clear. The day of judgment had not yet arrived, though the demons apparently thought so. It "was believed that at the final judgment Satan (the devil) and all demons would be gathered up and cast into a bottomless abyss (see Rev 20:3; *1 Enoch* 16:1; *Jubilees* 10:5-11). Water, into which the swine plunged, was often associated with the Abyss. Note also that it was believed that the demons sought 'waterless places' (11:24)" (C. A. Evans 1990:137). Jesus here is presented as conquering a whole group of demonic forces, perhaps foreshadowing his final conquest over demonic powers at the end of time. "Christ, by his act, foreshadows the coming conquest of the kingdom of God over the demonic realm" (Ellis 1981:129).

The upshot of the encounter was wonderful for the restored man but tragic for the community. They rejected the greatest opportunity they had ever received and "begged Jesus to go away and leave them alone, for a great wave of fear swept over them" (8:37). Evidently, they placed a higher value on their pigs than on people! Yet, as F. W. Farrar pointed out long ago, "the freeing of the neighbourhood from the peril and terror of this wild maniac was a greater benefit to the whole city than the loss of this herd" (1890:174). Sadly, they perceived Jesus as a threat: "Their fear may have been a superstitious reaction to the supernatural power that had so evidently been in operation. It may also have been associated with the material loss involved in the destruction of the pigs. If so, they saw Jesus as a disturbing person, more interested in saving people than in material prosperity. It was more comfortable to ask him to go" (Morris 1974:172).

The deliverance the man experienced led him quite naturally to desire to remain close to Jesus, his healer and benefactor. However, he was charged to tell the Good News to his own people—restoration was intended to lead to evangelism, the sharing of the story with others. Luke's closing of the scene is striking. After the man had been given the responsibility to relate all that "God" had done for him (8:39a), he went away and told of all "the great things Jesus had done for him" (8:39b). This is the Evangelist's way of reminding his readers that God was at work in the ministry of Jesus; people were experiencing God's healing and saving activity through Jesus' ministry and, consequently, sharing the Good News with others.

◆ DD. Jesus Heals in Response to Faith (8:40-56; cf. Matt 9:18-26; Mark 5:21-43)

⁴⁰On the other side of the lake the crowds welcomed Jesus, because they had been waiting for him. ⁴¹Then a man named Jairus, a leader of the local synagogue, came and fell at Jesus' feet, pleading with him to come home with him. ⁴²His only daughter,* who was about twelve years old, was dying.

As Jesus went with him, he was surrounded by the crowds. ⁴³A woman in the crowd had suffered for twelve years with constant bleeding,* and she could find no cure. ⁴⁴Coming up behind Jesus, she touched the fringe of his robe. Immediately, the bleeding stopped.

⁴⁵"Who touched me?" Jesus asked.

Everyone denied it, and Peter said, "Master, this whole crowd is pressing up against you."

⁴⁶But Jesus said, "Someone deliberately touched me, for I felt healing power go out from me." ⁴⁷When the woman realized that she could not stay hidden, she began to tremble and fell to her knees in front of him. The whole crowd heard her explain why she had touched him and that she had been immediately healed. ⁴⁸"Daugh-

ter," he said to her, "your faith has made you well. Go in peace."

⁴⁹While he was still speaking to her, a messenger arrived from the home of Jairus, the leader of the synagogue. He told him, "Your daughter is dead. There's no use troubling the Teacher now."

⁵⁰But when Jesus heard what had happened, he said to Jairus, "Don't be afraid. Just have faith, and she will be healed."

⁵¹When they arrived at the house, Jesus wouldn't let anyone go in with him except Peter, John, James, and the little girl's father and mother. ⁵²The house was filled with people weeping and wailing, but he said, "Stop the weeping! She isn't dead; she's only asleep."

⁵³But the crowd laughed at him because they all knew she had died. ⁵⁴Then Jesus took her by the hand and said in a loud voice, "My child, get up!" ⁵⁵And at that moment her life* returned, and she immediately stood up! Then Jesus told them to give her something to eat. ⁵⁶Her parents were overwhelmed, but Jesus insisted that they not tell anyone what had happened.

8:42 Or *His only child, a daughter.* 8:43 Some manuscripts add *having spent everything she had on doctors.* 8:55 Or *her spirit.*

NOTES

8:42 His only daughter. See note on 7:12 concerning the significance Luke attached to the fact that she was an "only daughter."

8:43 A woman in the crowd had suffered for twelve years with constant bleeding. This woman would have been ostracized from her community—menstrual flow was unclean (Lev 15:19-28), and so the poor woman had virtually become a leper. It is hard to imagine her suffering, which was as much socioreligious as physical. Jesus' healing ended her isolation and restored her to the religious and social life of the community.

This reading has the textual support of 𝔓75 B (D) 0279 syrˢ cop^sa. As noted in the NLT mg, some mss (ℵ A C L W 038 040 044) add "having spent everything she had on doctors." It is included in UBS⁴ but set in brackets to show the editors' doubts about its place in the original text. The omission of the phrase about doctors, if correct, strengthens the case that Luke (whom Paul described as "the beloved doctor" in Col 4:14) toned down the criticism of doctors implicit in Mark 5:26. On the other hand, Luke, like Matthew, might simply have omitted the material in the interest of conciseness.

8:44 Immediately, the bleeding stopped. In both the healing of the woman with the issue of blood and the healing of the twelve-year-old girl, Luke notes that the deliverance took place "immediately" (*parachrēma* [ᵀᴳ3916, ᶻᴳ4202]; 8:44, 47, 55). In Luke's view, this was another indication of the power that was characteristic of Jesus' ministry (cf. Acts 10:38).

8:50 have faith. The command to Jairus to "have faith" is closely linked to the commendation of the woman's faith in 8:48. She, a woman, is therefore a model of faith for the synagogue ruler, something unheard of in the Jewish world.

8:54 My child, get up! Mark's account of the raising of Jairus's daughter uses the Aramaic words *talitha qumi* and then translates them "Little girl, get up!" (Mark 5:41; cf. Mark 7:34; 14:36; 15:34). Luke, writing for Gentiles, never cites Aramaic words and phrases but rather translates them into Gr. (cf. 22:42 with Mark 14:36).

COMMENTARY

The deliverance of the Gerasene demoniac had taken place on the eastern shore of the Sea of Galilee. It was followed by a return trip by boat across the lake (8:37, 40). Large crowds had gathered, hoping that Jesus would come back to engage in further ministry in Galilee. Hopes were high, for the Jewish people were "expecting the Messiah to come soon" (3:15). After his imprisonment, John the Baptist had sent messengers to Jesus to pose the vital question: "Are you the Messiah we've been expecting, or should we keep looking for someone else?" (7:19-20). This element of expectancy seemed to be present on the return to Galilee as the crowds waited for Jesus on the other side of the lake.

Two remarkable events are mentioned here side by side, as in the account in Mark (Mark 5:21-43; cf. Matt 9:18-26). While Jesus was en route to heal a girl who was about twelve years old, a woman who had suffered from a serious hemorrhage for twelve years simply touched the "fringe" (8:44) of his robe (the only reference to such a contact in Luke). The link in the reader's mind between the woman and the girl is the reference to the twelve years: the woman had suffered for twelve years, and Jairus's daughter was twelve years old. Furthermore, Jesus' address to the afflicted woman as "daughter" binds the two stories together (cf. 8:42, 49 with 8:48). Mark was particularly fond of linking stories with some common element (e.g., Mark 2:1-

12; 3:1-6, 20-35; 5:21-32; 11:12-14; 14:1-11), and here, Luke followed him in making use of the same device.

When the distressed woman touched Jesus' robe, the bleeding ceased immediately. Then, Jesus raised the question of the identity of the woman: "Who touched me?" (8:45). When everyone denied it and Peter reminded Jesus of the crowd pressing up against him, Jesus insisted this was no casual, meaningless jostling: "Someone deliberately touched me, for I felt healing power go out from me" (8:46). Jesus wanted an open acknowledgement from the person who had been so wonderfully healed. The public declaration was both for the woman's benefit and for the crowd, who heard her testimony to the power of the one who had healed her.

Luke's account follows Mark's quite closely but has some special features. Like Mark, Luke mentions Jairus's name and position as a "leader of the local synagogue" (8:41). The request is a poignant one, Luke noting that the man was pleading for his "only" daughter (see note on 8:42). The interruption caused by the suffering woman's healing must have been frustrating for Jairus, but no mention is made of any word of complaint at the delay. Luke's account makes less than Mark does of the failure of the doctors to cure the woman, and this might point to his sensitivity to the members of his own profession (see note on 8:43; cf. Mark 5:26).

"When the woman realized that she could not stay hidden" (8:47), she came trembling and fell down before Christ, explaining her plight, acknowledging his healing touch, and noting the instantaneous nature of her healing. Her reluctance to speak was understandable, for she had suffered from an embarrassing condition that had made her ceremonially unclean for twelve long years. In this condition, she was unable to touch others without also rendering them unclean (see Lev 15:19-30). Her action in coming forward to bear public witness to her healing thus required courage and determination. She was reassured by the loving words of Christ: "Daughter, . . . your faith has made you well. Go in peace" (8:48). It should be noted that this is the only place in the Gospels where an individual is so addressed (see also the parallel accounts in Matt 9:22; Mark 5:34), thereby suggesting the kindness, compassion, and sensitivity of Jesus to the needs of this woman.

At this juncture in the narrative, word comes about the little girl's death. In the opinion of those who bore the message, this development rendered it pointless to trouble Jesus anymore—the case had passed the point of any meaningful intervention. Jesus, however, counseled Jairus to trust in his power to intervene and restore life: "Don't be afraid. Just have faith, and she will be healed" (8:50). When Jesus arrived at the house, he entered the dead girl's room, taking with him the girl's parents and three of his closest confidants—Peter, James, and John. These three apostles would also be present with him on other special occasions such as the Transfiguration (9:28), when they caught a glimpse of the glory of Christ on "the holy mountain" (2 Pet 1:18). On this occasion, they witnessed not only the traditional weeping and wailing, but also the decisive intervention of the divine Christ restoring life to a dead girl.

Luke's account, like Mark's, notes that the child was given something to eat, perhaps to show the skeptics that she was truly restored to life again. In a similar way, Jesus himself ate a piece of broiled fish after his resurrection (24:41-43). The girl had really died (8:53), but Jesus had raised her up. Her parents were amazed and overwhelmed by this miracle, "but Jesus insisted that they not tell anyone what had happened" (8:56; cf. Mark 5:43). He did not want to be understood merely as a wonder worker, "for the Son of Man came to seek and save those who are lost" (19:10). His ministry was a comprehensive one, bringing healing, wholeness, salvation, and peace. The response he asked for was faith—an openhearted response to him and a confidence in his power to intervene and deliver. In spite of Jesus' prohibition about telling others (8:56), the raising of Jairus's daughter spread Jesus' fame: "The report of this miracle swept through the entire countryside" (Matt 9:26).

◆   EE. Jesus Sends Out the Twelve Disciples (9:1-6; cf. Matt 10:1, 7-11; Mark 6:7-13)

One day Jesus called together his twelve disciples* and gave them power and authority to cast out all demons and to heal all diseases. ²Then he sent them out to tell everyone about the Kingdom of God and to heal the sick. ³"Take nothing for your journey," he instructed them. "Don't take a walking stick, a traveler's bag, food, money,* or even a change of clothes.

⁴Wherever you go, stay in the same house until you leave town. ⁵And if a town refuses to welcome you, shake its dust from your feet as you leave to show that you have abandoned those people to their fate."

⁶So they began their circuit of the villages, preaching the Good News and healing the sick.

9:1 Greek *the Twelve;* other manuscripts read *the twelve apostles.*   9:3 Or *silver coins.*

NOTES

9:1 *twelve disciples.* The Gr. text, according to the best evidence (𝔓75 A B D W), reads "the Twelve" (cf. NLT mg). Other mss (א C* L 038 040 044 0291) add "apostles," a scribal addition taken from 6:13.

9:2 *Then he sent them out to tell everyone about the Kingdom of God.* Preaching is important in Luke's presentation of the gospel, as shown in this passage (note 9:6, "preaching the Good News"). He mentions it as an activity of John the Baptist (announcing "the Good News to the people," 3:18), of Jesus (4:18, 43-44; 8:1), of the apostles (9:6), and of the early church's ministry in the book of Acts (Acts 8:4, 12; 10:36; 11:19-20; 15:35; 20:25; 28:31). For the terminology, see Runia 1978.

heal the sick. The early church continued the ministry of Jesus by caring for the sick and suffering (Acts 3:1-10; 5:12-16; 8:6-7; 9:32-42; 14:8-10; 28:7-9).

9:3 The instructions given by Jesus are essentially repeated when he sends out the larger group of workers in the next chapter (10:4) and then reversed shortly before he is betrayed (22:35-38). Walking sticks are still commonly in use by hikers to ease travel over rough terrain and ease the strain on one's legs, and the traveler's bag was employed to hold personal effects for a journey. An extra shirt and food would be minimal requirements for food and shelter. Jesus forbade all these items, for the missioners were to be subject to the provisions given them by their hosts, receiving whatever was offered them.

COMMENTARY

The close associates of the Lord had been with him for some time. They had witnessed his healing of the sick, his raising of the dead, his exorcising evil spirits, and his preaching the Kingdom of God. On the first tour of Galilee, Jesus had enlisted the four fishermen (5:1-11). On the second tour, all twelve apostles had accompanied him. On the third tour, Jesus traveled alone, after sending the Twelve out two by two (Mark 6:12). Now, the Twelve, the members of the inner circle of Jesus' disciples, were summoned to take an active part in his work. They had his approval and his blessing; in fact, they were specifically given "power and authority" by the Master himself "to cast out demons and to heal all diseases" (9:1). They were to serve as heralds announcing the coming of the Kingdom of God (9:2). The healings, which they were to carry out by Christ's authority, would serve as evidence that the messianic age had arrived (cf. 7:22).

The mission was an urgent one and required their active participation. They were told to travel light, for extra baggage would impede their rapid movement from place to place. They were even forbidden to carry the customary provisions for a journey (9:3), trusting simply in God and depending, like the wandering, peripatetic teachers of the Cynics, entirely on the people who would feed, clothe, and lodge them. They were not to move from house to house but rather to stay in one place until their ministry in that community had been completed. If the people refused to welcome them, they were to leave that place, shaking the dust off of their feet as a sign that they had discharged their missionary obligation and that, henceforth, the people must bear their own responsibility for what they had done with the Christian message. It was literally a "testimony against them," a symbolic action that, as the NLT translates, showed that they had "abandoned those people to their fate" (9:5).

The twelve apostles began their ministry in Galilee, moving about from village to village, "preaching the Good News and healing the sick" (9:6). Their ministry was a continuation of the ministry of Jesus, and it was exercised at his command and with his power and authority. Mark's parallel account notes that they called people to repentance and "cast out many demons and healed many sick people, anointing them with olive oil" (Mark 6:13).

Passages like these, wherein the disciples of Jesus are pictured as wandering teachers, have motivated certain scholars to say the same about Jesus—namely, that he was nothing more than a peripatetic teacher, wandering from place to place. Some modern scholars, such as John Dominic Crossan (in *Jesus: A Revolutionary Biography*) and Burton L. Mack (in *The Lost Gospel*), have presented Jesus as a Cynic sage who was simply a traveling "teacher of unconventional wisdom." As such, they have tried to explain Jesus in terms of the Hellenistic world of the first century. To make their case, they attack the historical value of the four Gospels and depend instead mainly on a hypothetical document called "Q" and the Gnostic *Gospel of Thomas*. These speculative reconstructions have been thoroughly analyzed and critiqued by Gregory A. Boyd in *Cynic, Sage, or Son of God?* (1995).

◆ FF. Herod's Confusion (9:7-9; cf. Matt 14:1-2; Mark 6:14-16)

⁷When Herod Antipas, the ruler of Galilee,* heard about everything Jesus was doing, he was puzzled. Some were saying that John the Baptist had been raised from the dead. ⁸Others thought Jesus was Elijah or one of the other prophets risen from the dead.

⁹"I beheaded John," Herod said, "so who is this man about whom I hear such stories?" And he kept trying to see him.

9:7 Greek *Herod the tetrarch.* Herod Antipas was a son of King Herod and was ruler over Galilee.

NOTES

9:7 *Herod Antipas, the ruler of Galilee.* Antipas ruled in Galilee until AD 39. He was one of three of Herod the Great's sons who inherited part of his kingdom when he died in 4 BC. As such, he was designated a tetrarch (lit., "ruler of a fourth part") along with his two siblings and Lysanius (3:1). The other two Herods of Jesus' time were Philip (Mark 6:17) and Archelaus (Matt 2:22), though Archelaus was deposed in AD 6. It was Herod Antipas who took Philip's wife (3:19) and eventually had John the Baptist put to death (Mark 6:27; cf. Matt 14:10). For an excellent study on this man, see Hoehner (1972). Recent archaeologists have excavated Herod's impressive palace in Tiberias. Almost a hundred sites where such digging has been done are discussed in *Excavations and Surveys in Israel* (vol. 15, 1996), published by the Israel Antiquities Authority.

COMMENTARY

News of Jesus' activities reached the ears of Herod Antipas, the ruler of Galilee and Perea, who was disturbed by the reports of Jesus' miracles. He wondered if John the Baptist had returned to life, as some people were saying (Mark 6:16; cf. Matt 14:2). The ministry of Jesus gave him cause for concern, for under pressure he had personally ordered the decapitation of John the Baptist, and perhaps he might have suffered some qualms of guilt over having taken the life of a righteous man. Other people were suggesting that Jesus was really a latter-day Elijah, who was viewed as the herald announcing the Messiah's coming (Mal 4:5; cf. Matt 11:14); still others were suggesting that Jesus was to be identified with "one of the other prophets risen from the dead" (9:8). While there is no indication that Jesus ever preached in Tiberias, Herod Antipas's capital on the western side of the Sea of Galilee, Herod was clearly interested in seeing Jesus. This expectation was to be satisfied later, in Jerusalem, when Pilate gave Herod the opportunity to examine Jesus and check out his claims for himself (23:6-12). Tragically, Herod—"that fox," as Jesus called him (13:32)—wanted to put him to death (13:31). Evidently, Herod's position meant more to him than the message of a Galilean prophet whose activities were proving rather troublesome and disconcerting.

◆ GG. Jesus Feeds Five Thousand (9:10-17; cf. Matt 14:13-21; Mark 6:30-44; John 6:1-15)

¹⁰When the apostles returned, they told Jesus everything they had done. Then he slipped quietly away with them toward the town of Bethsaida. ¹¹But the crowds found out where he was going, and they followed him. He welcomed them and taught them about the Kingdom of God, and he healed those who were sick.

¹²Late in the afternoon the twelve disciples came to him and said, "Send the crowds away to the nearby villages and farms, so they can find food and lodging for the night. There is nothing to eat here in this remote place." ¹³But Jesus said, "You feed them." "But we have only five loaves of bread and two fish," they answered. "Or are you expecting us to go and buy enough food for this whole crowd?" ¹⁴For there were about 5,000 men there.

Jesus replied, "Tell them to sit down in groups of about fifty each." ¹⁵So the people all sat down. ¹⁶Jesus took the five loaves and two fish, looked up toward heaven, and blessed them. Then, breaking the loaves into pieces, he kept giving the bread and fish to the disciples so they could distribute it to the people. ¹⁷They all ate as much as they wanted, and afterward, the disciples picked up twelve baskets of leftovers!

NOTES

9:13 *You feed them*. Divine feeding has a background in the OT, as in the special provision of the manna in the wilderness (Exod 16:14-36; Num 11:7-9; Deut 8:3; Josh 5:12; Ps 78:24; cf. John 6:31). The nearest OT parallel to this particular incident is found in 2 Kgs 4:42-44, where the prophet Elisha provides food for a hundred men. There were also, in the Jewish celebrations, the regular feasts, or festivals, such as Passover (Exod 12:34), Pentecost (Exod 34:22; Lev 23:15), Tabernacles (Exod 23:16; Lev 23:3), Purim (Esth 3:7; 9:15-32), and Dedication (John 10:22). The messianic feast is also mentioned in OT prophecy (Isa 25:6-9; cf. Jer 31:12-14) and vividly described later in *2 Baruch* 29:5-7.

9:14 *there were about 5,000 men there*. It is useful to study this passage in a harmony of the four Gospels—such as Aland (1987:sec. 146); Daniel (1986:sec. 72); Swanson (1975:secs. 33, 29, 38, 12, respectively). In contrast to Luke's account, it becomes apparent that only Mark mentions the "green grass" (Mark 6:39, pointing to the springtime and the Passover season); only Matthew records the instruction of Jesus about bringing to him the five loaves and the two fish (Matt 14:18) and the comment that the hungry people need not go away (Matt 14:16); and only John notes the fact of the "five barley loaves" (cheap food, used by the poor, John 6:9) and the test question Jesus put to Philip (John 6:5-7).

***groups of about fifty*.** The seating in groups of fifty was probably simply dictated by "convenience in serving" (Morris 1974:167). Mark's account may suggest "military overtones [cf. Exod 18:21; Deut 1:15; 1 Sam 8:12] which are not in Luke" (Summers 1972:107). In any case, when those who decided to use this occasion to force Jesus to become a Jewish messiah and king, he "slipped away into the hills by himself," thereby thwarting their attempt at military or political action (John 6:15).

9:17 *twelve baskets of leftovers!* The closest OT parallel to this incident is found in 2 Kgs 4:42-44, Elisha's feeding of 100 men with 20 loaves of barley bread and some ears of new grain. In that case, also, "there was plenty for all and some left over" (2 Kgs 4:44).

COMMENTARY

The miracle of Jesus feeding the 5,000 is the only miracle recorded in all four Gospels. The feeding of the five thousand made a profound impression on all four Evangelists because it was such a striking piece of evidence supporting the claims of Christ.

Matthew and Mark place this event after the death of John the Baptist. While Luke does not directly describe John's death, it is mentioned in the speech of Herod Antipas, who bluntly confesses, "I beheaded John" (9:9). In addition to mentioning

John's death, Luke connects the incident with the previous reference to the apostles' mission (9:1-6). Jesus had sent out the Twelve, who had then returned to give an account of their missionary activities (9:10). The Master perceived their need for some peace and quiet after this time of intense activity.

In search of solitude, Jesus "slipped quietly away with them toward the town of Bethsaida" (9:10) on the northern end of the Sea of Galilee, on the other side of the Jordan from Capernaum. The town itself is noteworthy here, as Bethsaida was the hometown of Peter, Andrew, and Philip (John 1:44). The withdrawal involved a boat trip on the lake: "They left by boat for a quiet place" (Mark 6:32). It appears that they retired to a secluded area near the town, for the location is described as a "remote place" (9:12). The Greek word used here is *erēmos* [TG2048/A, ZG2245], literally, "a wilderness" or "uninhabited region." This is significant here because "it echoes the feeding of the children of Israel in the wilderness in Moses' day and is enriched by that memory" (Craddock 1990:124).

The eager crowds determined to follow Jesus and his apostles on foot to this new setting and "ran ahead along the shore and got there ahead of them" (Mark 6:33). Jesus seized this as an opportunity for proclaiming the gospel. Matthew and Mark both note that on this occasion, Jesus reached out with compassion to the people. Mark gave a reason for this expression of concern—they were "like sheep without a shepherd" (Mark 6:34). The Master "welcomed them and taught them about the Kingdom of God, and he healed those who were sick" (9:11) As the day drew to a close, the disciples expressed a concern for the needs of the people. They wanted Jesus to dismiss the crowds so that they could have time to find food in the surrounding villages and countryside and an opportunity to secure lodging for the night (only Luke mentions the concern for lodging, 9:12).

Instead of acceding to their request, Jesus replied with a challenge: "You feed them" (9:13). They were overwhelmed by the size of the crowd and the paucity of their own resources: "We have only five loaves of bread and two fish" (9:13). The economic magnitude of the challenge is expressed in Mark's account by the apostles: "It would take 200 denarii to buy food for all these people!" (Mark 6:37, NLT mg; a denarius was equivalent to a full day's wage). However, at Jesus' command, they seated the people in groups of about fifty.

The action of Jesus in taking the food, thanking God, breaking it, and giving it to the disciples is described in terms that are very similar to the Lord's Supper (9:16; cf. 22:19) and seems to have strong Jewish overtones. In fact, some scholars (e.g., Fitzmyer 1981:768) think that, on this occasion, Jesus might have used the traditional Jewish prayer formula "Baruch Adonai" ("Blessed be the Lord"); he cites as "an example of such a prayer that Jesus may have uttered on such an occasion: 'Blessed be you, O Lord our God, King of the world, who causes bread to come forth from the earth'" (also noted by C. A. Evans 1990:146, citing *m. Berakhot* 6:1). Evans also notes that the feeding incident reveals the sufficiency of Jesus to meet human need (1990:143). For readers of Luke's Gospel, the feeding is also reminiscent of the account of the postresurrection meal in the Emmaus story (24:30).

As in the other accounts of this event, Luke says the people "ate as much as they wanted, and afterward, the disciples picked up twelve baskets of leftovers!" (9:17; cf. Matt 14:20; Mark 6:42-43). The collection of the surplus food in the hampers was both an example of avoiding waste and also an indication that everyone had been amply fed and satisfied. John's Gospel notes that the people were so impressed with the miracle that "they intended to come and make him king by force." This proposed action led Jesus to "withdraw again to a mountain by himself" (John 6:15, NIV). Jesus would not be compelled or driven by the wishes of others!

◆   HH. Peter's Declaration about Jesus (9:18-20; cf. Matt 16:13-20; Mark 8:27-30; John 6:68-69)

¹⁸One day Jesus left the crowds to pray alone. Only his disciples were with him, and he asked them, "Who do people say I am?"

¹⁹"Well," they replied, "some say John the Baptist, some say Elijah, and others say you are one of the other ancient prophets risen from the dead."

²⁰Then he asked them, "But who do you say I am?"

Peter replied, "You are the Messiah* sent from God!"

9:20 Or *the Christ. Messiah* (a Hebrew term) and *Christ* (a Greek term) both mean "the anointed one."

NOTES

9:20 *Messiah.* Gr., *Christos* [TG5547, ZG5986] (anointed one, Christ, Messiah). This figure was the deliverer predicted in Heb. prophecy and eagerly expected as the one who would bring in the Kingdom of God (e.g., Isa 9:6-7; 11:1-5; Jer 23:5-6; cf. Acts 1:6), particularly in times when the Jews were being oppressed by foreign powers. On the issue of messianic titles and functions, see de Jonge 1966; Fitzmyer 1981:192-219; Hengel 1983:65-77; P. R. Jones 1970; Tuckett 1997:72-93; NIDNTT 2.334-343.

COMMENTARY

Luke does not say where this incident occurred. Matthew and Mark place the incident in the region of Caesarea Philippi, located in the north, outside of Herod Antipas's territory at the foot of Mount Hermon. There were two cities named Caesarea in New Testament times. One was Caesarea Maritima, the splendid city built by Herod the Great on the Mediterranean, some 40 miles northwest of Jerusalem. This city served as capital for the Roman procurators who ruled Judea and Samaria. The other city was Caesarea Philippi, located north of the Sea of Galilee, near the slopes of Mount Hermon. Originally called Paneas after the Greek god Pan, it was rebuilt by Herod's son Philip, who renamed it after Tiberius Caesar and himself. It was a place with strong pagan associations. The ancient site is known today as Banias, a derivative of the old name Paneas (see McRay 2000; Wilson and Tsaferis 1998; ABD 1.803).

Luke does not specify the precise time of this event, being content to speak of it's occurring "one day" (9:18) during the ministry of Jesus. Luke tells his readers that Jesus was alone and praying when he approached his disciples and asked them the vital question about his identity (9:18). As we have seen, Luke was conscious of the prayerfulness of Jesus and drew attention to it at critical points in his narrative, such as the baptism, the choosing of the apostles, the giving of the Lord's Prayer, the special intercession for Peter, the agony in the garden, and the cross (3:21; 6:12; 11:1; 22:32, 41; 23:46). So it was most fitting that Jesus should be praying as he pondered the nature of his vocation and the manner in which he would carry it out.

When Jesus asked the disciples who the people thought he was, the disciples voiced some popular identifications: John the Baptist, Elijah, or one of the ancient prophets who had come back to life. John the Baptist had led the national back-to-God movement that paved the way for Jesus (3:1-20). Similarly, in Old Testament days, Elijah had spoken boldly for God, challenging the prophets of Baal in a dramatic contest (1 Kgs 18:1-40); his ministry later became associated with his role in the last days, such that he was considered a harbinger of the return of the Messiah (Mal 4:5). Other prophets were being mentioned as well, for the prophetic nature of Jesus' ministry was apparent to many.

While these were the opinions of the crowds, another question was necessary. This was the personal one that the disciples of Jesus had to answer for themselves: "Who do you say I am?" (9:20). The answer Peter gave is notable, for he plainly articulated the startling conviction that Jesus was the long-expected Messiah. It was a clear recognition that Jesus has a unique place in the plan of God and is in fact the divinely promised deliverer who came to set his people free and establish the Kingdom of God in righteousness and peace (cf. Isa 9:6-7; 11:1-9; 40:5; 52:10; 61:1-2a; Dan 2:44). The Messiah had indeed come, and the anointed one would reign over his people as the angel had earlier told Mary before his birth (1:32-33). But the nature of his rule was to take him by way of suffering, death, and rejection, a point he would make clear in his ensuing passion prediction.

Peter's recognition of Jesus' unique role as Messiah is prominent in each of the Gospels but stated in slightly different words. In Mark, he says simply, "You are the Messiah" (Mark 8:29). In Matthew, Jesus' identity is spelled out more fully when Peter declares, "You are the Messiah, the Son of the living God" (Matt 16:16). In John, Peter tells Jesus, "You are the Holy One of God" (John 6:69). In Luke, Peter literally says, "You are the Messiah of God" (9:20). Jesus responded to this remarkable confession of faith with some special words of counsel to Peter and a comment that the knowledge of the Messiah's identity had been given to Peter as a divine revelation (Matt 16:17-19). Peter's answer shows that the disciples had come to the point where "they find it possible to accept Jesus as Messiah, not because he has shown any signs of conforming to the traditional conceptions of Messiah, but because by his words and works he has recast their inherited ideas in the mould of his own interpretation" (Caird 1963:129).

The messiahship of Jesus was important to Luke, and 9:20 is a key text in the development of his Christology. The popular speculations that Jesus was John the Baptist, Elijah, or one of the ancient prophets reveal that Jesus had made no direct claims to be Messiah (9:19). "In contrast to the people in general, Peter infers the true messianic significance of Jesus' acts. He thereby fulfils the Lord's earlier prophecy: 'to you it has been given' (8:10; cf. 5:10; Matt 16:17). Nevertheless, Peter and his colleagues see only one side of the coin: Jesus is Lord over sickness and demons and nature. Until the end, the apostles fail to understand that Messiah must 'be killed and on the third day be raised' and that the kingdom of God does not mean a political revolution but a revolution in the order of nature itself. In their eyes, Jesus' 'pessimism' is unwarranted: swords are available. If some end up on a Roman cross, the cause will surely triumph. But their failure to understand also is in the providence of God (cf. 17:25; 19:11; 22:37-38, 49; 24:5-6, 25-26)" (Ellis 1981:139-140).

◆   ## II. Jesus Predicts His Death (9:21-27; cf. Matt 16:21; Mark 8:31)

21Jesus warned his disciples not to tell anyone who he was. 22"The Son of Man* must suffer many terrible things," he said. "He will be rejected by the elders, the leading priests, and the teachers of religious law. He will be killed, but on the third day he will be raised from the dead."

23Then he said to the crowd, "If any of you wants to be my follower, you must turn from your selfish ways, take up your cross daily, and follow me. 24If you try to hang on to your life, you will lose it. But if you give up your life for my sake, you will save it. 25And what do you benefit if you gain the whole world but are yourself lost or destroyed? 26If anyone is ashamed of me and my message, the Son of Man will be ashamed of that person when he returns in his glory and in the glory of the Father and the holy angels. 27I tell you the truth, some standing here right now will not die before they see the Kingdom of God."

9:22 "Son of Man" is a title Jesus used for himself.

NOTES

9:22 *The Son of Man must suffer.* In response to Peter's confession of faith, Luke steers a middle course between the portrayal of Peter's failure in Mark 8:32/Matt 16:22 and his high praise in Matt 16:17. On the necessity of Jesus' death to fulfill the divine plan, note Luke's use of *dei* [TG1163, ZG1256] (it is necessary) in 2:49; 4:43; 9:22; 11:42; 12:12; 13:14, 16, 33; 15:32; 17:25; 18:1; 19:5; 21:9; 22:7, 37; 24:7, 26, 44. On this point, see Cosgrove 1984.

rejected. The Gr. term (*apodokimazō* [TG593, ZG627]) seems to be "a technical term for rejection after a careful legal scrutiny. It implies that the hierarchy would consider Jesus' claims but decide against him" (Morris 1974:185). Isaiah's prophecy would be fulfilled in the man from Nazareth, who was "despised and rejected—a man of sorrows, acquainted with deepest grief" (Isa 53:3). On the general theme of "the suffering of the Lukan Jesus," see Scheffler (1993:103-158).

9:27 *some standing here right now will not die before they see the Kingdom of God.* Though it is possible to understand this verse as a reference to the day of Pentecost and the rapid spread of the gospel described in the book of Acts, the context seems to favor the view that it is actually a prediction of the Transfiguration, seen in 9:28-36. This was a preview of Jesus' return in the power and glory of the Kingdom (21:27; cf. 2 Pet 1:16). Caird argues that "in view of the atmosphere of imminent violence which pervades the whole context, it is unlikely that Jesus was contemplating a far-off event due to happen in the extreme old age of the youngest bystanders; rather he was promising that, although some of them will share with him in the death which God has decreed for the Son of man, others will survive to see the triumph of God's kingdom which that death will secure" (1963:130).

COMMENTARY

Peter had rather boldly acknowledged Jesus' role as Messiah, but this was not the time and place to declare it openly. Thus, Jesus warned the disciples "not to tell anyone who he was" (9:21). The Jews often thought of their Messiah as a conquering hero like Judas Maccabaeus, a descendant of David who would shatter unrighteous rulers and wipe out their enemies, sweeping all before him (see *Psalms of Solomon* 17:21-25). Jesus did not want to present himself in militaristic terms. These inadequate views needed to be revised and corrected. As the Son of Man, he "must" fulfill his place as the servant of God, suffering many things of his enemies; being rejected by the elders, chief priests, and scribes of his nation; and dying an ignominious death. However, that was not the end of the story, for a resurrection was promised on the third day. Jesus was to be vindicated by God in this surprising reversal. The religious establishment, which had plotted his death, was not to have the last word. On the day of Pentecost, Peter acknowledged that Jesus had been put to death on the cross but insisted, "God released him from the horrors of death and raised him back to life, for death could not keep him in its grip" (Acts 2:23-24).

Luke 9:22 is Luke's first reference to the death of Christ as an event specifically predicted and described as part of the plan of God for the salvation of the world. Other predictions of the Passion would follow later in the Gospel (9:44; 12:50; 17:25; 18:31-33; cf. 24:7, 25-27). Similar passion predictions are found in Matthew and Mark (Matt 16:21; 17:22-23; 20:17-19; Mark 8:31; 9:31; 10:32-34; see DJG 630-633).

The wonderful confession of faith offered by Peter and the first prediction of the Passion were accompanied by the clear teaching that Jesus gave on the conditions of discipleship. Luke's account stresses that these conditions applied to all prospective disciples: "If any of you wants to be my follower, you must turn from your selfish ways, take up your cross daily, and follow me" (9:23). Jesus insisted that discipleship must be embraced on a daily basis. Jesus put the question pointedly to possible recruits: "What do you benefit if you gain the whole world but are yourself lost or destroyed?" (9:25). In other words, he placed supreme value on one's relationship with God. This was the most important issue, and in comparison to it, everything else was of lesser significance.

There was a fundamental paradox in the whole matter of discipleship, and Jesus laid it squarely before his hearers: "If you try to hang on to your life, you will lose it. But if you give up your life for my sake, you will save it" (9:24). Perhaps this is what Hudson Taylor, the famous missionary to China, meant when, after a life of tremendous sacrifice, he solemnly declared, "I never made a sacrifice." He had truly lost all for Christ but in return found his all in Christ. Like Paul, he could say, "I have discarded everything else, counting it all as garbage, so that I could gain Christ and become one with him" (Phil 3:8-9).

Taking on this commitment to Christ included accepting the reproach that was directed against the Lord and his movement (cf. Heb 13:13). It involved standing up for him and taking his side even when that was a dangerous or embarrassing thing to do: "If anyone is ashamed of me and my message, the Son of Man will be ashamed of that person when he returns in his glory" (9:26). Stephen faced that challenge, bravely gave his witness, and suffered as a martyr, believing that it was the right thing to do and that the Son of Man would welcome him into heaven (Acts 7:1-60; note especially 7:56). In sum, the public confession of Christ as Savior and Lord was a matter of great significance and carried eternal consequences.

◆   JJ. Jesus' Transfiguration (9:28-36; cf. Matt 17:1-8; Mark 9:2-8;
    2 Pet 1:16-18)

²⁸About eight days later Jesus took Peter, John, and James up on a mountain to pray. ²⁹And as he was praying, the appearance of his face was transformed, and his clothes became dazzling white. ³⁰Suddenly, two men, Moses and Elijah, appeared and began talking with Jesus. ³¹They were glorious to see. And they were speaking about his exodus from this world, which was about to be fulfilled in Jerusalem.

³²Peter and the others had fallen asleep. When they woke up, they saw Jesus' glory and the two men standing with him. ³³As Moses and Elijah were starting to leave, Peter, not even knowing what he was saying, blurted out, "Master, it's wonderful for us to be here! Let's make three shelters as memorials*—one for you, one for Moses, and one for Elijah." ³⁴But even as he was saying this, a cloud overshadowed them, and terror gripped them as the cloud covered them.

³⁵Then a voice from the cloud said, "This is my Son, my Chosen One.* Listen to him." ³⁶When the voice finished, Jesus was there alone. They didn't tell anyone at that time what they had seen.

9:33 Greek *three tabernacles.* 9:35 Some manuscripts read *This is my dearly loved Son.*

NOTES

9:29 *the appearance of his face was transformed.* Lit., "the appearance of his face became different" (*heteros* [TG2087, ZG2283]). Luke does not use the Gr. word "transfigure" (*metemorphōthē* [TG3339/A, ZG3565]), the term employed in Matt 17:2 and Mark 9:2. It seems Luke deliberately steered clear of a term that had negative associations in the pagan world, where apotheosis (the elevation of humans to divine status) was known. "Luke was aware of the danger of confusing Jesus with some polytheistic pagan notions (compare Acts 14:11 [NIV], where Paul and Barnabas are acclaimed in Lystra as 'the gods' who 'have come down to us in human form'). Jesus is not to be identified in Luke's mind with one of the Hellenistic deities. He is the unique bearer of the divine glory (9:32; cf. 2 Cor 4:7)," and no comparison with any Hellenistic figure is appropriate or illuminating (Hurst and Wright 1987:74). For literature on the Transfiguration, see DJG 834-841; NIDNTT 3.861-865; Trites 1987a.

9:31 *his exodus from this world, which was about to be fulfilled.* Jesus' "exodus" would be accomplished in his death. Luke, like the other Gospel writers, underscores the theocentric character of Jesus' death—it was a fulfillment of the divine plan. God's prearranged plan is noted elsewhere in Luke–Acts (22:22; 24:25-27, 44; Acts 2:22; 3:18; 10:42; 17:31).

9:34 *a cloud overshadowed them.* The cloud imagery is important in all three accounts and points to the divine presence (Exod 24:15-18; 1 Kgs 8:10-11; Ps 97:2). In the wilderness, the Lord guided the children of Israel by a "pillar of cloud by day" and a "pillar of fire by night" (Num 14:14; cf. Exod 13:21; 14:24). A cloud covered Mount Sinai when the covenant was established (Exod 19:16), and a cloud descended on the Tabernacle when Moses entered to commune with God (Exod 33:9-10; Deut 31:15). A cloud filled the Temple at its dedication (1 Kgs 8:10). Tragically, Ezekiel lived to see the cloud of glory leave the Temple, symbolically removing from it the presence of God (Ezek 10). The cloud motif was often noted in Jewish descriptions of last things (Isa 4:5; Ezek 30:3-4; Joel 2:2; Zeph 1:15; 2 Macc 2:8; Wis 5:21). In his vision, Daniel saw the Son of Man surrounded by clouds (Dan 7:13; cf. *2 Baruch* 53; *4 Ezra* 13:3). In the NT, a cloud receives Christ at the Ascension (Acts 1:9), and Christ's return will be "with the clouds" (Rev 1:7). Christ's enemies will see him "coming on the clouds of heaven" (Mark 14:62). In the Transfiguration, too, the reference to the cloud prepares the reader for the statement from heaven approving the Son.

9:35 *Then a voice from the cloud.* The heavenly voice certainly recalls the accounts of the Baptism, when Jesus was similarly addressed as God's Son, but with the important additional charge "Listen to him." Jesus was thereby divinely acclaimed and recognized. "He is addressed in terms which recall the anointed King of Ps 2:7, the Servant of the Lord of Isa 42:1, and the latter-day Moses of Deut 18:15, 18. The voice from the cloud attests Jesus as the Promised Prophet like unto Moses, unto whom God's people must hearken (cf. Acts 3:22, 23). Obedience to Jesus is given heavenly endorsement and made mandatory for disciples" (Trites 1994:36).

COMMENTARY

The next incident is the event that is beautifully described in German as "the Glorification" (*die Verklärung*). It is closely related to the previous teaching, in which Jesus had been acknowledged as Messiah by Peter and then had instructed his disciples about both the nature of discipleship and the necessity of the Son of Man's rejection and execution. The essential details are recorded in Matthew, Mark, and Luke—each writer highlighting the event in his own special way. The incident is also mentioned later in the New Testament, where the writer declares that the Christian faith is based, not on myths or cleverly devised stories, but on facts supported by eyewitnesses; one such event, he asserts, was the Transfiguration (2 Pet 1:16-18).

The Exodus and Moses' experiences at Sinai are especially important events to make note of in seeking to understand the import of this great event. The Exodus was God's divine act in delivering the Israelites from slavery and establishing them as his own people (Exod 12:31-39; 14:15-31; 34:9; Deut 6:21-23). This divine event, in which Moses played a central role, was recognized and celebrated as the beginning of Israel's national history (Deut 7:8, 19; 9:26; 26:8; Neh 9:9-11; Pss 105:24-44; 106:7-12). Moses was not only God's appointed leader in the Exodus, but he also led the people to the site of Mount Sinai, where God established the covenant of the law with his people. There, God's blessing and closeness were manifest in a cloud (Exod 24:15-18), and Moses' experiences of spiritual illumination and empowerment while he was in communion with God resulted in the transformation of his appearance so that his face glowed radiantly for a time (Exod 34:33-35; cf. 2 Cor 3:13-18).

In light of the conceptual framework this background forms, it is no surprise that for Peter, James, and John, this event was unforgettable and theologically profound, as they were eyewitnesses on the Mount of Transfiguration (2 Pet 1:16-18). They became aware in a new way of the unique role of Jesus in achieving the redemptive purpose of God. The parallels made it natural for the Gospel writers to speak of this special event in terms similar to Moses' experience. He, too, had gone up on a mountain to pray. He, too, had his face changed by communion with the Father. He, too, had been energized for his future task. But this time a new exodus was in process (9:31), and the Son of Man had to actually suffer, die, and rise again to realize it (cf. 9:22, 44; 18:31-33). The law was indeed "given through Moses, but God's unfailing love and faithfulness came through Jesus Christ" (John 1:17). A new exodus (9:31) and a new covenant (22:20) were coming to again establish a holy people (Eph 2:14-16; 1 Pet 2:10).

All three Evangelists agree that this was an actual experience in the historical life of Jesus. Despite the fact that in recent years it has been fashionable in some circles to dismiss the incident as mythological, to view it as a vision of Jesus or Peter, or to regard it as a postresurrection event misplaced by the Evangelists, no good reason exists to reject the event as a real one that happened shortly after the confession of Peter at Caesarea Philippi. In fact, it fits admirably in the context in which it is placed in each of the synoptic Gospels and is rich in its use of Old Testament imagery and symbolism (note the parallel with Moses' transfiguration on Sinai, Exod 24:9-18; 34:2, 29-35).

All three synoptic Gospels agree that the Transfiguration took place on a mountain (Matthew and Mark describing it as a "high mountain"; cf. 2 Pet 1:18, "the holy mountain"). Jesus selected Peter, James, and John, the inner circle of the apostolic band, to accompany him on this unforgettable trip. There is no similar account in the fourth Gospel, probably because the life of Jesus as a whole is viewed as an unveiling of the divine glory (John 1:14, 18); this is revealed in the miracles (John 2:11; 11:4, 40) but supremely in the death and resurrection of Christ (cf. John 11:25; 12:16, 28; 13:31-32; 17:1, 4-5, 24).

On the mountain, a remarkable change took place in the appearance of Jesus that was evident in both his face and his clothes. Moses and Elijah appeared on the scene and conversed with Jesus. Peter, impressed by the sight, offered to build three booths or shelters, perhaps recalling Israel's Feast of Tabernacles (Lev 23:33-43; cf. Exod 23:16). He proposed to erect a shelter for Jesus and one for each of the distinguished visitors from the past. A cloud appeared and overshadowed the disciples, and a voice was heard from the cloud affirming Jesus as God's "Son" (9:35) and counseling the trio to listen to him. After the voice had spoken, Jesus was seen alone.

Each Evangelist adds a few unique details. Matthew and Mark describe the striking transformation in Christ using a Greek verb that speaks of a "change in form," but Luke steers away from this language and makes the same point in words less likely to be misunderstood by his readers (see note on 9:29). Matthew and Mark both note the fact that the three apostles were frightened by the scene (Matt 17:6; Mark 9:6), and Luke specifies that this took place when the cloud enveloped Jesus and the heavenly visitors (9:34; cf. Knox's helpful translation: "They saw those others disappear into the cloud and were terrified"). The transcendent nature of the revelation was apparently too much for them. Mark also mentions Christ's clothes becoming "dazzling white, far whiter than any earthly bleach could ever make them" (Mark 9:3), thus underlining the numinous, otherworldly aspect of the event.

Matthew describes Christ's face as shining "like the sun" and observes that his clothes "became as white as light" (Matt 17:2). Peter addressed Jesus as "Lord" and indicated a willingness to defer to his Master's will: "If you want, I'll make three shelters as memorials—one for you, one for Moses, and one for Elijah" (Matt 17:4). Matthew records that Jesus reassured the disciples by telling them not to be afraid (Matt 17:7), and he notes that the cloud was a "bright" one (Matt 17:5), unlike the threatening appearance of Mount Sinai at the giving of the Ten Commandments (cf. Exod 19:16-20).

Luke's account places the incident in a wider time frame (eight days rather than six), mentions that Jesus was praying, and describes the alteration in Christ's countenance, which took place while he was praying. Luke, too, mentions the dazzling white clothes (using *exastraptō* [TG1823, ZG1993], "flash forth like lightning"), thus connecting the incident with similar references later to the Resurrection and the Second Coming (cf. 17:24; 24:4, where *astraptō* [TG797, ZG848] is used). Only Luke refers to Moses and Elijah's appearing "in glory," and only Luke employs the striking phrase "behold, two men" (a special phrase also found in his accounts of the Resurrection [24:4] and the Ascension [Acts 1:10]). Other details unique to Luke are the mention of Christ's "exodus," or "departure," as something that will be accomplished in Jerusalem (9:31), the drowsiness of the disciples, their rousing from sleep to see the Messiah's glory (9:32), and the linking of the fear of the disciples with entrance of the heavenly trio into the cloud (9:34). Luke also contains other unique features: the Son is called God's "Chosen One" (9:35), and Peter's enthusiasm to erect tabernacles is connected with the departure of Moses and Elijah (9:33).

Luke's account, then, provides some striking details. He was responsible for introducing into the story "two elements which have had a vast influence upon its interpretation. It was during the *prayer* of Jesus that the change took place, and the conversation of Moses and Elijah explicitly connects the Transfiguration with the *passion*" (Ramsey 1949:112). Each of these themes demands a word of explanation.

Notice first the importance attached to prayer. We are told that the express purpose of the journey up the mountain was for prayer—to intentionally reach out to the Father in communion and fellowship (9:28; cf. 3:21). Luke reminds us that the marvelous change in the appearance of Jesus and his garments took place while he was praying (9:29). We have already noted several times that prayer was a characteristic feature of Jesus' ministry (3:21; 5:16; 6:12; 22:32, 41, 44; 23:46). Luke's great interest in prayer is not only biographical and historical, but also didactic. He plainly wanted to teach his readers how to pray, so that they could be victorious, even as their Lord was, in meeting and mastering their trials and temptations (11:1-

4; 22:39-46). This is especially clear from the fact that Luke is the only Gospel that has prayer parables (11:5-8; 18:1-14). Luke quite intentionally drew attention to the topic to remind disciples of their need for constant prayer (18:1). Prayer changed things for Jesus, and it could also be a source of strength for his followers. This was exhibited in the radiant face of Stephen as he prayed for those who were stoning him (Acts 6:15; 7:59).

Another element to which Luke directed special attention is the "exodus" theme. The topic that Moses and Elijah discuss with Jesus is the "exodus" that Jesus was to accomplish at Jerusalem (9:31). As I have remarked elsewhere, "This seems to be a deliberate reference to Israel's experience under Moses. The first Exodus was out of bondage in Egypt; the second Exodus was out of bondage in sin. The former deliverance was effected by Moses; the latter [was accomplished] by Jesus of Nazareth. Freedom from Egyptian slavery came through the 'death' of the Red Sea (lit. 'the Sea of Reeds,' Exod 15:22); freedom from slavery to sin came through the death of the Cross. In that sense the water 'baptism' under Moses prefigured the 'blood' baptism of Golgotha (1 Cor 10:1- 2; Luke 12:50)" (Trites 1994:39). The subject matter was the great divine act of deliverance; no wonder Moses and Elijah faded from the picture so that the bewildered disciples were left to confront the Messiah in his entire splendor alone. On the way down the mountain, they were told not to speak of this revelation to anyone until the Son of Man had risen from the dead (Matt 17:9; Mark 9:9). Luke notes their obedience to this instruction (9:36).

In all three Gospels, Moses and Elijah appear prominently in the story. It was widely held in Jewish circles that leading figures of Israel's past would make their appearance again in the last days and play a vital part in the fulfillment of God's purposes (*4 Ezra* 14:9; *2 Baruch* 76:2; *Testament of Benjamin* 10:5-6). Enoch and Elijah were often mentioned (cf. Gen 5:24; 2 Kgs 2:11), and some Jews thought Moses had been taken into heaven without dying (see Josephus *Antiquities* 4.326). Certainly, Moses and Elijah are more frequently mentioned in the synoptic Gospels than any other Old Testament leaders (24 and 25 times respectively), and they also are noted in John's Gospel (Moses appears 12 times and Elijah twice).

Moses and Elijah were dominant figures in the thinking of the Judaism of the time. Each of them "had fasted for forty days (Exod 34:28; 1 Kgs 19:8), and subsequently had enjoyed a vision of the glory of God on the same mountain: Moses on Sinai (Exod 31:18; Exod 3:1; Deut 29:8) and Elijah on Horeb (1 Kgs 19:8), which are two names for the same mountain. Moses had proclaimed the law from a mountain (Exod 19:16-25; 20:1-17) and Elijah had prophesied from a mountain (1 Kgs 18:18-40). In addition, each of these men had no known grave and each had received a special intimation from God of his own departure from earth (Deut 32:49-52; 2 Kgs 2:3, 5). Then, in the closing of the Old Testament, the law of Moses and the coming of Elijah are mentioned together (Mal 4:4-6)" (Trites 1994:38). Also, the coming of Elijah is mentioned as an expectation of the last days (cf. Sir 48:10) and interpreted by Jesus as realized in the ministry of John the Baptist (Matt 17:10-13; Mark 9:11-13).

Moses and Elijah were powerful leaders at critical points in Israel's history. Each had served as a bold spokesman for God in the face of strong opposition. While the foundation of Israel's national life had been established under the leadership of Moses, the nation had been called under Elijah to renounce its apostasy and reaffirm its covenant with God.

To sum up, the Transfiguration is described in terms that are saturated with Old Testament imagery and symbolism. It was an experience that was clearly meaningful to Jesus, reaffirming him as the obedient Son of God who was on the right course of action and who would fulfill God's plan by dying in Jerusalem (9:31). It was also profoundly significant for Peter, James, and John. Their Master's impending journey of suffering, rejection, death, and resurrection had been divinely confirmed and supported by two of the most important figures of the old covenant. Even more, Jesus enjoyed the unique blessing and approval of the Father. He was indeed the "Chosen One"; the disciples were to "listen to him" (9:35), obey him, and work with him for the fulfillment of the divine purpose. The Son of Man "must" suffer, but, in doing so, he would bring many sons and daughters to share in his glory (cf. Heb 2:10). The Transfiguration seems to be a proleptic foretaste of the glory of Jesus, revealed in his mighty resurrection from the dead, his glorious ascension into heaven, and the dramatic events associated with Pentecost and the subsequent spread of the Kingdom of God through the Spirit-directed expansion of the Christian church. In conclusion, the words of Archbishop Ramsey (1949:101-102) about Jesus' transfiguration are insightful:

> The Transfiguration seems to stand at a watershed in the ministry of Jesus, and to be a height from which the reader looks down on one side upon the Galilean ministry and on the other side on the *Via Crucis* ("way of the Cross"). The story resembles the Baptism of Jesus, inasmuch as it culminates in a heavenly voice proclaiming the Sonship; and it resembles the agony of Gethsemane, inasmuch as it shows the three disciples witnessing a decisive moment in the relation of Jesus to the Father.

◆ ### KK. Jesus Heals a Disturbed Boy (9:37-43a; cf. Matt 17:14-21; Mark 9:14-29)

37The next day, after they had come down the mountain, a large crowd met Jesus. 38A man in the crowd called out to him, "Teacher, I beg you to look at my son, my only child. 39An evil spirit keeps seizing him, making him scream. It throws him into convulsions so that he foams at the mouth. It batters him and hardly ever leaves him alone. 40I begged your disciples to cast out the spirit, but they couldn't do it."

41Jesus said, "You faithless and corrupt people! How long must I be with you and put up with you?" Then he said to the man, "Bring your son here."

42As the boy came forward, the demon knocked him to the ground and threw him into a violent convulsion. But Jesus rebuked the evil* spirit and healed the boy. Then he gave him back to his father. 43Awe gripped the people as they saw this majestic display of God's power.

9:42 Greek *unclean*.

NOTES

9:41 *corrupt people.* Both Matthew and Luke underscore the perversity and stubbornness Jesus encountered (cf. Matt 17:17).

9:42 *Jesus rebuked the evil spirit and healed the boy.* This story is more an exorcism than a healing story, though it is both. On exorcisms, see note on 4:33. There are many examples of miracles in Luke's Gospel. Physical healings are often noted, including, thus far, the healing of a leper (5:12-15), a paralytic (5:17-20), a man with a shriveled hand (6:6-10), a centurion's highly valued slave who was near death (7:1-10), and a woman with an incurable hemorrhage (8:43-48). There were also a number of cases of exorcism—the casting out of evil spirits (4:31-37; 8:26-39; 9:37-43)—where Jesus was active in bringing deliverance from demonic forces.

9:43a *majestic display.* Luke uses the same word here to describe the power or "majesty" of God that is used elsewhere to describe the "majestic splendor" of Christ in the Transfiguration (*megaleiotēs* [TG3168, ZG3484]; 2 Pet 1:16). Evidently, the glory of God was apparent in Jesus both on the mountain and in the valley where he met rampant human need.

COMMENTARY

As Jesus descended from the Mount of Transfiguration on the next day, he met a large crowd. Among them there was a man who called out earnestly, seeking help for his only son (9:38-39; cf. 7:12; 8:42). The man evidently had confidence that Jesus could act helpfully in this desperate case, despite the fact that his impotent disciples had failed miserably to provide the needed aid (9:40). The disciples were powerless in the face of a desperate call for help. There is a real contrast between this scene and the previous one, a contrast that has been aptly described by Plummer in his commentary on Luke: "the chosen three blinded by the light, the remaining nine baffled by the power of darkness" (as quoted in Caird 1963:135).

This excorsim and healing story is found in the other synoptic Gospels (Matt 17:14-20; Mark 9:14-29). Mark's account is the fullest and gives a graphic description of the boy's condition. He had a speech problem (Mark 9:17). In addition, he apparently suffered from epilepsy, for he had attacks during which he foamed at the mouth, gnashed his teeth, and became rigid (Mark 9:18). The need of this child was great, and his father was naturally concerned to enlist assistance from a well-known healer and exorcist in the hope of relieving his pitiable condition.

The reply of Jesus reveals something of the strain their spiritual condition put upon him: "You faithless and corrupt people, . . . how long must I be with you and put up with you?" (9:41). This criticism was not directed primarily against the father, for he had exercised some faith in turning to Christ for help and had been honest in acknowledging his struggle with doubt (Mark 9:24). It must have been directed at the disciples, who were rebuked for their lack of prayer (Mark 9:29) and faith (Matt 17:20). It was also directed at the stubborn, unbelieving spectators who were content to engage in disputes over the claims of Christ (note Mark 9:14, which particularly mentions "some teachers of religious law" engaging in such arguments). Jesus' ministry was being impeded by the slowness and obtuseness of his disciples and their unbelieving contemporaries. He was eager to press on to his rendezvous with destiny in Jerusalem, where he would fulfill his appointed role (cf. 12:50; 13:33). Despite these unfavorable conditions, Jesus invited the man to bring his son forward.

The grievous nature of the boy's condition was apparent, for even as he was coming to Jesus, he suffered a convulsion. At this point, Jesus intervened, healed the boy, and restored him to his father. The large crowd observed the wonderful difference Jesus had made in this case, and they were all amazed at "this majestic display of God's power" (9:43). Jesus was truly mighty in word and deed, and his healings and exorcisms were bringing people into restored health and wholeness. Here was power, but it was being used graciously and unselfishly, bringing help and deliverance to suffering people.

◆   LL. Jesus Again Predicts His Death (9:43b-45; cf. Matt 17:22-23; Mark 9:30-32)

While everyone was marveling at everything he was doing, Jesus said to his disciples, 44"Listen to me and remember what I say. The Son of Man is going to be betrayed into the hands of his enemies." 45But they didn't know what he meant. Its significance was hidden from them, so they couldn't understand it, and they were afraid to ask him about it.

NOTES
9:44 *The Son of Man.* See note on 5:24.

COMMENTARY
At this crucial time, when everyone was impressed with everything Jesus was doing, Jesus spoke of his future suffering. This is Luke's second passion prediction and is also recorded in Matthew and Mark. Mark notes that Jesus left the region where he had healed the epileptic boy and traveled through Galilee (Mark 9:30a). His aim was to avoid all publicity, in order to "spend more time with his disciples and teach them" (Mark 9:31). The core of his teaching was an explanation of the disturbing things that awaited him in the immediate future as the Son of Man. He knew that he faced betrayal and death, and he must accordingly prepare them for these somber events. On the other hand, they could take heart, for he promised them that he would rise again on the third day (Mark 9:31; cf. Matt 17:23). This impending series of events was baffling and perplexing to the disciples, but "they were afraid to ask him what he meant" (Mark 9:32).

Luke, in contrast to Matthew and Mark, makes no reference here to the hopefulness of a resurrection on the third day. He concentrates on the bleak side of the future that was staring them in the face: "Listen to me and remember what I say. The Son of Man is going to be betrayed" (9:44). This was another prediction of Jesus' forthcoming death (cf. 9:22), pointing out the manner by which it would be brought to pass. It was intended to make the disciples think seriously about the costliness of the redemption that the Son of Man would accomplish in Jerusalem, for it came at a crucial time when "everyone was marveling at everything he was doing" (9:43b). It was a sober reminder that the Son of Man must indeed suffer to effect the great salvation. The risen Christ will expound on this theme later at the close of the Gospel (24:26, 46-47). In the meantime, the disciples did not understand what he was talking about.

Luke repeatedly draws attention to people's failure to understand Jesus. This includes the parents of Jesus, who were perplexed when he said to them, "Didn't you realize that I should be involved with my Father's affairs?" (2:49, NLT mg). Sadly, "they didn't understand what he meant" (2:50). Here, the disciples did not grasp what the betrayal of the Son of Man meant: "Its significance was hidden from them, so they couldn't understand it" (9:45). Luke makes a similar comment after the third passion prediction, which is more detailed and mentions the Son of Man's resurrection on the third day: "[The disciples] didn't understand any of this. The significance of his words was hidden from them, and they failed to grasp what he was talking about" (18:34). To the two on the road to Emmaus and subsequently to the disciples, the risen Lord explained these things, enlightening them so that they could understand the Christ-centered message of their sacred texts (24:26-27, 32, 45-47).

◆　　**MM. The Greatest in the Kingdom (9:46-48; cf. Matt 18:1-5; Mark 9:33-37)**

⁴⁶Then his disciples began arguing about which of them was the greatest. ⁴⁷But Jesus knew their thoughts, so he brought a little child to his side. ⁴⁸Then he said to them, "Anyone who welcomes a little child like this on my behalf* welcomes me, and anyone who welcomes me also welcomes my Father who sent me. Whoever is the least among you is the greatest."

9:48 Greek *in my name.*

NOTES
9:46 *his disciples began arguing.* The Gr. for "arguing" is the noun *dialogismos* [TG1261, ZG1369], a word that is used to denote arguing and controversy in passages such as Phil 2:14 and 1 Tim 2:8.

COMMENTARY
Luke places this account of the overweening self-confidence of the disciples—their argument about greatness—just after Jesus predicts his impending death in 9:43b-45. Their hubris stands in striking contrast to Jesus' humble acceptance of the painful road that lay before the Son of Man. All three synoptic Gospels include the dispute about greatness. Mark's account provides the fullest details. The argument occurred "on the road" as the disciples were traveling back to Capernaum (Mark 9:33). When they were "in [the privacy of] a house," Jesus questioned them about it, and they grew silent, ashamed to tell the Master the self-seeking thoughts that had occupied their minds (Mark 9:33-34). Jesus seized this as an opportunity to do some serious teaching, calling the Twelve back to the basics of Christian service:

"Whoever wants to be first must take last place and be the servant of everyone else" (Mark 9:35). It was an unpalatable lesson, but one that was desperately needed.

Luke highlights the confrontational nature of the incident, calling it an "argument" (see note on 9:46), and he alone notes that "Jesus knew their thoughts" (9:47). The Master confronted them directly, pointing out the incongruity of all self-seeking attitudes with true Christian service. He was calling them to be servants of the servants of God, and they were summoned to place the needs of others before their own (cf. Acts 20:28; 1 Cor 4:9; 1 Pet 5:2-4).

To make the point unmistakably clear, Jesus "brought a little child to his side" (9:47) and used him as an object lesson for the disciples. A child could not offer any favors or bestow any honors. To accept and welcome such a powerless person was an act of sheer love and grace. Kingdom men and women were to act in that fashion, reaching out to help weak, defenseless people and acting entirely without any concern toward using people as stepping-stones for personal advantage. It was a stunning rebuke to all worldly ambition and a call to humble, self-forgetting service in the name of Christ. As an example, one might think of Mother Teresa exemplifying this spirit of loving compassion to the poor of Calcutta.

◆   ## NN. Using the Name of Jesus (9:49-50; cf. Mark 9:38-41)

⁴⁹John said to Jesus, "Master, we saw someone using your name to cast out demons, but we told him to stop because he isn't in our group."

⁵⁰But Jesus said, "Don't stop him! Anyone who is not against you is for you."

NOTES

9:49 *Master, we saw someone using your name to cast out demons.* On exorcism, see Twelftree (1985, 1993). Cf. 4:31-37; 8:26-39; 9:37-43.

COMMENTARY

The apostle John presented Jesus with the case of the strange exorcist (see also the parallel passage in Mark 9:38-41). Here was a man operating independently, and this was offensive to John and his fellow disciples, because the person didn't belong to their group. The exorcist was using the name of Jesus, and John challenged the legitimacy of his action: "We told him to stop" (9:49). Jesus advocated a more charitable policy: "Don't stop him! Anyone who is not against you is for you" (9:50). In these verses, we move from "openness and tolerance for the weak and humble (vv. 46-48) [to] openness and tolerance for the outsider who does work in Jesus' name" (C. A. Evans 1990:158). The point is applicable to all of Jesus' disciples—there is a real danger of unwarranted exclusivity, and it is to be studiously avoided. Some tolerance and goodwill are called for. Later, Luke will record Jesus stating the converse truth: "Anyone who isn't with me opposes me, and anyone who isn't working with me is actually working against me" (11:23). Here, neutrality was not presented as an option.

In concluding this section of Luke, we turn to the comments of Caird, who offers a helpful summary of the four incidents that Luke has presented immediately following his account of the Transfiguration of Christ: "The magnificent isolation of Jesus in his moral and spiritual grandeur, symbolized by the vanishing of Moses and Elijah from the mount of vision, is now further emphasized by four incidents which betray the weak faith, the slow comprehension, the self-seeking, and the intolerance of the disciples" (1963:134). Caird adds a perceptive comment about this last incident:

> The episode of the unauthorized exorcist contains a rebuke not only to John, but to all those who in later days have sought by priestcraft or persecution, by Acts of Uniformity or sectarian tests, to confine the activity of God to the 'proper channels'. Jesus' refusal to question the stranger's credentials is consistent with his regular response to those who questioned his own: the word of God and the works of God are self-authenticating. He who really knows and loves God will always be ready to acknowledge as an ally anyone who is obviously doing God's work. (1963:135-136)

◆ V. Jesus' Journey to the Cross (9:51–19:44)
A. Opposition from Samaritans (9:51–56)

⁵¹As the time drew near for him to ascend to heaven, Jesus resolutely set out for Jerusalem. ⁵²He sent messengers ahead to a Samaritan village to prepare for his arrival. ⁵³But the people of the village did not welcome Jesus because he was on his way to Jerusalem. ⁵⁴When James and John saw this, they said to Jesus, "Lord, should we call down fire from heaven to burn them up*?" ⁵⁵But Jesus turned and rebuked them.* ⁵⁶So they went on to another village.

9:54 Some manuscripts add *as Elijah did.* 9:55 Some manuscripts add an expanded conclusion to verse 55 and an additional sentence in verse 56: *And he said, "You don't realize what your hearts are like.* ⁵⁶*For the Son of Man has not come to destroy people's lives, but to save them."*

NOTES

9:51 *As the time drew near for him to ascend to heaven.* The Gr. behind "ascend to heaven" is the word *analēmpsis* [TG354, ZG378], which is used only here in the NT, though a closely related word is used in 1 Tim 3:16. "As with the use of the word *exodus* in the Transfiguration story, so here Luke packs a whole theology into the word *analēmpsis,* which means an assumption, a reception up into heaven. The word contains a strong echo of the Elijah motif that has already figured so prominently in this Gospel (cf. 2 Kgs 2:9-11). But Luke uses the word here in a thoroughly Johannine fashion to cover the whole complex of events by which Jesus made the transit from earth to heaven—crucifixion, resurrection, and ascension (cf. John 3:14; 8:23; 12:32-34)" (Caird 1963:140).

COMMENTARY

At this point, Luke introduces another major section of his Gospel that is virtually unparalleled in the canonical Gospels. Having presented the ministry of Jesus in Galilee (4:14–9:50), he begins the description of a momentous trip that would take Jesus from Galilee to his death and resurrection in Jerusalem and, ultimately, to his reception in heaven. Jesus' journey required him to go to Jerusalem, but the goal of the journey was what Luke here describes as his ascent to heaven. The phrase has the same sense as it does in 1 Timothy 3:16. This travel narrative occupies the whole central section of the third Gospel (9:51–19:44; see note on 9:51; cf. Noël 2004:391). The framework of a journey is employed, and there are periodic reminders that Jesus is on his way to the city of destiny, Jerusalem (9:51-53; 10:38; 13:22, 32-34; 17:11; 18:31). The emphasis is more theological than geographical, for the journey to Jerusalem is really a journey to the cross, where Jesus will suffer, die, rise again on the third day, and ascend into heaven (see note on 9:51). This divine pattern is seen as foreshadowed in Scripture and carried out in fulfillment of the plan of God for the redemption of the world (note the frequent reference to things that "must" happen—9:22; 13:33; 17:25; 22:37; 24:7, 44). Jerusalem is the city that tragically kills the prophets (13:34). Nevertheless, Jesus must press on to that destination in faithfulness and determination: "Yes, today, tomorrow, and the next day I must proceed on my way. For it wouldn't do for a prophet of God to be killed except in Jerusalem!" (13:33).

The solemn shadow of Jesus' impending suffering and death hangs over this central section of Luke's Gospel. Jesus' journey to the cross was an important part of salvation history and was therefore related to the whole plan of redemption. Since it was essential, Jesus had to steadfastly make his way to Jerusalem, though this would inevitably bring him pain, suffering, and death. There was no other way to fulfill God's purposes, and no shortcuts were possible. The way of the cross did indeed lead home.

The salvation that was being worked out in the life, death, and resurrection of Jesus was costly, and those who would follow the Savior are called to walk on the same road of self-denial and sacrifice: "If any of you wants to be my follower, you must turn from your selfish ways, take up your cross daily, and follow me" (9:23). Luke's central section (9:51–19:44) will spell out, in detail, what the implications of the journey to the cross will be for Jesus and for his disciples. These chapters are very rich in their teaching on the nature, meaning, and demands of Christian discipleship.

In preparation for the trip to the holy city, Jesus sent messengers ahead of him to arrange accommodations in a Samaritan village (9:52). Jewish antipathy for the Samaritans was so common that many preferred to take the longer route across the Jordan and through Perea to avoid Samaritan territory altogether (see Josephus *War* 2.12.3). The Samaritans had their own place of worship on Mount Gerizim and regarded the Temple in Jerusalem as a false rival (cf. Deut 12:4-5, 11; John 4:20-24). Jesus' messengers encountered hostility in the Samaritan village and were turned away.

This rebuff did not sit well with the volatile sons of Zebedee, to whom Jesus had given the nickname "Sons of Thunder" (Mark 3:17). They were full of indignation at the slight given to Jesus and his mission and immediately suggested strong retaliatory action, as Elijah had done (2 Kgs 1:9-16). James and John accepted the rebuke Jesus gave them, recognizing his authority as outstripping that of the Old

Testament prophets, who knew of no other way than calling down a curse on their enemies. God was now revealing a more excellent way in his Son, and therefore his servants must listen to him (9:35). This is why Moses and Elijah had to fade from sight on the Mount of Transfiguration, leaving Jesus in solitary splendor to instruct the bewildered disciples. Instead of retaliating, they simply followed their Master "on the way" as he traveled onward toward Jerusalem.

◆   B. The Cost of Following Jesus (9:57-62; cf. Matt 8:19-22)

57As they were walking along, someone said to Jesus, "I will follow you wherever you go."

58But Jesus replied, "Foxes have dens to live in, and birds have nests, but the Son of Man has no place even to lay his head."

59He said to another person, "Come, follow me."

The man agreed, but he said, "Lord, first let me return home and bury my father."

60But Jesus told him, "Let the spiritually dead bury their own dead!* Your duty is to go and preach about the Kingdom of God."

61Another said, "Yes, Lord, I will follow you, but first let me say good-bye to my family."

62But Jesus told him, "Anyone who puts a hand to the plow and then looks back is not fit for the Kingdom of God."

9:60 Greek *Let the dead bury their own dead.*

NOTES

9:57-62 *I will follow you.* The Jewish background of the passage is evident in the Son of Man reference (cf. Matt 8:20 and note on 5:24) as well as the parental obligations such as making funeral arrangements (cf. Matt 8:21). The mention of a family farewell implies a delay in taking up the demands of discipleship, which Jesus insisted must be the first priority for his followers.

9:60 *Let the spiritually dead bury their own dead!* The NLT captures the force of Jesus' metaphor here. "The duty of burial took precedence over the study of the Law, the Temple service, the killing of the Passover sacrifice, the observance of circumcision and the reading of the Megillah (*b. Megillah* 3b). But the demands of the kingdom were more urgent still" (Morris 1974:180). Fitzmyer (1981:835) notes that the burial of the dead came to be viewed as an act of meritorious service (see Tob 4:3; 12:12, where burial of the dead is seen as one of the great demonstrations of piety).

9:62 *Anyone who puts a hand to the plow and then looks back is not fit for the Kingdom of God.* The comment of Turlington here is apt: "The word 'fit' (9:62) is most interesting. The verb from which it comes [*eutheteō*] was used of setting broken bones so that they were joined together properly. The man who wavers in his allegiance to the forward goals of the kingdom, sometimes reverting to old standards of hope and security, has not become properly molded into the life and work of the kingdom" (1967:67-68). James similarly warns in his epistle of the terrible danger of being double-minded (Jas 1:6; 4:8). Such unstable people can't make up their minds; they waver back and forth in everything they do (Jas 1:8).

COMMENTARY

It has already been noted that Jesus had "resolutely set out for Jerusalem" (9:51). On the way there, the conditions of discipleship would be unfolded. In this brief section (9:57-62), Luke presents three potential disciples.

The first candidate, described as "one of the teachers of religious law" in Matthew's Gospel (Matt 8:19), offers to follow Jesus in an unrestricted way (9:57). He is solemnly reminded that discipleship might involve the relinquishment of security. To accompany the Son of Man was to accept risk and to be vulnerable. Therefore, it was necessary to count the cost. This point will be spelled out more fully later in Luke's travel narrative, where Jesus places two searching parables before the crowds (14:25-33).

The second person was called by Jesus but offered an excuse that would defer or postpone discipleship in order to fulfill a filial obligation. Since there is no indication that the father was dead, this likely meant delaying the commitment until some indefinite time in the future. In effect, it was a denial of the lordship of Jesus, who demanded that his followers should seek "the Kingdom of God above all else" (Matt 6:33). This was to be the disciple's primary concern, and nothing else would do. Jesus confronted him directly with this truth: "Your duty is to go and preach about the Kingdom of God" (9:60). In comparison with that overriding concern, even traditional family obligations had to take second place or be left to others. Again, this point is stated quite bluntly at a later point in the travel narrative: "If you want to be my disciple, you must hate everyone else by comparison—your father and mother, wife and children, brothers and sisters—yes, even your own life. Otherwise, you cannot be my disciple" (14:26). The imperious demands of the Kingdom were inescapable for true disciples.

The third prospective disciple, like the first, volunteered his services but introduced a condition that he first bid farewell to those at home, just as Elisha had done when he left his family to follow Elijah (1 Kgs 19:20-21). At first glance, his request seems plausible and reasonable (cf. 5:29). However, someone greater than Elijah was here! Evidently, the man's response concealed some inner hesitation to make the decisive commitment, so he was warned that there is no place in the Kingdom for those who turn back when they are summoned to move forward. It seems that he was in danger of putting something else first—the affection and approval of his family. Here, we see a recognition of the strength of family ties and the difficulty of putting them aside in favor of the preeminent claims of Christ. While strongly affirming the value of marriage and family life (Mark 10:1-12; cf. Matt 19:1-9), Jesus insisted on the primacy of the Kingdom of God. The apostle Paul wrote in the same vein to the Corinthian believers who were troubled about marriage, celibacy, and similar issues: "I want you to do whatever will help you serve the Lord best, with as few distractions as possible" (1 Cor 7:35).

Caird helpfully summarizes the radical demands of Jesus presented in this section: "A man [or woman] must be prepared to sacrifice security, duty, and affection, if he [or she] is to respond to the call of the kingdom, a call so urgent and imperative that all other loyalties must give way before it. The most difficult choices in life are not between the good and the evil, but between the good and the best" (1963:141). For a challenging testament about the cost of discipleship, see Bonhoeffer's classic treatment, *The Cost of Discipleship* (1959).

◆ C. Jesus Sends Out His Disciples (10:1-20; cf. Matt 9:37-38; 10:7-16; 11:21-23)

The Lord now chose seventy-two* other disciples and sent them ahead in pairs to all the towns and places he planned to visit. ²These were his instructions to them: "The harvest is great, but the workers are few. So pray to the Lord who is in charge of the harvest; ask him to send more workers into his fields. ³Now go, and remember that I am sending you out as lambs among wolves. ⁴Don't take any money with you, nor a traveler's bag, nor an extra pair of sandals. And don't stop to greet anyone on the road.

⁵"Whenever you enter someone's home, first say, 'May God's peace be on this house.' ⁶If those who live there are peaceful, the blessing will stand; if they are not, the blessing will return to you. ⁷Don't move around from home to home. Stay in one place, eating and drinking what they provide. Don't hesitate to accept hospitality, because those who work deserve their pay.

⁸"If you enter a town and it welcomes you, eat whatever is set before you. ⁹Heal the sick, and tell them, 'The Kingdom of God is near you now.' ¹⁰But if a town refuses to welcome you, go out into its streets and say, ¹¹'We wipe even the dust of your town from our feet to show that we have abandoned you to your fate. And know this—the Kingdom of God is near!'

¹²I assure you, even wicked Sodom will be better off than such a town on judgment day.

¹³"What sorrow awaits you, Korazin and Bethsaida! For if the miracles I did in you had been done in wicked Tyre and Sidon, their people would have repented of their sins long ago, clothing themselves in burlap and throwing ashes on their heads to show their remorse. ¹⁴Yes, Tyre and Sidon will be better off on judgment day than you. ¹⁵And you people of Capernaum, will you be honored in heaven? No, you will go down to the place of the dead.*"

¹⁶Then he said to the disciples, "Anyone who accepts your message is also accepting me. And anyone who rejects you is rejecting me. And anyone who rejects me is rejecting God, who sent me."

¹⁷When the seventy-two disciples returned, they joyfully reported to him, "Lord, even the demons obey us when we use your name!"

¹⁸"Yes," he told them, "I saw Satan fall from heaven like lightning! ¹⁹Look, I have given you authority over all the power of the enemy, and you can walk among snakes and scorpions and crush them. Nothing will injure you. ²⁰But don't rejoice because evil spirits obey you; rejoice because your names are registered in heaven."

10:1 Some manuscripts read *seventy;* also in 10:17.   10:15 Greek *to Hades.*

NOTES

10:1 *seventy-two other disciples.* This reading has the support of 𝔓75 B D 0181 syrᶜˢ copˢᵃ. The fact that this list includes one of the earliest papyri strengthens the case for "seventy-two" (𝔓45 has a lacuna here, but see 10:17). Other mss (ℵ A C L W 038 040 f¹·¹³ 𝔐) have the number as "seventy." The number "seventy-two" is favored by most modern translations (NIV, NEB, REB, JB, TEV, NLT) and has slightly better manuscript support. The number "seventy" is retained in some versions (RSV, NRSV). Since there were seventy elders who helped Moses (Exod 24:1, 9; Num 11:16, 24-25), some have seen this reference as pointing to Jesus as a second Moses. Others favor the number "seventy-two" because it "appears to be symbolic of the nations of the world, a view the Jews based on Genesis 10, where there are seventy names in the Heb. text and seventy-two in the LXX [the Greek text of the Old Testament used by the early Christians]. Whatever the truth behind these conjectures, Jesus sent the disciples ahead of him in pairs. Such a large group of forerunners shows that he had a busy itinerary ahead of him" (Morris 1974:198). On the textual issues, see Metzger (1971:150-151).

10:2 *The harvest is great, but the workers are few.* The harvest image is often found in the Gospels (see also Matt 9:37-38; John 4:35). It is frequently used in the parables of Jesus. Note as examples the parable of the growing seed (Mark 4:26-29), the parable of the weeds (Matt 13:24-30, 36-43), and the parable of the wicked tenants (20:9-19; Matt 21:33-46; Mark 12:1-12). See EDNT 2.144-146; TDNT 3.132-133 on "harvest" (*therismos* [TG2326, ZG2546]).

10:3 *I am sending you out as lambs among wolves.* The mention of "wolves" (*lukoi* [TG3074, ZG3380]) points to a similar reference in Acts, where Paul warns the Ephesian elders at Miletus about the coming of false teachers who, in their fierce, destructive, and rapacious ways, will act like "vicious wolves" not sparing the flock (Acts 20:29; cf. John 10:12).

10:4 These instructions for the wider mission are parallel to those in 9:3-5.

10:13 *What sorrow awaits you.* Lit., "Woe to you." The NLT thus conveys the force of the mournful interjection "woe" in anticipation of coming judgment.

repented. The Gr. is *metanoeō* [TG3340, ZG3566], meaning "change one's mind." It is a key word in Luke–Acts: see 10:13; 11:32; 13:3, 5; 15:7, 10; 16:30; 17:3-4; Acts 5:31; 11:18; 13:24; 19:4; 20:21; 26:20.

10:17 *seventy-two disciples.* The same textual diversity occurs here as in 10:1 (see note), but here, the case for "seventy-two" is further strengthened by the fact that the two earliest papyri (𝔓45 𝔓75), along with B D syrˢ copˢᵃ, support the reading "seventy-two."

COMMENTARY

The mission of Jesus required the partnership of others. Initially, he had sent out the apostles and given them authority to perform miracles and to announce the coming of the Kingdom of God (9:1-5; cf. Mark 6:7-11). Now, a larger body of disciples would be called upon to share in this great work. As in the case of the Twelve, these representatives were personally appointed by Jesus (10:1; cf. 6:13). The missionary task was vast and daunting, and the workers were few. Thus, others needed to be enlisted, and these had to be sent into the work at the direction of God: "So pray to the Lord who is in charge of the harvest; ask him to send more workers into his fields" (10:2b; cf. Acts 13:1-3). The workers would face strong and aggressive opposition, so they were forewarned of the difficulties and the savage attacks they would encounter (10:3). But their work was urgent and imperative; it demanded immediate action. Therefore, they were to travel light, carrying no purse, no travel bag, and no sandals. There was no time to waste, for that would delay the mission, so there could be no visits along the way and no lengthy greetings. Traditional oriental courtesies had to be put aside.

The appointment of the seventy-two is mentioned only in Luke, though similar instructions are given in the sending out of the Twelve in the other Synoptics (Matt 10:7-16; Mark 6:7-11). The number might be suggestive of the world mission, for there were traditionally thought to be seventy or seventy-two nations in the world (see note on 10:1), but the emphasis here is on a thoroughgoing campaign in Jewish territory, as the workers are sent in pairs into all the towns and villages Jesus planned to visit (10:1; cf. Matt 10:5-6). The news of the Kingdom of God was of the utmost importance. The message of the Messiah had to be offered to the Jewish people by his duly appointed representatives.

Detailed instructions were given to these workers. When they entered a home, they were to give it a blessing. Though they brought a gracious offer of heavenly peace, it depended upon the proper reception of the message. They were not to move from house to house but to remain instead in the first one that welcomed them, "eating and drinking what they provide" (10:7). As mendicants living solely on the gifts of others, they were thus not to be fussy about what was offered but rather to accept with gratitude the hospitality provided (10:8). They were encouraged with the reminder that "those who work deserve their pay" (10:7). This principle is cited elsewhere in the New Testament, often to justify material provisions for spiritual leaders (Matt 10:10; 1 Cor 9:14; 1 Tim 5:18).

In their preaching, teaching, and healing, the missionaries were announcing the presence of the Kingdom of God drawing near in Christ. When the message was repudiated, they were to leave that place, symbolically shaking off the dust from their feet so as to indicate that they had fully discharged their spiritual obligations to the people in that place (10:11; cf. 9:5; Matt 10:14; Mark 6:11; Acts 13:51). The Kingdom of God had been duly proclaimed, and those who had heard the proclamation must now bear their own responsibility. Tragically, Jesus was aware that Korazin, Bethsaida, and Capernaum, privileged cities in Galilee that had been exposed to his ministry and mighty works, had failed to change. Their sin was more culpable than that of the Syrian cities of Tyre and Sidon, for they had sinned against greater light and in spite of the active ministry of Jesus in their midst. The failure of those Galilean places to "repent" was sure to bring them down. They would have to answer for their reprehensible conduct on judgment day (10:13-15). These same woes (see note on 10:13) directed against the unrepentant cities are also mentioned in Matthew's Gospel (Matt 11:20-24).

The disciples received real encouragement from Jesus as they set out. He reminded them of the principle of agency, namely, that "the one who goes is as him who sent him." The words of John's Gospel come to mind, where the risen Jesus says to his disciples, "As the Father has sent me, so I am sending you" (John 20:21). In like manner, Jesus here reminded the disciples that they would go in his name and carry his authority: "Anyone who accepts your message is also accepting me. And anyone who rejects you is rejecting me. And anyone who rejects me is rejecting God, who sent me" (10:16; cf. Matt 10:40; John 5:23; 15:23).

Eventually, the disciples returned and reported to the Master the response that they had received. They were filled with joy at the success they had experienced and buoyantly proclaimed, "Lord, even the demons obey us when we use your name!" (10:17). Evidently, their exorcisms had been effective and impressive. In response, Jesus told them that, in observing their ministry, he was, literally, "continuing to view" (note the imperfect tense of the Gr. verb here: *etheōroun* [TG2334, ZG2555]) Satan falling from heaven as a flash of lightning (10:18; cf. John 12:31). Through their preaching, teaching, and healing, the Kingdom of God was advancing, and the kingdom of evil was retreating. Once again, Jesus reminded them that they were exercising spiritual power, and that involved the conquest of the devil: "I have given you authority over all the power of the enemy" (10:19). Their victories were pushing back the frontiers of evil.

The reference to snakes and scorpions (10:19) is to be taken metaphorically, for there is no evidence that Christians literally and intentionally walked on snakes and scorpions without suffering harm (though Paul miraculously withstood a poisonous snakebite [Acts 28:3-5]; the practice is known in some cultic groups today, probably based on their reading of the longer and textually uncertain ending of Mark's Gospel, Mark 16:9-20). The main point is that God will protect his people and give them victory over the evil one. Their joy was not to reside in their powers of exorcism but rather in their personal relationship with the living God.

◆   D. Jesus' Prayer of Thanksgiving (10:21-24; cf. Matt 11:25-27)

²¹At that same time Jesus was filled with the joy of the Holy Spirit, and he said, "O Father, Lord of heaven and earth, thank you for hiding these things from those who think themselves wise and clever, and for revealing them to the childlike. Yes, Father, it pleased you to do it this way.

²²"My Father has entrusted everything to me. No one truly knows the Son except the Father, and no one truly knows the Father except the Son and those to whom the Son chooses to reveal him."

²³Then when they were alone, he turned to the disciples and said, "Blessed are the eyes that see what you have seen. ²⁴I tell you, many prophets and kings longed to see what you see, but they didn't see it. And they longed to hear what you hear, but they didn't hear it."

NOTES

10:21 *Jesus was filled with the joy of the Holy Spirit.* On the importance of joy and rejoicing in Luke–Acts, see the Introduction and the comments on 1:39-45. See also Navone 1970:71-87; Morrice 1985.

O Father, Lord of heaven and earth, thank you for hiding these things from those who think themselves wise and clever. On the contents of this prayer, Spencer (1990:121) writes, "This whole prayer is a public confession. Consequently, Jesus naturally moves from the first to the third person. Jesus publicly and gratefully praises the Father in the presence of his disciples (v. 21). Then he speaks about their relationship in the third person, 'Son and Father' (v. 22). Finally, he speaks directly to the disciples (vv. 23-24)."

10:22 *no one truly knows the Father except the Son and those to whom the Son chooses to reveal him.* This passage has a high Christology in that it emphasizes the unique place of Jesus and his special role in communicating knowledge and experience of God to human beings. It recalls a prominent theme in John's Gospel, which emphasizes the idea that Jesus was "sent" from the Father to reveal God to humankind (John 4:34; 5:23-24, 30, 36-37; 6:29, 39; 7:16, 28; 8:16, 26; 12:44, 49; 14:24; 15:21; 16:5; 17:3; 20:21). This text also sheds light on the NT expression "God, the Father of our Lord Jesus Christ" (2 Cor 1:3; Eph 1:3; Col 1:3; 1 Pet 1:3).

COMMENTARY

This is a beautiful passage, encapsulating in exultant praise many of the themes of Jesus' teaching. In intimate language, like the fourth Gospel, it speaks eloquently of the Son of God's fellowship with his heavenly Father (see John 10:17-18, 28-30; 17:1-8, 25-26). The prayer reflects the spiritual communion Jesus had enjoyed with the Father throughout his life (2:49, 52; 3:21; 5:16; 6:12; 9:28-36). There is intimacy, trust, and confidence in this prayer of thanksgiving to God the Father, the "Lord of heaven and earth" (10:21). He is the one who ultimately reveals and conceals spiritual truth. His revelation is imparted not to the learned and sophisticated, "those who think themselves wise and clever" (10:21), but rather to helpless people, spiritual "infants" (*nēpioi* [TG3516/A, ZG3758]), those who in simple, childlike faith admit their total dependence upon the love and care of someone who is greater, wiser, and stronger than themselves. Jesus was grateful to the Father for his method of revelation and the persons to whom this divine revelation was disclosed. Jesus recognized the sovereignty of God in this and affirmed his "good pleasure" (*eudokia* [TG2107, ZG2306]; 10:21; cf. Eph 1:5, 9).

The prayer reveals the unique role of Jesus in the plan of God. The Father and the Son share a deep mutual knowledge of one another. The Son has received authority over everything from the Father (10:22; cf. Matt 11:27; 28:18; John 3:35; 13:3). He was aware of his special relationship with the Father and his awesome responsibility: "No one truly knows the Son except the Father, and no one truly knows the Father except the Son and those to whom the Son chooses to reveal him" (10:22). Jesus was conscious of his unrivaled knowledge of the Father and his unique role in communicating this divine knowledge to others. He was acutely aware that the Father had "sent" him for this purpose (cf. 4:18, 43; 9:48; 10:16).

When the disciples were alone, Jesus reminded them of the great blessings they had enjoyed through their association with him. They had been privileged to see the Messiah in person and in action. They had been eyewitnesses of his mighty works, and they had been earwitnesses of the words of life from the Savior of the world (cf. 1 John 1:1-3). What devout prophets and Israel's leaders had anticipated for centuries was now in the process of fulfillment right before their eyes (cf. 1 Pet 1:10-12). Luke had already noted that Simeon and Anna had served as prophets; they had expressed delight in living to see the long-promised Christ (2:25, 37; cf. 24:21). The disciples were truly favored to be participants in the messianic age, and they were reminded of the incredible opportunity that God had bestowed upon them (cf. Matt 13:16-17, where the "righteous" are linked with the "prophets" in longing for the time of consummation). This sense of privilege is reflected in other New Testament writings (cf. John 1:14; 4:42; 2 Pet 1:16-18; 1 John 1:1-3; 4:14).

A similar note of expectancy is sounded in 1 Peter: "This salvation was something even the prophets wanted to know more about when they prophesied about this gracious salvation prepared for you" (1 Pet 1:10). The disciples of Jesus were highly honored to live in the time of realization of the promises that God's people had fervently looked forward to in faith for centuries. They were fortunate to be alive and present for the prime events in the redemption of the world, which Peter described as "Christ's suffering and his great glory afterward" (1 Pet 1:11). With this matchless privilege came an accompanying responsibility to bear witness after they had received the Spirit's power to carry the gospel to the ends of the earth (24:46-49; Matt 28:18-20; John 15:27; Acts 1:8).

◆   E. The Most Important Commandment (10:25-29; cf. Matt 22:35-40; Mark 12:28-31)

²⁵One day an expert in religious law stood up to test Jesus by asking him this question: "Teacher, what should I do to inherit eternal life?"

²⁶Jesus replied, "What does the law of Moses say? How do you read it?"

²⁷The man answered, " 'You must love the LORD your God with all your heart, all your soul, all your strength, and all your mind.' And, 'Love your neighbor as yourself.'"*

²⁸"Right!" Jesus told him. "Do this and you will live!"

²⁹The man wanted to justify his actions, so he asked Jesus, "And who is my neighbor?"

10:27 Deut 6:5; Lev 19:18.

NOTES

10:25 *expert.* Such specialists in religious law were technically called "scribes." They became a guild or class of leaders who served as copyists and expounders of the Jewish law. Their wrong interpretations, changes, and innovations are exposed and denounced in the Gospels along with those of the priests (5:30; Matt 23:1-33; Mark 7:5-13).

10:27 *You must love the LORD your God.* Jesus commends the lawyer for giving the right answer (10:28) and challenges him to act on it. The parable of the Good Samaritan that follows unpacks the emphasis on doing, using an unlikely person to make the point. For a practical application of this passage to Christian discipleship today, see Scot McKnight's *The Jesus Creed;* he astutely points out that Jesus revised the *Shema* of Judaism in two ways: "loving others is added to loving God and loving God is understood as following Jesus" (2004:11). On the general importance of the love commandment, see Stern 1966; Furnish 1972; Hamilton 1988.

COMMENTARY

A lawyer, an expert in religious law (*nomikos* [TG3544A, ZG3788]), posed a question in a deliberate attempt to test (*ekpeirazō* [TG1598, ZG1733]) Jesus. The Master returned the question to the man who asked it, requiring the lawyer to give a biblical answer in terms of the Torah. The man was called upon to offer his own interpretation of the Scriptures, and he replied by quoting from the *Shema,* the basic words employed by pious Jews on a regular basis to confess their monotheistic faith (Deut 6:4-9; cf. Matt 22:37-39; Mark 12:29-30). The lawyer gave a comprehensive answer, combining Deuteronomy 6:5 and Leviticus 19:18, and Jesus commended him for his orthodox reply, going on to insist that this truth must be put into practice (10:28). The following parable drives home the practical point and shows the close connection that exists between the love of God and the love of neighbor. To borrow words from the First Epistle of John: "For if we don't love people we can see, how can we love God, whom we cannot see?" (1 John 4:20).

Luke's discussion about the love commandment is similar to that found in Matthew and Mark, but the setting and details are rather different (cf. Matt 22:35-40; Mark 12:28-31). Luke's direct treatment of the great commandment is the most concise, and it is illustrated in an unforgettable way by the parable of the Good Samaritan that follows. Luke's account is the only one that raises the ethical question in terms of salvation: "What should I do to inherit eternal life?" (10:25). Apparently, this was a common question (cf. 18:18). The form of the question seems to indicate a concept of salvation that depends upon works rather than on the grace of God (cf. Eph 2:8-9; Titus 3:5). The emphasis appears to be on what is *required* of human beings rather than on what God *gives* to those who reach out to him with a sense of need (cf. 18:13-14). However, the fact that Jesus commended him for this answer points to the conclusion that gift and demand must always be kept in balance. Salvation is a gracious gift of God, but a proper response must be forthcoming in grateful, loving service to God, expressed in keeping his commandments (6:46-49; cf. Matt 7:21).

A different setting is presupposed in the parallel passages. In Mark, one of the scribes heard Jesus on one occasion debating with other Jewish leaders and realized that Jesus had answered well. This prompted his penetrating question about the most important commandment (Mark 12:28). Jesus gave the answer straightforwardly, adding to Deuteronomy 6:5 the message of Leviticus 19:18 to make it clear that love for neighbor is the natural and logical expression of one's love for God. In Matthew, the question is raised in a series of controversies where the authority of Jesus had been questioned (Matt 21:23-27), the paying of taxes to Caesar had been raised (Matt 22:15-22), and the nature of marriage at the resurrection pondered (Matt 22:23-33). The answer Jesus had given concerning the resurrection had silenced the Sadducees (Matt 22:34), so this prompted the Pharisees to come together in a united fashion to "trap" Jesus by having one of their experts in the law pose the question about the greatest commandment (Matt 22:35-36). These differences between Matthew and Mark, on the one hand, and Luke, on the other, have led some commentators to view Luke as referring to a different incident. In any case, Luke agrees with the other Evangelists in identifying the two great commandments as central elements in the teaching of Jesus.

Mark and Luke speak of loving God with all the heart, soul, mind, and strength (10:27; Mark 12:30), while Matthew follows both the Hebrew and Greek texts of Deuteronomy 6:5 and speaks simply of loving God with all the heart, soul, and mind (Matt 22:37). Whether there is reference to three or four elements, the commandment to love God is clearly seen as embracing the whole of human life and personality.

◆ ## F. Parable of the Good Samaritan (10:30-37)

[30]Jesus replied with a story: "A Jewish man was traveling on a trip from Jerusalem to Jericho, and he was attacked by bandits. They stripped him of his clothes, beat him up, and left him half dead beside the road.

[31]"By chance a priest came along. But when he saw the man lying there, he crossed to the other side of the road and passed him by. [32]A Temple assistant* walked over and looked at him lying there, but he also passed by on the other side.

[33]"Then a despised Samaritan came along, and when he saw the man, he felt compassion for him. [34]Going over to him, the Samaritan soothed his wounds with olive oil and wine and bandaged them. Then he put the man on his own donkey and took him to an inn, where he took care of him. [35]The next day he handed the innkeeper two silver coins,* telling him, 'Take care of this man. If his bill runs higher than this, I'll pay you the next time I'm here.'

[36]"Now which of these three would you say was a neighbor to the man who was attacked by bandits?" Jesus asked.

[37]The man replied, "The one who showed him mercy."

Then Jesus said, "Yes, now go and do the same."

10:32 Greek *A Levite.* 10:35 Greek *two denarii.* A denarius was equivalent to a laborer's full day's wage.

NOTES

10:30 Two aspects of the parable should be noted: the shocking reversal of the normal experience (a characteristic of the parables [e.g., Matt 20:1-16]) and the common error of interpreters in the past who attempted to allegorize the details (e.g., Augustine).

a trip from Jerusalem to Jericho. The trip from Jerusalem to Jericho would be familiar to many pilgrims traveling to Jerusalem for the great Jewish festivals. The trip involved a descent of about 3,300 feet in just 17 miles. The road descended through wild, rocky, desolate country, in which lonely travelers could easily be attacked by ruthless bandits and abandoned in the desert.

10:33 *Then a despised Samaritan came along.* The widespread antipathy between the Jews and the Samaritans in Jesus' time is recognized in John's Gospel (John 4:9). A useful summary on the NT references to the Samaritans is found in ABD 5.940-947: "Jesus had trouble in the Samaritan villages (9:52-53) and instructed his disciples not to go there (Matt 10:5-6). Nevertheless, he talked to the Samaritan woman (John 4) and used Samaritans as favorable characters in some of his stories, particularly the account of the 10 lepers (17:11-19) and the parable of the Good Samaritan (10:29-37). Samaria was an early mission field for the growing church (Acts 8)." Just prior to his ascension, Jesus included Samaria as one of the areas in which the Good News was to be shared by his witnesses (Acts 1:8). (See also Purvis 1985; DJG 724-728.)

10:34 *the Samaritan soothed his wounds with olive oil and wine.* The medicinal properties of oil were well known (Mark 6:13; Jas 5:14; cf. Isa 1:6, "softened with oil," NRSV). Wine is often mentioned with oil in the Scriptures (Num 18:12; Deut 7:13; 1 Chr 9:29; 2 Chr 11:11; Ezra 6:9; Neh 5:11; Hag 1:11; Rev 6:6; 18:13). Wine could be mixed with certain drugs to increase its strength and to help ease pain, as happened when Jesus was dying on the cross (Mark 15:23; cf. Ps 69:21).

an inn. This word (*pandocheion*), used only here in the NT, refers to a "public place for receiving all comers and a more pretentious caravanserai than a *kataluma* [lodging, guest room] like that in Luke 2:7" (Robertson 1930:154).

10:35 *two silver coins.* The silver coin was a denarius, each of which had the value of a day's wages at that time (cf. Matt 20:1-16). These two coins would be sufficient evidence of good faith to secure adequate care for the wounded man, as Danker (1974:132) has pointed out: "Innkeepers were not known for their humanitarian sentiments. Therefore the Samaritan makes a generous down payment of what amounts to two-days' normal wages, with the assurance that he will pay the balance on his return. The pronoun I is emphatic: 'I, not the man, will pay.' He takes all precautions to insure good service for the wounded man."

COMMENTARY

The lawyer involved in the previous discussion "wanted to justify his actions," so he asked Jesus to define the concept of "neighbor" (10:29). Jesus did not answer his question directly but instead told a story involving three memorable characters—a priest, a Levite (or "Temple assistant"), and a Samaritan. The first two figures were obviously deeply involved in the practice of their Jewish religious faith and in maintaining the Temple worship in the holy city, Jerusalem. They were naturally concerned with pleasing God by walking in all the commandments and ordinances of the Lord blamelessly, like Zechariah and Elizabeth (1:6). Since the robbers had left the wounded man "half dead" (10:30), only by touching the person could one ascertain whether he was really dead or alive. The priest in the story, following the normal ritual concerns, could not afford to take the chance of contact with a dead body, for this would render him ceremonially unclean and consequently unable to perform his religious duties in the Temple (Lev 21:1-4). Therefore, he "crossed to the other side of the road and passed him by" (10:31). The Levite was governed by similar considerations, so he, too, "passed by on the other side" (10:32; cf. Num 19:11, 16).

The Samaritan, by contrast, was a despised foreigner (cf. 17:18), whose people advocated worship at Mount Gerizim, a rival site, while Jews worshiped at the Temple in Jerusalem (cf. John 4:20). There was a long-standing animosity between the Jews and the Samaritans (cf. 9:51-55; John 4:9), and feelings of mutual aversion ran deep. In spite of the barriers of race, religion, and culture, the Samaritan in the story stepped in to help. The hated foreigner was the only one who showed compassion, intervening to bind up the Jewish man's wounds, take him safely to an inn, and make ample provision to pay for his future expenses on the road to recovery. This is a story where the last becomes first and the first last.

It is perfectly obvious here that the man who is praised by Jesus was not the punctilious priest, nor the scrupulous lay worker in the Temple, but a caring outsider whose love was not limited to national boundaries nor confined by traditional prejudices. Jesus was inculcating a love that outstripped these cultural and ethnocentric limitations. Jesus insisted that the love we have for God must be practically reflected in the way in which we reach out to care for others, even when this involves a cost to ourselves. The neighbor clearly is the person who stands in need of the help that we can offer. Our faith in God, to be authentic, must be one that expresses itself in loving concern and helpfulness to our fellows (cf. Gal 5:6).

After presenting the story, Jesus invited the lawyer to make his own judgment on the case: "Now which of these three would you say was a neighbor to the man who was attacked by bandits?" (10:36). The expert in the law replied somewhat obliquely, as if the conclusion embarrassed him, "The one who showed him mercy" (10:37a). Then, Jesus pressed home the application: "Go and do the same" (10:37b).

The dialogue between Jesus and the lawyer is illuminating. It "illustrates the difference between the ethics of law and the ethics of love. To the lawyer, eternal life is a prize to be won by the meticulous observance of religious rules; to Jesus, love to God and neighbour is in itself the life of the heavenly kingdom, already begun on earth. The lawyer wants moral duties limited and defined with a rabbinical thoroughness; Jesus declines to set any limits to the obligations of love. Religion to the one is a set of restrictive regulations, to the other a boundless series of opportunities" (Caird 1963:148).

◆   G. Jesus Visits Martha and Mary (10:38-42)

[38]As Jesus and the disciples continued on their way to Jerusalem, they came to a certain village where a woman named Martha welcomed him into her home. [39]Her sister, Mary, sat at the Lord's feet, listening to what he taught. [40]But Martha was distracted by the big dinner she was preparing. She came to Jesus and said, "Lord, doesn't it seem unfair to you that my sister just sits here while I do all the work? Tell her to come and help me." [41]But the Lord said to her, "My dear Martha, you are worried and upset over all these details! [42]There is only one thing worth being concerned about. Mary has discovered it, and it will not be taken away from her."

NOTES

10:38 *they came to a certain village where a woman named Martha welcomed him.* This reading has the support of the excellent mss 𝔓45 𝔓75 B cop^{sa}. Other mss add "into the house" (א C L 33) or "into her house" (A D W 044 070 𝔐). Scribes added these phrases to soften the bare "welcomed him" (Metzger 1971:153).

welcomed. Luke uses a graphic verb (*hupodechomai,* meaning "receive" or "welcome as a guest") to depict the favorable reception given to Jesus by Mary and Martha here and later by Zacchaeus (10:38; 19:6; cf. Acts 17:7). He does not use this word to describe Jesus' meal with a Pharisee, because that was a less friendly, indeed hostile, occasion (11:37-54). Jesus urged his followers to practice hospitality (14:12-14; Matt 25:31-46), and the early church perpetuated this (Rom 12:13; 16:1-2; 1 Tim 3:2; 5:10; Tit 1:8; Heb 13:2; 1 Pet 4:9; 3 John 1:5-8).

10:41 *My dear Martha.* Lit., "Martha, Martha." The reply of Jesus is sensitive and tender and perhaps indicates a tendency for Jesus to occasionally use doubled words (note "Simon, Simon" in 22:31). There are several instances in the Bible where a name is repeated in a significant manner for emphasis: Abraham (Gen 22:11), Jacob (Gen 46:2), Moses (Exod 3:4), Samuel (1 Sam 3:4, 10), and Saul (Acts 9:4; 26:14).

10:42 *There is only one thing worth being concerned about.* This reading (lit., "but one thing is necessary") has the manuscript support of 𝔓45 𝔓75 A C* W, whereas other manuscripts (𝔓3 א B C^2 L) read "but few things are needful—or only one." Whatever reading we adopt, Jesus is saying that Martha is worried over too many things. Caird has a helpful discussion of the textual variants of the passage (1963:149-150).

COMMENTARY

This story is found only in Luke's Gospel and is one of Luke's banqueting scenes (see "Major Features and Themes" in the Introduction). "Luke appears not to have placed it in chronological sequence, for Bethany was near Jerusalem and at a later time Jesus was still far from the capital (17:11). He might have placed it immediately after the preceding parable as a safeguard against any of his readers coming under the misapprehension that salvation is by works. He makes the point that waiting quietly on the Lord is more important than bustling busy-ness" (Morris 1974:209). Jesus repeatedly warned his disciples against undue anxiety, as he does Martha. They were not to worry about the cares of everyday life (12:22; cf. Matt 6:25, 34), for this is unproductive and incompatible with faith in a loving heavenly Father, who cares for the needs of his children (12:23-30). Even in the face of trials, disciples were not to "worry about how to defend yourself or what to say" (12:11-12; cf. Matt 10:19-20); God would supply all their needs if they would make his Kingdom their primary concern (12:31; cf. Matt 6:33; Phil 4:6-7; 1 Pet 5:7).

This memorable incident is placed by Luke in the journey of Jesus to Jerusalem—a point brought out nicely in the NLT's rendering (10:38). Jesus and his disciples were welcomed into a place where he was loved and honored. The story in Luke focuses on Martha, not Mary. Elsewhere, we are told that the two women lived in Bethany, a village just east of Jerusalem (John 11:1). Martha, probably the older of the two sisters, was apparently in charge of the house and responsible for acting as hostess. She made elaborate preparations for a big dinner party, while Mary sat at the Lord's feet, quietly absorbing his teaching. The fact that Martha complained to Jesus about her sister's lack of help in preparing the meal indicates that her "work," or "service" (*diakonia* [TG1248, ZG1355]; 10:40), had become a burden, lacking in joy and fulfillment. Her hospitality had become a source of anxiety and trouble, distracting her from paying personal attention to the guest of honor, Jesus. Mary, by contrast, had taken time for Jesus personally, making him feel at home and listening to his teaching with appreciation and delight. Jesus reproved Martha for developing an unkind, critical spirit that was marring her otherwise commendable service.

Few Gospel stories have been subjected to greater mishandling than this one. Through the centuries, Mary has often been idealized at the expense of Martha, and in the Middle Ages, Mary was used as a model to exalt the contemplative life over the active one. However, that is to misuse the text and to misunderstand the context. "Martha need not be criticized for her ambitious behavior. For her actions reveal her loyalty to the Lord Jesus. Her true character is displayed in her honesty and steadfast faith" (Gardner 1995:444).

Mary's rightful role as a listener in this incident is significant. In Jesus' day, it was not considered appropriate for a Jewish woman to be instructed by a teacher; her role was largely restricted to domestic life, and thus, it was not expected that she should assume the role of a disciple, listening as a pupil to her teacher. Thus, Jesus' instruction here is clearly countercultural: "This strong affirmation of a woman's right to listen to the Lord speak and to be concerned with spiritual matters gives a clear indication that the Kingdom of God is for all who will listen and believe in Jesus. Luke's Gospel often mentions how people from all types of different backgrounds and minority groups needed to hear the Gospel of the Kingdom of God. Here is one of the clearest statements that Jesus intended women also to be recipients of his teaching and his rule" (Gardner 1995:448). The main point of the passage is about women as disciples. Like all believers, they are called to "serve the Lord . . . with as few distractions as possible," as Paul reminded the Corinthians (1 Cor 7:35).

◆ H. Teaching about Prayer (11:1-13; cf. Matt 6:9-13; 7:7-11)

Once Jesus was in a certain place praying. As he finished, one of his disciples came to him and said, "Lord, teach us to pray, just as John taught his disciples."

²Jesus said, "This is how you should pray:*

"Father, may your name be kept holy.
May your Kingdom come soon.
³Give us each day the food we need,*
⁴and forgive us our sins,
    as we forgive those who sin
    against us.
And don't let us yield to temptation.*"

⁵Then, teaching them more about prayer, he used this story: "Suppose you went to a friend's house at midnight, wanting to borrow three loaves of bread. You say to him, ⁶'A friend of mine has just arrived for a visit, and I have nothing for him to eat.' ⁷And suppose he calls out from his bedroom, 'Don't bother me. The door is locked for the night, and my family and I are all in bed. I can't help you.' ⁸But I tell you this—though he won't do it for friendship's sake, if you keep knocking long enough, he will get up and give you whatever you need because of your shameless persistence.*

⁹"And so I tell you, keep on asking, and you will receive what you ask for. Keep on seeking, and you will find. Keep on knocking, and the door will be opened to you. ¹⁰For everyone who asks, receives. Everyone who seeks, finds. And to everyone who knocks, the door will be opened.

¹¹"You fathers—if your children ask* for a fish, do you give them a snake instead? ¹²Or if they ask for an egg, do you give them a scorpion? Of course not! ¹³So if you sinful people know how to give good gifts to your children, how much more will your heavenly Father give the Holy Spirit to those who ask him."

11:2 Some manuscripts add additional phrases from the Lord's Prayer as it reads in Matt 6:9-13.   11:3 Or *Give us each day our food for the day;* or *Give us each day our food for tomorrow.*   11:4 Or *And keep us from being tested.*   11:8 Or *in order to avoid shame,* or *so his reputation won't be damaged.*   11:11 Some manuscripts add *for bread, do you give them a stone? Or [if they ask].*

NOTES

11:1 *Jesus was in a certain place praying.* Many aspects of prayer are represented in the prayers of Jesus in Luke's Gospel. Jesus made prayers of adoration and thanksgiving (10:21), communion (3:21; 5:16; 9:28-29), petition (22:42), and intercession (22:32). The one aspect that is lacking is confession, for there is no suggestion that Jesus needed to confess any sin; in fact, the NT repeatedly affirms the sinlessness of Christ (23:41; John 8:46; 2 Cor 5:21; Heb 4:15; 7:26; 1 Pet 2:22; 1 John 3:5). However, Jesus plainly taught his disciples that they should pray for the forgiveness of their sins (11:4). For an examination of Luke's vocabulary and theology of prayer, see O'Brien 1973, Spencer 1990:111-147, Trites 1978, and DJG 617-625.

11:8 *he will . . . because of your shameless persistence.* Note the NLT mg, which gives the alternate rendering "in order to avoid shame." I think this is the better rendering of this verse. The use of the word *anaideia* [TG335, ZG357] (shamelessness) can reasonably be translated either as in the NLT text or as in the mg, but the ancient Middle Eastern cultural context strongly favors the idea of avoiding shame. As Bailey has pointed out: "The cultural elements of the parable [of the Friend at Midnight, 11:5-8] fall into place once the key word *anaideia* ("avoidance of shame") is properly understood [this is a rare word, found only here in the NT]. The parable teaches that God is a God of honor and that man can have complete assurance that his prayers will be heard. . . . The parable climaxes around the question of the 'sense of honor' or 'blamelessness' of the man asleep, which leads him in the night to fulfil the [inconvenient] request" (1976:119). If a Middle Eastern man would go to such trouble for an unexpected guest to maintain his own sense of honor, then surely a gracious, faithful God could be counted on to meet the needs of his people who cry to him for help! It is an interesting argument from the lesser to the greater.

11:12 *if they ask for an egg, do you give them a scorpion?* Scorpions are mentioned occasionally in the OT, often in contexts that stress the element of pain. When Ezekiel was commissioned, he was reminded that his opponents would sting like scorpions (Ezek 2:6). Several times, scorpions are noted in connection with the harsh measures proposed by King Rehoboam ("My father beat you with whips, but I will beat you with scorpions!" 1 Kgs 12:11,14; 2 Chr 10:11,14). The children of Israel were called to remember how God had led them "through the great and terrifying wilderness" with its "poisonous snakes and scorpions" (Deut 8:15). In the NT, Jesus gave encouragement to the seventy-two workers he had sent out as missionaries, declaring, "I have given you authority over all the power of the enemy" (10:19). This included the conquest of snakes and scorpions, which were to be trampled and crushed—apparently a symbolic reference to the disciples' spiritual victory over the forces of evil. In the NT, the power and pain inflicted by scorpions are noted in the fearsome description of the locust plague in the book of Revelation (Rev 9:3-10).

11:13 *how much more will your heavenly Father give the Holy Spirit to those who ask him.* In Luke's thinking, the Holy Spirit is God's supreme gift to God's people, giving them spiritual wisdom, energy, and power to accomplish the will of God in the world. On the role of the Spirit in the life of Jesus, see TDNT 6.389-455; DJG 341-351; and Turner 1981, 1991. On possible links with Paul's conception of the Spirit, see Jackson 1989.

COMMENTARY

The third Gospel has already made a good deal of the importance of prayer, particularly in highlighting the prayerfulness of Jesus (3:21; 5:16; 6:12; 9:18, 28-29; 10:21; 23:46). Now the subject is quite properly introduced again in the training of the disciples; later, it will appear in the prayer parables that are unique to Luke (11:5-8; 18:1-14)

The setting is instructive. Jesus had been praying "in a certain place" (11:1). Evidently, the reality of Jesus' communion with the Father was apparent to the disciples, so they were anxious to gain similar strength and blessing by learning from Jesus how to have more meaningful fellowship with the living God. They were aware that John the Baptist had provided instruction on the topic to his disciples, and they sought similar guidance from their Master. In response, Jesus first gave them the model prayer (11:2-4) and then additional counsel and direction on the art of communicating with God.

The prayer, which has been widely used by Christians through the centuries, is given in its simplest form in Luke and in a longer version in Matthew (Matt 6:9-13). The preface to the model prayer in Luke assumes that Christian disciples will pray. The counsel given was not intended as a prohibition of free prayer, but rather as a general guideline and pattern for communicating with God: "This is *how* you should pray" (11:2). As such, it is invaluable for all those who take their fellowship with God seriously, for prayer surely lies close to the heart of Christian experience, and without it one's relationship with God withers and fades (cf. 18:1, 7-8; 22:40, 46).

The prayer has a strong God-centered focus. It begins with God and expresses genuine concern for the honoring of his holy name and desire for the coming of his Kingdom. Then it moves on to embrace human needs for daily food, forgiveness, and help in conquering temptation. The prayer is directed to a loving God who is approached humbly but confidently in his capacity as "Father"—a title that suggests access and intimacy while, at the same time, recognizing God's transcendence and power. God is acknowledged as having a purpose for the world, and true disciples are encouraged to pray for the realization of his Kingdom in its fullness in history.

The prayer begins with a simple, trustful address to God as "Father." The Aramaic word behind this invocation of God is *abba*; the use of the Aramaic term itself is recorded in Mark 14:36, and the address was evidently used by the early church in its prayers (Rom 8:15; Gal 4:6). On the lips of Jesus, it clearly spoke of a filial relationship between himself and the Father (cf. 10:21-22; 23:46; Matt 11:25-26; John 11:41-42). By calling on God as Father, Jesus intended to teach his followers to regard their heavenly Father in a close, intimate way, as one who knew, loved, and cared for them (cf. Ps 103:13; Mal 3:17; 1 Pet 5:7).

We are to pray to God the Creator, Preserver, and Sovereign of the world. God is the one and only person to whom human beings are to give their worship, adoration, and obedience. So the prayer gives the very greatest prominence to God, to whom disciples owe everything. God is to be given the highest place in the life of his people. A holy God must be treated in an appropriate way, and the prayer insists on placing God absolutely first. It takes us back to the first commandment: "You must not have any other god but me" (Exod 20:3; Deut. 5:7).

The second petition is also focused on God: "May your Kingdom come soon" (11:2c). If God is to be held in highest respect and esteem, then it follows logically that the divine Kingdom, or Reign, must be the chief concern of all true disciples. Above and beyond all personal concerns is to see God's purposes triumph and to pray and work for the coming of his Kingdom in its fullness in history. This means there must be confidence that God can answer prayer and bring about the consummation of the Kingdom for which devout believers pray. All true prayer is to be measured by these two fundamental petitions, which seek the full and proper recognition of God and the complete realization of God's sovereignty in the universe. Then and then only is it proper to pray for one's personal need. Hence Jesus' words: "Seek the Kingdom of God above all else, and live righteously, and he will give you everything you need" (Matt 6:33).

The third petition is directed toward material needs, but these are seen within the corporate context: "Give *us* each day the food we need" (11:3). As one looks to God for the meeting of one's own practical needs, so one bears in mind the needs of others for the same things. The same Lord is over all and is rich to all who call upon him (cf. Rom 10:12), so there is a summons here to bear in mind the needs of others as well as one's own. This suggests an element of loving sympathy and compassion for those who are in need of such necessities as food, clothing, and shelter. A loving God is aware of the needs of his children, and his people should share his concern for all who are suffering from a lack of the basic provisions to sustain human life.

The fourth petition points to another widespread concern—the universal human need for forgiveness. Since we are all sinners, we all stand in need of God's forgiveness. The fundamental presupposition here is that only God can forgive sin, a point raised elsewhere in the Gospels (5:21; Mark 2:7). Genuine admission of sinfulness must take the form of acknowledging and confessing it before God (cf. 1 John 1:9). However, it is clear that one cannot pray this prayer effectively and yet fail to forgive others. To experience this divine forgiveness with integrity, one is called upon to exercise the same attitude of genuine forgiveness that God has shown to us toward others (11:4; cf. 6:37; Gal 6:1; Eph 4:32; Col 3:13).

The final petition reaches out for divine help in facing temptation. Anyone who has honestly prayed for the forgiveness of sin must be concerned to avoid moral failure in the future. The Greek word *peirasmos* [TG3986, ZG4280] can mean "testing" as well as "temptation." As in the case of Christ himself (4:1-13; Matt 4:1-11; Mark 1:12-13; cf. Heb 4:15), God allows us to be tempted (cf. John 17:15; Rev 3:10) so as to test and purify us. We only succumb to our temptations when we are drawn away by our own lust and enticed (James 1:14). While temptation is common to all people, God has promised not to permit his servants to be tempted beyond the point of endurance, but rather to provide for them a way of escape (1 Cor 10:13; see Trites 1978:178).

Jesus' teaching on prayer placed great emphasis on God's honor, and that element comes to the fore in the parable of the friend at midnight (11:5-8). The setting of this parable is a small Palestinian village with no stores. Bread would be baked according to the needs of the day, and it would not be uncommon to run out after the last meal. Travelers in the Middle East often traveled in the early morning or late in the day to avoid the intense heat, so they would arrive tired and hungry, but three small loaves would be enough to satisfy a guest. The unexpected arrival of a late visitor meant that the person had to be fed if the traditional courtesies of oriental hospitality were to be observed (cf. Gen 18:1-15; 19:1-3). It was viewed as a disgrace to refuse to welcome even such an unexpected guest, and this explains the great lengths to which the man went to feed his visitor. There appears to be a touch of humor here, for the man who was approached for help had gotten his children settled down for the night in his poor one room house and had gone to bed himself. To answer the plea for help, he had to break the peaceful sleep of the whole family! The request for help was not initially met because it was highly inconvenient and meant the disruption of the whole household. However, "in order to avoid shame" (see note on 11:8), the man roused himself from bed, disturbed his whole family, and granted the request.

The parable offers great encouragement for boldness and persistence in prayer. It rests upon an argument that moves from the lesser to the greater, and this type of approach often appears in the New Testament (e.g., 11:13; 12:28; Matt 7:11; Rom 11:12; 1 Cor 6:3; Heb 10:28-29). The point here is straightforward: if a reluctant friend will rise to give three loaves of bread to a needy neighbor to avoid shame, how much more will a loving, gracious, all-powerful God act to help his needy children when they expectantly seek his aid! "The problem is not that man has to overcome the reluctance of God to hear and answer his prayers. To the contrary, the problem is located in the one who prays. If God does not respond immediately and on his terms, then the individual is apt to lose faith, either in God's existence or in his character as a loving Father. Persistence in prayer is an act of faith, a testimony to our belief in a loving personal God" (Tolbert 1970:98).

The message is applied quite directly to the practice of unceasing prayer: "And so I tell you, keep on asking, and you will receive what you ask for. Keep on seeking, and you will find. Keep on knocking, and the door will be opened to you" (11:9-10; cf. Matt 7:7-8). God is faithful in meeting the needs of his people when they urgently turn to him and persistently seek his intervention. Moreover, God's gifts are good. If sinful people bestow good gifts on their children, how much more will a loving God bestow his best gifts on those who ask him? And for Luke, God's supreme gift is his Holy Spirit (11:13), the one who energizes Christians, giving them the strength to bear witness to their Lord, power to perform mighty works, and courage to face persecution and suffering. All of these qualities Luke will amply illustrate as the Spirit works in the lives of Spirit-filled men and women in the book of Acts (e.g., Acts 2:44-45; 4:8-13, 23-37; 5:12-16; 6:8; 8:4-8; 9:27).

◆   I. Jesus and the Prince of Demons (11:14-28; cf. Matt 12:22-30; Mark 3:22-27)

[14]One day Jesus cast out a demon from a man who couldn't speak, and when the demon was gone, the man began to speak. The crowds were amazed, [15]but some of them said, "No wonder he can cast out demons. He gets his power from Satan,* the prince of demons." [16]Others, trying to test Jesus, demanded that he show them a miraculous sign from heaven to prove his authority.

[17]He knew their thoughts, so he said, "Any kingdom divided by civil war is doomed. A family splintered by feuding will fall apart. [18]You say I am empowered by Satan. But if Satan is divided and fighting against himself, how can his kingdom survive? [19]And if I am empowered by Sa-

tan, what about your own exorcists? They cast out demons, too, so they will condemn you for what you have said. [20]But if I am casting out demons by the power of God,* then the Kingdom of God has arrived among you. [21]For when a strong man like Satan is fully armed and guards his palace, his possessions are safe—[22]until someone even stronger attacks and overpowers him, strips him of his weapons, and carries off his belongings.

[23]"Anyone who isn't with me opposes me, and anyone who isn't working with me is actually working against me.

[24]"When an evil* spirit leaves a person, it goes into the desert, searching for rest. But when it finds none, it says, 'I will re-

turn to the person I came from.' ²⁵So it returns and finds that its former home is all swept and in order. ²⁶Then the spirit finds seven other spirits more evil than itself, and they all enter the person and live there. And so that person is worse off than before."

²⁷As he was speaking, a woman in the crowd called out, "God bless your mother—the womb from which you came, and the breasts that nursed you!" ²⁸Jesus replied, "But even more blessed are all who hear the word of God and put it into practice."

11:15 Greek *Beelzeboul;* also in 11:18, 19. Other manuscripts read *Beezeboul;* Latin version reads *Beelzebub.*
11:20 Greek *by the finger of God.* 11:24 Greek *unclean.*

NOTES

11:15 *Satan.* According to several Gr. mss (𝔓45 𝔓75 A C D L W 038 044 33 𝔐), the title is *Beelzeboul* (Eng. spelling "Beelzebul"). This reading has far better support than the reading *Beezeboul* (so ℵ B). Latin versions read *Beelzebub* (cf. NLT mg—the variants also appear in 11:18, 19). See Penney and Wise 1994, Evans and Porter 2000:269-273, and comments on exorcism at 4:31-37. The name probably goes back to Baal-zebub, the god of Ekron, the northernmost of the five main Philistine cities (2 Kgs 1:2-3, 6, 16). Baal-zebub means "lord of the flies," whereas the similar sounding name used by the Jews was Baalzebul, "lord of dung," probably a Jewish way of referring to the pagan god whose title was subsequently transferred to a demon and possibly to the Devil himself. Jesus clearly understood Beelzebul to be a reference to Satan, the archenemy of God. It is interesting that the name Baalzebul also appears in the Ras Shamra tablets, where it is used of a Canaanite deity and seems to have the meaning "lord of the high place" or "lord of the dwelling."

11:19 *if I am empowered by Satan, what about your own exorcists?* The point here is that in accusing Jesus of using Satanic power, the Jews were condemning their own people of doing the same. This effective use of logic turned the argument of Jesus' opponents back against them.

11:20 *the Kingdom of God has arrived.* The exorcisms performed by Jesus provided strong evidence that God's Kingdom, long anticipated and hoped for, had at last entered history in a transforming way. In fact, the words and works of Jesus as a whole revealed the fact that the Kingdom of God had actually arrived in the person of Jesus of Nazareth (cf. Jesus' answer to John the Baptist's questions in 7:22; Matt 11:5). Yet, there was still the future time when the purposes of God would be fully realized and consummated, and so the disciples were taught to pray, "May your Kingdom come soon" (11:2; Matt 6:10). The Kingdom's nearness and imminence (Mark 1:14-15) called for repentance in preparation for its final realization, when the Son of Man would come in power (Mark 14:62; Matt 26:64; cf. Luke 21:36; 22:69). Both the "already" and the "not yet" dimensions of the Kingdom must be affirmed and kept in careful balance to do justice to the present and future dimensions of the Kingdom theme. For further discussion see Beasley-Murray (1986).

COMMENTARY

As we have seen, exorcism (the casting out of evil spirits) has already been prominently featured in Luke's account of Jesus' ministry (4:31-37; 8:26-39; 9:37-43a). The casting out of the evil spirit in this case was striking, for the man's affliction had affected his speech (in Matthew's account, the man is also blind and regains his sight as well [Matt 12:22]). When Jesus delivered him, he regained his voice and the power of communication was restored. The miracle was impressive, and the "crowds were amazed" (11:14; cf. Matt 12:23), a feature noted in other stories where Jesus intervenes (4:36; 5:26; 8:25; 9:43). This incident raised a question about the exorcist: was he operating under divine sanction, or could his work be attributed to demonic agency (cf. Matt 12:22-30; Mark 3:22-27)? Some critics were disposed to accept the latter explanation, so they boldly asserted, "No wonder he can cast out demons. He gets his power from Satan, the prince of demons" (11:15). Since they could not deny the reality of what had taken place, they sought to repudiate it by claiming it was the work of the devil, which should be rejected as spurious. Others, trying to test Jesus, demanded "a miraculous sign from heaven to prove his authority" (11:16; cf. 1 Cor 1:22).

Jesus was aware of their hostile thoughts. In Mark's account, we are told that he summoned the hostile scribes and spoke to them in parables (Mark 3:23). In his similar response in Luke, Jesus declared that a divided home or a divided kingdom was doomed, for it had sown the seeds of its own destruction. So too in the spiritual realm: "If Satan is divided and fighting against himself, how can his kingdom survive?" (11:18). Jesus also showed that this question must be asked about the exorcisms that the followers of his accusers performed. Under whose auspices were they carried out? To question Jesus was, in effect, to question them as well: "They cast out demons, too, so they will condemn you for what you have said" (11:19). Their rejection of Jesus' exorcisms alone was based upon sheer prejudice and was untenable.

Despite their caviling, Jesus made a bold claim, namely, that in his ministry he was actually exercising the power of God, and, in the casting out of evil spirits, the mighty Kingdom of God had arrived among them as a present reality (11:20; cf. Matt 12:28). Matthew's account describes the exorcisms as the work of the Spirit of God, while Luke attributes them to the "finger of God" (NLT: "power of God"; 11:20), probably recalling the divine activity in the Exodus experience, where the Ten Commandments were "written by the finger of God" (Exod 31:18; Deut 9:10) and "where the acts of God are shown to be beyond the power of the Egyptian magicians to duplicate" (Tolbert 1970:99, citing Exod 8:19).

The illustration Jesus used was the forceful seizure of a property by a stronger power. Satan, the strong man, was being attacked and his stronghold stripped of its weapons and possessions. Jesus, the one who was stronger than Satan, was able to invade his territory and carry off his treasures. The Son of God was setting people free, and the exorcisms were an important part of his overall ministry that was bringing healing, wholeness, and deliverance. The spiritual battle was a real one, and Jesus was pushing back the frontiers of evil and advancing the Reign of God.

Then follows a striking remark that appears, in the context, to have been directed to Jesus' critics, but which certainly has a wider application: "Anyone who isn't with me opposes me, and anyone who isn't working with me is actually working against me" (11:23). Neutrality was impossible. The teachers of religious law had plainly revealed their hostility to Jesus by alleging that his power to cast out demons had come from Satan. They were thereby unmasked as opponents. This is not to deny the principle stated in Luke 9:50 ("anyone who is not against you is for you"), for there the worker was evidently a believer who was acting in the name of Jesus, although belonging to a different group (9:49).

Jesus gave further teaching on the return of the evil spirit (the wording in Matthew's Gospel is almost identical; cf. 11:24-26 and Matt 12:43-45). Just as nature abhors a vacuum, so does the spiritual world. It was commonly thought that when a demon was cast out of a person, it would attempt to settle inside someone else (just as the demons took possession of the pigs in 8:32). It was believed that when they left a person, they went into arid places, for they were associated with the desert and solitary places (cf. 8:29). The point of Jesus' teaching here is clear. It was not enough for a person to be a passive recipient of God's blessing in the expulsion of an evil spirit. It was "also necessary for him as well as those who witnessed the mighty deed of God to respond positively to the proclamation of the kingdom. By faith they could be filled with the power of God that would arm them against any future assaults by demons" (Tolbert 1970:100).

While Jesus had been speaking, a woman in the crowd, evidently moved by the display of divine power that she had seen, declared: "God bless your mother—the womb from which you came, and the breasts that nursed you!" (11:27). Only Luke records this incident, one which reminds us of another exchange with the women of Jerusalem, who were weeping and wailing as Jesus was being led to his crucifixion (23:27-29). Luke was deeply interested in the thoughts and feelings of women (cf. Acts 9:39) and particularly in portraying Jesus as deeply concerned for them. In response to the woman's emotional statement, Jesus replied, "But even more blessed are all who hear the word of God and put it into practice" (11:28). Physical relationship to Jesus had its place, and Luke had already recognized it in recording the exultant words of Elizabeth to Mary: "God has blessed you above all women, and your child is blessed" (1:42). However, a spiritual relationship to Jesus is definitely more important and is available to all genuine believers: "My mother and my brothers are all those who hear God's word and obey it" (8:21; cf. Mark 3:33-35; Matt 12:46-50).

◆ J. The Sign of Jonah (11:29-32; cf. Matt 12:28-42)

29As the crowd pressed in on Jesus, he said, "This evil generation keeps asking me to show them a miraculous sign. But the only sign I will give them is the sign of Jonah. 30What happened to him was a sign to the people of Nineveh that God had sent him. What happens to the Son of Man* will be a sign to these people that he was sent by God.

31"The queen of Sheba* will stand up against this generation on judgment day and condemn it, for she came from a distant land to hear the wisdom of Solomon. Now someone greater than Solomon is here—but you refuse to listen. 32The people of Nineveh will also stand up against this generation on judgment day and condemn it, for they repented of their sins at the preaching of Jonah. Now someone greater than Jonah is here—but you refuse to repent.

11:30 "Son of Man" is a title Jesus used for himself. 11:31 Greek *The queen of the south.*

NOTES

11:29 *the only sign I will give them is the sign of Jonah.* There are some details in Matthew's record about the sign of Jonah that supplement Luke's account (Matt 12:38-42). He notes that: (1) the sign was called for by the Jewish religious leaders (Matt 12:38; cf. Paul's comment on Jews requiring "signs from heaven" in 1 Cor 1:22); (2) the generation is literally described as "adulterous," that is, "faithless" or "unfaithful" to God, its covenant partner; and (3) Jonah's three days in the belly of the great fish are presented as analogous to the three-day sojourn of the Son of Man in the heart of the earth (Matt 12:40). Thus, in Matthew's Gospel, the sign of Jonah serves not only to address the vital issue of repentance (as it does in Luke), but also to symbolize the resurrection of Jesus on the third day. For a full treatment of this passage, see Edwards 1971 and DJG 754-757.

COMMENTARY

Having dealt with the accusation that he was the agent of Beelzebul, Jesus then turned to consider the issue of a sign (cf. 11:16). He offered the sign of Jonah as the only one that would be given: "What happened to him was a sign to the people of Nineveh that God had sent him. What happens to the Son of Man will be a sign to these people that he was sent by God" (11:30). "These people" is, more literally, "this generation," a generation that Jesus had just characterized as an "evil" or wicked one, standing under the judgment of God and in desperate need of repentance (11:29). That was why the sign of Jonah was such an eminently suitable sign. The people of Nineveh were called to repent at the preaching of Jonah, and the contemporaries of Jesus were being similarly called to repent at the preaching of Jesus, the Son of Man. If repentance was called for in the former case, how much more now, for "someone greater than Jonah is here" (11:32)!

The tragedy confronting Jesus was their stubborn impenitence: "You refuse to repent" (11:32). Again, the argument runs from the lesser to the greater: both Solomon (1 Kgs 10:1) and Jonah (Jonah 3:5-6) had received positive responses from the people they ministered to; therefore Jesus, who was greater than either of these, should receive an immeasurably greater positive response—but the people were recalcitrant. In a similar fashion, John's Gospel carefully describes the disappointing reception accorded to Jesus: "He came to his own people, and even they rejected him" (John 1:11). In the book of Acts, Stephen similarly criticizes his hearers with bold words: "You stubborn people! You are heathen at heart and deaf to the truth. Must you forever resist the Holy Spirit?" (Acts 7:51).

Later in his Gospel, Luke will highlight Jesus' sadness over the terrible unbelief he had to contend with in the holy city: "O Jerusalem, Jerusalem, the city that kills the prophets and stones God's messengers! How often I have wanted to gather your children together as a hen protects her chicks beneath her wings, but you wouldn't let me" (13:34). Jerusalem was to pay a horrible price for this unreceptive attitude—the destruction of the city and its Temple, which took place in AD 70 (see DJG 172-176, 811-817).

◆ K. Receiving the Light (11:33-36; cf. Matt 6:22-23)

33"No one lights a lamp and then hides it or puts it under a basket.* Instead, a lamp is placed on a stand, where its light can be seen by all who enter the house.

34"Your eye is a lamp that provides light for your body. When your eye is good, your whole body is filled with light. But when it is bad, your body is filled with darkness. 35Make sure that the light you think you have is not actually darkness. 36If you are filled with light, with no dark corners, then your whole life will be radiant, as though a floodlight were filling you with light."

11:33 Some manuscripts omit *or puts it under a basket.*

NOTES

11:34 When your eye is good. The Gr. word for "good" is *haplous* [TG573, ZG606], an adjective meaning "sound, healthy, clear." The point is that if the eye is "good" (*haplous*), then the light streams in so that the whole body is "filled with light." As Craddock has noted, "to the person of integrity and openness to light, Jesus' message is clear enough and able to give the light of God to one's life" (1988:1030). The struggle between good and evil forces is graphically depicted in both the DSS (e.g., "The War of the Sons of Light and the Sons of Darkness"; see Vermes 1997:120-142) and John's Gospel, where the struggle between good and evil is also presented in terms of light and darkness: "God's light came into the world, but people loved the darkness more than the light, for their actions were evil" (John 3:19-21).

COMMENTARY

In view of the resistance to Jesus and his teaching seen in the previous verses, Luke now gives Jesus' exhortation on the proper reception of his teaching ("the light"). Obviously, a lamp is meant to provide illumination, and it thus requires correct placement in a location where it can be observed and shed its light. This speaks of the necessary public character of Christian witness, and it points to the need for a pure witness: "When your eye is good, your whole body is filled with light. But when it is bad, your body is filled with darkness" (11:34). It is also a plain warning against a believer harboring darkness within and thus nullifying the light. By contrast, a faithful disciple of Christ is encouraged and promised abundant divine blessing: "If you are filled with light, with no dark corners, then your whole life will be radiant, as though a floodlight were filling you with light" (11:36). In this case, the promise given to the psalmist has been abundantly fulfilled: "Those who look to him for help will be radiant with joy" (Ps 34:5). The genuine Christian life, lived in the light and with integrity, is attractive and winsome (cf. Matt 5:16; Phil 2:15). The sad fact that this is not always the case is implied by Jesus, speaking of a body that is "filled with darkness" (11:34).

◆ L. Jesus Criticizes the Religious Leaders (11:37-54; cf. Matt 23)

37As Jesus was speaking, one of the Pharisees invited him home for a meal. So he went in and took his place at the table.* 38His host was amazed to see that he sat down to eat without first performing the hand-washing ceremony required by

Jewish custom. ³⁹Then the Lord said to him, "You Pharisees are so careful to clean the outside of the cup and the dish, but inside you are filthy—full of greed and wickedness! ⁴⁰Fools! Didn't God make the inside as well as the outside? ⁴¹So clean the inside by giving gifts to the poor, and you will be clean all over.

⁴²"What sorrow awaits you Pharisees! For you are careful to tithe even the tini-est income from your herb gardens,* but you ignore justice and the love of God. You should tithe, yes, but do not neglect the more important things.

⁴³"What sorrow awaits you Pharisees! For you love to sit in the seats of honor in the synagogues and receive respectful greetings as you walk in the market-places. ⁴⁴Yes, what sorrow awaits you! For you are like hidden graves in a field. People walk over them without knowing the corruption they are stepping on."

⁴⁵"Teacher," said an expert in religious law, "you have insulted us, too, in what you just said."

⁴⁶"Yes," said Jesus, "what sorrow also awaits you experts in religious law! For you crush people with unbearable reli-gious demands, and you never lift a finger to ease the burden. ⁴⁷What sorrow awaits you! For you build monuments for the prophets your own ancestors killed long ago. ⁴⁸But in fact, you stand as witnesses who agree with what your ancestors did. They killed the prophets, and you join in their crime by building the monuments! ⁴⁹This is what God in his wisdom said about you:* 'I will send prophets and apostles to them, but they will kill some and persecute the others.'

⁵⁰"As a result, this generation will be held responsible for the murder of all God's prophets from the creation of the world— ⁵¹from the murder of Abel to the murder of Zechariah, who was killed between the altar and the sanctuary. Yes, it will cer-tainly be charged against this generation.

⁵²"What sorrow awaits you experts in religious law! For you remove the key to knowledge from the people. You don't enter the Kingdom yourselves, and you prevent others from entering."

⁵³As Jesus was leaving, the teachers of religious law and the Pharisees became hostile and tried to provoke him with many questions. ⁵⁴They wanted to trap him into saying something they could use against him.

11:37 Or *and reclined.* 11:42 Greek *tithe the mint, the rue, and every herb.* 11:49 Greek *Therefore, the wisdom of God said.*

NOTES

11:37 *invited him home for a meal.* This is the rare word *aristaō* [TG709, ZG753] (eat a meal, dine). (Cf. 11:38; 14:12, where the cognate noun is used. For other examples, see Gen 43:25 LXX; Josephus *Antiquities* 6.362; 8.240; and esp. Luke 15:29 in Codex Bezae.) The verb is used in John 21:12, where Jesus offers breakfast to the disciples by the Sea of Gali-lee: "Now come and have some breakfast!" On Jesus' table fellowship with his contempo-raries, see Neyrey 1991:361-387 and Smith 1987.

11:39 *You Pharisees are so careful to clean the outside of the cup and the dish, but inside you are filthy.* There is a strong contrast drawn in the Gr. language in this passage between the "outward" and the "inward" dimensions of human life by the repeated use of *exōthen* [TG1855B, ZG2033] and *esōthen* [TG2081A, ZG2277] in 11:39-40. This distinction recalls the OT notion that "people judge by outward appearance, but the LORD looks at the heart" (1 Sam 16:7; cf. 1 Kgs 8:39; 1 Chr 28:9; 2 Chr 16:9; Ps 7:9; 139:2; Prov 15:11; 16:2; Jer 11:20), a point that is also reiterated in the NT (Acts 1:24; Heb 4:13; Rev 2:23).

11:40 *Fools! Didn't God make the inside as well as the outside?* This is the first of several passages in Luke where Jesus refers to people in strong language as "fools" (*aphrōn* [TG878, ZG933]). Jesus attacked the Jewish religious leaders for their rapacity and wickedness. The same word is used again in the story of the rich fool (12:20), where God castigates the self-centered farmer for his total absorption in personal gain. A different word is used to describe the two unenlightened disciples Jesus conversed with on the walk to Emmaus, where they are said to be "foolish people" (*anoētos* [TG453, ZG485], 24:25), lacking in understanding of all that the prophets wrote in the Scriptures about the sufferings of the Messiah.

11:41 *So clean the inside by giving gifts to the poor.* On almsgiving and charitable giving, see Hiebert 1975. Jesus certainly forbade ostentatious charity (Matt 6:1-4), but encouraged his followers to give to the needy generously and with spiritual motives (11:41; 12:33). The early church and the apostle Paul also carried on with the practice (Acts 4:32-35; 6:1-6; 9:36; Rom 15:25-27; 1 Cor 16:1-2; 2 Cor 8–9).

11:42 *tithe.* Tithing was the giving of a tenth of what one possessed to God. It was commanded in the Mosaic legislation (Lev 27:30; Num 18:21-28), and commended in the OT (Neh 10:37-39; 12:44; 13:10-12; Mal 3:8). Even before Moses, it was practiced, for Abraham offered a tithe to Melchizedek, "a priest of God Most High" (Gen 14:17-20; cf. Heb 5:5-10; 7:1-10). Tithing is rarely noted in the NT, and when it is, it occurs in passages that suggest the abuse of the practice, in the form of legalism or self-congratulation (18:12; Matt 23:23).

There are only three references to tithing in the Gospels, and each occurs in an unfavorable context (11:42; 18:12; Matt 23:23). The most concise treatment of the principles of Christian giving does not speak of tithing and is found in 1 Cor 16:2, where Paul teaches that giving is to be regular, personal, proportionate, and preventive or orderly (Lindsell 1965:1719). The fullest teaching on Christian giving is found in 2 Cor 8–9, where Paul describes its spirit and motivations at length but again does not speak of tithing, or giving in tenths.

COMMENTARY

As Jesus was speaking on this occasion, he was given an invitation to share a meal with a Pharisee (11:37). The very mention of such an event is significant in Luke, who highlights Jesus' table talk more than any other Gospel (e.g., 5:29-35; see the Introduction). Luke presented these occasions of sharing meals as teaching opportunities, when searching questions could be asked and Jesus could meet the lawyers and others on a face-to-face basis. These were times when dynamic teaching was possible because of the interactive nature of the communication. The discussion could be pitched at the appropriate level, and due attention could be given to the feedback of the questioner. Jesus raised the hackles of the Pharisees on this occasion because he had not observed the usual ceremonial washings. Mark's Gospel notes these detailed customs in describing the tradition of the elders (Mark 7:3-4; cf. Matt 15:1-9). This was not the only time, of course, that Jesus clashed with the Pharisees (see 7:36-50; John 7:45-52; 9:40, 41). Matthew's Gospel includes a whole chapter of accusations that Jesus made against the scribes and Pharisees (see Matthew 23, where they are rebuked as "blind guides"). The criticisms against the Pharisees that are noted in Luke are placed in a different setting than in Matthew. In Luke's account the "scribes" mentioned in Matthew's Gospel are called "experts in religious law" (11:46, 52), a more suitable term to describe these professional Jewish leaders for Gentile readers. Both Matthew and Luke note that Jesus castigated these religious and professional people as those who were failing to give the leadership expected of them. While Luke deals more briefly with these Jewish leaders, the thrust of his material is essentially the same as Matthew.

Luke, like Matthew, calls attention to the unfortunate contrast between "the outside" and "the inside," thereby underscoring Jesus' concern that there should be a true correspondence between the appearance of piety and its substantial inward reality: "Didn't God make the inside as well as the outside?" (11:40). Luke adds a positive note to the teaching of Jesus here that is not found in the parallel passage in Matthew: "So clean the inside by giving gifts to the poor, and you will be clean all over" (11:41). The radical nature of Jesus' instruction demanded an interior transformation.

Both Matthew and Luke note the denunciations connected with stewardship. The Pharisees were noted for their meticulous observance of tithing, including giving one tenth of vegetable herbs such as mint and rue (Matthew mentions mint, dill and cumin—Matt 23:23, NLT mg). However, their scrupulous attention to such matters was no substitute for basic ethical issues involving social justice and the love of God (11:42). Once again, Jesus' strong ethical concern is highlighted, as we have seen elsewhere (e.g., 4:18-21; 6:20-26; 10:25-37).

Another point of criticism noted is that of self-centeredness. Concern for the best seats in the synagogue and elaborate greetings in the marketplaces was telling evidence of this selfish tendency (11:43). Further, it was a sad but tragic fact that unsuspecting people would be apt to be contaminated by them without knowing it, just as they would be by walking over unmarked graves! They were putting folks at risk (11:44).

Only Luke's account makes reference to the feedback Jesus received from this pointed attack directed against the religious leadership of his nation: "'Teacher,' said an expert in religious law, 'you have insulted us, too, in what you just said' " (11:45). The establishment felt itself under severe scrutiny, and the experience was painful. The Jewish scribes, or lawyers, were told by Jesus that they were placing heavy burdens on their own people, and they were rebuked for their woeful failure to lift the burdens or lighten the loads they had so rigorously imposed (11:46; cf. Matt 23:4). Their inhumanity and lack of compassion were thus unmercifully exposed, and they winced at the revelation of their own character.

Lamentably, the only Jewish leaders they cared to recognize were dead ones, who would pose no threat to their position or influence (11:47; cf. Matt 23:29-31). Their actions had provided sufficient evidence that they were actually consenting to the murderous deeds of their ancestors and then hypocritically erecting memorial sepulchres to cover up their duplicity (11:47-48). It was a small wonder, then, that they should be accused of the blood of the martyrs that had been shed throughout Jewish history. The time period that spanned from Abel to Zechariah (11:51) covered the whole of their history, running from the first book of the Jewish Bible to the last (see Gen 4:8; 2 Chr 24:20-21).

Zechariah was "the son of Jehoida the high priest whose murder is recounted in 2 Chronicles 24:17-22. Since Chronicles is the last book of Hebrew Scripture in the

Masoretic text, all the martyrs of the Old Testament are included in the span from 'Abel to Zechariah.' The perversity and rebellion seen in Jewish history is thought of as reaching its climax in the treatment of Jesus and the first Christian witnesses" (Tolbert 1970:104). Jesus' hostile contemporaries were accountable for their actions and were guilty sinners in the eyes of a just God who would recompense them on the final day of judgment.

One of the most searching criticisms is left to the end, where the lawyers (called "teachers of religious law. . . Hypocrites!" in Matt 23:13) are indicted: "For you remove the key to knowledge from the people. You don't enter the Kingdom yourselves, and you prevent others from entering" (11:52; cf. Matt 23:13). Instead of showing openness and responsiveness to the teaching of Jesus, they were opposing it and obstructing those who were under their spiritual authority (cf. the parable of the evil farmers in Matthew 21:33-46, where we are told that "when the leading priests and Pharisees heard this parable, they realized he was telling the story against them," Matt 21:45). This was a damnable abuse of their leadership position, one for which they had to assume responsibility. It is not surprising that these religious leaders would retaliate against such trenchant attacks. Luke noted their attempts to get back at Jesus, counterattacking and seeking to trap him into saying something that they could use to rebut his accusations (11:53-54). They were neither receiving the light, nor letting those who looked to them for guidance see it!

◆ M. A Warning against Hypocrisy (12:1-12; cf. Matt 10:26-33)

Meanwhile, the crowds grew until thousands were milling about and stepping on each other. Jesus turned first to his disciples and warned them, "Beware of the yeast of the Pharisees—their hypocrisy. ²The time is coming when everything that is covered up will be revealed, and all that is secret will be made known to all. ³Whatever you have said in the dark will be heard in the light, and what you have whispered behind closed doors will be shouted from the housetops for all to hear!

⁴"Dear friends, don't be afraid of those who want to kill your body; they cannot do any more to you after that. ⁵But I'll tell you whom to fear. Fear God, who has the power to kill you and then throw you into hell.* Yes, he's the one to fear.

⁶"What is the price of five sparrows—two copper coins*? Yet God does not forget a single one of them. ⁷And the very hairs on your head are all numbered. So don't be afraid; you are more valuable to God than a whole flock of sparrows.

⁸"I tell you the truth, everyone who acknowledges me publicly here on earth, the Son of Man* will also acknowledge in the presence of God's angels. ⁹But anyone who denies me here on earth will be denied before God's angels. ¹⁰Anyone who speaks against the Son of Man can be forgiven, but anyone who blasphemes the Holy Spirit will not be forgiven.

¹¹"And when you are brought to trial in the synagogues and before rulers and authorities, don't worry about how to defend yourself or what to say, ¹²for the Holy Spirit will teach you at that time what needs to be said."

12:5 Greek *Gehenna.*   12:6 Greek *two assaria* [Roman coins equal to ¹⁄₁₆ of a denarius].   12:8"Son of Man" is a title Jesus used for himself.

NOTES

12:1 *Beware of the yeast of the Pharisees—their hypocrisy.* This is the first and only use of the noun for "hypocrisy" in Luke (*hupokrisis* [TG5272, ZG5694]); for other NT uses, see Matt 23:28; Mark 12:15; Gal 2:13; 1 Tim 4:2; 1 Pet 2:1. For some observations on the "hypocrites" mentioned in the Gospels, see the comments on Luke 6:37-42.

12:5 *hell.* Lit., "Gehenna," an "English transliteration of the Greek form of an Aramaic word, which is derived from the Hebrew phrase the 'Valley of [the son(s) of] Hinnom.' The name properly designates a deep valley delimiting the territories of the tribes of Benjamin and Judah" (TBD 516). This place was "the name of a valley near Jerusalem with repulsive associations. In ancient times, children were sacrificed here to the god Molech (Jer. 7:31-32), which may have prompted the conversion of the place into a desolate trash and garbage heap (2 Kgs 23:10). It was an appropriate symbol of a place of God's punishment" (Mark 9:43-48; Rev 14:7-13; see Craddock 1990:161).

he's the one to fear. In biblical thinking, to "fear" God is to render the proper respect and reverence that is due to God (Deut 6:1, 13, 24; Ps 15:4; 22:23; 33:8; 118:4; Prov 1:7; 9:10; 14:26; Eccl 12:13). The counsel of this verse "follows vv. 1-3 as a warning not to practice hypocrisy of the Pharisees out of fear or out of a felt need to impress those who have authority. It is far wiser to please God, whose authority greatly exceeds that of any mortal, than it is to please people and thereby incur God's wrath" (Evans 1990:194).

12:6 *What is the price of five sparrows—two copper coins?* The copper coin here is an *assarion* [TG787, ZG837], a Roman coin worth 1/16th of a denarius. As Bilkes (2000:915) has noted: "Sizable transactions were made in the denomination of the talent (Matt 18:24; 25:14-28) or the mina (19:13-25). The debtor of Jesus' parable owed alternatively 10,000 talents (Matt 18:24) or 500 denarii (7:41). The smaller denominations (the *chalkos, lepton, assarion,* and *quadrans*) were used in more daily affairs, for which a purse would be carried (22:36)."

12:8 *everyone who acknowledges me publicly here on earth, the Son of Man will also acknowledge.* Into this call for open confession, Luke has drawn together material (usually attributed to Q) that occurs separately in Matthew (cf. Matt 10:19-20, 26-33; 12:32). These verses contain both commands and promises and embrace both the present and future. Sometimes the confession of Christ would entail persecution. In extreme cases, open witnessing that acknowledged Jesus publicly could lead to martyrdom. On the general subject of Christian confessions or testimonies, see Neufeld 1963 and more recently, Longenecker 1999. For examples of recent Christian martyrs, see James and Marti Hefley 1979.

12:9 *anyone who denies me here on earth will be denied before God's angels.* On the role of angels, see the comments on Luke 1:11-17; see also EDNT 1.13-16.

12:10 *Anyone who speaks against the Son of Man can be forgiven.* This idea is difficult, for it seems to contradict the teaching Jesus had earlier given in sending out his disciples: "Anyone who accepts your message is also accepting me. And anyone who rejects you is rejecting me. And anyone who rejects me is rejecting God, who sent me" (10:16). Hebert has remarked, "Though he who rejects me rejects him that sent me, yet not all who seem to reject have really rejected. They may have been misinformed" (1960:32).

anyone who blasphemes the Holy Spirit will not be forgiven. Luke's version needs to be contrasted with the different setting of the saying found in Matthew and Mark, where blaspheming the Spirit is clearly tied to saying that Jesus' exorcisms were the work of the devil (Matt 12:32; Mark 3:29-30). Luke's general parallel to the exorcisms noted in Matthew and Mark is found in Luke 11:17-23. He has chosen to place the blasphemy saying in a section that contains a strong warning against hypocrisy, including the failure to acknowledge one's faith under pressure (12:1-12). Fear could immobilize Christians and keep them from openly witnessing to their faith in the Son of Man. The Lukan context suggests that believers were not to capitulate in such circumstances and attribute the work of the Holy Spirit to evil forces rather than to God. Instead, they were reminded that in such trying conditions "the Holy Spirit will teach you at that time what needs to be said" (12:11-12). This is a solemn passage as it speaks of an unforgivable sin. Lindsell's comment (1965:1499) is noteworthy: "To commit [the unpardonable] sin one must consciously, deliberately, and maliciously reject the testimony of the Spirit to the deity and saving power of the Lord Jesus. Since only the Holy Spirit can convince and convert the unsaved, a continuous and final rejection of His wooing and His witness shuts off the only possible avenue whereby the saving work of Christ is applied to the sinner in his need." Hebrews 6:4-6 and 10:26-31 give similar warnings elsewhere in the NT regarding the saving power of Jesus and the work of the Holy Spirit.

COMMENTARY

At this point in his ministry, Jesus found it necessary to give his disciples warning about the religious leaders' hypocrisy. Though they seemed to be devout, they really were not. Nothing is hidden from God; as the writer of Hebrews declares, "Nothing in all creation is hidden from God. Everything is naked and exposed before his eyes" (Heb 4:13). The future will reveal the secret things of people's hearts, and people will be called to account before an all-seeing and all-knowing God.

Jesus instructed the disciples to be aware of the insidious teaching of the Pharisees, for it was capable of spreading as silently and pervasively as yeast (12:1). Yet, the disciples were not to be afraid of those who desired to put them out of action by persecution and death. Their enemies were only able to hurt them physically, not spiritually, for their lives were ultimately in the hands of a loving Father who knew them intimately and valued them highly. The point is presented, as is often the case, in an argument from the lesser to the greater: if God is mindful of every little sparrow, how much more is he aware of the needs of his own servants, whose "very hairs" on their heads are all numbered (12:6-7). Their welfare is safe in God's providential care.

The Swiss Reformer, Ulrich Zwingli, said, "this is a world in which nothing whatsoever occurs by chance, nothing takes place which God has not foreseen and willed in his supreme goodness. It is a world in which divine knowledge of the sparrow's fall (Matt 10:29) and the number of hairs on every head (12:7) witness to a Deity for whom nothing is of too little value for God's providence to have a care of it" (cited in Farley 1988:148).

In light of such encouraging considerations, their only fear should be God alone: "Dear friends, don't be afraid of those who want to kill your body. . . . Fear God, who has the power to kill you and then throw you into hell" (12:4-5). Perhaps a passage such as this helps one to understand what was said in the sixteenth century of John Knox, the bold Scottish leader: "He feared the face of God so much that he feared not the face of any man."

It would be necessary in times of pressure and persecution to act with eternity's values in view, knowing that one's actions on earth had transcendental, heavenly consequences. Open earthly confession of Jesus, the Son of Man, would bring open, heavenly confession of the believer by Christ himself in the presence of God's angels (12:8; cf. Matt 10:32). The converse is also inescapably true: "Anyone who denies me here on earth will be denied before God's angels" (12:9; Matthew's parallel version speaks of the person being denied or repudiated "before my Father in heaven," Matt 10:33).

In the book of Acts, the case of the dying Stephen stands as a striking instance of this promise being fulfilled in the life of a faithful believer. The devout Stephen faithfully confessed his Lord in a bold witness before his peers on earth and was subsequently martyred. As he was dying, he saw the heavens opened and the Son of Man standing in the place of honor at God's right hand (Acts 7:56). This inspiring example would bring encouragement to those who might be called to face similar situations; they were not to fret about the consequences when they were brought to trial in hostile courts, whether Jewish or Gentile (12:11). In such threatening times, divine aid was promised as forthcoming: "The Holy Spirit will teach you at that time what needs to be said" (12:12).

The importance of the Holy Spirit is repeatedly stressed in both Luke's Gospel and the book of Acts. Jesus' whole ministry was seen as "filled with the Spirit's power" (4:14; see also 4:1). He preached in the power of the Holy Spirit (4:18-21, quoting Isa 61:1-2). The Spirit was promised by Jesus as a wonderful gift to those who made this matter an earnest request (11:13), and the disciples were instructed to wait in Jerusalem "until the Holy Spirit comes and fills you with power from heaven" (24:49).

Similarly, in Acts, the Spirit's role is stressed well over fifty times. Again, the disciples were told to remain in the holy city and wait for the Spirit (Acts 1:4), and the Spirit came in power, as promised, at Pentecost (2:1-4). It was through the Spirit that "signs and wonders" were carried out in Jesus' name by the apostles and their associates (4:29-31; 8:13; 14:3). The Holy Spirit is active throughout the book of Acts in guiding the church, empowering its witness, and furthering the ever-advancing mission of the church in the world (4:8; 6:3-5; 7:55; 8:29; 9:17; 11:24; 16:6-7; 20:28).

◆   **N. Parable of the Rich Fool (12:13-21)**

¹³Then someone called from the crowd, "Teacher, please tell my brother to divide our father's estate with me."

¹⁴Jesus replied, "Friend, who made me a judge over you to decide such things as that?" ¹⁵Then he said, "Beware! Guard against every kind of greed. Life is not measured by how much you own."

¹⁶Then he told them a story: "A rich man had a fertile farm that produced fine crops. ¹⁷He said to himself, 'What should I do? I don't have room for all my crops.' ¹⁸Then he said, 'I know! I'll tear down my barns and build bigger ones. Then I'll have room enough to store all my wheat and other goods. ¹⁹And I'll sit back and say to myself, "My friend, you have enough stored away for years to come. Now take it easy! Eat, drink, and be merry!"'

²⁰"But God said to him, 'You fool! You will die this very night. Then who will get everything you worked for?'

²¹"Yes, a person is a fool to store up earthly wealth but not have a rich relationship with God."

NOTES
12:15 *Beware! Guard against every kind of greed. Life is not measured by how much*
you own. Luke's Gospel vividly depicts the concern of Jesus for all people on the periphery
of society—the poor, the maimed, the lame, the blind, the ill, and those who cannot repay
any kindness or help they have received (see 14:13, 21). Luke's first beatitude, for example,
pronounces a blessing on the "poor," without qualifying it by an additional phrase (6:20;
cf. Matt 5:3). In addition, Luke presents "a number of stories that contrast people who are
rich and powerful with others who are poor or otherwise outside the mainstream of society's benefits. Wealth that is simply amassed as a hedge against the future or a source of
security is condemned (6:24-26; 12:13-21; 16:1-13, 19-31). 'Alms-giving' as the redistribu-
tion of wealth and not a charitable dole is presented as an important expression of one's
discipleship or following of Jesus" (Ringe 1995:9).

12:21 *Yes, a person is a fool to store up earthly wealth but not have a rich relationship*
with God. Note how careful Luke is to expose "the position of the man who hoards for
himself but fails to become rich where God is concerned" (Schonfield 1958:168). His
warning is blunt: "Beware! Guard against every kind of greed" (12:15).

COMMENTARY
In this passage, the use and abuse of wealth are clearly highlighted. Luke, like his
Lord, was keenly aware of the dangers of selfishness and covetousness. He presented this story from the teaching of Jesus to indicate the utter folly of the rapacious entrepreneur's course of action. The moral that Jesus pointed to is quite plain,
a moral that is as relevant in the twenty-first century as it was in the first: "A person
is a fool to store up earthly wealth but not have a rich relationship with God"
(12:21). The evangelist had just underscored this point in Jesus' encounter with the
expert in religious law (10:25-28), and here again Luke reiterates its importance.

Then, as now, the reality of personal greed was often present as a source of contention and dispute in the settlement of family estates. Jesus was asked to mediate
in a dispute where the disposition of a deceased father's assets was in question.
Moses had intervened centuries before when he saw a case of injustice and had
landed himself in a lot of trouble, including the charge of murder that forced him
into exile (Exod 2:11-15). Possibly, Jesus was thinking of this or of a similar incident of rapacity when he replied, "Friend, who made me a judge over you to decide
such things as that?" (12:14). It is always risky to interpose oneself, and, in any case,
the selfish desire for acquiring more wealth is always an ever-present danger to be
zealously guarded against (12:15). Real life is not to be measured by one's material
possessions! (Note also the parable of the rich man and Lazarus, Luke 16:19-31.)

◆ O. Teaching about Money and Possessions (12:22-34)

²²Then, turning to his disciples, Jesus
said, "That is why I tell you not to worry
about everyday life—whether you have
enough food to eat or enough clothes to
wear. ²³For life is more than food, and
your body more than clothing. ²⁴Look at
the ravens. They don't plant or harvest or
store food in barns, for God feeds them.
And you are far more valuable to him
than any birds! ²⁵Can all your worries add
a single moment to your life? ²⁶And if
worry can't accomplish a little thing like

that, what's the use of worrying over bigger things?

[27]"Look at the lilies and how they grow. They don't work or make their clothing, yet Solomon in all his glory was not dressed as beautifully as they are. [28]And if God cares so wonderfully for flowers that are here today and thrown into the fire tomorrow, he will certainly care for you. Why do you have so little faith?

[29]"And don't be concerned about what to eat and what to drink. Don't worry about such things. [30]These things dominate the thoughts of unbelievers all over the world, but your Father already knows your needs. [31]Seek the Kingdom of God above all else, and he will give you everything you need.

[32]"So don't be afraid, little flock. For it gives your Father great happiness to give you the Kingdom.

[33]"Sell your possessions and give to those in need. This will store up treasure for you in heaven! And the purses of heaven never get old or develop holes. Your treasure will be safe; no thief can steal it and no moth can destroy it. [34]Wherever your treasure is, there the desires of your heart will also be.

NOTES

12:28 *Why do you have so little faith?* All four Gospels stress the problem of inadequate faith. Matthew was fond of using the word *oligopistoi* [TG3640/A, ZG3899] ("people of little faith"; see Matt 6:30; 8:26; 14:31; 16:8) to rebuke lack of faith on the part of the disciples. Mark makes strong use of unbelief as a foil to show the great faith and character of Jesus (see Thompson 1989). All three evangelists note the disciples' lack of faith in the stilling of the storm incident (8:25; Matt 8:27; Mark 4:41), and all mention the lack of faith of people who are held accountable for their stubbornness and perversity (9:41; Matt 17:17; Mark 9:19).

12:33 *Sell your possessions and give to those in need.* Wealth and poverty are prominent themes in the synoptic Gospels, but not in John's Gospel. While Mark has some material on the subject (e.g., Mark 12:41-44), the "vast majority of the teaching is found in Q material, blocks of which occur in Matthew 6 and Luke 6, 12, and 16. Of the two Gospels, Luke has both more material than Matthew and a stronger form of the material which both include. For example, Luke includes woes along with his Beatitudes (6:20-26), which sharpen the teaching by explicitly stating the obverse. Therefore, it can be said fairly that Luke has a special interest in the topic, although the same general attitude is shared by Matthew and perhaps also by Mark. The three Evangelists give a consistent picture of Jesus' attitude toward wealth and poverty" (DJG 705). Note also Kim (1998), who attempts to relate the ideas of wealth and poverty with the theme of discipleship in Luke–Acts, stressing the importance in Luke's theology of Christians acting as stewards in the use of their wealth and practicing almsgiving to the poor both inside and outside the Christian community.

COMMENTARY

Jesus knew that material things often occupy the thoughts of most people, much of the time. Luke had already drawn attention to this tendency to absorption in material issues in the parable of the sower (8:11-15; cf. Matt 13:18-23; Mark 4:13-20). In the interpretation of that parable, disciples are warned that it is possible for the divine word to be "crowded out" or "choked" by the cares and riches and pleasures of this life (8:14b). The result of this stifling is the sad failure to achieve their expected potential: "And so they never grow into maturity" (8:14c). The exercise of patience was required to bring forth this productive, excellent fruit from the good soil: "The seeds that fell on the good soil represent honest, good-hearted people who hear God's word, cling to it, and patiently produce a huge harvest" (8:15).

Here, we have further teaching and a pertinent reminder that life consists of far more than food and clothing (12:23). Admittedly, these items are always needed by people, especially by those who are barely making ends meet in an economy where the rich are getting richer and the poor are being badly oppressed and exploited. But Jesus taught his followers not to worry about everyday life.

An illustration from the natural world was valuable and instructive. Jesus invited his disciples to consider the "raven," or common crow (in the NT, the Gr. word *korax* [TG2876, ZG3165] is used only in Luke 12:24). Once again, he was speaking in a familiar pattern, arguing from the lesser to the greater, one of his favorite ways of making a teaching point. Common observation taught the disciples that God, their Creator, provided for the birds. Although the birds failed to plant seed or harvest crops or store up provisions in barns for their future requirements, God was looking after their real needs and providing for them.

If God is truly looking after the material needs of the birds, then how much more would he care for the genuine needs of those who are far more valuable to him— those who are in a relationship with his Son! Worrying cannot contribute anything to one's well-being. Obviously, worrying cannot increase one's life span. Recent studies by psychologists reinforce Jesus' teaching on the counter-productive effects of worry on longevity.

The Master reinforced his teaching by once again resorting to analogies from the natural world with which his disciples were familiar. They knew that "lilies" (*krinon* [TG2918, ZG3211], the attractive, wild flowers growing in profusion in Galilee), like the birds just mentioned, made no effort to "work or make their clothing" (12:27), and yet, in actual fact, they far outstripped Solomon in all the splendor of his dazzling royal court. The paucity of faith exercised by the disciples was plainly at variance with the beneficent character of the God they served. The flowers that covered the shores of the Sea of Galilee were transient (cf. Isa 40:6), yet they were bountifully bedecked in loveliness by their Creator. Once more, we have an illustration of the argument from the lesser to the greater: "If God cares so wonderfully for flowers . . . , he will certainly care for you" (12:28).

In similar fashion, Jesus told his disciples not to worry about matters of food and drink. While these things dominate the thoughts of most people, they must remain secondary for Christian disciples, whose implicit trust is in a loving heavenly Father, one already aware of their needs and actively working to provide for them. In the words of the hymn, those who trust God fully find him fully true. The promise was clear and unequivocal: he will give people all they need from day to day if they make the Kingdom of God their primary concern (12:31).

This teaching is also plainly announced in the Sermon on the Mount in Matthew's Gospel (Matt 6:33). It is worth noting that the apostle Paul taught the same thing about living without worry: "Don't worry about anything; instead, pray about everything. Tell God what you need, and thank him for all he has done" (Phil 4:6). It appears that the early church took the instructions Jesus had given them about worry-free living with great seriousness.

The Master reassured his followers by reminding them that they were a "little flock," tenderly under the loving care of the great Shepherd (a point spelled out with great clarity in John 10:1-18; cf. Heb 13:20). The shepherd image evokes a sense of safety and confidence that the benevolent Father would take care of them. In fact, they were to take comfort in the fact that "it gives your Father great happiness to give you the Kingdom" (12:32). The promised blessings of the Reign of God were a gift from their heavenly Father. Later on, Luke will draw attention to the demands that the Kingdom of God will make of those who accept the Father's gracious gift (e.g. 14:25-33). The gospel involved both gift and demand, and Luke gives a balanced presentation of both features in his account of Jesus' teaching.

Luke highlighted the open-handed generosity taught by Jesus. In a world filled with real need, it was incumbent upon those who would follow the "man from Nazareth" to reach out in compassion and minister to those in distress (12:33-34). Instead of just being concerned to build up a store of treasure for oneself (as in the parable of the rich fool, 12:13-21), there was to be a willingness to part with possessions in order to meet the pressing needs of others, a point stressed by Jesus and buttressed by wonderful promises of blessing in the good time coming (Matt 19:29). In the stories of Acts, we see striking examples of people like Barnabas, the generous-hearted man from Cyprus who willingly shared his possessions for the sake of needy members of the Jerusalem church (Acts 4:34-37). By contrast, there were also people like Ananias and Sapphira who fell into the trap of duplicity; they wanted to appear to be generous, and so they deceptively inflated their account of what they had given. Their sad hypocrisy was revealed and exposed, with sobering results (Acts 5:1-11). By contrast, genuine concern on the part of disciples to meet the down-to-earth needs of people in the present life is to be viewed in the light of eternity, for "the purses of heaven never get old or develop holes" (12:33; cf. 6:38) Jesus spoke the revealing and exposing truth: "Wherever your treasure is, there the desires of your heart will also be" (12:34). If one's heart is on the eternal treasures, they will be more giving during their life on earth.

◆   P. Be Ready for the Lord's Coming (12:35-48; cf. Matt 24:43-51)

³⁵"Be dressed for service and keep your lamps burning, ³⁶as though you were waiting for your master to return from the wedding feast. Then you will be ready to open the door and let him in the moment he arrives and knocks. ³⁷The servants who are ready and waiting for his return will be rewarded. I tell you the truth, he himself will seat them, put on an apron, and serve them as they sit and eat! ³⁸He may come in the middle of the night or just before dawn.* But whenever he comes, he will reward the servants who are ready.

³⁹"Understand this: If a homeowner knew exactly when a burglar was coming, he would not permit his house to be broken into. ⁴⁰You also must be ready all the time, for the Son of Man will come when least expected."

⁴¹Peter asked, "Lord, is that illustration just for us or for everyone?"

⁴²And the Lord replied, "A faithful, sensible servant is one to whom the master

can give the responsibility of managing his other household servants and feeding them. ⁴³If the master returns and finds that the servant has done a good job, there will be a reward. ⁴⁴I tell you the truth, the master will put that servant in charge of all he owns. ⁴⁵But what if the servant thinks, 'My master won't be back for a while,' and he begins beating the other servants, partying, and getting drunk? ⁴⁶The master will return unannounced and unexpected, and he will cut the servant in pieces and banish him with the unfaithful.

⁴⁷"And a servant who knows what the master wants, but isn't prepared and doesn't carry out those instructions, will be severely punished. ⁴⁸But someone who does not know, and then does something wrong, will be punished only lightly. When someone has been given much, much will be required in return; and when someone has been entrusted with much, even more will be required.

12:38 Greek *in the second or third watch.*

NOTES

12:36 *Then you will be ready to open the door and let him in the moment he arrives and knocks.* Jesus encouraged believers to be ready for his return at any time but to act responsibly and faithfully in the present, knowing that the best preparation for the final day is in conscientious attention to tasks at hand (12:42-43).

12:46 *cut . . . in pieces.* This Gr. word (*dichotomeō* [ᵀᴳ1371, ᶻᴳ1497]) is a strong, graphic verb that connotes severe punishment. (It is also used in Matt 24:51 as part of the Olivet Discourse, Matt 24:1–25:46).

COMMENTARY

The service offered by disciples was to be governed by the motto that has become associated in the last hundred years with the Boy Scouts: "Be prepared" (12:35). The biblical image used to describe this is that of a man getting ready to go on a journey and, therefore, gathering up his long, flowing robes so as to prepare for vigorous action (cf. the similar figure of speech in 1 Pet 1:13). Christian service is to be given in the context of uncertainty about the date or time of the second coming of Christ: "He may come in the middle of the night or just before dawn" (12:38; lit., "in the second or third watch"; cf. Matt 24:36; Mark 13:32). This lack of knowledge on the part of the disciples would require constant alertness and readiness, and those suitably perceptive and prepared would be treated to special favor or "reward" on the part of the Master when he returned (12:38; cf. 1 Sam 2:30). Thus eschatology (the study of last things) is closely related to ethics (Christian conduct). Jesus stressed the necessary connection between them. Thinking about the future was not a matter of idle speculation, but a common sense issue of making the proper preparations so as not to be ashamed before the Lord at his coming (cf. 1 John 2:28). Instead of people regarding the lack of clarity of the divine timetable as a problem, they should see the Lord's imminent coming as an incentive to constant faithfulness. Every true servant of God should live and work in the consciousness that he or she is personally accountable for living responsibly, just as one would do who knew exactly when a burglar was to make his entrance: "You must be ready all the time, for the Son of Man will come when least expected" (12:40; cf. 1 Thess 5:2-4; 2 Pet 3:10).

To be forewarned is to be forearmed. The whole point of the instruction is quite practical and is later repeated in Jesus' teaching devoted to eschatology: "Don't let that day catch you unaware, like a trap . . . Keep alert at all times" (21:34-36; cf. Mark 13:35-37). The end will be sudden and unexpected; it will affect everyone living on the earth (21:35). Just as any trustworthy household steward will duly manage the household and care for its needs, so the faithful Christian servant will act appropriately and diligently at all times (12:42). For such a person, the Master's return will offer no embarrassment, and his conscientious service will certainly be duly recognized (12:43). The reward for such painstaking service will be increased responsibility, for "the master will put that servant in charge of all he owns" (12:44). By contrast, carelessness or negligence, expressed by such irresponsible acts as drunkenness, partying, and exercising power unjustly in oppressing the other servants will be severely punished and lead to the banishment of the servant with the unfaithful (12:45-47). Stubborn disobedience will not go unchallenged, though mitigating circumstances will allow for clemency in the case of ignorance; people who are not aware that they are doing wrong will be punished only lightly (12:48a). Jesus enunciated a clear and unmistakable principle that is of permanent value for all Christian leadership, stewardship, and service: "When someone has been given much, much will be required in return; and when someone has been entrusted with much, even more will be required" (12:48b). The apostle Paul gives a good summary of the accountability Jesus demanded: "We must all stand before Christ to be judged. We will each receive whatever we deserve for the good or evil we have done in this earthly body" (2 Cor 5:10).

◆   ## Q. Jesus Causes Division (12:49-59; cf. Matt 10:34-36)

⁴⁹"I have come to set the world on fire, and I wish it were already burning! ⁵⁰I have a terrible baptism of suffering ahead of me, and I am under a heavy burden until it is accomplished. ⁵¹Do you think I have come to bring peace to the earth? No, I have come to divide people against each other! ⁵²From now on families will be split apart, three in favor of me, and two against—or two in favor and three against.

⁵³'Father will be divided against son
    and son against father;
mother against daughter
    and daughter against mother;
and mother-in-law against daughter-
    in-law
    and daughter-in-law against
        mother-in-law.'*"

⁵⁴Then Jesus turned to the crowd and said, "When you see clouds beginning to form in the west, you say, 'Here comes a shower.' And you are right. ⁵⁵When the south wind blows, you say, 'Today will be a scorcher.' And it is. ⁵⁶You fools! You know how to interpret the weather signs of the earth and sky, but you don't know how to interpret the present times.

⁵⁷"Why can't you decide for yourselves what is right? ⁵⁸When you are on the way to court with your accuser, try to settle the matter before you get there. Otherwise, your accuser may drag you before the judge, who will hand you over to an officer, who will throw you into prison. ⁵⁹And if that happens, you won't be free again until you have paid the very last penny.*"

12:53 Mic 7:6.   12:59 Greek *last lepton* [the smallest Jewish coin].

NOTES

12:51 *I have come to divide people.* The Gr. word *diamerismos* [TG1267, ZG1375] (division) is found only here in the NT. Matthew has "sword" in the parallel passage. Ellis thinks the word "division" serves "as a clarification of the original [figurative] word, 'sword' (Matt 10:34)" (1981:183). An interesting attempt to write a popular portrait of Jesus built around this passage, which presents Christ as "the great divider," is France 1975. John's Gospel also stresses the division that Jesus produced (John 7:43; 9:16; 10:19-21; cf. 1:11-12; 3:18-21).

12:52 *From now on families will be split apart, three in favor of me, and two against— or two in favor and three against.* In Matthew, the context is Jesus' instructions in sending out the twelve apostles, where they are warned of the hostility they will face as his followers (Matt 10:22); sadly, sometimes this would reach into their own family circle: "Your enemies will be right in your own household" (Matt 10:36). They were encouraged to remain faithful and persevere in their discipleship, confident in the assurance that "everyone who endures to the end will be saved" (Matt 10:22). In Luke, the fact that the gospel message will divide families is similarly acknowledged, and true disciples are called to face up to the critical nature of the times in which they live and to act appropriately.

12:56 *You fools!* Lit., "hypocrites." This is one of the three times Luke used the word "hypocrite" (*hupokritēs* [TG5273, ZG5695]) to castigate a false approach to the issues of life, the other two being 6:42 and 13:15. See the notes on these passages and on 6:37.

COMMENTARY

The incendiary nature of Jesus' ministry was a fact to be reckoned with. It was to involve challenges to the status quo that had revolutionary implications for the Jewish people and for the launching of the Christian church (12:49). The igniting of this divine fire upon the earth was to be accomplished by immense suffering on the part of Jesus, and he forthrightly acknowledged that he was "under a heavy burden until it [was] accomplished" (12:50). Luke had already indicated the determination with which Jesus set out on his journey to Jerusalem (9:51). The signs of opposition were staring him in the face.

Luke, like the other Gospel writers, drew attention to this stubborn resistance. Indeed, he had already presented Jesus as challenging those among the Jewish nation who loved to have "the seats of honor in the synagogues and receive respectful greetings" in public (11:43; cf. Matt 23:6-7; Mark 12:38-39). Hostility from such leaders was not unexpected and was to be carefully taken into account: "What blessings await you when people hate you and exclude you and mock you and curse you as evil because you follow the Son of Man" (6:22). The ironic thing about this antagonism to Jesus was the tragic dimension of it, in that it would even set people within a family circle in direct opposition to one another and cause bitter strife and contention: "Father will be divided against son and son against father; mother against daughter and daughter against mother; and mother-in-law against daughter-in-law and daughter-in-law against mother-in law" (12:53; cf. Mic 7:6; Matt 10:21-22). Different members in the same family would treat Jesus differently; some would become devoted Christian disciples and some would remain unconvinced, even standing against the claims advanced for Jesus and promoted by his followers. The lines would become clearly and painfully drawn.

The ministry of Jesus produced a crisis in the nation of Israel. John's Gospel sounded the same note, for there, too, Jesus posed a crisis for the world: "The time for judging this world has come" (John 12:31). "According to these sayings, God is so acting toward the world in Jesus of Nazareth that a crisis is created, that is to say, Jesus is 'making a difference,' even within families [cf. Matt 10:34-37]. Historically, this has been proven true, and it will be finally true in the eschaton" (Craddock 1990:166).

The contemporaries of Jesus were able to read the signs of impending changes in the weather patterns and act accordingly, but they were not showing the same sagacity in spiritual matters. Jesus criticized their failure in perception: "You fools [the Greek text reads, "You hypocrites"]! You know how to interpret the weather signs of the earth and sky, but you don't know how to interpret the present times" (12:56). This dullness was to have decisive consequences, both for the Jewish people and for the subsequent world mission of the church. Note, for instance, the later comment in Acts given to the Jewish leaders who oppose Barnabas and Paul in Pisidian Antioch: "It was necessary that we first preach the word of God to you Jews. But since you have rejected it and judged yourselves unworthy of eternal life, we will offer it to the Gentiles" (Acts 13:46). The plan and purpose of God would not be ultimately frustrated by human opposition.

The teaching in the final paragraph of Luke 12 is found in a different context in Matthew's Gospel, where it appears in the Sermon on the Mount (Matt 5:25-26 parallels Luke 12:57-59). Real choices would have to be made and wise decisions arrived at if one were dealing with an accuser who was intent on securing a jail sentence for his enemy or opponent. When the courts were in operation, an accuser could take a person before the magistrate, and if a conviction was obtained, the judge could hand a person over to the police officer and incarceration would follow. Rather than landing a full term in prison, it would be expedient to come to agreement with one's legal opponent in an out-of-court settlement and avoid all of these negative consequences. Luke saw the relevance of placing this paragraph in close proximity to verse 53, where hostility to the gospel message was clearly in evidence, even in the family circle.

◆   ## R. A Call to Repentance (13:1-5)

About this time Jesus was informed that Pilate had murdered some people from Galilee as they were offering sacrifices at the Temple. ²"Do you think those Galileans were worse sinners than all the other people from Galilee?" Jesus asked. "Is that why they suffered? ³Not at all! And you will perish, too, unless you repent of your sins and turn to God. ⁴And what about the eighteen people who died when the tower in Siloam fell on them? Were they the worst sinners in Jerusalem? ⁵No, and I tell you again that unless you repent, you will perish, too."

NOTES

13:1 *Pilate had murdered some people from Galilee as they were offering sacrifices at the Temple.* Bock (1996:1205) draws attention to five incidents noted by the Jewish historian Josephus that have been variously proposed for Pilate's attack on the Galileans mentioned here: (1) Some Jews marched to Caesarea to protest the display of effigies of Roman rulers

(*War* 2.169-174; *Antiquities* 18.55-59), but this incident was too late in time. (2) Some Jews were massacred in the building of an aqueduct in Jerusalem (*War* 2.175-77; *Antiquities* 18:60-62). This event was not in the Temple, and it concerns Judeans, not Galileans. (3) Samaritans were attacked on Mount Gerizim in AD 36 (*Antiquities* 18.85-87). The date is too late, and the place and victims do not fit the historical situation described by the text. (4) Archelaus slaughtered 3000 Jews in 4 BC, but the date is too early and the ruler is a different person than Pilate. (5) The murder of 6000 Jews was carried out by Alexander Janneus (*Antiquities* 13.372), but this event seems much too early (1st century BC) to fit, and, again, the ruler is a different person.

While none of these incidents seem to fit the historical situation given by Luke here, they all indicate the type of violence that frequently broke out in those turbulent times (Fitzmyer 1985:1005-1007; Marshall 1978:553). This particular incident, unrecorded by Josephus, presented Jesus with an ideal opportunity to comment on the pressing need for his hearers to clean up their acts in genuine turning to God in the light of disturbing recent events. As Talbert has astutely observed, Jesus is dealing with two forms of tragedy here: tragedy due to human causes (the massacre), and tragedy due to a natural cause (the collapse of the tower). "Tragedy, says Jesus, is not the measure of one's sinfulness and one's need to repent. Those whose lives are tranquil likewise need to repent" (1989:145).

13:3 repent. Repentance (*metanoia* [TG3341, ZG3567]) is a vital theme both in Luke's Gospel and in Acts (e.g., 16:30; Acts 5:31; 8:22; 20:21; cf. Rom 2:4; 2 Tim 2:25). John the Baptist insisted on it (3:3, 8), as did Jesus (5:32), and it is a basic component of the apostolic message that was to be communicated to the world (24:47). People were strongly urged by Jesus to repent (13:3, 5), and repentance was connected with producing heavenly joy (15:7, 10). The book of Acts continues to stress repentance as a divine requirement for both Jews (Acts 2:38; 3:19; 5:31) and Gentiles (Acts 17:30; 20:21; 26:20). For more on repentance, see NIDNTT 1.353-362; EDNT 2.415-419.

COMMENTARY

Luke connects the events of 13:1-5 with the preceding teaching chronologically, using the phrase, "About this time" (13:1). This is a reminder of the troubled times in which Jesus and his disciples lived. Pilate had been guilty of slaying some Galileans as they were sacrificing at the Temple in Jerusalem (13:1). However, this did not mean that these Galileans were more morally culpable than other people from Galilee. Rather, it was an event that should have caused people to pause and think of their own sin and to turn in repentance to God, humbly seeking his forgiveness and cleansing. Jesus took such recent events as the bloody Galilean episode and the collapse of the Tower of Siloam in Jerusalem as relevant examples that were on the minds of his contemporaries and used them as a springboard for his summons to an appropriate response: "No, these folk were *not* worse sinners than others around them, and I tell you again that unless you repent, you will perish, too" (13:5, paraphrased). As Wright has pointed out: "Jesus' warnings about imminent judgment were intended to be taken as denoting socio-political events, *seen as the climactic moment in Israel's history*, and in consequence, as constituting a summons to *national* repentance" (2002:49).

The slowness of God to execute his judgment was, in fact, an evidence of divine grace, giving people time to rethink their actions and turn back in contrition to God. The same point is later made clearly in 2 Peter, where the reader is reminded that the Lord's delay is prompted by his patience: "He does not want anyone to be destroyed, but wants everyone to repent" (2 Pet 3:9).

◆   S. Illustration of the Barren Fig Tree (13:6-9)

⁶Then Jesus told this story: "A man planted a fig tree in his garden and came again and again to see if there was any fruit on it, but he was always disappointed. ⁷Finally, he said to his gardener, 'I've waited three years, and there hasn't been a single fig! Cut it down. It's just taking up space in the garden.'

⁸"The gardener answered, 'Sir, give it one more chance. Leave it another year, and I'll give it special attention and plenty of fertilizer. ⁹If we get figs next year, fine. If not, then you can cut it down.' "

NOTES

13:6 *story.* Lit., "parable." The parables of Jesus were the principal means he used to communicate his message of the in-breaking Kingdom of God. They were ideally suited for teaching mixed audiences that included disciples, less committed followers, interested crowds and hard-core opponents, all of whom were attracted to this well-known healer and compelling storyteller. For more on the parables of Jesus, see Blomberg 1990; Boucher 1977; Crossan 1973; Dodd 1961; McArthur and Johnson 1990; DJG 591-600.

A man planted a fig tree in his garden. The fig tree is a prominent image in the Bible. It is the first fruit tree mentioned in Scripture (Gen 3:7), and it obviously had a significant role in the economy of Palestine throughout biblical times. It was frequently used metaphorically in the OT as a symbol of prosperity (Isa 36:16; Mic 4:4; Zech 3:10). In the NT, the principal use of the fig tree is metaphorical (6:44; Matt 7:16; Jas 3:12). The most problematic passages about fig trees in the synoptic Gospels refer to Jesus' cursing of the barren fig tree (Matt 21:18-22; Mark 11:12-14, 20-25), but they are not directly parallel to this passage in Luke.

COMMENTARY

Jesus' call to repentance was followed by an illustration drawn from agriculture. People of the Mediterranean world during the first century AD would be familiar with fig trees, for they were common and useful. Any tree that was inspected repeatedly and proved to be perpetually unproductive would be questioned as to its continuing usefulness. So the man in the example naturally raised the question of the tree's utility: "Cut it down. It's just taking up space in the garden" (13:7) There might be a hint here that the mission to the Jews, like the fig tree, was disappointing in its yield, and something else like the Gentile mission may well prove to be more productive. The point is made that one more chance must be given, and only then would it be permissible for the barren fig tree to be replaced. Divine patience is here suggested, in that the gardener was reluctant to concede that the fig tree would remain unproductive (13:8).

◆   T. Jesus Heals on the Sabbath (13:10-17)

¹⁰One Sabbath day as Jesus was teaching in a synagogue, ¹¹he saw a woman who had been crippled by an evil spirit. She had been bent double for eighteen years and was unable to stand up straight. ¹²When Jesus saw her, he called her over and said, "Dear woman, you are healed of your sickness!" ¹³Then he touched her,

and instantly she could stand straight. How she praised God! ¹⁴But the leader in charge of the synagogue was indignant that Jesus had healed her on the Sabbath day. "There are six days of the week for working," he said to the crowd. "Come on those days to be healed, not on the Sabbath."

¹⁵But the Lord replied, "You hypocrites! Each of you works on the Sabbath day! Don't you untie your ox or your donkey from its stall on the Sabbath and lead it out for water? ¹⁶This dear woman, a daughter of Abraham, has been held in bondage by Satan for eighteen years. Isn't it right that she be released, even on the Sabbath?"

¹⁷This shamed his enemies, but all the people rejoiced at the wonderful things he did.

NOTES

13:10 *One Sabbath day.* Controversies over the observance of the Sabbath were frequent, and all the Gospels note them (6:6-11; Matt 12:1-14; Mark 2:23-27; 3:1-6; John 5:1-10). For a discussion of the issues involved in these controversies between Jesus and his opponents, see Bacchiocchi 1977; Banks 1975:113-131; Carson 1982; Riesenfeld 1970:111-137; Evans and Porter 2000:1031-1035.

13:13 *How she praised God!* Theissen (1983:69-72), in his study of the synoptic Gospels and Acts, notes that the giving of glory to God is a typical conclusion to a miracle story, particularly in Luke–Acts (8:47; 9:43; 13:13, 17; 18:43; 23:47; Acts 3:9). This type of conclusion usually consists of two standard reactions: namely, fear (2:9; 7:16; 8:35; cf. Matt 17:6; 27:54; Mark 4:41) and amazement (4:36; cf. Matt 8:27; Mark 1:27; 5:42; 6:51).

13:16 *This dear woman . . . has been held in bondage by Satan.* Coogan's incisive remark is worth citing: "Jesus relates the physical disorder of the woman to the work of Satan (cf. 11:14). Such afflictions conflict with God's purpose of salvation in his covenant with Abraham and are the concern of Jesus' ministry (4:18)" (2001:124).

COMMENTARY

This incident concerns a woman healed on the Sabbath. As in other cases, Jesus was roundly criticized for violating the traditional taboos associated with that sacred day (13:14; cf. Mark 2:23-28, 3:1-6). This story, found only in Luke, has several features that are notable: First, the woman had suffered from a horrible deformity, having been hunched over for eighteen years (13:11, 16). Jesus attributed her condition to satanic oppression, and his intervention was seen as an act of delivering a "daughter of Abraham" from a "bond" (13:16; cf. the deliverance of Zacchaeus, who is called a "son of Abraham" in 19:9). Second, Luke noted the tender intervention of Jesus, who touched her and restored her "instantly" to an upright condition (13:12-13a). Third, as is typical in Luke, he noted the response of praise and thanksgiving offered to God (13:13b; cf. 2:28, 38; 17:15; 24:53; Acts 2:47; 3:8-9; 4:21). Fourth, the fact that the incident was located in a synagogue is significant, showing the hostility Jesus experienced from that quarter. By contrast, the deliverance offered on that occasion produced a joyful response on the part of the common people, who rejoiced at the "wonderful things" (*endoxa* [^{TG}1741/A, ^{ZG}1902]) he was doing (13:17). Fifth, this healing of a woman on the Sabbath is paralleled by the healing of a man on the Sabbath in the next chapter (cf. 14:1-6).

A conflict was brewing between the leaders, who quibbled over Jesus' ministry, and those who were impressed by his mighty acts of healing. Jesus' retort to his critics on this occasion was to accuse them of blatant hypocrisy. They were quite prepared to rescue an animal from thirst on the Sabbath, making sure that their ox or donkey was released from confinement and allowed to drink the water the animal required (13:15). If this action were permissible to meet the physical needs of an animal, how much more was it legitimate to free "this dear woman" from a lengthy, satanic bondage (13:16). This bold answer of Jesus rightly "shamed his enemies," whose brazen inconsistency and heartless dehumanization of the woman were exposed.

◆   ## U. Parables of the Mustard Seed and the Yeast (13:18-21; cf. Matt 13:31-33; Mark 4:30-32)

[18]Then Jesus said, "What is the Kingdom of God like? How can I illustrate it? [19]It is like a tiny mustard seed that a man planted in a garden; it grows and becomes a tree, and the birds make nests in its branches."

[20]He also asked, "What else is the Kingdom of God like? [21]It is like the yeast a woman used in making bread. Even though she put only a little yeast in three measures of flour, it permeated every part of the dough."

NOTES

13:19 *mustard.* *sinapeōs* [TG4615, ZG4983]. "The word appears only in the sayings of Jesus, in his parable of the mustard seed (13:19; Matt 13:31; Mark 4:31) and in his simile concerning faith (17:6; Matt 17:20). In the parable the emphasis is upon the growth of the kingdom (or the spread of the gospel?) from small beginnings to the large, world-embracing events of the future, similar to the tiny mustard seed which grows so rapidly into a large plant. In the other saying the power of faith is likened to the commonly observed possibilities intrinsic within the tiny mustard seed" (IDB 3.476).

grows and becomes a tree. "The mustard seed (*sinapis nigra*) is black and grows predominantly in the southern and eastern areas of Mediterranean countries, Mesopotamia and Afghanistan. It is the smallest seed of the three or four varieties of mustard plants. The mustard plant could attain a height of ten or twelve feet, thus justifying the term 'tree'" (Kistemaker 1980:46).

a tree. This is the reading of 𝔓75 ℵ B L 070. Other mss (𝔓45 A W 038 044 f³ 33 𝔐) read *dendron mega* [TG3173, ZG3489], "a great tree." On this point, Metzger writes: "Although copyists may have deleted *mega* to harmonize Luke with the prevailing text of Matthew (Matt 13:32), it is much more probable that, in the interests of heightening the contrast between a mustard seed and a tree, *mega* was added—as it was added also to a few witnesses in the Matthean parallel" (1971:162).

13:21 *It is like the yeast a woman used.* Luke balanced the first illustration, relating to a man planting a tiny mustard seed (13:19) with one about a woman using yeast in making bread (13:21). Jesus' ministry appealed to both men and women to repent and enter the Kingdom. This fits into Luke's emphasis on the universality of the gospel.

COMMENTARY

As we have seen, the Kingdom of God was the principal theme of the teaching of Jesus (4:43; 6:20; 8:1, 10; 9:2, 9-11, 27, 60, 62; cf. Matt 13:1-50; Mark 4:1-34). He tried to explain it to his hearers again and again, working from the known to the unknown (e.g., Matt 13:31-33). He took things from nature and Palestinian life that would be familiar to his contemporaries and used them as illustrations and analogies to point to the transcendent Kingdom that was the grand subject of his teaching (cf. 6:39-42; Matt 6:25-33). Thus, it was quite appropriate for Jesus to select something that was small or minute in the beginning and impressively large and conspicuous in the end. The mustard seed suited Jesus' illustrative purpose well, because, like the seed, the Kingdom of God appeared tiny and infinitesimally small at the start but large and expansive in the end. It contained life, and that life must organically express itself in growth and development that would be noticeable and impressive.

The reference to the birds nesting in the branches is suggestive, hinting at the ultimate strength of the Kingdom (note the allusions to Ezek 17:32; 31:6; Dan 4:12, 21). As Kistemaker comments:

> The passage from Daniel was well known to his audience because it referred to Nebuchadnezzar's dream of a tree that became so strong that its top reached to heaven. Under that tree beasts of the field found shade, and on its branches the birds of the air came to perch. Jesus, who speaks the words of God (John 3:34), teaches Scripture indirectly by way of a verbal allusion, and calls attention to a Messianic parable in Ezekiel 17:23: "On the mountain heights of Israel I will plant it; and will produce branches and bear fruit and become a splendid cedar. Birds of every kind will nest in it; they will find shelter in the shade of its branches." (1980:46)

The spread of the gospel is still in progress and will continue until the end, when the tree is fully grown and the gospel of the Kingdom has been preached to all nations (Matt 24:14). In Luke, there is no emphasis on the smallness of the mustard seed at the beginning (unlike both Mark and Matthew). Here the key point is crystal clear: "Jesus wanted mainly to emphasize the ultimate universality of God's rule . . . the birds 'nesting in the branches of the tree' . . . [captures] the main point, i.e. inclusion of the nations of the world" (Gundry 1993:233). The future magnitude of God's rule will include the Gentiles, who are "represented by the birds in Daniel [4:12, 21] and Ezekiel [17:23]" (Gundry 1993:230; Gundry cites in support Zech 2:11 LXX; *1 Enoch* 90:30; *Joseph and Asenath* 15:6 v. l.; *Midrash Psalms* 104:13).

Here, as in the parable of the yeast that follows it, we have, as Craddock-has pointed out, "an excellent example of interpretation by location, a method that preachers and teachers could well learn from Luke . . . [Instead of placing them in a collection of parables, like Matthew and Mark, see Matt 13:31-33; Mark 4:30-32], Luke has placed these parables in the tension-filled journey to Jerusalem, immediately after a Sabbath healing and controversy and immediately before Jesus is asked, 'Lord, will those who are saved be few?' (v. 23)" (1988:1032). Jesus was going to his cross, and it was very important for the disciples to understand that the Kingdom of God, though now small and apparently insignificant, would one day be impressive and well-established. They were being asked to place their faith in something that was not yet fully visible, but only in its incipient stages. The growth and development would duly come in God's own time and way.

The hiddenness of the Kingdom of God, together with its mysterious power, is highlighted in the parable of the yeast (13:20-21). The yeast illustrates the pervasiveness of the divine enterprise. While it might be unobserved and unnoticed by humans at the beginning, it is quietly and mysteriously at work just like leaven, which penetrates a whole lump of dough. So human beings, acting as laborers with God (cf. 1 Cor 3:9), can sow the seed of the gospel with confidence, knowing that it will be quietly working and effecting wondrous changes in the whole of society, just as a little leaven eventually penetrates a large amount of flour. In ways unknown to humankind, God has been at work, and his Kingdom will grow and prosper despite its insignificant beginnings.

◆ V. The Narrow Door (13:22-30; cf. Matt 7:22)

²²Jesus went through the towns and villages, teaching as he went, always pressing on toward Jerusalem. ²³Someone asked him, "Lord, will only a few be saved?"

He replied, ²⁴"Work hard to enter the narrow door to God's Kingdom, for many will try to enter but will fail. ²⁵When the master of the house has locked the door, it will be too late. You will stand outside knocking and pleading, 'Lord, open the door for us!' But he will reply, 'I don't know you or where you come from.' ²⁶Then you will say, 'But we ate and drank with you, and you taught in our streets.'

²⁷And he will reply, 'I tell you, I don't know you or where you come from. Get away from me, all you who do evil.'

²⁸"There will be weeping and gnashing of teeth, for you will see Abraham, Isaac, Jacob, and all the prophets in the Kingdom of God, but you will be thrown out. ²⁹And people will come from all over the world—from east and west, north and south—to take their places in the Kingdom of God. ³⁰And note this: Some who seem least important now will be the greatest then, and some who are the greatest now will be least important then.*"

13:30 Greek *Some are last who will be first, and some are first who will be last.*

NOTES

13:22 *Jesus went through the towns and villages . . . always pressing on toward Jerusalem.* Luke noted that Jesus continued the exodus toward Jerusalem (see 9:51). Moessner writes, "Luke's Central Section (9:51–19:44) is the story of the journeying salvation of the New Exodus prophesied by Moses to the people of the Horeb covenant as the fulfillment of the promises to Abraham and his descendants. As Jesus reaches the Temple and later enters the city of Jerusalem to die on behalf of this people, the people of the 'new covenant' is established at the place which the Lord had chosen out of all Israel. The credo of Deut 26:1-11 has achieved its goal" (1989:290).

13:23 *will only a few be saved?* Danker remarks about the speculations that were taking place in Jewish circles: "According to 4 *Ezra* 8:3, 'Many are created, but few saved.' Some rabbis, on the other hand, taught that only a few in Israel would enjoy the blessings of heaven immediately after death. The rest would wait in Gehenna. However, all Israel would share in the blessings of the world to come after the resurrection of the dead took place . . . Jesus refuses to enter into such inquiries. Instead he takes up the prophetic note of decisive commitment" (1974:160).

13:28 *There will be weeping and gnashing of teeth.* This unusual phrase is found six times in Matthew's Gospel (Matt 8:12; 13:42, 50; 22:13; 24:51; 25:30), sometimes termed "the stern Gospel" because of its solemn warnings and its note of judgment (cf. Matt 5:22; and the "Seven Woes" mentioned in Matt 23:13-36). This is the only passage where the phrase occurs in Luke, using a passage that is usually attributed to Q and also appears in Matt 8:12. The reference in Matthew points to Gehenna, the Heb. name for the garbage heap south of Jerusalem where child sacrifice had been practiced (2 Kgs 23:10; Jer 7:31). "In order to discourage any more human sacrifices, the city rubbish dump was established there, and the custom was to put there, among all kinds of garbage, the corpses of criminals . . . [T]his was the picture in the mind of Jesus when he uttered [such] terrible warnings of which there are echoes in our gospels [e.g., Mark 9:43-48; Matt 23:15, 33] . . . Those who were thus condemned would, of course, be bitterly sorry; in the traditional phrase, they would weep and gnash their teeth. . . . corpses of criminals and paupers who did not receive a proper burial in a family cave or other tomb . . . Maggots bred in the place, and an everlasting bonfire was needed" (Edwards 1969:54-55). In Luke's account, Gehenna is not explicitly mentioned. The emphasis is on exclusion from the Kingdom with the resulting bitterness of regret.

13:29 *people will come from all over the world.* This is the only passage in Luke–Acts where there is a specific reference to people coming into the Kingdom of God "from east and west, north and south." Matthew has a similar reference to many Gentiles coming "from all over the world—from east and west" and sitting down at table in the Kingdom of Heaven "with Abraham, Isaac, and Jacob" (Matt 8:11; cf. Deut 28:64; 30:3).

C O M M E N T A R Y

This second stage in Jesus' travel itinerary is marked by Luke's mention of the section's theme, Jesus' deliberate travel to Jerusalem (13:22; cf. 9:51). The teaching found in this second stage is intended to prepare the reader for the meaning of Jesus' final actions in the holy city.

The determination of Jesus is evident in Luke's account as he continues his itinerant teaching ministry through the Palestinian towns and villages, doggedly "pressing on toward Jerusalem" (13:22). This strong sense of direction was not new. Luke signaled its importance in chapter 9: "As the time drew near for him to ascend to heaven, Jesus *resolutely* set out for Jerusalem" (9:51). From that time onward, Luke saw Jesus moving unflinchingly to his death in Jerusalem at the hands of his enemies. The holy city, the city of destiny, lay before him, and he refused to be diverted from its beckoning call: "Yes, today, tomorrow, and the next day I must proceed on my way. For it wouldn't do for a prophet of God to be killed except in Jerusalem" (13:33). He would not attempt to escape his God-given appointment as he proceeded southward from Galilee to Judea.

Since Jesus expected his followers also to take up their crosses, just as he shouldered his (9:23), it was not surprising that he should stress the rigors that lay ahead. Many would-be disciples were uncertain about the strength of their commitment, so they asked, "Lord, will only a few be saved?" (13:23). In response, Jesus reminded them of the stringent demands of discipleship and of the need to respond positively to the grace of God: "Work hard to enter the narrow door to God's Kingdom" (13:24). God's grace carried with it a bracing challenge; it was not the offer of what Dietrich Bonhoeffer called "cheap grace." Rather it entailed proper human response, which involves intense effort (the Gr. *agōnizomai* [TG75, ZG76] means "struggle" or "fight"). The daunting potential of failure was real, and they were so warned. Like the Corinthians, the disciples were warned not to receive the grace of God in vain (2 Cor 6:1). A long, steady, unrelenting obedience in the same direction that Jesus was taking was called for on the part of his true disciples.

It was not enough to use the right words, calling Jesus "Lord." People could do that and yet not have a real relationship with the Savior. Personal contact, symbolized by such friendly activities as eating and drinking, did not guarantee that they were bona fide believers. Neither did sharing Christian teaching with others substitute for their own direct knowledge of God, experienced in their personal relationship with Jesus. Such activities, devoid of spiritual connection with the Son of God himself, would not do. These persons who just superficially went through the motions did not pass muster. They were weighed in the divine balances and found wanting: "Get away from me, all you who do evil" (13:27). This sham piety was a subterfuge for refusal to meet the high demands of true discipleship and genuine knowledge of the Lord Jesus himself.

Though Luke's Gospel is loving and revels in the grace and loving-kindness of God, a somber note of tragedy and missed opportunity is sounded here: "There will be weeping and gnashing of teeth" (see note on 13:28). A similar sinister note is sounded frequently in Matthew's Gospel, often termed "the stern Gospel" (see Matt 8:12; 13:42; 50; 22:13; 24:51; 25:30). Proverbs speaks of just such a catastrophic end to a person who refuses to heed the warnings given: "Whoever stubbornly refuses to accept criticism will suddenly be destroyed beyond recovery" (Prov 29:1). The gospel message presents both *gift* and *demand,* and the two are nicely balanced in the third Gospel.

The reference to the patriarchs Abraham, Isaac, and Jacob is significant and indicates a link between true believers in Jesus and those foundational ancestors of the faith who have gone before them in holy history. The people of God, by divine intention, will ultimately include a transnational, transethnic group composed of both Jews and Gentiles, all of whom share the faith of Abraham and his son and grandson, who were repeatedly promised that through them all the families on earth would be blessed (Gen 12:1-3; 17:4; 22:18; 26:2-4). However, "the majority of that generation of Jewish people will, through their unbelief and the fact that they let the time of grace slip past, endure inexpressible afflictions and pangs of conscience when, at the end of the age while they themselves are rejected, they see their pious ancestors inherit the rich blessings of the kingdom of God" (Geldenhuys 1961:380).

Those who failed to meet the stringent conditions set out by Jesus would be certainly "thrown out" (13:28), despite the fact that they were persistently "knocking and pleading" to gain admission (13:25). Into this select, holy people of God that was then taking shape through Jesus' ministry would come people from all points of the compass, and they would be welcomed as genuine members who were qualified by divine appointment "to take their places in the Kingdom of God" (13:29). The standard of evaluation would be quite different than the prevailing worldly view because God looks at things differently than humans; as Isaiah put it, "'My thoughts are nothing like your thoughts,' says the LORD" (Isa 55:8). In the final reckoning, there would be some surprises: "Some who seem least important now will be the greatest then, and some who are the greatest now will be least important then" (13:30). It was vitally important for sincere followers not to let themselves be deceived!

◆   **W. Jesus Grieves over Jerusalem (13:31-35; cf. Matt 23:37-39)**

³¹At that time some Pharisees said to him, "Get away from here if you want to live! Herod Antipas wants to kill you!"

³²Jesus replied, "Go tell that fox that I will keep on casting out demons and healing people today and tomorrow; and the third day I will accomplish my purpose. ³³Yes, today, tomorrow, and the next day I must proceed on my way. For it wouldn't do for a prophet of God to be killed except in Jerusalem!

³⁴"O Jerusalem, Jerusalem, the city that kills the prophets and stones God's messengers! How often I have wanted to gather your children together as a hen protects her chicks beneath her wings, but you wouldn't let me. ³⁵And now, look, your house is abandoned. And you will never see me again until you say, 'Blessings on the one who comes in the name of the LORD!*'"

13:35 Ps 118:26.

NOTES

13:31 *some Pharisees said to him, "Get away from here if you want to live! Herod Antipas wants to kill you!"* Marshall comments, "The motives of Herod and the Pharisees are uncertain. Herod liked tranquility (Josephus *Antiquities* 18:245 [18.7.2]) and may simply have wished to quietly get rid of a possible trouble-maker; he may have had hopes that a threat would be sufficient. As for the Pharisees, it is most likely that their action here is motivated by malice, and that they were trying (like Herod) to get Jesus to make himself scarce" (1978:571).

13:32 *that fox.* "In Palestine the fox is an insignificant predator next to the lion, the king of beasts. Jesus will be done in by greater powers than Herod. Some readers may have caught an allusion to Ezekiel 13:4, which speaks of foxes among the ruins. Herod governs in a land which is soon to experience terrible disaster" (Danker 1974:161). See note on 13:35.

I will keep on . . . today and tomorrow; and the third day I will accomplish my purpose. The triple time reference here is "a Semitic idiom for a short indefinite time followed by an imminent and certain event" (Ellis 1981:190).

13:34 *O Jerusalem, Jerusalem, the city that kills the prophets! . . . How often I have wanted to gather your children together, . . . but you wouldn't let me.* On the tragic element in the Jewish rejection of Jesus, as presented by Luke, see Tannehill 1985. He links the four texts of Luke which speak of Jerusalem, its rejection of Jesus, and its coming destruction (chs 13, 19, 21, 23), and he notes Stephen's speech in Acts 7 on the history of Israel as displaying a story of the tragic reversal of fortune.

13:35 *your house is abandoned.* Jesus viewed the terrible destruction of Jerusalem as abandonment by God for its impenitence and unbelief in the face of the privileges it had enjoyed and the message it had been offered. There are allusions to such passages as 1 Kgs 9:7-8; Jer 12:7; 22:5; and Ps 69:25. "Here the reference is to the Romans' destruction of

Jerusalem. This is evident from 19:42-44 and 21:6, where the same verb is used to describe Jerusalem's fall in AD 70, as well as from the fact that Luke's readers knew from hindsight of this tragic event" (Stein 1992:384). For more discussion of the fall of Jerusalem, see Horsley 1981.

COMMENTARY

After speaking of the stringent conditions of discipleship (13:22-30), Jesus received a solemn warning of danger from some seemingly friendly Pharisees, who suggested a quick exit from the area if he wanted to live (13:31). The source of apparent danger was perceived to be Herod Antipas, the crafty ruler of Galilee and Perea. While Jesus was quite aware of the real danger posed by Herod, he refused to let it interfere with his mission of preaching, teaching, and healing. He had set his course "resolutely" for Jerusalem (9:51), and he would not be dissuaded from it. Instead of cowering in fear and being overcome by paranoia, Jesus turned to those who warned him and told them of his fixed determination to persevere: "I will keep on casting out demons and healing people today and tomorrow; and the third day I will accomplish my purpose" (13:32). The mention of the "third day" here is a strong pointer to Jesus' coming resurrection. "Luke's readers undoubtedly would call to mind the Lord's resurrection. This meaning is confirmed by the following word, 'finish' [or 'accomplish,' NLT]" (Ellis 1981:190).

God's plan for his Son's life had been given, and Jesus would follow it through until the very end. In his great high priestly prayer in John's Gospel, Jesus declared, "I brought glory to you here on earth by completing the work you gave me to do" (John 17:4). Later, on the cross, he cried, "It is finished!" (John 19:30). There was to be no pulling back when the storm clouds of opposition loomed heavy with danger. Rather, there was a steady faithfulness called for, as the Son of Man kept to his predetermined course of preaching, teaching, and healing, inexorably moving onward "today, tomorrow, and the next day" (13:33). He would inflexibly proceed on his way to the city of destiny. There in Jerusalem, he would meet his divinely appointed destiny, "for it wouldn't do for a prophet of God to be killed except in Jerusalem" (13:33). It was the capital city, and there, opposition to God's purpose would reach its zenith. There the suffering Servant of God would make his last appeal to the holy city and be despised, rejected, and executed.

There is a peculiar poignancy and pathos in Luke's account. Truly Jesus was going to meet disappointment, and this would be most evident in the holy city: "He came into the very world he created, but the world didn't recognize him" (John 1:10). No wonder he grieved over Jerusalem with such passionate concern (13:34-35). Despite his earnest aspirations and efforts to "gather" her people into the new covenant he was establishing, he had to face stubbornness and opposition (13:34). Tragically, this was to mean the people's own rejection and abandonment. Later, looking back after the destruction of the city and its Temple in AD 70, it was all too evident to Christians that the fall of Jerusalem had been a costly event for the Jewish people (see also Josephus *War* 4-6, which describes the devastation of the city).

In the near future, Jesus would be blessed by his followers, who would enthusiastically acclaim him. When he entered the holy city on the last week of his life, he was joyfully recognized by his supporters and hailed with appropriate shouts of praise (19:37-38). On the other hand, the King was to face cruel opposition and rejection as Jesus plainly recognized: "It wouldn't do for a prophet of God to be killed except in Jerusalem" (13:33).

◆   X. Jesus Heals on the Sabbath (14:1-6)

One Sabbath day Jesus went to eat dinner in the home of a leader of the Pharisees, and the people were watching him closely. ²There was a man there whose arms and legs were swollen.* ³Jesus asked the Pharisees and experts in religious law, "Is it permitted in the law to heal people on the Sabbath day, or not?" ⁴When they refused to answer, Jesus touched the sick man and healed him and sent him away. ⁵Then he turned to them and said, "Which of you doesn't work on the Sabbath? If your son* or your cow falls into a pit, don't you rush to get him out?" ⁶Again they could not answer.

14:2 Or *who had dropsy.*   14:5 Some manuscripts read *donkey*

NOTES

14:1 *Jesus went to eat dinner in the home of a leader of the Pharisees.* On the banquet theme in Luke, see "Major Features and Themes" in the Introduction and the notes on 5:29 and 14:15.

14:3 *Is it permitted in the law to heal on the Sabbath day, or not?* Proper Sabbath observance was a subject of controversy between Jesus and his opponents (cf. 6:1-10; 13:10-17 and notes).

14:5 *If your son or your cow.* The best evidence supports the reading "son" (𝔓45 𝔓75 A B W 𝔐 it^e syr^{h,p} cop^{sa}). Other mss (ℵ K L 044 f$^{1.13}$ 33) read "donkey." Though some argue that this was a transcriptional error—scribes mistaking *huios* [TG5207, ZG5626] for *onos* [TG3688, ZG3952], it is more likely that "son" was purposely changed to "donkey" to get a better pairing—animal with animal, instead of animal with human (Comfort 2007:[Luke 14:5]).

your cow falls into a pit. In the interest of keeping the Sabbath holy, as a day of rest, the Jews had expanded on the OT Sabbath laws, developing 39 rules concerning activities forbidden on the Sabbath (cf. Exod 34:21). This set of restrictions became a point of tension between Jesus and the Pharisees, who accused the man from Nazareth of violations of the Sabbath (e.g., Mark 2:23-3:6; Matt 12:9-14; Luke 6:1-5). In their system, healings were forbidden on the Sabbath, but Jesus' opponents implicitly acknowledged the notion that a cow would be rescued if it fell into a pit on the Sabbath day (a contrasting view is shown in CD 11:13-17). The reasoning pattern used by Jesus is a familiar one for him, arguing from the lesser to the greater (cf. Matt 7:11 with Luke 11:13; Matt 6:30 with Luke 12:28): if a Jew could quite properly rescue a cow falling into a pit on the Sabbath, how much more should Jesus be able to heal a sick person on the Sabbath (cf. 13:15)! The heartless application by Jesus' opponents of legalistic regulations in the face of human need was thereby exposed.

COMMENTARY

Luke 14:1-24 collects together several different teachings of Jesus that are connected by the common use of dining imagery and vocabulary. All three incidents also show Jesus in dialogue with the Pharisees.

This first incident presents Jesus in the home of a leader of the Pharisees for dinner; the occasion is specifically noted as occurring on the Sabbath (14:1). The critics of Jesus were present, waiting to pounce on anything that they might attack as a violation of their sabbatical principles. A man afflicted with dropsy, suffering from swollen arms and legs, was near Jesus (14:2). The merciless application of Pharisaic interpretations of keeping the Sabbath stood in the way of giving relief to such a suffering person.

The law of Moses had not given a specific definition of work, so it became a matter of concern to the Jewish rabbis to spell out for the people what was considered work in order to provide a hedge around the Law; "healing had been included in the things which were prohibited" (Summers 1972:175). The Sabbath healing performed in a Pharisee's house certainly recalls a previous incident where Jesus had healed a man with a withered hand on the Sabbath (6:10-11). The incident here in 14:1-6 is found only in this Gospel, and serves as "a literary device to provide a setting for the sayings" (Creed 1930:188) that follow in Jesus' comments at the dinner table (14:7-24). Jesus' intervention in this case to heal a man, and his defense of his actions for healing on the Sabbath "cast him once again in the role of a heaven-sent messenger or a teacher acting with authority. Again the episode reminds the reader of the way the evangelist has presented Jesus in 6:5 as the 'Lord of the Sabbath.' Implicitly, Jesus also criticizes his contemporaries for their lack of concern for a fellow human being" (Fitzmyer 1985:1039-1040).

The healing, like the four other healings on the Sabbath recorded in Luke (4:31-37, 38-39; 6:6-11; 13:10-16), is clearly an expression of the compassion of Christ. When the question of the legality of such a healing on the Sabbath day was put directly to the Pharisees and the experts in religious law, they refused to answer so that the ludicrous nature of their position would not become evident to the bystanders. Then, Jesus boldly touched the sick man and healed him in the presence of these critics. In defense of his action, Jesus reminded his hostile audience that they would surely have done something to help a son or an animal out of a pit. How much more they should have been prepared to assist a fellow human being in time of need! As Jesus said on another occasion, "The Sabbath was made to meet the needs of people, and not people to meet the requirements of the Sabbath" (Mark 2:27; cf. Matt 12:1-8; Luke 6:1-5).

◆   Y. Jesus Teaches about Humility (14:7-14)

7When Jesus noticed that all who had come to the dinner were trying to sit in the seats of honor near the head of the table, he gave them this advice: 8"When you are invited to a wedding feast, don't sit in the seat of honor. What if someone who is more distinguished than you has also been invited? 9The host will come and say, 'Give this person your seat.' Then you will be embarrassed, and you will have to take whatever seat is left at the foot of the table!

10"Instead, take the lowest place at the foot of the table. Then when your host sees you, he will come and say, 'Friend, we have a better place for you!' Then you will be honored in front of all the other guests. ¹¹For those who exalt themselves will be humbled, and those who humble themselves will be exalted." ¹²Then he turned to his host. "When you put on a luncheon or a banquet," he said, "don't invite your friends, brothers, relatives, and rich neighbors. For they will invite you back, and that will be your only reward. ¹³Instead, invite the poor, the crippled, the lame, and the blind. ¹⁴Then at the resurrection of the righteous, God will reward you for inviting those who could not repay you."

NOTES

14:10 *Instead, take the lowest place at the foot of the table.* In place of self-assertion and aggressiveness, Jesus advocated a spirit of humble service (see Mark 10:35-45), and modeled it himself (22:24-27; John 13:1-17), even to the extent of the total self-giving and obedience that led to the cross (Phil 2:5-8). Here, that attitude is played out in seating arrangements, which were a sign of status. In the Jewish etiquette of the time, one was expected to take an inconspicuous place and only move to a more prominent position if the host invited him to do so.

COMMENTARY

The dining theme continues in the parable of the marriage feast (14:7-14). There are two parts here: one describing the proper etiquette for those invited to a marriage party (14:7-11) and the other outlining the principles of hospitality for the host who invites the guests (14:12-14). The marriage story and the instructions to the hosts are clearly "metaphorical and teach a general attitude toward self and others appropriate to members in God's kingdom (cf. 14:15). Meekness and humility are basic to the proper attitude believers should display in their relationship toward God, and service to the needy is characteristic of the proper attitude one should have toward others" (Stein 1992:388). Unselfish concern for the disadvantaged would be recognized and rewarded "at the resurrection of the righteous" (14:14).

The teaching moment came out of the selfish jockeying for "seats of honor near the head of the table" (14:7). Weddings were occasions of great celebration, and, perhaps naturally, those invited would covet the best seats. However, it was always possible that someone more distinguished might turn up as an invited guest, and then the aggressive person would be forced to give way to the guest with higher status. It was far better to take the lowest place at the foot of the table and then be summoned by the host to a superior position than to assume too much and subsequently be forced to take the lowliest place at the table after being disgraced and publicly shamed before the whole banqueting party. The moral in all this dining etiquette was clear and pointed to the general requirement of humility on the part of all true disciples: "For those who exalt themselves will be humbled, and those who humble themselves will be exalted" (14:11). It was a basic lesson that Jesus would make unforgettable when he washed his disciples' feet, an incident recorded in John 13:1-17. Luke's Gospel also records Jesus' later reminder to his disciples of his own incomparable example of unselfish service: "I am among you as one who serves" (22:27). Jesus was trying to teach them a fundamental lesson that "slaves are not greater than their master" (John 13:16).

This counter-cultural message was applied specifically to the host (14:12-14). In this case, the man in question was advised not to give a luncheon or banquet for his peers and cohorts—that is, his natural contacts such as friends, relatives, colleagues, and neighbors. These people would undoubtedly reciprocate, and, following the laws of conventional courtesy, in the course of time, repay the hospitality in a similar way. It would be essentially a *quid pro quo* arrangement, and no one would lose anything in the long run. However, in Jesus' view, the incoming Reign, or Kingdom, of God was to topple this pattern. "Instead, invite the poor, the crippled, the lame, and the blind" (14:13; note that it is these same people who are specially summoned to the great banquet in 14:21). These disadvantaged, handicapped people would not be able to return the hospitality they had been given. It was an act of sheer compassion and grace to do something kind and loving for them. Yet they were people with worth and value in their own right. God would not forget the unselfish beneficence shown to these poor and helpless people. With eternity's values in view, it made sense in the long run: "Then at the resurrection of the righteous, God will reward you for inviting those who could not repay you" (14:14). The standards of the Kingdom of God transcend and outstrip the rules of conventional hospitality.

◆   Z. Parable of the Great Feast (14:15-24; cf. Matt 22:1-10)

15Hearing this, a man sitting at the table with Jesus exclaimed, "What a blessing it will be to attend a banquet* in the Kingdom of God!"

16Jesus replied with this story: "A man prepared a great feast and sent out many invitations. 17When the banquet was ready, he sent his servant to tell the guests, 'Come, the banquet is ready.' 18But they all began making excuses. One said, 'I have just bought a field and must inspect it. Please excuse me.' 19Another said, 'I have just bought five pairs of oxen, and I want to try them out. Please excuse me.' 20Another said, 'I now have a wife, so I can't come.'

21"The servant returned and told his master what they had said. His master was furious and said, 'Go quickly into the streets and alleys of the town and invite the poor, the crippled, the blind, and the lame.' 22After the servant had done this, he reported, 'There is still room for more.' 23So his master said, 'Go out into the country lanes and behind the hedges and urge anyone you find to come, so that the house will be full. 24For none of those I first invited will get even the smallest taste of my banquet.' "

14:15 Greek *to eat bread.*

NOTES

14:15 *to attend a banquet.* On feasting in the NT, see ABD 4.788-791. Smith (1987) argues that the banquet theme in Luke's Gospel is one which is rooted in a rich Greco-Roman tradition of table fellowship as a literary motif, going back to the Gr. archetypes of the genre like the *Symposia* of Plato and Xenophon. Luke drew on this rich heritage to develop this prominent literary motif.

14:23 *Go out into the country lanes and behind the hedges and urge anyone you find to come, so that the house will be full.* The widespread search to invite outsiders suggests an outreach to others who had hitherto not been welcomed—i.e. Gentiles. They too were to enjoy the privilege of having a share in the Kingdom of God (14:15). On Luke's treatment of "Jews, Gentiles and Judaism," see Tuckett (1997:50-71).

COMMENTARY

The final dining incident concerns the parable of the great feast (14:15-24), a parable that resembles a similar one in Matthew's Gospel (Matt 22:1-10). In Matthew, it is a royal invitation to a king's banquet, for the king is giving a marriage feast for his son. A notable feature of Matthew's account is the anger of the king, who sends troops that destroy the murderers and burn their city (Matt 22:7). This seems to be Matthew's depiction of God's terrible judgment awaiting Jerusalem should it fail to heed the strong warnings it had been given (cf. Matt 23:37-38, and esp. 24:2, where Jesus gives dire words predicting Jerusalem's complete destruction). In addition, Matthew noted that those who are brought into the banquet include "good and bad alike," and the outcome was that "the banquet hall was filled with guests" (Matt 22:10). However, one person was thrown out of the banquet for improper dress (Matt 22:11-14). As France has noted, "entry to God's kingdom may be free, but it is not without expectations" (2003:108). Gift and demand are presented in delicate balance.

Both versions of the parable recognize excuses that are offered to escape attendance at the special banquet to which they have been graciously invited. When one considers the excuses given, it is clear that the first two were economic, and the third one was domestic. It is interesting that the non-canonical *Gospel of Thomas* (Saying 64) adds a fourth, similar objection and concentrates its negative conclusion on the "tradesmen and merchants," who put their own interests above those of the one who issued the invitation which they had earlier accepted! As Craddock observed, "The economic pressures felt by the first two and the recent wedding of a third (the threefold pattern was common in storytelling) were honored in most societies. In fact, marriage exempted one from military duty in Israel (Deut 20:7; 24:5). The forces against which God's offer has priority are not simply over our worst but also over our best agendas" (1990:179).

In Luke, some special notes should be observed. One is the urgency with which the invitation to the banquet is pressed: "Go out into the country lanes and behind the hedges and urge anyone you find to come, so that the house will be full" (14:23). The whole passage is highly suggestive of the Gentile mission, though there is nothing here to justify the idea of forcibly compelling people to become disciples in a way that would be disrespectful to them as responsible persons. When the original people—the respectable, law-abiding Jews—turned down the invitation, the call was then extended to others, for "there is still room for more" (14:22). The hint of judgment is there for those who turned down the gracious offer: "For none of those I first invited will get even the smallest taste of my banquet" (14:24).

This parable was directed against the Pharisees, and it shattered the self-confident Pharisaic complacency:

> The kingdom of God is not an other-worldly prospect to be contemplated with unctuous sentiment, but a present reality calling for immediate response; the banquet is now ready and, according to Jewish custom, the

guests are being summoned by a servant to take their place at the table; and those who, having previously accepted the invitation, now discover other more pressing engagements, will lose their opportunity and find their place filled by others (Caird 1963:177).

◆   AA. The Cost of Being a Disciple (14:25-35)

²⁵A large crowd was following Jesus. He turned around and said to them, ²⁶"If you want to be my disciple, you must hate everyone else by comparison—your father and mother, wife and children, brothers and sisters—yes, even your own life. Otherwise, you cannot be my disciple. ²⁷And if you do not carry your own cross and follow me, you cannot be my disciple.

²⁸"But don't begin until you count the cost. For who would begin construction of a building without first calculating the cost to see if there is enough money to finish it? ²⁹Otherwise, you might complete only the foundation before running out of money, and then everyone would laugh at you. ³⁰They would say, 'There's the person who started that building and couldn't afford to finish it!'

³¹"Or what king would go to war against another king without first sitting down with his counselors to discuss whether his army of 10,000 could defeat the 20,000 soldiers marching against him? ³²And if he can't, he will send a delegation to discuss terms of peace while the enemy is still far away. ³³So you cannot become my disciple without giving up everything you own.

³⁴"Salt is good for seasoning. But if it loses its flavor, how do you make it salty again? ³⁵Flavorless salt is good neither for the soil nor for the manure pile. It is thrown away. Anyone with ears to hear should listen and understand!"

NOTES

14:26 *If you want to be my disciple.* Luke 14:25-33 consists of a group of sayings in which Jesus insists that discipleship requires total dedication. The preeminent place demanded by Jesus is to outstrip the natural love of one's own family members (14:26). The vivid Semitic idiom of "hate" is used to show the overriding place of Jesus in a disciple's life and priorities (cf. Mal 1:2-3). Disciples must not place ultimate value even on their own lives (cf. John 12:25).

14:27 *if you do not carry your own cross and follow me, you cannot be my disciple.* The stringency of the demands placed upon a true disciple of Jesus is further pressed home in this verse. In Galilee, the disciples had likely seen a man "take up his cross" in the company of a small band of Roman soldiers, and they knew what it implied: in effect, Jesus' disciples were asked to consider themselves already dead. This was the ultimate in self-denial. On an earlier occasion, Jesus had spoken of self-denial in the context of taking up the costly challenge of discipleship on a daily, ongoing basis (9:23).

14:28-33 This passage further develops the theme of the cost of discipleship by introducing two striking parables: the tower builder (14:28-30) and the warring king (14:31-33). On these and parables in general, see the notes on 5:36 and 8:11.

14:35 *Anyone with ears to hear should listen and understand!* Jesus had posted a warning that was to be taken seriously. This is not the first time Luke had challenged his readers on the importance of hearing and heeding the gospel message (Lk 8:8). Note also Jesus' earlier direct command to his disciples: "Listen to me and remember what I say" (Lk 9:44).

COMMENTARY

The radical nature of following Jesus is carefully spelled out in this section. To be a true disciple, everything else has to be put into a subsidiary position. This is made clear by the use of the Jewish idiom of hating something—that is, putting it in a secondary place in view of what one loves supremely. Jesus claimed the right to exercise this commanding place in the believer's life: "If you want to be my disciple, you must hate everyone else by comparison—your father and mother, wife and children, brothers and sisters—yes, even your own life" (14:26a). To insist that the Master stood ahead of one's nearest and dearest relatives, family, and friends was to insist on something that was nonnegotiable and mandatory: "Otherwise, you *cannot* be my disciple" (14:26b). Even one's own life was to be surrendered to the pressing demands of discipleship. This costly burden of discipleship was called the cross, a fitting metaphor and symbol of the old life that had been put to death. The apostle Paul uttered this reality when he said, "My old self has been crucified with Christ. It is no longer I who live, but Christ lives in me" (Gal 2:19-20). The very repetition of the comment "you cannot be my disciple" in 14:26 and 14:27 highlights the stringency of the demands Jesus was putting upon his followers.

To make his demands crystal clear, Jesus used two illustrations that stress the need to consider the matter carefully before making a profession of faith. The first case put up for consideration is that of a builder. Naturally, he must count the cost of construction before commencing building. If he has insufficient resources to complete the project, he will not start building. In the untimely event that he should run out of money just after finishing the foundation, he would expose himself to public shame and criticism: "There's the person who started that building and couldn't afford to finish it!" (14:30). His folly would be obvious to all.

The second illustration was drawn from political life and international affairs. One king contemplating war with another king would surely consider the resources available to win the war. If it turned out that he was facing a superior force and was outnumbered two to one, he would probably sit down with his advisers and calculate the difficulties. After carefully counting the cost and deciding that the odds were overwhelming, the king would send a delegation to discuss terms of peace while his enemy was still a long way away. Once again, the analogy Jesus used made clear the need to weigh carefully the demands of discipleship. It is not a matter to be entered into lightly, but soberly and thoughtfully, after a full consideration of the issues at stake.

In closing, Jesus stresses again that disciples must persevere—they must always maintain the distinctive qualities that belong to true disciples of Christ, just as salt must retain its saltiness to be of any value. Otherwise, they become worthless (14:35). The admonition of the difficult nature of discipleship should be heeded by all (14:35b; see note).

◆ BB. Parable of the Lost Sheep (15:1-7)

Tax collectors and other notorious sinners often came to listen to Jesus teach. ²This made the Pharisees and teachers of religious law complain that he was associating with such sinful people—even eating with them!

³So Jesus told them this story: ⁴"If a man has a hundred sheep and one of them gets lost, what will he do? Won't he leave the ninety-nine others in the wilderness and go to search for the one that is lost until he finds it? ⁵And when he has found it, he will joyfully carry it home on his shoulders. ⁶When he arrives, he will call together his friends and neighbors, saying, 'Rejoice with me because I have found my lost sheep.' ⁷In the same way, there is more joy in heaven over one lost sinner who repents and returns to God than over ninety-nine others who are righteous and haven't strayed away!

NOTES

15:4 *If a man has a hundred sheep and one of them gets lost, what will he do?* Sheep were common in the ancient Middle East, and there are scores of references to them in the Bible. Accordingly, shepherds are often mentioned (Gen 29:8; Exod 2:17-19; Luke 2:8, 15, 18). The shepherd metaphor became a primary one for God as "caretaker for his people [Ps 23:1-4], the king as leader and protector of the nation, or the priest as spiritual leader of the covenant community [see the references to the leaders as the 'shepherds of Israel' in Jer 23:1; Ezek 34:2]. With such a rich background, it was natural that early Christians poured this shepherd imagery into their portrait of Jesus and their expectation of the spiritual leaders in the Christian church" (Mills 1990:819).

COMMENTARY

The three parables presented in Luke 15 concentrate on the same theme—the peril of being lost and the joy of being found. This motif appears in the Parable of the Lost Sheep (15:1-7), the Parable of the Lost Coin (15:8-10), and the Parable of the Lost Sons (15:11-32). Each of these parables has its own unique contribution to make, but they all underscore the serious nature of the predicament.

It is important to know that the parables of Jesus, as has often been observed, were frequently used as weapons of controversy. This seems to be the case for these parables because they were offered by Jesus to explain and defend his actions. He had been reaching out to the people on the fringes of society, and his friendliness, not surprisingly, was attracting some people who had rather questionable credentials, including "tax collectors and other notorious sinners," who would come "to listen to Jesus teach" (15:1). This was offensive to the Jews who were concerned with purity issues, and they found much to criticize in such contacts. In addition, quite possibly, they might have been jealous that this unauthorized teacher from Galilee was gaining a following that they could not match, although this element is not stated here (though it is in John 12:19). In any case, the methods of Jesus and the nature of his audience were attracting criticism: the Pharisees and teachers of religious law were critical that Jesus "was associating with such sinful people—even eating with them" (15:2). It was this hostility on the part of his critics that prompted Jesus to put forward these parables.

The first parable presents a situation that was readily understood in a land where shepherds and sheep were well known. It supposes a missing sheep, and describes the shepherd leaving the ninety-nine sheep to go out in search of the one that is lost. It notes the persistence of the shepherd, who carries on the search until it is successful. Jesus mentioned the joy at the moment of discovery and the shared happiness and celebration that accompanies the return of the lost sheep. This illustration is used as an earthly story with a heavenly meaning, for it illuminates the divine joy "over one lost sinner who repents and returns to God" (15:7). It suggests that God is like the faithful shepherd in his love, persistence, joy, and concern that the lost should be found. It is a profound picture of the love of God, in terms that ordinary people can understand and appreciate.

◆   CC. Parable of the Lost Coin (15:8-10)

8"Or suppose a woman has ten silver coins* and loses one. Won't she light a lamp and sweep the entire house and search carefully until she finds it? 9And when she finds it, she will call in her friends and neighbors and say, 'Rejoice with me because I have found my lost coin.' 10In the same way, there is joy in the presence of God's angels when even one sinner repents."

15:8 Greek *ten drachmas*. A drachma was the equivalent of a full day's wage.

NOTES

15:8 *suppose a woman has ten silver coins and loses one.* The Gr. text speaks of 10 drachmas. Each drachma would be roughly equal to a full day's pay. The Palestinian life situation presupposed by the parable is that of someone living right on the edge of extreme poverty with barely enough resources to maintain sustenance. The presence of a dirt floor in the Palestinian home explains why the poor woman has to "sweep" the floor to recover the precious lost coin. As Jeremias has shown in his famous book on *The Parables of Jesus* (1975), the parables of Jesus reflect real life conditions in first century Palestine. In Galilee, for instance, we know that much of the land was in the hands of wealthy absentee landlords who exploited the local tenant farmers and made life very difficult and marginal for them (see also Theissen and Merz 1998:162-183).

15:10 *there is joy in the presence of God's angels.* On Luke's interest in angels, see the Introduction and the comments on 1:11-17.

COMMENTARY

In this parable we observe a literary feature that is characteristic of Luke: he liked to match a story of a man with a story of a woman. In this case, a woman in search of a lost coin matches the story of a shepherd in search of a lost sheep. A few other pairings may be noted: Jesus healed a centurion's servant and then a widow's son (7:1-17). On different Sabbath days, Jesus healed a woman who was "bent double" (13:10-17) and, in the next chapter, a man suffering from swollen arms and legs (14:1-6). Similarly, we read of a farmer who plants a mustard seed and of a woman who works yeast into her meal (13:18-21). Unquestionably, Luke wanted to show the value of women and their importance in the early company of those who followed Jesus (see Johnson 1991:56).

This parable also echoes some of the same themes we noted in the previous parable: the concern for something lost; the earnest, persistent search for its recovery (note the parallels between "until he finds it" and "until she finds it" in 15:4 and 15:8); the joy in discovery of the missing item; and the communal sense of celebration (15:6, 9). Once again, there is a transcendent meaning of eschatological significance to the followers of Jesus: "There is joy in the presence of God's angels when even one sinner repents" (15:10).

Through this parable and the others in this chapter, Luke bears witness to Jesus' ministry to "Israel's outcasts and to their entering God's kingdom. Through the parable Jesus both censured and appealed to his opponents: 'The lost of Israel are finding forgiveness; sinners are finding salvation. It is time to rejoice. In heaven God rejoiced over this. Why don't you enter into this joy?' The second parable makes this point using in its picture a woman who has lost a silver coin and finds it" (Stein 1981:401).

◆   ## DD. Parable of the Lost Sons (15:11-32)

[11]To illustrate the point further, Jesus told them this story: "A man had two sons. [12]The younger son told his father, 'I want my share of your estate now before you die.' So his father agreed to divide his wealth between his sons.

[13]"A few days later this younger son packed all his belongings and moved to a distant land, and there he wasted all his money in wild living. [14]About the time his money ran out, a great famine swept over the land, and he began to starve. [15]He persuaded a local farmer to hire him, and the man sent him into his fields to feed the pigs. [16]The young man became so hungry that even the pods he was feeding the pigs looked good to him. But no one gave him anything.

[17]"When he finally came to his senses, he said to himself, 'At home even the hired servants have food enough to spare, and here I am dying of hunger! [18]I will go home to my father and say, "Father, I have sinned against both heaven and you, [19]and I am no longer worthy of being called your son. Please take me on as a hired servant."'

[20]"So he returned home to his father. And while he was still a long way off, his father saw him coming. Filled with love and compassion, he ran to his son, embraced him, and kissed him. [21]His son said to him, 'Father, I have sinned against both heaven and you, and I am no longer worthy of being called your son.*'

[22]"But his father said to the servants, 'Quick! Bring the finest robe in the house and put it on him. Get a ring for his finger and sandals for his feet. [23]And kill the calf we have been fattening. We must celebrate with a feast, [24]for this son of mine was dead and has now returned to life. He was lost, but now he is found.' So the party began.

[25]"Meanwhile, the older son was in the fields working. When he returned home, he heard music and dancing in the house, [26]and he asked one of the servants what was going on. [27]'Your brother is back,' he was told, 'and your father has killed the fattened calf. We are celebrating because of his safe return.'

[28]"The older brother was angry and wouldn't go in. His father came out and begged him, [29]but he replied, 'All these years I've slaved for you and never once refused to do a single thing you told me to. And in all that time you never gave me even one young goat for a feast with my friends. [30]Yet when this son of yours comes back after squandering your money on prostitutes, you celebrate by killing the fattened calf!'

³¹"His father said to him, 'Look, dear son, you have always stayed by me, and everything I have is yours. ³²We had to celebrate this happy day. For your brother was dead and has come back to life! He was lost, but now he is found!' "

15:21 Some manuscripts add *Please take me on as a hired servant.*

NOTES

15:12 *I want my share of your estate now.* The father would have normally retained his possessions until he died. The younger son's demand said, in effect, "To me you're dead," and thus disgraced his father before the whole community.

divide his wealth. Jewish inheritance laws dictated that the right of the firstborn be honored (Deut 21:15-17).

15:13 *A few days later.* Lit., "not many days later." Luke used a figure of speech called a litotes (making a positive statement by means of an understated negative; e.g. "he's not bad looking" to mean "he's handsome") to indicate the haste of the son to get away as rapidly as possible. The same figure of speech is used in Acts 1:5; 12:18; 15:2; 17:4, 12; 19:11, 23-24; 20:12.

this younger son packed all his belongings and moved to a distant land. Kistemaker notes a somewhat similar parable to that of the prodigal son coming from Rabbi Meir, cited from *The Midrash, Deuteronomy* 1961:53: "This can be compared to the son of a king who took to evil ways. The king sent a tutor to him who appeared to him saying, 'Repent my son.' The son, however, sent him back to his father with the message, 'How can I have the effrontery to return? I am ashamed to come before you.' Thereupon his father sent back word, 'My son, is a son ever ashamed to return to his father? And is it not to your father that you will be returning?'" (1980:216).

and there he wasted all his money in wild living. Danker comments on an interesting parallel to this story from an Egyptian letter of a man, Antonios Longinus, to his mother, in which he asked his mother Neilus humbly to forgive him: "I was ashamed to go to Kanaris because I am so shabby. I am writing to tell you that I am naked. I plead with you, forgive me. I know well enough what I have done to myself. I have learned my lesson. I know that I made a mistake." Jesus' story, as told by Luke, goes beyond the experience of a wayward son and envisages also an elder brother, a "young man whose body stayed home, but whose heart was lost in misunderstanding a father's love" (1974:170).

15:16 *even the pods he was feeding.* Pods and seeds taken from the locust or carob tree served as fodder for pigs and cattle. In hard times, these were sometimes consumed by the poor.

15:29 *All these years I've slaved for you.* "In this speech [15:29-30] the elder brother shows that he also has, all along, been an unworthy son, serving his father not out of love but in the spirit of a hireling. The fact that he would have liked to enjoy himself 'with his friends' and away from his father, proves that he too was at heart a prodigal! And at heart the Pharisees and Scribes (v. 2) were also wanderers from God" (Weymouth 1912:207).

COMMENTARY

This is probably the most famous parable Jesus ever taught, and it has worked its way into general parlance in the Western world and other places that have been introduced to the Christian tradition. It was originally given with the two preceding parables in the context of criticism from the Pharisees and the scribes, who were grumbling about Jesus' methods and the questionable company he was keeping (15:2). All three parables, as we have suggested, advocate the importance of seeking, finding, and restoring the lost. The third parable is the most memorable and developed of the three. It was introduced "to illustrate the point further" (15:11a). "Unlike the lost sheep and lost coin, which were not responsible in any way for being lost, the lost son is lost because of his own wayward actions. If anyone deserved what he got, it would have to be this ungrateful, selfish, and wasteful young man. Jesus graphically portrays the ingratitude, sin, and degradation of this person" (Evans 1990:232).

The wayward son's escapades are described first. He seems to be completely selfish, egocentric, and anxious to move far away from his father's influence and authority and, probably, from Jewish restrictions and limitations. Moreover, although it was normal to wait until the father died before dividing the father's assets, this young man wanted his share of the estate immediately, showing no concern for his father's welfare and no interest in the management of the family holdings. Bailey writes that if "we were to read the parable of the prodigal son without realizing that the son's initial request for his share of the inheritance would be heard, within peasant village culture, as expressing the shocking wish that his father were dead, [our] entire reading of the parable would get off on the wrong foot" (1976:161).

The son's profligacy is indicated by the reference to "wild living" and the fact that he "wasted all his money" (15:13). His squandering of resources was accompanied by the onset of hard times as "a great famine swept over the land, and he began to starve" (15:14). In such desperate circumstances, the prodigal was reduced to feeding pigs. We must recall here that eating pigs was clearly something that was totally forbidden by the Jewish dietary laws (Lev 11:7; Deut 14:8; cf. Lev 5:2; Acts 10:14); in fact, Jewish tradition despised the work of a pig farmer ("cursed be the man who raises pigs," *b. Bava Qamma* 82b, cited by Fitzmyer 1985:1088). But the son's degradation went further, for he was reduced by hunger pangs to the point that he even ate the "pods he was feeding the pigs" (15:16). In respectable, law-abiding Jewish eyes, he had reached the lowest level of humiliation and shame.

At this point, he finally "came to his senses" (15:17), which is a Semitic way of speaking of repentance. He prepared a penitent speech, acknowledged his desperate need, and hoped to escape the pangs of hunger by returning to his father, apologizing for his sinfulness, asking his forgiveness, and requesting humble employment "as a hired servant" (15:19).

At this point, the focus of the parable turns to the father, who took the initiative in seeking his son's reconciliation and restoration to the family. In a way quite out of keeping with the dignified oriental father, this merciful father saw the son at a great distance and ran out to meet him. Filled with love and compassion, the father welcomed him as he embraced, kissed, and forgave his wayward son (15:20). The son was then invested with tokens of honor and acceptance:

> The best robe was a sign of position and the ring also, especially if, as many hold, a signet ring is meant (cf. Gen 41:42; Esth 3:10; 8:2; [Zech 3:4]). . . . In his destitution his son went barefoot. But this was fitting only for a slave and the [sandals] marked him out as a freeman. The fattened calf was clearly an animal carefully looked after for some special occasion. (Morris 1974:266)

Another point needs to be made here, and that is the fact that the third parable starts by telling us: "A man had *two* sons" (15:11b). Despite the fact that the parable has been generally described as that of "the prodigal son," there is considerable interest in the elder brother, who is the focus of attention in 15:25-32. What would he do when the younger son repented and came home? Would he join in the father's joy and participate in the celebrations, or would he sulk and remain outside the party? The father obviously loved both sons; indeed, he reminded the complaining older son of his loving provision for him: "Everything I have is yours" (15:31).

The parable reveals the anger of the older son, who had been working in the fields and returned home to the sounds of "music and dancing in the house" (15:25). When he learned the cause of the celebration, he vented his anger on the forgiving father, declaring: "All these years I've slaved for you and . . . you never gave me even one young goat for a feast with my friends" (15:29). There is a certain nastiness and vindictiveness in the older son's words that runs completely contrary to the compassionate attitude of his father, who forgave the one son and "came out and begged" the other to come inside and share in the family party (15:28). In addition, the cranky older brother attributed the worst possible interpretation on his brother's misfortune, attributing it to reckless "squandering" of his father's inheritance "on prostitutes" (15:30).

There was evidently an ungenerous spirit that Jesus perceived in his critics, the scribes and Pharisees, who had found fault with his contacts with tax collectors and "sinners"—people like the tax collector Zacchaeus, whom he would meet a little later (19:1-10; cf. 5:27-32), and "the poor, the crippled, the lame, and the blind," whom Jesus was reaching out to and inviting into the Kingdom's joys and blessings (14:13, 21; cf. 7:22-23). God was plainly active in the ministry of Jesus, forgiving and restoring sinners like the prodigal son, who had slipped into the greatest shame and degradation and had no claim on the father's resources. Divine grace was not appreciated by the critics, who wanted to earn God's favor and had no sympathy for those like the prodigal, who had to come back humbly to seek the Father's mercy when they didn't deserve it.

This parable, then, was clearly a weapon of controversy used by Jesus to challenge his critics to acknowledge the error of their ways, to see in his ministry God's beneficent grace for sinners, and to enter with joy and celebration into life in the heavenly Father's Kingdom, sharing in the party. Would they come in or stay outside? The choice was theirs, and the parable does not answer the question. If the Kingdom of God were like a party, would it not be tragic to remain outside? Jesus' critics were given a choice.

◆ EE. Parable of the Shrewd Manager (16:1-18)

Jesus told this story to his disciples: "There was a certain rich man who had a manager handling his affairs. One day a report came that the manager was wasting his employer's money. ²So the employer called him in and said, 'What's this I hear about you? Get your report in order, because you are going to be fired.'

³"The manager thought to himself, 'Now what? My boss has fired me. I don't have the strength to dig ditches, and I'm too proud to beg. ⁴Ah, I know how to ensure that I'll have plenty of friends who will give me a home when I am fired.'

⁵"So he invited each person who owed money to his employer to come and discuss the situation. He asked the first one, 'How much do you owe him?' ⁶The man replied, 'I owe him 800 gallons of olive oil.' So the manager told him, 'Take the bill and quickly change it to 400 gallons.*'

⁷"'And how much do you owe my employer?' he asked the next man. 'I owe him 1,000 bushels of wheat,' was the reply. 'Here,' the manager said, 'take the bill and change it to 800 bushels.*'

⁸"The rich man had to admire the dishonest rascal for being so shrewd. And it is true that the children of this world are more shrewd in dealing with the world around them than are the children of the light. ⁹Here's the lesson: Use your worldly resources to benefit others and make friends. Then, when your earthly possessions are gone, they will welcome you to an eternal home.*

¹⁰"If you are faithful in little things, you will be faithful in large ones. But if you are dishonest in little things, you won't be honest with greater responsibilities. ¹¹And if you are untrustworthy about worldly wealth, who will trust you with the true riches of heaven? ¹²And if you are not faithful with other people's things, why should you be trusted with things of your own?

¹³"No one can serve two masters. For you will hate one and love the other; you will be devoted to one and despise the other. You cannot serve both God and money."

¹⁴The Pharisees, who dearly loved their money, heard all this and scoffed at him. ¹⁵Then he said to them, "You like to appear righteous in public, but God knows your hearts. What this world honors is detestable in the sight of God.

¹⁶"Until John the Baptist, the law of Moses and the messages of the prophets were your guides. But now the Good News of the Kingdom of God is preached, and everyone is eager to get in.* ¹⁷But that doesn't mean that the law has lost its force. It is easier for heaven and earth to disappear than for the smallest point of God's law to be overturned.

¹⁸"For example, a man who divorces his wife and marries someone else commits adultery. And anyone who marries a woman divorced from her husband commits adultery."

16:6 Greek *100 baths . . . 50 [baths].* 16:7 Greek *100 korous . . . 80 [korous].* 16:9 Or *you will be welcomed into eternal homes.* 16:16 Or *everyone is urged to enter in.*

NOTES

16:1 *story.* Lit., "parable."

wasting . . . money. The same verb is used here that is used of the prodigal son who squandered his resources in dissolute living (*diaskorpizō* [TG1287, ZG1399]; 15:13). The initial picture of the steward, then, is of a man who was dismissed for mismanagement, not dishonesty. So this is a parable about worldly shrewdness (the "rich man" in 16:8 is neither God nor Jesus), and 16:8b is Jesus' explanation.

16:6 *800 gallons of olive oil . . . 400 gallons.* The Gr. word *batos* [TG943, ZG1004] (often transliterated "bath") was "a liquid measure of 65 pints or 8.1 gallons" (Neuman 1971:32). The NLT references to 800 gallons and 400 gallons respectively are clear and reasonably accurate (cf. NRSV, which speaks of "a hundred jugs of olive oil" reduced to "fifty").

16:7 *1,000 bushels of wheat . . . 800 bushels.* The Gr. word *koros* [TG2884, ZG3174] (often transliterated "kor") was a dry measure of about 10 to 12 bushels. The NLT is roughly accurate in speaking of a "1000 bushels of wheat" and "800 bushels" respectively (cf. NRSV, which speaks of a "hundred containers of wheat" reduced to a debt of "eighty"). As Dever (1985) has commented: "it must be observed that our reconstruction of ancient weights and measures, while more extensive and accurate than it was just fifteen or twenty years ago, is still provisional and may change with further archaeological discoveries" (see also Freedman 2000:1373-1376).

16:10 *If you are faithful in little things, you will be faithful in large ones.* Craddock has remarked, "Verses 10-12 contain sayings all of which are framed on what logicians call an argument *a fortiori*, that is, an argument from the lesser to the greater. The life of a disciple is one of faithful attention to the frequent and familiar tasks of each day, however small and insignificant they may seem" (1990:191).

16:13 *You cannot serve both God and money.* This puts God and money in an antithetical relationship to one another, stating that to be devoted to one is to rule out the pressing claims of the other. Each demands a commanding position that "calls the shots" and dominates one's life, but real, practical devotion to both is impossible. Material things have their place and can be used to advance spiritual ends, but they must be subordinated so that one keeps "first things first" (see Matt 6:33; 1 Tim 6:17-19). Believers are called to be astute in their use of material resources to advance the Kingdom of God.

16:16 *Until John the Baptist, the law of Moses and the messages of the prophets were your guides.* This is an important verse in exploring Luke's conception of holy history. Conzelmann believed that Luke had divided history into three epochs or eras. The first period, Conzelmann thought, ran from creation to the appearance of John the Baptist (referred to above in 16:16a). The second period, mentioned in Luke 16:16b, is thought of as the period of Jesus, when "the Good News of the Kingdom of God is preached," and the third period is the time of the church (see Acts 1:6-8). However, further study has cast doubt on whether this tripartite scheme is adequate, for Luke tends to support a twofold scheme of promise and fulfillment (see 24:25-27, 44-47). It is also highly questionable that Jesus and his church should be separated from one another in such a radical way. For a critique of Conzelmann's position, see Stein (1992:418), who observes, "It now is generally agreed that if Conzelmann had included Luke 1–2 as part of the Gospel, he would not have been able to argue so strongly for placing John [the Baptizer] in the OT era." Stein also notes there that "Matthew 11:12, the parallel to Luke 16:16, portrays John as part of the NT age." Wright offers a plausible reading of Luke 16:16 that has been endorsed by Ben Witherington III: "Jesus is referring obliquely to the fact that the Zealots, violent men, are trying to hijack the kingdom of God for their own nationalistic ends" (1999:263).

the Good News of the Kingdom of God is preached, and everyone is eager to get in. Luke speaks of the Kingdom being "preached" (*euangelizetai* [TG2097/A, ZG2294]) rather than using the wording in Matt 11:12, which says the Kingdom has been "forcefully advancing" (*biazetai* [TG971/A, ZG1041]). Luke's wording indicates that he understood that "the kingdom had burst upon the scene with the arrival of Jesus" (Wright 1996:468). The next clause, "everyone is eager to get in," does, however, use the word *biazetai*, and here its meaning is crucial. Note the NLT mg, which reads the passive meaning here: "Everyone is urged to enter in." A plausible case can be made for this interpretation as Schweitzer (1984:258) and Fitzmyer (1985:1117) have shown. Likewise, Bock argues "Why is Jesus warning and exhorting his opponents so constantly? Because he is attempting to persuade them to respond morally. In a sense, his mission is bound up in his proclamation to and effort toward those most opposed to him. . . . People may think that they can take or leave the kingdom message, but the warnings are necessary because the message will leave them, depending on how they respond. Thus the need to urge insistently [that they enter the kingdom]" (1996:1353). The time of messianic fulfillment has arrived and all are strongly invited to share in the Good News offered in Christ.

16:17 *that doesn't mean that the law has lost its force.* Apparently, Luke was aware that some people would fear that living under God's grace might lead to moral laxity, mistakenly supposing that the law belonged totally to the past. This is not the case, as Jesus reminded his audience that the law was to be fulfilled in the Good News. "Jesus never cast doubt on the validity of the Law. It was the way it was interpreted, particularly by the Pharisees, that drew his criticism" (Morris 1974:250).

16:18 *a man who divorces his wife and marries someone else commits adultery.* For a succinct treatment of marriage in the Bible, see von Allmen 1958. The subject of divorce is also discussed in Matt 5:31-32; 19:3-9; and Mark 10:11-12. For a brief analysis of Jesus' treatment of divorce, see Guthrie, who notes, "In both Mark and Luke there is prohibition of divorce, whereas in both the Matthew passages an exceptive clause is introduced (except for unchastity). Many regard the clause in Matthew as a later addition to the more rigorous form of the saying found in the other Gospels. A further point that Mark includes is the saying that a woman who divorces her husband and marries another man commits adultery, while all the Gospels contain a similar statement about divorced husbands who remarry. In both Mark (Mark 10:9) and Matthew (Matt 19:6), the creation story (Gen 1:27) is cited in support of the teaching, but Matthew also includes the comment that Moses allowed a bill of divorcement because of the hardness of the hearts of the people" (1981: 949-950). When the Christian message radically changes the hearts of people, then the original purpose of God for the institution of marriage can be fulfilled.

COMMENTARY

The striking difference between this parable and the preceding one (15:11-31) is well explained by Gooding:

> The first of the two parables teaches us that if we sinfully waste our lives and then, even at the eleventh hour, come back to God in true repentance and faith, the fact that we have wasted our lives will make no difference at all to the pardon we shall receive or to our acceptance with the Father. The second parable puts the other side of the story: if we waste our lives, it will in another sense make an eternal difference. (1987:272-273)

The second parable (16:1-9) raises several puzzling questions because it seems to contemporary Christians that Jesus here is commending dishonesty (though actually 16:1 tells us that the steward was dismissed because of mismanagement rather than dishonesty). First, they ask, why would the rich man praise a dishonest manager? Second, why would Jesus commend the actions of the dishonest steward? The answers to these questions seem to lie in an understanding of the profit-taking arrangements under which the dishonest manager worked (see Derrett 1961). He was doing nothing unethical in decreasing the amounts due him, but simply providing for his future with wise planning and prudent action. The steward's culpability lay not in his dishonesty, but rather in the fact that he had been guilty in squandering his master's resources (16:1), and he must now pay the price of dismissal. The wily steward, for prudential reasons, decided to cancel the commissions that he would have taken, and thus put himself in a favorable position with the landlord's creditors, who would be open to helping him in the future. It was a calculated decision involving short-term pain for long-term gain (so Caird 1963:185-188). Understood in this way it is easier to understand why Jesus saw fit to commend the sagacious manager as a worthy example for his followers. What Jesus was commending was the manager's *shrewdness*, a thing that worldly people are often good at achieving (note 16:8—"the children of this world are *more shrewd* in dealing with the world around them than are the children of the light"). There is a certain prudential quality about the shrewd manager that reminds us of some maxims in the book of Proverbs (e.g., Prov 18:15; 22:3; 27:12).

In normal commercial affairs, most business people can be expected to look out for themselves by exercising prudence and "providing for a rainy day." That is the case envisaged here, where a steward of an estate, probably working for an absentee landlord, was found guilty of mismanaging his position. In this situation, he faced certain loss of employment and dismissal because he had abused the trust that had been placed in him. In such critical circumstances, he was confronted by an uncertain future and contemplated his uncomfortable choices: "I don't have the strength to dig ditches, and I'm too proud to beg" (16:3). He had to decide on a course of action that was prudent in light of the circumstances, and he had to take responsibility for his own future before his position of trust was finally terminated. He did such a prudent, skillful assessment that he was commended, not for his squandering of resources, but for his sagacity. He had the common-sense wisdom to size up the situation and make prompt, suitable plans for the future.

The argument Jesus used here is clearly *from the lesser to the greater*. As we know from other examples, Jesus often couched his teaching in this format (see 11:11-13; 12:24, 28; Matt 7:11; 10:25; 12:12). If worldly people have that degree of wisdom in planning for a temporal and secular future, how much more should the people of God make appropriate plans for their eternal future!

The sayings in 16:10-13 are independent of the parable that precedes them, but they reinforce its teaching. They have a familiar ring about them because they appear several times in the teaching of Jesus and in different contexts: "If you are faithful in little things, you will be faithful in large ones" (16:10; cf. 19:17; Matt 25:21-23). The converse, sadly, was also true, and could be applied to eternal matters: "If you are untrustworthy about worldly wealth, who will trust you with the true riches of heaven?" (16:11). Earthly life is a testing ground for heavenly life, and the moral conditions that require faithfulness here and now are of vital significance to one's eternal position. A responsible, faithful attitude is required because there will be lasting consequences. As Caird has noted:

> All the opportunities of this world are tests of character, and by his behaviour in small matters a man shows whether or not he is fit for larger responsibility. In particular, worldly wealth is given to men on trust; it does not belong to them, but by their use of it they can show whether or not they are fit to be entrusted with real wealth, the wealth of the heavenly kingdom. (1963:188)

Verse 13, like verses 10-12, is a saying that stands somewhat independent of the parable that precedes it, but it also serves to reinforce the basic teaching of the parable that was aimed directly at the disciples (see 16:1). Instead of the movement from the lesser to the greater, it comes as a blunt, uncompromising remark that was highly disturbing to some of the listeners of Jesus: "You cannot serve both God and money" (16:13). This all-or-nothing comment was apparently highly unwelcome to the Pharisees, and Luke himself inserts a note of criticism here: they "dearly loved their money" (16:14). To be fair, we should note Caird's comment:

> There is no evidence that they were addicted to avarice to the same extent as either the Sadducees or the tax gatherers, but they did tend, with ample justification from the Old Testament, to regard prosperity, or at least their own prosperity, as the reward of godliness. The word "abomination" [translated in the NLT as "detestable"] always connotes idolatry; the pursuit of human recognition is idolatry in God's eyes. (1963:188)

The Pharisees indeed regarded wealth as a sign of God's approval and blessing (cf. Deut 28:1-4; 1 Sam 2:6-7; Ps 37:22; 107:38; 113:7-8; Prov 10:22; Eccl 3:10-13). Such an either-or choice was obviously painful and pointed to the danger that their covetousness presented (cf. the searching passage on the "peril of riches" repeated in each of the synoptic Gospels—Matt 19:16-30; Mark 10:17-31; Luke 18:18-30). It is no wonder that the Pharisees "scoffed at him" (16:14). Jesus had attacked their insincerity and duplicity (cf. the seven woes directed against the scribes and Pharisees in Matt 23). While they could put on a good performance of piety before their Jewish contemporaries, God knew what was really in their hearts (16:15), and they couldn't deceive him. There was a profound difference between what the world praised and what God esteemed. Worldly values and estimates are in total contradiction to the transcendent claims of the Kingdom of God!

Of course, John the Baptist had prepared the way for this Kingdom, and, before John the Baptist, they had been given the law of Moses and the messages of the prophets to guide them in the divinely appointed way (16:16a). But holy history had moved to the time of fulfillment, and the Kingdom of God had entered human history. The Good News was being offered to the Jewish people, and earnest seekers were anxious to gain entrance to it (16:16b). This did not mean that the law had lost its force; on the contrary, it was the divinely given preparation for the coming of the Good News. It had a permanent place in the plan of God, and its full force was *not* to be overturned by humans for their own convenience (in a similar vein, see Matt 5:17-20)!

Jesus cited a classic example of the law's ongoing relevance by referring to the divine institution of marriage (for fuller development of his teaching on sexuality and marriage, see Matt 19:1-12; Mark 10:1-12). Marriage, by divine intention, was to be a lifelong union of a man and a woman, and was viewed as a permanent, covenantal agreement. It was therefore not to be entered into casually, thoughtlessly, or carelessly, but soberly, thoughtfully, and in the reverent fear of God. The ideal was a solemn covenant that was viewed as binding and unbreakable. To break it in order to take up with someone else was considered a violation of a solemn agreement that had been made before God and the community. The law was certainly relevant here, for it held up the permanent divine ideal of a lifelong commitment between a man and his wife: "This explains why a man leaves his father and mother and is joined to his wife, and the two are united into one" (Gen 2:24). To violate this union deliberately was to fracture the divine commandment and to fall under judgment.

◆   **FF. Parable of the Rich Man and Lazarus (16:19-31)**

¹⁹Jesus said, "There was a certain rich man who was splendidly clothed in purple and fine linen and who lived each day in luxury. ²⁰At his gate lay a poor man named Lazarus who was covered with sores. ²¹As Lazarus lay there longing for scraps from the rich man's table, the dogs would come and lick his open sores.

²²"Finally, the poor man died and was carried by the angels to be with Abraham.* The rich man also died and was buried, ²³and his soul went to the place of the dead.* There, in torment, he saw Abraham in the far distance with Lazarus at his side.

²⁴"The rich man shouted, 'Father Abraham, have some pity! Send Lazarus over here to dip the tip of his finger in water and cool my tongue. I am in anguish in these flames.'

²⁵"But Abraham said to him, 'Son, remember that during your lifetime you had everything you wanted, and Lazarus had nothing. So now he is here being comforted, and you are in anguish. ²⁶And besides, there is a great chasm separating us. No one can cross over to you from here, and no one can cross over to us from there.'

²⁷"Then the rich man said, 'Please, Father Abraham, at least send him to my father's home. ²⁸For I have five brothers, and I want him to warn them so they don't end up in this place of torment.'

²⁹"But Abraham said, 'Moses and the prophets have warned them. Your brothers can read what they wrote.'

³⁰"The rich man replied, 'No, Father Abraham! But if someone is sent to them from the dead, then they will repent of their sins and turn to God.'

³¹"But Abraham said, 'If they won't listen to Moses and the prophets, they won't listen even if someone rises from the dead.' "

16:22 Greek *into Abraham's bosom.* 16:23 Greek *to Hades.*

N O T E S

16:19 *There was a certain rich man.* This parable is introduced by the same words as the parable of the shrewd manager: "There was a certain rich man" (16:1). This strongly suggests that, in both of these parables, there is an intention to teach the proper use of wealth.

splendidly clothed in purple and fine linen. The clothing mentioned was that of royalty, and the implication is that the rich man lived like a king (cf. Prov 31:22; Luke 7:25). Leaney (1958:225-226) wonders if the rich man in view was King Herod Antipas, ruler of Galilee and Perea, who had five brothers when the parable was originally composed, a possibility cited by Evans (1990:250), though there is no necessary reference to a historical person and generally parables do not name their characters (even though Lazarus is mentioned here).

16:20 *At his gate lay.* The Gr. verb *ebeblēto* [TG906, ZG965] translated here as "lay" is pluperfect passive: "He had been placed there and was still there" (Rienecker and Rogers 1977:190).

a poor man. There is a great deal in the Bible on the needs of the poor. The OT legal texts seek to protect the poor, orphans, widows, or strangers (Lev 19:9-10; 25:25, 35; Deut 15:7-11; 24:19-21). The prophets show a real concern for those who are exploited and warn against oppressing the poor (Isa 3:14-15; 5:8; Amos 2:7; 4:1; 5:11). The Psalms speak of God as the defender of the poor (Pss 22:26; 35:10; 40:17; 70:5). "The Gospel of Luke shows an empathy for the poor and hostility toward the rich that is more pronounced than in the other Gospels [note Luke 6:20; cf. Matt 5:3]" (Freedman 2000:1071). For more details, see DJG 701-710; Davids 1980:4-58.

16:21 *Lazarus.* Another point of contrast between the rich man and Lazarus is that only Lazarus is given a name—that is, significance. His name means "God has helped," and this feature might point to the contrast with his earthly life, when human help was in scarce supply. The parable has been rightly seen as in keeping with one of Luke's key themes: "Eschatological reversal is central in Luke's understanding of the final coming of the reign of God. . . . The story . . . is here used by Luke to address Pharisees who loved wealth and scoffed at Jesus' position on the subject (v. 14)" (Craddock 1992:195).

16:22 *the poor man died and was carried by the angels.* An accepted idea among the Jews was that angels carried the dead to their eternal destination (see *The Testament of Asher* 6:4-6). This belief might also be found in *The Shepherd of Hermas* (Vision 2.2.7; Similitudes 9:25). On the role of angels, see Gardner 1995:44-49 and the comments on 1:11-17; 2:8-20; 4:10.

to be with Abraham. Lit., "into Abraham's bosom" (cf. NLT mg). The Gr. word *kolpos* [TG2859, ZG3146] is the noun used here to denote "chest" or "bosom" (cf. John 1:18). Abraham's bosom was equated in Jewish tradition with paradise (see *b. Qiddushin* 72a-b; cf. Luke 23:43) as the abode of the righteous dead, who stayed there in a place of rest, honor, and blessedness while awaiting future vindication by God. "In using *kolpos,* 'bosom,' it may suggest either a place of honor for a guest at a banquet at the right of the host (see John 13:23) or an association of intimacy (see John 1:18)" (Fitzmyer 1985:1132). Notice that Abraham is mentioned as participating in the messianic banquet in Luke 13:28, so "to be with Abraham" means "that the beggar's place was right next to the father of all Israel, in his bosom, at the place of honor" (Tolbert 1970:132).

The rich man also died and was buried. The marked contrast continues in this verse, for no burial rites are mentioned for the wealthy man, while Lazarus has been borne by angels to paradise. At death there is a decided reversal of roles.

16:23 *the place of the dead.* Gr., *hadēs* [TG86, ZG87] (Hades). In the LXX, *hadēs* is used over 100 times, usually to translate the Heb. word *she'ol* ([TH7585, ZH8619]), the place that receives the dead. It is viewed as a place of darkness and gloom, where God is not remembered (Job 10:21-22; 26:5; Pss 6:5; 30:9; Prov 1:12; 27:20; Isa 5:14). *hadēs* occurs 10 times in the NT, appearing only in Matthew, Luke, Acts, and Revelation. It is found within the earth (Matt 11:23; Luke 10:15; cf. Matt 12:40). Like a city, it is pictured with gates (Matt 16:18, KJV). It is viewed as only a temporary place, for it must give up its dead again at the Resurrection (Rev 20:13). "According to Acts 2:27, 31 and Luke 16:23, 26, all the dead are in Hades" (TDNT 2:207).

Many readers view the two compartments spoken of in 16:22-23 as an actual depiction of postmortem conditions. However, this story is not intended to give a concrete description or revelation of the way things are after death or the state of the OT saints (Craddock 1992:195). Details such as this and the angels in 16:22 were characterized by Jesus according to local color to make the contrast between the two men vivid and memorable. Rather, the description of the two places points clearly to "an unbridgeable gulf between the locale of bliss and that of torment" (Fitzmyer 1985:1133). People are accountable for their relationships to their fellows (see 10:27; Lev 19:18; Matt 22:39), and in the final analysis are answerable for their actions to God (cf. Heb 9:27).

16:24 dip the tip of his finger in water and cool my tongue. While Paradise was favored with abundant water, hell (Hades) was depicted in Jewish tradition as hot and dry, as in 2 Esdr 8:59, which says, "so the thirst and torment which are prepared await them." (Cf. 2 Esdr 7:79-87, which describes the "torments" of those "who have not kept the way of the Most High, who have despised his law and hated those who fear God.")

I am in anguish in these flames. The notion of fire in hades, as Evans has pointed out, can probably be traced back to Isa 66:24, "which is quoted in Mark 9:48 (see also Rev 20:4-15). The anguish now experienced by the rich man is similar to (but more severe than) the burning pain the poor man had experienced because of his ulcerous condition" (1990: 251).

16:26 great chasm. The reference to a great chasm fixed "is no doubt a pictorial detail, but it means that in the afterlife there is no passing from one state to the other" (Morris 1974:254; see related note on 16:23). Fitzmyer calls this "an unbridgeable gulf between the locale of bliss and that of torment" and notes that the phrase itself is used with a different meaning in 2 Sam 18:17, LXX (1985:1133).

16:30 if someone is sent to them from the dead. No external evidence alone is adequate to compel faith. On this verse, note the perceptive remark of Siebald (1992:208): "The climactic statement has to do with one who 'rose from the dead,' an evident allusion to the resurrection of Jesus, which suggests that the story is also a polemic directed against those who refuse the gospel, failing to heed 'Moses and the prophets.'"

then they will repent. The importance of repentance, or "turning from sin," is a frequent theme in Luke–Acts (10:13; 16:30; 17:3-4; Acts 3:19; 17:30; 20:21). Repentance is a major element in the preaching of John the Baptist (3:3, 8), Jesus (5:32; 13:3-5; 24:47), and in the preaching of the early church (Acts 2:38; 5:31; 8:22; 11:18; 26:20).

COMMENTARY

The parable on the rich man and Lazarus continues the teaching on the right and wrong uses of money presented in the opening verses of chapter 16. God intended that material resources be shared with others, and those in desperate need were to be cared for ("use your worldly resources to benefit others," 16:9). This was common Jewish thinking, but covetous people often rejected it. Aggressive landlords employing rapacious business practices fleeced the poor (cf. Job 22:6-11; 29:11-16; Isa 58:7-8; Ezek 18:5-9, 14-18; Amos 8:4-6). Mark 12:40, for instance, expresses Jesus' condemnation of the scribes and Pharisees for just this offence: "They shamelessly cheat widows out of their property and then pretend to be pious by making long prayers in public. Because of this, they will be more severely punished."

The parable of the rich man and Lazarus does not describe such a vicious, deliberate exploitation of the poor. Rather, it is presented as an illustration of the proper use of material resources in the face of conspicuous human need. If Jeremias is correct, it adapts a popular Egyptian folk-tale of the journey of Si-Osiris to the underworld, which concludes with the words: "He who has been good on earth, will be blessed in the kingdom of the dead, and he who has been evil on earth, will suffer in the kingdom of the dead." Jeremias suggests that Alexandrian Jews brought the tale to Palestine where it became popular. He argues that Jesus was familiar with the story, noting that he used it in "the parable of the Great Supper" (14:15-24; 1963:183). Similarly, Fitzmyer notes "seven other tales about retribution in the afterlife from rabbinic sources of later date, the earliest of which is found in two forms in the Palestinian Talmud (*y. Sanhedrin* 6.23d and *y. Hagigah* 2.77d)— scarcely before AD 400" (1985:1126).

In Luke, the parable is really a drama in two acts, and it is the only parable given by Jesus in which one of the characters is actually named. Further:

> The picture of the fate in store for the good and the evil after death is also drawn from traditional Jewish sources (cf. *2 Enoch* 9:10). But it was not the intention of Jesus to propagate a strict doctrine of rewards and punishments (nothing is said about the piety of Lazarus), or to give a topographical guide to the afterworld. As he tells it, the point of the story is to be found in the character of the rich man and in the reasons for his failure to use the two kinds of opportunity granted to him, the first by his wealth, the second by his religion. (Caird 1963:191)

Act I presents the figure of Lazarus, a person with dire human need, who was literally at the door of the rich man, and yet whose pressing needs went unmet. The rich man, who remains unnamed, but is often called "Dives" from the Latin Vulgate version meaning "rich man," was daily confronted with a poor man "covered with sores" (a use of precise medical language). Dives, who enjoyed a lavish lifestyle, ignored Lazarus' repulsive condition. He basked every day in luxury and wore splendid clothing (16:19). He was quite unprepared to go out of his way to minister to the physical condition of a weak, helpless man at his door. There was no expression of compassion offered, despite the poor man's "longing for scraps from the rich man's table" (16:21). Luke painted a sad picture of two virtual solitudes—one rich and luxurious, the other poor and pitiable. No contact was made between the two men.

Things were different after death. In Act II, the affluent man died and received a proper Jewish burial. (No burial is mentioned in Lazarus' case.) The rich man's earthly life was over, and all the luxury and extravagance of his selfish lifestyle were behind him. Luke tells us that his soul went to the "place of the dead" (*hadēs* [TG86, ZG87]; see note on 16:23). When the poor man died, he was carried by the angels to be with Abraham, the great father of the Jewish people who had been given a divine promise that in him and in his family all the families of the earth would be blessed (Gen 12:1-3; 22:17-18). Lazarus was now in the place of comfort in the "bosom" of Abraham, the great patriarch of the people of God. While Lazarus had faced all manner of difficulties in his earthly existence, things were totally changed. Eschatological reversal had taken place, and death changed the situation for both men.

The situations of the two men had been dramatically reversed in the afterlife, though the metaphysical details of that life are not described. The point made is that God's view of things differs from man's earthly perspective. Lazarus was now in the blessed company of Father Abraham, while the rich man was "in torment" (16:22-23). Dives was seeking pity because he was "in anguish," so he made an earnest request that Lazarus be sent over to ease his pain (16:24). His request was met with a reminder that "during [his] lifetime" he had all kinds of opportunities to enjoy "everything [he] wanted," but those opportunities were over now (16:25). "A great chasm" separated those in fellowship with Abraham from those suffering anguish and torment, and there was no possibility of bridging that gulf (16:26). God had pronounced judgment on the destinies of the two men; it was final and irreversible.

The parable concludes with an epilogue in which Dives begs for an opportunity to send Lazarus to alert his five brothers to the similar danger that they faced (16:27-28). Despite the natural concern that Dives had to spare his brothers his own unenviable destiny, he was reminded that they had actually received sufficient warning already in the Scriptures: "Moses and the prophets have warned them. Your brothers can read what they wrote" (16:29). Dives's urgent, repeated request for a personal word of warning was rejected. The lesson is clear to Jesus' critics and the skeptics: if people refuse to give heed to the teachings of Scripture and find themselves out of favor with God in the future life, then they have only their own stubbornness and impenitence to blame. Even if one were to come back from the dead to speak to them (an apparent reference to those who later refused the evidence of the resurrection of Jesus), it would not be enough to convince and change them (16:31). The wheels of God's justice may "grind slowly, but they grind exceedingly fine" (Sextus Empiricus *Adversus Mathematicus* 1.287). The ultimate day of reckoning was coming, and adequate notice had been given of the need to be prepared! Once again, Luke's Gospel stresses the importance of genuine repentance and turning to God, and warns about the dangers of neglect and carelessness.

Jesus' point in the parable is not to give a guided tour of the afterlife, nor to teach a strict doctrine of rewards and punishments (note that nothing is said about the godliness of Lazarus), nor to answer speculation about things that God has not chosen to reveal to his servants, but to encourage practical action in the face of obvious human need (cf. Deut 29:29; Jas 2:14-17). Jesus stressed the character of the rich man and exposed his failure to use the opportunities he was given through both his material resources and his religious inheritance in the Law and the Prophets. And one might add that a third factor in the opportunities given him was his proximity—the needy man was placed right before him and called out for help.

The parable has two important lessons for the modern reader, as Hunter has pointed out: First, it clearly points to the requirement that believers meet pressing human needs such as feeding the hungry, clothing the naked, visiting prisoners, and ministering to the helpless (cf. Matt 25:34-45). Second, it insists that human beings must act on the revelation of God's purposes they have been given and not demand some supernatural sign before they act (11:29; cf. Matt 12:39; 16:4; 1971:170).

◆   ## GG. Teachings about Forgiveness and Faith (17:1-10; cf. Matt 18:6-7, 15; Mark 9:42)

One day Jesus said to his disciples, "There will always be temptations to sin, but what sorrow awaits the person who does the tempting! ²It would be better to be thrown into the sea with a millstone hung around your neck than to cause one of these little ones to fall into sin. ³So watch yourselves!

"If another believer* sins, rebuke that person; then if there is repentance, forgive. ⁴Even if that person wrongs you seven times a day and each time turns again and asks forgiveness, you must forgive."

⁵The apostles said to the Lord, "Show us how to increase our faith."

⁶The Lord answered, "If you had faith even as small as a mustard seed, you could say to this mulberry tree, 'May you be uprooted and thrown into the sea,' and it would obey you!

⁷"When a servant comes in from plowing or taking care of sheep, does his master say, 'Come in and eat with me'? ⁸No, he says, 'Prepare my meal, put on your apron, and serve me while I eat. Then you can eat later.' ⁹And does the master thank the servant for doing what he was told to do? Of course not. ¹⁰In the same way, when you obey me you should say, 'We are unworthy servants who have simply done our duty.' "

17:3 Greek *If your brother.*

NOTES

17:2 *millstone.* Millstones were used for grinding grain and could be large or small. Some were driven by animals and some were worked by women (for OT examples, see Num 11:8; Jdg 9:53; Deut 24:6; Isa 47:2). The one envisaged in Luke 17:2 (also in Matt 18:6; Mark 9:42) is that of a very heavy millstone turned by an animal. (For descriptions and uses of millstones, see NBD 776; EDNT 2.445.) In the ancient world, as in the modern world, the reference to a millstone around the neck became proverbial for an inescapable, heavy burden leading to one's death.

17:4 *Even if . . . asks forgiveness.* The "if" clause used here in Greek expresses a probable future condition. "Asks forgiveness" is literally, "saying 'I repent.'" The sentence points to the probability of the person falling short again in the future and therefore needing to turn again in repentance.

forgive. On the forgiving (*aphiēmi* [TG863, ZG918]), see DJG 241-243; EDNT 1.181-183. The importance of forgiveness is frequently emphasized in the NT via commands (Matt 5:23-24; 6:14-15; 18:21, 35; Mark 11:25; Luke 11:4; 17:4; 2 Cor 2:7; Eph 4:32; Col 3:13; Jas 2:13). The forgiveness of enemies was taught by both Jesus and Paul (Matt 5:44; Luke 6:27; Rom 12:14). This is an important and much-needed theme in our contemporary society, where an unrelenting insistence on rights often leads to an unforgiving attitude toward those who have wronged their fellow citizens.

17:5 *apostles.* See 6:12-16; 9:1-6 and comments.

17:6 *faith even as small as a mustard seed.* See note on 13:19.

17:9 *the servant.* The Gr. word here is *doulos* [TG1401, ZG1528], meaning "bond slave." Paul frequently used this term to describe his willing captivity and submission to his Lord Jesus Christ (Rom 1:1; Gal 1:10; Phil 1:1). Luke was especially fond of this word, too, for he used it over 25 times (e.g., 2:29; 12:37, 42; 14:17; 19:13, 15, 17, 22).

COMMENTARY

Chapter 17 continues Jesus' instruction to his disciples regarding the meaning and nature of discipleship, a thematic feature in Luke's record of the journey to Jerusalem. In this context, it was appropriate that vital issues of true commitment be addressed, as Jesus traveled to Jerusalem to suffer and die.

Luke recorded four sayings of Jesus here that pertain to important matters such as causing a fellow believer to sin, forgiveness, faith, and duty. Some of these sayings appear in other contexts in Matthew and Mark (see Matt 18:6-7, 15; Mark 9:42), but the saying concerning the servant's wages is unique to Luke (17:7-10).

The first saying concerns "things that cause people to sin" (NIV). Certainly, temptations are an ever-present reality that disciples must face in this world, and Jesus felt the need to prepare his disciples to meet them (see 17:23; 21:8; John 16:33). He wanted to challenge those who loved and followed him not to be the means of bringing about the downfall of others. Jesus warned that sorrow was awaiting "the person who does the tempting" (17:1). It is a serious, terrible thing to be responsible for the moral failure of "one of these little ones" (17:2)—presumably another believer who is less developed in faith and discipleship.

Naturally, such inexperienced persons would look to either older or more mature Christians to set for them a worthy example. If, on the other hand, they let them down, leading the vulnerable ones into temptations, the failure of of those vulnerable ones is a most reprehensible sin (17:2). The corruption of children would be included here, as well as those young in faith. The challenge that Jesus issued to his disciples was a summons to spiritual vigilance and alertness: "Watch yourselves" (17:3a). A similar warning is given later in Luke's Gospel in an apocalyptic section where Jesus is speaking of the future and trying to prepare his disciples to act responsibly: "Watch out! Don't let your hearts be dulled by carousing and drunkenness, and by the worries of this life. Don't let that day catch you unaware" (21:34). Here, the emphasis is not on the future but on careful, sensible living that calls for constant self-discipline and perpetual vigilance.

The second saying gives balance to the first as well as another perspective (17:3b-4). Christians are not expected to be sinless, and there has to be some real provision for human weakness and failure. As the letter of First John reminds us, "If we claim we have no sin, we are only fooling ourselves and not living in the truth" (1 John 1:8). While a sinful course of action could and should be challenged (cf. Gal 2:11; 1 Tim 5:20; 2 Tim 3:16), the way has to be held open for forgiveness and restoration to the Christian community (Gal 6:1; cf. 2 Cor 7:8-10). This means the maintenance of a delicate balance of recognizing the sin and correcting the person who has fallen, while at the same time holding open the way back into fellowship ("if there is repentance, forgive," 17:3). No strings should be attached to that forgiveness. It involves a loving acceptance of a person who has failed repeatedly but still wants to be restored: "Even if that person wrongs you seven times a day and each time turns again and asks forgiveness, you *must* forgive" (17:4).

In Matthew's version of the Lord's Prayer, this teaching on forgiveness immediately follows a request for one's own forgiveness by God: "If you forgive those who sin against you, your heavenly Father will forgive you. But if you refuse to forgive others, your Father will not forgive your sins" (Matt 6:14-15). Later, at least in one textual tradition (though not included in many ancient mss), Luke will record the loving words of forgiveness of the dying Savior to those who were putting him to death: "Father, forgive them, for they don't know what they are doing" (23:34). Similar words are recorded in the martyrdom of Stephen, who died, like his Lord, with a prayer of forgiveness on his lips for those who were stoning him to death: "Lord, don't charge them with this sin!" (Acts 7:60)

The third saying fits right into the issues of discipleship Jesus was presenting (17:3b-5). In view of the reality of temptations to sin, their own moral failures, problems in relating to other believers who had sinned, and an increasing awareness of their own fragility as disciples, the disciples recognized that they needed help. Thus the apostles cried out for the Master's assistance: "Show us how to increase our faith" (17:5). It was an earnest appeal for aid addressed to "the Lord" (a title Luke often applied to Jesus—see 5:8, 12; 6:46; 7:13, 19; 9:54; 10:1; 11:1; 13:15, 23). Jesus told his disciples that the benefits of the minutest amount of faith, "even as small as a mustard seed," were incalculable, and the possibilities of faith were limitless (17:6). Faith must be exercised in service if it is to grow. As disciples attempt to do things for God, their capacity for expectant faith will increase, for they will see God work in remarkable, outstanding ways to answer their prayers and efforts. The letter to the Ephesians makes a similar remark about God's inexhaustible power that is unleashed in believing: "Through his mighty power at work within us, [he is able] to accomplish infinitely more than we might ask or think" (Eph 3:20).

The fourth saying is found only in Luke (17:7-10). The instruction given is an important reminder of the servant status of true followers of Jesus. Their Master's needs must come before their own concerns. Their supreme interest is to wait on their Lord and put him first, just as any Palestinian servant would do for his earthly master. In their case, conscious as they undoubtedly were of their own shortcomings and limitations, they were to serve humbly, aware of the imperfections of their service and the undeniable fact that they were simply performing their duties as expected (17:10). They would never cease being servants, and the Lord's call upon them for lifelong service made mandatory what Eugene Peterson has called "a long obedience in the same direction."

◆   ## HH. Ten Healed of Leprosy (17:11-19)

[11]As Jesus continued on toward Jerusalem, he reached the border between Galilee and Samaria. [12]As he entered a village there, ten lepers stood at a distance, [13]crying out, "Jesus, Master, have mercy on us!"

[14]He looked at them and said, "Go show yourselves to the priests."* And as they went, they were cleansed of their leprosy.

[15]One of them, when he saw that he was healed, came back to Jesus, shouting, "Praise God!" [16]He fell to the ground at Jesus' feet, thanking him for what he had done. This man was a Samaritan.

¹⁷Jesus asked, "Didn't I heal ten men? Where are the other nine? ¹⁸Has no one returned to give glory to God except this foreigner?" ¹⁹And Jesus said to the man, "Stand up and go. Your faith has healed you.*"

17:14 See Lev 14:2-32.   17:19 Or *Your faith has saved you.*

NOTES

17:12 *lepers.* On leprosy in the Bible, see note on 5:12 and see DJG 463-464. Buchanan (1993:431) remarks, "Those who had been diagnosed as lepers by the priest were required to separate themselves from the community [note Num 5:2: 'Command the people of Israel to remove anyone from the camp who has a skin disease' (traditionally rendered 'leprosy')]. . . . The priest had no technique for healing lepers; he only determined whether or not they had been healed ('cleansed'). When he considered the affliction healed, he then offered the correct sin and guilt offerings so that the former leper might be atoned for this impurity" (cf. 5:12-16; Matt 8:1-4; Mark 1:40-45).

17:14 *Go show yourselves to the priests.* This accords with Lev 14:2-32, which required that the proper officials be consulted to certify that a cure had taken place and a person was thus fit to enter normal life and activities in the community again. Interestingly, we learn in 17:16 that one of these lepers was a Samaritan. Bock suggests that a local priest is probably in view for the verification of healing, but that if sacrifices were to be offered, this would require a trip to Jerusalem—or quite possibly to Mount Gerizim in the case of the Samaritan (1996:1402).

17:16 *Samaritan.* See 9:51-56; note on 10:33; Coggins 1993. "In both Luke and John it is surprising how positively the Samaritans are portrayed given the negative evaluation by 1st-century Judaism. They illustrate that Jesus and his message were not bound by cultural, religious, or ethnic stereotypes" (Gardner 1995:578).

17:18 *this foreigner.* The word employed here (*allogenēs* [TG241, ZG254]) is a common word used in the LXX to denote a "foreigner" (Exod 12:43; Lev 22:25; Job 15:19; 19:15; Isa 60:10; 61:5; Ezek 44:7-9; Zech 9:6). It is also the word used in the inscription discovered near the inner court of the Temple, which threatened Gentiles with death for proceeding beyond the warning point.

COMMENTARY

This is the second healing narrative (cf. Luke 13:10-17) "and the fourth healing incident in the 'teachings' division. Cf. 11:14; 14:4; 18:35. In each case the theme of the episode is not the miraculous act but the teaching-word arising from it" (Ellis 1981:209). In keeping with his universal outlook of a gospel for the whole world, Luke had already recounted one of Jesus' parables in which a Samaritan was a key figure (10:30-37), and here a Samaritan is the principal figure in a real-life episode.

The healing of the ten lepers takes place in the context of the journey to Jerusalem, a point flagged by Luke in noting that "Jesus continued on toward Jerusalem" (17:11). The geography makes it clear that this was a boundary situation, and yet the love of the Lord reached out to touch Jews and outsiders alike. In a real sense, all of these people were outsiders because they were ostracized by their disease from life in the community and were compelled to stand "at a distance" (17:12). The Jewish laws of purity dealt with skin problems of many kinds and spelled out conditions whereby lepers were excluded from the community. They also set forth the conditions under which they could be readmitted to the community (Lev 13:1-46;

14:1-32). Leprosy covered a wide range of diseases, and there was a concern to regulate it so as to protect the society and keep the ritual laws of purity. For the lepers, the terrible cost was exclusion from the life of the community and a resulting sense of social isolation.

The ten lepers here are pictured as crying out in desperation for help from the healer who was passing by: "Jesus, Master, have mercy on us!" (17:13). The response Jesus made to their request showed a clear recognition of the Jewish laws of purification, which required inspection by a priest, certification of a cure, and then readmission to the community. Jesus was not challenging the rules, but was announcing their healing by his powerful intervention. "As they went, they were cleansed of their leprosy" (17:14).

The emphasis of the story falls not so much on the healing but rather on the lepers' response to it. Ten men had been healed, but only one came back to Jesus to offer praise to God as an expression of his gratitude (17:15). He acknowledged the intervention of Jesus, "thanking him for what he had done" (17:16). The others were quite content to go on their way, heedless of the fact that they had been restored to health and community once again. Jesus challenged the thoughtlessness and ingratitude of the nine Jews with a rhetorical question addressed to the lone person returning to express appreciation: "Where are the other nine?" (17:17).

The incongruity of this situation is reflected in Jesus' reply to the healed Samaritan: "Has no one returned to give glory to God except this foreigner?" (17:18). This is the only place in the New Testament where the word "foreigner" (*allogenēs* [TG241, ZG254]) appears. Because the gospel was made available to "foreigners" as well as to Jews, Luke included this trenchant remark of Jesus. Earlier, Luke had used the cosmopolitan remark of Jesus that "people will come from all over the world—from east and west, north and south—to take their places in the Kingdom of God" (13:29). Luke thus presents the breadth of God's mercy; by divine intention "all people will see the salvation sent from God" (3:6).

The whole incident was significant for Luke, who saw the Christian message as one for all people who would receive it—including Jews, Samaritans, Gentiles, the clean and the unclean. Part of full restoration to health and wholeness was acknowledgement of the one who had performed the healing, so the closing words of the paragraph are significant: "Your faith has healed you" (17:19).

◆ II. The Coming of the Kingdom (17:20-37; cf. Matt 24:37-39; Mark 13:21)

²⁰One day the Pharisees asked Jesus, "When will the Kingdom of God come?"

Jesus replied, "The Kingdom of God can't be detected by visible signs.* ²¹You won't be able to say, 'Here it is!' or 'It's over there!' For the Kingdom of God is already among you.*"

²²Then he said to his disciples, "The time is coming when you will long to see the day when the Son of Man returns,* but you won't see it. ²³People will tell you, 'Look, there is the Son of Man,' or 'Here he is,' but don't go out and follow them. ²⁴For as the lightning flashes and lights up the

sky from one end to the other, so it will be on the day when the Son of Man comes. 25But first the Son of Man must suffer terribly* and be rejected by this generation.

26"When the Son of Man returns, it will be like it was in Noah's day. 27In those days, the people enjoyed banquets and parties and weddings right up to the time Noah entered his boat and the flood came and destroyed them all.

28"And the world will be as it was in the days of Lot. People went about their daily business—eating and drinking, buying and selling, farming and building—29until the morning Lot left Sodom. Then fire and burning sulfur rained down from heaven and destroyed them all. 30Yes, it will be 'business as usual' right up to the day when the Son of Man is revealed. 31On that day a person out on the deck of a roof must not go down into the house to pack. A person out in the field must not return home. 32Remember what happened to Lot's wife! 33If you cling to your life, you will lose it, and if you let your life go, you will save it. 34That night two people will be asleep in one bed; one will be taken, the other left. 35Two women will be grinding flour together at the mill; one will be taken, the other left.*"

37"Where will this happen, Lord?"* the disciples asked. Jesus replied, "Just as the gathering of vultures shows there is a carcass nearby, so these signs indicate that the end is near."*

17:20 Or by your speculations. 17:21 Or is within you, or is in your grasp. 17:22 Or long for even one day with the Son of Man. "Son of Man" is a title Jesus used for himself. 17:25 Or suffer many things. 17:35 Some manuscripts add verse 36, Two men will be working in the field; one will be taken, the other left. Compare Matt 24:40. 17:37a Greek "Where, Lord?" 17:37b Greek "Wherever the carcass is, the vultures gather."

NOTES

17:20 When will the Kingdom of God come? On the coming of the Kingdom, note 19:11; 21:7-11; Acts 1:6; see also Franklin 1975:8-47 and Ridderbos 1962.

17:21 the Kingdom of God is already among you. The Gr. phrase entos humōn can be taken in one of two ways—either as "within you" (the more common meaning of the preposition entos [TG1787, ZG1955]) or "in your midst" (the way preferred by most scholars as doing greater justice to the Kingdom theme in the Gospels). "Thus on the lips of Jesus this could mean that the kingdom is an inward reality, or that it has started to come into history with his own mission. For Luke it could mean that the kingdom is present in the church through the gift of the Spirit" (W. Baird 1972:696). The phrase in Luke 17:21 is probably best interpreted as "in your midst," as this makes better sense of the question posed by the Pharisees, who were looking for outward, visible phenomena that were observable (cf. the reply of Jesus to John's disciples in 7:22-23).

17:22 when the Son of Man returns. Luke offers his readers two eschatological discourses: one here in 17:20-37 and one in ch 21. Chapter 17 is more apocalyptic in character, while ch 21 includes specific references to the coming destruction of Jerusalem.

17:24 as the lightning flashes and lights up the sky from one end to the other. This image of the flashing lightning, also used in Matthew's teaching on last things (Matt 24:27), indicates that the coming of the Son of Man will be sudden, unexpected, and discernable to all people.

17:31 a person out on the deck of a roof. Generally, houses in the ancient Near East had flat roofs. Rooftops were frequently favorite sites for rest in the warm part of the day. In addition, they served as meeting places or for meals. Roofs are often mentioned in the Bible and were usually protected by parapets (Deut 22:8; Matt 24:17; Mark 13:15; Acts 10:9).

COMMENTARY

The healing of the ten lepers might have stirred eschatological expectations on the part of the Pharisees, for healing was one of the signs associated with the last days and the coming of the Messiah (Isa 35:5-6; 42:7; 43:8). In any case, this topic came up one day when the Pharisees presented the question quite directly to Jesus: "When will the Kingdom of God come?" (17:20). This was an important matter in their thoughts, for the Jews were under foreign occupation by the Romans and consequently dreamed of a glorious day in the future when they would be free of foreign domination and rule. One of Jesus' followers—Simon—had been a Zealot, a keen patriot who had devoted himself to a Jewish freedom fighter group whose aim was the complete overthrow of the Roman government in the holy land (6:11; cf. Matt 10:4; Mark 3:18). The political issue was in the minds of Jesus' first disciples, too, because they were Jews and participated in the general interest in these matters and discussed them frequently (e.g., Acts 1:6, where the disciples ask Jesus the question, "Lord, has the time come for you to free Israel and restore our kingdom?").

In Jesus' response to the Pharisees, he refused to set out a list of external phenomena that could be observed and chronicled. It would not be possible for people to calculate the day of the final advent of God's Kingdom with precision and say, "Here it is!" (17:21). Mysteriously, the Kingdom of God had *already* arrived in the person and work of Jesus, as he had already announced (4:18-21; Matt 4:12-17; Mark 1:14-15). They were reminded of the wonderful intervention God had already made into the world in the coming of Jesus, who declared the long-promised Reign of God was already present in their midst (17:21). Nonetheless, Jesus balanced a realized eschatology (17:21) with a strong futuristic one (17:24), as is also the case in Luke 21. The Kingdom had definitely come into history in the person of Jesus, and the Kingdom would be consummated and completed in the end time by the coming of Jesus as King.

Naturally enough, some people want to make startling predictions of the last day, but the followers of Jesus were not to be taken in by such speculation. Despite the appeal of such prognosticators, Jesus said to the disciples, "Don't go out and follow them" (17:23). This was false teaching and purely speculative. Any idea of a secret appearance of the Son of Man was ruled out, for his future coming was to be public, universally recognizable, and known to all (17:24). The reference to the Son of Man in this passage is important, for this was the mysterious title Jesus often used to describe himself (see note on 5:24). It is noteworthy here that the passage speaks of both *suffering* and *glory*, linking the two ideas together. While the disciples and their contemporaries were taken up with speculation about last things, they were reminded that the glorious return of the Son of Man had to be preceded by something painful and ignominious: "First the Son of Man must suffer terribly and be rejected by this generation" (17:25). The divinely planned destiny for him *must* come by way of the suffering and rejection by his contemporaries (note the key word "must" in 17:25). Yet this did not rule out the eschatological events they were so interested in. The Son of Man would bring many sons and daughters to glory (Heb 2:10), but *first* he must suffer and die for them and their salvation.

Jesus gave them a couple of familiar illustrations from their own Scriptures that would help them to prepare for this expected time "when the Son of Man returns" (17:26). Both of them are drawn from the book of Genesis and were well-known biblical stories. The first is the antediluvian tale of the Flood (Gen 6:6-8). Although Noah had warned people of the coming deluge and invited people to seek the safety of the ark, life went on as usual with people showing no concern for the future but instead simply enjoying "banquets and parties and weddings right up to the time Noah entered his boat" in utter disregard of the impending catastrophe (17:27). Because they had made no preparation, the flood came upon them and destroyed them all except Noah and his family, who entered the ark and were delivered (Gen 7:22-24). This frightening scenario was a foretaste of what could be expected at the final appearance of the Son of Man, and the danger should be noted—judgment could come upon them too!

The second illustration was the tragic story of Lot, who had to flee the destruction of Sodom and the neighboring cities of the plain (Gen 19). Once again, people carried on with life as usual, "eating and drinking, buying and selling, farming and building," acting as if there was no crisis to face (17:28). But as soon as Lot had cleared out of Sodom in accordance with divine directions, there was a catastrophe of cataclysmic proportions which utterly wiped out the cities of the plain: "Fire and burning sulfur rained down from heaven and destroyed them all" (17:29). Jesus told his hearers that people will be acting in the same way when the Son of Man returns at the final consummation. This will be a crisis situation, and there will be no time for dallying. It will definitely *not* be "business as usual"!

The notable person who got lost in the tragedy at the destruction of Sodom was Lot's wife (17:32; cf. Gen 19:26). She had been duly warned and urged to flee the coming destruction, but she had not acted with the urgency that the situation demanded and so lost her life in the enveloping destruction. The same kind of thing could happen again if people were unprepared for the sudden advent of the Son of Man!

In this apocalyptic context, the paradoxical words of discipleship certainly present a real challenge: "If you cling to your life [as Lot's wife did] you will lose it, and if you let your life go, you will save it" (17:33). The same paradox about losing and finding is repeated in a number of places in the Gospels and in different contexts, showing how vital it was to the teaching of Jesus (Matt 10:39; 16:25; Mark 8:35; Luke 9:24; John 12:25). Discipleship certainly demanded appropriate action in the face of the coming consummation of all things. When the final end came, it would be too late to make a decision. An eternal judgment would divide people, and it would be irrevocable—"one will be taken, the other left" (a point repeated for emphasis in 17:34-35; cf. Matt 24:40-41). The mention of a nighttime activity and a daytime one in Luke's account suggests the unknown time of the final end but the inescapable need to be ready.

The "vultures" mentioned by Jesus are birds of prey waiting to pounce on dead carcasses (17:37; cf. Job 39:30), not the Roman eagles used on the imperial standards that conquered Jerusalem (cf. Luke 21:20). As Ellis has pointed out, "In this context (and in Matt 24:28) the proverb refers to the last judgment. Judgment will occur when it is required, i.e., universally. Cf. Hab. 1:8" (1981:212). The imminence of the end requires vigilance. Indeed, all three synoptic Gospels stress the importance of watchfulness (Matt 24:42; 25:13; Mark 13:35-37; Luke 21:31).

◆   JJ. Parable of the Persistent Widow (18:1-8)

One day Jesus told his disciples a story to show that they should always pray and never give up. ²"There was a judge in a certain city," he said, "who neither feared God nor cared about people. ³A widow of that city came to him repeatedly, saying, 'Give me justice in this dispute with my enemy.' ⁴The judge ignored her for a while, but finally he said to himself, 'I don't fear God or care about people, ⁵but this woman is driving me crazy. I'm going to see that she gets justice, because she is wearing me out with her constant requests!' "

⁶Then the Lord said, "Learn a lesson from this unjust judge. ⁷Even he rendered a just decision in the end. So don't you think God will surely give justice to his chosen people who cry out to him day and night? Will he keep putting them off? ⁸I tell you, he will grant justice to them quickly! But when the Son of Man* returns, how many will he find on the earth who have faith?"

18:8"Son of Man" is a title Jesus used for himself.

NOTES

18:1 *always pray and never give up.* On the importance of prayer in Luke, see the Introduction, the note on 3:21, and the comments on 9:28-36 and 11:1-13. See also Conn 1972; Harris 1967; O'Brien 1973; Spencer 1990:40-83.

18:2 *a judge . . . who neither feared God nor cared about people.* Corrupt judges, like corrupt rulers, priests, and prophets (see Isa 28:7-8, 14-15), were nothing new. In OT times, the prophets pronounced God's judgments on such people for unjust practices (e.g., Amos 2:6-7; 5:10-13; Isa 10:1-2; 29:21; cf. Prov 28:21).

18:3 *widow.* On the role of widows in ancient Israel, see Freedman 2000:1377-1378; on their role in the NT, see Freedman 2000:1378, who states, "In the NT Luke associates Jesus of Nazareth with the prophet Elijah and with the Lord's care for widows by having him restore to life a widow's only son (7:11-17 [cf. 1 Kgs. 17:8-24; Luke 4:25-26]). Widows also appear in the parables as embodiments of generosity (Mark 12:41-44) and persistence (18:1-8). The Jerusalem [church] community provided food for widows (Acts 6:1), and the Greek Dorcas wins praise for having made clothing for them (Acts 9:39)." Care for widows is enjoined in James as a mark of religious commitment (Jas 1:27), and rules for the support of widows by the local church are set out in the Pastoral Epistles (1 Tim 5:3-16). By the second century, the role of widows in the church had been institutionalized. Later in his Gospel, Luke will note the sacrificial offering of a poor widow in the Temple (21:1-4; cf. Mark 12:41-44) and the callous exploitation of widows by the scribes (20:45-47; cf. Matt 23:13-14; Mark 12:38-40).

18:5 *she is wearing me out.* Luke uses the rare word *hypōpiazō* [ᵀᴳ5299, ᶻᴳ5708], "wear somebody out," only here. The only other place the word is used in the NT is in 1 Cor 9:27, where Paul speaks of punishing or disciplining his body "like an athlete" for the sake of his Christian witness.

COMMENTARY

Luke, alone of the four Gospel writers, provided Jesus' parables about prayer: the parables of the Friend at Midnight (11:5-8) and the Persistent Widow (18:1-8), as well as the Parable of the Pharisee and the Tax Collector (18:9-14). These are important in unpacking Jesus' teaching on prayer and highlight the need for importunity and persistence, something that Jesus strongly emphasized in his teaching (e.g., he told his disciples to keep on asking, seeking and knocking in Luke 11:9; Matt 7:7).

Having dealt in some detail with the need for readiness in the face of the unexpected coming of the Son of Man, Jesus provided a parable to encourage his disciples to engage in constant prayer (18:1). As there would certainly be difficulties in maintaining a posture of faith, the followers of Jesus needed encouragement to persevere in the way of discipleship. The Parable of the Persistent Widow that Jesus shared with them was designed to meet these needs.

This parable is arresting in that Jesus mentions an unjust judge as a way of relating a truth about God. Jesus argued from the lesser to the greater. "If an unjust judge would yield to the repeated appeals of an unknown widow for such a selfish reason, how much more will a loving God, the helper of widows and of all in distress, reward the unremitting cries of his own people? (18:7)" (Trites 1978:176).

The story is a familiar one. A helpless widow seeks justice and appeals to an unscrupulous judge. He is without religious convictions, and he has no particular empathy or compassion for people, including widows, who were among the most powerless members of ancient Palestinian society (cf. 20:47; 21:1-4; Job 22:9; Isa 9:17; 10:2; Jer 15:8; Lam 5:3; Ezek 22:25). In these unfavorable circumstances, she put her case before the judge with such determination and persistence that at last he gave in to her and granted her request for legal action, simply worn down by her ceaseless badgering. Though the judge is without strong religious or social convictions, he yields to her unrelenting entreaties because, as he says, "this woman is driving me crazy" (18:5). He grants her justice simply to gain some peace and quiet, "because she is wearing me out with her constant requests!" (18:5). As we have noticed elsewhere in the teaching of Jesus, he presents a compelling argument, working from the lesser to the greater (cf. 11:13; 12:28). If such a heartless judge could perform this act of justice when pestered by a persistent woman, how much more will a loving, gracious, and compassionate God act for the help of his needy people who earnestly make their unremitting requests to him!

The moral of this little story is pointed out by Jesus to his disciples: "So don't you think God will surely give justice to his chosen people who cry out to him day and night? Will he keep putting them off?" (18:7). The use of the rhetorical question here (indicated by the Greek) expects the answer, "Of course not!"

In this parable, the Lord offers encouragement to hard-pressed disciples. They are not to give up—ever! The remedy for problems is constant prayer, a reaching out to God for the needed strength to persist in the face of delays and difficulties. God will meet his earnest, hard-pressed servants and "grant justice to them," and the needed aid will arrive "quickly"—that is, in timely fashion to meet their critical circumstances (18:8).

The real question is not the adequacy of God but the perseverance of his servants. To his followers, Jesus raised the burning question about the coming of the Son of Man at the end of time: how many people "will he find on the earth who have faith?" (18:8). The end times would unquestionably bring stress, testing the loyalty and faithfulness of professed disciples. The need for persistence in discipleship would remain a perennial imperative until the very end (cf. Matt 10:22; 24:13; Mark 13:13).

◆   **KK. Parable of the Pharisee and Tax Collector (18:9-14)**

⁹Then Jesus told this story to some who had great confidence in their own righteousness and scorned everyone else: ¹⁰"Two men went to the Temple to pray. One was a Pharisee, and the other was a despised tax collector. ¹¹The Pharisee stood by himself and prayed this prayer*: 'I thank you, God, that I am not a sinner like everyone else. For I don't cheat, I don't sin, and I don't commit adultery. I'm certainly not like that tax collector! ¹²I fast twice a week, and I give you a tenth of my income.'

¹³"But the tax collector stood at a distance and dared not even lift his eyes to heaven as he prayed. Instead, he beat his chest in sorrow, saying, 'O God, be merciful to me, for I am a sinner.' ¹⁴I tell you, this sinner, not the Pharisee, returned home justified before God. For those who exalt themselves will be humbled, and those who humble themselves will be exalted."

18:11 Some manuscripts read *stood and prayed this prayer to himself.*

NOTES

18:10 *a despised tax collector.* Those who gathered taxes were thoroughly detested by the rank and file of the Jewish people. "It is evident in the Gospels that the title itself is a term of abuse (Matt 5:46; 18:17) or a foil to the hypocrites (3:12; 7:29; 8:10-14). Elsewhere it is joined in vituperative apposition to 'prostitutes' (Matt 21:31-32) and, most commonly, 'sinners' (e.g., Mark 2:15; Luke 15:1). This attitude was universal: the rabbis joined tax collectors with 'robbers'" (DJG 805).

18:11 *The Pharisee stood by himself and prayed.* This reading has the support of A W f¹³ 𝔐. Better ms attestation (𝔓75 ℵ² B L T 038 044) supports the reading, "the Pharisee stood and prayed this prayer to himself" (so NLT mg).

18:12 *I fast twice a week.* The law of Moses required fasting on only one day of the year, the Day of Atonement (Lev 16:29), which occurred in September/October in the ancient Hebrew lunar calendar. The Pharisee in the parable, and no doubt others like him, fasted twice a week, on Mondays and Thursdays, and undoubtedly was proud of the fact that he was going beyond the requirements of the law. There are other references to the stress on fasting by the Pharisees and John the Baptist's disciples (5:33; Matt 9:14; Mark 2:18). Cf. the comments on 5:33-39.

COMMENTARY

This passage presents the third of Luke's prayer parables (the other two are in 11:5-8 and 18:1-8). Luke was deeply interested in the theme of prayer. This was a key feature of Jesus' own life (3:21; 5:16; 6:12; 9:18, 28; 11:1), and it was the intention of the evangelist, following his Lord's peerless example and teaching, to stress the central role prayer should play in the life of every Christian disciple. Prayer, in Luke's view, was clearly the divine solution to discouragement and giving up, a point made by the immediately preceding Parable of the Persistent Widow (18:1-8).

The present parable is a critique of those who pray with a self-righteous attitude (18:9-14). In the story Jesus told, the Pharisee exhibits great confidence in his own righteousness and scorns other people whom he views as unworthy (18:9). He was proud and cocky about his own achievements. In the scenario envisaged, he told God rather pretentiously, "I am not a sinner like everyone else. For I don't cheat, I don't sin, and I don't commit adultery" (18:11). He waxed eloquent in a mood of self-congratulation that praised his ability to keep the basic ethical commandments of the law of Moses. He knew that every pious Jew was required to fast only one day of the year, the Day of Atonement (Lev 16), but he prided himself in his punctilious ways, fasting twice a week and dutifully giving a tithe of his income as required by Jewish law (18:12; cf. Lev 27:30-33; Deut 14:22-24). He thought himself to be righteous and noted with evident satisfaction the vast difference between him and the other character who appeared at the Temple to pray, the despised tax collector (18:10).

In contrast with this arrogant man who was so pleased with himself is his counterpart, the sinful tax collector. He sensed his unworthiness and didn't even dare to "lift his eyes to heaven," so conscious was he of his sinfulness (18:13). But he was penitent, beating his chest as a true expression of sorrow (18:13; see 23:48 [NLT mg]; cf. Nah 2:7; Isa 32:12) and asking God in humility for mercy and forgiveness. The unforgettable point of this prayer parable is the insistence that sincerity is absolutely necessary in coming before God. All things are naked and exposed to God when we pray, and no pretense will do. The high and mighty Pharisee was not praying to God but was really offering a soliloquy to himself (cf. 18:11, NLT mg).

This was important teaching for the disciples, who sometimes were arrogant, on occasion even trying to correct or rebuke their Master (10:40; Matt 16:22; Mark 4:38; 8:32; John 13:6-8). Certainly, there was no place for such conceit in prayer and absolutely no grounds for comparison with another person also seeking divine favor. Here, the consciousness of one's sin should make one come humbly before God, penitently seeking help. It was a forceful lesson on effective prayer that Jesus drove home to the hearts and minds of his disciples. They were told in no uncertain terms which man's prayers were heard: "This sinner, *not the Pharisee*, returned home justified before God" (18:14).

The general principle was then plainly stated, a point that had already been made in another passage in Luke's Gospel also trying to inculcate humility: "Those who exalt themselves will be humbled, and those who humble themselves will be exalted" (18:14b; cf. 14:11). Evidently, this upside-down principle was frequently on the lips of Jesus, for he also used it in warning the religious leaders and in teaching his disciples lessons on the nature of leadership (Matt 23:12). The importance of humility in the people of God is often noted throughout the sacred writings (cf. Job 5:11; 22:29; Prov 3:34; 29:23; Jas 4:6; 1 Pet 5:5). The deuterocanonical book Ben Sirach puts it succinctly: "The greater you are, the more you should humble yourself; then you will find favor with the Lord. The Lord is great and powerful, but he is honored by the humble" (Sir 3:18-20).

◆   **LL. Jesus Blesses the Children (18:15-17; cf. Matt 19:13-15; Mark 10:13-16)**

[15]One day some parents brought their little children to Jesus so he could touch and bless them. But when the disciples saw this, they scolded the parents for bothering him.

[16]Then Jesus called for the children and said to the disciples, "Let the children come to me. Don't stop them! For the Kingdom of God belongs to those who are like these children. [17]I tell you the truth, anyone who doesn't receive the Kingdom of God like a child will never enter it."

NOTES

18:15 *some parents brought their little children to Jesus.* Jesus was approached by some parents who wanted Jesus to lay hands on their children and bless them. Obviously, the parents had heard of Jesus' feats of healing and blessing the people who came to be taught and helped, and they longed for a blessing from this popular Nazarene who had gained a considerable following in Galilee.

COMMENTARY

The incident of Jesus blessing the children is recorded in all three synoptic Gospels in very similar words. Mark, probably our earliest source, stressed Jesus' displeasure with the disciples for restraining the people (Mark 10:14). He added a graphic touch when he noted that Jesus "took the children in his arms and placed his hands on their heads and blessed them" (Mark 10:16). Matthew preserved the saying about the need to "turn . . . and become like little children" in a different setting (Matt 18:3), though it is generally similar to Mark.

In Luke, the incident is introduced rather loosely as occurring on "one day" (note similar references in 9:18; 11:14; 14:1; 17:1, 20; 18:1). Evidently, Luke did not have access to a detailed chronology of every day of Jesus' life, so he resorted to a general phrase that would serve as a suitable connective when a direct chronological sequence could not be given. In this way, he sought to honor his stated aim to provide an "orderly account" of Christian origins (1:3; "a careful account," NLT).

Luke's account, the shortest of the three in the synoptic Gospels, notes "they were bringing *even infants* to him" (18:15, RSV, NRSV; "little children," NLT). The disciples objected. Doubtless, they had seen Jesus thronged and pressed on previous occasions (e.g., 5:1; 8:19, 45; Mark 2:2; 3:9-10; 5:24, 27-28), and now they desired to save him from this unsought intrusion. This is often the case with famous men whose followers are apt to screen people to see if they warrant their leader's time and attention. In the eyes of the disciples, these children were an unimportant nuisance and could be dispensed with (18:15).

However, Jesus took a different view than the disciples. He invited the children to come to him and receive his blessing (18:16). The disciples were rebuked for their rejection of the children, who were not considered by Jesus as "bothering him" (18:15). In fact, they were to be encouraged, for "the Kingdom of God belongs to those who are like these children" (18:16). In their openness, simplicity, and faith, children are veritable pictures of what it means to become children of God. They served, in fact, as a paradigm of faith and receptivity to God. The tragedy is when one refuses to come to God on such humble terms: "Anyone who doesn't receive the Kingdom of God like a child will never enter it" (18:17).

◆ MM. The Rich Man (18:18-30; cf. Matt 19:16-30; Mark 10:17-31)

18Once a religious leader asked Jesus this question: "Good Teacher, what should I do to inherit eternal life?"

19"Why do you call me good?" Jesus asked him. "Only God is truly good. 20But to answer your question, you know the commandments: 'You must not commit adultery. You must not murder. You must not steal. You must not testify falsely. Honor your father and mother.'*"

21The man replied, "I've obeyed all these commandments since I was young."

22When Jesus heard his answer, he said, "There is still one thing you haven't done. Sell all your possessions and give the money to the poor, and you will have treasure in heaven. Then come, follow me."

23But when the man heard this he became very sad, for he was very rich.

24When Jesus saw this,* he said, "How hard it is for the rich to enter the Kingdom of God! 25In fact, it is easier for a camel to go through the eye of a needle than for a rich person to enter the Kingdom of God!"

26Those who heard this said, "Then who in the world can be saved?"

27He replied, "What is impossible for people is possible with God."

28Peter said, "We've left our homes to follow you."

29"Yes," Jesus replied, "and I assure you that everyone who has given up house or wife or brothers or parents or children, for the sake of the Kingdom of God, 30will be repaid many times over in this life, and will have eternal life in the world to come."

18:20 Exod 20:12-16; Deut 5:16-20. 18:24 Some manuscripts read *When Jesus saw how sad the man was.*

NOTES

18:18 *religious leader.* Luke, like Matthew, followed Mark quite closely in this passage, but Luke introduced some interesting details (cf. Mark 10:17-31; Matt 19:16-30). He noted that the man was "a religious leader" (*archōn* [TG758, ZG807], "ruler"), who was perhaps a man serving as a magistrate.

18:19 *"Why do you call me good?" Jesus asked him. "Only God is truly good."* This enigmatic remark has been interpreted by some as if Jesus were denying that he were God, and by others as an oblique reference to his deity, which was possibly being recognized by the inquiring ruler. Luke, like Mark, notes that the man prefaced his question by addressing Jesus as "Good Teacher" (18:18). Jesus replied by raising the question, "Why do you call me good? . . . Only God is truly good" (18:19; cf. Mark 10:18). Matthew, on the other hand, phrases Jesus' response as, "Why ask me about what is good? . . . There is only One who is good" (Matt 19:17). Either form of the reply emphasizes a cardinal OT truth about the goodness of God (Pss 34:8; 100:5; 106:1; 1 Chr 16:34). However, "Jesus is not implying that he himself is not good" (Evans 1990:276), but rather posing a question to the man as a "spiritual director." The fact that Jesus challenged the religious leader in an authoritative way to radical stewardship in his life and then summoned him personally to "follow me" as a disciple indicates that an oblique reference to Jesus' deity is the Gospel writers' intent (see also the parallels, Matt 19:17 and Mark 10:17, where Mark noted that the man deferentially "knelt down" before Jesus). The tragedy in the situation was the man's refusal to make the costly commitment required, the entrapment in his own wealth, and his consequent unwillingness to share it to meet the needs of others.

18:20 the commandments. In reciting the commandments dealing with duties to other people, Luke omitted the prohibition "you must not cheat" (as found in Mark 10:19), probably because it does not appear in precisely this form in the Ten Commandments (cf. Exod 20:3-17; Deut 5:6-21). It is worthy of note that cheating or defrauding is explicitly mentioned in some NT passages as a practice forbidden to Christians (1 Cor 6:6-10; 1 Thess 4:6; for a more detailed analysis, see DJG 132-136).

18:22 Sell all your possessions and give the money to the poor. Luke, very concerned with the oppressed members of society, showed that Jesus did not forget the poor. Luke mentioned the need to exercise compassion to those less fortunate (16:19-31). He underscored the dangers of wealth, rapacity, and greed (12:13-21). He is the sole evangelist to mention Jesus' command to "sell your possessions and give to those in need" (12:33) and to "invite the poor" and other disadvantaged people to a meal (14:13). Luke included Jesus' beatitude to the poor (6:20) and Jesus' concern for the poor in his Nazareth sermon (4:18). The needs of the poor are also addressed in Zacchaeus' repentance, where he dedicated half of his wealth to the poor (19:8). It is significant that Luke drew attention to acts of unselfishness and generosity on the part of the early Christians who were seeking to follow their Lord's teaching and instruction (Acts 2:44-46; 4:32-37). On the issues of poverty and riches, see notes on 6:20-23; 12:13-21; and 16:19-31.

18:28 We've left our homes to follow you. This statement prepares the reader for the comprehensive answer given by Jesus in the next two verses—a passage that mentions the pain of giving up "house or wife or brothers or parents or children" in order to live as a disciple of Jesus (18:29-30).

COMMENTARY

This well-known story is essentially the same in each of the synoptic Gospels. A man came to Jesus and asked what he must do to inherit eternal life (Matthew's version says "have" eternal life). Jesus replied by saying, "You know the commandments" (18:20), and then Jesus recited several of the Ten Commandments, noting especially the ones relating to one's duties to others. The inquirer responded, claiming to have kept the commandments from the time of his youth. Jesus put his sincerity to the test by challenging his wholehearted commitment: "There is still one thing you haven't done. Sell all your possessions and give the money to the poor, and you will have treasure in heaven. Then come, follow me" (18:22).

We must face squarely the question posed by this passage: was Jesus stating that one could inherit eternal life by keeping the commandments? The answer must surely be an emphatic "No," for already both Mark and Luke had just declared that "only God is truly good" in an unqualified sense (18:19; Mark 10:18). Human beings are sinners standing in need of divine forgiveness, and, as has already been noted, forgiveness is a prominent theme in both Luke's Gospel and the book of Acts (5:23; 7:47-48; 11:4; 12:10; Acts 5:31; 8:22; 13:38; 26:18).

The trouble Jesus identified was the ruler's covetousness and self-centeredness (cf. Exod 20:17). He was not prepared to love his neighbor as himself, for his possessions were more important to him than sharing unselfishly with others. When he heard this radical demand upon his resources, he refused to distribute his goods and went away sorrowful, "for he was very rich" (18:23) and his riches meant too much to him for him to take part in meeting the needs of others in a serious way.

All three accounts spell out the point that God will amply compensate his people for any sacrifices undertaken in the interest of the divine Kingdom. All three accounts underscore the adequacy of God's care for his people, who "will be repaid many times over in this life, and will have eternal life in the world to come" (18:30). There is a helpful comment on this passage furnished in the apocryphal *Gospel of the Hebrews* (cited in Origen's Latin commentary on Matt 15:14, as quoted in Throckmorton 1973:130), where the rich man is challenged in searching words: "How can you say 'I have fulfilled the law and the prophets,' when it is written in the law: You shall love your neighbor as yourself; and lo, many of your brothers, sons of Abraham, are clothed in filth, dying of hunger, and your house is full of many good things, none of which goes out to them?" This connects with Luke's earlier story of the rich man and Lazarus, where the rich man is guilty of seeing such a needy man right on his doorstep and doing nothing to alleviate his suffering (16:19-31).

Something is lacking when a person professes to love God and yet is unwilling to share what he or she has to meet the desperate needs of others. If we are called to love God and our neighbor, then it is incongruous for us to claim to be in right relation with God and at the same time be in total disregard of the needs of our brother or sister. Much the same point is made later in the first letter of John: "If someone has enough money to live well and sees a brother or sister in need but shows no compassion—how can God's love be in that person?" (1 John 3:17).

Jesus noted the stringent requirements of entering the Kingdom of God—conditions that, for rich people who are wrapped up in their own possessions, seem very hard to meet. He used the ludicrous picture of a camel going through the tiny hole of a needle to make his point (18:25). This seems to be utterly impossible in human terms, and yet "what is impossible for people is possible with God" (18:27).

◆ NN. Jesus Again Predicts His Death (18:31-34; cf. Matt 20:17-19; Mark 10:32-34)

³¹Taking the twelve disciples aside, Jesus said, "Listen, we're going up to Jerusalem, where all the predictions of the prophets concerning the Son of Man will come true. ³²He will be handed over to the Romans,* and he will be mocked, treated shamefully, and spit upon. ³³They will flog him with a whip and kill him, but on the third day he will rise again."

³⁴But they didn't understand any of this. The significance of his words was hidden from them, and they failed to grasp what he was talking about.

18:32 Greek *the Gentiles*

NOTES

18:31 *all the predictions of the prophets concerning the Son of Man will come true.* These predictions would include those concerning the suffering Servant, such as Isa 52:13–53:12 (cf. 24:25-27; Ps 22; 1 Pet 1:10-12). Other predictions of the passion in Luke include 5:35; 12:50; 13:32-33; 17:25.

18:33 *They will flog him with a whip and kill him, but on the third day he will rise again.* This is one of the most specific predictions Jesus made concerning his death, including a prediction of being flogged and rising from the dead specifically on the third day.

COMMENTARY

This is oftentimes referred to as the third passion prediction in Luke's Gospel, though there are more predictions in Luke than three (see note on 18:31). The first definite prediction in Luke is found in 9:22 and the second in 9:43-45. It was important in Luke's concept of holy history that the death of the Messiah had been predicted in the Scriptures centuries before (Ps 22; Isa 53; Zech 13:7; cf. 24:27; Matt 26:24, 31, 54). Luke noted that Jesus himself had repeatedly talked about his impending suffering, humiliation, and death.

In these predictions Jesus called himself "the Son of Man." This title was Jesus' preferred, but mysterious, way of referring to himself. Though some scholars have refused to attribute the use of this title to Jesus himself or have been sceptical of certain uses of it, there seems to be no adequate reason to deny the authenticity of the designation. In fact, it combines just those features which were so crucial to Jesus' self-understanding: his identification with humanity in the rough and tumble of daily life (e.g., 7:34; 9:58); his humiliation, betrayal, and death in the holy city (17:25; 22:22, 48; cf. 24:7); his subsequent resurrection on the third day according to the Scriptures (18:31; cf. 24:7); and his triumphal appearance in glory at the consummation of God's plan for the world (12:40; 17:22, 24, 30; 18:8; 21:27; 22:69). The passion predictions underscore the cardinal importance of this title (cf. DJG 775-781; Mercer 1990:846-848).

Jesus, the Son of Man, plainly told his disciples that he would fulfill his destiny as predicted (note the angels confirming this in 24:6-8). There would be some distasteful aspects to his earthly ministry, for he would fall into the hands of the Romans and would suffer mockery, shameful treatment, and rejection. He would endure a cruel flogging and then be put to death. Wonderfully, however, he would rise again on the third day as predicted.

The death and the resurrection of Jesus were not understood by the twelve disciples but were solemnly affirmed by the Master himself. Luke candidly says that the meaning of these solemn words was hidden from them at the time. The subsequent events of Jesus' life would eventually make it all clear, and they would go forth boldly to proclaim this good news after they had received the enabling power of the Holy Spirit on the day of Pentecost (Acts 2; cf. 4:13, 33).

The failure of Jesus' contemporaries in understanding the meaning of important events in redemptive history is noted by Luke on a number of occasions. When Jesus spoke with the teachers in the Temple, for example, he upset his parents who had been frantically searching for him. In response to their reproachful questioning, he replied that he must be in his Father's house (2:49). The text then says that his parents "didn't understand what he meant" (2:50). The same reaction recorded in Luke 18:34 is mentioned in the second passion prediction in Luke: "Its significance was hidden from them, so they couldn't understand it" (9:45). Later, the two on the road to Emmaus were rebuked by Jesus for finding it "hard to believe all that the prophets wrote in the Scriptures" (24:25). They needed illumination in order to understand the significance of Jesus' life, death, and resurrection. Jesus gave all the disciples the needed clarification after the resurrection: "He opened their minds to understand the Scriptures" (24:45). Before that moment, the disciples were kept from recognizing the risen Lord (24:16).

◆ OO. Jesus Heals a Blind Beggar (18:35-43; cf. Matt 20:29-34; Mark 10:46-52)

[35]As Jesus approached Jericho, a blind beggar was sitting beside the road. [36]When he heard the noise of a crowd going past, he asked what was happening. [37]They told him that Jesus the Nazarene* was going by. [38]So he began shouting, "Jesus, Son of David, have mercy on me!"

[39]"Be quiet!" the people in front yelled at him.

But he only shouted louder, "Son of David, have mercy on me!"

[40]When Jesus heard him, he stopped and ordered that the man be brought to him. As the man came near, Jesus asked him, [41]"What do you want me to do for you?"

"Lord," he said, "I want to see!"

[42]And Jesus said, "All right, receive your sight! Your faith has healed you." [43]Instantly the man could see, and he followed Jesus, praising God. And all who saw it praised God, too.

18:37 Or *Jesus of Nazareth.*

NOTES

18:35 *a blind beggar was sitting beside the road.* Luke's geographical setting differs from that in Matthew and Mark. Robertson explains the difference as follows: "It is probable that Mark and Matthew refer to the old Jericho, the ruins of which have been discovered, while Luke refers to the new, Roman Jericho. The two blind men were apparently between the two towns. Mark (Mark 10:46) and Luke (18:35) mention only one blind man, Bartimaeus" (1930:1.163). Craig Evans posits a reasonable editorial suggestion for Luke's different way of referring to Jericho: "The reason that Luke wants to leave the impression that Jesus is not leaving Jericho when he heals the blind man is to accommodate the Zacchaeus episode that follows (19:1-10), which also takes place in Jericho. Jesus could hardly be in the process of leaving Jericho when he heals the blind man and then be back in Jericho again when he meets Zacchaeus" (1990:278).

18:38 *Jesus, Son of David.* The title "Son of David" was "a royal, kingly title also associated with healing in Matthew (Matt 9:27; 12:23)" (Coogan 2001: NT 38). It is one of Matthew's favorite Christological titles for Jesus (Matt 9:27; 12:23; 15:22; 21:9, 15), probably recalling Jewish hopes of a time when God would "raise up a righteous descendant from King David's line" (Jer 23:5; cf. Zech 3:8); but Luke much less frequently employed it in writing for Gentile readers (18:38-39). It is occasionally used in Mark (10:47-48; 12:35).

Clearly it was a "messianic title which recalled God's fidelity to the promises he made to King David (2 Sam 7:12-16; Pss 2:7; 110; Isa 9:1-7; 11:1, 10; 55:3; Luke 1:32; cf. Rev 21:7). His contemporaries acclaimed Jesus of Nazareth with this title . . . Likewise the church confessed its faith in Jesus Christ (Rom 1:3; 2 Tim 2:8), thereby articulating Jesus' rootedness in Israel (Matt 1:1; Luke 3:31; John 7:42) while also proclaiming that he was David's Lord (Matt 22:42-45; Mark 12:35-37; Luke 20:41-44; Acts 2:25; 13:36; Rev 3:7; 5:5; 22:16)" (Léon-Dufour 1980:378-379).

18:43 *Instantly the man could see, and he followed Jesus, praising God.* The restoration of sight happened "instantly," and the result was that the man became a disciple, following Jesus, "praising God" (18:43). Luke often notes that praising God is the proper response that people should make to God when he has blessed them (19:37; 24:53; Acts 2:47; 3:8).

COMMENTARY

On the last leg of his final journey to Jerusalem, Jesus had to pass through Jericho (18:35). As he approached the "city of palms," he met a blind beggar sitting by the roadside and seeking alms, an incident mentioned in all three synoptic Gospels. When the blind man inquired of the excitement that had stirred up the crowd, he was informed that Jesus of Nazareth was passing by (18:36-37). Since he had heard tales of wonderful healings and exorcisms performed by the Nazarene, his hopes were raised that this stranger could do something for him. Boldly he cried out, "Jesus, Son of David, have mercy on me!" (18:38).

His boisterous cries did not sit well with the bystanders, who told him to be quiet in no uncertain terms (18:39). This attempted put-down only made the man more determined to gain the attention of Jesus, such that he "only shouted louder," repeating his request with ever-increasing earnestness (18:39). His dogged persistence had the desired effect: Jesus stopped and had "the man . . . brought to him" (18:40). When he was asked what his request was, he plainly declared, "I want to see!" (18:41). His request was answered immediately; his sight was restored (18:43).

Mark's account is the fullest of the three Gospel writers. He alone mentioned the man's name—Bartimaeus; and he unpacks its Aramaic derivation as "son of Timaeus" for his non-Jewish readers (Mark 10:46). Mark included a human-interest feature by noting that once Jesus called for the blind man, the bystanders encouraged him: "Cheer up. . . . Come on, he's calling you!" (Mark 10:49). Mark also added the details of the man's enthusiastic response: "Bartimaeus threw aside his coat, jumped up, and came to Jesus" (Mark 10:50).

Matthew's account follows Mark. Like Mark, he described Jesus as performing the healing as he was leaving Jericho (Matt 20:29). While Mark concentrates on the spokesman who cried out so vociferously for healing, Matthew notes the number of people who were healed—two men. His Gospel reveals his interest in the Jewish principle of multiple witness, whereby every matter was established by at least two witnesses to count as legally acceptable evidence (Deut 17:6; 19:15; John 8:17; 1 Tim 5:19; cf. Matt 18:15-18). Another interesting feature of Matthew's account is its reference to the compassion of the Savior in touching the men's eyes (Matt 20:34).

Luke's account also has some special features. It alone locates the miracle as taking place as Jesus was drawing near to Jericho, perhaps pointing to the archaeological fact that there were a couple of miles between Old Testament and New Testament Jericho (see note on 18:35) and suggesting that there were legitimately different perspectives on the geographical location of the incident. In addition, Luke specially mentions the multitude passing by and creating considerable noise that prompted the blind man's curiosity. Luke also uses his preferred term of address for Jesus by disciples: Lord, "probably meaning no more than 'Sir,' but for Luke the word in this context should be 'Lord,' since the blind man will be commended for his faith, faith that Luke probably understands as at least incipiently Christian" (Evans 1990:279). Finally, Luke notes that the healed man "glorified" or "praised" God—a typical point in Luke's miracle accounts (5:26; 7:16; 13:13; 17:15; 23:47; Acts 4:21; 11:18; 21:20).

The accounts of Jesus healing Bartimaeus reveal both traditional and redactional features and are useful passages for understanding some of the special features and interests of each of the three synoptic Gospel writers. Having acknowledged this, it should be noted that the three accounts also have much in common. They all note the features of blindness, begging by the roadside, the geographical connection with Jericho, the urgent call for help to the Son of David, the specific question put by Jesus, the words of healing spoken to him, the immediate nature of the healing, and the definite healing that ensued.

◆ PP. Jesus and Zacchaeus (19:1-10)

Jesus entered Jericho and made his way through the town. ²There was a man there named Zacchaeus. He was the chief tax collector in the region, and he had become very rich. ³He tried to get a look at Jesus, but he was too short to see over the crowd. ⁴So he ran ahead and climbed a sycamore-fig tree beside the road, for Jesus was going to pass that way.

⁵When Jesus came by, he looked up at Zacchaeus and called him by name. "Zacchaeus!" he said. "Quick, come down! I must be a guest in your home today."

⁶Zacchaeus quickly climbed down and took Jesus to his house in great excitement and joy. ⁷But the people were displeased. "He has gone to be the guest of a notorious sinner," they grumbled.

⁸Meanwhile, Zacchaeus stood before the Lord and said, "I will give half my wealth to the poor, Lord, and if I have cheated people on their taxes, I will give them back four times as much!"

⁹Jesus responded, "Salvation has come to this home today, for this man has shown himself to be a true son of Abraham. ¹⁰For the Son of Man* came to seek and save those who are lost."

19:10"Son of Man" is a title Jesus used for himself.

NOTES

19:2 *There was a man there named Zacchaeus.* In Maccabean times, there was an officer in the army of Judas Maccabeus who had this name (2 Macc 10:19). The name itself means "pure," though the tax collector known to Jesus was clearly described by his contemporaries as a "sinner" (19:7).

the chief tax collector in the region. Tax collectors were often grouped with prostitutes and other questionable figures as "sinners," for it was necessary for them to collaborate with the Roman occupation government and serve imperial ends. Tax collectors were also notorious for exploiting the people with exacting excessive taxes that served to "feather their own nest" as, at the same time, they served Rome. Zacchaeus fit this description; he was "the chief tax collector in the region, and he had become very rich" (19:2). As the head administrator of the region, he got a cut of everyone's tax profits (contrast Matthew, a local tax collector— Matt 10:3; Mark 2:14; Luke 5:27). Zacchaeus and other tax collectors were highly unpopular and suspicious characters at the time of Jesus, and their occupation was thoroughly despised by the rank and file of the Jewish people.

19:4 *sycamore-fig tree.* "The sycomore-fig (sycamore, RSV [JB, NRSV]), *Ficus sycomorus*, L., [was] a sturdy tree 10–13 meters [30–40 feet] high, with a short trunk, widely spreading branches, and evergreen leaves. It was, and still is, abundant in Egypt and the lowlands of Palestine (1 Kgs 10:27; 2 Chr 1:15; 9:27). The fruits are edible and were sufficiently important for King David to appoint an overseer to look after the olive trees and sycamore trees (1 Chr 27:28)" (NBD 1217). They are mentioned in Ps 78 in a warning not to forget the historical judgments of God on his people in the past, when God "destroyed their grapevines with hail and shattered their sycamore-figs with sleet" (Ps 78:47). They are noted in Amos, where the prophet is described as one who takes care of sycamore-fig trees (Amos 7:14).

COMMENTARY

This story, found only in Luke's Gospel, is one of the unforgettable vignettes that make Luke's work so well loved and remembered. He had a gift for telling a story in such a way that he implanted it in the minds and hearts of his readers. Who can forget the stories of the prodigal son, the rich man and Lazarus, or the parables of the lost coin or the rich fool? Luke, a master storyteller, helped bring the teaching of Jesus alive for his readers by his skill in narration. (For further discussion on the literary aspects of this passage, see O'Toole 1991.)

In this case, the setting is the well-known Hellenistic city of Jericho, some 17 miles northeast of Jerusalem near the Jordan River, a mile south of ancient Jericho (Marshall 1978:693) and just north of the point where the river empties into the Dead Sea. With a rich supply of water, it had been inhabited from ancient times as an oasis town blessed with an abundance of vegetation, palms, and sycamore-fig trees. Its location made it an important customs post in Jesus' time. Into this lush setting Jesus came, making "his way through the town" (19:1). Since Jesus was by this time well-known as a preacher and healer, it was not surprising that crowds should line the streets to catch a glimpse of this remarkable person (19:3). One of those interested in Jesus was a man named Zacchaeus. His profession was that of tax collector, and he had developed a big enterprise as "the chief tax collector in the region" (19:2). Such a man was naturally despised in Palestinian society, for the Jews were under the heel of the Roman Empire and therefore had to pay taxes to hated foreigners. This made Zacchaeus's job unacceptable to virtually all his fellow Jews and put him in a socially unacceptable position with the Jewish people. Moreover, he was in a position, as a chief tax collector in that region, to farm out tax concessions to others who would collect the taxes and enable him to rake off a vast surplus for himself. He was an entrepreneur who had profited from the system and had made himself both very wealthy and very much despised by the Jewish people he had exploited.

Into this situation came Jesus, and somehow this little man's curiosity was piqued. "He tried to get a look at Jesus, but he was too short to see over the crowd" (19:3). In his eagerness, Zacchaeus ran ahead and climbed into a sycamore tree on the route Jesus would travel, and thus he was in a position to see the famous stranger pass by when Jesus finally came that way (19:4). Jesus reached out to this lonely, despised man. Jesus called him by name and invited himself as a guest to meet the man in his home that very day (19:5). While Zacchaeus was full of "great excitement and joy" at the prospect of such an unexpected encounter (19:6), the people around him in the crowds complained and voiced their evident displeasure, charging Jesus with keeping bad company as "the guest of a notorious sinner" (19:7).

At this point in the narrative, the text says, "Zacchaeus stood before the Lord and said, 'I will give half my wealth to the poor, Lord, and if I have cheated people on their taxes, I will give them back four times as much!' Jesus responded, 'Salvation has come to this home today'" (19:8-9a). Most commentators have taken this passage to mean that Zacchaeus had a conversion experience when he met Jesus, which resulted in his salvation. However, Evans has argued against the usual interpretation of Zacchaeus's conversion by pointing out that the Greek words in his answer are in the present tense and therefore suggest that he was claiming to be giving up half of his wealth to the poor *already* and was prepared to restore any illegitimate profits fourfold, even as the law required. On this reading, Evans understands 19:8 to be "the statement of Zacchaeus as an immediate protest against the muttering crowd which disapproved of Jesus' intention to dine with him and which had referred to the tax collector as a 'sinner' (v.7). In other words, Zacchaeus has responded to the sting of being called a sinner for no other reason than the mere fact of his occupation. He has protested, in effect, that whereas other tax collectors may cheat and gouge their fellow citizens, he, Zacchaeus, regularly contributes to the poor and whenever he (accidentally) collects too much (not necessarily 'cheated'), he always makes fourfold restitution" (1990:280).

Evans's interpretation does not appear to be the most natural way of reading the passage, for Luke seems to be pointing to the life-changing nature of this encounter of Zacchaeus with Jesus. Notice particularly how Jesus declared to him, "Salvation has come to this home *today*" (19:9). His relationship with Jesus had changed his values, and, in genuine repentance, he had promised to both make restitution to those whom he had wronged and to be generous with his resources, giving away half of his wealth to meet the needs of the poor whom he had hitherto exploited. Zacchaeus made an ethical response that exceeded the demands of the Torah: "The Hebrew law (Exod 22:1) required a fivefold, fourfold, or double restoration in special cases . . . Usually it was equal restitution plus 20 per cent for damages (Lev 6:5; Num 5:6ff). Zacchaeus vows the harder, fuller penalty" (Grant 1962: 295). His contact with Jesus had made a real difference, and he was no longer the same self-centered man. By his proper response to God, he had demonstrated his genuine faith and revealed himself as "a true son of Abraham" (19:9), the father of the faithful with whom God had made a covenant (Gen 15; cf. Gen 12:1-3; 22:15-18). And so, the passage closes with the memorable words on the lips of Jesus that epitomize the message of Luke: "For the Son of Man came to seek and save those who are lost" (19:10).

◆ **QQ. Parable of the Ten Servants (19:11-27; cf. Matt 25:14-30)**

[11]The crowd was listening to everything Jesus said. And because he was nearing Jerusalem, he told them a story to correct the impression that the Kingdom of God would begin right away. [12]He said, "A nobleman was called away to a distant empire to be crowned king and then return. [13]Before he left, he called together ten of his servants and divided among them ten pounds of silver,* saying, 'Invest this for me while I am gone.' [14]But his people hated him and sent a delegation after him to say, 'We do not want him to be our king.'

[15]"After he was crowned king, he returned and called in the servants to whom he had given the money. He wanted to find out what their profits were. [16]The first servant reported, 'Master, I invested your money and made ten times the original amount!'

[17]"'Well done!' the king exclaimed. 'You are a good servant. You have been faithful with the little I entrusted to you, so you will be governor of ten cities as your reward.'

[18]"The next servant reported, 'Master, I invested your money and made five times the original amount.'

[19]"'Well done!' the king said. 'You will be governor over five cities.'

[20]"But the third servant brought back only the original amount of money and said, 'Master, I hid your money and kept it safe. [21]I was afraid because you are a hard man to deal with, taking what isn't yours and harvesting crops you didn't plant.'

[22]"'You wicked servant!' the king roared. 'Your own words condemn you. If you knew that I'm a hard man who takes what isn't mine and harvests crops I didn't plant, [23]why didn't you deposit my money in the bank? At least I could have gotten some interest on it.'

[24]"Then, turning to the others standing nearby, the king ordered, 'Take the money from this servant, and give it to the one who has ten pounds.'

[25]"'But, master,' they said, 'he already has ten pounds!'

[26]"'Yes,' the king replied, 'and to those who use well what they are given, even more will be given. But from those who do nothing, even what little they have will be taken away. [27]And as for these enemies of mine who didn't want me to be their king—bring them in and execute them right here in front of me.' "

19:13 Greek *ten minas;* one mina was worth about three months' wages.

NOTES

19:11 *he told them a story.* Jesus frequently used parables and stories to communicate his message about the Kingdom of God to the crowds of people who came to hear him (Matt 13, 22; Mark 4; Luke 8)

to correct the impression that the Kingdom of God would begin right away. On Luke's carefully nuanced, balanced approach to eschatology, see Franklin 1975:9-47 and Guy 1997. On the Kingdom theme, see notes on 4:42-44. On the ways in which scholars have understood Luke's views about Jews and Judaism, see Tyson 1999.

19:12 *A nobleman was called away to a distant empire to be crowned king and then return.* Schonfield has suggested an interesting historical allusion here: "Luke's version of the story told in Matt 25:14-30 seems partly to have been influenced by the history of Archelaus, Herod the Great's successor, who went to Rome to be confirmed in the kingship by Augustus. His people sent a deputation to oppose him (see Josephus *War* 2.6.1)" (1958:179).

19:13 *ten pounds of silver.* Lit., "ten minas," roughly 20 to 25 dollars in modern currency (Fitzmyer 1985:1235). One mina, or silver pound, was equal to about three months' wages. In Matthew's account, the servants receive "talents," a much larger unit of money. It took 60 minas to equal the value of one talent. The small amount in Luke "perhaps reflects Luke's view that although many of those in the church are poor, they are, nevertheless, expected to be good stewards with what they do have" (Evans 1990:287).

19:27 *as for these enemies of mine who didn't want me to be their king—bring them in and execute them.* J. T. Sanders (1981) indicates that these remarks are anti-Semitic. But Evans objects to the charge, arguing as follows: "The parable says that only those who have opposed the king will be slain (v.27; cf. Deut. 18:19, quoted in Acts 3:23). And, in the light of Acts, the Jews of Jerusalem are given many opportunities to repent (see Tannehill [1985; 1986:161]). Moreover, to argue that the parable teaches that the king will slay all his subjects is nonsensical. Who are the good servants (vv.13, 15b-19)? They are just as Jewish as the subjects who opposed the king. Consequently, there is no justification to distinguish Jews from Gentiles (or Christians). The question of race has nothing to do with the parable" (1990:286).

COMMENTARY

The final days in Jesus' earthly ministry were looming on the horizon, and, as he approached Jerusalem, Jesus was concerned with teaching the people some important lessons about last things. This was necessary because many incorrect ideas were circulating, and Jesus wanted "to correct the [false] impression that the Kingdom of God would begin right away" (19:11). He had an attentive audience, and the occasion was right to share such timely instruction.

The vehicle he chose to use was a parable about ten servants who were left in charge of a nobleman's estate during his protracted absence. The servants were summoned together before their master's proposed trip and challenged to invest the resources entrusted to them during the unspecified time of their master's absence. They did different things with what had been entrusted to them, and eventually they were called to account for their stewardship upon the return of their newly crowned king (19:15).

A number of allegorical features appear in this parable. Note that the master is described as a "nobleman" called away "to a distant empire" in order to be "crowned king" and then make his "return" (19:12). Notice also that there was opposition to this figure, for "his people hated him" and bluntly opposed his kingship (19:14; cf. John 1:11). All of these elements seem to suggest that this story is pointing to Jesus, who was despised and rejected by his people, bitterly opposed when his kingship was announced, and called away for a time in his death, resurrection, and exaltation to the Father. In God's time, he would return again in power and glory and then demand an accounting of those to whom he had entrusted substantial resources.

The servants in the parable made different use of what they had been given, and they were recognized fairly and with sensitivity. The first one had invested his allotted money productively and had experienced a tenfold profit (19:16). He was commended for his effectiveness as a good servant and duly rewarded with increased responsibility over a much larger field of endeavor (19:17). In similar fashion, the second servant reported that he had been successful and had gained a fivefold profit. The master approved of his stewardship as well and responded, "Well done!
. . . You will be governor over five cities" (19:19). Both of these servants had been fruitful in their management of resources, had seen substantial development and growth, and, accordingly, had been recognized and given increased opportunities of usefulness in enlarging fields of service.

The third man was different and, by contrast, totally unproductive. He was anxious to excuse himself by blaming his course of action on the nobleman, alleging that the master was "a hard man" and utterly ruthless and unscrupulous in his actions (19:21). According to the commonly used "law of end stress" in parables, the story makes it clear that the focus is on the last man—the unfaithful servant who had squandered his master's resources: " 'You wicked servant!' the king roared" (19:22). He was condemned out of his own mouth by his own words and rebuked for a culpable offense (19:23). He was convicted for a gross dereliction of duty, and his money was stripped from him and given to the most highly productive servant (19:24). This rather shocking settlement was questioned by some (19:25); however, the principle of stewardship was emphatically stated by the king: "To those who use well what they are given, even more will be given" (19:26). Unfortunately, the converse is also true, as this parable so forcefully reminds us: "But from those who do nothing, even what little they have will be taken away" (19:26b).

The parable stresses the fact that Christians are accountable to the Lord for their lives. The time of the King's return is unknown, but its uncertainty calls for faithfulness and diligence in the use of resources. When the nobleman returns as King, all those to whom he has given resources must give a careful account of their stewardship. Those who have been faithful will be amply recognized and commended, and those who have been negligent will be called to account for what they have failed to do. The story closes on a solemn note of terrible punishment for the King's enemies, who, in the story, had opposed his kingship and authority—they will be brought to judgment in no uncertain terms (19:27).

> [This parable on stewardship] fits well with other teachings found elsewhere in Luke. We have a similar parable in 12:35-40 in which faithful stewardship is described as being "watchful" (12:37) and "ready" (12:38). In this parable faithful stewardship is also intimately connected to the parousia. . . . Within the parable also are present two additional themes. One involves Jesus' kingship. . . . Also associated with this parable is an emphasis on Jesus' rejection by the Jewish nation. Luke's references to this in the parable (19:14, 27) are not found in the Matthean parable [Matt 25:14-30] but are unique to him. (Stein 1992:475)

In conclusion, it should also be noted that Matthew's version of this parable contains a number of distinct differences in detail. Matthew mentions three servants, whereas Luke notes ten servants (19:13). Matthew describes the person in charge as a "man" who is called "the master" (Matt 25:14, 19, 21, 26), whereas in Luke it is a "nobleman" who goes to receive a "kingdom" and returns as a "king" who has the right to carry out executions for treasonable conduct (19:12, 15, 22, 26-27). In Matthew, the servants receive talents (Matt 25:15, NLT mg), an amount worth perhaps as much as fifty times that of the minas, or "pounds of silver," mentioned in Luke (19:13, NLT mg). Matthew's second servant receives the same words of commendation as the first (Matt 25:21, 23), while in Luke there is less lavish praise for the less productive servant (19:17, 19). In Matthew, nothing is said when the talent is taken from the unproductive servant and given to the servant who already had the ten talents (Matt 25:28), whereas in Luke there is a word of complaint (19:25). In Matthew's version the worthless servant is cast into the outer darkness "where there will be weeping and gnashing of teeth" (Matt 25:30), while in Luke the "enemies" are slain before the King and the rebellion quelled (19:27). Both versions of the parable appear in eschatological settings. In Matthew, the story is preceded by the story of the ten bridesmaids and followed by the teaching on the final judgment, and in Luke the setting is clearly to prepare the disciples as they neared Jerusalem and to revise their timetable of last things (19:11).

◆   RR. The Triumphal Entry (19:28-40; cf. Matt 21:1-9; Mark 11:1-10)

28After telling this story, Jesus went on toward Jerusalem, walking ahead of his disciples. 29As he came to the towns of Bethphage and Bethany on the Mount of Olives, he sent two disciples ahead. 30"Go into that village over there," he told them. "As you enter it, you will see a young donkey tied there that no one has ever ridden. Untie it and bring it here. 31If anyone asks, 'Why are you untying that colt?' just say, 'The Lord needs it.' "

32So they went and found the colt, just as Jesus had said. 33And sure enough, as they were untying it, the owners asked them, "Why are you untying that colt?"

34And the disciples simply replied, "The Lord needs it." 35So they brought the colt to Jesus and threw their garments over it for him to ride on.

36As he rode along, the crowds spread out their garments on the road ahead of him. 37When he reached the place where the road started down the Mount of Olives, all of his followers began to shout and sing as they walked along, praising God for all the wonderful miracles they had seen.

38 "Blessings on the King who comes
      in the name of the LORD!
   Peace in heaven, and glory in
      highest heaven!"*

39But some of the Pharisees among the crowd said, "Teacher, rebuke your followers for saying things like that!"

40He replied, "If they kept quiet, the stones along the road would burst into cheers!"

19:38 Pss 118:26; 148:1.

NOTES

19:29 *Bethphage.* "In Talmudic literature Bethphage (Beth Pagi) marked the eastern limits of Jerusalem. . . . The name means 'the house of unripe or early figs'" (Freedman 2000:175). Matt 21:1 and Mark 11:12 also name Bethphage as the starting point for the Triumphal Entry.

19:33 *Why are you untying that colt?* Jesus' entry into the holy city on a specially chosen animal is noted in all three Synoptic accounts. The Gospels go into considerable detail in recounting the events of Passion week, and all record Jesus' entry into Jerusalem, which is seen in terms of the fulfillment of prophecy (Matt 21:4-5; John 12:15; cf. Zech 9:9). Luke's presentation highlights Jesus' joyful entry into the city in terms of God's peace (*shalom*) and glory, heralded by shouts of glad acclaim and recognition of Jesus as the promised "King who comes in the name of the LORD" (19:38; cf. John 12:12). In this way Luke relates this event to both the message of the angels at the nativity and to the universal proclamation of "peace" through Jesus Christ (cf. 2:8-14; Acts 10:36).

19:37 *praising God.* Luke's Gospel, like the book of Acts, often notes the praise and worship of God's people. In the nativity stories, for example, Luke stressed the note of joy in the births of John the Baptist and Jesus and gave his readers some beautiful hymns in the songs of Mary, Zechariah, the heavenly host, and Simeon (1:46b-55, 67-80; 2:14, 29-35). Now, once again, the note of praise is conspicuously sounded upon the entrance of Jesus to Jerusalem, as the crowds of his disciples acclaim him in messianic terms on the road that descended "down the Mount of Olives" (19:37). On Luke's interest in "praise" (*aineō* [TG134, ZG140]), see 2:13, 20; 19:37; 24:53; Acts 2:47; 3:8-9.

19:38 *Blessings on the King who comes in the name of the LORD!* There are clear echoes of Ps 118:25-26 and Zech 9:9 (cf. Isa 62:11) here that are also present in the parallel accounts (see Matt 21:9; Mark 11:9-10). Matthew and Mark include the acclamation "Hosanna" (a transliteration of the Heb. in Ps 118:25 that means "Please, Lord, save us") and the recognition of Jesus as the Son of David and, therefore, the rightful King whose sovereignty is to be heralded and acclaimed. Since Luke was writing for a larger audience, he naturally highlighted the general theme of the kingship of Jesus without using the Jewish vocabulary and associations that would be less familiar to Gentile readers.

19:39 *Teacher, rebuke your followers.* Only Luke mentions this attempt by some of the hostile Pharisees to stifle the boisterous welcome that accompanied Jesus into the holy city. This reference to the opposition serves as a preparation for the rejection that Jesus will shortly experience in Jerusalem.

19:40 *If they kept quiet, the stones . . . would burst into cheers!* The reply of Jesus about the stones crying out "indicates that his kingship is a reality whether it is recognized by people or not. The inhabitants of Jerusalem may not accept their true king, but the very stones of which the city is built do" (Evans 1990:289). There is probably a textual echo of Hab 2:11 here, where the prophet spoke of the stones crying out against the wicked Chaldeans.

COMMENTARY

The Passion story has often been considered in seven phases or stages. First, there is the "Triumphal Entry"; secondly, the cleansing of the Temple. Third, there is the betrayal planned by Judas and the anointing that takes place at Bethany. Fourth, the Last Supper is instituted as the Lord's Supper, followed by the agony and arrest of Jesus in the garden of Gethsemane. Sixth, there are the various trials of Jesus before Jewish and Roman officials; and seventh, there is the account of the crucifixion itself. Each of these events is related to the others, but each has its own integrity and importance to Luke's overall presentation of the Passion.

The first event is often termed the "Triumphal Entry", but this description is somewhat deficient and inaccurate. Ultimately, of course, Christians look forward to the "triumph" of Jesus at the consummation of history and anticipate with joy the Second Coming of Christ as the time of his final triumph and victory. Accordingly, Jesus declared at his trial before the high priest that the Jewish people could expect something special at the end of time, when "the Son of Man will be seated in the place of power at God's right hand" (22:69; cf. Matt 26:64; Mark 14:62). Clearly, the Palm Sunday event is not the final victory of Jesus, but it prefigures it. There is a fleeting but valuable recognition of Jesus as King before he suffers and dies as "King of the Jews" (23:37-38).

Luke shows that while Jesus is King, his kingship must be first exercised by way of the cross. In order to fulfill the divine plan, he "must suffer many terrible things. . . . He will be rejected by the elders, the leading priests, and the teachers of religious law. He will be killed, but on the third day he will be raised from the dead" (9:22). As I have noted elsewhere, "Luke follows Mark in stressing the divinely ordained role which Jesus fulfills as the righteous sufferer, but he adds his own contribution even when he appropriates Mark" (Trites 1987b:34). Only Luke prefaces the third Passion prediction by noting Jesus' comment to the disciples: "We're going up to Jerusalem, where all the predictions of the prophets concerning the Son of Man will come true" (18:31-33; cf. Matt 20:17-19; Mark 10:32-34). In Luke's presentation, "Christ's suffering and his great glory afterward" are intimately connected, as is the case in the first letter of Peter (1 Pet 1:11).

The Triumphal Entry ironically leads to the commencement of the Passion Story, for it directly introduces the final leg of Jesus' trek to Jerusalem. Significantly, on the road to the city of destiny, Jesus was "walking ahead of his disciples" (19:28). They began to climb up the hills of the Judean wilderness as they worked their way westward toward Jerusalem. Eventually, Jesus and the apostles arrived at the Mount of Olives, on the outskirts of the city, where the towns of Bethany and Bethphage were located. Bethany was the home of Mary, Martha, and Lazarus (10:38-42; John 11:1); see the note on 19:29 on Bethphage.

Jesus gave orders for two of his disciples to go ahead into the adjacent village (Matthew only mentions Bethphage, probably to avoid geographical confusion here) and secure the use of a young donkey, the animal Jesus proposed to ride as he made his significant entrance into Jerusalem. It was to be an unbroken colt—one on which no one had ever ridden before; and it was to be used by the Lord after it had been untied and brought to him by the disciples who had been sent to fetch it (19:30). The colt was to be released on a pre-arranged signal—"Just say, 'The Lord needs it'" (19:31).

The two disciples entered the village and found the colt, "just as Jesus had said" (19:32). They carried out his instructions in untying the donkey and gave the expected password to the owners, thereby gaining the use of the animal (19:33-34). They fulfilled their mandate, returning with the colt to Jesus and then casting their garments over it as a saddle on which Jesus could ride (19:35). Jesus was astride the animal, quite intentionally riding into the holy city on a beast of peace, not a war charger. This was the manner in which Solomon had entered Jerusalem as the successor to his father, King David (1 Kgs 1:33, 38). It was a symbolic way of announcing the peaceful character of his reign, and Jesus was intending a similar message—a point brought out in Matthew's use of the messianic quotation from Zechariah (Matt 21:5, quoting Zech 9:9). The crowds in the Lukan narrative were very receptive and "spread out their garments on the road ahead of him" in open recognition of his kingship (19:36). At the point of descent down the western slope of the Mount of Olives, the adoring throng exploded into joyous praise: "All of his followers began to shout and sing as they walked along, praising God for all the wonderful miracles they had seen" (19:37). They used a cry of acclamation that springs from Psalm 118:25-26, part of the *Hallel*, a prayer of thanksgiving, consisting of Psalms 113–118, recited during Passover (19:38; cf. Matt 21:9; Mark 11:9-10).

The proclamation "peace in heaven, and glory in the highest heaven" comes from Psalm 148:1; it is singularly appropriate here. At Jesus' birth, the angels sang the beautiful words, "Glory to God in highest heaven, and peace on earth to those with whom God is pleased" (2:14). It was the turn of human beings to praise God, and once again the *gloria in excelsis deo* is sounded (19:38). Both heaven and earth offered their praises to Jesus, the King and promised Savior.

The reaction of some of the Pharisees was not surprising, given their previous hostility and skepticism (see 5:30; 7:30, 34, 39; 15:2). They wanted such enthusiastic remarks to be restrained, for the praise suggested a messianic excitement that they obviously did not share (19:39). Jesus refused to yield to his critics, insisting on the legitimacy of this warm praise and acclamation (19:40), for it was the willing recognition of the followers of Jesus that he was worthy of their praise and adoration.

◆   SS. Jesus Weeps over Jerusalem (19:41-44)

⁴¹But as he came closer to Jerusalem and saw the city ahead, he began to weep. ⁴²"How I wish today that you of all people would understand the way to peace. But now it is too late, and peace is hidden from your eyes. ⁴³Before long your enemies will build ramparts against your walls and encircle you and close in on you from every side. ⁴⁴They will crush you into the ground, and your children with you. Your enemies will not leave a single stone in place, because you did not accept your opportunity for salvation."

N O T E S

19:41 *saw the city . . . began to weep.* This passage is sometimes described as the "Prediction of the Destruction of Jerusalem" because it lays out in painful detail the impending doom that Jesus forecasted for the holy city. In ch 21 Jesus speaks in greater detail of the coming devastation. He was passionately involved in the destiny of his people, and like Jeremiah, "the weeping prophet" (Jer 9:1; 13:17; 48:32; Lam 1:16), he longed for the repentance of the people and the removal of the terrible cloud of judgment that was about to descend upon the holy city (cf. 2 Chr 7:14).

COMMENTARY

As Jesus came over the hill and began to descend from the Mount of Olives, he looked right onto the city just ahead and was overcome with emotion. He began to weep over it, predicting its coming destruction and desolation (19:43-44). Sadly and tragically, the Jewish people had chosen the wrong course of action, and their general rejection of his claims would cost them dearly. They had not opted for "the way of peace," and now it was too late (19:42). They faced the utter destruction of their city by military siege and the total breakdown of its defenses and fortifications (19:43-44). All of this devastation was attributable to the leaders' failure to respond appropriately to Jesus (19:39, 47).

In Jesus' person and ministry, God had been "visiting" his people. A couple of Old Testament passages shed light on the notion of God "visiting" his people. Jeremiah 29:10 speaks of God coming graciously to "visit" after the seventy years of Babylonian exile, and Zephaniah 2:7 says, "For the LORD their God will visit his people in kindness and restore their prosperity again." The tragedy of the Jewish people in Jesus' day was that they did not respond positively to their golden "opportunity for salvation" (19:44). Jesus knew the result would be an awful judgment on his beloved city, for the leaders there were about to put him to death in just a few days. Jesus' proclamation alludes to certain Old Testament passages that describe the devastation of the holy city by its enemies as a divine judgment upon its ways: "I will be your enemy, surrounding Jerusalem and attacking its walls. I will build siege towers and destroy it" (Isa 29:3; see also Isa 37:33; Ezek 4:1-3).

◆ VI. The Passion Story (19:45–24:53)
   A. Jesus Clears the Temple (19:45–48; cf. Matt 21:12–13;
      Mark 11:15–19; John 2:13–17)

⁴⁵Then Jesus entered the Temple and began to drive out the people selling animals for sacrifices. ⁴⁶He said to them, "The Scriptures declare, 'My Temple will be a house of prayer,' but you have turned it into a den of thieves.'"*

⁴⁷After that, he taught daily in the Temple, but the leading priests, the teachers of religious law, and the other leaders of the people began planning how to kill him. ⁴⁸But they could think of nothing, because all the people hung on every word he said.

19:46 Isa 56:7; Jer 7:11.

NOTES

19:45 *Then Jesus entered the Temple.* The Temple had an important place in Luke's thinking, though Stephen's address in Acts makes it clear that ultimately God " doesn't live in temples made by human hands" (Acts 7:48), perhaps suggesting that the Temple had become something of an idol standing in the way of a direct relationship with God. The Temple was originally chosen to have a unique place in God's plan for his people, as was clear in King Solomon's great prayer at the dedication of the Temple (2 Chr 6:14-42). It was the place where the people of Israel were to call on God in all times of difficulty and he would meet them in grace and forgiveness.

began to drive out the people selling animals for sacrifices. The cleansing of the Temple is recorded in all four Gospels (19:45-48; Matt 21:12-17; Mark 11:15-19; John 2:13-17). John places it near the beginning of Jesus' public ministry, where it serves as a kind of frontispiece to his Gospel, showing the cleansing, or catharsis, that Jesus will bring to the institutions of Judaism (John 2:13-22). A comparison of John's account with the Synoptics shows its differences from them in particular vocabulary, the animals mentioned, and the details of Jesus' actions (cf. Morris 1971:188-189). Matthew's account has an interesting detail not found in Mark and Luke about Jesus healing in the Temple at this time (Matt 21:14). Some interpreters have argued that the official place for money changing was on the Mount of Olives, just east of Jerusalem, beyond the Kidron Valley. If this view is correct, then the Sadducees deliberately had a rival place in the Temple for the sole purpose of profit (cf. Evans 1990:296).

19:47 the leading priests, the teachers of religious law, and the other leaders of the people began planning how to kill him. On the dimensions of conflict between Jesus and the Jewish authorities, see the study by Gransgaard 1999. It is striking that Luke presents the religious leaders as being cared for and pitied by Jesus (note esp. 19:39-44; cf. Powell 1990). On the suffering of Jesus in Luke, see Scheffler 1993:103-158.

COMMENTARY

Luke has prepared the reader for the final part of his account. After his initial opening in the form of a preface (1:1-4), the evangelist has introduced the preparation and setting for the ministry of Jesus (1:5-4:13). He has conducted us through the first major division of his Gospel by exploring the ministry of Jesus in Galilee (4:14-9:50). Then, in the second major division, he has presented the ministry of Jesus on the journey from Galilee to Jerusalem (9:51-19:44), during which Jesus carefully outlined not only his own impending suffering and death, but also the conditions of discipleship that his people must follow as they walk in his steps. Now, in the last major division of his Gospel, he unfolds the ministry of Jesus in Jerusalem (19:45-23:56).

The story of Jesus' earthly ministry drew to an appropriate close in Jerusalem. Luke had been presenting Jesus as moving inexorably to the holy city where the climax of redemption would be worked out according to the divine plan. Jesus had been preparing his disciples for his death all through this trip (9:51-19:44). The awful events of humiliation and crucifixion that had been predicted would be unfolded one by one. Beyond that time of pain and heartache would come his vindication in his resurrection and exaltation to glory.

The Johannine account of the cleansing of the Temple occurs at the beginning of John's Gospel and differs from the Synoptic accounts with several points of interest. In John, the clearing of the Temple involves Jesus taking some ropes and making a whip, or scourge, which he used to remove the money changers and those who sold animals (John 2:15). Jesus' criticism of those who were abusing the place of worship and exploiting the Temple was direct and blunt: "Get these things out of here. Stop turning my Father's house into a marketplace!" (John 2:16; cf. Matt 21:13). The remarkable zeal of Jesus in carrying out this public demonstration was later remembered by the disciples and interpreted as a fulfillment of the Scripture: "Passion for God's house will consume me" (John 2:17; cf. Ps 69:9). This incident was important to the disciples in hindsight because it strengthened and confirmed their faith in Jesus and the Scriptures (John 2:22).

It might be that there was only this one Temple cleansing, which took place during Passion Week, and that John moved it forward in his narrative for theological reasons, especially to show God's judging work in the Messiah's ministry. However, John's unique details, mentioned above, cause some commentators to propose two Temple cleansings (e.g., Morris 1971:188-191; Plummer 1896:453). This would mean there was one cleansing early in Jesus' ministry, during the first few months (seen only in John), and another one during the last week of his ministry, attested by the Synoptic Gospels. A few commentators hold views other than these two (e.g., Bammel and Moule 1984:455-460; Nolland 1993:93), but the view that there were the two cleansings is slightly more satisfactory than any of the others, though none is without difficulties.

The Synoptic Gospels place the incident at the close of Jesus' public ministry. Mark's account is the most detailed. He notes the strong authority Jesus exercised in the incident: "He stopped everyone from using the Temple as a marketplace" (Mark 11:16). Mark saw the threat Jesus posed to the leading priests and the scribes by his decisive action, noting that when they heard what Jesus had done, "they began planning how to kill him" (Mark 11:18a). His open confrontation with the religious establishment provoked fear in them "because the people were so amazed at his teaching" (Mark 11:18). Jealousy of this popular—and therefore dangerous—teacher was a factor in their determination to get rid of him (cf. John 12:19).

Matthew's account is similar to Mark's but has some significant additions. He also mentions the attempted expulsion of the money changers and all those who bought and sold in the Temple, including the seats of those who sold pigeons (Matt 21:12; cf. Mark 11:15; Luke's account doesn't mention the pigeons). Matthew's account also includes healings in the Temple after this event (21:14).

When we turn to Luke's version, we see that as soon as Jesus entered the holy city, he entered the Temple. The tragedy in Jesus' day was the perversion that happened in that sacred place. The house of God was certainly intended by God to be a place of worship and prayer, but it had been desecrated by crass commercialism. A vigorous religious business of selling animals for sacrifices (19:45) took place in the Court of the Gentiles, the only place in the sacred precincts where Gentiles were allowed to worship. Moreover, pilgrims came from many far away places to the Temple and had to exchange their profane coins to make their offerings in acceptable Temple currency. The priests also required that their sacrificial animals be purchased there because they stipulated that only these offerings met the standards as laid out in the book of Leviticus (1:1–7:21). Jesus protested against this business exploitation in the Temple and "began to drive out the people" engaged in it (19:45). It was a travesty of the divine purpose for which the Temple had been created, and Jesus rebuked the practice in strong, biblical terms: "The Scriptures declare, 'My Temple will be a house of prayer,' but you have turned it into a den of thieves" (19:46; cf. Isa 56:7; Jer 7:11).

Jesus' trenchant criticism had partly come from the prophecy of Isaiah that had pointed out the divine purpose to bring blessing to all people: "My Temple will be called a house of prayer for all nations" (Isa 56:7). That holy purpose had been negated by the practices that had been permitted in the Court of the Gentiles, and Jesus raised a vigorous protest against it. The other passage he cited was from Jeremiah's famous Temple sermon (Jer 7). In that sermon, Jeremiah had assaulted the self-satisfaction of people who assumed that going through the motions of religion was enough: "Don't be fooled into thinking that you will never suffer because the Temple is here. It's a lie!" (Jer 7:8). Religion without ethics was a perversion of God's ways: "Don't you yourselves admit that this Temple, which bears my name, has become a den of thieves? Surely I see all the evil going on there. I, the LORD, have spoken" (Jer 7:11). Jesus' reference to Jeremiah's address effectively exposed the manipulative, unscrupulous practices that were taking place in the Temple.

It is no wonder that Luke, following Mark, noted that the leading priests and the scribes were anxious to destroy Jesus and were making their plans accordingly (19:47; cf. Mark 11:18). He was plainly a threat to them, and his daily teaching in the Temple made the contrast between his methods and theirs immediately obvious (19:47). Despite the animosity of the leaders, they could not find any grounds for public criticism "because all the people hung on every word he said" (19:48).

◆ ## B. The Authority of Jesus Challenged (20:1-8; cf. Matt 21:23-27; Mark 11:27-33)

One day as Jesus was teaching the people and preaching the Good News in the Temple, the leading priests, the teachers of religious law, and the elders came up to him. ²They demanded, "By what authority are you doing all these things? Who gave you the right?"

³"Let me ask you a question first," he replied. ⁴"Did John's authority to baptize come from heaven, or was it merely human?"

⁵They talked it over among themselves. "If we say it was from heaven, he will ask why we didn't believe John. ⁶But if we say it was merely human, the people will stone us because they are convinced John was a prophet." ⁷So they finally replied that they didn't know.

⁸And Jesus responded, "Then I won't tell you by what authority I do these things."

NOTES

20:1 *Jesus was teaching the people and preaching.* In Luke 20, the context is clearly the Temple, which Jesus had just cleansed (19:45-46) and which thereby became a suitable place for his teaching and preaching (19:47-48; 20:1). This scene introduces the first of five debates between Jesus and the Jewish leaders in ch 20, and it is paralleled by similar controversies in the other synoptic Gospels (Matt 21:23-27; 22:15-45; Mark 11:27-33; 12:13-37). The debates appear in the same order in each of the three Gospels: the question about authority, the question about tribute to Caesar, the question about the resurrection, the question about the great commandment, and the question about David's son. These controversies show the strong opposition Jesus faced from the Jewish religious establishment. He was perceived as a threat to their position of leadership, both in the Jewish community and in the larger Roman context (cf. John 11:45-57). The debates were designed to stir up public opposition to Jesus, to entrap him and make it easier to get rid of him with public support. The final debate, the paradoxical question about David's son, was initiated by Jesus to put his enemies on the defensive. It was followed by Jesus' strong denunciation of the scribes (Luke 20:45-47; cf. Matt 23:1-7; Mark 12:38-40).

COMMENTARY

The question about Jesus' authority is found in all three Synoptics, with Luke's version being the shortest. In all three Gospels the persons involved in raising the question are essentially the same leaders who had been opposing Jesus in previous instances: the chief priests, the scribes, and the elders of the people (though Matthew omits the scribes, or teachers of religious law, here). The question they pose is fundamentally the same in each Gospel, and Jesus' counterquestion is the same, shifting the *onus probandi* from his shoulders to theirs. Each Gospel notes the internal debate that took place among these leaders before they gave their considered reply.

Several features of Mark's account are noteworthy. First, in Mark, Jesus insisted that his critics respond to his searching theological question about the baptism of John. Jesus, the controversialist, could hold his own in debate, a point that has been argued at length by Stott on a whole range of issues (1970). Second, while all three Synoptics indicate the widespread respect that John the Baptist enjoyed from the Jewish people, Mark's Gospel highlights the esteem in which the rank and file of Jewish people held John, saying they "considered John to have been a prophet indeed [Gr. *ontōs* (TH3689, ZH3953)]" (Mark 11:32 NASB). Tragically, the members of the Sanhedrin were out of touch with the religious sentiments of the people they were charged with leading.

Matthew's account is largely the same as Mark's. He too placed the question about Jesus' authority right after the incident of the withered fig tree (Matt 21:20-22; cf. Mark 11:12-14, 20-25). Both writers stress the importance of faith in God, and both offer definite encouragement to supplicate God boldly in believing prayer. The fig tree is not mentioned here in Luke, probably because Luke had already provided in his Gospel an illustration of a barren fig tree whose lack of productivity had raised questions about its continued usefulness (13:6-9).

As we have already noted, his bold act in cleansing the Temple made Jesus a man to be noticed. His decisive words and actions had been performed in public, and they were duly challenged by the Jewish authorities, including the "leading priests, the teachers of religious law, and the elders" (20:1). They confronted this Galilean teacher whose activities were so questionable in their eyes: "By what authority are you doing all these things? Who gave you the right?" (20:2). Jesus' intelligent response was to ask a counterquestion, putting them on the defensive and shifting the burden of proof to them (20:3-4). He put them on the spot concerning John the Baptist's authority: was it heavenly in its origin, or did it come from a merely human source (20:4)? It was not an easy question for his opponents to answer, for it put them on the horns of a dilemma. If the origin of John's authority was from God, then the inescapable question would be why they didn't believe in him (20:5). If they attributed John's baptism to a merely human source, they would be despised and persecuted by the common people, who were truly persuaded of John's role as a prophet (20:6). After pondering this delicate issue among themselves (20:5), they gave a noncommittal reply, claiming they didn't know the truth of the matter (20:7). Jesus the controversialist had beaten his malicious opponents at their own game and, hence, was still in charge. He did not have to disclose to them the source of his authority.

◆   ## C. Parable of the Evil Farmers (20:9-19; cf. Matt 21:33-46; Mark 12:1-12)

⁹Now Jesus turned to the people again and told them this story: "A man planted a vineyard, leased it to tenant farmers, and moved to another country to live for several years. ¹⁰At the time of the grape harvest, he sent one of his servants to collect his share of the crop. But the farmers attacked the servant, beat him up, and sent him back empty-handed. ¹¹So the owner sent another servant, but they also insulted him, beat him up, and sent him away empty-handed. ¹²A third man was sent, and they wounded him and chased him away.

¹³"'What will I do?' the owner asked himself. 'I know! I'll send my cherished son. Surely they will respect him.'

¹⁴"But when the tenant farmers saw his son, they said to each other, 'Here comes the heir to this estate. Let's kill him and get the estate for ourselves!' ¹⁵So they dragged him out of the vineyard and murdered him.

"What do you suppose the owner of the vineyard will do to them?" Jesus asked. ¹⁶"I'll tell you—he will come and kill those farmers and lease the vineyard to others."

"How terrible that such a thing should ever happen," his listeners protested.

¹⁷Jesus looked at them and said, "Then what does this Scripture mean?

'The stone that the builders rejected
has now become the cornerstone.'*

¹⁸Everyone who stumbles over that stone will be broken to pieces, and it will crush anyone it falls on."

¹⁹The teachers of religious law and the leading priests wanted to arrest Jesus immediately because they realized he was telling the story against them—they were the wicked farmers. But they were afraid of the people's reaction.

20:17 Ps 118:22.

NOTES

20:9 *A man planted a vineyard, leased it to tenant farmers, and moved to another country.* Recent study has shown that wealthy absentee landlords owned much of Galilee's land. They let out the working of the land to tenant farmers, who eked out a subsistence living. There was much resentment directed against such absentee figures, coupled with a smoldering animosity against the Romans who occupied the country and saddled the people with heavy taxes and custom duties (Freyne 1980; Horsley 1985).

Luke's parable of the wicked tenants is closely paralleled in the other two Synoptic accounts (Matt 21:33-46; Mark 12:1-12). There is a shorter version of this parable in the *Gospel of Thomas* (Saying 65); there, the theme of rejection is continued in Saying 66.

Kistemaker (1980:90) viewed the parable as "a portrayal of Israel's ecclesiastical history" (see Isa 65:2; cf. Rom 10:21). In addition, he noted "the people surrounding Jesus understood the story, for they responded to the parable by saying 'May this never be' (20:16 ['How terrible,' NLT]). Moreover, the Pharisees, chief priests and the teachers of the law knew that this parable was directed against them" (20:19; cf. Matt 21:45). On the meaning of the parable viewed in terms of the vineyard parable of Isa 5:1-7, see Evans 1984. For a study of the variations in the Synoptic accounts, see Newell 1972.

20:14 *Here comes the heir to this estate. Let's kill him and get the estate for ourselves!* It is helpful to set this parable in the context of the ancient Middle East. "In oriental custom, the coming of the only son suggests that the owner had died and that the heir had to come to claim his inheritance. The tenants resolved to kill the heir, thus removing the last obstacle to their complete control of the vineyard" (Summers 1972:241). It is noteworthy here that the murderers cast the son out of the vineyard (20:15); to the early Christians, it was theologically important that Jesus' death took place outside the city walls of Jerusalem (Heb 13:11-13).

20:17 *The stone that the builders rejected has now become the cornerstone.* This is a quotation of Ps 118:22, followed by allusions to Isa 8:14 and Dan 2:34 in the next verse. Dodd argued that early Christians used such passages as Isa 8:14, Dan 2:34, and Ps 118:22 in developing a "testimony-book" of Old Testament passages that they believed were particularly helpful in presenting the claims of Christ (Dodd 1952). Jesus was accepted by Christian believers as "the stone that the builders rejected" but whom God had placed as the cornerstone (see 1 Pet 2:6-8, which links together Ps 118:22 and Isa 8:14 in speaking of Christ as the capstone or cornerstone). For an early foreshadowing of the rejection of Christ as a stumbling block to those who refuse to believe, note the prophecy of Simeon (2:34).

COMMENTARY

Many of Jesus' parables were weapons of controversy, which is obviously the case in this parable about the evil farmers. This parable has allegorical features that emphasize the hostility of the Jewish leaders toward Jesus (20:11). The claims of Jesus were unacceptable to the original tenants of the Lord's vineyard (the Jews), who had treated God's servants (the prophets) shamefully. As a last resort, God had sent his Son, but he did not receive the respect to which he was entitled. As a result, the owner of the vineyard (God) would judge the wicked tenants and give the vineyard to others. The allegorical features of the story make plain the rejection of Jesus by the wicked tenants (the Jews, represented by their hostile leaders) and the opportunity that was being extended to new tenants (the Gentiles). The spread of the Christian message to the Gentile world is a major theme in the book of Acts (Acts 1:8; 9:15; 10:42-43; 26:19-20).

There are unique points in each of the Synoptic accounts of this parable, and Mark and Matthew provide a few more details than Luke about the vineyard, noting the hedge placed around it and the building of a tower, presumably for security purposes. All three accounts mention that the vineyard is let out to tenants while the owner departs for another country, though Luke's version alone observes that the departure was for an extended period of time (20:9). This emphasis on a considerable delay seems to be part of Luke's eschatology, whereby he prepares disciples for a long period in which faithfulness to the Lord is required before he finally returns in glory (cf. 18:8, where the searching question is posed: "When the Son of Man returns, how many will he find on the earth who have faith?")

In all three Gospels the owner eventually returns and sends one or more of his servants to receive some of the fruit of the vineyard. The appointed "time" (*kairos* [TG2540, ZG2789] is used in all three accounts) for the grape harvest is mentioned, and a settlement of business claims is anticipated. The shameful treatment of the servants is noted in all three accounts, as well as the climactic sending of the son. Interestingly, this person is described in both Mark and Luke as a "beloved son," pointing the attentive reader to earlier references to the accounts of the baptism and transfiguration, where that language is applied to Jesus (Matt 3:17; 3:22; 9:35; Mark 1:11; 9:7; in some mss). Similarly, all three accounts hold open the possibility of "respect" for this son (20:13; Matt 21:37; Mark 12:6), though this fails to materialize and the son is killed for purely selfish reasons (see note on 20:14). Regarding the respect for the son, Luke uniquely uses the qualifying adverb *isōs* [TG2481, ZG2711] meaning "perhaps" or "it may be," here translated in the NLT as "surely" (20:13).

All these features comprise an allegory with clear ties to Isaiah's Song of the Vineyard (Isa 5:1-7), where the owner of the vineyard is God and the tenants are his people:

> The nation of Israel is the vineyard of the LORD of Heaven's Armies. The people of Judah are his pleasant garden. He expected a crop of justice, but instead he found oppression. He expected to find righteousness, but instead he heard cries of violence. (Isa 5:7)

After presenting the allegory, Jesus asked what the owner of the vineyard would do with the wicked tenants (20:15). In Matthew, Jesus' question goes directly to his critics, the religious leaders, who reply: "He will put the wicked men to a horrible death and lease the vineyard to others who will give him his share of the crop after each harvest" (Matt 21:41). Thus, the Jewish leaders are made to pronounce the sentence out of their own mouths and thus convict themselves. This is similar to instances in the Old Testament where a person pronounces sentence on a case and unwittingly stands convicted by his own admission (as in the parable of the little ewe lamb recorded in 2 Sam 12:1-7 and the case presented by the wise widow of Tekoa in 2 Sam 14:1-14).

In Luke's account, Jesus answers his own question quite directly and forcibly with a strong word of judgment: "He will come and kill those farmers and lease the vineyard to others" (20:16). Jesus' listeners should have been appalled at the prospect of losing their favored status and being summarily replaced by others who might be more productive and fruitful. After pronouncing judgment on them, Jesus quoted to them a significant prophetic passage: "The stone that the builders rejected has now become the cornerstone" (20:17, quoting Ps 118:22). Though the Messiah would be rejected by the religious leaders, God would make him the cornerstone in God's new building, the church.

Then Jesus said, "Everyone who stumbles over that stone will be broken to pieces, and it will crush anyone it falls on" (20:18). This passage alludes to Isaiah 8:14-15 (where the Jewish people were told to trust in God because in reverencing, or fearing, him, there was nothing else to fear) and to Daniel 2:34-35 (a passage that made mention of a rock cut from a mountain by supernatural means that would crush to pieces opposing forces and overcome the ungodly kingdoms of the world). In the event that Israel failed to heed the call to trust the Lord, they were warned, "He will be a stone that makes people stumble, a rock that makes them fall" (Isa 8:14). The pointed reference to Jesus as the "stone" was a link between 20:17 (the citation of Ps 118:22) and 20:18 (which refers to Isa 8:14-15 and Dan 2:34-35). Those who chose to reject Jesus as the promised Son whom God had sent would experience destruction. As in the days of Isaiah, "stumbling" over the "rock" God had provided for security meant utter devastation—being broken to pieces.

The message of the parable was apparent to the religious leaders and priests. They had opposed Jesus vigorously and perceived the ominous note of judgment that was being sounded. Their response was to try "to arrest Jesus immediately because they realized he was telling the story against them" (20:19). They had been identified in no uncertain terms as the wicked tenants, but they were cautious in carrying out their plans because of their fear of popular opposition.

◆ D. Taxes for Caesar (20:20-26; cf. Matt 22:15-22; Mark 12:13-17)

20Watching for their opportunity, the leaders sent spies pretending to be honest men. They tried to get Jesus to say something that could be reported to the Roman governor so he would arrest Jesus. 21"Teacher," they said, "we know that you speak and teach what is right and are not influenced by what others think. You teach the way of God truthfully. 22Now tell us—is it right for us to pay taxes to Caesar or not?"

23He saw through their trickery and said, 24"Show me a Roman coin.* Whose picture and title are stamped on it?"

"Caesar's," they replied.

25"Well then," he said, "give to Caesar what belongs to Caesar, and give to God what belongs to God."

26So they failed to trap him by what he said in front of the people. Instead, they were amazed by his answer, and they became silent.

20:24 Greek *a denarius.*

NOTES

20:20 *the leaders sent spies.* The word used here to describe a "spy" (*enkathetos* [TG1455, ZG1588]) is found only here in the NT. In the LXX it is used of a person lying in wait for someone (Job 19:12; 31:9). The word in Luke suggests the devious and underhanded methods of the opponents of Jesus.

20:22 *is it right for us to pay taxes to Caesar or not?* On the surface, the question seemed legitimate, for the bitterness of an oppressed people made the payment of taxes to a hated foreign power understandable, but the motives of those who asked it turned out to be questionable. On taxes, see France 2003:109 and the notes on Luke 18:10 and 19:2.

20:24 *Roman coin.* Gr., *dēnarion* [TG1220, ZG1324] (denarius). Merely by having such an idolatrous coin (one bearing the image of the emperor) the Jewish leaders implicated themselves. Coins have been in use in Israel since roughly the late fifth century. Coins from the Hellenistic period have been identified, including some bearing portraits of the Ptolemies. Hasmonean coins, the first issued by Jewish kings on their own authority, have also been found, often carrying symbols such as those noted on Seleucid coins, such as the lily, star, palm branch, and pomegranate.

COMMENTARY

The vexatious issue of Roman taxation was a sore point with Palestinian Jews in the time of Jesus. They were an oppressed people who were very conscious of being under the power and jurisdiction of imperial Rome. Therefore, it is not surprising that all three synoptic writers would describe this contentious encounter that Jesus had with his enemies during the closing days of his ministry in Jerusalem (20:20-26; Matt 22:15-22; Mark 12:13-17). As France has pointed out: "Jesus came from Galilee, where taxes were paid to a local ruler, Herod Antipas. But in Judea, the Romans had imposed a poll tax paid directly to Rome, and the people hated it. When it was first imposed some 20 years before, it had led to a serious revolt and bloodshed, and Jewish nationalists still claimed that to pay taxes to a pagan king was disloyalty to Israel's God. So what did the visiting teacher think about it?" (2003:109).

This was the second issue that the opponents of Jesus had put up to entrap him, the first being the question about the source of Jesus' authority (see 20:1-8). While they made a pretense of honesty, their question was really motivated by a desire to trick Jesus into making an admission that could be used to discredit him. Then he could be reported to the Roman governor to secure his arrest (20:20). Once again, Jesus had proven equal to the challenge presented by his enemies.

The three accounts in the synoptic Gospels are very similar. However, the Lukan account is slightly shorter in Jesus' request to be shown the coin and slightly longer in its introduction, noting the spies who were sent to watch Jesus and their duplicitous efforts to pretend to be sincere or honest in their intentions (20:20). Both Matthew and Mark point to "some Pharisees and supporters of Herod" planning to entrap Jesus (Mark 12:13; see also Matt 22:15). All three writers mention that Jesus was addressed in a deferential way as "Teacher" and praised as a man of integrity and impartiality, possibly to get his defenses down so that an opponent could find a weak spot to attack. All three pose the same question to Jesus about the lawfulness of paying tribute to the emperor. All three recognize the speciousness of the question, with both Matthew and Luke noting the hypocrisy behind it, and Luke pointing out the trickery (20:23). Matthew and Mark view the challenge as a deliberate attempt to put Jesus to the test. Matthew draws attention to their malice, and Luke points out that they were "pretending to be honest men" (20:20). In Matthew, Mark, and Luke, Jesus asks the same question about the coin: "Whose picture and title are stamped on it?" (20:24; Matt 22:20; Mark 12:16). And all three versions present the same basic challenge by Jesus to his questioners: "Give to Caesar what belongs to Caesar, and give to God what belongs to God" (20:25; Matt 22:21; Mark 12:17). All three accounts close out the incident with a reference to the response of amazement that Jesus' answer provoked on the part of his critics (though

Mark uses a different Gr. word here than Matthew and Luke). Matthew observes that "they went away," apparently unsuccessful in their attempt to entangle him in his talk (Matt 22:22). Luke also indicates that "they failed to trap him . . . in front of the people . . . and they became silent" (20:26).

Several points of this encounter should be highlighted: (1) The state has been instituted by God and was intended to provide for the peace, order, and stability of society. (2) Normally, the state has a legitimate claim on a citizen's loyalty and obedience. Barclay has noted the benefits of the *Pax Romana* for the Roman empire: "It is beyond question that the Roman government brought to the ancient world a sense of security it never had before. For the most part, except in certain notorious areas, the seas were cleared of pirates and the roads of brigands, civil wars were changed for peace and unpredictable and capricious tyranny for Roman impartial justice. . . . The principle is still true that no one can honorably receive all the benefits which living in a state confer upon him and then opt out of all the responsibilities of citizenship" (1965:299). (3) The ultimate claim, however, upon every person's life, belongs to God, not the state. In other words, there is a clear limit. "The coin had Caesar's *image* upon it, and therefore belonged to Caesar. Man has God's *image* upon him—God created man in his own image (Gen 1:26-27)—and therefore belongs to God" (Barclay 1965:299). It is no wonder that the enemies of Jesus were silent after such a brilliant answer (20:26).

◆   E. Discussion about Resurrection (20:27-40; cf. Matt 22:23-33; Mark 12:18-27)

27Then Jesus was approached by some Sadducees—religious leaders who say there is no resurrection from the dead. 28They posed this question: "Teacher, Moses gave us a law that if a man dies, leaving a wife but no children, his brother should marry the widow and have a child who will carry on the brother's name.* 29Well, suppose there were seven brothers. The oldest one married and then died without children. 30So the second brother married the widow, but he also died. 31Then the third brother married her. This continued with all seven of them, who died without children. 32Finally, the woman also died. 33So tell us, whose wife will she be in the resurrection? For all seven were married to her!"

34Jesus replied, "Marriage is for people here on earth. 35But in the age to come, those worthy of being raised from the dead will neither marry nor be given in marriage. 36And they will never die again. In this respect they will be like angels. They are children of God and children of the resurrection.

37"But now, as to whether the dead will be raised—even Moses proved this when he wrote about the burning bush. Long after Abraham, Isaac, and Jacob had died, he referred to the Lord* as 'the God of Abraham, the God of Isaac, and the God of Jacob.'* 38So he is the God of the living, not the dead, for they are all alive to him."

39"Well said, Teacher!" remarked some of the teachers of religious law who were standing there. 40And then no one dared to ask him any more questions.

20:28 See Deut 25:5-6. 20:37a Greek *when he wrote about the bush. He referred to the Lord.*
20:37b Exod 3:6.

NOTES

20:28 *Teacher, Moses gave us a law that if a man dies, leaving a wife but no children, his brother should marry the widow and have a child.* This was probably a stock example used by the Sadducees in their debates with Pharisees as an attempt to show that believing in the resurrection was misguided (see Acts 23:8). It is important in dealing with the Sadducees' question to understand the Hebrew principle of levirate law. This law "states that if two brothers live together, and one of them dies without leaving a male heir, his brother shall marry his widow, and the first son of the union shall take the name of the brother who died. If the brother refuses to marry the widow, she shall bring him before the elders of the city and in their presence remove a sandal from his foot and spit in his face. The purpose of the law obviously was to provide an heir for the dead brother (Deut 25:5-10)" (Barabas 1975). If the nearest kinsman failed to exercise this right, another member of the family could take up the right as the kinsman redeemer after the proper legal process had been carried out (see Ruth 4:1-12).

COMMENTARY

The third question raised during the day of questions concerned the issue of the resurrection, and it appears in all three Gospels. The accounts are very similar, and the common source seems to be Mark's Gospel. All address Jesus respectfully as "Teacher," all pose the same question about the implications of levirate marriage for life "in the resurrection," and all of them are told that in the resurrection from the dead they "will neither marry nor be given in marriage" (20:28-35; Matt 22:24-30; Mark 12:19-25). Different conditions will prevail in the resurrection than have been known in earthly life (note the comment in 20:34 that "marriage is for people here on earth"). The people present in that new era will enter into a new dimension where "they will never die again" (20:36a). "In this respect they will be like angels" (20:36b), a point noted in the other accounts as well, where both Matthew and Mark describe resurrected believers being like "the angels in heaven" (Matt 22:30b; Mark 12:25b). The wonders of such a glorious life in heaven are only hinted at, for God's people are described as "children of God and children of resurrection" (20:36c).

While the question about tribute had been raised by some of the Pharisees and the Herodian party, the Sadducees—"religious leaders who say there is no resurrection from the dead"—raised this provocative question (20:27). Their beliefs are summarized in the book of Acts as those who claimed that there is "no resurrection or angels or spirits," in contrast with the Pharisees, who affirmed all three of these things as realities (Acts 23:8). It is clear that the Sadducees were out to disgrace or embarrass Jesus if they could, seeking to make his views on the future life look ludicrous or ridiculous. They made reference to the Old Testament law that required, under certain conditions, that a man marry the wife of his deceased brother and thus perpetuate the name of his brother in the covenant community (see Deut 25:5-10; see note on 20:28). There is a striking instance of this law in operation in the book of Ruth, where Boaz marries the widow Ruth and fulfills the role of the kinsman redeemer (Ruth 4:1-12).

While the Sadducees refused to accept the notion of the future resurrection, Jesus told them they were out of harmony with their own professed loyalty to the law of Moses, presented in the first five books of the Scriptures. Jesus pointed to the Pentateuch, which told the story of Moses' encounter with God at the burning bush (Exod 3:1-12). In that memorable event, God addressed Moses as the God of his ancestors—"the God of Abraham, the God of Isaac, and the God of Jacob" (Exod 3:6, cited in 20:37, Matt 22:32, and Mark 12:26). Jesus deduced from this famous passage the vital eschatological conclusion that the Sadducees were denying: "So he is the God of the living, not the dead, for they are all alive to him" (20:38; cf. Matt 22:32). In other words, Abraham and Isaac and Jacob were, from God's perspective, still alive.

In Mark's version, Jesus castigated the Sadducees for a scriptural mistake they should not have made: "He is the God of the living, not the dead. You have made a serious error" (Mark 12:27). Matthew noted that the crowds were impressed or "astounded" at Jesus' teaching on this occasion (Matt 22:33). Luke observed that some of the scribes recognized that Jesus had spoken well (20:39). In the end, Jesus' words had silenced all his opponents, such that "no one dared to ask him any more questions" (20:40). As we will see in the next passage (20:41-44), Jesus is about to turn the tables and ask his opponents a question that they are not able to answer.

◆   F. Whose Son Is the Messiah? (20:41-47; cf. Matt 22:41-46; Mark 12:35-37a)

⁴¹Then Jesus presented them with a question. "Why is it," he asked, "that the Messiah is said to be the son of David? ⁴²For David himself wrote in the book of Psalms:

'The LORD said to my Lord,
  Sit in the place of honor at my
    right hand
⁴³until I humble your enemies,
  making them a footstool under
    your feet.'*

⁴⁴Since David called the Messiah 'Lord,' how can the Messiah be his son?"

⁴⁵Then, with the crowds listening, he turned to his disciples and said, ⁴⁶"Beware of these teachers of religious law! For they like to parade around in flowing robes and love to receive respectful greetings as they walk in the marketplaces. And how they love the seats of honor in the synagogues and the head table at banquets. ⁴⁷Yet they shamelessly cheat widows out of their property and then pretend to be pious by making long prayers in public. Because of this, they will be severely punished."

20:42-43 Ps 110:1.

NOTES

20:41 *Why is it . . . that the Messiah is said to be the son of David?* The question about David's son is presented in all three Synoptic accounts. Mark located the incident during Jesus' teaching in the Temple (Mark 12:35a). Matthew said Jesus posed the question when he was "surrounded by the Pharisees" (Matt 22:41), who had been impressed by his refutation of the Sadducees. Now that the discussion about the resurrection had been addressed, Jesus thought it was appropriate to pose a question to the Pharisees.

20:42 *Sit in the place of honor at my right hand.* On the use of Ps 110 in early Christianity, see Hay, who finds 33 quotations and allusions to this psalm in the NT (5 in Hebrews alone) and seven more in other Christian writings from before the middle of the second century (1973:15; see his Appendix for the references: 163-166). Psalm 110 was probably the basic proof text for the resurrection and exaltation of Jesus (see Acts 2:34-35; 1 Cor 15:25; Eph 1:20; Heb 1:13; 10:13).

20:45-47 Luke's account follows Mark very closely at this point and includes the warning Jesus issued to the crowds who were intently listening to his teaching (20:45-47; Mark 12:37b-40). Most of this material is spelled out in greater detail in Matthew in the section known as "Woes against the Pharisees" (Matt 23:1-36, note esp. 23:6-7).

20:46 *how they love the seats of honor in the synagogues and the head table at banquets.* In this striking condemnation of the scribes, the argument moves "from their craving for honor to a concrete example of their exploitation of the poor" (Coogan 2001: NT 82). Both their self-centeredness and their rapacity were attacked by Jesus.

20:47 *they shamelessly cheat widows out of their property.* These aggressive people took advantage of vulnerable people such as widows. Widows received special consideration in the OT; exploitation of widows was forbidden and condemned (see Exod 22:22-24; Deut 10:18; 14:29; 25:5-10). Myers notes that the kindly treatment of widows in the NT is in harmony with that found in the OT: "The Hebrews' regard for the plight of widows is reaffirmed in the New Testament (e.g., James 1:27). Luke singled out virtuous widows (2:36-38; Acts 9:39-41). Jesus used them as examples (Mark 12:42-43; Luke 18:3; 21:2-3); he exhibited special concern for them (7:12-15) and sharply denounced their oppressors (Mark 12:40; Luke 20:47). Acts 6:1-6 records a problem (and its resolution) concerning the charitable distribution of food to needy widows" (1987:1056).

COMMENTARY

Jesus had been badgered by various groups of Jewish opponents—Pharisees, Sadducees and Herodians, all of whom had hostile intentions according to the Evangelists. So he turned the tables on his enemies by posing a question to them that made them face the question of his true identity. It was a question about the relationship of the Messiah to King David: how could David's "Lord" be David's son? In the opening verse of Psalm 110, the psalmist, here identified as David, addresses the Lord Messiah in glowing terms, invites him to sit in the place of honor at his right hand, and anticipates the defeat of his enemies (Ps 110:1, cited in 20:42-43). The fact that David called the Messiah his Lord posed an exegetical and interpretive problem for Jesus' questioners.

The question stumped them. How could one who came historically later on the scene be superior to Israel's beloved king? The answer lay in the respective roles that David and Jesus had been appointed to fulfill in holy history. David, after he had served his own generation by the will of God, died (Acts 13:36). But before his death, David had served as a prophet of the messianic age. He had predicted that the Messiah would be exalted and occupy the throne of God's Kingdom, sitting at God's right hand, the place of acknowledged power and authority (Ps 110:1). Jesus, on the other hand, was to be raised by God from death and be made alive forever (cf. Rom 6:9-10). The question Jesus posed was completely unanswerable, unless Jesus' opponents admitted that David's "Lord" was truly the divine Son of God. Later, Paul recognized this when he declared that Jesus Christ "was shown to be the Son of God when he was raised from the dead by the power of the Holy Spirit" (Rom 1:4).

After stumping the Jewish leaders with his question, Jesus turned to the crowd that was listening and proceeded to warn them about the religious leaders. Despite the impressive dress of these teachers of religious law, it was evident that they were wrong and therefore were misleading the people who looked to them for spiritual guidance. In fact, the answers Jesus had given to the Pharisees, Sadducees, scribes, and Herodians had shown them to be in error on many points. They loved to have people act deferentially towards them as they walked about in the market places, paraded "in flowing robes," and proudly took up "the seats of honor in the synagogues and the head table at banquets" (20:46; cf. Mark 12:38-39). But these ostentatious acts could not cover up the fact that they made it a practice to "cheat widows out of their property and then pretend to be pious by making long prayers in public" (20:47a; cf. Mark 12:40). God was aware of their duplicity and hypocrisy, and these serious violations of the moral law would certainly lead to their judgment by God (20:47b). Jesus, acting boldly as a prophet, exposed the religious pretense of these leaders and solemnly warned the Jewish people to be wary of them.

◆   G. The Widow's Offering (21:1-4; cf. Mark 12:41-44)

While Jesus was in the Temple, he watched the rich people dropping their gifts in the collection box. ²Then a poor widow came by and dropped in two small coins.*

³"I tell you the truth," Jesus said, "this poor widow has given more than all the rest of them. ⁴For they have given a tiny part of their surplus, but she, poor as she is, has given everything she has."

21:2 Greek two lepta [the smallest of Jewish coins].

NOTES

21:2 *two small coins.* The monetary unit of the two small coins "would have been a Greek *lepton* [ᵀᴳ3016, ᶻᴳ3321], a tiny bronze coin weighing just over half a gram" (Evans and Porter 2000:222-224). It took 128 lepta, the coins mentioned here, to equal one denarius, a silver coin worth a day's wages, so two lepta represented a very small amount financially.

21:3 *poor widow.* Luke used three different words in this passage to emphasize the widow's poverty and thereby bring out the sacrifice, represented in her giving, that pointed to the spiritual value of her gift in contrast with the others, whose larger gifts cost them nothing in terms of costly self-denial. He describes her as "poor" or "needy" (*penichra* [ᵀᴳ3998, ᶻᴳ4293]; 21:2, and used only there in the NT); "poor," perhaps "pitiable" (*ptōchē* [ᵀᴳ4434, ᶻᴳ4777]; 21:3); and as being in "want" or in "deficiency" (*husterēma* [ᵀᴳ5303, ᶻᴳ5729]; 21:4), lacking some of the basic necessities of life.

21:4 *poor as she is.* Here we see, as in the Song of Mary (1:46-55) and the Song of Zechariah (1:68-79), another reason why Luke has been called "the evangelist of the poor" (Johnson 1991:13).

COMMENTARY

In the Temple area, one proceeded from the outside into the Court of the Gentiles (where Jesus drove out the money changers), then into the Court of the Women, where Anna undoubtedly prayed (2:37) and where Jesus observed the poor widow offering her sacrificial gift at the collection boxes (21:4), then into the Court of the Israelites, and finally into the Temple itself. Gentiles were confined to the outer court and could proceed no further on pain of death; in fact, two actual Greek inscriptions prohibiting Gentiles from entering the inner precincts have been found, and these state quite bluntly, "No foreigner may enter within the barricade which surrounds the Temple and enclosure. Anyone who is caught doing so will have himself to blame for his death" (Bruce 1962:434). The women could proceed no further than the Court of the Women. Jewish men could proceed into the Court of the Israelites, if they satisfied the conditions of ritual purity. This court appears to be "the narrative setting of the Pharisee praying (18:11), for the disciples praying (24:53) and, of course, for Jesus standing before the altar (Mark 11:11). No one but priests could continue on to enter the Temple building itself [which contained the Court of the Priests and the Holy of Holies]" (DJG 812).

Luke's story of the widow's offering appears to come from Mark, who has a slightly longer account (Mark 12:41-44). Mark noted that many rich people contributed large sums to the Temple treasury, and he mentioned the insignificant amount offered by the widow as just "two small copper coins, which are worth a penny" (Mark 12:42 NRSV). He presented Jesus as deliberately using the occasion by calling his disciples to him and teaching them a lesson about true stewardship. Obviously, Luke wanted to draw attention to the widow as well and made her an illustration of true sacrificial giving that was both radical and exemplary.

Luke had already shown a great deal of interest in the role of widows. He described the devout Anna, who greeted the infant Jesus in the Temple and prophesied, praising God and talking about Jesus to those who "had been waiting expectantly for God to rescue Jerusalem" (2:36-40). He noted the remarkable encounter that Elijah had with a Gentile woman, a widow from Zarephath (4:25), and recorded the intervention of Jesus for a widow whose only son was restored to life (7:11-17). Luke had also used a widow as an example of persistence in prayer in a parable (18:1-8), and he mentioned the exploitation of widows by some teachers of religious law (20:45-47). In this pericope (21:1-4), he mentions a poor widow's unselfish generosity in contributing to the collection box that was placed in the Temple to help with the cost of maintaining the religious establishment.

The thrust of this passage is to highlight the difference in the patterns of giving that Jesus observed in the Temple. While there was undoubtedly a contrast between the large gifts that wealthy people were offering and the small gift that this woman gave, the former gifts represented "a tiny part of their surplus" (21:4), and therefore they were offered without sacrifice or essential cost to the lifestyle of the person who gave them. Their own affluent manner of life continued unimpeded. By contrast, the poor widow was extolled as one who had "given everything" she had (21:4). Her "two small coins" (21:2), meager though they were, were all that she had to give. So her offering was praised by Jesus and held up for commendation by Luke.

◆   H. Jesus Foretells the Future (21:5-38; cf. Matt 24:4-36; Mark 13:5-37)

⁵Some of his disciples began talking about the majestic stonework of the Temple and the memorial decorations on the walls. But Jesus said, ⁶"The time is coming when all these things will be completely demolished. Not one stone will be left on top of another!"

⁷"Teacher," they asked, "when will all this happen? What sign will show us that these things are about to take place?"

⁸He replied, "Don't let anyone mislead you, for many will come in my name, claiming, 'I am the Messiah,'* and saying, 'The time has come!' But don't believe them. ⁹And when you hear of wars and insurrections, don't panic. Yes, these things must take place first, but the end won't follow immediately." ¹⁰Then he added, "Nation will go to war against nation, and kingdom against kingdom. ¹¹There will be great earthquakes, and there will be famines and plagues in many lands, and there will be terrifying things and great miraculous signs from heaven.

¹²"But before all this occurs, there will be a time of great persecution. You will be dragged into synagogues and prisons, and you will stand trial before kings and governors because you are my followers. ¹³But this will be your opportunity to tell them about me.* ¹⁴So don't worry in advance about how to answer the charges against you, ¹⁵for I will give you the right words and such wisdom that none of your opponents will be able to reply or refute you! ¹⁶Even those closest to you—your parents, brothers, relatives, and friends—will betray you. They will even kill some of you. ¹⁷And everyone will hate you because you are my followers.* ¹⁸But not a hair of your head will perish! ¹⁹By standing firm, you will win your souls.

²⁰"And when you see Jerusalem surrounded by armies, then you will know that the time of its destruction has arrived. ²¹Then those in Judea must flee to the hills. Those in Jerusalem must get out, and those out in the country should not return to the city. ²²For those will be days of God's vengeance, and the prophetic words of the Scriptures will be fulfilled. ²³How terrible it will be for pregnant women and for nursing mothers in those days. For there will be disaster in the land and great anger against this people. ²⁴They will be killed by the sword or sent away as captives to all the nations of the world. And Jerusalem will be trampled down by the Gentiles until the period of the Gentiles comes to an end.

²⁵"And there will be strange signs in the sun, moon, and stars. And here on earth the nations will be in turmoil, perplexed by the roaring seas and strange tides. ²⁶People will be terrified at what they see coming upon the earth, for the powers in the heavens will be shaken. ²⁷Then everyone will see the Son of Man* coming on a cloud with power and great glory.* ²⁸So when all these things begin to happen, stand and look up, for your salvation is near!"

²⁹Then he gave them this illustration: "Notice the fig tree, or any other tree. ³⁰When the leaves come out, you know without being told that summer is near. ³¹In the same way, when you see all these things taking place, you can know that the Kingdom of God is near. ³²I tell you the truth, this generation will not pass from the scene until all these things have taken place. ³³Heaven and earth will disappear, but my words will never disappear.

³⁴"Watch out! Don't let your hearts be dulled by carousing and drunkenness, and by the worries of this life. Don't let that day catch you unaware, ³⁵like a trap. For that day will come upon everyone living on the earth. ³⁶Keep alert at all times. And pray that you might be strong enough to escape these coming horrors and stand before the Son of Man."

³⁷Every day Jesus went to the Temple to

teach, and each evening he returned to spend the night on the Mount of Olives.

³⁸The crowds gathered at the Temple early each morning to hear him.

21:8 Greek *claiming, 'I am.'* 21:13 Or *This will be your testimony against them.* 21:17 Greek *on account of my name.* 21:27a"Son of Man" is a title Jesus used for himself. 21:27b See Dan 7:13.

NOTES

21:5 *the majestic stonework of the Temple.* On the majestic appearance of the Temple, Josephus (*War* 5.222 [5.5.6]) "relates that the entire facade of the Temple was covered with gold plates. When the sun rose the reflection was nearly blinding. On a clear day the brilliance of the Temple was visible from a considerable distance outside Jerusalem. And this brilliance was not due to gold alone; the upper parts of the Temple were pure white, probably marble. Once a year the priests applied whitewash to this upper section. At the very top gold spikes lined the roof" (DJG 812-813). Josephus reports that the stones were enormous, almost 40 feet long and 12 feet high (*Antiquities* 15:421 [15.11.3]). Some of these enormous stones still remain at the base of the Temple mount today.

21:6 *The time is coming when all these things will be completely demolished.* This prediction of judgment is somewhat parallel to the judgment Matthew and Mark record in the cursing of the fig tree (Matt 21:18-19, 20-22; Mark 11:12-14, 20-25). "It is probably true that Luke uses fewer apocalyptic images than Matthew in conveying the significance of Jesus' death and resurrection. But it is not true that the future return of the Son of Man is a minor emphasis in Luke and Acts. Luke includes various apocalyptic-type passages as well as two lengthy discourses on the end: the so-called Q Apocalypse (17:20-37) and 21:5-36, which is substantially parallel to the discourses of Mark 13 and Matt 24. The Luke 17 material clearly betrays both a realized (v. 21) and a futurist (v. 24) perspective. In ch 21, Luke, more so than the other evangelists, seems to distinguish between the historical events surrounding the fall of the Temple (21:8-9, 12-24) and the eschatological events that will take place at a later time (21:10-11, 25-36). . . . The kingdom is portrayed in Luke as already and not yet, just as it is in the other Gospels, even though differences in emphasis can be detected" (DJG 25). On the apocalyptic discourse of Luke 21 and its parallels in Mark 13 and Matt 24, see Marshall 1990:57-69.

21:7 *when will all this happen? What sign will show us that these things are about to take place?* The synoptic Apocalypse is found in 21:5-36, with its parallels in Matt 24:1-36 and Mark 13:1-37. All three accounts record the teaching as taking place in the environs of the Temple and being prompted by the disciples' comments about the wonderful stones and buildings that made the Temple establishment so impressive. This misplaced admiration for the Temple led Jesus to predict its complete destruction, when there would not remain one stone upon another, for all would be thrown down (21:5-7; cf. Matt 24:1-3; Mark 13:1-4). In Mark, the question the disciples asked was focused on the destruction of Jerusalem and of the Temple (Mark 13:4). In Matthew, often called "The Teacher's Gospel," a distinction is made between the destruction of Jerusalem and the sign of the Parousia; in addition to asking about the destruction of the holy city, there was a related but different question: "What sign will signal your return and the end of the world?" (Matt 24:3). In Luke, in addition to the destruction of Jerusalem, a time period is mentioned when "Jerusalem will be trampled down by the Gentiles until the period of the Gentiles comes to an end" (21:24). The adverb "then" (*tote* [^{TG}5119, ^{ZG}5538]) in 21:27 suggests some indeterminate subsequent time when everyone will see the Son of Man coming. Thus, the two eschatological events are related but given separate consideration.

21:9 *the end won't follow immediately.* According to this passage, it is an error to record the number of wars, earthquakes, etc., as evidence for the nearness of the end as many prophecy preachers are fond of doing.

21:17 *everyone will hate you because you are my followers.* "The NT contains frequent references to persecution (Mark 10:30; Luke 11:49-51; Gal 6:12). Jesus was persecuted (4:29; John 5:16) and suffered mocking, beating, and crucifixion. He told his followers to expect similar treatment (Matt 10:23; 24:9; Mark 13:9; Luke 21:12; John 15:20; 16:2). These occasions were not to be feared, for the Holy Spirit would give them courage (12:11-12; 21:15; Acts 1:8)" (Freedman 2000:1030).

21:22 *the prophetic words of the Scriptures will be fulfilled.* On the theme of fulfillment in Luke's Gospel, see Bock 1987, and note Helyer (1993), who finds a number of texts in Luke that focus on the "fulfillment of prophecy" theme. He argues that God did not abandon the national and political dimensions of Israel's restoration but simply put them on hold until the time was right for their fulfillment (cf. Acts 1:6-7; 3:19-21). This theme appears again in the Emmaus account (24:25-27, 42-44).

21:25 *And here on earth the nations will be in turmoil, perplexed by the roaring seas and strange tides.* For a helpful book on disturbed weather patterns, see Davies 1999.

21:26 The Son of Man's coming will take place after the shaking of the heavens, that is, the appearance of the cosmic signs (note the use of apocalyptic language; see Isa 34:4; Ezek 32:7,8; Joel 2:31; cf. Matt 24:29; 2 Pet 3:10). These cosmic disturbances are spelled out more fully in the book of Revelation (note chapters 6–20). The signs will create massive fear among those who reject the Christian message but should produce expectant joy in believers, because they herald that the time of promised salvation is "near" (21:28).

21:32 *this generation will not pass from the scene until all these things have taken place.* The phrase "this generation" has been taken to mean: "(1) Jesus' own generation, (2) the Jewish people, (3) humans in general, (4) the last generation in history, and (5) Luke's contemporaries. . . . The third suggestion appears to be the best option. Elsewhere in Luke, this expression is used to describe sinful humanity, unresponsive to God and oblivious to the possibility of immediately encountering him (cf. 12:16-21, 35-40; 17:26-37). 'This generation,' which ignored the coming of the kingdom in Jesus' ministry, continues in its rejection of the gospel message until the very end. Thus, 'this generation' of 21:32 stands in continuity and solidarity with 'this generation' of Jesus' day" (Stein 1992:526-527).

21:36 *Keep alert at all times.* Unending vigilance and a higher level of ethical obedience are urged in light of the Lord's return, when Christians will give an account of their lives as they "stand before the Son of Man" (21:36; cf. 2 Cor 5:10). This theme is emphasized further in the parables of Matt 24:42–25:46, and in virtually every passage on the Lord's return in the rest of the NT (e.g., Rom 13:11-14; 1 Cor 7:29-31; Eph 5:14-18; 6:13-20; Col 3:1-10; 1 Thess 5:5-11; 2 Tim 4:1-8; Tit 2:11-14; Heb 12:22-29; 1 Pet 1:13; 4:7; 2 Pet 3:8-14).

COMMENTARY

The springboard for the Temple discourse is the remark that some of Jesus' disciples made as they walked about the Temple precincts and took in the impressiveness of the stonework and the "memorial decorations on the walls" (21:5; see note). The whole appearance and design of the structure that proceeded inward and upward was intended to point to the transcendent, heavenly, pure, and holy God whose earthly home it symbolized. Tragically, as Jesus saw very clearly, it had become for many an idol, taking the place of God himself. Jesus therefore pointed to the Temple's transience: "The time is coming when all these things will be completely demolished" (21:6).

This utter devastation was boldly predicted by Jesus (21:5-7; cf. Matt 24:1-3; Mark 13:1-4) and was sadly fulfilled in the terrible destruction of Jerusalem that took place a generation later in AD 70, when the Roman armies under Titus burned and destroyed the city and its beautiful Temple. There is a vivid description of the siege and capture of Jerusalem by the historian Josephus (*War* 5–6). Herod's Temple had been completed in AD 64, and it was destroyed just six years later in the Jewish War.

Such news, of course, was totally unwelcome to Jesus' disciples, who looked on Jerusalem as the holy city and the Temple as the most sacred place on earth. There is no indication that they doubted the truthfulness of Jesus' remark, but they were deeply interested in preparing for such a cataclysmic event. Naturally, they were anxious to place this event in the calendar of holy history, so they asked: "*When* will all this happen? *What sign will show us* that these things are about to take place?" (21:7; cf. Matt 24:3; Mark 13:4).

Jesus did not attempt to provide a precise timetable (cf. Mark 13:32; Matt 24:36), though often, in subsequent church history, Christians have mistakenly supposed that he gave them a blueprint such that they could pinpoint the time of the end. Instead, he warned them against the possibility of false messiahs. Indeed, a number of such messianic pretenders could be expected to trumpet their claims in the coming days, asserting that it was the end time and that they were the promised leader, or Messiah (21:8; cf. Matt 24:5; Mark 13:5-6). To be forewarned was to be forearmed: "Don't believe them," Jesus counselled his followers (21:8). Frightening events such as wars and political upheavals were not to produce, in genuine believers, utter chaos and confusion: "Don't panic. Yes, these things must take place first, but the end won't follow immediately" (21:9).

God would bring in his Kingdom in the end, but the messianic woes had to come first. These would include political disturbances, nations attacking other nations, and there would also be unsettling things like serious food shortages; epidemics; widespread natural disasters, such as earthquakes; and great cosmic signs in the heavens (21:10-11). However, before all of this there was to be "a time of great persecution" (21:12). This was not to take them by surprise. Believers would be hauled into synagogues and shut up in prisons, and some would find themselves being attacked in courts of law, where they would "stand trial before kings and governors" because of their utter loyalty to Jesus (21:12). This threatening time was also a wide open door of challenge and opportunity for a bold witness in unfavorable and unlikely settings.

Such testing times were common experiences in the days of the early church (e.g., Acts 4:16-20; 5:28-29, 40-42). The book of Acts is full of wonderful stories where Christians gave their witness faithfully and courageously, and the heroic story of Stephen, the Spirit-filled man with the face of an angel, comes immediately to mind (Acts 6:8-15). He addressed the Jewish council with a bold Christian witness, suffered arrest for his testimony, and ultimately died with a prayer on his lips for those who were martyring him (Acts 7:59-60). Even more prominent in Acts is the witness of Saul of Tarsus, who, following his encounter with the risen Lord on the road to Damascus, was told that he is God's "chosen instrument to take [God's] message to the Gentiles and to kings, as well as to the people of Israel" (Acts 9:15). The subsequent course of the evangelistic and missionary work of the apostle Paul reveals the abundant fulfillment of that divinely given commission, and the story is told in glowing terms in the book of Acts.

The coming persecution had a positive side to it, for it would furnish golden opportunities for the followers of Jesus to confess their allegiance to him and take his side before his enemies, whether they were Jewish or Gentile: "This will be your opportunity to tell them about me" (21:13). The disciples were instructed to remain steadfast in spite of the coming difficulties. The problems confronting them would be met with abundant divine help: "So don't worry in advance about how to answer the charges against you, for I will give you the right words and such wisdom that none of your opponents will be able to reply or refute you!" (21:14-15). The hard times were coming, and one of the hardest elements to cope with would be the betrayal by those closest to them—their family, relatives, and people they had hitherto loved and trusted as friends (21:16). Nevertheless, the Lord was with them and would protect them, enabling them to bear a faithful witness to the end. Martyrdom was a possibility, and some of their number, like Stephen, James, and Antipas, would indeed die for their faith (see Acts 7:58-59; 12:2; cf. Rev 2:13). Yet, the reality of God's ruling and overruling providence was to be accepted: "But not a hair of your head will perish!" (21:18). Such faithful witnesses were under God's overarching care and would fulfill their mission.

The challenge given to the servants of Jesus was a daunting one, for their witness had to be delivered in hostile circumstances and they would be exposed to real antipathy and enmity because they were Jesus' followers (21:17). Sustaining faith in such perilous times would demand real perseverance and fidelity: "By standing firm, you will win your souls" (21:19; cf. Matt 10:22; 24:13; Mark 13:13; Rev 2:10). These are the "honest, good-hearted people who hear God's word, cling to it, and patiently produce a huge harvest" (8:15).

The fate of Jerusalem was naturally in the minds of Christ's disciples as he discussed the last things, so it was proper that he should address this concern. He told them that Jerusalem would be "surrounded by armies" (21:20; cf. the previous reference to Jesus' weeping over the city and speaking of its terrible devastation, 19:43-44). The language used to describe its siege is typical of biblical language for the destruction of a city by hostile armies (Isa 29:3; Jer 51:14; Ezek 4:1-4; 21:22-23). This encompassing of the city was to be the promised signal that "the time of its destruction" had arrived (21:20). At that time, they should depart from the city before it was too late, and those in the outskirts in Judea should flee to the hills for safety (21:21). In these apocalyptic times, the inhabitants of the holy city were to get out, and those at work in the fields were not to return to Jerusalem (21:21-22).

The reasons for such flight were entirely pragmatic and prudential, for the city would be under divine judgment for its sin, and the devastating predictions of Scripture about the city's downfall would be in the process of realization (21:22). Apparently, some of the early Christians heeded the admonition to depart from

Jerusalem and possibly fled into Transjordan to the Hellenistic city of Pella, located about seven miles southeast of Beth-shan, but the evidence for this is inconclusive (Eusebius *History* 3.5). It is interesting that Luke did not record the counsel of Jesus, "Pray that your flight will not be in winter" (Mark 13:18; cf. Matt 24:20). Possibly, he omitted this because he was writing after the siege of Jerusalem in AD 70, and the siege had taken place between April and August and not in the winter.

Jesus expressed sensitivity to those especially vulnerable in this impending time of crisis, such as "pregnant women" and "nursing mothers," for the disaster would overtake these helpless people and serve as an expression of God's "great anger" against a disobedient nation (21:23). In this overwhelming event, people would "be killed by the sword or sent away as captives to all the nations of the world" (21:24). In the devastation that ensued, the holy city would be brutally "trampled down by the Gentiles until the period of the Gentiles comes to an end" (21:24; cf. Zech 12:1-3). In Luke's thinking, this was evidently the time between the first appearing of Christ in the incarnation and his final coming in glory at the climax of history. The destruction of Jerusalem and the end of the world were not to be confused, and the period between the two events was the significant and valuable period for the church's witness. Christ's followers were to engage in that task until the final advent of Christ in power and great glory.

Luke, like Matthew and Mark, warned believers against being deceived by false prophets making Messianic claims (21:8; cf. Matt 24:4-5; Mark 13:5-6), though the other Evangelists more fully develop the seductive enticements provided by the false prophets (Matt 24:23-25; Mark 13:21-23). In Luke, Jesus had already warned believers about them (17:21-23).

Another feature of the end times will be cosmic disturbances (21:25-28; cf. Matt 24:29-31; Mark 13:24-27). Jesus taught that the cosmic signs in heaven and on earth will produce general panic and terror. Believers, however, have no reason to be upset or alarmed by them. In fact, these cosmic woes really will serve as heralds of the coming of the Son of Man in glory. "But if the signs spell panic for the rest of mankind, they are the signal for the disciples to take fresh heart, for the coming of the Son of Man will bring them redemption" (Marshall 1978:774).

In the heavens, there will be uncommon, strange phenomena that will be noted in the "sun, moon, and stars" (21:25a). Similarly, on the earth there will be unusual natural events, including "roaring seas and strange tides" (21:25c), suggesting a disruption of normal weather patterns that drastically alter human life. These natural disasters will be accompanied by political disturbances and upheavals, involving conflicts among the nations and a state of widespread unrest and turmoil (21:25b). These unsettled conditions will scare people, who "will be terrified at what they see coming upon the earth, for the powers in the heavens will be shaken." (21:26). At this difficult, uncertain time, the apocalyptic conditions will be ripe for the final predicted advent of the Son of Man "coming on a cloud with power and great glory" (21:27). The reference to the cloud points to the coming one as a vindicated, triumphant heavenly figure who comes to bring in the final time of consummation (cf. Dan 7:13-14; Acts 1:9; Rev 1:7; 11:12). This grand climax will begin to unfold as promised, and in that time the longed-for Day of the Lord will come, bringing to fulfillment the glorious salvation and ultimate deliverance of the people of God (21:28).

The anticipation of the nearness of this time heightened Christian expectation. The illustration Jesus gave of the fig tree was intended to be helpful to the disciples (21:29; cf. Matt 24:32-33; Mark 13:28-29). Jesus presented first a similitude (21:29-30), followed by an application to challenge Jesus' hearers with the fact that the Kingdom of God was near (21:31). They were then reminded that "this generation" will not pass away until "all these things have taken place" (21:32) and were solemnly warned that the words of Jesus would not pass away (21:33). In the case of the fig tree, the leaves came out first and thereby pointed to the approaching summer. So, "in the same way," Jesus suggested to the disciples, "when you see all these things taking place, you can know that the Kingdom of God is near" (21:31). This would be the time of the final wrap-up of history, and it was a serious time for a sinful humanity that had not repented and responded to God with faith and obedience. That Kingdom had come near in the preaching of Jesus and the announcement of Good News (Mark 1:14-15). Now that Kingdom would reach its final realization and completion. The amazing thing that Jesus declared was that, in some way, the fulfillment of these apocalyptic events would happen within "this generation" (see note on 21:32), though the precise time was unspecified (21:32). While earthly and heavenly realities would change and disappear, Jesus solemnly declared, "my words will never disappear" (21:33). These were staggering claims.

The point to remember about last things was the perennial call to alertness. The uncertainty of the exact time called for constant watchfulness (21:34). If one were to be ready and waiting, there was obviously no place for carelessness or reckless behavior: "Don't let your hearts be dulled by carousing and drunkenness, and by the worries of this life" (21:34). Prudent action was called for on the part of believers; they were not to be taken by surprise but to stay focused. The final day would come, but they were not to be caught unprepared and unready. It was not meant to be a "trap" that one would fall into by accident or mistake. In fact, the predicted day of disclosure was to be a universal, public event, and would "come upon everyone living on the earth" (21:35). It was the final day of reckoning and called for unfailing vigilance and preparation (21:36a). Jesus counselled his disciples to pray for the strength to escape "these coming horrors" of the last day (21:36b). They clearly needed divine strength if they were to "stand before the Son of Man" at the end, when each of them would give a final account for his life (21:36c).

Luke presented this teaching as taking place in the Temple and noted the return of Jesus to the Mount of Olives every evening to spend the night (21:37; cf. 21:5-6). Even though his crucifixion was only a few days away, Jesus still was enjoying a large following, for every morning "the crowds gathered at the Temple" to hear him (21:38).

◆ I. Judas Agrees to Betray Jesus (22:1-6; cf. Matt 26:1-5, 14-16; Mark 14:1-2, 17-21)

The Festival of Unleavened Bread, which is also called Passover, was approaching. ²The leading priests and teachers of religious law were plotting how to kill Jesus, but they were afraid of the people's reaction.

³Then Satan entered into Judas Iscariot, who was one of the twelve disciples, ⁴and he went to the leading priests and captains of the Temple guard to discuss the best way to betray Jesus to them. ⁵They were delighted, and they promised to give him money. ⁶So he agreed and began looking for an opportunity to betray Jesus so they could arrest him when the crowds weren't around.

NOTES

22:1 *The Festival of Unleavened Bread, which is also called Passover.* The Passover, together with Pentecost and Tabernacles, was one of the three great national festivals in Israel (Lev 23:4-8, 15-22, 33-43; Num 28:16-30; 29:12-39; Deut 16:1-17). It marked one of the three times each year that all Israelite men were called to appear before the Lord in the central place appointed for worship (Deut 16:16). The celebration of Passover came to be combined with the Festival of Unleavened Bread and the celebration ran from Nisan 15-21 (March/April on our Western, Gregorian calendar).

22:3 *Then Satan entered into Judas Iscariot.* "Where this Gospel differs from the other Synoptics is in omitting the story of the anointing from the passion narrative (but cf. Luke 7:36-50) and in adding to their account of the plot an explanation of what prompted Judas to [betray Jesus]: 'then Satan entered into Judas' (22:3)" (DJG 406).

Judas Iscariot. The name *Judas* is the Gr. equivalent of "Judah," from the Heb. *yehudah* [TH3063, ZH3373]. *Iscariot* has been interpreted by some as meaning "man of Kerioth," which was a town in Judea. If this view is correct, this would make Judas the only Judean, which might have been a possible source of friction in the apostolic band, since all the other apostles came from Galilee. Judas was chosen as one of the twelve apostles after Jesus had spent a whole night in prayer (6:12). In all the lists of the apostles, he is always mentioned last, along with a note of his betrayal of Jesus (6:12-16; Matt 10:1-4; Mark 3:13-19).

22:6 *an opportunity.* This word (*eukairia* [TG2120, ZG2321], "opportune time") occurs only here and in Matt 26:16 in the NT. The devil had departed from Jesus in the Temptation encounter "until the next opportunity came" (4:13); now in Judas, there was again an opportune moment for attack.

COMMENTARY

The conspiracy against Jesus is noted in all four Gospels, with John providing the fullest account and Luke the briefest (22:1-2; cf. John 11:45-52). John noted the insecurity of the Jewish religious leaders who conferred in the high council (or Sanhedrin) and concluded: "If we allow him to go on like this, soon everyone will believe in him. Then the Roman army will come and destroy both our Temple and our nation" (John 11:48). John also mentioned the high priest's prophecy that Jesus "would die for the entire nation" (John 11:51); John noted Jesus' prediction of his betrayal by Judas a little later (John 13:18-30).

Mark tells us that the betrayal took place two days before the Passover and the Festival of Unleavened Bread, and it was engineered by the leading priests and "the teachers of religious law" (often translated "scribes") who were actively "looking for an opportunity to capture Jesus secretly and kill him" (Mark 14:1). The only thing that was hindering them was the timing, for Passover was a time of Messianic excitement, and they didn't want the large crowds of people assembled for the festival to get upset and be provoked into creating a disturbance by any precipitous action on their part (Mark 14:2).

Matthew's account follows Mark quite closely but adds a few details of its own. It links the setting with the previous teaching of Jesus on the last judgment (Matt 25:31-46) and records Jesus uttering another Passion prediction on the very threshold of the Passover celebration. It thus heightens the tension as the decisive hour draws near, and solemnly declares the betrayal and the ensuing crucifixion (Matt 26:1-2). In addition, Matthew notes that the plot to kill Jesus was hatched "at the residence of Caiaphas, the high priest" (Matt 26:3), thus highlighting the fact that Jesus came to his own people, and yet they tragically rejected him (cf. John 1:11), even planning his execution in the house of the high priest.

Luke's short account names the festival that provided the setting and the principal players involved in seeking to put Jesus to death. Interestingly, Luke says that the cause of the Jewish leaders' reluctance to act was their fear of the people's reaction (22:2). The parallel accounts in Mark and Matthew explain more fully the apprehension of the leading priests and teachers of religious law. They advocated stealth and careful timing, so they remarked, "Not during the Passover celebration, . . . or the people may riot" (Matt 26:5; Mark 14:2). The same kind of assessment of the volatile political situation is reflected in John 11:48-51. There was a risk that any ill-considered action on their part could provoke a riot among the people and thus bring on Roman military intervention.

All three synoptic Gospels detail the betrayal by Judas Iscariot (22:3-6; Matt 26:14-16; Mark 14:10-11; cf. John 6:70-71; 13:2). Matthew and Mark simply relate that he went to the leading priests and offered his services at a price, while Luke notes the demonic element, attributing the betrayal to the initiative of Satan (22:3; cf. John 13:27). Matthew's account brings out the calculated nature of the offer: "How much will you pay me to betray Jesus to you?" (Matt 26:15). Mark noted that when the priests received the offer of assistance they were "delighted" and promised to pay him money (Mark 14:11). Only Matthew mentioned the amount as "thirty pieces of silver," which was roughly a month's wages. This amount is also significant in its relation to Zechariah 12:12-13, where the prophet portrays a good shepherd rejected by his sheep and sold for thirty pieces of silver, the amount mentioned in the Old Testament as the price of a slave (Exod 21:32).

Judas was one of the twelve men chosen by Jesus and called as an apostle (6:12-16; cf. Matt 10:1-4; Mark 3:13-19; John 6:70-71). According to John's Gospel, he acted as treasurer of the apostles and pilfered some of the proceeds for personal use (John 12:6). The mercenary interests of Judas are also revealed in the Johannine account of the anointing of Jesus at Bethany (John 12:1-8; cf. Mark 14:3-9). Because he was familiar with the movements of Jesus during this period (21:37; 22:39; cf. John 18:2), he would be able to lead the Temple guard to a secluded spot where

Jesus could be apprehended privately. He was promised that he would be given a reward for his efforts.

All three Synoptic accounts note that Judas agreed to the commercial arrangement struck with the leading priests and began looking for an opportunity to apprehend Jesus. Matthew and Luke both used the rare word *eukairia* [TG2120, ZG2321] to refer to the "opportune moment" for the betrayal (22:6; Matt 26:16). Luke indicated that the consultation with the leading priests included the "captains of the Temple guard," who were later involved in the actual arrest in the Garden of Gethsemane (22:4, 52). In addition, Luke noted the deliberate intention of the officials, in planning the arrest, to carry it out discreetly, "when the crowds weren't around" (22:6).

The reason for Judas's betrayal of Jesus is unclear. Some have suggested that he carried it out after he became convinced that Jesus planned to die (Mark 14:3-9; cf. Luke 14:10-11), or because he wanted the money (Matt 26:14-16; cf. John 12:4-6), or because he was disappointed in the manner in which Jesus was carrying out his messianic program (cf. 7:18; Matt 11:3; John 6:14-15). In any case, "Scripture informs us that Christ knew that Judas would betray Him even before he was chosen as a disciple (see John 6:64, 70-71). It is difficult to reconcile the freedom that Judas exercised in betraying Christ and the divine foreordination that assured that he would do so (Acts 1:15-17, 20). Yet, both are affirmed in the Scriptures. Christ announced that it would have been better for that man if he had not been born (Matt 26:24)" (Lindsell 1965:1483).

◆ J. The Last Supper (22:7-30; cf. Matt 26:17-19, 26-29; Mark 14:12-16, 22-25)

7Now the Festival of Unleavened Bread arrived, when the Passover lamb is sacrificed. 8Jesus sent Peter and John ahead and said, "Go and prepare the Passover meal, so we can eat it together."

9"Where do you want us to prepare it?" they asked him.

10He replied, "As soon as you enter Jerusalem, a man carrying a pitcher of water will meet you. Follow him. At the house he enters, 11say to the owner, 'The Teacher asks: Where is the guest room where I can eat the Passover meal with my disciples?' 12He will take you upstairs to a large room that is already set up. That is where you should prepare our meal."

13They went off to the city and found everything just as Jesus had said, and they prepared the Passover meal there.

14When the time came, Jesus and the apostles sat down together at the table.*

15Jesus said, "I have been very eager to eat this Passover meal with you before my suffering begins. 16For I tell you now that I won't eat this meal again until its meaning is fulfilled in the Kingdom of God."

17Then he took a cup of wine and gave thanks to God for it. Then he said, "Take this and share it among yourselves. 18For I will not drink wine again until the Kingdom of God has come."

19He took some bread and gave thanks to God for it. Then he broke it in pieces and gave it to the disciples, saying, "This is my body, which is given for you. Do this to remember me."

20After supper he took another cup of wine and said, "This cup is the new covenant between God and his people—an agreement confirmed with my blood, which is poured out as a sacrifice for you.*

21"But here at this table, sitting among

us as a friend, is the man who will betray me. ²²For it has been determined that the Son of Man* must die. But what sorrow awaits the one who betrays him." ²³The disciples began to ask each other which of them would ever do such a thing.

²⁴Then they began to argue among themselves about who would be the greatest among them. ²⁵Jesus told them, "In this world the kings and great men lord it over their people, yet they are called 'friends of the people.' ²⁶But among you it will be different. Those who are the greatest among you should take the lowest rank, and the leader should be like a servant. ²⁷Who is more important, the one who sits at the table or the one who serves? The one who sits at the table, of course. But not here! For I am among you as one who serves.

²⁸"You have stayed with me in my time of trial. ²⁹And just as my Father has granted me a Kingdom, I now grant you the right ³⁰to eat and drink at my table in my Kingdom. And you will sit on thrones, judging the twelve tribes of Israel.

22:14 Or *reclined together.*   **22:19-20** Some manuscripts omit 22:19b-20, *which is given for you . . . which is poured out as a sacrifice for you.*   **22:22** "Son of Man" is a title Jesus used for himself.

NOTES

22:8 *Go and prepare the Passover meal, so we can eat it together.* The Passover meal itself was eaten on the 15th of Nisan. It was the great annual commemoration of the divine rescue of Israel's firstborn, their deliverance from slavery in Egypt, and the miraculous crossing of the Red Sea (Exod 13:18; 15:22). The Passover was observed in haste, with unleavened bread and in recognition that it was Yahweh, Israel's mighty covenant-making God, who had delivered his people with a mighty hand and an outstretched arm from bondage (Exod 12) and had led them through the great and terrible wilderness into the land of promise, the land "flowing with milk and honey" (Deut 26:8-9). For details of typical Passover preparations in Jewish homes today, see Alony 1969; for Christian liturgical use of the Passover, see Rubin and Rubin 1994.

22:11 *The Teacher.* The Gr. term *didaskalos* [TG1320, ZG1437] is used 14 times to address Jesus in Luke's Gospel (e.g., 3:12; 7:40; 11:45; 20:21, 28, 39).

22:14 *Jesus and the apostles sat down together.* The Lukan presentation of the Lord's Supper is laid out in 22:14-20, including Jesus' opening comments (22:15-16), the taking of the first cup (22:17-18), and the meal itself and its symbols (22:19-20)—the bread (relating to Christ's body) and the "third" cup (relating to Christ's blood and establishing the new covenant).

This Passover meal was Jesus' last meal with the apostles prior to his crucifixion. Meal times and table fellowship were important to Luke (see the Introduction, "Fondness for Meal Scenes"). Together in fellowship, Jesus and the Twelve recall the Exodus of Israel out of Egypt. Now Jesus introduces a new meaning to the Passover celebration, "the first hint of which is Jesus' vow to refrain from Passover and wine until the consummated kingdom. His desire to fellowship with his disciples is related to this special moment. The approaching suffering will be followed by victory." (Bock 1996:1717). In this passage there are two striking images of salvation—the Exodus and the death of Jesus. "The bread pictures Jesus' body given for all who believe. The wine pictures Jesus' blood shed for the new covenant. This meal [the Passover] becomes an occasion to recall Jesus' death and the inauguration of the new covenant." (Bock 1996:1717-1718)

22:15 *I have been very eager to eat this Passover meal with you.* Lit., "With desire have I desired to eat this Passover with you." This Hebraism emphasizes Jesus' intense feelings about this occasion.

22:17 *he took a cup of wine.* In Luke, the cup of wine is mentioned first, and then the bread, followed by a second cup of wine. "Some Jewish meals included prayers over the cup of wine, and several such prayers might be offered during the meal (see v. 20). Luke's order of events may be related to this practice, or to a variation among early Christians in the way they remembered and observed the 'Lord's supper.' Jesus transformed a Jewish devotional meal into a continuing expression of association with himself in death and victory" (Coogan 2001: NT 139).

22:19b-20 *which is given for you . . . a sacrifice for you.* As the NLT mg indicates, some mss do not include this section—namely a few Western ones (D it^(a, d, i, l)) and the Didache. The ms evidence in favor of the longer text is outstanding: 𝔓75 ℵ A B C L T^(vid) W 038 040 044 f^(1.13) it^c syr^p cop^(sa, bo). On the complicated textual issues raised by Luke 22:19b-20, see Metzger (1971:173-177), who favors the longer reading in order to keep the traditional bread/cup pattern. Comfort's comments on this issue are helpful:

> All Greek manuscripts except D testify to the presence of Luke 22:19b-20 in the account of the Last Supper. Very likely, the Bezan editor was puzzled by the cup/bread/cup sequence, and therefore deleted this portion but in so doing was left with the cup/bread sequence, contrary to Matt 26:26-28, Mark 14:22-24, and 1 Cor 11:23-26. As far as we know, the Bezan order is found only in the Didache 9.2-3 and some Old Latin manuscripts. The other four variants show translators' attempts to resolve the same problem of cup/bread/cup, but their deletions and transpositions produce the more usual bread/cup sequence. The Bezan editor, Latin translators, and Old Syriac translators must not have realized that the cup mentioned in 22:17 was the cup of the Passover celebration, occupying 22:15-18. Going back to 22:16, it seems clear that the food of the Passover is implied when Jesus speaks of never again eating it until the Kingdom of God is realized. Then, according to 22:17-18, Jesus passed around a cup of wine, again saying that he would not drink of it until the Kingdom of God came. Thus, 22:16-18 has its own bread/cup sequence as part of the Passover meal. Following this, 22:19-20 has the bread/cup sequence of the new covenant. (Comfort 2007:[Luke 22:19-20])

There is a difference between Mark/Matthew/Paul and Luke on the sequence of the words of institution used in the Lord's Supper, or Eucharist (cf. 22:19-24 with Matt 26:26-29; Mark 14:22-25; 1 Cor 11:23-26). The first three mention first the bread, and then the cup, while Luke's order—if the longer text is accepted—is cup, bread, and cup; but this difference can be explained when the ritual of the Passover meal is understood. The reference to a second cup would not seem unusual to Jews of the time because there were four cups to drink in the course of the Passover meal (cf. *m. Pesahim* 10.1-7). Jesus' words in 22:17-18 might be a simple summary of his comments on the significance of the Passover meal, not something intended as part of a new institution. "Rather than looking back to the Exodus, Jesus is looking forward to the kingdom of God" (Evans 1990:317).

Jesus, Luke noted, greatly desired to celebrate this Passover meal with his disciples before his Passion (22:15), not because he reveled in the suffering entailed in his death (see 22:42), but because it symbolized the "new covenant" that would be established by his "blood"—that is, his death upon the cross (20:20). His life was to be "poured out as a sacrifice" to confirm this new agreement between God and his people (22:20; cf. Jer 31:31-33). And every time his followers took the cup and ate the bread, they were to think of their Lord's death and remember his sacrifice to reestablish the broken relationship between God and sinners.

22:24-30 Some Bibles and commentators regard this as a separate section and describe it as "the dispute about greatness," in which Jesus defines "greatness in the Kingdom of God" (cf. Matt 20:25-28; Mark 10:42-45).

22:25 *friends of the people.* The term "benefactor" (*euergetēs* [TG2110, ZG2309]) "renders a Gr. word that served as a title for rulers in Syria and Egypt" (Danker 1974:222).

COMMENTARY

At last the Passover season had arrived, as well as the time for the Passover meal. For this occasion, Jesus sent two of his most trusted men ahead of him, instructing Peter and John to make all the necessary arrangements for this highly significant meal that he would eat with the apostles (22:7-8). Anxious to carry out his instructions properly, the two apostles inquired about the place. They were given the information required and were told that they would see the unusual site of a man carrying a pitcher of water immediately upon entrance to the city (22:10; this was a task usually performed by women). This was to be the signal to follow the guide to a Jerusalem guest room that had been arranged for the Passover meal. It was an upstairs room of ample size to accommodate Jesus and the apostles, and it was to be made available to them on the agreed terms (22:11). Evidently, the owner of the house respected "the Teacher" and was favorably disposed to accommodate him for this occasion. Clearly, the arrangements had been made beforehand, for Peter and John "found everything just as Jesus had said, and they prepared the Passover meal there" (22:13).

This special meal also fits with Luke's thematic element of table fellowship. This time, it was a Passover observance, rich in symbolic meaning for Jesus and for his disciples who gathered with him since it recalled the great deliverance of the people of God out of Egypt through God's special intervention (see Exod 12). Jesus felt deeply about this meal with his disciples (see note on 22:15). He was conscious that this would be the last time he would share in this sacred occasion before his impending suffering (22:15). Its meaning was certainly given an eschatological coloring when he told the apostles that the meaning of this last supper would only be fulfilled, or realized, in the Kingdom of God (22:16). In other words, Jesus was looking beyond the meal itself to a celebration in some future time when the hopes of the Kingdom of God would be fully realized (cf. 13:28-29; 14:15; 22:28-30). Beyond the time of suffering, there would be glory.

Luke highlighted the connection between the last supper and the final coming of the Kingdom of God; in fact, the Kingdom theme is noted twice in a three-verse span to underscore its importance (22:16, 18). Jesus thanked God for the cup and invited the disciples to share it with one another (22:17). The meal, they were reminded, would be the last one they would share before the final time of fulfillment (22:16, 18). As the disciples received the bread from Jesus, he gave it a very personal reference to himself by declaring, "This is my body, which is given for you. Do this to remember me" (22:19). In saying this, he was implying that what he was going to do was to deliver his people, just as God had delivered his people from ancient Egypt. They were to remember this new Exodus and thank God for the deliverance Jesus was going to effect in Jerusalem (cf. 9:31).

God was establishing in the death of Christ a new covenant, or agreement, between God and the people of God (see Heb 10:12-16; cf. Jer 31:31-34). With the words about the bread, we have the "institution" of the Lord's Supper. "The *bread* is broken and described by Jesus as his *body given for* his followers. All Christians are called to observe this ritual *in remembrance of* Jesus. Likewise, Jesus described the *new covenant in* his *blood* [as that] *which is poured out for* his followers (Mark 14:24). . . . Jesus will shed his blood (perhaps an allusion to Isa 53:12) in order to establish a new covenant" (Evans 1990:317).

In the midst of this meal, Jesus announced that a betrayer sat among them. Luke does not record Judas' being identified during the meal, but does name him earlier (22:3-6). Such perfidy would not defeat the plan of God, for "the Son of Man" had been given a role in holy history by divine appointment (22:22). The plan of God would not be defeated, but the one who would betray him would fall under terrible judgment (22:22; cf. Matt 26:24). The disciples were dumbfounded that anyone among them would do such a dastardly thing (22:23).

But the disciples passed from this item of concern to another one; specifically, they became involved in heated debates "about who would be the greatest among them" (22:24). In this regard, the Synoptic texts present the aggressiveness and competitiveness of the apostles and show them in a very selfish light, particularly at that ominous time when the death of their Lord was looming before them. Once again, Jesus reminded them that they were really summoned to be the servants of servants. Self-serving action has no place in the Kingdom he had come to establish. This was not a common way of looking at things in a secular, Hellenistic world, where kings and other patrons were sometimes called "friends of the people" or "benefactors" (see note on 22:25). In Jesus' controversial Kingdom, these values are reversed (22:26).

The measure of greatness was not to be self-assertiveness but humble service: "Those who are the greatest among you should take the lowest rank, and the leader should be like a servant" (22:26). Jesus pointed to himself as the perfect example of such humble service that puts the needs of others ahead of one's own needs: "For I am among you as one who serves" (22:27). In just a few hours, he would submit to suffering, humiliation, and death as the faithful servant of God who would fulfill God's plan to establish the new covenant between God and his people. When would the disciples ever learn the way of the cross?

Despite their waywardness and slowness to understand Jesus and his message, Jesus was patient and gracious with them. He acknowledged their connection to him and was grateful for their support when others had slipped away (22:28; cf. John 6:66). In spite of their frailty and weakness, Jesus made solemn promises to them that were related to God's coming theocratic reign: "Just as my Father has granted me a Kingdom, I now grant you the right to eat and drink at my table in my Kingdom. And you will sit on thrones, judging the twelve tribes of Israel" (22:29-30). God was in the process of establishing his Kingdom through the life, death, and resurrection of Jesus, and the apostles were figures of cardinal importance in that process. A new Israel was in the offing, and they were to play key roles in that exciting development of holy history.

◆   **K. Jesus Predicts Peter's Denial (22:31-38; cf. Matt 26:30-35; Mark 14:26-31; John 13:36-38)**

31"Simon, Simon, Satan has asked to sift each of you like wheat. 32But I have pleaded in prayer for you, Simon, that your faith should not fail. So when you have repented and turned to me again, strengthen your brothers."

33Peter said, "Lord, I am ready to go to prison with you, and even to die with you."

34But Jesus said, "Peter, let me tell you something. Before the rooster crows tomorrow morning, you will deny three times that you even know me."

35Then Jesus asked them, "When I sent you out to preach the Good News and you did not have money, a traveler's bag, or extra clothing, did you need anything?"

"No," they replied.

36"But now," he said, "take your money and a traveler's bag. And if you don't have a sword, sell your cloak and buy one! 37For the time has come for this prophecy about me to be fulfilled: 'He was counted among the rebels.'* Yes, everything written about me by the prophets will come true."

38"Look, Lord," they replied, "we have two swords among us."

"That's enough," he said.

22:37 Isa 53:12.

NOTES

22:31 *Simon, Simon, Satan has asked to sift each of you like wheat.* This statement is found only in Luke. (For a detailed study of the material in Luke 22 not found in the other Gospels, see Soards 1987.) The repetition of Peter's name adds emphasis and urgency. The image of sifting as grain is sifted in a sieve comes from Amos 9:9, which reads, "For I will give the command and will shake Israel along with the other nations as grain is shaken in a sieve, yet not one true kernel will be lost." A sieve "was a type of winnowing tool usually with a coarse mesh. . . . In the sifting process the grain would fall to the ground and the stones, chaff, and other unwanted material would be retained in the sieve" (ISBE 4.505). The same image is used again in Isa 30:28, where it is said that God "will sift out the proud nations," leading them off to their destruction. According to 22:31, Satan desired to test the disciples (the Gr. "you" is in the plural, cf. NLT "each of you"), something Jesus compared to the sifting process.

22:32 *But I have pleaded in prayer for you, Simon.* Jesus here explicitly recognized Peter's vulnerability and acknowledged that he had made this a personal matter of intercession before the Father.

So when you have repented and turned to me again. The verb *epistrephō* [TG1994, ZG2188] is used to describe the idea of "turning," "returning," or "turning back" (e.g., 11:25; Matt 10:13; 12:44; 24:18; Mark 5:30; 8:33; John 21:20), and is used in the NT especially of one's relationship with God (1:16; Mark 4:12; Acts 9:35; 11:21; 2 Cor 3:16).

strengthen. This verb (*stērizō* [TG4741, ZG5114], "strengthen, establish") is often used in the NT to describe helping Christians grow strong and firm in their faith (Rom 1:11; 16:25; 1 Thess 3:2, 13; 2 Thess 2:17; 2 Pet 1:12).

22:36 *And if you don't have a sword, sell your cloak and buy one!* The reference to buying a sword here is difficult. As Stein has noted: "Attempts to interpret this literally as a Zealot-like call to arms, however, are misguided and come to grief over the saying's very 'strangeness.' Understood as a call to arms, this saying not only does not fit Jesus' other teachings but radically conflicts with them . . . The 'sword' is best understood in some metaphorical sense as indicating being spiritually armed and prepared for battle against the spiritual foes [cf. Eph 6:10-18]. The desperate need to be 'armed' for these future events is evident by the command to sell one's mantle, for this garment was essential to keep warm at night" (1992:555).

COMMENTARY

This passage, a particularly tender one, is significant because it depicts Jesus' role as a prevailing intercessor for Peter (cf. the role of Moses as an intercessor for Aaron and for Israel, Deut 9:20, 23-29). The solicitous care of Jesus for one of his leading apostles is clearly marked by the repetition of his name ("Simon, Simon," 22:31). The reality of satanic attack is presupposed here, and the importance of resisting it has already been taught in the Model Prayer by the petition, "And don't let us yield to temptation" (11:4; cf. Matt 6:13, which adds, "but rescue us from the evil one"). The prominence given to Jesus' "pleading in prayer" for a weak and fallible disciple was intended to encourage the readers of the Gospel as they reflected upon their own weakness and frailty (cf. Heb 7:25). If Jesus could do so much for a disciple who had fallen so grievously, could he not also help them?

In addition, the future recovery of Peter was anticipated following his repentance, and he was urged to pick up the task of leadership once again and strengthen other members of the believing community. The whole experience of temptation would be a testing one; it is compared to the sifting of grain to separate what is desired from what is of no use (cf. the winnowing imagery in 3:17 and the note on 22:31). Jesus prayed for Peter's safe passage through the trial that was upon him, and he was restored in time to his place of service and usefulness.

Peter did not have any sense of needing Jesus' help at this point. He confidently affirmed his willingness to go to prison and even to death in his loyalty to Jesus (22:33). Jesus rebuffed this cockiness, telling Peter something about himself and predicting his imminent threefold denial of Jesus (22:34). Jesus then spoke to the twelve apostles, asking them a serious question about the adequacy of the provision they had known as his followers: "When I sent you out to preach the Good News . . . did you need anything?" (22:35). When they recalled the strict conditions under which he had sent them out on an urgent mission (9:1-6; cf. 10:1-12, where Jesus sends out 72 other disciples), they could only marvel that their basic needs had been adequately met and confessed this. God had provided through the help of friendly people, but the conditions they were to face in the future would be different (the "but now" of 22:36 marks an emphatic contrast):

> On their early mission the disciples went out without provisions and depended entirely on the hospitality of their hearers. In the new situation brought about by Jesus' death (22:37), they must go equipped and be prepared to face hostility and persecution. This involved their purchasing a "sword" because what the Scriptures said about the death of God's Son was about to be fulfilled. The opposition to Jesus that had been mounting was about to come to its culmination, and the end was very near. To Jesus' frustration, however, the disciples failed to grasp his meaning in the use of the sword metaphor, and he concluded the conversation. (Stein 1992:554-555)

In his own near future, Jesus was about to be treated as a rebel and executed. This treatment was in accordance with Scripture and was a fulfillment of prophecy (note particularly that Isa 53:12 is quoted here from one of the great Servant Songs of the book of Isaiah). Indeed, Jesus viewed his whole life in terms of a divine pattern:

"Yes, everything written about me by the prophets will come true" (22:37; cf. 24:25-27, 44-48).

◆ **L. Jesus Prays on the Mount of Olives (22:39-46; cf. Matt 26:36-46; Mark 14:32-42)**

39Then, accompanied by the disciples, Jesus left the upstairs room and went as usual to the Mount of Olives. 40There he told them, "Pray that you will not give in to temptation."

41He walked away, about a stone's throw, and knelt down and prayed, 42"Father, if you are willing, please take this cup of suffering away from me. Yet I want your will to be done, not mine." 43Then an angel from heaven appeared and strengthened him. 44He prayed more fervently, and he was in such agony of spirit that his sweat fell to the ground like great drops of blood.*

45At last he stood up again and returned to the disciples, only to find them asleep, exhausted from grief. 46"Why are you sleeping?" he asked them. "Get up and pray, so that you will not give in to temptation."

22:43-44 Verses 43 and 44 are not included in many ancient manuscripts.

NOTES
22:43-44 The NLT mg rightly notes that these verses are not included in many ancient mss and other witnesses, namely 𝔓69vid 𝔓75 ℵ¹ B T W itf syrs cops a, some Greek mss (according to Anastasi), mss (according to Jerome), some Greek and Old Latin mss (according to Hilary), Marcion, Clement, and Origen. This is an impressive array of witnesses (nearly all the early mss). The verses are found in the following witnesses: ℵ² D L 038 044 0171vid 0233 f 𝔐, most Greek mss (according to Anastasius), mss (according to Jerome), mss (according to Epiphanius, Hilary), Justin Irenaeus Hippolytus Eusebius. Several other manuscripts include the verses but mark them with obeli thereby noting their obtrusion into the text (Comfort 2007:243-245).

For further discussion of the textual evidence, see Metzger, who thinks the verses "were added from an early source, oral or written, of extra-canonical traditions concerning the life and passion of Jesus" (1971:177). Similarly Ellis argues that they belong to a "genuine extra-canonical tradition," but are not Lukan (1981:258). As I have noted elsewhere: "This tradition at least is in full agreement with the Epistle to the Hebrews, which speaks of Jesus offering up 'prayers and supplications, with loud cries and tears' (Heb 5:7)" (Trites 1978:175).

COMMENTARY
The arrest in the garden is preceded in Matthew, Mark, and Luke by a vivid account of Jesus in prayer on the Mount of Olives. Each Gospel has special features that are worthy of brief mention, though the main story line is the same in each account.

All three evangelists mention that Jesus found repeatedly that the disciples were "asleep," despite his dependence on their support at this critical time (22:45; Matt 26:40; Mark 14:37). All three speak of the personal request that Jesus uttered to the "Father" for the "cup" of suffering to be removed if it were in keeping with the Father's will, though Jesus offered his complete submission to that will (22:42; Matt 26:39; Mark 14:36). All three note the command of Christ to alertness and prayer (22:40, 46; Matt 26:38; Mark 14:38).

Both Matthew and Mark observe that Jesus prayed three times and was disappointed by the disciples in each instance when he came to check up on them (Matt 26:40, 43, 44-45; Mark 14:37, 40, 41). In addition, Matthew and Mark note that the place was called "Gethsemane" (Matt 26:36; Mark 14:32), and both mention the presence of Peter, James, and John on the occasion (Matt 26:37; Mark 14:33; Matthew here referring to the latter two as "the sons of Zebedee"). Matthew and Mark specifically note that Jesus was experiencing deep distress at this critical time, when he felt "crushed with grief to the point of death" (Matt 26:37-38; Mark 14:33-34) and sought the garden location as a suitable place for intense prayer, simply asking that the disciples "sit" in the area while he withdrew a short distance for prayer (Matt 26:36; Mark 14:32). Both accounts record the failure of the disciples to stay alert ("They couldn't keep their eyes open"; Matt 26:43; Mark 14:40) and that they suffered a mild rebuke for "still sleeping" and taking their rest (Matt 26:45; Mark 14:41). Both accounts show Jesus referring to himself as the Son of Man who was about to be betrayed, and they both close out the incident with Jesus telling the disciples to rise and be going, for his betrayer was at hand (Matt 26:45b-46; Mark 14:41b-42).

Luke's account is the shortest Synoptic account of Jesus' last struggle in prayer before his arrest and eventual crucifixion. Luke did not mention the garden of Gethsemane, but located the incident on the Mount of Olives, noting that Jesus left the upstairs room where the Last Supper had been celebrated and "went as usual" to this familiar place of retreat (22:39). This serves to connect the institution of the Last Supper with the subsequent events. In one textual tradition, there is mention of the role of a special angel here: "Then an angel from heaven appeared and strengthened him" (22:43). Some textual critics have doubted the genuineness of verses 43 and 44, but a case can be made for taking them seriously, even if their canonicity is questioned (see note on 22:43-44).

As the Evangelist of prayer, Luke called attention to two special features in this time of intense prayer. First, he noted the great reverence and seriousness of Jesus' prayer on this occasion (22:41-42); and second, he used the incident to underscore the transfer value of earnest prayer for Christian discipleship (notice the repetition of the command to pray at both the beginning and the end of the Lukan account in 22:40 and 22:46). Luke intended the reader to notice the pedagogic value of Jesus' prayer for believers in their times of trial. This event served to "show that they should always pray and never give up" (18:1), however severe the trial might be. Prayer is the divinely appointed way of meeting and conquering temptation.

◆   M. Jesus Is Betrayed and Arrested (22:47-53; cf. Matt 26:47-56;
       Mark 14:43-52; John 18:2-11)

[47]But even as Jesus said this, a crowd approached, led by Judas, one of the twelve disciples. Judas walked over to Jesus to greet him with a kiss. [48]But Jesus said,

"Judas, would you betray the Son of Man with a kiss?"

[49]When the other disciples saw what was about to happen, they exclaimed, "Lord,

should we fight? We brought the swords!" ⁵⁰And one of them struck at the high priest's slave, slashing off his right ear. ⁵¹But Jesus said, "No more of this." And he touched the man's ear and healed him. ⁵²Then Jesus spoke to the leading priests, the captains of the Temple guard, and the elders who had come for him. "Am I some dangerous revolutionary," he asked, "that you come with swords and clubs to arrest me? ⁵³Why didn't you arrest me in the Temple? I was there every day. But this is your moment, the time when the power of darkness reigns."

NOTES

22:47 *a crowd approached, led by Judas.* The actions of Judas could suggest his disappointment with the manner in which Jesus was carrying out his messianic vocation. "It is possible that Judas was attracted by the objectives of the Zealots (cf. Mark 3:18ff). Even if it is likely that his surname means 'man (Heb. *'ish* [TH376, ZH408]) from Kerioth' (in southern Judea), it is still conceivable that Judas, being very disappointed by Jesus' inactivity, made contact with old friends among the opponents of Jesus in order to force him into action at last and thus set events in motion. Nevertheless, these ideas are no more than conjectures which are at best merely probabilities" (Schweizer 1970:292).

22:52 *revolutionary.* This is a good translation of the Gr. term *lēstēs* [TG3027, ZG3334] (cf. 23:19; Mark 15:7). Josephus was aware of such brigands, for the procurator "Felix took Eleazar the arch-robber and many that were with him, when they had ravaged the country for twenty years, and [he noted] another sort of robbers in Jerusalem, which were called Sicarii, who slew men in the daytime, and in the midst of the city; this they did chiefly at the festivals, when they mingled themselves with the multitude, and concealed daggers under their garments, with which they stabbed those that were their enemies" (*War* 2.13. 2-3). The times were rife with revolutionary activity. Jesus knew that his opponents were going to try to lay charges on him as a political revolutionary against Rome and remonstrated with the guards, who had come out to apprehend him with a show of force uncalled for by Jesus' previous actions (22:52-53; cf. Mark 14:48-49; Matt 26:55; note also John 18:20-21).

COMMENTARY

The Gospels are very detailed in their accounts of Passion Week. Each one includes a section on the betrayal and arrest of Jesus (Matt 26:47-56; Mark 14:43-52; Luke 22:47-53; John 18:2-11). Once again, the Synoptic accounts are very similar to one another. They record the arrival of the crowd, and all note that Judas, one of the twelve, was leading them (22:47; Matt 26:47; Mark 14:43; John 18:3). Matthew and Mark note the presence of "swords and clubs," obviously suggesting that the authorities were prepared to use force if necessary (Matt 26:47; Mark 14:43). These two Gospels also indicate that Judas had arranged a definite signal (the kiss) so that the soldiers would know the one whose arrest had been planned, and seize him with a minimum of difficulty at the agreed time and place (Matt 26:48; Mark 14:44).

Luke presented Judas with some distinctive elements. First, he noted that Judas consulted with the chief priests because Satan had entered into him (22:3). Second, he stressed the fact that the perfidious act took place at the table, the place of fellowship, acceptance, and friendship: "But here at this table, sitting among us as a friend, is the man who will betray me" (22:21). Third, he shortened the account of Judas'

betrayal but put into bold relief the treachery of the action by a direct word addressed to the perpetrator: "Judas, would you betray the Son of Man with a kiss?"
(22:48). Fourth, in the book of Acts, he provided some unique information:

> According to Acts 1:15-20, the apostle Peter, speaking to the believers some
> time after the death and resurrection of Jesus, pointed out that Judas' betrayal
> and death were a fulfillment of David's words (in Pss 69:25; 109:8). This
> passage includes an account of the circumstances surrounding Judas' death
> that differs from the narrative in Matthew [27:1-10]. Possible harmoniza-
> tions have been suggested, but it is difficult to reconstruct the details with
> certainty. (Gardner 1995:388)

According to Matthew, Judas approached Jesus with bold words of recognition:
"Greetings, Rabbi!" (Matt 26:49). The reply he received from Jesus shows both
kindness and yet clear knowledge of the dastardly deed that has been planned to destroy him: "My friend, go ahead and do what you have come for" (Matt 26:50).
Luke's account brings out the tragic, traitorous element in the encounter, for Jesus
said to him, "Judas, would you betray the Son of Man with a kiss?" (22:48). The awful treachery of the human heart seems to be revealed in this act of betrayal. Luke
also noted the provocative element in the arrest in the eyes of Jesus' supporters who
asked, "Lord, should we fight? We brought the swords!" (22:49). Evidently, they
had not grasped the metaphorical nature of the reference to swords that Jesus had
previously taught them just a short while before (22:36-38), nor had they taken in
the unique nature of his Kingdom (see John 18:36). Foolishly, they were eager to
defend their Master, and one of them struck the servant of the high priest and cut off
his ear. With characteristic concern for detail, Luke noted that it was his right ear, a
point also noticed by John, who also tells us that the man's name was Malchus
(John 18:10).

Jesus put a stop to this retaliation and use of force; then, with characteristic kindness and charity toward his enemies, Jesus touched and healed the man's ear
(22:51). Earlier he had taught his disciples what to do with their opponents: "Love
your enemies! Do good to them. . . . [Then] you will truly be acting as children of
the Most High, for he is kind to those who are unthankful and wicked. You must be
compassionate, just as your Father is compassionate." (6:35-36). In the moment of
crisis, Jesus practiced what he preached.

With moral courage, Jesus confronted "the leading priests, the captains of the
Temple guard, and the elders who had come for him" (22:52). He exposed the
incongruity of their procedure, for they had acted as if he were some "dangerous
revolutionary" advocating the violent overthrow of the religious or political establishment (22:52). He challenged them: "Why didn't you arrest me in the Temple?"
(22:53). He had taught there quite openly, and every day they had had ample
opportunities to apprehend him in a public place in full view of the assembled
crowds. "The reason was clear to Luke's readers—the people would have opposed
them (19:47-48; 20:19; 22:2; cf. also John 18:20). The very fact that Jesus taught
daily and openly in the Temple distinguished his activity from that of the revolu-

tionaries, who operated in the mountains and had to be hunted down. Jesus did not operate in the darkness, as his opponents were presently doing, but in the light" (Stein 1992:562). Jesus was exposing their moral cowardice in resorting to a clandestine arrest on the Mount of Olives. Nevertheless, Jesus knew that this was their "moment" or "hour" (hōra [TG5610, ZG6052]; 22:53; also a key word in the fourth Gospel—see John 12:23, 27; 13:1; 17:1); at that moment, his enemies were fulfilling the redemptive purposes of God.

◆ N. Peter Denies Jesus (22:54-65; cf. Matt 26:57-75; Mark 14:53-72)

54So they arrested him and led him to the high priest's home. And Peter followed at a distance. 55The guards lit a fire in the middle of the courtyard and sat around it, and Peter joined them there. 56A servant girl noticed him in the firelight and began staring at him. Finally she said, "This man was one of Jesus' followers!"
57But Peter denied it. "Woman," he said, "I don't even know him!"
58After a while someone else looked at him and said, "You must be one of them!" "No, man, I'm not!" Peter retorted.
59About an hour later someone else insisted, "This must be one of them, because he is a Galilean, too."

60But Peter said, "Man, I don't know what you are talking about." And immediately, while he was still speaking, the rooster crowed.
61At that moment the Lord turned and looked at Peter. Suddenly, the Lord's words flashed through Peter's mind: "Before the rooster crows tomorrow morning, you will deny three times that you even know me." 62And Peter left the courtyard, weeping bitterly.
63The guards in charge of Jesus began mocking and beating him. 64They blindfolded him and said, "Prophesy to us! Who hit you that time?" 65And they hurled all sorts of terrible insults at him.

NOTES

22:60 *I don't know what you are talking about.* As to the issue of Peter's denial, Ellis has commented helpfully: "Two meanings are implicit here: (1) to dispute, refuse to recognize, and (2) to abandon, deny solidarity with someone. The church uses the term in the latter sense as the opposite of 'confession.' Thus, it indicates apostasy from the faith or from Christ (cf. 12:8ff; 2 Tim 2:12). The theological meaning underscores the gravity of Peter's sin. But it also gives assurance to the penitent apostate that his is not an unforgivable sin. This story, then, is a counterbalance to the warning in 12:9. It would have been especially relevant at a time when the penitent apostate posed a problem for the church" (1981:260).

22:61 *the Lord.* For a helpful article on the nuances of Jesus as Savior and Lord in Luke and Acts, see Bock (1986:146-154), who argues that the early church (including Luke) understood "Jesus as Lord" to mean that Jesus is "the divine Mediator and Dispenser of Salvation" (9:20; Acts 4:12; 16:30-31). However, this confession is only a part of saving faith, for it also demands a life lived in submission and obedience to Jesus, as the abysmal failure of Peter and his subsequent repentance make clear (cf. 22:31-32, 61-62).

22:65 *all sorts of terrible insults.* Luke's expression here (noting that they were lit. "blaspheming") makes it clear that he was offended and repulsed by the blasphemous things that were directed against Jesus. "Conceptually, the passage recalls OT texts about rejection of the righteous (Isa 50:6; 53:3; Ps 69:6-12)" (Bock 1996:1790).

COMMENTARY

The denial of Jesus by Peter, which probably took place on Thursday night, is mentioned in all four Gospels (cf. John 18:19-24). It occurs in the setting of the residence of the high priest (22:54) with all the members of the Sanhedrin assembled together, a point noted by both Matthew and Mark (Matt 26:57, 59; Mark 14:53, 55). All three Synoptic accounts mention the fact that Peter followed "at a distance" (*makrothen* [TG3113, ZG3427]; 22:54; Matt 26:58; Mark 14:54), and Mark notes that he "went right into the high priest's courtyard" (Mark 14:54). Matthew remarks that, at this point, Peter sat with the guards in the courtyard "and waited to see how it would all end" (Matt 26:58). Since it was nighttime and somewhat chilly, he was warming himself at the fire as he sat with the guards (Mark 14:54). Luke observes that those who had seized Jesus and brought him to the high priest's house had kindled a fire "in the middle of the courtyard and sat around it, and Peter joined them there" (22:55). One of the maids, a servant girl, stared intently at Peter when she saw his face reflected in the fire's light and boldly declared: "This man was one of Jesus' followers!" (22:56). This was a serious charge at a volatile moment when the Master himself was before the Jewish supreme council facing a death sentence.

To extricate himself, Peter flatly repudiated the accusation, claiming that he didn't even know Jesus (22:57). But someone else, after an interval, raised the same charge, insisting that Peter was "one of them"—that is, a follower of Jesus (22:58). Once again, Peter flatly denied the charge (22:58). The accusation surfaced a third time about an hour later when someone else insisted that Peter was definitely "one of them, because he is a Galilean, too"—he was from the northern province with which Jesus was identified (22:59). For a final time, Peter vehemently denied the charge, once again, repudiating any connection with Jesus and saying, "I don't know what you are talking about" (22:60). Then the rooster crowed immediately, and Peter remembered the solemn words of Jesus predicting his defection just a day before (22:34, 61). Earlier, he had insisted he would be completely true to his Lord, even if he had to go to prison or death for him (22:33). Now as he recalled his self-confident words and his repeated failures, he had to face up to the fact that he had denied his Lord openly and blatantly. He went out "weeping bitterly" (22:62). He acknowledged how greatly he had disappointed his Master in his cowardice and weakness. Perhaps he also recalled the fact that Jesus had prayed for him and had hinted that he would be forgiven and restored (22:32).

Though Peter's denials are carefully recorded in each of the Gospels, Luke's account has some distinctive features. First, only he directly noted that it was the "home" of the high priest (22:54, the word *oikia* [TG3614, ZG3864] does not appear in the Greek text of the other Gospels here; cf. Matt 26:57; Mark 14:53); perhaps he wanted to implicate the Jewish leadership more explicitly in the miscarriage of justice. Second, he mentioned that both sexes asked Peter about his relationship to Jesus (a woman in 22:56-57, and two men in 22:58, 60). Third, he drew careful attention to the time element ("after a while," 22:58; "about an hour later," 22:59), perhaps an indication of his historical concern for accuracy and chronology (cf. 1:1-4; 3:1-3). Fourth, Luke noted that "the Lord turned and looked at Peter" (22:61), thereby triggering his memory that Jesus had predicted the denials, and his subsequent sorrow expressed in "weeping bitterly" (22:62).

In the last chapter of John's Gospel, there is a sequel to this incident, wherein Peter is reconciled to Jesus. In response to Jesus' thrice repeated question, "Do you love me?" Peter answered, "Yes, Lord, . . . you know I love you" (John 21:13-17; cf. 18:15-27). The leading disciple had grievously fallen, but he was fully restored by affirming his genuine love of Jesus: "Lord, you know everything. You know that I love you" (John 21:17).

Meanwhile, the guards who were in charge of Jesus began to mock him and beat him. They played blindman's bluff (if you will), insulting him, hitting him, and asking him to identify those who poked at him (22:63-65). Only Luke's account gives us the whole picture. Matthew records the mocking question, "Who hit you?" but does not record the blindfolding, and Mark notes the blindfolding but doesn't cite the question. Luke alone, of the Evangelists, placed the mockery of Jesus *before* he was presented to the Jewish Council. It was common for the soldiers of that time to badger and humiliate an apprehended person: "Brutal hazing of prisoners often preceded official interrogation" (O'Day and Peterson 1999:124).

All three accounts describe a process of the strongest rejection and contempt, Matthew and Mark both calling attention to the spitting and striking of Christ (Matt 26:67; Mark 14:65), and all three mentioning the disrespectful demand that he "prophesy" (22:64; Matt 26:68; Mark 14:65). Apparently, the Evangelists saw the prophecy in Isaiah coming to some kind of gruesome fulfillment, for there it had been said that the Servant of God "was despised and rejected—a man of sorrows, acquainted with deepest grief" (Isa 53:3). The writer of the epistle to the Hebrews saw value in our reflecting on the abuse that Christ suffered: "Think of all the hostility he endured from sinful people; then you won't become weary and give up" (Heb 12:3). A similar point is made in 1 Peter, where the exemplary nature of Christ's suffering is mentioned to inspire heroic living on the part of suffering believers (1 Pet 2:21-25).

◆   O. Jesus before the Council (22:66-71; cf. Matt 26:57-68; Mark 14:53-65)

⁶⁶At daybreak all the elders of the people assembled, including the leading priests and the teachers of religious law. Jesus was led before this high council,* ⁶⁷and they said, "Tell us, are you the Messiah?"

But he replied, "If I tell you, you won't believe me. ⁶⁸And if I ask you a question, you won't answer. ⁶⁹But from now on the Son of Man will be seated in the place of power at God's right hand.*"

⁷⁰They all shouted, "So, are you claiming to be the Son of God?"

And he replied, "You say that I am."

⁷¹"Why do we need other witnesses?" they said. "We ourselves heard him say it."

22:66 Greek *before their Sanhedrin.*   22:69 See Ps 110:1.

NOTES

22:66 *Jesus was led before this high council.* This is the only use of the term *sunedrion* [TG4892, ZG5284] in Luke's Gospel to refer to the Sanhedrin or "high council" of the Jews. This august body was composed of about 70 elders of the Jewish people, including the leading priests and teachers of religious law, and was presided over by the high priest. It constituted the ruling body in Judaism and controlled political and religious life until the overthrow of Jerusalem and the Temple in AD 70. The apostles would also eventually be examined by this body (Acts 4:15-18; 22:30; 23:1-10).

In Luke, there are five items to be observed in the trial narratives: (1) the mocking and beating of Jesus (22:63-65), (2) the trial before the Jewish Sanhedrin (22:66-71), (3) the trial before Pilate (23:1-5), (4) the trial before Herod (23:6-16), and (5) the death sentence given by Pilate (23:17-25). There is no clandestine night trial scene in Luke and no reference to the accusation introduced by the false witnesses, who alleged that Jesus had uttered threats about destroying the Temple (Matt 26:60-61; Mark 14:56-59). Since the council was not permitted to meet officially at night (*m. Sanhedrin* 4:1), this was probably a preliminary information-gathering meeting held in the high priest's palace to assemble evidence to present to Pilate. Apart from 23:13 (which implies a break or recess before the convening of the formal judgment session), the hearings are not marked with clear indications of a time sequence. Still, when the Gospels are put together, the "trials" of Jesus probably took most of the night.

Jesus' formal trial before the Sanhedrin was convened at daybreak, for it was necessary to assemble after daylight to make the legal decision recommending the death penalty (*m. Sanhedrin* 4:1). Matthew's account remarks, "All the chief priests and the elders of the people came to the decision to put Jesus to death" (Matt 27:1 NIV). Since they, like Rome's other subject peoples, did not have the power to carry out the death penalty directly (cf. John 18:31), they bound Jesus "and took him to Pilate, the Roman governor" (Matt 27:2). "The restriction was important, for otherwise Rome's supporters could be quietly removed by local legal executions" (Barker 1985:1633). The Jews were, however, permitted to execute Gentiles who trespassed into the Temple, and Steven's execution was apparently overlooked. In the case of the Gospel trials, the Jewish preliminaries were over at this point, and now Jesus stood before the prefect. For more details on the trials of Jesus, including Jewish and Roman sources, NT witnesses, Passion narratives, legal issues, and theological significance, see DJG 841-853.

22:70 *are you claiming to be the Son of God?* Jesus being the Son of God is vitally important to the life of the church, as Tolbert has pointed out: "The church's conception of Jesus as God's Son has its foundation in his own consciousness of a unique relationship with God expressed, for example, in the way he spoke of God as his Father [see Luke 10:21-22]. For him, this was no abstract, metaphysical dogma of the Trinity. It was an existential conviction that his life belonged uniquely to God. . . . The conviction that Jesus is the Son of God may mean much that we cannot grasp. But at least it means that there is not, nor can there be, any other revelation of God in history so clear and so profound as this. Jesus is the key to our understanding of God and the world, of ourselves and our fellow men, of history and the future" (1970:174).

COMMENTARY

Luke's interest in Jesus' trial was to establish his innocence and righteousness. (Of course, ultimately, his resurrection was his vindication.) Some interpreters understand the presentation of Jesus here in terms of the suffering righteous one seen in the Psalms, Isaiah, and in the book of Wisdom (Ps 22:1-21; 25:16-19; 31:1-18;

69:6-12, 14-15, 19-21; Isa 50:6; 53:2-12; Wis 2:10-22; 12:20-22). In this view, Jesus' passion is presented by Luke as "the suffering and death of God's Righteous Sufferer who goes to his death in spite of his innocence but is subsequently vindicated by God. This view makes sense of the innocence motif in the passion story, dovetails well with the 'contrast formulae' in the speeches in Acts (e.g., 'you nailed him to a cross and killed him. [24]But God released him from the horrors of death and raised him back to life' Acts 2:23-24) and demonstrates in Jesus' life how God overturns injustice—an important theme in Luke–Acts" (DJG 161). This view, however, does not take sufficient account of the theocentric passages in Luke that insist on the divine necessity of the cross in terms of salvation history (e.g., 9:22; 17:25; 24:7, 26, 44; Acts 17:3).

In any event, the interrogation of Jesus had gone on during the night when it was illegal to conduct a Jewish trial, according to the rules laid down in the Mishnah (Sanhedrin 4.1). When the time came, the whole assembly of the Jewish leaders gathered together, "including the leading priests and the teachers of religious law" (22:66). The Sanhedrin was the ruling supreme council of the Jews and consisted of 70 members, plus the presiding high priest. Jesus was brought into this assembly to answer questions and make his defense before the high council.

Omitting the preliminary investigation in Mark and Matthew, where testimony was sought that might merit a death sentence for Jesus, Luke gets right to the point. The elders' question was direct and barbed: "Tell us, are you the Messiah?" (22:67). Jesus did not directly answer their question, knowing that they were set on incriminating him. And he countered that they would be quite unwilling to answer a question that he might put to them about the nature of the ambiguous term Messiah (22:67-68). Instead he gave a reply about the Son of Man, his preferred term, asserting, "From now on the Son of Man will be seated in the place of power at God's right hand" (22:69). In saying this, Jesus boldly alluded to Daniel 7:13, a passage where the mysterious figure, "the Son of Man," is given authority, honor, and royal power over all the nations of the world. The irony of the scene is that, while the Sanhedrin thought they were sitting in judgment on him, the roles were reversed: he was the judge who would judge them and their nation.

In response, members of the Jewish high council were quick to ask Jesus, point blank, whether he was "the Son of God" (22:70). "Whether Jesus' implicit claim of messiahship, his self-designation as Son of Man, or both, prompt this question is uncertain. Since the latter title is related to Psalm 110:1, which was probably understood as a messianic Psalm, the title Son of Man would also have been understood in a messianic sense" (Evans 1990:332).

According to Luke's wording, Jesus avoided self-incrimination by refusing to give a direct affirmation of his identity as Son of God (note the oblique words, "You say that I am," 22:70). Jesus' opponents here "are asking whether Jesus claims a special relationship to God. His reference to the Son of Man and to the place at God's right hand must have seemed to them a claim to a higher place than that which they understood the Messiah to occupy. For them a claim to be Messiah might be a mistake, but it was not blasphemy. But this was something different. Jesus' reply means something like, 'That is your word, not mine. I would not have put it like that, but since you have, I cannot deny it' " (Morris 1974:318). Plainly, Jesus' view of his divine sonship was different from theirs, but he could not disown the term—he was, in very truth, the Son of God. By contrast, Mark's version of Jesus' response to the high priest is unequivocally affirmative. When asked, "Are you the Messiah, the Son of the Blessed One [God]?" Jesus responded, "I AM" (Mark 14:61-62). As such, it is one of the clearest references to Jesus affirming his own divine, messianic identity.

For the Jewish high council, that ended the matter. They were not interested in any qualifications Jesus might want to make. In their eyes he had incriminated himself by this damaging admission. Since they had heard the words from his own lips, they required no further testimony.

◆   **P. The Trials of Jesus before Pilate and Herod (23:1-25; cf. Matt 27:1-2, 11-14; Mark 15:1-5; John 18:33-38)**

Then the entire council took Jesus to Pilate, the Roman governor. ²They began to state their case: "This man has been leading our people astray by telling them not to pay their taxes to the Roman government and by claiming he is the Messiah, a king."

³So Pilate asked him, "Are you the king of the Jews?"

Jesus replied, "You have said it."

⁴Pilate turned to the leading priests and to the crowd and said, "I find nothing wrong with this man!"

⁵Then they became insistent. "But he is causing riots by his teaching wherever he goes—all over Judea, from Galilee to Jerusalem!"

⁶"Oh, is he a Galilean?" Pilate asked. ⁷When they said that he was, Pilate sent him to Herod Antipas, because Galilee was under Herod's jurisdiction, and Herod happened to be in Jerusalem at the time.

⁸Herod was delighted at the opportunity to see Jesus, because he had heard about him and had been hoping for a long time to see him perform a miracle. ⁹He asked Jesus question after question, but Jesus refused to answer. ¹⁰Meanwhile, the leading priests and the teachers of religious law stood there shouting their accusations. ¹¹Then Herod and his soldiers began mocking and ridiculing Jesus. Finally, they put a royal robe on him and sent him back to Pilate. ¹²(Herod and Pilate, who had been enemies before, became friends that day.)

¹³Then Pilate called together the leading priests and other religious leaders, along with the people, ¹⁴and he announced his verdict. "You brought this man to me, accusing him of leading a revolt. I have examined him thoroughly on this point in your presence and find him innocent. ¹⁵Herod came to the same conclusion and sent him back to us. Nothing this man has done calls for the death penalty. ¹⁶So I will have him flogged, and then I will release him."*

¹⁸Then a mighty roar rose from the crowd, and with one voice they shouted, "Kill him, and release Barabbas to us!" ¹⁹(Barabbas was in prison for taking part in an insurrection in Jerusalem against the government, and for murder.) ²⁰Pilate argued with them, because he wanted to release Jesus. ²¹But they kept shouting, "Crucify him! Crucify him!"

²²For the third time he demanded, "Why? What crime has he committed? I have found no reason to sentence him to death. So I will have him flogged, and then I will release him."

23But the mob shouted louder and louder, demanding that Jesus be crucified, and their voices prevailed. 24So Pilate sentenced Jesus to die as they demanded. 25As they had requested, he released Barabbas, the man in prison for insurrection and murder. But he turned Jesus over to them to do as they wished.

23:16 Some manuscripts add verse 17, *Now it was necessary for him to release one prisoner to them during the Passover celebration.* Compare Matt 27:15; Mark 15:6; John 18:39.

NOTES

23:4 the crowd. On the fickleness of crowds see the interesting comments of Leaney, who distinguishes the "entire council" of 23:1 (*plēthos* [TG4128, ZG4436], "crowd"), who were the members of the house of the high priest that had condemned the Lord, from the "crowds" (*ochlos* [TG3793, ZG4063]) of the ordinary people who "are mentioned here in the Passion Narrative of this gospel for the first time." Nevertheless, he insists that "this is only literary: Luke is well aware that the whole people were responsible and makes this point with emphasis at Acts 3:13ff. The last point in the narrative when the people were an effective defence for the Lord was 22:2" (Leaney 1958:279).

23:8 Herod was delighted at the opportunity to see Jesus. The appearance of Jesus before Antipas is recorded only in Luke 23:6-12. This material might have come from Joanna, wife of Chuza, Herod's steward (8:3). For a useful study on Herod, see Hoehner 1972.

23:16 I will have him flogged. The Roman method of flogging was notorious for its brutality. "Roman scourging ignored the limits of the Mosaic law (which restricted the number of strokes applied to a victim to 40 [Deut. 25:1-3; in practice, to 39 strokes, cf. 2 Cor 11:24]) and varied the severity according to the status of the victim. A freed man, like Paul, could be beaten with rods (*rhabdos* [TG4464, ZG4811]) of elm or birch by Roman lictors (Acts 16:22; 2 Cor 11:25). Slaves or non-Romans could be scourged with straps (*mastix* [TG3148, ZG3465]) or whips of leather cords knotted at the ends and weighted with pieces of metal or bone in Matt 27:26 (cf. verb *phragelloō* [TG5417, ZG5849]) and in John 2:15 (cf. noun *phragellion* [TG5416, ZG5848])" (Freedman 2000:1173). These thongs imbedded with pieces of metal or bone would leave painful marks on the back and the buttocks, scoring the flesh with ugly scars and bloody wounds.

23:16b-18 "I will release him." Then a mighty roar rose from the crowd, and with one voice they shouted, "Kill him, and release Barabbas to us!" As noted in the NLT mg, several mss add verse 17: "Now it was necessary for him to release one [prisoner] for them." However, the MS support for this inclusion (א W 038 044 f[1.13] 892[mg] 𝔐; D syr[c.s] insert the verse after 23:19) is exceedingly inferior to those mss that do not include it (𝔓75 A B L T 070 892[txt] it[a] cop[sa]). Scribes borrowed from Mark 15:6 to let readers know about a custom of prisoner release during the Passover, the background for the demand to release Barabbas.

23:19 Barabbas was in prison for taking part in an insurrection. Luke used the word *stasis* [TG4714, ZG5087] to describe a rebellion or revolt (so also 23:25). The word appears in Acts in the charges laid by Tertullus against Paul: "We have found this man to be a troublemaker who is constantly stirring up *riots* among the Jews all over the world" (Acts 24:5; cf. 19:40 concerning the riot or commotion raised by the silversmiths in Ephesus against Paul).

23:25 insurrection and murder. Instead of Jesus, Pilate responded to the crowd's demands and released Barabbas, a notorious prisoner mentioned in all four Gospels (23:18-19; Matt 27:16-26; Mark 15:7-15; John 18:40). Barabbas was a known criminal and is again called a "murderer" in Acts 3:14. "In making such a choice, and the fact that the religious leaders led the people in that choice, we find the ultimate rejection of God's Messiah, the 'Holy and Righteous One' [Acts 3:14]" (Gardner 1995:74).

COMMENTARY

The trial scene of Jesus before Pilate is related in all the Gospels (23:1-25; Matt 27:11-16; Mark 15:2-15; John 18:28–19:16). Interestingly, there seem to be some parallels between Luke's account of the trial of Jesus and John's. Both repeatedly note that the charges against Jesus were unfounded, and both mention the flogging. (On possible links between Luke and John's Gospel in the Passion narrative, see Matson 2001).

This first trial was precipitated by "the entire council" bringing Jesus before the Roman governor (23:1). It turned into an occasion where the Jewish leaders could make public charges against Jesus that would incriminate him in the eyes of the Roman authorities, alleging that he had instigated Jewish opposition to Rome "by telling them not to pay their taxes to the Roman government and by claiming he is the Messiah, a king" (23:2). The claim to be a king would be seen in political terms as an act of treason against Rome, and the alleged attack on taxes would be viewed as undermining Roman authority and fomenting rebellion against the occupying power.

Pilate took up the charge of kingship by asking him directly if he was "the king of the Jews" (23:3a). Jesus' puzzling answer—"you have said it" (23:3b)—leaves the onus of responsibility on Pilate to make up his own mind. In Luke's account, as in John's, Pilate pronounced Jesus innocent of the charges raised by his accusers, and this was publicly stated by Pilate to the leading priests and members of the crowd— not once but *three* times (23:4, 14, 22; cf. John 18:38; 19:4, 6).

But the first word of the governor clearing Jesus of the charges was not accepted by the Jewish leaders, who continued to press hostile charges against Jesus, alleging that he was fomenting civil unrest, "causing riots by his teaching wherever he goes—all over Judea, from Galilee to Jerusalem" (23:5). They were persistent in their determination to make political accusations against Jesus that would hold up in Roman eyes. Pilate recognized the mention of Galilee as an opportunity to push the decision on the case into another jurisdiction. On determining that Jesus was from Galilee, Pilate "sent him to Herod Antipas, because Galilee was under Herod's jurisdiction, and Herod happened to be in Jerusalem at the time" (23:7). Herod was undoubtedly in Jerusalem for Passover. Pilate hoped that Herod would handle this contentious matter, and thus Pilate would escape the badgering of these Jewish leaders who were determined to get rid of their Galilean opponent.

The trial scene before Herod is unique to Luke's account (23:6-12). Herod Antipas was the son of the famous King Herod (Herod the Great), who was the ruler of the Jews at the time of Jesus' birth (Matt 2:1). As tetrarch, he was the ruler of Galilee and Perea, and thus politically in charge of Galileans. The information on this trial might have been provided by Chuza, who was the manager of Herod's household and whose wife, Joanna, was among the supporters and helpers of Jesus when he went about Galilee on a preaching mission (8:1-3). We know that Herod's headquarters was in Tiberias, and there is no reference in the Gospels to Jesus ever visiting that city. It seems that he had deliberately steered clear of Herod, who had shut John up in prison and eventually beheaded him (3:19-20; 9:7-9; cf. Mark 6:14-29).

Herod Antipas, who had heard of Jesus' remarkable preaching, teaching, and healing, was "delighted at the opportunity to see Jesus" (23:8a). He had learned of his mighty works from others, and for a long time he had been curious to see him personally at work, "hoping . . . to see him perform a miracle" (23:8b). This was the opportunity that he had been waiting for.

Herod Antipas plied Jesus with questions, but Jesus was unwilling to answer, preferring to remain silent (23:9; cf. Isa 53:7, where the portrayal of the Righteous Sufferer includes silence in the midst of oppression and harsh treatment). This silence was remarkable because the determined enemies of Jesus, the leading priests and teachers of religious law, were loud and persistent in "shouting their accusations" against him (23:10). Vehemently, they assaulted him verbally, while the soldiers poked fun at him, using the occasion to mock and ridicule Jesus, and even Herod joined in their banter (23:11a). As a final insult, they "put a royal robe on him and sent him back to Pilate" (23:11b).

As despicable as the incident was, Luke cites it as healing a broken relationship between Herod and Pilate (23:12). They had been at odds with each other as political rivals, and the rift between them was bridged that day (23:12). As Fitzmyer has noted: "The relationship is carried further in the *Gospel of Peter,* where in 2:5 Herod addresses the Roman prefect as 'Brother Pilate'" (1985:482). The original cause of the enmity is not stated, though the fact that Pilate put to death Galileans while they were offering their sacrifices in the Temple at Jerusalem (13:1) might be the principal explanation of the tension that had existed between Herod Antipas and Pilate. Another contributing factor might have been the incident of the gilded shields mentioned by Philo (*Embassy* 299–305), which served as the basis of an appeal to the emperor Tiberius by the four sons of Herod the Great (Marshall 1978:857). As Danker has observed: "The incident is one of many that display Luke's keen perception of the opportunism that infects much political activity in both secular and religious spheres" (1974:233).

After this, Pilate assembled the Jewish priests and other religious leaders who were clamoring for Jesus' death on the alleged grounds "of leading a revolt" against Rome (23:14a). Pilate repeated his verdict: "I have examined him thoroughly on this point in your presence and find him innocent" (23:14b). He supported his finding by drawing attention to the report of Herod Antipas, who came to the same conclusion Pilate reached and had returned the prisoner to his jurisdiction. Pilate stated quite unequivocally that there were no grounds for the death penalty (23:15). His plan was to have Jesus flogged, possibly as a public example to warn any would-be messianic pretenders of the danger of opposing Rome, and then to release Jesus in view of the lack of substance in the malicious charges that had been raised against him (23:17).

The uproar that followed was remarkable, for the whole crowd of the leading priests, teachers of the law, and their religious supporters shouted out in unison, "Kill him, and release Barabbas to us!" (23:18). Ironically, Jesus' enemies were bound and determined to get their pound of flesh, even if it meant releasing

Barabbas, a known insurrectionist who had taken part in acts of violence against the government and who had committed murder (23:19). Pilate saw both the danger and the injustice in their proposal and accordingly argued with them, "because he wanted to release Jesus" (23:20). Craddock has noted the strangeness of the crowd's attitude: "The contradiction in such behavior is lost on them; when minds are made up, there is no room for reason. One cannot avoid recalling the countless champions of freedom who have acted violently to deny freedom in the name of freedom" (1990:270). The united force of their opposition and their vociferous cries were insistent and unrelenting: "Crucify him!" (23:21).

Despite their repeated cries for execution, Pilate was reluctant to grant their demands. He challenged the nature of Jesus' supposed crime, raising serious questions about it. Once again, he insisted that he found no reason "to sentence him to death" (23:22). Partially to appease them, he proposed a second time that he would have Jesus beaten and then let him go (23:22). Though Pilate had given his verdict, the boisterous shouts of the mob continued to demand that Jesus be crucified (23:23), and, at length, Pilate capitulated and "sentenced Jesus to die as they demanded" (23:24). The Roman historian Tacitus (*Annals* 15.44) also notes that Pilate ordered the crucifixion of Jesus. Pilate did this reluctantly, under pressure from the Jewish leaders who pressed the point that if he released Jesus he was "no 'friend of Caesar'" (John 19:12). Clearly this was a blatant "threat of blackmail by accusing Pilate of permitting rebellion against the emperor" (Coogan 2001: NT 178). Pilate acceded to their request and released Barabbas. Once again, Luke ironically noted that this man was a notorious criminal who was "in prison for insurrection and murder" (23:25; cf. 23:19). A gross miscarriage of justice had taken place.

◆   **Q. The Crucifixion of Jesus (23:26-43; cf. Matt 27:32-44; Mark 15:21-32; John 19:16-27)**

²⁶As they led Jesus away, a man named Simon, who was from Cyrene,* happened to be coming in from the countryside. The soldiers seized him and put the cross on him and made him carry it behind Jesus. ²⁷A large crowd trailed behind, including many grief-stricken women. ²⁸But Jesus turned and said to them, "Daughters of Jerusalem, don't weep for me, but weep for yourselves and for your children. ²⁹For the days are coming when they will say, 'Fortunate indeed are the women who are childless, the wombs that have not borne a child and the breasts that have never nursed.' ³⁰People will beg the mountains, 'Fall on us,' and plead with the hills, 'Bury us.'* ³¹For if these things are done when the tree is green, what will happen when it is dry?*"

³²Two others, both criminals, were led out to be executed with him. ³³When they came to a place called The Skull,* they nailed him to the cross. And the criminals were also crucified—one on his right and one on his left.

³⁴Jesus said, "Father, forgive them, for they don't know what they are doing."* And the soldiers gambled for his clothes by throwing dice.*

³⁵The crowd watched and the leaders scoffed. "He saved others," they said, "let him save himself if he is really God's Messiah, the Chosen One." ³⁶The soldiers mocked him, too, by offering him a drink

of sour wine. [37]They called out to him, "If you are the King of the Jews, save yourself!" [38]A sign was fastened to the cross above him with these words: "This is the King of the Jews."

[39]One of the criminals hanging beside him scoffed, "So you're the Messiah, are you? Prove it by saving yourself—and us, too, while you're at it!"

[40]But the other criminal protested, "Don't you fear God even when you have been sentenced to die? [41]We deserve to die for our crimes, but this man hasn't done anything wrong." [42]Then he said, "Jesus, remember me when you come into your Kingdom."

[43]And Jesus replied, "I assure you, today you will be with me in paradise."

23:26 *Cyrene* was a city in northern Africa. 23:30 Hos 10:8. 23:31 Or *If these things are done to me, the living tree, what will happen to you, the dry tree?* 23:33 Sometimes rendered *Calvary*, which comes from the Latin word for "skull." 23:34a This sentence is not included in many ancient manuscripts. 23:34b Greek *by casting lots.* See Ps 22:18.

NOTES

23:26-56 Luke's account of the crucifixion and burial of Jesus is presented in five sections: 1) Jesus is on the way to Calvary (23:26-31), 2) he is crucified (23:32-38), 3) the penitent thief cries out for help (23:39-43), 4) Jesus dies (23:44-49), and 5) he is laid in a tomb (23:50-56). Some themes in the Lukan story continue throughout this section, such as the compassion of Jesus for the Daughters of Jerusalem and the penitent thief (23:27-31, 41-42), the forgiveness theme (if the text of 23:34 is accepted; see the NLT mg and the textual discussion in the note below), the role of Jesus as "King" (23:37, 42), and the filial trust of Jesus in his heavenly Father as he expires, quoting Ps 31:5. In addition, several times Luke draws attention to the gross miscarriage of justice in the death of Jesus (23:41, 47), but also the faithfulness and loyalty of Jesus' friends, "including the women who had followed him from Galilee" (23:49; cf. 8:3). The irony of the death of Jesus is that he saved others, but he could not have done so if he had saved himself (23:35, 37, 39).

23:26 *Simon, who was from Cyrene.* Cyrene was a major city of Libya in North Africa and had a large Jewish population. Simon might have come to Jerusalem as a pilgrim to celebrate the Passover, or he might have been a permanent resident in the city, where there were Greek-speaking Jews from the Dispersion who worshiped in synagogues in Jerusalem, where their numbers were sufficiently large to allow services to be conducted in Greek (Acts 6:9). According to Mark's Gospel, he was "the father of Alexander and Rufus," two men who were known to the Marcan community (Mark 15:21). There is a good chance that Simon was converted as a result of being forced to carry the cross, for Mark 15:21 mentions his sons, one of whom, Rufus, is probably the man who was later a Christian leader at Rome (Rom 16:13).

The soldiers seized him and put the cross on him. The "Roman army had the power to requisition assistance from civilians (Matt 5:41). Simon was pressed into service to carry not the whole cross, which would have been too much for any one man, but the *patibulum* or cross-bar, to which the condemned man was fastened either by ropes or by nails before it was hoisted into position on the upright post" (Caird 1963:249).

23:28 *Daughters of Jerusalem, don't weep for me, but weep for yourselves and for your children.* Luke's passion account centers on Jerusalem, the capital city and site of the Jewish Temple. The death of Jesus took place in Jerusalem, and the message of forgiveness of sins and new life through a crucified, risen Savior was to be taken to the world from Jerusalem to "the ends of the earth" (Acts 1:8). Since Jerusalem was tremendously important in holy history, Luke showed how much Jesus loved the city (9:51; 13:22, 33-34; 17:11; 18:31; 19:11, 28, 41-44). On the importance of Jerusalem in holy history, see Walker 1992 and 1996.

23:34 Jesus said, "Father, forgive them, for they don't know what they are doing." Several important ancient mss do not include this prayer of Jesus, including 𝔓75 א¹ B D* W 038 070 itᵃ syrˢ copˢᵃ. Many other mss do include it: א*.² (A) C D² L 044 0250 f¹.⁽¹³⁾ 𝔐 syrᶜʰᵖ. The documentary evidence favors its omission as the combination of 𝔓75 א¹ B D* W itᵃ syrˢ copˢᵃ is far stronger than the opposing witnesses. This support is both early and geographically diverse. Some scholars, however, appeal to the continuity between this verse and Acts 3:17 and 7:60 as evidence that it might have been original (Caird 1963:251; Ellis 1981:267-268), though such an argument is inconclusive. For further discussion, see Comfort (2007: Luke 23:34) and Metzger (1971:180), both of whom point out the strong textual evidence against its genuineness. Though the words were most likely not written by Luke, the words probably came from an authentic oral tradition. Indeed, Westcott and Hort considered these words and 22:43-44 to be "the most precious among the remains of the evangelic tradition which were rescued from oblivion by the scribes of the second century" (1882:67).

23:38 This is the King of the Jews. The superscription, like the taunts directed against Jesus (23:35, 37, 39) is another unconscious testimony to the real truth of the scene. The kingship of Jesus is highlighted in the Gospels, particularly in Matthew and John (see Matt 2:2; Matt 27:11; John 1:49; 12:13; 18:33, 37, 39). The kingship of Jesus continued to be a theme in the apostolic preaching (Acts 17:7; cf. 28:31).

23:42 Jesus, remember me when you come into your Kingdom. The robber's appeal was probably based on the charge against Jesus that he claimed to be the King of the Jews (23:2-3, 38).

23:43 I assure you, today you will be with me. Jesus' death is salvific, as Stein has pointed out: "[That Jesus] died as a 'Savior' is clear (23:35-37, 39). The criminal was able to be saved precisely because Jesus did not save himself. Jesus' cross is intimately involved in his being able to 'seek and to save what was lost' (19:10) and to forgive sins (5:20-26; 7:36-50; Acts 10:39-43); in this account he is able to save even the 'most lost.' Tax collectors, prostitutes, the poor, the blind, and even criminals being executed for their crimes are able in the eleventh hour to find in Jesus an all-sufficient Savior" (1992:593).

paradise. This word (paradeisos [ᵀᴳ3857, ᶻᴳ4137]) came into Gr. as a loan word from the Persian language and occurs in two other places in the NT (2 Cor 12:4; Rev 2:7). "The original meaning was *enclosed park* or a *pleasure ground*, but it came to be used in the LXX as a term for the Garden of Eden [e.g., Gen 2:8-10; 13:10] and in the intertestamental period for a superterrestial place of blessedness [e.g., *Testament of Levi* 18:10-11]. As it is used here, it can mean only heaven or the presence of God" (Lindsell 1965:1579). Eventually, the word came to be used for the home of the righteous dead as well (2 Cor 12:4; Rev 2:7; cf. 22:1-2).

COMMENTARY

Roman execution by crucifixion involved an elaborate procedure. Usually the victim would be scourged; this in itself was a brutal and dehumanizing operation carried out by hardened soldiers. This was frequently followed by the victim carrying the crossbeam through the streets to the site of execution, which was always a public place. The person was then stripped and his clothing given to the executioners. Next, the victim was tied or nailed to the cross beam, after which the beam was lifted up and the feet secured. Finally, there was the posting of the superscription over the cross to indicate the person's offence for all passersby to see and take as a warning.

Martin Hengel has described the procedure in his monumental study, *Crucifixion in the Ancient World and the Folly of the Message of the Cross* (1977). The person crucified naturally suffered from the beating, exposure to the elements, loss of blood, maltreatment, dehydration, insects, and impaired circulation, and ultimately died of shock or asphyxiation as the process of breathing became increasingly difficult and exhausting. It was a horrible and slow way to die. Often the person was refused burial as a further disgrace, and the body was left on the cross to rot or to be food for birds of prey. Josephus, an eyewitness account of a Roman siege of Jerusalem, "observes how hundreds of Jewish prisoners were 'scourged and subjected to torture of every description . . . , and then crucified opposite the city walls.' Hoping that the gruesome sight might induce the Jews to surrender the city, Titus, the Roman commander, gave his soldiers freedom to continue the crucifixions as they pleased. 'The soldiers out of rage and hatred amused themselves by nailing their prisoners in different positions [Josephus War 5.11.1]'" (DJG 147).

The account of Jesus' crucifixion is quite simple and straightforward in the Synoptic accounts (23:26-32; Matt 27:32-44; Mark 15:21-32; cf. John 19:16-37). All three mention the role of Simon of Cyrene, who was seized by the soldiers and forced to carry the cross. Simon, a man from Cyrene in North Africa, was passing by as Jesus was carrying his cross. Mark notes that he was coming into the city of Jerusalem from the countryside (Mark 15:21). The soldiers seized him and compelled him to carry the cross (23:26; cf. Matt 5:41). Luke describes a considerable crowd that followed the procession to the place of execution, with many "grief-stricken women" among them (23:27), and he alone gave details of Jesus' conversation with the wailing women (23:27-31).

Luke notes the concern Jesus exercised for these upset women, as he predicted that terrible days were coming to the holy city and told them that they should weep for themselves rather than for him (23:28). They and their children would have to face apocalyptic conditions in the future that would be frightening. In the coming days, when Jerusalem would be invaded and surrounded by armies, they would beg the mountains, "Bury us," and plead with the hills, "Fall on us," because of the disastrous conditions they would meet and seek to escape (23:30; cf. Hos 10:8). The Roman masters of Jerusalem were crucifying Jesus in the spring, while the trees were green (23:31a), but what would happen later, when they became dry (23:31b)? "Spring is the time of sowing; fall, the time of reaping. Jerusalem is sowing seeds now that will bear a harvest of bitter fruits. Only three crosses pierced the landscape on that fateful day. But we are informed that the Roman conquerors crucified an untold number of Jews after the fall of Jerusalem" (Tolbert 1970:179). Tough times were indeed coming to the holy city, and the people were warned of the painful conditions that were about to descend upon them in consequence of their actions. Remember the words Jesus had spoken just a few days before: "Your enemies will not leave a single stone in place, because you did not accept your opportunity for salvation" (19:44).

The crucifixion scene reveals two others who were put to death with Jesus, both of them "criminals" (kakourgos [TG2557, ZG2806]; used only in 23:32-33 and in 2 Tim 2:9 in the NT). The three men who were being executed were taken to "a place called

The Skull" (sometimes called "Calvary," from *calvaria*, the Latin word for "skull"), a name probably suggested by the shape of the hill. John's Gospel also notes the "Place of the Skull," which in Hebrew is called "Golgotha" (John 19:17; cf. *gulgoleth* [TH1538, ZH1653]). The Romans were familiar with this cruel method of execution, which they had derived from the Persians and the Greeks, and had perfected as a means of torture and as a painful reminder to a subjugated people of the terrible consequences if they got out of line. The *titulus* or "signboard" over the cross usually contained the charge against the person and was a means of warning people not to commit similar offences lest they suffer the same fate.

In this case, the three men were nailed directly to the cross. Though sometimes ropes were used to tie those being executed, the actual word for "nail" (*hēlos* [TG2247, ZG2464]) is found twice in John 20:25 with reference to Jesus' crucifixion, thereby indicating that these victims were nailed to the cross. The two criminals were put to death by crucifixion too, one placed on each side of Jesus (23:33). It was an agonizing way to die, and sometimes people lasted for days on their crosses before they expired.

As Jesus was being executed, he prayed for the forgiveness of those who were putting him to death, declaring, "They don't know what they are doing" (see note on 23:34). In a very deep sense this was true, for they were putting to death the Savior of the world. He had come to his own people, and they had rejected him (John 1:11), and now he was dying "despised and rejected—a man of sorrows, acquainted with deepest grief," to borrow language from the fourth Servant Song of Isaiah (Isa 53:3).

One of the perks that came to the Roman executioners was taking possession of the garments of those they had executed. To do this, the soldiers on duty "gambled for his clothes by throwing dice" (23:34). All three Evangelists refer to the dividing of his garments and the casting of lots in an apparent allusion to Psalm 22:18 and its description of a righteous sufferer.

The irony of the whole gruesome scene came out as the crowd watched the grim spectacle and the leaders scoffed at the apparently helpless figure on the central cross. They jeered and hurled taunts at him, urging him to save himself just as he had delivered others in the past (23:35). But this is the irony that Luke depicts in the situation: it is precisely because he is the Savior that he had to give himself to the point of death. He is truly "God's Messiah, the Chosen One" (23:35, a point Luke has already noted in the Transfiguration, 9:35; cf. 3:22; 9:20), and he would prove to be the righteous Servant of the Lord, who poured out his life unto death.

The soldiers joined the taunting alongside Jesus' enemies, and then eventually they offered him a drink of sour wine or vinegar alongside their mockery (*oxos* [TG3690, ZG3954], a wine vinegar which was a favorite drink of soldiers and the lower classes of society). Such an act is mentioned in Psalm 69:21. Offers of wine mixed with myrrh or gall are mentioned in the other Gospel accounts where Matthew and Mark show that Jesus refused to take the wine which would dull the pain, thereby accepting the pain of his death fully (Matt 27:34; Mark 15:22-23). It is unclear whether Luke here refers to the same offer of a drink. In John's account, Jesus seemingly requests a drink and is given the *oxos* (John 19:28-29). John has several other additional details in the scene, including Jesus' commitment of his mother to the care of the beloved disciple (John 19:26-27), the anguished cry "I am thirsty" (John 19:28), and the highly significant remark of Jesus after he had tasted the sour wine, "It is finished!" (John 19:30).

All three Synoptic accounts note that the inscription of the charge over the cross referred to Jesus as "the King of the Jews" (23:38; Matt 27:37; Mark 15:26), and the same title appears in John's Gospel (John 19:19). The stubborn Roman governor, Pontius Pilate, refused to yield when challenged by the leading priests, who had demanded that he change the charge to read, "He said, I am the King of the Jews" (John 19:21-22).

All three Synoptics observe the railing and reviling Jesus endured from the other prisoners who were being executed at the same time. Only Luke mentions the debate between the two criminals, one demanding that Jesus release them, and the other confessing his sins, acknowledging the justice of the sentence against him, and humbly asking Jesus for mercy (23:39-43). Perceiving Jesus as one who had done no wrong, this penitent criminal asked, "Jesus, remember me when you come into your Kingdom" (23:42). This seems to be a tacit recognition that Jesus' Kingdom is "not of this world"—a point explicitly recognized in John 18:36. The response of Jesus was significant in that it recognized both the fact of their imminent deaths and the assurance that the penitent man would be with him after death (23:43). Paradise, the destination promised to the penitent thief, was the place where the righteous went at the time of their death and was associated with blessedness (cf. 16:22-23, where the reference is lit. to "Abraham's bosom").

◆ **R. The Death of Jesus (23:44-49; cf. Matt 27:45-56; Mark 15:33-41; John 19:28-37)**

⁴⁴By this time it was noon, and darkness fell across the whole land until three o'clock. ⁴⁵The light from the sun was gone. And suddenly, the curtain in the sanctuary of the Temple was torn down the middle. ⁴⁶Then Jesus shouted, "Father, I entrust my spirit into your hands!"* And with those words he breathed his last.

⁴⁷When the Roman officer* overseeing the execution saw what had happened, he worshiped God and said, "Surely this man was innocent.*" ⁴⁸And when all the crowd that came to see the crucifixion saw what had happened, they went home in deep sorrow.* ⁴⁹But Jesus' friends, including the women who had followed him from Galilee, stood at a distance watching.

23:46 Ps 31:5.   23:47a Greek *the centurion.*   23:47b Or *righteous.*   23:48 Greek *went home beating their breasts.*

NOTES

23:45 *The light from the sun was gone.* An ancient historian named Thallus composed a history of the Eastern Mediterranean world covering the period from the Trojan War to his own time. While his writing has been lost, some fragments of it occur in the citations of other writers, including Julius Africanus, who wrote around AD 220. Africanus, speaking of the crucifixion of Jesus and the darkness that enveloped the land during this event, refers to the account of Thallus and asserts: "Thallus, in the third book of his histories, explains away the darkness as an eclipse of the sun—unreasonably, as it seems to me" (as cited in Bruce 1960:1130). As Habermas has commented: "Julius Africanus objected to Thallus' rationalization concerning the darkness which fell on the land at the time of the crucifixion because an eclipse could not take place during the time of the full moon, as was the case during the Jewish Passover season" (1984:93-94). The passage might recall Amos 8:9, which says, "I will make the sun go down at noon and darken the earth while it is still day." See also Joel 2:31, a passage that is quoted by Peter on the day of Pentecost (Acts 2:20).

the curtain in the sanctuary of the Temple was torn down the middle. Sylva (1986) has pointed out that in Luke's account, the Temple curtain being torn precedes Jesus' death, while in Mark the curtain is torn after Jesus' death. He thinks Luke's purpose for this change was not to indicate the Temple's destruction but rather to present the last moment of Jesus' life as one of communion with his Father in the Temple.

23:46 *Father, I entrust my spirit into your hands!* This final proclamation comes from Ps 31:5. "The suitability of this psalm to Jesus' passion is obvious: Jesus, the son of David (1:32; 18:38), has been falsely accused, entrapped, scorned, betrayed, and now, hanging on the cross, faces death. . . . The specific verse that the Lukan Jesus has quoted was employed as a prayer before going to sleep (*Numbers Rabbah* 20:20; *Midrash Psalms* 25.2). It was a prayer that God protect one's spirit until one awakens. 'Sleep' could mean either literally sleep or figuratively death. . . . Thus understood, Ps. 31:5 is particularly suitable for the dying Jesus" (Evans 1990:344).

23:47 *Surely this man was innocent.* Morris is correct to say that "Matthew and Mark have 'Son of God', but the sense in which a Roman would have used the term is better given in Luke's words. Plummer paraphrases, 'He was a good man, and quite right in calling God His Father'" (1974:330). Luke's form of the centurion's statement once again affirms the innocence of Jesus, "an innocence recognized by a second Roman (Pilate being the first, see vv. 4, 13-16, 22)" (Evans 1990:343).

COMMENTARY

The phenomena accompanying the death of Jesus are mentioned in all three Synoptic accounts. Matthew is the fullest account and mentions the tearing of the Temple veil, an earthquake, the opening of the tombs, the restoration of some of God's people who had died, the entrance of these resuscitated saints into Jerusalem, and their appearance to many in the city (Matt 27:51-53), drawing attention in this way to the cataclysmic nature of what had taken place in the resurrection of Jesus and its accompanying signs.

All three Synoptic accounts note the unusual darkness over the whole land from the sixth hour until the ninth hour (that is, from noon to 3 p.m.). Evans has noted, "This darkness is probably a vivid illustration of Jesus' reference to his arrest as an 'hour when darkness reigns' (22:53). It may also be a portent that foreshadows the strange phenomena that accompany Jesus' return as 'Son of Man' (21:25)" (1990:343-344). At this time, "the curtain in the sanctuary of the Temple was torn down the middle"—a striking feature that is noted in all three accounts (23:45; Matt 27:51; Mark 15:38). The Letter to the Hebrews also notes the rending of the veil or curtain in the Temple and relates it theologically to the notion that Jesus' death provided a new way of access to God (Heb 9:7-8; 10:19-22).

All three accounts also note the response of the centurion (and other soldiers, in Matthew) to the remarkable events he had witnessed. In Mark's version, the remarks of the centurion serve as the climax of the whole Gospel, and, significantly, his insight was gained at the crucifixion as he saw how Jesus had died. "This man," he declared, "truly was the Son of God!" (Mark 15:39). The light dawned on the Roman official at the foot of the cross. Matthew's treatment is very similar and links the crucifixion with the terror that had come "by the earthquake and all that had happened" leading to the same magnificent confession: "This man truly was the Son of God!" (Matt 27:54). Luke's version stresses the innocence of Jesus, who had died as the Righteous Sufferer: "Surely this man was innocent" (23:47). This strong declaration that Jesus was not guilty of the charges laid against him agrees with the earlier threefold declaration of Jesus' innocence—a point of agreement in both Luke and John (23:4, 14, 22; John 18:38; 19:4, 6).

Matthew and Mark both mention Jesus' agonizing cry of dereliction, Matthew citing it in Hebrew and Mark in Aramaic, both drawing on the opening words of Psalm 22, a psalm describing a righteous sufferer, which ends in praise to God and salvation offered to all (Ps 22:22-31). Christian interpreters have long understood this psalm as messianic, depicting Jesus as the "good shepherd," who "sacrifices his life for the sheep" (John 10:11). Matthew and Mark observe that some of the bystanders interpret the cry as a call to Elijah; indeed, Mark's graphic account notes the comment of one observer at the scene of the crucifixion, "Wait! . . . Let's see whether Elijah comes to take him down!" (Mark 15:36). At this point in both Matthew and Mark, Jesus uttered another loud cry and breathes his last (Matt 27:50; Mark 15:37). Luke's account notes the loud cry or shout, which included Jesus' prayer of final commitment, "Father, I entrust my spirit into your hands!" (23:46).

This final prayer from the cross is biblical, rooted in Psalm 31:5, a prayer of lamentation and thanksgiving (see note on 23:46). According to a long tradition, this was the seventh and last of Jesus' utterances during his crucifixion. Those utterances are:

1. the word of forgiveness: "Father, forgive them." (23:34)
2. the word of salvation: "Today you will be with me in paradise." (23:43)
3. the word of affection: "Woman, here is your son," and "Here is your mother." (John 19:26-27)
4. the word of despair: "My God, my God, why have you abandoned me?" (Matt 27:46; Mark 15:34)
5. the word of physical torment: "I am thirsty." (John 19:28)
6. the word of triumph: "It is finished!" (John 19:30)
7. the word of committal: "Father, I entrust my spirit into your hands!" (23:46)

Before concluding the section on Jesus' death, Luke added a touching note to his account. He related that the multitudes who had witnessed the crucifixion of Jesus returned to their homes literally "beating their breasts" in deep sorrow (23:48; cf. NLT mg). The reference to Jesus' friends, "including the women who had followed him from Galilee" (23:49), recalls the women mentioned earlier in Jesus' tour of the towns and villages of Galilee, when a number of women are named as accompanying Jesus, namely, Mary Magdalene, Joanna, Susanna, and others (8:1-3). These followers had been helpful in contributing their own resources to support Jesus and his disciples, and they had trudged along loyally as Jesus entered Jerusalem for the final time. They stood at a distance watching the whole gruesome scene, sad at the execution of the one on whom they had pinned their hopes (cf. 24:21).

◆ S. The Burial of Jesus (23:50-56; cf. Matt 27:57-61; Mark 15:42-47; John 19:38-42)

⁵⁰Now there was a good and righteous man named Joseph. He was a member of the Jewish high council, ⁵¹but he had not agreed with the decision and actions of the other religious leaders. He was from the town of Arimathea in Judea, and he was waiting for the Kingdom of God to come. ⁵²He went to Pilate and asked for Jesus' body. ⁵³Then he took the body down from the cross and wrapped it in a long sheet of linen cloth and laid it in a new tomb that had been carved out of rock. ⁵⁴This was done late on Friday afternoon, the day of preparation,* as the Sabbath was about to begin.

⁵⁵As his body was taken away, the women from Galilee followed and saw the tomb where his body was placed. ⁵⁶Then they went home and prepared spices and ointments to anoint his body. But by the time they were finished the Sabbath had begun, so they rested as required by the law.

23:54 Greek *It was the day of preparation.*

NOTES

23:53 *he took the body down . . . and laid it in a new tomb.* The customary Jewish interment procedure following death is well known. It included the closing of the eyes and binding of the mouth of the deceased, and the washing and anointing of the body (cf. *Gospel of Peter* 6:24; *m. Sanhedrin* 13:5). "The warm climate dictated a speedy burial, with the use of spices necessary to counter the stench of decomposition. The deceased were buried in their own clothes or in specially prepared wraps (cf. Mark 15:46; John 19:40; *Gospel of Peter* 6:24). The tomb was closed off by a large rock held in place by a smaller stone. After a twelve-month period of decomposition, the bones were collected and placed in an ossuary" (DJG 88-92). For more information on what Jewish burial practices reveal about the beginning of the Christian movement, see Evans 2003.

23:54 *This was done late on Friday afternoon, the day of preparation.* This was the day on which Jews made the required preparations for the observance of the Sabbath, a day when no work was permitted (cf. Matt 27:62; Mark 15:42; John 19:42). The Jewish Sabbath began at sundown, so the burial of Jesus was completed before the sun went down on Friday.

COMMENTARY

All four Gospels record the death of Jesus. John took particular care to underscore the fact that the death was verified by a Roman soldier whose professional responsibility included the certification of death before the crucifixion was completed (John 19:34-35). Mark's description is the longest, partly because he, like John, wanted to affirm that Pilate had inquired from the Roman military officer that Jesus was dead and had carefully checked out this matter with the centurion in charge of the execution, before releasing the body to Joseph of Arimathea, an honored member of the Jewish high council (Mark 15:42-45; cf. John 19:38).

All four Gospels refer to the role of Joseph of Arimathea (a town in Judea) in taking possession of the body of Jesus and providing a burial place for him. They all describe Joseph in favorable terms. Mark said he was a respected leader (Mark 16:43), Matthew considered him a "disciple of Jesus" (Matt 27:57), and John said he was a "secret disciple" (John 19:38). Luke described the character of Joseph, calling him "a good and righteous man," and specifically excluded him from consenting to the council's decision to execute Jesus (23:50-51). His spiritual sensitivity was also noted, for "he was waiting for the Kingdom of God to come" (23:51; cf. 2:25-32, 36-38).

All the Gospel accounts except Mark mention the fact that the tomb was a new one, never used before (23:53; Matt 27:60; John 19:41). The Synoptics speak with one voice in noting that the tomb was hewn out of the rock (23:53; Matt 27:60; Mark 15:46), and John added that the "place of crucifixion was near a garden" (John 19:41). Each of the Synoptics describe the linen shroud that Joseph used to wrap around the body of Jesus (23:53; Matt 27:59; Mark 15:46), and both Luke and John talk of the spices that were used, John noting that this was customary in Jewish burial practice (John 19:39-40) and Luke referring to the women from Galilee returning to the tomb after they had prepared spices and ointments (23:56–24:1). Rarely do the canonical Gospels come closer to one another than in their recounting of the death and burial of Jesus. Significantly, Luke rounded out his account by noting that after the women had prepared the spices, "they rested as required by the law" in order to respect the Sabbath (23:56; cf. Exod 20:8-10; 31:14; 35:2-3).

◆   T. The Resurrection of Jesus (24:1-12; cf. Matt 28:1-10;
    Mark 16:1-8; John 20:1-10)

But very early on Sunday morning* the women went to the tomb, taking the spices they had prepared. ²They found that the stone had been rolled away from the entrance. ³So they went in, but they didn't find the body of the Lord Jesus. ⁴As they stood there puzzled, two men suddenly appeared to them, clothed in dazzling robes. ⁵The women were terrified and bowed with their faces to the ground. Then the men asked, "Why are you looking among the dead for someone who is alive? ⁶He isn't here! He is risen from the dead! Remember what he told you back in Galilee, ⁷that the Son of Man* must be betrayed into the hands of sinful men and be cruci-

fied, and that he would rise again on the third day."

⁸Then they remembered that he had said this. ⁹So they rushed back from the tomb to tell his eleven disciples—and everyone else—what had happened. ¹⁰It was Mary Magdalene, Joanna, Mary the mother of James, and several other women who told the apostles what had happened. ¹¹But the story sounded like nonsense to the men, so they didn't believe it. ¹²However, Peter jumped up and ran to the tomb to look. Stooping, he peered in and saw the empty linen wrappings; then he went home again, wondering what had happened.

24:1 Greek *But on the first day of the week, very early in the morning.*   24:7 "Son of Man" is a title Jesus used for himself.

NOTES

24:1 *very early on Sunday morning the women went to the tomb.* The four Gospels all place the women at the tomb of Jesus early on Sunday morning, where they see the evidence of his resurrection (24:1; Matt 28:1; Mark 16:2; cf. John 20:1, which has only Mary Magdalene at the tomb). Comparison of the accounts of all four Gospels, however, raises many questions due to differences in the accounts. None of the Gospels claims to be exhaustive; rather, the accounts should be taken to supplement one another. Further, there are differences due to the differing perspectives of the Evangelists and their unique literary styles and themes; each chose to include certain events or aspects of the resurrection accordingly.

As an example, we may note that Luke mentions "two men" (24:4), Mark "a young man" (Mark 16:5), Matthew "an angel" (Matt 28:5), and John speaks of "two white-robed angels" (John 20:12). Matthew, stressing the supernatural, transcendent element, noted the power and splendor of the angel and the overwhelming force of "a great earthquake" (Matt 28:2-4). Mark included a note that showed the Lord's concern for Peter (Mark 16:7). Luke highlights the phrase "behold two men" (24:4 RSV) to link together the Transfiguration, the Resurrection, and the Ascension (see 9:30; 24:4; Acts 1:10 [Trites 1987a:78]). John, by contrast, mentions the undisturbed condition of the grave clothes, a point that impressed him as having evidential value (John 20:5-9).

Many more issues and influencing factors for the differences could be considered, but it suffices to say here that a reasonable case can be made for the reliability of the resurrection accounts while we must, at the same time, affirm that these historical documents are each shaped by unique literary and theological concerns. For a detailed, judicious assessment of the evidence furnished by the Gospels, see Osborne 1984.

24:7 *he would rise again on the third day.* The predicted resurrection of the Son of Man is mentioned repeatedly in the Gospels (e.g., 12:50; 17:25; John 2:19-22) and is strongly asserted in the passion predictions (Matt 16:21; 17:22; 20:18-19; Mark 8:31; 9:31; 10:33-34). This theme is certainly present in Luke's passion predictions (9:22, 44; 18:31-33). Repeatedly in these passages, there is a constant expectation of a resurrection on "the third day." The OT background for the idea of the third day includes Jonah 1:17 (cf. 11:29-30; Matt 12:40) and Hos 6:2. For more on the resurrection theme, see Longenecker 1998; Osborne 1984; Perkins 1984a; Wright 1992:320-334. For up-to-date summaries of current thinking, see DJG 673-688. For a simple, clear presentation of the apologetic grounds for Christian belief in the resurrection of Jesus, see Stott 1968:45-59.

24:11 *the story sounded like nonsense.* While some commentators have pointed out that the testimony of women was not acceptable in Jewish courts of law (Josephus *Antiquities* 4.219; *m. Rosh Hashana* 1:8), clearly the women weren't testifying in court here but simply passing on a message to the apostles. Nonetheless, the apostles thought they had hallucinated. Craddock's comment here is helpful: "That the apostles did not believe the report should not be explained by saying it was because the report was given by women (24:11). There has been too much of such flippancy; no doubt men bringing the same report would have met the same unbelief. Their faith waits on a confirming experience of the risen Christ, an experience that was not without its own element of unbelief (24:41). In the meantime, v. 11 reminds all of us who celebrate Easter so easily what a burden the resurrection of the dead places on faith, even among those close to Jesus" (1990:283).

so they didn't believe it. Concerning the strong unbelief noted in this account, Luke uses the rare word *apisteō* [TG569, ZG601] ("refuse to believe") three times, twice to underscore the apostles' refusal to exercise faith (24:11, 41) and once at the end of Acts, where Paul meets the Jewish leaders and convinces some, while others "did not believe" (Acts 28:24). When Jesus appeared later to the disciples in Jerusalem, he challenged their doubts by asking,

"Why are your hearts filled with doubt?" (24:38). Unbelief after the resurrection is also noted in Matt 28:17 (cf. Mark 16:11, 14).

24:12 *Peter jumped up and ran to the tomb to look. Stooping, he peered in.* Codex Bezae alone excludes this verse. Westcott and Hort thought this omission and others in Luke (24:3, 36, 51, 52) were "Western non-interpolations" and therefore original. Nearly all textual critics refute this notion. Indeed, all the other witnesses (including the earliest, namely 𝔓75 ℵ B A W) include 24:12 and the other verses.

C O M M E N T A R Y

In theological terms, the resurrection of Jesus was God's vindication of Jesus in four vital respects: (1) it "vindicated the messiahship of Jesus" (cf. Mark 14:61-62; Acts 2:31-32; 3:13-15; 4:10-11; 1 Pet 1:3); (2) it "vindicated and confirmed the sonship of Jesus" (cf. Matt 11:27; 27:4; Rom 1:3-4; 1 Pet 1:21); (3) it "vindicated the work of Jesus" (cf. John 19:30; Acts 5:31; 1 Tim 3:16); and (4) it "vindicated his followers and his Father" (cf. Mark 10:28; Luke 22:28; Acts 13:34; 1 Cor 15:20). (For further elaboration on these four points, see M. Harris 1990:165-170.)

The conviction that Jesus conquered death and was raised by the Father on the third day is basic to Christianity, as Paul clearly saw: "If our hope in Christ is only for this life, we are more to be pitied than anyone in the world. But in fact, Christ has been raised from the dead" (1 Cor 15:19-20). It was on the strength of this conviction that Paul gave himself so utterly and completely to the declaration of the risen Lord throughout the Roman world.

The evidence for the resurrection of Jesus stands on the basis of five great convictions that are of the greatest apologetic significance: (1) the tomb was empty; (2) the grave clothes of Jesus were undisturbed; (3) Jesus was seen alive by multiple people after his crucifixion (cf. Mark 16:1-8; Matt 28:16-20; Luke 24:13-24; 1 Cor 15:5-8); (4) the disciples were changed; and (5) the church has survived (Stott 1968:45-59). We will explore these assertions, particularly noting how they are reflected in Luke's writings.

One item (point 2) should be noted at the outset here, and that concerns the undisturbed condition of the grave clothes. This feature is explored principally in John's Gospel, but briefly noted in Luke's account. In Luke, Peter runs to investigate the tomb, where he stoops, peers into the tomb, sees the empty linen wrappings, and then goes home again, "wondering what had happened" (Luke 24:12). In John's Gospel, an unnamed disciple who had run to the tomb just ahead of Peter finally goes in and is impressed by the remarkable condition of the linen wrappings lying there, since grave robbers would not have left the wrappings behind. The evidence of the cocoon-like shape of the empty grave clothes convinced this man that a miracle had taken place—namely, Jesus' conquest over death: "He saw and believed" (John 20:3-9).

Regarding point 4, the change in the disciples becomes evident in the book of Acts after they receive the Spirit and power promised by Jesus before his ascension (see Acts 1:8). Before Pentecost, the disciples were fearful, apprehensive, and lacking in courage to share their message about the risen Christ. After Pentecost, they were empowered to communicate their faith as Jesus had promised. It was the power of the risen Lord at work in the lives of the disciples that was observed in their boldness, courage, and tenacity in the book of Acts.

On the survival of the church (point 5), we have the fact that the living Lord has been with his people throughout the ups and downs of two thousand years of church history, vindicating his promise to the disciples that he would build his church and "all the powers of hell" would not "conquer it" (Matt 16:18; cf. Matt 28:20). The book of Acts offers an important piece of evidence here. It shows the presence of the risen Lord with his people in the days of the early church, energizing and equipping them by his mighty Spirit and enabling them to work unflinchingly in the interest of the Great Commission (see Acts 1:8; cf. 9:15; 23:11; 26:15-18).

Now, let us examine the key evidence—the empty tomb (point 1). While the women had obeyed the Sabbath commandment (23:56b), their spices had already been prepared before the Sabbath had commenced (23:56a), so they were anxious to finish their embalming of the body very early on the first day of the week (a Sunday, 24:1). In the early morning, they arrived at the tomb with their spices and found, to their surprise, that "the stone had been rolled away from the entrance" (24:2). Taking an opportunity to go inside the tomb, they were confronted with its emptiness, for "they didn't find the body of the Lord Jesus" as they had expected (24:3). In the midst of their perplexity, they saw two men dressed in "dazzling robes" (24:4), which suggests their mysterious nature; indeed, they were angels whose visages looked like men. Apparently, Luke was fond of the phrase, "behold two men" (a literal rendering), for he had already used it with reference to the appearance of Moses and Elijah at the Transfiguration of Jesus (9:30), and he uses it again of the two angels at the beginning of Acts, in his account of the Ascension (Acts 1:10). In 24:4, the presence of the two men suggests that the principle of multiple witness, which is important generally in the Bible, was being honored once again (cf. Num 35:30; Deut 17:6; 19:15; John 5:31; 2 Cor 13:1; 1 Tim 5:19; Heb 10:28). Clearly it was a matter of the greatest importance that the resurrection of Jesus should be properly attested and the Jewish rules of evidence satisfied.

Luke drew attention to the fear the women experienced when they found the tomb empty and met the mysterious men who confronted them in dazzling robes. In their timidity, they "bowed with their faces to the ground" (24:5). Such a posture is expressed elsewhere in the Bible in the face of an overwhelming divine revelation (Ezek 1:28; Dan 8:18; 10:8-9, 17-19; Rev 1:17). They were challenged by the two men not to waste their time looking for "someone who is alive" among the dead (24:5) and were told forcefully that Jesus wasn't there, but had risen from the dead (24:6). Indeed, they were reminded of the previous words of Jesus—that the whole scenario of his betrayal, crucifixion, and resurrection on the third day was part of the divine plan for the Son of Man (24:6-7). Despite their evident perplexity, God's purposes were proceeding according to plan, and this jogging of their memories helped them recall that their Lord had, in fact, prepared them in advance during his Galilean ministry for all that had happened in recent days (24:8; cf. 9:22; 18:31-33).

As the women recalled the things Jesus had told them, which had now been ful-filled, they were naturally eager to share the news of the empty tomb with the eleven disciples and their friends, for the truth of the resurrection was beginning to grip them (24:10). These messengers of the good news of the risen Lord who are men-tioned—the two Marys, Joanna, and several others—probably are the same group of women mentioned in Luke 8:1-3 (those women who accompanied Jesus and the disciples during their Galilean ministry and helped to support them with their con-tributions). Susanna is not mentioned here directly, unless she is included in the general reference "and several other women" (24:10). Sadly, their message was ini-tially met with unbelief by the apostles, who thought the women were suffering from delusions after the crucifixion had apparently put an end to their messianic hopes (see note on 24:11). It should be noted that women were not permitted to serve as witnesses in Jewish courts of law (*m. Rosh HaShanah* 1:8). Despite this, and in contrast with Paul's list of post-resurrection appearances (1 Cor 15:3-9), the role of women as witnesses is specifically mentioned in each of the Gospel resurrection accounts. The fact that there is no attempt to mask the fact that women were the first witnesses of the risen Lord points to the authenticity of the resurrection accounts.

◆ U. The Walk to Emmaus (24:13-34)

¹³That same day two of Jesus' followers were walking to the village of Emmaus, seven miles* from Jerusalem. ¹⁴As they walked along they were talking about everything that had happened. ¹⁵As they talked and discussed these things, Jesus himself suddenly came and began walk-ing with them. ¹⁶But God kept them from recognizing him.

¹⁷He asked them, "What are you dis-cussing so intently as you walk along?"

They stopped short, sadness written across their faces. ¹⁸Then one of them, Cleopas, replied, "You must be the only person in Jerusalem who hasn't heard about all the things that have happened there the last few days."

¹⁹"What things?" Jesus asked.

"The things that happened to Jesus, the man from Nazareth," they said. "He was a prophet who did powerful miracles, and he was a mighty teacher in the eyes of God and all the people. ²⁰But our leading priests and other religious leaders handed him over to be condemned to death, and they crucified him. ²¹We had hoped he

was the Messiah who had come to rescue Israel. This all happened three days ago.

²²"Then some women from our group of his followers were at his tomb early this morning, and they came back with an amazing report. ²³They said his body was missing, and they had seen angels who told them Jesus is alive! ²⁴Some of our men ran out to see, and sure enough, his body was gone, just as the women had said."

²⁵Then Jesus said to them, "You foolish people! You find it so hard to believe all that the prophets wrote in the Scriptures. ²⁶Wasn't it clearly predicted that the Messiah would have to suffer all these things before entering his glory?" ²⁷Then Jesus took them through the writings of Moses and all the prophets, explaining from all the Scriptures the things con-cerning himself.

²⁸By this time they were nearing Emma-us and the end of their journey. Jesus acted as if he were going on, ²⁹but they begged him, "Stay the night with us, since it is getting late." So he went home with

them. ³⁰As they sat down to eat,* he took the bread and blessed it. Then he broke it and gave it to them. ³¹Suddenly, their eyes were opened, and they recognized him. And at that moment he disappeared! ³²They said to each other, "Didn't our hearts burn within us as he talked with us on the road and explained the Scriptures to us?" ³³And within the hour they were on their way back to Jerusalem. There they found the eleven disciples and the others who had gathered with them, ³⁴who said, "The Lord has really risen! He appeared to Peter.*"

24:13 Greek *60 stadia* [11.1 kilometers]. 24:30 Or *As they reclined.* 24:34 Greek *Simon.*

NOTES

24:13 *two of Jesus' followers were walking to the village of Emmaus.* This is another travel narrative with a theological message—leave in defeat, return in triumph and joy— told by Luke with consummate literary skill. Freedman explains the importance of this post-resurrection recognition story that appears only in Luke:

> [It] conveys a distinctive Lukan emphasis on the appearance of Jesus: Luke combines Jesus' appearance with a meal and prophecy. Jesus appears without being recognized, and the disciples' eyes are opened only when Jesus takes, blesses, breaks, and distributes bread (cf. Luke 9:16; 22:19; also 24:41-43). Yet Jesus does not share the meal; he vanishes when the pair recognize him. Other Lukan passages also show Jesus attending meals (9:10-17; 22:14-38; Acts 10:41), and the table provides a key gathering place for the Church (Acts 2:42, 46; 20:7; 27:33-36). . . . The Emmaus account also emphasizes the importance of prophecy. The disciples remember Jesus as a prophet mighty in deed and word and recall their disappointment that he had been killed. But Jesus rebukes them, explaining that the Messiah's suffering had been indicated by Moses and the prophets. (2000:405)

seven miles from Jerusalem. The Emmaus story begins and ends in Jerusalem; Luke alone among the Synoptics places all the post-resurrection appearances in the vicinity of the holy city. As the NLT mg indicates, the Gr. text refers to 60 stadia, a distance of 11.1 kilometers.

24:16 Note that God sovereignly ordained when they should recognize Jesus. Cf. 24:31.

24:18 *Cleopas.* This is the sole mention of Cleopas in the Bible, unless one interprets John 19:25 as referring to the same man named Clopas, whose wife was Mary. However, Evans is linguistically correct in asserting that Cleopas is "shortened of the Greek name *Cleopatros,* not to be confused with Clopas (a Semitic name) found in John 19:25" (1990:352). Cleopas was one of the disciples of Jesus (note the implication of their recognizing him in "breaking the bread" in 24:35 and the possibility of their recalling Jesus' feeding of the 5,000 in 9:10-17), and he had, with his companion, a memorable conversation with Jesus on the road to Emmaus after the resurrection. The other person who was with Cleopas is not named, but the fact that they apparently shared a common home (24:29) has suggested the possibility that the unknown person was Cleopas's wife. The two disciples were despondent when Jesus joined them on the walk, but Jesus' explanation of the Scriptures brought them enlightening instruction, and later, awestruck recognition.

24:25 *all that the prophets wrote in the Scriptures.* The fulfillment theme is strongly presented in 24:6-7, 25-27, 44. The "Scriptures" Jesus referred to might have included Pss 16:9-11; 132:11; Isa 7:14; 9:6-7; 40:10-11; 50:6; 52:13-53:12; Jer 23:5-6; 33:14-16; Dan 9:24-26; Mic 5:2-4; Zech 9:9. The fulfillment motif is important in the preaching of Acts as well (Acts 2:16-21, 25-35; 13:27; 26:22-23; 28:23-28).

24:27 *Then Jesus took them through the writings of Moses and all the prophets, explaining from all the Scriptures the things concerning himself.* "Speaking to faithful Jews, Jesus worked right through the Law (Genesis to Deuteronomy) into the prophets to show that it was actually necessary for the Christ to suffer and die (24:25-27). The necessity of Jesus, the Messiah, to come to die for his people and thus redeem them from their sin has become a foundation stone of classical Christianity" (Gardner 1995:104-105). On the methods Jesus used in handling the Scriptures, see Kimball (1994).

COMMENTARY

This incident, unique to Luke's Gospel, is placed on the same day as Jesus' resurrection (24:5-7). The village of Emmaus was located some seven miles northwest of Jerusalem (24:13). Two followers of Jesus were walking on this road and conversing quite naturally "about everything that had happened" in Jerusalem, particularly the sad and gruesome crucifixion of the Nazarene to whom they had given their allegiance, and from whom they expected the messianic deliverance to come (24:14). Jesus, unrecognized, joined them and began traveling on foot with them as they made their way toward Emmaus. He engaged them in conversation and drew out their thoughts on recent events concerning the man from Nazareth who had so recently been put to death.

From the perspective of Cleopas and his unnamed companion, Jesus "was a prophet who did powerful miracles, and he was a mighty teacher in the eyes of God and all the [Jewish] people" (24:19). Unfortunately, he had been persecuted by the religious authorities who had urged his death at the hands of the Roman officials (24:20). To the two erstwhile followers of Jesus, this had been a great disappointment, for it had ostensibly dashed all their high hopes for deliverance: "We had hoped he was the Messiah who had come to rescue Israel" (24:21). Their faith had slipped into the past tense, and they were disconsolate. However, some women from the Nazarene's followers had visited the tomb early that morning and had reported the amazing absence of Jesus' body from the tomb. They alleged that "they had seen angels who told them Jesus is alive!" (24:23). When the story was checked out by some men in the disciples' group, they affirmed that the body of Jesus was indeed "gone, just as the women had said" (24:24). This puzzling state of affairs had not quelled their disquiet (cf. 24:21), so they remained troubled and anxious, without an explanation that satisfied them or resolved their doubts.

At this point, Jesus intervened and rebuked their slowness to believe and their lack of understanding, since all of the recent events were in accordance with the teachings of the prophets as outlined in the Scriptures: " 'You foolish people! . . . Wasn't it clearly predicted that the Messiah would have to suffer all these things before entering his glory?' Then Jesus took them through the writings of Moses and all the prophets, explaining from all the Scriptures the things concerning himself" (24:25-27).

In the Pentateuch, Moses had predicted the coming of the prophet Messiah, who would bring deliverance to God's people: "The LORD your God will raise up for you a prophet like me from among your fellow Israelites. You must listen to him" (Deut 18:15, 18). Interestingly, this passage is quoted in Peter's second sermon in Acts 3:22 and given a strongly Christocentric interpretation as well. Jesus must have also recited and explained such passages as the Servant Songs of Isaiah (e.g., Isa 52:13–53:12). The Servant's glorious vindication would come in time, but, first, the suffering and humiliation must be accepted and endured.

The Messiah was to be understood not as a triumphal conqueror that would wipe out their enemies but as God's obedient servant, who would be humiliated, rejected, and killed. And yet, in some mysterious way, he would bring the redemption God had promised to his people and, ultimately, offer a message of Good News for the whole world (see Ps 22; Isa 53; Zech 13:7; cf. Acts 1:8; 2:23-32; 4:24-31; 9:15).

The journey to Emmaus was drawing to a close, and the two conversation partners invited the mysterious stranger to join them, when he would have gone on his way. They urged him to stay for the night, "since it was getting late," and he agreed to accept their invitation (24:29). As they began to share a meal together, Jesus "took the bread and blessed it. Then he broke it and gave it to them" (24:30). Obviously, there was something characteristic about his actions at the supper that triggered their memories, for immediately "their eyes were opened, and they recognized him" (24:31a). "The memories which Jesus' actions evoked must have been of other meals which he had held with his friends, perhaps, like the last supper, as anticipations of the messianic banquet of the kingdom" (Caird 1963:259).

Mysteriously, as soon as they perceived who Jesus was, he disappeared (24:31b). This unusual encounter with the one whom they had loved and followed and who had now revealed himself to them at the table was thrilling. They burst out in stunned amazement: "Didn't our hearts burn within us as he talked with us on the road and explained the Scriptures to us?" (24:32). Things began to make sense as they remembered the actual events of Jesus' life and recalled the wonderful scriptural background of the Messiah's ministry, which he had unfolded to them on that memorable walk from Jerusalem to Emmaus. Shortly, they were once again on the road, returning to Jerusalem to share with the eleven disciples and the other followers of Jesus the incredible encounter they had experienced with the risen one. But first they were greeted by a welcome report from the apostolic company who told them, "The Lord has really risen! He appeared to Peter" (24:34).

When the two from Emmaus had an opportunity to share their news, they told the story of Jesus' appearance to them on the road from Jerusalem to their village and how they had finally recognized him as he broke the bread. Doubtless, this encounter reminded them of earlier occasions when Jesus had fed the multitudes by the Sea of Galilee and when he had celebrated that last Passover with them and instituted the Lord's Supper (see 9:16; 22:15-20).

◆　V. Jesus Appears to the Disciples (24:35-49)

35Then the two from Emmaus told their story of how Jesus had appeared to them as they were walking along the road, and how they had recognized him as he was breaking the bread. 36And just as they were telling about it, Jesus himself was suddenly standing there among them. "Peace be with you," he said. 37But the whole group was startled and frightened, thinking they were seeing a ghost!

³⁸"Why are you frightened?" he asked. "Why are your hearts filled with doubt? ³⁹Look at my hands. Look at my feet. You can see that it's really me. Touch me and make sure that I am not a ghost, because ghosts don't have bodies, as you see that I do." ⁴⁰As he spoke, he showed them his hands and his feet.

⁴¹Still they stood there in disbelief, filled with joy and wonder. Then he asked them, "Do you have anything here to eat?" ⁴²They gave him a piece of broiled fish, ⁴³and he ate it as they watched.

⁴⁴Then he said, "When I was with you before, I told you that everything written about me in the law of Moses and the prophets and in the Psalms must be fulfilled." ⁴⁵Then he opened their minds to understand the Scriptures. ⁴⁶And he said, "Yes, it was written long ago that the Messiah would suffer and die and rise from the dead on the third day. ⁴⁷It was also written that this message would be proclaimed in the authority of his name to all the nations,* beginning in Jerusalem: 'There is forgiveness of sins for all who repent.' ⁴⁸You are witnesses of all these things.

⁴⁹"And now I will send the Holy Spirit, just as my Father promised. But stay here in the city until the Holy Spirit comes and fills you with power from heaven."

24:47 Or *all peoples.*

NOTES

24:36 *Jesus himself was suddenly standing there among them.* There are a total of ten or eleven post-resurrection appearances recorded in Scripture. Mark, followed by Matthew and Luke, mentions the appearance of Jesus to the women in Jerusalem (24:1-10; Matt 28:1-10; Mark 16:1-8). Luke, in addition, speaks of both the encounter on the road to Emmaus near Jerusalem and the special appearance to Peter (24:13-32, 34; cf. 1 Cor 15:5). John, in addition to the appearances to Mary Magdalene, the disciples at a commissioning scene behind locked doors, and Thomas, notes Simon Peter and another disciple running to check out the empty tomb in Jerusalem (John 20:1-10, 11-18, 19-23). Matthew records a great commission in Galilee (Matt 28:16-20; possibly the same occasion mentioned in 1 Cor 15:6), while John has an epilogue in which Jesus appears to seven disciples beside the Sea of Galilee (John 21:1-23). To sum up, there are appearances in Jerusalem and there are appearances in Galilee with John and Matthew having both, and there is no reason to affirm one set of appearances at the expense of the other. Acts 1:3 says they occurred over a forty-day period, which would help to account for the differences, seeing that each Evangelist would have recorded the events that fit his particular theological perspective (note, for instance, that 24:34ff closely parallels, but is different than, John 20:19ff).

24:39 *Touch me and make sure that I am not a ghost, because ghosts don't have bodies, as you see that I do.* "The bodily resurrection of Jesus is clearly set forth as a historical event in the New Testament. The Resurrection was necessary (1) to make possible the forgiveness of sins (1 Cor 15:17); (2) to fulfill the Scriptures (24:45-46); (3) to afford justification for believers (Rom 4:25; 8:34); (4) to furnish a solid basis for Christian hope (1 Cor 15:19)" (Lindsell 1965:1581).

24:42 *They gave him a piece of broiled fish.* On the possible apologetic significance of Jesus' eating a piece of broiled fish, as well as the significance of other physical details in Luke's Gospel, see Talbert 1966.

24:44 *everything written about me in the law of Moses and the prophets and in the Psalms must be fulfilled.* This theme has appeared frequently in Luke's Gospel. For instance, Jesus specifically predicted his ignominious suffering and death in Jerusalem, "where all the predictions of the prophets concerning the Son of Man will come true" (18:31-32). The predictions of the prophets also included the promise that "on the third day he will rise again" (18:33).

The OT Scriptures spoke of the Messiah's resurrection, and the NT made abundant use of this material in its preaching and teaching: see Ps 2:7 (cf. Acts 13:32-33); Ps 16:8-11 (Acts 2:25-31; 13:35-37); Hos 6:2 (1 Cor 15:4); Isa 53:10-12; 55:3 (cf. Acts 13:34); Jonah 1:17 (Matt 12:40). The "third day" is an idiom meaning, "after three days" (9:22; 13:22; 18:33; 24:7, 21, 46; Matt 20:19; Mark 9:31; 10:34; Acts 10:40; 1 Cor 15:4).

24:47 this message would be proclaimed in the authority of his name to all the nations. The great commission accounts of 24:46-49 and Acts 1:8 are formulated on the basis of the servant themes of Isaiah (e.g., Isa 42:1-9; 45:22; 49:6; 50:4-9). These themes are discussed by T. S. Moore (1997), who argues that this is Luke's way of showing that Jesus' mission as servant is continued by the disciples as they testify to God's saving actions in Christ.

COMMENTARY

For a full spectrum of the post-resurrection appearances of Jesus, the reader needs to look at all four Gospel accounts; a few other New Testament passages are also relevant. Matthew recorded two appearances: the first to Mary Magdalene and another Mary near the empty tomb outside Jerusalem, and the second to the eleven disciples on the mountain in Galilee (Matt 28:1-10, 16-20).

All the appearances mentioned in the Gospel of Mark occur in the textually suspect longer ending—namely, the appearances to Mary Magdalene at the tomb, to the disciples in the upper room, and to the disciples on the mountain in Galilee (Mark 16:9-11, 14, 15-18). These later additions to Mark are discussed by Metzger, who sums up a detailed discussion of the textual problem by concluding that "on the basis of good external evidence and strong internal considerations it appears that the earliest ascertainable form of the Gospel of Mark ended with 16:8" (1971:122-126).

John recorded four appearances: to Mary Magdalene at the tomb, to the ten disciples in the upper room, to the eleven disciples in the upper room, and to seven disciples fishing on the Sea of Galilee (John 20:11-18, 19-25, 26-31; 21:1-23).

Luke recorded Jesus' appearances to the two travelers on the road to Emmaus, to Peter in Jerusalem, to the gathering of disciples in Jerusalem, and at the Ascension on the Mount of Olives, thus having a total of four encounters, each of them located in the vicinity of Jerusalem (24:13-32, 34, 36-49, 50-53). In 1 Corinthians, Paul also indicates that the tradition passed down to him included four appearances—namely, to Peter, to the eleven disciples, to more than 500 at one time, and to James—plus the unique appearance to Paul "last of all" (1 Cor 15:5-8). There must have been other appearances, because Luke noted at the beginning of Acts that Jesus "appeared to the apostles from time to time, and proved to them in many ways that he was actually alive" (Acts 1:3). Acts also includes the Ascension, the last of the public appearances of Jesus (Acts 1:6-11; cf. Luke 24:50-53).

We have already commented on two of the four appearances mentioned in Luke—one to the two disciples on the way to Emmaus and one to Peter. The present passage recounts Jesus' appearance to the disciples gathered in Jerusalem. After the report of the first two appearances, the disciples' hopes were beginning to overcome the doubt and skepticism that had greeted the women when they came back from the empty tomb and the encounter with the angels (24:11). The message rang out strong and clear: "The Lord has really risen! He appeared to Peter" (24:34). And he had appeared to the two en route to Emmaus in just as convincing a fashion (24:35; see also 24:13-34 and the commentary on those verses).

Just as these two were relating their encounter with Jesus (24:35), the risen Lord showed himself, "suddenly standing there among them" (24:36). Apparently the Risen One was not bound by the same conditions that had characterized his earlier life, for now, once again, he appeared "suddenly," even as he had "suddenly" revealed himself in the Emmaus episode and immediately had disappeared (cf. 24:36 with 24:31). There was an element of transcendence and mystery in these encounters, so it was not surprising that the apostolic group was "startled and frightened, thinking they were seeing a ghost" (24:37). To borrow words from Rudolf Otto, they were exposed to a *mysterium tremendum et fascinans*—a mystery that produces both fear and awe, a mystery that attracts and repels by its very majesty. They were beholding the glory of God in the face of Jesus Christ (see 2 Cor 4:6).

Jesus confronted their fear and asked for the reason that had prompted it (24:38). He also perceived the doubt that yet remained in their hearts, despite the appearances he had graciously given his disciples. They were boldly challenged to consider the empirical evidence that he offered them: "Look at my feet. . . . Touch me. . . . Ghosts don't have bodies, as you see that I do" (24:39). These were evidential encounters they could not afford to miss. The Risen One took the initiative to reveal himself to them: "He showed them his hands and his feet," even as he addressed them and called them to check out the tangible evidence for themselves (24:39-40). Though the disciples were filled with joy and wonder, the presence of the risen Jesus was too much for them to grasp (24:41).

Faced with their disbelief, Jesus continued to present himself to them as a credible, living person. Wishing to make it clear that he was alive and had a real body, Jesus requested something to eat (24:41). This partaking of real food was a detail that had some apologetic significance for Luke, who notes that Jesus ate the broiled fish he was offered "as they watched" (24:43). The eyewitnesses present could vouch for the fact that this post-resurrection appearance was no delusion or apparition but a real encounter with an actual person who had eaten in their midst and whose reality could accordingly be attested by witnesses.

At this point in the episode, Jesus gave a second Scripture talk analogous to the one he had given to the two on the Emmaus road (24:44-49; cf. 24:25-27). All three parts of the Hebrew Bible were called upon in this master class of biblical exegesis— the Law of Moses, the Prophets, and the Writings (the third division of the Scriptures whose largest book is Psalms). Once again, Jesus stressed the fulfillment of the Scriptures, and once again he stressed his cardinal role in that fulfillment (24:44). This Christocentric focus was the grand theme of the lesson, and it resulted in opening their minds to understand that Christ himself, as Luther once said, was "Lord and King" of Scripture. The divine revelation given over the centuries anticipated and prepared the way for the coming of Christ, indicating that "the Messiah would suffer and die and rise from the dead on the third day" (24:46; see Ps 2:7; 16:8-11; Isa 53:10-12; 55:3; Hos 6:2; Jonah 1:17).

God was keeping his word to his people. Moreover, this message was to be proclaimed in Jesus' name "to all nations" as a redemptive story of universal significance (24:47). The starting point of outreach was Jerusalem, where it had all begun, but it would extend to all people (cf. Acts 1:8). Accordingly, the apostolic message proclaims good news for all who meet the conditions of faith and repentance: "There is forgiveness of sins for all who repent" (24:47; cf. Acts 2:38).

Then Jesus told the apostles, "You are witnesses of all these things" (24:48). They had been eyewitnesses of the whole public ministry of Jesus from the baptism of John to the Ascension, so they were qualified to certify the principal facts of the gospel story (cf. Acts 1:21-22). They were chosen by Christ to be the people who would valiantly endeavor to convince others of the truth of the gospel message and persuade them to repent and believe it for themselves so that they might know the joy of having their sins forgiven and of life in the family of God (cf. 1 John 1:2-3).

Jesus told these timid disciples to wait for the coming of the Holy Spirit, the energizer whom the Father had promised (24:49; cf. 11:13). To that end, they were instructed to remain in the city of Jerusalem "until the Holy Spirit comes and fills you with power from heaven" (24:49). That promise was fulfilled in a mighty way on the day of Pentecost, as Luke made abundantly clear in his second volume (Acts 2:1-13).

In the book of Acts, great emphasis is given to the Holy Spirit, who is mentioned well over fifty times. The Spirit's coming was indispensable to the church's mission and growth. Just prior to the Ascension, Jesus had told the apostles: "You will receive power when the Holy Spirit comes upon you. And you will be my witnesses, telling people about me everywhere—in Jerusalem, throughout Judea, in Samaria, and to the ends of the earth" (Acts 1:8). The Spirit's power came upon the prayerful company of 120 on the day of Pentecost (Acts 2:1-4) and was demonstrated in a large response to the gospel, with 3,000 people being "added to the church" (Acts 2:41). The Spirit's direction was evident in the choosing of Spirit-filled leaders (Acts 6:1-7) and in the launching of the mission to the Gentiles from Antioch, after fasting, worship, and prayer (Acts 13:1-5). Christian workers such as Philip and Stephen were energized by the Spirit and preached with divine power (Acts 6–8). Similarly, Paul's ministry, right from the start, was marked by his being filled with the Holy Spirit (Acts 9:17). In short, all the development and growth of the Christian community was guided, directed, and empowered by the Holy Spirit (e.g., Acts 2:4; 4:31; 5:32; 8:15-17, 29; 9:31; 10:44-46; 15:28; 16:6-7).

◆   W. The Ascension of Jesus (24:50-53; cf. Acts 1:6-11)

50Then Jesus led them to Bethany, and lifting his hands to heaven, he blessed them. 51While he was blessing them, he left them and was taken up to heaven.* 52So they worshiped him and then returned to Jerusalem filled with great joy. 53And they spent all of their time in the Temple, praising God.

24:51 Some manuscripts do not include *and was taken up to heaven.*

NOTES

24:50 Luke outlines at least five post-resurrection encounters: First, the frightened women encounter the two men in dazzling robes, run back to tell the eleven disciples, and then Peter and another disciple check out the tomb (24:1-12). Second, on that same day (Easter Sunday), the two travelers on the road to Emmaus have their unforgettable encounter with the risen Lord (24:13-32). Third, also on that same day, the eleven disciples report to the community that the Lord has appeared to Peter (24:34). The fourth appearance takes place that same Sunday evening to the ten disciples in the upper room (24:36-43). The fifth encounter Luke records takes place forty days later; it is the last appearance to the eleven disciples and their associates on the Mount of Olives (24:44-49; Acts 1:3-8). Luke tells his readers that during this forty-day period, Jesus "appeared to the apostles from time to time, and he proved to them in many ways that he was actually alive"; the theme of his conversation was "the Kingdom of God" (Acts 1:3).

24:51 *While he was blessing them, he left them and was taken up to heaven.* The Ascension is only related at the end of Luke's Gospel and at the beginning of the book of Acts, and this is one of many indications of the link between the two books. (On the issue of the unity of Luke–Acts, see Parsons and Pervo 1993, an examination of the generic unity, the narrative unity, and the theological unity of the two books—though, in an unwarranted fashion, they consider Acts a work of fiction). The Ascension provided a final occasion for commissioning the apostles (Acts 1:6-11; cf. Luke 24:45-53). Those who witnessed it returned to Jerusalem with a sense of praise, joy, and exhilaration (24:52). They believed their risen Lord would return again in power and great glory (Acts 1:11; cf. Matt 24:30; Mark 13:26; John 13:3). On Luke's use of the Ascension theme, see Heuschen 1965; Maile 1986; Parsons 1987.

COMMENTARY

It is worth comparing and contrasting the two Lukan accounts of the Ascension. In Luke, the Ascension is placed in Bethany, and Jesus leaves the disciples while blessing them and ascending up to heaven. Jesus is worshiped as he is received up, and the Gospel closes with the leaders returning to Jerusalem filled with great joy and spending their time praising God in the Temple (24:51-52). In Acts, the Ascension is discussed more fully. Jesus has demonstrated the reality of his physical resurrection for a period of forty days (Acts 1:3) and ascends "after giving his chosen apostles further instructions" (Acts 1:2). He promises to send the Holy Spirit to equip them for an ever-enlarging witness that will eventually spread through the whole world (Acts 1:8). After his ascension, two white-robed men (presumably angels) inform the apostles that Jesus has been taken into heaven, but will return at the appointed time to consummate the purposes of God (Acts 1:9-11).

The two accounts are complementary. The first account brings Luke's Gospel to a close on a characteristic note of joy and praise. The Gospel that begins with Zechariah in the Temple appropriately ends in the same place. Acts begins with a fitting reference to Theophilus that links the two volumes together (Acts 1:1; cf. Luke 1:1-4). It then places the Ascension in the context of a world mission, where the Spirit-endued apostles and their associates will carry out a bold witness for their Lord that will reach the ends of the earth. The ascended Lord will preside over his church in heaven until he comes again "for the time of the final restoration of all things" (Acts

3:21). The two accounts fit their contexts beautifully and offer helpful perspectives that supplement one another.

It is striking that the actual ascension of Jesus is recorded only at the end of Luke's Gospel and at the beginning of Acts, and nowhere else in the New Testament. This is one of many indications of links between the two books. In addition to the main passages in Luke and Acts, "there must be added the statements of Jesus recorded in the gospel of John which specifically anticipate the Ascension ([John] 6:62; 20:17 using *anabainō* [TG305, ZG326]) or which imply it through reference to the lifting up and glorification of Jesus ([John] 3:14; 7:39). In addition, the writer to the Hebrews insists that Jesus has entered the heavenly sanctuary as the High Priest ([Heb] 4:14; 6:19- 20; 9:12, 24)" (Toon 1984:6).

The ascension of Jesus is significant for several reasons: (1) this event is the last of the post-resurrection appearances of Jesus to the eleven (there was, of course, the special appearance to Paul, mentioned in 1 Cor 15:8); (2) it presents a final commissioning service for the apostles; (3) it marks the beginning of a mighty spiritual ministry in the age of the Spirit; (4) it depicts Christ going up to heaven, thereby suggesting his elevation to a position of supreme power and authority; (5) it anticipates the Christian's own glorious entrance into the presence of God, where our forerunner has gone (Heb 6:20; cf. John 12:26; 2 Cor 5:4; Phil 3:21); and (6) it reminds us of the promised return of Jesus Christ (Acts 1:11; see Trites 1984:23-24).

The conclusion of Luke's Gospel accords with his Christ-centered focus throughout. It closes with the Savior lifting up his hands to bless his people, even as he departs from them into heaven (24:50). Jesus was worshiped by his followers, who then returned to Jerusalem "filled with great joy" (24:52), a theme found throughout Luke (see Introduction). The angels had announced a message of "great joy to all people" (2:10). Now that message was about to wing its way out of Jerusalem into a needy and sin-filled world. It was a message that the world desperately needed, and the story would be told by Spirit-filled, passionate disciples, who would carry it as witnesses to the ends of the earth. The second volume of Luke's story would begin to unpack the grand scope of that message to the uttermost parts of the earth (Acts 1:8).

Theologically, the Ascension indicates Christ's elevation to the place of supreme power and authority (Eph 1:19-23; Phil 2:9-11). It is also closely tied to both his intercession on behalf of believers (Rom 8:34; Heb 7:25; 1 John 2:1) and the gift of the Spirit (John 7:39; 16:7), two sources of confidence and blessing for the church. The idea of Jesus' going to the Father is mentioned frequently in the New Testament, especially in John (John 3:13; 6:62; 13:1-3; 14:3, 28; 16:10, 16, 28; 20:17; Eph 4:8-10). As promised, the Ascension triggered the beginning of a powerful ministry in the Christian community energized by the Holy Spirit—one whose benefits the Lord's people can enter into even today in anticipation of the "final restoration of all things" (Acts 3:21).

BIBLIOGRAPHY

Abbott-Smith, G.
1923 *A Manual Greek Lexicon of the New Testament.* Edinburgh: T & T Clark.

Abel, E. L.
1973 The Genealogies of Jesus ho Christos. *New Testament Studies* 20:203-210.

Aberbach, M.
1966 *The Roman-Jewish War AD 66-70: Its Origins and Consequences.* London: R. Golub.

Achtemeier, P. J.
1978 The Lukan Perspective on the Miracles of Jesus: A Preliminary Sketch. Pp. 153-167 in *Perspectives in Luke-Acts.* Editor, C. H. Talbert. Danville, VA: Association of Baptist Professors of Religion.
1985 (Editor) *Harper's Bible Dictionary.* San Francisco: Harper & Row.

Agnew, F.
1986 The Origin of the New Testament Apostle-Concept: A Review of Research. *Journal of Biblical Literature* 105:75-96.

Aland, K., editor
1987 *Synopsis of the Four Gospels.* New York: United Bible Societies.

Alexander, C. A. L.
1985 Luke's Preface in the Context of Greek Preface-Writing. *Novum Testamentum* 28:48-74.
1993 *Preface to Luke's Gospel: Literary Convention and Social Context in Luke 1:1-4 and Acts 1:1.* Society of New Testament Studies Monograph Series 78. New York: Cambridge University Press.

von Allmen, J.-J., editor
1958 Marriage. Pp. 253-258 in *Vocabulary of the Bible.* London: Lutterworth.

Alon, G.
1980 *The Jews in Their Land in the Talmudic Age.* Jerusalem: Humanities Press.

Alony, M. A.
1969 *All about Pesach.* Southport: Shaffer Brothers.

Aune, D. E., editor
1972 *Studies in New Testament and Early Christian Literature: Essays in Honor of A. P. Wikgen.* Leiden: Brill.

Averbeck, R. E.
1980 The Focus of Baptism in the New Testament. *Grace Theological Journal* 1:265-301.

Bacchiocchi, S.
1977 *From Sabbath to Sunday: A Historical Investigation of the Rise of Sunday Observance in Early Christianity.* Rome: Pontifical Gregorian University Press.

Badia, L. F.
1980 *The Qumran Baptism and John the Baptist.* Lanham, MD: University Press of America.

Bailey, K. E.
1976 *Poet and Peasant: A Literary Cultural Approach to the Parables in Luke.* Grand Rapids: Eerdmans.

Baird, J. A.
1969 *Audience Criticism and the Historical Jesus.* Philadelphia: Westminster.

Baird, W.
1972 Luke. Pp. 672-706 in *The Interpreter's One-Volume Commentary on the Bible.* Editor, C. M. Laymon. London: Collins.

Bammel, E. and C. F. D. Moule, editors
1984 *Jesus and the Politics of His Day.* Cambridge: Cambridge University Press.

Banks, R.
1975 *Jesus and the Law in the Synoptic Tradition.* Society for New Testament Studies Monograph Series 28. Cambridge: Cambridge University Press.

Barabas, S.
1975 Levirate Law. P. 912 in vol. 3 of *Zondervan Pictorial Encyclopedia of the Bible.* Editor, M. C. Tenney. Grand Rapids: Zondervan.

Barclay, W.
1965 *The Gospel of Mark.* Edinburgh: St. Andrews Press.
1967 *The Lord's Supper.* Nashville: Abingdon.
1974 *Educational Ideals in the Ancient World.* Grand Rapids: Baker.
1975 *And He Had Compassion on Them.* Edinburgh: St. Andrews Press.

Barker, K., editor
1985 *The NIV Study Bible.* Grand Rapids: Zondervan.

Barrett, C. K.
1978 *The Gospel according to St. John,* 2nd ed. London: SPCK.

Barth, M.
1988 *Rediscovering the Lord's Supper.* Atlanta: John Knox.

Bauckham, R. J.
1998 Life, Death, and the Afterlife in Second Temple Judaism. Pp. 80-95 in *Life in the Face of Death.* Editor, R. N. Longenecker. Grand Rapids: Eerdmans.
1999 *The Fate of the Dead: Studies on the Jewish and Christian Apocalypses.* Leiden: Brill.

Bauer, J. B., editor
1981 *Encyclopedia of Biblical Theology.* New York: Crossroad.

Beasley-Murray, G. R.
1954 *Jesus and the Future.* London: Macmillan.
1962 *Baptism in the New Testament.* London: Macmillan.
1986 *Jesus and the Kingdom of God.* Grand Rapids: Eerdmans.
1987 *John.* Waco: Word.
1989 *Christian Character in the Gospel of Luke.* London: Epworth.

Beavis, M. A.
1992 Ancient Slavery as an Interpretative Context for the New Testament Servant Parables with Special Reference to the Unjust Steward. *Journal of Biblical Literature* 111:37-54.

Best, E.
1981 *Following Jesus.* Sheffield: JSOT Press.

Bilde, P.
1979 The Causes of the Jewish War according to Josephus. *Journal for the Study of Judaism* 10:179-202.

Bilezikian, G.
1985 *Beyond Sex Roles: A Guide for the Study of Female Roles in the Bible.* Grand Rapids: Baker.

Black, M.
1950 The Aramaic Spoken by Christ and Luke 14.5. *Journal of Theological Studies* 1:60-62.

Blair, E. P.
1987 Luke. Pp. 247-253 in *The Illustrated Bible Handbook.* Nashville: Abingdon.

Blevins, J. L.
1981 *The Messianic Secret in Markan Research.* Washington, DC: University Press of America.

Blomberg, C. L.
1990 *Interpreting the Parables.* Downers Grove: InterVarsity.
1999 *Neither Poverty nor Riches: A Biblical Theology of Material Possessions.* Grand Rapids: Eerdmans.

Bock, D. L.
1986 Jesus as Lord in Acts and in the Gospel Message. *Bibliotheca Sacra* 143:146-154.
1987 *Proclamation from Prophecy and Pattern: Lucan Old Testament Christology.* Journal for the Study of New Testament Supplement Series 12. Sheffield: Sheffield Academic Press.
1992 Gospel of Luke. Pp. 495-510 in *Dictionary of Jesus and the Gospels.* Editors, Green, McKnight, and Marshall. Downers Grove: InterVarsity.
1992, 1994 *Luke,* 2 vols. Chicago: Moody.
1994 *Luke 1:1–9:50.* Grand Rapids: Baker.
1996 *Luke 9:51–24:53.* Grand Rapids: Baker.

Boice, J. M.
1972 *The Sermon on the Mount.* Grand Rapids: Zondervan.

Bonhoeffer, D.
1959 *The Cost of Discipleship*, 2nd ed. New York: Macmillan.

Boslooper, T.
1962 *The Virgin Birth*. London: SCM.

Boucher, M.
1977 *The Mysterious Parable*. Washington, DC: The Catholic Biblical Association of America.

Bovon, F.
2002 *Luke 1: A Commentary on the Gospel of Luke 1:1–9:50*. Minneapolis: Fortress.

Boyd, G. A.
1995 *Cynic, Sage, or Son of God?* Wheaton: Victor Books.

Brawley, R. L.
1991 *Centering on God: Method and Message in Luke–Acts*. Louisville: Westminster/ John Knox.

Brindle, W.
1994 The Census and Quirinius: Luke 2:2. *Journal of the Evangelical Theological Society* 27:43-52.

Brodie, T. L.
1986 Towards Unraveling Luke's Use of the Old Testament: Luke 7:11-17 as an *Imitatio* of 1 Kings 17:24. *New Testament Studies* 32:247-267.

Bromiley, G. W., editor
1985 *Theological Dictionary of the New Testament: Abridged in One Volume*. Grand Rapids: Eerdmans.

Brown, C.
1984 *Miracles and the Critical Mind*. Grand Rapids: Eerdmans.

Brown, R. E.
1967 *The Lord's Supper*. Nashville: Abingdon.

1973 *The Virginal Conception and Bodily Resurrection of Jesus*. New York: Paulist Press.

1977 *The Birth of the Messiah*. London: Geoffrey Chapman.

1986 Gospel Infancy Narrative Research from 1976 to 1986, Part 2 (Luke). *Catholic Biblical Quarterly* 48:660-680.

Brown, R. E., K. P. Donfried, and J. Reumann, editors
1973 *Peter in the New Testament*. Minneapolis: Augsburg.

Brown, R. M.
1984 *Unexpected News: Reading the Bible with Third World Eyes*. Philadelphia: Westminster.

Bruce, F. F.
1960 *The New Testament Documents: Are They Reliable?* London: Oxford InterVarsity Fellowship.

1962 *The Book of Acts*. London: Marshall, Morgan & Scott.

1968 *The New Testament Development of Old Testament Themes*. Grand Rapids: Eerdmans.

1984 Render to Caesar. Pp. 249-263 in *Jesus and the Politics of His Day*. Editors, E. Bammel and C. F. D. Moule. Cambridge: Cambridge University Press.

1990 *The Acts of the Apostles: the Greek text with introduction and commentary*. Grand Rapids: Eerdmans.

Brunt, P. A.
1990 *Roman Imperial Themes*. Oxford: Clarendon Press.

Buchanan, G. W.
1959 Mark 11:15-19: Brigands in the Temple. *Hebrew Union College Annual* 30:169-177.

1993 Leprosy. Pp. 431-432 in *The Oxford Companion to the Bible*. Editors, Bruce Metzger and Michael Coogan. Oxford and New York: Oxford University Press.

Bultmann, R.
1958 *Jesus Christ and Mythology*. New York: Scribner.

1963 *The History of the Synoptic Tradition*. Translator, J. Marsh. Oxford: Blackwell.

Byrsborg, S.
2000 *Story as History—History as Story: The Gospel Tradition in the Context of Oral History*. Tübingen: Mohr Siebeck.

Cadbury, H. J.
1919-1920 *The Style and Literary Method of Luke*. 2 vols. Cambridge, MA: Harvard University Press.

1961 *The Making of Luke–Acts*. London: Macmillan.

Caird, G. B.
1955 *The Apostolic Age.* London: Duckworth.
1963 *Luke.* The Pelican Gospel Commentaries. Baltimore: Penguin Books.
1980 *The Language and Imagery of the Bible.* Philadelphia: Fortress.

Campbell, R. A.
1996 Jesus and His Baptism. *Tyndale Bulletin* 47/2:191-214.

Cargounis, C. C.
1986 *The Son of Man.* Tübingen: J. C. B. Mohr.
1989 Kingdom of God, Son of Man and Jesus' Self-understanding. *Tyndale Bulletin* 40:3-23, 223-238.

Carson, D. A.
1978 *The Sermon on the Mount.* Grand Rapids: Baker.
1982 *Sabbath to Lord's Day: A Biblical, Historical, and Theological Investigation.* Grand Rapids: Zondervan.

Carson, D. A., D. Moo, and L. Morris
1992 *An Introduction to the New Testament.* Grand Rapids: Zondervan.

Carter, W.
1988 Zechariah and the Benedictus (1:68-79), "Practising What He Preaches." *Biblica* 69:239-247.
1992 *Studies in Q.* Edinburgh: T. & T. Clark.

Charlesworth, J. H.
1983 *The Old Testament Pseudepigrapha.* Garden City: Doubleday.
1987 *The Messiah.* Minneapolis: Fortress.
1991 *Jesus' Jewishness.* New York: Crossroad.

Cheong, C-S. A.
2001 *A Dialogic Reading of The Steward Parable (16:1-9).* New York: Lang.

Chilton, B. and J. I. H. McDonald
1987 *Jesus and the Ethics of the Kingdom.* Grand Rapids: Eerdmans.

Coggan, F. D.
1970 *The Prayers of the New Testament.* London: Hodder & Stoughton.

Coggins, R. J.
1975 *Samaritans and Jews: The Origins of Samaritanism Reconsidered.* Atlanta: John Knox.
1993 Samaritans. Pp. 671-673 in *The Oxford Companion to the Bible.* Editors, Bruce Metzger and Michael Coogan. Oxford and New York: Oxford University Press.

Cohen, S. J. D.
1989 Crossing the Boundary and Becoming a Jew. *Harvard Theological Review* 82:13-33.

Comfort, P. W.
2007 *New Testament Text and Translation Commentary.* Carol Stream: Tyndale House.

Conn, H. M.
1972 Luke's Theology of Prayer. *Christianity Today* 17:6-8.

Conzelmann, H.
1960 *The Theology of St. Luke.* Translator, G. Buswell. London: Faber and Faber.

Coogan, M. D., editor
2001 *The New Oxford Annotated Bible,* 3rd ed. Oxford: Oxford University Press.

Coppan, P. and C. A. Evans, editors
2001 *Who Was Jesus?* Louisville: Westminster/John Knox Press.

Cosgrove, C.
1984 The Divine *DEI* in Luke-Acts: Investigations into the Lukan Understanding of God's Providence. *Novum Testamentum* 26:168-190.

Cox, J. W.
1992 The Sermon on the Mount. *The Review and Expositor* 89:165-278.

Craddock, F. B.
1988 Luke. Pp. 1010-1043 in *Harper's Bible Commentary.* Editor, J. L. Mays. San Francisco: Harper & Row.
1990 *Luke.* Interpretation Commentary. Louisville: John Knox Press.

Cranfield, C. E. B.
1988 Some Reflections on the Subject of the Virgin Birth. *Scottish Journal of Theology* 41:177-198.

Creed, J. M.
1930 *The Gospel according to St. Luke.* London: Macmillan.

Crossan, J. D.
1973 *In Parables.* New York: Harper & Row.

Cullmann, O.
1962 *Peter: Disciple, Apostle, Martyr,* 2nd ed. Philadelphia: Westminster.

Danby, H.
1924 *The Mishnah.* Oxford: Oxford University Press.

Daniel, O. E.
1986 *Interwoven Harmony of the Gospels.* Perrysburg, OH: Welch.

Danker, F. W.
1974 *Jesus and the New Age.* St. Louis: Clayton.

Davids, P. H.
1980 New Testament Foundations for Living More Simply. Pp. 4-58 in *Living More Simply.* Editor, R. J. Sider. Downers Grove: InterVarsity.

Davies, A. F.
1999 *Biblical Weather.* Belleville: Essence Publishing.

Davies, W. D.
1964 *The Setting of the Sermon on the Mount.* New York: Cambridge University Press.

Davies, W. D. and D. C. Allison, Jr.
1988 *Matthew.* International Critical Commentary. 2 vols. Edinburgh: T & T Clark.

Derrett, J. D. M.
1961 Fresh Light on St. Luke xvi.l. The Parable of the Unjust Steward. *New Testament Studies* 7:198-219.

1970 *Law in the New Testament.* London: Longman and Todd.

1977 The Zeal of the House and the Cleansing of the Temple. *Dunside Review* 95:79-94.

1978 Law in the New Testament: The Palm Sunday Colt. Pp. 165-177 in *Studies in the New Testament,* vol. 2. Leiden: Brill.

Dever, W. D.
1985 Weights and Measures. P. 1131 in *Harper's Bible Dictionary.* Editor, P. J. Achtemeier. San Francisco: Harper & Row.

Dillon, R. J.
1981 Previewing Luke's Project from His Prologue. *Catholic Biblical Quarterly* 43:205-227.

Dodd, C. H.
1936 *The Apostolic Preaching and Its Developments.* London: Hodder and Stoughton.

1947 The Fall of Jerusalem and the Abomination of Desolation. *Journal of Roman Studies* 37:47-54.

1961 *The Parables of the Kingdom.* London: Fontana.

1965 *According to the Scriptures.* London: Fontana.

Dollar, H.
1996 *St. Luke's Missiology: A Cross-Cultural Challenge.* Pasadena: William Carey Library.

Donahue, J. R.
1989 Two Decades of Research on the Rich and Poor in Luke–Acts. Pp. 129-144 in *Justice and the Holy.* Editors, Knight and Paris. Atlanta: Scholars Press.

Donne, B. K.
1983 *Christ Ascended: A Study in the Significance of the Ascension of Jesus Christ in the New Testament.* Greenwood, NC: Attic Press

Dunn, J. D. G.
1970 *Baptism in the Holy Spirit.* Philadelphia: Westminster.

1975 *Jesus and the Spirit.* Philadelphia: Westminster.

Earl, D.
1990 Prologue-Form in Ancient Historiography. Pp. 842-846 in *Aufstieg und Niedergang der romischen Welt,* vol. 1, part 2. Editors, Temporini and Haase. Berlin.

Edwards, D.
1969 *The Last Things Now.* London: SCM Press.

Edwards, R. A.
1971 *The Sign of Jonah in the Theology of the Evangelists and Q.* London: SCM.

Ehrenberg, V. and A. H. M. Jones
1976 *Documents Illustrating the Reigns of Augustus and Tiberius.* Oxford: Clarendon.

Ellis, E. E.
1972 *Eschatology in Luke.* Philadelphia: Fortress.
1981 *The Gospel of Luke.* The New Century Bible Commentary. Rev. ed. London: Marshall, Morgan & Scott.
2000 Present and Future Eschatology in Luke. Pp. 129-146 in *Christ and the Future in New Testament History.* Leiden: Brill.

Elwell, W. A., editor
1988 *The Marshall Pickering Encyclopedia of the Bible.* London: Marshall, Morgan and Scott.

Eppstein, V.
1964 The Historicity of the Gospel Account of the Cleansing of the Temple. *Zeitschrift für Neutestamentliche Wissenschaft* 55:42-58.

Erickson, R. J.
1993 The Jailing of John and the Baptism of Jesus: Luke 3:19-21. *Journal of the Evangelical Theological Society* 36:455-466.

Evans, C. A.
1984 On the Vineyard Parables of Isaiah 5 and Mark 12. *Biblische Zeitschrift* 28:82-86.
1989 Jesus' Action in the Temple: Cleansing or Portent of Destruction? *Catholic Biblical Quarterly* 51:237-270.
1990 *Luke.* New International Biblical Commentary. Peabody, MA: Hendrickson.
2003 *Jesus and the Ossuaries.* Waco: Baylor University Press.

Evans, C. A. and S. E. Porter, editors
2000 *Dictionary of New Testament Background.* Downers Grove: InterVarsity.

Evans, C. F.
1957 The Central Section of St. Luke's Gospel. Pp. 37-53 in *Studies in the Gospels.* Editor, D. E. Nineham. Oxford: Blackwell.

Evans, M. J.
1983 *Women in the Bible: An Overview of All Crucial Passages on Women's Roles.* Downers Grove: InterVarsity.

Farley, B. W.
1988 *The Providence of God.* Grand Rapids: Baker.

Farrar, F. W.
1890 *The Gospel according to St. Luke.* Cambridge: Cambridge University Press.

Farris, S. C.
1985 *The Hymns of Luke's Infancy Narratives.* Journal for the Study of the New Testament, Supplement 9. Sheffield: JSOT Press.

Fisher, F. L.
1964 *Prayer in the New Testament.* Philadelphia: Westminster Press.

Fitzmyer, J. A.
1981 *The Gospel according to Luke,* vol. 1. Anchor Bible. Garden City: Doubleday.
1985 *The Gospel according to Luke,* vol. 2. Anchor Bible. Garden City: Doubleday.
1989 *Luke the Theologian.* New York: Paulist Press.

Ford, D.
1979 *The Abomination of Desolation in Biblical Eschatology.* Washington, DC: University Press of America.

France, R. T.
1975 *I Came to Set Fire on the Earth.* Downers Grove: InterVarsity.
1987 *Matthew.* Tyndale New Testament Commentary. Grand Rapids: Eerdmans.
2003 Encounter with God. *Scripture Union Notes,* Jan–Mar, 108-116.

Franklin, E.
1975 *Christ the Lord: A Study in the Purpose and Theology of Luke–Acts.* London: SPCK.

Freedman, D. N., editor
2000 *Eerdman's Dictionary of the Bible.* Grand Rapids: Eerdmans.

Freyne, S.
1980 *Galilee from Alexander the Great to Hadrian.* Notre Dame: University of Notre Dame.

Furnish, V. P.
1972 *The Love Command in the New Testament.* Nashville: Abingdon.

Gardner, P., editor
1995 *The Complete Who's Who in the Bible.* London: Marshall Pickering.

Garland, D.
1987 Matthew's Understanding of the Temple Tax (Matt 17:24-27). *Society of Biblical Literature Abstracts and Papers* 26:190-209.

Garrett, S. R.
1989 *The Demise of the Devil: Magic and the Demonic in Luke's Writings.* Minneapolis: Fortress.

Gaston, L.
1970 *No Stone on Another: Studies in the Significance of the Fall of Jerusalem in the Synoptic Gospels.* Society for New Testament Studies Monograph Series 23. Leiden: Brill.

Geddert, T. J.
1989 *Watchwords: Mark 13 in Markan Eschatology.* Sheffield: JSOT Press.

Geldenhuys, N.
1961 *Commentary on the Gospel of Luke.* London: Marshall, Morgan & Scott.

Gooding, D.
1987 *According to Luke.* Grand Rapids: Eerdmans.

Goodman, M.
1982 The First Jewish Revolt: Social Conflict and the Problem of Debt. *Journal of Jewish Studies* 33:417-427.

1983 *State and Society in Roman Galilee, AD 132–212.* Totowa, NJ: Rowman & Allanfield.

1997 *The Roman World 44 BC–AD 180.* London: Routledge.

Gransgaard, B. R.
1999 *Conflict and Authority in Luke 19:47 to 21:4.* New York: Peter Lang.

Grant, F.C., editor
1962 *Matthew–Acts.* Vol. 6 in Nelson's Bible Commentary. New York: Thomas Nelson & Sons.

Grant, M.
1971 *Herod the Great.* New York: American Heritage.

Grassi, C. M. and J. A. Grassi
1986 *Mary Magdalene and the Women in Jesus' Life.* Kansas City: Sheed & Ward.

Green, J. B.
1988 *Death of Christ.* Tübingen: J. C. B. Mohr.

1989 Jesus and a Daughter of Abraham (13:10-17): Test Case for a Lucan Perspective on Jesus' Miracles. *Catholic Biblical Quarterly* 51:643-654.

1995 *The Theology of the Gospel of Luke.* New York: Cambridge University Press.

1997 *The Gospel of Luke.* The New International Commentary on the New Testament. Grand Rapids: Eerdmans.

Green, M.
1989 *Matthew for Today.* Dallas: Word.

Grenz, S. J.
1995 *Women in the Church.* Downers Grove: InterVarsity.

Guelich, R. A.
1982 *The Sermon on the Mount: A Foundation for Understanding.* Waco: Word.

Gundry, R. H.
1967 *The Use of the Old Testament in St. Matthew's Gospel.* Novum Testamentum, Supplement 18. Leiden: Brill.

1993 *Mark: A Commentary on Its Apology for the Cross.* Grand Rapids: Eerdmans.

1994 *Matthew: A Commentary on His Literary and Theological Art.* Grand Rapids: Eerdmans.

Guthrie, D.

1981 *New Testament Theology.* Downers Grove: InterVarsity.

Guy, L.

1997 The Interplay of the Present and Future in the Kingdom of God (19:11-44). *Tyndale Bulletin* 48:119-137.

Habermas, G. R.

1984 *Ancient Evidence for the Life of Jesus.* Nashville: Thomas Nelson.

Halas, R. B.

1946 *Judas Iscariot, A Scriptural and Theological Study of His Person, His Deeds and His Eternal Lot.* Washington, DC: Catholic University of America.

Halley, H.

1952 *Halley's Bible Handbook.* Chicago: Halley.

Hamilton, G. J.

1988 The First Commandment: A Theological Reflection. *New Blackfriars* 69:174-181.

Hamilton, N. Q.

1964 Temple Cleansing and Temple Bank. *Journal of Biblical Literature* 83:365-372.

Hansen, K. C. and D. E. Oakman

1998 *Palestine in the Time of Jesus: Social Structures and Social Conflicts.* Minneapolis: Fortress.

Harrington, W. J.

1968 *The Gospel of St. Luke.* London: Geoffrey Chapman.

Harris, L. O.

1967 Prayer in the Gospel of Luke. *Southwestern Journal of Theology* 10:59-69.

Harris, M. J.

1985 *Raised Immortal: Resurrection and Immortality in the New Testament.* Grand Rapids: Eerdmans.

1990 *From Grave to Glory: Resurrection in the New Testament.* Grand Rapids: Zondervan.

Hay, D. H.

1973 *Glory at the Right Hand.* Nashville: Abingdon.

Head, P. M.

2001 The Role of Eyewitnesses in the Formation of the Gospel Tradition. *Tyndale Bulletin* 52:275-294.

Hebert, A. G.

1960 Blaspheme, Blasphemy. P. 32 in *A Theological Word Book of the Bible.* Editor, A. Richardson. New York: Macmillan.

Hefley, J. and M. Hefley

1979 *By Their Blood: Christian Martyrs of the 20th Century.* Milford, MI: Mott Media.

Helyer, L. R.

1993 Luke and the Restoration of Israel. *Journal of the Evangelical Theological Society* 36:317-329.

Hendrick, H.

1996 *The Third Gospel for the Third World,* vol. 2B (Lk 7:1-9:50). Collegeville, MN: Liturgical Press.

Hengel, M.

1971 *Was Jesus a Revolutionist?* Philadelphia: Fortress.

1977 *Crucifixion in the Ancient World and the Folly of the Message of the Cross.* London: SCM.

1983 *Between Jesus and Paul.* London: SCM.

Hennecke, M., W. Schneemelcher and E. M. Wilson, editors

1963 *New Testament Apocrypha,* vol. 1. Philadelphia: Westminster.

Herron, R.W.

1983 The Origin of the New Testament Apostolate. *Westminster Journal of Theology* 45:101-131.

Herzog, W. R., III

2000 *Jesus, Justice, and the Reign of God.* Louisville: Westminster/John Knox.

Heuschen, J.

1965 *The Bible on the Ascension.* De Pere, WI: St. Norbert Abbey.

Hiebert, D. E.
1975 Alms, Almsgiving. Pp. 109-110 in vol. 1 of *Zondervan Pictorial Encyclopedia of the Bible.* Editor, M. C. Tenney. Grand Rapids: Zondervan.

Hieke, T.
2001 *Q 6:20-21: The Beatitudes for the Poor, Hungry and Mourning.* Leuven: Peeters.

Hiers, R. H.
1971 Purification of the Temple: Preparation for the Kingdom of God. *Journal of Biblical Literature* 90:82-90.

1973 *The Historical Jesus and the Kingdom of God.* Gainesville: University of Florida.

Higgins, A. J. B.
1980 *The Son of Man in the Teaching of Jesus.* Cambridge: Cambridge University Press.

Hock, R. F.
1987 Lazarus and Micyllus: Greco-Roman Backgrounds to Luke 16:19-31. *Journal of Biblical Literature* 106:447-463.

Hoehner, H. W.
1972 *Herod Antipas.* Society for New Testament Studies Monograph Series 17. Cambridge: Cambridge University Press.

1977 *Chronological Aspects of the Life of Christ.* Grand Rapids: Zondervan.

Hood, R. T.
1961 The Genealogies of Jesus. Pp. 1-15 in *Early Christian Origins, Festschrift for H.R. Willoughby.* Editor, A. Wikgren. Chicago: Quadrangle Books.

Hopkins, K.
1980 Taxes and Trade in the Roman Empire 200 BC—AD 400. *Journal of Roman Studies* 70:101-125.

Hoppe, L. J.
2004 *There Shall Be No Poor among You: Poverty in the Bible.* Nashville: Abingdon.

Horsley, R. A.
1981 Banditry and the Revolt against Rome AD 66-70. *Catholic Biblical Quarterly* 43:409-432.

1993 *Jesus and the Spiral of Violence: Popular Jewish Resistance in Roman Palestine.* Minneapolis: Fortress.

1995 *Galilee: History, Politics, People.* Valley Forge: Trinity.

Horsley, R. A. and J. S. Hanson
1985 *Bandits, Prophets, and Messiahs.* Minneapolis: Winston.

Howard, J. K.
2001 *Disease and Healing in the New Testament: An Analysis and Interpretation.* Lanham, MD: University Press of America.

Hull, W. E.
1967 A Teaching Outline of the Gospel of Luke. *Review and Expositor* 64:426-432.

Hunter, A. M.
1960 *Interpreting the Parables.* London: SCM.

1971 *The Parables Then and Now.* London: SCM.

Hurst, L. D. and N. T. Wright, editors
1987 *The Glory of Christ in the New Testament.* Oxford: Clarendon.

Inch, Morris A.
1988 Gospel of Luke. *The Marshall Pickering Encyclopedia of the Bible.* Editor, Walter A. Elwell. London: Marshall, Morgan & Scott.

Ingholt, H.
1953 The Surname of Judas Iscariot. Pp. 152-162 in *Studia Orientalia Ioanni Pedersen.* Copenhagen: K. Munksgaard.

Irudhayasamy, R. J.
2003 *A Prophet in the Making: A Christological Study on Lk 4, 16-30.* New York: Peter Lang.

Jackson, D.
1989 Luke and Paul: A Theology of One Spirit from Two Perspectives. *Journal of the Evangelical Theological Society* 32:335-343.

James, M. R.
1924 *The Apocryphal New Testament.* Oxford: Oxford University Press.

Jeffrey, D. L., editor
1992 *A Dictionary of Biblical Tradition in English Literature.* Grand Rapids: Eerdmans.

Jeremias, J.
1960 *Infant Baptism in the First Four Centuries.* London: SCM.
1966 *The Eucharistic Words of Jesus.* London: SCM.
1975 *The Parables of Jesus.* New York: Charles Scribner's Sons.

Johnson, L. T.
1977 *The Literary Function of Possessions in Luke–Acts.* Missoula: Scholars Press.
1982 The Lukan Kingship Parable (Lk 19:11-27). *Novum Testamentum* 24:139-159.
1991 *The Gospel of Luke.* Sacra Pagina. Collegeville, MN: Liturgical Press.

Johnson, M. D.
1969 *The Purpose of the Biblical Genealogies with Special Reference to the Setting of the Genealogies of Jesus.* Society for New Testament Studies Monograph Series 8. Cambridge: Cambridge University Press.

Jones, D.
1970 The Title *christos* in Luke–Acts. *Catholic Biblical Quarterly* 32:69-76.

Jones, P. R.
1982 *The Teaching of the Parables.* Nashville: Broadman.

de Jonge, M.
1966 The Use of the Word 'Anointed' in the Time of Jesus. *Novum Testamentum* 8:132-148.

Kaiser, C. B.
1982 *The Doctrine of God.* Westchester, IL: Crossway.

Karris, J.
1978 Poor and Rich: The Lukan *Sitz im Leben.* Pp. 112-125 in *Perspectives on Luke–Acts.* Editor, C. H. Talbert. Danville, VA: Association of Baptist Professors of Religion.

Keck, L. E. and J. L. Martyn, editors
1966 *Studies in Luke–Acts.* Philadelphia: Fortress.

Kee, A.
1969 The Question about Fasting. *Novum Testamentum* 11:161-173.

Kee, H. C.
1983 *Miracle in the Early Christian World.* New Haven: Yale University Press.

Keeley, R., editor
1982 *Eerdmans' Handbook to Christian Belief.* Grand Rapids: Eerdmans.

Kim, K.
1998 *Stewardship and Almsgiving in Luke's Theology.* Sheffield: Sheffield Academic Press.

Kim, S.
1983 *The Son of Man as the Son of God.* Grand Rapids: Eerdmans.

Kimball, C. A.
1994 *Jesus' Exposition of the Old Testament in Luke's Gospel.* Sheffield: JSOT Press.

Kingsbury, J. D.
1983 *The Christology of Mark's Gospel.* Philadelphia: Fortress.

Kistemaker, S.
1980 *The Parables of Jesus.* Grand Rapids: Baker.

Klassen, W.
1980 The Role of Jesus in the Transformation of Feminine Consciousness. *Journal of Comparative Sociology and Religion* 7:82-210.

Koet, B. J.
1989 Today This Scripture has been Fulfilled in Your Ears: Jesus' Explanation of Scripture in Luke 4,16-30. Pp. 24-55 in *Five Studies on Interpretation of Scripture in Luke–Acts.* Leuven: Leuven University Press.

Kopas, J.
1986 Jesus and Women: Luke's Gospel. *Theology Today* 43:192-202.

Kraeling, E.
1951 *John the Baptist.* New York: Scribner.

Kraybill, D. B.
1978 *The Upside-Down Kingdom.* Scottdale, PA: Herald.

Kummel, W. G.
1961 *Promise and Fulfilment,* 2nd ed. Studies in Biblical Theology 23. Naperville, IL: Allenson.

Kurz, W. S.
1993 *Reading Luke-Acts.* Louisville: Westminster/John Knox.

Kvalbein, H.
1987 Jesus and the Poor. *Themelios* 12:80-87.

Ladd, G. E.
1974 *The Presence of the Future.* Grand Rapids: Eerdmans.
1975 *I Believe in the Resurrection of Jesus.* Grand Rapids: Eerdmans.

Laymon, C. M., editor
1971 *The Interpreter's One-Volume Commentary on the Bible.* Nashville: Abingdon.

Leaney, A. R. C.
1958 *A Commentary on the Gospel of St Luke.* London: A & C Black.

Léon-Dufour, X.
1980 *Dictionary of the New Testament.* San Francisco: Harper & Row.

Levine, A., editor
2002 *A Feminist Companion to Luke.* New York: Sheffield Academic Press.

Lindars, B.
1983 *Jesus Son of Man.* Grand Rapids: Eerdmans.

Lindsell, H., editor
1965 *Harper Study Bible.* Grand Rapids: Zondervan.

Longenecker, R. N.
1981 *Acts.* Pp. 205-573 in *The Expositor's Bible Commentary,* vol. 9. Editor, F. Gaebelein. Grand Rapids: Zondervan.
1998 *Life in the Face of Death.* Grand Rapids: Eerdmans.
1999 *New Wine into Fresh Wineskins: Contextualizing the Early Christian Confessions.* Peabody, MA: Hendrickson.
2001 *Into God's Presence: Prayer in the New Testament.* Grand Rapids: Eerdmans.

van der Loos, H.
1965 *The Miracles of Jesus.* Leiden: Brill.

Lull, D. J., editor
1989 *Society of Biblical Literature 1989 Seminar Papers.* Atlanta: Scholars Press.

Luz, U.
1989 *Matthew 1-7: A Commentary.* Minneapolis: Fortress.

Machen, J. G.
1930 *The Virgin Birth.* Grand Rapids: Baker.

Maile, J. F.
1986 The Ascension in Luke-Acts. *Tyndale Bulletin* 37:29-59.

Mandell, S.
1984 Who Paid the Temple Tax When the Jews Were Under Roman Rule? *Harvard Theological Journal* 77:223-232.

Marshall, I. H.
1967 The Development of Christology in the Early Church. *Tyndale Bulletin* 18:77-93.
1969 Tradition and Theology in Luke (8-15). *Tyndale Bulletin* 20:56-75.
1970 *Luke: Historian and Theologian.* London: Paternoster.
1975 *The Origins of New Testament Christology.* London: InterVarsity.

1978 *The Gospel of Luke.* The New International Greek Testament Commentary. Exeter: Paternoster.
1980 *Last Supper and Lord's Supper.* Grand Rapids: Eerdmans.
1990 *Jesus the Saviour.* Downers Grove: InterVarsity.
1992 *The Acts of the Apostles.* Sheffield: JSOT Press.

Martin, H.
1949 *Luke's Portrait of Jesus.* London: SCM.

Matson, M. A.
2001 *In Dialogue with Another Gospel? The Influence of the Fourth Gospel on the Passion Narrative of the Gospel of Luke.* Society of Biblical Literature Dissertation Series 178. Atlanta: Society of Biblical Literature.

Matthewson, D. L.
1995 The Parable of the Unjust Steward (16:1-13): A Reexamination of the Traditional View in Light of Recent Challenges. *Journal of the Evangelical Theological Society* 38:29-40.

Mattill, A. J., Jr.
1979 *Luke and Last Things.* Dillsboro: Western North Carolina Press.

McArthur, H. K. and R. M. Johnson
1990 *They Also Taught in Parables.* Grand Rapids: Zondervan.

McKnight, S.
1991 *A Light among the Gentiles: Jewish Missionary Activity in the Second Temple Period.* Minneapolis: Fortress.
2004 *The Jesus Creed: Loving God, Loving Others.* Orleans, MA: Paraclete.

McRay, J. R.
2000 Caesarea Philippi. Pp. 178-79 in *Dictionary of New Testament Background.* Editors. C. A. Evans and S. E. Porter. Downers Grove: InterVarsity.

Meijr, F. and O. van Nijf
1992 *Trade, Transport and Society in the Ancient World: A Sourcebook.* London: Routledge.

Mercer, C.
1990 Son of Man. Pp. 846-848 in *Mercer's Dictionary of the Bible.* Editor, W. E. Mills. Macon, GA: Mercer University Press.

Metzger, B. M.
1971 *A Textual Commentary on the Greek New Testament.* New York: United Bible Societies.

Metzger, B. M. and M. D. Coogan, editors
1993 *The Oxford Companion to the Bible.* Oxford and New York: Oxford University Press.

Millar, F.
1981 *The Roman Empire and Its Neighbors.* London: Duckworth.

Miller, D.
1959 *Luke.* The Layman's Bible Commentary. Atlanta: John Knox Press.

Mills, W. E., editor
1990 *Mercer Dictionary of the Bible.* Macon, GA: Mercer University Press.

Moessner, D. P.
1989 *Lord of the Banquet: The Literary and Theological Significance of the Lukan Travel Narrative.* Minneapolis: Fortress.

Moody, D.
1953 God's Only Son. *Journal of Biblical Literature* 72:213-219.

Moore, A. L.
1966 *The Parousia in the New Testament.* Leiden: Brill.

Moore, T. S.
1997 The Lucan Great Commission and the Isaianic Servant. *Bibliotheca Sacra* 154:47-60.

Morrice, W. G.
1985 *Joy in the New Testament.* Grand Rapids: Eerdmans.

Morris, L.
1971 *John.* The New International Commentary on the New Testament. Grand Rapids: Eerdmans.

1974 *The Gospel according to St. Luke.* Grand Rapids: Eerdmans.

Moule, C. F. D.
1977 *The Origin of Christology.* New York: Cambridge University Press.

Mounce, R. H.
1960 *The Essential Nature of New Testament Preaching.* Grand Rapids: Eerdmans.

Muto, S. A.
1984 *Blessings That Make Us Be.* New York: Crossroad.

Myers, J. M., O. Reimer and H. N. Bream, editors
1969 *Search the Scriptures. New Testament Studies in Honor of Raymond T. Stamm.* Leiden: Brill.

Navone, J.
1970 *Themes of St. Luke.* Rome: Gregorian University Press.

Neufeld, V. H.
1963 *The Earliest Christian Confessions.* Grand Rapids: Eerdmans.

Neuman, B. M., Jr.
1971 *A Concise Greek-English Dictionary of the New Testament.* London: United Bible Societies.

Neusner, J.
1973 *The Idea of Purity in Ancient Judaism.* Leiden: Brill.
1989 Money-Changers in the Temple: The Mishnah's Explanation. *New Testament Studies* 35:287-290.

Newell, J. E. and R. R.
1972 The Parable of the Wicked Tenants. *Novum Testamentum* 14:226-237.

Neyrey, J., editor
1991 *The Social World of Luke–Acts: Models for Interpretation.* Peabody, MA: Hendrickson.

Nineham, D. E., editor
1957 *Studies in the Gospels.* Oxford: Blackwell.

Nolland, J.
1989 *Luke,* vol. 1. Dallas: Word.
1991 *Luke,* vol. 2. Dallas: Word.
1993 *Luke,* vol. 3. Dallas: Word.

O'Brien, P. T.
1973 Prayer in Luke–Acts. *Tyndale Bulletin* 24:111-127.

O'Day, G. R. and D. Peterson, editors
1999 *The Access Bible.* Oxford: Oxford University Press.

van Ommwern, N. M.
1991 Was Luke an Accurate Historian? *Bibliotheca Sacra* 148:57-71.

Osborne, G. R.
1982 Numismatic Windows into the Social World of Early Christianity: A Methodological Inquiry. *Journal of Biblical Literature* 101:195-223.
1984 *The Resurrection Narratives: A Redactional Study.* Grand Rapids: Baker.
1989 Women in Jesus' Ministry. *Westminster Journal of Theology* 51:259-291.

O'Toole, R. F.
1991 The Literary Form of Luke 19:1-10. *Journal of Biblical Literature* 110:107-116.

Overstreet, R. L.
1981 Difficulties of New Testament Genealogies. *Grace Theological Journal* 2:303-316.

Packer, J. I., Merrill C. Tenney, and William White, Jr., editors
1982 *All the People and Places of the Bible.* Nashville: Nelson.

Parsons, M. C.
1986 A Christological Tendency in P75. *Journal of Biblical Literature* 105:463-479.
1987 *The Departure of Jesus in Luke–Acts: The Ascension Narratives in Context.* Sheffield: JSOT Press.

Parsons, M. C. and R. I. Pervo
1993 *Rethinking the Unity of Luke and Acts.* Minneapolis: Fortress.

Payne, J. B.
1973 *Encyclopedia of Biblical Prophecy.* New York: Harper & Row.

Penney, D. L. and M. O. Wise
1994 By the Power of Beelzebub: An Aramaic Incantation Formula from Qumran (4Q560). *Journal of Biblical Literature* 113:627-650.

Perkins, P.
1984a *Resurrection: New Testament Witness and Contemporary Reflection.* New York: Doubleday.
1984b Taxes in the New Testament. *Journal of Religious Ethics* 12:182-200.
1990 *Jesus as Teacher.* New York: Cambridge University Press.

Perrin, N.
1963 *The Kingdom of God in the Teaching of Jesus.* Philadelphia: Westminster.

Pervo, R. L.
1987 *Profit with Delight: The Literary Genre of the Acts of the Apostles.* Philadelphia: Fortress.

Pilgrim, W. E.
1981 *Good News for the Poor.* Minneapolis: Augsburg.

Plummer, A.
1896 *A Critical and Exegetical Commentary of the Gospel according to St. Luke.* New York: Scribners.

Pobee, J. S.
1987 *Who Are the Poor? The Beatitudes as a Call to Community.* Geneva: World Council of Churches.

Pokorny, P.
1973-1974 The Temptation Stories and Their Intention. *New Testament Studies* 20:115-127.

Porter, Calvin
1962 Papyrus Bodmer XV (P75) and the Text of Codex Vaticanus. *Journal of Biblical Literature* 81:363-376.

Pousma, R. H.
1975 Diseases of the Bible. Pp. 132-142 in Vol. 2 of *The Zondervan Pictorial Encyclopedia of the Bible.* Editor, M. C. Tenney. 5 Vols. Grand Rapids: Zondervan.

Powell, M. A.
1989 *What Are They Saying About Luke?* New York: Paulist Press.
1990 The Religious Leaders in Luke: A Literary-Critical Style. *Journal of Biblical Literature* 109:93-110.

Pummer, R.
2002 *Early Christian Authors on Samaritans and Samaritanism: Text, Translation, and Commentary.* Tübingen: Mohr Siebeck.

Purvis, J. D.
1985 Samaritans. Pp. 898-900 in *Harper's Dictionary of the Bible.* Editor, P. J. Achtemeier. San Francisco: Harper & Row.
1986 The Samaritans and Judaism. Pp. 81-98 in *Early Judaism and Its Interpreters.* Editors, Kraft and Nickelsburg. Philadelphia: Fortress.

Ragg, Lonsdale
1922 *Luke.* Westminster Commentaries. London: Methuen.

Ramsey, A. M.
1949 *The Glory of God and the Transfiguration of Christ.* New York: Longmans, Green & Co.

Reicke, B.
1972 Synoptic Prophecies on the Destruction of Jerusalem. Pp. 111-134 in *Studies in New Testament and Early Christian Literature: Essays in Honor of A. P. Wikgren.* Editor, D. E. Aune. Leiden: Brill.

Rhoads, D. M.
1976 *Israel in Revolution 6-74 CE.* Philadelphia: Fortress.

Rice, G. E.
1982 Luke 5:33-6:11: Release from Cultic Tradition. *Andrews University Seminary Studies* 20:127-132.

Richard, E., editor
1990 *New Views on Luke and Acts.* Collegeville, MN: Liturgical Press.

Richardson, P.
2002 *City and Sanctuary: Religion and Architecture in the Roman Near East.* London: SCM.

Ridderbos, H. S.
1962 *The Coming of the Kingdom*. Philadelphia: Presbyterian and Reformed Publishing.

Rienecker, F. and C. L. Rogers, Jr.
1977 *A Linguistic Key to the Greek New Testament*. Grand Rapids: Zondervan.

Riesenfeld, H.
1970 *The Gospel Tradition*. Philadelphia: Fortress.

Ringe, S. H.
1995 *Luke*. Westminster Bible Companion. Louisville: Westminster/John Knox.

Robbins, V.
1978 By Land and By Sea: The We-Passages and Ancient Sea Voyages. Pp. 215-242 in *Perspectives on Luke-Acts*. Editor, C. H. Talbert. Danville, VA: Association of Baptist Professors of Religion.

Robertson, A. T.
1922 *A Harmony of the Gospels*. New York: Harpers.
1930 *Word Pictures in the New Testament*, 6 vols. Nashville: Broadman.

Roth, C.
1960 The Cleansing of the Temple and Zechariah. *Novum Testamentum* 4:174-181.

Rubin, B. and S. Rubin
1994 *The Messianic Passover Haggadah*. Baltimore: Messianic Jewish Resources International.

Runia, K.
1978 What is Preaching according to the New Testament? *Tyndale Bulletin* 29:3-48.

Russell, D. S.
1964 *The Method and Message of Jewish Apocalyptic*. London: SCM.

Russell, L. M., editor
1985 *Feminist Interpretation of the Bible*. Philadelphia: Westminster.

Sabourin, L.
1986 *The Divine Miracles Discussed and Defended*. Rome: Catholic Book Agency.

Safrai, S., M. Stern, D. Flusser, and W. C. van Unnik, editors
1974-1976 The Province of Judea. Pp. 308-376 in *The Jewish People in the First Century*. Compendia Rerum Iudaicarum ad Novum Testamentum, sec. 1. Amsterdam: Van Gorcum.

Sanders, E. P.
1985 *Jesus and Judaism*. Philadelphia: Fortress.
1990a *Jewish Law from Jesus to the Mishnah: Five Studies*. Philadelphia: Trinity.
1990b *Judaism: Practice and Belief*. Philadelphia: Trinity.

Sanders, J. T.
1981 The Parable of the Pounds and Lucan Anti-Semitism. *Theological Studies* 42:660-668.

Scheffler, E.
1993 *Suffering in Luke's Gospel*. Zürich: Theologischer Verlag.

Schiffman, L. H.
1985 Anoint. P. 32 in *Harper's Dictionary of the Bible*. Editor, P. Achtemeier. San Francisco: Harper & Row.

Schnabel, E. J.
2004 *Early Christian Mission*. 2 vols. Downers Grove: InterVarsity.

Schonfield, H. J.
1958 *The Authentic New Testament*. New York: Mentor Books.
1984 *The Good News according to Luke*. Atlanta: John Knox.

Schweizer, E.
1970 *The Good News according to Mark*. Translator, D. Madvig. Atlanta: John Knox.
1984 *The Good News according to Luke*. Translator, D. Green. Atlanta: Westminster/John Knox.

Scobie, C. H.
1964 *John the Baptist*. Philadelphia: Fortress.

Seccombe, D. P.
1982 *Possessions and the Poor in Luke–Acts*. Linz: Studien zum Neuen Testament und seiner Umwelt.

Seitz, O. J.
1969 Love Your Enemies. *New Testament Studies* 16:39-54.

Siebald, M.
1992 Dives and Lazarus. Pp. 208-210 in *A Dictionary of Biblical Tradition in English Literature.* Editor, D. L. Jeffrey. Grand Rapids: Eerdmans.

Siker, J. S.
1992 First to the Gentiles: A Literary Analysis of Luke 4:16-30. *Journal of Biblical Literature* 111:73-92.

Smith, D. E.
1987 Table Fellowship as a Literary Motif in the Gospel of Luke. *Journal of Biblical Literature* 106:613-638.

1989 The Historical Jesus at Table. Pp. 466-489 in *Society of Biblical Literature 1989 Seminar Papers.* Editor, D. J. Lull. Atlanta: Scholars Press.

Smith, R. H.
1964a The Household Lamps of Palestine in Old Testament Times. *Biblical Archaeologist* 27:1-31.

1964b The Household Lamps of Palestine in Intertestamental Times. *Biblical Archaeologist* 27:101-124.

1966 The Household Lamps of Palestine in New Testament Times. *Biblical Archaeologist* 29:1-27.

Soards, M.
1987 *The Passion according to Luke. The Special Material of Luke 22.* Sheffield: JSOT Press.

1994 *The Speeches in Acts: Their Content, Context, and Concerns.* Louisville: Westminster/John Knox.

Souter, A.
1953 *Pocket Lexicon.* Oxford: Oxford University Press.

Spencer, W. D. and A. B. Spencer
1990 *The Prayer Life of Jesus.* Lanham, MA: University Press of America.

Sproston, W. E.
1987 'The Scripture' in John 17:12. Pp. 24-36 in *Scripture: Meaning and Method.* Editor, B. P. Thompson. Hull: University Press.

Stagg, F.
1955 *The Book of Acts: The Early Struggle for an Unhindered Gospel.* Nashville: Broadman.

1967 The Journey toward Jerusalem in Luke's Gospel. *Review and Expositor.* 64:499-512.

Stagg, F. and E. Stagg
1978 *Woman in the World of Jesus.* Philadelphia: Westminster.

Stanton, G. N.
1973 On the Christology of Q. Pp. 27-42 in *Christ and Spirit in the New Testament.* Editors, Lindars and Smalley. Cambridge: Cambridge University Press.

1990 *The Gospels and Jesus.* Oxford: Oxford University Press.

Stein, R. H.
1981 *An Introduction to the Parables of Jesus.* Philadelphia: Westminster.

1983 Luke 1:1-4 and Traditionsgeschichte. *Journal of the Evangelical Theological Society* 26:421-430.

1992 *Luke.* The New American Commentary. Nashville: Broadman.

Stegner, W. R.
1985 The Parable of the Good Samaritan and Leviticus 18:5. Pp. 27-38 in *The Living Text: Festschrift for E. W. Saunders.* Editors, Groh and Jowett. Washington, DC: University Press of America.

Stern, J. B.
1966 Jesus' Citation of Dt 6,5 and Lv 19,18 in the Light of Jewish Tradition. *Catholic Biblical Quarterly* 28:312-316.

Stevenson, J., editor
1963 *A New Eusebius.* London: SPCK.

Stonehouse, N. B.
1951 *The Witness of Luke to Christ.* London: Tyndale.

Stott, J. R.
1961 *The Preacher's Portrait: Some New Testament Word Studies.* London: Tyndale.

1968 *Basic Christianity.* Grand Rapids: Eerdmans.

1970 *Christ the Controversialist.* London: Tyndale.

1978 *The Message of the Sermon on the Mount.* Downers Grove: InterVarsity.

Summers, R.
1972 *Commentary on Luke.* Waco: Word.

Swanson, R. J.
1975 *The Horizontal Line Synopsis of the Gospels.* Dillsboro: Western North Carolina Press.

Sylva, D.
1986 The Temple Curtain and Jesus' Death in the Gospel of Luke. *Journal of Biblical Literature* 105:239-250.

Talbert, C. H.
1966 *Luke and the Gnostics.* Nashville: Abingdon.

1974 *Literary Patterns, Theological Themes and the Genre of Luke–Acts.* Society of Biblical Literature Manuscript Series 20. Missoula, MT: Scholars Press.

1978 *Perspectives on Luke–Acts.* Danville, VA: Association of Baptist Professors of Religion.

1984a *Acts.* Knox Preaching Guides. Atlanta: John Knox Press.

1984b *Luke–Acts: New Perspectives for the Society of Biblical Literature Seminar.* New York: Crossroad.

1989 *Reading Luke: A Literary and Theological Commentary on the Third Gospel.* New York: Crossroad.

Taylor, Vincent
1962 Gospel of Luke. Pp. 180-188 in *The Interpreter's Dictionary of the Bible.* Editor, G. A. Buttrick. Nashville: Abingdon Press.

Tannehill, R.
1985 Israel in Luke–Acts: A Tragic Story. *Journal of Biblical Literature* 104:69-85.

1986 *The Narrative Unity of Luke–Acts: A Literary Interpretation,* vol. 1. Philadelphia: Fortress.

Theissen, G.
1983 *The Miracle Stories of the Early Christian Tradition.* Philadelphia: Fortress.

Theissen, G. and A. Merz
1998 *The Historical Jesus.* London: SCM.

Thielman, F.
1994 *Paul and the Law.* Downers Grove: InterVarsity.

Thompson, G. H.
1960 Called-Proved-Obedient: A Study in the Baptism and Temptation Narratives of Matthew and Luke. *Journal of Theological Studies* 11:1-12.

Thompson, M. N.
1989 *The Role of Disbelief in Mark.* New York: Paulist Press.

Throckmorton, B. H., Jr.,
1973 *Gospel Parallels: A Synopsis of the First Three Gospels.* Nashville: Nelson.

Tiede, D. L.
1980 *Prophecy and History in Luke–Acts.* Philadelphia: Fortress.

Tolbert, M. O.
1970 *Luke.* Pp. 1-187 in *Broadman Bible Commentary,* vol. 9. Editor, C. J. Allen. Nashville: Broadman.

1979 *Perspectives on the Parables: An Approach to Multiple Interpretations.* Philadelphia: Fortress.

Toon, P.
1984 *The Ascension of Our Lord.* Nashville: Thomas Nelson.

Trites, A. A.
1977 *The New Testament Concept of Witness.* Society for New Testament Studies Monograph Series 31. Cambridge and New York: Cambridge University Press.

1978 The Prayer Motif in Luke–Acts. Pp.168-186 in *Perspectives on Luke–Acts.* Editor, C. H. Talbert. Danville, VA: Association of Baptist Professors of Religion.

1983 *New Testament Witness for Today's World.* Valley Forge: Judson Press.

1984 The Ascension. *Atlantic Baptist* 20/4:23-24.

1987a The Transfiguration in the Theology of Luke: Some Redactional Links. Pp. 71-81 in *The Glory of Christ in the New Testament.* Editors, L. D. Hurst and N. T. Wright. Oxford: Clarendon.

1987b Teaching Resources. *Baptist Leader,* March, 34-36, 40-42, 46-48, 52-54, 58-60.

1992 The Blessings and Warning of the Kingdom (Matthew 5:3-12; 7:13-27). *Review and Expositor,* 89/2:179-196.

1994 *The Transfiguration of Christ: A Hinge of Holy History.* Hantsport, NS: Lancelot.

1995 Luke. Pp. 422-428 in *The Complete Who's Who in the Bible.* Editor, P. Gardner. London: Marshall Pickering.

1996 Church Growth in the Book of Acts. Pp. 44-54 in *Vital New Testament Issues.* Editor, R. Zuck. Grand Rapids: Kregel.

1997 The Resilient Christ. Pp. 43-54 in *What's Cooking? [A Festschrift in Celebration of the 75th Birthday of Mary Ella Milham].* Editor, J. S. Murray. Fredericton: University of New Brunswick.

Tuckett, C. M.

1982 *The Messianic Secret.* Philadelphia: Fortress.

1997 *Luke.* New Testament Guides. Sheffield: Sheffield Academic Press.

Turlington, H. E.

1967 *Luke's Witness to Jesus.* Nashville: Broadman.

Turner, M. B.

1981 Jesus and the Spirit in Lucan Perspective. *Tyndale Bulletin* 32:3-42.

1991 The Spirit and the Power of Jesus' Miracles in the Lucan Conception. *Novum Testamentum* 33:124-152.

Twelftree, G. H.

1985 *Christ Triumphant: Exorcism Then and Now.* London: Hodder & Stoughton.

1993 *Jesus the Exorcist.* Wissenschaftliche Untersuchungen zum Neuen Testament 54. Tübingen: Mohr Siebeck.

Tyson, J. B.

1986a *The Death of Jesus in Luke–Acts.* Columbia: University of South Carolina Press.

1986b *Luke–Acts and the Jewish People: Eight Critical Perspectives.* Minneapolis: Augsburg.

1999 *Luke, Judaism, and the Scholars: Critical Approaches to Luke–Acts.* Columbia: University of South Carolina Press.

Verhey, A.

1984 *The Great Reversal: Ethics and the New Testament.* Grand Rapids: Eerdmans.

Vermes, G., translator

1997 *The Dead Sea Scrolls.* London: Penguin Books.

Via, D. O., Jr.

1967 *The Parables: Their Existential and Literary Dimension.* Philadelphia: Fortress.

1985 *The Ethics of Mark's Gospel—In the Middle of Time.* Philadelphia: Fortress.

Vielhauer, P.

1966 On 'Paulinism' in the Acts of the Apostles. Pp. 33-50 in *Studies in Luke–Acts.* Editors, L. E. Keck and J. L. Martyn. Nashville: Abingdon.

Wainwright, G.

1980 *Doxology: The Praise of God in Worship, Doctrine and Life.* New York: Oxford University Press.

Walker, P. W., editor

1992 *Jerusalem Past and Present in the Purposes of God.* Cambridge: Tyndale House.

1996 *Jesus and the Holy City: New Testament Perspectives on Jerusalem.* Grand Rapids: Eerdmans.

Wansbrough, H., editor

1990 *The New Jerusalem Bible.* New York: Doubleday.

Watty, W. W.

1981–1982 Jesus and the Temple—Cleansing or Cursing? *Expository Times* 93:235-239.

Weber, H.

1979 *Jesus and the Children.* Geneva: World Council of Churches.

Wenham, D.

1984 *The Rediscovery of Jesus' Eschatological Discourse.* Sheffield: JSOT

Wenham, D. and C. Blomberg, editors

1986 *Gospel Perspectives 6: The Miracles of Jesus.* Sheffield: JSOT Press.

Wenham, J. W.
1991 The Identification of Luke. *Evangelical Quarterly* 63:3-44.

Westcott, B. F., and F. J. A. Hort
1882 *The New Testament in the Original Greek.* New York: Harper & Bros.

Westerholm, S. and C. A. Evans
1978 *Jesus and Scribal Authority.* Lund: CWK Gleerup.

Westermann, C.
1990 *The Parables of Jesus in the Light of the Old Testament.* Minneapolis: Fortress.

Weymouth, R. F.
1912 *The New Testament in Modern Speech.* London: James Clarke.

White, R. E. O.
1979 *The Mind of Matthew.* Philadelphia: Westminster.
1987 *Luke's Case for Christianity.* Harrisburg: Morehouse.

Wiedemann, T.
1989 *Adults and Children in the Roman Empire.* London: Routledge.

Wikgren, A., editor
1961 *Early Christian Origins.* Festschrift for H. R. Willoughby. Chicago: Quadrangle Books.

Wilcock, M.
1979 *Savior of the World: The Message of Luke's Gospel.* Downers Grove: InterVarsity.

Williams, Charles B.
2000 *The New Testament in the Language of the People.* Millennium ed. Montreat, NC:
    Sprawls Educational Publishing.

Willis, W., editor
1987 *The Kingdom of God in 20th Century Interpretation.* Peabody, MA: Hendrickson.

Wilson, J. and V. Tsaferis
1998 Banias Dig Reveals King's Palace. *Biblical Archaeological Review* 24:54-61.

Wilson, R. R.
1977 *Genealogy and History in the Biblical World.* New Haven: Yale University.

Wink, W.
1968 *John the Baptist in the Gospel Tradition.* Cambridge: Cambridge University Press.

Winter, B. W. and A. D. Clarke, editors
1993 *The Book of Acts in Its Ancient Literary Setting.* Grand Rapids: Eerdmans.

Witherington, Ben, III
1984 *Women in the Ministry of Jesus.* Society for New Testament Studies Monograph Series 51.
    Cambridge: Cambridge University Press.
1990 *The Christology of Jesus.* Minneapolis: Fortress.
1999 *Jesus the Seer: The Progress of Prophecy.* Peabody, MA: Hendrickson.
2002 On the Road with Mary Magdalene, Joanna, Susanna, and Other Disciples. Pp. 133-139 in
    A Feminist Companion to Luke. Editor, A. Levine. New York: Sheffield Academic Press.

Wren, M.
1984 Sonship in Luke: The Advantage of a Literary Approach. *Scottish Journal of Theology* 37:310-311.

Wright, N. T.
1992 *The New Testament and the People of God.* Minneapolis: Fortress.
1996 *Jesus and the Victory of God.* Minneapolis: Fortress.
2002 *The Contemporary Quest for Jesus.* Minneapolis: Fortress.

Young, B. H.
1989 *Jesus and His Jewish Parables.* New York: Paulist Press.

Young, N. H.
1983 The Commandment to Love Your Neighbor as Yourself and the Parable of the Good Samaritan
    (10:25-37). *Andrews University Seminary Studies* 21:265-272.

Zerwick, M.
1988 *A Grammatical Analysis of the Greek New Testament.* Rome: Pontifical Biblical Institute.

Zwiep, A. W.
1997 *The Ascension of the Messiah in Lukan Christology.* Leiden: Brill.

Acts

WILLIAM J. LARKIN

INTRODUCTION TO
Acts

THE BOOK OF ACTS is more than first-century church history; it is a narrative about the Triune God on an unstoppable mission to the ends of the earth. The book of Acts intends to evangelize us by persuading us that the second half of the gospel— salvation for all the nations (Luke 24:47)—is true. God "on mission" not only means that all three of the Trinity initiate the mission but also that they are the direct agents of mission. The Father "calls" both Jew and Gentile to himself (2:39). What Jesus "began to do and teach" (1:1), as recorded in Luke's Gospel, he continues—only now from heaven—and the Spirit bears direct witness (5:32). The momentum of Acts is ever outward, not only geographically, as promised in Jesus' final words (1:8), but also ethnically—from Jews to Samaritans to God fearers to pagan Gentiles. And that momentum extends beyond the book's last verse, as it draws us, the evangelized, into the company of those on mission, who also evangelize boldly (28:31).

AUTHOR

The author of the book of Acts did not identify himself, but he did claim to have been a traveling companion of Paul. The reader discovers this through the "we passages" scattered throughout the second part of the book (16:10-17; 20:5-15; 21:1-8; 27:1–28:16); these uses of the first person plural indicate that the writer was a participant in certain events recorded in the book.[1]

The author's reference to the "first book" he wrote (see Acts 1:1) is undoubtedly a reference to the third Gospel. The same addressee, Theophilus; similarities of interest (for example, salvation of the Gentiles); and similar language and style lead to the conclusion that he also authored the Gospel of Luke. Church tradition, from the second century onward, consistently testifies that the author is Luke, the beloved physician (Col 4:14), and often associates him with the church of Syrian Antioch (Carson, Moo, Morris 1992:186). By using other patristic evidence and reasoning from the content of Luke–Acts and Paul's letters, John Wenham (1991) has proposed that the references in the New Testament to Luke, whether formal (*Loukios* [TG3066, ZG3372]; cf. 13:1; Rom 16:21) or familiar in spelling (*Loukas* [TG3065, ZG3371]; cf. Col 4:14; 2 Tim 4:11; Phlm 1:24), are all to the same person, who is also the author of Luke–Acts. This identification further fills out the author's profile. He is from Cyrene and is Paul's blood relative. Luke, then, was a Hellenistic Jew and not a proselyte or a Gentile. This means that the author of Acts was at one and the same time "a Jew, steeped in the traditions of his fathers, having the fullest entré into the institutions of the Jewish faith" and that he, as a founder and leader in the church at Syrian Antioch, was "partly instrumental in starting a movement of the church towards the Gentiles, which was as important as Peter's baptism of Cornelius" (Wenham 1991:38-40).

DATE

Acts should be dated sometime between the last events recorded in Acts (AD 62) and the terminus of the expected life span of Paul's traveling companions (AD 85). Scholars have normally opted for either the early sixties or sometime in the seventies to mid eighties.

There are seven "historical silences" in Acts that, together with the content Luke presents, suggest that the book predates certain historical events (Mehat 1992:174-175). These point to a date in the early sixties. Luke does not tell his readers about the following mid- to late-sixties events: (1) the outcome of Paul's trial; (2) the death of James, the brother of Jesus; (3) Nero's persecution around AD 64; (4-6) the deaths of Peter, Paul, and Nero; (7) the Jewish revolt (AD 66) and the fall of Jerusalem in AD 70. The book's use of evaluations by Roman authorities as an apologetic for Christianity's innocence, Luke's concern with the reception of Gentile Christians into a predominantly Jewish Christian church, and the prominence of Paul in the narrative also indicate a time before these events.

Acts devotes so much space to the events of the three years immediately preceding its seemingly abrupt conclusion (chs 20–28) that it is likely the events had just occurred. The accuracy of its geographical, political, and sociocultural details is best explained if the work was produced close to the events. These facts could not have been recovered through library research at a later time since there were no such reference works in the first century.

An early sixties date makes the ending of Acts understandable both in terms of its apparent abruptness and its appropriateness as a fitting conclusion. Luke reports the course of early church history only as far as he knows it. This does not include Paul's death, even though the circumstances Luke portrays prepare his readers for it (20:25-28). The date in the early sixties does, however, bring the narrative to a point where Paul is able, though a prisoner, to preach boldly and without hindrance the Kingdom of God and teach about the Lord Jesus Christ (28:31), thus confirming the truth of a gospel that had claimed that God's message of repentance unto the forgiveness of sins in the Messiah was for all nations (Luke 1:4 [implicit in that Theophilus is not a Jewish name]; 24:46-47; Acts 1:8; 28:31). Such a conclusion communicates most effectively if it was written in a time when Christianity experienced relative freedom and official protection—namely AD 62–63. At this time the Jews had not revolted, and Christians would have still been considered a sect of Judaism, granting them official protection. Further, it was in AD 64 that Nero used Christians as scapegoats for a fire he had set in the capital.

AUDIENCE

Luke dedicated his work to "most honorable Theophilus" (Luke 1:3; cf. Acts 1:1). The honorific title could indicate the equestrian rank in Roman society. Moberly (1993:23) thinks so, for he identifies Theophilus as a "man of Roman citizenship and Equestrian rank, possibly another Roman governor or ex-governor." At the least, the title points to a person of elite social standing. The equestrian rank in the imperial Roman society was the second aristocratic order, ranking only below the senatorial rank in status. It provided the officer corps for the Roman army and a wide range of civil administrators.

Recent studies concerning the audience implied by Luke's writings indicate that Luke wrote to an ethnically and socially mixed group that lived in an urban setting (Esler 1987). Some scholars proceed further, based on the content of Luke–Acts, to characterize the elite element as either "elite periphery" or "isolates," "in-between" people "restricted by prestige and rank but enabled by money and circumstance" (Moxnes 1994:387; Botha 1995:155). Though some see the evidence from the details of Luke–Acts as pointing to any of the urban centers of the eastern Mediterranean (Moxnes 1994:380), others see Luke writing within and to the setting of urban Rome (Domeris 1993). Given the evidence I will present for the occasion and purpose of writing (discussed below), Rome does seem the most likely location for the audience. Theophilus, then, is representative of the literate, upper-middle-class Roman public for which Luke wrote; it was a "sophisticated audience" who would have "an appreciation of subtlety" (Soards 1990:47).

Many scholars (including all those cited so far) heavily favor seeing Luke's audience as Christian, though there has been consistent recognition that the works could be directed to non-Christians. Downing (1995:91) gives this carefully nuanced assessment: "If Christian Luke has Theophilus as a friend or patron (or friendly patron), he is most likely at least a sympathizer, more likely a member of the group." Since I will argue for an evangelistic purpose for the book, I see Acts' audience as basically non-Christian. Downing's (1995:94-96) proposal of symposia and dinner settings for the readings of the works accords with such an audience and purpose, though he again sees it happening within a Christian context.

OCCASION AND PURPOSE OF WRITING

The occasion for Acts should, then, be found in the encounter of the Roman upper-middle class with the Christian faith. This audience had been informed of Christianity in an environment where many voices contested Christianity's value. The Jewish community in Rome, according to Suetonius, "constantly made disturbances at the instigation of *Chrestus*" during Claudius's reign (*Claudius* 25.4). Evidently, Christian missionary activity in the Jewish community caused public disorder (taking *Chrestus* as a variant form of *Christus*). Claudius issued an edict that the Jews be expelled. This seems to have been implemented to the extent of the expulsion of the ringleaders and a prohibition of assembly (18:2; *Dio Cassius* 60.6.6). The attention the emperor gave to the Jewish-Christian controversy and the influential position Jews held in Roman society makes it likely that their negative evaluation of Christianity would have had some impact on inquiring, non-Christian Romans. As Acts and Romans and Philippians (works written to or in the Roman context of the late fifties and early sixties) bear witness, unbelieving Jews branded Christianity as a disorderly sect, hardly innocent before the state and unworthy of the attention of law-abiding Romans (Luke 23:4-5, 13-16, 22, 47; Acts 17:5-9; 18:13; 24:4-5; Rom 13:1-7).

The initial natural reaction of this level of society would be to despise the Christian faith as an eastern cult (16:20-21; 25:18-20; cf. Rom 1:15-16). When Tacitus and Suetonius describe the persecution of Christians under Nero in the middle sixties, they term Christianity "a pernicious superstition . . . a disease . . . horrible or shameful; a new and mischievous superstition" (Tacitus, *Annals* 15.44; Suetonius *Nero* 16.2). Moberly (1993:23) judges that Luke's work would have seemed "subversive, anti-social, and foolish" to most men of the equestrian class. This negative assessment of Christianity was so pervasive among the general populace that Nero was able to accuse and punish Christians for his own incendiary acts. Tacitus indicates that Christians were "loathed for their vices" and that they "were convicted, not so much on the count of arson as for hatred of the human race" (*Annals* 15:44). Not only did their worship of Jesus threaten to corrupt, if not obliterate, native forms of Roman worship, but their refusal to invoke the Roman gods and make offerings to the emperor's statue was a treasonous act, which undermined the empire's security (cf. Pliny *Letters* 10.96). Thus, their crime in Roman eyes was *odio humani generis*—"hatred of the human race."

Some in the Roman upper-middle class, initially informed about the claims of the Christian gospel, then, may have heard of Paul's case. If the negative assessment of Christianity by the Jewish community or by their own native biases had not given them pause to embrace the gospel, at the least it would have created some confusion. A final element to add to the confusion was the church's internal debate over the nature of salvation by grace through faith. Judaizers were attacking the legitimacy of a salvation by grace for the Gentiles (Luke 18:9; Acts 15:1-2; 21:20-21; Rom 10:1-21; Phil 3:1-16).[2] What was the truth about this Christian gospel? Was it certain? Was it for a Roman?

If this is the occasion, what is Luke's purpose in writing Luke–Acts? Is it edification or evangelism? A recently published assessment of Acts (Green 1997:17) lists seven views (with chief proponents) concerning purpose: (1) defense of the Christian church to Rome; (2) defense of Rome to the Christian church; (3) apology for Paul against Judaizers; (4) edification providing an eschatological corrective; (5) edification providing reassurance of the truth of the gospel; (6) edification to assist the church in legitimizing itself over against Judaism; and (7) edification to encourage Christians in allegiance to Jesus, which involves a basic social and political stance within the empire. Our framing of the question is intended to set the discussion as a choice between a variant of number one—an evangelistic purpose—and numbers four through seven. (Numbers two and three are less likely as a purpose since they are centered on a purpose particular to Acts and/or Paul and therefore are not comprehensive enough to encompass both the third Gospel and Acts.) Was Luke providing certainty to those who had embraced the faith (edification), or was he providing proof of the truth of the faith so that they would embrace it (evangelism)?

The soundest way to pursue this discussion is to assess four factors in Luke's writing that all scholars agree must be examined if we are to arrive at a satisfactory answer concerning Luke's purpose: Luke's preface (Luke 1:1-4), appropriate details, central themes, and literary genre (Gasque 1978:119; for discussion of literary genre see "Literary Style," p. 369). Luke explicitly gives us his purpose in the clause: "so you can be certain of the truth of everything you were taught" (Luke 1:4). The kind of knowledge (*epiginōskō* [TG1921, ZG2105]; NLT "be certain") Luke desires for his readers includes both recognition of the truth about facts (cf. 4:13) and Spirit-aided insight (cf. usage in Luke 24:31). Luke wanted his readers to be reassured of "the truth" of all they had been taught. This truth is a certainty based on a clear understanding of the evidence (21:34; 22:30) and also the firm assurance that such truth has personal significance for the reader (2:36).

The interpretation of the last phrase of Luke's purpose statement helps to determine whether this certainty of knowledge is for the edification of the church or the evangelism of non-Christians. The NLT rendering "so you can be certain of the truth of everything you were taught" (cf. *katecheō* [TG2727, ZG2994], "taught") suggests an edifying purpose because Theophilus is represented as having already made a decision and been catechized. Although *katecheō* eventually became a technical term in the church for the instruction of new believers, in biblical usage it can also refer simply to informing someone about something. Luke uses it both ways in Acts ("taught," 18:25; "have been told," 21:21).

This range of meaning opens up the possibility that Luke 1:4 may be referring to the fact that Theophilus has simply been introduced to information about the Christian faith in evangelistic contacts. Luke's writing, then, would aim to provide confirmation to Theophilus concerning what he has been informed of, in order to persuade him to embrace the gospel. I would argue that the use of similar vocabulary in Acts 21-23 provides appropriate parallels to Theophilus's situation. Just as Jewish Christians in Jerusalem had received information—albeit incorrect information—about Paul's encouragement of Diaspora Jews to apostatize from Judaism (21:21, 24), so Theophilus had received information about the Christian faith. As Paul acted to correct the misinformation by his actions, Luke sought to confirm the truth of the Christian Good News through writing his Gospel. And just as the tribune sought to know the truth about the cause of the Temple disturbance (21:34; 22:30; cf. 23:28), so Luke desired to help Theophilus understand the truth of the gospel of which he had been informed.

If this use of *katecheō* to mean "inform" points to an initial exposure to Christianity, then the "everything" (*logon* [TG3056, ZG3364]) refers to the content of the gospel. That gospel, summarized in Luke 24:46-48, has two parts: (1) *salvation accomplished*—Jesus said, "It was written long ago that the Messiah would suffer and die and rise from the dead on the third day," and (2) *salvation applied*—"this message would be proclaimed in the authority of his name to all the nations, beginning in Jerusalem: 'There is forgiveness of sins for all who repent.' You are witnesses of all these things." The Gospel of Luke was written to confirm the truth of "salvation accomplished." Luke penned Acts to provide a basis for certainty that the "salvation applied" portion of the gospel was true and applied to his contemporaries. Understanding Luke 1:4 in this way requires that we see Theophilus as the object of evangelism, not catechesis.

A number of details in Acts point to its evangelistic purpose and a Roman reading public. For example, no matter the numbers or ethnicity involved, each conversion account focuses on the desired response to the gospel and in that way fulfills an evangelistic purpose. This is achieved rhetorically in Acts 2, through a citation of Old Testament promise (Acts 2:21, citing Joel 2:32), descriptions of the crowd's internal and external reactions (Acts 2:37, 41), and through Peter's explanation of the correct response to the salvation offer (2:38-40). The Pentecost account serves not simply as a model to edify Christian witnesses but as an evangelistic call to non-Christians, in this case a Jewish group. Paul's conversion experience, reported three times throughout Acts (chs 9; 22; 26), includes a commissioning to missionary service. This might lead us to place material about Paul in the category of contributions to a missionary model and to regard these accounts as oriented to the church's edification (Kurz 1990b). However, each successive account, while not abandoning the theme of Paul's commissioning, progressively brings out more aspects of the gospel's "salvation applied" content (22:14-16; 26:16-18; cf. 26:22-23). By the time we get to Acts 26:29, Paul stands as a very explicit model of conversion (Brawley 1988).

The other conversion experience reported multiple times concerns Cornelius, his household, and his friends (10:1–11:18). Through commands in angelic visions and the Spirit's speaking, God takes the initiative in gathering the Cornelius group and bringing the messenger Peter to them. Each successive telling of the vision gives more of the "salvation applied" content, including the values and responses worth emulating (10:4-8, 22, 32; 11:14). The climax of Peter's speech links the Cornelius group to the evangelistic purpose of Acts (10:42-43). The Holy Spirit affirms their reception of the message by coming upon them while Peter was still speaking (10:44). Peter's spirited defense of his witness at Caesarea and his use of it to settle the dispute over circumcision also leave in the reader's mind a positive impression of this Gentile audience and its response to the gospel (11:1-18; 15:7-11).

When these case studies are combined with a survey of the other conversion accounts (particularly those of individual Romans in Acts 16) and the trial scenes of chapters 24–26, it becomes increasingly clear that Luke recounts these events in order to evangelize his reader. What is highlighted in each is not the example of the witness but its reception. In other words, the scenes provide more detail about Lydia, the Philippian jailer, Felix, Festus, and Agrippa in their respective responses to the gospel message than they do about Paul in his method of witness. Luke includes many accounts that highlight individual non-Jews, particularly non-

Christian Romans, who often respond positively to the early church's missionary message (S. Wilson 1973:ch 7). In this way, he demonstrates the truth of the "salvation applied" portion of the gospel. Repentance and forgiveness of sins have been proclaimed effectively in Christ's name among all the nations because it is for all nations—including all of Luke's readers.

The distinctive theological themes of Acts have to do with the gospel message, but especially with its "salvation applied" portion: proper response, salvation blessings, and universal offer. Luke consistently presented the "salvation accomplished" portion of the saving message: the divinely ordained mission of the Messiah in suffering and rising in fulfillment of Scripture (2:23-32; 3:18; 4:11; 5:30; 7:52; 10:39, 43; 13:32-39; 17:3; 26:22-23). But just as consistently he developed his theme of repentance as the proper response to God's offer of salvation—mainly in preaching portions of Acts (2:38; 8:22; 17:30; 20:21; 26:18; cf. 9:35; 14:15). The promise of salvation blessings (2:38; 3:26; 4:12; 5:31; 10:43; 13:38; 22:16; 26:17-18) and the universal scope of the salvation offer (2:39; 3:25; 10:43; 13:39, 46-48; 17:30-31; 22:15, 21; 26:17, 23) also occur often in the speeches of Acts. These themes definitely advance an evangelistic purpose.

CANONICITY AND TEXTUAL HISTORY

There is firm evidence that from the early fourth century Acts was listed among the acknowledged books of the canon (Eusebius *History* 3.4.1; 3.2.5). This is confirmed in the subsequent canonical lists found in Athanasius's 39th Festal Letter (AD 367) and in Jerome's *Lives of Illustrious Men* 7. Earlier, from the mid-second- to early third-century church fathers, we find allusions or references to Acts in Tertullian (*Against Marcion* 5.2; *Prescriptions against Heretics* 22); Clement of Alexandria (*Miscellanies* 5.12-13); and Irenaeus (e.g., *Against Heresies* 1.15.1-3). In each case, false teaching is being countered with an authoritative appeal to the content of Acts.

The earliest evidence for the canonicity of Acts is mixed in terms of the certainty it yields. On the one hand, Justin Martyr (AD 100–165) has a number of possible allusions, which at best keep open the possibility he knew Acts (Barrett 1994:41-44). The strongest allusion is in his *Apology* (39.3): "From Jerusalem there went out into the world men, twelve in number, and they were uninstructed (*idiōtēs* [TG2399, ZG2626]; same word as in 4:13), unable to speak [cf. 4:13, where a similar concept is conveyed by a different Greek word], but by the power of God they indicated to the whole human race that they had been sent by Christ to teach all men the word of God" (as translated in Barrett 1994:41; note Justin's factual divergence from the Acts account of the apostles' role in the prosecution of the church's missionary task). Another group of early witnesses, which were once thought to date from the latter half of the second century, are the Anti-Marcionite Prologues. These mention that Luke wrote Acts. "They are now held to have been neither directed against Marcion, nor written so early, nor even to be of the same date" (Cross and Livingstone 1997:77). This leaves the Muratorian Canon of the late second century as the first clear statement to place Acts among the books of the New Testament canon. It reads, "But the acts of all the apostles are written in one book. For the 'most excellent Theophilus,' . . . Luke . . . summarizes the several things that in his own presence have come to pass, as also by the omission of the passion of Peter he makes quite clear, and equally by (the omission) of the journey of Paul, who from the city (of Rome) proceeded to Spain" (Hennecke 1963:1.43-44). In this statement we see the canonicity of Acts is clear and unequivocal, and we may conclude that the church acknowledged it as part of the canon from the end of the second century forward.

If establishing the canonicity of Acts is fairly straightforward, untangling its textual history is not (see Metzger 1994:222-236; Barrett 1994:2-29). There are two distinct forms of the Greek text of Acts: the Alexandrian text type, the one traditionally regarded as the authentic text of Acts; and the Western text type. The Alexandrian is supported by 𝔓41, 𝔓45, 𝔓50, 𝔓53, 𝔓74, ℵ, A, B, C, Y, 0189, 33, 81, 104, 326, 1175, 1739. The Western text is supported in the main by Codex Bezae (also noted as D), 𝔓38, 𝔓48, syr^h (readings marked by * or mg), African Old Latin (it^h), and citations in Cyprian and Augustine. The difference between the two text forms, first of all, is length. The Western text is 8.5 percent longer than the Alexandrian text form (19,983 words versus 18,401 words). According to Metzger (1994:223), the Western text is generally more picturesque and circumstantial, while the Alexandrian text form is more colorless and in some places more obscure. There is not much difference between the text types in terms of date. Both appeared very early so that we cannot expect on the assessment of the age of manuscripts alone "to say which emerged before the other" (Barrett 1994:27; in fact, Barrett says we cannot determine this at all). In the early period, the Alexandrian text seems to be focused in northern Egypt (hence "Alexandrian"), while the Western text appears in various localities of the Greco-Roman world.

Metzger (1994:223-232) surveys nine theories of the origin of the Western text form and finds each in one way or another defective. This is mostly because each chooses a different aspect of the problem on which to concentrate. None, therefore, gives a comprehensive explanation. He basically approves of Haenchen's (1971:50-60) characterization of the Western differences and their probable origin: (1) A great number of minor variants seem to be present to clarify, explain, or smooth over the text. These do not indicate the work of an editor but a text form widely current in the church, as evidenced by its use by those who do not normally support the Western text form: Marcion, Tatian, Irenaeus, and others. (2) Another group of variants reflect the work of an early reviser who eliminated textual gaps and added historical, biographical, and geographical details (see also Aland 1985; Comfort 1992:112). (3) There are variants that belong only to Codex Bezae (D) and point to the work of two scribes.

How shall we understand and assess these phenomena so that we can decide at any given point in Acts what is the probable wording of the original text? Metzger (1994:235) calls for a measured, eclectic approach. It might be better to think in terms of Western *texts* rather than the Western *text*. It might be better to think in terms of a Western text form tendency rather than a Western editor at one point in the process. As Strange (1992:37) points out, "It is legitimate to refer to *the* Western text, as long as it is understood that what is meant is a broad stream of textual tradition, and a way of handling the text, rather than a coherent recension of the text created at a specific time."

It is necessary to remember that Codex Bezae has its own history as well, and this must be factored into any assessment of its witness at any point (see Parker 1992). All these cautions mean, in practical terms, that each textual problem must be decided on its own merits, bringing fully into play transcriptional and intrinsic probabilities in dialogue with the extrinsic probabilities. The Western text at any given point could possibly contain the original wording. Then, again, there may be times when it contains factual material that is accurate but not part of the original text. In those cases the Alexandrian reading is preferable. In fact, as Metzger (1994:235) reviewed the work of the UBS committee, he saw "that more often than not the shorter, Alexandrian text was preferred." This commentary will follow the same kind of eclectic approach, judging each variant unit on the merits of its own particular evidence, utilizing the assessment of all three probabilities. Attention will also be given to Western text material that, though not regarded as part of the original text, does appear to contain accurate factual information.

LITERARY STYLE

David Aune (1987:139) classifies Luke–Acts as "general history," analogous to general and antiquarian histories, which "focused on the history of a particular people (typically the Greeks or Romans) from mythical beginnings to a point in the recent past, including contacts (usually conflicts) with other national groups in various geographical theaters." Many scholars see the basic genre of Luke–Acts as history, whether general or specialized—historical monograph, political history, or apologetic historiography (Green 1997:8; Downing 1995:99). There have been, however, different suggestions: biography (Talbert 1974), novel (Pervo 1987), and technical treatise (Alexander 1993).[3] Alexander has made a strong case for the Lukan prefaces being in the tradition of "scientific treatises"—technical and professional writing on medicine, mathematics, engineering, etc. Downing's reflections (1995:100), in part, provide a way to wed such prefaces with the historical content of Luke–Acts. Luke, a physician, uses a preface from a genre with which he is familiar to introduce a "non-professional history," not unlike Calliphorous, surgeon with the Fifth Lancers, to whom Lucian refers (*How to Write History* 16). In the case of Acts, this is an "apologetic history," which Moberly (1993:7) consistently labels "a missionary brief." Such a genre would serve well an evangelistic purpose that sought to persuade Romans of the truth and universal relevance of the Christian gospel.[4]

If Acts is the second half of an apologetic history/missionary brief and is written to evangelize an upper-middle-class Roman reading public, how, then, did Luke proceed to accomplish this purpose? He used a variety of methods: programmatic statements, pointing to an overarching organizing principle; summary statements to create "panels" of episodes; parallelism and patterns on various levels; allocation of space and the use of repetition; and variation of the scope of focus from individual to group.

Acts 1:8 gives an organizing principle for Acts in terms of geography: "You will be my witnesses, telling people about me everywhere—in Jerusalem, throughout Judea, in Samaria, and to the ends of the earth." In general terms, the narrative does seem to play out in that fashion (chs 1–5—Jerusalem; 6:1–11:18—Judea and Samaria; 11:19–28:31—the ends of the earth). But because Acts ends in Rome, which for a first-century Mediterranean inhabitant was at the center (not at the ends) of the earth, geography is not a completely satisfying way to look at the structure of Acts. Some also point out that Acts also organizes the church's outward movement in ethnic terms. The gospel goes across various cultural thresholds to persons increasingly ethnically distant from the Jewish people. It comes first to the Hebrew-speaking Jew (chs 1–5), then to the Hellenistic Jew (chs 6–7), the Samaritan (8:1–25), a God-fearing eunuch (or proselyte, 8:26-40), the God-fearing Gentile (10:1–11:18), and, finally, the pagan Gentile (11:19ff). While this perspective, in combination with the geographical, produces more satisfying results, there is still much of Acts that must be accounted for (e.g., the audience 2:5-11 does not fit under the "Hebrew-speaking" rubric).

If we think in terms of the contexts and agents of mission, we can bring the whole of Acts into perspective. Chapters 1–12 show the Jerusalem church in its establishment (chs 1–2); its growth, including witness in Jerusalem and Judea, and the witness of its Hellenistic Jewish-Christian members in Samaria and to a God-fearing eunuch (or proselyte, chs 3–9). The Jerusalem church's mission then extends to the Gentiles, first God-fearing, then pagan (chs 10–12). Chapters 13–28 give us, first, the Syrian Antioch church's witness to Cyprus and central Asia Minor (Paul's first missionary journey, chs 13–14) and the resolution of the multi-ethnic church problems that resulted from Christianity's expansion among the Gentiles (15:1–16:5). Then, there is Paul's mission to Greece and west Asia Minor during his second and third missionary journeys (16:1–19:20). Finally, Luke recounts Paul's Palestinian ministry in chains (19:21–26:32) and his journey to Rome (chs 27–28).

Luke's use of the programmatic statements in Luke 4:16-30 and 22:35-37, together with the travel narrative (Luke 9:51–19:27), to provide structural and thematic unity for his Gospel has long been recognized. It is more difficult, however, to find such clear programmatic statements in Acts beyond what is in Acts 1:8. This may be because the Gospel of Luke follows the ministry of the Son of God, who was able to declare his divinely destined purposes throughout his ministry and then fulfill them. The believers in Acts seek to follow their Lord but with little certainty about what lies ahead. The Pentecost speech and the description of early church life in Acts 2 indeed provide gospel themes that reverberate throughout Acts 1–12, and the word of the Lord to Ananias about Paul's mission (9:15-16) certainly finds fulfillment in the events of his missionary journeys. There are also prophetic promises (23:11; 27:23-24) and repeated themes, such as Paul's standing trial for his belief in the Resurrection and his legal innocence (23:6, 9, 29; 24:15, 21; 25:18-19, 26-27;

26:23, 30-32), that do drive the action forward and unify the narrative during Paul's apostleship in chains. Still, for Acts, unity and movement must be found in another literary device: the summary statement.

At six points in the Acts narrative, Luke summarizes the action to that point, indicating that in spite of internal dissension or external opposition, the word of God was continuing to grow, the number of disciples was increasing, and the church was showing itself mature (6:7; 9:31; 12:24; 16:5; 19:20; 28:31; Longenecker 1981:234). These statements divide the narrative of Acts into six panels that coincide nicely with advances in the geographical or ethnic context of witness or changes in the agent of witness (cf. the divisions outlined above). These statements, then, should provide the basic guidance to discerning the structure of Acts.

As we compare the content of these panels with one another and with the Gospel of Luke, we become immediately aware of the degree to which Luke has made use of parallelism. Tannehill (1986, 1990) and Talbert (1974) have done much work to show parallel content between Luke and Acts. Within Acts the parallels between Peter's and Paul's ministries are especially striking: speeches, miracles, opposition faced, imprisonment, and status in the Christian community (Liefeld 1995:38).

Luke brought out what is important to him in the narrative in at least two ways: the relative amount of space he allocates to a given topic and his use of "functional redundancy" (seen in his telling and retelling of certain events). As to space allotment, Luke was more interested in the church's being a witness to the world than in the church's internal life and order. Thus, of the fifteen speeches of Acts, only three are addressed to Christians (1:15-22; 15:1-35; 20:16-38).

When repetition is one of the reasons for space allocation, the event's importance is particularly heightened. For example, there are two events that are consciously repeated in Acts: Paul's conversion (chs 9; 22; 26), and Cornelius's conversion, elements of which are repeated three to four times within a chapter and a half, and the whole of which is alluded to several chapters later (10:1–11:18; 15:7-11). Luke, by space allocation and repetition, then, was showcasing these two events: the inauguration of the Gentile mission through Peter and the conversion and call of Paul the apostle to the Gentiles. These events, more than any others, prove true his contention that "salvation applied" means salvation blessings are for all people, including Theophilus and his readers.

Another Lukan technique is variation in the scope of focus in relating evangelistic encounters. Sometimes he emphasized the crowd (cf. in the main, the conversions of the first missionary journey, chs 13–14). Sometimes he focused on individuals (Sergius Paulus, Lydia). Among these he sometimes gave the dialog that led to conversion and the faith response that embodied it (Cornelius, Paul, the Philippian jailer). As noted above, it is often Romans about whom the most detail is given. Through these models of conversion, Luke evangelized Theophilus and his fellow countrymen.

Luke's use of repetition also includes presenting the advance of the church's witness according to a discernible dynamic. In the early chapters of Acts, as the church is established and grows initially, God acts in miraculous power (2:1-11;

3:1-10; 5:12-16); the apostles interpret these acts (2:14-36; 3:12-26); opposition—mainly official—arises to God's initiatives and is thwarted (2:13; 4:1-22; 5:17-40); and the bold witness continues to advance (2:40-42, 47; 4:23-31; 5:41-42). In the middle chapters (the missionary journeys) the pattern includes: (1) gospel witness (with or without divine miraculous acts, 13:16-41; 14:1; 17:1-3, 11-12; 18:5); (2) division among the Jews, as well as between Jew and Gentile, arising in response to the message (13:42-45; 14:4; 17:4, 13; 18:6); (3) the by-and-large Jewish rejection of the message (13:45; 14:5; 17:5, 13; 18:6); (4) withdrawal of the Christian witnesses from the Jewish religious community (13:46-47, 51; 14:6; 17:14; 18:6-7); and (5) further progress in Christian witness (13:48-49, 52; 14:6-7; 17:10-12, 14, 16-31; 18:8-11). In the sequences of both the early and middle sections, the unstoppable nature of the church's mission under God comes out clearly. Nothing will keep the "salvation applied" portion of the gospel from being realized throughout the world.

Luke records the church's advance by presenting itineraries in episodic fashion, punctuated with speeches and summary statements. As we have seen with evangelistic encounters, it is his general practice to vary his lens constantly, if you will, sometimes giving us a very tight shot with much detail and at other times zooming out to a panoramic overview. As such, Luke rarely engages in sustained plot development. From Acts 21:27 to 28:31, however, he did take such an opportunity: He builds tension by recording a number of threats to Paul's physical well-being, each successively more life-threatening. The Jewish crowd is beating him to death (21:27-31), only to have Paul rescued by a Roman commander, who then wants to interrogate him through scourging his already pummelled body (22:24). Only an appeal to his Roman citizenship saves him from the scourging (22:25). Paul's appearance before the Sanhedrin leads to his being almost torn limb from limb, only to be rescued again by the commander (23:10-11). Safe in custody, he hears of an ambush plot against his life and has to be spirited away to Caesarea under heavy guard (23:12-35). Left in jail when Felix vacates the governorship (24:27), he must appeal to Caesar in order to avoid another ambush plot (25:3-5, 9-12). Packed off to Rome, he endures a two-week winter storm at sea and a shipwreck. He and the passengers and other prisoners survive in spite of the crew's attempt to abandon ship and the soldiers' plan to kill all the prisoners (27:27, 31-32, 42). Then, when Paul arrives safely on Malta, he is bitten by a poisonous snake but remains unharmed (28:3-5). Luke's narrative so carries us along that we breathe a sigh of relief (along with Paul, we imagine) when Rome is at last in sight and fellow believers from Rome have come to greet him. We, with Paul, thank God and take courage (28:15).

HISTORICAL RELIABILITY

Since Luke's purpose is to evangelize Theophilus and his compatriots through a thoroughly investigated, orderly account of events demonstrating the truth of the gospel, the historical reliability of Acts is foundational to the author's aims (Luke 1:1-4). Luke is not alone in this. We find ancient historians introducing their works with claims of accurate investigation and goals of presenting "the truth as it actually happened" (Lucian *How to Write History* 49–50; cf. Diodorus Siculus *Works* 1.4.4; Josephus *Against Apion* 5.1-5; Hemer 1989a:90-91). Unless we redefine historical writing so that a mixture of fabrication and fact is acceptable (Johnson 1992:7), we must continue to judge Luke's claims to historical reliability by an uncompromising standard of truthfulness. This we do by answering two questions: Did Luke have access to the events reported so that he had the capacity to write reliable history? Did Luke write an account that contradicts either itself, other biblical witnesses to the events, namely Paul's letters, or other ancient literary or archaeological evidence?

Luke did have access to the events. First, he participated in many of them. If he is Lucius of Cyrene, he could have participated in the life of the Hellenistic Jewish Christian community within the Jerusalem church. This would have placed him at events at least from Pentecost until the dispersion of Hellenistic Jewish Christians at the martyrdom of Stephen (Acts 2:1–8:3). He also could well have participated in the founding and early history of the church at Antioch (11:19-30; 13:1-3, 14:26-28). A more explicit claim to authorial participation, of course, is found in the "we passages" present from the second missionary journey forward (16:10-17; 20:15-17; 21:1-8; 27:1–28:16). Although scholars have offered other explanations of the origin and nature of the "we passages" such as an outside source, a travel journal coming to Luke, or the use of a literary device (Praeder 1987), the understanding that best explains all the features of this phenomenon in Acts is still authorial participation (Longenecker 1981:224).

Luke tells us that he depended on sources as well. These were "the eyewitness reports circulating among us from the early disciples" (Luke 1:2; the use of *hupēretēs* [TG5257, ZG5677], which emphasizes service that strictly follows orders, in conjunction with *autoptēs* [TG845, ZG898], "eyewitness," points to the accuracy of the witnesses [cf. 13:5; 26:16]). It is not possible to isolate literary sources in Acts, given the uniformity of Luke's style and the lack of extant potential source documents (Dupont 1964). For every section of Acts, however, there are identifiable personal acquaintances of Luke who were eyewitnesses to the events recorded:

Passages in Acts	Eyewitness(es)
Chapters 1–5	Mark and Barnabas
6:1–8:40	Philip [cf. 21:8] and Paul
9:1-31	Paul
10:1–11:18	Peter (transmitted to Luke through Mark)
11:19-30; 13:1-4; 14:26-28	The congregation of the Antioch church
12:1–13:13	Mark
12:25–28:31	Paul
16:10-17; 20:5-15; 21:1-8; 27:1–28:16, [the "we passages"]	Luke himself

As to internal consistency, many scholars claim the differences among the three reports of Paul's conversion experience (chs 9; 22; 26) show that Luke was not interested in writing a historically accurate account (Haenchen 1971:323; Lake 1979:195; Lohfink 1976; Hedrick 1981). Others claim this is evidence of history writing, which may be characterized as "narrative shaped by the author's imagination," as well as a "report of substantial historical information" (Johnson 1992:5-7; Witherington 1996a:343). Close analysis of the differences shows, however, that neither assessment is correct. The differences are not historical contradictions, which would point to the author's imagination. They can, indeed, be harmonized so that the details of the one event behind the reports can be reconstructed. The differences involve features well suited to each historical setting: original telling, defense before a Jewish mob, and defense before a Gentile governor (Bruce 1988:188, 419). "Functional redundancy" is also at work, in which, for rhetorical effect, certain features are withheld for later retellings (Witherup 1992).

There is no final contradiction between the picture we get of Paul in Acts and in his letters. The concerns about discrepancies in theology and behavior (Vielhauer 1966; Haenchen 1971:112-116) and in the description of major events (e.g., the collection for Jerusalem and Acts 21; Galatians 2 and Acts 15 [resolved if Acts 11:30–12:25 encompasses the events of Gal 2:1-10; cf. Morgado 1994]) have been satisfactorily addressed by Gasque (1978) and Bruce (1976). The differences are no more than what one would expect between Paul's self-portrait and Luke's appreciative picture, painted for a different audience and purpose. The negative assessment of Acts in this matter, however, continues (Krodel 1986:14; Tyson 1985:10-11; Johnson 1992:7; Barrett 1998:xxxv-xlii).

Luke is given high marks by even skeptical critics for his "factual fastidiousness" when it comes to geographical, social, and political minutiae (Koester 1982:2.50). It is anachronistic to take this accuracy simply as the result of the kind of research a good historical novelist would do (so Johnson 1992:5). In the first century there were no reference works that would make such research possible. Eyewitness participation in the events remains, according to Hemer, the "easiest . . . most satisfying hypothesis. It is the only basis on which I feel able to account for certain features which need a sufficient explanation" (1977a:39).

The speeches of Acts have consistently been understood as Lukan compositions and hence historical fabrications (Tyson 1985:10-11). Some stake out a middle ground in which Luke, with historical realism and based on traditional material, writes the speeches (Pillai 1979:111). Green (1997:11), following Gempf (1993a), seeks to recast this position in terms of "historical appropriateness" and overcome the impasse between those who see Luke's speeches as the author's compositions and those who see them as reports, if only in precis or summary form, of what was actually said on a particular occasion. The shift of categories does not overcome the problem because it has not dealt with the more basic issues of truth and the source of the content of the speeches. However, given the content, vocabulary, and style of each speech, there is still no impediment to taking the speeches as containing in verbatim, precis, or summary form the substance of what was said on the occasion cited (Bruce 1974). In sum, for all of Acts, Luke succeeded in writing a historically reliable work.

MAJOR THEOLOGICAL THEMES

A theological perspective on the book of Acts must take into account what God is doing, as well as what he is saying.[5] God's activity and purpose, the *missio dei*, play an important role in Acts. Luke clearly presents "God on mission," applying his salvation among all nations to the end of the earth.

The Mission of the Triune God through the Apostles. It is common to recognize that Luke's presentation of mission in Acts is less about the "Acts of the Apostles" than about the "Acts of the Holy Spirit," less about the mission of the church than about the mission of God (Wilson 1973:242; Gaventa 1982:414-416). Detailed study reveals how true these characterizations are. Luke's narrative portrays each person of the Godhead as a "sending one," both in commissioning and promoting mission. Each person of the Trinity is also a direct agent of mission, as well as a participant working through human agents.

In Luke the apostles' commission does not come only from the words of the risen Jesus, such as those found in Luke 24:46-48 and Acts 1:8. Each of these "commissioning" statements is formulated as a command and a prophetic promise (Barrett 1994:79). The first (Luke 24:46-48) is a statement of gospel content as the fulfillment of Scripture that includes the declaration: "Beginning in Jerusalem . . . You are witnesses of all these things" (Luke 24:47-48). Acts 1:8 is a future-tense formulation: "You will be my witnesses, telling people about me everywhere." Later, Peter tells Cornelius that divinely chosen eyewitnesses of the Resurrection were commanded by the risen Jesus to warn everyone of the coming judgment (10:42; cf. Luke 24:47). Paul and Barnabas boldly announce to the hostile Jews at Antioch that "the Lord [Jesus] gave us this command" to declare the Good News to the Gentiles and even to the end of the earth (13:47; cf. 1:8; Luke 24:47). Paul was constantly aware of his divine commission (20:24; 26:16-18) and aware that the Father and the Spirit were involved in it (13:2, 4; 22:14-15). Peter, too, was aware of a divine commissioning at a key point during his ministry. God had chosen that through his mouth the Gentiles might hear the word of the gospel and believe (15:7). As Luke recounts the divine commissioning, it is the Spirit who tells Peter to go with the emissaries from Cornelius, not asking any questions, for he has sent them (10:19-20). The book of Acts climaxes with Paul's declaration through a divine passive that "this salvation from God has also been offered to the Gentiles" (28:28, cf. *apostellō* [TG649, ZG690], lit., this salvation "has been sent").

The Triune God is the sending one par excellence, enabling and guiding faithful witnesses through adversity, through hesitation in crossing cultural thresholds, and through any other impediment to advancing the gospel to the ends of the earth. The Lord Jesus appeared to Ananias and sent him to Paul in order to confirm and empower him in his conversion and calling (9:10, 17). By his angel, the Lord led Peter out of prison so that he could go to "another place," presumably to continue his witness (12:17). Twice when Paul was facing adversity, Jesus appeared to him and encouraged him to keep on witnessing (18:9; 23:11). God the Father declared the ritual purity distinctions null and void, and from this Peter learned that God desires to remove any ethnic barrier to the hearing of the gospel (10:15, 28). God also guided a mission onto a new continent, when Paul (and his co-workers) interpreted the vision of the Macedonian's call for help as God calling them to preach the Good News there (16:10). Indeed, God the Holy Spirit is most active in guiding the church across cultural and geographical boundaries (8:29, 39; 16:6-7; 19:21).[6] The Spirit also facilitates this unstoppable mission in the face of impending adversity by preparing the witnesses to be bold (20:22-24; 21:4, 11, 13-14).

Luke lets his readers know from the very first verses of Acts that the agents of mission will be both divine and human. Luke's description of his Gospel as being about "everything Jesus began to do and teach" (1:1) creates the expectation that the reader will see Jesus continue this mission in the second volume. Luke also almost immediately introduces human agents (1:2) and often describes a divine-human synergism in the carrying out of the mission (e.g., 2:4; 4:8, 29-31; 13:9; 19:11). As the narrator unfolds the advance of the church in mission, the Triune God is consistently present, directly applying salvation blessings.

It is the exalted Lord who grants repentance and forgiveness to Israel (5:31) and pours out the Spirit (2:33). Luke describes conversion as the Lord opening an individual's heart (16:14), as the Lord's hand being with his witnesses (11:21), and as the Lord adding daily those being saved (2:47). The divine passive (a passive verb where the unnamed subject or actor is God) occurs in descriptions concerning large numbers of people who "were brought to the Lord" (5:14; 11:24). Jesus validates the apostles' "preaching boldly about the grace of the Lord" with miracles (14:3). So directly is he involved with these salvation blessings that the human agent will say to the sick: "Jesus Christ heals you!" (9:34). Moreover, Jesus is there in judgment as the hand of the Lord is against those who oppose the progress of the mission (13:11).

The apostolic preaching sees the Father in mission as he "commands everyone everywhere to repent of their sins and turn to him" (17:30) and "calls" Jew and Gentile to himself (2:39). Salvation blessings come directly from him, whether repentance or the Holy Spirit or the miraculous (3:13; 11:17-18; 15:8; 19:11). Of particular interest to Luke is the Father's involvement in the Gentile mission. Using Old Testament salvific terminology, James told how God first "visited" to take a people from among the Gentiles (15:14). Luke never tired of celebrating what God had done during the first missionary journey and beyond, opening a door of faith for the Gentiles (14:27; 15:4, 12; 21:19).

Luke presented the work of the Holy Spirit synergistically as witnesses filled with the Spirit spoke the saving message—and the response, whether positive or negative, manifested that God was at work (2:4, 37-41; 4:8-13; 6:5, 10; 7:54, 57-58). One time, however, through Peter's proclamation, the claim is made that when the gospel is preached the Spirit is bearing direct parallel witness (5:32).

A final divine agent of mission is "the word of the Lord." Luke characterizes the advance of mission as the word of the Lord growing, especially in the context of human opposition (6:7; 12:24; 13:48-49; 19:20). This image does not simply describe the spread of God's word; it points to the life-giving power of the message of the gospel. Legrand (1990:92) notes, "The church is animated by this Word living within it. The latter impels it to the fore. It finds its identity and cohesion in this Word, and this continual new beginning to the point that Luke unconsciously interchanges the terms . . . church . . . and . . . the Word."

If Luke wants us to see what God is doing (i.e., his mission), he also wants us to hear what he is saying: the good news of salvation accomplished and applied. Luke's summary of the gospel message, thus, provides a helpful framework for expounding his theology. "Yes, it was written long ago that the Messiah would suffer and die and rise from the dead on the third day. It was also written that this message would be proclaimed in the authority of his name to all the nations, beginning in Jerusalem: 'There is forgiveness of sins for all who repent.' You are witnesses of all these things" (Luke 24:46-48).

"Yes, it was written long ago," asserts that the gospel message's origin is not human religious tradition but divine revelation. It was promised first through the prophets and is now fulfilled in the death and resurrection of Christ and the church's worldwide evangelistic mission. Although the impact of such an argument is greatest on the Jews, whose forefathers received the prophetic promises (2:17, 21, 39; 10:36; 13:32; 15:16), its effect is not lost on Gentiles. They, too, would be impressed with a message about saving events promised long ago but now fulfilled. From this initial theme flows Luke's theology of God the Father, the Scriptures, history, and the end times.

In the proclamation of the gospel to Gentile audiences, Luke presents God the Father as transcendent and immanent (17:28-29), as Creator (14:15; 17:24; cf. 4:24), and as sustainer and controller of history, particularly salvation history (14:17; 17:26; cf. 1:7). In preaching to the Jews, he highlights God's active intervention in history to accomplish his saving purposes (7:2-47; 13:17). The climax of God's saving acts is bringing Jesus the Messiah to Israel in fulfillment of the promises he made through the prophets (13:23, 33). He legitimized Jesus' person and work through signs and wonders (2:22; 10:38). By his "prearranged plan" Jesus is handed over to suffering and death (2:23; 4:28), and by his power he raises Jesus from death (2:32; 3:26; 13:34; 17:31). He gave to the Son the promise of the Spirit who, poured out on Pentecost, validates the claim that Jesus is both Messiah and Lord and empowers the church in its worldwide witness (1:4, 8; 2:33, 36). He has appointed Jesus as judge of all at the end of time, giving his resurrection as proof (17:31).

God's intervention in space and time to accomplish his salvation necessarily molds Luke's view of history. The present is a time of the continuance of Jesus' ministry (1:1), though in a different form: by the Spirit through the church. And it is "the last days," for it is the time of the Spirit's outpouring "on all people" and the universal proclamation of the gospel (2:17, 21). Luke also has the end in view, especially in terms of final resurrection and judgment at Christ's second coming (1:11; 3:21; 17:31; 23:6; 24:15, 25; 26:6-8), but what is in the forefront of his presentation is this current period of salvation history, "the last days." The gospel message itself binds the two main features of "the last days"—Jesus' ministry and the church's mission (Luke 24:46-48)—together under the rubric of scriptural fulfillment.

The Lord Jesus Christ and His Salvation. The gospel message focuses first on a Messiah who suffered and rose from the dead on the third day (Luke 24:46). Luke developed his Christology in terms of titles by emphasizing that the Scriptures prophesy both the death of the Messiah, the Son of David, and his resurrection (2:31; 17:3). Christian witnesses argue forcefully for Jesus' identity as the Messiah (9:22; 18:5). Luke uses other messianic titles: "A Prophet," "this holy, righteous one," and "his servant" are used to highlight the culpability of the Jews and to link Jesus' completed suffering to his present glory, as manifest in his resurrection and miraculous activity through the church (3:13-14, 22, 26; 4:30). In Acts, the term *Son of God* is used sparingly (9:20; cf. 13:33), and the term "Lord" predominates. It refers to Jesus in his resurrected, exalted position as Lord of all (10:36; cf. 2:36). The "Lord" is the source of salvation for all those who will believe in him (2:21; 9:42; 16:31). It is the "word of the Lord" that is preached and spreads (8:25; 12:24; 13:49). The Lord himself guides the church's mission and enables it to advance (2:47; 9:10). Though many titles are used, they compose a unified portrait of "the 'Messiah-Servant' who is seen, as the story progresses, to be a 'more than Messiah' figure in that he is the Lord" (Marshall 1989:54).

In terms of the Messiah's work, Luke focused on Jesus' earthly ministry, death, resurrection, ascension and exaltation, current reign, and return. He emphasized that God, according to his messianic promise, brought to Israel a Savior, Jesus (13:23). This man, announced by John the Baptist and divinely anointed with the Spirit's power, conducted a public healing ministry including the conquest of demons (2:22; 10:38-39; 13:24-25). Such miraculous doing of good demonstrated God's approval. Though he was the holy, righteous one, innocent of any wrongdoing, the Jewish people and especially their leaders rejected him and had him put to death by crucifixion (2:23; 3:13-15; 4:10; 5:30; 7:52; 10:39; 13:28). Yet all this was according to God's saving plan as announced by the prophets (2:23; 3:18; 4:11; 8:32-35; 10:43; 13:29; 26:22-23). This salvation is a key theme in Luke's writing.

Luke emphasized Christ's resurrection as the central event in God's saving purposes. Of all of Christ's work, it is the immediate source of salvation blessings (2:33-39; 3:26; 4:10-12; 5:31; 13:37-39). Not only was the Messiah's resurrection prophesied in Scripture (2:24-32; 13:32-37; 17:3; 26:23), it had been realized as an objective historical event for which there were eyewitnesses (1:3, 22; 10:40-41; 13:31). In fact, the main task of the apostles is to bear witness to this resurrection and its saving significance, especially as a prototype of the coming resurrection (1:22; 3:15; 5:32; 10:40-41; 13:31; 22:14-15; 23:6; 24:15, 21). This witness also serves as a warning that the resurrected Lord will come as final judge (10:42; 17:31).

Christ's ascension and exaltation place him in the position of "Lord of all." From the right hand of the Father he pours out salvation blessings and actively empowers and guides the church in its witness (2:33-36; 9:10). Luke will use the "name" of Jesus to stand for his active presence as he seeks to describe the spiritual effects of his unseen presence when the church acts in his authority (2:38; 3:16; 4:10, 12, 30; 8:12, 16; 10:43, 48; 16:18). Christ's imminent return will involve a final resurrection and judgment (1:11; 3:20-21; 17:31; 23:6; 24:14-15; 26:6-8).

The Reception of the Gospel of Salvation. The second focus of the gospel message (the first is discussed in the prior section) introduces the conditions for and results of receiving salvation, as well as the human method and scope of its dissemination (Luke 24:47): "It was also written that this message would be proclaimed in the authority of his name to all the nations, beginning in Jerusalem: 'There is forgiveness of sins for all who repent.'" As Luke's Gospel substantiates the first half of the gospel message, so Acts validates the truthfulness of the second half. It shows Theophilus that the gospel message he has heard is the same one with which the Lord Jesus charged his disciples.

Though it is not expressed in this summary, Luke does use faith as the general term for the whole process of responding to the gospel. Faith is so central to the message that "believer" is a very common term to denote a Christian (see 2:44; 4:32; 15:5; 18:27; 21:25). God's grace and election are at work in producing saving faith (13:48; 15:11). Several times faith is mandated as the proper condition for salvation (10:43; 13:39; 16:31). It is the word of God, the gospel message, to which persons must respond in faith (4:4; 8:12; 11:21; 15:7; 18:8). When they come to saving faith in response to miracles, Luke usually notes that the preaching of the word was also present (8:12-13; 13:12; 19:10-11, 19-20); Acts 5:14 and 9:42 are exceptions. Luke makes explicit that the way of faith must be followed by Gentiles, as well as Jews (15:11).

Faith involves a commitment characterized by repentance and conversion. This also is a divine gift to men (5:31; 11:18, 21). It is a universal condition that all must meet if they are to avoid final judgment (17:30-31). *Repentance* and the related term *conversion* describe a complete turn from sin, darkness, Satan's authority, and idols, to God, light, God's Kingdom, and the Lord (8:22; 9:35; 14:15; 20:21; 26:18). In his final articulation of the gospel message, Luke notes that true repentance will issue in deeds worthy of repentance (26:20).

Open confession of faith and baptism are other aspects of receiving salvation. Though these are not mentioned every time a conversion is described in Acts, they are commanded at the beginning (2:38). Further, they are mentioned at significant junctures in the church's advance in mission to different ethnic groups and as a practice throughout all of Paul's missionary journeys (8:12-13, 36, 38; 10:47; 16:15, 33; 18:8; 19:5). Acts presents a mixed pattern concerning the sequence of factors in conversion: personal response of faith and repentance, outward manifestation of the Spirit, and water baptism (8:12, 15; 10:44-48; 19:2-6). Further, the outward manifestation of the Spirit is not consistently presented as an identifiable, second experience separated in time from conversion. This mixture in sequential pattern—sometimes the Spirit comes before water baptism (10:47; 11:15; 15:8-9) and sometimes afterward, separated in time from conversion (8:15-17)—is probably due to God's initiative in mercifully persuading Jewish Christians, through the outward sign of the Holy Spirit's coming on various Gentile ethnic groups (including the Samaritans), that he had indeed regenerated them. These outward manifestations of the Spirit at the initial implementation of the mission to all nations had a limited purpose, which they achieved. This fact, together with the mixed sequential pattern in which we observe them, probably indicates that these manifestations are not necessarily normative for all Christians in all ages.

With the phrase, "forgiveness of sins," Luke captures the results of salvation. When combined with other words Luke frequently associates with salvation, such as *grace* and *joy*, we arrive at a comprehensive picture of salvation blessings. From the very beginning of Acts the concept of salvation serves as an overarching theme. In explaining the Spirit's coming at Pentecost, Peter concludes his quotation from the prophet Joel with the promise, "Everyone who calls on the name of the LORD will be saved" (2:21). Luke consistently presents the spiritual rescue of people, which is known as "being saved" (2:47; 11:14; 16:31). Jesus, the Savior, is the only source of salvation (4:12; 5:31; 13:23). When describing healings, *being saved* can be used for restoration of physical wholeness. When it occurs in Acts, such restoration is always a sign of the spiritual wholeness available in the name of Jesus (4:10, 12; 14:9, 15).

Grace portrays salvation benefits in two ways: It is the divine enablement for a person to believe and receive salvation (15:11; 18:27). It is that divine power and quality of life that manifest themselves in the lives of believers so that they may be described as having great grace resting on them or as being full of grace (4:33; 6:8; 11:23).

Joy refers to the portion received by those who believe the gospel message, especially Gentiles (8:8, 39; 13:48, 52; 16:34). Luke says their joy is in response not only to the liberation they find in Christ but also particularly to the knowledge that this salvation is intended for them, too (13:46-48).

The Church. It is in the church that these salvation blessings come to fullest expression. Spiritual qualities find expression in patterns of living. The early church's unity and grace are seen in the fellowship it practiced, especially the breaking of bread. They took meals together regularly, even daily, which probably also included the celebration of the Lord's Supper (2:42, 46; 20:7, 11). This fellowship further overflowed in the practical compassion of Dorcas (9:39), the hospitality of Lydia (16:14-15; cf. 10:48; 16:33-34), and the Jerusalem church's sharing of goods with those in need (2:42-47; 4:32-37; 6:1-6).

The churches showed the spiritual quality of trust—total dependence on the Lord (16:5; cf. 6:5 and 11:24 for descriptions of individuals). They did this by the consistent practice of prayer, both individually and corporately (1:14; 2:42; 6:4; 10:9; 13:2; 16:25; 20:36; 21:5). In fact, in two important summary statements

Luke highlights prayer as an essential of church life and one of the church leaders' main duties (2:42; 6:4). Specific occasions for prayer included the advance of the church's mission, whether in preparation, confirmation, commissioning, empowerment, or deliverance (1:14; 4:24-30; 6:6; 8:15; 9:40; 12:5, 12; 13:3; 14:23; 28:8).

Luke stressed the teaching activity of the church, which had both an evangelistic and an edifying dimension (evangelism—4:2, 18; 5:21, 28, 42; 15:35; 20:20; 28:31; edification—11:26; 16:4-5; 18:11). He consistently noted the way that teaching and words of encouragement resulted in the church's being strengthened (11:23; 14:22; 15:32, 41; 18:23).

Because Luke focused almost exclusively on the church's outwardly directed mission, there is little discussion and little detail about its internal life and organization. No particular polity emerges as normative, although some spiritual characteristics of organization emerge. The church manifests an organic unity so that its multiple expressions in a region can be described by a phrase with the singular form: "the church . . . throughout Judea, Galilee, and Samaria" (9:31). A local expression is termed "the church in/at _____" (8:1; 13:1). Such unity is grounded in spiritual equality. All Christians view other members as their brothers (11:29; 15:23; cf. the Gr. of 15:1, 36; 17:10, 14). This includes the leaders, who exercise their authority collegially, following the humble, servant-leader role commanded by Christ (Luke 22:24-30). The decision-making process preserves all these traits. Each party, leader, and congregation fulfills its role—submitting its action to the other and neither moving ahead without the approving consensus of the other (6:1-6; 15:22-29). The premier manifestation of God's salvation in the individual and the church is the presence of the Holy Spirit to empower and guide (2:4; 4:8, 31; 8:29; 10:19; 16:6-7).

For Luke the church is a missionary church. Christ commands that this salvation message "be proclaimed in the authority of his name to all the nations" (Luke 24:47). Three key concepts capture Luke's teaching on the church's mission: proclamation/witness, "the word" as the gospel message, and the Spirit.

Luke makes clear from the very climax of his Gospel and the opening of Acts that the church's main mission is proclamation/witness (Luke 24:44-48; Acts 1:8). He reiterated the themes at key points in the church's advance: Philip's mission to Samaria (8:5), Paul's first public act as a Christian (9:20), Paul's description to the Ephesian elders of his activities among them (20:21, 24-25), and the climax of Acts—Paul at Rome "proclaiming the Kingdom of God" (28:31). Luke summarized the content of the church's witness as the Resurrection, the person of Christ, salvation blessings, and the kingdom of God (2:32; 3:15; 5:32; 8:25; 9:20; 10:41-42; 18:5; 19:13; 20:21, 24-25; 22:15; 28:23, 31). Luke stresses eyewitnesses bearing witness to the truth of the facts of the salvation story (1:22; 5:32; 10:40-42; 13:31; 26:16; cf. 26:26).

The Word of God. The word of God is a key theological concept in the book of Acts. It is the means by which salvation is proclaimed. God takes the initiative in sending this word of salvation to Israel (10:36; 13:26). It is "the word" that Christian witnesses speak, evangelize, and announce (4:31; 8:4, 25; 11:19; 13:5, 46; 14:25; 15:7, 35-36; 16:6, 32; 17:13). Converts are saved by hearing and believing, receiving, and glorifying that word (2:41; 4:4; 8:14; 10:44; 11:1; 13:7, 44, 48; 17:11; 19:10). So central is "the word" to the church's mission that the apostles make their priority the ministry of the word and prayer (6:2, 4), and Luke can describe the church's growth as the word of the Lord spreading and growing (6:7; 12:24; 13:49; 19:20). God's empowerment of "the word" to saving effect can sometimes be accompanied by signs and wonders that bear witness to it (4:33; 14:3). The word of God proclaimed is truly the bridge between salvation accomplished and salvation applied.

The Power of the Holy Spirit. When Jesus commissioned the apostles (1:8), he told them that they would be empowered by the Holy Spirit. The Holy Spirit is the promised gift from the Father and from the exalted and reigning Son. He is first poured out at Pentecost on all who repent and believe in the Lord Jesus for salvation. The Holy Spirit's presence is the blessing of salvation. Speaking in tongues can be an outward manifestation of his presence, a sign of regeneration or empowerment for witness. As I pointed out under the heading "The Reception of the Gospel of Salvation," the lack of a consistent pattern of conversion and outward manifestation makes it unlikely that Luke sees such outward manifestation as normative for all Christian conversion or ministry.

In the church's life, the Spirit does provide power for witness. There is general enablement, boldness, and convincing conviction when Christians full of the Spirit testify (2:4, 17-18; 4:8, 13, 31; 5:32; 6:5, 10; 18:24-25). Also, the Spirit supplies further guidance, especially as it is related to the advance of the church's mission (8:29, 39). He gave specific instruction in combination with supernatural communication in order to overcome ethnic hesitation and moved Peter to preach the gospel to Gentiles (10:19-20; 11:12). He guided Paul into his Gentile mission both in its inauguration through the Antioch church and in its further thrust into Macedonia. The Spirit can indicate God's purposes both positively and negatively (13:2, 4; 16:6-7). He can warn of the negative circumstances surrounding an action. When Paul purposes "in the Spirit" to minister at Jerusalem and Rome (19:21), the Holy Spirit subsequently warns Paul of the persecution and suffering awaiting him. This enables Paul to persevere (20:22-24; 21:4, 11, 13-14). Finally, the Spirit's presence promotes church unity. At the Jerusalem Council, the source of the decision that promoted Jewish-Gentile Christian spiritual equality and harmony is reported as, "It seemed good to the Holy Spirit and to us" (15:28).

In church life, the Holy Spirit also facilitates edification. He fills leaders for service, shepherding, and prophesying (6:3, 5; 11:24, 28; 20:28). Accountability to him is central in discipline (5:3, 9). No better picture of the Spirit's role in the church's growth and maturity can be found than in Luke's summary statement about the church in Judea, Galilee, and Samaria. It "had peace . . . and it became stronger as the believers lived in the fear of the Lord. And with the encouragement of the Holy Spirit, it also grew in numbers" (9:31).

The Worldwide Scope of the Gospel. That the gospel message will be preached "to all the nations" raises several important issues in Luke's theology: the legitimacy of the Gentile mission, the relationship of Israel and the church, and the relationship of the Christian to the law. Luke establishes the Gentile mission's legitimacy by showing how God's hand of blessing attended the witness to the Gentiles (10:45; 11:17; 13:48; 14:27; 15:3, 8, 12; 21:19). At a critical juncture (Peter's witness to Cornelius), God gave the Spirit just like at Pentecost. This enabled the apostles to understand and effectively argue for a gospel of grace that had come in the same way to Jew and Gentile alike. Luke points out that the Gentile mission is a fulfillment of God's purposes articulated in the Old Testament (13:47; 15:15-16). He repeatedly refers to Paul's commission to take the gospel to the Gentiles and his obedience to it (9:15; 13:46; 18:6; 22:21; 26:17). In his last summary of the gospel message, he clearly presents the Gentile mission as part of its content (26:23).

If the Gentile mission is legitimate, what is the relationship between Israel and the church? Luke acknowledges the special place of the Jews in God's salvation plan. When preaching to Jewish audiences, the apostles stressed that according to the promise made to their fathers, God gave Israel a Savior and made them the first recipients of the gospel message (3:26; 10:36; 13:23, 46). Luke customarily used the word *people* (*laos* [TG2992, ZG3295]) as a designation of the Jews in their special relationship to God (e.g., 2:47; 3:12; 13:24). There were two times when Luke used it to designate Gentiles who would respond to the gospel (15:14; 18:10) and thereby claim to be part of God's people (11:14; 15:7-11). Luke presents the continuity and discontinuity between Israel and the church by viewing the church as the true Israel, responsive to God's fulfillment of his salvation promises in Jesus the Messiah (20:21, 28). Historically, the church started out as a predominantly Jewish group that integrated the fruit of the Gentile mission into its company; that integration transformed the church into the new people of God—composed of both Jew and Gentile (11:26; cf. Eph 2:14-16).

The church and individual Christians relate to the law in the context of the freedom of grace (15:10-11, 19). Nevertheless, freedom in love must be used to promote fellowship across ethnic lines (15:19). In all, ethnic diversity is respected, though within the limits of the written law of God, while unity encompassing that diversity is pursued (15:23-29; 21:25).

With this stance the scope of the gospel message's audience, "all the nations," Jew and Gentile alike, is affirmed, and the mission to tell "people about [Jesus] everywhere . . . to the ends of the earth" continues until the King returns. By the time he read the entire book of Acts, Theophilus surely understood that the gospel message was true for him and for his compatriots, and even for all people (Luke 1:1-4). That same sure knowledge should be ours as well.

OUTLINE

E. Paul and Barnabas in Iconium (14:1-7)
F. Paul and Barnabas in Lystra and Derbe (14:8-20)
G. Paul and Barnabas Return to Antioch of Syria (14:21-28)
H. The Council at Jerusalem (15:1-21)
I. The Letter for Gentile Believers (15:22-35)
J. Paul and Barnabas Separate (15:36-41)
K. Paul Begins a Second Missionary Journey (16:1-5)
V. The Mission to Greece (Europe) and Western Asia Minor (16:6-19:20)
A. A Call from Macedonia (16:6-10)
B. Lydia of Philippi Believes in Jesus (16:11-15)
C. Paul and Silas in Prison (16:16-40)
D. Paul Preaches in Thessalonica (17:1-9)
E. Paul and Silas in Berea (17:10-15)
F. Paul Preaches in Athens (17:16-34)
G. Paul Meets Priscilla and Aquila in Corinth (18:1-17)
H. Paul Returns to Antioch of Syria (18:18-23)
I. Apollos Instructed at Ephesus (18:24-28)
J. Paul's Third Missionary Journey (19:1-7)
K. Paul Ministers in Ephesus (19:8-20)
VI. Paul's Witness in Chains: Jerusalem, Caesarea, Rome (19:21-28:31)
A. Riot in Ephesus (19:21-41)
B. Paul Goes to Macedonia and Greece (20:1-6)
C. Paul's Final Visit to Troas (20:7-12)
D. Paul Meets the Ephesian Elders (20:13-38)
E. Paul's Journey to Jerusalem (21:1-14)
F. Paul Arrives at Jerusalem (21:15-25)
G. Paul Is Arrested (21:26-36)
H. Paul Speaks to the Crowd (21:37-22:23)
I. Paul Reveals His Roman Citizenship (22:24-29)
J. Paul before the High Council (22:30-23:11)
K. The Plan to Kill Paul (23:12-22)
L. Paul Is Sent to Caesarea (23:23-35)
M. Paul Appears before Felix (24:1-27)
N. Paul Appears before Festus (25:1-22)
O. Paul Speaks to Agrippa (25:23-26:32)
P. Paul Sails for Rome (27:1-12)
Q. The Storm at Sea (27:13-26)
R. The Shipwreck (27:27-44)
S. Paul on the Island of Malta (28:1-10)
T. Paul Arrives at Rome (28:11-16)
U. Paul Preaches at Rome under Guard (28:17-31)

ENDNOTES

1. In critical matters concerning authorship, Praeder (1987) gives a good summary of the current approaches to the "we passages" while Longenecker (1981:224) amply defends them as the product of an eyewitness participant in the events (cf. Green's [1997:16] concurrence). Donald Guthrie (1990:114-115) answers critiques of the ancient church tradition that Luke, the beloved physician, was the author of Acts. Barrett (1994:30-48) documents the evidence, though at the outset he maintains that internal evidence from Acts calls its conclusion into question. Marx (1980) gives valuable background on the status, training, and practice of physicians in ancient times, especially their activities as litterateurs.

2. Karris (1979:85-86) also sees opposition to Christianity as a key component in the situation of Luke's readers because, in his view, they are Christian missionary communities bearing witness in the late 70s. David J. Bosch (1991:85) proposes a setting in the 80s in which, again under Jewish and Gentile opposition from without and flagging enthusiasm from within, the church questions its identity and mission. To account for the intensity of Luke's concern with Judaism and Judaizing influences, a pre-AD 70 situation is still to be preferred.

3. See Green (1997) for a dictionary article and Winter and Clarke (1993) and Witherington (1996a) for essays that give a continuing discussion and assessment of genre options.

4. It is interesting to note that Green (1997:17) proposes a purpose that, while presented as edifying, could just as easily be—and in the light of evidence offered is more likely to be—evangelistic. Luke writes "to strengthen the Christian movement in the face of opposition by ensuring them in their interpretation and experience of the redemptive purpose of God and by calling them to continued faithfulness and witness in God's salvific project. The purpose of Luke–Acts would thus be primarily ecclesiological, centered on the invitation to participate in God's project." To invite someone to participate in God's project, when he or she has not before embraced the Christian faith, is to evangelize.

5. Marshall and Peterson (1998) offer the most comprehensive treatment of all aspects of Luke's theology in one volume to date.

6. On the ambiguity of the reference to "spirit" (Paul's spirit or the Holy Spirit) in Acts 19:21, see Larkin 1995:279. It should be noted that the commentary sections on 17:16-34; 18:1-17; 19:21-41; 20:13-38; 21:26-36; 23:12-22; 24:1-27; 27:1-12; 28:11-16, though reworked and supplemented, rely heavily on Larkin's work, entitled *Acts* in the IVP New Testament Commentary series.

COMMENTARY ON
Acts

◆ **I. The Jerusalem Church's Establishment and Mission in the City (1:1–6:7)**

A. The Promise of the Spirit (1:1-5)

In my first book* I told you, Theophilus, about everything Jesus began to do and teach ²until the day he was taken up to heaven after giving his chosen apostles further instructions through the Holy Spirit. ³During the forty days after his crucifixion, he appeared to the apostles from time to time, and he proved to them in many ways that he was actually alive. And he talked to them about the Kingdom of God.

⁴Once when he was eating with them, he commanded them, "Do not leave Jerusalem until the Father sends you the gift he promised, as I told you before. ⁵John baptized with* water, but in just a few days you will be baptized with the Holy Spirit."

1:1 The reference is to the Gospel of Luke.   1:5 Or *in;* also in 1:5b.

NOTES

1:1 *my first book.* Acts 1:1-11 is the preface to this second volume. Barrett (1994:61) extends it to v. 14. According to the consistent practice of "scientific treatises" (e.g., Dioscorides *Materia Medica* 2, 3, 4, 5; see Alexander's discussion [1993:143]), Luke recapitulated the events of his first volume, particularly Luke 24:44-53. This practice is also seen in historical works (e.g., Josephus *Antiquities* 7.380-382; 8.1). Acts is not a letter but the second part of an "apologetic history" or "missionary brief."

Theophilus. He was either the work's patron or a representative of the intended audience. See discussion under "Audience" in the Introduction.

1:3 *forty days.* Acts 1:1-11 recapitulates Luke 24:36-53. The transitional *de* [TG1161, ZG1254] (now, then) at Luke 24:44 allows for a break in time sequence and does not demand that the Ascension happen on Easter evening. In this way we can harmonize the two accounts and see Acts as providing the specifics of the timing of the Ascension (Moule 1982:63).

1:4 *when he was eating with them.* This renders *sunalizomenos* [TG4871, ZG5259]. The NASB translates this "gathering them together," and RSV translates it "while staying with them." Of these three possibilities, "eating with them" is the best option. For more detail on the three options and the issues involved here, see BDAG 964.

1:5 *with water . . . with the Holy Spirit.* In the Gr., it is possible to take both phrases as either instrumental (NLT text) or locative, "in" (NLT mg). The NLT rendering is preferred since the grammatical construction here is the same as in Luke 3:16 (perhaps indicating adherence to a traditional form of this statement) and parallels the use of the Hebrew preposition *bet* with "Spirit" in 1QS 4:21 (cf. Barrett 1994:74).

COMMENTARY

God is on mission! What Jesus began to do and teach, he continues by his Spirit through the church (4:10; 9:15; 18:10; 23:11). By the Spirit he instructed his apostles, whom he had chosen during his earthly ministry (Luke 6:13). They were to be his agents, sent on mission with his authority. In Jewish thought, the "apostle of God" was applied to the priesthood, Moses, Elijah, Elisha, and Ezekiel, "because there took place through them things normally reserved for God" (TDNT 1.419). In Acts, the apostles guarantee the message about the "words and works of Jesus," especially the truth of the Resurrection (1:22; 10:41-42). Over a forty-day period, Jesus appeared to them, showing them the necessary evidence or "undeniable proofs" (tekmērion [TG5039, ZG5447]; cf. Quintilian Institutio oratoria 5.9), from which one could draw no other conclusion than that he was alive. During his resurrection appearances, Jesus talked to them about the Kingdom of God (1:3). Here we have more than a code word for the content of the early church's preaching (cf. 8:12; 19:8; 28:31). The salvation accomplished in Jesus' death and resurrection and applied in the proclamation and reception of the gospel meant the initial arrival of the final reign of God (Isa 24:23; Zech 14:9; Luke 11:20).

Jesus' command that the apostles not embark on the mission until the Holy Spirit came (Luke 24:49; Acts 1:4-5) serves as a reminder to us that, though the mission is prosecuted through human agents, it is primarily God's mission. Jesus gave this command during a solemn meal in which the eleven probably renewed their commitment to their Lord (1:4, cf. sunalizomenos [TG4871, ZG5259], lit. "eating salt"; cf. the Semitic background of a "covenant of salt," in the NLT mg of Num 18:19; 2 Chr 13:5; Ezra 4:14; see also ISBE 4.286).

Placing the promise in eschatological perspective, Jesus declared that John's water baptism of repentance in preparation for the coming of the Kingdom will be superseded by a "Spirit and fire" baptism of fulfillment. This will happen soon, at Pentecost, which will initiate salvation blessings: the gift of the Spirit at conversion and his filling for empowerment in witness (2:38; 4:8). This, however, was only the foreshadowing of the promised end-time deluge of the Spirit and fire (2:1-13; Joel 2:28; cf. Isa 66:15; Ezek 36:25-27; 39:29). The future encounter with God's "Spirit and fire" will be like an angry sea engulfing and sinking a boat, or like a massive surge of floodwater suddenly sweeping down on a man and overwhelming him as he attempts to cross a river. It will be immense, majestic, and devastating (Turner 1981:51).

◆   B. The Ascension of Jesus (1:6-11)

⁶So when the apostles were with Jesus, they kept asking him, "Lord, has the time come for you to free Israel and restore our kingdom?"

⁷He replied, "The Father alone has the authority to set those dates and times, and they are not for you to know. ⁸But you will receive power when the Holy Spirit comes upon you. And you will be my witnesses, telling people about me everywhere—in Jerusalem, throughout Judea, in Samaria, and to the ends of the earth."

⁹After saying this, he was taken up into a cloud while they were watching, and they could no longer see him. ¹⁰As they strained to see him rising into heaven, two white-robed men suddenly stood among them.

¹¹"Men of Galilee," they said, "why are you standing here staring into heaven? Jesus has been taken from you into heaven, but someday he will return from heaven in the same way you saw him go!"

NOTES

1:7 *The Father alone has the authority to set those dates and times.* Jesus' response corrects the disciples mainly about the timing of the coming Kingdom. When he returns, Jesus will exercise a universal reign as the Davidic Messiah over a redeemed ethnic Israel (3:21; McLean 1994).

1:8 *you will receive power when the Holy Spirit comes upon you.* The Spirit empowers the believers to bear witness to forgiveness of sins in Jesus' name (Luke 24:46-47); it indicates a different kind of reign by Jesus, king of peace. As servant-king, he will take away "the burden of sin, law and corruption to lead [people] into freedom" (Legrand 1989:19).

ends of the earth. Ellis (1991:132) convincingly identifies this as Spain (the city of Gades in particular, since the Gr. phrase is in the sg.). According to ancient geography, Spain was the western "end of the earth" (Diodorus Siculus *History* 25.10.1; cf. Isa 49:6 and Acts 13:47). Luke, through the use of this term, "signals his knowledge of a (prospective) Pauline mission to Spain and his intention to make it part of his narrative" (Ellis 1991; cf. Rom 15:24, 28; 1 *Clement* 5:6).

1:9 *he was taken up.* The Ascension was the second stage of Jesus' three stage movement to heaven after his death (Resurrection, Ascension, and session at the divine right hand— see 2:32-34). Luke's account of the Ascension is not a figurative depiction of Jesus' spiritual exaltation, identical with his resurrection (contra Baird 1980:5), nor is it his previous departure to heaven, from which he came for every post-Resurrection appearance after his spiritual resurrection-exaltation to the Father's right hand (contra Harris 1983:84). Rather, for Luke the Ascension is a distinct event after the Resurrection, the second stage of Jesus' progress to the Father's right hand. The account does not depend on the first-century cosmology of a three-story universe (Gooding 1980:113); in fact, a cloud intervenes at the point of Jesus' actual entrance into the presence of God in heaven.

COMMENTARY

Jesus' talk of the Spirit's promised coming and the Kingdom of God (1:3, 5) made the apostles' ears tingle. Everything in their understanding of the arrival of the age to come, even corrected by the Messiah's suffering and resurrection, told them that nothing stood in the way of the full realization of the reign of God in Israel on earth. So they kept asking Jesus whether he would restore the Kingdom and liberate Israel then and there (Jer 16:15; 23:8; Hos 11:11; Joel 3:1).

Jesus' response focused the apostles' attention on the time before the final consummation and on their mission in it. History is fully in God the Father's hands (2:23; 3:21; 17:30). He sets the dates and determines the seasons but does not reveal the precise timing to humans (not even the Son; cf. Mark 13:32). As Peter will preach later, Jesus must be exalted to heaven for a period of time before "the final restoration of all things" (3:21). What Jesus revealed is a task that must be performed until the last day: witness to Jesus' saving power must be borne to the ends of the earth (Luke 21:13; 24:47; cf. Matt 24:14).

God would pursue his mission through these agents once they received the Holy Spirit. When the Holy Spirit came upon them, they would be equipped to do the work of bold, effective witness (2:37; 4:7-8, 31, 33; 6:5, 8, 10; 7:51, 55; 8:13; 18:24-25; 19:10). As we will soon learn from Peter, the outpouring is not only from the Father who promised it (1:4) but also from the Son because he, exalted to the Father's right hand, would receive from God the promised Holy Spirit, which he then would pour out (2:32-35). The empowerment for mission comes from the Triune God.

Jesus had told his disciples that the message of repentance and forgiveness of sins in his name would be taken to the ends of the earth and that beginning from Jerusalem, they were to be witnesses of these things (Luke 24:47-48). Through their personal knowledge of the facts and significance of Jesus' ministry, they would be able to bear witness (14:2-3; 22:14-21; 23:11; 26:16). God would so closely attend this witness with his Spirit that, at points, Luke will say that in the Christian's witness the Holy Spirit or the Lord is witnessing (5:32; 26:23).

The extent of the witness is summarized geographically here, though it is also detailed ethnically in the accounts of Acts. God empowers his witnesses, sending them forth with a centrifugal momentum to Palestinian and Hellenistic Jews in Jerusalem (2:1-8:3), then on to the Samaritans, a pious Ethiopian eunuch, and a group of God-fearing Gentiles in Judea and Samaria (8:3-11:18; see esp. 8:5, 27; 10:3), and finally to pagan Gentiles beyond Palestine in a movement from east to west—Syria, Cyprus, central Asia Minor, west Asia Minor, Greece, Italy, and "the ends of the earth" (11:19-28:31).

As if to punctuate the point of the connection between earth and heaven in this great mission, Jesus was lifted up, and a cloud carried him out of their sight immediately after he had pronounced the mission (cf. Exod 40:34; Dan 7:13; Luke 21:37). Thereafter, he would direct his mission from the Father's right hand in heaven (2:32-34), though he would always be active on earth bringing salvation, encouragement, and guidance to his people (16:10, 14; 18:9). The angels' rebuke of the disciples' paralyzed stare at the sky (the word translated "sky" and "heaven" in these verses is the same Gr. word) gives as its immediate reason (in the form of a promise) the fact that the end will come when Jesus visibly returns.

◆ ### C. Matthias Replaces Judas (1:12-26)

¹²Then the apostles returned to Jerusalem from the Mount of Olives, a distance of half a mile.* ¹³When they arrived, they went to the upstairs room of the house where they were staying.

Here are the names of those who were present: Peter, John, James, Andrew, Philip, Thomas, Bartholomew, Matthew, James (son of Alphaeus), Simon (the Zealot), and Judas (son of James). ¹⁴They all met together and were constantly united in prayer, along with Mary the mother of Jesus, several other women, and the brothers of Jesus.

¹⁵During this time, when about 120 believers* were together in one place, Peter stood up and addressed them. ¹⁶"Brothers," he said, "the Scriptures had to be fulfilled concerning Judas, who guided those who arrested Jesus. This was predicted long ago

by the Holy Spirit, speaking through King David. ¹⁷Judas was one of us and shared in the ministry with us."

¹⁸(Judas had bought a field with the money he received for his treachery. Falling headfirst there, his body split open, spilling out all his intestines. ¹⁹The news of his death spread to all the people of Jerusalem, and they gave the place the Aramaic name *Akeldama*, which means "Field of Blood.")

²⁰Peter continued, "This was written in the book of Psalms, where it says, 'Let his home become desolate, with no one living in it.' It also says, 'Let someone else take his position.'*

²¹"So now we must choose a replace-ment for Judas from among the men who were with us the entire time we were traveling with the Lord Jesus—²²from the time he was baptized by John until the day he was taken from us. Whoever is chosen will join us as a witness of Jesus' resurrection."

²³So they nominated two men: Joseph called Barsabbas (also known as Justus) and Matthias. ²⁴Then they all prayed, "O Lord, you know every heart. Show us which of these men you have chosen ²⁵as an apostle to replace Judas in this min-istry, for he has deserted us and gone where he belongs." ²⁶Then they cast lots, and Matthias was selected to become an apostle with the other eleven.

1:12 Greek *a Sabbath day's journey.*   1:15 Greek *brothers.*   1:20 Pss 69:25; 109:8.

NOTES

1:12 *distance of half a mile.* Lit., "a Sabbath day's journey" (see NLT mg). This was two thousand cubits or three quarters of a mile, about 1,100 meters. The rabbis ingeniously calculated this distance by interpreting Exodus 16:29 in the light of Numbers 35:5. Josephus placed the Mount of Olives at five or six stadia (960–1,152 meters, a stadion is 192 meters; *Antiquities* 20.169; *War* 5.70) from Jerusalem.

1:13 *upstairs room.* Because of differences in vocabulary, it is difficult to identify this place with the site of the Last Supper (Luke 22:11-13), the Resurrection appearances (Luke 24:36), or John Mark's mother Mary's house (12:12).

Simon (the Zealot). He was probably a member of the nationalistic Jewish faction who were the spiritual heirs of the Hasmonean insurgents (Josephus *War* 2.651; 4.160; 1 Macc 2:27).

1:14 *several other women.* The Western text with its addition "and children" (*kai teknois* [TG5043, ZG5451]) sees *gunaixin* [TG1135, ZG1222] (women) as referring to the apostles' wives (and so Barrett 1994:89) rather than the faithful band of female disciples (Luke 8:1-3). The word order and Luke's consistent reference to that band as witnesses of Jesus' sufferings and resurrection probably indicate their presence here (Luke 23:49, 54-56; 24:1-10, 22; Johnson 1992:34; Luter 1995:184).

1:15 *about 120.* The group's imprecise number and mixed gender probably indicate it is not intended as a populace over which the twelve apostles (according to the ratio of 1:10) served as a ruling council, analogous to the synagogue or Sanhedrin.

1:16 *the Scriptures.* This is lit. "the Scripture" and may be either an allusion to Psalm 41:10 (Barrett 1994:96) or a reference to the first of the two OT quotations in v. 20 (Johnson 1992:35).

1:18 *Judas had bought a field. . . . Falling headfirst . . . his body split open, spilling out all his intestines.* Luke and Matthew's accounts (Acts 1:18-19 and Matt 27:3-10) may be harmonized if one understands the Jewish leaders' purchase of land as done in Judas' name. Further, Judas may have attempted suicide by hanging himself but actually died when the rope broke and he fell headlong and his body ruptured, an explanation which goes all the way back to Augustine (Polhill 1992:92; Gordon 1971:98). Finally, there is no need to assert that the act of "falling headlong" and "bursting open" necessarily assumes falling from a building on the property, an action inconsistent with the picture of the property as an undeveloped field (contra Johnson 1992:36).

field. The word used here, *chōrion* [TG5564, ZG6005], is synonymous with *agros* [TG68, ZG69] (Matt 27:7-8, 10; Josephus *Antiquities* 9.119; cf. 5:1, 3, 8-9).

1:19 *news of his death spread.* Luke does not emphasize the rapidity but the extent to which Judas' death and its link to the "field of blood" were common knowledge.

Akeldama. This transliteration, Gr., *hakeldamach*, represents the Aramaic word combination: *khaqel* (field) + *dema'* (blood); cf. Derrett 1995:130.

1:20 *This was written.* The validity of Peter's interpreting the maledictions against the oppressors of the righteous in Pss 69 and 109 as referring prophetically to Judas has often been questioned or excused (e.g., Longenecker 1981:266; Barrett 1994:100; Bruce 1990:110). Peter's interpretation is valid when these psalms are understood messianically, based on the Davidic authorship titles for both, a literal reading of them (e.g., the use of Judas's homestead as a cemetery [Matt 27:7-8] meant no living person dwelled there, Ps 69:25), and Jesus' own use of Ps 69 to describe his passion (Ps 69:4/Jn 15:25; cf. Ps 69:9/Jn 2:17; Ps 69:21/Jn 19:29; cf. Ps 69:9/Rom 15:13).

position. The Gr. is *episkopē* [TG1984, ZG2175], ("oversight," cf. 20:28), which, when combined with *diakonia* [TG1248, ZG1355] ("ministry," 1:17, 25; cf. 6:4) as it is in this context, conveys what Luke means by *apostolē* [TG651, ZG692] ("apostle," 1:25).

1:21, 22, 24 *We must choose . . . chosen . . . chosen.* Except for the phrase addressed to the Lord Jesus in prayer, "you have chosen" (1:24), there is no explicit Gr. wording for "choice" behind the vocabulary of selection used in these verses. Though the NLT's use of the passive does place the initiative with God, the rendering "we must choose" (1:21) puts more stress on human activity than Luke seems to intend. Luke's concern throughout the narrative is to describe the divine necessity according to OT prophecy and the divine activity in selection through dependent prayer and the casting of lots.

1:22 *from the time he was baptized by John.* This clause could mean "from the time when John began his ministry" (cf. 10:37; 13:24).

1:23 *Barsabbas.* This could mean "son of the Sabbath" (born on the Sabbath); "son of an old man" (one born in one's old age); or "son of Saba" (cf. Barrett 1994:102). Judas (also called Barsabbas; 15:22) is possibly Joseph's brother.

1:26 *cast lots.* Given the OT background and practice (Lev 16:8; Num 26:55; 33:54; Josh 19:1-40; Jonah 1:7-8), it was not a mistake to cast lots. It does not seem, however, to be a method that became normative in the early church after Pentecost (Marshall 1980:67).

Matthias was selected. Some have thought that this was a mistake because Paul should have been assigned this place and Matthias is not mentioned anywhere else in the NT. Paul, however, did not meet the requirements and recognized the "abnormality" of his apostolic calling (1 Cor 15:8; Longenecker 1981:166).

COMMENTARY

The preparation God desires of those whom he empowers to carry out his mission is persistent prayer and restored integrity. Responding to the angels' mild rebuke and being obedient to Jesus' directive, the apostles and those with them (cf. 1:15) returned to Jerusalem to await the Spirit's coming. Jerusalem is a key place theologically for Luke. Not only is it where the Messiah must suffer (Luke 13:31-35), it is also the place from which the Lord said his mission must commence (Luke 24:47; cf. Acts 22:17).

In an evidently spacious upstairs room, suitable for large gatherings and for prayer, the apostles and others gathered for continuous prayer as they awaited the Spirit's coming. Luke presented the nucleus of the New Testament church as he enumerated the Twelve minus Judas, mentioned female disciples, and noted that Mary and Jesus' siblings were part of his spiritual family (1:13-14). In so doing, not only does he introduce the first two spiritual generations of Jerusalem church leadership—Peter and James, the half-brother of Christ (12:12; 15:13; 21:18)—he also stresses the continuity of this praying band of believers with the Messiah's earthly ministry and with God's people Israel.

The group's persistent, united prayer was a foretaste of a crucial aspect of their common life after the Spirit came (2:42, 46; 6:4). Unity and corporate prayer indeed would mark them (2:42, 46; 4:24, 29; 5:12; 12:5; 15:25). Their prayer life included petitioning the Lord to pour out his power upon them (4:29-31; cf. 8:15). In waiting for the coming of the Spirit, they had learned from their Lord's life and teaching (Luke 3:21-22; 11:13; 18:1-8). It underlined their belief that God was directing the entire course of history for his good purposes and that the application of salvation blessings were his doing (Plymale 1991:76).

During this period, Peter took the initiative (1:15, 20) to mend the tear in the apostolic leadership left by Judas's defection. Judas literally "was one of us and shared in the ministry with us" (1:17). At the same time, he was the traitor (Luke 22:3, 47, 54). Peter described this contradictory situation as being within the purview and control of God's sovereign, saving purposes (1:16; cf. Luke 22:22). As with the suffering and death of Jesus himself, the Spirit's predictions in the Old Testament about Judas had now come to fulfillment (2:23; 4:25-28; 13:27).

Since the Scripture Peter cited assumes knowledge of Judas's remorse and bloody end, Luke parenthetically lets his audience in on the rest of the story (1:18-19). With the reward for his treachery Judas purchased a field. His bloody suicide on the southern slope of the valley of Hinnom turned this property into cursed ground, twice defiled (Matt 27:7-8; cf. Num 35:33; Deut 21:22-23). It became a cemetery for the ceremonially unclean. Judas's death itself is in character with the end of the unrighteous dead in Israel (2 Chr 21:18-20; cf. Josephus *War* 7.453). The infamy of this place spread through all Jerusalem, for all knew this macabre "tourist attraction" as "Akeldama"—the field of blood. Such details serve as a sobering warning of divine judgment on wrongdoing (cf. 5:1-11; 8:20-23; 13:10-11).

The end of Judas and his property fulfills Psalm 69:25: "Let their homes become desolate and their tents be deserted." In what may be the center of a chiasm (a reverse parallelism), Peter immediately proceeds to cite another Scripture text, which is fulfilled in what follows (the chiasm would thus be: event, 1:18-19; Scripture, 1:20a; Scripture, 1:20b; event, 1:21-26). The statement "let someone else take his position" (Ps 109:8) provides the warrant for the assembly's action in selecting Judas's replacement. It shows that the action is part of the divinely predicted judgment on Judas and is therefore not a precedent for a practice of apostolic succession. It also shows that God sees the restoration of the full quota of apostles as a positive necessity for the fulfillment of God's saving purposes to bring salvation to Israel and the nations (Luke 22:28-30; Acts 1:8).

Peter then goes on to speak of the divine necessity (*dei* [TG1163, ZG1256]) of finding one to become "with us" a witness to the resurrection (1:21). He states the qualifications: one who had accompanied Jesus' disciples the whole time he engaged in his public ministry, from the time of John the Baptist's ministry until Jesus' ascension (1:21-22). This time period contained the events covered in the early church's gospel preaching (e.g., 10:37-43; 13:23-41) and the Gospel of Mark. Such a person would be qualified to serve as an apostolic guarantor, not only of the Resurrection but also of the words and works of Jesus. Being a witness to the Resurrection was a key apostolic qualification and role because that event, and that event alone, makes possible the application of salvation blessings.

The assembly, or possibly the apostles, set forth two candidates: Joseph Barsabbas, with the Roman name Justus, and Matthias (1:23). Neither is mentioned again in Scripture, though Judas called Barsabbas (15:22) might have been Joseph's brother. The assembly, or again possibly the apostles, addressed the Lord Jesus in prayer. They thereby showed their dependence on the Lord to guide them in important decisions concerning leadership and the prosecution of the mission (9:11; 13:1-3; 22:17). They asked Jesus to do from heaven what he once did on earth: pick disciples and give them instruction (Luke 6:13; Acts 1:2). Both men were equally qualified outwardly. But the assembly needed Christ's mind as the "divine knower of all hearts" to identify the person qualified inwardly (Acts 15:8; Deut 8:2; Pss 7:9; 64:6; 139:23). They wanted to make sure that another Judas, one into whose heart Satan could enter (Luke 22:3), was not chosen.

The assembly described the position as a "place of ministry and apostleship." Jesus declared in his farewell discourse in Luke that the apostles will sit on "thrones, judging the twelve tribes of Israel" as part of the Kingdom (Luke 22:30). The places were set, but Judas by his defection left one vacant. Though divinely determined and predicted, Judas by his own choice experienced the "sorrow" of Luke 22:22. The assembly, under divine guidance, must fill this place. Though the place involves authority and leadership, the one who fills it is to do the service of apostleship (Luke 22:26-27; Acts 6:4). Apostles are servants of God's word for the benefit of the people of God.

The assembly cast lots (1:26). In this process, each candidate's name was written on a stone that was placed in a container. The container was shaken and turned upside down until one of the stones sprang or fell out, thus indicating the Lord's choice (*m. Yoma* 3.9; 4.1; ISBE 3:173). This method had a long history in Israel (Josh 18:6; 1 Chr 24:5; Prov 16:33). The lot fell on Matthias, and he was enrolled with the eleven apostles, thereby restoring the integrity of the leadership.

By united, persistent prayer, by declaration of divinely predicted scriptural fulfillment, by focused prayer appealing to the Lord Jesus to indicate his choice, and by the casting of lots, which was understood as a means of providentially revealing God's will, Luke demonstrates that God was active in preparing his people for the mighty outpouring of his Spirit.

Such an account helps Theophilus and us by giving a basis for embracing the truth of the events of "salvation accomplished" and the realities of "salvation applied." The events of salvation accomplished were communicated by the apostolic band of eyewitnesses chosen by the Lord. Salvation applied comes by the power of God applied to the lives of those who embrace the gospel. The early community's model life of prayer awaiting the inaugural outpouring of the Spirit points to the true source of effectiveness in mission. The replacement of Judas demonstrates that nothing will thwart the complete fulfillment of God's saving purposes.

◆   **D. The Holy Spirit Comes (2:1-13)**

On the day of Pentecost* all the believers were meeting together in one place. ²Suddenly, there was a sound from heaven like the roaring of a mighty windstorm, and it filled the house where they were sitting. ³Then, what looked like flames or tongues of fire appeared and settled on each of them. ⁴And everyone present was filled with the Holy Spirit and began speaking in other languages,* as the Holy Spirit gave them this ability.

⁵At that time there were devout Jews from every nation living in Jerusalem. ⁶When they heard the loud noise, everyone came running, and they were bewildered to hear their own languages being spoken by the believers. ⁷They were completely amazed. "How can this be?" they exclaimed. "These people are all from Galilee, ⁸and yet we hear them speaking in our own native languages! ⁹Here we are—Parthians, Medes, Elamites, people from Mesopotamia, Judea, Cappadocia, Pontus, the province of Asia, ¹⁰Phrygia, Pamphylia, Egypt, and the areas of Libya around Cyrene, visitors from Rome ¹¹(both Jews and converts to Judaism), Cretans, and Arabs. And we all hear these people speaking in our own languages about the wonderful things God has done!" ¹²They stood there amazed and perplexed. "What can this mean?" they asked each other.

¹³But others in the crowd ridiculed them, saying, "They're just drunk, that's all!"

2:1 The Festival of Pentecost came 50 days after Passover (when Jesus was crucified).   2:4 Or *in other tongues.*

NOTES

2:1 *On the day of Pentecost.* The Western reading expands this: "And it came to pass in those days of the arrival [fulfillment] of the day of Pentecost" (see Ropes 1979:10). This heightens this introduction of a key salvation history fulfillment event by adding Semitic narrative features (Barrett 1994:112-113).

The relevant theological background of Pentecost for the Spirit's coming is probably its original significance; the firstfruits of the wheat harvest (Exod 23:16; Lev 23:15-21; Deut 16:9-12) applied to the fulfillment of both OT and NT prophecies about the coming of the Spirit, who is the firstfruits of the eschatological harvest (Luke 24:49; Acts 1:4-5, 8; Isa 32:15; Joel 2:28-32; cf. Rom 8:23; Witherington 1998:131). The later significance in Jewish tradition, which celebrated Pentecost as the anniversary of the giving of the law on Sinai (*b. Pesaḥ* 68b; Talbert 1997:42), is not developed by Luke. The reversal of Babel (Gen 11:1-9) may be a subtheme (Barrett 1994:112) but in a nuanced way that affirms cultural diversity (D. Smith 1996:184-186).

2:3 *flames or tongues of fire.* Lit., "divided/dividing tongues like fire." As described in the NLT, they were individual tongues resting on each one, not a fireball dividing itself and coming to rest on each (contra Polhill 1992:98; Dunn 1996:25).

2:4 *filled with the Holy Spirit.* There is not yet consensus among interpreters as to whether the gift was "the power and life of the church" received by individuals at conversion/initiation (Dunn 1970; cf. Atkinson 1995 for Pentecostal/charismatic response) or "the *donum superadditum,* the vocational empowerment for witness" (Stronstad 1984:53). It is probably best to see Luke's presentation of the baptism and filling with the Spirit in a comprehensive way (Turner 1998). The Spirit comes at Pentecost as both an initial, permanent endowment for the church (compare the way it serves as a benchmark event at 10:47; 11:17; 15:8) and as a particular instance of vocational empowerment for witness, a filling that may be repeated (4:8, 31; 9:17; 13:9).

other languages. Or, "in other tongues" (NLT mg). The NLT rightly translates *glōssais* [TG1100, ZG1185] in the text as intelligible human languages (contra Everts 1994). The miracle was that the languages were unknown to the Galilean speakers (cf. 2:7-8). Though there may have been exuberance in the speaking, so much so that it could be mistaken for drunkenness (Witherington 1998:133), it was not the ecstatic speech of 1 Cor 14 or Acts 10:46; 19:6 (Bruce 1990:115). Nor, given the list of nations (2:9-11) is it simply vernacular Aramaic or Greek within a diglossia setting where "Holy Hebrew" would have been expected (contra Zerhusen 1995).

Spirit gave them. "Gave" (*edidou* [TG1325, ZG1443]) is an iterative imperfect (lit., "was giving") and signifies the Spirit's endowment of each of the apostles with the ability to speak in another tongue.

2:5 *devout Jews.* Though *Ioudaioi* [TG2453/A, ZG2681] (Jews) is missing from ℵ and a few Old Latin mss, the vast majority of mss contain it. Explicitly describing "godly residents of Jerusalem from every nation" as "Jews" creates a number of surface problems of redundancy and dissonance, which probably led to the deletion (Metzger 1994:251).

2:6 *their own languages being spoken.* The Western reading, which adjusts the word order, makes clear, as does the NLT, that the miracle is in the speaking, not in the hearing (Ropes 1979:13).

2:7 *completely amazed.* This NLT phrase renders two verbs: *existanto* [TG1839/A, ZG2014] (be beside oneself, be astonished) and *ethaumazon* [TG2296, ZG2513] (be amazed). The former is a feeling of astonishment mingled with fear, the natural reaction to the totally unexpected, especially the miraculous (8:13; 9:21; 10:45; 12:16). The latter, "amazement, marveling," is often the reaction to a declaration of the mighty acts of God and the supernatural in Luke–Acts (e.g., Luke 2:33; 9:43; Acts 3:11; 4:13).

2:9-11 *Parthians, Medes, Elamites . . . Cretans and Arabs.* Many different origins for the list of nations have been proposed: Hellenistic history, geography, or astrology; a Roman list of provinces; a Jewish list of Diaspora regions; a pre-Lukan tradition of the regions of Christian mission (Linton 1974:44). Though the "Jewish list" explanation is currently the most popular (e.g., Barrett 1994:122; Talbert 1997:42), even it does not explain all the names. A historical report of the Pentecost event itself is the best explanation.

2:13 *They're just drunk, that's all!* The exclamation renders a Gr. phrase that contains the object *gleukos* [TG1098, ZG1183] (sweet, or new, wine). Since the yearly vintage would not occur until after Pentecost, the wine referred to probably would have been kept sweet throughout the year (see Bruce 1988:59 for ancient methods for preserving sweetness). New wine, sweet to the taste, would have been a ready cause of drunkenness (Witherington 1998:133).

COMMENTARY

God had prepared a time for fulfillment: the Day of Pentecost, a celebration of the "firstfruits" of the Promised Land, God's inheritance. What better time to send the

Spirit, "the eschatological firstfruits" of God's final salvation blessings. God had prepared his people. Obediently, in prayerful unity, the believers were meeting together in one place, probably the upper room, waiting for the Spirit's coming (1:4, 14).

God the Father marked the coming of the Spirit with his own presence. Suddenly there was a sound from heaven. Biblical theophanies are often accompanied by a loud sound (Exod 19:16, 19; 20:18; cf. Heb 12:19). That it is "from heaven" and is only "like" some earthly phenomenon points to its divine origin and supernatural character. The sound like the "roaring of a mighty windstorm" (pnoē [TG4157, ZG4466]; 2:2) is reminiscent of the Old Testament pnoē of God: the "breath of his nostrils, his snorting," which often brought devastating judgment (2 Sam 22:16; Job 4:9; 37:10; Isa 30:33). But here the sound fills the house in blessing, coming as the inescapable, overpowering, all-embracing presence of God.

God visibly signaled the Spirit's arrival by the appearance of flaming tongues. Though fire can often serve as a sign of divine presence (Exod 3:2; 13:21; Ps 18:12-13; Ezek 1:4), these tongues signify the Spirit in particular. Jesus, following John, promised that he would baptize with "the Holy Spirit and fire" (Luke 3:16; Acts 1:5). In the Old Testament the Spirit came selectively and often temporarily on God's people (1 Sam 11:6; 16:13-14; 2 Chr 24:20; Ezek 2:2). Now he would come indiscriminately and permanently, just as the tongues settled on each person gathered in the room.

God matched the outward sign with a corresponding inner reality. He filled all with the Spirit. This initial endowment of the church with its "power and life" as a "filling," which will be followed by other fillings, is also an empowerment for witness. The outward manifestation of this filling is yet another miracle: the ability to instantly speak a foreign language. This gift came at the Spirit's initiative and was inspired speech, as implied by the use of the Greek apophthengomai [TG669, ZG710] ("utter inspired speech"—see BAGD 102). This term is used sparingly but significantly in Acts (2:4, 14; 26:25; cf. Mic 5:11 LXX; Plutarch De Pythiae oraculis 23[405E]; Philo Moses 2:33). Through this miracle, the promised Spirit came to empower the believers to be witnesses to all peoples, even to the end of the earth (1:8).

What of Pentecost does God want the church to experience in its life today? What is repeatable? What is unrepeatable? Given the rest of Acts, it is best to think in terms of three categories of events: unique (unrepeatable), benchmark (repeatable at God's initiative), and normative (repeatable as God's mandate). The unique and unrepeatable aspects of Pentecost fulfilled their purpose in signifying the inauguration of the Spirit's empowering, missional presence indiscriminately among his people. The Spirit giving the early believers the ability to speak foreign languages fits this category (as in 2:4).

Benchmark events are featured repeatedly later in Acts and are analogous to some previous events. Pentecost is appealed to either by allusion or explicitly to legitimize claims that the Spirit is actually present in the lives of those experiencing the phenomena. What is important to note is that in each instance there is a specific, limited purpose for the presence of the feature, and the feature is not exactly but only analogously replicated. The shaking of the place where the believers are praying for the Spirit's aid is analogous to but not exactly the same as the effects of the "sound from heaven" (4:31; cf. 2:2). The speaking in tongues done by the God-fearing Gentiles and Ephesian disciples of John the Baptist, which is probably ecstatic speech similar to that mentioned in 1 Corinthians 14, is analogous to the miraculous speaking in foreign languages (10:46; 19:6; cf. 2:4).

What is normative (repeatable as God's mandate) is the filling of the Spirit. God desires that his people keep on being filled with—indeed, be full of—his Spirit so that they may be powerfully enabled to live for and bear witness to Christ and his gospel (Eph 5:18; cf. Acts 4:8; 7:55; Rom 12:11 mg).

Pious Diaspora Jews resident in Jerusalem were attracted to the "sound" and formed a crowd. They followed the believers, who had probably moved out of the house and through the city streets to the Temple. The attraction was immediately disorienting, however. The crowd was bewildered, beside themselves, and amazed at hearing these Galilean believers declare to each one, in his own language, the "wonderful things God has done!" (2:11). Galileans, with their indistinct pronunciation (confused or lost laryngeals and aspirates), were notorious for their lack of linguistic ability (b. Eruvin 53a; b. Megillah 24b).

These events had such an impact that it took Luke five different words to express the crowd's reaction. At first, the crowd was bewildered or confused (2:6, cf. the condition of the Ephesian and Jerusalem mobs described in 19:32 and 21:31). Then, when the full impact of the miracles struck them, they were beside themselves with wonder (see note on 2:7). After reflecting on the event (2:12), the crowd was still amazed (actually "astonished," existanto [TG1839/A, ZG2014] is used again), and they were either perplexed or mocking in their assessment of what was happening (2:12-13).

The crowd's bewilderment or confusion points to a reversal of Babel and makes for an interesting, contrasting parallel. According to Genesis, God confused the languages so that the people would not understand (Gen 11:7, 9 LXX suncheōmen . . . sunecheen [TG4797, ZG5177], "confound"). In Acts 2:6 the Spirit brings understanding, which causes the crowd to be confused (sunechuthē [TG4797, ZG5179], the same word as in Gen 11, LXX). But the confusion is a function of the continuing effects of Babel. The crowd was expecting language barriers, not the miraculous suspension of them through a Spirit-empowered affirmation of linguistic—and hence cultural—diversity. Yes, this miracle affirms the universality of the gospel proclamation among all nations, but it does so in such a way that the integrity of each culture is embraced. God's original design for humankind in the creation and post-Flood mandate was to spread out and fill the earth with a harmonious patchwork of diverse cultures (Gen 1:28; 9:7; 10:5). Now the Good News must be proclaimed and applied by his Spirit to persons in all those cultures.

As the people in the crowd enumerated their nationalities and places of origin, the true universal scope of the application of salvation comes clearly into focus.

They began with the far eastern border of the Roman Empire: "Parthians, Medes, Elamites," and moved westward through "Mesopotamia and Judea" (i.e., Israel, according to its God-given boundaries per Gen 15:18; Josh 1:4). The list then encompasses regions of Asia Minor in a circular, counterclockwise order, commencing with the east: "Cappadocia, Pontus, the province of Asia, Phrygia, Pamphylia." It next notes southern regions of the empire: "Egypt" and west of it, "the areas of Libya toward Cyrene." Completing the list and enhancing its comprehensiveness is "Rome," the empire's center, and inhabitants of two geographical extremities: "Cretans" (island dwellers) and "Arabs," (denizens of the desert; cf. Ezek 30:5).

This miraculous ability of the apostles to speak in foreign languages enables all to hear in his or her own tongue the "wonderful things God has done" (*ta megaleia tou theou*). Often, Old Testament ascriptions of praise referred to God's mighty acts of delivering his people with the word *megaleia* [TG3167, ZG3483] (LXX of Deut 11:2; Pss 71[70]:19; 105[104]:21; cf. 1 QS 1:21). Now his witnesses sound forth his mighty acts in accomplishing salvation through the death and resurrection of his Son and applying it through the gift of his Spirit.

Those in the crowd quickly developed either an open or a closed stance toward what was happening. Some were thoroughly "perplexed" (*diaporeō* [TG1280, ZG1389], cf. Luke 9:7; Acts 5:24; 10:17). They admitted their inability to explain either the source or the significance of what they were seeing and hearing. But they were open to an explanation because they asked, "What can this mean?" Others, for whom much of the speech was gibberish, interpreted the believers' exuberance cynically, mocking them for being drunk with sweet wine at this early hour. Such varied reactions, none of which show an understanding of the miracle, demonstrate graphically the communicative limits of the simple occurrence of a mighty deed of God. Without interpretation, the people were clueless and prone to misunderstanding.

◆   E. Peter Preaches to a Crowd (2:14-42)

14Then Peter stepped forward with the eleven other apostles and shouted to the crowd, "Listen carefully, all of you, fellow Jews and residents of Jerusalem! Make no mistake about this. 15These people are not drunk, as some of you are assuming. Nine o'clock in the morning is much too early for that. 16No, what you see was predicted long ago by the prophet Joel:

17'In the last days,' God says,
    'I will pour out my Spirit upon
        all people.
    Your sons and daughters will
        prophesy.
    Your young men will see visions,
    and your old men will dream dreams.

18In those days I will pour out my
        Spirit
    even on my servants—men and
        women alike—
    and they will prophesy.
19And I will cause wonders in the
        heavens above
    and signs on the earth below—
    blood and fire and clouds of smoke.
20The sun will become dark,
    and the moon will turn blood red
    before that great and glorious day
        of the LORD arrives.
21But everyone who calls on the name
        of the LORD
    will be saved.'*

²²"People of Israel, listen! God publicly endorsed Jesus the Nazarene* by doing powerful miracles, wonders, and signs through him, as you well know. ²³But God knew what would happen, and his prearranged plan was carried out when Jesus was betrayed. With the help of lawless Gentiles, you nailed him to a cross and killed him. ²⁴But God released him from the horrors of death and raised him back to life, for death could not keep him in its grip. ²⁵King David said this about him:

'I see that the LORD is always with me.
I will not be shaken, for he is right
    beside me.
²⁶No wonder my heart is glad,
    and my tongue shouts his praises!
    My body rests in hope.
²⁷For you will not leave my soul among
    the dead*
    or allow your Holy One to rot in
    the grave.
²⁸You have shown me the way of life,
    and you will fill me with the joy of
    your presence.'*

²⁹"Dear brothers, think about this! You can be sure that the patriarch David wasn't referring to himself, for he died and was buried, and his tomb is still here among us. ³⁰But he was a prophet, and he knew God had promised with an oath that one of David's own descendants would sit on his throne. ³¹David was looking into the future and speaking of the Messiah's resurrection. He was saying that God would not leave him among the dead or allow his body to rot in the grave.

³²"God raised Jesus from the dead, and we are all witnesses of this. ³³Now he is exalted to the place of highest honor in heaven, at God's right hand. And the Father, as he had promised, gave him the Holy Spirit to pour out upon us, just as you see and hear today. ³⁴For David himself never ascended into heaven, yet he said,

'The LORD said to my Lord,
    "Sit in the place of honor at my
        right hand
³⁵until I humble your enemies,
    making them a footstool under
        your feet."'*

³⁶"So let everyone in Israel know for certain that God has made this Jesus, whom you crucified, to be both Lord and Messiah!"

³⁷Peter's words pierced their hearts, and they said to him and to the other apostles, "Brothers, what should we do?"

³⁸Peter replied, "Each of you must repent of your sins and turn to God, and be baptized in the name of Jesus Christ for the forgiveness of your sins. Then you will receive the gift of the Holy Spirit. ³⁹This promise is to you, and to your children, and even to the Gentiles*—all who have been called by the Lord our God." ⁴⁰Then Peter continued preaching for a long time, strongly urging all his listeners, "Save yourselves from this crooked generation!"

⁴¹Those who believed what Peter said were baptized and added to the church that day—about 3,000 in all.

⁴²All the believers devoted themselves to the apostles' teaching, and to fellowship, and to sharing in meals (including the Lord's Supper*), and to prayer.

2:17-21 Joel 2:28-32. 2:22 Or *Jesus of Nazareth.* 2:27 Greek *in Hades;* also in 2:31. 2:25-28 Ps 16:8-11 (Greek version). 2:34-35 Ps 110:1. 2:39 Or *and to people far in the future;* Greek reads *and to those far away.* 2:42 Greek *the breaking of bread;* also in 2:46.

NOTES

2:14 *eleven other apostles.* The Western reading, "ten apostles," suggests a source for the account that "either disregarded or was ignorant of the election of Matthias" (Metzger 1994:255). In addition, the Western reading has *prōtos* [ᵀᴳ4413, ᶻᴳ4755] (first) modifying Peter's activity, which points to the participation of the others (Barrett 1994:134). Finally, the Western text has *eipen* [TG3004, ZG3306] (speak, say) in place of *apophthengomai* [TG669, ZG710] ("utter inspired speech"—see BAGD 102), to convey Peter's speech. If D (the Western text) is original, then copyists have brought over *apophthengomai* from 2:4 (Barrett 1994:134). If not, then some emphasis on the Spirit-filled nature of Peter's speech is lost.

2:16 *what you see was predicted.* Peter's appropriation of Joel for Pentecost is legitimate. The details in the Joel passage—"the day of the LORD" and a final gathering of Israel for salvation and of the nations for judgment—tie the events to the consummation of human history (Joel 2:31-3:2; Treier 1997:15). There was a general Jewish expectation, often appealing to Joel 2, that an indiscriminate outpouring of the Spirit, manifesting itself in "all Israel prophesying," would characterize the age to come (*Deuteronomy Rabbah* 6:14; *Numbers Rabbah* 15:25; cf. Num 11:29; Ezek 39:29; Zech 12:10).

2:17-21 *In the last days.* This wording in the quote from Joel 2:28-32 differs from the LXX. Acts 2:17 has *en tais eschatais hēmerais* ("in the last days") where the LXX (reflecting the MT) has *meta tauta* ("after these things") and then introduces "God says." It also reverses two lines of Joel 2:28. Acts 2:18 adds "and they will prophesy" to Joel 2:29. Acts 2:19 adds "above . . . signs . . . below" to Joel 2:30. These changes are appropriate inferences from the immediate context or legitimate expansions for greater clarity and impact (Archer and Chirichigno 1983:149).

The Western text shows a universalizing tendency: it applies Joel to the Gentiles as well as the Jews by making "all flesh" plural, changing "your sons . . . your daughters" to "their sons . . . their daughters," and changing "your young men . . . your old men" simply to "young men . . . old men." The same motivation may be behind the switch from second person to first person pronouns in verse 39, thus identifying salvation as a gift for spiritual Israel—both Jew and Gentile (Metzger 1994:257). The Western text does not contain "blood and fire and clouds of smoke." Either a copyist saw the details as irrelevant to Peter's points, or he committed a parablepsis—that is, his eye skipped from *katō* [TG2736, ZG3004] (below) to *kapnou* [TG2586, ZG2837] (smoke) so that he failed to copy the line in between (Metzger 1994:258).

2:19-20 *signs on the earth below.* These "signs" may be eschatological portents, the miracle-working ministry of Jesus (including his resurrection-ascension-session, cf. 2:22), the gift of the Spirit (2:33), apostolic signs and wonders (2:43; 4:16, 30-31; 5:12), or a complex referent including all of these with a focus on Jesus' ministry on through his exaltation (Sloan 1991:234). The reverse parallelism ties "signs on the earth" with "blood and fire and clouds of smoke." This probably points to the sociopolitical upheaval of the "last days" (Luke 21:9-10; Rev 18:9; cf. Judg 20:40; Zech 11:1).

2:24 *death could not keep him in its grip.* Lit., "birth pangs of death" (*ōdinas* [TG5604, ZG6047] *tou thanatou* [TG2288, ZG2505]). The interchange of Heb. *khebel* [TH2256A, ZH2475] (cord) and *khebel* [TH2256C, ZH2477] (birth pangs), in the way the LXX translates Ps 18 [17]:5 and Ps 116 [114]:3, results in a remarkable mixed metaphor in which death is regarded as being in labor and unable to hold back the Messiah's resurrection.

2:22-36 Peter's interpretation of Pss 16 and 110 is logical and coherent given his starting points: literal interpretation and a messianic understanding of first-person Davidic psalms. The warrant for adopting such starting points is the Christocentric interpretive practice of Jesus himself (cf. Luke 20:41-44 and Ps 110:1; Luke 24:25-27, 44-48).

Though the rabbis related some of Ps 16 to the messianic age, there is only a fleeting reference to the Messiah. For them, it is David's corpse that is incorruptible (*Midrash Psalms* 16:9-11; Strack and Billerbeck 1978:2.618).

2:27 *to rot in the grave.* The NLT supplies the phrase "in the grave," which picks up on nuances from the previous line's "among the dead" (this is *hadēs* [TG86, ZG87] in the Gr., representing the *she'ol* [TH7585, ZH8619], "pit" or "grave," of the MT). The Gr. (from the LXX) simply speaks of "rot" or "decay" (via the word *diaphthora* [TG1312, ZG1426], "decay" or "corruption"; [cf. Ps 30[29]:9; 35[34]:7; 55[54]:23]; the LXX's stereotyped equivalent to *shakhat* [TH7845, ZH8846] "corruption," the word used in the MT). Peter keys in on *diaphthora* to establish his point concerning resurrection.

2:29 *his tomb is still here.* The tomb of David was probably extant in the days of Jesus and the apostles (Josephus *Antiquities* 7.392-394; 13.249; 16.179-183; *War* 1.61).

2:36 *made this Jesus . . . to be both Lord and Messiah.* This is not Adoptionistic Christology (contra Barrett 1994:152). Jesus did not become someone he was not before (see Luke 2:11). Rather, by his resurrection and exaltation God "instates" him in a unique, lofty position from which he functions as the exclusive medium of salvation, the Messiah and Lord over all (3:20; 4:10-12; 5:31; 10:36, 42-43; Hurtado 1997:171).

2:37 *pierced their hearts.* Lit. "they were cut [divine passive] to the heart." The verb here is *katanussomai* [TG2660, ZG2920], the same as used in Isa 6:5 LXX.

2:38 *repent . . . be baptized . . . forgiveness . . . receive the . . . Holy Spirit.* Luke gives us, in a single complex, the four normative ingredients in receiving salvation: repentance, baptism, forgiveness, the Holy Spirit. These should never be reduced to a mechanistic pattern, which would turn baptism into a work or make the reception of the Spirit a separate second experience (Polhill 1992:116; cf. Tanton 1990; Dunn 1996:33).

2:39 *Gentiles.* Lit., "to those far away" (so NLT mg). Scholars, arguing from Joel's Jewish referent for "all flesh" (Joel 2:28; cf. Acts 2:17), the Jewish mind-set, and the failure of the apostles to immediately embrace the Gentile mission, contend that Peter and Luke (Witherington 1998:141), if not Peter only (Longenecker 1981:286), have the diaspora Jews in mind here. But Peter, and Luke following him, alludes to the last line of Joel 2:32 here, making a point of including the nuance of the first line of Joel 2:32 (cf. Acts 2:21) by using "those far away" in place of the LXX's *euangelizomenoi* [TG2097/A, ZG2294] ("messengers")—a choice possibly influenced by Isa 57:19. Luke introduces in the immediate context a list of nations. For Peter and Luke, then, the "all people" (2:17) and the "everyone who calls" (2:21), and finally "all who have been called" (2:39) include the Gentiles (van de Sandt 1990:70).

2:41 *believed.* Interestingly, both the Western text (*pisteusantes* [TG4100, ZG4409], "believing") and the NLT render the people's response "more precisely and theologically" than the NA²⁷ reading, *apodechomai* [TG588, ZG622], "receiving" (Barrett 1994:161).

about 3,000. Although critical scholars believe a large response is reasonable, they still dismiss the number's accuracy. Dunn (1996:34) calls it "impressionistic (propagandistic)." Reinhardt's recent study (1995:237), however, places Jerusalem's first-century population at 60,000 to 120,000. Festival crowds, of course, swelled it. The Temple courts could accommodate 200,000. This size of response could have been accommodated by any of the common modes of baptism.

2:42 *fellowship.* This idea of "fellowship" (*koinōnia* [TG2842, ZG3126]) is not the Pauline "shared participation in the Spirit" (contra Dunn 1996:35) or in a broad range of activities (Blue 1998:489), which "the Lord's Supper" and "prayer" may further define (contra Witherington 1998:160). Rather, given the word play on *koinos* [TG2839, ZG3123] ("shared," 2:44) and the further descriptions of the community in 4:32-36, Luke was referring primarily to sharing in material things that flow from a community fellowship grounded in a common acceptance of the apostles' message and a oneness in the Spirit (Barrett 1994:164; cf. 1QS 5:1-4; D. Williams 1985:39).

the Lord's Supper. Lit., "the breaking of the bread." Breaking of bread, the signal to begin an ordinary meal, also served as a metonymy for the whole meal (see 27:35). The phrase can also refer to the Lord's Supper. This double significance and the specification "after supper" in the words of institution (Luke 22:19-20) may point to an early Christian practice of taking an ordinary meal bracketed by the Lord's Supper (Fernando 1998:121).

COMMENTARY

Peter addressed the crowd's perplexity, "What can this mean?" (2:12), by speaking to the question, "Why did this happen?" In doing so, he unfolds for us how all three members of the Trinity are at work in accomplishing and applying salvation.

Peter "shouted to the crowd" (lit. "lifted up his voice and uttered inspired speech," *apephthenxato . . . rhēma* [TG669/4487, ZG710/4839], cf. 2:4; 5:20, 32; 10:22, 44; 11:14, 16; 13:42; 26:25; 28:25). With good humor, he dismissed the mockers' explanation by saying it was much too early for drunkenness. Later rabbinic tradition identifies 10 a.m. as Jewish breakfast time (*b. Bava Metzia'* 83b), on Sabbaths at noon (Josephus *Life* 279). Cicero declared that even the worst debauchery did not begin until 9 a.m. (*Philippics* 2.41.104). The real cause and significance must be found in what God had previously declared through the prophet Joel (Joel 2:18-32).

Peter made it explicit that God is the source of Joel's prediction ("God said"). God is the master of the timing for its fulfillment (1:6-7). He says he will pour out his Spirit "in the last days," in the last epoch of history—a time which is integrally related to, but not the same as, the final day of judgment and redemption (see Isa 2:2; Mic 4:1; 1 Tim 4:1; 2 Tim 3:1). In Joel's imagery, the vivifying impact of a Near Eastern torrential downpour on parched earth pictures the Spirit's coming. As the prophets foretold, the Spirit's outpouring marks a people repentant (Zech 12:10) and restored (Ezek 39:29). Joel's prophecy especially highlights the indiscriminate scope of the outpouring. Gender, age, and socio-economic condition are not barriers to receiving the Spirit (Acts 2:17-18). As the speech progresses, we learn the universal scope of God's offer of salvation (2:21, 39).

The outpouring is for prophesying, for receiving dreams and visions. Visions and dreams were common experiences by which a prophet would receive revelation (Num 12:6). In Acts they occur regularly, especially in promoting the advance of the Christian mission (e.g., 9:10, 12; 10:3, 17, 19; 11:5; 16:9; 18:9). While some would limit early Christian prophecy to "episodic, oracular utterances that are spoken on the basis of supernaturally given revelation via dreams, visions, and angelic visitors," others see prophecy in Acts as occurring across a continuum of varying degrees of divine intervention (Giles 1997b:971). Indeed, the "prophesying" of Joel 2:28 is fulfilled at Pentecost in "witnessing with power" (1:8) and in being "filled with the Holy Spirit" to declare miraculously in foreign languages the "wonderful things God has done" (2:4, 11). Throughout Acts, we meet this same range of Spirit-aided proclamation: from oracular prediction or assurance (11:28; 18:9-10; 21:11; 23:11) to special revelation passed on later (10:30-33), episodic immediate inspiration (4:18-31; 13:9; 21:11), speaking in tongues (2:4; 10:46; 19:6), words of exhortation and encouragement (14:22; 15:32, 41), and boldly preached expository sermons with Spirit-given interpretation and application of Scripture (4:8-12; 7:2-52; 13:16-41). By the power of the

Spirit, God's witnesses will make known his wondrous deeds: how he has accomplished and now intends to apply his salvation.

God's work "in the last days" also includes heavenly wonders and earthly signs. These are the conditions right before the conclusion of human history, which comes with the arrival of the "great and glorious Day of the Lord." Signs on earth, particularly scenes of bloodshed and destruction, will mark the unsettling and ever accelerating fraying of the national and international social fabric. Wonders in the heavens also will be unsettling: an eclipsed sun (Joel 3:15; Amos 5:18-20; Zeph 1:15; Luke 21:25-26) and a bloodred moon, possibly the result of earthquakes (Jer 4:23-24). The natural order's being out of joint will not only mirror the world's moral order, so long out of joint at the hands of sinful humankind, it will also presage the inevitable end: divine judgment in the Day of the Lord (Isa 13:6, 9; Ezek 30:3; Zeph 1:14-15). The significance of this Pentecost event, then, is its decisive inauguration of the last days, which offers the promise of salvation blessings now and will conclude with the Judgment Day of the Lord. For now there is hope; there is still time. The Lord promises that anyone who calls on his name will be saved by him (note the divine passive; cf. 2:36-40, 47; 4:12; 16:30-31).

Peter proceeded to argue in the rest of his sermon that Jesus of Nazareth, in his resurrection and in his exaltation, was the immediate cause of the outpouring of the Spirit and salvation blessings. Peter moved through four phases in establishing the truth of the resurrection and the exaltation: proclamation (2:22-24, 36), Scripture proof (2:25-28 with Ps 16:8-11; Acts 2:34-35 with Ps 110:1), interpretation (Acts 2:29-31, 34), and witness (2:32-33). All of this occurs within the early church's understanding of the gospel and salvation history: Jesus' earthly mission, his resurrection, and his exaltation—the Ascension and session at God's right hand.

As Peter gave his proclamation of Jesus' earthly ministry, death, and resurrection, he placed God's purpose and action at the forefront. In human history, with public knowledge (26:26), God the Father "endorsed" Jesus of Nazareth (as Messiah, as we shall later learn, 2:36) through "miracles, signs, and wonders" that he did through him (cf. Luke 4:18 with Isa 61:1; Luke 7:21-22 with Isa 35:5; Acts 10:38). Though not mentioned explicitly, we may infer from Luke's Gospel that these works were a result of God's Spirit resting on Jesus (Luke 3:22; 4:18).

According to God's "prearranged plan" (lit. "determined purpose and foreknowledge," cf. 3:18; 4:28; 13:29), Jesus was handed over, first by Judas (Luke 22:21-22, 48) and then by the Jews, to the Gentiles (Luke 23:1), and finally again figuratively handed over by Pilate to the Jews as he implemented their will (Luke 23:25). Balancing this divine sovereign purpose is human responsibility: Jews with the help of Gentiles put Jesus to death. The significance of Jesus' death as vicarious atonement is not brought out as explicitly here as in the Pauline summary of the kerygma (the apostolic proclamation, 1 Cor 15:3). Later, in the "salvation applied" portion, "forgiveness of sins" will assume it (Acts 2:38). Still, all the objective elements of the message about Jesus are present: a righteous Jesus endorsed by God, murdered—but according to God's plan.

Humans may have killed Jesus, but it is God who "raised him back to life again."
He dealt with death's "horrors" (2:24); he acted so decisively that the impotence of
death's grip in the face of *Christus Victor* is demonstrated once and for all.

Since, in Jewish thought, the Messiah was destined for an uninterrupted eternal
reign (2 Sam 7:13; Ps 132:12; Isa 9:7), Peter had to give proof from Scripture that
God also had the Messiah's resurrection in his sovereign saving plans. Peter quoted
from Psalm 16:8-11, where David says with confidence, "I see that the LORD is always with me. I will not be shaken, for he is right beside me." God's presence is at
his right hand as a protector against any of his enemies who would unsettle him.
This brings joy and a sense of security. Peter continued with David's words: "My
body rests in hope. For you will not leave my soul among the dead." The reason for
this peace is that God would not abandon his soul to the place of the dead. God
would not permit his Holy One "to rot in the grave" (see note on 2:27). This protection is for God's Holy One, his *khasid* [TH2623A, ZH2883] ("a person who lives in covenant loyalty and knows God's covenant loyalty and blessing"; cf. Pss 86:2; 89:18).
To him God makes known "the way of life" and fills him with joy in his presence.

With increasing identification with his audience, "Jews . . . People of Israel . . .
Dear brothers" (2:14, 22, 29), Peter moved to an interpretation of Psalm 16 that explained how it could be speaking of the Messiah's resurrection (saving out of
death), as opposed to David's earthly protection (saving from death). By a process
of elimination and assuming a literal interpretation of "rotting in the grave," Peter
pointed to David's tomb as evidence that the psalm could not be speaking of
David's own experience (see note on 2:29). The threefold basis for the new interpretation is David's status as a prophet, the promise of an eternal reign he received for
one of his descendants, and his prophetic ability to see beforehand the resurrection
of the Messiah as he spoke about neither being abandoned to the place of the dead
nor his flesh seeing decay (cf. 2:31 with Ps 16:10). First-century Jews viewed David's
anointing by the Spirit as indicative of his prophetic status (cf. 11QPs 27:11 with
2 Sam 23:1-3; Josephus *Antiquities* 6.166 with 1 Sam 16:13), and they recognized
that the descendant who reigned eternally was the Messiah (2 Sam 7:12-13; Ps
132:12; 4QFlor 1:10-11). The underlying logic is, for a Messiah to both suffer and
reign forever, he must be resurrected; and that a prophet, who is the recipient and
conveyor of a promise that will be fulfilled in one of his descendants (lit. "from his
loins"), may legitimately use first-person expression to speak for and describe that
Messiah's experience.

One final point marked the climax of the argument as Peter moved from interpretation to witness: Jesus fulfilled this prophecy, since God raised him from the
dead. The apostles were all witnesses to this fact (1:3, 8, 22; 3:15; 5:30-32; 10:40-41;
13:31). If the apostles were witnesses to the first stage of Jesus' exaltation, the crowd
had just become witnesses to the reality of its completion at God's right hand. They
had seen and heard, in the coming of the Spirit and the miracle of tongues and in
Peter's message, evidence that Jesus was installed in that position. By terming God
"Father," it is now clear that all three members of the Trinity were involved in this

inaugural act of applying salvation blessings to humans. The Father gives the Spirit to Jesus, his Son, who mediates it to humankind (John 14:16, 26; 16:7).

No one has observed this transaction—only what Peter claims are its results. Interpretation of scriptural proof must establish it. Again by a process of elimination, assuming literal interpretation and the possibility of reading this first-person Davidic psalm messianically, Peter declared that David had not ascended into heaven. Therefore, the person that Psalm 110 presents—the one commanded by God to sit at his right hand until he makes his enemies a footstool for his feet— must be David's greater son, the Messiah (Ps 110:1; compare the messianic interpretation Jesus assumes in his riddle, Luke 20:41-44). The Father promised an unstoppable reign for his Son, though evidently not without opposition. So, in Acts the progress of the church is constant, though not without obstacles in spiritual warfare (8:18-21; 13:9-11; 19:11-20) and persecution (see 4:20, 31; 9:1-31; 12:1- 25). Yet, in every case, God fulfills his promise, deals with the opposition, and empowers his messengers so that to the very end they keep on "boldly proclaiming the Kingdom of God and teaching about the Lord Jesus Christ" (28:31).

The crowd should have embraced with certainty this proclamation: Jesus whom you crucified "God has made . . . both Lord and Messiah!" (2:36). God has given Jesus two titles, which reveal his true nature and role. He is Messiah, the exclusive mediator of salvation (4:10-12; 5:31; 10:42-43), and he is Lord, not just the ruler over all (10:36) but actually God incarnate. The Old Testament promised salvation in the last days by the Messiah (Zech 9:9) and by the Lord God (Isa 56:1). Now we know that it is brought by one and the same person!

By the Spirit (John 16:8-11) "Peter's words pierced their hearts" (2:37). For Luke, in continuity with Old Testament thought, the heart (the inner life) is the source of all the thoughts, motivations, intentions, and plans of sinful human beings (Luke 6:45; 12:34; Acts 5:3-4; 8:21-22; 28:27). If Jesus were Lord and Messiah, the only source of salvation, and they were responsible for his death, what could they do? Their sin had already doomed them for that "great and glorious day of the LORD" (2:20).

Peter made a general call for repentance (*metanoeō* [ᵀᴳ3340, ᶻᴳ3566]), followed by a parenthetic, individualized instruction to be baptized (*baptisthētō hekastos humōn,* "let each of you be baptized"). Baptism in the name of Jesus the Messiah shows that the individual has been united to the Messiah and belongs to the renewed people of God who live in the "last days" (cf. 2:17). This commitment has saving consequences: "forgiveness of sins" and "the gift of the Holy Spirit." While repentance is indeed a necessary condition (Luke 13:3, 5; 15:7; 16:30; 24:47; Acts 3:19; 17:30; 20:21; 26:20), it and these blessings are still gifts of grace (3:19; 5:31; 13:38; 15:8). The "gift of the Spirit" here should be understood as an epexegetical genitive, which is to say that the gift is the Spirit himself, who regenerates, indwells, and transforms lives. All the fruit and ministry gifts flow from the one gift.

The unlimited scope of the salvation offer encompasses all generations and cultures, "those far away" (see note on 2:39; cf. Isa 57:19; Eph 2:13). God declares that everyone he calls to himself will experience salvation. As such, salvation is God's doing and depends finally on his effective call (13:48; 16:14).

Peter strongly urged the people: "Save yourselves (lit. "be saved," divine passive) from this crooked generation" (2:40; Deut 32:5; Ps 78:8). Israel's stubborn, rebellious, and unrepentant wilderness generation knew God's judgment. So also, this present generation faced the certain judgment of the Day of the Lord if they did not repent. Those in the crowd and among the readers of Acts who heed Peter's warning will allow themselves to be rescued from such a fate.

Luke characterizes the response quantitatively and qualitatively. Three thousand "believe" the word and are baptized. But again, their being "added to their fellowship" (divine passive) was God's doing (2:47; 5:14; 11:24). Qualitatively, the new believers made four commitments: to learn, to care, to fellowship, and to worship. Devotion to the apostles' teaching probably included learning an account of Jesus' life and ministry, a collection of his ethical and practical teachings, the Christocentric Old Testament hermeneutic, and above all, Jesus' gospel. It was a commitment to both evangelism and edification (4:2; 5:42; 15:35). Fellowship and the breaking of bread involved sharing of possessions and lives in common meals. "Prayer" pointed to a patterned practice of prayer by the assembly. Prayer is central to the church's life (4:24; 6:4; 12:5; 13:3; 20:36); it provides the key link between the exalted Lord in heaven and his body on earth, for by it he guides and strengthens his people, especially in mission (4:29-31; 6:6; 8:15; 14:23; 28:8).

◆ **F. The Believers Meet Together (2:43-47)**

[43]A deep sense of awe came over them all, and the apostles performed many miraculous signs and wonders. [44]And all the believers met together in one place and shared everything they had. [45]They sold their property and possessions and shared the money with those in need. [46]They worshiped together at the Temple each day, met in homes for the Lord's Supper, and shared their meals with great joy and generosity*—[47]all the while praising God and enjoying the goodwill of all the people. And each day the Lord added to their fellowship those who were being saved.

2:46 Or *and sincere hearts.*

NOTES

2:44, 47 *together . . . to their fellowship.* The Gr. phrase here, *epi to auto* (lit., "upon the same," used elsewhere to mean "together"), is uniquely used as a quasi-technical term for "community in church fellowship" and created a number of difficulties for copyists. The phrase is also found in Ps 122[121]:3 LXX where the MT has *yakhad* [TH3162/A, ZH3480] (cf. 1QS 1:12). The confusion of the copyists is perhaps most evident to English readers through a comparison of the NLT with the KJV, which relies on a Gr. text that has added the word for *church* to 2:47 and ended the sentence, leaving the phrase *epi to auto* to begin 3:1, which results in "Peter and John went up *together.*"

2:45-47 *They sold . . . shared . . . worshiped.* The Western text (D) adds *hosoi* [TG3745, ZG4012] (those who); this indicates that not all Christian property owners sold their property. It also moves *kath' hēmeran* [TG2250, ZG2465] (each day) from describing Temple attendance

(2:46) back to characterizing the distribution of money (*diamerizō* [TG1266, ZG1374], 2:45). The Western text also heightens the community's devotion by adding *pantes* [TG3956, ZG4246] ("all"; 2:46) to read "all worshiped . . . and shared their meals," and it expands the church's approval from the "goodwill of all the people" to "goodwill of the whole world" (*kosmos* [TG2889, ZG3180]).

COMMENTARY

The miraculous events and the Spirit-filled preaching (2:17, 20-21, 38-40) worked a continuing "fear" (*phobos* [TG5401, ZG5832], not "awe" as in NLT) in those who had not received the word. God intensified this sense as he consistently worked miraculous signs through the apostles ("miraculous embodiments of spiritual truth") and wonders ("astonishing, significant portents that point to God's presence"; see Larkin 1995:55).

The Christians' unity, grounded in their reception of the apostles' teaching, is a mark of the restored community of the last days (Mic 2:12; cf. Isa 11:6-7; 1QS 5:1-3). Sharing "everything they had" expresses the extent to which their unity embraced the apostles' "fellowship." In phrasing reminiscent of the ancient proverbial definition of friendship ("to have all things in common"; Plato *Laws* 5:739b-c), Luke pictures a model of church care that moves far beyond the ancient ideal of reciprocity among equals to an unassuming, self-giving meeting of physical needs across all socioeconomic boundaries (Mitchell 1992:255-272). The implementation manifests the free working of the Spirit, as individuals voluntarily sold property and goods and contributed to a fund that could be drawn on as any had need (compare and contrast the mandatory practices in the Qumran communities, 1 QS 6:13-23; CD 14:12-17; Josephus *War* 2.122; Philo *Hypothetica* 11.10-11; see Capper 1995:323-356).

The community lived out its commitment to prayer (2:42) by worshiping "at the Temple each day" (2:46). And there was also devotion to instruction ("the apostles' teaching") in Solomon's Colonnade at the eastern end of the court of the Gentiles (5:12; cf. 5:20-21, 42, and Jesus' practice in Luke 20:1; 21:37).

Daily the community broke bread together in homes—sharing a meal and probably combining it with the Lord's Supper, by beginning the meal with the bread and ending it with the cup (Luke 22:19-20; 24:35; Acts 20:7, 11). God was present in their table fellowship, as marked by their joy (2:46; 8:8; 13:52; 16:34), issuing in praise to God, and a simple piety (2:46; lit., "singleness of heart"; NLT, "generosity") that was favorable to the people of Israel (Longenecker 1981:291). Through it all, the Lord was "on mission" fulfilling his saving purposes—daily adding "to their fellowship" those who were being saved (2:47).

◆ G. Peter Heals a Crippled Beggar (3:1-11)

Peter and John went to the Temple one afternoon to take part in the three o'clock prayer service. ²As they approached the Temple, a man lame from birth was being carried in. Each day he was put beside the Temple gate, the one called the Beautiful

Gate, so he could beg from the people going into the Temple. ³When he saw Peter and John about to enter, he asked them for some money.

⁴Peter and John looked at him intently, and Peter said, "Look at us!" ⁵The lame man looked at them eagerly, expecting some money. ⁶But Peter said, "I don't have any silver or gold for you. But I'll give you what I have. In the name of Jesus Christ the Nazarene,* get up and* walk!"

⁷Then Peter took the lame man by the right hand and helped him up. And as he did, the man's feet and ankles were instantly healed and strengthened. ⁸He jumped up, stood on his feet, and began to walk! Then, walking, leaping, and praising God, he went into the Temple with them.

⁹All the people saw him walking and heard him praising God. ¹⁰When they realized he was the lame beggar they had seen so often at the Beautiful Gate, they were absolutely astounded! ¹¹They all rushed out in amazement to Solomon's Colonnade, where the man was holding tightly to Peter and John.

3:6a Or *Jesus Christ of Nazareth.*   3:6b Some manuscripts omit *get up and.*

NOTES

3:1 *Peter and John.* John, though he performed no active role in the healing, functioned as the second of two witnesses to validate testimony to Jesus (cf. Deut 19:15; Luke 10:1; 2 Cor 13:1).

one afternoon. This phrase is not in the original, which simply says "the ninth hour." The ninth hour was "three o'clock," and this addition eases the transition from 2:47. Compare the additon found in the Western text (D): "now in these days" (*en de tais hēmerais tautais*).

3:2 *Temple gate.* Luke used *hieron* [TG2411, ZG2639] (temple) flexibly to refer to the entire Temple-mount area, including the court of the Gentiles (Luke 19:45), as well as the sanctuary precincts, beginning with the court of women (Luke 2:37).

Beautiful Gate. Because no ancient Jewish source names a Temple gate "Beautiful," the gate's identity and location is a matter of conjecture. There are two likely candidates: the Shushan gate, which was the eastern entrance to the outer court of the Gentiles (*m. Middot* 1:3; *m. Kelim* 17:9), and the Nicanor gate positioned either in the eastern wall of the court of women (providing access from the court of the Gentiles; Josephus *War* 5.201, 204-205) or in its western wall (providing access to the court of Israel; *b. Sotah* 40b; *m. Middot* 2:3; cf. Josephus *War* 2.411; 6.293). The renowned beauty of the Nicanor gate's Corinthian bronze decoration (Josephus *War* 5.201) and the greater access it afforded to the city crowds have convinced many, beginning with Lake and Cadbury (1979:32), that it is Luke's "Beautiful Gate." However, the presentation of the apostles' movements through the gate and presumably immediately into "Solomon's Colonnade" argues for the Shushan gate. Cowton (1996:475) asks whether a quieter gate (the Shushan) might not be just as attractive in the competitive atmosphere of alms seeking. In the end, the Nicanor gate location fits better with the healed beggar's strong response: excitedly joining in the worship of Israel from which his prior condition had excluded him (*m. Shabbat* 6:8 [66a]).

3:6 *Nazarene.* The reference is geographical, not connected to the Nazirite vows of Num 6 (Barrett 1994:183; contra Johnson 1992:66).

get up. Although ℵ B D cop^sa do not contain *egeire kai* [TG1453, ZG1586] ("arise and"), it is present in other mss of all families. Luke probably recorded it in conscious parallel to Jesus' healing of a paralytic (Luke 5:23; Johnson 1992:66). Barrett (1994:183) disagrees; he assigns it to a copyist's filling out of the narrative.

3:7-8 *Peter took the lame man by the right hand and helped him up.* Commentators differ on whether it was the apostles' faith alone that was the basis of the healing (see Talbert's [1997:54] reading of Acts 3:16), or the faith of both the apostles and the man who was healed, evidenced by Peter's initiative and the man's lack of resistance to being helped.

3:9 *All the people.* Instead of seeing this as "typical storyteller's hyperbole" (Dunn 1996:44), the theological point of *pas ho laos* [^{TG}2992, ^{ZG}3295] should be noted. The miracle occurs in the presence of Israel, the people of God, as a whole (Barrett 1994:185).

C O M M E N T A R Y

Luke now relates a particular instance of the apostles' "signs and wonders" ministry (2:43). In it we learn the scope of divine salvation: the whole person. We learn the means by which heaven touches earth—not by magic but by a Christocentric faith in God's power as a sovereign gift. And we learn the purpose of signs: to be an indisputable, public witness to Jesus Christ, who by his resurrection and exaltation now gives salvation blessings.

Peter and John, living out their commitment to worship (2:42, 46) via religious custom rooted in Old Testament regulation, went to the Temple for the afternoon sacrifice, one of the Jews' traditional times of daily prayer (Exod 29:38-40; Num 28:1-8; Dan 6:10; 9:21; Josephus *Antiquities* 14.66; *m. Tamid* 5:1; 6:4). As they arrived, a man, "lifeless" in his legs due to a birth defect, was being carried to his accustomed begging place. He could not have been more helpless. Grounded in the Old Testament law regarding the poor (Deut 24:10-22), charitable support of the poor was one of the three pillars of the Jewish religion, along with Torah study and worship, and it fit very naturally with other acts of piety.

Peter looked intently at the man and asked the same attention in response. He reoriented the man's focus away from the expected gift to one unexpected, and yet, more welcome. He turned the man away from the power of the material, the silver and gold, to sustain a poor beggar a few more days, to the power of heaven. "In the name of Jesus Christ the Nazarene, [i.e., by the power and authority of the crucified and risen Jesus of Nazareth, who is the Messiah] get up and walk!" (3:6). Jesus was still doing his saving work—so much so that Peter would later say to the ailing Aeneas, "Jesus Christ heals you" (9:34). Yet, this is no magic formula by which the apostle controls the supernatural. As Peter went on to explain, uttering such a command comes from faith, which itself has been received as a gift because it is worked "through Jesus" (3:16; cf. 1:8).

Having commanded the man to walk, he grabbed the lame man by the right hand to help him get up. "As he did," instantaneously, his "feet" were strengthened (divine passive). Jumping up, he stood for the first time in his life. He tried out his new freedom by walking around; then, in a response natural to a person who realized he had been touched by God's power, he moved into the court of women and then the court of Israel, "walking, leaping, and praising God" (3:8; cf. 2:47). He had become the living embodiment of the messianic age as predicted in Isaiah 35:6, "The lame will leap like a deer."

This sign, then, was no isolated supernatural incident. It signified that God's grand saving purposes, promised through the prophets, were being fulfilled, not only in Jesus' ministry (Luke 5:25; 7:22), but also in the lives of the Spirit-filled apostles. This sign graphically demonstrated that those saving purposes involve the whole person. Bodily health comes as a foretaste of the resurrection of the body just as conversion is the firstfruits of ultimate redemption from sin (Talbert 1997:54). Viewed as comprehensively as possible, the goal of this salvation is a restored people praising God (2:46; 3:8). This sign is also a witness that God has indeed raised up Jesus from the dead and exalted him to his right hand so that he might give salvation blessings until he comes. Miracles don't happen in the name of dead men.

Should we expect such miracles today? True, the apostles are no longer with us, and miracles seemed to cluster around them as signs that the "last days" had truly dawned. But even in the first century, miraculous signs were not everyday occurrences (cf. 19:11), and Jesus still is present by his Spirit in the church. So we should not be surprised if we hear reports of miracles today, but a healing miracle in the New Testament sense must have the following marks: It must be an instantaneous and complete deliverance from a grave organic condition. It must occur in response to a direct command in the name of Jesus, and it must be publicly acknowledged as indisputable (Larkin 1995:65-66; Stott 1990:103).

The crowd's response was recognition, amazement, and attraction. They became witnesses of the miracle's authenticity (4:16), for they knew him in his prior condition and then saw him walking and heard him praising God. Their recognition gives way to being "absolutely astounded" (lit. "filled with amazement and astonishment"); it was the awe known in the presence of divine activity (Luke 4:36). They had been lifted out of their habitual life and thought by a direct encounter with the power of God (Haenchen 1971:200). This sight quickly drew a crowd that rushed out to Solomon's Colonnade to get a closer look at the rejoicing man and his healers.

◆   H. Peter Preaches in the Temple (3:12-26)

[12]Peter saw his opportunity and addressed the crowd. "People of Israel," he said, "what is so surprising about this? And why stare at us as though we had made this man walk by our own power or godliness? [13]For it is the God of Abraham, Isaac, and Jacob—the God of all our ancestors—who has brought glory to his servant Jesus by doing this. This is the same Jesus whom you handed over and rejected before Pilate, despite Pilate's decision to release him. [14]You rejected this holy, righteous one and instead demanded the release of a murderer. [15]You killed the author of life, but God raised him from the dead. And we are witnesses of this fact!

[16]"Through faith in the name of Jesus, this man was healed—and you know how crippled he was before. Faith in Jesus' name has healed him before your very eyes.

[17]"Friends,* I realize that what you and your leaders did to Jesus was done in ignorance. [18]But God was fulfilling what all the prophets had foretold about the Messiah—that he must suffer these things. [19]Now repent of your sins and turn to God, so that your sins may be wiped away. [20]Then times of refreshment will come from the presence of the Lord, and he will again send you Jesus, your appointed Messiah. [21]For he must remain in heaven until the time for the final restoration of all things, as God promised long ago through his holy prophets. [22]Moses said, 'The LORD your God will raise up for you a Prophet like me from among your own people. Listen carefully to everything he tells you.'* [23]Then Moses said, 'Anyone who will not listen to that Prophet will be completely cut off from God's people.'* [24]"Starting with Samuel, every prophet

spoke about what is happening today.
25You are the children of those prophets,
and you are included in the covenant God
promised to your ancestors. For God said
to Abraham, 'Through your descendants*

all the families on earth will be blessed.'
26When God raised up his servant, Jesus,
he sent him first to you people of Israel,
to bless you by turning each of you back
from your sinful ways."

3:17 Greek Brothers.   3:22 Deut 18:15.   3:23 Deut 18:19; Lev 23:29.   3:25 Greek your seed; see Gen 12:3;
22:18.

NOTES

3:13, 17 Gentile anti-Semitism has been alleged as the reason for the Western text's longer
readings in these verses (most recently, Witherington 1998:183; following Epp 1966:41ff.).
This motivation is supposed to be evident in the following changes: To "This is the same
Jesus whom you handed over" (3:13), the Western text adds, "for judgment." It also adds
that Pilate "wanted to release Jesus." Both additions bring out clearly the Jewish responsibility. In 3:17, the Western text's insertion of *poneron* [TG4190/B, ZG4505] (evil deed) also
seems to heighten Israel's guilt. Heimerdinger (1995:271-273), however, has convincingly
shown that such wording, along with *Christon* [TG5547, ZG5986] (Christ) after "Jesus" in v. 13
(so D) and the substitution of *ebarunate* [TG925, ZG986] (you oppressed) for *ernesasthe* [TG720,
ZG766] (you denied) in v. 14 are thoroughly Jewish, match Targumic expression, and probably represent the rendering closer to the original.

3:13 *has brought glory to his servant Jesus by doing this.* Given its place in the speech,
the NLT rightly identifies the miracle, not the Resurrection, as the event in which Jesus is
glorified (contra Barrett 1994:195; see Hamm 1984:202). "Servant" (*pais* [TG3816, ZG4090];
cf. Isa 52:13–53:12 LXX) can involve an allusion to Christ's vicarious atonement work if we
see the objective elements for it in the description of the unjust treatment of the Holy and
Righteous One (3:13-14; contra Polhill 1992:131).

3:14 *holy, righteous one.* While these descriptors may simply relate Jesus' innocence in
contrast to the murderer (Johnson 1992:67), it is interesting that both give some "hint of
messianic status" (Barrett 1994:196): "Righteous one" more so (Isa 53:11; Jer 23:5; 33:15;
Zech 9:9) and "Holy one" less so (Ps 16:10; Isa 41:14). They are both also connected with
the OT description of God (Ps 129:4; Isa 6:3; see especially Isa 5:16).

3:15 *author of life.* While most commentators take *archegos* [TG747, ZG795] as "originator,
founder" (e.g., Barrett 1994:198), Johnston (1981) makes a solid case for the other nuance,
"leader," in Acts (here and 5:31) and in the OT when the LXX uses it to refer to Messiah as
Davidic crown prince (*nasi'* [TH5387, ZH5954], "leader"; Ezek 34:24; 37:25; cf. Marshall and
Peterson 1998:273).

3:17 *in ignorance.* Normally, this declaration is seen as a softening of Peter's indictment
(Polhill 1992:133; Dunn 1996:45). Barrett (1994:201) calls it a partial excuse. When
understood against the background of the sin of ignorance in the OT (cf. *shagah* [TH7686,
ZH8706], *shegagah* [TH7684, ZH8705], or *shegi'ah* [TH7691, ZH8709]; Lev 4:22; Num 15:27-31; Ps
19:12-13 [13-14]), Peter was not so much excusing the people as explaining to them how
they were guilty of murdering the Messiah, even though they did not recognize Jesus as the
Messiah (cf. Luke 23:34; note Gentile culpability expressed in similar terms, 17:23, 30).
A sin of ignorance in the OT was to be confessed and atoned for by sacrifice. Then, forgiveness could be declared (Num 15:28; NIDOTTE 4.42-43).

3:20-21 *times of refreshment . . . final restoration of all things.* These phrases do not
refer to the same thing (contra Polhill 1992:134). The former is the "last days," marked
periodically by conversions and miracles, as the plural "times" and the word *anapsuxeos*
[TG403, ZG433] ("refreshment, temporary respite," cf. Exod 8:10, 15) indicate (Barrett

1994:205). The latter is the final day of salvation—characterized by the creation of new heavens and earth at Christ's return—but not the salvation of all men (contra Barrett 1994:207; cf. TDNT 1.389 for secular evidence but set within a cyclic cosmology).

3:22-23 The text form of the OT quotation (Deut 18:15-16, 19) follows neither the LXX nor MT but a Palestinian text tradition found in the Dead Sea Scrolls and the Targum (DeWaard 1971).

3:22, 26 raise up . . . raised up. *anistēmi* [TG450, ZG482]. Although Luke used this word and cognates frequently in reference to Christ's resurrection (see Polhill [1992:136] at verse 22), we should understand the verb in vv. 22 and 26 as pointing to his incarnation. That was when God fulfilled his promise by bringing the Messiah onto the stage of human history (Barrett 1994:213). A play on the two uses of the word may be present, especially in v. 26 (Hamm 1984:214).

3:25 descendants. Lit., "seed" (*sperma* [TG4690, ZG5065]). This may refer to Christ via a midrashic treatment of the singular (Spencer 1997:49; cf. Gal 3:16), though most commentators, like the NLT translation, take it as referring only to the collective Hebrew stock (e.g., Johnson 1992:70).

COMMENTARY

Peter seized the opportunity to interpret for the crowd not only the miracle but also their amazement. He quickly set aside a human cause: "Why stare at us as though we had made this man walk by our own power or godliness (*eusebeia* [TG2150, ZG2354], 'piety')?" (3:12). They did not claim to have such virtue that God would have to answer them if they were to ask him for a miracle (compare the reputation of the Jewish charismatic, Honi the circle maker, *m. Ta'anit* 3:8). Rather, "the God of Abraham, Isaac, and Jacob [cf. Exod 3:6, 15] . . . has brought glory to his servant Jesus" (Acts 3:13). With its allusions to God as the God of the patriarchs and to Jesus as the Suffering Servant of Isaiah (see Isa 52:13–53:12), this declaration places the miracle and the crowd's astonishment within the framework of past, present, and future salvation history. God has promised and has brought to fulfillment both the suffering and the glory of Messiah Jesus and the application of salvation blessings or judgment that are determinative of each person's human destiny (Luke 24:25-27).

Peter immediately alleged the Jews' culpability in handing over and rejecting Jesus (see Luke 9:44; 18:32; 22:21-22; 23:25). The strong contrast between Pilate's decision to release Jesus (Luke 23:4, 14, 22) and the Jews' persistent rejection of the "holy, righteous one," together with the exchange for Barabbas the murderer (Luke 23:18-19) not only emphasizes the Jews' sin and their blindness to the work of God but also presents the objective realities on which understanding Christ's death as a salvific vicarious atonement is based. This innocent, "holy, righteous one" had not died for his own sins (Luke 23:47), yet he was rejected and reckoned as a sinner, as the swap for Barabbas graphically showed. What can make sense of this grave miscarriage of justice other than the fact that, according to God's plan, Jesus died not for his own sins but for the sins of others (Isa 53:12; Luke 22:35-37)?

Yes, the Jews killed the crown prince of life (cf. 5:20; 11:18; 13:46, 48, for "life" as a synonym for salvation). He is the leader who guides those who follow him into eternal life. "But God raised him from the dead" (3:15). The Resurrection is the essential link between Jesus' past suffering and death and his present glorification in this miracle. The apostles were witnesses to that event in space and time (see 1:22; 2:32; 4:10; 10:40-41; 13:30-31).

In a compressed fashion Peter declared how, in this miracle, heaven had touched earth. In a reverse parallelism, we meet the objective power of the name of Jesus (Jesus himself present in his resurrection power) and the subjective operation of faith—not only as a human activity, but also as a divine gift. Peter's announcement starts with "faith in his name," repeated twice (3:16). In this way we gain a comprehensive view of the dynamic involved in the healing and, at the same time, are again steered away from any thought of magic. As with the Resurrection (1:3, 21-22; 13:31), this healing was publicly attested by those who knew the man's prior condition: "and you know how crippled he was before . . . before your very eyes" (3:16). The man was made completely well (*holoklēria* [TG3647, ZG3907]). For the first time in his life, he was as fit for worship as unblemished sacrifices would be.

Peter then assessed the responsibility for Jesus' death from human and divine angles. What was a culpable sin of ignorance on the part of people and leaders (see note on 3:17) was part of a plan God both declared beforehand through all the prophets and then fulfilled (Luke 24:25-27, 46-47; Acts 2:23; 8:35; 13:27-29; 17:2-3; 26:22-23). The theme of the Messiah's suffering can be traced through three of the four major prophets and one minor prophet (Isa 53; Jer 11:19; Dan 9:26; Zech 13:7).

Peter's strong call for repentance, "repent of your sins and turn to God" (3:19; *metanoēsate . . . epistrepsate* [without explicit objects]), comprehensively pictures conversion. Luke uses *metanoeō* [TG3340, ZG3566] for conversion—the decision of the whole person to turn around (Luke 3:8; 5:32)—focusing at one time or other on turning from sin (8:22; 17:30) and to God (20:21). When the word is used in combination with *epistrephō* [TG1994, ZG2188] (turn), *metanoeō* indicates the "turning from" aspect (3:19; 26:20). In the LXX, *epistrephō* is used consistently to translate the Old Testament word for repentance (see Hos 5:4; 6:1; Amos 4:6). According to Luke, it refers to the whole process of turning from sin to God (14:15; 26:18), as well as focusing on the positive aspect of the process (9:35; 11:21; 15:19; 26:20; see Larkin 1995:68).

Three purposes for obeying this command embrace present and future salvation blessings; they apply to us as well as to Peter's audience. In the present, sins will be blotted out. As writing on ancient scrolls was erased by washing away the ink, so our account before God will be a clean sheet (see Ps 51:1, 9; Isa 43:25; Rev 3:5; 21:4). This is possible only because the "holy, righteous one" died for us (Acts 3:13-14). Additionally, God will send us "times of refreshment" (3:20; cf. *4 Ezra* 11:46), soothing our parched souls with spiritual renewal as a "breath of fresh air" or "cooling water" heals the body (cf. Hippocrates *Fractures* 25 [2.81.20, Kühlewein]; Euripides *Iphigeneia at Aulis* 421). And in the future, God will again send the Messiah, whom he has "made ready to act" (*prokecheirismenon* [TG4400, ZG4741]) in the role of messianic Savior. But there will be a delay because, according

to God's determination, Christ "must" (*dei* [TG1163, ZG1256], a word denoting necessity) "remain" in heaven until the time when he restores all things. This, too, was
foretold by the prophets (Isa 65:17; 66:22; Dan 7:13-14).

Peter then gave a sense of urgency and relevance to his appeal, as again through
promise and fulfillment he tried to persuade his audience to repent and embrace this
salvation. Moses did prophesy that God would raise up a prophet like himself,
whom the people would be responsible to hear and obey (Lev 23:29; Deut 18:15-16,
19). Taking the passage literally and messianically, first-century Jews looked for that
one prophet *par excellence*, like Moses, to arrive at the end of time (John 1:21; 4:25;
6:14; 4QTest 5-8; 1QS 9:11). Peter proclaimed that when God raised up his servant
Jesus, he brought onto the stage of human history "the prophet like Moses" (3:26).
But such good news has a decisive urgency to it. If the crowd did not heed that
prophet's words, as spoken through his apostles, they would forfeit their right to be
part of the people of God. Their penalty would be to be "completely cut off" by
God—a premature and sudden death at the hands of God (Lev 23:29). Peter reinforced his point by contending that every prophet from Samuel onward prophesied
about the last days, when there would be the call to heed the words of the "prophet
like Moses" and embrace forgiveness and "times of refreshment" (cf. Joel 2:32 with
Acts 2:21; Isa 49:8 with 2 Cor 6:2; Isa 61:1 with Luke 4:18; Ps 95:7 with Heb 4:7-11).

Peter emphasized the relevance of all these promises for the Jews by stressing the
unbroken continuity between them and their fathers—"You are the children of the
prophets, and you are included in the covenant" (cf. Luke 1:72; 1QM 17:8). They
were rightful heirs of the promises—the covenant blessings and their fulfillment. So
Peter concluded with God's words to Abraham (the promise of covenant blessing in
its most pristine form), concentrating on the means and scope of the blessing:
"Through your descendants [lit. 'seed'] all the nations of the earth will be blessed"
(Gen 22:18). Through the "seed," who is the Messiah, the blessing was intended to
extend beyond the Jews to the Gentiles, but the Jews still had priority in receiving
the fulfillment, for God raised up his servant Jesus and sent him "first" to them
(3:26). Through the full course of his incarnate ministry and up to the present, especially in his vicarious suffering and victorious glorification, the Messiah is able to
bring blessing. Not only does he blot out sin (3:19) and bring "times of refreshment" (3:20), but he also actually enables his redeemed people to live restored lives
in righteousness (3:26; 26:20, 23).

◆   I. Peter and John before the Council (4:1-22)

While Peter and John were speaking to
the people, they were confronted by the
priests, the captain of the Temple guard,
and some of the Sadducees. 2These leaders were very disturbed that Peter and
John were teaching the people that
through Jesus there is a resurrection of
the dead. 3They arrested them and, since
it was already evening, put them in jail
until morning. 4But many of the people
who heard their message believed it, so
the number of believers now totaled
about 5,000 men, not counting women
and children.*

⁵The next day the council of all the rulers and elders and teachers of religious law met in Jerusalem. ⁶Annas the high priest was there, along with Caiaphas, John, Alexander, and other relatives of the high priest. ⁷They brought in the two disciples and demanded, "By what power, or in whose name, have you done this?"

⁸Then Peter, filled with the Holy Spirit, said to them, "Rulers and elders of our people, ⁹are we being questioned today because we've done a good deed for a crippled man? Do you want to know how he was healed? ¹⁰Let me clearly state to all of you and to all the people of Israel that he was healed by the powerful name of Jesus Christ the Nazarene,* the man you crucified but whom God raised from the dead. ¹¹For Jesus is the one referred to in the Scriptures, where it says,

'The stone that you builders rejected has now become the cornerstone.'*

¹²There is salvation in no one else! God has given no other name under heaven by which we must be saved."

¹³The members of the council were amazed when they saw the boldness of Peter and John, for they could see that they were ordinary men with no special training in the Scriptures. They also recognized them as men who had been with Jesus. ¹⁴But since they could see the man who had been healed standing right there among them, there was nothing the council could say. ¹⁵So they ordered Peter and John out of the council chamber* and conferred among themselves.

¹⁶"What should we do with these men?" they asked each other. "We can't deny that they have performed a miraculous sign, and everybody in Jerusalem knows about it. ¹⁷But to keep them from spreading their propaganda any further, we must warn them not to speak to anyone in Jesus' name again." ¹⁸So they called the apostles back in and commanded them never again to speak or teach in the name of Jesus.

¹⁹But Peter and John replied, "Do you think God wants us to obey you rather than him? ²⁰We cannot stop telling about everything we have seen and heard."

²¹The council then threatened them further, but they finally let them go because they didn't know how to punish them without starting a riot. For everyone was praising God ²²for this miraculous sign—the healing of a man who had been lame for more than forty years.

4:4 Greek *5,000 adult males.* 4:10 Or *Jesus Christ of Nazareth.* 4:11 Ps 118:22. 4:15 Greek *the Sanhedrin.*

NOTES

4:1 *priests.* The mss B and C read "chief priests." In terms of the cult there was only one high priest at a time, but a plural designation is accurate, whether pointing to members of the high priest's family, including former active high priests, or to the sociological reality of a priestly aristocracy (Chilton 1992:403).

4:2 *teaching the people that through Jesus there is a resurrection of the dead.* D (the Western text) renders the phrase as *anangellein ton Iēsoun en tē anastasei tōn nekrōn* ("to proclaim Jesus by the resurrection of the dead"). Metzger (1994:274) labels this "curious." The difficulty in understanding the relationship between Jesus and the Resurrection in the phrasing of the other mss may partially account for the changes. They read *katangellein en tō Iēsou tēn anastasin tēn ek nekrōn* ("to proclaim in Jesus the resurrection from the dead"). It is best to take "in Jesus" as instrumental (Barrett 1994:220); through telling the story of Jesus' ministry, death, and resurrection, the apostles were proclaiming the reality of the resurrection from the dead.

4:4 *about 5,000 men.* See the note on 2:41 for a comment on the accuracy of such numbers in the light of first-century Jerusalem demographics.

4:6 Annas . . . Caiaphas, John, Alexander. Annas served as high priest during AD 6–15 (Luke 3:2). His son-in-law Caiaphas was presiding high priest from AD 17–36. Both figured prominently in Jesus' trial (John 18:13-14, 24, 28). Alexander and John are otherwise unidentifiable unless the Western reading *Iōnathas* [TG2493.1, ZG2728] is correct. This would be a reference to Jonathan, son of Annas, who served as high priest from AD 36 to 37. Bruce (1990:150) proposes Annas's grandson John, son of Theophilus, as a possibility for the non-Western reading.

4:11 The stone . . . cornerstone. The text form for this citation of Ps 118:22 does not follow the LXX, as Luke 20:17 does. It probably reflects an old tradition, possibly a testimony book (Barrett 1982:69)—that is, a collection of Old Testament quotations used by the early Christians as proof texts. The differences in wording—*humōn* [TG4771, ZG5148] ("you," pl.) inserted in apposition to "builders" and *exoutheneō* [TG1848, ZG2024] ("scorned") instead of *apodokimazō* [TG593, ZG627] ("rejected")—drive home the application, while heightening and personalizing the reference to persecution (Luke 23:11; D. Williams 1985:67; Barrett 1994:230).

Psalm 118:22 itself provides no definitive information on the identity of the stone or the builders. Is it Israel being rejected by the nations? Is it the king being despised by the heathen or by skeptics in Israel? Among the Jews, interpretations ranged from Abraham to Jacob to David (Strack and Billerbeck 1978:1.876; e.g., *Midrash Psalms* 118:20). In Jewish thought, religious leaders in Israel, both true and false, were seen as builders (CD 4:12, 19). Jesus, however, is the source and validator of the interpretation: stone = Messiah; builders = Jewish leaders (Luke 20:17, 19).

4:12 There is salvation in no one else! This verse's exclusivistic claims have, in the current climate of religious pluralism, consistently been softened by some through minimizing exegesis (Stendahl 1981; Pinnock 1991). Among evangelicals the softening often takes the form of admitting the uniqueness of Christ in the objective accomplishment of salvation but saying that the text does not teach that it is essential to hear the good news about Jesus' saving work and consciously call on his name (Sanders 1988; 1992:62). This dichotomy will not maintain itself in the face of Luke's teaching in the immediate and larger context. The universal scope of the statement (lit., "under heaven, given to [or, among] men") extends to all human beings and is in line with Luke's missionary purpose and the complex of OT ideas about an exclusive, divine "name" that saves those who call on it (Sandnes 1998). Ten of the 32 references to the name in chs 2–4 imply conscious acknowledgement of that name for salvation (Fernando 1998:165). Luke's explicit teaching in the immediate and remote contexts is that salvation is applied by calling on and believing on the name of the Lord Jesus Christ (Luke 24:47; Acts 2:21, 38; 3:16; 11:17; 16:31; cf. Larkin 1995:80).

4:13-16 The Western text, D, gives "an amplification of the darker side of Jewish faults" (Witherington 1998:196, n. 133), increased emphasis on the leader's frustration, and a lessening of the depreciation of the apostles (Metzger 1994:277-278). It omits *kai idiōtai* [TG2399, ZG2626] ("ordinary men," 4:13); inserts *poiēsai ē* [TG4160/2228, ZG4472/2445] after *eichon* [TG2192, ZG2400] ("the council had nothing *to do or* say," 4:14); substitutes *apachthēnai* [TG520, ZG552] ("to be led away") for *apelthein* [TG565, ZG599] ("to go aside"); and uses the comparative adj. *phanerōteron* (comparative as elative—"it is all too clear") for *phaneron* [TG5318, ZG5745] ("it is clear").

4:13 ordinary men . . . no special training. These represent the Gr. *idiōtai* [TG2399, ZG2626] and *agrammatoi* [TG62, ZG63] respectively and may be helpfully understood in terms of ancient Greco-Roman culture generally as an appropriate means for communicating with Theophilus and fellow readers (de Villiers 1990; Witherington 1998:195). But given the original Jewish historical context, it is best to take the phrases to mean: "ordinary men" =

laymen (not credentialed to practice scribal law); "no special training" = no scribal training in Torah (*m. Sanhedrin* 10:2 [105a]; *m. Moed Katan* 1:8; Barrett 1994:234).

4:15 *the council chamber.* The NLT mg supplies the transliteration "Sanhedrin" for *sunedrion* [TG4892, ZG5284], usually a reference to the body of leaders, though it can refer to the room where they met (so the NLT; cf. P. Oxyrhynchus 717.8, 11 [II BC]; *Berlin Greichische Urkunden [BGU]* 540.25).

Christian sympathizers in the Sanhedrin, such as Nicodemus or Joseph of Arimathea, or others (e.g., Paul, Gamaliel's pupil), could have later supplied Luke with information on the Sanhedrin's "closed-door" session (Kistemaker 1990:159). This scene is not a matter of Luke's employing "the sovereign perspective of the storyteller" (contra Dunn 1996:51).

4:19 *Do you think God wants us to obey you rather than him?* This choice is one in a pattern of "brave opposition to tyranny" since Socrates (Plato *Apology* 29D-E; Johnson 1992:79). There are, however, OT and Jewish expressions of divine allegiance that provide the more immediate background (1 Sam 15:22; Jer 7:22; 2 Macc 7:2; Josephus *Antiquities* 17.158-159; 18.268; contra Witherington [1998:197], who sees Christianity being presented as a noble philosophy).

COMMENTARY

The mission of God does not advance unopposed (cf. Luke 8:13; 12:11-12; 21:15). Any call to repentance that included a recognition of Jesus as the messianic "prophet like Moses," the source of all present and future salvation blessings (3:19, 20-21, 26), was bound to challenge any competing religious authority, even those grounded in biblical revelation. As Peter and John obediently continued their Spirit-filled witness before the Sanhedrin, we see how God's work in the face of opposition is undeniable and unstoppable.

The sudden, dramatic appearance of hostile officials interrupted the apostles' preaching. The "priests" (Sadducean in conviction), the "captain of the Temple guard" (a member of the high priest's family charged with Temple security), and "Sadducees" (probably aristocratic laymen) were "very disturbed" (*diaponeomai* [TG1278, ZG1387], lit., "worn out," implying irritation and exasperation). Peter and John's teaching and proclaiming to the people, on the authority of Jesus, the "resurrection of the dead" not only challenged the Sadducean party's claim to be Israel's sole authority for interpreting Scripture but also Sadducean doctrine, which held that there would be no resurrection.

The Sadducees, the priestly and lay aristocracy, ruled the Jews in religious, social, and political matters at the behest of foreign overlords since Hasmonean times. They viewed any messianic movement, which the early church clearly was (2:36; 3:13-15, 20), as politically seditious, posing a threat to their comfortable position. Doctrinally, they considered themselves traditional, holding only to the written Torah and the interpretation of Israel's biblically constituted authority: the high priest. They rejected the Pharisees' rival authority and interpretation embodied in the oral Torah, the sayings of the fathers. They did not teach the resurrection (Josephus *Antiquities* 18.16-17; *b. Sanhedrin* 90b). The "resurrection from the dead" looked to the salvation blessings of a future messianic age, while the Sadducees placed their hope in this life. They believed that correct worship in the Temple would bring with it material prosperity. Many Sadducees successfully lived out that principle (see McCready 1992:79-97).

Though the apostles were placed in custody until a hearing the next day (due to the lateness of the hour), God was not thwarted in the advance of his saving work. In a summary statement, Luke tells us that five thousand males (not counting women and children) heard their message and believed it.

The next day the Sanhedrin convened in its "rock hewn chamber" on the south side of the Temple's inner forecourt precincts (m. Middot 5:4; m. Sanhedrin 11:2). This highest legislative and judicial body in Israel consisted of seventy-one members from three groups: "elders" from the landed gentry; "teachers of religious law," professional Torah scholars who taught, expounded, and applied the law, as well as argued it in court; and "priests," particularly the high priest and priestly officials from his family (m. Sanhedrin 1:6). The chief priest was the presiding officer. To heighten the role of the Sadducean party in the hearing, Luke gives us the names of four of the chief priests (cf. Josephus Antiquities 18.26-35, 95).

Placing the apostles in their midst (the Sanhedrin sat in a semicircle—m. Sanhedrin 4:3), they demanded to know by what "power" (source, cf. 1:8; 3:12; 4:33) and "name" (authority, 3:6, 16; 4:10, 12, 17-18, 30) they had done this. The apostles' ministry and message had challenged these leaders' spiritual authority, just as Jesus' did (Luke 20:2). The emphatic placement of "you" in the question shows the contempt with which they held these "ordinary men" with "no special training" (4:13). Their apparent lack of awareness of God's presence (see 4:19) and their decided opposition to Christ's disciples indicates they had disqualified themselves from the leadership of Israel, if not even cut themselves off from the true people of God (3:23).

Peter, empowered through the Spirit's intense presence (4:31; 13:9), gave witness before the court in fulfillment of Jesus' promise (Luke 12:11-12; 21:15). He was well aware of the seriousness of the situation, as he reframed the interrogation question. They wanted to know the means of healing (lit. "how this one has been saved"). By introducing the word sōzō [TG4982, ZG5392], which can refer to rescue from both physical dangers and afflictions (Luke 7:50; 17:19; 23:35-37; Acts 14:9) and to rescue from eternal death at the Last Judgment (Luke 19:10; Acts 2:21, 40, 47; 4:12; 11:14; 15:11; 16:31), Luke initiated a wordplay that he completes in 4:12.

As Jesus said it would, Peter's answer, framed as an evangelistic proclamation, did turn into an opportunity to bear witness (Luke 21:13). Peter wanted all those gathered and all the "people" (laos [TG2992, ZG3295]) of Israel to know that, by the name of Jesus Christ of Nazareth, the crippled man "was healed" (lit. "stands before you well"—received present salvation blessings). In explaining why the name of an "absent" Jesus can have such power, Peter indicted his listeners: it is this "man you crucified but whom God raised from the dead" (4:10; cf. 2:23-24, 36; 3:15, 17).

As at Pentecost (2:23-24), Peter addressed the scandal of Jesus' sufferings, but this time he focused particularly on the leaders' role. How could they have been so wrong? As his Lord did, Peter declared a coherent truth, interpreting their actions to them in terms of Psalm 118:22. The "builders" had certainly rejected Jesus, and now standing before them was proof positive that Jesus had "become the cornerstone" (lit. "head of the corner," probably pointing to the "capstone," which completes a building and, possibly, holds it all together).

Peter climaxed his answer with an urgent truth: this exalted Jesus is the only way of salvation for all humankind. If the leaders, or anyone else, would be saved from the generation of humans who, in disobedient rebellion, face the certain judgment of the day of the Lord (2:20, 40; 3:23), then they must repent, turn to the only Savior and Lord, and call upon him to be saved (2:21; 3:19, 26). In this one statement, Peter both exclusively particularizes salvation in Jesus—"salvation in no one else" (4:12; cf. Isa 43:11-12; 45:21-22; Hos 13:4)—and universalizes the scope of its application—(lit. "under heaven," an idiom for "the whole earth," Deut 2:25; 4:19; Job 28:24). Indeed, the only way of salvation is for people to call on the name of the Lord Jesus.

While the crowd was amazed at the miracle (3:11-12), the council was amazed at Peter and John's boldness. They spoke the whole truth before authorities "without fear or favor" (cf.13:46; 14:3; 26:26). Such courage came from supernatural empowerment, as a part of the outpouring of the Spirit from the risen exalted Lord, the "head of the corner" and only Savior. It was not from their credentials or training (see note on 4:13). Though the leaders were unwilling to recognize this as from the Lord (contrast Ps 118[117]:22 LXX), they took into account that these disciples had been with Jesus (1:21; Luke 8:1; 22:14, 56).

If the manner of witness amazed people, the result of the ministry is undeniable. A former cripple, having been healed and standing before them, was living proof that Jesus was risen and exalted to God's right hand (cf. 2:33). To this "there was nothing the council could say" (4:14; cf. Luke 21:15). The Sanhedrin conferred in closed session over their dilemma. Jesus' followers and their message were unacceptable, yet they had performed a "miraculous sign," known to everyone in Jerusalem (4:16; cf. 1:8; 2:5). The leaders sensed the miracle's import, for they labeled it a "sign"—a miracle that points beyond itself to make claims for the dawn of the age of salvation in Jesus (cf. 4:22; 8:6; Luke 11:29-30). There was no denying the reality of this miracle; but how would they keep the message of its saving significance from spreading? Silence the messengers. Warn them not to speak any longer in Jesus' name.

Calling the apostles back in, the council, in the strongest possible terms, ordered them to never again let the name of Jesus cross their lips, let alone teach in that name. To be silenced in this way would effectively quash any instruction about "resurrection from the dead." Invoking the presence of God (cf. 2:25; 10:33), Peter and John declared that allegiance to God and man are distinguishable and sometimes in competition (cf. Luke 20:25). The council, to the contrary, would expect such untrained laymen to accept its will as the will of God. The apostles asked the council to decide the just thing in this instance: to obey (lit., "heed," *akouein* [TG191, ZG201], cf. 3:23) a human council or God? Then they declared their own decision. "We cannot stop telling about everything we have seen and heard" (4:20). Their witness to the risen Lord and his message is unstoppable (Luke 24:48; Acts 1:8; 3:15; 2 Pet 1:16-18). With further warning the council released them. The disciples were not punished because of the people's positive regard—they had praised God for the miracle (cf. Luke 5:26; 7:16).

Luke triumphantly concluded his account with a reminder of the greatness of the miracle mirrored in how long the man had been lame: "for more than forty years." Labeling the healing "this miraculous sign" he again reminded his readers that this wonder points beyond itself to the one in whose name alone all the salvation blessings for the restored people of God are available (Luke 24:47; Acts 3:20-21, 26; 4:12; cf. Isa 35:6).

◆ J. The Believers Pray for Courage (4:23-31)

23As soon as they were freed, Peter and John returned to the other believers and told them what the leading priests and elders had said. 24When they heard the report, all the believers lifted their voices together in prayer to God: "O Sovereign Lord, Creator of heaven and earth, the sea, and everything in them—25you spoke long ago by the Holy Spirit through our ancestor David, your servant, saying,

'Why were the nations so angry?
Why did they waste their time with futile plans?
26The kings of the earth prepared for battle;
the rulers gathered together against the LORD
and against his Messiah.'*

27"In fact, this has happened here in this very city! For Herod Antipas, Pontius Pilate the governor, the Gentiles, and the people of Israel were all united against Jesus, your holy servant, whom you anointed. 28But everything they did was determined beforehand according to your will. 29And now, O Lord, hear their threats, and give us, your servants, great boldness in preaching your word. 30Stretch out your hand with healing power; may miraculous signs and wonders be done through the name of your holy servant Jesus."

31After this prayer, the meeting place shook, and they were all filled with the Holy Spirit. Then they preached the word of God with boldness.

4:25-26 Or his anointed one; or his Christ. Ps 2:1-2.

NOTES

4:23 *the other believers.* Lit., "their own" (*tous idious* [cf. TG2398, ZG2625]), i.e., "their own people" in the sense of Christian family (cf. 24:23). The Christian community as a whole (not just the other apostles; contra Johnson 1992:83) both prays and is filled with the Spirit for witness (cf. 4:31; Polhill 1992:148).

4:24b-30 In its structure and some of its vocabulary this prayer parallels Hezekiah's petition for deliverance in a crisis situation (2 Kgs 19:15-19; Isa 37:16-20): an invocation and praise ascription with two divine attributes (4:24b-28), and a two-petition entreaty (4:29-30; Plymale 1991:80-82). Both constructions are reverse parallelisms, Trinitarian in focus with Christ at the center (von Wahlde 1996).

4:25 The introduction to the quotation from Psalms here exhibits rough syntax (LeRoux 1991; von Wahlde 1995; cf. the smoothing over of it in the NLT and ms tradition; Metzger

1994:279-281). A satisfying stylistic explanation for this is found if we view it as a chiastic construction centering around the divine and human agents (i.e., the Holy Spirit and the mouth of David). To achieve the construction, the wording uses hyperbaton (a deliberate departure from normal word order for effect, here the words for "our father" are pushed forward, out of order) and zeugma, as "through" (*dia* [TG1223, ZG1328]) does double duty, serving as a preposition for both "Holy Spirit" and "mouth of David." Understood in this way, we may take the more difficult reading as "authentic and clear."

4:27 Herod . . . Pilate . . . Gentiles . . . people of Israel. The prayer probably correlates "Herod" and "Pilate" with "the kings" of Acts 2:26/Ps 2:2, since "rulers plot together" probably matches the Jewish leaders' activity mentioned in the immediate and larger contexts (4:5; Luke 22:66). The other option is to correlate "Herod" with "kings" and "Pilate" with "rulers" (Witherington 1998:202). "Gentiles" correlates with "nations" (Acts 4:25/Ps 2:1) and "the people of Israel" correlates to *laoi* ("peoples"; NLT translates "they") in Acts 4:25/Ps 2:1. Though "peoples" customarily points to a non-Jewish referent, Israel's disobedience in rejecting Jesus, the Lord's anointed, rightly qualifies her for this "Gentile" label here (cf. 3:23; Hos 2:23).

your holy servant. Kilgallen (1998b) gives a comprehensive and insightful exposition of the complex Christology found in this phrase (contra Polhill's [1992:149] more restricted assessment).

4:30 Stretch out your hand with healing power. In the Gr. this is not a separate request (contra Fernando 1998:169) but an accompanying infinitive phrase: lit., "while you stretch out your hand in healing." It expresses confidence that God, at his initiative, will provide a "dual testimony" in word and deed to the truth about his Messiah (Talbert 1997:62).

the name. As in the OT, it denotes "the transcendent deity's personal, active, and authoritative presence among his people" (Buckwalter 1998:119; cf. its thematic use throughout 3:1–4:31, esp. 3:6-7, 16; 4:7, 10, 12, 17-18).

COMMENTARY

Opposed by the council yet determined to obey their Lord, the apostles reported to their fellow believers the commands and threats of the Sadducean priests and elders (4:17-18, 21). The body of believers immediately went to prayer. In united, corporate prayer, they addressed God as "Sovereign Lord" (*despotēs*, [TG1203, ZG1305]; cf. Luke 2:29; Jude 1:4; Rev 6:10; Josephus *War* 7.323). In praising God as creator of all things (Exod 20:11; Ps 146:6) and as speaker and fulfiller of a prophetic word (his certain, purposeful, saving involvement in the affairs of history), the believers proclaimed the scope of his control, even over the threats of the Sanhedrin (cf. Ps 2:1-2). Emphatically, both Father and Spirit speak through the mouth of David, who is, at once, "our ancestor" (the church is in continuity with the true people of God, cf. 3:26) and "your servant." God predicted that opposition against him and his anointed one, though militant and united (Ps 2:2), would in the end be only a "futile plan" (Ps 2:1).

The prayer declares fulfillments of Psalm 2, first in Jesus' sufferings and then in the church's. Herod Antipas (Luke 23:6-12), Pontius Pilate (contrast 3:13), the Gentile Roman soldiers (Luke 23:36-37; Acts 2:23), and the Jewish throngs (Luke 23:23-25; Acts 2:23, 36; 3:13-15) were "all united against Jesus," as were the Sanhedrin, who also opposed the church. Luke's phrasing, "Jesus, your holy servant, whom you anointed" (4:27), brings together Christ's roles as Isaianic servant (*pais* [TG3816, ZG4090]) and Davidic Messiah—the latter understood in terms of Jesus' obedient servanthood (cf. 13:22), his Spirit-anointed earthly ministry (Luke 3:21-22; 4:18; Acts 10:38), and his innocent suffering (Luke 2:34-35; 22:37; 24:25-27—the basis for a vicarious death).

The church's praise climaxed by celebrating God's active accomplishment of his plan, as even his enemies act according to his predetermined will and "plan" (*hē boulē* [TG1012, ZG1087], here this is possibly an ironic wordplay since this was also a common designation for the Sanhedrin in session; see Josephus *War* 2.641). The church requested empowerment to implement God's promise to the Messiah in Psalm 2:8: "Only ask, and I will give you the nations as your inheritance, the whole earth as your possession" (Bolt 1998:201). The first petition, "hear their threats" (4:29), asks that God take notice of them, probably in such a way that he will not let them thwart the advance of his saving purposes (cf. Exod 3:7). The second petition, "give us, your servants, great boldness in preaching," calls for divine enablement to bring the message to the nations effectively so that they may embrace it and become part of the restored people of God, the Messiah's inheritance and possession. Labeling themselves "servants" places them in continuity with David and Messiah Jesus (4:25, 27, 30) and marks them as bearers of the Spirit-filled prophetic witness of the last days (2:18). The church, then, rightly views itself as fulfilling Scripture.

The "great boldness," or candor, the believers asked for is not only the freedom of speech of a Greek citizen versus a slave (Demosthenes *Orations* 9.3) but also the courage that stands up to all those who would limit the right to reveal the truth (Dio Chrysostom *Discourses* 32.26-27). Peter had already demonstrated such Spirit-filled boldness in declaring the whole truth to the Sanhedrin (4:8, 13).

As God with Moses saw the plight of his people (Exod 3:7), raised his mighty hand to save (Exod 3:19-20; 7:4-5), and did signs and wonders through Moses (Deut 34:10-12), who spoke through Moses (Exod 5:23), so also the believers in Acts 4, who had heeded the message of Jesus ("the prophet like Moses" [3:22-26]), assume that God will hear and there will be accompanying healings, signs, and wonders in the name of God's holy servant Jesus.

The believers' prayers are answered immediately, directly, and unmistakably. In reverse order, God, through an earthquake, did a "wonder"—an astonishing sign that pointed to his presence. They were all then filled with the Spirit so that they spoke with spontaneity and boldness beyond normal speech (4:31; cf. 4:8). And they were unstoppable, for they kept preaching God's message. Regarding the effect of the place being shaken, Chrysostom observed: "That made them [the disciples] the more unshaken" (*Homilies on Acts*, 11).

◆ **K. The Believers Share Their Possessions (4:32-37)**

³²All the believers were united in heart and mind. And they felt that what they owned was not their own, so they shared everything they had. ³³The apostles testified powerfully to the resurrection of the Lord Jesus, and God's great blessing was

upon them all. [34]There were no needy people among them, because those who owned land or houses would sell them [35]and bring the money to the apostles to give to those in need. [36]For instance, there was Joseph, the one the apostles nicknamed Barnabas (which means "Son of Encouragement"). He was from the tribe of Levi and came from the island of Cyprus. [37]He sold a field he owned and brought the money to the apostles.

NOTES

4:32 *All the believers were united in heart and mind.* The Western text has some enhancements. D adds *kai ouk ēn diakrisis* [TG1253, ZG1360], "and there were no distinctions." E has the final word as *chorismos* ("divisions"). The enlargement is, "and there was no quarrel (division) among them at all." This emphasizes the primitive church's unity (Metzger 1994:283).

united in . . . mind. Lit., "one soul" (*psuchē* [TG5590, ZG6034]), a concept strikingly reminiscent of Aristotle's description of friendship as "a single soul dwelling in two bodies" (Diogenes Laertius, *Lives of the Eminent Philosophers* 5.20).

4:32, 34 *they shared everything they had.* Lit., "they had all things in common." As such, there was no poverty among them. Bartchy (1991) and Capper (1995) have persuasively demonstrated these descriptions' basic historicity within the first-century Palestinian context (cf. Horn [1998:375-378], who is still not persuaded). These statements mirror idealistic pagan and OT expressions (Plato *Republic* 5.46 2c; Aristotle *Nicomachian Ethics* 1168B; Cicero *De Officiis* 1.16.51; Deut 15:4). This activity is best understood as the voluntary, occasional, but "just in time," disposal of discretionary personal capital to meet others' needs (4:34-37). Luke views this kind of sharing as normative (Horn 1998:382; Witherington 1998:207; Marshall and Peterson 1998:499-518).

4:33 *testified powerfully.* The power was probably not just miracles (so Polhill 1992:152) or effectiveness of proclamation (so Johnson 1992:86). Given the phrase's ambiguity (a simple dative *dunamei megalē* [TG1411/3173, ZG1539/3489]), it probably refers to both (Barrett 1994:254).

4:36 *Joseph.* The NKJV, following 𝔐, has "Joses" (*Iōsēs* [TG2501, ZG2737]), a spelling that reflects the Byzantine scribes' replacement of *ph* with *s* to arrive at a Greek-sounding word ending (Metzger 1994:284).

Barnabas (which means "Son of Encouragement"). In Aramaic, *bar* [TA1247, ZA10120], as a prefix, means "son of." The derivation and significance of *nabas* is notoriously difficult (see Polhill [1992:154] for a list of options). Some take "encouragement" (*paraklēsis* [TG3874, ZG4155]), according to Luke's usage, to refer to some sort of speech activity, often "preaching, exhortation" (13:15; 15:31; cf. the verb, 2:40; 11:23; 14:22; Barrett 1994:258). The whole phrase would then be "son of exhortation" = "preacher," with *nabas* derived from *nabi'* [TH5030, ZH5566] ("prophet"). Others, drawing on the Syriac Peshitta, find the link in the first person imperfect (*nBy'*) of an Aramaic verb (*By'*) "to comfort" (Brock 1974; but note Barrett's [1994:258] critique).

COMMENTARY

Another evidence of God working in the believers' midst was their Spirit-filled unity: a divine gift of the last days (Jer 32:39). In a phrase that masterfully brings together the Graeco-Roman ideal of friendship, "a single soul dwelling in two bodies" (see note on 4:32) and the Old Testament ideal of total loyalty (1 Chr 12:38[39]; cf. Deut 6:5; 10:12), Luke tells us that "all the believers were united in heart and mind." From this unity came a mind-set: "They felt that what they owned was not their own." Each member chose to see his possessions as being available for sharing. The church's common life of caring for its needy, indeed, begins with and is sustained by united hearts, souls, and mind-sets intent on sharing (see Luke 9:24; 12:22, 34; 14:26; Acts 2:46).

That this was of God is reinforced by the reminder that, in answer to prayer that confidently assumed God would stretch out his hand in healings and signs and wonders (4:29-30), the apostles "testified powerfully to the resurrection of the Lord Jesus" (4:33; cf. 1:8, 22; 3:15; 5:32). Indeed, the foundational good news is of a risen and exalted Lord who now pours out his Spirit from heaven, bringing times of refreshment in a community whose unity and care for one another approximate the community and friendship ideals of Gentile and Jew alike. So God's "great favor" (lit. "great grace," cf. Acts 6:8; 11:23; 20:32; Exod 33:13; Ps 84:11) does rest on all the believers in the form of the united "heart and soul" of sharing. As Luke goes on to explain (*gar* [TG1063, ZG1142], "for," introduces verse 34), "There were no needy people among them" (4:34; cf. Deut 15:4). This phrase does not indicate an eradication of poverty but, as the next explanatory statement clarifies, the reality that Christians who were in need were soon provided for.

What was the church's ongoing practice? The Greek of Acts 4:34-35 consistently uses the iterative or customary imperfect tense (lit., "selling," "were bringing and were placing," and "were distributing"). The implication is that there was a pattern where persons of means in the community would on occasion voluntarily sell land or houses, for which they evidently had no immediate use, and would bring the sale price to the apostles (lit. "to the apostles' feet"). Such language signals a humble, self-giving stance in submission to the leaders' authority (Ps 110:1). Normally, in first-century society such contributors would be honored as "patrons" for such contributions and given a place of privilege over the rest, their clients. But these believers placed their funds at the disposal of the apostles: their inferiors both economically and socially (cf. Cicero [*De Officiis* II.50-51] who socially ranks the work of agriculturalists at the top and fishermen at the bottom).

Joseph, known to us more familiarly as Barnabas ("Son of Encouragement" or "Son of Exhortation") is a particular example of such humility and care. From the "tribe of Levi" and a native of Cyprus with its large Jewish population (Philo *Legatio ad Gaium* 282), he had wealth in land, one piece of which he sold and "brought . . . to the apostles." For Luke, Joseph embodies the fully integrated life of witness, as both a "Son of Exhortation" (11:23) and one who took care of the church's needs.

◆ L. Ananias and Sapphira (5:1-11)

But there was a certain man named Ananias who, with his wife, Sapphira, sold some property. ²He brought part of the money to the apostles, claiming it was the full amount. With his wife's consent, he kept the rest.

³Then Peter said, "Ananias, why have you let Satan fill your heart? You lied to

the Holy Spirit, and you kept some of the money for yourself. ⁴The property was yours to sell or not sell, as you wished. And after selling it, the money was also yours to give away. How could you do a thing like this? You weren't lying to us but to God!"

⁵As soon as Ananias heard these words, he fell to the floor and died. Everyone who heard about it was terrified. ⁶Then some young men got up, wrapped him in a sheet, and took him out and buried him.

⁷About three hours later his wife came in, not knowing what had happened. ⁸Peter asked her, "Was this the price you and your husband received for your land?"

"Yes," she replied, "that was the price." ⁹And Peter said, "How could the two of you even think of conspiring to test the Spirit of the Lord like this? The young men who buried your husband are just outside the door, and they will carry you out, too."

¹⁰Instantly, she fell to the floor and died. When the young men came in and saw that she was dead, they carried her out and buried her beside her husband. ¹¹Great fear gripped the entire church and everyone else who heard what had happened.

NOTES

5:1-11 In the account of Ananias and Sapphira, biblical parallelism has been noted by various scholars for the following features: embezzlement and discovery (Achan in Josh 7; Johnson 1992:91); immediate divine judgment resulting in death with removal of the bodies (Nadab and Abihu in Lev 10:1-5; Witherington 1998:214); husband-wife conspiracy with respect to property (Ahab and Jezebel in 1 Kgs 21; Talbert 1997:66); Satan's filling a heart for Jesus' betrayal (Judas in Luke 22:3, 21-22; Acts 1:18-19; O'Toole 1995:204); Jesus' temptation (O'Toole 1995:205-206), and—less likely—Adam and Eve's fall (Gen 3; contra Marguerat 1993a).

Ananias who, with his wife, Sapphira. The name *Ananias* may mean "The LORD is gracious" (*khananyah* [TH2608, ZH2863]) or "the LORD answers" (*'ananyah* [TH6055, ZH6731]). *Sapphira,* from the Heb. *shiprah* [TH8235/8236, ZH9185/9186], means "beautiful."

5:4-5 Codex Bezae (D) makes 5:4 more vivid by adding *poiēsai ponēron touto* ("to do this evil"). D also heightens dramatic effect in 5:5 by inserting from 5:10 the adverb *parachrēma* [TG3916, ZG4202] ("immediately").

5:4 *The property . . . give away.* There is not sufficient detail present (contra Capper 1995:339) to reconstruct a procedure for the early church's participation in the community of goods, parallel to Qumran's approach with its two-step probationary period (1QS 6:13-23; Barrett 1994:263). Nor does its voluntary nature create a necessary contradiction with 4:34 but rather interprets it (Witherington 1998:216; contra Barrett 1994:267).

lying . . . to God. This was a sin against God and merited severe punishment, not just because it challenged the apostles' authority (contra Johnson 1992:92) but because it happened in the presence of a community in which the Spirit dwelt (Witherington 1998:215; involved an oath (Havelaar 1997:71); and created a breach in the unity and purity of the fellowship (Polhill 1992:161). Peter's role was not to pronounce a sentence of death (contra Dunn 1996:64) but to speak a prophetic, explanatory word, responding in "anguish and anger" to so serious a crime (O'Toole 1995:194; Witherington 1998:218).

5:5, 10 *fell to the floor and died.* Their deaths are a direct act of God—"death at the hands of heaven" (Derrett 1977:197)—and not simply the result of natural causes, such as a heart attack triggered by the psychological impact of being found out (contra Witherington 1998:216, 218). For Luke, the fear (5:5, 11) is terror in the presence of the supernatural (cf. 2:43; 19:17; Luke 5:26; 7:16; 8:37). In contrast to Simon Magus (8:20-24), the couple were probably regenerated Christians (Polhill 1992:160-162), though Luke did not editorialize on this feature (Witherington 1998:219).

5:6, 10 *buried him . . . buried her.* This disgraceful summary burial, without traditional rituals of mourning, befits the sin and the punishment (Derrett 1977:198; contra Barrett 1994:269).

5:10 *carried her out and buried her.* D adds *susteilantes* [TG4958, ZG5366] ("wrapping up") here. This is taken from 5:6 and is clearly secondary since, according to Jewish custom, women could wrap both men and women, but men could wrap men only.

COMMENTARY

Showing their unity with the believers, Ananias and Sapphira sold some real estate (cf. 5:3). Ananias brought money to the apostles as Barnabas had done (4:36-37). The difference was that the couple agreed together to "hold back" some of the money and only bring part of it to the apostles but apparently claim it was the full amount (*nosphizomai* [TG3557, ZG3802]; cf. the use of this word in LXX Josh 7:1 for Achan's actions).

Peter, as a Spirit-filled apostle with prophetic insight (cf. Luke 5:22; 9:47; 24:38), exposed the fraud and labeled the sin as having come from Satan. Peter sought to help Ananias see clearly what the cause of the fraud was. Satan had filled Ananias's heart with the prospect of receiving praise for his generosity while keeping a secure nest egg for his wife. The real estate may have been a *ketubah*, a sum paid to a wife in case of a unilateral divorce or her husband's death (*m. Ketubbot* 4:7–5:1).

Ananias lied to the Holy Spirit when he perjured himself before the Spirit-filled community. It was not a lie to humans but to God (note: the Spirit's deity and personality are clearly affirmed, cf. 5:9). Ananias was fully responsible because throughout the whole process he had complete control over his property and the sale price in the community's voluntary approach to "having all things in common" (2:44; 4:32). In a premeditated fashion he had planned this deception. "How could you do a thing like this?" (lit. "Why is it that you have placed this matter in your heart?" 5:4).

"As soon as Ananias heard these words, he fell to the floor and died" (5:5; *exepsuxen* [TG1634, ZG1775], "expired, breathed his last"). Ananias had violated the sanctity of the Christian community: the complete integrity and transparent unity it shared. So, God, the knower of all hearts, immediately and physically cut Ananias off from God's people. This "death at the hands of heaven" had the intended effect: "Everyone who heard about it was terrified" (5:5). The hasty, unceremonious burial of Ananias showed that the believers recognized it as God's judgment (see Lev 10:6). The young men (young in age, not office) covered Ananias's eyes and wrapped his body in a shroud. Without mourning rituals, they took the corpse outside the city and buried it.

Three hours later Sapphira arrived, ignorant of what had transpired. Peter's query was not a trap but an opportunity for her to confess her sin. But Sapphira perpetuated the lie about the amount of the sale, and Peter exposed her sin with another *why* question. Why had she and her husband agreed together to put the Spirit of the Lord to the test? Their harmonious conspiracy was a hypocritical mockery of the Christian community's Spirit-filled unity of sharing. As with Israel's unbelief and murmurings against God in the wilderness, the couple's sin was actually putting

God to the test to see how far they could go before he would act in judgment (Num 14:20-23; Ps 95:7-11; cf. Acts 15:10; Deut 6:16). Peter notes this time that it was the Holy Spirit of the Lord Jesus whom they had lied to and put to the test; he would not be mocked (5:9; Gal 6:7-8; cf. Acts 16:6-7).

Peter's prophetic word declared the immediacy and certainty of judgment: the young men who buried her husband were at the door and would carry her out too. "Instantly" Sapphira expired at Peter's feet, ironically giving obeisance in death, where, in life, there was only the mock submission of a fraudulent contribution (5:2). A second dishonorable burial immediately followed, as the young men did their grisly duty and buried her beside her partner in crime.

"Great fear gripped the entire church"—here is the first reference in Acts to the body of Christians as the "church" (ekklēsia [TG1577, ZG1711]). This term, though used in secular Greek to describe citizen assemblies (cf. 19:32, 39), derives its special theological meaning from its use in the LXX as a consistent translation of the Hebrew qahal [TH6951, ZH7736], the "assembly" or "congregation" of God's people (e.g., Deut 4:10; 9:10; Ps 26[25]:12; cf. Deut 31:12). For Christians to use this word to describe their corporate identity was to claim to be the true people of God, the rightful heirs of God's promised salvation blessings. To find it at the climax of this passage only heightens the seriousness of Ananias and Sapphira's sin and gives explicit justification for the severity of the punishment. Luke lets us know that the dread extended to non-Christians, as well.

◆ M. The Apostles Heal Many (5:12-16)

12The apostles were performing many miraculous signs and wonders among the people. And all the believers were meeting regularly at the Temple in the area known as Solomon's Colonnade. 13But no one else dared to join them, even though all the people had high regard for them. 14Yet more and more people believed and were brought to the Lord—crowds of both men and women. 15As a result of the apostles' work, sick people were brought out into the streets on beds and mats so that Peter's shadow might fall across some of them as he went by. 16Crowds came from the villages around Jerusalem, bringing their sick and those possessed by evil* spirits, and they were all healed.

5:16 Greek unclean.

NOTES

5:12-13 the believers were meeting regularly. Though there is no expressed subject, the NLT correctly presents the unified gathering as believers, not only the apostles (cf. 2:46; 4:24, 33; contra Johnson 1992:95).

no one else dared to join them. "No one else" probably refers to non-Christians (Haenchen 1971:242), not everyone else impacted by Ananias and Sapphira's deaths (contra Johnson 1992:95; cf. 5:11). It does not point to believers frightened by the Sanhedrin's warning (4:18; see Witherington 1998:225-227) or to Jewish sympathizers (see Schwartz 1983). These non-Christians "dared" not "join them" (kollasthai [TG2853, ZG3140]); they dared not "come into the Christian community" (Krodel 1986:123; see Acts 17:34).

5:15 *Peter's shadow*. As in the OT and Jesus' life and ministry, the presence and power of God come as an "overshadowing" (cf. the power of "the name," 3:16). On Luke's part, there is no animistic thinking (contra Talbert 1997:67).

Codex Bezae (D) adds at the end of the verse: *apēllassonto gar apo pasēs astheneias hōs eichen hekastos autōn* ("for they were being set free from every sickness, such as each of them had"). E and some old Latin mss add *kai rusthōsin apo pasēs astheneias hēs eichon* ("and they were delivered from any sickness that they had"). Both expansions magnify the image of Peter and anticipate the use of *astheneis* [TG772, ZG822] (sick) in 5:16 (Witherington 1998:227; Johnson 1992:96).

COMMENTARY

The church's mission continued to advance through the apostles' performance of miraculous signs and wonders among the people. The special role signs and wonders play in salvation history—their clustering around key redemptive events and new epochs of revelation, and the fact that mainly the leaders do them—should circumscribe our expectations of such exceptional events today. Still, we must not lose sight of Luke's perspective of "God on mission." He does not so much distinguish between natural and supernatural occurrences as between God's active working out of his saving purposes through his ordinary providence and his exceptional interventions. In fact, Luke so presented the progress of the church as a continuous mighty work of God that it is consequently difficult to pick out the miraculous from the nonmiraculous in Luke's story (Lampe 1965:171).

Just as miraculous is the church's continued unity in the wake of the Ananias and Sapphira incident. They "were meeting regularly" (lit., "were together"—*homothumadon* [TG3661, ZG3924], with one mind, purpose, and impulse, 1:14; 2:46; 4:24) in Solomon's Colonnade at the Temple for worship, teaching, and evangelism (cf. 2:42; 4:33; 5:25).

The aura of God's presence in and through the Spirit-filled apostles and community both repelled and attracted those outside. In the face of the miraculous preservation of the community's integrity and transparent fellowship, some dared not join them, evidently unready to count the cost of authentic discipleship. Yet, "everyone" (lit. "the people"—*ho laos* [cf. TG2992, ZG3295]) had "high regard for them" (5:13; cf. 2:10, 46; 19:17). Nevertheless, crowds of both men and women who believed (cf. 2:44; 4:4, 32) "were brought to the Lord" (5:14)—literally, "they were added to the Lord." To join the church, Christ's body, is to be added to the Lord.

The apostles' ministry resulted in further attraction. The sick were brought to them, even laid in the streets to intercept them, as in Jesus' early Galilean ministry (Luke 4:40-41; 6:17-19). There was heightened expectation, the hope that at least the shadow of Spirit-filled Peter might fall on someone as he passed by. The scope of the church's mission was broadening. Though still a centripetal dynamic, the church entered its mission's second phase, becoming "witnesses in all Judea" as crowds from the villages around Jerusalem streamed in, bringing their sick and demon possessed to be healed. The result was complete: "They were all healed" (5:16).

◆ N. The Apostles Meet Opposition (5:17-42)

¹⁷The high priest and his officials, who were Sadducees, were filled with jealousy. ¹⁸They arrested the apostles and put them in the public jail. ¹⁹But an angel of the Lord came at night, opened the gates of the jail, and brought them out. Then he told them, ²⁰"Go to the Temple and give the people this message of life!"

²¹So at daybreak the apostles entered the Temple, as they were told, and immediately began teaching.

When the high priest and his officials arrived, they convened the high council*— the full assembly of the elders of Israel. Then they sent for the apostles to be brought from the jail for trial. ²²But when the Temple guards went to the jail, the men were gone. So they returned to the council and reported, ²³"The jail was securely locked, with the guards standing outside, but when we opened the gates, no one was there!"

²⁴When the captain of the Temple guard and the leading priests heard this, they were perplexed, wondering where it would all end. ²⁵Then someone arrived with startling news: "The men you put in jail are standing in the Temple, teaching the people!"

²⁶The captain went with his Temple guards and arrested the apostles, but without violence, for they were afraid the people would stone them. ²⁷Then they brought the apostles before the high council, where the high priest confronted them. ²⁸"Didn't we tell you never again to teach in this man's name?" he demanded. "Instead, you have filled all Jerusalem with your teaching about him, and you want to make us responsible for his death!"

²⁹But Peter and the apostles replied, "We must obey God rather than any human authority. ³⁰The God of our ancestors raised Jesus from the dead after you killed him by hanging him on a cross.*

³¹Then God put him in the place of honor at his right hand as Prince and Savior. He did this so the people of Israel would repent of their sins and be forgiven. ³²We are witnesses of these things and so is the Holy Spirit, who is given by God to those who obey him."

³³When they heard this, the high council was furious and decided to kill them. ³⁴But one member, a Pharisee named Gamaliel, who was an expert in religious law and respected by all the people, stood up and ordered that the men be sent outside the council chamber for a while. ³⁵Then he said to his colleagues, "Men of Israel, take care what you are planning to do to these men! ³⁶Some time ago there was that fellow Theudas, who pretended to be someone great. About 400 others joined him, but he was killed, and all his followers went their various ways. The whole movement came to nothing. ³⁷After him, at the time of the census, there was Judas of Galilee. He got people to follow him, but he was killed, too, and all his followers were scattered.

³⁸"So my advice is, leave these men alone. Let them go. If they are planning and doing these things merely on their own, it will soon be overthrown. ³⁹But if it is from God, you will not be able to overthrow them. You may even find yourselves fighting against God!"

⁴⁰The others accepted his advice. They called in the apostles and had them flogged. Then they ordered them never again to speak in the name of Jesus, and they let them go.

⁴¹The apostles left the high council rejoicing that God had counted them worthy to suffer disgrace for the name of Jesus.* ⁴²And every day, in the Temple and from house to house, they continued to teach and preach this message: "Jesus is the Messiah."

5:21 Greek *Sanhedrin;* also in 5:27, 41. 5:30 Greek *on a tree.* 5:41 Greek *for the name.*

NOTES

5:17 *jealousy.* The Gr. here draws on the use of the OT word for jealousy (*qin'ah* [TH7068, ZH7863]). Here it indicates "a passionate, consuming zeal focused on God" (TDNT 2.878), which, in defense of God's honor, can lead to violence. This is the Sanhedrin's fervent but misguided reaction (Phinehas, Num 25:11, 13; Elijah and Jehu, 1 Kgs 19:10, 14; 2 Kgs 10:16; cf. Acts 13:45; TDNT 2.880).

5:24 *wondering where it would all end.* The NLT rightly identifies the officers' perplexity over the outcome (Haenchen 1971:250), not over the cause (Longenecker 1981:320) or the significance (Spencer 1997:60) of the missing prisoners.

5:26 *stone them.* This is not an example of capital punishment for blasphemy (contra Johnson 1992:97) but mob violence in which people throw stones at unpopular individuals (ISBE 4.630).

5:30 *raised Jesus from the dead after you killed him.* Lit., "raised up Jesus whom you killed." It is possible to interpret *egeirō* [TG1453, ZG1586] ("raised") as a reference to the Resurrection (so the NLT, which adds "from the dead" and "after"). However, the expression "God of our ancestors," the verb's placement at the beginning of a description of Jesus' saving work, and the fact that all other uses pointing to the Resurrection are either explicitly qualified (3:15; 4:10; 13:30; 26:8) or involve contextual pointers (10:40; 13:37), suggest another sense: "brought on the scene" (13:22; cf. 3:26; Fernando 1998:212).

5:32 *the Holy Spirit.* His witness is displayed not in the gift in salvation (contra Marshall 1980:120), or in outward miraculous manifestations that salvation has come (8:15-17; 10:44-47; 15:8; contra Polhill 1992:170), but as an indwelling of those who obey God so that their witness is characterized by boldness and persuasive conviction (Dunn 1996:70; cf. 4:8, 31, 33-34; 6:5, 10; 7:55; John 16:8).

5:33-39 *Gamaliel . . . said . . . "take care what you are planning to do to these men!"* Though all scholars agree that Luke viewed the Pharisees and Gamaliel ironically, some see the irony as part of a positive appraisal. Gamaliel's words are "sound Pharisaic doctrine" (Fernando 1998:213; *Pirke Aboth* 4:14). They even articulate a "truth test" for the Christian movement: Does the witness have an unstoppable, overcoming character? (5:39; Rapske 1998:237). Such a view, except as Rapske states it, could be open to the charge of being un-Lukan because of its pragmatic triumphalism (Lyons 1997:38-39). Gamaliel does not become a Christian (Gowler 1991:279).

An ironic, negative assessment of Gamaliel and the Pharisees is more congruent with Luke's presentation throughout Luke–Acts (Darr 1998). Gamaliel, a member of the Sanhedrin, is more problematic than heroic (contrast Luke's treatment of Joseph of Arimathea, Luke 23:51; Darr 1998:125). As a Pharisee, he was part of a sect that, although not violently opposed to Jesus and his movement as the Sadducees were, still "remains wholly inimical to the outworking of God's purpose on earth" (Darr 1998:134; cf. Luke 19:39). In his speech, he remained more oblivious than insightful about the presence of the plan of God in Christ and his followers (cf. Luke 7:30, 39-47; 13:31-35).

5:36-37 *Theudas . . . Judas of Galilee.* Gamaliel referred to a revolutionary Theudas who was active before the time of Judas the Galilean (AD 6; Josephus *War* 2.117-118). If we identify this Theudas with the revolutionary referred to by Josephus (active under Cuspus Fadus AD 44–46; *Antiquities* 20:97-98), then Luke committed a historical error of order and created an anachronism, for Gamaliel presumably gave this speech in the early 30s. Johnson (1992:99) says that the lack of independent controls makes it impossible to harmonize or to utterly dismiss either version. Many would view the "modest proposal" of two persons named Theudas as possible but not probable since Luke probably mishandled Josephus (Mason 1992:211) or whatever information he had (Barrett 1994:295). Still, there are good grounds for concluding that Luke was accurately referring to another Theudas, a revolutionary active at Herod the Great's death (4 BC). Luke is at least as historically trustworthy as Josephus and on some matters more so (Witherington 1998:239). Josephus should not be seen as the standard or source for Luke, especially in matters of chronology (Witherington 1998:239; cf. Cohen 1979). Josephus reported many uprisings at Herod's death (*Antiquities* 17.269). Theudas, a contracted form of names such as Theodorus, Theodotus, and Theodosius, was a common name in antiquity, as inscriptions and papyri show (Bruce 1990:176).

he [Judas] was killed. Codex Bezae's reading *dieluthē autos di' hautou* ("he was destroyed by himself") points to suicide and may further support the explanation that Josephus and Luke refer to two different Theudases, since Josephus's Theudas was beheaded by the Romans (Witherington 1998:239).

5:38-39 The Western text presents a "vigorous and attractive paraphrase" of these verses (Lake and Cadbury 1979:62). With the chief expansions italicized, it reads as follows (using the NLT): "So, *brothers*, my advice is, leave these men alone. Let them go *without defiling your hands.* If they are planning and doing these things merely on their own, it will soon be overthrown. (39) But if it is from God, you will not be able to overthrow them— *neither you nor kings nor tyrants. Therefore keep away from these men.* You may even find yourselves fighting against God."

If they are planning . . . merely on their own . . . If it is from God. The class three "future more probable" condition (*ean ē,* "if it might be") followed by a class one "real" condition (*ei estin,* "if it is") has led some commentators to find here a possible indication of Gamaliel's own view (Witherington 1998:235). Darr (1998:138), following Zerwick, rightly sees the "real" condition as not necessarily representing the speaker's view of the matter. The apostles' contention was so concrete that when it is discussed as a supposition, it is placed in a first-class "real" condition. Further, the psychological impact of the assertion: that the movement might actually be from God—the more actual and pressing alternative—requires a "real" condition to express it.

5:42 *Temple . . . house to house . . . teach and preach.* Polhill (1992:174) has pointed out a reverse parallelism: Temple—homes, and teach—preach. This parallelism has attracted some support (Fernando 1998:214; Witherington 1998:240) and can tend to distinguish teaching and evangelizing depending on the nature of the audience. Luke's almost interchangeable use of "preaching" and "teaching," however, should tell us that they are pointing to the same basic activity (Barrett 1994:301). The early church's evangelizing centered around teaching the truth of the gospel. And the early church's teaching was never without an evangelistic thrust (cf. 3:12).

COMMENTARY

The success of the apostles' witness and healing ministry (4:33; 5:12-16) caused the Sadducean high priest and "his officials" to be filled with jealousy. Instead of being filled with the Spirit and rejoicing at salvation blessings (2:4, 46; 4:31; 13:52; cf. Luke 15:7, 10), the leaders' blind zeal for God (cf. 13:45; 17:5) leads to violent action. They arrested the apostles, not just Peter and John (4:2-3), and placed them in a public jail to hold them for a hearing the next day.

For the first time since Pentecost, we encounter direct intervention from heaven. An "angel of the Lord" (5:19) delivered the apostles. In a very matter of fact way, Luke tells us the angel opened the prison doors at night, led the incarcerated apostles out, and commissioned them: "Go to the Temple and give the people this message of life!" (5:20). Although Theophilus and his readers would probably be familiar with nighttime-escape stories, a favorite way among pagans to affirm that the deity and his movement were unstoppable (e.g., Euripides *Bacchae* 1.346-357, 510-519, 615-640; Philostratus *Apollonius of Tyana* 8.30; 7.38), this account is different because the escapees are sent right back into the precincts of their captors. They were to go to the Temple, Israel's worship center and the place for greatest exposure to the largest number of people, take their stand, and speak to the people the message of life (5:20). "Life," with or without the adjective *eternal,* is one way Luke refers to salvation blessings (3:15; 11:18; 13:46; Luke 10:25; 18:18, 29-30). This command presents the truth that by God's word the salvation blessing of eternal life can be appropriated now and that beyond death there is life in which God's salvation will be fully known forever (Deut 8:3; 32:47; Job 19:25-26).

Heeding the angelic guidance, the apostles returned early in the morning to the Temple to teach the people. Ignorant of the apostles' liberation, the "high council," the full Sanhedrin, convened and told the Temple guards to get the prisoners. But the "Temple guards" discovered and then reported that no one was inside the fully secured jail. The authorities were "perplexed." This is a natural, human response to supernatural occurrences when no interpretation is present (cf. Luke 9:7; 24:4; Acts 2:12; 10:17), but they *had* received an interpretation. Had not these same apostles declared that they would continue to obey God rather than men by speaking of what they had seen and heard (4:19-20)? The leaders' perplexity, then, is actually all the more damning, for if they had heeded the apostles' message at the first hearing, they would know and not now be "wondering where it would all end" (5:24).

Another surprise was in store for them, however. Someone arrived and announced, "The men you put in jail are standing in the Temple, teaching the people" (5:25). The Sanhedrin's humiliation was complete. Not only had God frustrated their attempt to detain the apostles, but he had also emboldened and enabled them to continue their mission. Those publicly jailed were publicly taking their stand and teaching in the Temple.

Springing into action, the captain and officers rearrested the apostles, who offered no resistance. The officers used no violent force, in contrast to their customary behavior, as memorialized in a Jewish street ballad: "For they are the high priests, and their sons the treasurers: their sons-in-law are Temple-officers, and their servants beat the people with their staves" (*b. Pesahim* 57a; *t. Menahot* 13:21). Since the church was still experiencing the people's favor (5:26), the populace would start throwing stones at the Temple police if they handled the apostles roughly. Since the apostles went peaceably, no violence broke out.

The chief priest began his interrogation with a strong question introduced by the Hebraic expression "with a command did we not command you?" (5:28). He was concerned about the apostles' disobedience to the Sanhedrin's previous prohibition (4:18). Disdainful throughout his interrogation, he did not let Jesus' name cross his lips, referring only to "this man's name" (lit. "this name") and "his death" (lit. "the blood of this man"). The chief priest made two charges: Contrary to the prohibition, the apostles had filled Jerusalem with their teaching, and they apparently had a vendetta against the leaders, intending to blame them for Jesus' death (lit., "bring down on us the blood of this man"—an OT expression for divine retribution for murder of an innocent person; cf. Judg 9:24 LXX; Jer 6:19; Ezek 18:13; 33:2-4).

It is true that the apostles in their boldness did not hold back the truth that the leaders were responsible for Jesus' death (3:17; 4:10). Ironically, the objective basis for the gracious, vicarious atonement they proclaimed—the portrayal of an innocent servant suffering an unjust death (3:13-15)—only served to emphasize the leaders' culpability. Even so, these facts were always accompanied by the good news of the offer of salvation (3:19, 26; 4:12) rather than any call to take action against the leaders.

Peter's defense (5:29) immediately took the form of an aggressive witness. First, he proclaimed the basis for their civil disobedience—the priority of divine over human authority. "We must obey God rather than any human authority" (5:29; cf. 4:19-20; Luke 20:25). Second, he answered the vendetta issue by pointing the Sanhedrin to the grand sweep of salvation history. As the God of our ancestors raised up Moses, Joshua, Samuel, and David, so now he has raised up and brought onto the stage of human history Jesus (3:13, 25; 13:22; see note on 5:30). But the leaders did not recognize him and killed Jesus by crucifying him (lit. "hanging him on a tree," Luke 23:21). With this language Peter referred to Deuteronomy 21:23 ("anyone who is hung is cursed in the sight of God"); it showed the depth of contempt with which the leaders had held Jesus. They had asked for a death that would place Jesus under God's curse (cf. 10:39; 13:29; Gal 3:13). Again, Peter did not back away from this incontrovertible fact: the leaders were responsible for Jesus' death (3:15; 4:10). But by hastening to tell what God did to Jesus, Peter removed any sense of vendetta. God "put him in the place of honor at his right hand" (5:31; Ps 110:1), as the messianic, Davidic "prince" (*archēgos* [TG747, ZG795], see comment on 3:15), Israel's final "Savior" (cf. Luke 2:11; Acts 2:36; 4:12). Jesus' position at God's right hand and his title of "Savior" point to his deity. The Old Testament is marked by the parallel themes that God will bring the final salvation and that the Messiah will bring this salvation (Ps 106:47; 118:25-26; Isa 63:8; Jer 17:14; Joel 2:32). The apostles revealed that God and the Messiah are both present in one person, namely the Savior Jesus (2:21, 36, 38-40).

God's purpose in Jesus' exaltation is for him to give Israel salvation blessings: repentance and forgiveness of sins (2:38; 3:19-20, 26). Every aspect of applying salvation, the human response (repentance) and the salvation benefit (forgiveness of sins), is a gift of the risen and exalted Lord (3:26; 11:18; 15:9). Though these blessings are not given exclusively to Israel, it is appropriate to proclaim that the people whose ancestors received the promises now receive the fulfillment (3:26; 13:46).

Peter then answered the charge that they had filled all Jerusalem with their teaching with another bold declaration grounded in salvation history (5:32). Peter claimed to fulfill the divinely commissioned role of "witness" to the God who decrees, acts, and saves. The prophet Isaiah said this role would be given to the restored people of God in the last days (Isa 43:10; 44:8; see 43:8-44:8 for many themes present in Peter's brief gospel summary). Thus, it is not "his" (Peter's) teaching either in terms of source or content. He was simply obeying the commission of the risen, ascended, and exalted Lord (1:8), to tell others of everything he had seen and heard (4:20). Furthermore, God the Holy Spirit was a second witness (cf. Isa 43:10), empowering those who were obeying God (cf. 3:23) with such boldness and convincing conviction that Jerusalem was indeed filled with their effective teaching (5:14).

Peter's defense violated the council's prohibition and boldly declared the council to be on the wrong side of salvation history. The Sanhedrin was furious and wanted to do away with him (cf. Luke 22:2). It is evident that they took Peter's statement about Christ being at God's right hand as Prince and Savior as a blasphemous confession of Jesus as God (cf. Luke 22:69-71); otherwise they had no basis for the death penalty here.

In the midst of the furor "a Pharisee named Gamaliel, who was an expert in religious law and respected by all the people," took the floor. But before he spoke, he had the apostles removed so that the Sanhedrin could deal privately with the matter. The Pharisees (their name meaning "separated ones") were a lay movement promoting strict adherence to the written and oral Torah. Though a minority in the council, their voice carried great weight, often overruling the Sadducees, because of the favor the Pharisees had with the people (Josephus *Antiquities* 13.298; 18.17). Gamaliel urged cautious noninvolvement (5:35, 38-39). He referred to two contemporary examples of failed revolutionary movements: Theudas (4 BC, see note on 5:36-37) and Judas the Galilean (AD 6/7). The former had either claimed to be a prophet or was a messianic pretender. The latter upbraided his fellow countrymen for paying taxes to the Romans (Josephus *War* 2.118). He founded the Zealot movement, whose credo was reminiscent of Peter's words in 5:29. Josephus tells us, "They have a passion for liberty that is almost unconquerable, since they are convinced that God alone is their leader and master" (*Antiquities* 18.23). Gamaliel's negative estimate of the Christian movement comes across in the choice of failed movements as examples (the Maccabees had been a success). Luke heightens it with an ironic use of vocabulary, which elsewhere he applies to Jesus and his followers. Both Theudas and Judas "arise" (*anistēmi* [TG450, ZG482], NLT "there was"; 5:36; cf. 2:32; 3:22) and are killed (*anaireō* [TG337, ZG359], 2:23; 5:33, 36) or destroyed (*apoluō* [TG630, ZG668], Luke 13:33).

Gamaliel's counsel in 5:38-39 appears, on the surface, to be sound Pharisaic rabbinic thinking (*m. Avot* 4:11). He strongly advised, "Leave these men alone." Then he gave two options for the source of the conception of the Christian movement: man or God. Clearly, the reader knows that it was God's own design that brought the movement into being (4:8-12, 16).

Gamaliel's "wait and see" attitude was salubrious for the church because it put a brake on the Sadducees' misguided zeal. Still, for Luke, Gamaliel was an ironic, tragic figure. His noninvolvement was a rejection of the saving work of God. Holding out the possibility that this is "of God" was probably only a way to score points theologically against the Sadducees. The Sadducees believed only in human causation in history, while the Pharisees affirmed the work of both human beings and God (Josephus *Antiquities* 13.171-173; 18.12-15).

"The others accepted his advice" (5:40) and in the process completed the irony by continuing to "obey men rather than God" (see 5:29). They took the counsel of one who purported to guide them in discerning God's will. Calling the apostles back in, the council had them "flogged" (*derō* [TG1194, ZG1296], probably a scourging with a whip 39 times; *m. Makkot* 3:10-15; cf. Luke 22:63; Acts 16:37; 22:19), and they ordered them not to speak anymore in Jesus' name (cf. 4:17-18; 5:28). Then the council "let them go." Having the spiritual eyes to see what it meant to suffer for the name of Jesus, the apostles responded to their physical suffering with joy. As far as Luke is concerned, two things should bring Christians joy: contemplating salvation and the honor of being dishonored for Jesus' sake (Luke 10:20; Acts 8:39; 11:23; 13:48).

In a brief summary statement Luke tells us that in the Temple courts and in homes (2:46-47) the believers continued teaching and evangelizing daily with the message: "Jesus is the Messiah" (5:42). This central confession, a key point of debate among the Jews (17:3; 18:5), is the heart of the Good News. Salvation has been accomplished and is now being applied in Jesus, who is the Lord's Anointed One (2:38; 3:6).

◆　**0. Seven Men Chosen to Serve (6:1-7)**

But as the believers* rapidly multiplied, there were rumblings of discontent. The Greek-speaking believers complained about the Hebrew-speaking believers, saying that their widows were being discriminated against in the daily distribution of food.

²So the Twelve called a meeting of all the believers. They said, "We apostles should spend our time teaching the word of God, not running a food program. ³And so, brothers, select seven men who are well respected and are full of the Spirit and wisdom. We will give them this responsibility. ⁴Then we apostles can spend our time in prayer and teaching the word."

⁵Everyone liked this idea, and they chose the following: Stephen (a man full of faith and the Holy Spirit), Philip, Procorus, Nicanor, Timon, Parmenas, and Nicolas of Antioch (an earlier convert to the Jewish faith). ⁶These seven were presented to the apostles, who prayed for them as they laid their hands on them.

⁷So God's message continued to spread. The number of believers greatly increased in Jerusalem, and many of the Jewish priests were converted, too.

6:1 Greek *disciples;* also in 6:2, 7.

NOTES

6:1-7 *select seven men.* There is no final inconsistency between the seven being appointed to physical service and then engaging in Spirit-empowered preaching (contra Johnson 1992:111; cf. Stephen in 6:8, 10; 6:15-7:60; Philip, 8:5, 35). The apostles were not the only Spirit-filled preachers (Hill 1997:464-465; Acts 4:31). There is also precedent for combining physical and spiritual service in the Essene leader known as the "Guardian" or "Inspector" (CD 13:7-14:2; Capper 1995:354).

6:1 *Greek-speaking believers.* *Hellēnistēs* [TG1675, ZG1821] means "Greek speaker" (9:29; 11:20). The context determines the exact meaning (Reinbold 1998:98-99). Here it is Hellenistic Jewish Christians—Jerusalem residents who spoke primarily Greek—many of whom hailed from the Diaspora.

Hebrew-speaking believers. Gr. *Hebraios* [TG1445, ZG1578], meaning "Hebrew- or Aramaic-speaker." These were predominantly Palestinian Jewish Christians, who spoke only a Semitic language. It is doubtful they spoke Greek, though some could (Fiensey 1995:235). See Witherington 1998:240-247 for a complete discussion of the distinctions between these two elements of the Jerusalem church.

daily distribution. Although Capper (1995:356) is correct that this was probably closely tied to the daily meal fellowship (2:46; 5:42), his use of the Essene pattern to posit a two-tier approach to charity in the Jerusalem church skews the reconstruction of the church's practice. The initial "community of goods" probably covered both Greek-speaking and Aramaic-speaking segments and was a voluntary contribution from the sale of disposable wealth, not a compulsory surrendering of daily wages.

6:3 *seven.* The decision to appoint this number of men does not correspond to any political institution in Scripture or Josephus (Pearce 1995; contra Talbert 1997:465). It may have been chosen as a subset of "seventy" (elders; Num 11:16-25, Pearce 1995:483) or "twelve" (apostles; Thiessen 1996:328), or as a number appropriate to a subgroup within the whole church.

6:6 *These seven were presented to the apostles, who prayed for them as they laid their hands on them.* Lit., "whom they presented to the apostles. And as they prayed, they laid hands on them." Both D (which inserts *hoitines* [TG3748, ZG4015], "whoever, who") and the NLT imply that it was the apostles who prayed and laid their hands on the seven men, while the natural, though not totally unambiguous, reading is that the congregation did this (Barrett 1994:315).

COMMENTARY

As the apostles taught and evangelized (5:42), the multiplication of "believers" frayed the church's welfare program. Hellenistic ("Greek-speaking") Jewish Christian widows "were being discriminated against" (lit. "overlooked") in the daily food distribution (6:1). The church, from its very inception, was culturally diverse (2:5-11, 41). The Greek-speaking segment had previously congregated in its own synagogues (6:9) with their own communal or private welfare system for widows and orphans. Now they probably met in their own Greek-speaking house churches and were dependent on a centralized welfare system administered by Aramaic-speaking Jewish Christians, who discriminated against them. Although all first-century Jews in Palestine, no matter their language, faced the same strong Hellenizing influences, they often judged each others' responses to this threat to their shared Jewish identity. Exacerbated by language barriers, such concerns could and, in the Jerusalem church, did foster suspicion, distrust, prejudice, discrimination, and discord (contrast 2:44, 46; 4:32; 5:12).

"The Twelve called a meeting of all the believers" (6:2), and they pointed out another threat to the church's health. Until now, the apostles had administered the reception of welfare funds (4:35, 37; 5:1-2) but evidently had no direct involvement in dispersing them—that is, "running a food program." They declared that for them to do so would be to "abandon the word of God" (*kataleipsantas ton logon tou theou* [TG2641, ZG2901]; 6:2). While a holistic gospel values both kinds of service (Luke 7:11-17; Acts 9:36-42; cf. Luke 9:1-6, 10-17; 22:14-27), neither should be practiced to the exclusion of the other (cf. Luke 10:38-42). A division of labor may sometimes be necessary, as the apostles proposed.

Addressing the entire assembly as "brothers" (familial imagery stressing unity in spite of language and cultural differences), they called them to look around and select seven men. They were to be moral, "well respected" (10:22; 16:2; 22:12), spiritual ("full of the Holy Spirit"), and practical—to have the "wisdom" of knowing the right decisions to make. Meanwhile, the apostles would "spend their time" (lit. "be devoted to," 1:14; 2:42, 46) in "prayer and in preaching and teaching the word." The apostles' prayer ministry was exercised both in public leadership and in private, collective, and individual intercession. Prayer is central to the church's vitality and advancement (cf. Jesus' life and teaching, Luke 5:16; 6:12; 9:18, 28; 11:1; 22:41; see 18:1). "Teaching and preaching" (lit. "service of the word") are equally essential to the church's quantitative and qualitative growth.

The original proposal sought to agree with what pleases God (6:2); the final decision pleased "the whole group"—Greek-speaking and Aramaic-speaking Jewish Christians alike. They brought forward seven men, whose Greek names and spiritual qualities may indicate they were already exercising leadership among the Hellenistic Jewish Christians. Only Stephen, Philip, and possibly Nicolas are mentioned elsewhere in Scripture (6:9–7:60; 8:4-40; 21:8; Rev 2:15).

The assembly presented the seven to the Twelve, who confirmed their choice; but it was the assembly that, through the "laying on of hands," accompanied by prayer, showed their submission to and solidarity with these seven, commissioning them and asking God's blessing for them in their new task (cf. Num 27:18-23).

By doing the right thing in the right way, the church experienced the continued blessing of God: growth (6:7). As such, the word of God, the message of salvation, grew in ever widening circles. As the seed possesses the power of growth, so "the word has in itself the power of life. . . . This independent force of the word of God makes it the preeminent instrument of salvation" (Kodell 1974:506). Luke's combination of "grew" and "increased" (multiplied) echoes the Old Testament command, "Be fruitful and multiply," which was incorporated into covenant promises about the people of God (Lev 26:9; Jer 3:16; 23:3; cf. Gen 1:28; Exod 1:7). Even from among the priests there were converts. These converts probably came from the 2,000 rank-and-file members who resided in Jerusalem (Fiensy 1995:228) and were disaffected from the priestly Sadducean ruling hierarchy (Josephus *Antiquities* 20.181; *War* 2.409).

◆ II. The Jerusalem Church's Mission in Judea and Samaria (6:8-9:31)
A. Stephen Is Arrested (6:8-15)

⁸Stephen, a man full of God's grace and power, performed amazing miracles and signs among the people. ⁹But one day some men from the Synagogue of Freed Slaves, as it was called, started to debate with him. They were Jews from Cyrene, Alexandria,

Cilicia, and the province of Asia. ¹⁰None of them could stand against the wisdom and the Spirit with which Stephen spoke. ¹¹So they persuaded some men to lie about Stephen, saying, "We heard him blaspheme Moses, and even God." ¹²This roused the people, the elders, and the teachers of religious law. So they arrested Stephen and brought him before the high council.*

¹³The lying witnesses said, "This man is always speaking against the holy Temple and against the law of Moses. ¹⁴We have heard him say that this Jesus of Nazareth* will destroy the Temple and change the customs Moses handed down to us." ¹⁵At this point everyone in the high council stared at Stephen, because his face became as bright as an angel's.

6:12 Greek *Sanhedrin;* also in 6:15.   6:14 Or *Jesus the Nazarene.*

NOTES

6:9 *Synagogue of Freed Slaves . . . Jews from Cyrene, Alexandria, Cilicia, and the province of Asia.* The difficult syntax may point to one synagogue of five groups (Barrett 1994:323) or four groups (NLT; Polhill 1992:184), depending on whether "Freed Slaves" is a head term describing the synagogue or actually designates a particular group within it—possibly prisoners of war under Pompey taken to Rome and later freed (Tacitus *Annals* 2.85; Josephus *Antiquities* 17.300; Suetonius *Tiberius* 36; Philo *Embassy* 155). Or, more likely, given the repetition of the definite article *tōn* (*tōn ek tēs sunagōgēs . . . tōn apo Kilikias*), there were two synagogues, one of "Freed Slaves" from North Africa and one of Diaspora Jews from Asia Minor (Spencer 1997:68; cf. Talbert 1997:76; Johnson 1992:108). Riesner (1995) has effectively answered Kee's (most recently, 1997:37-39) contention that there were no organized synagogues or meeting places in first-century Palestine (positive evidence for synagogues in Jerusalem includes the "Theodotus inscription" [Lake and Cadbury 1979:67]; *t. Megilah* 3:6; *y. Megilah* 3:1 [73d]; *b. Megilah* 26a).

6:13 *lying witnesses.* Using Jesus' teaching and Stephen's speech, it is possible to sort out truth from error in their false claims (Dunn 1996:87; see Witherington 1998:257-259; contra Hill 1992:57-58). Jesus said the Temple would be destroyed, not that he would do it (Luke 21:6; John 2:19-22), and Stephen questioned not the legitimacy but the necessity of the Temple (7:48-50). Jesus declared divinely orchestrated changes in the law economy and in the law's proper interpretation and application (Matt 5–7; Luke 6:20-49; 16:14-18). Stephen pointed out that unbelieving Jews, not Christians, are the true lawbreakers (7:51-53; Blomberg 1998:403).

6:14 *customs.* In parallel with "Moses" (6:11) and "law" (6:13), "customs" refers to both the written and oral law in a way the Jewish law was usually explained to Gentiles (Hill 1992:63; Josephus *Antiquities* 14.213, 216, 223; 15.268; contra Johnson 1992:110).

COMMENTARY

Stephen embodies God's "ever outward" momentum in mission. He, a Greek-speaking Jewish Christian, bore witness to the gospel among Diaspora Jews who were resident in Jerusalem and met opposition and death. Yet, in the process, Stephen became a catalyst for the gospel to spread (via his Greek-speaking fellow believers) to Judea and Samaria, where it would reach the marginalized "half-breed" Samaritans and a God-fearing Ethiopian as well (ch 8).

We already know of God's hand on Stephen (6:3, 5), but now Luke portrays him, not unlike the apostles, as "full of God's grace and power," performing "amazing miracles and signs among the people" (6:8; cf. 2:43; 4:33; 5:12). This gracing, though expressly focused on miraculous deeds, probably included his Spirit-empowered preaching (6:9-10; cf. 14:26; 15:40; 20:32). In fulfillment of the Lord's promise, those of the synagogues of Diaspora Jews debated with Stephen but had no answer to his Spirit-inspired wisdom (7:55; Luke 12:12; 21:15; John 16:8-11).

Unsuccessful in debate, Stephen's opponents resorted to subterfuge. In an underhanded and fraudulent manner, they put some men up to making accusations. Luke labeled them "lying witnesses" (6:13). We read the charges three times (6:8, 11, 13-14). Each mention is more intense and more specific: Stephen "blaspheme[s] Moses, and even God . . . speak[s] against the holy Temple and against the law of Moses . . . say[s] that this Jesus of Nazareth will destroy the Temple and change the customs Moses handed down to us." Jesus had been accused of blasphemy for taking to himself divine prerogatives (Matt 26:65; Luke 5:21; John 10:30); now Stephen was accused along similar lines. He allegedly taught that in the future Jesus would exercise further divine prerogatives: destroy the Temple, the holy place where God said he would cause his name to dwell (Deut 12:5, 11; 2 Chr 6:18), and change God's inviolable, eternal law (cf. Dan 7:25; 1 Macc 1:49; contrast Exod 27:21; Lev 24:8; Num 15:15). Though Stephen's arguments conquered their minds, their wills remained unconquered, and they were not led to repentance and conversion.

Stephen's "Temple criticism" (6:11, 13), as recorded in 7:2-53, actually seems to be directed against the distorted perspective of zealous Jews, especially Diaspora Jews who had taken up residence in Jerusalem so they could take part in daily Temple worship. Their love of and pride in the Temple had eclipsed a true worship of God. They were so busy concentrating on what they were doing for God in worship that they failed to acknowledge God as the One who took the initiative in every generation of promise to speak, act, and save (7:2, 8-9, 17, 30, 34, 45-47). Stephen's alleged "criticism of the law" is not very evident, for he consistently treated the law positively in his sermon (7:38, 44, 53; see the note on 6:13 for more on the charges, especially as they relate to Jesus' teaching).

Stephen's Greek-speaking Jewish opponents stirred up the people (6:12). This is the first reported opposition of the common people to the Christian community (contrast 2:47; 4:21; 5:13, 26). They also aroused the "elders" (predominantly Sadducees, cf. 4:1) and "the teachers of religious law" (predominantly Pharisees, cf. 5:34; contrast 5:38-39). They violently came upon Stephen and snatched him away by force to the "high council," the Sanhedrin. A formal trial ensued, with the required hearing of multiple witnesses reporting what they had heard (m. Sanhedrin 7:5). But in Stephen's case these were "lying witnesses" (see note on 6:13).

Stephen was a wonder to behold. The council members could not take their eyes off him (6:15; cf. 1:10; 3:4, 12; 7:55). As with Moses and Jesus (Exod 34:29, 35; Luke 9:29), Stephen was in such communion with God and so full of the Spirit with wisdom, faith, grace, and power, that the glory of God shone from his face. There can be no doubt who was speaking through Stephen in the speech that followed.

◆   B. Stephen Addresses the Council and Is Martyred (7:1–8:1a)

Then the high priest asked Stephen, "Are these accusations true?" ²This was Stephen's reply: "Brothers and fathers, listen to me. Our glorious God appeared to our ancestor Abraham in Mesopotamia before he settled in Haran.* ³God told him, 'Leave your native land and your relatives, and come into the land that I will show you.'* ⁴So Abraham left the land of the Chaldeans and lived in Haran until his father died. Then God brought him here to the land where you now live.

⁵"But God gave him no inheritance here, not even one square foot of land. God did promise, however, that eventually the whole land would belong to Abraham and his descendants—even though he had no children yet. ⁶God also told him that his descendants would live in a foreign land, where they would be oppressed as slaves for 400 years. ⁷'But I will punish the nation that enslaves them,' God said, 'and in the end they will come out and worship me here in this place.'* ⁸God also gave Abraham the covenant of circumcision at that time. So when Abraham became the father of Isaac, he circumcised him on the eighth day. And the practice was continued when Isaac became the father of Jacob, and when Jacob became the father of the twelve patriarchs of the Israelite nation.

⁹"These patriarchs were jealous of their brother Joseph, and they sold him to be a slave in Egypt. But God was with him ¹⁰and rescued him from all his troubles. And God gave him favor before Pharaoh, king of Egypt. God also gave Joseph unusual wisdom, so that Pharaoh appointed him governor over all of Egypt and put him in charge of the palace.

¹¹"But a famine came upon Egypt and Canaan. There was great misery, and our ancestors ran out of food. ¹²Jacob heard that there was still grain in Egypt, so he sent his sons—our ancestors—to buy some. ¹³The second time they went, Joseph revealed his identity to his brothers,*

and they were introduced to Pharaoh. ¹⁴Then Joseph sent for his father, Jacob, and all his relatives to come to Egypt, seventy-five persons in all. ¹⁵So Jacob went to Egypt. He died there, as did our ancestors. ¹⁶Their bodies were taken to Shechem and buried in the tomb Abraham had bought for a certain price from Hamor's sons in Shechem.

¹⁷"As the time drew near when God would fulfill his promise to Abraham, the number of our people in Egypt greatly increased. ¹⁸But then a new king came to the throne of Egypt who knew nothing about Joseph. ¹⁹This king exploited our people and oppressed them, forcing parents to abandon their newborn babies so they would die.

²⁰"At that time Moses was born—a beautiful child in God's eyes. His parents cared for him at home for three months. ²¹When they had to abandon him, Pharaoh's daughter adopted him and raised him as her own son. ²²Moses was taught all the wisdom of the Egyptians, and he was powerful in both speech and action.

²³"One day when Moses was forty years old, he decided to visit his relatives, the people of Israel. ²⁴He saw an Egyptian mistreating an Israelite. So Moses came to the man's defense and avenged him, killing the Egyptian. ²⁵Moses assumed his fellow Israelites would realize that God had sent him to rescue them, but they didn't.

²⁶"The next day he visited them again and saw two men of Israel fighting. He tried to be a peacemaker. 'Men,' he said, 'you are brothers. Why are you fighting each other?' ²⁷But the man in the wrong pushed Moses aside. 'Who made you a ruler and judge over us?' he asked. ²⁸'Are you going to kill me as you killed that Egyptian yesterday?' ²⁹When Moses heard that, he fled the country and lived as a foreigner in the land of Midian. There his two sons were born.

³⁰"Forty years later, in the desert near Mount Sinai, an angel appeared to Moses in the flame of a burning bush. ³¹When Moses saw it, he was amazed at the sight. As he went to take a closer look, the voice of the LORD called out to him, ³²'I am the God of your ancestors—the God of Abraham, Isaac, and Jacob.' Moses shook with terror and did not dare to look.

³³"Then the LORD said to him, 'Take off your sandals, for you are standing on holy ground. ³⁴I have certainly seen the oppression of my people in Egypt. I have heard their groans and have come down to rescue them. Now go, for I am sending you back to Egypt.'*

³⁵"So God sent back the same man his people had previously rejected when they demanded, 'Who made you a ruler and judge over us?' Through the angel who appeared to him in the burning bush, God sent Moses to be their ruler and savior. ³⁶And by means of many wonders and miraculous signs, he led them out of Egypt, through the Red Sea, and through the wilderness for forty years.

³⁷"Moses himself told the people of Israel, 'God will raise up for you a Prophet like me from among your own people.'* ³⁸Moses was with our ancestors, the assembly of God's people in the wilderness, when the angel spoke to him at Mount Sinai. And there Moses received life-giving words to pass on to us.*

³⁹"But our ancestors refused to listen to Moses. They rejected him and wanted to return to Egypt. ⁴⁰They told Aaron, 'Make us some gods who can lead us, for we don't know what has become of this Moses, who brought us out of Egypt.' ⁴¹So they made an idol shaped like a calf, and they sacrificed to it and celebrated over this thing they had made. ⁴²Then God turned away from them and abandoned them to serve the stars of heaven as their gods! In the book of the prophets it is written,

'Was it to me you were bringing
    sacrifices and offerings
during those forty years in the
    wilderness, Israel?
⁴³No, you carried your pagan gods—
    the shrine of Molech,
    the star of your god Rephan,
    and the images you made to
        worship them.
So I will send you into exile
    as far away as Babylon.'*

⁴⁴"Our ancestors carried the Tabernacle* with them through the wilderness. It was constructed according to the plan God had shown to Moses. ⁴⁵Years later, when Joshua led our ancestors in battle against the nations that God drove out of this land, the Tabernacle was taken with them into their new territory. And it stayed there until the time of King David. ⁴⁶"David found favor with God and asked for the privilege of building a permanent Temple for the God of Jacob.* ⁴⁷But it was Solomon who actually built it. ⁴⁸However, the Most High doesn't live in temples made by human hands. As the prophet says,

⁴⁹'Heaven is my throne,
    and the earth is my footstool.
Could you build me a temple as good
        as that?'
    asks the LORD.
'Could you build me such a resting
        place?
⁵⁰   Didn't my hands make both heaven
        and earth?'*

⁵¹"You stubborn people! You are heathen* at heart and deaf to the truth. Must you forever resist the Holy Spirit? That's what your ancestors did, and so do you! ⁵²Name one prophet your ancestors didn't persecute! They even killed the ones who predicted the coming of the Righteous One—the Messiah whom you betrayed and murdered. ⁵³You deliberately disobeyed God's law, even though you received it from the hands of angels."

⁵⁴The Jewish leaders were infuriated by Stephen's accusation, and they shook their fists at him in rage.* ⁵⁵But Stephen,

full of the Holy Spirit, gazed steadily into heaven and saw the glory of God, and he saw Jesus standing in the place of honor at God's right hand. 56And he told them, "Look, I see the heavens opened and the Son of Man standing in the place of honor at God's right hand!"

57Then they put their hands over their ears and began shouting. They rushed at him 58and dragged him out of the city and began to stone him. His accusers took off their coats and laid them at the feet of a young man named Saul.* 59As they stoned him, Stephen prayed, "Lord Jesus, receive my spirit." 60He fell to his knees, shouting, "Lord, don't charge them with this sin!" And with that, he died.

CHAPTER 8

Saul was one of the witnesses, and he agreed completely with the killing of Stephen.

7:2 *Mesopotamia* was the region now called Iraq. *Haran* was a city in what is now called Syria.   7:3 Gen 12:1.
7:5-7 Gen 12:7; 15:13-14; Exod 3:12.   7:13 Other manuscripts read *Joseph was recognized by his brothers.*
7:31-34 Exod 3:5-10.   7:37 Deut 18:15.   7:38 Some manuscripts read *to you.*   7:42-43 Amos 5:25-27 (Greek version).   7:44 Greek *the tent of witness.*   7:46 Some manuscripts read *the house of Jacob.*   7:49-50 Isa 66:1-2.   7:51 Greek *uncircumcised.*   7:54 Greek *they were grinding their teeth against him.*   7:58 *Saul* is later called Paul; see 13:9.

NOTES

7:1-53 Stephen's speech, the longest in Acts, plays a role in the overall structure of Luke–Acts, as it presents "the ancestors and dates of settlement" portion of a history of a people, namely the people of God (cf. Dionysius of Halicarnassus *Roman Antiquities* 1.9-70; Balch 1990b:11-13). In the context of Acts, this speech functions as a history lesson and catalyst for a significant change in the direction of the church's mission: from Jerusalem (thrust out by persecution) to Samaria and the ends of the earth (compare similar selections in Herodotus *Persian Wars* 9.26-27; Thucydides 1.3.68-70; 2.6.35-47; Josephus *War* 5.376-419; note also biblical and Jewish retellings of Israel's history, especially as paraenetic historical review, Neh 9:5-37; Pss 78, 106; Ezek 20; Genesis Apocryphon; Jubilees; cf. Josephus *War* 5.376-419; Philo *Abraham, Moses;* Johnson 1992:120; Neudorfer 1998:281). In terms of rhetorical analysis, the speech is probably epideictic, a speech of blame or censure (Penner 1996:355), not a forensic defense (contra Witherington 1998:260). This explains why the charges are not dealt with directly.

7:2-3 *Haran.* The reference to a call in Mesopotamia, not Haran (using the wording of Gen 12:1), is not, in the final analysis, a discrepancy with the Genesis account (Gen 11:31; contra Johnson 1992:115; Barrett 1994:341). We need not view the problem as intractable (contra Neudorfer 1998:235) or conclude that OT evidence is conflated here (D. Williams 1985:118) or that Stephen relies on a variant Jewish tradition (Krodel 1986:140; Kistemaker 1990:239; cf. Josephus *Antiquities* 1.154; Philo *Abraham* 70-72). If we keep in mind the OT testimony to a divine call in Ur of the Chaldees (Gen 15:7; Neh 9:7) and the fact that the waw consecutive imperfect verb that introduces the quote in Gen 12:1 can be translated as a perfect with the pluperfect meaning, "had said," there is no difficulty with Stephen's statement.

7:4 *until his father died.* If Terah was 70 years old when Abraham was born (Gen 11:26) and Abraham was 75 when he left Haran for Canaan (Gen 12:4), and this occurred after Terah's death, we must conclude that Terah was 145 when he died. But Gen 11:32 says he was 205. How do we account for the 60 years? It is not necessary to see the discrepancy as due to Luke's dependence on a variant textual tradition (Polhill 1992:190; cf. Samaritan Pentateuch Gen 11:32; Philo *Migration* 177) or as an example of the simple sequential reading of the text (Litke 1996:159). Gleason Archer's (1983:378) solution overcomes the difficulty. If we take Abraham as Terah's youngest son, not as his eldest (though he is mentioned first because of his prominence in the narrative), it is possible to propose that he was born some time after Terah was 70, even 60 years later—that is, Terah turned 70 before fathering Nahor, later had Haran, and then finally, when he was 130, had Abram. This would account for the missing 60 years and harmonize the passages.

7:6 *400 years.* Was Israel in Egypt 400 or 430 years (Gen 15:13; Exod 12:40)? Either the same time period was reported in Scripture both as a round and as a more precise number (Kistemaker 1990:242), or the period was calculated in one case from the time of Isaac's birth and in the other from the giving of the promise (so the rabbis; see Strack and Billerbeck 1978:2.668-671).

7:7 *worship me here in this place.* Many see this phrase as taken from Exod 3:12 (e.g., Johnson 1992:116; Barrett 1994:345; Witherington 1998:266). The switch of referents from Mt. Horeb to Canaan has been explained as conflation or telescoping (Bruce 1988:134); as a reapplication of referent under the rubric "a promise of freedom to worship God" (Polhill 1992:190); or as an unproblematic transfer since Jews and Christians viewed worship at Horeb as a provisional arrangement (Larsson 1993:386). The phrase, however, may be inferred from the immediate context of Gen 15 (esp. v. 16; Marshall 1980:136). There is, then, no necessary allusion to Exod 3:12 here, though that verse and Stephen's words are "related in sense" (Archer and Chirichigno 1983:7).

7:12 *grain.* The TR (H P many minuscules) reads *sita* [TG4621, ZG4992] ("grain," pl. form), whereas 𝔓74 ℵ A B C D E read *sitia* [TG4618.1, ZG4989] ("food which is made from grain," pl. form), which occurs only here and in the LXX at Prov 30:22. Copyists have assimilated this rarely occurring word to the more common *sitos* [TG4621, ZG4992], "grain" (Metzger 1994:301-302).

sons—our ancestors. Stephen refers to the patriarchs as "our ancestors" in order to maintain a parallelism between their mistreatment of Joseph and his audience's rejection of Jesus and the Christian movement (cf. 7:52). For the sake of clarity, the NLT refers to them as "sons" of Jacob.

7:14 *seventy-five persons.* Did seventy (MT tradition Gen 46:27; Exod 1:5) or seventy-five (LXX tradition Gen 46:27; Exod 1:5, followed by Acts) go down to Egypt with Jacob (cf. Philo *Migration* 199-201, which uses both numbers)? As Archer explains it, both numbers can be taken as correct, depending on whether or not we count the descendants born to Joseph in Egypt as part of the family entourage (Archer and Chirichigno 1983:378-379).

7:16 *in Shechem.* Genesis 23:3-20 describes Abraham's purchase of the cave of Machpelah at Hebron for a burial site. Genesis 33:19 tells of Jacob's purchase at Shechem, where Joseph was later buried (Josh 24:32). Acts 7:16 says Abraham bought the property at Shechem. We need not conclude that Luke was confused or mistaken (Stott 1990:134; contra Johnson 1992:119; Neudorfer 1998:285-286) or that he has again conflated two accounts (contra Witherington 1998:268). Rather, a case can be made that Abraham purchased the site at Shechem originally (cf. Gen 12:6-7) and then forfeited his claim through his nomadic movements. Jacob then repurchased it in Genesis 33, just as Isaac had to do with wells (21:27-30; 26:26-32). Thus Archer concludes that, though the detail is not recorded in Genesis, Stephen was aware of a reliable oral tradition that said Abraham bought a tract of land at Shechem near the oak of Moreh, where he had built an altar when first entering the land (Archer and Chirichigno 1983:380).

The text at this point has four major variant readings: (1) *en Suchem* [TG4966, ZG5374] ("in Shechem") in ℵ* B C; (2) *tou Suchem* ("of Shechem") in 𝔓74 D 044 𝔐; (3) *tou en Suchem* ("of the one in Shechem") in ℵ² A E; (4) omitted in syrᵖ. The variants reflect two OT uses for "Shechem"—a person's name (if so here, it reverses the father-son relationship with Hamor), and a place-name. The place-name usage is the most satisfactory, has the best external evidence, and should be followed (Metzger 1994:301-302).

7:18 *a new king*. While this ruler is often identified as Ramses II (nineteenth dynasty, c. 1290–1223 BC; Bruce 1990:196), Archer understands the oppression as occurring over a number of dynasties starting in the later Hyksos period and extending to Thutmose I (c. 1600–1514 BC; Archer 1964:215-221).

***throne of Egypt*.** Lit., "over Egypt." NLT overcomes the possible redundancy with "in Egypt" (7:17) by this phrasing, just as a number of copyists representing a Western reading appear to have overcome it by omitting the phrase: 𝔓45^vid D E Old Latin syr^h (Metzger 1994:302-303).

7:20 *a beautiful child in God's eyes*. Gr., *asteios* [TG791, ZG842] *tō theō*. Though Witherington (1998:269) says this refers to character traits approved by God (cf. Kee 1997:319), Barrett (1994:353) is probably correct that the phrase indicates "an entirely satisfactory child without mental or physical handicaps" (Plutarch *Themistocles* 5.4 [114]).

7:22 *powerful in both speech and action*. Moses' protests in Exod 4:10 do not finally contradict this picture, for they are either Moses' self-interested self-deprecations with little basis in fact (Marshall 1980:140) or point to an early lack of eloquence that he overcame later (Bruce 1990:198). If Moses' protests have a modicum of truth to them, then, "mighty in . . . speech" may be limited to skillfulness in the written word (Polhill 1992:195).

7:30, 35 *angel*. Should we understand this as a reverent way of describing a theophany of the transcendent God (Bruce 1988:140; Marshall 1980:141) or a Christophany (Calvin 1965:190)? Barrett (1994:360) thinks not. It is better to see Stephen following the description of characters in the OT narrative, which presents an angel "who bears the presence and authority of God himself" (Kistemaker 1990:258; cf. Exod 3:2; 23:20-23).

7:38 *life-giving words*. The law is *logia zōnta* [TG3051/2198, ZG3359/2409] (living oracles) not in the sense of "life-giving" (contra NLT, Spencer 1997:96), but in the sense of being Israel's very life—oracles that determined their lives (Dunn 1996:95; Deut 30:19-20; 32:46-47).

7:42 *turned away*. Barrett (1994:368), like the NLT, takes *estrepsen* [TG4762, ZG5138] (turn) as intransitive, but Johnson (1992:131), seeing a close parallelism with the *paredōken* [TG3860, ZG4140] (gave them up) that follows, takes it as transitive: "He caused them to turn."

Was it to me you were bringing sacrifices . . . ? The LXX and the NT correctly understand that the question in Amos 5:25 expects a negative answer because idolatry had replaced the true worship of God in the wilderness (McComiskey 1985:316; contra Barrett 1994:369).

7:43 *shrine of Molech*. This LXX rendering is a legitimate pointing of the Heb. consonants *skkth mlk* as *sukkath* [TH5521, ZH6109], "booth of"; *molek* [TH4432, ZH4891], "Molech" (Archer and Chirichigno 1983:151). The phrase points to an accoutrement of false worship, which in the MT is in chiastic parallel with "Kaiwan (of) your images." The LXX rendering probably also reflects the Jewish practice of deliberately distorting the names of false gods "your king God" (cf. "king"; *melek* [TH4428, ZH4889]) reproduced as "Molech" (this is *melek*, but using the vowels of *bosheth* [TH1322, ZH1425], "shame") in disrespect and abhorrence of even taking the name of a false god on one's lips (cf. Lev 20:2-4; BDB 574).

***Rephan*.** Gr., *Rhaiphan* [TG4481A, ZG4818] renders the Heb. *kiyun* [TH3594A, ZH3962], probably from Assyrian *kaivanu*, meaning "Saturn" (BDB 475). Rephan is the Egyptian deity of the planet Saturn. Another way of understanding *kiyun* is as a common noun meaning "pedestal" (*kyn*). It would then be in parallel with "booth" of the previous line. This explanation of the derivation of the term is less likely since it destroys the chiastic construction and does not satisfactorily account for *kiyun* being the basis for a god's name in the LXX.

***as far away as Babylon*.** Stephen's substitution of "Babylon" for "Damascus" (Amos 5:27, MT and LXX) is not so much an accommodation to a postexilic audience located in Judah (contra Polhill 1992:201) as it is Luke's literary way of creating a balance between the exile into Mesopotamia (Babylon) with the call out of Mesopotamia (7:4; contra Richard 1982:42). Stephen made a dramatic jump in that he directly linked Israel's initial "golden calf" apostasy with the apostasy that spelled the end to Israel as a nation (Dunn 1996:96).

7:46 God of Jacob. Some mss read, "the house of Jacob" (see NLT mg). Internal evidence, especially preparation for 7:48, favors "God" (Johnson 1992:132). Indeed, the other reading seems not simply more difficult but, in the minds of some, nonsensical and therefore probably a primitive corruption (Longenecker 1981:347). Yet, transcriptionally, it is hard to see why a copyist would have substituted "house" for "God" (Larsson 1993:393). External evidence—major Alexandrian and Western witnesses, together with a similar thought in the Qumran literature (1QS 9:3-6)—persuades me to take the more difficult marginal reading, "house of Jacob," as the original (see Metzger 1994:308-309). The potential influence of Ps 132[131]:5 on the other reading should not be overlooked.

7:47-48 But . . . However. Gr., *de . . . alla* [TG1161/0235, ZG1254/0247]. Though many scholars still maintain that Stephen's speech embodies a radical criticism of the law and the Temple (Dunn 1996:97; Spencer 1997:78; Fernando 1998:261; cf. Barrett's 1994:373-374 nuanced approach), Larsson (1993) and Hill (1997) have convinced others that such a critique is not present (e.g., Brehm 1997; Witherington 1998:263). Stephen is positive toward the law (7:38, 53; Hill 1997:466), appeals to it throughout his narrative, and even indicts his accusers for not keeping it (7:53). He refers to David's desire to build being fulfilled in Solomon's action using an ascensive, not adversative *de* [TG1161, ZG1254] (meaning he says something in addition to the previous rather than in contrast to it), and gives no clear Temple criticism (7:46-47; Larsson 1993:390). In the strongly contrasting statement of 7:48, what the NLT has as "temples made by human hands" in the Gr. is simply *cheiropoiētois* [TG5499A, ZG5935], "things made by human hands." Luke lifts the discussion away from tent and Temple (house) to a more generic level (cf. 17:23, 29; 19:26, 37). Through his Isaiah quote, he refocused attention on the nature of God and how he is present in the world. From this come the implications for the way he is to be worshiped. As a result, we see his criticism is not of the Temple cult per se but of its abuse by the Temple hierarchy, who would define and control the nature and location of God's presence (Witherington 1998:274).

7:53 you received it from the hands of angels. Lit., "you received it at the direction of angels." The idea is that the angels are mediators, passing on God's directions that the law be handed on to Israel (BAGD 189; cf. Deut 33:2 LXX; Gal 3:19; Heb 2:2).

7:54 shook their fists at him in rage. Lit., "they were grinding their teeth against him" (see NLT mg). The NLT text rightly captures the significance of the action. In the OT, it is always an expression of hate coupled with a desire to destroy, usually by sinners against the righteous (Job 16:10; Pss 35:16; 37:12; 112:10; Lam 2:16 LXX; TDNT 1.641). The note "grinding their teeth" gives accurately the concrete action: a gobbling noise but without food (Barrett 1994:382).

7:55-56 Jesus standing . . . the Son of Man standing in the place of honor at God's right hand! The significance of "standing" versus "sitting" at God's right hand (cf. Ps 110:1) has been variously identified in terms of posture (see Barrett's [1994:384-385] comprehensive listing of eleven options and Talbert's [1997:79] collage of four connotations). Was Jesus standing to worship, as the angels do, or to welcome the martyr Stephen (Plevnik 1991:340)? Was he coming to Stephen in a personal parousia (Barrett 1994:385), serving as his advocate confessing his name before the Father (Bruce 1990:210; Luke 12:8), or affirming Stephen's witness and that of the early church (Spencer 1997:82)? Or was he acting as judge (Polhill 1992:208) or overseeing an interim salvation history before the church age, with its Gentile mission, truly dawns (Longenecker 1981:350)? Is this the conventional posture of figures appearing in biblical visions (Légasse 1990)? Given the crowd's reaction, the most important implication of Stephen's statement is probably a matter not of posture but of position (cf. 7:33; Richard 1978:295). Stephen was emphatically confessing Jesus' transcendent place in heaven.

7:58 *dragged him out of the city and began to stone him.* A formal trial turned into a lynching, leaving the legalities of the situation moot, either in terms of the Sanhedrin operating under a Roman military governor or their own procedures for capital punishment by stoning (*m. Sanhedrin* 6:1-6; Witherington 1998:276). Though the trial did not conclude in an orderly fashion, with the typical announcement of a verdict on the following day, the details present do support the conclusion that Stephen was executed for blasphemy (Dunn 1996:100; Lev 24:13-16; Deut 17:1-7). Stephen was thrust out of the city and experienced stoning as a form of execution (*lithoboleō* [TG3036, ZG3344]), as opposed to just a mob action of pelting with stones (*lithazō* [TG3034, ZG3342]; Barrett 1994:385 does not grant this distinction; see note at 5:26); witnesses were prominent in the execution.

at the feet of a young man named Saul. Given the designation "young man" and the menial duties traditionally assigned to those designated as such (5:6, 10), it is better to see Saul as "a valet to the stoning squad" (Spencer 1997:82) than as the leader in the opposition to Stephen (Johnson 1992:140). Saul could have been anywhere from 24 to 40 years old (Josephus *Antiquities* 18.197; Longenecker 1981:352).

COMMENTARY

The high priest, probably Caiaphas (active as high priest until AD 36; see 4:6), the Sanhedrin's presiding officer, asked Stephen whether the charges of blasphemy were true (7:1). As with other Christian defense speeches at court in Acts, Stephen's reply answered the charges only indirectly (cf. 5:29-32; 26:2-23). Rather, through a review of Israel's history, he gave positive witness (Luke 21:13) to a God who calls in promise and, in fulfillment, delivers and provides an inheritance; declares his will in the law and plans for worship; and makes his sovereign presence known (7:2-50). At the same time, Stephen outlined the ways Israel had always rejected its God-appointed deliverers, disobeyed God's law, and substituted idolatry for true worship. As Stephen applied this history to his own situation, the audience stood condemned of the same sins as evidenced by their mistreatment of Jesus the Messiah (7:51-53).

Stephen began respectfully ("Brothers and fathers," cf. 22:1) but with authority: "listen to me" (2:22; 3:22-23; Deut 18:15-16, 19). He begins with the facts that the sovereign "glorious God" (lit., "God of glory," 7:2; cf. Ps 29[28]:3) takes the initiative, appearing to Abraham and calling him. In contrast to his accusers' concern with a particular place and structure (6:13-14), Stephen declared that the glorious God's presence is not so confined. He can appear outside Palestine and apart from a tabernacle (Exod 40:34-38) or Temple (Ezek 43:5).

What Stephen stressed in Abraham's initial call is God's command of radical displacement: "Leave your native land and your relatives" (7:3; cf. Gen 12:1-3). This called for faith-filled obedience—a total dependence on God to supply what he promises. In fact, the only part of the Genesis 12 promise that Stephen repeats is "the land that I will show you." Its identity, and presumably its possession, would depend totally on God. Abraham obeyed this call in stages (Gen 11:31–12:6). First he traveled from Mesopotamia (southern region of modern Iraq, as NLT mg) to

Haran. Then, after his father died, he traveled from Haran, a flourishing city in the upper Euphrates valley at the intersection of important trade routes (located in modern Syria, as NLT mg), to Canaan. Stephen reports that Abraham obeyed but then emphasizes that it was God who resettled him in Palestine, "the land where you now live" (7:4). Stephen thereby reminded his accusers, Diaspora Hellenistic Jews resettled in Palestine (cf. 2:9), how similar their experience was to Abraham's. In this way he presented "displaced Abraham" as a model of faithful obedience and radical dependence on God.

Stephen deepened the sense of Abraham's dependence on God's covenant faithfulness by reporting that four hundred years would pass before Abraham's seed would be in the land of inheritance (Gen 15:13-14). During this time, the resident aliens would experience enslavement and mistreatment. Eventually, God would punish (lit. "judge") the enslaving nation and provide liberation so that Israel could "come out and worship [God] here in this place" (7:7). As worship had been the proper response to receiving the covenant promise (Gen 12:7; 13:18) so it would also be proper when Abraham's descendants received its fulfillment.

Stephen concluded his rehearsal of God's covenant promises to Abraham by announcing the outward covenant sign: circumcision (7:8). This part of the covenant also contained a transgenerational fulfillment quality, for it was to be applied to one's sons. Again, God's initiative and work are strongly implied. Stephen closely linked the sign, given before the child of promise was born (Gen 17:1-16; 21:1-5), with the birth that followed: "So when Abraham became the father of Isaac, he circumcised him on the eighth day" (7:8).

In 7:9-16, Stephen recounts the circumstances that lead to the fulfillment of the prophecy concerning the nation's sojourn in another country (7:6). In doing so, he employs the twin themes of Israel's rejection of God-ordained deliverers and God's faithfulness to accomplish his saving purposes.

In jealousy the patriarchs sold their brother Joseph as a slave into Egypt (Gen 37:11, 28). "But God was with him" (7:9; see Gen 39:2-3, 21, 23). God delivered Joseph from his anguish (*thlipsis* [TG2347, ZG2568], "affliction;" cf. Gen 42:21 LXX). God gave him "favor" and "wisdom" before Pharaoh, first manifested in the interpretation of dreams and then in civil administration (Gen 41:37-39; cf. 39:4). Pharaoh "appointed him governor over all of Egypt and put him in charge of the palace" (7:10; Gen 41:40-41). Then, when famine struck Canaan, as well as Egypt, Jacob and his family were on the point of starvation. The covenant promises were on the verge of dying out in the fourth and fifth generations, but the patriarchs gained relief by sending to Egypt for food (cf. Gen 41:54, 57; 42:2, 5). Not only did Joseph keep them alive, but on the second visit he also revealed himself to them (7:13; Gen 45:1-15). In a possibly foreboding detail, Stephen tells us that Joseph's "race" (*genos* [TG1085, ZG1169], "stock, family") became known to Pharaoh (cf. NLT's "they were introduced to Pharaoh" in 7:13; Gen 45:16).

Stephen concluded this portion of Israel's history with the note that Joseph sent for Jacob and the whole family, seventy-five souls, and so they settled in Egypt

(7:14; Gen 46:5-7). He tells us of the patriarchs' deaths (Exod 1:6) and of their burial in Shechem (Samaritan territory for Stephen's listeners) in Canaan. So God was accomplishing his purposes—both his eternal covenant with Abraham to build a great nation and his prophecy that there would be a sojourn in another country. Though trouble and separation from the Land of Promise seem to put the fulfillment of the promise even further away, the patriarchs had faith. Their final instructions were to have their bones buried in the land (cf. the patriarch's requests, Gen 47:30; 49:29; 50:25), and this their sons did in hope.

Stephen returned to his promise-and-fulfillment framework with the emphatic, dynamic time-marker: "As the time drew near when God would fulfill his promise to Abraham" (7:17). The promise personified is actively moving to fulfillment. At this time, the Hebrew nation experienced numerical increase—one of the blessings of the covenant (Gen 12:2; 17:2, 6; 35:11; 46:3; Exod 1:7)—until the time of a Pharaoh "who knew nothing about Joseph" (7:18; Exod 1:8). "Plotting against" them, he "harmed" the people, fulfilling what God had told Abraham (cf. 7:6; Exod 1:11). He sought to subdue the Hebrews through infanticide (*ektithēmi* [TG1620, ZG1758], a technical term for infanticide by exposure; cf. Philo *Moses* 1.12; Diodorus Siculus *Library of History* 2.4.3), applied to all male babies. Again, human circumstances threatened the fulfillment of God's covenant promise of descendants, generation after generation. God had miraculously opened barren Sarah's womb to guarantee conception. He had sent Joseph ahead to preserve, in the face of famine, the third through fifth generations. How would he counter population control through infanticide?

Stephen immediately gives us the answer: "At that time," in that season (*kairos* [TG2540, ZG2789]) of exposed newborns Moses was born, "a beautiful child in God's eyes" (7:20; Exod 2:2). And God sovereignly preserved him from an early death, for though he was "abandoned" ("exposed") after three months, Pharaoh's daughter "adopted him" (lit. "took him up"; *aneilato* [TG337A, ZG359], 7:21). This is the verb used in the LXX to explain the derivation of Moses' name: "I lifted him out of the water" (Exod 2:10). It is also a technical term for adopting a foundling (Papyri Oxyrhynchus 37.6; 38.6).

Pharaoh's daughter reared Moses as her own son (Exod 2:10). In line with ancient rhetorical biographical practice (cf. 22:2-3), we learn of Moses' birth, rearing, and finally education in "all the wisdom of the Egyptians" (7:22; cf. parallels in Jewish tradition, though not the OT: Philo *Moses* 1.21-24; Josephus *Antiquities* 2.236; Heb 11:25-26). Thus, he became "powerful in both speech and action" (7:22; cf. Jesus [Luke 24:19] and Apollos of Alexandria [Acts 18:24]). God again worked out his purposes in alien territory. He displayed his supreme sovereign power by using the daughter of Israel's oppressor to rescue the Hebrew baby boy who would grow up to lead God's people out from under that oppression.

Stephen, who had been dealing in centuries and generations of salvation history (7:6, 8, 15), suddenly focused on hinge events between the first third and second third of one man's life (for the division of Moses' life into equal thirds see rabbinic tradition, e.g., *Genesis Rabbah* 100.10). Paying such attention to Moses was entirely warranted since he is a type for Jesus, the prophet like Moses (3:22-23; 7:37). Stephen wanted his audience to see their own treatment of Jesus clearly mirrored in their ancestor's treatment of Moses.

Moses "decided to visit his relatives" (7:23; lit. "his brothers, the sons of Israel"—the nation, not just his extended family). Moses probably intended more than an inspection tour because the expression "to visit" (*episkeptomai* [TG1980, ZG2170]) in biblical parlance is to show concern and to bring aid (esp. of God to his people in distress, cf. Exod 3:16; 4:31; Luke 1:68; 7:16). Indeed, when he encountered injustice Moses defended an oppressed Jew and avenged him by slaying the Egyptian oppressor (Exod 2:11-12).

Stephen, moving outside the Exodus account, tells us Moses' thought about the legitimacy and significance of this act. It is linked to Moses' sense of calling—that God was going to give salvation to the people through Moses. Though the promise had been given in negative terms—"God said, 'I will punish the nation'"—there was an implied liberation in the declaration of Israel's subsequent departure: "They will come out" (7:6-7). Stephen made this explicit in the thinking of Moses. Moses "assumed" that his fellow countrymen would understand, but they did not—just as their first-century descendants would not understand the mission of Jesus, the "prophet like Moses" (Luke 2:50; 18:34, cf. Acts 3:17; 28:26-27; Mark 10:34).

This lack of understanding led to rejection (7:26-29; Exod 2:13-15). "The next day" Moses attempted to mediate between two Hebrews. He "tried to be a peacemaker" (lit. "reconcile them"), a characteristic of Jesus' ministry and the church's life (Luke 1:79; 2:14, 29; 19:42; Acts 9:31; 10:36; 15:33). But someone "pushed Moses aside" and rhetorically questioned the source of his authority and his motive—did he intend to murder him as he had done the Egyptian?

At this word Moses banished himself to Midian, a region east of Aqaba in northwest Arabia. He lived as a foreigner and had two sons. The name of one, Gershom (meaning "foreigner"), commemorates Moses' alien status (Exod 2:21-22). In many ways Acts 7:29 is the nadir of the time of promise. God had brought to Israel a savior, but Israel had not realized it and therefore rejected him. The deliverer was self-exiled as a common criminal, and Israel continued to face oppression under a genocidal Pharaoh.

But God would not be thwarted. He acted to fulfill his promise to Abraham at the hinge between the second and third portions of Moses' life, "forty years later" (7:30). Again, Stephen showed through fulfillment language that God had sovereignly marked off Moses' life into orderly periods (7:17, 23). As with Abraham (7:2), there was a supernatural appearance in a place outside the "Holy Land." "In the desert near Mount Sinai an angel appeared to Moses in the flame of a burning bush." Stephen called this a "vision" (7:31; NLT "the sight")—a supernatural sight experienced while one is awake or asleep (cf. 10:3, 19). Interestingly, the occurrence of visions in Acts consistently deals with guidance for those carrying on God's mission of salvation through their witness (9:11-12; 10:3, 17, 19; 11:5; 16:9-10; 18:9).

And here, the "vision" with the accompanying commission (7:31-32, 34) would send Moses to accomplish God's salvation for his people.

The vision so attracted Moses' attention that he marveled and approached it to make careful observation. As he did this, "the voice of the LORD" came to him declaring his divine presence and identity: "I am the God of your ancestors—the God of Abraham, Isaac, and Jacob"—the covenant-making and covenant-keeping God of generations (7:2, 8). Immediately Moses understood that he was standing in the palpable presence of God. Moses shook with terror, not daring to look (Exod 3:6; cf. Exod 19:21; 33:20-23; Heb 12:21). God's immediate command and rationale showed Moses that it was a transcendently holy yet approachable God in whose presence he stood (7:33). Sandals are notorious for having dust clinging to them, which inevitably would be the dust of ritually unclean places (*m. Berakhot* 9:5). Since to stand in God's very presence sanctifies the place where one stands as "holy ground," one's sandals must be shed. By calling this patch of ground outside the Holy Land, "holy ground," God once again relativized the Jewish claim to the Temple as the one and only "holy place" (6:13). Wherever God chooses to make his presence known is a "holy place."

Israel's trials were not only part of God's foreknowledge; they were also part of his conscious oversight, which necessarily led to action (Exod 3:7-8). He had seen the "misery" of his people; he had heard their groans. And when he heard their groans, he remembered his covenant and came down to rescue his people through Moses.

As Stephen makes the transition from the "promise" and "groundwork for fulfillment" portions of salvation history (7:1-8, 9-34) to God's implementation of fulfillment (7:35-50), his style and his focus change perceptibly. The theme present in the previous sections: Israel's jealous and malicious rejection of God's deliverers (7:9, 26-28) becomes predominant. Staccato-like syntax, such as the demonstrative "this" referring to Moses five times, punctuates Acts 7:35-38 (cf. NASB) in a reverse parallelism that places Moses' redeemer and lawgiver roles (miraculously carried out) within the context of Israel's initial rejection of his leadership and their initial apostasy with the golden calf (7:35-41). Indeed, the whole history of Israel's worship practice from wilderness to final Babylonian exile stands under the ringing indictment of the prophet Amos (Amos 5:25-27) and rises through Isaiah's "Temple critique" (7:48-50; Isa 66:1-2) to a final judgment of the present audience along with their ancestors (7:51-53).

Stephen reminded his audience of Israel's rejection of Moses's leadership on his first visit (Exod 2:14; cf. Acts 7:27-28). But he immediately proceeded from a divine and human perspective to affirm Moses's work of deliverance (Acts 7:35-36). God had sent him to act as ruler and savior (*lutrōtēs* [TG3086, ZG3392], "redeemer") in association with the work of the angel. Through them, God would "judge" Egypt, the oppressor nation. An enslaved people would be able to "come out" and worship God in the inherited land (7:7). As Exodus 6:6 (LXX) relates: "I will redeem you with my exalted arm and great judgment." From the human perspective "this" Moses would have a forty-year career (the final third of his life, cf. Acts 7:23, 30) of leading the people out with signs and wonders in Egypt, through the Red Sea, and in the wilderness (Exod 7–11; 14:21; Num 14:22). Stephen's characterization of Moses as one rejected by men but accepted and used by God to accomplish his saving purposes coincides with the pattern of expression and vocabulary concerning the Messiah, Jesus (3:15-16; 5:30-31).

Stephen made a direct connection between Moses and the Messiah by quoting the "prophet like Moses" prophecy (7:37; cf. Deut 18:15 and Acts 3:22-23). The main parallel Stephen drew between Jesus and Moses was Israel's mistreatment and rejection of him (7:23-29, 39, 51-53). This is a powerful argument for Jesus' messianic claims and strengthens the warning to the leaders to turn from their sin.

Moses's work as mediator of God's deliverance was matched by his work as mediator of the law (7:38). He was with the "assembly of God's people" (*ekklēsia* [TG1577, ZG1711], often rendered "church" in English translations of the NT). This probably points to the "day of assembly" when the people gathered to receive the law (Deut 4:10; 9:10; 18:16). Stephen heightened the importance of the law and in the process showed that accusations against him about blasphemy of the law were false (6:11, 13). Twice he declared that the law came through the mediation of angels (7:38, 53)—thereby pointing to its heavenly origin (see note on 7:53). Here he also called them "life-giving words," the very life of the people of God (see note on 7:38).

Though Moses was the mediator of the law from God through angels to the people, Stephen pointed out their rebellion in idolatrous apostasy. The people "rejected" Moses (lit., "did not want to obey and shoved away from themselves," 7:39). In their hearts they returned to Egypt (Exod 13:17). They re-embraced the pagan worldview, calling on Aaron their priest to construct idols who would lead them (Exod 32:1, 23). They determined to operate only "by sight." To them "this Moses," absent on the mountain hearing from God, was just a man who led them out of Egypt and had now disappeared. But it was truly God who had become totally absent from their thoughts (contrast 7:34, 36). So with gusto they fashioned a golden calf, sacrificed to it, and rejoiced in "what they had made" (lit., "the works of their hands," 7:41; cf. Acts 7:48; 17:24-25, 29; Exod 32:4-6). Such festive celebration should be reserved for God alone (Lev 23:40; Deut 12:7, 18). Rejection of God's deliverer will lead to disobedience of his law, which will lead to false worship. Could it be that just as Israel in the wilderness in the absence of Moses embraced idolatry, so now their children, in the physical absence of Jesus, "the prophet like Moses" (at present, ascended and sitting at God's right hand), had also lapsed into idolatry of the Temple "made with hands"? Were they, like their ancestors, refusing to obey God's Spirit-empowered word through his messengers while accusing them of blasphemy against their God, law, and holy place?

For the first time since his report of Moses' commissioning (7:35), Stephen presented God taking direct action, but now in judgment (7:42-43). Whereas the covenant promise was that his people would worship him in the Land of Promise, God turned away from them and gave them up to the consequences of their apostasy (cf.

Rom 1:24, 26): to serve as gods the "host of heaven" (*stratia tou ouranou* [TG4756/3772, ZG5131/4041]). The Pentateuch and the prophets agree that Israel practiced idolatry, even star worship, in the wilderness (Lev 18:21; 20:2-5; Deut 4:19; Ezek 20:10-26; Hos 9:10). By using Amos's eighth-century indictment with its mid-second-millennium wilderness-wanderings reference, and by identifying the final judgment as the Babylonian exile, Stephen wrote *idolatry* over the entire course of the nation's worship life (2 Chr 36:16-18). A shrine to Molech, who among the Ammonites was known as Venus's star, and images of Rephan (see note on 7:43) were the worship accoutrements of the nation, which at the same time was being led by Moses with signs and wonders for forty years. And all this while God had provided the accoutrements for true worship among them: "the Tabernacle," (lit., "tent of witness"; 7:44 NLT mg). This contained the Ark of Testimony, a box holding stone copies of the Ten Commandments (Exod 25:10, 16, 21-22; 31:7). In fact, it was during the very time when Moses was receiving instructions about these items on the mountain that Israel made the golden calf (Exod 24:18–27:21; 32–33). Stephen made sure we couldn't miss the irony as he used Amos's idolatry vocabulary, speaking of the "shrine" (*skēnē* [TG4633, ZG5008]) of Molech and the "images" (*tupos* [TG5179, ZG5596]) for the "Tabernacle" (*skēnē*), constructed according to the "plan" (*tupos*) God showed Moses (Exod 25:9, 40).

Stephen traced God's initiative and saving work in yet another generation when he spoke of Joshua and the conquest generation having received the Tabernacle in turn and bringing it into the land (7:45; cf. Josh 18:1). They were able to do this because "God drove out" the Gentiles. The promise of Abraham's descendants worshipping in the land (7:7) finally came true and continued down to the days of David.

Like Joseph and Moses, David found favor with God (2 Sam 7:3, 8-9), and he asked for the "privilege of building a permanent Temple for the house of Jacob" (7:46 NLT mg; see note on 7:46). Although "permanent Temple" represents David's intentions as 2 Samuel and 1 Chronicles relate them (2 Sam 7:2-16; 1 Chr 17:1-14), Stephen used a more general term: *skēnōma* [TG4638, ZG5013], "dwelling place" (cf. Ps 132[131]:5). This term, along with the fact that David finds favor with God and that the building is for the "house of Jacob" as a worship center (Pss 23:6; 27:4; 52:8), shows that Stephen approved of David's initiative. Still, to directly grant the request would have violated God's covenant dynamic, in which he sovereignly takes initiative and does the essential work of making a way for his people to approach and worship him. So, in the original Old Testament narrative, God denied David's request and replaced it with two promises: He would establish David's dynasty, and David's son would build a house for God's name (2 Sam 7:11-16). Stephen also indicates the change of initiative: "But it was Solomon who actually built it" (7:47).

But lest even this work be misunderstood as an idolatrous "doing for God," Stephen climaxed his discourse with a strongly contrasting word, a thundering, Old Testament prophetic word (7:48-50; see note on 7:47-48) that focuses on the nature of God and what that means for our worship of him. When Stephen makes the generic statement that the Most High doesn't dwell in "things made with human hands" (*cheiropoiētois* [TG5499A, ZG5935]), he employs a word that was usually applied to idols and idol worship (Lev 26:1, 30; Isa 2:18; 10:11; 31:7; Dan 5:4, 23). To infer this of, or actually apply it to, the Temple would certainly have jolted, if not enraged, his listeners.

Stephen's thinking, however, was quite biblical, as the subsequent Old Testament quote shows (Isa 66:1-2; cf. 1 Kgs 8:27). God is not only transcendent, the "Most High" (cf. Luke 2:14; 19:38), he is "immense." He so fills heaven and earth that figuratively heaven is his throne and the whole earth is but his footstool. God asks, "Could you build me a temple as good as that?" (lit., "What kind of house will you build for me?"). It is impossible, given who God is in relation to his creation, for any of his creatures to construct an edifice that could shelter, let alone confine him. And since God is Creator of all, it is nonsense for his creatures to think they could meet any of his needs, like providing a "resting place" for him (17:24-25). Stephen, however, did not balance these negative statements with a positive one, so that we could know what replaces the Temple. God's transcendence, his reign in heaven above, as Stephen will shortly see and testify to, must be the controlling perspective for any proper use of a house of worship (7:55-56; 1 Kgs 8:17-20, 27-53; see Sylva 1987:261-275).

Stephen effectively answered the second charge against him—that he spoke blasphemy against "God" and "the holy Temple" (6:11, 13). In so doing, he identified the real blasphemers as anyone who so venerated the Temple that it ceased to be a place where the transcendent God was glorified and instead became a place where self-glorying men took pride in what they had done "for God."

Stephen then declared his audience's guilt in continuity with Israel's guilt historically (7:51-53). He began with their will, moved to the heart and mind, and concluded with their behavior. The people were "stubborn" (lit. "stiff-necked," refusing to bow to God's authority; cf. Exod 33:3, 5; 34:9—all in the context of their idolatrous worship of the golden calf, Acts 7:39-41). They were "heathen at heart and deaf to the truth" (lit. "uncircumcised in heart and ears"). Though they were physically circumcised, outwardly loyal to their ethnic-religious heritage, their hearts' values, affections, and purposes were no different from an uncircumcised heathen's (Lev 26:41; Jer 9:26). Their ears were indeed "deaf to the truth," as though they were covered with uncircumcised foreskin (Jer 6:10), and this unrepentant, unregenerate condition manifested itself in consistent resistance to the Holy Spirit (cf. Isa 63:9-10). They resisted God's Spirit-anointed messengers, Jesus and his followers, as the ancestors had done with Moses.

Israel had always acted out this resistance through persecution of the prophets (2 Chr 36:16; Luke 6:23; 11:49; 13:34) and even the assassination of those who "predicted the coming of the Righteous One—the Messiah" (7:52; see 3:14). The generation Stephen addressed had finished the job: betraying and murdering the Messiah himself (Luke 9:44; 18:32; 22:4, 6; 24:7; Acts 3:14). They stood condemned of the very charges they leveled at Stephen. By doing away with the Lord's Anointed, God's one provision for salvation, they showed themselves to be truly against God and his presence. They were also against Moses' law, altering its authority through selective obedience (Exod 20:13, 16). In fact, they kept their manmade traditions, "customs Moses handed down to us," (6:14) intact, even if it meant violating the plain command of the law (Matt 15:3-6). Yes, they received the law at the direction of angels (cf. 7:38), yet they had not kept this divinely given standard.

Stephen's indictment so penetrated their uncircumcised hearts that the Jewish leaders "were infuriated" (lit. "sawn through in their hearts," cf. 5:33) and reacted with blood-curdling hostility against the messenger (7:54; see note). In stark contrast, Stephen was "full of the Spirit," so totally yielded to the Spirit's control (cf. 6:5, 8, 15) that he received a prophet's vision, gazing directly into heaven (7:55; atenizō [TG816, ZG867], "gaze," is consistently used for viewing a supernatural sight, 1:10; 3:4, 12; 6:15). He saw "the glory of God" (either a circumlocution for God the Father or the shekinah glory that both conceals and reveals the divine presence, cf. 7:2; 22:11) and Jesus. Here was stunning proof of Stephen's contention: God dwells in heaven, not in temples made with hands (7:48-50).

Stephen declared that he saw "the heavens opened and the Son of Man standing in the place of honor at God's right hand!" (7:56). "Son of Man," a phrase otherwise present primarily on the lips of Jesus during his earthly ministry, could refer to Jesus in his incarnation, saving death and resurrection, heavenly exaltation, universal dominion, or glorious future reign (Ps 110:1; Dan 7:13; Matt 8:20; Luke 9:22, 44; 18:31; 19:10; 21:27, 36; 22:69). Here, with the Daniel 7 background most prominent and with Stephen's prayer, committing his spirit to God in death and requesting Jesus' forgiveness of others (7:59-60), the divine nature of the figure is most clearly in view. By this confession, Stephen and Luke invite us to see Jesus for who he really is and in that vision to recognize him as worthy of worship, complete devotion, and obedience even to death.

To the Sanhedrin, Stephen's announcement that Jesus was at God's right hand was blasphemy (Luke 22:66-71), which their shouts must drown out and their hands must prevent from entering their ears (so rabbinic practice, b. Ketubim 5a). Like a herd of stampeding animals (cf. Luke 8:33), yet intent on one purpose, they rushed together against Stephen, dragged him out of the city, and began to stone him (7:57-58; see note on 7:58). With a deft touch in his reference to the "valet of the execution squad," Luke introduces us to "a young man named Saul," who will figure prominently in Luke's account of the church's advance in the near and long term (8:3; chs 9, 13–28).

Jewish custom, which was probably not followed in this lynch-mob atmosphere, prescribed that the condemned be given an opportunity to confess his sins on his way to execution so that he might have "a share in the world to come" (m. Sanhedrin 6:2). Stephen's declarations revealed his innocence and his Christian grace to those who had wronged him. In prayer he called on Jesus to take him into his presence at death (cf. 2:21). He echoed his Lord's words of confident trust on the cross but prayed them to him (cf. Luke 23:34, 46). Whether falling under the weight of the stoning or deliberately kneeling in prayer, Stephen cried out with a loud voice, asking that Jesus not count this sin of his executioners (Rom 10:3; cf. Luke 23:34). How could this happen? If they repented and received the Good News (Luke 24:47; Acts 2:38; 3:19; 5:31; 10:43), then their sins would be forgiven and they would not have to face the final punishment for a sin standing against them. We know of one person for whom this prayer was answered: Paul, who was a witness of Stephen's death and completely agreed with it.

◆ C. Persecution Scatters the Believers (8:1b-3)

A great wave of persecution began that day, sweeping over the church in Jerusalem; and all the believers except the apostles were scattered through the regions of Judea and Samaria. ²(Some devout men came and buried Stephen with great mourning.) ³But Saul was going everywhere to destroy the church. He went from house to house, dragging out both men and women to throw them into prison.

NOTES

8:1b *all the believers except the apostles.* While Greek-speaking Jewish Christians, compatriots of Stephen, were probably targeted first for persecution (Witherington 1998:278), the note "except the apostles" does not necessarily indicate that Hebrew-speaking Christians were exempt because they did not share the Hellenistic Jewish Christians' radical anti-law and anti-Temple views (contra Polhill 1992:211). Rather, the apostles were being good pastors by staying with the threatened flock (Barrett 1994:391). Furthermore, their standing in the Jewish community as powerful miracle workers may have insulated them from attack (Witherington 1998:278; cf. 2:43; 4:21; 5:26).

COMMENTARY

In the wake of Stephen's martyrdom, the Jerusalem church experienced a "great wave of persecution," which was the context and catalyst for God to make a great advance in mission. Previously leaders had been targeted (4:1; 5:17), but now the whole church received the brunt of persecution (8:1b). This is pictured as a ferocious attempt at devastation (8:3, *lumainomai* [TG3075, ZG3381], Ps 79:14 LXX; cf. 2 Chr 16:10). Saul violated house church precincts, violently dragging out both men and women to throw them into jail (cf. 14:19), even as Jesus warned (Luke 21:12-19).

In spite of the adversity, God's mission advanced. For as the believers were scattered abroad (*diaspeirō* [TG1289, ZG1401], "were scattered, dispersed"), they began evangelizing (8:4; cf. Luke 8:5-8, 11) and in so doing entered the second theater of the Great Commission's fulfillment: Judea and Samaria (1:8). The apostles' continuing presence in Jerusalem provided a stable "center." Stephen's proper burial with public mourning from godly people, probably not yet believers (cf. Luke 2:25; Acts 2:5; 22:12), indicated that God was still at work in the "center."

◆ D. Philip Preaches in Samaria (8:4-25)

4But the believers who were scattered preached the Good News about Jesus wherever they went. 5Philip, for example, went to the city of Samaria and told the people there about the Messiah. 6Crowds listened intently to Philip because they were eager to hear his message and see the miraculous signs he did. 7Many evil* spirits were cast out, screaming as they left their victims. And many who had been paralyzed or lame were healed. 8So there was great joy in that city.

9A man named Simon had been a sorcerer there for many years, amazing the people of Samaria and claiming to be someone great. 10Everyone, from the least to the greatest, often spoke of him as "the Great One—the Power of God." 11They listened closely to him because for a long time he had astounded them with his magic.

12But now the people believed Philip's message of Good News concerning the Kingdom of God and the name of Jesus Christ. As a result, many men and women were baptized. 13Then Simon himself believed and was baptized. He began following Philip wherever he went, and he was amazed by the signs and great miracles Philip performed.

14When the apostles in Jerusalem heard that the people of Samaria had accepted God's message, they sent Peter and John there. 15As soon as they arrived, they prayed for these new believers to receive the Holy Spirit. 16The Holy Spirit had not yet come upon any of them, for they had only been baptized in the name of the Lord Jesus. 17Then Peter and John laid their hands upon these believers, and they received the Holy Spirit.

18When Simon saw that the Spirit was given when the apostles laid their hands on people, he offered them money to buy this power. 19"Let me have this power, too," he exclaimed, "so that when I lay my hands on people, they will receive the Holy Spirit!"

20But Peter replied, "May your money be destroyed with you for thinking God's gift can be bought! 21You can have no part in this, for your heart is not right with God. 22Repent of your wickedness and pray to the Lord. Perhaps he will forgive your evil thoughts, 23for I can see that you are full of bitter jealousy and are held captive by sin."

24"Pray to the Lord for me," Simon exclaimed, "that these terrible things you've said won't happen to me!"

25After testifying and preaching the word of the Lord in Samaria, Peter and John returned to Jerusalem. And they stopped in many Samaritan villages along the way to preach the Good News.

8:7 Greek *unclean.*

NOTES

8:5 *the city of Samaria.* The external evidence is strong for the presence of the definite article: 𝔓74 ℵ A B 69 181 460* 1175 1898. Yet an anarthrous phrase: "a city of Samaria" is the more natural antecedent to v. 8: "that city." Luke's consistent use of "Samaria" to denote a region and the anarthrous *polin* [TG4172, ZG4484] "a city," as opposed to *tēn polin,* "the city" (i.e., the main city), render the phrase "a city of Samaria" imprecise. A number of cities could be meant: the governmental center, previously called *Samaria* but renamed *Sebaste* by Herod the Great (Talbert [1997:84] accepting the reading with the definite article); the Samaritans' religious center, Neapolis (Nablus); the ancient Shechem (Bruce 1988:165); or Gitta, Simon Magus's home (according to Justin Martyr [*Apology* 1.26], who himself hailed from the region).

8:9 *Simon.* Simon the sorcerer is probably identical with the alleged founder of a Gnostic heresy, the Simonians (*Acts of Peter* 4–32; Justin Martyr *Apology* 1.26; *Dialogue with Trypho* 120.6; Pseudo-Clement *Homilies* 2.22-24; Irenaeus *Against Heresies* 1.23; Hippolytus

Refutation of All Heresies 6.2, 4-15; R. Wilson 1979), but Maynard-Reid (1997:1077) strongly doubts this identification. Some see Simon as a genuine pre-Christian teacher of Gnosticism (e.g., Lüdemann 1987). Others see him as a representative of Samaritan Christian heterodoxy (von Dobbeler 1996:20-21, following Berger 1995). But most see Simon as a magician, not a Gnostic, who was later co-opted by the Simonians in order to root their views in the NT (Polhill 1992:215; cf. Johnson 1992:146; Barrett 1994:405).

8:10 *the Great One—the Power of God.* Lit., "This is the power of God, the (power) that is called 'Great.'" The awkward *kaloumenē* [TG2564, ZG2813], "called," is omitted by the later Byzantine text (cf. NKJV, "This man is the great power of God") or replaced by *legomenē* [TG3004, ZG3306] in a number of minuscules (Metzger 1994:313-314). The confession may be read as an explicit claim to deity, though Barrett (1994:40) thinks not. "The Power" or "the Powerful One" is a favorite rendering of the tetragrammaton in the Samaritan Targum traditions (Witherington 1998:284). More likely, it confesses Simon to be a subordinate supernatural being, "The Great Power" (cf. inscriptional evidence from Lydia and Samaria in Horsley 1983:22; 1981:105-107; cf. D. Smith [1996:145-151]; Origen *Against Celsus* 6.11; 7.9; *Clementine Recognitions* 1.54).

8:16 *The Holy Spirit had not yet come.* The Spirit's postponed arrival to these baptized Samaritans does not support the classic Pentecostal and charismatic view that the gift of the Spirit is a *donum superadditum* empowerment for witness subsequent to conversion, since the "not yet . . . had only" in this explanatory note implies that the normal expectation was that baptism and the Spirit would be closely connected (Turner 1998:338). In fact, Acts contains no one pattern for the order of occurrence of conversion, baptism, and coming of the Spirit in conversion-initiation that could be used to validate any particular human scheme, whether confirmationist, sacramental, or charismatic (2:38; 8:16-17; 10:44-48; 19:6; Polhill 1992:218). While v. 16 assumes a close relationship between baptism and the coming of the Spirit, and hence would tend to support the sacramental approach (cf. Das 1993), still the Lukan presentation of the Spirit's coming as an answer to prayer and totally under God's control is incongruent with this view (Witherington 1998:288). Interpreting the passage via the normative conversion—initiation understandings of Dunn and the Reformed tradition (i.e., the Spirit regenerates at conversion), requires accounting for the delay in the Spirit's arrival as either an indication that the Samaritans had a deficient faith (Dunn 1970:63-68) or that they silently received the Spirit at regeneration with an outward manifestation later (Kistemaker 1990:301). Both of these understandings do not let the anomaly of the passage stand. One labels the Samaritans with a false faith when Luke does not; and the other assumes a coming of the Spirit that v. 16 does not seem to allow for.

It is more satisfactory to see the conversion of the Samaritans as a process over time and to explain the delay in the Spirit's coming as appropriate for a benchmark event in salvation history; the Spirit's manifestation at the initial salvation of a non-Jewish people and the overcoming of the historic enmity between Jew and Samaritan was delayed until the Jerusalem apostles came to validate Philip's mission (Dunn 1996:111).

8:17 *laid their hands upon.* This was not a transfer of power (as Johnson 1992:107) or a universal gesture of blessing (as Barrett 1994:412) but a show of solidarity and fellowship as the apostles fulfilled their purpose in coming: to validate that this new movement did authentically flow from Jesus himself (Dunn 1996:111; Spencer 1997:88; cf. Barrett 1994:409).

8:21 *no part in this.* Lit., "(no) part or portion in this matter" (*meris oude klēros en tō logō toutō*). The expression *tō logō toutō* ("this matter") refers not to "ministry" (as Witherington 1998:286 pointing to Luke's use of *klēros* [TG2819, ZG3102] in Acts 1:26) but to salvation (Polhill 1992:220; Fernando 1998:274; cf. Deut 12:12; 14:27). Bruce (1990:222) suggests we see here the Jewish concept of "portion in the age to come" (*m. Sanhedrin* 10:1-4).

8:23 *full of bitter jealousy*. This phrase does not point to either Simon's evil effect in the church (as Williams 1985:143) or a bitter attitude (as Kistemaker 1990:306). Rather, the phrase *cholēn pikrias*, [TG5521/4088, ZG5958/4394] (bitter poison), refers to his unregenerate condition manifested by his animistic proposal (cf. Deut 29:17 LXX; Barrett 1994:416).

8:24 *Pray to the Lord for me*. D adds *hos polla klaiōn ou dielimpanen*, "who did not stop weeping copiously," which suggests, according to Metzger (1994:314), "tears of remorse and perhaps of repentance." Polhill (1992:220), based on the request for prayer from others and the fear of judgment, argues for remorse. Johnson (1992:153) and Barrett (1994:417) more charitably argue for repentance. In the Clementine literature, Simon's tears are tears of rage and disappointment (*Clementine Homilies* 20.21; *Clementine Recognitions* 10.63).

C O M M E N T A R Y

As the believers scattered, they preached "the Good News about Jesus." As Philip carried out his mission to Samaria, we see the way God's Kingdom advanced in a religious environment dominated by the forces of evil. It is the preaching of the word, accompanied by God's signs, that conquers self-assertive and self-serving occult magic (8:5-8, 13). The gift of the Spirit, which God's apostles refused to equate with magical power, marked the advance (8:18-23).

The Samaritans' syncretism and mixed race (2 Kgs 17:24-41), together with the reciprocal reprisals against their respective worship centers in intertestamental times (Josephus *Antiquities* 13.255-58; 18.29), so heightened the prejudice and animosity between Jew and Samaritan, that the best that could be said for their relations in the first century was "Jews refuse to have anything to do with Samaritans" (John 4:9).

Instead of the Davidic Messiah, the Samaritans looked forward to the coming of the *Taheb*, "the restorer" (Deut 18:18), a herald of the last day—a day of final judgment, of vengeance and reward, when the temple of Gerizim would be restored, the sacrifices reinstated, and the heathen converted (ISBE 4.307). Philip "proclaimed" to them "the Messiah" (Acts 8:5). The deliverer they were expecting had already come and begun to reign; his name is Jesus Christ (8:12). Philip did "miracles" (lit. "signs"), tokens that Jesus' messianic kingdom was, indeed, advancing into enemy territory with its false worship inspired by regnant "evil spirits" (lit. "unclean spirits," so called because they are ritually unclean and made those whom they possess unclean). As in Jesus' ministry, evil spirits left their victims with angry screams (8:7; Luke 4:41) and the "paralyzed and lame were healed" (Isa 35:3, 6; cf. Luke 5:24-25; 7:22; Acts 9:33-34). Therefore, the people "listened intently" to what Philip had to say (cf. 16:14), and they experienced joy when they embraced the Good News (cf. Luke 8:13; Acts 8:39; 13:48, 52).

The nature of this first-time advance of the gospel across the cultural threshold to Samaria may primarily account for the presence of signs. But the fact that Philip faced a situation of spiritual encounter, not unlike what pioneer church planters among unreached peoples face today, should encourage us to expect the powerful working of the gospel in these situations as well.

Luke now shows the magnitude of the kingdom's triumph by relating its effects in Simon the sorcerer's life. For a long time, his self-assertive practice of magical arts had astonished people and gained him the constant attention of everyone from "the least to the greatest" among "the Samaritans." The people confessed him to be an angelic being or lesser deity: "the Great One—the Power of God" (8:10). Philip, by contrast, was a recently arrived refugee sharing the good news about the presence and advance of the divine reign in Jesus Christ (8:12). Indeed, wherever demonic forces are directly confronted, it is God's reign that is proclaimed (19:8; 20:25; cf. 28:23, 31). The "name of Jesus Christ" (8:12) is consistently invoked when his powerful presence is needed in messianic salvation blessings, whether physically, in healing, or spiritually, in the sealing of baptism (2:38; 3:6; 4:10). And here the Samaritans believed and were baptized, trading their false confession of Simon, a man making himself divine, for the true confession of Jesus: God become man. Though not mentioned in every account of a conversion, Luke does mention baptism at most crossings of cultural and even geographical thresholds: the Pentecost crowd of Hebrew- and Greek-speaking Jews in the church's advance in mission (2:38, 41); half-Jew Samaritans (8:12-13); a god-fearing Ethiopian Eunuch (8:36, 38); a God-fearing Gentile (10:47-48); and Roman colonists in Europe (16:15, 33).

Simon believed, was baptized, and "began following Philip wherever he went" (8:13). The one who astonished the Samaritans (8:9, 11) was now continually astonished at Philip's signs and great miracles (*dunameis megalas* [TG1411/3173, ZG1539/ 3489] cf. his title, *dunamis tou theou . . . Megalē*, 8:10). Luke, however, left us clues that Simon's conversion may not have been genuine, for he did not tell us the content of his faith, and he emphasized that his devotion to Philip was from fascination with the miracles and signs he observed (cf. 3:16). Not only must divine signs be rightly interpreted through the accompanying "word of God" (cf. 2:11-21; 3:6-8, 12-16), their significance must be rightly appropriated by a transformed mind and heart. Simon needed to turn from his fascination with magic to the true God, who grants salvation blessings when and where he will (Luke 16:29-31; John 2:23-25).

The Samaritans welcomed "God's message" (8:14; cf. Luke 8:13; Acts 11:1; 17:11). This gospel and what people do with it, then, continue to be the central dynamic of the mission (2:41; 4:4, 29, 31; 6:2, 4; 8:4, 25). When they heard of Samaria's response, the apostles sent down Peter and John. Thus they fulfilled their supervisory role as validators of each new development in the church's mission (cf. Luke 22:29-30; Acts 9:27; 11:2, 15, 22-24; 18:22). Peter and John discovered that the Spirit had not come upon the baptized Samaritan believers, who were the first non-Jewish group to receive the gospel. As a result, Peter and John prayed for them to receive the Holy Spirit.

Since the clear teaching of the apostles and their customary practice is that the giving of the Spirit is a spiritual birthright for every Christian, received at conversion (2:38; 1 Cor 12:3, 13; see note on Acts 8:16), the delay here is a benchmark event but not a precedent-setting event. God delayed the Spirit's coming in order to preserve the unity of the church and the integrity of the church's cross-cultural mission to all nations in the face of the longstanding animosity between Jew and Samaritan. If God had not withheld his Spirit until the Jerusalem apostles came, converts on both sides of the cultural barrier might have found Christ without finding each other. Neither Samaritan nor Jewish Christians would have been assured that the Samaritans were truly regenerate and spiritual equals of regenerate Jews (cf. 15:8-11). What Luke teaches us, then, is that the unity of the church and the unhindered advance of its mission into all cultures are so important to God that he will delay giving to a converted people what is their birthright, the salvation blessing of the Spirit, in order to ensure that these realities will be fully preserved.

Simon, however, continued to deal in matters of "sight." He observed the human instrumentality of the Spirit's coming in "the laying on of hands of the apostles" (8:18). His unconverted magical mind-set led him to covet and then offer to purchase with money this "power," or authority (*exousia* [TG1849, ZG2026], "authority"; contrast 26:18). He desired to buy the priestly office, subordinate to that of the apostles, so that whomever he placed his hands on, would receive the Spirit.

Peter's condemnatory reply (8:20-23) told Simon the truth about what God thought of his request and what that request reveals about Simon's spiritual condition. In a "curse formula," ironically similar to those found in pagan magical papyri, Peter placed both Simon and his money under a ban, consigning both to eternal destruction (8:20; cf. Josh 6:17-18; 7:13-15). His rationale was Simon's presumption that he could obtain the gift of God through money (cf. 2:38; 10:45; 11:17). To pay money for God's power violates its essential nature as a gift of the sovereign God who always has the receiver in his control and is not controlled by any human.

Peter declared Simon unregenerate (8:21; see note) and gave as his reason: "Your heart is not right with God." Unlike some of the ancient kings of Israel, who manifested an uprightness before the Lord through their reforms, which included the removal of idolatry (1 Kgs 15:11; 2 Chr 14:2-3; cf. Ps 7:11), Simon's request revealed that the understandings, affections, and purposes of his heart had never been converted from the false worship of a magical, animistic worldview (cf. 7:39, 51).

True to the gospel message of repentance unto the forgiveness of sins (Luke 24:47), Peter called on Simon to repent from his wickedness and pray that perhaps God might forgive his heart's "evil thoughts" (8:22). Peter perceived in Simon an unregenerate condition, like "bitter and poisonous fruit" (Deut 29:18). He was indeed "held captive by sin" (8:23; Isa 58:6, 9).

Peter was so aware of Simon's magical mind-set that he had to state his promise of forgiveness very provisionally, lest Simon approach it with the same presumption and garner to himself cheap and false grace. In his repentance and pleading, Simon must cast himself totally on the mercy of God. But Simon's plea (8:24, see note) still focused on the human instruments, as he asked Peter to pray for him that nothing the apostle had spoken would happen to him. He was concerned with avoiding his sin's consequences, perishing and having no part in eternal life (8:20-21), and the only way that could happen is if he repented and pled for forgiveness. Though he did not give any direct indication that he would take such steps, they were probably implied in his request to Peter to escape judgment. Peter, by implication, was being asked to pray that the whole process of turning from sin would be successful.

The initial mission to Samaria concluded as it had begun (8:4, 25), with God's messengers broadly sharing the "word of the Lord" in the city and preaching "the Good News" in many villages. The "testifying" (8:25; *diamarturamenoi* [TG1263, ZG1371], "warning") probably included the warning about the consequences of not embracing the gospel wholeheartedly (cf. 2:40; 10:42).

◆　E. Philip and the Ethiopian Eunuch (8:26-40)

26As for Philip, an angel of the Lord said to him, "Go south* down the desert road that runs from Jerusalem to Gaza." 27So he started out, and he met the treasurer of Ethiopia, a eunuch of great authority under the Kandake, the queen of Ethiopia. The eunuch had gone to Jerusalem to worship, 28and he was now returning. Seated in his carriage, he was reading aloud from the book of the prophet Isaiah.

29The Holy Spirit said to Philip, "Go over and walk along beside the carriage."

30Philip ran over and heard the man reading from the prophet Isaiah. Philip asked, "Do you understand what you are reading?"

31The man replied, "How can I, unless someone instructs me?" And he urged Philip to come up into the carriage and sit with him.

32The passage of Scripture he had been reading was this:

"He was led like a sheep to the slaughter.
And as a lamb is silent before the shearers,

he did not open his mouth.
33He was humiliated and received no justice.
Who can speak of his descendants?
For his life was taken from the earth."*

34The eunuch asked Philip, "Tell me, was the prophet talking about himself or someone else?" 35So beginning with this same Scripture, Philip told him the Good News about Jesus.

36As they rode along, they came to some water, and the eunuch said, "Look! There's some water! Why can't I be baptized?"* 38He ordered the carriage to stop, and they went down into the water, and Philip baptized him.

39When they came up out of the water, the Spirit of the Lord snatched Philip away. The eunuch never saw him again but went on his way rejoicing. 40Meanwhile, Philip found himself farther north at the town of Azotus. He preached the Good News there and in every town along the way until he came to Caesarea.

8:26 Or *Go at noon.* 8:32-33 Isa 53:7-8 (Greek version). 8:36 Some manuscripts add verse 37, "*You can,*" *Philip answered, "if you believe with all your heart." And the eunuch replied, "I believe that Jesus Christ is the Son of God."*

NOTES

8:26 **Go south.** Or, "Go at noon" (NLT mg). Though *kata mesēmbrian* [TG2596/3314, ZG2848/3540] can indicate a direction (Josephus *War* 5.505; so here, Johnson 1992:154; Kee 1997:110), it may also be a time marker (so regularly in the LXX: Deut 28:29; 2 Kgs 4:20; Ps 36:6; Isa 18:4). Since few travelers would be on the road in the harsh midday sun, this makes the command all the more unusual and its purpose and fulfillment all the more dependent on divine providence (Barrett 1994:423).

8:27 *the treasurer of Ethiopia, a eunuch of great authority.* In ancient times "eunuch" could mean a castrated male (Lev 21:20; Deut 23:1); a castrated male who served in high government office, particularly under a woman ruler or in duties involving women (such as oversight of a harem, Esth 2:3, 14-15; 4:4-5) or in a treasury (Plutarch *Demetrius* 25.5); or any male high-government official (as in Jer 29:2[36:2]; 52:25). Since *dunastēs* [TG1413, ZG1541] ("of great authority," NLT) immediately following *eunouchos* [TG2135, ZG2336] (eunuch) points to his being an official, "eunuch," probably indicates his physical condition (Marshall 1980:162; contra Wilson 1973:171). Identified ethnically as an "Ethiopian," he is probably not Jewish by birth. And since eunuchs could not become proselytes (Deut 23:1), he is probably a God fearer, a Gentile who worshiped the one true God and identified with the Jewish synagogue in ethic and piety (cf. Levinskaya 1990). In his case, Jewish regulations prevented him from converting to Judaism. The tension created by the presence of this Gentile convert before the celebrated account of the conversion of Cornelius (often considered the first Gentile convert 10:1–11:18), need not be resolved either by saying Luke viewed him as a proselyte (as Wilson 1973:171-172) or that Luke intentionally presents him as the first Gentile convert in parallel with Cornelius (Polhill 1992:222). Rather, the eunuch's conversion is part of a triad of conversions dealing with the inauguration of the Gentile mission: the eunuch (8:26-40); Paul (9:1-31); and Cornelius (10:1–11:18). Although its placement allows Luke to complete his discussion of Philip's mission (Barrett 1994:426), it also forcefully indicates the divine initiative with regard to the Gentile mission, even without apostles, and permits Philip to serve as a precursor of Peter (cf. 8:40; Witherington 1998:301).

8:32-33 Scripture he had been reading. Luke reported the eunuch's reading of the Septuagint, which deviates from the MT at a number of points (see Archer and Chirichigno 1983:123). An increasing number of scholars view the resulting ambiguity for interpretation as an occasion to propose, however tentatively, that the early church and Luke saw v. 33, in whole or part, as actually declaring Jesus' vindication: "his justice" = "his condemnation" (*hē krisis autou* [TG2920, ZG3213]) had been removed. "Who can speak of his descendants?" (i.e., because they are so many); "his life was taken from" = "taken up from the earth in resurrection-exaltation" (*airetai* [TG142, ZG149]); cf. Johnson 1992:156; Polhill 1992:225; Spencer 1992:158; Talbert 1997:90-91; Witherington 1998:298-299, but see Barrett's (1994:431) disagreement. Still, a negative understanding of the verse preserves a greater continuity in meaning between the MT and the LXX and actually would heighten the eunuch's concern about someone who would suffer such an unjust, childless, premature death (Gage and Beck 1994:37). The Isaiah 53 quote begins after and closes before the passage's explicit reference to vicarious atonement. As a function of writing history, Luke was reporting what Philip heard as he approached the eunuch (Witherington 1998:298); Luke was not intentionally avoiding the concept (contra Parsons 1998:115-117). Luke does present a vicarious atonement soteriology explicitly elsewhere (Luke 22:19-20; Acts 20:28), but here, as we have seen in other speeches, he was satisfied to assume it and simply present its objective basis: the righteous sufferer (e.g., Luke 22:37; Acts 3:14-15; 7:52; see Larkin 1977; Marshall and Peterson 1998:99).

8:36-37 Some mss add v. 37 (see NLT mg). Most late mss, the earliest being E (6th century), include this verse. There is also a second-century reference to this confession in Irenaeus *Against Heresies* 3.12.8. Since the verse's style is not Lukan and there is little motive for removal and sufficient motive for a copyist to insert a confession that was mandatory in his own church's practice, it makes sense to see this verse as not originally part of Acts. The mss that exclude it are early and diverse: 𝔓45 𝔓74 ℵ A B C 044 33^vid syr^p cop^sa, bo.

8:39-40 the Spirit of the Lord snatched Philip away. Some scholars consider it unnecessary to see Philip's removal as a "supersonic ride of miraculous velocity" (Stott 1990:162; Kistemaker 1990:321; cf. Dunn 1996:115; contrast Krodel 1986:171). However, the fact that the eunuch suddenly did not see Philip anymore, though he had arrived on foot, and the use of the verb *harpazō* [ᵀᴳ726, ᶻᴳ773] ("rapture"; cf. 2 Cor 12:2; 1 Thess 4:17; cf. also 1 Kgs 18:12; 2 Kgs 2:16; Ezek 3:14; 8:3) indicates that we are dealing with a miraculous relocation.

COMMENTARY

God is on mission, making sure his salvation is applied to all nations and all sorts of people (1:8; Luke 24:47). This intent is clearly shown in this first part of Acts. Indeed, from this point on, with greater frequency, Luke tells us how God will directly intervene, through angel, Spirit, and visions of the risen Lord, to direct his witnesses outward across geographical and religio-ethnic boundaries with the Good News (e.g., just in these three chapters, 8:26, 29, 39; 9:3-6, 10-16; 10:3-6, 19-20).

Through an angel, God took the initiative and directed Philip to take the road south from Jerusalem to Gaza. The direction of the mission continued outward, away from the center (8:1, 4), but this time it involved greater intentionality on the part of Philip and more specific geographical guidance from God. A "desert" or wilderness road (probably the northern route from Jerusalem to Gaza) at noontime (see note on 8:26) would be primarily populated only by those whom God wanted Philip to meet. Philip displayed instant, unquestioning, complete obedience to the command, "Get up and go": he got up and went.

Indeed, under God's providence at that time and place, he encountered an Ethiopian eunuch, who was simultaneously exotic and disgraceful, powerful and pious. Greeks and Romans were particularly fascinated with dark-skinned Africans (Diodorus Siculus *Library of History* 3.8.2-3; Strabo *Geography* 17.2.1-3; Heliodorus *An Ethiopian Story*; Philostratus *Life of Apollonius* 3.20). Two expeditions were conducted into the region: a military one in 23 BC and a scientific one in AD 62 (Dio Cassius 54.5; Pliny the Elder *Natural History* 6.35; Seneca *Natural Questions* 6.8.3). However, being a eunuch—physically castrated—placed this man among the despised and derided of both Graeco-Roman and Jewish ancient society (Herodotus 8.104-106; Lucian *The Eunuch* 6-11; t. *Megilah* 2.7; Josephus *Antiquities* 4.290-291; Philo *Special Laws* 1.324-325). But he was also very powerful, the treasurer of the Kandake, the Queen Mother and ruling monarch of the ancient kingdom of Meroe (this title is spelled "Candace" in many versions and has been misunderstood as a proper name). This kingdom covered what is now northern Sudan, from south of Aswan to Khartoum, between the first and sixth cataracts of the Nile. It was a wealthy kingdom with its iron smelting, gold mining, and strategic trading position. It served as a conduit for goods from the rest of the continent (Pseudo-Callisthenes *Life of Alexander of Macedon* 3.18-23).

But piety is what especially marked this complex figure. Though his physical condition barred him from becoming a proselyte and entering fully into the worship of Israel (see note on 8:27), he was trying to understand the Scriptures. Philip encountered him returning from a pilgrimage to Jerusalem for one of the feasts, "seated in his carriage," a simple four-wheeled vehicle, probably ox-drawn, reading aloud the prophet Isaiah (8:28). Reading aloud was a common practice in ancient times and was especially necessary because words were commonly strung together on a manuscript without spacing or punctuation.

At the Spirit's direction (cf. 13:2, 4; 16:7-8), Philip approached the wagon, walked briskly alongside, and engaged the eunuch in conversation about his reading. God in his mercy had provided not only the text but also the interpreter, a Spirit-filled evangelist. Luke consistently tells us that reading and understanding Scripture are not the same thing, especially for those who do not have the Christocentric hermeneutical key held in the gospel (Luke 24:25-27, 44-48; cf. Acts 13:27; Luke 6:3; 10:26). Correct, enlightened understanding of the Scriptures is a divine gift that comes only to those who, like the eunuch, admit they don't understand (cf. 17:19, 20; Luke 8:9). Urgently but politely, the eunuch asked for guidance.

God's timing is perfect, even down to the very words of Isaiah the Ethiopian was reading as Philip approached (Isa 53:7-8). The prophet Isaiah was describing an innocent sufferer in the starkest of terms. This picture arrested the eunuch's attention and stirred his sympathy. He identified with the sufferer who, like himself, would have no offspring: "Who can speak of his descendants?" (8:33). Yet, this sufferer's childless, premature death, uncomplainingly accepted, was a severe miscarriage of justice. To whom had this happened and why? The eunuch did not realize it yet, but, as Philip will declare, this description is a portrayal of the Messiah's vicarious atonement. Luke had already pictured Jesus in his passion in these terms: silent before authorities (Luke 23:9), deprived of justice, a man declared innocent, handed over to a death penalty (Luke 23:4, 15, 22, 47; cf. Acts 2:22-23; 3:14), his life taken (Luke 23:18; Acts 3:15).

The eunuch's request for the identity of the sufferer is most understandable since sometimes this sufferer, the Servant, is presented in the first person (Isa 49:5; 50:4), although the prophet had children (Isa 8:3). Sometimes he is Israel (Isa 44:1ff), while at other times he is distinguished from Israel (Isa 49:5; 53:1-3). For the Jew in the first century, the suffering Servant of Isaiah 53 was either the humiliated but vindicated "righteous sufferer" of the apocalyptic and wisdom traditions (Isa 53:11; *1 Enoch* 46, 62, 63; Wis 2:12–5:23; Sir 11:13 [cf. Isa 52:13-15]), or, as the Targum has it, wicked Gentile nations suffering at the hands of the victorious Messiah, who would vindicate his people (*Targum* Isaiah 53:7-8; note Israel suffers in *Targum* Isaiah 52:14; 53:2, 4, 10, and the wicked Gentile nations in 53:3, 7-9, 11). The messianic interpretation was original with Jesus (see Luke 22:37 and Isa 53:12).

Beginning with this text, Philip told the eunuch the "Good News" about Jesus. Through his resurrection and ascension to God's right hand, Jesus had become victorious over his enemies and that victory—salvation blessings—was made available to all who repent (cf. Luke 24:46-48; Acts 13:38-39). Philip may have simply expounded the rest of Isaiah 53, or he may have linked it to the teaching on baptism in Isaiah 54:9-10 and the Good News in Isaiah 56:3-8 that, in the last day, foreigners and eunuchs will participate in the worship of the people of God. Or he may have gone farther afield in Scripture via early Christian testimonies to show how all the Scriptures spoke of Jesus and his salvation (e.g., Pss 22; 34; 69; 118).

God again so ordered events in time and space that Philip's exposition came to such a point as they approached some water that the eunuch remarked on its suitability for baptism (8:36; probably at *Ein Yael,* five miles south of the old City of Jerusalem on the northern route to Gaza [Rapuano 1990:48]). "Why can't I be baptized?" This question reveals that Philip's Christocentric, kerygmatic interpretation has done its work, for the eunuch understood and welcomed the gospel's liberating message. Indeed, Luke consistently shows there are now no hindrances to receiving the good news of salvation, not age (Luke 18:16), religious tradition (Luke 9:49-50; 11:52), race or ethnic origin (Acts 10:47; 11:17), or physical condition (8:36).

Whether by immersion or some other mode (the account accommodates all understandings), Philip baptized the eunuch. This act signifies that in God's eyes he was cleansed of his sins and whole, no matter his physical condition. And he was incorporated into the fellowship of those who receive Christ's salvation blessings (2:38-39; 10:47-48; 16:31-33).

Though Philip was taken from him suddenly, the eunuch went on his way rejoicing. His joy from salvation (8:8; Luke 6:23; 10:20) and the presence of the Spirit (Acts 13:52) was all the greater because he had not only been introduced to a saving understanding of Scripture; he had also experienced full acceptance among the people of God. God's plan for inclusive salvation overcomes physical defect, ethnic/racial barriers, and geographical remoteness (cf. Ps 68:31; Zeph 3:10).

The episode ends as it began, with divinely guided, but now miraculously transported, outreach. As with the prophets of old (see note on 8:39-40), the Spirit instantly moved Philip over thirty miles to the seacoast town of Azotus (Ashdod). God completed the evangelization of Judea to the coast by Peter's witness in places like Lydda and Joppa (cf. 9:32-43; 10:5-23) and Caesarea, farther north (cf. 21:8).

◆ **F. Saul's Conversion (9:1-19a)**

Meanwhile, Saul was uttering threats with every breath and was eager to kill the Lord's followers.* So he went to the high priest. ²He requested letters addressed to the synagogues in Damascus, asking for their cooperation in the arrest of any followers of the Way he found there. He wanted to bring them—both men and women—back to Jerusalem in chains.

³As he was approaching Damascus on this mission, a light from heaven suddenly shone down around him. ⁴He fell to the ground and heard a voice saying to him, "Saul! Saul! Why are you persecuting me?"

⁵"Who are you, lord?" Saul asked.

And the voice replied, "I am Jesus, the one you are persecuting! ⁶Now get up and go into the city, and you will be told what you must do."

⁷The men with Saul stood speechless, for they heard the sound of someone's voice but saw no one! ⁸Saul picked himself up off the ground, but when he opened his eyes he was blind. So his companions led him by the hand to Damascus. ⁹He remained there blind for three days and did not eat or drink.

¹⁰Now there was a believer* in Damascus named Ananias. The Lord spoke to him in a vision, calling, "Ananias!"

"Yes, Lord!" he replied. [11]The Lord said, "Go over to Straight Street, to the house of Judas. When you get there, ask for a man from Tarsus named Saul. He is praying to me right now. [12]I have shown him a vision of a man named Ananias coming in and laying hands on him so he can see again."

[13]"But Lord," exclaimed Ananias, "I've heard many people talk about the terrible things this man has done to the believers* in Jerusalem! [14]And he is authorized by the leading priests to arrest everyone who calls upon your name."

[15]But the Lord said, "Go, for Saul is my chosen instrument to take my message to the Gentiles and to kings, as well as to the people of Israel. [16]And I will show him how much he must suffer for my name's sake."

[17]So Ananias went and found Saul. He laid his hands on him and said, "Brother Saul, the Lord Jesus, who appeared to you on the road, has sent me so that you might regain your sight and be filled with the Holy Spirit." [18]Instantly something like scales fell from Saul's eyes, and he regained his sight. Then he got up and was baptized. [19]Afterward he ate some food and regained his strength.

9:1 Greek *disciples.*   9:10 Greek *disciple;* also in 9:26, 36.   9:13 Greek *God's holy people;* also in 9:32, 41.

NOTES

9:1, 10 *followers.* Lit., "disciples." The NLT renders with varying degrees of freedom the same term *mathētēs* [TG3101, ZG3412], "a person who is a disciple or follower of someone" (L&N 1.471).

9:2 *requested letters.* Saul's credentialing by the Sanhedrin to extradite Jews in Damascus lacks immediate first-century parallels (Barrett 1994:446), but there is precedent (Josephus *Antiquities* 14.190-195; *War* 1.474). The Romans did allow the Jews freedom in governing their religious affairs, and the Sanhedrin's direct governance from Jerusalem in Judea could well have extended across the whole of the province of Syria, including Damascus (Sherwin-White 1963:100; Kee 1997:115). If these were simply letters of introduction and commendation, which asked permission to arrest Jews (possibly refugees from Jerusalem), the Sanhedrin was exerting its influence over Diaspora Jews through moral suasion (Schürer 1973:218; Safrai 1974:204; Barrett 1994:446).

9:4 *me.* The link between Jesus and his followers is probably not rooted in the theological constructs of the body of Christ (contra Fernando 1998:296) or the filling up of Christ's sufferings (contra Witherington 1998:317) or the fact that Paul's persecution was motivated by personal hostility to Jesus and the claims made for him (contra Dunn 1996:122). Rather, for Luke the connection is the simple identification of the follower with the leader who sent him (Luke 10:16; Johnson 1992:163; Talbert 1997:99).

9:5 *lord.* Because he was inquiring into a heavenly being's identity, this is more than a polite "sir" (Polhill 1992:234), but it is not a Christian confession of Jesus as "Lord" (contra Kistemaker 1990:332; cf. Rom 10:9-10; 1 Cor 12:3; Fernando 1998:296).

9:8, 18 Though Bullock (1994) has drawn interesting parallels between the symptoms of a person struck by lightning and what happened to Paul, such symptoms do not account for a number of key elements in the account, particularly what Paul saw and heard and what the bystanders encountered.

he was blind. His blindness is not a punishment (contra Spencer 1997:97), or an indication of divine disfavor (contra Hedrick 1981:419), or simply a concrete proof of the vision (contra Haenchen 1971:323). An acted parable, it shows Saul the true nature of his spiritually bankrupt pre-Christian condition, mirrored in his present powerlessness, brokenness, and lack of understanding of what he was called to do (cf. Barrett 1994:452; Polhill 1992:235; Kee 1997:115).

9:9 did not eat or drink. This abstinence, during which Paul prays (9:11), should not be understood as the effects of the event, either physically, psychologically (contra Polhill 1992:236), or existentially (i.e., Paul reduced to nothingness so God can refashion him *ex nihilo*; contra Marguerat 1995:142). Prayer and abstinence from food may point to penitence (Talbert 1997:98) but more certainly signal preparation for further revelation (Johnson 1992:164; cf. Luke 6:12-16; Acts 1:4, 14).

9:10-19a Saul is my chosen instrument. There was probably a mutually confirming relationship between the direct revelation on the Damascus Road (Acts 26 and Gal 1) and the word of the Lord through Ananias in Judas's house (Acts 9 and 22; Bruce 1988:188). If so, there is no final contradiction between Paul's insistence that he received his gospel and apostleship directly from Christ and Luke's portrayal of Ananias's role (Acts 9:10-18; 22:12-16; Gal 1:1, 11-12; Lake 1979:191). Contrast Barrett (1994:450-451), who says Luke does not do justice to the tension found in Paul's Epistles between where Paul got his gospel and his relation to the churches. Ananias functioned as a prophet speaking a direct revelation of Christ (Williams 1985:158).

Paul and Luke do not differ on the basic facts about Paul's apostleship. Paul had seen the risen Lord and had received his gospel and apostleship from him (9:17; 22:14; 26:15-18; 1 Cor 9:1; 15:8; Gal 1:1, 11-12, 15-16). Yet there is an irregularity: Paul did not meet the qualifications of "the Twelve" (1:21-22; 1 Cor 15:9). Luke dealt with the irregularity by reserving the term *apostolos* [TG652, ZG693] almost exclusively for "the Twelve" and only occasionally calling Paul an apostle, and then in company with Barnabas (14:4, 14). "The Twelve," having been with Jesus from the baptism of John to the Ascension (1:22), guaranteed the gospel facts and provided the authoritative exposition of their significance (Luke 24:44-48). Paul shared with them the second function (Marshall and Peterson 1998:189).

9:15 take my message. Lit., "bear my name." This does not point to confessing Christ as a Christian, especially in trial testimony (contra Polhill 1992:237), but, as in the NLT, it presents Paul's missionary calling (Marguerat 1995:145; cf. Acts 9:27-28).

9:17 the Lord Jesus, who appeared to you. Lit., "The Lord sent me, Jesus who appeared to you." The NLT smooths it over; similarly, *Iēsous* [TG2424, ZG2652] (Jesus) is omitted in a number of mss (H L P).

COMMENTARY

In the midst of a series of divinely initiated individual conversions that push across geographical and ethnic boundaries to a Samaritan magician Simon, an Ethiopian eunuch, and a God-fearing Roman Gentile Cornelius (8:9-11:18), Luke turned to focus on a character who had demonstrated the most extensive opposition to the church to that point: Saul of Tarsus (7:58; 8:1, 3). In relating his conversion at this point, Luke shows us not only God's direct intervention to convert and call his chief missionary to all nations, but he also displays the overwhelming power of the gospel, which can turn a persecuting antagonist into a persecuted protagonist and convert a reluctant church to embrace their former archenemy.

With Old Testament imagery for anger—snorting through distended nostrils (Ps 18:8, 15)—Luke builds on his picture of Saul as a wild beast on the rampage against the Lord's followers (9:1; cf. 8:3). His threats are followed by more than just an eagerness to arrest Christians, for Luke tells us he is also breathing out "murder" (*phonou* [TG5408, ZG5840]; cf. 8:1; 26:10). Other than this hostility, we do not receive any further indication of Saul's inner thoughts and motives before, during, or after his conversion (but see 26:9-11; Rom 7:7-12; Gal 1:13-14; Phil 3:4-11).

Going to the high priest Caiaphas (4:6), Saul requested letters of introduction to the synagogues of Damascus, requesting their permission and possibly their aid in arresting Christians (9:2). Damascus, 135 miles north-northeast of Jerusalem, was a prosperous commercial center astride the main trade route between Egypt and Mesopotamia. It was also part of the Decapolis: a league of ten free cities (Pliny *Natural History* 5.74). Its Jewish population numbered in the tens of thousands (Josephus *War* 2.561; cf. 7.368). So, possibly because the synagogues were receptive to Sanhedrin leadership, Saul planned to pursue and arrest "followers of the Way" there. While it may have been a scornful label among the Jews (cf. 24:14), for a Christian to be "of the Way" meant an identity grounded in a life of discipleship, embarking on the way of salvation by following Jesus who said, "I am the Way" (John 14:6; cf. Acts 16:17; cf. Qumran's "way," which meant strict adherence to the Mosaic law, 1QS 8:12-15; 9:17-18).

Saul's encounter with Christ probably occurred at Kaukab, fifteen kilometers southwest of Damascus on the Jerusalem road (Meinardus 1981:58). As Paul traveled, a brilliant light from heaven suddenly shone down, or better, "flashed around" (the verb here is related to *astrapē* [TG796, ZG847], "lightning"). As light and lightning signal God's presence in biblical theophanies (Exod 3:16-17; Ps 97:4), and lightning can be a divine weapon of conquest (Ps 18:14; 144:6), so this enveloping, flashing light from heaven threw Saul to the ground.

Then, as at the burning bush (Exod 3:4), a voice came from the supernatural sight—heard by all but addressed and intelligible only to Saul (9:4-7; 22:9). The question, "Saul! Saul! Why are you persecuting me?" revealed that Saul was on the wrong side of salvation history (5:39). His misapplied zeal for God had actually placed him in the long line of persecutors of God's messengers (Luke 11:49; 21:12; Acts 7:52). The "why" exposes Saul's persecution project as a sin of "ignorance and unbelief" (1 Tim 1:13). Saul had not understood the true identity of the object of his hostility—the risen Lord identified with his church.

Once the Lord identified himself, Saul realized that Jesus of Nazareth was risen from the dead! Stephen was telling the truth when he bore witness to the Son of Man standing at God's right hand (7:56). Jesus was the Messiah, the Son of God, the Savior, the Lord (9:20, 28). Jesus then commanded Saul to go to the city and await further divine instructions: "You will be told [divine passive] what you must do" (9:6). From now on Saul would live to do the will of Jesus.

The Lord's appearance to Saul impacted his travel companions, who were probably a number of wayfarers banded together in a caravan for protection on the journey. They "stood speechless," hearing the sound of a voice but not understanding the words, seeing the light but not Jesus (9:7; cf. 22:9). The appearance was at once objective and very personal. These witnesses saw and heard something, but only Saul saw Jesus and conversed with him (cf. 7:56; John 12:29-30).

This encounter's physical effects on Saul were devastating (9:8-9). As he got up from the ground and opened his eyes, he discovered he couldn't see anything. The one who was determinedly pursuing God's people to bind and destroy them now found himself bound in darkness, broken and powerless, so much so that his companions had to lead him by the hand into Damascus. The one who had self-confidently planned out his every move must now, for three days, fast and pray, awaiting further instructions (cf. 1:14). The spiritual effects on Saul would last a lifetime. The spiritual significance of a Jewish rabbi's being physically blinded by the light of the glory of God in the face of Jesus Christ was not lost on Saul or Luke (2 Cor 4:4-6). Through a "double vision," actually a vision within a vision (9:10, 12), the risen Lord completed the conversion and commissioning of Saul. He laid the groundwork for overcoming the church's reluctance to embrace its former chief persecutor (9:13-16). At one and the same time, he preserved Saul's integrity as an apostle who received his gospel by revelation (Gal 1:12) and made sure Saul's Gentile mission would be the church's mission (13:1-4; cf. other visions that guide the church's advance, 10:3, 17; 16:9-10; 18:9-10).

The Lord then appeared to Ananias, a resident of Damascus and a devout disciple (22:12). He directed him to "Straight Street" and the house of Judas to look for Saul of Tarsus (9:11). This main east-west thoroughfare of Damascus was fifty feet wide and had great porches and gates at each end and colonnades for commerce running along each side. With added notes that Saul was praying and had seen a vision in which Ananias healed him, the Lord mercifully gave Ananias enough evidence that he had nothing to fear from this notorious persecutor Saul.

But Ananias objected, citing Saul's past persecution in Jerusalem and his projected assault on the church at Damascus (9:13-14). In the process he undercut his own objection, for he not only addressed the exalted Jesus as "Lord," implying his sovereign rule over the affairs of humankind, but he also identified the Lord's saving relationship with his people as he called them "believers" (lit., "saints"; cf. 9:32, 41; 26:10) and "everyone who calls upon your name" (9:14; see 2:21; 7:59; 22:16).

The Lord did not directly answer Ananias's misgivings; he simply repeated his command, though he did add the rationale of his personal interest in Saul's conversion and commissioning. He told Ananias that Saul was "*my* chosen instrument" or "choice vessel" (emphasis added) one the Lord had singled out and fashioned for special service (Rom 16:13; 2 Cor 4:7; 2 Tim 2:20-21). This service was a divine mission: "to take *my* message to the Gentiles and to kings, as well as to the people of Israel" (emphasis added; see note on 9:15). In broad terms, this was the way Saul executed his mission in the rest of Acts: Gentiles (13–19); kings (24–26); people of Israel (28:17-27). Furthermore, Jesus made it very clear that Saul would have to suffer for the sake of making the name of Jesus known.

Ananias obeyed, found Saul, and showed his and the church's acceptance of him by addressing him as a fellow Christian: "brother Saul" (9:17). Though in completing Saul's conversion the Lord was using a human instrument, Ananias let Saul know that the Lord had sent him so that Saul would regain his sight and also be filled with the Holy Spirit. This phrasing, answered as it is by the results—Saul regained his sight and was baptized—probably points to the coming of the Spirit as a salvation blessing (2:38) as part of a conversion-initiation. In Saul's case, this involved some unique events over a four-day period: the Damascus road appearance, blinding, and healing. The use of the term *to fill* focuses the reader on that aspect of the Spirit's coming that is most germane to Saul's commission: empowerment for witness (cf. 2:4; 4:8, 31).

◆   G. Saul in Damascus and Jerusalem (9:19b-31)

Saul stayed with the believers* in Damascus for a few days. [20]And immediately he began preaching about Jesus in the synagogues, saying, "He is indeed the Son of God!"

[21]All who heard him were amazed. "Isn't this the same man who caused such devastation among Jesus' followers in Jerusalem?" they asked. "And didn't he come here to arrest them and take them in chains to the leading priests?"

[22]Saul's preaching became more and more powerful, and the Jews in Damascus couldn't refute his proofs that Jesus was indeed the Messiah. [23]After a while some of the Jews plotted together to kill him. [24]They were watching for him day and night at the city gate so they could murder him, but Saul was told about their plot. [25]So during the night, some of the other believers* lowered him in a large basket through an opening in the city wall.

[26]When Saul arrived in Jerusalem, he tried to meet with the believers, but they were all afraid of him. They did not believe he had truly become a believer! [27]Then Barnabas brought him to the apostles and told them how Saul had seen the Lord on the way to Damascus and how the Lord had spoken to Saul. He also told them that Saul had preached boldly in the name of Jesus in Damascus.

[28]So Saul stayed with the apostles and went all around Jerusalem with them, preaching boldly in the name of the Lord. [29]He debated with some Greek-speaking Jews, but they tried to murder him. [30]When the believers* heard about this, they took him down to Caesarea and sent him away to Tarsus, his hometown. [31]The church then had peace throughout Judea, Galilee, and Samaria, and it became stronger as the believers lived in the fear of the Lord. And with the encouragement of the Holy Spirit, it also grew in numbers.

9:19 Greek *disciples;* also in 9:26, 38.   9:25 Greek *his disciples.*   9:30 Greek *brothers.*

NOTES

9:19 *believers.* Lit., "disciples" (see NLT mg).

9:20 *Son of God.* Though many scholars see this as a royal messianic title, synonymous with v. 22 and grounded in Ps 2:7 and 2 Sam 7:13-14 (Hurtado 1997:171; Dunn 1996:124), the Jewish audience's astonishment, Saul's Damascus road experience and his own Christological witness (Gal 2:20; Rom 1:1-4), together with Luke's consistent Christology of divine sonship make it probable that Saul was proclaiming that Jesus is divine (Luke 1:32, 35; 3:22; 8:28; 9:35; 22:70; Spencer 1997:100; Buckwalter 1998:112; cf. Witherington 1998:321).

9:22 *Saul's preaching became more and more powerful.* Lit., "he became more powerful." The NLT specifies the verb's subject, as do a few mss (C E it[h, p]). Saul became more powerful, not physically (cf. Metzger 1994:321; Acts 9:19a) but spiritually, particularly in the effectiveness of his apologetic preaching, which is made clear by what follows (Longenecker 1981:376).

9:23-25 Compare 2 Cor 11:32-33. Although the precise political relationship between Nabatea and Damascus at this time is not certain (Barrett 1994:466; contrast D. Williams [1985:160-61] who is certain Aretas IV controlled the city through an ethnarch), a cooperative endeavor against Saul by both Nabateans (2 Corinthians) and Jews (Acts) is plausible, especially if Saul had been proclaiming the gospel while he was in Arabia and thereby annoyed the authorities (Marshall 1980:174; Fernando 1998:300).

9:25 *believers.* Lit., "his disciples" (see NLT mg). Though the NLT mg gives us the oldest reading extant in the mss (*hoi mathētai autou*, "his [Saul's] disciples"; supported by 𝔓74 ℵ A B C 81*), it goes against Lukan and NT usage. Johnson (1992:172) and Witherington (1998:322) note the difficulty but still prefer the reading. Though a number of grammatical explanations have been put forward, it is best to see this reading as an early scribal error (Metzger 1994:321-22), which the NLT note has cited but appropriately corrected in the text.

9:26-27 *but they were all afraid of him.* When we consider that Saul has been away in Arabia (here, modern-day Jordan) a good portion of that time and that a persecuted community was naturally suspicious of any good news about its most violent adversary (Dunn 1996:126), it is plausible that after three years (cf. Gal 1:18) the Jerusalem Christians still would be fearful of Saul, unaware or unconvinced of his conversion and call (contrast Barrett 1994:468).

9:27 *the apostles.* This generalizing plural gives the general picture, while Gal 1:18-20 gives the particulars. Saul saw Peter and James, the Lord's brother (Hemer 1977a:81; contrast Johnson 1992:172).

9:28-29 *Saul stayed with the apostles and went all around Jerusalem with them.* This description may be reconciled with Saul's limited contact with the churches of Judea (Gal 1:22) if we take into account the church's continuing fear or shunning of Paul and his public ministry focus—evangelization of Hellenistic Jews (Witherington 1998:325; contrast Barrett 1994:471).

9:31 *church.* A variant reading is *ekklēsiai* [TG1577, ZG1711] (churches), which is followed by the KJV and NKJV and is in line with Luke's normal practice (15:41; 16:5), though less well attested ([E] most minuscules it syr^h). However, it's more likely that this originated through copyist adjustment than that it was original (Metzger 1994:322-323). Giles (1985) suggests that the variant *ekklēsia* (found in Ψ) with plural verbs be given serious consideration.

Scholars continue to struggle with the singular as the copyists did. Some take it to stand for a single unit: the Jerusalem church in dispersion or in its witness extended throughout these areas (Bruce 1988:196; Polhill 1992:244). Others see groups of churches across the single territory of ancient Israel (Dunn 1996:127) or the church represented in its universality and unity (Lake and Cadbury 1979:107; cf. Acts 20:28).

encouragement. Gr., *paraklēsis* [TG3874, ZG4155] (appealing to, exhorting, encouraging, comforting), probably should be rendered "exhortation," indicating Holy Spirit-empowered preaching, and linked to the church's numerical growth: "By the exhortation of the Holy Spirit [the church] was multiplied." This is permissible in the Greek syntax (*tē paraklēsei tou hagiou pneumatos eplēthuneto* [TG4129, ZG4437]).

COMMENTARY

Saul's initial ministry experience in Damascus and Jerusalem shows us that "God on mission" can include the total conquest of the church's enemies. God thoroughly undid the harm Saul had done so that the church was left tranquil, healthy, and growing (9:31).

The believers took Saul into their fellowship, and he immediately engaged in Spirit-filled, Jesus-centered preaching in the synagogues (9:19b-20). Just as instantaneous as his healing was his fulfillment of the calling God had given him (9:15, 18, 20). Without training or a probationary period, he proclaimed on numerous occasions, "Jesus is the Son of God."

Only here and at Acts 13:33 (quoting Ps 2:7) did Saul proclaim Jesus "the Son of God." Within a messianic and monotheistic framework (2 Sam 7:14-16; Ps 2:7), this title, like "Son of Man," both conceals and reveals who Jesus is. Jews can hear it and understand nothing more than the messianic title of the ideal king, royal David's son (cf. 4QFlor 1:10-11; *1 Enoch* 105:2; *4 Ezra* 7:28-29). Yet when understood literally in terms of essence, it indicates participation in the divine nature (Luke 1:35, 38; 20:41-44; 22:69; cf. Ps 110:1; Dan 7:13). Saul, who has just seen Jesus in all his glory as the risen and exalted Lord, made this the theme of his first sermons (9:3-5; cf. Rom 1:1-4; Gal 1:16).

God's way with this "persecutor turned proclaimer" was to make him ever more powerful in his apologetic preaching. Saul would set the details of Jesus' life and ministry side by side with Old Testament prophecies and in that way provided "proofs that Jesus was indeed the Messiah" (9:22; 17:3; 18:5; 26:23). So strong was his Spirit-filled argumentation that it "threw into confusion" (*sunechunnen* [TG4797A, ZG5179]; NLT renders "[they] couldn't refute") the unbelieving Jews. They had another "Stephen" on their hands (cf. 6:10).

Luke indicates the end of Saul's time in Damascus with the imprecise phrase "when many days were being fulfilled" (9:23; NLT: "After a while"). Not only does this allow for Saul's three-year stay in Arabia (Gal 1:17; modern-day Jordan); it also shows that the plot and Saul's inelegant exit from Damascus were actually part of God's sovereign plan for his witness (cf. 7:23, 30). Evidently, Saul's preaching was so effective that the Jews plotted to do away with him (cf. Luke 22:2; 23:32; Acts 2:23; 5:33, 36, 38). In collusion with forces of the governor under Nabatean King Aretas IV, the Jews sought to ambush Saul at the city gate when he left the city (see 2 Cor 11:32-33). Saul learned of the plot (cf. 23:12-16), and at night the disciples put him in a large woven hamper (*spuris* [TG4711, ZG5083]; cf. *sarganē* [TG4553, ZG4914], "basket" in 2 Cor 11:33) and lowered him through a window in the city wall. He fled to Jerusalem.

Saul's arrival in Jerusalem was a further step in God's undoing of his previous career (9:26). Those whom he persecuted he now attempted to "meet with" (i.e., "associate with and join," *kollaomai* [TG2853, ZG3140], cf. 17:34), yet he faced a situation created by his life as a persecutor. Whereas previously the disciples were fearless and the Jewish leaders and populace fearful (4:19-20, 31; 5:12-14, 26, 28-29), now even three-year-old reports of Saul's conversion could not remove the suspicion and fear of this foe. As Ananias needed God's help to embrace Saul, the church's former archenemy, so did the Jerusalem church and its leadership (9:13-14). The two parties were brought together by a bridge person—Barnabas ("son of encouragement, exhortation"; 11:22, 25; 15:22, 25, 35)—rather than by a vision. Barnabas took Saul and brought him to the apostles. In this, God had ironically reversed Saul's original intent, which had been to bring Christians, bound, to the high priests (9:2, 21). The apostles, who were the guarantors of the church's message and mission (8:14-15; 11:1-17; 15:1-29), heard a summary of the Lord's calling of Saul from Barnabas. This summary of his calling was congruent with the marks of the apostleship of the Twelve. Saul had seen the risen Lord, although he did not accompany him during his earthly ministry and it was a post-Ascension appearance (22:14; 1 Cor 9:1; Gal 1:12; cf. Acts 1:21-22). Barnabas reported "how the Lord had spoken to Saul" (9:27). Saul, too, had received a commission, although again in post-Ascension circumstances (cf. Luke 24:46-48; Acts 1:8). Like the apostles, Saul was filled with the Spirit (9:17) and had "boldly preached in the name of Jesus" (9:28; cf. 4:8, 13, 31, 33).

Saul, whose mission would extend to the nations, was accepted by the founding leaders, providing the unity and continuity essential for the church's advance. What God enabled Saul to do in Damascus he also did in Jerusalem: he preached "boldly in the name of the Lord" (9:28). "In the name of the Lord" signals "God on mission" through Saul because it is in Jesus' authority, through his power, and in his person, that salvation blessings come (Luke 24:47; Acts 2:38; 4:12; 9:15-16; 10:48; 19:5; 22:16).

Saul picked up where Stephen left off, debating with "Greek-speaking Jews," which probably included compatriots in his hometown synagogue (6:9; 9:29). The reaction was the same—a plot to do away with the witness (cf. 6:11-12)—but the result was different. Believers, getting wind of the plot, spirited Saul away to the seaport Caesarea and then off by ship to Tarsus in Cilicia, his hometown (9:11; 22:3). As Luke will later relate, God, in a vision, had let Saul know that such a departure was according to his divine plan for the apostle's work (22:17-21; cf. 9:15).

In a summary statement (9:31; cf. 2:42; 6:7; 12:25), which looks backward and forward, Luke tells us of the outward circumstances and inner health of a church that was the fruit of "God on mission"—completing the first stages of the great commission (1:8). In a reverse parallelism, Luke begins and ends with the outward circumstances, which in the NLT read, "The church then had peace . . . [and] also grew in numbers" (9:31). This circumstance of peace and growth is a foretaste of what heirs of the messianic kingdom will one day enjoy (Jer 3:16; 23:3; 33:6; Ezek 37:26). The central expression ("believers lived in the fear of the Lord" 9:31) shows us how essential the church's piety and obedience are to its well-being and advance.

◆ III. The Jerusalem Church's Mission to the Gentiles (9:32–12:25)
   A. Peter Heals Aeneas and Raises Dorcas (9:32-43)

32Meanwhile, Peter traveled from place to place, and he came down to visit the believers in the town of Lydda. 33There he met a man named Aeneas, who had been paralyzed and bedridden for eight years. 34Peter said to him, "Aeneas, Jesus Christ heals you! Get up, and roll up your sleeping mat!" And he was healed instantly.

³⁵Then the whole population of Lydda and Sharon saw Aeneas walking around, and they turned to the Lord. ³⁶There was a believer in Joppa named Tabitha (which in Greek is Dorcas*). She was always doing kind things for others and helping the poor. ³⁷About this time she became ill and died. Her body was washed for burial and laid in an upstairs room. ³⁸But the believers had heard that Peter was nearby at Lydda, so they sent two men to beg him, "Please come as soon as possible!" ³⁹So Peter returned with them; and as soon as he arrived, they took him to the upstairs room. The room was filled with widows who were weeping and showing him the coats and other clothes Dorcas had made for them. ⁴⁰But Peter asked them all to leave the room; then he knelt and prayed. Turning to the body he said, "Get up, Tabitha." And she opened her eyes! When she saw Peter, she sat up! ⁴¹He gave her his hand and helped her up. Then he called in the widows and all the believers, and he presented her to them alive. ⁴²The news spread through the whole town, and many believed in the Lord. ⁴³And Peter stayed a long time in Joppa, living with Simon, a tanner of hides.

9:36 The names *Tabitha* in Aramaic and *Dorcas* in Greek both mean "gazelle."

NOTES

9:32 *traveled from place to place.* This general statement (*dierchomenon* [TG1330, ZG1451] *dia pantōn*, lit. "traveling through all") probably points to the entire region mentioned in 9:31 (Haenchen 1971:338), not just the territory between Jerusalem and Lydda (contra Bruce 1990:246) or in the Sharon—the coastal plain between Lydda/Joppa and Caesarea (contra Spencer 1997:105).

to visit the believers. Most commentators (e.g., Johnson 1992:177; Dunn 1996:128; Fernando 1998:309) view Peter's travels "from place to place" as a visitation to the churches for the sake of edification. If the *kai* [TG2532, ZG2779] ("and, also, even") that introduces his coming to the Lord's people at Lydda ("*and* he came"; NLT) is not taken as a simple "and" it could imply that his itineration was evangelistic missionary work among non-Christians (Polhill 1992:245; cf. Witherington 1998:328-329).

Lydda. Lydda and Joppa are not far away from the Azotus-Caesarea road; as such, Philip could have planted churches there (8:40; Witherington 1998:328). They need not have originated from the witness of either the Pentecost Christians or the Greek-speaking Christians scattered at Stephen's death (2:9; 8:1, 3; contra Longenecker 1981:381).

9:33 *bedridden for eight years.* Though many note that *ex* [TG1537, ZG1666] *etōn oktō* can be read "for eight years" or "from the age of eight," most prefer the former (e.g., Barrett 1994:480).

9:34 *Jesus Christ heals you!* The verb *iatai* [TG2390, ZG2615] may be accented either as present, "heals" (so the NLT), or perfect tense, "has healed," as is demonstrated by the scribal rendering in B (*eiatai* [a spelling that seems to imply the perfect tense, with the accent on the first syllable], cf. Metzger 1994:323). Barrett (1994:481, contra Metzger) takes *eitai* as a common itacism (i.e. a spelling error based on the fact that in NT times *ei* and *i* were pronounced the same in Greek). The present tense better fits the context, and itacism is a plausible explanation.

9:35 *the whole population.* Some see the "all" in *pantes hoi katoikountes* [TG2730, ZG2997], "all those dwelling," as hyperbolic (Fernando 1998:310; Witherington 1998:330), yet still pointing to a large response, a "people movement" (Wagner 1995:59).

9:37-38 Some commentators assume the burial had been delayed in the hope that Peter would raise Dorcas (Haenchen 1971:339; Marshall 1980:179). Others see the practice of burial the same day as the death as the motive for the urgency in calling Peter (9:38; Deut 21:23; Kee 1997:126; Keener 1993:349; contrast Barrett [1994:484], who says the urgent appeal is to overcome Peter's reluctance to go to Joppa, a Greek city). The delay, however, is not outside normal Jewish burial practice (cf. *Leviticus Rabbah* 34:10). In fact, outside Jerusalem, burial was not necessarily carried out on the same day, especially if the shroud or the coffin needed to be prepared (Safrai 1976:776).

9:43 *Simon, a tanner of hides.* Luke uses the detail that Simon was a tanner of hides simply to distinguish him from his guest, Simon Peter the apostle. Tanning was a ritually unclean trade, since it dealt in the skins of dead animals; thus some have seen Peter's choice of accommodation and Luke's note of it as foreshadowing Peter's leadership role in taking the gospel to the Gentiles (Kee 1997:127; cf. Dunn 1996:130). Barrett (1994:487) doubts it, for it undercuts the following vision. Furthermore, one wonders whether the religious significance of this detail would have registered with a Gentile audience (Johnson 1992:179).

COMMENTARY

In these paired accounts of the miraculous restoration of a male and female disciple, we meet God's direct intervention to maintain "peace" for his people. When his prophetic agents depend totally on him, there is a foretaste of the full eschatological salvation, which issues in further evangelistic advance.

Peter, who had been evangelizing Samaritan villages on his return to Jerusalem (8:25), engaged in even more extensive outreach in Judea, Galilee, and Samaria (9:31). The apostle arrived at Lydda, the Old Testament city of Lod, twenty-five miles northwest of Jerusalem at the intersection of highways from Egypt to Syria and from Jerusalem to the coastal port Joppa. The capital of a toparchy, or administrative district, in an ethnically mixed region, its populace was predominantly Jewish (1 Macc 11:34; Pliny the Elder *Natural History* 5.70; Josephus *War* 3.55).

"There," that is, among the Lord's people, not the population in general, he met Aeneas, who had been paralyzed for eight years, confined to sitting on a mat (9:33; cf. Luke 5:18-26; Acts 3:2; 14:8-10). Peter declared, "Jesus Christ heals you!" The exalted Christ was directly intervening to apply to Aeneas a foretaste of eschatological salvation blessings: the full restoration of the whole person. Aeneas's healing served as a "sign," an acted-out parable, of the empowerment and freedom that turning to the Lord can mean (cf. Acts 28:26-27; Isa 6:9-10 LXX). The risen Christ commanded Aeneas to arise, as having become a participant in his resurrection power. Aeneas, "healed instantly" of his eight-year condition, got up immediately.

Luke pointed to this miracle's effect on the church's evangelistic witness. In Lydda and the coastal plain of Sharon, stretching from Joppa to Mount Carmel beyond Caesarea, all who "saw Aeneas walking around . . . turned to the Lord" (9:35). Luke adopted a nuanced approach to the relationship between miracle working and evangelism. Miracles do not automatically lead to saving faith; they are not irresistible proof (2:13; 3:12; 4:16-17; 5:13; 6:8-12; 8:18-19; 14:11-18; 19:13-14). An unregenerate worldview may continue to blind people to a miracle's true origin and significance. Still, miracles have a legitimate role as authenticators of the gospel witness and as encouragements to faith for those who have "eyes to see" and "ears to hear."

Eleven miles farther northwest, in Joppa, once the ancient seaport for Jerusalem (Josh 19:46) but by this time a Greek city (Josephus *War* 3.56), lived "Tabitha (which in Greek is Dorcas)." Luke's semitic/Hellenistic rendering of her name may point to the locale's ethnically mixed nature (Josephus *War* 4.145). Dorcas, a "believer" (lit. "female disciple" *mathētria* [TG3102, ZG3413]), was famous for her kindness to the poor. She lived in the fear of the Lord (9:31) by adopting correct values concerning material things (cf. Luke 12:33; Acts 10:2, 4; 20:35; 24:17). While Peter was ministering in Lydda, Dorcas became sick and died. She was "washed for burial" (9:37). According to Jewish practice, funeral arrangements begin with the cleansing of the body with oil and rinsing it clean with water (*m. Shabbat* 23:5). Her friends placed her in an "upstairs room," which may also have been the Christians' meeting place (cf. 1:13; 20:8). With Lydda so close (11 miles away, a three- or four-hour journey by foot each way), the believers dispatched two men to Peter, urging him to come as soon as possible.

When Peter arrived and was taken to the upstairs room, the noisy wailing of widows greeted him (cf. Luke 7:13; 8:52). They were probably among the Christian poor Dorcas had helped (cf. 6:1 and Jesus' special interest in widows in his teaching ministry: Luke 4:25-26; 7:12; 18:1-8; 20:47; 21:1-4). In fact, they showed him some of "the coats and other clothes"—outer garments and inner garments (*chitōnas kai himatia* [TG5509/2440, ZG5945/2668])—she used to make for them (*epoiei* [TG4160, ZG4472], "was making," customary imperfect). The death of Dorcas, benefactress to these economically most vulnerable, had shattered them.

Peter's actions show his total dependence on God. Ordering everyone out of the room (Mark 5:40), he fell on his knees in total submission to God (cf. Luke 22:41; Acts 7:60). He asked for a foreshadowing of the final eschatological salvation. This corpse's resuscitation pictures the Resurrection (*anastasis* [TG386, ZG414], 24:15; Luke 14:14; 20:36), the inaugural event of the final salvation. Then, turning to the body, Peter issued a simple command: "Get up, Tabitha" (9:40). In a reversal of the first act of preparation for burial—closing the eyes of the deceased (*m. Shabbat* 23:5; *Semahot* 1.4), Dorcas opened her eyes and, seeing Peter, sat up.

After giving her his hand and helping her up (*anestēsen* [TG450, ZG482], a verb often related to resurrection), Peter called "the widows and all the believers" (9:41, lit. "the saints"). Not only did he, by this act, reunite her with the community and restore to the widows their source of support, but by showing them "that she was alive," he also turned the community members into public witnesses to the objective reality of this miracle. And again, reports of the miraculous promote saving faith, for as Dorcas's return to life became well known, "many believed in the Lord" (9:42; cf. 4:4; 9:35). Wholeness and numerical growth again marked the church in which God was at work (9:31). Peter stayed on many days in Joppa in the house of Simon the tanner. He was now strategically positioned to answer the next call of God: a summons to witness to a Gentile (10:1–11:18).

◆ B. Cornelius Calls for Peter (10:1-8)

In Caesarea there lived a Roman army officer* named Cornelius, who was a captain of the Italian Regiment. ²He was a devout, God-fearing man, as was everyone in his household. He gave generously to the poor and prayed regularly to God. ³One afternoon about three o'clock, he had a vision in which he saw an angel of God coming toward him. "Cornelius!" the angel said. ⁴Cornelius stared at him in terror. "What is it, sir?" he asked the angel.

And the angel replied, "Your prayers and gifts to the poor have been received by God as an offering! ⁵Now send some men to Joppa, and summon a man named Simon Peter. ⁶He is staying with Simon, a tanner who lives near the seashore." ⁷As soon as the angel was gone, Cornelius called two of his household servants and a devout soldier, one of his personal attendants. ⁸He told them what had happened and sent them off to Joppa.

10:1 Greek *a centurion;* similarly in 10:22.

NOTES

10:1 Italian Regiment. Previously, inscriptional evidence placed the *Cohores II Miliaria Italica Civium Romanorum* in Syria in AD 69 (*Inscriptiones Latinae Selectae* 9168; note *Corpus Inscriptionum Latinarum* 11.6117 may place it there earlier, though the inscription is difficult to date). Recently cataloged numismatic evidence—twenty countermarked pieces of Judean provincial coinage, made suitable for military pay, dating from AD 31/32–41—places the regiment there at a time congruent with Luke's chronology (Lönnqvist 1992).

10:2 God-fearing man. So the NLT renders *phoboumenos ton theon* [TG5399/2316, ZG5828/2536]. "God fearer" was a semitechnical term for a category of Gentile sympathizers who, to a greater or lesser extent, embraced the theology and practice of Judaism short of becoming proselytes (2 Chr 5:6 LXX; inscriptions at Aphrodias [Schürer 1986:25-26, 166]; Bosporan kingdom inscriptions [Levinskaya 1996:ch 6; appendix 3]; Juvenal *Satires* 14.96-107; cf. deBoer 1995; Cohen 1989:14).

10:4 Your prayers. This is just part of his practice of piety (Dunn 1996:136); it was not a specific request that he be fully incorporated into the fellowship of the people of God (contra Wagner 1995:72).

10:6 A few mss (69ᵐᵍ 1611 several Latin mss) and the Textus Receptus (hence the KJV and NKJV) end the sentence with *houtos lalēsei soi ti se dei poiein,* "this one will tell you what you must do." This is probably modeled on Acts 9:6. Several minuscules (321 322 436 453 466 467) add from 11:14 the words *hos lalēsei rhēmata pros se, en hois sōthēsē su kai pas hō oikos sou,* "who will speak to you words by which you and all your household will be saved" (Metzger 1994:325-326). Such additions do not reckon with Luke's literary technique of selectively increasing the information he gives us in each retelling of an event (Witherup 1993:52). The first telling always has the least information and in this case, heightens the focus on God's mysterious will at work and Cornelius's immediate and unquestioning obedience.

10:8 what had happened. This translates *hapanta* [TG537, ZG570] (all), which with its meaning and emphatic position, stresses the comprehensive report Cornelius gave (Williams 1985:172).

sent them off to Joppa. Some have supposed that the thirty-mile distance meant they rode there (Marshall 1980:184). Others suggest that a determined march through the night, with rest stops, would permit them to arrive about noon the next day (Haenchen 1971:347; cf. 10:9, 17).

COMMENTARY

If the conversions of Samaritan Simon, the Ethiopian eunuch, and persecutor Saul each took a decisive step toward making salvation available to all people, the "conversion" of Peter (in his thinking) and the conversion of the God-fearing Gentile Cornelius in Acts 10:1–11:18 (cf. 15:7-11) are the final steps in the inauguration of that mission. The first stage (10:1-8) within this final step presents most graphically how essential God's initiative and direct intervention and a human's obedient response are to the fulfillment of God's saving purposes in a universal context.

At Caesarea, a mainly Gentile city (and the residence of the Roman proconsul from AD 6 onward), lived Cornelius, "a Roman army officer" (10:1). As "captain (*hekatontarchēs* [TG1543, ZG1672], "centurion") of the Italian Regiment," he was in charge of sixty to one hundred men, the equivalent of a modern-day army company. His regiment (see note at 10:1) had ten companies and was equivalent to a modern military battalion.

Cornelius and his "entire household," which would have included household servants and military orderlies and their families, were "devout"—that is, they were marked by religious reverence (10:2; cf. Luke 2:25; Acts 2:5; 8:2). They were "God fearers" (*phoboumenos ton theon* [TG5399/2316, ZG5828/2536], see note on 10:2; cf. 10:22, 35; 13:16, 26, 43, 50; 16:14; 17:4, 17; 18:7). So strong was Cornelius's sympathy with Judaism that his spiritual disciplines included two of the three pillars of Jewish piety: almsgiving (Tob 1:16; Sir 7:10; 16:14) and regular prayer (the Jewish practice was three times a day; *m. Berakhot* 4:1; cf. 1 Chr 16:40; Dan 6:10; the third pillar was fasting; cf. Matt 6:1-14; Tob 12:8). As an army captain, however, he also would have participated publicly in the idolatrous polytheism of the imperial forces.

"One afternoon about three o'clock" (10:3; lit., "the ninth hour," the Jewish afternoon hour of prayer at the time of the evening sacrifice), Cornelius saw a vision of an angel approaching him and addressing him by name. The combination of prayer, vision, and angelic messenger brings together those ways of divine direct intervention God uses to guide the advance of his mission. God employed this combination here either because he was taking the initiative and communicating his plans or because he must deal with human resistance or uncertainty.

Reacting quite naturally to an experience of the supernatural, "Cornelius stared at him in terror" (10:4) and asked, "What is it, sir?" (The Greek for "sir," *kurie* [TG2962, ZG3261], suggests more than a courteous "sir"; it probably gives some worshipful acclaim.) The angel told Cornelius that his "prayers and gifts to the poor" had risen (as the aroma of the meal offering rose) as a memorial before God (10:4; see Lev 2:2, 9; Ps 141:2; Heb 13:15-16; Tob 12:12; 1QS 8:1-9). With such phrasing, God communicated that he had already begun to overcome the barrier between Jew and Gentile, for though Cornelius's ritual uncleanness prevented him from offering sacrifices in the Temple, God in his grace was receiving and accepting his acts of piety as such. Yet, as the angel's directive to summon Peter implies, Cornelius lacked something. His faithfulness to the revelation he had did not yet place him in a saving relationship with God. Rather, it would lead to more revelation (cf. 10:33; 11:14).

With very precise instructions (10:5-6), which again emphasize God's initiative in this move, the angel called for men to be sent to Joppa, 30 miles south, and to summon Simon Peter, who was staying with "Simon, a tanner who [lived] near the shore." The men would find him in an industrial district, which would have the goodly supply of water needed for his trade and be segregated from the general population (shielding them from the sights and smells of this "aesthetically revolting" and ritually unclean trade).

This directive reveals that salvation comes to all people in the same divinely commanded and enabled way: through human messengers who proclaim the gospel (Luke 24:47). In light of Jesus' commission that his messengers take the message to all nations (1:8), the fact that Peter had to receive a summons via an angelic command reveals that something was not yet right in the apostles' implementation of their mission.

In immediate, unquestioning obedience, Cornelius called "two of his household servants and a devout soldier, one of his personal attendants" (10:7), told them all that had happened, and sent them off to Joppa. Cornelius's immediate obedience to limited information provides a model of the kind of faith that will truly receive salvation—faith that depends on God's word of promise alone.

◆   C. Peter Visits Cornelius (10:9-33)

[9]The next day as Cornelius's messengers were nearing the town, Peter went up on the flat roof to pray. It was about noon, [10]and he was hungry. But while a meal was being prepared, he fell into a trance. [11]He saw the sky open, and something like a large sheet was let down by its four corners. [12]In the sheet were all sorts of animals, reptiles, and birds. [13]Then a voice said to him, "Get up, Peter; kill and eat them."

[14]"No, Lord," Peter declared. "I have never eaten anything that our Jewish laws have declared impure and unclean.*"

[15]But the voice spoke again: "Do not call something unclean if God has made it clean." [16]The same vision was repeated three times. Then the sheet was suddenly pulled up to heaven.

[17]Peter was very perplexed. What could the vision mean? Just then the men sent by Cornelius found Simon's house. Standing outside the gate, [18]they asked if a man named Simon Peter was staying there.

[19]Meanwhile, as Peter was puzzling over the vision, the Holy Spirit said to him,

"Three men have come looking for you. [20]Get up, go downstairs, and go with them without hesitation. Don't worry, for I have sent them."

[21]So Peter went down and said, "I'm the man you are looking for. Why have you come?"

[22]They said, "We were sent by Cornelius, a Roman officer. He is a devout and God-fearing man, well respected by all the Jews. A holy angel instructed him to summon you to his house so that he can hear your message." [23]So Peter invited the men to stay for the night. The next day he went with them, accompanied by some of the brothers from Joppa.

[24]They arrived in Caesarea the following day. Cornelius was waiting for them and had called together his relatives and close friends. [25]As Peter entered his home, Cornelius fell at his feet and worshiped him. [26]But Peter pulled him up and said, "Stand up! I'm a human being just like you!" [27]So they talked together and went inside, where many others were assembled.

²⁸Peter told them, "You know it is against our laws for a Jewish man to enter a Gentile home like this or to associate with you. But God has shown me that I should no longer think of anyone as impure or unclean. ²⁹So I came without objection as soon as I was sent for. Now tell me why you sent for me."

³⁰Cornelius replied, "Four days ago I was praying in my house about this same time, three o'clock in the afternoon. Suddenly, a

man in dazzling clothes was standing in front of me. ³¹He told me, 'Cornelius, your prayer has been heard, and your gifts to the poor have been noticed by God! ³²Now send messengers to Joppa, and summon a man named Simon Peter. He is staying in the home of Simon, a tanner who lives near the seashore.' ³³So I sent for you at once, and it was good of you to come. Now we are all here, waiting before God to hear the message the Lord has given you."

10:14 Greek *anything common and unclean.*

NOTES

10:10 *fell into a trance.* Later texts (E L P many minuscules, followed by the Textus Receptus and NKJV) contain *epepesen* [ᵀᴳ1968, ᶻᴳ2158] (fell on), which avoids the repetition of *egeneto* [ᵀᴳ1096, ᶻᴳ1181] (happen) in the verse (Metzger 1994:326). This clause, however, should read *egeneto ep' auton ekstasis,* "a trance came upon [happened] to him."

10:12 *all sorts of animals.* This probably refers to both clean and unclean (Johnson 1992:184), not just unclean (contra Haenchen 1971:348; Marshall 1980:185). Peter's refusal in 10:14 is not nonsensical (contra Barrett 1994:507) when we take into account the function of the imagery: to evoke the completeness of God's household (Humphrey 1995:81).

10:14 *No, Lord.* Peter, given his previous practice (1:21, 24), probably takes the heavenly voice as Jesus' (Spencer 1997:110-111; contrast Witherington [1998:350] who says Peter addresses God or at least a heavenly messenger; cf. Fernando [1998:320]). Still, he refuses to eat, not because he takes it as the devil's temptation (contrast Roloff 1981:169) or a divine test (contrast Talbert 1997:107), but because he is making an unthinking but characteristic outburst (Matt 16:22; Luke 22:33; Fernando 1998:320; cf. Barrett 1994:507).

impure and unclean. In Lev 11 and Deut 14, the clean-unclean distinction marks what the holy people of God are and are not permitted to eat. Wenham (1981) closely critiques and finds inadequate all the suggested rationales for the distinction: hygiene, association with idolatry, carnivores as unclean, and ethical symbolism. He proposes an overarching symbolism of purity understood as integrity and wholeness. Animals that do not seem to fit their class are unclean (e.g., those having more legs and wings than normal, Lev 11:20-23). Wenham applies this to Israel's relation to God. Their diet was limited to certain meats because God had restricted his choice among nations to Israel. It reminded them of their calling to be a holy nation.

10:17 *the gate.* Barrett (1994:510), following Haenchen (1971:348), sees this (*pulōn* [ᵀᴳ4440, ᶻᴳ4784]) as an ordinary door to a house, since a tanner would not have a grand house with a gate, gatehouse, and courtyard leading to a main building. Witherington (1998:350-351), Keener (1993:351), and the NLT understand it in accord with its more common meaning (gate) and envision that larger building complex.

10:19 *the Holy Spirit said.* One must be careful neither to reduce the Spirit's communication to "growth of inward conviction" (contra Marshall 1980:187) nor to lump the angel (10:3), the heavenly voice, and the Spirit into one divine reality that "is both exegetically and experientially difficult, if not impossible, to draw any sharp lines between" (contra

Longenecker 1981:389; cf. Dunn 1996:138). While there is certainly a unity of purpose and action from the Triune God, the distinct methods of communication must not be ignored (cf. 8:26, 29; 13:2; 16:6, 7).

10:20 *without hesitation.* Gr., *mēden diakrinomenos.* The verb in this phrase, *diakrinomai* [TG1252A, ZG1359], is in the middle, or passive, voice, so it can mean either "to take issue with" or "to be at odds with oneself, to doubt, to waver, to have misgivings" as it is understood here by many (Barrett 1994:511; Kistemaker 1990:382; cf. Rom 14:23; Jas 1:6). But since Peter's objections were really based on continuing prejudicial distinctions between Jew and Gentile, and the vision, as he came to properly interpret it, has to do with removing such distinctions (10:28), it seems best to take the verb here as an intensified form of its active meaning: "to make a distinction, to differentiate" (cf. 11:12; 15:9; Marshall 1980:187). Johnson (1992:185) says both meanings are picked up here.

10:22, 33 *hear your message . . . the message the Lord has given you.* In these instances Johnson (1992:185, 191) asserts that the speaker either expands what the angel said or assumes that Peter is bearing a message. If, however, we take into account the literary device of functional redundancy, Luke introducing new information in multiple retellings, then we can see that the angel told Cornelius the purpose of Peter's mission and on that basis Peter stated his readiness to receive God's message (Witherup 1993:55-56; cf. 11:14).

10:24 *They arrived.* This rendering agrees with the reading of 𝔓74 ℵ A C E 𝔐, which is *eisēlthon* (third person pl.). This may be an assimilation to the plurals that precede and follow it (*sunēlthon* [TG4905, ZG5302], "go together"; and *autous,* "them"). Cf. Metzger 1994:329. Other mss (B D 044) read *eisēlthen* [TG1525, ZG1656] (he arrived).

10:25-26 *Cornelius fell at his feet and worshiped him.* The NLT rightly represents Cornelius's action as worship (Dunn 1996:138; Barrett 1994:513; Witherington 1998:352), which Peter refused. Contrast Fernando (1998:322) and Talbert (1997:107), who think it is customary oriental obeisance to an important person.

10:28 *I should no longer think of anyone as impure or unclean.* The alleged discrepancy between a vision about clean and unclean animals (10:11-16) and Peter's statement about clean and unclean humans need not be explained by a redaction of disparate traditions (contra Barrett 1994:497). Rather, for the Jews, historically and hermeneutically, the food laws were a part of a larger complex of prohibitions limiting social intercourse with Gentiles (Scott 1991:479; Dunn 1996:139; see Spencer [1997:111] for a description of this in socio-anthropological terms; cf. Lev 20:24-26). Literarily, the parabolic (Fernando 1998:321) or polyvalent (Humphrey 1995:81) nature of the vision's imagery was the catalyst for Peter's legitimate application of it to Jew-Gentile relations. Indeed, the narrative graphically illustrates "the correlation of codes governing food and eating, domestic relations, spatial and ethnic boundaries, and social identity." By it Luke demonstrates the unity of the issues of "communal inclusivity, commensality, and co-salvation of all who believe" (Elliott 1991:107).

10:30 *Four days ago . . . three o'clock.* The NLT smooths out the awkward time marker, which is, lit., "from the fourth day until this hour I was at the ninth hour praying." Though the Textus Receptus (cf. NKJV), supported by a diversified and respectable array of witnesses (𝔓50 A² D 044 𝔐), introduces fasting (*nēsteuōn* [TG3522, ZG3764]) as Cornelius's activity over the four days and some mss are concerned with correlating the number of days with the rest of the narrative, none actually deals with the heart of the awkwardness: the fourth day set between the two prepositions. So, Metzger (1994:331) proposes the time marker is "colloquial koine" or "Semitized Greek" (cf. Barrett [1994:517] who says it may be an idiom not yet found in other literary texts or papyri).

COMMENTARY

By giving Peter a vision synchronized with Cornelius's messengers' arrival and the Spirit's instructions, God overcame the Jewish religio-ethnic barriers, producing Peter's obedient response in taking God's mission to all nations.

"About noon" the following day, as "Cornelius's messengers were nearing the town," Peter mounted the outside staircase to the "flat roof" to pray, modeling an apostle's devoted prayer life (10:9; cf. 2:42; 6:4). The rooftop provided solitude, possibly an awning for shade, and the refreshment of breezes off the Mediterranean. During prayer, "a trance" came on Peter. He did not lose consciousness or fall asleep (contrast Gen 2:21 LXX). Rather, God brought a "visionary state" upon Peter while he was wide awake (cf. 11:5; 22:17). God communicated with him visually and audibly.

Peter witnessed one of those rare instances of the free intercourse between heaven and earth (cf. 1:10-11; 2:2; 7:55-56; 9:3-6), as he saw heaven opened (10:11; cf. Luke 3:21; Rev 4:1; 19:11; NLT "sky open"). "Something like a large sheet" (*othonēn* [TG3607, ZG3855]; used in *Martydom of Polycarp* 15.2 of a ship's sails) was "let down by its four corners." This action indicates that what is to be said and done in the vision comes from God and has universal implications (cf. "four corners of the earth," Rev 7:1). The categories of animals the sheet contains correspond to a comprehensive Old Testament cataloging of the animal kingdom on land and in the air (Gen 1:24; 7:14; 8:19; Lev 11; see note on 10:12). Sound is added to sight as a "voice" commands Peter to slaughter these animals and eat them (*thuson* [TG2380, ZG2604], "slaughter," is a verb used in sacrificial and meal contexts; 2 Chr 29:22; Lev 19:5-6; Deut 12:15-16; *m. Hullin*).

In the strongest possible terms, Peter refused (10:14; cf. Ezek 4:13-15). He declared his continuing commitment to live distinctively as a Jew, maintaining ritual purity—i.e., not eating anything "common and unclean" (10:14 NLT mg; Lev 10:10; 11:1-47; Deut 14:3-21). Divinely prohibited food is "common" (*koinos* [TG2839, ZG3123]) because it is permitted to every human being except those who are God's "own," the people who claim distinctive allegiance to him (*idios* [TG2398, ZG2625], "one's own," is the opposite of *koinos*; cf. 4:32). Divinely prohibited food is "unclean" because ingesting it renders the person ritually defiled and unfit, apart from ritual cleansing, to come into God's presence in worship. These distinctions in diet, along with circumcision and Sabbath observance, then, were the concrete boundaries that first-century Jews zealously observed in maintaining their distinctive religio-ethnic identity.

The voice came again, this time with the rationale: "Do not call something unclean if God has made it clean" (10:15). Divine revelation had imposed the boundary between clean and unclean simply based on divine fiat (see note on 10:14). Divine revelation, by a subsequent fiat, removed it. Both the visual image and the divine command from heaven assumed the boundary had been erased. This divine pronouncement declared it to be so and made clear that any continuing human maintenance of it can claim no divine support. Jewish thought said that the

Messiah, in his kingdom, would remove the distinction between clean and unclean food (*Midrash Psalms* 146 § 4 [268]). Jesus' teaching and behavior had prepared the way for such a declaration (Mark 7:14-23; Luke 11:39-41), and the cross provided its salvific basis (Eph 2:14-15; Col 2:14). Though none of the prohibited foods were ever unclean in and of themselves (Gen 1:31), with their boundary-marking role set aside, their essential goodness could be clearly affirmed (1 Tim 4:3).

The threefold occurrence of the vision emphasizes the authority of its message; at the same time, it anticipates the resistance to its truth by Peter, the church, and Pharisaic Christians (11:3; 15:5). It also sadly parallels Peter's other threefold denial (Luke 22:34, 54-62).

Peter was "very perplexed" by the vision (10:17). He could not sort out the evident contradiction in the heavenly command to disregard divinely given food laws. Even if he were to accept the validity of this subsequent revelation, what implications did this boundary removal have for his identity and behavior as a Jew who had become a Christian?

Just as he was puzzling over the vision, by providential coincidence, Cornelius's men stood outside at the gate of Simon the tanner's house. In the midst of Peter's "puzzling" (*dienthumoumenou* [TG1326.1, ZG1445]—that is, thorough or serious thinking about something) the Spirit spoke to him (10:19-20). Again, God was taking the initiative, giving guidance in the outward movement of his mission across ethnic boundaries (cf. 8:29; 13:2). He told Peter that three men were seeking him, and he instructed him to go with them without making prejudicial distinctions (NLT "without hesitation"; see note 10:20). He was preparing Peter for what he would learn soon enough: These men were Gentiles! Divine fiat is again the rationale: "I have sent them." The command and rationale from the Spirit and from the vision mutually illumine each other. If he was not to keep on calling common what God had declared clean, he was to treat Gentiles without prejudicial distinction even to the extent of enjoying their hospitality.

Peter met the men and was unconsciously ironic in his greeting: "I'm the man you are looking for. Why have you come?" (10:21). An apostle, sent to proclaim the gospel to all nations, must be "sought" and, when found, was still without a clue about his mission!

The messengers described Cornelius's social and ethnic identity as being "righteous" toward both God and man and as being a God-fearing man with a good reputation among "all the Jews." They then related the holy angel's instruction. God's initiative in the matter of the gospel coming to Cornelius, then, is total. He commands the intended audience to summon the gospel messenger. He commands the gospel messenger to obey that summons. So strong was the prejudice, that if God had not acted to remove the boundary and overcome the distance between Jew and Gentile, it would never have happened. But God was determined that his mission would be fulfilled continuously, moving from its inaugural center among the Jewish people of promise across every ethnic and geographical boundary. So determined was he that he took the extraordinary steps of providing visions for Jew and

Gentile and issuing the Spirit's command as part of providential "coincidences" to make sure the boundaries came down.

Peter invited the men to be his guests (10:23), which does not go beyond what a law-abiding Jew might do. Still, because of their visit's purpose, Peter's hospitality was a sign that he agreed to their request, which was not permitted for a Jew. God continued to use human means to accomplish his mission. Even his direct intervention from heaven must be matched by human obedience.

Peter may have sensed the precedent-setting nature of his visit to Cornelius (cf. 15:7). He was certainly aware of the possible concern the visit would be to Jewish Christians back in Jerusalem. So he set out with a delegation of six believers from Joppa. They symbolized the church's crossing this next boundary in mission, and they served as witnesses (10:23; 10:45; 11:12). While they were traveling, Cornelius magnanimously gathered his own delegation of "relatives and close friends"—his immediate and extended household including retainers with various business and military reciprocity relations (10:24; Josephus *Antiquities* 7.350; cf. Acts 11:14). His eager anticipation parallels that of the Old Testament people of God toward the final salvation (Luke 3:15; 7:19-20; 12:46).

There was some understandable awkwardness when Peter and Cornelius met as the soldier fell at the apostle's feet "and worshiped him." Cornelius may well have been filled with awe at meeting the one whom an angelic vision said to summon. Peter would have none of this (10:26). Pulling him to his feet, Peter let Cornelius know that he himself was only a human being. Not only was Peter affirming a biblical monotheism in which God alone receives worship (Exod 20:3-5; Deut 5:7-9; Rev 19:10; 22:8-9) but he was also placing himself on the same footing with Cornelius. He acknowledged the level ground of creation: "I'm a human being just like you." This implicitly undercut any claims of ethnic superiority of Jews over Gentiles.

Luke focused on Peter's dramatic step of entering a Gentile's house. When Peter said, "It is against our laws for a Jewish man to enter a Gentile home like this," he used phrasing that emphasized complete separation from foreigners, which involved no association with them (10:28; cf. 5:13; 17:34; 18:2; Demosthenes *Orations* 24.176; 22.69). This principle of separation from Gentiles undergirded the food laws from the very beginning of Israel's national life (Lev 20:24-26) and intensified in postexilic and intertestamental times (cf. Ezra 10:11; *Letter of Aristeas* 139-142; Philo *Moses* 1.278). Gentile writers commented on it (Diodorus Siculus *Bibliotheca Historia* 63.2; Tacitus *Histories* 5.5; Philostratus *Life of Apollonius* 5.33; Juvenal *Satires* 14.104). Rabbinic law extended the separation by proscribing Jewish acceptance of hospitality in Gentile homes (*m. Avodah Zarah* 5:5; *m. Teharot* 7:6).

Despite this deep-seated taboo, Peter announced he had learned the lesson of the complex of divine initiatives. Stated concisely, he said, "God has shown me that I should no longer think of anyone as impure or unclean." No human being is to be viewed as "common," beyond the reach of God's grace to choose him as part of his own people. No human being is to be viewed as unclean (cf. Jesus' example, Luke 5:30; 7:34; 15:1).

Peter's immediate response demonstrates he had learned the vision's lesson. Then he wanted to know why he had been called to Cornelius's house. Peter's understanding continued to develop incrementally. He knew God had erased the boundary between clean and unclean, and he was very comfortable in his divinely-directed association with Gentiles. But what was he supposed to do in Cornelius's company? Cornelius's response indicates that God had orchestrated this historic meeting, including its purpose. This second retelling of Cornelius's vision and subsequent obedience affirmed to Peter that it was God who had brought Cornelius and him together. As in worship, they were present "before God to hear the message the Lord has given you" (10:33). The message, too, would be of divine origin.

◆ **D. Gentiles Hear the Good News (10:34-43)**

[34]Then Peter replied, "I see very clearly that God shows no favoritism. [35]In every nation he accepts those who fear him and do what is right. [36]This is the message of Good News for the people of Israel—that there is peace with God through Jesus Christ, who is Lord of all. [37]You know what happened throughout Judea, beginning in Galilee, after John began preaching his message of baptism. [38]And you know that God anointed Jesus of Nazareth with the Holy Spirit and with power. Then Jesus went around doing good and healing all who were oppressed by the devil, for God was with him.

[39]"And we apostles are witnesses of all he did throughout Judea and in Jerusalem. They put him to death by hanging him on a cross,* [40]but God raised him to life on the third day. Then God allowed him to appear, [41]not to the general public,* but to us whom God had chosen in advance to be his witnesses. We were those who ate and drank with him after he rose from the dead. [42]And he ordered us to preach everywhere and to testify that Jesus is the one appointed by God to be the judge of all—the living and the dead. [43]He is the one all the prophets testified about, saying that everyone who believes in him will have their sins forgiven through his name."

10:39 Greek *on a tree.* 10:41 Greek *the people.*

NOTES

10:35 *accepts.* In Gr. this is the adjective *dektos* [TG1184, ZG1283], meaning "pertaining to that which is pleasing in view of its being acceptable" (L&N 1:299). Some say Luke presents Cornelius in the Jewish category of "righteous Gentile," one accepted by God and enjoying salvation (Talbert 1997:109; cf. Barrett 1994:521; see Bassler's [1985] argument for this understanding within the framework of Greco-Roman universalism). Others see Peter's declaration as support for the principle that God will judge the heathen by the light they have, not according to "the light that did not reach them" (Pinnock 1990:367; Anderson 1970:102). These views are not congruent with either the immediate or larger context. The angelic announcement of the purpose for Peter's visit (11:14) would have made the visit redundant at best and irrelevant at worst if Cornelius was already saved, "accepted" by God. In fact, Peter's message is thoroughly evangelistic, climaxing with an announcement of forgiveness of sins for all those who believe in Jesus (10:43; Fernando 1998:334). Not only does Luke declare elsewhere that salvation only comes by believing in Jesus' name (4:12; 16:30-31; cf. Witherington 1998:359) but he also makes very clear

that salvation and right standing with God do not come through works of the law
(13:38-39; Kilgallen 1998a:301). It is best, then, to understand *dektos* [TG1184, ZG1283]
as "acceptable, welcome" to God (Bayer 1998:268), not "accepted, saved."

10:36-38 The NLT has smoothed out the rough syntax of these verses by rendering an
introductory accusative of respect followed by a relative clause (10:36; *ton logon hon*, lit.,
"the word, which he sent") as a predicate noun introduced by "this is" (note the textual
critical uncertainty concerning the relative pronoun, cf. Metzger 1994:333) and by introducing a connective and main verb, "And you know" (10:38), to anchor a subordinate
clause. The resulting thought flow permits v. 36 to stand independently of either what
precedes or what follows. Thus, the word of the gospel does not stand clearly in apposition to the impartiality and acceptability statements (10:34-35; so Polhill 1992:261;
Witherington 1998:356), creating the possibility of misunderstanding the salvation
status of pre-evangelized Cornelius. Neither is it clearly linked to v. 37, which prevents
v. 37 from properly functioning as proof of the sermon's theme contained in v. 36
(Burchard 1985:293; cf. Luke 2:15, 17). Treated independently, v. 36 contains the gospel
message on the pattern of its first announcement to the shepherds (Luke 2:10-14). The
NLT permits such a reading, though it does de-emphasize both God's role in sending the
message and the Christological confession at the verse's climax (*houtos estin pantōn kurios*
[TG2962, ZG3261], "this one is Lord of all") by making it a relative clause: "who is Lord
of all."

COMMENTARY

Peter's speech provides the interpretive climax for this stage of "God on mission." In
Jesus, Lord of all people regardless of race or ethnicity, forgiveness is found by all
who believe (10:36, 43). Peter's speech proceeds in three stages; an introduction
presents the theme, "Jesus Christ, who is Lord of all" (10:34-36); a statement of the
kerygma proves the theme (10:37-41); and a conclusion applies Christ's judicial,
saving lordship to the hearers (10:42-43).

Peter announced his newly acquired understanding that, in matters of race or
ethnicity, "God shows no favoritism." It is not that he is tolerant of different religions but that he is an impartial judge (Deut 10:17; 2 Chr 19:7). He "accepts," or
rather "welcomes" (see note on 10:35) from every "nation," including the Jews,
those who reverence him (Deut 10:12) and "do what is right" (lit. "produce righteousness"). "Nation" (*ethnos* [TG1484, ZG1620]) points to any racial, ethnic, or cultural
grouping by which humans distinguish themselves.

Peter and Luke are seeking to avoid two extremes here: the Jews' ethnic pride and
prejudice, which saw no Gentile as a fit object of God's saving call, and the view that
the religions of all cultures are equally valid bases for being acceptable to God. In
turning away from idols to the one true God, Cornelius demonstrated belief in
God's existence; in turning away from pagan immorality to doing "what is right,"
according to Old Testament ethic and piety, he showed his earnestness in seeking
God (Heb 11:6). These first steps of repentance did not save him but showed that
he was making positive pre-evangelistic moves so that, in his case, God's promise
to gather the Gentiles to himself would be fulfilled (Isa 56:6-8).

In wording reminiscent of Psalm 107:20 and Isaiah 57:2, Peter stated the theme
of his sermon (10:36). God had sent a message to the people of Israel, the Good

News of peace through Jesus Christ. This Jesus Christ is Lord of all people (cf. Rom 10:12). Cornelius learned of the universal scope of salvation blessings in Jesus. God's original intention is now clear (Luke 2:10, 14).

Jesus' ministry "throughout Judea, beginning in Galilee," after John the Baptist's preparatory mission, was such public knowledge that evidently Cornelius and his household knew about it. God anointed Jesus "with the Holy Spirit and with power" (cf. Luke 4:18; 10:21); his lordship's power was manifest in his going around "doing good" (*euergetōn* [TG2109, ZG2308], a word related to a title given to Hellenistic monarchs in their roles as "public benefactors," cf. 22:25; *Papyri Strass* 7.637, lines 10-11). More precisely, he exercised his lordship in healing through releasing the oppressed from the devil's power (Luke 13:16). Indeed, "God was with him." What Luke especially focused upon was the credibility of Peter's witness to Jesus' earthly ministry and death (10:39; cf. Luke 1:4).

Peter's declaration, that the Jews put Jesus to death by crucifixion (lit. "hanging on a tree"—a death under curse, Deut 21:22), again, creates the objective grounds for a salvific understanding of Jesus' death as vicarious atonement. His death is the basis for an offer of forgiveness of sins (10:43; cf. 3:13-14; 5:30). Peter then recounts that after Jesus' crucifixion, God raised him to life three days later and "allowed him to appear" (lit. "gave him to be manifest"). As the Greek word *emphanē* [TG1717, ZG1871] was used, in legal circles, of evidence provided in open court (Antiphon 5.34; Euripides *Electra* 1109) so Jesus' post-Resurrection manifestations evidenced his victory over death.

Peter realized that Jesus was not seen by all the people, but this was not a deficiency. For God chose those who would see the risen Lord, thus indicating that their witness not only had his approval but also an origin in divine initiative (cf. Luke 6:13-16; Acts 1:2). Peter further testified to the Resurrection's historical authenticity by saying that during the post-Resurrection period the apostles "ate and drank with" Jesus—that is, they experienced Jesus with their senses (10:41; cf. Luke 24:30, 39-43; Acts 1:3-4; John 20:19-23, 27; 21:12).

Peter's conclusion applies Christ's universal lordship to his audience (10:42-43). In Jesus they face both a final accounting and a unique opportunity. God appointed Jesus the judge of all humankind. The theme of final judgment occurs consistently in speeches to Gentiles (17:31; 24:25), and the Resurrection is the key event establishing Jesus as universal lord and judge. For, only the one whom God raised, conquering the power of death, is qualified to be a divinely appointed judge of all humankind, living or dead. He alone qualifies to render verdicts of eternal death or life.

Peter then announced the Good News that through the name of this universal lord, Jesus, all have the unique opportunity to receive forgiveness of sins. He grounded this offer of salvation blessings in the witness of all the Old Testament prophets (Isa 33:24; 53:4-6, 11-12; Jer 31:34; Dan 9:24; cf. Luke 24:25-27, 44-47). He moved from the particular, the Jewish prophets' witness, to the universal, the promise "that everyone who believes in him" receives forgiveness.

◆ E. Gentiles Receive the Holy Spirit (10:44-48)

⁴⁴Even as Peter was saying these things, the Holy Spirit fell upon all who were listening to the message. ⁴⁵The Jewish believers* who came with Peter were amazed that the gift of the Holy Spirit had been poured out on the Gentiles, too. ⁴⁶For they heard them speaking in tongues and praising God.

Then Peter asked, ⁴⁷"Can anyone object to their being baptized, now that they have received the Holy Spirit just as we did?" ⁴⁸So he gave orders for them to be baptized in the name of Jesus Christ. Afterward Cornelius asked him to stay with them for several days.

10:45 Greek *The faithful ones of the circumcision.*

NOTES

10:44 *Even as.* This interruption is not simply a literary device of Luke (contrast Johnson 1992:193, 195; Talbert 1997:110) but a reflection of the true history of the event in which God shows that he was continuing to take the initiative in bringing the gospel to the Gentiles (Polhill 1992:263; Witherington 1998:255).

10:45 *Jewish believers.* Lit., "the faithful ones of the circumcision" (cf. NLT mg). This probably refers not to Jewish Christians generally (so Barrett 1994:529; NLT) but to a Jewish Christian party within the church who "continued to regard circumcision as the most distinctive feature of the covenant people" (Dunn 1996:145; cf. Acts 11:2; 15:1, 5).

10:46 *speaking in tongues.* The precise nature of this phenomenon is difficult to decide since, on one hand, tongues is briefly described in terms of glossolalia (*lalountōn glōssais* [TG1100, ZG1185], cf. 1 Cor 14:2-3, 39)—that is, ecstatic utterance requiring equally inspired interpretation—yet on the other hand, the phenomena is presented as analogous to the xenolalia—the speaking and hearing of a foreign language—of Acts 2. (Note the Western witnesses here, which incorporate various modifiers that would make the text say that they spoke with "other tongues," i.e., human languages, Metzger 1994:336). While most scholars see the phenomenon of Acts 10:46 as ecstatic utterance (Esler 1992:141; Kee 1997:143; Witherington 1998:360), some opt for a direct correlation with the xenolalia of Acts 2 (Dunn 1996:146). Still others are more cautious, either saying they are uncertain (Kistemaker 1990:400) or using a more generic category of inspired speech: "a language not the speaker's own" (Barrett 1994:116).

COMMENTARY

The Spirit's falling on Cornelius and his household could be called a "Gentile Pentecost." Simultaneous with Peter's preaching, the Holy Spirit fell on all who "were listening to the message" (10:44). Luke affirmed the normal pattern for reception of salvation blessings: they come to those who hear and heed the gospel message (cf. Luke 8:15; Acts 4:4; 11:19; 15:7). At the same time, he showed that the event was a unique benchmark by presenting it as a divine interruption. It was all of God, for Peter had not even finished his sermon, let alone given the invitation. God demonstrated that he had not only welcomed the Gentiles but also regenerated them, apart from any Jewish initiation ritual. With suddenness and intensity, the Spirit fell on the Gentiles.

For any Jewish Christian, but especially for those with a commitment to circumcision, it was astonishing that the Holy Spirit had been poured out on uncircumcised Gentiles. Indeed, the presence of the Spirit in Israel and his absence among the Gentiles was one of the distinctive marks of God's holy people.

The conversion of Cornelius and his household represents a divinely initiated "class action." The gospel had definitively crossed the cultural threshold to the Gentiles (15:7). As they spoke in tongues and praised God, just as happened at Pentecost (cf. 2:4, 11), they gave convincing evidence that they were authentically experiencing God's complete salvation (2:28, 33). Indeed, the experience of salvation always evokes praise to the Giver of salvation. As happened at Pentecost (2:11) and in Ephesus, the last evangelized area of Paul's missionary journey, the newly converted or newly filled-with-the-Spirit magnified God.

Peter asked, "Can anyone object (lit. "prevent/hinder water [to be brought]") to their being baptized?" (cf. 8:36). In other words, God has acted: "They have received the Spirit just as we did." It would not have been right to withhold from them baptism, that outward physical sign of full incorporation into the church, the company of the saved. So Peter ordered them to be baptized. This call for baptism, along with the Joppa Christians' witness, shows that the Gentiles' reception of salvation was to be recognized in the whole church, not seen as an idiosyncratic aberration of one apostle. As often occurs in Acts, those who experience saving grace show their gratitude immediately to the gospel messengers, so Cornelius invited Peter and presumably the others to enjoy his hospitality "for several days" (10:48).

◆   ## F. Peter Explains His Actions (11:1-18)

Soon the news reached the apostles and other believers* in Judea that the Gentiles had received the word of God. ²But when Peter arrived back in Jerusalem, the Jewish believers* criticized him. ³"You entered the home of Gentiles* and even ate with them!" they said.

⁴Then Peter told them exactly what had happened. ⁵"I was in the town of Joppa," he said, "and while I was praying, I went into a trance and saw a vision. Something like a large sheet was let down by its four corners from the sky. And it came right down to me. ⁶When I looked inside the sheet, I saw all sorts of small animals, wild animals, reptiles, and birds. ⁷And I heard a voice say, 'Get up, Peter; kill and eat them.'

⁸"'No, Lord,' I replied. 'I have never eaten anything that our Jewish laws have declared impure or unclean.*'

⁹"But the voice from heaven spoke again: 'Do not call something unclean if God has made it clean.' ¹⁰This happened three times before the sheet and all it contained was pulled back up to heaven.

¹¹"Just then three men who had been sent from Caesarea arrived at the house where we were staying. ¹²The Holy Spirit told me to go with them and not to worry that they were Gentiles. These six brothers here accompanied me, and we soon entered the home of the man who had sent for us. ¹³He told us how an angel had appeared to him in his home and had told him, 'Send messengers to Joppa, and summon a man named Simon Peter. ¹⁴He will tell you how you and everyone in your household can be saved!'

¹⁵"As I began to speak," Peter continued, "the Holy Spirit fell on them, just as he fell on us at the beginning. ¹⁶Then I thought of the Lord's words when he said, 'John baptized with* water, but you will be baptized with the Holy Spirit.' ¹⁷And since God gave these Gentiles the same

gift he gave us when we believed in the Lord Jesus Christ, who was I to stand in God's way?" [18]When the others heard this, they stopped objecting and began praising God. They said, "We can see that God has also given the Gentiles the privilege of repenting of their sins and receiving eternal life."

11:1 Greek *brothers*. 11:2 Greek *those of the circumcision*. 11:3 Greek *of uncircumcised men*. 11:8 Greek *anything common or unclean*. 11:16 Or *in*; also in 11:16b.

NOTES

11:2 *the Jewish believers*. Lit., "those of the circumcision" (cf. NLT mg). Some take this as a reference to the whole church, either noting the natural antecedent, "the apostles and other believers" in v. 1 (Rapske 1998:240), or the fact that the crowd was so readily mollified (11:18; Barrett 1994:529, 536). Since it is redundant to call an entirely Jewish Christian church, "those of the circumcision," it is best to see the objectors as a more or less well-defined faction within the Jerusalem church for whom circumcision was fundamental to their identity (Dunn 1996:149; Polhill 1992:266). Maloney (1991:73) contends that, in order to forward his Jerusalem church unity motif, Luke gives an inaccurate picture of a circumcision party faction. Maloney thinks the whole church was objecting to Peter's action. This does not square with the full evidence in Acts. There was a range of responses in the Jerusalem church to various ethnic groups' receptions of the gospel (cf. Acts 15 and 21).

11:11 *we were staying*. The ms evidence for this reading, *ēmen* [TG1510, ZG1639] (we were), is 𝔓74 ℵ A B D; the variant reading *ēmēn* (I was) has the support of 𝔓45 E 044 33 1739 𝔐 syr cop. Thus, the evidence is evenly divided. The reading with the first person singular shows an interest in Peter and is probably an assimilation to v. 5 (Barrett 1994:540; Metzger 1994:339). The plural reading implicates the Joppa Christians from the very beginning of Peter's contacts with Cornelius's emissaries (Johnson 1992:197).

11:12 *not to worry that they were Gentiles*. While some witnesses (𝔓45[vid?] D syr[h]) omit *mēden diakrinanta* [TG1252, ZG1359] ("not making distinctions"; cf. L&N 30.113), the older and better attested reading includes it—per ℵ(*) A B (E Ψ) 33 1739. The majority of mss (incl. Textus Receptus) read *mēden diakrinomenon* [TG1252A, ZG1359], meaning "not doubting, worrying, objecting" (L&N 31.37). Though some seek to preserve both meanings and thus maintain an ambiguity or double entendre (Johnson 1992:198; Dunn 1996:150; see NLT), it is best to follow the manuscript evidence and take the active, "not making distinctions," as original and the Majority Text reading as an assimilation to 10:20.

11:14 This verse is neither a Lukan literary device whereby he read back into 10:5-6 the content of 10:22, 33 (so Johnson 1992:198), nor an example of storyteller's license in which Peter's ministry is introduced in terms of the results it produced (so Dunn 1996:150). Rather, it is an example of "functional redundancy" in which Luke withholds the divinely intended purpose of Peter's visit so that it may have the maximum literary impact in the final of a series of retellings (Witherup 1993:57). Historically, it makes sense of Cornelius's expectation as declared in 10:22, 33.

11:15 *As I began to speak*. This does not contradict Acts 10, where Peter had preached for some time before the Spirit fell (10:43-44; contrast Barrett 1994:541; Kurz 1997:580). "Began" may not be a strict time marker here (Kilgallen 1990). Both passages affirm that Peter was interrupted (10:44; 11:15). It may be that Peter "was just getting started" in the sense that he introduced his gospel in summary form and intended to develop it further in discussions with his audience in the days ahead (cf. Kistemaker 1990:413).

11:16 *John baptized with water, but you will be baptized with the Holy Spirit*. The dative *hudati* [TG5204, ZG5623] (water) and the phrase *en pneumati hagiou* [TG1722/4151/40, ZG1877/4460/41] (in the Holy Spirit) probably differ only for the sake of stylistic variation (Lake and Cadbury 1979:126). Though the NLT mg gives the locative option for both, the text's instrumental rendering is probably correct. It points to the impersonal means by which the baptism takes place (Wallace 1996:435).

11:17 *when we believed*. Grammatically and logically, the immediate context permits us to take the participle *pisteusasin* [TG4100, ZG4409] (to the ones who believed) with either or both "them" (the Gentiles) or "us" (the Jewish believers). Barrett (1994:542) notes this view; the NLT takes it with "us." A number of scholars say that to take it with "us," though it strengthens the point of comparison (Maloney 1991:77), is to say that the apostles came to faith on Pentecost Sunday. Dunn (1996:151), with his thoroughgoing conversion-initiation approach to the gift of the Spirit, is positive about this prospect. Talbert (1997:113) is negative on this option because it eliminates seeing the coming of the Spirit at Pentecost as an empowering of those who already believed. It is better, logically, to take it with "them," and see Peter explicitly linking faith in Christ with the Spirit's coming (cf. 10:43-44; Barrett 1994:542). The first part of this verse, then, would be better translated, "And since God gave these Gentiles, when they believed in the Lord Jesus Christ, the same gift he gave us. . . ."

COMMENTARY

In Peter's report of what God did to bring Jewish gospel messenger and Gentile audience together, we learn how Peter came to a clear recognition that salvation could be received directly by the Gentiles—without their having to become Jews.

News of this event reached the leaders and members of the mother church in Judea (11:1), and Peter immediately faced criticism when he arrived in Jerusalem (11:2). For some of the Jewish believers, the maintenance of the boundary markers between Jew and Gentile was vital (see note on 11:2), so they were criticizing Peter for exposing himself to almost certain ritual defilement by entering the home of the uncircumcised and eating with them (see 10:28 for Jewish regulations in this regard; cf. 10:48). Sadly, their prejudicial myopia prevented them from seeing and rejoicing in the salvation God had granted to the Gentiles (cf. Luke 5:30; 15:1).

In telling them exactly what had happened, Peter embarked on an explanatory discourse about a difficult matter of which they had a defective understanding (18:26; 28:23). And he did it in an orderly fashion, following a chronology governed by his firsthand experience. Peter focused on four divine initiatives, which led him from the very position of his critics to a stance of both preaching salvation directly to the Gentiles and incorporating them fully into the fellowship of the church.

Beginning with his own vision, Peter's retelling focuses on how the Lord had to overcome his (Peter's) resistance to removing the barrier between Jews and Gentiles. His critics, therefore, should fully identify with him, for he needed the same "conversion" in thinking that he would commend to them.

Peter had experienced an intersection of divine initiatives that disclosed to him God's intention: the scope of the application of God's saving purposes was to be universal (11:11-12; cf. Luke 24:47). The first divine initiative, the vision, had ended in a stalemate. Three times Peter's refusal to eat had been countered by the heavenly declaration that the boundary betweem clean and unclean had been removed and a warning to not keep on enforcing it. "Just then," three men sent from Caesarea stood at the house where Peter and the Joppa believers were. In this second divine initiative, the Spirit commanded Peter to go with these men, not making any distinctions (11:12, see note; contrast the critics' stance, 11:2-3).

Peter responded in obedience to the vision and the Spirit's command, accompanied by six brothers from Joppa. One can almost hear his critics gasp when Peter relates most plainly, "We soon entered the home of the man" (cf. 10:25; 11:3). Peter admitted the accusation but in such a way that he showed its irrelevance to the new situation. In the third and fourth divine initiatives—Cornelius's vision and the Spirit's outpouring—Peter continued to focus on God's action. He passed over the circumstances of his initial encounter with Cornelius, as well as the sermon (contrast 10:25-29, 34-43). He concentrated on Cornelius's report of what he had seen and heard and the fact that the Spirit came upon the Gentiles.

As to Peter's report about Cornelius's vision, Peter concentrated on three items. He pointed out that Cornelius had an angel appear to him in his house (11:13; cf. 10:3). Rarely is the messenger's location described in reports of visions (cf. *Joseph and Aseneth* 6:2; 14:5-8). Its significance here is that God had crossed the boundary between clean and unclean by sending his holy angel to enter and stand in an uncircumcised man's house even before he commanded Peter to do so. Peter zeroed in on two things Cornelius heard: the command to summon Peter and the purpose of Peter's coming—"He will tell you how you and everyone in your household can be saved!" (11:14, see note). Disclosed for the first time, Peter lets us know that God had a salvific intent in removing religio-ethnic identity boundary markers and in forbidding prejudice against other human beings, no matter their race or ethnic group. The means (hearing the message) and the conditions of salvation (the believing embrace of that message) were the same for Jew and Gentile (cf. 2:21, 38-40; 10:42-43; 15:11). God's removal of the barriers insured that the Jewish gospel messengers would get to the Gentiles. God's removal of the barriers would also insure that the Gentiles would come into the church without having to become Jews.

In an abrupt, unlooked for, but thoroughly analogous fashion to what happened at Pentecost, the Spirit fell on Cornelius and his household just as Peter was getting started with his speech. By remembering a prophecy of the risen Lord, Peter interpreted what was happening: "John baptized with water, but you will be baptized with the Holy Spirit" (11:16; cf. 1:5; Luke 3:16). This "Gentile Pentecost" opened Peter's eyes to see that "you" includes both Jew and Gentile fully participating in salvation blessings on the same basis. God gives Gentiles who believe in the Lord Jesus the same gift of the outpoured Spirit that he gave to Jews at Pentecost (see note on 11:17; cf. 2:38; 10:45; 15:8). Indeed, each member of the Trinity was active at Pentecost and at the conversion of these Gentiles (2:33, 38-39; 11:17).

Peter's conclusion was simple: "Who was I to stand in God's way?" (11:17; lit. "Who am I to hinder God?"). In other words, Peter said that God had demonstrated that the Gentiles who believe in the Lord Jesus Christ should be treated as full members of God's holy people. If Peter continued to treat them as unholy by withholding baptism (10:47), let alone association and table fellowship with them, he would actually be trying to hinder God's saving purposes (cf. 5:39).

At this, those listening to Peter, literally, "became quiet" (11:18). Some were satisfied, but as subsequent events show, others seemed only to acquiesce to Peter at this point (15:1, 5; cf. Luke 14:4; Acts 21:14). This was followed by praise to God that the Gentiles' faith was genuine. Such praise usually occurs in Luke and Acts in response to a miracle or to news of the success of the Gentile mission (Luke 5:25-26; 13:13; 18:43; 23:47; cf. 2:20; Acts 13:48; 21:20). They said, "We can see that God has also given the Gentiles the privilege of repenting of their sins and receiving eternal life." The phrasing indicates that the Jewish believers understood the paradigm shift that had occurred. It was not just an isolated God-fearing man's household but "the Gentiles," all non-Jews, to whom the door of salvation was wide open. Further, this salvation is a gift from God to the Gentiles, just as it was to the Jews (3:26; 5:31).

◆　G. The Church in Antioch of Syria (11:19-30)

[19]Meanwhile, the believers who had been scattered during the persecution after Stephen's death traveled as far as Phoenicia, Cyprus, and Antioch of Syria. They preached the word of God, but only to Jews. [20]However, some of the believers who went to Antioch from Cyprus and Cyrene began preaching to the Gentiles* about the Lord Jesus. [21]The power of the Lord was with them, and a large number of these Gentiles believed and turned to the Lord.

[22]When the church at Jerusalem heard what had happened, they sent Barnabas to Antioch. [23]When he arrived and saw this evidence of God's blessing, he was filled with joy, and he encouraged the believers to stay true to the Lord. [24]Barnabas was a good man, full of the Holy Spirit and strong in faith. And many people were brought to the Lord.

[25]Then Barnabas went on to Tarsus to look for Saul. [26]When he found him, he brought him back to Antioch. Both of them stayed there with the church for a full year, teaching large crowds of people. (It was at Antioch that the believers* were first called Christians.)

[27]During this time some prophets traveled from Jerusalem to Antioch. [28]One of them named Agabus stood up in one of the meetings and predicted by the Spirit that a great famine was coming upon the entire Roman world. (This was fulfilled during the reign of Claudius.) [29]So the believers in Antioch decided to send relief to the brothers and sisters* in Judea, everyone giving as much as they could. [30]This they did, entrusting their gifts to Barnabas and Saul to take to the elders of the church in Jerusalem.

11:20 Greek *the Hellenists* (i.e., those who speak Greek); other manuscripts read *the Greeks.* 11:26 Greek *disciples;* also in 11:29. 11:29 Greek *the brothers.*

NOTES

11:20 *Gentiles. Hellēnistas* [TG1675, ZG1821] (Hellenists); other mss read *Hellēnas* [TG1672, ZG1818] (Greeks). Some scholars, following 𝔓74 ℵ[2] A D*, support *Hellēnas* ("Greeks"; e.g., Dunn 1996:154; Kee 1997:322). Metzger (1994:341-342) finds the evidence stronger for *Hellēnistas* (Hellenists)—B D[2] E Ψ 1739 𝔐. The reading *euangelistas* [TG2099, ZG2296] (evangelists), found in ℵ*, though corrected to *Hellēnas* (Greeks), seems to assume the presence of *Hellēnistas* in the text. "The Hellenists" is the more difficult reading because in this context, if original, it must mean Gentiles, in contrast to "Jews" (11:19), whereas prior uses

indicate Greek-speaking Jews whether Christian (6:1) or non-Christian (9:29). If the referent of *Hellēnistas* (Hellenists) is always determined by its immediate context (Barrett
1994:550; contra Spencer [1997:119] and Dunn [1996:154] who see it as referring to
Jews), then here it points to Gentiles—i.e., "Greek speaking persons." The term *Hellēnas*
means "a Greek"—i.e., a native of Greece. This change by scribes was a transcriptional clarification in the light of the prior Lukan usage.

11:26 Christians. *Christianous* [ᵀᴳ5546, ᶻᴳ5985] is a Latin transliteration of a name coined by
adding to the proper name "Christ" the suffix *-ianos*, meaning "belonging to" and designat-
ing a follower of a political or military leader (e.g., *Augustiani* designated partisans of Nero,
Suetonius *Nero* 25.1; Tacitus *Annals* 15.14). Dunn (1996:156), however, sees no political
connotations in the term. Though Luke does not identify the source, the term was probably
coined by Roman authorities in Antioch (see Taylor 1994:82 for arguments for other
options: Christians, Jews, Gentile populace at Antioch or Rome). Further support for this
conclusion is that the suffix has negative overtones (Johnson 1992:204); its earliest uses in
Scripture and extra-biblically are by outsiders (26:28; 1 Pet 4:16; Dio Cassius 60.6.6;
Suetonius *Claudius* 25.4; Tacitus *Annals* 15.44.2; Josephus *Antiquities* 18.63-64). Furthermore, the verb *chrēmatizō* [ᵀᴳ5537, ᶻᴳ5976] (called) in the expression "called Christians" is
consistently used in the papyri of "naming" as an official designation (MM 1930:692).
Though Taylor (1994:86-94) sees the occasion for coining the term as public disturbances
among the Jews over the Christian movement (during which the Jews used "Christ" as a
politically charged title), the most that Luke tells us is that a major influx of Gentiles
directly into the church so changed its complexion vis-à-vis Judaism that outsiders had to
coin a new designation (Spencer 1997:12).

11:28 a great famine . . . during the reign of Claudius. The frequent famines of Claudius's reign (AD 41–54; Suetonius *Claudius* 18; Tacitus *Annals* 12.43) and the great famine
of Palestine (AD 46–48; Josephus *Antiquities* 20.51, 101) adequately fulfills the prophecy
(Johnson 1992:205), especially when we remember that crop shortages in one region (e.g.,
Egypt, the empire's breadbasket) would create an empire-wide food shortage, especially for
the lower classes (Witherington 1998:372-373).

11:30 entrusting their gifts to Barnabas and Saul. This famine relief visit is distinct from
Paul's collection visit (Acts 20–21; Rom 15:25-28; 1 Cor 16:1-4; 2 Cor 8–9; Witherington
1998:374; contra Johnson 1992:209). It is to be identified with Paul's second visit to Jerusalem, reported in Gal 2:1-10 (Morgado 1994:66; Witherington 1998:92-93). The conclusion that Gal 2:1-10 refers to the Jerusalem Council (Acts 15), while still the majority view
among scholars, is not satisfactory, for either one has to say that Paul had purposely left
one of his visits unreported (Polhill 1992:275) or that Luke has made a doublet out of
the visit mentioned in Gal 2, reporting part of it in Acts 11 and part in Acts 15 (Barrett
1994:559; Dunn 1996:158). The differences between Acts 11:30 and Gal 2:1-10 in the
meeting participants (elders or apostles) and its purpose (validation of the gospel to the
Gentiles or famine relief) are distinct but not mutually exclusive (cf. Gal 2:10 for an allusion to care for the poor). And there are strong similarities: both are a second visit; are
prompted "by revelation"; show a concern for the poor; and have a pre-Jerusalem Council
date, which in the case of Galatians better explains the report of Peter's backsliding (Gal
2:11-14) and the silence on the council decrees.

C O M M E N T A R Y

Picking up the story line from Acts 8:4, Luke relates how Greek-speaking Jewish
Christians, who had been scattered because of persecution, were actually spreading
the life-giving seed of the "word" as they went about preaching "the Good News"

(11:19). They evangelized the Jews of Phoenicia, a coastal, somewhat mountainous strip of land seven and a half miles wide and 185 miles long that extended from Mount Carmel north to Mount Cassius. Today, this area lies mostly in modern Lebanon. Congregations in Tyre, Sidon, and Ptolemais were the fruit (21:4, 7; 27:3). They extended their mission to Cyprus with its very large Jewish colony (Philo *Embassy* 282; cf. Acts 4:36) and then on to "Antioch on the Orontes" in Syria. This city was 300 miles from Jerusalem and 15-20 miles east of the Mediterranean at the crossroads of trade routes south to Palestine and Egypt, east to Persia, and west to the Asia Minor peninsula.

Of the sixteen cities built by the Seleucid general Seleucus I Nicator and named for his father Antiochus, Syrian Antioch was the largest and most prosperous. With its population of 300,000 (Strabo *Geography* 16.2.5), including a Jewish colony of 22,000-65,000 (Josephus *War* 7.43; noteworthy also for its Jewish proselyte population, 7.45), and its thriving economy, due to its strategic position, Josephus justly ranked it as the third greatest city of the Roman Empire, behind Rome and Alexandria (Josephus *War* 3.29). This free city, capital of the Roman province of Syria, was a cosmopolitan melting pot of East and West.

To such a city came Greek-speaking Jewish Christians from Cyprus and Cyrene (an area on the Mediterranean coast of modern Libya with a Jewish population; cf. Josephus *War* 7.437-450). They directly evangelized Gentiles in addition to their outreach to Jews (11:20; the Gr. here uses *kai* [TG2532, ZG2779], "also"). Luke gives us neither the motive nor the date of this new mission. Since Peter was the inaugurator of the church's Gentile mission (15:7, referring to 10:1-11:18), and since the church sent Barnabas, not the apostles, to investigate, it appears that this witness followed Peter's preaching to Cornelius.

While many in their day were trying to find salvation through the "lords" of various mystery cults, e.g., "Lord Sarapis" (*Papyrus Fayum* 1275), the Christian gospel messengers announced the Good News (*euangelizomenoi* [TG2097A, ZG2294]) about the only Savior, "the Lord Jesus" (cf. 8:4; 10:36; 16:31; 20:21; 28:31; Isa 40:9-11; 60:6). The Gentiles responded in "large numbers" and were converted (11:21; cf. 4:4; 6:7; 9:24, 35; 10:27; 14:15; 15:19; 26:18, 20). Luke gives this, not signs and wonders, as evidence that the hand of the Lord was with this witness (cf. Luke 1:66; Ezra 7:6; Isa 66:14; contrast Acts 4:30).

Luke used the divine title "Lord" interchangeably for the Father and the Son. If all the uses in Acts 11:19-26, however, speak of Jesus, we learn how the Lord Jesus himself is "on mission," bringing salvation directly to the Gentiles. He is the gospel's content, power, and goal. He is the object of loyalty and the central identity of those who are saved.

The Lord went out ahead of the church in the mission to proclaim salvation to all nations. Some in the Jerusalem church evidently only acquiesced to the divine initiative to and through Peter (11:18). So, when news of the direct Gentile mission came, the Jerusalem church sent Barnabas to investigate. Barnabas validated this direct Gentile mission by his initial joyful response to the "evidence of God's blessing" (11:23). The "evidence" of God's grace in the presence of authentic salvation is probably primarily quantitative, not qualitative (cf. 2:41; 11:21). Joy is heaven's response, and should be ours, when salvation has been effectively given, especially across cultural thresholds (Luke 15:7, 10; Acts 15:3; cf. 21:20).

Barnabas lived up to his name ("Son of Exhortation/Encouragement") by encouraging the Antioch believers to "stay true to the Lord" (11:23; lit. "with purpose of heart to remain with the Lord"). The way they began their Christian lives—with the Lord opening, cleansing, and enabling their hearts to understand the Good News (15:9; 16:14; 28:27)—is how they should continue. For it is not the external marks of circumcision and Jewish practice that seal one's identity as a member of God's people but rather the perseverance in a discipleship relationship with Christ, who has transformed one from the inside out.

In a narrative aside, Luke affirmed Barnabas's validation of the direct Gentile mission. God's Spirit had filled a person of "good" character, a man strong in faith, to testify that he was convinced that the successful direct Gentile mission was indeed God's work, a fulfillment of the salvation offer's universal scope (cf. Luke 24:47; Acts 2:21, 39). And the Lord further validated this mission, for as with the Jerusalem church subsequent to Pentecost (2:47; 4:4; 5:14; 6:7), there was even more divinely spawned growth: "And many people were brought to the Lord" (11:24; lit. "were added to the Lord").

In the meanwhile, Barnabas traveled northwest to Tarsus in Cilicia, in eastern Asia Minor, "to find Saul" in his hometown (the term implies a thorough search; cf. Luke 2:44-45; Acts 9:30; 21:39; 22:3). On their return, they "stayed with the church" (lit. "gathered together in the church," which points to hospitality and church gatherings in which fellowship and worship took place—see 4:31; 14:27; 15:30; 20:7-8). Their primary responsibility for an entire year was teaching, helping the church learn what to believe and how to act as disciples of Christ (cf. 2 Tim 1:11), who were called "Christians" (by outsiders; see note on 11:26).

During these days, Agabus, one of the itinerant prophets from Jerusalem, "stood up in one of the meetings" (11:28) and delivered a predictive oracle (see comment at 2:17 for other types of prophetic speech in Acts). By the Spirit, he revealed that "a great famine was coming upon the entire Roman world" (11:28). Luke tells us this prediction was fulfilled during Claudius's reign (see note on 11:28). The church responded. From discretionary income ("everyone giving as much as they could" 11:29), the church decided to set aside funds for a collection (see Rom 15:31; 2 Cor 8:4). This interchurch relief involved a mixed Jewish and Gentile congregation serving a Jewish assembly. It demonstrates a unity based on the conviction that the church is a body greater than any single congregation within any particular culture. This unity carries with it a responsibility for the well-being of all disciples, wherever they are. Barnabas and Saul were commissioned to take this collection to the "elders of the church in Jerusalem," (11:30) who had evidently emerged as the administrators of physical aid after the dispersal of the "Seven" subsequent to Stephen's martyrdom.

◆ H. James Is Killed and Peter Is Imprisoned (12:1-5)

About that time King Herod Agrippa* began to persecute some believers in the church. ²He had the apostle James (John's brother) killed with a sword. ³When Herod saw how much this pleased the Jewish people, he also arrested Peter. (This took place during the Passover celebration.*) ⁴Then he imprisoned him, placing him under the guard of four squads of four soldiers each. Herod intended to bring Peter out for public trial after the Passover. ⁵But while Peter was in prison, the church prayed very earnestly for him.

12:1 Greek *Herod the king*. He was the nephew of Herod Antipas and a grandson of Herod the Great.
12:3 Greek *the days of unleavened bread.*

NOTES

12:2 *killed with a sword.* It is not clear whether the execution was by beheading (Johnson 1992:211). Beheading was a shameful death involving desecration of the body, a punishment worthy of murderers, idolaters, and apostates (*m. Sanhedrin* 7:2; 9:1). Polhill (1992:278) notes the alternative possibility that he was simply thrust through with a sword. At the least it was a governmental action, possibly for a political crime (see Barrett 1994:575).

12:3-4 *during the Passover celebration.* Lit., "the days of unleavened bread" (NLT mg). The NLT has rightly understood Luke's interchangeable use of "Passover" and "Days of Unleavened Bread" (cf. Luke 22:1). Technically, Passover is 14 Nisan and the Days of Unleavened Bread are 15–21 Nisan.

12:3 *this pleased the Jewish people.* It was not the manner of execution (contra Johnson 1992:211) but the fact that action was taken against Christians that was pleasing to the Jews. The church's unqualified reception of Gentiles was a repugnant betrayal of Jewish loyalty, especially in a time when the Roman emperor Caligula was practising a flagrant disregard for Jewish religious sensibilities (Josephus *Antiquities* 18.262-264, 266, 268-269, 274-275; Polhill 1992:278).

12:4 *bring . . . out for public trial.* Lit., "bring out to the people." Given Herod's summary execution of James, this could just as well mean "bring out for public execution" (so Barrett 1994:577) as "bring out for public trial" (Keener 1993:356; Witherington 1998:385).

COMMENTARY

Herod Agrippa I (10 BC–AD 44; cf. 12:1 NLT mg) spent his childhood and some of his adult life in the highest imperial circles in Rome. He had recently returned to Palestine to rule over territory that by AD 41 extended as far as his grandfather's kingdom (see Schürer 1973:442-454 for a complete description of Agrippa's life and reign). A client king loyal to Rome, with Hasmonean blood ties to Judaism, Agrippa I was a pious observer of Judaism but lived a thoroughly Greco-Roman lifestyle when away from Palestine (Josephus *Antiquities* 19.292-293).

At his own initiative, Herod began to persecute believers from the church (cf. 4:3; 5:18; 21:27). Luke does not tell us why, but he does give the results: the execution of James, son of Zebedee, brother of John (Luke 5:10). The times of tranquility commencing with Paul's conversion (9:31) were over. For the first time since Jesus' crucifixion, Roman authorities took direct action against the church and that with the utmost severity and impact. One of the "Twelve," Jesus' inner circle, had been removed from the scene. Nothing was there to stop Herod from dismembering the entire movement, for the action pleased the Jewish people (contrast 5:26).

Next he arrested Peter, placing him under a secure guard of "four squads of four soldiers each" (12:4). These would rotate in three-hour shifts throughout the night so that fresh, alert personnel would always be on duty (Vegetius *De Re Militari* 3.8). Ever scrupulous in his Jewish observance, Herod left Peter in prison during the seven-day Feast of Unleavened Bread, which immediately followed Passover.

As often happens in Acts, when the activities of the church's enemies are chronicled, we are shown only the action on the human plane. There is no mention of God at work (cf. 4:1-22; 5:17-42; 6:9-15). Luke, then, skillfully juxtaposed the power of the state ("But while Peter was in prison") and the power of the church ("the church prayed very earnestly for him," 12:5). In continuous, earnest, united prayer, the church petitioned God concerning Peter. Prayer is the only weapon the church has, but it is more than enough.

◆   I. Peter's Miraculous Escape from Prison (12:6-19)

⁶The night before Peter was to be placed on trial, he was asleep, fastened with two chains between two soldiers. Others stood guard at the prison gate. ⁷Suddenly, there was a bright light in the cell, and an angel of the Lord stood before Peter. The angel struck him on the side to awaken him and said, "Quick! Get up!" And the chains fell off his wrists. ⁸Then the angel told him, "Get dressed and put on your sandals." And he did. "Now put on your coat and follow me," the angel ordered.

⁹So Peter left the cell, following the angel. But all the time he thought it was a vision. He didn't realize it was actually happening. ¹⁰They passed the first and second guard posts and came to the iron gate leading to the city, and this opened for them all by itself. So they passed through and started walking down the street, and then the angel suddenly left him.

¹¹Peter finally came to his senses. "It's really true!" he said. "The Lord has sent his angel and saved me from Herod and from what the Jewish leaders* had planned to do to me!"

¹²When he realized this, he went to the home of Mary, the mother of John Mark, where many were gathered for prayer. ¹³He knocked at the door in the gate, and a servant girl named Rhoda came to open it. ¹⁴When she recognized Peter's voice, she was so overjoyed that, instead of opening the door, she ran back inside and told everyone, "Peter is standing at the door!"

¹⁵"You're out of your mind!" they said. When she insisted, they decided, "It must be his angel."

¹⁶Meanwhile, Peter continued knocking. When they finally opened the door and saw him, they were amazed. ¹⁷He motioned for them to quiet down and told them how the Lord had led him out of prison. "Tell James and the other brothers what happened," he said. And then he went to another place.

¹⁸At dawn there was a great commotion among the soldiers about what had happened to Peter. ¹⁹Herod Agrippa ordered a thorough search for him. When he couldn't be found, Herod interrogated the guards and sentenced them to death. Afterward Herod left Judea to stay in Caesarea for a while.

12:11 Or *the Jewish people.*

NOTES

12:7 *struck him on the side*. The verb is softened in the Western text (D it gig Lucifer): *nuxas* [TG3572, ZG3817] (nudged).

12:10 *first and second guard posts*. Guards were probably stationed at entryways (Marshall 1980:209; so the NLT) but may have been patrolling one corridor (Haenchen 1971:384).

The Western text (D) says Peter and the angel, upon exiting the prison, "walked down seven steps." Though this has a "verisimilitude that reflects local knowledge of Jerusalem" (Metzger 1994:347), it is right to be cautious, even negative, about the authenticity of the detail (Longenecker 1981:412). Further, the precise identity of the prison is unknown, though many suggest the Antonia fortress adjacent to the Temple. Large homes, such as Mary's (12:12-17), probably in the Upper City, would be readily accessible from the Antonia fortress.

12:11, 17 *the Lord*. There is an admitted ambiguity in the use of "Lord" (*kurios* [TG2962, ZG3261]); it might refer to Father or Son (Dunn 1996:164). If one agrees that the consistent referent in the previous context is Jesus (11:20-21, 23-24), then it is natural to see him referred to here (cf. Wall 1991:637; contrast Maloney 1991:104).

12:12 *home of Mary, the mother of John Mark*. Whether this was the site of the upper room (1:13) is disputed. Harrison (1986:203) says perhaps; Marshall (1980:210) says there is no positive evidence; Barrett (1994:583) says such a conclusion is without foundation or value. Though some see this verse as evidence of close association between Peter and John Mark, Black (1998:102) points out that the mention of John Mark and Peter in this context does not establish a connection between them, since the purpose of referring to John Mark here is to identify his mother, who was Peter's influential patron (cf. Barrett 1994:583).

12:13 *servant girl*. Barrett (1994:584) takes *paidiskē* [TG3814, ZG4087] as "young woman, member of the church," but based on Rhoda's activity in the context and the use of the term throughout the NT (cf. Luke 12:45; 22:56; Gal 4:22-23, 30-31), most commentators understand it as the NLT does, implying her place as a servant (Spencer 1997:127; Witherington 1998:383).

12:15 *It must be his angel*. A component of Jewish angelology included personal guiding and guardian angels (Gen 48:16 LXX; Tob 5:4, 17, 22; cf. Matt 18:10), even those who resembled the one they protected (*Genesis Rabbah* 78 [50a], Gen 33:10 interpreted in the light of Gen 32:22-32). Since it is hard to think of a guardian angel leaving his charge, a better background for this exclamation is the Jewish understanding of the intermediate state of the departed dead as being like angels (2 *Baruch* 51:5, 10; cf. Luke 20:36; 24:37; Acts 23:8; Daube 1990:494; Maloney 1991:114). The further belief that the departed spirit would hover near the body for a few days immediately after death (cited in commentators without primary references, e.g., Polhill 1992:282) would create the basis for drawing such a conclusion about the appearance of Peter's angel. Such an understanding is not Christian, as the Western reading (D syrP) shows with the addition of *tuchon* [TG5177A, ZG5593] (perhaps). This reading, also, both heightens the naivete and softens the definiteness (Metzger 1994:349).

12:17 *Tell James*. Though James may have been coming into prominence as a church leader at this time (Witherington 1998:388), this instruction is not an indicator that James was already the undisputed leader (so Bruce 1988:239), nor is it a commissioning of James in a transfer of authority (so Wall 1991:641). It is simply a command to alert another segment of the church, the Hebrew-speaking Jewish Christian house churches (if Mary's house church was composed of Hellenistic Jewish Christians), about Peter's release (Maloney 1991:105).

the other brothers. These were probably members of the community (Maloney 1991:105), not apostles or elders, whom Luke could have more precisely identified (contra Harrison 1986:205; cf. 11:1, 30).

another place. This "place" has been variously identified as follows: (1) an unknown hiding place (Fernando 1998:363); (2) one of the coastal plain cities of the mission described in 9:32-43 (these were still within Herod's territory); (3) Syrian Antioch (Gal 2:11-14; Marshall 1980:211); (4) north-central Asia Minor (1 Pet 1:1; Williams 1985:203); or (5) Rome (Wenham 1972; the Roman Catholic tradition). It is best to take this statement for the little it does imply—Peter so completely escaped Herod's clutches that there is no record of where he went. This feature cannot be used as the basis for Wall's (1991) proposal that Peter's imprisonment and escape experience, followed by further mission, was being portrayed as a passion-exaltation typology parallel to that of Jesus. While attracting some support (Spencer 1997:128), this understanding of Luke's intentions overreaches the evidence (Witherington 1998:388).

COMMENTARY

On the eve of Peter's being "brought out," probably for summary execution rather than for public trial (so NLT, see note at 12:4), and in the midst of tight security (the detachment of four guards fully deployed), God went into action. The Lord sent an angel, who "suddenly" came upon Peter. In Luke's writings, the angel of the Lord not only provides deliverance for God's witnesses (5:19) but also gives strength (Luke 22:43), brings judgment (12:23), and, above all, reveals God's will about the advance of his saving purposes (Luke 1:11; 2:9; Acts 8:26; 10:3).

This escape was all God's doing—from the angelic arousal of Peter with a proverbial swift kick in the ribs, to the miraculous falling away of the manacles from his wrists, to the orders: "Get dressed and put on your sandals" with the subsequent exit (12:7-8, 10). Peter, still drowsy and somewhat disoriented, still followed orders. As if to underscore this, Luke tells us that Peter thought his experience was a vision (12:9). Just as during waking hours he, during a trance, participated in a vision in which he received heavenly commands (10:10-16), so he concluded the angel's guidance and his obedient response were simply part and parcel of a visionary encouragement from heaven. Verses 11 and 12 chronicle his progressive realization of what was really happening.

Luke described the actual escape in the most matter of fact terms (12:10). The angel, with Peter following, passed two guard posts and approached the final barrier to freedom: "the iron gate leading to the city." Luke is silent on the guards' reaction to all these doings. He only tells us of the great commotion in the morning "about what had happened to Peter" (12:18). This simply heightens the impression that the Lord was directly at work in this undetected escape.

With the angel gone, Peter finally realized what had happened (12:11). He affirmed the reality, the source, and the result of the rescue. Christianity is indeed a faith that confesses that its Lord can and will act in history on behalf of his witnesses. As Peter says, "It's really true!" In other words, "Now I know this has *really happened!*" The Lord has the same power to rescue now as he did when he delivered Israel from Egypt (Exod 3:8).

A solution to the theological and moral puzzle of why Peter was rescued while James was executed may be found in Luke's use of the term "saved" (*exeilato* [TG1807A, ZG1975], "rescued"; 12:11). Acts 26:17 uses the word to describe God's protecting hand on his witnesses to make sure they fulfill his purposes for them. As long as it is necessary that a particular servant of the Lord be actively deployed in accomplishing Christ's mission, he or she will be rescued. Any martyrdom is still a mark of God's sovereignty, not of his weakness. His gracious purposes may be traced in it. Any rescue is a sign of the triumphant advance of God's mission and a mark that nothing—especially the expectations of the opponents of that mission—can thwart the accomplishment of his purposes.

After his escape, Peter went to the home of Mary, the mother of John Mark (on John Mark, cf. 12:25; 13:5, 13; 15:37; Col 4:10; 2 Tim 4:11; Phlm 1:24; 1 Pet 5:13). From the description of the home's entryway (Peter knocks at "the door in the gate") and the "many" gathered there, we learn that the house was spacious. Its layout included at least a main building separated from a gatehouse or vestibule by an open court.

In the first of a number of details that continue to highlight God's total sovereignty in taking the initiative and accomplishing Peter's liberation, Luke tells us that Peter came to the house while the church was still praying (12:12). A maidservant named Rhoda (meaning "rosebud"), charged with answering the door, was so overcome with joy at the sound of Peter's voice that she left him standing there while she rushed in to announce his arrival. While the church members argued over the truthfulness of her report, Peter was left knocking, for they did not believe it and called Rhoda crazy. When she stuck to her story, they concluded that Peter's "angel," probably his ghost, had come to them (12:15; see note). Such excitement—blocking even the most basic clearheaded thinking—further emphasizes for the reader that Peter's escape was the Lord's work for the church, which was praying for the escape but not prepared to embrace it when it happened! But in this case "seeing is believing," for when they went to investigate and "opened the door," they saw him and were beside themselves with astonishment.

Motioning with his hand for silence (cf. 13:16; 19:33; 21:40), Peter briefly recounted his rescue in terms of its ultimate source, process, and concrete results (12:17). He briefly narrated the escape, letting the church know that it was the Lord who had freed him. Peter then instructed them to tell these things to "James and the other brothers." James, the half-brother of Jesus, had some form of administrative leadership along with the apostles by the mid-30s AD (Gal 1:19; 2:9), presided at the Jerusalem Council in AD 49 (Acts 15:13) and by the late 50s was head of the Jerusalem church (21:18). Though this was not a transfer of authority, this message to James provided encouragement that the Lord was actively and triumphantly prosecuting his mission, even in the face of opposition. The Lord liberated Peter, not to continue ministry in their midst, but to direct him "to another place." In the final analysis, the church must place confidence in the Lord and look to him for guidance for its further advance.

In the morning there was a "great commotion" (12:18) among the guards over Peter's whereabouts. Herod Agrippa made a "thorough search" for Peter and came up empty. He "interrogated the guards" and "sentenced them to death" (12:19; lit. "ordered them to be led away," presumably to execution; cf. Luke 23:26). According to Roman custom, the guard suffers the same penalty that the escapee would have faced (*Code of Justinian* 9.4.4). Thoroughly mystified and frustrated by the divine intervention, Herod Agrippa left "Judea" (understood in its narrower sense—"the environs of Jerusalem") and went to Caesarea, his administrative capital on the Mediterranean.

◆ J. The Death of Herod Agrippa (12:20-25)

²⁰Now Herod was very angry with the people of Tyre and Sidon. So they sent a delegation to make peace with him because their cities were dependent upon Herod's country for food. The delegates won the support of Blastus, Herod's personal assistant, ²¹and an appointment with Herod was granted. When the day arrived, Herod put on his royal robes, sat on his throne, and made a speech to them. ²²The people gave him a great ovation, shouting, "It's the voice of a god, not of a man!"

²³Instantly, an angel of the Lord struck Herod with a sickness, because he accepted the people's worship instead of giving the glory to God. So he was consumed with worms and died.

²⁴Meanwhile, the word of God continued to spread, and there were many new believers.

²⁵When Barnabas and Saul had finished their mission to Jerusalem, they returned,* taking John Mark with them.

12:25 Or *mission, they returned to Jerusalem.* Other manuscripts read *mission, they returned from Jerusalem;* still others read *mission, they returned from Jerusalem to Antioch.*

NOTES

12:20 *they sent a delegation.* The NLT explicitly represents the implicit idea of a representative delegation appearing before Herod and avoids the impression that the entire population of Tyre and Sidon approached the king (contrast NASB, NIV, ESV).

12:21 *an appointment with Herod . . . the day.* Verse 21 begins simply with *taktē* [TG5002, ZG5414] *de hēmera,* "on the appointed day." In a fashion similar to the NLT's rendering, the Western text inserts, between vv. 21 and 22, the phrase *katallagentos de autou tois Turiois* [TG2644, ZG2904], "and on the occasion of his reconciliation with the Tyrians" (see Metzger 1994:349). This explicitly ties Herod's appearance to the controversy with Tyre (and Sidon).

12:23 Josephus (*Antiquities* 19.343) places this event at "spectacles in honor of Caesar," either during the ninth celebration (AD 44) of the March 5 festival (which was held every five years in honor of the founding of Caesarea and its namesake Augustus and inaugurated by Herod the Great; Josephus *War* 1.415) or the one instituted by Herod Agrippa himself to celebrate Claudius's August 1 birthday (Suetonius *Claudius* 2.1). Since Passover fell after March 5 that year, depending on which festival is adopted, Peter would have been imprisoned either in AD 43 or 44.

12:25 *When Barnabas and Saul had finished their mission to Jerusalem, they returned.* The harder reading, ". . . mission, they returned to Jerusalem," is supported by the earliest and best witnesses (Metzger 1994:351). Later mss change "to Jerusalem" *eis Ierousalēm*

[TG1519/2419, ZG1650/2647] to read "from" Jerusalem (using *ek* [TG1537, ZG1666] or *apo* [TG575, ZG608], cf. NLT mg). This is not as well attested and is manifestly a secondary resolution of the difficulty.

COMMENTARY

Tyre and Sidon, coastal cities of northwest Palestine, depended on the breadbasket of Judea for grain (12:20; cf. Ezek 27:17). Luke tells us they had made the king "very angry," but he does not tell us why (see Josephus *Antiquities* 18.147-150 for earlier, personal difficulties he had in the region). Nor does Luke give us the precise nature of the king's reprisal, though the note about the region's dependence on Herod's realm for food points to an economic boycott involving foodstuffs. The situation was serious enough that the cities sent a delegation to Herod to request peace. In a sense Herod was exercising divine prerogatives over these cities. He presumed to grant or withhold their physical sustenance, which God alone supplies (14:17). Herod was the one they had to approach for peace, while it is God and God alone who can give peace (9:31; 10:36).

The delegation approached the king by winning the support of "Blastus, Herod's personal assistant" (12:20), possibly through bribery. Blastus was the king's "chamberlain" (lit. "the one in charge of his bedroom"), the one entrusted with the most intimate matters of his life, and, presumably, the most influential with him (cf. Suetonius *Domitian* 16).

As Josephus reports it, on the day of the appointment with Herod (12:21), during games held in honor of Caesar, "clad in a garment woven completely of silver so that its texture was indeed wondrous, he (Herod) entered the theatre at daybreak. There the silver, illumined by the touch of the first rays of the sun, was wondrously radiant and by its glitter inspired fear and awe in those who gazed intently upon it" (*Antiquities* 19.343-344; the whole account is in 343-359). Herod assumed a divine posture, bedecking himself in a splendor fit for a heavenly being (cf. Luke 9:29) and sitting on his throne. It is no wonder that as he made his speech the assembly gave him a great ovation: "It's the voice of a god, not of a man!" (12:22).

In the most serious derogation of divine prerogatives, Herod received their worship. "Instantly, an angel of the Lord struck Herod . . . he was consumed with worms" (12:23). He experienced pain in his heart and stomach—possibly peritonitis from a perforated appendix, combined with intestinal roundworms, ten to sixteen inches long. (Bunches of these can obstruct the intestines, causing severe pain, copious vomiting, and finally death.) This excruciating condition continued for five days until he died (see note on 12:23). Luke explicitly links the trespass of divine prerogative and the Lord's immediate judgment. The angel struck him "because he accepted the people's worship instead of giving the glory to God" (12:23; cf. Luke 2:14; 19:38). God, indeed, will not share his glory with another (Isa 42:8; 48:11).

With poignant contrast Luke summarized the Lord's victory over opposing political powers. Worms spread and devoured Herod's body. The word of God, the Christian message, also spread and multiplied. Herod was cut off just four years into his reign, but God's mission knows no such incompleteness in any aspect. In the end, this passage teaches us that Herod Agrippa's demise graphically portrays the truth that those who usurp God's place will face his swift and certain judgment and will by no means thwart the advance of his mission (12:23-24).

◆ IV. Paul's First Missionary Journey and the First Church Council at Jerusalem (13:1–16:5)
A. Barnabas and Saul Are Sent Out (13:1-3)

Among the prophets and teachers of the church at Antioch of Syria were Barnabas, Simeon (called "the black man"*), Lucius (from Cyrene), Manaen (the childhood companion of King Herod Antipas*), and Saul. ²One day as these men were wor- shiping the Lord and fasting, the Holy Spirit said, "Dedicate Barnabas and Saul for the special work to which I have called them." ³So after more fasting and prayer, the men laid their hands on them and sent them on their way.

13:1a Greek *who was called Niger.*   13:1b Greek *Herod the tetrarch.*

NOTES

13:1 *called "the black man."* Lit., "who was called Niger" (so NLT mg). *Niger* [TG3526, ZG3769] is a Latin loanword meaning "black." Although Barrett (1994:603) dissents (based on Josephus *War* 2.520, but Witherington [1998:392] disagrees with Barrett's use of Jo- sephus), in the light of Simeon's pairing in the list with Lucius from Cyrene, most commentators see this as a nickname referring at the least to Simeon's ethnic and geographical origin: Africa (Johnson 1992:220; Kee 1997:159; Fernando 1998:373), if not to his race (Dunn 1996:171; Talbert 1997:126).

King Herod Antipas. Lit., "Herod the tetrarch" (cf. NLT mg). In order to distinguish him from his nephew, Herod Agrippa I (Acts 12), Luke refers to Antipas, a son of Herod the Great who received a quarter of his realm including Galilee, as "Herod the tetrarch" (cf. Luke 3:19; 9:7).

13:2 *these men.* The NLT rightly understands the natural antecedent of *autōn* [TG846, ZG899] ("they," occuring in a genitive absolute participial construction) as the leaders listed in v. 1 (Witherington 1998:393), not the entire community (contra Spencer 1997:137 and Fernando 1998:374).

COMMENTARY

As we enter the second half of Acts with its focus on mission to the ends of the earth (1:8), we see that God took the initiative in deploying human agents for his mis- sion. Through his Spirit, God spoke to spiritually gifted ("prophets and teachers," 13:1), multicultural leaders. "Barnabas," a Levite from Cyprus (4:36), labored alongside the African "Simeon" (nicknamed "the black man") as well as with "Luci- us (from Cyrene)," also from that continent (cf. 11:20). "Manaen," who in his youth was chosen as a companion to a prince, Herod Antipas, ministered with "Saul," a Pharisee from Cilicia in southeast Asia Minor (22:3; Phil 3:5).

As they engaged in worship (lit. "ministering as priests to the Lord") and fasting, the Holy Spirit spoke to them. Though we are not told how, presumably it was through one of the prophets (cf. 11:28; 21:11). His directive manifests the supreme claim God has on his missionaries. When the church dedicated Barnabas and Saul to God, they were placing them completely at God's disposal to do the work he had called them to do.

The church leaders promptly obeyed. With earnest intercession (more fasting and prayer) and by the "laying on of hands," they not so much ordain as commission Barnabas and Saul, commending them to God's grace and blessing to a particular work, evidently of limited duration (14:26).

◆   ## B. Paul's First Missionary Journey (13:4-12)

4So Barnabas and Saul were sent out by the Holy Spirit. They went down to the seaport of Seleucia and then sailed for the island of Cyprus. 5There, in the town of Salamis, they went to the Jewish synagogues and preached the word of God. John Mark went with them as their assistant.

6Afterward they traveled from town to town across the entire island until finally they reached Paphos, where they met a Jewish sorcerer, a false prophet named Bar-Jesus. 7He had attached himself to the governor, Sergius Paulus, who was an intelligent man. The governor invited Barnabas and Saul to visit him, for he wanted to hear the word of God. 8But Elymas, the sorcerer (as his name means in Greek), interfered and urged the governor to pay no attention to what Barnabas and Saul said.

He was trying to keep the governor from believing.

9Saul, also known as Paul, was filled with the Holy Spirit, and he looked the sorcerer in the eye. 10Then he said, "You son of the devil, full of every sort of deceit and fraud, and enemy of all that is good! Will you never stop perverting the true ways of the Lord? 11Watch now, for the Lord has laid his hand of punishment upon you, and you will be struck blind. You will not see the sunlight for some time." Instantly mist and darkness came over the man's eyes, and he began groping around begging for someone to take his hand and lead him.

12When the governor saw what had happened, he became a believer, for he was astonished at the teaching about the Lord.

NOTES

13:6 *Afterward they traveled from town to town.* This rendering of a single participle, *dielthontes* [TG1330, ZG1451] ("having passed through"), picks up a Lukan use of the term to describe preaching tours (9:32; 13:14; 14:24; cf. 8:4, 40, where the preaching is explicit; Polhill 1992:292; see Gill [1995] for the probable route). Witherington (1998:396) is not convinced any hint of missionary work is present here.

13:7 *Sergius Paulus.* While the inscriptional evidence regarding governors on Cyprus is not clear enough to definitely refer to him (cf. Johnson 1992:222; Polhill 1992:292; Kee 1997:161), Witherington (1998:400), following Nobbs (1994), concludes that, taken cumulatively, the evidence clearly places members of the Sergii Pauli family (the *nomen* and *cognomen*, i.e., clan and family name) on the island of Cyprus; and it is quite feasible that one of their number gave public service as both curator of the Tiber and proconsul on Cyprus.

13:8 *Elymas, the sorcerer (as his name means in Greek).* When scholars take "Bar-Jesus" (13:6) as the antecedent of "name," they rightly identify an intractable problem: how can the non-Greek word "Elymas" be in any way a Greek translation of "Bar-Jesus"? (Barrett 1994:615; Spencer 1997:139). More naturally, as implied in the NLT, the translation equation is between "Elymas" and "the sorcerer." The two most favored solutions take "Elymas" as a transliteration for Arabic *'alim* ("wise"; "magician") or Aramaic *haloma* ("interpreter of dreams"; Klauck 1994:97).

13:9 Saul, also known as Paul. "Paul" was actually Paul's *cognomen,* his family name. (We don't know either his clan or personal names—*nomen* or *praenomen;* see Bruce 1988:249). "Saul" was probably his *signum,* a nickname used among other Jews. The introduction of the name *Paul* here has to do with the environment in which he would now minister— the Greco-Roman world (Marshall 1980:220)—and not his assumption of leadership (cf. Polhill 1992:295).

13:11 struck blind. This is not simply a traditional punishment for wickedness (as Talbert 1997:128) nor a counter hex, which beats a sorcerer at his own game (as Spencer 1997:139), but rather a physical exteriorization of his spiritual blindness, possibly a concrete example of the prophecy in Isa 6:9-10 (cf. Acts 28:26-27; Kilgallen 1997:229).

13:12 he was astonished. The carefully worded description of the impact of both miracle and teaching does not mask a presentation of superior magic or thaumaturgy (contra Johnson 1992:224-225) but rather shows Luke's understanding that miracle and teaching are part of a single whole (Dunn 1996:177; cf. Polhill 1992:295).

COMMENTARY

"Sent out by the Holy Spirit," Barnabas and Saul began the special work God had commissioned them to do (13:4; cf. Luke 4:1). Traveling to Seleucia, a Mediterranean port of Syrian Antioch (16 miles west and 5 miles north of the mouth of the Orontes), the missionary band embarked for Cyprus. Landing at Salamis, an eastern port and administrative center (about 130 miles west of the Syrian coast), they went to the Jewish synagogues (13:5). As Saul followed his theologically-grounded plan of going to the Jews first (cf. 13:46; 18:6), Saul and Barnabas engaged in the primary task of God's mission: preaching God's message of grace and salvation (13:7, 44, 46, 48). John Mark assisted them (13:5; cf. 12:25), probably both in practical matters (24:23) and in the ministry of the word (cf. 15:37).

After a preaching tour that took them along 115 miles of the southern coastal route, they arrived at Paphos, the official capital of this senatorial province (13:6). There they experienced a mixed reception. There was opposition from "Bar-Jesus" (Aramaic for "son of Jesus"), a "Jewish sorcerer" (*magos* [TG3097, ZG3407]) whom Luke labeled a "false prophet." Sergius Paulus, the "governor" (or, "proconsul") of this senatorial province, however, was receptive (13:7). He not only summoned Saul and Barnabas to court but he "wanted to hear the word of God." Luke pointed out that Sergius was "an intelligent man" (13:7) and thereby commended this high Roman official as a positive model of the proper response to hearsay about Christianity.

Luke's characterization of Elymas, together with Saul's denunciation of him (13:10), presents the picture of a court astrologer with demonic powers who, while wrongly claiming to be a medium of divine revelation, used magic formulas to break the bonds of fate and give the governor control over the future (cf. Philo *Special Laws* 3.100-101; Josephus *Antiquities* 20.141-142; Strabo *Geography* 16.2.3; Pliny *Natural History* 30.11). In the face of the truth of the "word of God," Elymas was withstanding its preachers (13:8; the verb *anthistato* [TG436, ZG468] describes imperfect continuous action: "kept on standing against them"). His aim was to turn the governor away from the Christian faith (cf. 6:7; 14:22).

Saul (now called Paul for the first time in Acts; see note on 13:9) was "filled with the Holy Spirit" (cf. 9:17) and empowered with divinely-inspired prophetic insight into the true nature of people. As such, he had the authority to declare God's judgment or blessing (cf. Peter's similar prophetic powers, 5:1-11; 8:20-24). Fixing his attention on the sorcerer (13:10; cf. 3:4; 14:9), he exposed the sorcerer's true character, nature, and activities. Elymas was "full of every sort of deceit and fraud." He intended to obtain fraudulent gain by his deceptive practices (cf. 1 Thess 2:3). His practice in the occult magical arts showed him to be no "Bar-Jesus" (most likely a transcription of the Aramaic, meaning "Son of [bar] Jesus [Joshua]") but in truth a "son of the devil," the father of lies and ruler of the demonic hosts of darkness. In withstanding the gospel messengers, he was an "enemy of all that is good" (lit., "of all righteousness"). In total contrast to John the Baptist, the last true prophet before Christ, Elymas would "never stop perverting the true ways of the Lord" (13:10; cf. Luke 3:3-6).

Paul declared the divine judgment on Elymas as coming from the sovereign "hand of the Lord." For Luke, this hand directs the Lord's saving purposes in history (4:28) and otherwise directly intervenes in healing and salvation blessing (4:30; 11:21). For Elymas, this would mean temporary blindness. Since it was temporary, it may have been intended to bring the sorcerer to repentance. But when the blindness came on him, it was instantaneous. The once imperious "seer" had to grope about "begging for someone to take his hand and lead him" (13:11).

The event produced saving results: the governor "believed" (4:4; 11:21). When Sergius Paulus saw what had happened, he believed. Luke tells us that what brought about belief was the governor's astonishment because of the teaching about the Lord.

◆ **C. Paul Preaches in Antioch of Pisidia (13:13-43)**

¹³Paul and his companions then left Paphos by ship for Pamphylia, landing at the port town of Perga. There John Mark left them and returned to Jerusalem. ¹⁴But Paul and Barnabas traveled inland to Antioch of Pisidia.*

On the Sabbath they went to the synagogue for the services. ¹⁵After the usual readings from the books of Moses* and the prophets, those in charge of the service sent them this message: "Brothers, if you have any word of encouragement for the people, come and give it."

¹⁶So Paul stood, lifted his hand to quiet them, and started speaking. "Men of Israel," he said, "and you God-fearing Gentiles, listen to me.

¹⁷"The God of this nation of Israel chose our ancestors and made them multiply and grow strong during their stay in Egypt. Then with a powerful arm he led them out of their slavery. ¹⁸He put up with them* through forty years of wandering in the wilderness. ¹⁹Then he destroyed seven nations in Canaan and gave their land to Israel as an inheritance. ²⁰All this took about 450 years.

"After that, God gave them judges to rule until the time of Samuel the prophet. ²¹Then the people begged for a king, and

God gave them Saul son of Kish, a man of the tribe of Benjamin, who reigned for forty years. [22]But God removed Saul and replaced him with David, a man about whom God said, 'I have found David son of Jesse, a man after my own heart. He will do everything I want him to do.'*

[23]"And it is one of King David's descendants, Jesus, who is God's promised Savior of Israel! [24]Before he came, John the Baptist preached that all the people of Israel needed to repent of their sins and turn to God and be baptized. [25]As John was finishing his ministry he asked, 'Do you think I am the Messiah? No, I am not! But he is coming soon—and I'm not even worthy to be his slave and untie the sandals on his feet.'

[26]"Brothers—you sons of Abraham, and also you God-fearing Gentiles—this message of salvation has been sent to us! [27]The people in Jerusalem and their leaders did not recognize Jesus as the one the prophets had spoken about. Instead, they condemned him, and in doing this they fulfilled the prophets' words that are read every Sabbath. [28]They found no legal reason to execute him, but they asked Pilate to have him killed anyway.

[29]"When they had done all that the prophecies said about him, they took him down from the cross* and placed him in a tomb. [30]But God raised him from the dead! [31]And over a period of many days he appeared to those who had gone with him from Galilee to Jerusalem. They are now his witnesses to the people of Israel.

[32]"And now we are here to bring you this Good News. The promise was made to our ancestors, [33]and God has now fulfilled it

for us, their descendants, by raising Jesus. This is what the second psalm says about Jesus:

'You are my Son.
Today I have become your Father.'*

[34]For God had promised to raise him from the dead, not leaving him to rot in the grave. He said, 'I will give you the sacred blessings I promised to David.'* [35]Another psalm explains it more fully: 'You will not allow your Holy One to rot in the grave.'* [36]This is not a reference to David, for after David had done the will of God in his own generation, he died and was buried with his ancestors, and his body decayed. [37]No, it was a reference to someone else—someone whom God raised and whose body did not decay.

[38]*"Brothers, listen! We are here to proclaim that through this man Jesus there is forgiveness for your sins. [39]Everyone who believes in him is declared right with God—something the law of Moses could never do. [40]Be careful! Don't let the prophets' words apply to you. For they said,

[41]'Look, you mockers,
     be amazed and die!
For I am doing something in your own day,
     something you wouldn't believe
     even if someone told you about it.'*"

[42]As Paul and Barnabas left the synagogue that day, the people begged them to speak about these things again the next week. [43]Many Jews and devout converts to Judaism followed Paul and Barnabas, and the two men urged them to continue to rely on the grace of God.

13:13-14 *Pamphylia* and *Pisidia* were districts in what is now Turkey. 13:15 Greek *from the law.* 13:18 Some manuscripts read *He cared for them;* compare Deut 1:31. 13:22 1 Sam 13:14. 13:29 Greek *from the tree.* 13:33 Or *Today I reveal you as my Son.* Ps 2:7. 13:34 Isa 55:3. 13:35 Ps 16:10. 13:38 English translations divide verses 38 and 39 in various ways. 13:41 Hab 1:5 (Greek version).

NOTES

13:13 *John Mark left them.* Luke does not tell us why Mark left (see Polhill 1992:296 for a list of possibilities). Based on the pejorative nuances of *apochōreō* [TG672, ZG713] ("desert," 3 Macc 2:33; "turn back in fear or cowardice," Jer 46:5 [26:5, LXX]) and Acts 15:38, John

Mark's return may have been sparked by a disagreement with Paul over the validity of a direct Gentile mission (Kee 1997:165).

13:14 *Antioch of Pisidia.* This rendering inadvertently appears to reflect the reading *tēs - Pisidias*, which has the support of D E 044 33 1739 𝔐 and is sometimes rendered "Antioch in Pisidia." This reflects a later boundary under Diocletian (after AD 295; Barrett 1994:627). The better reading is the adjectival *tēn Pisidian* [TG4099A, ZG4408], which means "Pisidian" or "toward Pisidia" (𝔓45 𝔓75 ℵ A B C; cf. Strabo, *Geography* 12.6.4; Acts 16:6; 18:23). This reading distinguishes this Antioch in the adjacent ethnic territory of Phrygia from another Phrygian Antioch on the Maeander River.

Some scholars suggest, however tentatively, that Paul bypassed Perga and traveled inland to Pisidian Antioch to recuperate from illness (cf. Gal 4:13; Dunn 1996:178). Commentators (Witherington 1998:403; cf. Nobbs 1994:287; Keener 1993:359) cite the connection between the Sergii Pauli family (13:7) and Pisidian Antioch (they owned a large estate in the area).

13:18 *He put up with them.* Other mss read, "he cared for them" (cf. NLT mg). The difference in textual variants is one Greek letter, π (*p*) versus φ (*ph*). The text has *etropophorēsen* [TG5159, ZG5574] (put up with); the variant has *etrophophorēsen* [TG5162.1, ZG5578] (care for). Each reading has equal strength in ms support (Johnson 1992:231). The same textual variants occur in the Deut 1:31 LXX, with *etrophophorēsen* ("care for") being better attested. This translates *nasa'* [TH5375, ZH5951], meaning "bear, carry" and having within its range both nuances: "bear with" and "bear up, care for." The positive reading "cared for" is more congruent with the immediate context's narrative of God's saving work on behalf of ancient Israel (so Johnson 1992:231 and Witherington 1998:410) but may have been introduced both for that reason and under the influence of the LXX. The more difficult reading, "put up with," is, however, congruent with the increasingly explicit description of Israel's sin throughout the rest of the speech (13:21, 24, 27-29, 38-41).

13:20 *All this took about 450 years.* Johnson (1992:231) and Barrett (1994:634) both note this verse's awkward Greek syntax and the difficulty of correlating "450 years" with Israel's chronology. The Textus Receptus reverses the time marker and the note about the giving of judges, probably to overcome the possible misunderstanding that the conquest of the land took four and a half centuries (Metzger 1994:359). The correction makes the period of the judges 450 years long, which agrees with Josephus *Antiquities* 8.3.1 but differs widely from 1 Kgs 6:1. It is better to follow the Alexandrian reading (𝔓74 ℵ A B C 33), as the NLT does, and see the "450" as a round, cumulative number covering 400 years (Israel in Egypt) + 40 years (wilderness wandering) + 10 years (possessing the land; Keener 1993:359).

13:22 *He will do everything I want him to do.* This is not an allusion to Isa 44:28 (contra Johnson 1992:232) but probably to the *TargumJonathan* paraphrase set next to the literal rendering of a portion of 1 Sam 13:14, "a man after my [God's] own heart" (cf. *1 Clement* 18:1; Bruce 1987:72).

13:33 *God . . . by raising Jesus.* Given the immediate context, many see *anastēsas Iēsoun* [TG450/2424, ZG482/2652] (raising up Jesus) and hence Ps 2:7 as referring to Christ's Resurrection (Johnson 1992:234; Dunn 1996:180; Talbert 1997:130-131; Marshall and Peterson 1998:302-303). In Luke's usage it can just as well refer to God bringing a person onto the stage of human history (3:22 [Deut 18:15-16], 26; 7:37). Given the way the phrase is introduced from v. 32 and its parallels in vv. 22-23, this is its meaning here (Barrett 1994:645). God's promise "has come true" in Christ's entire messianic mission: his Incarnation, earthly ministry, suffering, death, Resurrection, and exaltation.

Today I have become your Father. This could also be rendered, "Today I reveal you as my Son" (cf. NLT mg; cf. Ps 2:7). Both the NLT text and mg reflect a metaphorical understanding of *gegennēka* [TG1080, ZG1164] (I give birth). This verb renders the Hebrew verb *yalad* [TH3205, ZH3528], which, when "God" is the subject, is metaphorical for intimacy with his people or an adoptive relation with the king (Deut 32:18; Ps 2:7; NIDOTTE 2.456). On the day of the king's enthronement, when he was "born" into a new relationship of sonship with Yahweh, God named him "my Son" and God "became" his father or "revealed" him as his Son.

The Jews and the early church came to understand this psalm messianically (*Psalms of Solomon* 17:21-23; Strack and Billerbeck 1978:3.675-677; Acts 4:25-26 [Ps 2:1-2]; Heb 1:5; 5:5 [Ps 2:7]). This reference is neither to the Resurrection nor to the baptism but more properly to the Incarnation itself (Luke 1:35). The Gr. *gegennēka* [TG1080, ZG1164] (give birth) should then be understood literally, yet in such a way that both the reality of the virgin birth and the full deity of the Son, including his eternity, are preserved. The Nicene Creed's phrase "begotten, not made" captures this truth.

13:34-35 *sacred blessings*. In assessing Luke's use of the rabbinic *gezerah shawah* link-word method of interpretation (*ta hosia* [TG3741B, ZG4008], "sacred blessings" . . . *ton hosion* [TG3741/A, ZG4008], "Holy One"), some commentators see either a violation of meaning in the original context (Barrett 1994:647) or strained logic (Dunn 1996:181) in Luke's use of Isa 55:3 combined with Ps 16:10. But, if the "sacred blessings I promised to David" are the blessings of his Son's "forever reign," then there is a natural, indeed necessary, connection between the promise in Isa 55 and the promise in Ps 16—that the mediator of those eternal blessings will be resurrected (Marshall and Peterson 1998:304).

13:38-39 The NLT smooths out the syntax of a few clauses in the Greek that have left a number of scholars with the impression that, when compared with Paul's letters, Luke has "less than a full understanding" of Pauline theology (Barrett 1994:650; Dunn 1996:181). The difference in audience, however, (speech to unbelievers, letters to believers) and the stage of Paul's ministry (early versus mature thought) may explain the difference in expression (Witherington 1998:414). This is thoroughly Pauline content, and its manner of expression can be paralleled in his letters ("forgiveness of sin," Rom 4:7; "everyone who believes," Rom 10:4; "declared right with God," Rom 6:7; law's inability, Rom 8:3; DeSilva 1994:46-47).

13:41 *Look, you mockers, be amazed and die!* Luke's text form for Hab 1:5, following the LXX, differs from the MT in addressing "mockers" (*kataphronētai* [TG2707, ZG2970]) versus "nations" and inserting the command "die" (*aphanisthēte* [TG853A, ZG906]). The first difference may indicate that the Heb. text used by the LXX translator differed from the MT and read *bogedim* [TH898, ZH953] (treacherous ones) instead of *ba-ggoyim* [TH871.2/1471, ZH928/1580] (at the nations; cf. 1QpHab 2:1, 3, 5; see Archer and Chirichigno 1983:159).

Paul's typological appropriation of God's action is not so much direct (implying judgment on Israel) as it is a correlation between the the the surprising character of God's work then and now, particularly in its encompassing of Gentiles. Just as it was surprising to a proud Jew (Habakkuk) that God would use Gentiles (Babylonians) to judge Israel, so it could be surprising to the Diaspora Jew that the benefits of the Messiah's saving work in Jesus should be offered, apart from the law, to "everyone who believes," including the Gentiles (DeSilva 1994:47).

13:42 The Gr. does not specify who "left" the synagogue or who asked to hear more about the apostles' message. The TR supplies *tōn Ioudaiōn* [TG2453/A, ZG2681] (the Jews) and *ta ethnē* [TG1484, ZG1620] (the Gentiles), and the KJV, therefore, reads, "when the Jews were gone out of the synagogue, the Gentiles besought that these words might be preached to them." The NLT more correctly identifies "Paul and Barnabas" as the ones leaving and "the people," both Jewish and Gentile synagogue attenders, as those "begging" to hear more.

COMMENTARY

"Paul and his companions" (pointing to his leadership; cf. 13:2, 7) set sail from Paphos for the province of "Pamphylia," the south central coast of Asia Minor 160 miles away (13:13). Though not mentioned, they evidently disembarked at the seaport of Attalia (cf. 14:25) and proceeded 12 miles inland either by land or by rivercraft via the Cestrus river valley to Perga, five miles from the river (the NLT rendering "landing at" favors rivercraft, but either is possible). At this point John Mark left the group and returned to Jerusalem.

Not stopping to evangelize Perga, Paul and his party headed 100 miles inland to Pisidian Antioch on the central Anatolian plateau, having an elevation over 3,600 feet. They probably took the western route on the spur of the broad Via Sebaste (built 6 BC), following the flat alluvial valleys of the lake region through the Roman colony of Comana, passing the western edge of the lakes Burdur and Egridir, before turning east to Antioch.

Pisidian Antioch was founded by Seleucus I Nicator in the early third century BC. Designated a Roman colony in 25 BC and settled with army veterans and their families, it was a main garrison city for a number of Roman outposts, set up to pacify the notoriously hostile mountain region to its south. The city center with its temple, impressive colonnade, and square was a major center for the imperial cult. The leading families also supported the local cult of the god, Men. Members of Antiochene families served in important military and administrative posts throughout the empire (cf. the governor of Cyprus from the Sergii Pauli family, 13:7) and, in fact, were the first families from the eastern portion of the empire to gain entrance to the Roman senate. Josephus reports that 2,000 Jewish families had settled in Lydia and Phrygia in the third century BC (Josephus *Antiquities* 12.147-153). The population, then, was a diverse mixture of Phrygian, Greek, Jewish, and Roman.

Luke's fascinating glimpse of a diaspora synagogue service focuses on the readings from the five books of Moses and the prophets (usually with a oral paraphrase in the vernacular) and the sermon (13:15-16). This was the heart of the service, preceded by an initial recital of the Shema ("Listen, [O Israel]. . ."; Deut 6:4-9) and prayers (e.g., the Eighteen Benedictions), and followed by the priestly benediction (*m. Megillah* 4:3; Philo *Special Laws* 2.62; *b. Megillah* 23b-32a). "Those in charge of the service" (lit., "the leaders of the synagogue") were wealthy patrons and benefactors in their financial support as well as supervisors of the service, choosing the participants. They invited one person out of Paul's group to give the sermon. Those gathered were expecting a "word of encouragement" both to exhort and to comfort them as they lived in faithful obedience to the law and waited for the final salvation of Israel (Luke 2:25; 1 Macc 12:9).

Addressing both Jews and God-fearing Gentiles, Paul began with a recital of four key events in God's mighty saving acts, which forever marked the Jews as God's people (13:17-20). Each year, when they offered the firstfruits of their produce to the Lord, pious Jews would recite them (Deut 26:1-10; cf. Exod 23:14-17). God first acted in unconditional love to choose a particular ethnic stock, "our ancestors" (cf.

Deut 4:37-38). Thus, it was not a matter of Israel's merit vis-à-vis the other nations. Second, he blessed Israel during its sojourn in Egypt (Exod 1:7). In making them prosper, God demonstrated his supreme sovereignty—for God brought them to a place of superior status within another nation. The Egyptians' oppressive response (not mentioned by Paul, but made explicit by the NLT) is also evidence of their superior status (Exod 1:8-14). Third, God powerfully and decisively led them out of Egypt (Deut 26:8). Fourth, God, after overthrowing seven nations in Canaan, caused Israel to inherit those nations' lands (Josh 3:10; 24:11). Though God had to "put up with" Israel's murmuring, idolatrous rebellion, and lack of faith in the wilderness, he still fulfilled his saving purposes for them through his providence and protection during those forty years (Num 14:34; Deut 1:31). A decade of conquest in Canaan culminated four and one half centuries of divine working to fulfill his covenant promises to Abraham (Gen 15:13-14; Num 14:34; Josh 14:10).

Paul then briefly extended his discussion to include the judges, Samuel, Saul, and David, finally jumping all the way to the last prophet of the old covenant, John the Baptist (13:20-25). God's sovereign control and care was again communicated by the recitation of his action in an orderly sequence of time periods. God gave judges until the last judge and first prophet Samuel (3:24; 13:20; 1 Sam 3:20; 7:6, 15). God also gave the people Saul as a king but removed him after a forty-year reign (cf. Josephus *Antiquities* 6.378), and replaced him with David (13:22).

Paul subtly insinuated the dark subplot of man's sin. From the Old Testament we know it is because the people rejected the God-ordained rule that they "begged" Samuel for a king (1 Sam 8:4-9). The Old Testament also informs us that this king was subsequently removed because of his willful disobedience. Though God had superintended their national life, there was still a need for salvation. So God raised up David. God said he had found "a man after my own heart, for he will do everything I want him to do" (1 Sam 13:14; Ps 89[88]:21, LXX). David, though far from perfect, did submit to God's will (Ps 40:8; 143:10). To such a one, God gave a promise of a seed, under whose eternal reign his people would know God's covenant blessings of salvation (2 Sam 7:12-16; cf. 22:51; Pss 89:29, 36; 132:11, 17).

As if he could not hold the good news back, Paul made only passing mention of the promise but immediately declared its fulfillment: as promised, God has given Israel a Savior—Jesus (13:23). Here, Paul avoided the use of the term "Messiah" and its wrong connotations of a purely political leader. He heightened expectations about this Savior by his description of how John the Baptist prepared the way for him (13:24-25). John preached a baptism of repentance in preparation for participation in the Messiah's holy Kingdom, the final salvation (Luke 3:3-16). This ritual washing was a visible sign of a person's turning away from sin and to God.

The way Paul presented John in relation to Jesus gave certain clues that the latter is no mere man. The timing of John's appearance is given in language that recalls Malachi 3:1, where God announces that he is sending his messenger to prepare the way before him, and that the Lord himself will then come (cf. Luke 7:27-28). The question of the Messiah's identity and nature is captured in the question, denial, and declaration John made repeatedly—"I am not the Messiah" (cf. John 1:19-21). In fact, the Messiah would be so much greater than John that the prophet was not worthy to perform the most menial of tasks: "untie the sandals on his feet" (13:25). The rabbi Levi said the most devoted disciple of a rabbi should do everything for his teacher that a slave would do, except "take off his sandals" (b. Ketubbot 96a). Such is the distance between the Savior Jesus and the man he called "more than a prophet. . . . of all who have ever lived, none is greater than John" (Luke 7:26-28).

In the next section (13:26-41), Paul proclaims the message of salvation to the Jews and God-fearing Gentiles of Antioch. This salvation involves three significant facts. First there is Jesus' scandalous condemnation and death, which fulfilled Old Testament Scripture and thus were part of God's plan (13:27-29; cf. 2:23; 3:17-18; 4:28). Ironically, the people living in Jerusalem and their leaders, in ignorance, fulfilled the Scriptures that they read every Sabbath. Indeed, it was a complete fulfillment of all the prophecies (cf. Luke 12:50; 18:31; 22:37; 24:44). Second, Jesus died as an innocent sufferer, the objective basis for salvific vicarious atonement (13:27-28). Paul straightforwardly maintained Jesus' innocence: "no legal reason to execute him" (13:28). Pilate declared as much three times during the proceedings (Luke 23:4, 14-15, 22; cf. Acts 3:13-14). Even Jesus' receiving a proper burial speaks of his innocence (13:29; cf. Luke 23:53, 55). At the same time, Paul portrayed Jesus' suffering as that of a criminal—in that he was condemned by the Jews, who requested a Roman execution for him, and he was crucified (hanging on the "tree"; xulon [TG3586, ZG3833]), a cursed death (cf. 5:30; 10:39; Deut 21:23; Gal 3:13). Third, Paul emphasized the historical veracity of these events. They actually happened in space and time, and there were witnesses. The reality of the events shows that salvation can be objectively known in space and time, as well as in eternity; the salvation Paul proclaimed was more than a subjective experience. Jesus' burial affirmed the reality of his physical death, a truth on which many ancient and modern heresies stumble (cf. 1 Cor 15:4). Then, with powerful simplicity, Paul announced, "God raised him from the dead!" (13:30). While God had used ignorant Jerusalemites, their leaders, and Pilate to accomplish the "death phase" of his redemptive plan, he had acted alone in accomplishing what only he could accomplish—the defeat of death in Jesus' Resurrection (cf. 3:15; 10:40; 13:37; Rom 10:9; Gal 1:1; Eph 1:20; Col 2:12; 1 Thess 1:10). Paul then noted that Jesus "appeared to those who had gone with him from Galilee to Jerusalem" (13:31). They were eyewitnesses who could not be easily misled. These multiple witnesses had multiple opportunities to see Jesus because he appeared over "a period of many days" (1:3).

Paul then moved to the present moment and reiterated the New Testament kerygma, the "Good News." The promises made to the ancestors (Gen 12:1-3; 2 Sam 7:12-16) had now been fulfilled. He declared the "salvation accomplished" aspect of the gospel in terms of Scriptural proof—proof that establishes the truth of the arrival of God's Son on the stage of human history and the truth of his bodily Resurrection (13:33-37). Paul affirmed that the Scriptures—specifically Psalm 2:7,

16:10, and Isaiah 55:3—speak of Jesus' divine sonship as proved by his Resurrection (cf. Rom 1:3-4; Gal 4:4). God raised him from the dead never again to die (13:34-35; cf. Isa 55:3; Ps 16:10). Isaiah 55 gives us the saving results of the Messiah's Resurrection in promise form: "I will give you the sacred blessings I promised to David." The link between these blessings and the Messiah's Resurrection involves this interpretational reasoning: If the Messiah must undergo an atoning death for the sins of the people and reign forever, a Resurrection must decisively intervene. Just as importantly, if that "eternal reign" is to be characterized by full and final salvation from the presence, power, and penalty of sin, then the Savior-King, who will grant such blessings to participants in his Kingdom, must experience a Resurrection that will so transform him that "he will never die again."

Paul continued his discussion of the Resurrection by proving that it must happen to the Messiah. Following a literal hermeneutic and conducting a search for the appropriate referent through a process of elimination (cf. Peter's speech at Pentecost, 2:27-32), Paul explained that "after David had done the will of God in his own generation, he died" (13:36; *idia genea hupēretēsas tē tou theou boulē ekoimēthē* [TG2837, ZG3121]; note that the word order allows "according to the will of God" to go with the verb "to die," emphasizing even more that it was God's will that David not be the one to receive the promise of Ps 16:10). With maximum effect, Paul set the dignified imagery for David's death and burial (lit., "he fell asleep and was added to his fathers") next to the jarring statement, "his body decayed." But the good news is that this psalm is referring to "someone whom God raised and whose body did not decay" (13:37). Paul had already identified this person as Jesus (13:23, 33-34).

The sermon reached its climax as Paul solemnly declared salvation blessings and warned of judgment. Placing it at the beginning and end of his declaration (13:23, 38), Paul stressed Jesus as the mediator of these blessings. The blessings themselves are couched in the familiar terms of Lukan gospel essentials (e.g., "the forgiveness of sins"; Luke 24:47; Acts 2:38-39; 10:43) but with a distinctively Pauline characterization. The believer is thereby "declared right with God," which no one could ever accomplish by trying to keep the Mosaic Law (cf. 15:7-11; Gal 2:16; 3:11). The final notable emphasis is the offer's universal scope, again at both the declaration's beginning and the end. The good news is for both Jews and Gentiles.

Paul was aware that this "Good News" was not only good but in many respects startling. So he warned his audience about failing to recognize it (13:40-41; Hab 1:5). God's surprise move is that through his incarnate and risen Son Jesus he makes salvation blessings available to all who will believe, including Gentiles—apart from the law! For legalistic, ethnocentric Jews and even for God-fearing Gentiles this might indeed be unbelievable, perhaps even outrageous and offensive.

Here, however, there was an initial positive response to Paul's sermon. The congregation asked him back next week (13:42), and there were converts from among the Jews and proselytes—the "devout converts to Judaism" (13:43). They "followed" Paul and Barnabas (this is the only use of the verb *akaloutheō* [TG190, ZG199] in Acts that indicates Christian commitment; cf. Luke 5:27; 9:23, 59; 18:22). In response, Paul and Barnabas "urged them to continue to rely on the grace of God" (13:43). Given the way salvation blessings were offered (13:38-39) and the parallel thought at 13:23, Paul and Barnabas were encouraging them to remain in the salvation offered in the gospel (13:23, 26, 38-39) and to not return to performance-based thoughts of salvation through obedience to the Old Testament law and Jewish tradition. This encouragement was needed, especially when we remember the attacks these churches subsequently sustained from Judaizers (cf. Gal 1:6-7; 3:1-6; 5:7-12; 6:11-13).

◆　## D. Paul Turns to the Gentiles (13:44-52)

44The following week almost the entire city turned out to hear them preach the word of the Lord. 45But when some of the Jews saw the crowds, they were jealous; so they slandered Paul and argued against whatever he said.

46Then Paul and Barnabas spoke out boldly and declared, "It was necessary that we first preach the word of God to you Jews. But since you have rejected it and judged yourselves unworthy of eternal life, we will offer it to the Gentiles. 47For the Lord gave us this command when he said,

'I have made you a light to the Gentiles,

13:47 Isa 49:6.　13:52 Greek the disciples.

to bring salvation to the farthest corners of the earth.'*"

48When the Gentiles heard this, they were very glad and thanked the Lord for his message; and all who were chosen for eternal life became believers. 49So the Lord's message spread throughout that region. 50Then the Jews stirred up the influential religious women and the leaders of the city, and they incited a mob against Paul and Barnabas and ran them out of town. 51So they shook the dust from their feet as a sign of rejection and went to the town of Iconium. 52And the believers* were filled with joy and with the Holy Spirit.

NOTES

13:45 *jealous*. The newcomer's comparative success may have sparked this envy (Marshall 1980:229), though behind it was opposition to the direct mission to the Gentiles and what that would mean for the Jewish minority's social links to the larger society via God-fearing Gentiles of high standing (Longenecker 1981:429; Levinskaya 1996:124-125).

slandered Paul. Although some see the "slander" as directed against Paul (Marshall 1980:227-228), more precisely, it characterizes the opposition to Paul's message.

13:47 *I have made you a light to the Gentiles*. In the Gospel of Luke, this was applied to Jesus as the Servant-Messiah, bringing salvation to the Gentiles (Luke 2:32). Paul here appealed to it as authority for the Lord Jesus' commission of his disciples to a worldwide mission (1:2, 8). This appeal rests not on a "solidarity principle" producing parallel missions (contra Krodel 1986:248; Polhill 1992:307), nor on a "completion theory": the church fulfills a mission given originally to Israel (contra Dunn 1996:184; Witherington 1998:416) or to Christ (contra Longenecker 1981:430). The deity of Christ also does not satisfactorily explain the appropriation here. Dennis Johnson, who holds the deity view (1990:353), asserts, "Luke discloses the identity of Jesus, . . . [portraying] the risen Lord Jesus acting and speaking with the authority that belongs uniquely to Yahweh himself." Given the placement of the *houtōs* [TG3779, ZG4048] (thus) at the very beginning of the sentence, a more satisfactory approach is to see the Isaiah passage as originally directed to the Messiah (i.e., Jesus). Paul asserted that the Lord Jesus then used it as the warrant for his commission to his disciples.

13:48 *thanked the Lord for his message.* Lit., "glorified the word of the Lord." This expression is adjusted in a number of directions in the manuscript tradition. Codex Bezae (D) reads "received the word of the Lord." Codices B and E read, "they were glorifying the word of God." Some minuscules read, "they were glorifying God." The NLT rendering brings out the essential components of this brief expression (cf. Barrett 1994:658).

13:50 *influential religious women.* Given Luke's normal use of *phoboumenos* [TG5399, ZG5828] to designate God-fearing Gentiles, Johnson (1992:242) is unsure whether this phrase (Gr., *tas sebomenas gunaikas tas euschēmonas*) should be understood as referring to that same class of Gentiles who sympathized with Judaism. Levinskaya (1996:122-123) argues strongly for it, however, based on indicators in the immediate context.

COMMENTARY

The following week almost the entire city turned out to hear the word of the Lord. The message about the Lord Jesus Christ was central to the church's missionary enterprise and advance (cf. 8:4, 14, 25; 10:44; 11:19; 13:5, 26). But the Jews were jealous of this Christian success, especially because it was attracting an important segment of society—namely, high-society God-fearing Gentiles (cf. 5:17; Phil 3:6). In a blasphemous way, they contradicted what Paul was saying (13:45, see note; cf. 18:6; 28:19, 22). Their divisiveness was indeed blasphemous because they opposed the message about God's Son.

In a decisive withdrawal from the Jews, Paul and Barnabas—by the power of the Spirit and in the face of opposition—boldly declared that the gospel, first declared to the Jews but rejected by them, would now go to the Gentiles (13:46; cf. 4:8, 13, 29, 31; 9:27-28). The gospel messengers spoke first to those who had originally received the promises (13:46; cf. 3:26; 13:32-33; Rom 1:16-17). But the Jews rejected the message, deeming it "unworthy" of their commitment. In reality, Paul declares, they were judging themselves "unworthy" of eternal life (cf. 5:20; 11:18). Habakkuk 1:5 would indeed come true for them (Acts 13:40-41).

Given the universal scope of the Lord's mandate (Luke 24:47; Acts 1:8), Paul was not thwarted by this rejection. It was simply the occasion for "turning to the Gentiles," in step with the centrifugal momentum of God's mission. Since the Lord God had appointed his Servant-Messiah as a "light to the Gentiles," his witnesses could only obey that Servant-Messiah's command to declare his salvation to "the farthest corners of the earth" (13:47; Isa 49:6).

In contrast to the Jewish jealousy that blasphemed and rejected the message, the Gentile reception was evidenced by joy, praise, and belief (13:48). Wherever God's salvation is embraced there is joy, and as Luke makes clear, this joy is the fruit of the Holy Spirit (13:52; cf. Luke 2:10; Acts 8:8, 39; 15:31). There is literally a "glorifying of the Word of the Lord," especially for the ethnic inclusiveness of the scope of its offer. And there is faith—God's work in those he has predestined—among "all who were chosen for eternal life." (The expression "were chosen" is a perfect passive functioning as a periphrastic divine passive with emphasis on the continuing validity of

God's completed, fixed decree. For similar passive constructions, see Luke 10:20; Isa 4:3; Dan 12:2; Rev 20:12-15; 21:27.) This reception helped the advance of God's mission. Through personification and by way of pointing to the life-giving quality of the gospel message, Luke tells us "the Lord's message spread throughout that region" (13:49; cf. 6:7; 12:24; 19:10).

In response to these events, the Jews stirred up "influential religious women" (God-fearing Gentiles who had remained loyal to Judaism) and "leaders of the city," possibly their husbands who were either of the local aristocracy or Roman magistrates (13:50; cf. Josephus *Antiquities* 2.34-35, 38). Instead of believing the message, they "incited a mob" (lit., "raised up a persecution") against the messengers, and they ran the chief messengers out of town.

This rejection would lead only to the further advance of the gospel but not before the missionaries for a third time placed the Jews on notice of the final judgment they would face for rejecting God's message (13:51; cf. 13:40-41, 46). According to the Lord's instruction, as a sign of disassociation from a community doomed to destruction, they "shook the dust from their feet as a sign of rejection." While Paul and his missionary band then took the gospel eighty miles southeast to Iconium, the believers in Antioch of Pisidia were filled with joy and with the Holy Spirit.

◆　E. Paul and Barnabas in Iconium (14:1-7)

The same thing happened in Iconium.* Paul and Barnabas went to the Jewish synagogue and preached with such power that a great number of both Jews and Greeks became believers. ²Some of the Jews, however, spurned God's message and poisoned the minds of the Gentiles against Paul and Barnabas. ³But the apostles stayed there a long time, preaching boldly about the grace of the Lord. And the Lord proved their message was true by giving them power to do miraculous signs and wonders. ⁴But the people of the town were divided in their opinion about them. Some sided with the Jews, and some with the apostles.

⁵Then a mob of Gentiles and Jews, along with their leaders, decided to attack and stone them. ⁶When the apostles learned of it, they fled to the region of Lycaonia— to the towns of Lystra and Derbe and the surrounding area. ⁷And there they preached the Good News.

14:1 *Iconium*, as well as *Lystra* and *Derbe* (14:6), were towns in what is now Turkey.

NOTES

14:2-3 *But the apostles stayed there.* The narrative tension between opposition (14:2) and continued ministry (14:3) caused difficulties for Western text copyists. The scribe of D added, "But the Lord quickly gave them peace" to serve as a transition between the verses (Metzger 1994:370-371). The introductory phrase *men oun* [TG3303/3767, ZG3525/4036] is usually rendered "therefore," thus contributing to the tension. The transition should not be labeled "obscure narrative logic" (contra Johnson 1992:246) or a clumsy source adaptation to a pattern of mission advance established at Pisidian Antioch (contra Barrett 1994:669). Rather, we should take the connective *men oun* as the adversative "but," as the NLT does (Witherington 1998:419; cf. Acts 25:4; 28:5). The opposition mentioned in v. 2 provides the occasion for the lengthy stay: to support the embattled disciples as well as to display the Lord's power in that context (Polhill 1992:311).

14:4 *apostles*. Here and at 14:14 (not in the NLT, but introduced at vv. 6 and 13) are the two times in Acts that "apostle" does not refer to the Twelve. Are these Luke's conscious or unconscious uses of an Antiochene source in which Paul and Barnabas are styled as church agents or church missionaries, a use at variance with Luke's normal reference to "the Twelve"? (See Witherington 1998:419; Barrett 1994:666-667; Polhill [1992:311] says Luke may be following customary usage.) Or, are they Luke's support for Paul's understanding of himself as an apostle, if only in an impressionistic way (Spencer 1997:149; cf. Witherington 1998:419)? Or, given the Holy Spirit's sending, the "signs and wonders" ministry, and the parallels between Peter's and Paul's ministries, is this a heightened use of the term (Barrett 1994:666-667) in which Paul and Barnabas fulfill, with respect to the nations, the commission originally given to the eleven apostles (compare 13:2, 4; 14:3 with 5:12; 14:8-10 with 3:1-10; 13:47; Isa 49:6 with 1:8; cf. Marshall and Peterson 1998:183-185)? The most justice is done to Luke's usage if we understand that Luke, like Paul, uses "apostle" both in the restricted sense for "the Twelve" chosen by Christ and in a broader sense for "missionaries," commissioned messengers of the gospel (cf. 2 Cor 8:23; Gal 1:19; Phil 2:25). The latter sense occurs here.

COMMENTARY

Phrygian Iconium was a Greek city-state with Hellenistic culture (cf. 14:1 where the non-Jews [NLT, "Gentiles"] are referred to as *Hellēnōn* [TG1672, ZG1818], "Greeks"). With orchards on a fruitful plain and a thriving wool industry, it was a prosperous commercial and agricultural center at the border between Phrygia and Lycaonia.

Following their strategy of going to the Jews first, Paul and Barnabas went to the synagogue (cf. 13:5, 14). They preached with such power that a "great number of both Jews and Greeks became believers." Luke often expressed the advance of God's mission in terms of quantitative growth. But lest we forget that this advance also means spiritual warfare, Luke immediately tells us of opposition. Some of the Jews, whose forebears rebelled against God's word in the wilderness (Deut 9:7, 23-24), "spurned" God's message (*apeithēsantes* [TG544, ZG578], lit., "disobeyed") and "poisoned the minds of the Gentiles against Paul and Barnabas" (lit., "the brothers"). Though the focus of the attack was probably Paul and Barnabas (so NLT), "the brothers" probably included all the newly converted (cf. 1 Thess 1:6).

Paul and Barnabas responded to the opposition by preaching with persevering boldness. Just as earlier preaching with boldness had been a mark of Spirit-filled witness, so now also such preaching continued because God bore witness to the truth of his message of grace by granting miraculous signs and wonders through the hands of the messengers (14:3). And these miracles further served to authenticate the message of God's grace, for they gave a foretaste of the fullness of salvation blessings yet to come (5:12; 15:12; Joel 2:30; Gal 3:4-5).

The opposition mounts from a standoff to mob action (14:4-5). With uncontrolled, irrational, violent intent, a mob of both Jews and Gentiles, together with civic and religious leaders, decided to attack, even to stone, Paul and Barnabas (cf. 7:57-58; 19:29). In God's protecting providence, they learned of the plot and "fled for their lives" into the ethnic region of Lycaonia. On the Via Sebaste they traveled eighteen miles south and a little west to the Roman colony of Lystra and then sixty miles southeast on an unpaved track to Derbe "and the surrounding area" (14:6).

Their flight meant further advance for God's mission because their escape not only thwarted the opposition but it also provided new opportunities to preach. Luke tells us simply, "There they preached the Good News" (an imperfect periphrastic construction emphasizing the continuous character of their efforts).

◆ F. Paul and Barnabas in Lystra and Derbe (14:8-20)

⁸While they were at Lystra, Paul and Barnabas came upon a man with crippled feet. He had been that way from birth, so he had never walked. He was sitting ⁹and listening as Paul preached. Looking straight at him, Paul realized he had faith to be healed. ¹⁰So Paul called to him in a loud voice, "Stand up!" And the man jumped to his feet and started walking.

¹¹When the crowd saw what Paul had done, they shouted in their local dialect, "These men are gods in human form!" ¹²They decided that Barnabas was the Greek god Zeus and that Paul was Hermes, since he was the chief speaker. ¹³Now the temple of Zeus was located just outside the town. So the priest of the temple and the crowd brought bulls and wreaths of flowers to the town gates, and they prepared to offer sacrifices to the apostles.

¹⁴But when the apostles Barnabas and Paul heard what was happening, they tore their clothing in dismay and ran out among the people, shouting, ¹⁵"Friends,* why are you doing this? We are merely human beings—just like you! We have come to bring you the Good News that you should turn from these worthless things and turn to the living God, who made heaven and earth, the sea, and everything in them. ¹⁶In the past he permitted all the nations to go their own ways, ¹⁷but he never left them without evidence of himself and his goodness. For instance, he sends you rain and good crops and gives you food and joyful hearts." ¹⁸But even with these words, Paul and Barnabas could scarcely restrain the people from sacrificing to them.

¹⁹Then some Jews arrived from Antioch and Iconium and won the crowds to their side. They stoned Paul and dragged him out of town, thinking he was dead. ²⁰But as the believers* gathered around him, he got up and went back into the town. The next day he left with Barnabas for Derbe.

14:15 Greek *Men.* 14:20 Greek *disciples;* also in 14:22, 28.

NOTES

14:10 *the man jumped to his feet.* Some see Paul's miracle as an instance of "power evangelism" demanded by his pioneering work in this pagan context, a type of ministry to be expected both then and now (Wagner 1995:177). Standard dispensational and Reformed theology limits the working of signs and wonders to the apostolic age (Edgar 1988; Gaffin 1996:23-64). Luke, rather, sees miracles as a secondary part of preaching and teaching, demonstrating the irresistible nature of God's word and authorizing the witness (Jervell 1984:87; cf. Hamblin 1974:34).

14:11-12 *Zeus . . . Hermes.* Barrett (1994:677) simply finds the Ovid account (*Metamorphosis* 8.611-724) "not inconsistent" with this response and the inscriptional evidence for worship of Zeus and Hermes in this area. Breytenbach (1993:405-407) finds strong evidence that the local Lycaonian Hittite-Luwan deity—the weather god and god of vegetation—was worshiped as Zeus and that the worship included Hermes, his messenger. There is no need to conclude a misidentification, even for the purpose of clearer communication with a broader Greco-Roman audience, when Luke uses "Zeus" and "Hermes" (contra Martin 1995:154; Witherington 1998:424, n. 281). Though it is attractive to some to see the significance of "Zeus" and "Hermes" as gods of ambassadors and guarantors of emissaries and their missions (Martin 1995, followed by Marshall and Peterson 1998:307-308; Witherington 1998:425), Breytenbach (1993) has solidly grounded them in the local agricultural fertility cult and shown how Paul's speech (14:14-17) is most congruent with that type of cult.

14:13 *the town gates.* Given the location of the temple outside the town (the verse describes the priest as the priest of "Zeus before the city"), most commentators favor this understanding of the ambiguous *epi tous pulōnas* [TG4440, ZG4784], "at the gates" (e.g., Talbert 1997:133-134; Johnson 1992:248). Since Lystra did not have walls at this time, this probably refers to the gates of the sacred precincts to the temple (Gill 1994a:82). Bruce (1990: 322) says it refers to the house gates where Paul and Barnabas were staying.

14:14 The NLT omits "apostles," as do Western witnesses D it^gig. h syr^p. See note at 14:4 for Luke's meaning for the term here.

14:16 *he permitted all the nations to go their own ways.* While many commentators see this as excusing the nations for past idolatry (Haenchen 1971:428; Polhill 1992:316; Barrett 1994:681), a number say the verse is silent about culpability (Breytenbach 1993:398) or, the difference between indicting or excusing the nations for their past is negligible, if not irrelevant, to Luke's purpose (Lin 1998:260). I think there is an implied indictment here when the passage is understood in the light of the preceding call to conversion (14:15) and the further exposition of Acts 17:30 and Rom 1:18-23.

14:17 While Barnes (1997) makes a strong case for rabbinic exegesis of Pss 65:13[14]–66:1 with a link to Ps 146:6 as the background here (*Deuteronomy Rabbah* 7:7), it is better to see these themes as present in a number of OT passages and the wording as tailored to address adherents of the local Lycaonian cult (Breytenbach 1993:405, 408; cf. Bruce 1987:74; Johnson 1992:249).

14:19 *They stoned Paul.* Since both Jews and Gentiles were involved, the stoning here and at Acts 14:5 must be understood as an act of mob violence (Polhill 1992:311), not the carrying out of a Jewish judicial death sentence (contra Kee 1997:171; Keener 1993:363).

COMMENTARY

At Lystra, a Roman colony, frontier outpost, and thriving town in the Lycaonian hill country, Paul announced the gospel to the general populace. During his preaching he encountered a totally helpless man. He was crippled from birth, "so he had never walked" (14:8; cf. 3:2 and a number of parallel features in 3:1-26). Luke marked the divine working through Paul by three features in 14:9-10. With spiritual insight Paul looked into the man's heart and realized that the man had "faith to be healed" (cf. 8:23; 13:10, 46). With a loud voice, Paul issued a restorative command: "Stand up!" (14:10). The man then experienced a healing that was instantaneous, complete, and lasting, for he "jumped to his feet and started walking."

As Luke described the man's readiness, he not only signaled the importance of faith in receiving God's gracious work of healing (cf. Luke 8:36; 17:19; Acts 3:16), but he also pointed to the miracle as a sign of the holistic salvation God desires to apply now. He also referred to the potential healing in 14:9 as being "saved" (*sōzō* [TG4982, ZG5392]; cf. "be healed" in NLT), thus linking the healing with the salvation Paul had been proclaiming.

The crowd's response demonstrates that unless a miracle is witnessed and understood from within a worldview that believes in the one true God, creator and sustainer of all things, there may be total excitement with little if any comprehension. Unless there is interpretation, the sign by itself is powerless to point convincingly to God and his saving acts (cf. Luke 16:27-31; 24:25-27). So, the crowd cried out in Lycaonian, the local dialect, "These men are gods in human form!" (lit., "the gods, having become like men, have come down to us"). Such a notion was not only common among ancient pagans (Homer *Odyssey* 17.485-487) but there was also a local legend of a previous visitation by Zeus and Hermes to the Phrygian region. They came in human form and inquired at one thousand homes, but none showed them hospitality. Only a poor elderly couple, Baucis and Philemon, took them in. The pair was rewarded by being spared when the gods flooded the valley and destroyed its inhabitants. The couple's shack was transformed into a marble-pillared, gold-roofed temple, and they became its priests. The crowd's reaction to Paul and Barnabas, then, is understandable. They wanted to avoid punishment and garner any blessings that the gods may desire to dispense.

While we glimpse some of the significance of Zeus through Paul's ensuing corrective (14:17), Luke explained that the crowd labeled Paul "Hermes" because he was the "chief speaker" (14:12; cf. Iamblichus *Egyptian Mysteries* 1.1; Gal 4:14). "Hermes" was a messenger god who preferred oral persuasion to force of arms; he was the patron god of orators. The priest of the temple of Zeus prepared sacrifice on a grand scale—a bull festooned with garlands of flowers (14:13; cf. Lucian *Sacrifices* 3, 12; Pausanias *Description of Greece* 7.22.11).

Reacting with intense dismay, Paul and Barnabas tore their clothes in revulsion at the blasphemous false worship, and then they rushed out into the crowd, insisting that the worship stop. As Paul sought to provide the proper interpretive framework for viewing the miracle, he had to first dismantle their animistic, polytheistic view. He assumed common ground with his audience, a place from which they could together evaluate these actions. He pointed out his common humanity with them, which obviously disqualified him from being treated as a theophany. The people's misidentification called into question the legitimacy of the whole religious superstructure of polytheistic, idolatrous worship that had fostered it. Paul labeled idolatry as "worthless" (*mataios* [TG3152/A, ZG3469]). Idols are worthless, empty, indeed deceitful, because they do not produce the effect they promise (cf. Jer 2:5). Paul then reminded his audience that "the living God" is the one "who made heaven and earth, the sea, and everything in them" (14:15; cf. Exod 20:11; 2 Kgs 19:15-16). If the true God is living, then the idols must be dead; if the true God is creator of everything, then there is no room for the idols as deity. In fact, to worship them is to rob God of the glory due him.

Paul then tied God to these Lycaonians' history in such a way that he resolved the puzzle regarding how it could be that the Lystrans hadn't known about the one true God and had instead been worshiping these "worthless things." God's providence, which either permits or hinders men and nations, had allowed all nations "to go their own ways" (cf. 16:7). God combined his permissive providence in history with an ongoing witness to his existence through general revelation. In particular, he revealed himself in his doing good for all people, in sustaining life by providing "rain" from heaven, "good crops . . . food, and joyful hearts" (14:17; cf. Pss 104:13-15; 147:8; Jer 14:22; Matt 5:45). Interestingly, Paul's positive message again points to these pagans' misidentification of the true source of divine working, for Zeus was a weather god and the god of vegetation. From inscriptions from this region and contiguous parts we know he bore such titles as *Zeus Kalagathios* ("Zeus Doer of Good") and *Zeus Karpophoros* ("Zeus of Fruitful Crops"; see note on 14:11-12). With such words Paul only slightly dampened their enthusiasm for sacrificing to him.

Although Antioch was upwards of 100 miles away, Jews from Antioch and Iconium came and persuaded the crowds to violently oppose Paul, even to stone him (2 Cor 11:25; Gal 6:17; 2 Tim 3:10-11). They dragged him out of the city, discarding what they thought was a corpse (14:19). But God was not through with his witness. In the barest of terms, Luke tells us how the believers gathered around Paul until he recovered. He "got up and went back into the town" (14:20). It was a quiet victory, but a victory nonetheless, for not only was the recovery as instantaneous as the healing but there was also freedom of movement in hostile territory and a further advance in witness 50 to 60 miles down the road at Derbe.

◆   **G. Paul and Barnabas Return to Antioch of Syria (14:21-28)**

[21]After preaching the Good News in Derbe and making many disciples, Paul and Barnabas returned to Lystra, Iconium, and Antioch of Pisidia, [22]where they strengthened the believers. They encouraged them to continue in the faith, reminding them that we must suffer many hardships to enter the Kingdom of God. [23]Paul and Barnabas also appointed elders in every church. With prayer and fasting, they turned the elders over to the care of the Lord, in whom they had put their trust. [24]Then they traveled back through Pisidia to Pamphylia. [25]They preached the word in Perga, then went down to Attalia.

[26]Finally, they returned by ship to Antioch of Syria, where their journey had begun. The believers there had entrusted them to the grace of God to do the work they had now completed. [27]Upon arriving in Antioch, they called the church together and reported everything God had done through them and how he had opened the door of faith to the Gentiles, too. [28]And they stayed there with the believers for a long time.

NOTES

14:22 *we must suffer many hardships to enter the Kingdom of God.* Luke views discipleship from a cosmic and personal eschatological perspective (Witherington 1998:428; Polhill 1992:319; cf. 1 Cor 6:9-10; 15:10) rather than seeing it in basically existential terms (contra Johnson 1992:253).

14:23 *appointed elders.* Though the verb *cheirotoneō* [TG5500, ZG5936] (to extend the hand) originally described democratic appointment by vote, it also came to indicate appointment by an authority, as here (Barrett 1994:687; cf. Lucian *Death of Peregrinus* 41). There is no implication of "the laying on of hands" (contra Johnson 1992:254). The congregation's role in Paul and Barnabas's activity must be conjectured based on other passages (e.g., 6:1-7; cf. Polhill 1992:319).

The use of "elder" is not an anachronism in which Luke reads the church government of a later time back into Paul's ministry (contra Barrett 1994:666, 688; Bruce 1990:326; Dunn 1996:193 among others). Giles (1997a:222-223) has convincingly shown that Jewish community and Jewish synagogue governance (municipal elders, synagogue leaders, and assistants) provided the model for early church officers: church elders, house church overseers, and deacons. Though none of Paul's uncontested letters use "elder" to designate church leaders (only 1 Tim 5:17, 19; Titus 1:5), there is evidence he did appoint institutional leaders (1 Cor 16:15-18; 1 Thess 5:12-13). Paul's nonuse of "elder" may be a result of both his desire to clearly distinguish church from synagogue and his tendency to describe leadership in terms of function, not office (Rom 12:8; 1 Thess 5:12; cf. 1 Tim 5:17).

COMMENTARY

The witness at Derbe and the return trip bring into bold relief the reality that God is truly "on mission" through these missionaries. And his mission is more than just evangelization; it is the formation and strengthening of disciples in such a way that they persevere and so, through many tribulations, enter the Kingdom of God.

In the eastern provincial border town of Derbe (Lycaonian for "juniper tree"), sixty miles east of Lystra, in a further advance of the mission, Paul and Barnabas preached the Good News and made many disciples (14:21). Since Paul's goal in church planting was, at the coming of Christ, to present disciples to God, "perfect in their relationship to Christ," it is not surprising that, instead of moving straight eastward to his hometown, Tarsus (150 miles east), he retraced his steps, revisiting Antioch, Iconium, and Lystra (cf. Rom 15:16; Col 1:28; 1 Thess 2:17-20). His purpose was, literally, "to strengthen the souls of the disciples," making them more firm and unchanging in their heart-commitment to Christ (14:22; cf. Luke 9:24; 21:19; 22:32; Acts 15:32, 41). He engaged in a verbal ministry of encouragement (cf. 11:23; 13:43); these believers had known persecution and would continue to experience the pressure of Judaizers' attempts to turn them from the way of faith back to works (Gal 1:6-7; 3:1-3; 6:12-13). As it was Christ's divinely appointed destiny to suffer before entering his time of glory (Luke 24:26), so his followers must enter into the Kingdom of God through many tribulations (14:22; cf. Rom 8:7; Phil 3:10-11; Col 1:24). The "many tribulations" are, primarily, persecutions for the sake of the Good News (5:41; 11:19; 20:23; cf. Luke 9:23). "Entering the Kingdom" is tantamount to experiencing the full enjoyment of salvation blessings, whether at death (Luke 23:42; 2 Tim 4:18) or at Christ's return (Luke 13:29; 22:30).

Paul and Barnabas also strengthened the churches by appointing elders (14:23). Such appointments were accompanied by prayer and fasting because the elders would have a particularly spiritual ministry; God would surely work through them (cf. 13:1-3; 20:28; 1 Tim 4:14; 5:17). These appointments placed the leaders "on deposit" with God, entrusting them into his protection, guidance, and empowerment (20:32; cf. 2 Tim 1:12, 14). The Lord is certainly worthy of such a trust, and he was the very one in whom they had trusted for forgiveness of sins and eternal life (13:38-39, 46, 48).

Paul and Barnabas made their way southward through wild, mountainous Pisidia to the fruitful alluvial plain of Pamphylia to preach for the first time at Perga, a major Greek city near the coast (14:24-25; cf. 13:13). Departing from the port city Attalia, eight miles southwest, they sailed almost 400 miles by sea back to Syrian Antioch and their sending church (14:26).

From the missionaries' perspective, it had been a mission of divine-human synergism. As the prophets and God's people of old, they announced God's mighty deeds (Pss 64:10; 71:17; Isa 2:3; 53:2; Jer 46:14; Amos 4:13). These were, literally, the "many things God did with them." They were more than just "instruments"; they were co-workers with God throughout the mission (14:3; 15:4; cf. 11:21; 1 Cor 3:9). Wherever they went, God was the one who, for the Gentiles, swung wide open the door for salvation blessings to be embraced by faith (13:12, 43, 46-48; 14:1).

◆　## H. The Council at Jerusalem (15:1-21)

While Paul and Barnabas were at Antioch of Syria, some men from Judea arrived and began to teach the believers*: "Unless you are circumcised as required by the law of Moses, you cannot be saved." ²Paul and Barnabas disagreed with them, arguing vehemently. Finally, the church decided to send Paul and Barnabas to Jerusalem, accompanied by some local believers, to talk to the apostles and elders about this question. ³The church sent the delegates to Jerusalem, and they stopped along the way in Phoenicia and Samaria to visit the believers. They told them—much to everyone's joy—that the Gentiles, too, were being converted.

⁴When they arrived in Jerusalem, Barnabas and Paul were welcomed by the whole church, including the apostles and elders. They reported everything God had done through them. ⁵But then some of the believers who belonged to the sect of the Pharisees stood up and insisted, "The Gentile converts must be circumcised and required to follow the law of Moses."

⁶So the apostles and elders met together to resolve this issue. ⁷At the meeting, after a long discussion, Peter stood and addressed them as follows: "Brothers, you all know that God chose me from among you some time ago to preach to the Gentiles so that they could hear the Good News and believe. ⁸God knows people's hearts, and he confirmed that he ac-

cepts Gentiles by giving them the Holy Spirit, just as he did to us. ⁹He made no distinction between us and them, for he cleansed their hearts through faith. ¹⁰So why are you now challenging God by burdening the Gentile believers* with a yoke that neither we nor our ancestors were able to bear? ¹¹We believe that we are all saved the same way, by the undeserved grace of the Lord Jesus."

¹²Everyone listened quietly as Barnabas and Paul told about the miraculous signs and wonders God had done through them among the Gentiles.

¹³When they had finished, James stood and said, "Brothers, listen to me. ¹⁴Peter* has told you about the time God first visited the Gentiles to take from them a people for himself. ¹⁵And this conversion of Gentiles is exactly what the prophets predicted. As it is written:

¹⁶'Afterward I will return
　　and restore the fallen house*
　　of David.
I will rebuild its ruins
　　and restore it,
¹⁷so that the rest of humanity might
　　seek the LORD,
　　including the Gentiles—
　　all those I have called to be mine.
The LORD has spoken—
¹⁸　he who made these things known
　　so long ago.'*

¹⁹"And so my judgment is that we should not make it difficult for the Gentiles who are turning to God. ²⁰Instead, we should write and tell them to abstain from eating food offered to idols, from sexual immorality, from eating the meat of strangled animals, and from consuming blood. ²¹For these laws of Moses have been preached in Jewish synagogues in every city on every Sabbath for many generations."

15:1 Greek *brothers;* also in 15:3, 23, 32, 33, 36, 40. 15:10 Greek *disciples.* 15:14 Greek *Symeon.* 15:16 Or *kingdom;* Greek reads *tent.* 15:16-18 Amos 9:11-12 (Greek version); Isa 45:21.

NOTES

15:1, 3 believers. Lit., "brothers" (so also in 15:3, 23, 32, 33, 36, 40—so NLT mg).

15:7 some time ago. Though the immediate reference in terms of fulfillment is to the Cornelius incident (Acts 10:1–11:18; Witherington 1998:453), the phraseology used (*aph' hēmerōn archaiōn* [TG744, ZG792] (from ancient days) points not just to the early days or the beginning of the Christian movement (contra Barrett 1998:713; Dunn 1996:200) but also to God's first promises to save the Gentiles in the ancient past (Deut 4:32; Ps 44:1 [43:2]; Isa 37:26; cf. Acts 15:14, 18; Maloney 1991:138-39; van de Sandt 1992:85, 97).

15:10 why are you now challenging God? Lit., "putting God to the test." This might refer to questioning God's power to save the Gentiles without circumcision (Williams 1985:253; cf. NLT). By analogy to Israel's resistance in the wilderness (Exod 17:2; Deut 6:16), this might also be equivalent to "putting God to the test" by seeing how far one can go in rebelling against his plan (Johnson 1992:262; Polhill 1992:327; Barrett 1998:717), testing his patience, and inviting his judgment (Fernando 1998:416). It is more likely, though, that this "testing" refers to tempting God to inflict punishment, even eternal condemnation, by placing the Gentile convert back "under the law," that futile "law performance" way of trying to relate to God.

burdening the Gentile believers. If the "burdening" is understood as making the law a requirement for salvation (cf. Nolland 1980), then there is no final contradiction with Peter's Jewish piety (10:14; 11:18; contra Barrett 1998:719). Here we have no unhistorical "Paulinism," for it accords well with the heart of Peter's gospel: salvation blessings as forgiveness of sins received by faith (2:38; 10:43).

15:11 We believe that we are all saved the same way, by the undeserved grace of the Lord Jesus. The expression *pisteuomen sōthēnai* [TG4100/4982, ZG4409/5392] (we believe in order to be saved) is an infinitive of purpose (Barrett 1998:719-720). The "grace" is not Jesus as the gift (as Johnson 1992:263) nor God's sovereign activity in saving whomever and however he will (as Polhill 1992:327); rather, from God's perspective, grace is the necessary and sufficient basis and means of salvation for both Jew and Gentile (Dunn 1996:201).

15:16-17 The wording of the quotation varies significantly from the MT of Amos 9:11-12. The change of introductory phrasing in 15:16, "Afterward I will return," is probably an allusion to Hos 3:5 and Jeremiah 2:15 (Bauckham 1996:157). At Amos 9:12, the MT reads, "Israel will possess what is left of Edom," while Acts and the LXX read, "the rest of humanity might seek" (Acts has the object "the Lord"). This is not an example of Luke following the LXX for the sake of his Greek readers, while still establishing his point via that part of the verse in which MT and LXX agree, as Polhill (1992:329) posits; nor is it the exercise of a prerogative in Jewish exegesis (*'al tiqre*), the use of any alternative reading at hand to further one's point (as Bauckham 1996:161; cf. Bruce 1988:293-294). Rather, the MT is likely a corruption of the Hebrew text that stands behind the LXX and Acts (cf. CD 7:16; 4QFlor 1:12; Archer and Chirichigno 1983:155; Braun 1977:117). The Hebrew *yidreshu* [TH1875, ZH2011] (they shall seek) could easily have been copied as *yireshu* [TH3423, ZH3769] (they shall possess), the *daleth* and *yod* often being confused in transmission (Braun 1977:117). The object, which may have fallen out, may have originally been either "him" or "me," both referring to God. The string of consonants here—*aleph, daleth, mem*—can be pointed to spell either *'adam* [TH120, ZH132] (humanity) or *'edom* [TH123, ZH121] (Edom), and the *matres lectionis* added later to facilitate the MT reading, "Edom."

15:16 *Afterward.* Polhill (1992:329), by noting that the quote's function is to substantiate the Gentile mission, has effectively critiqued the dispensational interpretation that takes "afterward" as a time-marker separating the gospel dispensation to the Gentiles (15:14-15) from the future restoration of the Davidic kingdom in the Millennium.

restore the fallen house of David. The raising up of "David's fallen tent" is fulfilled in Jesus' entire messianic mission (cf. Jewish messianic interpretation of the passage: CD 7:16; 4QFlor 1:11-13; *b. Sanhedrin* 96b-97a; Polhill 1992:329; Barrett 1998:726; Bolt 1998:204; cf. Talbert [1997:140] who focuses on Jesus' Resurrection or in the Christian community, particularly as God's eschatological temple (Jer 12:14-17; Amos 5:26/9:11 in CD 7:14-16; *Sibylline Oracles* 5.414-434; Bauckham 1996:158-160; cf. Kee 1997:181). If the prophecy includes Peter's role, then the rebuilt Davidic tent is a restored Israel made up of the Jewish Christians whom God chose to inaugurate the Gentile mission (15:7, 14; Longenecker 1981:446).

15:20, 29 The apostolic decree comes in three forms in the manuscript tradition. (1) 𝔓74 ℵ B and various Byzantine manuscripts have the four items as present in the NLT. (2) In 15:20 and 29, D and other Western witnesses delete *tou pniktou* [TG4156/A, ZG4465] (the strangled thing) and place a converse Golden Rule after "immorality": "Do not do to others what you would not want them to do to you." The result is that *haima* [TG129, ZG135] ("blood"; NLT, "consuming blood") can be understood as "bloodshed," forming a list of three ethical demands followed by a summarizing principle. (3) The word *porneia* [TG4202, ZG4518] (sexual immorality) is omitted from 15:20 by 𝔓45 (which is not extant at 15:29 or 21:25) and from 15:29 by one Vulgate manuscript, Origen, Vigilius, and Gaudentius. The resulting list involves ritual purity prohibitions. Since both shorter lists can be accounted for as attempts to ease the difficulties of the four-item list, the four-item list should be taken as original (Metzger 1994:379-383).

Scholars have understood this decree against various backgrounds and have interpreted the particulars accordingly. Is it an expression of the Jewish ethical expectations of all Gentiles, or possibly of proselytes, which came to be embodied in the Noachide commandments against idolatry, sexual immorality, and bloodshed (Borgen 1988; Bockmuehl 1995)? Is it the obverse of this—namely, non-negotiable Jewish distinctives in a pagan context (Barrett 1998:734)? Is it prohibitions against further involvement in idolatry, particularly pagan temple worship and feasts (Wedderburn 1993; Witherington 1998:460-64)? (If so, *porneia* [TG4202, ZG4518] is temple prostitution [2 Macc 6:4-5]; *pnikta* [TG4156/A, ZG4465] are "stews" made from sacrifices; and *haima* [TG129, ZG135] is "blood" drunk from sacrifices; cf. Philo *Special Laws* 4.119, 123, 125.) Is it a list of dietary and sexual mores regulations from Lev 17-18, originally for Israel and resident alien Gentiles living in Israel, now applied to Gentile Christians as minimum requirements for association with Jewish Christians, who continued to practice their traditional piety (Callan 1993; Bauckham 1996:172; Kee 1997:182; Talbert 1997:141)? (This reads the word *porneia* as either sexual immorality or marriage within kinship lines [Lev 18:6-18, 26], and *pnikta* as the negative corollary of meat whose blood is drained [Lev 17:13].) Is it simply *ad hoc* practical wisdom for Jewish-Gentile Christian interaction (Blomberg 1998:408-410)?

While each proposed background and the explanation of particulars is not without its difficulties, especially within the context of Paul's law-free gospel, this last option seems best. The decree seems to respond particularly to the issue of Jewish-Gentile interaction, especially table fellowship (11:3; 15:5; Gal 2:11-14). Giving practical wisdom grounded in OT law (Lev 17–18), it encourages Gentile Christians to use their freedom to serve their Jewish Christian brothers and sisters. In not going beyond God's original design and arrangement for the Israelites and the foreigners who lived among them, it is a reasonable, even necessary, request of Gentile Christians (cf. Acts 15:19, 28).

15:21 *These laws of Moses have been preached . . . in every city on every Sabbath.* The rationale for the decree is not intended to proclaim Mosaic authority (as van de Sandt 1992:93) nor the availability of teaching on the law, nor to tell persons who want the law where to find it (as Fernando 1998:419), nor to give assurance that these restrictions don't threaten dissemination of knowledge of the law (as Dunn 1996:206), but rather to show that they are simply necessary due to the unavoidability of contact with pious Jews in the Diaspora (Talbert 1997:142).

COMMENTARY

Many Bible readers want to know if Acts 15 and Galatians 2:1-10 are speaking of the same event. When Acts 15 and Galatians 2:1-10 are viewed as reporting the same event, the discrepancies between them often lead to a negative evaluation of Luke's historical reliability (cf. Johnson 1992:269-270; Kee 1997:184; Barrett 1998:xxxviii-xlii). Attempts to harmonize the two accounts have proven unsatisfactory since they often have to explain away evidence (e.g., the lack of reference to the Acts 11:30 visit in Galatians; Peter's and Barnabas's curious withdrawal from table fellowship at Antioch after the decree; cf. Gal 2:11-14). A more satisfying solution is to equate Acts 11:30 and 12:25 with Galatians 2:1-10 and conclude that Acts 15 reports a subsequent event after the writing of Galatians (Longenecker 1981:405, 440; Morgado 1994:61-65; Witherington 1998:440-449; see the Introduction to Galatians in the Cornerstone Biblical Commentary series).

At the literary and theological center of his work, Luke's Jerusalem Council account teaches us that God's mission will advance to the ends of the earth (Acts 16–28) only when the church recognizes that God, by grace through faith, is calling out a "people for himself" from every ethnic group. He desires that they be united on an equal footing into one body characterized in its common life by a respect for cultural diversity.

During the lengthy reunion at Antioch of Syria, some men came down from Judea and began to teach in the strongest possible terms the necessity of circumcision for salvation (15:1). We may also be reading about their arrival in Galatians 1:11-14, though from what we learn about Peter's and James's approach at the council, those from Judea should not be organically linked to either or be viewed as official church representatives (15:24). They were probably part of the "believers who belonged to the sect of the Pharisees," reflecting as they do the same teaching of a "proselyte model" of Gentile conversion (15:5). This was most natural for pious Jews steeped in the aspect of Old Testament thought that predicted the Gentiles would stream to Israel in the end times (Isa 2:2-3; 25:6-8; 56:6-7; 60:2-22; Zech 8:23).

So fundamental was this issue that Paul and Barnabas were forced to withstand them in such a way that the resulting discord (15:2) prompted an argument in which neither side could work for a resolution and still maintain its position. What was at stake was nothing short of grace-based salvation, received by faith, and the inclusion of all ethnic groups in the church on an equal footing with Jewish Christians (13:38-39, 43, 48; 14:27). To achieve clarity, which would preserve doctrinal purity and restore unity and peace, the church wisely ordered Paul and Barnabas and some others to go to the Jerusalem church about this question. Since the Jerusalem church was the source of both the teachers of circumcision and the founders of the Antioch church (11:19-21)—not to mention the "church of the apostles"—it was the natural venue for settling the dispute.

What began as a standoff would end in vindication for Paul's law-free gospel. The Antioch church sent out Paul and Barnabas as their delegates, even escorting them on their journey. As they passed through the Phoenician coastal plain and the hill country of Samaria, they shared with other believers in detail about the conversion of the Gentiles, bringing great rejoicing. Unlike the skeptical circumcision party, they gave the correct response to reports of God's saving work among other ethnic groups (cf. Luke 15:7, 10, 32; Acts 11:23). In Jerusalem, where Paul and Barnabas again announced what God had done with them, they were welcomed (15:4). The opposition, however, did not let this Good News go uncontested. These opposers still identified themselves as Pharisees (NLT implies they had been but did not continue to be; contrast 23:6; 26:5). These men declared the necessity of the "proselyte model" for Gentile conversion to Christianity—not only the initiation rite of circumcision but also a lifestyle governed by the ritual, as well as the moral, components of "the law of Moses." Both sides claimed divine sanction for their approach. How would the apostles and elders arrive at a satisfying resolution?

When the leaders, "apostles and church elders," probably in the presence of the whole assembly (cf. 15:12), gathered to decide the question, there was much debate, leading again to a standoff. Peter intervened with a word which effectively quelled the debate (15:7-12). He described three divine acts which, taken together, demonstrated conclusively that God's intent is that both Gentiles and Jews embrace salvation on the same basis of grace and faith. As God chose Israel to be his people (13:17; Deut 4:37; 7:7; Josh 24:15), so he chose from ancient days that through Peter's mouth the Gentiles might hear the word of the gospel and believe (Acts 15:7, see note). First, it was God who had ordained and even promised in the prophets, the outward means by which Gentiles would embrace salvation. This began to be fulfilled when Cornelius and his household believed the gospel preached by Peter, a Jewish Christian (10:22, 33, 36, 42-43; 11:14). Second, God confirmed this Gospel by giving the Spirit to the Gentiles, as he had at Pentecost (15:8). Third, God did an inner work of regeneration (15:9). Refusing to make distinctions, as he had shown Peter (10:20; 11:14; cf. 10:34), God directly "cleansed" the Gentiles' hearts, a move completely in line with his removal of the "clean/unclean" distinction (10:15; 11:9; cf. 10:28). The "yoke of the law," the "performance way" of trying to relate to God, though prized by the Jews as a discipline pleasing to God, was really an unbearable burden in all generations. It left everyone guilty and was futile for achieving salvation (Acts 13:38-39; Gal 3:10-12). Thus, Peter declared that it is by means of the special favor of the Lord Jesus—his saving grace (11:23; 13:43; 14:3)—that Jews and Gentiles are enabled to believe so as to be saved.

With the assembly quiet after Peter's explanation, Paul and Barnabas added their own evidence to confirm that God directly accepts Gentiles for salvation (15:12). God did "miraculous signs and wonders" at the Exodus to redeem the Jews from among a Gentile nation (Deut 4:33-34; 34:11); he did them when he gathered to himself Jews to be Jewish Christians, a "restored Israel," people of God; and now Paul and Barnabas reported the "miraculous signs and wonders" God had done through them among the Gentiles (14:3, 9-10). By analogy, then, Paul's mission and message—the law-free gospel of grace—had the same divine legitimacy as Peter's.

James, the half-brother of Jesus, probably the presiding elder, stood and gave his assessment of the evidence and offered a solution to the controversy. Interpreting Peter's experience with Cornelius as a major event in salvation history, he used biblical language which placed the inauguration of the Gentile mission on par with God's saving acts toward Israel (see Luke 1:68, 78; 7:16; Exod 3:16; 4:31; Jer 39:41 LXX). Using phrasing that closely echoes God's choice of Israel, James heightened the radical nature of the new thing God had done (Exod 19:5; Deut 7:6). God would now take "a people for himself" from among the Gentiles (cf. Zech 2:1-5). It is still one people of God but now expanded in terms of the number of ethnic groups from which it would be drawn—"all nations" (Luke 24:47). James made it clear through the quotation of Amos that one does not have to become a Jew in order to become a Christian.

This radically new move for these first-century Jews was not new to God. "What the prophets predicted" was in agreement with this. What was happening among the Gentiles was so much a part of the fulfillment of God's plan that James could say the Old Testament prophets agreed with it (see notes for the multiple OT allusions in the quote from Amos 9:11-12). The Old Testament quotation is programmatic for the remainder of Acts and comprehensively presents God's work through Jewish Christians to bring Gentiles into the church (Wall 1998:449). The Lord would return and restore "the fallen house of David" (15:16; Amos 9:11). This occurred in Jesus' messianic mission when he rebuilt Israel through a reconstituted leadership, the twelve apostles (Luke 22:28-30; Acts 1:25). They, in turn, were directed to be witnesses to and for the King, to all nations to the end of the earth (Luke 24:47; Acts 1:8; 2:39). In that way, "the rest of humanity" could seek the Lord. James tells his hearers that this fulfills God's sovereign plan, for he has already marked out for his possession from among the Gentiles those, literally, "on whom my name has been called on them" (cf. Deut 28:10; 2 Chr 7:14; Jer 4:19). In fact, Amos says the Lord is doing these things. In an allusion to Isaiah 45:21, James points out that this new multi-ethnic shape of God's people is a thing "known long ago"—it was part of God's eternal counsels.

How then shall Jew and Gentile live together as this new people of God? First, Jewish Christians should accept Gentiles who are turning to God and not harass them by making circumcision and the yoke of the law a necessary condition or sign of their salvation. Second, Gentile converts need to show sensitivity to Jewish cultural taboos but not necessarily going beyond what God originally required of Gentile aliens living alongside Jews in the land (Lev 17–18). They should "abstain from eating food offered to idols" (cf. Lev 17:7-8); "sexual immorality" (Lev 18:6-18, 26); "consuming blood" (Lev 17:10); or "eating the meat of strangled animals" (Lev 17:13). They should do this because there was a widespread, law-observing Jewish population of long standing in the Diaspora (15:21).

◆ I. The Letter for Gentile Believers (15:22-35)

²²Then the apostles and elders together with the whole church in Jerusalem chose delegates, and they sent them to Antioch of Syria with Paul and Barnabas to report on this decision. The men chosen were two of the church leaders*—Judas (also called Barsabbas) and Silas. ²³This is the letter they took with them:
"This letter is from the apostles and elders, your brothers in Jerusalem. It is written to the Gentile believers in Antioch, Syria, and Cilicia. Greetings!
²⁴"We understand that some men from here have troubled you and upset you with their teaching, but we did not send them! ²⁵So we decided, having come to complete agreement, to send you official representatives, along with our beloved Barnabas and Paul, ²⁶who have risked their lives for the name of our Lord Jesus Christ. ²⁷We are sending Judas and Silas to confirm what we have decided concerning your question.

²⁸"For it seemed good to the Holy Spirit and to us to lay no greater burden on you than these few requirements: ²⁹You must abstain from eating food offered to idols, from consuming blood or the meat of strangled animals, and from sexual immorality. If you do this, you will do well. Farewell."

³⁰The messengers went at once to Antioch, where they called a general meeting of the believers and delivered the letter. ³¹And there was great joy throughout the church that day as they read this encouraging message.
³²Then Judas and Silas, both being prophets, spoke at length to the believers, encouraging and strengthening their faith. ³³They stayed for a while, and then the believers sent them back to the church in Jerusalem with a blessing of peace.* ³⁵Paul and Barnabas stayed in Antioch. They and many others taught and preached the word of the Lord there.

15:22 Greek *were leaders among the brothers.*   **15:33** Some manuscripts add verse 34, *But Silas decided to stay there.*

NOTES

15:26 *risked their lives.* Since here it cannot not indicate martyrdom, *paradedōkosi* [TG3860, ZG4140] (they handed over) could point to Paul and Barnabas's commitment to Christ (Johnson 1992:276; Barrett 1998:743). The idea that they "risked their lives" is a better interpretation than they "handed over their lives." The Western text's explanatory gloss, "in every trial," reveals this interpretive stance.

15:33-34 As it states in the NLT mg, some mss add v. 34, "But Silas decided to stay there." The mss that add this verse are later and were followed by the Textus Receptus, which includes this verse. Codex D has it in a longer version: "But it seemed good to Silas that they remain, and Judas journeyed alone." In the judgment of many textual critics, the verse was inserted to account for Silas's presence at v. 40 (Metzger 1994:388).

COMMENTARY

James's final judgment at the Jerusalem council prevailed. The Judaizers were marginalized, but they still continued to exert their influence (cf. 21:20-25). The council chose official representatives to accompany Paul and Barnabas and to deliver a letter and give a report of the decision to the Antioch church (15:22; cf. 15:25, 27). "Judas (also called Barsabbas)" is possibly the brother of Joseph Barsabbas (1:23), though the patronymic (= son of Saba, Seba, or Sabbath) was common. "Silas" (also known as "Silvanus," the diminutive of "Saul") later became a traveling companion of Paul (15:40; 1 Thess 1:1). Both were "church leaders" (cf. Luke 22:26) and "prophets" (15:32) and possibly representatives, respectively, of the Hebrew-speaking Jewish and Hellenistic Jewish wings of the church.

The letter's very address shows a careful balance between unity in Christ and respect for diverse cultural identities. "The apostles and elders, your brothers," addressed Christian brothers and sisters in Antioch, Syria, and Cilicia, recognizing their ethnic identity: "to the Gentile believers." Though the letter only lists these three cities in the address, it is evident the decree was intended for the whole church (cf. 16:4).

The body of the letter communicates the council's decisions on the two key issues: the spiritual status of uncircumcised Gentiles who had converted to Christianity (15:24-27) and the regulations for their table fellowship with Jewish Christians (15:28-29). Although the council did not reiterate the direct acceptance of Gentiles into salvation by grace through faith, it did indicate its position on this matter in several ways. It assumed the Gentile Christians' standing in Christ, when it labeled the Judaizers' teaching as a serious threat to their spiritual health. In the strongest terms, the apostles said it not only "troubled" (*tarassō* [TG5015, ZG5429], cf. Gal 1:7; 5:10) them but also "upset" them, literally "devastated their souls" (*anaskeuazontes tas psuchas* [TG384, ZG412]). As destructive as an army's devastation of enemy territory (Josephus *Antiquities* 14.406) and an orator's destructive argument (Aristotle *Rhetoric* 2.24.4[1401b]; Quintillian *Institutio oratoria* 2.4.18), it left Gentile Christians questioning their understanding of the gospel and their standing in Christ. The council totally disassociated itself from the Judaizers by saying that though they had come from the Jerusalem assembly, they were not following the apostles' and elders' instructions when they taught their "yoke of the law" gospel.

In fact, by this letter and the "official representatives" who carried it, the council displaced the Judaizers' unwelcome influence. The unanimous decision showed that it was the work of the Spirit bringing unity to the church (15:25, 28). The representatives would give verbal attestation to the letter's content and in that way provide secure, dual witness to the council's decision. They would be accompanied by Paul and Barnabas, whom the leaders commended as their own valued co-workers of the highest integrity (15:25-26).

Either because of the Spirit's prior witness to the Gentiles' salvation by grace through faith in a law-free gospel (15:8; cf. 10:19, 44; 13:2), or taking their unanimity as evidence that they were acting in accordance with the Spirit, the council declared itself Spirit-led in dealing with the second issue through a decree (15:28-29). Because there were Jews everywhere with scruples in these matters (15:21), the Gentile believers had to use their freedom in Christ to love and serve their Jewish brothers by observing these few requirements. It was normative practical wisdom, applicable as a matter of courtesy to cultural sensitivities about table fellowship. Embedded in this practical wisdom, of course, was a universal ethical norm: abstinence from sexual immorality.

With "great joy" the Antioch church received the letter and its encouraging message (15:31; cf. 9:31). Where there had been terror (15:24) there was now rejoicing. And rightly so, for the Gentile converts knew where they stood with reference to salvation and Judaism and Jewish Christian believers. Affirmations of the direct availability of salvation always bring joy, especially among the Gentiles (cf. 13:48).

Being prophets, Judas and Silas were supernaturally gifted, like their Old Testament counterparts, to apply the word of God to the personal and corporate circumstances of God's people (cf. 1 Cor 14:3, 31). They began a ministry of encouraging and strengthening the believers. They repaired the damage done by the Judaizers (15:24) and enabled the saints to build the church on a firm foundation (cf. 14:22).

The prophet-envoys eventually took their leave of the Antioch church "with a blessing of peace" (15:33). The letter and their ministry had restored harmony within and among the churches (cf. 9:31). The church, with renewed vigor, engaged in outreach in the further advance of its mission (15:35). Paul and Barnabas and "many others" were teaching and preaching the word of the Lord, "evangelizing." The outward momentum of sharing the Good News, last seen in the middle of the first missionary journey, is thereby resumed (14:7, 15, 21).

◆ ## J. Paul and Barnabas Separate (15:36–41)

[36]After some time Paul said to Barnabas, "Let's go back and visit each city where we previously preached the word of the Lord, to see how the new believers are doing." [37]Barnabas agreed and wanted to take along John Mark. [38]But Paul disagreed strongly, since John Mark had deserted them in Pamphylia and had not continued with them in their work. [39]Their disagreement was so sharp that they separated. Barnabas took John Mark with him and sailed for Cyprus. [40]Paul chose Silas, and as he left, the believers entrusted him to the Lord's gracious care. [41]Then he traveled throughout Syria and Cilicia, strengthening the churches there.

NOTES

15:36-41 Those who equate Gal 2:1-10 with Acts 15 see the disagreement over table fellowship (Gal 2:11-14) as the source of Paul's and Barnabas's quarrel (e.g., Johnson 1992:287; Barrett 1998:756). Since that disagreement probably preceded the Jerusalem council and was settled by it, we should not see Luke either masking the true nature of the Paul-Barnabas rift (as Spencer 1997:158) or presenting a false impression by showing that Paul had continuing cordial relations with Antioch (15:40; as Dunn 1996:211).

15:39 *they separated.* Though it is too much to say with Johnson (1992:287) that Luke presents both Barnabas and John Mark as committing a kind of apostasy, Luke's neutral portrayal of their work does give a hint of disapproval. Since we do not meet Barnabas and John Mark again in Acts and since Luke focuses exclusively on Paul's mission, beginning with the Antioch church commending him to "the Lord's gracious care," it is also too much to say that Luke shows a divinely orchestrated doubling of mission coming from division (contra Talbert 1997:145).

15:40 *the Lord's gracious care.* Lit., "the Lord's grace." Alexandrian and Western witnesses attest *kuriou* [TG2962, ZG3261] (Lord's): 𝔓74 ℵ A B D 33 it^d cop^sa. Other witnesses, some ancient (𝔓45 C E 044 𝔐 syr cop^bo) read *theou* [TG2316, ZG2536] (God's), probably in scribal assimilation to 14:26 (cf. NKJV; Metzger 1994:388-89). Dunn (1996:211) is unsure whether Jesus (cf. 15:11) or the Father (cf. 14:26) is the referent behind "Lord." Barrett (1998:757) judiciously comments that while Luke does not say that "the Lord (Jesus) is God," he writes in such a way as to suggest the possibility to his readers.

COMMENTARY

With some sense of urgency, or at least pastoral concern, Paul suggested to Barnabas a follow-up visit to the new believers of the recently planted churches (15:36; cf. 14:21-23; 18:23; 19:21; 20:1-6 for Paul's practice of follow-up). Although he had made one immediate follow-up visit for the purpose of exhorting them to persevere in the midst of trials, the effect of Judaizers on the churches required another personal visitation (cf. Gal 1:6-7; 3:1; 4:11, 19-20; 5:7).

Barnabas concurred, and he "wanted" (in the sense of "desired and planned") to take along John Mark (Acts 15:37). Luke does not tell us why. What we do know is that from Paul's perspective, John Mark's desertion in the midst of the first missionary journey rendered him unfit for the second (13:13; cf. Luke 8:13; 1 Tim 4:1). Luke does not tell us why John Mark deserted, but if his phrasing of Paul's rationale for rejecting him is any clue (John Mark "had not continued with them in their work"), we can surmise that his defection not only revealed the character flaw of unreliability but also his disagreement with God's mission of opening the "door of faith" to the Gentiles (14:26-27; cf. 13:2, 41). John Mark's presence, then, could have proven to be more of a liability than an asset on a journey to shore up Gentile Christians in the face of Judaizers.

After a "sharp disagreement," indeed a heated conflict of opinions, Paul and Barnabas separated, sacrificing unity for peaceful coexistence at a distance. Barnabas took John Mark and sailed for his homeland, Cyprus (4:36). Paul chose Silas, probably summoning him from Jerusalem. A spiritually gifted prophet (15:32) and a Roman citizen (16:37), Silas would prove to be a valuable coworker (cf. 2 Cor 1:19; 1 Thess 1:1; 2 Thess 1:1). God's ruling and overruling in the Paul-Barnabas dispute resulted in Paul having at his side a person even more qualified than Barnabas, for as one of the Jerusalem church's two official letter carriers and verbal witnesses to the council's decision, Silas could speak for the Jerusalem church in the face of Judaizing claims, which often claimed the mother church's authorization (15:22, 27).

As Paul departs, Luke focuses on his leadership, the Lord's empowerment, and the mission's positive impact: Paul, after choosing Silas, was handed over to the Lord's grace, went out, and passed through Syria and Cilicia, strengthening the believers there. He affirmed the good foundation of the law-free gospel lived out in a community which should be both united and respectful of cultural diversity (cf. 14:22; 15:32). The Jerusalem council decree strengthened his hand in this.

◆ **K. Paul Begins a Second Missionary Journey (16:1-5)**

Paul went first to Derbe and then to Lystra, where there was a young disciple named Timothy. His mother was a Jewish believer, but his father was a Greek. ²Timothy was well thought of by the believers* in Lystra and Iconium, ³so Paul wanted him to join them on their journey. In deference to the Jews of the area, he arranged for Timothy to be circumcised before they left, for everyone knew that his father was a Greek. ⁴Then they went from town to town, instructing the believers to follow the decisions made by the apostles and elders in Jerusalem. ⁵So the churches were strengthened in their faith and grew larger every day.

16:2 Greek *brothers;* also in 16:40.

NOTES

16:1 *Timothy.* All commentators think that Luke viewed Timothy as an uncircumcised Jew, with his ethnicity being traced through his mother; however, not all see this as historically accurate (Barrett 1998:761-762; Johnson 1992:289). Barrett and Johnson follow Cohen (1986) who traced the rabbinic practice of counting descent matrilineally only back to the second century AD (*m. Qiddushin* 3:12; *m. Yevamot* 7:5). Acts, however, is evidence that such an approach existed among the Jews in the first century, before the rabbis officially sanctioned it in the second (Blomberg 1998:410-411).

16:3 *Paul . . . arranged for Timothy to be circumcised.* Barrett (1998:761) says it is a bare possibility, though by no means probable, that Paul would have done this. It flies in the face of the book of Galatians, especially the reports of Paul's resistance to Titus's circumcision and his confrontation with Peter and Barnabas (Gal 2:3-5, 11-14; cf. 5:1; 1 Cor 7:18). So long as there was not soteriological significance, however, Paul maintained a flexible approach to Jewish practices (1 Cor 9:19-20). He continued to practice Jewish piety and encouraged his fellow Jewish Christians to do the same (18:18; 20:16; 21:23-26; Rom 14:1–15:13; 1 Cor 7:18; 2 Cor 11:24; Gal 5:6; 6:15). Paul's report of his opponents' accusations may also hint at this (Gal 5:11). Here, as part of a missionary strategy for evangelizing the Jews, Paul regularized Timothy's Jewish status through circumcision.

COMMENTARY

In this section we see how God's mission was advanced by a culturally sensitive approach to proclaiming the law-free gospel. With an element of providential surprise (*kai idou* [TG2532/2400, ZG2779/2627] "and behold," not rendered in NLT), Paul encountered his replacement for John Mark at Lystra. Timothy was a disciple of good character (Phil 2:20-22; cf. Acts 6:3; 1 Tim 3:7) with a reputation known to the believers in Iconium, a day's journey away (16:2). But he was of mixed parentage (16:1), and his father, possibly deceased (the tense in 16:3 may be taken to indicate this), had evidently refused to permit Timothy's circumcision. Paul took steps to fully regularize Timothy's Jewish status through circumcision. In this way, he removed a team member's uncircumcised status as an impediment to evangelizing unbelieving Jews of the region (cf. their previous hostility, 14:5, 19). At the same time, he reinforced the "cultural respect" component of the Jerusalem decree. Just as the church's law-free gospel does not mean that Gentiles must Judaize in order to be Christians, so, conversely, Jews do not have to "Gentilize."

Lest we lose sight of the mutual cultural respect required of the multi-ethnic people of God, Luke immediately tells us that, as Paul and Silas retraced some of the steps of the first missionary journey, they "were handing over" to the churches (*paredidosan* [TG3860, ZG4140], stronger than NLT's "instructing"; cf. 6:14; Luke 1:2) the Jerusalem council's decree (16:4).

In a summary statement, which not only closes the Jerusalem council account (15:1-35) but also the book's fourth panel—"The Church in Antioch's Mission to Cyprus and Western Asia Minor" (13:1-16:5)—Luke reiterated those marks of church health which showed that God was attending to his mission (16:5). The embrace of the Jerusalem council's decisions produced churches "strengthened [divine passive] in their faith." The decrees clearly were not at odds with, but rather undergirded, the truly salvific "faith way" of relating to God through Christ (13:38-39; 14:22, 27; 15:9). As such, the church grew daily in numbers. Such daily additions (cf. 2:47) are a mark of God's fulfillment of his saving purposes in applying salvation. (Cf. Luke's emphasis on quantitative growth at 2:41; 4:4; 5:14; 11:21; especially at summary statements which conclude literary sections: 6:7; 9:31; 12:24.)

◆ V. The Mission to Greece (Europe) and Western Asia Minor (16:6-19:20)
A. A Call from Macedonia (16:6-10)

⁶Next Paul and Silas traveled through the area of Phrygia and Galatia, because the Holy Spirit had prevented them from preaching the word in the province of Asia at that time. ⁷Then coming to the borders of Mysia, they headed north for the province of Bithynia,* but again the Spirit of Jesus did not allow them to go there. ⁸So instead, they went on through Mysia to the seaport of Troas.

⁹That night Paul had a vision: A man from Macedonia in northern Greece was standing there, pleading with him, "Come over to Macedonia and help us!" ¹⁰So we* decided to leave for Macedonia at once, having concluded that God was calling us to preach the Good News there.

16:6-7 *Phrygia, Galatia, Asia, Mysia,* and *Bithynia* were all districts in what is now Turkey. 16:10 Luke, the writer of this book, here joined Paul and accompanied him on his journey.

NOTES

16:6-7 The NLT mg says, "Phrygia, Galatia, Asia, Mysia, and Bithynia were all districts in what is now Turkey." More precisely, Phrygia was an ethnic region, the western portion being the Roman province of Galatia, which itself covered the central portion of the Asia Minor peninsula. Hemer (1976, 1977c) has provided the literary and epigraphic evidence. Barrett (1998:767) doubts it, given the improbable geography from such a use in the immediate context; the NLT rendering of the participle as causal overcomes the difficulty (cf. Hansen 1994:378-79). Asia was the province west of Galatia extending to the coast, though the term could refer more restrictively to its western coastlands on the Aegean (Polhill 1992:344). Mysia, adjacent to Phrygia, was an ethnic region comprising the northern portion of the province of Asia, including Troas. Bithynia, adjacent to Mysia, was a Roman province covering territory northwest of Asia.

16:7 *the Spirit of Jesus did not allow them to go there.* French (1994:57) argues that the divine prohibition was actually a periphrasis for Paul's discretion and trepidation, as he sought to avoid further Roman official trouble by not using the major public roads in Asia. Jewett (1997) points out, however, that the archeological evidence for ancient roadways from Dorylaeum in Phrygia to Troas has not been thoroughly investigated. A network of Roman roads probably existed. The presence of a mining industry in the Scamander and Macestus valleys and a sufficient number of Roman towns and cities would have warranted it. The information from ancient itineraries also points to it. Therefore, the lack of information should not lead us to adopt French's conclusion that, lacking a direct route to Troas, Paul headed there only because he intended to embark for Macedonia (cf. Witherington 1998:479).

16:10 *we decided to leave for Macedonia.* As the NLT mg indicates, Luke (the author) here joined Paul and accompanied him on his journey. (See discussion under "Author" in the Introduction.)

COMMENTARY

In this prelude to the Macedonian phase of the second missionary journey, Paul and his team became aware that, though they might strategize their next moves in line with the centrifugal trajectory of the divinely mandated mission, God retained the prerogative to give precise direction for the next steps.

Paul probably had just completed his tour of the Galatian churches and was at Pisidian Antioch, just inside the Phrygian region of the Roman province of Galatia. Given his penchant for pursuing the Gentile mission in ever-widening contiguous regions (Rom 15:19), he probably intended next to make his way straight west into the Roman province of Asia on the Via Sebaste, 150 miles to Colossae and then 150 more to Ephesus. We are not told how, but the Holy Spirit "prevented them from preaching the word in the province of Asia at that time" (16:6). While the Lord's purposes are always for the gospel to be preached and for all persons to fully embrace it (cf. Luke 18:16; Acts 8:36; 10:47; 11:17; 28:31), in this instance, he sovereignly redirected his servants to another area—probably a place where none had heard.

Paul and his party headed north to Dorylaenum at the northwest border of Phrygian Galatia within the Mysian region of the province of Asia. They attempted to move northeast into the province of Bithynia, ever advancing outward in their mission, but again the Spirit of Jesus (which is the same as the Holy Spirit—cf. 16:6 and 16:7) did not let them enter. As before in 16:6 we are not told how. Jesus not only sovereignly directed the mission in its general scope and direction, but he also directed it geographically, ethnically, and socially (1:8; 9:4-6, 15). When he chose to, he managed critical details, guiding his witnesses even more specifically, though they were already being most obedient to the general scope and sequence of his directive.

Ever moving forward, outward, "to the end of the earth," Paul "went on through" Mysia and came down to Troas, a large seaport and commercial center on the coast, with an estimated population of 100,000. As it was in the province of Asia, Paul was not to evangelize there.

Positive guidance was not long in coming; in a vision at night (cf. 9:12; 18:9; 22:17; 26:16), Paul met a man from Macedonia who begged him to come over and help. The group's need was expressed not only in the "pleading" but also in the specified call for "help." The text then says that "we . . . concluded that God was calling us to preach the Good News there" (16:10; as the NLT mg note observes, the author, Luke, participates in the journey from here). Again God was out ahead of them in time and place, summoning them to carry out his mission of evangelizing all the nations. Their obedience was immediate.

◆ B. Lydia of Philippi Believes in Jesus (16:11-15)

¹¹We boarded a boat at Troas and sailed straight across to the island of Samothrace, and the next day we landed at Neapolis. ¹²From there we reached Philippi, a major city of that district of Macedonia and a Roman colony. And we stayed there several days.

¹³On the Sabbath we went a little way outside the city to a riverbank, where we thought people would be meeting for prayer, and we sat down to speak with some women who had gathered there. ¹⁴One of them was Lydia from Thyatira, a merchant of expensive purple cloth, who worshiped God. As she listened to us, the Lord opened her heart, and she accepted what Paul was saying. ¹⁵She was baptized along with other members of her household, and she asked us to be her guests. "If you agree that I am a true believer in the Lord," she said, "come and stay at my home." And she urged us until we agreed.

NOTES

16:12 *a major city of that district of Macedonia.* This rendering of *prōtē* [TG4413, ZG4755] *tēs meridos Makedonias polis* follows the oldest witnesses: 𝔓74 ℵ A C 81 (Metzger 1994:393-395). The UBS³ editorial committee preferred an emendation reconstructed from ancient versions which reads, "a city of the first district of Macedonia" (itᶜ vgᵐˢˢ slav; *prōtēs* [TG4413, ZG4755] *meridos tēs Makedonias polis*). This is geo-politically more accurate on the surface. Thessalonica was the capital of the province of Macedonia, and Amphipolis was the seat of government for the first district, the one in which Philippi was located. If Philippi is designated as "first city" not politically but as a matter of civic pride (so the NLT's "major"), the difficulty is removed (Ascough 1998; cf. Dio Chrysostom *Orations* 38-39). If "of Macedonia" is a partitive genitive, not a genitive of apposition, as the definite article which precedes it indicates, and if the definite article before "district" is taken as a demonstrative ("a major city of that district of Macedonia"), another potential inaccuracy—identifying the province Macedonia as a district—is removed (Barrett 1998:778; Witherington [1998:489] suggests *meris* [TG3310, ZG3535] be taken not as a technical term, "district," but simply as "portion, part").

COMMENTARY

With providential efficiency that matched the missionary team's prompt response to divine guidance (Acts 16:10), Paul, Silas, Timothy, and Luke took a 156-mile, two-day sea voyage on a straight line to Samothrace (a mountainous island that served as a navigational marker with its 5,577-foot Mount Fengari) and then on to Neapolis on the Macedonian coast (16:11; note that the reverse trip took five days, 20:6). Using the Egnatian Way, the Roman road that stretched across the northern portion of the Greek peninsula from the Adriatic to the Aegean, they proceeded some ten miles inland over some hills to Philippi on the central Macedonia plateau. By identifying Philippi as "a major city of that district of Macedonia and a Roman colony," Luke brought out not only its relative importance in the region but also its distinctive political, judicial, and cultural characteristics. Since its founding by Philip II of Macedon, it had been a commercial center dealing in the agricultural produce of the rich plain and the gold and silver mined from the surrounding mountains. More recently, it had been settled as a Roman colony by army veterans after the decisive battle of the second civil war (42 BC, Strabo *Geography* 7, frag. 41) and by Italian colonists in 30 BC (Dio Cassius *Roman History* 51.4.6). As a colony, with its core of Roman citizens, it enjoyed *libertas*, the right of autonomous government; *immunitas*, freedom from normal provincial tribute or taxation; and *Ius Italicum*—the whole legal system was the same as that on Italian soil. Culturally, the city was thoroughly Romanized, with Latin being the standard language.

Pursuing his strategy of going to the Jews first (13:5, 14; 14:1), Paul, on the Sabbath, looked for a Jewish "place of prayer" (a synagogue) outside the gate of the city by a riverbank (cf. Josephus *Life* 54; *Antiquities* 14.258; Philo *Against Flaccus* 6.41; 7.45, 47-9, 53). What he found was a gathering of women, probably in the open air. Always alert to every opportunity, Paul and his team shared the gospel with them.

Luke focused on Lydia, a God-fearing Gentile and wealthy business woman—"a merchant of expensive purple cloth"—from Thyatira in Asia. The dye extracted from the root of the Eurasian madder, an herb plentiful in the area around Thyatira, made Thyatira a production center for such cloth which the wealthy and royalty prized (*Inscriptiones Graecae* 10.2.1.291; Luke 16:19; 1 Macc 10:62). As God had cleansed the hearts of the Gentile Cornelius and his household by faith (Acts 15:9), so here the Lord opened the heart of Lydia, a Gentile, to "accept" (*prosechein* [TG4337, ZG4668], "to pay attention to, follow"; cf. Acts 8:6, 11) the gospel message. This divine direct intervention is essential if the unregenerate heart, always slow to believe—if not antagonistic to the gospel message—is to positively embrace it in an "honest, good-hearted" way (Luke 8:15; Acts 7:51, 54; 24:25; 28:27).

Confessing her faith in the Lord, she was baptized—along with her household (16:14). Because ancient households were united in a common religious cult, the conversion of the head of household had necessary religious, and in this case spiritual, implications for the other household members. Lydia's action of inviting the missionary team to stay in her home validated the Jerusalem council's decision to promote unity between Jewish Christians and Gentile Christians, even in the matter of table fellowship.

◆   ## C. Paul and Silas in Prison (16:16-40)

[16]One day as we were going down to the place of prayer, we met a demon-possessed slave girl. She was a fortune-teller who earned a lot of money for her masters. [17]She followed Paul and the rest of us, shouting, "These men are servants of the Most High God, and they have come to tell you how to be saved."

[18]This went on day after day until Paul got so exasperated that he turned and

said to the demon within her, "I command you in the name of Jesus Christ to come out of her." And instantly it left her.

[19]Her masters' hopes of wealth were now shattered, so they grabbed Paul and Silas and dragged them before the authorities at the marketplace. [20]"The whole city is in an uproar because of these Jews!" they shouted to the city officials. [21]"They are teaching customs that are illegal for us Romans to practice."

[22]A mob quickly formed against Paul and Silas, and the city officials ordered them stripped and beaten with wooden rods. [23]They were severely beaten, and then they were thrown into prison. The jailer was ordered to make sure they didn't escape. [24]So the jailer put them into the inner dungeon and clamped their feet in the stocks.

[25]Around midnight Paul and Silas were praying and singing hymns to God, and the other prisoners were listening. [26]Suddenly, there was a massive earthquake, and the prison was shaken to its foundations. All the doors immediately flew open, and the chains of every prisoner fell off! [27]The jailer woke up to see the prison doors wide open. He assumed the prisoners had escaped, so he drew his sword to kill himself. [28]But Paul shouted to him, "Stop! Don't kill yourself! We are all here!"

[29]The jailer called for lights and ran to the dungeon and fell down trembling before Paul and Silas. [30]Then he brought them out and asked, "Sirs, what must I do to be saved?"

[31]They replied, "Believe in the Lord Jesus and you will be saved, along with everyone in your household." [32]And they shared the word of the Lord with him and with all who lived in his household. [33]Even at that hour of the night, the jailer cared for them and washed their wounds. Then he and everyone in his household were immediately baptized. [34]He brought them into his house and set a meal before them, and he and his entire household rejoiced because they all believed in God.

[35]The next morning the city officials sent the police to tell the jailer, "Let those men go!" [36]So the jailer told Paul, "The city officials have said you and Silas are free to leave. Go in peace."

[37]But Paul replied, "They have publicly beaten us without a trial and put us in prison—and we are Roman citizens. So now they want us to leave secretly? Certainly not! Let them come themselves to release us!"

[38]When the police reported this, the city officials were alarmed to learn that Paul and Silas were Roman citizens. [39]So they came to the jail and apologized to them. Then they brought them out and begged them to leave the city. [40]When Paul and Silas left the prison, they returned to the home of Lydia. There they met with the believers and encouraged them once more. Then they left town.

NOTES

16:16 *demon-possessed slave girl.* Lit., the girl had *pneuma puthōna* [TG4436, ZG4780], "a Python spirit." This was not a fraudulant exercise of ventriloquism (contra Barrett 1998:785; cf. Plutarch *Moralia* 414e) but actually, as Luke and Paul treat it, an instance of demon possession (cf. Maurizio 1995). "Python" here is a reference to what could be called a "Pythian spirit," one expected to predict the future according to Greek myth (see discussion below).

16:17 *These men are servants of the Most High God, and they have come to tell you how to be saved.* Some have thought that the woman had a syncretized, pagan misunderstanding of God as the Highest One in a pantheon and the gospel as just one way of salvation among others (Trebilco 1989). Levinskaya (1996:83-104) has convincingly shown that the religious context for such a misunderstanding does not exist. There is no clear and abundant evidence for *hupistos theos* [TG5310A/2316, ZG5736/2536] (Most High God) as a common pagan religious title. The slave girl tells the truth with biblical and Jewish language (Gen 14:18ff [cf. Philo *Embassy* 3.83; his interpretation guards the title against polytheism]; Deut 32:8; Pss 56:2 LXX; 78:56; Dan 4:26, 32; Tob 1:4, 13; *Sibylline Oracles* 3.519, 580; cf. Levinskaya [1996:95-97] for Jewish inscriptional evidence).

16:18 *Paul got so exasperated.* Paul's exasperation was with the demonic source of the girl's assertion, which would serve at the least to confuse and at the most to discredit the message (cf. Luke 4:34, 41; 8:28; Levinskaya 1996:100; Kee 1997:195, 197).

16:22 *A mob.* The NLT and most commentators (e.g., Johnson 1992:296; Witherington 1998:496) see the crowd as "unstable rabble," ready to riot. Rapske (1994a:122), however, sees its role in the social context of ancient jurisprudence, as that body of "participant observers" who support the charges in an articulate, orderly, yet forceful fashion (cf. 24:9).

16:23-24 *they were thrown into prison.* The incarceration was part of summary justice, a severe punishment meted out to individuals whom the magistrates considered persons of low judicial and social standing—Jewish strangers (Rapske 1994a:125). According to Rapske (1994a:126), the "inner dungeon" and the "stocks" were reserved for the worst crimes and the lowest class of felons as a form of demoralizing, humiliating punishment— they were more than added security. Paul and Silas, then, were not imprisoned as a part of binding them over to the proconsul for trial, as Sherwin-White (1963:82) suggests, for to dignify their case by referral would not only be an insult to their accusers but an annoyance to provincial authorities (Rapske 1994a:129).

16:25-34 What Haenchen (1971:501) called a "nest of improbabilities" still challenges commentators. The selective effects of the earthquake (the foundations shook but the roof did not fall in) are not credible to some (Barrett 1998:776, 799) yet credible to others in terms of the strength of the tremor (Witherington 1998:497). The earthquake's miraculous character consisted in both its timing and its targeted effects. Further, some contend that the jailer seemingly acted irrationally. He prepared to commit suicide without first trying to round up the prisoners or remembering that he would not be punished for escapes occasioned by an "act of God" (Justinian *Digest* 48.3; Barrett 1998:795; Johnson [1992:300] labels "threat of suicide" a novelist theme). Still, the psychological impact of the earthquake on a person with an "honor/shame" mentality could reasonably cause such a reaction (Dunn 1996:222; Witherington 1998:497). Dunn (1996:222) labels as novelistic Paul's "omniscient" shout of comfort, which seems to know both the jailer's intentions and the location of all the prisoners. Witherington (1998:497), however, says the layout of the prison could account for it.

16:26 *the chains . . . fell off!* The earthquake did not simply shake loose the chains' staples from the wall so that the prisoners were free, though still attached to their chains (so Polhill 1992:355; Witherington 1998:497). Luke claims, rather, that the manacles actually fell off the prisoners (Barrett 1998:794).

16:30 *Sirs, what must I do to be saved?* The question could be completely secular: "What must I do to escape the punishment for a lapse in security?" (Kee 1997:199; cf. Polhill [1992:355] who eliminates this option since no one had escaped). Or it could be religious—from within a pagan animistic and polytheistic worldview: "What must I do to escape this natural calamity with the help of the gods or to escape the punishment of the deity who is angry with me for incarcerating his servants?" (Witherington 1998:148, 153; Barrett 1998:797). Or it could have a greater or lesser Christian tinge, depending on how much one presumes the jailer knows of Paul's message and how much Luke's theological use of the term "saved" is in play (cf. Johnson 1992:301; Dunn 1996:223). As with Acts 4:9, 12, we are probably dealing with a play on words, in which Paul picks up at the very most a reference to divine rescue from calamity in this life and transforms it into an offer of eternal salvation (16:31).

16:31 *Believe in the Lord Jesus.* Barrett (1998:797) contends that this form of Christian belief is "neither profound or exalted." Yet, Luke left clues that *kurios* [TG2962, ZG3261] in this phrase, analogous to the pagan designations of deity—"Lord Osiris," "Lord Sarapis," "Lord Caesar"—may be a bridge concept for establishing Christ's full deity with pagans, just as it had been with the Jews (cf. 2:21, 36). In the immediate context, Luke summed up faith in the Lord Jesus as believing in God (16:31). In the broader context, pointers to Jesus' deity are (1) his title among the Gentiles, "Lord of all" (10:36); (2) that preaching the Lord Jesus among the Gentiles was made possible by "the power of the Lord" bringing many to faith (11:20-21); (3) that Gentiles seeking the "Lord" is programmatic in the second half of Acts (15:17; see Amos 9:12).

16:33 *he and everyone in his household were immediately baptized.* While this verse, along with 16:15, is seen by some to offer no support for infant baptism (Polhill 1992:350, 356), most commentators conclude that the wording and the immediate context are too ambiguous to be used as clear support either for or against the practice (Dunn 1996:220; Barrett 1998:783, 797-798).

16:35 *Let those men go!* Luke is not explicit about the motive for the release, though the Western text is: "the city officials *assembled together in the market place, and recollecting the earthquake that had taken place, they were afraid; and* sent the police" (addition in italics; so D syr[h (mg)] Cassiodorus and Ephraem; Metzger 1994:398). The magistrates were not motivated by qualms about peremptory punishment (contra Dunn 1996:223) or the view that overnight incarceration was sufficient punishment (contra Rapske 1994b:129; Witherington 1998:499). Rather, the earthquake moved them to order the release (Barrett 1998:800).

16:37 *we are Roman citizens.* Although a number of commentators are agnostic on whether Paul was really a Roman citizen (Johnson 1992:300; Barrett 1998:802), his delay in declaring it should not be seen as part of the problematic evidence (Rapske 1994a:129-134). Paul's earlier silence was part of his mission strategy, for in doing so, he avoided losing time and money through protracted and costly litigation. Further, with Roman citizenship to the fore as a shield against suffering, the gospel's clear call, which involved repenting of many activities in Roman culture and being willing to suffer for doing so, would be seriously compromised. Now, having already been freed, Paul chose to reveal his citizenship in order to publicly undo the harm done to the church's reputation through his unjustified imprisonment.

COMMENTARY

Beneath the story line of Paul and his team's adventures, which could be understood simply in terms of ancient socio-religious and political history, Luke enables us to trace God's mission in Philippi. Demonic badgering, even with accurate truth claims, led to a liberating exorcism and summary justice: beating and imprisonment. But the latter was overturned, as a divinely timed and targeted earthquake became the occasion for the salvation of the jailer and his household, who washed the missionaries' wounds and received them at his table. The magistrates' subsequent public release of the missionaries and Paul's freedom to encourage the brothers and move on to other places completed the reversal of the situation and stamped the mission's victory as total.

As Paul continued his outreach to Jews and God fearers, he encountered a "demon-possessed slave girl," i.e., one with a "Python spirit" (16:16). "Python" referred originally to the serpent or dragon that guarded the abode of the Delphic Oracle, who predicted the future. Apollo slew the dragon and took to himself the power of prophecy so that he became known as the Pythian Apollo (Ovid *Metamorphosis* 1.438-447). The female priestesses at Delphi, who claimed to prophesy while being indwelt by him, were called "the Pythia" (Plutarch *Moralia* 404b-405a; 432c-433c). Rabbinic literature mentions Python explicitly when dealing with the demonic (e.g., *m. Sanhedrin* 7:7). As with Simon Magus (8:18-20), the occult and money are closely connected—this slave girl turned fortune-teller "earned a lot of money for her masters" (16:16).

Day after day, she told the truth about Paul and his companions. Through their verbal ministry, they demonstrated they were "servants of the Most High God" (cf. 2:18; 4:28). "Most High God" is the biblical way Gentiles referred to Israel's God as the one true God (*'el 'elyon* [TH410A/5945B, ZH446/6610]; see note on 16:17). Indeed, Paul and his companions had come to proclaim the way of salvation (13:5, 10, 26, 38, 47). The slave girl's declarations were as clear as any statements made by demons in Jesus' presence (Luke 4:34, 41; 8:28).

Paul's exasperation (cf. 4:2) with this confusing and potentially discrediting source of the truth led to liberating action: " 'I command you in the name of Jesus Christ to come out of her.' And instantly it left her" (16:18). As at Jerusalem and Judea (5:16) and in Samaria (8:7), so now in a move across the sea toward the end of the earth, the advance of the divine mission meant the extension of the Kingdom of God through a liberation of those under Satan's authority (26:18).

Jesus' and Paul's ministries of exorcism were similar in occasion and basic method. The demons were rebuked with a word of command—at which the demons immediately departed (Luke 4:35; 8:29; 9:42; 11:14). The ministries were significantly different, however, in that Paul's authority was derived from Christ (cf. 19:13, 17). Any exorcism ministry by Christians, then, must be approached with much care, humility, and prayer—it must rely on the power of Christ alone. There must also be bold confidence that Jesus is still bringing release to the captives (Luke 4:18).

When the demon left, so did the girl's handlers' "hopes of wealth." Grabbing Paul and Silas and dragging them before the local magistrates in the marketplace, the girl's masters pressed charges. In this colony, Roman local administration of civil and criminal cases rested with the *duoviri*, two *praetors* (Gr. *stratēgoi* [TG4755, ZG5130]) to whom were assigned two *lictors*, police escorts who carried the *fasces*, the symbol of their authority, a bundle of rods bound together with thongs.

Paul and Silas were charged with putting the whole city into a state of mental confusion and civic disorder (*ektarassousin* [TG1613, ZG1752], cf. Luke 23:2; Acts 15:24; Josephus *Antiquities* 17.253). The accusers played the "race card" by citing the missionaries' Jewishness. In addition to the pervasive anti-Semitism of ancient times (Philostratus *Life of Apollonius* 5.33), the recent decree of Claudius expelling Jews from Rome because of disturbances at the instigation of Chrestus (AD 49; Suetonius *Lives of the Caesars* 25.4; see commentary on 18:1-17) may have made the magistrates in this out-of-the-way Roman colony particularly sensitive to any Jewish involvement in an alleged disturbance. Making a further traditionalist and patriotic charge (Acts 16:21), the girl's masters appealed to the Roman sensibility that held that it was wrong for people to convert away from their own religion and customs (Livy *History* 39.16.8-9; Cicero *Pro Flacco* 69; see Josephus *Antiquities* 19.290-291 for Claudius's anti-proselytization warning to Jews).

As with the slave girl's cries, there was a kernel of truth in the charges. Augustus had made Apollo his special god, and after the Battle of Actium (31 BC) in this region, he vowed to build a temple to Apollo in Rome. In the exorcism of a slave girl possessed by a Pythian Apollo spirit, Paul had demonstrated the superiority of Jesus to Caesar's god. To proclaim the way of salvation in the name of (i.e., on the authority of) that same Jesus was, indeed, to urge new "customs" upon the Romans that necessarily entailed disloyalty to Rome.

The "mob" (better "crowd"; see note on 16:22) stood with the accusers, so the magistrates proceeded to administer rough summary justice, which shows the low esteem the missionaries had in their eyes (16:22). Though such measures were not used with Roman citizens (see notes on 16:35-40), the magistrates ordered Paul and Silas stripped and had the police apply the rod to their backs (2 Cor 11:25; 1 Thess 2:2). Though security seemed to be a strong motive, we should not lose sight of the demoralizing and humiliating treatment, fit only for low-class, dangerous felons, that their placement in the "inner dungeon" and in "stocks" truly was (*Martyrdom of Pionius* 11.3; Lucian *Toxaris* 150).

At midnight the missionaries followed their Lord's example, now embodied in the church and especially its leadership (Luke 6:12; 9:18; Acts 2:42; 3:1; 6:4; 9:11). They were "singing hymns to God" (probably OT psalms or new compositions along those lines) as they were praying (16:25). Praising in the midst of suffering became a witness in itself, for "the other prisoners were listening." With cheerful, faithful witnesses, even imprisonment did not stop God's mission.

"Suddenly" (cf. 2:2), God made his liberating presence known through a "massive earthquake" (16:26). Earthquakes were common in that part of the world and were, to the pagan, a sign of the work or visitation of a god, particularly Poseidon (cf. Ovid *Metamorphosis* 9.782-783; 15.668-678; Lucian *Lover of Lies* 22). For these Christian witnesses, it was the one true God who made his immediate presence known. The tremor was complete in its liberating effect: the prison was shaken at its very foundations, all its doors flew open, and all the prisoners' chains fell off.

The jailer's immediate, confused response to his "failed security" in the face of God's sovereign intervention places in bold relief the completeness of the divine triumph. Thinking only of the public humiliation and likely severe punishment he would experience for letting prisoners escape (*Code of Justinian* n9.4.4), the jailer drew his short sword (a dagger) and was about to plunge it into his neck or heart when Paul shouted to him, "Stop! Don't kill yourself! We are all here!" (16:28). Here, for the first time in Acts, a Christian meets the temporal need of a non-Christian.

Shaken by the presence of the supernatural (cf. 7:32), the jailer fell before Paul and Silas asking, "Sirs, what must I do to be saved?" He thereby makes the Macedonian's call for help more specific (16:9). By framing it openly and in the divine passive he admitted a need that only the divine can meet. Still, with an animistic mindset, he wanted to know what he could do to appease the gods or invoke their rescue from calamity.

Paul's answer was one simple command: "Believe in the Lord Jesus and you will be saved, along with everyone in your household" (16:31). The only thing the jailer could do was to "trust, rely on" what God had already done in providing a savior, Jesus (16:34; 17:12, 34; 18:8; cf. 17:4). Faith must be directed to the "Lord Jesus," which involves a recognition that if Jesus is truly Savior, he must also be Lord, even God (16:35; see note on 16:31). Indeed he would "be saved" (divine passive) but from more than he was asking for—he would be saved from the power, penalty, and presence of sin at the last day (cf. 2:20-21, 38-39; 10:43; 11:14; 13:26, 38-39). Just as God targeted households in his rescue of his people at the Exodus (Exod 12:27), so now in his calling a people to himself from among the Gentiles he would save the jailer's entire household (cf. 16:15). This was not automatic salvation but a gracious promise that God intended that as household members heard the word of the Lord, they would believe (16:32, 34) and become part of God's people.

God had released Paul and Silas from their stocks and manacles. The jailer took them out of the "inner dungeon" and into his company, where he washed their wounds. As baptism follows the washing, Chrysostom comments: "He washed and was washed, he washed them from their stripes, and was himself washed from his sins" (*Homilies on Acts* 36).

The jailer and his household were quintessential converts. They came to faith through hearing the word, were then baptized, experienced the great joy of salvation, and lived out their new life of grace by offering hospitality (2:42, 46; 16:15; 17:5; 18:7). As God's people of promise ate and rejoiced before the Lord in households at his command (Deut 12:7; 14:26; 15:20), so also those called out to be his people from among the Gentiles rejoiced (16:34).

One last aspect of the suffering had yet to be undone: the official summary justice. Though Luke does not explicitly draw the parallel (see note on 16:35), we see that just as a healing miracle, the populace's approval, and the impact of an angelic release had motivated the Jewish authorities to release the apostles in Jerusalem (4:21-22; 5:26, 39), so now a divinely targeted earthquake appeared to motivate the magistrates to release these prisoners. In proper administrative fashion, the magistrates sent word by their lictors for the jailer to release Paul and Silas. The jailer relayed the message and gave them his blessing: "Go in peace" (cf. 10:36). Paul, however, refused release until the official punishment was undone, not for his sake, but for the sake of the fledgling church's standing in the eyes of Roman authorities and society—that is, that they might have every opportunity to experience peace (cf. 9:31).

Paul announced his Roman citizenship and declared that two of his fundamental rights had been violated by the previous day's proceedings (16:22-23). The *Lex Valeria* (509 BC) and *Lex Porcia* (248 BC), reaffirmed in the *Lex Julia* (23 BC), shielded Roman citizens from humiliating punishments in public, such as beating with rods (Livy 10.9.4; Cicero *On Behalf of Rabirius Charged with High Treason* 12; Cicero

Against Verres 2.5.66). Further, a Roman citizen was always entitled to a trial before punishment was administered (Tacitus *Histories* 1.6; Cicero *Against Verres* 2.1.9). Paul demanded that the magistrates come and publicly escort them from prison.

On hearing that these traveling Jewish preachers were Roman citizens, the magistrates were "alarmed" (Acts 16:38). A magistrate might lose his office or, worse, be disqualified from ever serving in governmental administration again, if he mistreated a Roman citizen (Cicero *Against Verres* 2.5.66; Suetonius *Claudius* 25; cf. Acts 22:22-29). The magistrates did as Paul demanded; they came in person and "apologized." Escorting them out, they requested that Paul and Silas leave the city. Paul and Silas acceded to their request. Their release not only cleared their record but restored their freedom for further mission advance. They used it to meet with the church at Lydia's house and, if Paul's consistent practice in Acts and his letters is any indicator, they encouraged the brothers to stand firm even in the midst of suffering (16:40; cf. 14:22; 15:32; Phil 1:27-30; 2:1; 4:2).

Since the "we" sections of Acts stop after the Philippi episode and do not pick up again until Acts 20:5 (again at Philippi), many have conjectured that Paul left Luke there to strengthen the church.

◆   D. Paul Preaches in Thessalonica (17:1-9)

Paul and Silas then traveled through the towns of Amphipolis and Apollonia and came to Thessalonica, where there was a Jewish synagogue. ²As was Paul's custom, he went to the synagogue service, and for three Sabbaths in a row he used the Scriptures to reason with the people. ³He explained the prophecies and proved that the Messiah must suffer and rise from the dead. He said, "This Jesus I'm telling you about is the Messiah." ⁴Some of the Jews who listened were persuaded and joined Paul and Silas, along with many God-fearing Greek men and quite a few prominent women.*

⁵But some of the Jews were jealous, so they gathered some troublemakers from the marketplace to form a mob and start a riot. They attacked the home of Jason, searching for Paul and Silas so they could drag them out to the crowd.* ⁶Not finding them there, they dragged out Jason and some of the other believers* instead and took them before the city council. "Paul and Silas have caused trouble all over the world," they shouted, "and now they are here disturbing our city, too. ⁷And Jason has welcomed them into his home. They are all guilty of treason against Caesar, for they profess allegiance to another king, named Jesus."

⁸The people of the city, as well as the city council, were thrown into turmoil by these reports. ⁹So the officials forced Jason and the other believers to post bond, and then they released them.

17:4 Some manuscripts read *quite a few of the wives of the leading men.* 17:5 Or *the city council.* 17:6 Greek *brothers;* also in 17:10, 14.

NOTES

17:4 quite a few prominent women. The NLT mg indicates the variant reading: "wives of the leading men." The genitive phrase in the text *gunaikōn te tōn prōtōn* [TG4413, ZG4755] is strongly attested: 𝔓74 ℵ A B E 044. The reading is ambiguous, however, because the phrase can either directly modify "women" ("the first women"), or it can refer to their husbands ("women of the first"—that is, leading men). The Western text (D Old Latin mss Vulgate syr[p, h]) clarifies in the direction of the second understanding by inflecting "women" [cf. ᵀᴳ1135, ᶻᴳ1222] differently: *kai gunaikes tōn prōtōn*. Given the parallel in 17:12, where both the women's standing and the reference to men are distinct, the NLT understanding here of the better attested phrase is to be preferred.

17:5 the crowd. Or, as the NLT mg says, "the city council." The expression *ton dēmon* [ᵀᴳ1218, ᶻᴳ1322] may mean either, nontechnically, a "crowd" or "mob" (Polhill 1992:362; cf. Barrett [1998:814] who notes the meaning is disputed) or, technically, "a citizen assembly" (Johnson 1992:306; Witherington 1998:507). The NLT mg represents the latter possibility by "city council," which is overly restrictive and confusing because the same phrase is used to render *tous politarchas* [ᵀᴳ4173, ᶻᴳ4485], "the politarchs" or the body of local magistrates (17:8; cf. 17:6; Horsley 1994:419-432). Although Marshall (1980:278) reconstructs a plausible sequence of events based on the technical meaning, a simpler reading of the text involves only the Jewish opposition, the Gentile mob, the politarchs, and the Christians.

17:6 caused trouble all over the world. Stated in the most universal of terms, this is a social and cultural charge: "overturning established social and moral patterns that have come to characterize the human race" (Kee 1997:207; cf. Dunn 1996:228). More probably, in light of the more specific political charges which follow, it refers to "fomenting public disorder" (Witherington 1998:507; Barrett 1998:815; cf. Acts 21:38).

17:7 guilty of treason against Caesar. Lit., "practicing against the decrees of Caesar." Contra NLT, this is probably not a charge of "treason," since that involves Roman law, not imperial decree (Talbert 1997:157; Kee 1997:207; Johnson 1992:306). Rather, given Paul's politically charged language in his preaching to the Thessalonians about the coming of another king, Jesus (1 Thess 1:9-10; 2:12; 2 Thess 1:5-2:12), this charge probably invoked decrees that Roman emperors issued forbidding astrologers' and other prognosticators' predictions and inquiries into the death or change of rulers (Dio Cassius *Roman History* 56.25.5-6; 57.15.8; Dio Chrysostom *Orations* 57.15.8; Tacitus *Annals* 6.20; 12.52; cf. 14.9; Witherington 1998:508).

COMMENTARY

Proceeding southwest along the Egnatian Way, Paul and Silas traveled thirty miles to Amphipolis, the capital of the first district of Macedonia. They went a further twenty-seven miles to Apollonia and finally thirty-five miles to Thessalonica, the capital of both the second district and the whole province (17:1). Paul made a strategic choice by targeting Thessalonica, for this city was uniquely situated to serve as a center for the spread of the gospel to the whole Balkan peninsula (see Rom 15:19; 1 Thess 1:7-8). A seaport on the Thermaic Gulf, Thessalonica linked sea and land routes to the rich agricultural plain of the interior of Macedonia. Paul's evangelistic approach to Thessalonica again pursued the "to the Jew first" pattern, which Luke highlights with the facts that "for three Sabbaths in a row" Paul "used the Scriptures to reason with the people" in the synagogue (17:2).

Instead of presenting one of Paul's speeches, Luke gives us Paul's apologetic strategy (17:2b-3). Saved until the climax, the phrase, "This Jesus I'm telling you about is the Messiah" places all the reasoned discussion (17:2b) within the context of proclamation (cf. 13:5, 38; 16:21; 26:23). Paul, first and foremost, came declaring the Good News of salvation in Jesus (13:26). But there were barriers to the first-century Jews' accepting this message. Paul sought to remove these barriers when he "used the Scriptures to reason with the people." This means that Paul "reasoned, or discoursed argumentatively, either in the way of dialogue . . . or in that of formal and continuous discourse" (Kemler 1975:35). This process involved an "explaining" (lit., "opening"; cf. Luke 24:32) and a "proving." The Greek word for "proving" (*paratithemenos* [TG3908/A, ZG4192]) means "demonstrating by setting evidence side by side"—in this case Old Testament prophecy and New Testament facts from Jesus' suffering, death, and Resurrection. The two propositions to be handled in this way were the necessity of Messiah's death and Resurrection and the identity of Jesus as that Messiah (cf. Luke 24:44-48; for a sample of Paul's exposition and proof concerning Jesus, the dying and rising Messiah, see 13:23-37).

Using predestinarian "divine passives," Luke again reminds us that God was at work in Thessalonica. Some of the Jews, possibly Jason and Aristarchus (17:7; 20:4), "were persuaded." They subsequently "joined Paul and Silas" (cf. 2:47; 13:48; 16:14; 1 Thess 1:4; 2:13). The large response of God-fearing Greeks and "prominent women" points to God's quantitative and qualitative ingathering (cf. 4:32; 5:14; 13:50; 14:1; 17:12).

The Jews who did not believe became jealous, evidently of the mission's success among the Gentiles (cf. 5:17; 13:45). In stark contrast to the fledgling church, "they gathered some troublemakers from the marketplace." These were unemployed day laborers, always ready for mischief (Aristophanes *Frogs* 1015 [1047]; Plato *Protagoras* 347c). Once formed into a mob, they set the city in an uproar. Moving against the missionaries staying at Jason's house, the mob was frustrated to not find them there. Instead, they brought Jason and some of the other believers before the magistrates and lodged inflammatory political charges. They accused Paul and Silas of fomenting public disorder and violating Caesar's decrees that forbid any prediction of a monarch who would replace the currently reigning emperor (see note on 17:6). If Paul had been proclaiming and then proving that Jesus was the royal Davidic Messiah, who had suffered and risen (17:3), then his gospel message could not avoid declaring King Jesus' approaching return, when he would judge the whole world and reign exclusively forever (1 Thess 4:13–5:11; 2 Thess 1:4-10). Though not entirely without warrant, Paul's opponents could easily twist his eschatology into an inflammatory political prediction about a coming monarch who would displace Caesar. For Thessalonica, a free city (Pliny the Elder *Natural History* 4.38) whose quasi-independent status depended on loyalty to Caesar and maintenance of the civil peace, such accusations could not but disturb everyone in the city (17:8; cf. 15:24; 16:20; 19:23).

Ironically, as often happens in persecution, the civil authorities chose to listen to the Jews and the mob, who were the immediate cause of the disturbance, and to sanction those who had been labeled as its ultimate cause (cf. 19:25-28). In order to assure no further disturbance (i.e., to guarantee good behavior on the part of Jason and the believers, as well as Paul and Silas), the politarchs had Jason and the believers "post bond" (17:9). The situation was so volatile that the believers in Thessalonica thought it best for Paul and Silas to leave. The two were spirited out of the city that very night (17:10).

◆   E. Paul and Silas in Berea (17:10-15)

¹⁰That very night the believers sent Paul and Silas to Berea. When they arrived there, they went to the Jewish synagogue. ¹¹And the people of Berea were more open-minded than those in Thessalonica, and they listened eagerly to Paul's message. They searched the Scriptures day after day to see if Paul and Silas were teaching the truth. ¹²As a result, many Jews believed, as did many of the prominent Greek women and men.

¹³But when some Jews in Thessalonica learned that Paul was preaching the word of God in Berea, they went there and stirred up trouble. ¹⁴The believers acted at once, sending Paul on to the coast, while Silas and Timothy remained behind. ¹⁵Those escorting Paul went with him all the way to Athens; then they returned to Berea with instructions for Silas and Timothy to hurry and join him.

NOTES

17:14 on to the coast. All the manuscript traditions behind this text can be taken to indicate simply the direction of Paul's movement: (1) Alexandrian, *heōs* [ᵀᴳ2193, ᶻᴳ2401] *epi tēn thalassan*, "as far as to the sea," in 𝔓74 ℵ A B 33 88 1739; (2) Byzantine *hōs* [ᵀᴳ5613, ᶻᴳ6055] *epi tēn thalassan*, "as to the sea" in 𝔐 syrʰ; and (3) Western, *epi* [ᵀᴳ1909, ᶻᴳ2093] *tēn thalassan*, "to the sea," in D 049 itᵍⁱᵍ syrᵖ. Meers (1993), seeing the Alexandrian reading as un-Lukan and inserted under the influence of Acts 17:15, which reads *heōs Athēnōn*, argues for the Western reading as original. The UBS committee, however, sees the Alexandrian reading as Lukan [Luke 24:50; Acts 21:5; 26:11] and original (Metzger 1994:404). The "ruse" understanding of the Byzantine reading, "he made as to travel by sea, but actually traveled by land" (Bruce 1990:374) is not supported by any referent to port of embarkation or verbal indicators of land-travel in Acts 17:15 and is not favored by scholars (cf. Barrett 1998:819). Still, commentators display an uncertainty about whether Paul went by land or sea (Dunn 1996:229; Talbert 1997:158; Barrett 1998:819; Witherington 1998:510).

Silas and Timothy remained behind. Meers (1993:204) takes *ekei* [ᵀᴳ1563, ᶻᴳ1695] (lit., "[remained] there") as referring to "Macedonia," not "Berea." No reference to Timothy after Philippi may indicate that he remained there with Luke (cf. Acts 16:17). Given the bail bond at Thessalonica and the persecution at Berea, Silas may have been sent to Philippi; however, the more natural referent of *ekei* (there) is Berea (Kee 1997:209; Talbert 1997:158).

Some continue to see Timothy's movements according to Paul (Athens to Thessalonica per 1 Thess 3:2) as contradictory to those seen in Acts (remaining at Berea, rejoining Paul at Corinth per Acts 17:14; 18:5) and understand that only Paul was correct (Lüdeman 1989: 188). The two itineraries may be harmonized if we conclude that Luke did not tell us all of Timothy's movements: he went to Athens from Berea and then was dispatched to Thessalonica from whence he returned to Paul at Corinth (Polhill 1992:364; cf. Johnson's [1992:308] very positive estimate of the correspondence in detail between Acts 16–17 with 1 Thess 1–3).

COMMENTARY

The believers at Thessalonica, wanting to assure the terms of the bail bond (disturbance-free good behavior), sent away "that very night" Paul and Silas and, presumably, also Timothy (17:10). They traveled west-southwest along the Egnatian Way some twenty miles and then left it and headed south thirty more miles to Berea. This strategic withdrawal into the third district of Macedonia and to a city that Cicero labeled "off the beaten path" (*Against Piso* 36.89, probably because it was not on a main Roman road) was not a retreat but a means for further advance. Another populous city, indeed a "noble town" (Livy *History* 45.30), in another district of Macedonia would hear the gospel because of Paul's strategy of going "to the Jews first."

The Berean Jews and God fearers did not require a sustained proof from Scripture with Paul's proclamation (contrast 17:2-3). They were "more open-minded" (*eugenesteroi* [TG2104/A, ZG2302]; lit. "more noble"), willing to embrace and then evaluate the message without prejudice. In Greek and biblical understanding, to be *eugenēs* [TG2104, ZG2302] primarily was to be "of noble birth" (cf. Luke 19:12; 1 Cor 1:26) and, derivatively, to have qualities which go with "good breeding"—openness, tolerance, generosity.

"They listened eagerly to Paul's message." The proclamation and reception of God's message was the central activity of God's missionary advance through Paul (for the second missionary journey, cf. 16:6, 32; 17:11, 13; 18:5, 11, 15; 1 Thess 1:6; 2:13). The emphasis here is on the Bereans' eager reception. As God worked in the hearts of Israel at various points in its history to generously, willingly give their goods for the Tabernacle or Temple construction (cf. Exod 35:29; 1 Chr 29:14, 17; Ezra 1:6; 2:68), so now God, in calling out a people for himself from among the Gentiles, worked in them a noble "open-mindedness" which showed itself as "eagerness" (cf. Luke 8:15; Acts 16:14; Isa 32:8). Such an enthusiasm, however, was not gullibility. Their alacrity in embracing the message was matched by the perseverance of a thorough scrutiny of the Old Testament scriptures to validate Paul's claims concerning Jesus as the dying and rising Messiah. Their examination parallels the best in human jurisprudence—unbiased investigation to get at the truth. The result was a great harvest, both quantitatively and qualitatively. Many from among both Jews and Gentiles believed (cf. 16:34; 17:34; 18:8), particularly a large number of prominent Greek women and many Gentile men.

The whole of Paul's ministry is captured in a statement that highlights the centrality of his mission: "Paul was preaching the word of God in Berea" (17:13; cf. 16:32; 17:3, 23; 18:11). When some Jews in Thessalonica learned about this, they tried to stop it by coming to Berea, where they "stirred up trouble." Though we are not told why, the believers took Paul away to the coast before any arrest or judicial action could occur. Their escort of Paul provided protection and care on the journey.

This second consecutive withdrawal would prove to be another advance. Not only did Paul leave behind a newly-planted church to be nurtured by Silas and Timothy—his escape would take him to Athens, the center of Greco-Roman culture and Greek religion. Paul's progress was like wildfire. Trying to stamp it out in one place only sent its embers flying to ignite elsewhere.

◆   F. Paul Preaches in Athens (17:16-34)

16While Paul was waiting for them in Athens, he was deeply troubled by all the idols he saw everywhere in the city. 17He went to the synagogue to reason with the Jews and the God-fearing Gentiles, and he spoke daily in the public square to all who happened to be there.

18He also had a debate with some of the Epicurean and Stoic philosophers. When he told them about Jesus and his resurrection, they said, "What's this babbler trying to say with these strange ideas he's picked up?" Others said, "He seems to be preaching about some foreign gods." [19]Then they took him to the high council of the city.* "Come and tell us about this new teaching," they said. [20]"You are saying some rather strange things, and we want to know what it's all about." [21](It should be explained that all the Athenians as well as the foreigners in Athens seemed to spend all their time discussing the latest ideas.)

[22]So Paul, standing before the council,* addressed them as follows: "Men of Athens, I notice that you are very religious in every way, [23]for as I was walking along I saw your many shrines. And one of your altars had this inscription on it: 'To an Unknown God.' This God, whom you worship without knowing, is the one I'm telling you about.

[24]"He is the God who made the world and everything in it. Since he is Lord of heaven and earth, he doesn't live in man-made temples, [25]and human hands can't serve his needs—for he has no needs. He himself gives life and breath to everything, and he satisfies every need. [26]From one man* he created all the nations throughout the whole earth. He decided beforehand when they should rise and fall, and he determined their boundaries. [27]"His purpose was for the nations to seek after God and perhaps feel their way toward him and find him—though he is not far from any one of us. [28]For in him we live and move and exist. As some of your* own poets have said, 'We are his offspring.' [29]And since this is true, we shouldn't think of God as an idol designed by craftsmen from gold or silver or stone.

[30]"God overlooked people's ignorance about these things in earlier times, but now he commands everyone everywhere to repent of their sins and turn to him. [31]For he has set a day for judging the world with justice by the man he has appointed, and he proved to everyone who this is by raising him from the dead."

[32]When they heard Paul speak about the resurrection of the dead, some laughed in contempt, but others said, "We want to hear more about this later." [33]That ended Paul's discussion with them, [34]but some joined him and became believers. Among them were Dionysius, a member of the council,* a woman named Damaris, and others with them.

17:19 Or the most learned society of philosophers in the city. Greek reads the Areopagus.   17:22 Traditionally rendered standing in the middle of Mars Hill; Greek reads standing in the middle of the Areopagus.   17:26 Greek From one; other manuscripts read From one blood.   17:28 Some manuscripts read our.   17:34 Greek an Areopagite.

NOTES

17:18 *Jesus and his resurrection*. Some think Paul could have been misunderstood as referring to a male and female deity when he spoke of *ton Iēsoun kai tēn anastasin* [TG386, ZG414] (McRay 1994; Barrett 1998:830). Polytheistic Athenians, with no concept of resurrection, could readily have made this mistake (Johnson 1992:314; Winter 1996:80). Croy (1997:23) proposes that *Iēsous* [TG2424, ZG2652] might have been equated with *Iēsō* or *Iasō*, daughter of Asclepius and goddess of healing.

17:19, 22 *high council*. Lit., "the Areopagus" (cf. NLT mg). The NLT text correctly identifies the referent of *Areion Pagon* [TG697, ZG740] (Areopagus) as a deliberative body, not a place. The Areopagus was Athens' main administrative body (Cicero *De Natura Deorum* 2.29.74), overseeing such matters as religion and education (Charles 1995:52). "Areopagus" can also refer to the 370-foot outcropping northwest of the Acropolis, which was the council's traditional meeting place. The word is actually the transliteration of a phrase meaning either "hill of Ares" (the Gr. god of war; the Roman equivalent is Mars, hence the NKJV "Mars Hill") or "hill of the Arai," the Furies who avenged homicides and whose shrine was at its base (ISBE 1.287-288). The syntax of vv. 22 and 33 (lit., "Paul stood in . . .

went out of the midst of the Areopagus") seems to indicate the body. The meeting's location is uncertain (Gill 1994a:447).

Paul's appearance before the Areopagus was not so much a discussion to satisfy their intellectual curiosity (as Johnson 1992:314) or an informal inquiry of its education commission into Paul as a teacher (cf. Charles 1995:52). Rather, understanding vv. 18-20 in a technical, judicial way, we see here a serious pre-trial hearing in which Paul's message was being assessed for its introduction of new deities to Athens (Winter 1996:80-83; Witherington 1998:517).

17:22-31 Scholars on the whole now see the speech as an example of Hellenistic Jewish, and even Christian, apologetics against idolatry rather than as an expression of Greco-Roman, particularly Stoic, thought (Balch 1990a:72; Dunn 1996:231). Yet, they also view it as a Lukan composition (Johnson 1992:318; Dunn 1996:231), which for some inaccurately expresses Paul's theology (Barrett 1998:825; Wilson 1973:214). The lack of condemnation of pagan immorality other than idolatry in Acts 17 (Wilson 1973:214) is under- standable given the hearing's purpose. The speech's themes of ignorance, "groping," and repentance from idolatry render the Gentile idolater just as culpable as Paul's teaching in Rom 1 does (17:23, 30). The pursuit of a negative critique of idolatrous wisdom seen in Acts 17, without a positive proclamation of Christ crucified (Barrett 1998:825; 1 Cor 2:1-5), is congruent with the overall direction of Paul's missionary thrust among the Gentiles (1 Thess 1:9-10; Lindemann 1995:253). Again the speech's immediate purpose and its rhetorical strategy— a deliberative speech to a hostile audience operating by *insinuatio* (cryptic comments which intend to elicit more questions; Sandnes 1993:19)—explain the lack of reference to the cross. Both Acts 17:30 and Rom 3:26 describe the divine initiative overcoming God's impugned righteousness, one through Christ's Resurrection, one through his death. The speech is in no way incongruent with the theology of Paul's epistles (Gempf 1993a:51-54).

17:23 To an Unknown God. Van der Horst (1994:196), in his study of the literary and archaeological evidence, finds no clear example for this designation in the singular. But he concludes, "It is not improbable that there were altars with dedications in the singular, though it is likely that they were an exception to the rule, most dedications being in the plural." Neither conventional literary license (Philo *On Sobriety* 150; Hesiod *Works* 289-292) nor the Stoic and Epicurean use of the singular and plural of *theos* [TG2316, ZG2536] interchangeably (Diogenes Laertes *Lives of the Philosophers* 7.119; Winter 1996:84) explains Luke's use of the singular here.

There are reports of altars to unknown gods at Athens (Pausanias *Description of Greece* 1.1.4; Philostratus *Life of Apollonius* 6.3.5), but their origin is less certain. Were they part of the hero cult related to the Mycenaen tombs which surrounded the Athenian agora (as Wycherley 1968:621)? Were they the result of reuse or rededication of altars after wars or natural disasters or the result of other circumstances in which the god's name was not known (Bruce 1990:380-381; Witherington 1998:522)? Had a Gentile God fearer erected an altar to the God of Israel (van der Horst 1992; cf. Lucan *Pharsalia* 2.592-593; Josephus *Apion* 2.167)? Or, the most promising explanation, were these an example of how animistic, polytheistic Athenians sought to protect themselves by making sure that all possible gods, known and unknown, had been appeased (cf. Diogenes Laertes *Lives of the Philosophers* 1.110; Gempf 1993a:51)?

This God, whom you worship without knowing, is the one I'm telling you about. Some see this statement as a basis for contending that some non-Christian religionists, who were seeking God but didn't know his name, were in a saving relationship with him (Pinnock 1990:364; Richardson 1981:ch 1), and many find here an affirmation that the one true God was being worshiped, albeit in ignorance of his true nature (Winter 1996:89). Paul, however, made his point of contact between the one true God and what is worshiped at that altar in terms of "divine nature," not personal identity. He used the neuter, not the masculine pronoun: "that which (*ho* [TG3739, ZG4005]) you worship ignorantly, this (*touto* [TG3778, ZG4047]) I proclaim to you." He then immediately followed with the masculine gender: "the God (*ho theos* [TG2316, ZG2536]) who made the world"—a positive declaration of the personal identity of the one true God—as Paul proceeded to expound his true nature (17:24; cf. 14:15).

17:26 *nations.* The word *ethnos* [TG1484, ZG1620] might be better rendered "culture" since it is "the most general and therefore the weakest of [biblical] terms [for 'a people'], having simply an ethnographical sense and denoting the natural cohesion of a people in general" (TDNT 2.364-371). Witherington (1998:527), with his emphasis on the uniting of persons from these cultures into one universal people of God, does not view positively the cultural diversity in God's design.

he determined their boundaries. Some see the "boundaries" of nations in ways congruent with Stoic philosophy. The agricultural seasons and the existence of temperate geographical zones are evidence of divine providence in sustaining humankind (Dio Chrysostom *Orations* 12.32; Cicero *Tusculan Disputations* 1.28.68-69; cf. Acts 14:17; Barrett 1998:844). Most, like the NLT, see these categories historically—the nation's divinely predestined limits across time and space (Gen 10-11; Deut 32:8; Dunn 1996:235; Witherington 1998:527).

17:27 *perhaps feel their way toward him.* The Gr. word *psēlaphaō* [TG5584, ZG6027] can mean "feeling" or "groping." The "feeling" denotation means making physical contact in order to prove the reality or existence of a thing (Luke 24:39; 1 John 1:1; so here according to Külling 1993:112). At the least, since it is in the optative within a conditional clause, this would point to the possibility, though not the certainty, of humans finding God through general revelation and the natural theology it yields (Barrett 1998:844). This, however, is not congruent with the themes of uncertainty, ignorance, and repentance from idolatry found in the immediate and larger contexts. The negative meaning of the word—"groping," like a blind man feeling his way down a wall, or someone stumbling in the dark—better suits the context (Aristophanes *Women of the Assembly* 315; *Peace* 691; Plato *Phaedo* 99b; LXX of Deut 28:29; Judg 16:26; Job 5:13-14; 12:25; Isa 59:10; Witherington 1998:528). Sin has intervened so that God's original intent that people of all cultures find him is not attainable without special revelation, though God still remains within reach (Witherington 1998:529).

17:32, 34 *some laughed in contempt. . . . but some joined him and became believers.* Paul's mission was not a failure because he abandoned the simple gospel for an intellectual approach (1 Cor 2:2 is often appealed to). His rhetorical strategy designed to evoke requests for further information succeeded with some (17:32; Sandnes 1993:19). This "sincere, if somewhat hesitating, interest" set over against the mocking (*men . . . de* [TG3303/1161, ZG3525/1254]) and the report of converts, even from the Areopagus's membership (17:34), point to the mission's success (Croy 1997:26-27; Barrett 1998:854).

COMMENTARY

When Paul arrived at Athens in the province of Achaia, he came to an anomaly. Though its population was not more than 10,000, and it had been reduced to poverty and submission by its war with Rome (146 BC), Athens was still recognized as a cultural center in religion and education for Greece and the empire (Philo *Good Person* 140). The ubiquitous idolatry of Athens assaulted the eyes from every direction (Livy *History* 45.27.11). As Paul stood "in the public square" (*en tē agora* [TG58, ZG59], "market"), possibly standing in the Stoa Poikile, his immediate gaze would have fallen on temples devoted to the imperial cult, crowding the agora—the temple of Ares, the Stoa of Zeus Eleutherios, together with numerous small altars dedicated to Augustus. Lifting his eyes to the skyline, he would see the temple of Roma and Augustus. All these were but the most recent overlay of idolatrous religion, for they sat "cheek by jowl" with the temples of historic Athens—the temples of Hephaistos and on the Acropolis the Erectheion and Parthenon—each housing its own idol. What made Athens a veritable "forest of idols" were the many "hermes" (square pillars with the bust of Hermes, the god of roads, gateways, and the marketplace) everywhere guarding the entrances to houses, shrines and public places (Gill 1994a:443-445).

No wonder Paul was "deeply troubled." He experienced a paroxysm in his spirit, a provocation of anger or grief or both, because the glory due to God alone was being given to idols. God reacted the same way to idolatry in Israel (Deut 9:7, 18, 22; Ps 106:28-29; Isa 65:2-3), and so should we. Yet this deep emotional and spiritual revulsion, far from paralyzing Paul, spurred him to action. According to his strategy of going to the Jews first (17:2, 10; 18:4), he debated with the Jews in the synagogues about "Jesus and the resurrection." Paul also took his witness daily to the "public square," which was originally an open area where all the citizens could gather to decide political matters. As government buildings, businesses, and temples grew up around its periphery, connected by colonnades, or "stoa," the *agora* [TG58, ZG59] became the center for daily life. It was a place where people would gather to learn the latest news and discuss all kinds of subjects, a place where the intellectual elite and the philosophers, as well as traveling teachers, could converse and ply their trade.

Epicurean and Stoic philosophers, representatives of two of the three major philosophical schools of thought in Paul's day, reacted to his message. The Epicureans mocked, "What's this babbler trying to say with these strange ideas he's picked up?" (17:18). "Babbler" (*spermologos* [TG4691, ZG5066]) was a term of derision originally pointing to a seed-picking or scavenger bird and then applied to third-rate philosophers as "ragbag collectors of scraps of learning" (Dio Chrysostom *Orations* 32.9). They did not originate nor necessarily understand their material. The Stoics were curious: "He seems to be preaching about some foreign gods" (17:18; lit., "he's a herald of strange gods"). Luke went on to explain that this was in response to Paul's message about "Jesus and his resurrection" (see note on 17:18).

Epicureans, atomic materialists, viewed reality as an endless, chance combination and dispersion of atoms. Nothing of the human survived death; therefore, bodily resurrection was laughable (Epicurus *Epistle to Menoeceus* 127b-132). The Stoics, materialist pantheists, identified the divine as the principle of reason pervading all and governing all as inexorable fate. The human soul does continue after death but is not immortal. Rather, for the wicked the continued existence is short lived; while for the wise or righteous it maintains itself until the next great periodic conflagration of the cosmos, when human souls, along with everything else, are reabsorbed into the world's Oversoul (Diogenes Laertes *Lives of the Philosophers* 7.156-

157; Chrysippus *Fragment* 625). The Stoics' cyclic cosmic eschatology also had no room for the concept of physical resurrection. Thus, these groups did not comprehend or were not willing to accept Paul's gospel concerning "Jesus and his resurrection." Yet, as Paul would show in his sermon, these truths were what Epicureans and Stoics needed to hear the most, and so they were what the gospel messenger must boldly proclaim, not compromising the integrity of his message.

The Athenians had a reputation for an interest in the novel (Acts 17:21) and for incorporating alien deities into their pantheon (Chariton *Chaereas and Callirhoe* 1.11.67; Strabo *Geography* 10.3.18). They were also very vigilant to ensure that the "new" did not undermine their well-established religious beliefs (Josephus *Against Apion* 2.267). Note the way Paul was labeled: "the herald of foreign gods"; one who brings "startling, foreign things" to their ears (literal translation of Acts 17:18, 20; cf. Plato *Apology* 24b-c for similarly worded charges against Socrates). The Athenians engaged the Areopagus, their highest administrative body, to assess whether to introduce any particular "new gods" into their pantheon. The council looked into the legitimacy of the god's epiphany, its eagerness to join the pantheon, its good will and benefit to the people, and its herald's credentials. The Areopagus would determine practical matters such as the type of official recognition required, the provision of land and resources for erecting a temple and statue, and the designation of an annual official feast day.

For this purpose, Paul was taken before the council (cf. 16:17; 18:19). In judicial language the council declared its authority and intent (17:19-20). In essence they were saying, "We possess the right to judge this new teaching that is being spoken of by you. You are bringing 'strange [foreign] things' to our ears; we therefore wish to judge what it is being claimed [or 'decreed'] 'these things' are" (see note on 17:19).

Commencing his speech with irony, Paul gave his assessment of the Athenians. He noticed that they were "very religious" (*hōs deisidaimonesterous* [TG1174, ZG1273]). The Athenians' reputation for religious piety is well attested (Pausanias *Description of Greece* 1.17.1; 1.24.3; Strabo *Geography* 9.1.16). While the term may be understood positively (Aristotle *Politics* 5.9.15, p. 1315a; Xenophon *Cyropaedia* 3.3.58), among both Epicureans and Stoics it was understood negatively as "superstitious fear" of the gods and was part of their critique of popular religion (Lucretius *On the Nature of Things* 1.62-78; Strabo *Geography* 16.2.37). It should be noted that in both Stoic and Epicurean thought, there had also been an accommodation to the idolatry of popular religion (originally with the Epicureans [Philodemos *De Pietate* 1.765-772] reacted to by Lucretius; and secondarily among the Stoics, cf. Dio Chrysostom *Orations* 32). Paul's ambiguous assertion acknowledged a limited truth—their religiosity, but with a negative twist. The readers of Acts have already received this perspective (17:16), and Paul would develop it further (17:23, 30; cf. 25:19).

Paul's point of contact was a need that the Athenians unwittingly admitted in their worship. As he walked along he "saw" (lit., "looked at, carefully examined again and again") their many "altars" (lit., "objects of worship"—*sebasmata* [TG4574,

ZG4934]; this could include idols, cf. Josephus *Antiquities* 18.344; Wis 14:20; 15:17). Paul found an altar with the inscription, "To an Unknown God." Understood within the context of animistic, polytheistic idolatry, such an inscription reflects the fear of offending and the desire to appease whatever god may inhabit a given place (see note). Diogenes Laertes (*Lives of the Philosophers* 1.110) relates how once when Athens was plagued by pestilence in the sixth century BC and the city rulers had exhausted all their strategies to abate it, they sent to Crete, asking the prophet Epimenides to come and help. His remedy was to drive a herd of black and white sheep away from the Areopagus and, wherever they lay down, to sacrifice them to the god of that place. The plague was stayed, and Diogenes Laertes says that memorial altars with no god's name inscribed on them may consequently be found throughout Attica.

Paul picked up their admission of ignorance and applied it in a totally different direction. Their worship of an impersonal deity in self-confessed ignorance actually revealed the incorrectness of their whole approach to worship (cf. Jewish ignorance about God's work in Christ, 3:18; 13:27). They did not understand the true nature of deity (*to theion* [TG2304/A, ZG2521], cf. 17:29), and it is "this" (*touto* [TG3778, ZG4047]) that Paul would proclaim to them by declaring the excellencies of the one true personal God, who can be known (17:24-27).

Paul testified to "the God who made the world and everything in it . . . Lord of heaven and earth" (Deut 4:39; Ps 146:6; Isa 42:5), and he drew out the implication for worship: "He doesn't live in man-made temples" (Acts 17:24). Some Epicurean and Stoic thinkers would have agreed with Paul's implications for worship practice (Lucretius *On the Nature of Things* 5.146-154; Plutarch *Moralia* 1034B), but they would have done so based on a materialist, polytheistic deism or materialist pantheism, which Paul challenged with his affirmation of the one, transcendent personal God.

Paul moved immediately to another implication: "Human hands can't serve his needs—for he has no needs" (17:25). Service (*therapeuō* [TG2323, ZG2543]) is bringing anything to an idol, such as food, to sustain it as one would sustain a human being. God's self-sufficiency is affirmed in the Old Testament (Ps 50:7-15) and developed in Jewish prayer (2 Macc 14:35; 3 Macc 2:9). Stoics and Epicureans also agreed with the self-sufficiency of the divine, though again according to their pantheist and polytheistic deistic understandings (Plutarch *Moralia* 1052D; Lucretius *On the Nature of Things* 2.650; Philodemus *Peri eusebeias* [*De pietate*] fr. 38). Paul brushed aside the necessity, let alone the appropriateness, of idolatrous worship's servicing of the divine nature by affirming that, conversely, it is God who gives life and breath to everything (14:15; Gen 1:29; 2:7; 9:3; Isa 42:5; cf. the Stoic pantheistic Logos's "breathing in of life" to humans, Dio Chrysostom *Orations* 12.30, 31, 74). What good news Paul had for the Epicureans and Stoics, living as they did under impersonal chance or inexorable fate! Behind or within reality stands neither of these but rather a transcendant, gracious, personal Creator—the Ruler, and Sustainer of all.

Paul then focused on humankind. In contrast to the Stoics' pantheistic, metaphysical affirmation of a divine ancestral parent to humankind (Dio Chrysostom *Orations* 12.30, 42), Paul made the historical assertion that the transcendent, personal God "from one man . . . created all the nations throughout the whole earth" (17:26). It was God's design that from the first human being, every culture (*ethnos* [TG1484, ZG1620], see note on 17:25) of humans should dwell on all the face of the earth, covering it with a harmonious patchwork of diverse cultures (Gen 1:28; 9:1, 7; 10:5, 20, 31-32). That harmony is born of God's governance of the time period and the geographical territory each culture would inhabit (Deut 32:8; Ps 102:13; Dan 2:36-45; see note on 17:26). While Stoicism looked at humankind in its diversity and urged it to consider itself as one community, "even as a herd that feeds together and shares the pasturage of a common field" (Plutarch *Moralia* 329B), Paul affirmed both unity and diversity.

God's second design was "for the nations to seek after God" (17:27). This was not the Stoics' metaphysical longing of innate reason (Dio Chrysostom *Orations* 12.60-61; cf. 12.28) but the biblical understanding of the will directed to God in faith (Luke 11:9-10; 12:31; Ps 14:2; Prov 8:17; Isa 55:6; Jer 29:13; Amos 9:12 LXX; Heb 11:6). Yet sin had interjected itself into the human experience, so that the "seeking" had become "groping" with no certainty, nor indeed likelihood of success, even though God is "not far from any one of us" (cf. Ps 145:18; Jer 23:23-24; see note on 17:27). Epicureans and Stoics understand this separation metaphysically, either as deistic divine non-involvement or as a pantheistic loss over time of primordial contact with the divine (Epicurus *Epistle to Menoeceus* 123ff; Dio Chrysostom *Orations* 12.28). As Paul would make clear in his call to repentance (17:30), the separation is moral. Sin puts a person "far away" from God (cf. Luke 18:13); the nations, going their own way, were "far away" from God (2:39; 22:21; Eph 2:13, 17). Still this cultural distance is in tension with the reality of God's personal nearness to every human being, no matter the culture (cf. 14:17).

To reinforce God's nearness, and by inference humankind's culpability in not finding him, Paul asserted God's presence in terms of our dependence on him by saying, "For in him we live and move and exist" (17:28). Though the Stoics would take the expression "in him" (*en autō* [TG1722/846, ZG1877/899]) pantheistically (cf. Dio Chrysostom *Orations* 12.27, 43), Paul probably was thinking of it instrumentally. "By his power, in dependence on him," humans live, move, and are (Ps 3:3; Hos 1:7; 12:6 LXX; cf. Sophocles *Oedipus Coloneus* 1443). Paul then appealed to the fourth- and third-century Stoic Aratus for confirmation: "We are his offspring" (from *Phenomena* 5). Paul's introductory remark cleansed Aratus's quotation of both its reference to Zeus and its pantheistic metaphysic. The quote could then carry accurate meaning regarding the one true God, the transcendent, personal creator who sustains humans, who are "his offspring" (*tou genos* [TG1085, ZG1169]) in that they, like any human group ("race" or "nation"), have a common origin and social life—in this case, the source is God and they are made in his image (Gen 1:26-27; cf. Acts 4:36; 13:26; 18:2).

As twice before (17:24-25), Paul draws implications for worship from these truths about God. His basic line of argument, found often in Old Testament and Jewish literature, is that if like begets like, it is illogical to suppose that the divine nature (*to theion* [TG2304/A, ZG2521], NLT "God") that created living human beings is like an "idol" made of an inanimate substance, no matter how valuable (Deut 4:28; Isa 40:18-20; 44:9-20; Wis 13:10; 15:7-17). Not even the exquisite Athena Parthenos, or the impressive Hephaisteion Athena, "designed by craftsmen" (lit., "by the skill and imagination of humans"), could be the god who made its makers. Even a Stoic, who recognized the validity of idols as expressions of the divine spark within the idol-maker (Dio Chrysostom *Orations* 12.44-46), could not avoid reasoning in this direction, though his pantheism led him to incorrectly declare that the only image worthy of Zeus is the whole universe (12.80-81).

God overlooked people's former ignorance. In all those past generations from the first human beings until Christ (except Noah's generation, Gen 6:5-8; 9:11-17), God "overlooked" humankind's sin, especially false worship. This was not an excusing or failing to notice but rather a delay in punishing it as it deserved (14:16; Rom 3:25). "Now," however, God commands "everyone everywhere to repent of their sins and turn to him" (17:30). Each generation's problem is that its ignorant worship is culpable, rebellious, false worship. God's solution is not for humans to receive more information but to make a radical turn from idolatry to the one true God (14:15; 26:20). Formerly, humankind was "groping"—living in a sinful ignorance that God in his mercy passed over (cf. Wis 11:23). "But now" (17:30), since sin has been judged in Jesus' death and Resurrection, there comes the "day of salvation" in a gospel proclaimed in his name, calling for repentance and promising forgiveness. No matter their culture and religion, "everyone everywhere," living on this side of the "now," must embrace that salvation available only in Jesus' name (Luke 24:47; 2 Cor 6:2).

This call to repentance is urgent because the consequences for not repenting—a final judgment and eternal condemnation—are as horrific as they are inescapable and final. The judgment is definite ("he has set a day"; Luke 17:24, 30; 21:34-36) and universal ("for judging the world" or "whole inhabited world" *tēn oikoumenēn* [TG3625, ZG3876], 11:28; 17:6). It will be "in justice," not so much by any human conception of fairness but, more specifically, within the framework of the mutual obligations of covenant partners (Pss 31:1; 35:24; 45:8; Isa 26:2; 45:21). God made humans and providentially sustained their existence in cultures (17:26). He gave them the task of seeking him and relating to him in praise and thanksgiving (17:27; Rom 1:21). But humans turned to ignorant, idolatrous worship. If they do not repent of it, they will face judgment. The Epicurean denied all the elements of theodicy: the gods do not judge; the soul does not survive death; there is no postmortem judgment (Diogenes Laertes *Lives of the Philosophers* 10.133, 139). The Stoics affirmed all the elements but within a pantheistic, cyclic metaphysic with judgment occurring either within history or after death (Posidonius in Athenaeus *Deipnosophistae* 6.266ef; Plutarch *Moralia* 560F). For both, a judgment for all at the end of human history would be strange news.

Paul argued that God has indeed appointed one human being to be this universal judge (17:31). Jesus' Resurrection, itself established by many "undeniable proofs" in space and time (1:3), guarantees the reality of this event at the end of time. The Resurrection is, then, the linchpin for both potential ways of applying the death and Resurrection of the Christ to one's eternal destiny. It establishes both the warning of judgment and the promise of salvation blessings (2:32-33; 5:30-32; 10:40-42).

The mocking reaction of some, probably Epicureans, is most understandable (17:32). The Greeks viewed resurrection as impossible; it simply did not happen. Interestingly, Aeschylus said that at the inauguration of the court of the Areopagus, Apollo stated, "Once he [man] is slain; there is no resurrection" (*Eumenides* 648). The Stoics seemed to respond to Paul with jaded curiosity: "We want to hear more about this later." Though at other times during his missionary witness Paul was able to capitalize on people's genuine curiosity (13:42, 44; 17:2, 11), Luke does not tell us whether Paul ever had opportunity to take the Areopagites up on their request (cf. other instances of procrastination that do not lead to repentance, 24:25; 26:28).

On the other hand, some of Paul's hearers "joined him and became believers" (17:34; cf. 5:13; 9:26; 10:28; 16:34; 17:12). Luke names Dionysius, a member of the Areopagus council, and Damaris, possibly part of the listening crowd or a convert from earlier witness. God's mission in Athens was not without fruit.

Thus, Paul's preaching at Athens shows us how God's messenger made inroads into the very center of a culture's religious and intellectual life. A fearless proclamation of Jesus and the Resurrection within the framework of God's work as transcendent Creator, immanent sustainer, and righteous savior may have brought mockery, but it also yielded adherents (17:32-34).

◆ G. Paul Meets Priscilla and Aquila in Corinth (18:1-17)

Then Paul left Athens and went to Corinth.* ²There he became acquainted with a Jew named Aquila, born in Pontus, who had recently arrived from Italy with his wife, Priscilla. They had left Italy when Claudius Caesar deported all Jews from Rome. ³Paul lived and worked with them, for they were tentmakers* just as he was.

⁴Each Sabbath found Paul at the synagogue, trying to convince the Jews and Greeks alike. ⁵And after Silas and Timothy came down from Macedonia, Paul spent all his time preaching the word. He testified to the Jews that Jesus was the Messiah. ⁶But when they opposed and insulted him, Paul shook the dust from his clothes and said, "Your blood is upon your own heads—I am innocent. From now on I will go preach to the Gentiles."

⁷Then he left and went to the home of Titius Justus, a Gentile who worshiped God and lived next door to the synagogue. ⁸Crispus, the leader of the synagogue, and everyone in his household believed in the Lord. Many others in Corinth also heard Paul, became believers, and were baptized.

⁹One night the Lord spoke to Paul in a vision and told him, "Don't be afraid! Speak out! Don't be silent! ¹⁰For I am with you, and no one will attack and harm you, for many people in this city belong to me." ¹¹So Paul stayed there for the next year and a half, teaching the word of God.

¹²But when Gallio became governor of Achaia, some Jews rose up together against Paul and brought him before the governor for judgment. ¹³They accused Paul of "persuading people to worship God in ways that are contrary to our law."

¹⁴But just as Paul started to make his defense, Gallio turned to Paul's accusers and said, "Listen, you Jews, if this were a case involving some wrongdoing or a seri-ous crime, I would have a reason to accept your case. ¹⁵But since it is merely a question of words and names and your Jewish law, take care of it yourselves. I refuse to judge such matters." ¹⁶And he threw them out of the courtroom.

¹⁷The crowd* then grabbed Sosthenes, the leader of the synagogue, and beat him right there in the courtroom. But Gallio paid no attention.

18:1 *Athens* and *Corinth* were major cities in Achaia, the region in the southern portion of the Greek peninsula. 18:3 Or *leatherworkers.* 18:17 Greek *Everyone;* other manuscripts read *All the Greeks.*

NOTES

18:2 *Claudius Caesar deported all Jews from Rome.* While most commentators follow Orosius's date in placing this at AD 49 (*Historiae contra Paganos* 7.6.15-16; e.g., Dunn 1996:240; Kee 1997:200; Witherington 1998:541), Slingerland (1992), though too skeptical himself, has introduced appropriate caution. Coordination with "the Gallio inscription" date (see note on 18:12) is probably the best independent confirmation of Orosius's accuracy.

Some have thought that "all Jews" was a Lukan assumption because only ring-leaders were expelled (as Dunn 1996:241); others have thought this is rhetorical hyperbole for a very large number (as Witherington 1998:539). Given the number and importance of Jews to the life of the city, the decree's content may well have differed from the extent of its implementation (Harrison 1986:292).

18:3 *tentmakers.* Most commentators, in agreement with the NLT rendering, see *skēnopoios* [TG4635, ZG5010] as the tentmaking trade, but inclusive of anything fabricated of leather (Johnson 1992:322; Dunn 1996:241; Witherington 1998:545)—hence, the NLT mg, "leatherworkers." Szesnat (1993:395) effectively argues for a focus not on the material but on the product: "a building or structure without solid walls—tents, canopies, etc." What Paul produced could have been of leather, linen, or even *cilicium,* fabric of goat's hair from Paul's home region (Szesnat 1993:400). Rapske (1994a:7) opts only for leather, since the other materials would require weaving, thereby utilizing bulky looms impractical for a traveling teacher to carry.

18:7 *Then he left and went to the home of Titius Justus.* This does not mean that Paul changed residence; rather, it means that Paul began to use the house of Titius Justus for his place of teaching (Barrett 1998:867).

18:12 *Gallio . . . governor of Achaia.* Murphy-O'Connor (1993) has decisively answered Slingerland's (1991) skepticism about the precision of the "Gallio inscription" at Delphi for dating Paul's encounter with that governor. The inscription, the emperor's response to Gallio's inquiry, dates from the first half of AD 52 (Claudius's 12th year [after January 25, 52] and 26th acclamation [before August 1, 52—date of 27th acclamation]). Gallio probably took the request to Rome the previous summer or fall, when due to illness he returned to Rome after just beginning a one-year tenure or, perhaps, hardly finishing a previous two-year tenure (Seneca *Letters* 104.1; Pliny the Elder *Natural History* 31.62). Paul, then, would have appeared before him in AD 50 or 51.

18:15 *a question of words and names.* Winter (1999:219) takes *zētēmata [estin] peri logou kai onomatōn* as technical legal wording: "a legal claim" about a "declaration of legal immunity" and "professing of names." In other words, the accusers were saying that Christians, given their racial composition, did not qualify to be treated as Jews who had been granted legal immunity from the imperial cult because they were professing a name for Jesus— namely, "Messiah." Barrett (1998:874) and the NLT understand the comment in its plain sense rather than as technical legal language. Either way, Gallio declared the dispute intramural among Jews and, as a result, not a matter for direct Roman jurisdiction. He did so by applying the Roman legal principle that persons are liable for actions (which in 18:14 he found unobjectionable), not for the words they profess (Winter 1999:219).

18:17 *The crowd.* The Gr. is *pantes* [TG3956, ZG4246] (everyone), which has the support of 𝔓74 ℵ A B cop^bo. Another reading is *pantes hoi Hellēnes* [TG1672, ZG1818] (all the Greeks), which is strongly supported by other witnesses, chiefly Western and Byzantine witnesses (D E 044 33 1739 𝔐 syr cop^sa). This reading points to Gentile anti-Semitism countenanced by Roman authorities (Talbert 1997:170).

COMMENTARY

Paul left Athens and traveled thirty-seven miles south-southwest to Corinth. Situated on the three-and-a-half-mile-wide isthmus between the Peloponnesian peninsula and the Greek mainland, Corinth was, as the NLT mg indicates, "a major city"—in fact, the main city, economically and politically, for the region. Since 27 BC, Corinth had been the capital of the senatorial province of Achaia, which covered the central and southern portions of Greece (Peloponnese, Attica, Boeotia, Aetolia, Thessaly, and part of Epirus). Corinth (population 200,000) was also a key commercial center at the juncture of north-south roads and east-west sea routes. It boasted a cosmopolitan mix of Greeks, Romans, and Orientals, including a large number of Jews, living in a rip-roaring town, where, as Horace put it, "none but the tough could survive" (*Epistles* 1.17.36; cf. Pausanias *Description of Greece* 2.2.3– 2.4.7).

To this point in the Acts narrative, every believer we have encountered either has become a Christian as the narrative progresses (e.g., Paul) or has a conversion traceable to reported missionary activity (e.g., Timothy at Lystra). Paul's encounter with Aquila and Priscilla (18:2) introduces a new phenomenon. They were Christians whose conversion is not traceable to any of the reported missionary activity in Acts. Aquila was a native of Pontus—Bithynia, where Paul was not permitted to minister (16:7)—but he had recently arrived from Rome, which did have visitors present in the Pentecost audience (2:10). The advance of God's mission was more extensive than Acts directly reports.

God in his providence orchestrated their meeting through an imperial decree: Claudius's deportation of all the Jews from Rome. Suetonius tells why this deportation occurred: "since the Jews constantly made disturbances at the instigation of *Chrestus*" (*Claudius* 25.4). Though somewhat garbled, this probably refers to a dispute in the Jewish community over Jesus *Christus* (the names would have been pronounced similarly).

God provided Paul support in two ways: social and spiritual companionship of fellow Christians (he had come to Corinth alone), and an economic opportunity to work at his trade of tentmaking—or fabricating buildings or structures without solid walls, whether of *cilicium* (Pliny the Elder *Natural History* 6.143), leather, or linen (Cicero *Against Verres* 2.5.30, 80). Jewish rabbis were bivocational so that they would not have to charge for their teaching (*m. Avot* 2:2; cf. Acts 20:34-35; 1 Cor 4:12; 9:15, 18; 1 Thess 2:9; 2 Thess 3:8). Other traveling teachers in the Hellenistic world received remuneration for their lectures. Public speaking would have been considered prestigious, while, in Greco-Roman culture, the manual labor of the artisan class (e.g., tentmakers) was despised.

When Timothy and Silas arrived from Macedonia, probably bringing a monetary gift (2 Cor 11:9; Phil 4:15), they provided a form of providential support which freed Paul to spend "all his time preaching the word" (*suneicheto tō logō* [TG4912A/3056, ZG5309/3364], lit., "absorbed with, intensely engaged in the word"). Paul pursued his strategy of going to the Jews first and telling them that Jesus was the Messiah (18:4-5; cf. 17:2-3; 28:23).

The familiar pattern of Paul's confrontation with Judaism—proclamation, division, rejection, separation, further advance—occurs here in rapid succession (cf. 13:42). The Jewish opposition is stated in absolute terms: "they opposed and insulted." The "insults" (*blasphēmountōn* [TG987, ZG1059], "blasphemed") could well have been directed as blasphemous statements against the Lord Jesus Christ (cf. 13:45).

Paul rejected their rejection in such a way that he effectively proclaimed to them the seriousness of their refusal to embrace Jesus the Messiah and his salvation (18:6). He shook his garments, wanting to be rid of even the finest particles of dust that might link him to them. He knew that if they did not repent, the coming judgment would be so complete that not even the dust that clung to them would escape (Luke 9:5; 10:10-11; Acts 13:46, 51; Neh 5:13). With Old Testament phraseology, he declared himself free of responsibility for their eternal destiny, again pointing to the serious consequences of their continued rejection (2 Sam 1:16; Ezek 33:1-7; cf. Matt 27:24-25).

Through with his mission to the Jews in Corinth (he would continue it elsewhere; see Acts 18:19), Paul focused on the Gentiles. His new base of operations was the house of a God fearer, Titius Justus, next door to the synagogue (18:7). God placed his stamp of approval on this strategic withdrawal for further advance by a harvest that was both qualitative and quantitative (18:8; cf. 1 Cor 1:26; 3:6-9). In contrast to those of the synagogue who opposed and blasphemed, "Crispus, the leader of the synagogue"—holding the highly visible position of supervising Sabbath services and maintaining order—and "everyone in his household believed in the Lord" (cf. Acts 16:15, 33). Many others, when they heard the Good News, "were [also] believing and being baptized" (*episteuon kai ebaptizonto* [TG4100/907, ZG4409/966], iterative imperfect). Here and throughout this second missionary journey, God was indeed calling out a people to himself, who were responding in faith and identifying with the new people of God through baptism (16:15, 31, 33-34; 17:4; 1 Cor 1:14-17, 21; 2:3).

The Lord Jesus, ever the providential prosecutor of his mission by the Spirit through his witnesses, intervened directly with comforting guidance (cf. 9:12; 16:9-10). He gave a threefold command attached to a threefold promise, all expressed in Old Testament language like that directed to the prophets (18:9-10; cf. Deut 31:6; Josh 1:5; Isa 41:10; 43:5; Jer 1:7-9).

Don't be afraid! / I am with you.
Speak out! / No one will attack and harm you.
Don't be silent! / Many people in this city belong to me.

We are not told why Paul was afraid (cf. 1 Cor 2:3), but we are told the antidote: embracing the promise of Christ's presence (cf. Matt 28:20). The Lord directly affirmed Paul with the command, "Speak out! Don't be silent!" and the promise that though there would be opposition, Paul would not be harmed. The outcome of Paul's appearance before Gallio would be the promise's concrete fulfillment (18:12-17). Indeed, Paul should not "be silent," for the Lord had already chosen "many people" (*laos* [TG2992, ZG3295]; cf. 15:14) to belong to him in this city (cf. 2 Cor 6:16). The Lord's predestination (13:48) not only guaranteed a fruitful ministry but demanded that Paul responsibly fulfill his obligation to witness. He did so by "teaching the word of God" for the next eighteen months (18:11). Teaching the word—which for Luke includes evangelism as well as edification (5:42; 15:35)— was central to the mission.

The Jews "rose up together against Paul" (18:12; cf. 4:1; 6:12; 17:5), bringing him before Gallio the governor "for judgment." Lucius Junius Gallio, along with his brother, Marcus Annaeus Seneca, a Stoic philosopher, politician, dramatist, and tutor to young Nero, had participated in the highest and most influential circles of Roman society. Pursuing a career in government, Gallio, between his praetorship and admission to the consulate, served as the governor of the senatorial province of Achaia. Though a fussy hypochondriac, Gallio did have an affable personality, as Seneca attests: "No other human being is so charming to just one person as he (Gallio) is to all people" (*Naturales quaestiones* 4A, preface 11).

The Jews brought an ambiguous charge (Acts 18:13). Who were the "people" Paul was "persuading"? Were they Jews or Gentiles, even Roman citizens? What "law" was the resulting worship allegedly contrary to—Old Testament or Roman? If the former, it could still have been treated as a serious charge concerning a movement that had apostatized from Judaism, an officially recognized ancient religion. As a novelty, this Christianity might make inroads into traditional and civic cults and thus undermine civic functions and good order. Or, it could have been treated as a trivial intramural Jewish debate. If the latter, Christianity might be seen as violating Claudius's edicts that prohibited fomenting disturbances among the Jews (Josephus *Antiquities* 19.278-291).

Without any prompting from Christian witnesses (cf. Acts 16:37-39), the Roman governor fulfilled the Lord's promise that no harm would come to Paul (18:14-15). Using technical legal language (the clause *kata logon [an] aneschomēn* [TG430, ZG462] *humōn*, "I would be obliged to listen to you," i.e., "I would hear the case"), Gallio said that "some wrongdoing" (open or violent wrongdoing) or "serious crime"—an offense involving deception (cf. "persuasion by deception" in the charge, 18:13)—

would be a legitimate matter for his jurisdiction. The governor, however, immediately declined to hear the case because it was an intramural Jewish matter, a dispute about "words" versus "deeds," about "names"—professing Jesus as Messiah—and about matters of Jewish law (a law-free gospel for the Gentiles; cf. 18:5-8). Here we see precedent-setting divine protection. Christianity continued under the umbrella of Judaism, which the Romans viewed as a morally unobjectionable and politically innocuous ancient religion and which, because of Claudius's edicts, enjoyed protection from attack and rights of redress if attacked.

There was also a dark side to Gallio's lack of involvement, which revealed the self-destructive nature of the opposition (18:16-17). Not only did he drive the defendant and plaintiffs from the court—possibly by physical force through the lictors—but he also took no action when the Jews began to beat one of their own, Sosthenes, the leader of the synagogue. He was evidently the successor to Crispus (a recent Christian convert; 18:8) as synagogue administrator. His lack of success in persuading Gallio to adjudicate charges against Paul led to the violent attack by fellow Jews. For the first time in Acts, we see hostile internal dissension among the opposition.

◆   ## H. Paul Returns to Antioch of Syria (18:18-23)

¹⁸Paul stayed in Corinth for some time after that, then said good-bye to the brothers and sisters* and went to nearby Cenchrea. There he shaved his head according to Jewish custom, marking the end of a vow. Then he set sail for Syria, taking Priscilla and Aquila with him.

¹⁹They stopped first at the port of Ephesus, where Paul left the others behind. While he was there, he went to the synagogue to reason with the Jews. ²⁰They asked him to stay longer, but he declined. ²¹As he left, however, he said, "I will come back later,* God willing." Then he set sail from Ephesus. ²²The next stop was at the port of Caesarea. From there he went up and visited the church at Jerusalem* and then went back to Antioch.

²³After spending some time in Antioch, Paul went back through Galatia and Phrygia, visiting and strengthening all the believers.*

18:18 Greek *brothers;* also in 18:27.   18:21 Some manuscripts read "*I must by all means be at Jerusalem for the upcoming festival, but I will come back later.*"   18:22 Greek *the church.*   18:23 Greek *disciples;* also in 18:27.

NOTES

18:18 *he shaved his head according to Jewish custom, marking the end of a vow.* This rendering, which adds "according to Jewish custom," interprets Paul's action as the completion of a Nazirite vow (Dunn 1996:246). The paucity of evidence for Jewish regulations about completing a Nazirite vow outside Palestine leads some to take it as a private vow (Bruce 1988:355), even a vow according to the general customs of the ancient world (Tomes 1995:193). Yet there is rabbinic evidence for undertaking and ending a vow outside Palestine, though concluding sacrifices had to be offered in the Temple (*m. Nazir* 3:6; 5:4; *b. Nazir* 19b, 20a, 45b; Josephus *Wars* 2.313-314). Acts 18:18 is the first ancient evidence for cutting the hair outside Palestine (Horn 1997:122). If historically possible in terms of Jewish practice, the vow was also historically and theologically possible for Paul (Witherington 1998:557). He lived out his faith-commitment to Christ through voluntary acts of Jewish piety (1 Cor 9:20; 2 Cor 11:22-24; contra Barrett [1998:859] who sees this as unworthy of the apostle of the law-free gospel).

18:21 *I will come back later.* This reading has excellent support: 𝔓74 ℵ A B E 33 1739 it^d cop^sa. Another reading of this is, "I must by all means be at Jerusalem by the upcoming festival, but I will come back later." This has the support of Western and Byzantine mss: (D) 044 𝔐 it^gig, w, which witness to this explanation of Paul's rush to Jerusalem. The shorter text, however, does have strong Alexandrian, Western, and Byzantine witness. One must choose between copyist motivations: an insertion to explain Paul's hasty departure (Metzger 1994:412) or a deletion to avoid granting Pauline authority to Jewish practices (Ross 1992:349). The shorter reading is preferred. The longer reading is a copyist's clarification since it clears up the ambiguity at v. 22: which church did Paul go up to/come down from—Caesarea or Jerusalem? (see NLT text and mg; Kee 1997:224).

COMMENTARY

Protected by the authorities, Paul remained in Corinth "for some time" (18:18). Eventually he said goodbye to "the brothers and sisters" and "set sail for Syria." Paul took along with him the valuable husband-and-wife team, Priscilla and Aquila (Rom 16:3-4). Paul would leave them in Ephesus to plant the church (18:27)—another first for the advance of God's mission: apostolically deployed church planters. Previously, the only apostolic deployment was in follow-up (17:14-15; 18:5).

At Corinth's eastern port city, Cenchrea, seven miles southeast, Paul cut his hair, signaling the beginning of the end of a Nazirite vow (Num 6; *m. Nazir*). Luke did not tell us the circumstances of this act of Jewish piety. Possibly the uncertainties of this second missionary journey, which had occasioned divine guidance by visions (Acts 16:9-10; 18:9-10), moved Paul to take a vow as part of his earnest petition to God for success in the mission. Now in thanksgiving, recognizing that God had made good on his promises, Paul ended the vow.

The first leg of Paul's journey involved a quick visit to Ephesus (18:19), the leading city in the province of Asia, both politically and economically, having a population of more than 250,000, including a large contingent of Jews with Roman citizenship (Josephus *Antiquities* 14.228-230, 234, 236-240; 16:162-166, 171-173). Though Paul received a positive response to his "reasoning" in the synagogue (18:4, 20), he made a hasty departure. Perhaps he was intent on getting to Jerusalem by Passover. The sea lanes opened March 5–10, and in AD 52 Passover was in early April. Paul promised to come back later, "God willing" (18:21). Paul's personal understanding of the missionary "course" laid out for him seems to have been to witness progressively outward in contiguous regions (16:6-7; Rom 15:19). God had redirected him on this second journey to bypass Asia, the territory contiguous with Galatia, and go witness in Macedonia and Achaia. Now he hoped, but only if his desires matched God's will, to fill in his orderly progress by evangelizing Asia from Ephesus.

In a very abbreviated fashion (18:22), Luke describes Paul's arrival at Caesarea; his "going up" and "coming down" from Jerusalem (NLT rightly understands the destination; cf. 8:15; 11:2; 25:1, 6-7) after greeting the church there; and his return to Antioch. By these visits, Paul modeled considerate communication, promotion of the unity of the body, and continuity of mission.

Leaving Antioch, Paul began his 1500-mile journey with an orderly revisiting of the churches in Galatia and Phrygia. These were probably the churches of the

Lycaonian and Phrygian ethnic regions in the province of Galatia, the churches Paul had planted on the first missionary journey (Acts 13-14; 16:6). He strengthened the believers so they could withstand trials to their faith.

◆ **I. Apollos Instructed at Ephesus (18:24-28)**

²⁴Meanwhile, a Jew named Apollos, an eloquent speaker who knew the Scriptures well, had arrived in Ephesus from Alexandria in Egypt. ²⁵He had been taught the way of the Lord, and he taught others about Jesus with an enthusiastic spirit* and with accuracy. However, he knew only about John's baptism. ²⁶When Priscilla and Aquila heard him preaching boldly in the synagogue, they took him aside and explained the way of God even more accurately.

²⁷Apollos had been thinking about going to Achaia, and the brothers and sisters in Ephesus encouraged him to go. They wrote to the believers in Achaia, asking them to welcome him. When he arrived there, he proved to be of great benefit to those who, by God's grace, had believed. ²⁸He refuted the Jews with powerful arguments in public debate. Using the Scriptures, he explained to them that Jesus was the Messiah.

18:25 Or *with enthusiasm in the Spirit.*

NOTES

18:25 **with an enthusiastic spirit.** Given Luke's interest in God the Holy Spirit, *zeōn tō pneumati* [TG2204/4151, ZG2417/4460] should probably be understood spiritually—"aglow with the Spirit" (Rom 12:11; Dunn 1996:251; Barrett 1998:887)—not psychologically, as in the NLT rendering. The NLT mg is preferable: "with enthusiasm in the Spirit." Apollos, a figure standing astride a decisive transition in salvation history, was truly regenerate, had the Spirit, but was baptized only with John's baptism. Like the apostles at Pentecost, he did not need to receive Christian baptism (Dunn 1996:250; Turner 1998:338).

18:27 **those who, by God's grace, had believed.** Although the syntax, which places *dia tēs chariti* [TG1223/5485, ZG1328/5921] (by grace) at the end of the sentence, might be an emphatic way of modifying the main verb—"proved to be of great benefit" (Bruce 1990:404)—the NLT and Barrett (1998:890) rightly link it to the closer verb, "had believed."

COMMENTARY

Apollos (a short form of Apollonius), an Alexandrian Jew (lit., "a Jew, a native of Alexandria"; NLT simply says he "arrived from Alexandria"), had evidently taken advantage of the education of that city and especially its Jewish community (Pliny the Elder *Natural History* 5.62-63). Alexandria, known for its museum, library, and ancillary learning facilities, boasted a Jewish population containing scholars who had produced the Septuagint and later counted Philo the philosopher among their ranks (*Letter of Aristeas* 301-321; Philo *Against Flaccus*). Luke styled Apollos as "an eloquent speaker"; the Greek term *logios* [TG3052, ZG3360] meant he was either "learned" (Aristotle *Politics* 1267B) or "eloquent" (Lucian *The Cock* 2). Since ancient education focused on rhetoric, an interest of Luke's, the former would have included the latter. He was, literally, "mighty in the Scriptures," knowing them well (as the NLT says), but also powerful in the understanding and use of them in preaching and debate (18:26, 28). More than "with an enthusiastic spirit," Apollos was "aglow with the Spirit" (see note on 18:25), as he taught with accuracy the things concerning Jesus. Apollos was a Spirit-inspired, bold Christian preacher (18:26), who had been taught "the way of the Lord"—i.e., the way of salvation that leads to the Lord. This is the first indication that God's mission must have extended southward to Egypt (but cf. 8:36-39, the conversion of a eunuch on his way home to Ethiopia, south of Egypt).

Though accurate as far as it went, Apollos's understanding of the gospel was still deficient. "He knew only about John's baptism" (18:25). Was Apollos operating with an "under-realized eschatology"—understanding that Jesus was the fulfill-ment of messianic salvation promises but continuing to view him from John the Baptist's preparatory "promise" perspective (Luke 3:10-14)? If he had the Spirit, he understood and experienced more than the Ephesian disciples of John (19:1-7). Yet, if his praxis was limited to John's baptism, he did not yet fully understand the universal, Christocentric, present salvific meaning of salvation blessings, which in-corporation into the one people of God by Christian baptism signifies (2:38-39). Priscilla and Aquila took him aside and explained to him "the way of God even more accurately," presumably in the area of Christian baptism.

Once he was given complete understanding about the gospel, Apollos intended to go to Achaia (18:27). In the first indication that a church had been planted at Ephesus and in a further indication that the churches viewed themselves as part of a network that could proactively share personnel (cf. 15:30-33; 16:1), the Ephesian Christians encouraged Apollos and provided him with a letter of commendation (cf. 2 Cor 3:1). Apollos proved to be a "great benefit" to those in Achaia (Corinth) who had come by grace to believe in Christ (1 Cor 3:6; 16:12). The mission begun by God's grace (cf. Acts 11:23; 15:11) continued and proliferated through this Spirit-filled apologist, whose training had been completed by a husband-and-wife team of faithful teachers. Through a very effective apologetic ministry—completely refuting the Jews in public debate (cf. 6:10)—Apollos explained from the Scriptures that "Jesus was the Messiah" (18:28).

◆   J. Paul's Third Missionary Journey (19:1-7)

While Apollos was in Corinth, Paul trav-eled through the interior regions until he reached Ephesus, on the coast, where he found several believers.* 2"Did you receive the Holy Spirit when you believed?" he asked them.

"No," they replied, "we haven't even heard that there is a Holy Spirit."

3"Then what baptism did you experi-ence?" he asked.

And they replied, "The baptism of John."

4Paul said, "John's baptism called for repentance from sin. But John himself told the people to believe in the one who would come later, meaning Jesus."

5As soon as they heard this, they were baptized in the name of the Lord Jesus. 6Then when Paul laid his hands on them, the Holy Spirit came on them, and they spoke in other tongues and prophesied. 7There were about twelve men in all.

19:1 Greek disciples; also in 19:9, 30.

NOTES

19:1 *interior regions.* Since Paul said he had not met persons in the Lycus valley (Col 2:1), this phrase (*ta anōterika merē* [TG510/3313, ZG541/3538], "upper parts" either in terms of hinterland or elevation) probably points to a northerly interior route at higher elevations, not necessarily along the Pontic and Propontid upper coasts (as French 1994:55), but along the Cayster River, not the Lycus or Maeander Rivers, to Ephesus (Barrett 1998:893; contra Polhill [1992:398], who says Paul traveled through the Lycus and Maeander valleys but did not evangelize).

believers. Lit., "disciples," as also in 19:9, 30 (cf. NLT mg). Since the NLT consistently uses "believers" to indicate Christians, as is indeed the case in 19:9, 30, the note infers this is the case here. Some would agree that Luke presented them as Christians, an indication that he recognized that the convictions and experience of the new movement were by no means uniform (Kee 1997:229). Others see him as confused (Erickson 1993:465-466) or vague (Dunn 1996:255) about their status. Most, however, see them as disciples of John the Baptist (Keener 1993:378; Spencer 1997:184-185; Barrett 1998:893). They account for the ambiguity via Luke's nuanced use of terminology ("disciple"; "believed"), which requires an attention to immediate context (Paul's interrogation, their response, and his subsequent action, 19:2-6; Witherington 1998:570), to determine these persons' true spiritual condition.

19:5 *they were baptized in the name of the Lord Jesus.* Christian missionaries treat Apollos and these Ephesian disciples of John the Baptist differently, not because they saw their baptism from John differently (as Longenecker 1981:494), for there was a uniform view of the distinctive nature of Christian baptism (Witherington 1998:572). Rather, the presence or absence of the Spirit was the key to the treatment of these transitional figures (cf. Dunn 1996:255).

COMMENTARY

Traveling through the interior regions by the Cayster valley (see note on 19:1), Paul came to Ephesus. This city was an essential port for all sea lanes north, south, and west; the starting point for the two great trade routes east to the Euphrates; the judicial center and capital of the Roman province of Asia; and the religious and cultural center with its Artemis cult (cf. 19:27). Ephesus was, indeed, "the principal trading center of Asia" (Strabo *Geography* 12.8.15) and most strategic to Paul's evangelistic purposes (19:10, 26).

The gospel had already been preached there by Priscilla and Aquila and Apollos, who had moved on to Corinth (18:19, 24-27). Thus, it is not surprising that Paul encountered people that appeared to be "believers" (see note on 19:1). Finding no evidence of the Spirit's fruit or giftings, at least probably no talk of the Spirit, Paul asked, "Did you receive the Holy Spirit when you believed?" Paul's assumption, and Luke's, is that the gift of the Holy Spirit, however manifested, normally accompanies conversion (2:38; 10:47; 11:15-16; 15:8; cf. Eph 1:13-14; 4:4-5). The believers' (or better, "disciples'") response in 19:2 (which the NLT renders literally) probably should be taken to mean that they had not heard of the Holy Spirit's contemporary presence as a salvation blessing. Since they had received John's baptism and were his "disciples" (19:3), they would probably know of the Spirit's existence, if not from the Old Testament witness (Num 11:16-17, 24-29; Isa 63:10-11; Joel 2:28-32), then certainly through John's preaching (Luke 3:16). In fact, John closely tied together the Messiah's baptism "with the Holy Spirit" and the baptism "with fire" at the final judgment. John's disciples apparently still looked forward to the Spirit's coming. Unlike Apollos—who had the Spirit but not the whole truth about the universal, Christocentric, present salvific meaning of salvation blessings—they lacked both the truth and the reality of those blessings. Thus, it is fitting that Paul's third missionary journey began with helping these disciples of John the Baptist see that faith in Christ is intended to bring a present experience of the Spirit.

Paul placed John's baptism and their spiritual condition as his disciples in the context of the Christocentric focus of salvation history. John's self-proclaimed role as the precursor of the Messiah (Luke 3:16; 7:20) rendered his baptism preparatory and potentially obsolete after the arrival of the Messiah. Though the Gospels never explicitly state that John called for faith in Christ, the exalted status and role as savior and judge he gave to Jesus certainly imply it (Luke 3:16-17; John 1:27, 29; 3:23-30).

These disciples of John heard and believed the gospel, so it is right that they received Christian baptism "in the name of the Lord Jesus." By Paul's laying on of hands and the extraordinary manifestations of the Spirit parallel to Pentecost—speaking in tongues and prophesying, God mercifully gave these disciples the presence of the Spirit in their lives. Pentecost, again, served as a benchmark event. It binds together all Christians, no matter their prior understanding, in the one conversion-initiation experience: faith and repentance, baptism, and the reception of the Holy Spirit (2:38-39; Eph 4:3-6).

◆ ## K. Paul Ministers in Ephesus (19:8-20)

⁸Then Paul went to the synagogue and preached boldly for the next three months, arguing persuasively about the Kingdom of God. ⁹But some became stubborn, rejecting his message and publicly speaking against the Way. So Paul left the synagogue and took the believers with him. Then he held daily discussions at the lecture hall of Tyrannus. ¹⁰This went on for the next two years, so that people throughout the province of Asia—both Jews and Greeks—heard the word of the Lord.

¹¹God gave Paul the power to perform unusual miracles. ¹²When handkerchiefs or aprons that had merely touched his skin were placed on sick people, they were healed of their diseases, and evil spirits were expelled.

¹³A group of Jews was traveling from town to town casting out evil spirits. They tried to use the name of the Lord Jesus in their incantation, saying, "I command you in the name of Jesus, whom Paul preaches, to come out!" ¹⁴Seven sons of Sceva, a leading priest, were doing this. ¹⁵But one time when they tried it, the evil spirit replied, "I know Jesus, and I know Paul, but who are you?" ¹⁶Then the man with the evil spirit leaped on them, overpowered them, and attacked them with such violence that they fled from the house, naked and battered.

¹⁷The story of what happened spread quickly all through Ephesus, to Jews and Greeks alike. A solemn fear descended on the city, and the name of the Lord Jesus was greatly honored. ¹⁸Many who became believers confessed their sinful practices. ¹⁹A number of them who had been practicing sorcery brought their incantation books and burned them at a public bonfire. The value of the books was several million dollars.* ²⁰So the message about the Lord spread widely and had a powerful effect.

19:19 Greek 50,000 pieces of silver, each of which was the equivalent of a day's wage.

NOTES

19:8-20, 21-40 A number of commentators continue to find little verifiable history in these accounts of Paul's Ephesian ministry, though they find much accurate local detail (White 1995:36-38; Koester 1995:129; Kee 1997:229; Johnson 1992:342-343). Barrett (1998:902, 917) and Witherington (1998:585, 598) have cogently answered their objections and have affirmed, to a lesser or greater extent, the account's historical reliability.

19:9 *lecture hall.* Some have argued for *scholē* [TG4981, ZG5391] as "guild hall," with Tyrannus as its patron (Malherbe 1983:89-91). Others, based on its core meaning "leisure," see *scholē* indicating a "group of people meeting at leisure" under the aegis of Tyrannus (Horsley 1981:130). Even if Tyrannus is taken to be a philosopher rather than a patron/proprietor, the immediate context indicates it is better to see *scholē* as a building (Barrett 1998:904) than as only a social context.

That Paul preached daily in Tyrannus's lecture hall "from the fifth to the tenth hour" (i.e., "from 11 a.m. to 4 p.m.") is an interesting addition in the Western text, which, while not original (there is no reason for copyists to have deleted it), may preserve accurate information about Paul's daily schedule (Metzger 1994:417; contrast Johnson [1992:339], who sees it as no more reliable than the "seven steps" of Acts 12:10).

19:12 *handkerchiefs or aprons.* Gr., *soudaria ē simikinthia* [TG4676/4612, ZG5051/4980]. The former were actually probably rags worn around Paul's head during work to keep sweat out of his eyes (Keener 1993:378), and the latter were definitely not belts and not aprons in the typical sense, since neither stood in direct contact with Paul's skin. Rather, they were hand towels, sweat cloths carried in the hand as described in Ammonius *Fragmenta in Acta Apostolorum ad 19.12* (cf. Barrett 1998:907).

19:14 *Sceva, a leading priest.* Since no lists of first century "chief priests" among the Jews before AD 70 contain "Sceva" (Josephus *Antiquities* 18.34–20.179), some see an inaccuracy here (Kee 1997:229), though Keener (1993:379) says other texts and inscriptions point to irregularities in Jewish priestly claims outside of Palestine. Witherington (1998:581) demurs, saying Luke was capable of indicating such a renegade claim. Sceva is not "the chief priest" of the imperial cult (Polhill 1998:404; contra Fitzmyer 1998a:334), and Luke was not simply using the title for "hype" (contra Dunn 1996:259). Rather, as a general title (no definite article, so the NLT), "a leading priest" was a natural designation for exorcists who became involved in the occult, since the Jewish "chief priest" in Judaism was the only one permitted to enter God's presence on the Day of Atonement and utter his "unpronounceable name" (cf. Juvenal *Satires* 6.544, where a fortune-telling Jewess is labeled *magna sacerdos*; Barrett 1998:909; Witherington 1998:581).

19:18 *Many who became believers.* Or, "many who had believed." This is *pepisteukotōn* [TG4100, ZG4409] a perfect tense verb; these were established converts.

19:19 *incantation books.* The NLT has correctly identified the *biblous* [TG976, ZG1047] as codices or scrolls containing thaumaturgic formulae, incantations, hymns, and prayers. They are probably not the little scrolls on which the formulae were written to be placed in amulets and worn by the "patient" (contra Fernando 1998:517 following Keener 1993:379). The confusion may arise from the term "Ephesian letters." Originally these were exotic syllables/symbols engraved on the crown, girdle, and feet of statues of Artemis, which were woven and expanded into magical formulae (Frankfurter 1994:196; Plutarch *Moralia* 706E). Later, the "Ephesian letters" referred to books containing such formulae (Athenaeus *Deipnosophistae* 12.548; Clement of Alexandria *Stromata* 5.242).

several million dollars. The NLT mg reads, "Greek *50,000 pieces of silver,* each of which was the equivalent of a day's wage." Though the type of silver coin is not explicitly designated, a drachma is normally assumed. The books themselves were not worth millions of dollars, but their use could net a profit of such.

COMMENTARY

Keeping his promise (18:21) and pursuing his strategy of going to the Jews first, Paul "preached boldly" for three months in the synagogue. His bold preaching not only held nothing back of what was beneficial to his audience (20:20, 27)—it was Spirit-anointed. His methods were again "reasoning" and "persuasion" (cf. 17:2-4). His message was "the Kingdom of God"—the fact that God's promised Kingdom had finally come in Jesus (20:25; Eph 5:5; cf. Eph 1:18-23).

Some of the Ephesian Jews "rejected" God's word due to their stubbornness (cf. Heb 3:8, 13). These spoke publicly against the Way. This may have been a formal rejection, since "publicly" translates a phrase that literally means "before the assembly" (cf. 6:2; 15:12). Paul responded with a self-excommunication in which he "left the synagogue" and "took the believers with him" (cf. Luke 6:22).

This withdrawal, however, led to a further advance because over the next two years Paul preached daily at the lecture hall of Tyrannus. If the Western text gives us reliable tradition, this lecturing took place at midday, "from the fifth to the tenth hour" (11 a.m. to 4 p.m.)—during the Mediterranean siesta. Paul, who worked at his trade while in Ephesus (20:34), tirelessly shared the word of the Lord during what should have been for him "down time." What was the result? "People throughout the province of Asia—both Jews and Greeks—heard the word of the Lord" (19:10); this was probably via Paul's converts (Col 1:7; 2:1; 4:13). Some of the churches addressed in the Prison Epistles and the book of Revelation are probably the fruit of this mission (1 Cor 16:19; Eph 1:1; Col 1:2; Phlm 1:1; Rev 2-3; cf. 1 and 2 Tim). Whether described as Spirit-anointed preaching or the province-wide hearing of "the word of the Lord," Luke lets us know that proclaiming and embracing the gospel is the central dynamic of "God on mission."

God wed "unusual miracles" with the spread of his word, literally "doing them through Paul's hands" (19:11). So strongly was God's power present with Paul that people used to take away "handkerchiefs or aprons"—sweat cloths worn on his head or carried in his hand—and apply them to the infirm and the demon-possessed. Then the diseases and demons would depart (cf. Luke 8:43-48; Acts 5:15;). These evidences of the presence of the reign of God in giving liberating wholeness by "unusual" means point to God's merciful visitation. In fact, so far in the background is the human agent (Luke is silent even about Paul's approval or disapproval) that to think Luke wants us to mimic this practice doesn't only reduce the miraculous to impersonal magical manipulation, it fails to catch Luke's real point—these miracles were *God's* doing.

As with Simon Magus (8:19), some in the region tried to manipulate the power of "the name of the Lord Jesus" (19:13). Though the Old Testament expressly forbade dabbling in the occult, Jews in ancient times, legitimizing themselves through Solomon or high priestly prerogatives, played an important role in mediating the magical wisdom of the East to the Greco-Roman world (Lev 20:6, 27; Deut 18:10-11; Luke 11:19; Josephus *Antiquities* 8.45-49). The "sons of Sceva, a leading priest," followed the time-honored practice of piling name upon powerful name so as to create exorcistic incantations strong enough to require spirits to do one's bidding: "I command you in the name of Jesus, whom Paul preaches" (Acts 19:13-14; cf. Eph 1:21). One such conjuration goes, "I conjure you by the god of the Hebrews/Jesus, IABA, IAË ABRAÖTH AIA THÖTH ELE ELÖ . . ." (*Papyri Graecae Magicae* IV.3019-3020). This presents a spell found in one of the magical papyri; it illustrates the syncretism of the times, which included the use of Jesus' name and the Old Testament divine name.

Luke chose one "botched" exorcism to demonstrate (without human agent, Paul, or even direct divine action) the unquestionably superior power of the "Jesus, whom Paul preaches" (cf. 8:20-23; 13:9-11). The demons displayed true spiritual insight, knowing and recognizing the authority of both Jesus and Paul but not that of the magicians (cf. Luke 4:34, 41; 8:28). They added injury to insult by physically mastering the exorcists, thereby unmasking their total impotence. These exorcists could neither command nor resist demonic spiritual forces. The demon-possessed man "leaped on" them (*ephallomai* [TG2177, ZG2383], often indicating overpowering by superior spiritual beings; 1 Sam 10:6; 16:13, LXX). He so overpowered them that they fled the house "naked and battered" (19:16).

Luke emphasized the extent of the spread and impact of the report of this incident. It became known (same Gr. verb is used in 4:16; 9:42) "all through Ephesus, to Jews and Greeks alike." As with the experience or report of any supernatural visitation—especially one involving judgment—fear came on all who heard it (Luke 1:12; Acts 2:43; 5:5, 11). Removed from the vocabulary of incantation, Jesus' name was accorded the honor it deserves (cf. 5:13; 10:46). We hear of no conversions as a direct result of the incident, though a climate for a proper hearing of the gospel had been created (Luke 24:47). Conversions would come, as 19:20 summarizes (cf. 9:35, 42).

The real fruit of this "indirect" power encounter, however, was among the believers. It was not recent converts (as the NLT implies) but established believers who repented of their continued syncretistic practices (see note on 19:18). They turned from their use of magic by "confessing" and announcing publicly their magical spells (*anangellontes* [TG312, ZG334] *tas praxeis* [TG4234, ZG4552] *autōn*; cf. 14:27; 15:4; the NLT renders "confess" and "announce" as one verb and takes the object more generally—"sinful practices"). This public disclosure robbed the spells of their power. In fact, it assured no further use. Many of the Christians, who had practiced sorcery, brought their "incantation books" (see note on 19:19) and voluntarily burned them publicly. Their repentance was complete and costly. No longer would they be able to sell these formulae for protection, blessing, or cursing with the potential total profit of 50,000 days' wages (see note on 19:19).

In a summary statement closing his fifth panel (16:6-19:20), this time declaring the gospel's complete triumph over spiritual counterfeits, Luke again, through personification of the message, communicates that it was God who was on mission. "The message about the Lord spread widely and had a powerful effect" (6:7; 12:24; 19:10). Luke's theology places proclamation of the gospel message as the central dynamic of any "power advance" of the *missio dei*, and so should ours.

◆ VI. Paul's Witness in Chains: Jerusalem, Caesarea, Rome (19:21–28:31)
A. Riot in Ephesus (19:21–41)

21Afterward Paul felt compelled by the Spirit* to go over to Macedonia and Achaia before going to Jerusalem. "And after that," he said, "I must go on to Rome!" 22He sent his two assistants, Timothy and Erastus, ahead to Macedonia while he stayed awhile longer in the province of Asia.

23About that time, serious trouble developed in Ephesus concerning the Way. 24It began with Demetrius, a silversmith who had a large business manufacturing silver shrines of the Greek goddess Artemis.* He kept many craftsmen busy. 25He called them together, along with others employed in similar trades, and addressed them as follows:

"Gentlemen, you know that our wealth comes from this business. 26But as you have seen and heard, this man Paul has persuaded many people that handmade gods aren't really gods at all. And he's done this not only here in Ephesus but throughout the entire province! 27Of course, I'm not just talking about the loss of public respect for our business. I'm also concerned that the temple of the great goddess Artemis will lose its influence and that Artemis—this magnificent goddess worshiped throughout the province of Asia and all around the world—will be robbed of her great prestige!"

28At this their anger boiled, and they began shouting, "Great is Artemis of the Ephesians!" 29Soon the whole city was filled with confusion. Everyone rushed to the amphitheater, dragging along Gaius and Aristarchus, who were Paul's traveling companions from Macedonia. 30Paul wanted to go in, too, but the believers wouldn't let him. 31Some of the officials of the province, friends of Paul, also sent a message to him, begging him not to risk his life by entering the amphitheater.

32Inside, the people were all shouting, some one thing and some another. Everything was in confusion. In fact, most of them didn't even know why they were there. 33The Jews in the crowd pushed Alexander forward and told him to explain the situation. He motioned for silence and tried to speak. 34But when the crowd realized he was a Jew, they started shouting again and kept it up for two hours: "Great is Artemis of the Ephesians! Great is Artemis of the Ephesians!"

35At last the mayor was able to quiet them down enough to speak. "Citizens of Ephesus," he said. "Everyone knows that Ephesus is the official guardian of the temple of the great Artemis, whose image fell down to us from heaven. 36Since this is an undeniable fact, you should stay calm and not do anything rash. 37You have brought these men here, but they have stolen nothing from the temple and have not spoken against our goddess.

38"If Demetrius and the craftsmen have a case against them, the courts are in session and the officials can hear the case at once. Let them make formal charges. 39And if there are complaints about other matters, they can be settled in a legal assembly. 40I am afraid we are in danger of being charged with rioting by the Roman government, since there is no cause for all this commotion. And if Rome demands an explanation, we won't know what to say." 41*Then he dismissed them, and they dispersed.

19:21 Or *decided in his spirit.*   19:24 *Artemis* is otherwise known as Diana.   19:41 Some translations include verse 41 as part of verse 40.

NOTES

19:21 *compelled by the Spirit.* The alternate rendering is, "decided in his spirit" (NLT mg). The NLT has correctly identified two possible referents for *pneumati* [TG4151, ZG4460] in this phrase, though the marginal note more correctly translates the verb and the preposition which links "s/Spirit" to it. Barrett (1998:919) argues that *tithēmi* [TG5087, ZG5502] (to purpose) demands that the phrase refers to the subject's spirit (cf. Homer *Odyssey* 4.729). Though Johnson (1992:346) stresses the phrase's ambiguity, most commentators see the Holy Spirit referenced here (Dunn 1996:262; Kee 1997:233; Witherington 1998:588). They point to Luke's divine-purpose theme present in the *dei* [TG1163, ZG1256] of divine necessity in the immediate context ("I must go on to Rome!") as corroboration. A similar ambiguity occurs in 18:25.

19:22 *He sent his two assistants, Timothy and Erastus.* Timothy's and Titus's movements, as presented in the Corinthian letters (1 Cor 4:17; 16:10; 2 Cor 2:13), pre-date and do not historically contradict this deployment (Barrett 1998:920; contra Haenchen 1971:569-570). Though some continue to identify Erastus as the Corinthian city official (Rom 16:23; Keener 1993:379; Kee 1997:233), it is unlikely he would have become a traveling coworker of Paul, given an official's day-to-day responsibilities (Witherington 1998:589-590; cf. 2 Tim 4:20).

19:24 *silver shrines.* These were plaques, silver reliefs of the goddess within her temple. The New York Metropolitan Museum of Art has a first or second-century BC bronze matrix of Artemis in her temple (Reeder 1987). It is the form into which a sheet of silver or bronze was pressed to make such a plaque. These would serve local worshipers and pilgrims as votive offerings to be left in the Great Temple of Artemis or as family worship centers or grave decorations (Trebilco 1994:338).

Greek goddess Artemis. Artemis, a Greek goddess, had long been identified with Diana (cf. NLT mg), the ancient Italian goddess of women, particularly of childbirth and children. It is a commonplace to identify Artemis as a goddess of fertility, especially given the multiple bulbous objects on her chest which have been variously interpreted as "breasts, bee eggs, ostrich eggs, steer testicles, grapes, nuts, and acorns" (Arnold 1989:25-26; Keener 1993:381; Kee 1997:227). LiDonnici (1992), however, has made a strong case that the bulbous objects are a later adornment of the image. The later identification of Artemis with Isis and the motif of nursing led to these objects being incorporated into the form of the idol. As a sovereign of unsurpassed cosmic power over astrological fate, yet a virgin, Artemis possessed a non-eroticized significance to her femininity. She was nurturer, legitimate wife, and protectress of family and of political and cosmic stability (LiDonnici 1992:411; Trebilco 1994:319).

19:29 *Gaius and Aristarchus, who were Paul's traveling companions from Macedonia.* The majority of mss identify both Gaius and Aristarchus as "Macedonians" (*Makedonas* [TG3110, ZG3424]; so NLT). This clashes with 20:4, which says Gaius is from Derbe in Asia Minor. Some scribes tried to resolve this discrepancy by either making "Macedonians" singular and referring only to Aristarchus (36 307 453) or, in a Western reading at 20:4, listing Gaius's hometown as *Dobērios* (it^gig; D* *Doub[e]rios* [TG1395.1, ZG1523] and it^d *doberius*), a Macedonian post-town near Mt. Pangaios on the road from Philippi (Metzger 1994:422). Given the pairing of Gaius with Timothy of Lystra in Acts 20, it is better to conclude we are dealing with two different people named Gaius.

19:31 *officials of the province.* This phrase translates *Asiarchōn* [TG775, ZG825] (Asiarchs), a term that, until recently, was equated with the "high priest" of the provincial (Fitzmyer 1998b:334) or imperial cult (Keener 1993:380). Friesen (1993:92-113) and Kearsley (1994) have convincingly argued that the term refers to prominent wealthy persons who served as civic administrators for fixed terms and whose duties could have involved religious functions, including offering sacrifices, though they were not necessarily priests.

19:33 *The Jews in the crowd pushed Alexander forward and told him to explain.* Lit., the first sentence reads, "[Some] of the crowd instructed (*sumbibazō* [TG4822, ZG5204]) Alexander, the Jews having thrust him forward." The identity of the crowd (Jewish or Gentile), the meaning of *sumbibazō*, the sequence of events, the intentions of the crowd, the Jews, and

Alexander are all unclear (Johnson 1992:349; Barrett 1998:532). If we take the subject (*ek de tou ochlou* [TG3793, ZG4063], "some of the crowd") as disjunctive with the preceding majority (*hoi pleious* [TG4119/A, ZG4498]), "who didn't even know why they were there"; understand the verb *sumbibazō* according to its LXX meaning, "instruct" (e.g., Exod 4:12, 15; 18:16; Deut 4:9); and see the aorist participle (*probalontōn* [TG4261, ZG4582], "thrust forward") as action antecedent to the main verb, then the following understanding results: the Jews thrust Alexander forward to find out what was happening, and some of the crowd of Gentile Ephesians (not "Jews" as the NLT), who, unlike the majority, did know why they had assembled, instructed Alexander. He then stood to defend Judaism to the crowd and to distinguish it from, not to speak for, Christianity (Spencer 1997:189).

19:35 official guardian. This word, *neōkoros* [TG3511, ZG3753], is not an anachronistic reflection of the introduction of the *Sebastoi* imperial cult (AD 89/90; contra White 1995:37). Rather, as coinage from Nero's time demonstrates, and the "twice Neokoros" moniker from Domitian's time attests, Ephesus saw itself as the "official guardian" of Artemis (Friesen 1993:53-54).

whose image fell down to us from heaven. This phrase translates the term *diopetous* [TG1356, ZG1479] (the literal etymology of this term is "fallen from Zeus"). Because there is no other evidence for such beliefs about Artemis's origin (Trebilco 1994:351), the reference is ambiguous. Does it refer to a meteorite, perhaps shaped like a person (Barrett 1998:936)? Or does it refer to the mythical, heavenly origin of the image (Dunn 1996:264; cf. Euripides *Iphigeneia at Tauris* 87-88; cf. 1384)? Or could it refer to both, with the meteorite from the heavens serving as the image (Johnson 1992:349)?

19:38 officials. Lit., *anthupatoi* [TG446, ZG478] (proconsuls); each province had only one proconsul. It does not indicate a confused interregnum in Asia in the middle 50s (contra Keener 1993:381). Rather, this is a "generalizing plural" (as NLT), possibly under the influence of the preceding "courts" (Trebilco 1994:356).

19:39 legal assembly. Though Sherwin-White (1963:87) was quite sure of Chrysostom's (*Homilies* 42) specification of one regular and two extra sessions of the assembly a month, most scholars now doubt the value of Chrysostom's testimony, due to its fourth-century date (Keener 1993:381; Barrett 1998:938).

COMMENTARY

Luke introduced the "riot at Ephesus" by a transitional statement (19:21-22) that places Paul's movements under divine guidance, even divine necessity. "Afterward" is literally "now when these things had been fulfilled"; this points back to Paul's mission at Ephesus as having accomplished God's purpose. When Paul looked ahead, he now had internal positive divine guidance—he "felt compelled by the Spirit" (see note on 19:21)—whereas previously all positive guidance contained an external component (13:2, 4; 16:9; 18:9-10).

Paul again purposed to follow up the churches he planted, this time those of the second missionary journey (Luke does not tell us of the sorrowful visit to Corinth which preceded these moves, 2 Cor 2:1). As had been his custom in promoting unity by beginning each new advance back at the church's founding center(s) (13:1-3; 18:23; cf. 15:36, 40), Paul planned to return to the Jerusalem church. He declared himself to be under divine compulsion with regard to the goal of his new advance: "I must go on to Rome!" (19:21). What better way to fulfill a calling to all the nations, to "kings" and the small and the great, than to proclaim the message of the

Kingdom at the very center of it all, the capital of the empire? Through his converts, in centrifugal fashion, God's mission could then reach to the ends of the earth (1:8; 9:15; 26:22). Paul began to work his plan by sending Timothy and Erastus (see note on 19:22) as an advance party to Macedonia (cf. Luke 9:52).

"About that time," which was also near the end of Paul's ministry in Ephesus (cf. 20:1), "serious trouble," a disturbance, concerning the "Way" occurred. This general statement, though followed with the detail of a particular incident, points to the strong effect of the gospel's continued spread throughout Asia (19:10, 20). Christianity is a way of life—a new belief system with a new object of worship at its center—and it is a new set of mores and behavior patterns—in short, a new culture. Because every culture survives through the dynamic of coercive conformity, the presence of a new way, which claims to be "the Way," would by definition create a disturbance (*tarachos* [TG5017, ZG5431], "mental agitation, consternation" leading to "disorder"; cf. 12:8; 17:6-8, 13).

Demetrius, a silversmith with a number of craftsmen in his employ, manufactured "silver shrines of the Greek goddess Artemis" (see note on 21:24). It was a good living and integral to a central activity in Ephesus: the cult of Artemis. If religious processions and festivals are any indicator, the bi-weekly procession of hundreds of people and many statues of Artemis from her temple to the amphitheater and back again (*Die Inschriften von Ephesos* 27) and the annual month-long festival, Artemisa—a time of carnival and religious celebration, to which pilgrims flocked from all over the empire—reveal the cult's importance.

Calling together his workmen and those of "similar trades" (craftsmen of religious objects of the Artemis cult, whether in lead, marble, or semi-precious stones), Demetrius reviewed two facts about their situation: (1) the "wealth" which should come from the business and (2) the negative effect of Paul's polemic against polytheistic idolatry. Paul, in persuading many people, literally "had caused them to change positions"; he had brought them to a different mental and spiritual point of view. Many people had believed his message that "handmade gods aren't really gods at all" (14:15; 17:29-30; 1 Thess 1:9; cf. Isa 44:9-20; 46:1-7; 1 Cor 8:4-6; 10:20).

If the dissemination and reception of this message continued unchecked, there would be three dire consequences: (1) Economically, their portion of the business would suffer such a "loss of public respect" that orders and sales would dry up. (2) Religiously, the temple of the great goddess Artemis would "lose its influence"—be counted as "a zero" (*eis outhen logisthēnai* [TG3762D/3049A, ZG4032/3357]). Declared one of the seven wonders of the world, the temple's precincts covered an area 425 by 225 feet, four times the size of the Parthenon, with 127 columns 60 feet tall. It was a foremost worship center in Asia and a world-renowned bank (Pausanias *Description of Greece* 7.5.4; Dio Chrysostom *Orations* 31.54). Yet Demetrius declared it would soon be abandoned if more and more people decided that the image for which it was built was no goddess at all. (3) Ethnically, if the Christian witness succeeded, the goddess would be "robbed of" her regional, indeed worldwide, prestige—literally, "thrown down from her magnificence." Thirty-three Artemis worship sites have been located across the Roman empire from Spain to Syria (Strabo *Geography* 4.1.5). According to Pausanias, this cult received the most extensive and highest worship in the ancient world (*Description of Greece* 4.31.8). The Ephesians would take the loss of prestige very personally. They had a unique bond with the goddess that even the Romans recognized (Tacitus *Annals* 4.55; Dio *Roman History* 59.28.1).

The prospect of wounded ethnic and religious pride made Demetrius's audience boil in anger (cf. Acts 5:17; 13:45) and begin to shout a defiant chant of adoration: "Great is Artemis of the Ephesians!" (19:28; Xenophon *Ephesians* 1.11.5). These emotions, with their destructive mixture of mindless zeal and fury, ran so high that "the whole city was filled with confusion." The craftsmen and workers formed the core of a mob which, like a herd of wild animals, rushed violently into the amphitheater, snatching up two of Paul's traveling companions as they went.

The amphitheater (having a capacity for 24,000 people) was the largest and most impressive of the structures in ancient Ephesus. Built into the steep western slope of Mount Pion and facing the sea, its position at the intersection of the main north-south street and the broad street to the sea located it at the very center of the life of the city. It was used for citizens' assemblies, but Demetrius's gathering was an irregular, unofficial meeting of the city assembly at best and a riotous mob at worst.

Never one to miss an opportunity for witness, even to an angry, misguided crowd of false worshipers (14:14-18; 21:39), Paul wanted to go to the assembly, but fellow disciples, and even some provincial officials, "Asiarchs" (see note on 19:31), shielded him. They persuaded him not to "risk his life by entering the amphitheater" (19:30-31).

The assembly was divided—some shouting one thing, some another—confused and ignorant of its purpose. It was an apt picture of the disorienting nature of misguided religious fervor. In the end, the Artemis cult's opposition to the gospel degenerated into prolonged, irrational chanting. Eventually, the Jews in the crowd pushed forward a man named Alexander to determine the cause of the tumult (see note on 19:33). When some from the crowd told him it had to do with the Christian "Way," he tried to speak to the assembly to make a defense for the Jewish community, presumably to distance it from "the Way." The crowd would have none of it. Recognizing that Alexander was a Jew, their anti-Semitism (Josephus *Antiquities* 16:27-65) together with either their inability or unwillingness to draw a distinction between Jews and Christians (both held monotheistic and anti-idolatry views), moved them to use a common technique in riotous assembly—that is, they shouted down the opposition (Dio Chrysostom, *Orations* 7.25; 48.3). For two hours they chanted, "Great is Artemis of the Ephesians!"

A voice of moderation intervened. The "mayor" (or better, "clerk") quieted the crowd. As city registrar and chief executive officer of the citizens' assembly, he readily understood the irregularity of the gathering and the potential threat it was to the freedom of the city. He declared "undeniable facts" about Artemis and his judgment concerning the Christians' behavior (19:35-37) and their implications for the crowd (19:36, 38-39).

The clerk declared as an "undeniable fact" the universal reputation of Ephesus as "official guardian" of Artemis's cult and that her image fell from heaven (see note on 19:35). Such an affirmation speaks to both Demetrius's anxiety and Paul's polemic against gods made with human hands (19:26-27). The clerk announced that Ephesus's reputation was safe; in fact, Artemis did not fall into the category of idols that Paul was critiquing. The clerk consequently counseled that the Ephesians "should stay calm" (stated positively in the Gr., "be quiet," cf. 19:35) and not "do anything rash" (cf. Josephus *Antiquities* 5.106 reporting Josh 22:18).

The clerk declared the Christians by reputation innocent of any wrongdoing. They were not "temple robbers" (*hierosulous* [TG2417, ZG2645])—a term which came to mean "sacrilege" of any type (*Die Inschriften von Ephesos* 26.22-23; 27.217)—or "public blasphemers" of the goddess (cf. Josephus *Against Apion* 2.237; *Antiquities* 4.207 for Jewish sensitivity to such charges). If Paul's approach had been the same as at Athens, Paul's polemic involved reasoning on a generic level: the nature of deity and the worship appropriate to it from human beings who are its offspring. No direct attack on Artemis, a concrete case, was necessary. So there was no reason for this "kangaroo court" of an irregular assembly. The clerk suggested two legitimate means of redress: "the courts," and the legislature meeting in "a legal assembly" (*Die Inschriften von Ephesos* 27.203, 269, 468-469). Ephesus, as an assize district center, hosted the former on a regular basis (Pliny the Elder *Natural History* 5.105-126). It could handle any private financial disputes Demetrius and his fellow workers might have with Christians. The citizens' assembly could deal with an alleged attack on the city's prestige.

Having placed everything in proper perspective, he dismissed the crowd after warning them of the real danger (contrast 19:27)—being accused of rioting without cause—and its consequence: losing their "free city" status (19:40; Tacitus *Annals* 12.58; Suetonius *Augustus* 47). Indeed, there is no cause for "all this commotion" (*sustrophē* [TG4963, ZG5371] can have the sense of a seditious gathering; 23:12).

Without making a defense, fair-minded government officials vindicated the "law-abiding" Way vis-à-vis potentially disorderly pagan religion. The triumph of God's mission was complete as the liberating wholeness, peace, and innocence it engendered was clearly on display. The gospel message's confrontation with the Artemis cult, the most powerful and widespread religio-cultural phenomenon of its day, unmasked the brutishly hostile, confused, and even irrational character of pagan religion. It, not Christianity, threatened the Pax Romana.

◆ **B. Paul Goes to Macedonia and Greece (20:1-6)**

When the uproar was over, Paul sent for the believers* and encouraged them. Then he said good-bye and left for Macedonia. ²While there, he encouraged the believers in all the towns he passed through. Then he traveled down to Greece, ³where he stayed for three months. He was preparing to sail back to Syria when he discovered a plot by some Jews against his life, so he decided to return through Macedonia.

⁴Several men were traveling with him. They were Sopater son of Pyrrhus from

Berea; Aristarchus and Secundus from Thessalonica; Gaius from Derbe; Timothy; and Tychicus and Trophimus from the province of Asia. ⁵They went on ahead and waited for us at Troas. ⁶After the Passover* ended, we boarded a ship at Philippi in Macedonia and five days later joined them in Troas, where we stayed a week.

20:1 Greek *disciples.* 20:6 Greek *the days of unleavened bread.*

NOTES

20:1-6 Luke tells us nothing of the immediate circumstances surrounding Paul's movements into Macedonia and Greece. For his change of plans, the anxious frame of mind with which he moved to Troas and then into Macedonia as he looked for Titus and the news he brought of how the Corinthian church had responded to his "sorrowful letter" of correction, we must turn to 1 Cor 16:5-8 and 2 Cor 1:15–2:1; 2:12-13. Further, we learn nothing of Paul's probable activities during these travels: Titus's report and the writing of 2 Corinthians in Macedonia (2 Cor 7:5-16), the evangelistic mission along the Egnatian Way as far west as Illyricum (Rom 15:19; 2 Tim 4:10), the making of arrangements with the churches for a collection for the poor in the Jerusalem church (Rom 15:25-32; 1 Cor 16:1-4; 2 Cor 8–9), and the writing of Romans in Corinth (Rom 16:1, 21-23).

Most puzzling is that, except for an oblique reference in 24:17, there is a lack of explicit reference to the collection itself. It would have provided a motive for the plot against Paul's life (20:3), and for Paul's counter-tactics of dividing his party, traveling overland, and avoiding Ephesus—protecting the large sum from theft (20:3, 5-6, 13, 16). It would have explained the function of Paul's traveling delegation as representatives of the churches of the Gentiles (20:4) and given a central incentive for Paul's being anxious to get to Jerusalem by Pentecost so as to present the "firstfruits" from among the Gentiles to the mother church (20:16). Though a number of explanations have been offered (for a list, see Polhill 1992:417), the presumed negative reception of the collection by the Jerusalem church being the most popular (e.g., Witherington 1998:603, following Johnson 1992:357), Luke's and Paul's silence about the collection's reception prevents us from coming to any definite conclusions.

COMMENTARY

When the noise and confusion of the excited crowds had died down, Paul decided it was a good time to leave Ephesus. He called the disciples together for some encouragement (*parakaleō* [TG3870, ZG4151]). Growing out of the basic meaning "to call to one's side," this verb can mean "to appeal to or beseech," "to exhort," or "to comfort." Of particular relevance to New Testament usage are Old Testament eschatological contexts that highlight divine comfort through deliverance as a salvation blessing (Isa 40:1, 2, 11; 49:13; 57:18). Though the full comfort is not yet present (cf. Luke 2:25), the Spirit-filled witnesses exercised their verbal ministry to bring encouragement to the believers (9:31; 11:23; 15:32; cf. 14:22; 16:40; Eph 4:1). This strengthened the Christians to persevere in the faith in the face of trials, especially persecution, particularly in the absence of the apostolic church-planters. In leaving Ephesus (20:1) and in journeying through Macedonia and Achaia (20:2), Paul "encouraged the believers" with a strong verbal ministry. His three-month stay was probably due to winter, when sea travel was avoided (cf. 27:12; 28:11; Titus 3:12).

In the first intimation that Jerusalem would be a place of suffering, Paul discovered a plot, an organized conspiracy of the Jews against his life, just as he was preparing to sail back to Syria. Possibly the threat came from Jewish pilgrims, who would have been fellow passengers on a vessel bound for Jerusalem for Passover (cf. 21:27; 24:19). Paul abruptly changed plans, adopting a route back through Achaia and Macedonia. There was quite a band of traveling companions with Paul, including representatives of almost all the churches Paul had planted throughout his first three journeys (20:4). Macedonia's representatives were Sopater of Berea (cf. Rom 16:21) and Thessalonica's Secundus and Aristarchus (cf. 19:29; 27:2; Col 4:10; Phlm 1:24). Galatia provided Gaius of Derbe (see note on 19:29) and Timothy of Lystra (16:1). Asia's delegates were Tychicus and Trophimus (21:29; Eph 6:21; Col 4:7; 2 Tim 4:12, 20). Since the "we" passages, which left off in Philippi (16:11-15), pick up again there (20:6), many see Luke as representing Philippi. The ongoing tensions with the Corinthian church, as evidenced by the Corinthian letters, may explain why it had no representatives.

With further prudence, Paul divided his party, sending some (either the Asians, Tychicus and Trophimus, or all seven mentioned) on ahead to Troas with instructions to wait for him and the remainder of the group. With the time marker "after the Passover ended," Luke may be implying that Paul was continuing to live out his piety through Jewish traditions (the entire celebration, often simply designated "Passover," was one commemorative Passover meal followed by seven days of eating only unleavened bread—hence the NLT text and note; cf. Exod 12:14-20). After a five-day journey against contrary winds (the normal voyage this direction would take three to four days; cf. 16:11), Paul and Luke rejoined the party at Troas.

◆　C. Paul's Final Visit to Troas (20:7-12)

[7]On the first day of the week, we gathered with the local believers to share in the Lord's Supper.* Paul was preaching to them, and since he was leaving the next day, he kept talking until midnight. [8]The upstairs room where we met was lighted with many flickering lamps. [9]As Paul spoke on and on, a young man named Eutychus, sitting on the windowsill, became very drowsy. Finally, he fell sound asleep and dropped three stories to his death below. [10]Paul went down, bent over him, and took him into his arms. "Don't worry," he said, "he's alive!" [11]Then they all went back upstairs, shared in the Lord's Supper,* and ate together. Paul continued talking to them until dawn, and then he left. [12]Meanwhile, the young man was taken home unhurt, and everyone was greatly relieved.

20:7 Greek *to break bread.* 　20:11 Greek *broke the bread.*

NOTES

20:7 *share in the Lord's Supper.* Lit., "to break bread" (cf. NLT mg). The range of understandings for what the Christians were doing runs the gamut from a simple non-eucharistic church fellowship meal (Barrett 1998:950) to a full eucharistic liturgy including homily (Talbert 1997:182; Fitzmyer 1998a:667; cf. Kee 1997:237). The truth is probably somewhere in between. The Lord's Supper bracketed a Greco-Roman church fellowship meal—breaking the bread to commence and taking the cup to conclude (cf. Dunn 1996:268; Witherington 1998:606).

20:10 *he's alive!* Though most commentators are agreed that Luke was presenting a miraculous resuscitation of someone who had really died (Dunn 1996:268; Fernando 1998:531; Barrett 1998:950; Fitzmyer 1998a:668), a number are also unsure of the event's historical authenticity (Barrett 1998:954; Johnson 1992:356). The concreteness of detail, when combined with the spareness in describing the miracle itself (particularly the lack of adornment from literary parallels such as 1 Kgs 17:17-24 and 2 Kgs 4:34-35), commends the account to us as historically reliable.

20:12 *Meanwhile, the young man was taken home unhurt.* Luke presents Eutychus as being led back into the gathering, not "home" as the NLT suggests (Barrett 1998:956). However, the NLT's rendering of *ēgagon de ton paida zōnta* [TG2198, ZG2409] (lit. "now they led the youth/slave alive") correctly overcomes the narrative's disjointedness in delaying until this verse the report of Eutychus's full recovery. The delay in reporting this may be due to following the form typical of miracle stories, with the presentation of the crowd's reaction last (Witherington 1998:607). Depending on how *pais* [TG3816, ZG4090] is understood ("youth," 8–14 years old, Philo *On the Creation* 105; or "slave") and related to *neanias* [TG3494, ZG3733] (20:9, "young man," 24–40 years old, Diogenes Laertes *Lives of the Eminent Philosophers* 8.10; Philo, *Cherubim* 114), Eutychus is at least in his early teens, possibly in his twenties or thirties. If his sleep was caused as much by the toil of the day as by the soporific effects of smoky lamps and "long-winded" Paul, then he was probably an adult slave.

COMMENTARY

In chronicling Paul's progress to Jerusalem, Luke alternates between general travel summaries (20:1-6, 13-16; 21:1-8a, 15-16) and concrete episodes (20:7-12, 17-38; 21:8b-14, 18-26). In this first episode, which contains Paul's last miracle as a free man, the church experienced divine encouragement through the ordinary means of grace—the ministry of word and sacrament, as well as an extraordinary token of divine mercy in Eutychus's being raised from the dead.

At the end of a week's stay in Troas, Paul, his traveling companions, and local believers gathered on the evening of the "first day of the week" to "share in the Lord's Supper" (probably Sunday evening according to Roman daily reckoning, 2:5; 3:1). They participated in a fellowship meal that began and ended with the elements of the Lord's Supper (Luke 22:19-20; Acts 2:42, 46; 20:11; 1 Cor 10:16; 11:24; see note on 20:7). This earliest unambiguous reference to early church practice concerning Sunday worship shows how Christians, after completing what was for all a workday, hallowed it through corporate worship in celebration of Christ's Resurrection (Luke 24:1; cf. 1 Cor 16:2; Rev 1:10; *Didache* 14:1; *Epistle of Barnabas* 15:9; Pliny the Younger *Letters* 10.96.7).

We can see how integral, indeed central, the preaching of the word was to the worship. Luke stressed the preaching's unusually prolonged nature (till midnight and again to dawn), occasioned by Paul's imminent departure (20:7, 9, 11). This only heightened its importance, as Paul gave verbal exhortation that possibly involved discussion and conversation, though he probably did the lion's share of the talking.

In the midst of such an encouraging scene, tragedy struck. Eutychus (whose name means "good fortune"), probably a slave in his twenties or thirties (see note on 20:12), fell into a deep sleep. The low-ceilinged room's atmosphere must have been heavy with many small, smoking torches. He was perhaps trying to catch the night air by sitting on a windowsill, but weariness from the day's work, the lateness of the hour, the hypnotic effect of the flickering lights, and Paul's lengthy discourse all probably contributed to his drowsiness. Falling asleep, he lost his balance, fell out the window—probably no more than an open slit in the wall—and down three stories "to his death below" (cf. *Papyrus Oxyrhynchus* 3.475; Josephus *War* 5.220).

Like Elisha of old, Paul "bent over" (lit., "fell on") Eutychus and took him in his arms (see 2 Kgs 4:32-35; cf. 1 Kgs 17:19-24). The boy's life returned and Paul declared, "Don't worry . . . he's alive!" (lit. "his life, *psuchē* [TG5590, ZG6034], is in him"). Then, almost matter-of-factly, Luke tells us that Paul returned to the upper room, partook of the Lord's Supper, continued talking to them until daybreak, and then departed.

Eutychus was led back into their presence (see note on 20:12), and they were "greatly relieved." What a climatic statement of the proof of the power of God and of the ongoing comfort for Christians about to lose their leader but never to be bereft of their Lord.

♦ ## D. Paul Meets the Ephesian Elders (20:13-38)

¹³Paul went by land to Assos, where he had arranged for us to join him, while we traveled by ship. ¹⁴He joined us there, and we sailed together to Mitylene. ¹⁵The next day we sailed past the island of Kios. The following day we crossed to the island of Samos, and* a day later we arrived at Miletus.

¹⁶Paul had decided to sail on past Ephesus, for he didn't want to spend any more time in the province of Asia. He was hurrying to get to Jerusalem, if possible, in time for the Festival of Pentecost. ¹⁷But when we landed at Miletus, he sent a message to the elders of the church at Ephesus, asking them to come and meet him.

¹⁸When they arrived he declared, "You know that from the day I set foot in the province of Asia until now ¹⁹I have done the Lord's work humbly and with many tears. I have endured the trials that came to me from the plots of the Jews. ²⁰I never shrank back from telling you what you needed to hear, either publicly or in your homes. ²¹I have had one message for Jews and Greeks alike—the necessity of repenting from sin and turning to God, and of having faith in our Lord Jesus.

²²"And now I am bound by the Spirit* to go to Jerusalem. I don't know what awaits me, ²³except that the Holy Spirit tells me in city after city that jail and suffering lie ahead. ²⁴But my life is worth nothing to me unless I use it for finishing the work assigned me by the Lord Jesus—the work of telling others the Good News about the wonderful grace of God.

²⁵"And now I know that none of you to whom I have preached the Kingdom will ever see me again. ²⁶I declare today that I have been faithful. If anyone suffers eternal death, it's not my fault,* ²⁷for I didn't shrink from declaring all that God wants you to know.

²⁸"So guard yourselves and God's people. Feed and shepherd God's flock—his church, purchased with his own blood*—over which the Holy Spirit has appointed you as elders.* ²⁹I know that false teachers, like vicious wolves, will come in among you after I leave, not sparing the flock. ³⁰Even some men from your own group will rise up and distort the truth in order to draw a following. ³¹Watch out! Remember the three years I was with

you—my constant watch and care over you night and day, and my many tears for you. [32]"And now I entrust you to God and the message of his grace that is able to build you up and give you an inheritance with all those he has set apart for himself. [33]"I have never coveted anyone's silver or gold or fine clothes. [34]You know that these hands of mine have worked to supply my own needs and even the needs of those who were with me. [35]And I have been a constant example of how you can help those in need by working hard. You should remember the words of the Lord Jesus: 'It is more blessed to give than to receive.' "

[36]When he had finished speaking, he knelt and prayed with them. [37]They all cried as they embraced and kissed him good-bye. [38]They were sad most of all because he had said that they would never see him again. Then they escorted him down to the ship.

20:15 Some manuscripts read *and having stayed at Trogyllium.* 20:22 Or *by my spirit,* or *by an inner compulsion;* Greek reads *by the spirit.* 20:26 Greek *I am innocent of the blood of all.* 20:28a Or *with the blood of his own [Son].* 20:28b Greek *overseers.*

NOTES

20:13 *went by land.* Since Luke does not tell us why, there has been much speculation (see Fernando's [1998:531] and Trebilco's [1994:360] lists).

20:16 Luke tells us why Paul avoided Ephesus. Commentators propose a specific character-ization of the delay Paul was avoiding: the time needed to help the church (Trebilco 1994:362) or the slow progress of a coasting vessel versus a fast-sailing one (Fitzmyer 1998a:672). They also offer additional, unrecorded reasons: the opposition Paul would continue to face at Ephesus (19:23–20:1; 1 Cor 15:32; Dunn 1996:269; Fernando 1998:531) and his carrying a large sum of money (Barrett 1998:960).

20:17-35 The speech's setting and content cause some to question its historicity (Watson 1991:185; Barrett 1998:960, 966, 972, 979). The seeming incongruence between motive (avoiding Ephesus to hurry to Jerusalem) and actions (stopping at Miletus and sending for the Ephesian elders—a 60-mile round trip) is not an indication that Luke gives us the right setting (Miletus) but the wrong audience (contra Watson 1991:185). Rather, Miletus serves as a sort of compromise between Paul's pastoral concerns for the Ephesus church and his purpose in quickly traveling to Jerusalem: while he could not spare the time he anticipated that a full visit to Ephesus would entail, he fulfilled the longing and calling of his pastoral heart by arranging a meeting with the Ephesian elders in Miletus. Desire to avoid opposi-tion at Ephesus was not as significant a motivator as Paul's other concerns (contra Johnson 1992:356).

20:17 *elders of the church.* The reference to "elders" (20:17) is not a Lukan anachronism but reflects Paul's practice (14:23), though admittedly the term occurs rarely in Paul's let-ters (1 Tim 5:17, 19; Titus 1:5). It is congruent with the early church's ecclesiastical organi-zation, which flowed from the Jewish communal leadership structure, the *gerousia* [[TG]1087, [ZG]1172] ("board of elders"; cf. Giles 1997a:221-222). Other supposedly late-first-century features such as the foreboding about coming difficulties (20:29-30), the clear differentia-tion between heresy and orthodoxy, and parallels in language to the Pastorals (20:24, 28; Dunn 1996:210-271; Barrett 1998:979), may all be found in Paul's letters which predate or follow within a decade after this incident (foreboding about false teachers—Phil 3:2; differ-entiation of heresy and orthodoxy—Gal 1:8-9). Many commentators judge the speech's vocabulary to be thoroughly Pauline (cf. Fernando 1998:532; see Johnson [1992:367] and Witherington [1998:615] for lists). Further signs of historical authenticity are its presence in a "we" passage and its ignorance of Paul's further movements in the East after release from his first imprisonment (Witherington 1998:615-616; contrast Acts 20:25 with the Pastoral Epistles).

20:18-32 As to genre, this section is a "departure address," analogous to farewell discourses throughout Scripture (Luke 22:15-38; Gen 47:29–49:33; Deut 31:14–33:29; Josh 23:1–24:30; 1 Sam 12:1-25; 2 Kgs 2:1-14; Matt 28:18-20; John 13–17; 2 Tim; 2 Pet). Farewell discourses review the departing leader's life as an example for imitation and an apologetic for his conduct. There are warnings concerning future dangers to the faith, exhortations to faithfulness, and God's benediction in an affectionate, sorrowful, prayerful farewell. Since it is not strictly a last will and testament, this speech should not be seen as epideictic, an encomium to honor Paul (contra Watson 1991:208) but rather as deliberative, persuasive speech urging the elders to fulfill their duties in the light of Paul's departure (Witherington 1998:614). Though many structures have been discerned (see Watson's [1991:187-188] overview), scholars generally see vv. 25 and 28 as the central hinge points of the speech (Kilgallen 1994:116; cf. Talbert 1997:186 and O'Toole 1994:345-347). Rhetorically, Witherington's (1998:612-614) simple structure most clearly captures the flow of thought: *narratio,* circumstances with a climactic statement of his departure (20:18-25); *probatio,* arguments that he has fulfilled his duties, and they must do so also (20:26-30); and *peroratio,* conclusion with an urging to imitate Paul (20:31-35).

20:22 *by the Spirit.* The NLT mg offers two other possibilities: "by my spirit" or "by an inner compulsion." As at 19:21, *tō pneumati* [TG4151, ZG4460] (by the spirit) is potentially ambiguous (Barrett 1998:969-970), though most recent scholars—given the clear reference to the Holy Spirit in v. 23 and elsewhere in Acts to describe divine guidance of Paul's missionary activity (13:2; 16:6-7; cf. 19:21)—take it as the NLT text does (Johnson 1992:361; Dunn 1996:272; Fitzmyer 1998a:677; Turner 1998:334).

20:28 *God's flock—his church, purchased with his own blood.* This renders a phrase for which the external evidence is singularly balanced between *tēn ekklēsian tou theou* (the church of God) in ℵ B 614 syr^(p, h) cop^(boMS) Athanasius, Chrysostom and *tēn ekklēsian tou kuriou* (the church of the Lord) in 𝔓74 A C* D E 33 1739 (Metzger 1994:425). Stylistically, "church of God" agrees with Paul's general usage and "church (assembly) of the Lord" with LXX usage. In context, "church of God" is the more difficult reading. It raises the question—does God have blood?—which then is alleviated by a reference to the Lord Jesus. The NLT has correctly opted for the more difficult reading.

purchased with his own blood. Many Byzantine witnesses (𝔐 L P slav) avoided the "blood of God" difficulty by conflating the previous phrase into "church of God and Christ," reading here *idiou haimatos* [TG2398/129, ZG2625/135] ("his own blood"; Metzger 1994:427). The better attested *haimatos tou idiou* ("the blood of his own"; 𝔓74 ℵ A B C D E 044 33) also solves the difficulty, when understood as a term of endearment referring to Jesus (cf. Rom 8:32; Metzger 1994:426; Bolt 1998:207). Fitzmyer (1998a:680) calls this solution a "last ditch effort" to save a textual problem. While some see the more difficult reading ("his own blood" in NLT) as evidence of sloppy writing (Luke, when combining thoughts with two different subjects, was not careful to change referents, so Barrett 1998:974), it actually may reflect a high Christology in which Luke considered the actions of God the Father and the Son as so closely related that he moved from one to the other without explicit transition (Fitzmyer 1998a:680; Dunn 1996:273).

While some commentators continue to see no soteriological significance to Christ's death presented here (Dunn 1996:273; Barrett 1998:974), a growing number are positive on its contribution to a Lukan salvific interpretation of the cross, when understood in the covenantal language of an elect people bought by the divine Son's blood (Green 1998:98; Bock 1998:60; Witherington 1998:623).

elders. Lit., "overseers." The NLT text and mg note follow the NT's general use of "elder" and "overseer" without distinction, even interchangeably, with "overseer" (*episkopos* [TG1985, ZG2176]) emphasizing function (see 20:17, 28; Titus 1:5, 7; 1 Pet 5:1-2 [the verb]).

20:35 *the words of the Lord Jesus.* Not found elsewhere in the NT but present in variant wording in *1 Clement* 2:1, this *agraphon* (that is, a saying of Jesus not recorded in any of the four Gospels), though a sentiment found in various contexts in the ancient world, cannot be tied in both form and content to any other example (Plutarch *Moralia* 173D; 778C; Thucydides *History* 2.97.4). Kilgallen (1993) has effectively answered Plümacher's (1992) case for Thucydides as the saying's source. Its sapient form, its content's congruence with Jesus' teaching in Luke, and the reverential manner of introduction all indicate that it originated with the one to whom it is attributed, Jesus (Witherington 1998:626; O'Toole 1994:334-340; Hemer 1989a:82-83; cf. Luke 6:38).

COMMENTARY

Returning to a travel summary, Luke follows the progress of Paul and his companions down the west coast of Asia Minor (20:13-16). The party departed Troas by ship ahead of Paul, who gave them orders to wait for him and take him on board at Assos (20:13). Paul traveled the twenty-mile distance over land. Assos, a port city with the only good harbor on the north shore of the Adramyttian Gulf, was a "notable city," especially as the birthplace of the Stoic philosopher Cleanthes, and it was the venue for three years of Aristotle's teaching career (Strabo *Geography* 13.1.57-58, 66).

After the rendezvous, Paul and his companions proceeded 44 miles south to Mitylene (20:14), a chief city on the island of Lesbos, some 60 miles south of Troy. Its position near old trade routes, between the Hellespont and ports south and east, made it an important seaport. Mitylene, a free city, was a favorite resort for Roman aristocrats. The next day they passed the island of Kios (20:15). Shaped like a drawn bow facing Asia Minor, it is twelve miles from ancient Smyrna and five miles from the mainland. The birthplace of Homer, it was struck with a violent earthquake in the time of Tiberius, who helped rebuild it.

The following day, they "crossed to the island of Samos." One of the most famous of the Ionian islands, Samos lies at the mouth of the Bay of Ephesus, separated from the mainland by the mile-wide straight of Mycale. Samos was renowned not only for its works of art but also for its chief manufacture: pottery of a fine, smooth clay, deep red in color. The next day they put in at Miletus. This prosperous and influential Ionian seaport was situated on the south promontory of a gulf into which the Maeander River once emptied (Pliny *Natural History* 5.112).

Such an island-hopping method of travel was necessitated by the meteorological and topographical demands on navigation, given first-century technology. On the Aegean, summer winds customarily blew only during daylight hours, so sailing vessels could make no headway at night. Further, the narrow channels along the west coast of Asia Minor were so dotted with small islands that night navigation was dangerous.

Paul's shorter route from Kios to Samos to Miletus, which avoided cutting in along the Asiatic coast to Ephesus, certainly reflected his desire to hurry to Jerusalem for Pentecost, again to live out his piety according to Jewish custom (20:16; see Deut 16:16; cf. Acts 20:6). But at Miletus, his pastor's heart overcame his personal schedule, so he summoned the elders from Ephesus, who were about thirty miles away. On the model of Jewish community organization, these members of a council of elders for the Christian community in Ephesus supervised the spiritual progress of the cluster of house churches there (cf. 14:23; 15:6).

In 20:18-25, the *narratio* of a farewell-deliberative speech, Paul laid out the facts of his past (20:18-21) and the immediate future, both for him (20:22-24) and the Ephesian church (20:25). Based on these realities, he would seek to persuade the elders to pursue what was beneficial and should be imitated from his life as they exercised their own spiritual leadership. He emphasized their firsthand experience of a consistently modeled life and message (20:18). The model life was "[doing] the Lord's work"—literally, "serving the Lord as a slave" (20:19). Such a perspective on his life's work placed Paul in the only position possible for an agent of "God on mission." Standing in the train of the prophetic servants of God and the Messiah— servant of God par excellence—Paul spoke only the message of the sovereign Lord Jesus (cf. Acts 13:47; Isa 49:5-6). Such allegiance, especially when understood as embodying and entailing an imitation of his master, explains the character of Paul's model life. As he did the Lord's work "humbly," Paul exercised his spiritual author- ity as a servant-leader in stark contrast to cultural expectations (Luke 22:25-27; Eph 4:2; Epictetus *Discourses* 3.24.56; Plutarch *Moralia* 475E). In very practical socio- economic humility, Paul did not insist on his right, even in the gospel, to make his living from his teaching but avoided even the suggestion of materialistic covetous- ness by working with his own hands to supply his needs (20:33-34; cf. Acts 19:12; 1 Cor 9:12; Eph 4:28). Not unlike his Lord, the suffering servant (Luke 19:41-44; Isa 53:3-4), Paul showed intense empathy in his relationships, as with tears he bore witness to the gospel (which became an offense to his fellow Jews, 19:9) and cor- rected, even admonished and warned, the new converts of the dangers of continu- ing in a syncretistic understanding of the faith which accommodated magic (the situation assumed by 19:18-19). In the face of trials and plots from the Jews, he endured (Acts 9:24; 20:3; cf. Luke 22:28).

Paul, who lived this model life, was the bearer of a model message, characterized by comprehensiveness in its presentation and in its required response (20:20-21). Unlike false teachers, especially the intellectual forebears of the gnostics, Paul had not divided his audience and worked only with the *pneumatikoi* [TG4152/A, ZG4461] ("the spiritually enlightened ones"), but he taught "Jews and Greeks alike." Paul had not taught one thing in public and an esoteric teaching in private. No, in both venues and with a method of teaching in considerable detail, Paul did not shrink from telling them what they "needed to hear" (lit., "what was beneficial"). No future false teachings could justly claim that they had an essential supplement to Paul's teaching (cf. 20:27, 29-30).

Not unlike Romans 10:9-10, Paul's articulation of the desired response to the gospel here entails a complete change of allegiance—"repenting from sin and turn- ing to God"—and a new object of trust—"faith in our Lord Jesus," the only source of salvation (16:31; 19:4-5; Eph 1:15; 2:8; 3:17; 4:13). With surrender and trust, the journey on the path of grace into and in the Kingdom must be begun, continued, and completed (20:24-25).

Turning to his and their futures, Paul pointed to three divine dynamics at work in his progress to Jerusalem. Like Jesus on his last journey to Jerusalem, it was divine compulsion that drove him there (20:22; cf. Luke 9:51; 13:31-33). He went to Jerusalem, literally "bound by the Spirit," which was not so much an irresistible drawing as a Spirit-impelled driving. There may be a play on words, for the same verb is used for the divine necessity that compelled Paul and the "binding" of being handcuffed and incarcerated (deō [TG1210, ZG1313]; 21:11, 13, 33; 22:29; 23:11; 24:27; 27:24).

With divine enlightenment intended to test and strengthen his resolve, God the Holy Spirit, whether through a prophet or direct revelation, "in city after city," mercifully prepared his servant with news that "jail and suffering lie ahead" (20:23). Though Paul knew that trials, especially born of persecution, were the Christian's lot, and his in particular (9:16; 11:19; 14:22), God matched the divine inner compulsion with these warnings from the Holy Spirit in a mutually confirmatory way. Doing God's will may well involve suffering.

Paul assessed the relative value of his "life" in terms of physical self-preservation versus an investment in pursuing the Lord's transcendent purposes for him and, with determination, chose the latter. For Paul, "finishing the work assigned me by the Lord Jesus" entailed both finishing a race (cf. 2 Tim 4:17) and completing a task, thereby testifying to the gospel of the grace of God (Eph 2:5, 7-8; 3:2).

Paul concluded his *narratio* by speaking of their "Paul-less" future (20:25) and in the process again capsulized his entire ministry among them. It was, by its very nature, itinerant; hence, a final departure was not totally out of character. God's mission advanced as Paul moved on, heralding with decisive urgency the presence of God's reign and calling all to participate in it (28:31). For the Jew, this was the Good News of the messianic kingdom's salvation blessings (19:8); for the Gentile, a preaching of the only true saving power (19:13).

With a narrative of the past and immediate future clearly in mind, Paul then entered the *probatio*, or argumentation, phase of his speech in which he sought to persuade the elders of what was useful and should be imitated (20:26-30). Paul first asserted that he had fulfilled his responsibilities to them (20:26-27). Like the watchman of Ezekiel 33:9, Paul had no blood on his hands with regard to anyone's eternal destiny (see NLT mg on 20:26). He did not shrink back from "declaring all that God wants you to know"—literally, "announcing in detail the whole will of God." This divine plan involved not only salvation's accomplishment (cf. 2:23; 4:28; Eph 1:11) but also its application (Luke 24:46-47). When embraced with repentance and belief, it removed the "damnation" to which all humans are destined from birth (2:40; cf. 17:27. 30-31).

With Paul's example for imitation before their eyes, the elders now heard of their responsibilities (20:28) and the circumstances in which they must be fulfilled (20:29-30). They were to exercise pastoral leadership by guarding the flock. Paul further specified his charge with a call to "shepherd" the flock (*poimainō* [TG4165, ZG4477], NLT, "feed and shepherd"; cf. 1 Pet 5:2; John 21:16). The longstanding biblical image of leader and God's people as shepherd and flock suggests a spiritual caring for, feeding, guiding, and protecting (1 Chr 17:6; Pss 78:52, 71-72; Isa 40:11). As Paul fills out the command, he reminded the elders that it must be, indeed, a spiritual and a conscientious leadership. It was "the Holy Spirit" who had "appointed" them as "elders" ("overseers"; 13:2-4; 1 Cor 12:7-11; 1 Tim 4:14). They must undertake their work with a serious conscientiousness, matching the church's infinite worth as God's special covenant possession, purchased with "his own blood"—Jesus (see note on 20:28).

Paul's charge was all the more urgent because of future dangers. From without "false teachers" (Luke 21:8) and possibly also persecutors (21:12-18) would come in, spiritually ravaging the flock like "vicious wolves" (cf. Didache 16.3; Ignatius To the Philadelphians 2:1-2). From within, even from this leadership, heresy leading to schism would be the order of the day. (There are reports of its occurrence at Ephesus in 1 Tim 4:1-3; 2 Tim 1:15; and Rev 2:1-7.)

In reverse parallelism, Paul begins his peroratio—a concluding review and emotional appeal (20:31-35)—with a more specific charge to the elders: "Watch out!" In light of the predators, from without and within (cf. 1 Cor 16:13; 1 Pet 5:8), they were, like Paul, to engage in constant and heartfelt "watch and care" over the flock—exercising a correcting, admonishing, or warning influence to set believers' minds in order so as to believe and act as Christians (Rom 15:14; Eph 6:4; Col 1:28; 3:16; 1 Thess 5:12, 14).

Because his relationship with the Ephesians was at an end, both physically and spiritually, the only and, indeed, the best thing Paul could do about their future was offer a blessing in the form of a committal (20:32). He entrusted the elders to God and his message of grace. As such, the flock would experience spiritual growth (9:31). More important than the leaders' commitment to their charge was God's commitment to fulfilling his mission, for through it he actively works that grace in both leaders and laypeople which assures fruitful perseverance to the end.

With a concluding example for imitation and a word of the Lord, Paul climaxed his farewell with the attitude and conduct that should characterize all spiritual ministry in God's mission—grace and giving (20:33-35). This attitude requires a person to say "no" to covetousness, as Paul had not desired "anyone's silver or gold or fine clothes" (precious metals and clothing were standard forms of wealth in ancient times; see Matt 6:19; Jas 5:2). Such conduct negates the reciprocity principle of friendship, as Paul did not insist on his and his companions' rights to remuneration for teaching but rather worked with his hands to pay his own way for them and himself. This attitude would open the way to positive ministry that the elders must pursue: helping the poor by working hard and having Christ's attitude, "It is more blessed to give than to receive." This lifestyle of labor aims to have what is sufficient, not only for self-support, but also to help the poor, literally "the weak" (Eph 4:28). In Luke and Acts, "the weak" are normally the chronically, physically ill who come to Jesus or the apostles for healing—hence, they are those who are incapable of self-support through work (Luke 4:40; 9:2; Acts 9:37; 19:12). Throughout the speech, this attitude of grace, captured in Christ's saying, characterizes the disposition and the actions of the Father (20:24, 32) and the Son (20:28).

Paul then sealed his farewell with prayer. Falling on his knees, he acted out his total submission to the Lord (cf. Eph 3:14). The elders in their affectionate devotion to Paul, joined him in much weeping—weeping like the sound of mourning (Luke 7:13; 8:52; 23:28). Their embraces are literally described in the idiom "they fell on his neck"; they also repeatedly kissed Paul (Gen 33:4; 45:15). In ancient culture, a parting kiss on the cheek, forehead, shoulder, or hand was a sign of grateful respect and love (Luke 15:20; cf. Gen 50:1; 1 Kgs 19:20). The emotion of parting was especially heightened by the anguish of knowing they would not see Paul again. So they accompanied him to the ship, possibly also supplying provisions for the journey.

Paul's address to the Ephesian elders at Miletus (his one speech in Acts to a Christian audience) teaches us that God intends his mission to continue in the next spiritual generation through Spirit-appointed elders. They, in a self-giving way, should nurture the flock with God's word of grace and guard the church against divisive false teaching. They should always follow the example of the humble, compassionate, and brave service of those in the foundational generation, who faithfully lived and preached the whole counsel of God.

◆   E. Paul's Journey to Jerusalem (21:1-14)

After saying farewell to the Ephesian elders, we sailed straight to the island of Cos. The next day we reached Rhodes and then went to Patara. ²There we boarded a ship sailing for Phoenicia. ³We sighted the island of Cyprus, passed it on our left, and landed at the harbor of Tyre, in Syria, where the ship was to unload its cargo.

⁴We went ashore, found the local believers,* and stayed with them a week. These believers prophesied through the Holy Spirit that Paul should not go on to Jerusalem. ⁵When we returned to the ship at the end of the week, the entire congregation, including women* and children, left the city and came down to the shore with us. There we knelt, prayed, ⁶and said our farewells. Then we went aboard, and they returned home.

⁷The next stop after leaving Tyre was Ptolemais, where we greeted the brothers and sisters* and stayed for one day. ⁸The next day we went on to Caesarea and stayed at the home of Philip the Evangelist, one of the seven men who had been chosen to distribute food. ⁹He had four unmarried daughters who had the gift of prophecy.

¹⁰Several days later a man named Agabus, who also had the gift of prophecy, arrived from Judea. ¹¹He came over, took Paul's belt, and bound his own feet and hands with it. Then he said, "The Holy Spirit declares, 'So shall the owner of this belt be bound by the Jewish leaders in Jerusalem and turned over to the Gentiles.' " ¹²When we heard this, we and the local believers all begged Paul not to go on to Jerusalem.

¹³But he said, "Why all this weeping? You are breaking my heart! I am ready not only to be jailed at Jerusalem but even to die for the sake of the Lord Jesus." ¹⁴When it was clear that we couldn't persuade him, we gave up and said, "The Lord's will be done."

21:4 Greek *disciples;* also in 21:16.   21:5 Or *wives.*   21:7 Greek *brothers;* also in 21:17.

NOTES

21:2 *we boarded a ship sailing for Phoenicia.* Paul changed ships, not necessarily to avoid a plot or because the ship from Miletus only traveled the Aegean, but because he needed to exchange the smaller, relatively slower coastal vessel for a larger ship, which could handle the four-hundred-mile trans-Mediterranean route to Phoenicia (Lake and Cadbury 1979:265; Barrett 1998:988). Phoenicia was a Mediterranean coastal strip between Mount Carmel in the south and the Eleutherus River in the north of the province of Syria.

21:4 *prophesied through the Holy Spirit.* This is the NLT rendering of *elegon dia tou pneumatos* [TG4151, ZG4460] (were saying through the Spirit). The range of meaning of *dia* [TG1223, ZG1328] with the genitive, which extends all the way from efficient cause through modal, accompanying circumstance, to occasion and ultimate cause, permits us to see Luke's description as neither contradictory to 20:23 and 21:11, nor inadequate in expressing the process (Barrett 1998:990). Rather, this phrase combines the church's somewhat misguided, though understandable response to the Spirit's revelation (words urging Paul not to go up to Jerusalem) with its prophetic basis—the Spirit's revelation itself.

21:7-8 *next stop after leaving Tyre . . . The next day we went on to.* In v. 7 the NLT does not translate the circumstantial participial phrase *ton ploun dianusantes* [TG1274, ZG1382], which may mean "continuing or having completed the voyage" (Fitzmyer 1998a:685, 688). If it means the latter, then Paul went overland from Ptolemais to Caesarea (Witherington 1998:632). The attendant circumstance participle *exelthontes* [TG1831, ZG2002] (having gone out [of the city]) in v. 8 refers to a destination of harbor or ship or road, depending on the means of transport inferred from v. 7 (Barrett 1998:992). If the time marker *tē epaurion* [TG1887, ZG2069] (the next day) describes not only the beginning but the end of the journey to Caesarea (40 miles by land, 32 by sea), then the journey was probably by ship (Keener 1993:385).

21:9 *unmarried daughters.* Though in Hellenistic religion prophetesses were often virgins (Plutarch *Moralia* 405C; Pausanias *Description of Greece* 10.12.6), few see *parthenos* [TG3933, ZG4221] (young woman, unmarried, a virgin) as linked to their gift of prophecy here (Johnson 1992:369; Witherington 1998:632). It pertains more to age here (probably under 16) than to marital status (Keener 1993:385).

21:9-10 *gift of prophecy.* Most commentators would agree that Luke's focus in this phrase is on function as opposed to office (Johnson 1992:369), although some do hold that Luke is unclear, particularly about Agabus (Barrett 1998:995) or that he prevents us from making too rigid a distinction between function and office.

There continues to be uncertainty about the precise nature of New Testament prophecy: Was it inspired preaching or possibly ecstatic utterance (2:14; 19:6; Fitzmyer 1998a:689)? Or was it possibly prophetic prediction (19:6; 11:28; Kee 1997:246)? Witherington (1998:632) provides a comprehensive definition which combines "inspired preaching" (proclamation) and Spirit-illumined discernment into OT prophetic fulfillment with occasional new predictive prophecy. As Ellis (1970:67) phrases it, the NT prophet "is the Lord's instrument . . . who makes known (*gnōstos* [TG1110, ZG1196]) the meaning of Scripture, exhorts and strengthens the congregation, and instructs the community by revelations of the future."

21:11 *bound.* Some simply note the difference between the prophetic prediction (Paul bound by the Jews and handed over to the Gentiles) and its fulfillment (Paul bound by the Gentile Romans, after having been wrested from the Jews' clutches; 21:11, 30-33; Spencer 1997:201; Talbert 1997:191). Others attribute it either to Luke's lack of notice or care for neat formal correspondence (Barrett 1998:995) or his anti-Jewish bias (Dunn 1996:282-283) or a desire to formulate the prediction of Paul's sufferings in phrasing reminiscent of Jesus' passion predictions (Barrett 1998:995). Still others account for the differences by pointing to the large measure of poetic license in OT prophecy (Keener 1993:386) or to the qualitative difference between OT prophecy's divinely authoritative literal transcript of a direct word from the Lord and NT prophecy's less authoritative general content, which must be sifted (1 Cor 14:29-32; Witherington 1998:631, following Grudem 1982:29-30).

None of these explanations are necessary, for there is no final contradiction. Though Luke tells us that the Romans bound Paul (21:33), he is silent about any "binding" by the Jews when they arrested him. The verb *paradidōmi* [TG3860, ZG4140] (handed over) is a difficulty only if it is understood as involving only a voluntary "handing over." The Jews did hand Paul over, though unwillingly. It should be remembered, further, that the Jews consistently pursued Paul with accusations before the Gentiles during his Palestinian detention (Barrett 1998:995).

C O M M E N T A R Y

"After saying farewell to the Ephesian elders"—a separation he was loath to make—in God's providence, with the aid of a northeast wind, Paul was able to expeditiously finish the Aegean/Asia Minor leg of his journey by sailing on successive days "straight to the island of Cos" and then on to the island of Rhodes, probably stopping at the ports of the same name (Pliny the Elder *Natural History* 5.132-134). Finally, the party made it to Patara, a major port of Lycia and a favorite haven for large vessels traveling from the eastern Mediterranean to the Aegean (Herodotus 1.182.2).

Paul and his party changed ships, choosing a larger vessel for the four-hundred-mile trans-Mediterranean voyage to the Syrian province of Phoenicia (see note on 21:2). Two-thirds of the way into their journey, Cyprus, the site of Paul's first missionary campaign in Acts (13:4-12), came into view. Luke says they passed it and left it behind on their left (port side). After a journey of five days (so Chrysostom *Homilies* 43.1; evidently with a favorable wind, it was three days from Rhodes to Tyre; Xenophon of Ephesus 1.14.6), they put in at the "harbor of Tyre, in Syria" (21:3). Tyre was a city built on an island with its port on the south side. An earthen mole constructed by Alexander the Great connected the city to the mainland, and subsequent action of the harbor waters had left a sand beach.

During a week's layover to unload and load cargo, Paul and his party searched out and stayed with the local believers (21:4). This church was probably founded by Hellenistic Jewish Christians who had been scattered in the aftermath of Stephen's martyrdom (11:19; cf. the positive disposition of Tyrians to Jesus' ministry, Luke 6:17; 10:13-14). Paul may have previously visited it twice (12:25; 15:3).

The disciples in Tyre, inspired by the Holy Spirit, warned of his coming suffering (20:22-23), and the believers drew the conclusion that Paul should not go up to Jerusalem (see note on 21:4). Luke did not tell us Paul's response to this repeated warning and doubtless heartfelt pleading. He and his party's actions speak for themselves: "We returned to the ship at the end of the week" (21:5). The fellow believers subordinated their own desires to Paul's sense of divine calling and inner guidance, entrusting him to the will of God. Again, their actions tell us as much, for they prayed for the missionary. In united affection, "the entire congregation, including wives and children" escorted Paul and his companions to the shore and the ship. In intense, solemn, sincere prayer they knelt, calling on God for Paul's continued protection (21:5).

The party made a voyage of twenty-seven miles to Ptolemais (21:7), situated on a small promontory on the north side of a broad bay opposite the modern city of Haifa. Ptolemais, the site of ancient Acco (Judg 1:31) and modern Acre, was a prosperous metropolis and Roman colony with the best anchorage on that part of the central Syrian coast. Here, during a one-day stopover, Paul and his party greeted the believers in a church probably planted at the same time as Tyre's (11:19).

Sailing from Ptolemais to Caesarea, Paul found himself in the Roman provincial capital of Judea with its magnificent harbor. This was a city built by Herod the Great to serve as the port for Jerusalem, which Paul had passed through twice before (9:30; 18:22). This was the site of that benchmark event—the gospel coming to God-fearing Gentiles through Peter (10:1–11:18). Luke marked the continuity with the church's earliest days by noting that Paul stayed with "Philip the Evangelist, one of the seven" (21:8; cf. 8:40). This description not only distinguishes Philip from the apostle of the same name but points to the Spirit's presence in his life and ministry (6:3, 5; 8:6, 13). Interestingly, this is one of the three occurrences in the New Testament of the title "evangelist" (Eph 4:11; 2 Tim 4:5). Though it points to the core function of proclaiming the gospel to the unconverted (cf. Rom 10:15), it may apply to any minister of the gospel, for pastors like Timothy were to do the work of an evangelist (2 Tim 4:2, 5). That Philip's young daughters (see note on 21:9) had "the gift of prophecy" is the most explicit indication of the Spirit's presence. It shows that at Caesarea, in fulfillment of Joel 2:28, without regard to gender, God continued to pour out his Spirit, even to succeeding spiritual generations in this post-Resurrection time period called "the last days" (cf. 2:17).

The Holy Spirit had guided Paul in implementing God's mission, not only by initial positive guidance (13:2, 4), and negative, corrective intervention (16:6, 7), but most recently by an inner compulsion to minister in Jerusalem and Rome (19:21; 20:22). The latter had been matched by the Spirit's warnings of the suffering that lay ahead in Jerusalem (20:23; 21:4). What Luke gave us previously as Paul's report (20:23) or by third person narration (21:4), we now meet in a direct and climactic iteration. Agabus the prophet arrived from Judea (cf. 11:27-28) and, in an acted parable, gave Paul a final opportunity to renew his resolve to go to Jerusalem (21:10-11). The action and word together graphically communicated that God's prophetic word would indeed come to fulfillment (Isa 55:11; cf. 1 Kgs 11:29-40; Jer 13:1-11). Agabus took Paul's "belt," which was probably a long strip of cloth which he would wrap around himself several times, thus creating "pockets" in which he could carry money (cf. Matt 10:9). Agabus bound his own feet and hands with it and said, "The Holy Spirit declares, 'So shall the owner of this belt be bound by the Jewish leaders in Jerusalem and turned over to the Gentiles'" (21:11).

Though neither of these actions is recorded, both are assumed in what Luke tells us of the Jews' treatment and the Romans' handling of Paul (21:30-33; 24:1-9; cf. 28:17; see note on 21:11). The prophecy's wording, especially "turned over to the Gentiles" (21:11), parallels Jesus' predictions of his own suffering (Luke 9:44; 18:32; 24:7). Though throughout the whole account the theologically significant parallelism does extend to Paul's innocence (24:12-13; 25:10-11, 18; 26:31-32), what seems to be most sharply in focus here is the deep irony of the rejection by both Jew and Gentile of the bearer of God's Good News to both groups (9:15-16). Though Jewish opposition had perpetrated much against Paul, this would be the first time they would successfully hand him over to the Gentiles (contrast 18:12). The audience of Paul's mission, which had been so problematic for the Jews, was now, humanly speaking, to have total control of his destiny and, as the Jews hoped, be the agents of his demise.

Paul's fellow believers, including the traveling companions, reacted with tender affection and "begged" Paul "not to go on to Jerusalem" (21:12). They wanted to preserve the beloved apostle from physical harm, possibly death, and so keep him for themselves and the church. Paul responded with unwavering resolve as he told them the will of God in this matter. He wrestled with the impact of emotions on his resolve, asking, literally, "Why are you doing this—engaging in mournful weeping and pulverizing my heart?" (21:13; cf. Luke 23:38). He reached back to the calling that motivated his whole life: "for the sake of [the name of] the Lord Jesus" (21:13). The one under whom he served (20:19, 24) and in whose name he preached, healed, and baptized (9:27-28; 16:18; 18:15; 19:5) was the one for whose name he was willing to suffer—even die (cf. 5:41). Aside from his Lord's general prediction (Luke 21:12), had not Paul's own initial call included that as part of the program (9:16)? So the Spirit's inner prompting and his outer warning did not contradict, but they were mutually reinforcing opportunities for Paul to reaffirm his readiness to face whatever suffering lay ahead, even death in Jerusalem, like the prophets and Jesus before him (Luke 13:33-34). Paul would go through his own "Gethsemane" and thereby fulfill the will of the Lord.

◆   F. Paul Arrives at Jerusalem (21:15-25)

¹⁵After this we packed our things and left for Jerusalem. ¹⁶Some believers from Caesarea accompanied us, and they took us to the home of Mnason, a man originally from Cyprus and one of the early believers. ¹⁷When we arrived, the brothers and sisters in Jerusalem welcomed us warmly.

¹⁸The next day Paul went with us to meet with James, and all the elders of the Jerusalem church were present. ¹⁹After greeting them, Paul gave a detailed account of the things God had accomplished among the Gentiles through his ministry.

²⁰After hearing this, they praised God. And then they said, "You know, dear brother, how many thousands of Jews have also believed, and they all follow the law of Moses very seriously. ²¹But the Jewish believers here in Jerusalem have been told that you are teaching all the Jews who live among the Gentiles to turn their backs on the laws of Moses. They've heard that you teach them not to circumcise their children or follow other Jewish customs. ²²What should we do? They will certainly hear that you have come.

²³"Here's what we want you to do. We have four men here who have completed their vow. ²⁴Go with them to the Temple and join them in the purification ceremony, paying for them to have their heads ritually shaved. Then everyone will know that the rumors are all false and that you yourself observe the Jewish laws.

²⁵"As for the Gentile believers, they should do what we already told them in a letter: They should abstain from eating food offered to idols, from consuming blood or the meat of strangled animals, and from sexual immorality."

NOTES

21:15-25 Paul's own forebodings (Rom 15:30-31), the silence about the collection and about any aid from the Jerusalem leadership after his arrest, the possible communication of the Jerusalem council decree to him for the first time (21:25), and his agreement to do a law-observant action (21:24, 26-27)—all indicate for some that Luke's portrayal of peaceful relations between Paul and the Jerusalem leadership and his submissive Jewish orthopraxy are historically inaccurate (e.g., Johnson 1992:378; Barrett 1998:1000-1001; Fitzmyer 1998a:146, 692). They suggest that what really happened was the leadership's persuasion of Paul against his better judgment. At odds with Paul's unconditional acceptance of the Gentiles, they probably had ulterior motives: at best, discrediting Paul before Gentile Christians or, at worst, ensnaring him in a situation which they knew would provoke a riot (Barrett 1998:1000-1001).

Bauckham (1995:475-480), while granting that there may well have been tension between Paul and the Jerusalem church, sees Luke's presentation as historically plausible, particularly the stance of the Jerusalem leadership and Paul's action. Luke's silence on the collection was because it did not succeed as a unifying action (Witherington 1998:647). His silence on further aid after the arrest again was because of its probable lack of effectiveness (Bauckham 1995:478). The reiteration of the decree is to remind Luke's readers, not to inform Paul (Johnson 1992:376). Paul's "law-observant" actions were guided by his principles of cultural flexibility and avoiding offense (Rom 14:13; 1 Cor 9:19-29; Dunn 1996:284; Tomes 1995:197).

21:16 *they took us to the home of Mnason.* Given the distance between Caesarea and Jerusalem (67 miles), the Western text inserts a rest stop between Caesarea and Jerusalem: "at a certain village." "The distance between the two cities . . . cannot be traveled in a day. Thus, the reviser has Paul go from Caesarea to a certain village, where he stays with Mnason, and then on to Jerusalem the next day. That this is pure conjecture is indicated by the fact that the village is left unnamed" (Comfort 2007:[Acts 21:15]). If *episkeuasamenoi* [ᵀᴳ1980.1, ᶻᴳ2171] (21:15; "packed our things," NLT) is understood as "saddled horses" (Xenophon *Hellenica* 5.3), then a one-day journey is possible.

21:24 There are at least three options for understanding the status of the ceremonial law in Luke's thinking. Jacob Jervell claims that Luke had a conservative outlook: "By insisting on Jewish Christian universal adherence to the law he succeeds in showing that they are the restored and true Israel entitled to God's promises and to salvation" (1972a:147). Stephen G. Wilson (1983:102) argues against Jervell and ends at a mediating position. He says that living according to the law has no bearing on achieving salvation for Jew or Gentile, but Luke views it in a wholly positive light as a means of expressing piety. Blomberg goes further and says that, in addition to not speaking to the issue of law-keeping, this passage shows that Luke does not approve of Paul's actions, since the entire plan backfires (1998: 413). When Luke's work is viewed as a whole, Wilson has the most accurate understanding of Luke's approach.

21:24, 26 *join them in the purification ceremony . . . purification ritual.* Paul, having contracted ritual uncleanness from his time abroad in Gentile lands (*m. Ohalot* 2:3; 17:5; 18:6), had to make himself ritually pure through a seven-day ceremony (Num 19:12) so that he would be in a position to accompany the four and pay the expenses for the sacrifices by which they would complete their Nazirite vow (Num 6:13-20; *m. Nazir* 6:7). Though potentially confusing (cf. Johnson 1992:376; Barrett 1998:1018; Fitzmyer 1998a:694), the use of the same purification terminology (*hagnizō* [TG48, ZG49] and *hagnismos* [TG49, ZG50]) for these two different rites (here telescoped together) has precedent in LXX usage (Num 6:3, 5; 19:12; Witherington [1998:649] concurs). The four men's "purification," then, was not for defilement contracted during the vow (contra Barrett 1998:1015 and what NLT could imply) but for their completing of the vow.

COMMENTARY

Paul's meeting with the Jerusalem church leaders reveals that those who prosecute God's mission cross-culturally must both embrace a respect for individual cultures and prize the super-cultural unity born of the believer's radical new identity in Christ, no matter one's culture. For those like the "law-serious" Jewish Christians, who continued to view God's mission through myopic, monocultural lenses (21:20-21), such commitments would be a source of offense, suspicion, and misunderstanding.

In this travel summary (21:15-16), Paul made his way quickly in a sixty-mile journey overland to Jerusalem. Led by believers from Caesarea and, of course, with his mixed delegation of Jewish and Gentile Christians in tow, Paul found ideal accommodations in "the home of Mnason" (21:16). Mnason (an authentic Greek name, but possibly a Hellenized variant of "Manasseh") was a Cypriot and "one of the early believers" (21:16); he was a Hellenistic Jewish Christian. How far back he goes with the church is unclear. He might have been part of the original 120, part of the converted Pentecost throng, or someone converted by Barnabas or the evange-listic Hellenistic Jewish Christians (1:15; 2:5; 4:36; 6:8-10).

The final concrete episode of this journey presents us with Paul's mixed reception in Jerusalem. Generally, he was received positively. Luke summarizes, "When we arrived, the brothers and sisters in Jerusalem welcomed us warmly" (21:17). The next day there was a respectful reception by James, the half brother of Jesus and the church's chief elder (cf. 15:6, 13, 23). "After greeting them" (more precisely, after Paul greeted James, *aspasamenos* [TG782, ZG832]), Paul entered into a "detailed account of the things God had accomplished among the Gentiles through his ministry" (21:19; cf. 15:12, 14; 14:27; 20:24). The result was that all praised God for the salva-tion of the Gentiles (21:20; cf. 11:18; 13:48).

But not all in the Jerusalem church would be pleased with Paul's arrival or his ministry among the Gentiles. The elders, charged with the unity and edification of the church, immediately pointed out to Paul that a large segment of the Jerusalem church was Jewish and took "the law of Moses very seriously" (lit., "are zealots for the law"; 21:20). Possibly the converted Pharisees of 15:5, these Jewish Christians lived out their loyalty to God by combining ardent nationalism with strict obser-vance of the whole Mosaic code. Phinehas, Elijah, and the Maccabees were their worthy predecessors (Num 25:10-13; 1 Kgs 19:10, 14; Josephus *Antiquities* 12.271). Consequently, they were very susceptible to reports circulating in Jerusalem that Paul's proclamation of a "law-free gospel" in the Diaspora meant that he was in-structing Jews to "Gentilize"—that is, "turn their backs on the laws of Moses" (*apostasian* [TG646, ZG686] . . .*apo Mōuseōs* [TG575/3475, ZG608/3707], "apostasy from Moses"). Specifically, the rumor said Paul was telling parents to ignore the main

Jewish identity marker, circumcision, and the lifestyle according to "Jewish customs" (21:21). For Paul, since neither the circumcised condition or uncircumcised condition had any spiritual significance, it is highly unlikely that he would have taught Jews this "apostasy from the law"; it would have been like teaching Gentiles to take on the yoke of the law, something he opposed (see Rom 2:25-30; 1 Cor 7:18-19; Gal 5:6; 6:15). In fact, his circumcision of Timothy (16:3) and his respect for the weaker brother's conscience in matters of Jewish custom (Rom 14:1-15:7) demonstrate that he proclaimed his "law-free" gospel with a flexibility which aimed to violate no one's cultural identity. His "law-free" gospel, then, did not mean that Paul instructed persons in a "custom-free" life.

The elders' concern about the impact of Paul's arrival (21:22) and the remedy they prescribed (21:23-24) point to a probable fracturing of the church: (1) the leaders (some Hebrew-speaking Jewish Christians and Hellenistic Jewish Christians) siding with Paul, and (2) that larger segment, Pharisaic Hebrew-speaking Christians, siding against him.

Four pious but poor men in the congregation had taken on themselves a Nazirite vow of limited duration (Num 6). By abstaining from products of the vine, not cutting their hair, and avoiding ritual impurity, they had been showing thankfulness for past blessings, earnestness in petition, or strong devotion to God. The multi-animal sacrifice and cleansing ceremony at the end of the vow period, when the hair was cut and offered to God, was financially prohibitive. Paul was told to bear the expenses of the four. This was a commonly recognized act of piety (Josephus *Antiquities* 19.294). To do so, he had to go through a seven-day ritual of cleansing himself, because he had recently returned from Gentile lands (*m. Ohalot* 2:3; 17:5; 18:6; Num 19:12). The intended result was that the rumors about Paul would be shown to be baseless, and he would be seen to "observe the Jewish laws" (21:24). Lest Paul's action be misunderstood in another direction—as making Jewish custom normative for Gentile Christians—the elders hastened to add that the Jerusalem council decree was still in place: the Gentiles with Paul had no need to take up Jewish customs but should uphold a few basic standards to avoid offending their Jewish brothers (see commentary and notes on 15:20, 29).

♦   ## G. Paul Is Arrested (21:26-36)

²⁶So Paul went to the Temple the next day with the other men. They had already started the purification ritual, so he publicly announced the date when their vows would end and sacrifices would be offered for each of them.

²⁷The seven days were almost ended when some Jews from the province of Asia saw Paul in the Temple and roused a mob against him. They grabbed him, ²⁸yelling, "Men of Israel, help us! This is the man who preaches against our people everywhere and tells everybody to disobey the Jewish laws. He speaks against the Temple—and even defiles this holy place by bringing in Gentiles.*" ²⁹(For earlier that day they had seen him in the city with Trophimus, a Gentile from Ephesus,* and they assumed Paul had taken him into the Temple.)

³⁰The whole city was rocked by these accusations, and a great riot followed. Paul was grabbed and dragged out of the Temple, and immediately the gates were closed behind him. ³¹As they were trying to kill him, word reached the commander of the Roman regiment that all Jerusalem was in an uproar. ³²He immediately called out his soldiers and officers* and ran down among the crowd. When the mob saw the commander and the troops coming, they stopped beating Paul.

³³Then the commander arrested him and ordered him bound with two chains. He asked the crowd who he was and what he had done. ³⁴Some shouted one thing and some another. Since he couldn't find out the truth in all the uproar and confusion, he ordered that Paul be taken to the fortress. ³⁵As Paul reached the stairs, the mob grew so violent the soldiers had to lift him to their shoulders to protect him. ³⁶And the crowd followed behind, shouting, "Kill him, kill him!"

21:28 Greek *Greeks.* 21:29 Greek *Trophimus, the Ephesian.* 21:32 Greek *centurions.*

NOTES

21:26 *the next day.* The NLT correctly indicates the time sequence. Paul's purification preceded the men's completion of their vow (Witherington 1998:652; contra Marshall 1980:347). See note on 21:24, 26.

21:27 *seven days.* This was the period of Paul's purification (Num 19:12; Witherington 1998:652), not that of the men who had contracted uncleanness during the vow (Num 6:9; so Barrett 1998:1018).

21:30-31 *The whole city was rocked by these accusations, and a great riot followed.* This is not hyperbole (contra Fitzmyer 1998b:698-699), for Josephus consistently attests to "the volatility of the great crowds at the pilgrimage feasts, where a perceived slight against the ancestral customs could quickly generate a riot" (*War* 1.88-89; 2.223-227, 449-456).

21:31 *Roman regiment.* The *speirēs* [ᵀᴳ4686, ᶻᴳ5061] ("cohort," or "battalion") stationed at Jerusalem during festival times was at its full strength of 1,000 troops (760 infantry, 240 cavalry; Lake and Cadbury 1979:275) or possibly 600 troops total (Keener 1993:388; Josephus *Antiquities* 2.224).

21:32 *soldiers and officers.* The fact that the officers were *hekatontarchas* [ᵀᴳ1543, ᶻᴳ1672] (centurions), commanding 60–100 men each, does not necessarily mean that at least 160 men accompanied them (Barrett 1998:1022).

21:34 *he ordered that Paul be taken to the fortress.* Lit., Paul was ordered taken into "the barracks," which was located in the Antonia fortress.

21:36 *the crowd.* Lit., "the congregation of the people" (*plēthos tou laou* [ᵀᴳ4128/2992, ᶻᴳ4436/3295]), a technical term for the people of God, which is significant theologically for Luke (3:23; 4:10; 6:2; 10:42; 13:17; 15:14, 30). Here this term heightens the rejection of the gospel messenger by the Jews, the OT people of God.

COMMENTARY

What triggered the Jerusalem Jews' assault on Paul was his presence in the Temple. Following the directive of James and the elders (21:23-24), Paul began his own ritual purification and declared to the Temple authorities the date that the Nazirite vows would be completed through a sacrificial ceremony (21:26). It was toward the end of Paul's seven-day purification process (possibly the seventh day, when he would receive the "water of atonement") that Jews from Asia Minor saw him in the Temple. From the time of his witness in the Ephesian synagogue, Paul had faced constant opposition from Asian Jews, and now under cover of a Pentecost pilgrimage, they had apparently dogged his steps to Jerusalem (19:9; 20:19; cf. 6:9; 20:29). As Jews were accustomed to take public action against apostates, especially those who were thought to be false prophets (3 Macc 7:10-14), they "roused a mob" against Paul and seized him as they broadcast charges against him (21:27-28; cf. Luke 21:12; Acts 4:3; 5:18; 12:1).

These Jews of Asia Minor claimed that Paul's teaching contained comprehensive opposition to Judaism—"our people . . . Jewish laws . . . the Temple" (21:28; contrast Paul's own understanding of his stance toward Judaism in 24:14-16). While his preaching affirmed the Jews' divinely privileged place as God's people in salvation history (13:17, 24, 46), Paul also understood that God would take for himself a people from among the Gentiles (13:46-47; 18:10; cf. 15:14). Though he did not force Jews to become "custom-free," he did teach a "law-free" gospel, declaring that the law is unable to free from sin or bring forgiveness (13:39). Luke does not give us his views on the Temple, though his assertion in Athens—the true God "doesn't live in man-made temples" (17:24)—is akin to Stephen's critique of Jewish possessiveness with respect to their Temple (7:48-50).

The specific charge was that Paul had brought "Gentiles" (*Hellēnas* [TG1672, ZG1818] "Greeks") into the Temple and defiled it (21:28). His accusers had seen "Trophimus, a Gentile from Ephesus" in Paul's company (21:29; cf. 20:4; 2 Tim 4:20; the NLT mg, "Trophimus the Ephesian," indicates that the NLT text makes explicit Trophimus's non-Jewish ethnicity). The accusers wrongly assumed that Paul, who preached so strongly against maintaining the Jew-Gentile distinctions when it came to receiving Gentiles into the church, would not hesitate to "Gentilize" the Temple courts by bringing a non-Jew in beyond the court of the Gentiles to the Jews-only precincts.

Though Gentiles were welcome to worship in the outermost court, they were forbidden on penalty of death to enter beyond the balustrade into the two inner courts (*m. Kelim* 1:8). Josephus informs us, and archaeological evidence confirms, that at intervals there were signs posted in Greek and Latin saying, "No foreigner is to enter within the forecourt and the balustrade around the Sanctuary. Whoever is caught will have himself to blame for his subsequent death" (Josephus *Wars* 5.193; Segal 1989:79). This prohibition enforced Numbers 3:38.

Luke graphically takes us from the panoramic view of a whole city "rocked," to a "great riot" erupting, to the people forming themselves into a mob, to the man at the vortex—Paul—being "grabbed and dragged out" of the Temple's sacred courts to the court of the Gentiles. "And immediately the gates were closed behind him" (21:30).

Here we have the last major spiritual and geographical turning point in Acts. Never again would Paul return to Jerusalem for worship or witness. By shutting out the messenger and the message of salvation, Paul's opponents had sealed the city's doom (Luke 13:34-35; 21:6, 20). In permitting its ethnic pride to prevent it from fulfilling its divinely intended mission as "a light to the Gentiles" (Isa 49:6), the Jews not only rejected their place in the true people of God but robbed the Temple of the universal glory God planned for it as "a house of prayer for all nations" (Isa 56:7; cf. Luke 19:46).

After telling us the Jews "were trying to kill" Paul (21:31), Luke focused again on the big picture. Things had gotten so out of hand that a report came to the Roman commander in the Antonia fortress that "all Jerusalem was in an uproar." The Jews were about to enact a mob execution, dealing summary justice on Paul for his alleged Temple defilement; it would be "death at the hands of heaven" (Philo *Legatio ad Gaium* 212), and the people were about to dissolve into anarchy (19:29, 32, 40).

Adjacent to the Temple area—at the juncture of the western and northern porticoes that formed the outer boundary of the court of the Gentiles—was the Antonia fortress. It was the headquarters of the Roman garrison stationed at Jerusalem. This spacious, sixty-foot-tall building had the general appearance of a tower; turrets stood at its four corners, the one on the southeast being 105 feet high. From it, Roman soldiers commanded a view of the whole Temple area. Stairways into the northern and western porticoes gave direct access to the court of the Gentiles (Josephus *Wars* 5.192, 238-247; *Antiquities* 15.409).

The commander, with some centurions and soldiers, "ran down" the steps into the crowd (21:32). Their very presence brought a halt to the beating of Paul. The handcuffing of Paul by the two soldiers was effectively the same as "handing him over" to the Gentiles (cf. 20:23, 13; 21:11). So loud and confused, indeed irrationally incensed, was the crowd that the commander could not find out anything about Paul and his actions. Ironically, their religious fervor mirrors the animistic pagan frenzy at Ephesus (cf. 19:32). So strong was their brutish violence against Paul that soldiers had to lift him away from the press of the crowd if they were to make any progress back up into the fortress. The crowd was so intent on his death that they followed behind, shouting "Kill him!" (21:36; cf. Luke 23:18).

The mob action of Jerusalem Jews leading to Paul's arrest by the Romans reveals that even those who were historically the "people of God," but had opposed God's mission to all nations, would, in that very opposition, reduce themselves to a violent, confused, irrational, barely controllable mass of humanity—in short, "no people of God."

◆   ## H. Paul Speaks to the Crowd (21:37–22:23)

37As Paul was about to be taken inside, he said to the commander, "May I have a word with you?"

"Do you know Greek?" the commander asked, surprised. 38"Aren't you the Egyptian who led a rebellion some time ago and took 4,000 members of the Assassins out into the desert?"

39"No," Paul replied, "I am a Jew and a citizen of Tarsus in Cilicia, which is an important city. Please, let me talk to these people." 40The commander agreed, so Paul stood on the stairs and motioned to the people to be quiet. Soon a deep silence enveloped the crowd, and he addressed them in their own language, Aramaic.*

CHAPTER 22

"Brothers and esteemed fathers," Paul said, "listen to me as I offer my defense." 2When they heard him speaking in their own language,* the silence was even greater.

³Then Paul said, "I am a Jew, born in Tarsus, a city in Cilicia, and I was brought up and educated here in Jerusalem under Gamaliel. As his student, I was carefully trained in our Jewish laws and customs. I became very zealous to honor God in everything I did, just like all of you today. ⁴And I persecuted the followers of the Way, hounding some to death, arresting both men and women and throwing them in prison. ⁵The high priest and the whole council of elders can testify that this is so. For I received letters from them to our Jewish brothers in Damascus, authorizing me to bring the Christians from there to Jerusalem, in chains, to be punished.

⁶"As I was on the road, approaching Damascus about noon, a very bright light from heaven suddenly shone down around me. ⁷I fell to the ground and heard a voice saying to me, 'Saul, Saul, why are you persecuting me?'

⁸"'Who are you, lord?' I asked.

"And the voice replied, 'I am Jesus the Nazarene,* the one you are persecuting.' ⁹The people with me saw the light but didn't understand the voice speaking to me.

¹⁰"I asked, 'What should I do, Lord?'

"And the Lord told me, 'Get up and go into Damascus, and there you will be told everything you are to do.'

¹¹"I was blinded by the intense light and had to be led by the hand to Damascus by my companions. ¹²A man named Ananias lived there. He was a godly man, deeply devoted to the law, and well regarded by all the Jews of Damascus. ¹³He came and stood beside me and said, 'Brother Saul, regain your sight.' And that very moment I could see him!

¹⁴"Then he told me, 'The God of our ancestors has chosen you to know his will and to see the Righteous One and hear him speak. ¹⁵For you are to be his witness, telling everyone what you have seen and heard. ¹⁶What are you waiting for? Get up and be baptized. Have your sins washed away by calling on the name of the Lord.'

¹⁷"After I returned to Jerusalem, I was praying in the Temple and fell into a trance. ¹⁸I saw a vision of Jesus* saying to me, 'Hurry! Leave Jerusalem, for the people here won't accept your testimony about me.'

¹⁹"'But Lord,' I argued, 'they certainly know that in every synagogue I imprisoned and beat those who believed in you. ²⁰And I was in complete agreement when your witness Stephen was killed. I stood by and kept the coats they took off when they stoned him.'

²¹"But the Lord said to me, 'Go, for I will send you far away to the Gentiles!' "

²²The crowd listened until Paul said that word. Then they all began to shout, "Away with such a fellow! He isn't fit to live!" ²³They yelled, threw off their coats, and tossed handfuls of dust into the air.

21:40 Or *Hebrew.* 22:2 Greek *in Aramaic,* or *in Hebrew.* 22:8 Or *Jesus of Nazareth.* 22:18 Greek *him.*

NOTES

21:37–22:23 Some scholars question the historical authenticity of this entire scene, doubting whether Paul ever did deliver such a speech. Objections are that the speech does not answer the charges, it is questionable whether the tribune would permit Paul to speak, and it is unlikely the crowd would have actually quieted down enough to hear him (Fitzmyer 1998a:703; Johnson 1992:385; Barrett 1998:1027).

This speech, however, does fit the occasion, for in rhetorical form, it is a forensic speech with exordium, an introduction (22:1-2), and *narratio*—in this case, a lengthy statement of the facts of the case, given the hostile audience (22:3-21; Witherington 1998:667). Paul gave biographical details—both his loyalty to Judaism and his divine conversion and calling to evangelize the Gentiles—from which he could argue his *probatio*, proofs in answer to the specific charges (21:28). But he was interrupted before he could continue.

Though it might seem to the tribune's advantage to deny Paul's request and hustle him inside Antonia fortress, permitting Paul to speak had the potential to help restore order (Talbert 1997:196, citing Vergil *Aeneid* 1.148-153) or clarify his identity (Keener 1993:389). Was the tribune impressed with Paul's personality or was it his significant Hellenistic credentials—that is, the ability to politely address a superior in fluent Greek and being a citizen of the famous city of Tarsus (Johnson 1992:384; Witherington 1998:664)? Paul's intense personality (Barrett 1998:1027), not to mention his being Spirit-filled, and the presence of the tribune by his side (Witherington 1998:664) probably quieted the crowd when he waved for their attention.

21:38 *the Assassins.* This rendering of *sikariōn* [TG4607, ZG4974] points to guerrillas of the Jewish nationalistic movement (this Gr. word is from the Latin *sica* "short dagger," *sicarius* = "dagger men"). These guerrillas used such an easily concealed weapon to assassinate political opponents in the festival throngs in the Temple courts. They would then disguise themselves by crying out in indignation as their victims fell (Josephus *War* 2.252-256). Since there is not clear identification of these with the followers of the Egyptian false prophet in Josephus's writings (but note reference to them in *Antiquities* 20.185-188), the term may be being used generically for "terrorist" (Fitzmyer 1998a:701), but not necessarily anachronistically (contra Dunn 1996:290).

21:40; 22:2 *in their own language, Aramaic.* In both instances, the Gr. is *tē Hebraidi dialektō* [TG1446/1258, ZG1579/1365]. In 21:40, the NLT has correctly identified the translation options—"Hebrew" or "Aramaic," though at 22:2, it represents only one. The DSS give strong evidence for the currency of Hebrew in first-century Palestine, and Paul speaking the sacred language of Scripture would certainly have captured the audience's attention. But a Diaspora Jew speaking Aramaic would have been just as startling. Given the consistent NT practice of *Hebrais* accompanying transcriptions of Aramaic, it seems best to follow the vast majority of commentators and understand the reference as one to Aramaic (e.g., Barrett 1998:1028-1029; Fitzmyer 1998b:701; contra ISBE 1.233).

22:3 *zealous to honor God in everything I did.* The words *zēlōtēs* [TG2207, ZG2421] *tou theou* (a zealot for God), which while not un-Pauline (cf. Rom 10:2), are unusual enough for Acts (cf. 21:20) that Western readings smooth out the rendering: (1) 614 and codex Toletanus of the Vulgate omit *tou theou* [TG2316, ZG2536] (of God); (2) the Vulgate reads "[zealous of] the law"; (3) syr^h (mg) reads with an asterisk "[zealous of] my ancestral traditions" (cf. Gal 1:14; Metzger 1994:430).

22:4 *hounding some to death.* The NLT picks up the metaphorical use of the phrase *ediōxa achri thanatou* [TG1377/2288, ZG1503/2505] (I persecuted unto death), which some see as unlikely given the Roman prerogative in death penalty matters and the general absence of evidence elsewhere for Paul's murderous activities (Johnson 1992:388; Dunn 1996:294). However, Barrett (1998:1036) says that this is no exaggeration when we remember that synagogue beatings could be severe enough to kill (26:10). Most recognize that Paul, at the least, as in the case with Stephen, had taken action and cooperated in efforts that led to the death of various Christians (Witherington 1998:670; cf. Fitzmyer 1998b:705).

22:9 *The people with me . . . didn't understand the voice.* Lit., "they didn't hear the voice." This appears to contradict 9:7, which says that the men with Saul "heard the sound of someone's voice" (e.g., Witherup 1992:78; Johnson 1992:389; Dunn 1996:294; Barrett 1998:1038-1039; Fitzmyer 1998b:706). Often Luke's alleged lack of concern for or failure to notice this discrepancy is seen as its source (Dunn 1996:294; Barrett 1998:1038-1039). Wallace (1996:134) attributes the difference to Luke's reticence to change two traditions handed down to him. Though according to Wallace (1996:133) there are as many instances of exceptions as there are of this rule in the NT, the rule does still seem to obtain that *akouō* [TG191, ZG201] with the genitive means simply to hear a sound (9:7 is an example of this), while *akouō* with the accusative means to hear with understanding (22:9 is an example of this). Standard NT Greek grammars and recent studies apply this distinction to these passages and in that way harmonize them (Robertson 1934:506; Moulton 1908:1.66; 1963:3.233; contrast Moule 1977:36).

22:10 *What should I do, Lord?* Paul's response was not as a good Jew responding to divine revelation (contra Longenecker 1981:525); not as a person simply stupefied, realizing he must change (contra Marshall 1980:355); and not as stating openness to receive his commission (contra Witherington 1998:671), but like the Pentecost crowd (2:37), Paul realized he was under judgment and deliberated whether there was any remedy.

22:13 *'regain your sight' . . . I could see him!* It is unclear from the Gr. whether Ananias specifically commanded Paul to "look up" or to "see again." The NLT's rendering of the two occurrences of *anablepō* [TG308, ZG329], which can mean "see again" or "look up," removes the ambiguity of the second occurrence (*aneblepsa eis* [TG1519, ZG1650] *auton*, "I saw again with reference to him" or "I looked up at him"). Some mss also remove the ambiguity either by omitting the prepositional phrase (𝔓41) or using *blepō* [TG991, ZG1063] (𝔓74 A) or *emblepō* [TG1689, ZG1838] (056 1739 1891).

22:14 *his will.* Its content is not simply Paul's subsequent service or what would only be revealed as Paul lived in exceptionally intimate terms with God (contra Barrett 1998:1041). Rather, "his will" is the divine plan of salvation accomplished and applied, especially the role Paul played in it (Fitzmyer 1998b:707).

22:16 *be baptized. Have your sins washed away by calling on the name of the Lord.* As theological explanations of baptism, these last phrases point neither to a sacramental understanding, which makes baptism essential to salvation, nor to a post-regeneration entry into fellowship with Christ (contra Tanton 1991). Rather, guarding against a magical understanding, the phrases, especially the last one, say baptism mirrors the stance of faith and obedience directed to Christ in response to the washing from sins he has provided at conversion (Barrett 1998:1043; cf. Dunn 1996:296).

22:17-21 The fact that both Luke and Paul place Paul's commissioning to the Gentiles on the Damascus road (26:16-18; Gal 1:15-16) and are silent about a Temple visit and divine directive to leave Jerusalem during Paul's first visit (9:29-30; Gal 1:17-19) does not render this account historically unlikely (contra Barrett 1998:1027; Fitzmyer 1998b:708). Though the Gentiles were Paul's special focus, his initial commissioning, as Acts gives it, included both Jew and Gentile (9:15; 26:17). The Temple vision is not a delay in giving the Gentile mission, rather a further directive in deployment, much like the additional prayers of 13:3. The visit to Jerusalem in the Acts 9 account can accommodate the Temple vision, if we see the reasons for Paul's departure as a coincidence of divine direction and human actions (Bruce 1988:419). Note Morray-Jones's (1993) strong case for this incident being that of 2 Cor 12:1-12 and taking place during the first Jerusalem visit.

22:23 *threw off their coats, and tossed handfuls of dust into the air.* The actions were not a response to hearing blasphemy, for the cloaks are thrown or waved, not torn (contra Keener 1993:390). Rather, the crowd expresses its revulsion against Paul's unclean Gentile mission by treating him as an unclean Gentile, shaking out their cloaks as a pious Jew would do when he returned from Gentile lands (cf. 13:51; 18:6), and they throw dust since there are no stones at hand (Witherington 1998:675).

COMMENTARY

Just as Paul was about to be taken into the barracks, he made a polite request of the commander, evidently in Greek. "May I have a word with you?" (21:37). The commander tried to place Paul's identity. If he could speak Greek, he was probably not a Palestinian Jew. Maybe he was from the Diaspora. If he caused such a disturbance, maybe he was that Egyptian revolutionary of several years ago. Indeed, four or five years earlier (AD 54), an Egyptian false prophet had led a large band of terrorists into the desert and returned to the Mount of Olives. From there, he had promised his band that he would command the walls of Jerusalem to fall flat, leading to the easy subjugation of the city. Governor Felix's troops, however, took preemptive action and quashed the insurgency, scattering many, including the Egyptian (Josephus *War* 2.261-263; *Antiquities* 20.169-172).

Clearly distinguishing himself from the Egyptian, Paul declared he was a Jew and "a citizen of Tarsus in Cilicia" (21:39). On the Cydnus River, sitting astride the key east-west trade route and strategically commanding a key pass through the Taurus mountains to the central plateau of Asia Minor, Tarsus (population 500,000 at the height of its prominence) was an "important city"—a center of Hellenistic culture and learning, especially Stoic philosophy (Strabo *Geography* 14.5.13-15; Dio Chrysostom *Orations* 33.48; 44.3; Lucian *Octogenarians* 21).

Ever guided by his sense of mission—"telling others the Good News about the wonderful grace of God" (20:24)—Paul asks for permission to talk to "these people" (21:39; lit., "the people," *ton laon* [TG2992, ZG3295]; this is Luke's last use of this freighted theological term in reference to the Jerusalem crowd). As Luke presents it, this is Jerusalem's last opportunity to hear and receive the gospel (compare and contrast the Pentecost speech and response in ch 2). Permission granted, with an orator's wave of the hand for attention (cf. 13:16; 19:33), "a deep silence enveloped the crowd"—manifestly the work of the Spirit clearing the way for the gospel messenger to have a hearing (21:40). Paul addressed them in their native tongue, Aramaic (see note on 21:40).

In a brief exordium (his introduction, 22:1-2), Paul gained the respect and attention of the audience by addressing them as "brothers and esteemed fathers"—the latter being priests, any members of the Sanhedrin, and older members in the crowd—and by speaking in Aramaic. Further quiet resulted. At the same time, Paul was realistic about the crowd's disposition toward him, for he asked that they listen to his "defense" (*apologia* [TG627, ZG665]). The crowd had proceeded to summary execution without a trial. Now they would hear the defendant's case. When Luke recorded Jesus' preparation of his followers for persecution, he used trial, or court, language and stressed not only the opportunity for witness but the Spirit-inspired content of such defenses (Luke 12:11-12; 21:12-15). It is not surprising, then, that we find Paul evangelizing his audience here and in subsequent chapters (Acts 23–26), even as he laid out his defense before various authorities.

The remainder of Paul's speech is a lengthy *narratio* (22:3-21) in which Paul not only sought to establish his credentials as a loyal Jew but also to state the facts of the case. But because his speech was interrupted, Paul never got to state the facts about the immediate circumstances surrounding the Jewish tumult and their seizure of him. He began with the common biographical triad of one's formative years: birth, rearing, and education (22:3; cf. 7:20-22). Each in its own way brought out his loyalty to Judaism. He was a Diaspora Jew, a citizen of Tarsus by birth, which made his speaking in fluent Aramaic all the more impressive. His parents were devout Diaspora Jews, for they saw to it that he would be brought up in Jerusalem. His education had been most scrupulous with respect to "Jewish laws and customs," for he had studied at the feet of the Pharisee Gamaliel (22:3; cf. 5:34; 26:5; Josephus *Antiquities* 17.41). Through it all, he had become "very zealous to honor God," a passion that he affirmed his audience was displaying right then.

Paul proved his zeal for the Jewish God by a persecution of Christians—"followers of the Way" (22:4; cf. Phil 3:6), which encompassed men and women and extended to physical punishment, imprisonment, and even death (see note on 22:4). This could even be substantiated by Judaism's chief religious leaders, for with their authorization Paul proceeded to Damascus. Paul had made the strongest case possible that he once acted out his zeal for God against Christians in the same way his audience was acting against him.

This arrester of Christians, however, soon found himself arrested by God. On the road to Damascus, at midday, a very bright light "from heaven" so overpoweringly enveloped Paul that he fell to the ground (22:6). The question "Saul, Saul, why are you persecuting me?" challenged Paul to question whether his zeal might have been misguided all along (22:7). In biblical thought, "persecution" always signified oppression against the righteous innocent, including Israel's actions against true prophets (Luke 11:49; Pss 70:11; 118:84, 86; 2 Chr 36:19). The heavenly question unmasked Paul's persecution born of religious zeal for what it truly was—an oppression of the righteous innocent by the self-righteous wicked. And when Paul inquired after the heavenly being's identity, the answer came: "I am Jesus the Nazarene, the one you are persecuting" (22:8). The terrible realization dawned on Paul that his zeal for God had set him at war with God in the person of the risen and exalted Lord Jesus (cf. his teacher's warning, 5:39).

Paul assured his audience that this really did happen—it was an event in space and time—for he noted that his traveling companions objectively experienced both the sight and the sound. Though objective, Paul's encounter with Christ was in many respects private. His companions "saw the light" surrounding Paul but not the risen Lord who appeared to him (22:9, 14; 9:7). They heard a voice addressing Paul but were not privy to its message (see note on 22:9; cf. 9:7).

The Pentecost crowd had realized its guilt for slaying the Lord's Anointed One — their only hope for divinely accomplished salvation—and asked in perplexity, if not despair, "What should we do?" (2:37). Similarly Paul, having persecuted, even "hounding . . . to death" (22:4), the Lord's anointed agents for applying that salvation, asked, "What should I do, Lord?" (see note on 22:10). The Lord's indirect reply called for faith and obedience but still assured Paul that what had been ordained for him as part of God's eternal saving purposes would be fully made known to him. In an acted parable of his spiritual poverty and total mastery that his new Lord had over him, blind Paul had to be led by his companions into Damascus to await further orders. The "intense light" (22:11; lit., "the glory of the light") that blinded Paul was God's effective presence in the world (cf. 7:2)—in fact, it was the splendor of the exalted Lord Jesus appearing from heaven (Luke 24:26; 21:27; cf. Luke 2:9; 9:26, 31-32; Acts 7:55; 2 Cor 4:6).

Told from the perspective of Paul as an eyewitness, and with his Jewish audience in mind, this version of his encounter with Ananias gives Ananias a more limited role. Still, Ananias embodied the way Jewish Christianity is a bridge for pious Jews to the Christian faith. If a Jew with a broad reputation for his law-abiding piety could play such a key role in Paul's conversion to Christ, then being a pious Jew and a Christian convert were not necessarily mutually exclusive (22:12; cf. Luke 2:25; Acts 2:5; 6:3; 16:2).

In the plainest of descriptions, Paul told how Ananias arrived, "stood beside" him, announced, "Brother Saul, regain your sight," and how in that very hour he could see again (22:13). The lack of physical contact (contrast 9:17) and his sudden arrival at Paul's side point to God's work. The recovery of sight itself becomes another acted parable, this time of God's saving work. For, as we will discover, salvation was declared to Paul in terms of opening eyes and turning persons from darkness to light (26:18).

Ananias interpreted to Paul his Damascus road experience, placing it in the framework of God's saving purposes, linking it to the divine commission of Paul and the next steps in his Christian life (22:14-16). In continuity with his Old Testament heritage, Paul and his audience were to know that it was "the God of our ancestors" who had chosen, or foreordained, three things for Paul in his Damascus road encounter (3:13; 5:30; 7:32). First, he should "know his will"—God's eternal plan for accomplishing, and especially, applying salvation, particularly Paul's commission to be a witness to its message (22:14-15). We must wait until the third telling of Paul's conversion for the details on that revealed will (26:16-18, 22-23; cf. Luke 24:46-47). Still, much of the plan embodied in the gospel message is hinted at in this description of Paul's work as a witness and what he must do in completing his own conversion-initiation (22:15-16). Second, God predestined Paul to "see the Righteous One" (22:14; cf. 3:14; 7:52; Jer 23:5-6; 33:15; Zech 9:9). That sight demonstrates Jesus of Nazareth as the vindicated victim of an unjust death, whose vicarious atonement is the basis for having "sins washed away" (22:16). Third, God had chosen Paul to hear God speak the gracious words of the gospel and the commanding words of commission. Again, we must await 26:14-18, 22-23 for the specific content (cf. Paul's own testimony that his gospel was revealed from heaven in Gal 1:12, 15-16; cf. also Rom 10:9-10; 1 Cor 15:1-4). Paul's commission was the reason for his Damascus road encounter (22:15). Paul's focus was on his role as a witness to Jesus in continuity with the apostles (1:8; 1:22; 2:32; 3:15); the universal scope of his audience; and the origin in personal experience—"what you have seen and heard" (22:15)—of the testimony.

Ananias completed his mission by encouraging Paul to fulfill his responsibility in response to his conversion: "Be baptized." Through this rite he would complete the conversion-initiation process of being enfolded into the church (Matt 28:18-20; 1 Cor 12:13). He would be picturing—in that outward purification—the inward cleansing from his sins that had resulted from his calling on the name of the Lord for salvation (2:38, 21; 9:14, 21). Up to this point, Paul continued to evangelize his audience by his personal testimony. Paul not only modeled the possibility, indeed the necessity, of conversion for those living out a zeal for God driven by religioethnic pride, he also presented the steps to take in conversion.

Moving closer to the issue for which the crowd had first assaulted him, Paul related a subsequent encounter with the risen Lord in the Jerusalem Temple (22:17-21; see note). As did the early apostles, Paul continued to live out his piety by praying at the Temple (cf. 3:1; 5:42). On one occasion, he "fell into a trance" (22:17; lit., "was in an ecstasy, ecstatic vision"; cf. 10:10; 11:5; Gen 15:12; Philo *Heir* 249-265). He saw Jesus, the Lord of the Temple (Luke 19:45-48; cf. 2:46-49), and heard his command: "Hurry! Leave Jerusalem, for the people here won't accept your testimony about me" (22:18). With an urgency born of implied danger (cf. 9:30) or of the need to get the message to those who would embrace it, Jesus directed Paul into a centrifugal, outward-moving mode of mission (cf. 1:8 and note). In contrast to the first speech to a Jerusalem throng, where the message was received, now the verdict—and that from heaven—was that Jerusalem would not receive Paul's testimony about Jesus.

In a fine rhetorical move to gain his present audience's trust, Paul told them how he remonstrated with God. Surely his life as a persecutor and his service as an accomplice to Stephen's death would be enough evidence of his Jewish loyalty and would gain him a hearing (7:58; 8:1, 3; 9:2; 22:4). The Lord did not argue with Paul. He had already given his rationale. Israel's essential opposition was not to the messenger; it was not an issue of their taking his zeal for God in persecuting the church into account. Their opposition was to the message—the "testimony about me" (22:18). The person and work of Christ, especially the universal scope of his gracious offer of salvation, was the sticking point for any whose zeal burned to preserve a distinctive ethno-religious identity. All that remained was for the Lord to repeat the command and for Paul to obey: "Go, for I will send you far away to the Gentiles!" (22:21; cf. 2:39; 13:46; Eph 2:13, 17). The Gentile mission was always the final and, as Acts portrays it, the increasingly dominant horizon of Paul's ministry, yet always within a theologically grounded "to the Jew first" strategy (9:15; 13:46; 14:27; 15:3, 12; 21:19).

That a once crucified but now resurrected and exalted Messiah should, during a vision in the Temple, send Paul "to the Gentiles" was verbal defilement of the sacred precincts. As with Stephen's testimony to the same exalted Lord, they tried to drown it out with their own voices, as they shouted a united verdict: "Away with such a fellow! He isn't fit to live!" (22:22; cf. Luke 23:18; Acts 7:56-57; 21:36). In their blind zeal for the people, law, and Temple, they believed their suspicions about Paul were confirmed. He was consorting with Gentiles with no conscience about defiling the Temple precincts. He deserved "death at the hands of heaven."

"Throwing off" (possibly "shaking out") their cloaks and tossing dust in the air (22:23), they showed their extreme disgust as they foreswore all association with Paul, wanting not even the least particle of what touched him to touch them, lest they defile themselves (cf. Luke 9:5; 10:10-11; Acts 13:51; 18:6; *m. Ohalot* 17:5). Their rejection was complete.

◆ **I. Paul Reveals His Roman Citizenship (22:24-29)**

²⁴The commander brought Paul inside and ordered him lashed with whips to make him confess his crime. He wanted to find out why the crowd had become so furious. ²⁵When they tied Paul down to lash him, Paul said to the officer* standing there, "Is it legal for you to whip a Roman citizen who hasn't even been tried?"

²⁶When the officer heard this, he went to the commander and asked, "What are you doing? This man is a Roman citizen!" ²⁷So the commander went over and asked Paul, "Tell me, are you a Roman citizen?"

"Yes, I certainly am," Paul replied.

²⁸"I am, too," the commander muttered, "and it cost me plenty!"

Paul answered, "But I am a citizen by birth!"

²⁹The soldiers who were about to interrogate Paul quickly withdrew when they heard he was a Roman citizen, and the commander was frightened because he had ordered him bound and whipped.

22:25 Greek *the centurion;* also in 22:26.

NOTES

22:24-29 Some question the historicity of this scene, saying there is no good reason Paul would delay identifying himself as a Roman citizen until now (Barrett 1998:1048). To do so before the Jerusalem crowd, however, would have driven a highly destructive wedge between him and his audience (Rapske 1994b:142). It was only to the Roman authorities that he revealed his citizenship, for he did not want to undercut his identity as a Christian Jew (Rapske 1994b:143). He would use his citizenship at a point where it was needed for defense and was most likely to influence the conduct of the Romans.

22:25 *tied Paul down to lash him.* The Gr. wording may convey either a sense of instrumentality or purpose (*proeteinan auton tois himasin* [TG2438, ZG2666], "they stretched him out with/for lashes"). The majority of scholars choose purpose, i.e., "for the purpose of lashing" (Johnson 1992:391; Barrett 1998:1048; Witherington 1998:677; contrast Dunn 1996:298). Fitzmyer says the text is unclear (1998b:712). The NLT expresses the idea of purpose in its translation.

a Roman citizen who hasn't even been tried. The qualifier in this phrase, *akatakriton* [TG178, ZG185], can also mean "uncondemned," which accords with later Roman practice of setting aside the absolute prohibition in the light of conviction for certain crimes (Sherwin-White 1963:72-73).

22:28 *the commander muttered!* This is the NLT making explicit the implied cynicism or sarcasm on the commander's part. Though a common understanding, this probably masks the statement's role in "social/judicial damage assessment." If the tribune harmed a social superior (e.g., one born a Roman citizen), as indeed he had, then his crime for violating a Roman citizens' rights would be all the greater. (For detailed background on Paul's use of his Roman citizenship see Rapske 1994b:47-56, 135-145; Sherwin-White 1963: 72-73, 148-149.)

COMMENTARY

Presumably, the commander had exhausted all non-physically coercive means for finding out why Paul occasioned such a furor. He ordered interrogation with whips to extract information from him, if not a confession. In flogging, a whip of thongs— either knotted cords or wire having bristled ends, sometimes strung with knucklebones or lead pellets—was applied repeatedly to the back of a person positioned on the floor, at a pillar, or suspended from the ceiling. The person was stretched out with bound arms secured so he could not deflect the blows.

As the soldiers were stretching Paul out with thongs about his wrists to secure him for scourging, he asked a question of the centurion: "Is it legal for you to whip a Roman citizen who hasn't even been tried?" (22:25). From the Augustan age, the Lex Julia contained an absolute prohibition on binding or beating a Roman citizen (cf. 16:37). The qualification *akatakriton* [TG178, ZG185] (better translated "uncondemned") points to the later practice of administering beatings to citizens for certain crimes (see note on 22:25; the Romans also forbade punishment of citizens without due process). In dismay, the centurion questioned and entreated the tribune against the order to whip Paul (22:26). In his providence, God worked through human law to spare Paul.

The tribune verified Paul's Roman citizenship with a simple question that the apostle answered in the affirmative (21:27). To falsely claim Roman citizenship was a serious, even capital offense (Suetonius *Claudius* 25.3; Epictetus *Discourses* 3.24.41). As a regular traveler, Paul may have carried with him a copy of his birth registration.

Convinced, the tribune assessed the judicial damage of his order (22:28). He stated his status as a Roman citizen. He'd had to bribe intermediaries in the imperial secretariat or provincial administration to ensure that his name would appear on the list of candidates for enfranchisement. Achieving this status may have been part of his working his way up through the ranks, moving at last from the rank of centurion to tribune. If Paul came by his Roman citizenship in a way which would give him social status superior to the tribune's, then the commander would suffer more severely for having violated Paul's citizen rights. Paul's declaration, "I am a citizen by birth" (21:28), is just what he didn't want to hear because it meant that Paul was his social superior.

In God's providence, Paul was in as favorable a position as one could expect for someone who had been "turned over to the Gentiles" (21:11); he was a Roman citizen with superior social status to the arresting officer. So the interrogators "quickly withdrew," and the commander was "frightened" because of what he had done (21:29). The Roman orator Cicero exclaimed, "To bind a Roman is a crime, to flog him is an abomination, to slay him is almost an act of murder" (*Against Verres* 2.5.66).

Paul's revelation of his Roman citizenship and its consequences teach us that when the laws of the state truly reflect God's moral order (Rom 13:4), then God's servants may have an opportunity to gain protection and thereby advance God's mission.

◆   **J. Paul before the High Council (22:30–23:11)**

30The next day the commander ordered the leading priests into session with the Jewish high council.* He wanted to find out what the trouble was all about, so he released Paul to have him stand before them.

CHAPTER 23

Gazing intently at the high council,* Paul began: "Brothers, I have always lived before God with a clear conscience!"

2Instantly Ananias the high priest commanded those close to Paul to slap him on the mouth. 3But Paul said to him, "God will slap you, you corrupt hypocrite!* What kind of judge are you to break the law yourself by ordering me struck like that?"

4Those standing near Paul said to him, "Do you dare to insult God's high priest?"

5"I'm sorry, brothers. I didn't realize he was the high priest," Paul replied, "for the Scriptures say, 'You must not speak evil of any of your rulers.'*"

6Paul realized that some members of the high council were Sadducees and some were Pharisees, so he shouted, "Brothers, I am a Pharisee, as were my ancestors! And I am on trial because my hope is in the resurrection of the dead!"

7This divided the council—the Pharisees against the Sadducees—8for the Sadducees say there is no resurrection or angels or spirits, but the Pharisees believe in all of these. 9So there was a great uproar. Some of the teachers of religious law who were Pharisees jumped up and began to argue forcefully. "We see nothing wrong with him," they shouted. "Perhaps a spirit or an angel spoke to him." 10As the conflict grew more violent, the commander was afraid they would tear Paul apart. So he ordered his soldiers to go and rescue him by force and take him back to the fortress.

11That night the Lord appeared to Paul and said, "Be encouraged, Paul. Just as you have been a witness to me here in Jerusalem, you must preach the Good News in Rome as well."

22:30 Greek *Sanhedrin.*   23:1 Greek *Sanhedrin;* also in 23:6, 15, 20, 28.   23:3 Greek *you whitewashed wall.*
23:5 Exod 22:28.

NOTES

22:30 *The next day the commander . . . released Paul.* The potential historical difficulty of the delay in releasing a Roman citizen, Paul, may be resolved if we assume that Paul was released from his bonds immediately and that *elusen* [TG3089, ZG3395] (release) was a further slackening of custodial arrangements (Rapske 1994b:145). Paul was temporarily released from custody, though conducted by the commander, to go to the Sanhedrin (Witherington 1998:686).

ordered the leading priests into session with the Jewish high council. Here is another potential difficulty: how could a Roman commander order the Sanhedrin into session? This may be resolved when we see the Sanhedrin meeting as an informal hearing to interrogate Paul, not as a formal session placing him on trial (Barrett 1998:1053).

22:30; 23:1, 6, 15, 20, 28 *the Jewish high council.* Lit., "Sanhedrin" (cf. NLT mg). This is a transliteration of *sunedrion* [TG4892, ZG5284], which "means first the 'place of those who sit together' (*sunedroi* [TG4892.2, ZG5286]), then their 'session,' 'council,' 'governing body'" (TDNT 2.861). In first-century Jewish circles, it referred to the highest legislative and judicial body in Israel. It consisted of seventy-one members from three groups: "elders" from the landed gentry; "teachers of religious law," professional Torah scholars who taught, expounded and applied the law, and argued it in court; and "priests," particularly the high priest and priestly officials from his family (*m. Sanhedrin* 1:6). The chief priest was the presiding officer.

23:2 slap him on the mouth. Though not explicitly noted, the high priest's motive was probably not Paul's manner of speaking: his simple form of address, "Brothers" (Lake and Cadbury 1979:287); his speaking out of turn (Johnson 1992:396); or his use of Greek language or concepts—"conscience" (Dunn 1996:303). Rather, it was what he said—namely, his claim to a sincere conscience in living a life before God, which to the high priest was, at best, a "total untruth" (Kee 1997:262) and, at worst, a blasphemous assertion. Paul's conscientious life as a follower of Christ would actually be destroying Judaism as they understood it (Barrett 1998:1058).

23:5 I didn't realize he was the high priest. This was not true ignorance on Paul's part, whether from poor eyesight (contra Dunn 1996:304) or lack of familiarity with the priestly hierarchy due to his infrequent visits to Jerusalem (contra Fernando 1998:567) or the informal nature of the hearing in which the high priest would not necessarily sit in his accustomed place as the presiding officer or be wearing his distinctive robes (contra Keener 1993:391). Paul's retort (23:3) indicates he knew who the high priest was (Witherington 1998:689). Neither was Paul's response true irony, in which he declared the high priest's behavior as making him unrecognizable as such (contra Marshall 1980:364; Spencer 1997:212), for Paul did confess his true ignorance and guilt (Fitzmyer 1998b:717). Rather, Paul confessed a sin of ignorance that was a sin of omission. Paul confessed that he did not take into consideration the man's position when he made the declaration (Polhill 1992:469).

23:6 I am a Pharisee, as were my ancestors! Lit., a "Pharisee, son of Pharisees." This may point to the instruction he received under Gamaliel (Dunn 1996:305) or his character as the quintessential Pharisee (Barrett [1998:1063] lists this option), as well as his lineage (Johnson 1992:397).

I am on trial because my hope is in the resurrection. Paul's declaration about being on trial because of the Resurrection was not so much a "divide and conquer" tactic (contra Johnson 1992:398; Keener 1993:392; Dunn 1996:302), though it did have that effect. Rather, Paul was employing a rhetorical move during his defense in which he sought to redefine for the Romans what was at issue in the controversy. He wanted to move them away from thinking that he was charged with disrupting Judaism and toward viewing him as a protagonist in an intramural theological debate over eschatology (Tannehill 1992:259; Spencer 1997:213). The commander's letter (23:29) indicates Paul succeeded (Witherington 1998:684, 691).

23:8 angels or spirits. The immediate context does not permit these references to point to the Sadducees' lack of agreement with the Pharisees' developed angelology (contra Keener 1993:392), nor does it point to a monistic or dualistic understanding of resurrection with spirit beings, "spirit bodies," or souls moving into another body (contra Viviano and Taylor 1992), which Fitzmyer follows (1998b:719). Rather, this refers to two Jewish beliefs about the mode of existence in the intermediate state after death and before the resurrection (cf. 23:9; Daube 1990).

COMMENTARY

Having already removed his chains (see note on 22:30), the commander temporarily set Paul free the next day. Calling the "Jewish high council" into session, the commander tried to "find out what the trouble was all about" (22:30; lit., "what he [Paul] was being accused of by the Jews"). He was trying to solve his dilemma: how could he continue to keep in custody, even protective custody, a Roman citizen against whom there were no criminal charges?

Paul gazed intently (23:1; *atenizō* [TG816, ZG867]; cf. 13:9; 14:9) at the high council with the same spiritual discernment that accompanied God's miraculous work through him for salvation or judgment. Addressing the Sanhedrin as "Brothers," he treated them as peers (cf. 23:6). He confessed that he had lived a blameless life, "always lived [as a citizen] before God" (*pepoliteumai* [TG4176, ZG4488]; 23:1; Phil 1:27; 3:20). As the Jews appropriated this term for describing a life of piety, they expanded its scope of reference to the whole conduct of life (3 Macc 3:4; 4 Macc 5:16; cf. Gen 17:1). Paul both identified with his audience and yet held himself to a more comprehensive standard, for it was not simply "before the law," but "before God" that he had lived (23:1), just as his zeal was for God and not just for the law (22:3). Paul strengthened his confession by claiming that he had lived with "a clear conscience" (23:1; cf. 1 Cor 4:4; Phil 3:6; 2 Tim 1:3) his whole life. This statement was a reference to his being conscious of no wrongdoing in his self-righteous "blamelessness" before he became a Christian (cf. Rom 7:9-12; Phil 3:6; 1 Tim 1:13) and to his living with a renewed mind and cleansed conscience after his conversion (Rom 12:1-2; 2 Tim 1:3; cf. Heb 9:14). It was not a claim to sinlessness (1 Tim 1:15).

Instantly, Ananias ordered an assistant or one of the Temple police (cf. 5:22, 26) to "slap" Paul on the mouth. The mob had charged Paul with teaching apostasy from Judaism and aiding and abetting defilement of the Temple. If true, then Paul's confession was an offensive, insulting lie, deserving immediate censure. Ordering Paul to be slapped was very much in character for the high priest Ananias, son of Nedebaeus (or Nebedaeus), who served AD 47–59. He was both greedy and ruthlessly violent, using beatings to extort tithes from common priests' allotments and leaving them destitute (Josephus *Antiquities* 20.205-207).

Paul fired back a predictive curse: "God will slap you, you whitewashed wall!" (see NLT mg). Paul employed an Old Testament image for hypocrisy first uttered in the context of impending judgment. Ezekiel called false prophets "whitewashed walls," for they prophesied peace but could no more stand against the onrushing judgment of God than a stone wall, held together only by whitewash, can withstand an oncoming flood (Ezek 13:10-16). Paul's position was that one who presumed to sit in judgment against Paul according to the law was in violation of that same law because he was ordering punishment without due process. By this perversion of justice, he revealed his culpability and hypocrisy (Lev 19:15).

The assistants' remonstrance—"Do you dare to insult God's high priest?" (23:4)—points to the tension of this encounter between an apostle and the highest religious and political officer of the Jews, the high priest. Once Paul realized he was wrong, Paul confessed a sin of omission (see note on 23:5). His failure to consider Ananias's position left him open, through his hasty anger, to violate a basic biblical precept lived out by David in his dealings with Saul. Though an officeholder dishonors the office through his conduct, one does not have liberty to dishonor him (1 Sam 24:6; 26:9-11). "You must not . . . curse any of your rulers" (Exod 22:28). Paul had momentarily erred.

Paul then took the initiative to define the terms of his controversy with the Jews (23:6; cf. Quintillian *Institutio oratoria* 4.1.21). In so doing, not only did he seek to position himself before the Romans for a favorable disposition of his case, he also continued to participate in God's mission, testifying to the availability of salvation blessings in Jesus. The "trouble" was not that Paul had so attacked Judaism that he was culpable of violating Claudius's edicts of tolerance and non-molestation of the Jews (Josephus *Antiquities* 19:278-291). Rather, declaring himself a law-abiding and pious Jew—a Pharisee and a son of Pharisees—he shouted, "I am on trial because my hope is in the resurrection of the dead." Paul introduced the subject generally, seeking common ground with at least some of his audience. Many Jews, particularly the Pharisees, believed the inaugural event for participation in the messianic kingdom of the age to come was one's individual Resurrection (Dan 12:2; 2 Macc 7:14; *1 Enoch* 51:1-5; *Psalms of Solomon* 3:11-12). For the Christian, the firstfruits of this resurrection life could be experienced now because of Jesus' resurrection (2:32-33). With a bit of functional redundancy, Luke will show Paul developing this theme more and more fully through the defense speeches of the next several chapters (cf. 24:15, 21; 26:6-8, 22-23; cf. 25:19; 28:20).

Paul was on trial for declaring the hope of the resurrection as a present reality in its initial form, bringing salvation blessings to one restored people of God from all nations. Paul was on trial because of the Resurrection of Jesus. For if Jesus had not risen from the dead, he could not have appeared to Paul on the Damascus Road, or in the Temple, and commissioned him to take the gospel to the Gentiles (22:15, 21).

As Luke points out, and Josephus and other ancient Jewish literature documents, the Sadducees and Pharisees differed on what happens to human beings after death (23:8). The Pharisees affirmed both an intermediate state as "angels or spirits" and a final resurrection (Josephus *War* 2.163; *Antiquities* 18.14; see *2 Baruch* 51:5, 10 for evidence of Jewish belief in an intermediate state as angels; *1 Enoch* 22:3, 7; 103:3-4 for post-death existence as spirits). The Sadducees affirmed neither (Josephus *War* 2.165; *Antiquities* 18:16; cf. Luke 20:36). This led to a divided assembly and a "great uproar" befitting a mob scene (23:9; cf. 22:23). The Pharisees entered the verbal battle on Paul's side, declaring his innocence and the legitimacy of revelation from a "spirit" or an "angel." Such a tug of war ensued that Paul was about to be torn limb from limb, so the commander's troops intervened. How ironic that the one who had only twenty-four hours earlier ordered Paul to be stretched out for scourging should now snatch him out of the Jews' clutches, recognizing the prisoner as a Roman citizen and returning him to the barracks for safety.

What was to become of Paul? He had experienced the limits of the Spirit's warnings: bonds and afflictions in Jerusalem and being handed over to the Gentiles (20:22-23; 21:11). And he was in legal limbo with his case having little prospect of being clearly defined, let alone totally resolved. The commander had been thwarted at every turn in his attempt to get at the facts of the case. And the one court adequate to judge Paul's case, if it involved only an intramural debate about Jewish theology, had proved to be biased and out of control.

Mercifully, the Lord, in order to further encourage, guide, and direct Paul in his mission, appeared to him that night and told him: "Be encouraged, Paul. Just as you have been a witness to me here in Jerusalem, you must preach the Good News in Rome as well" (23:11). Paul then knew that the Lord approved of the witness he had borne and that he would, in the future, be a witness for Jesus in Rome.

◆ K. The Plan to Kill Paul (23:12-22)

¹²The next morning a group of Jews* got together and bound themselves with an oath not to eat or drink until they had killed Paul. ¹³There were more than forty of them in the conspiracy. ¹⁴They went to the leading priests and elders and told them, "We have bound ourselves with an oath to eat nothing until we have killed Paul. ¹⁵So you and the high council should ask the commander to bring Paul back to the council again. Pretend you want to examine his case more fully. We will kill him on the way."

¹⁶But Paul's nephew—his sister's son—heard of their plan and went to the fortress and told Paul. ¹⁷Paul called for one of the Roman officers* and said, "Take this young man to the commander. He has something important to tell him."

¹⁸So the officer did, explaining, "Paul, the prisoner, called me over and asked me to bring this young man to you because he has something to tell you."

¹⁹The commander took his hand, led him aside, and asked, "What is it you want to tell me?"

²⁰Paul's nephew told him, "Some Jews are going to ask you to bring Paul before the high council tomorrow, pretending they want to get some more information. ²¹But don't do it! There are more than forty men hiding along the way ready to ambush him. They have vowed not to eat or drink anything until they have killed him. They are ready now, just waiting for your consent."

²²"Don't let anyone know you told me this," the commander warned the young man.

23:12 Greek *the Jews.*   23:17 Greek *centurions;* also in 23:23.

NOTES
23:12-13 *a group of Jews.* As the NLT mg indicates, the Gr. reading is "the Jews." Although several mss indicate that not all the Jerusalem Jews plotted against Paul—only "some of the Jews" (*tines* [ᵀᴳ5100, ᶻᴳ5516] *tōn Ioudaiōn*: 𝔓48 𝔐 it syrᵖ copˢᵃ ᴹˢˢ)—better textual evidence supports the reading "the Jews" (*hoi Ioudaioi* [ᵀᴳ2453/A, ᶻᴳ2681]: 𝔓74 ℵ A B C E 33). In any event, it is evident that a group of Jews is in view, as 23:13 tells us that it was 40 or so Jews who conspired together.

got together . . . in the conspiracy. Though *sustrophē* [ᵀᴳ4963, ᶻᴳ5371] can mean simply a "gathering together" (cf. 19:40), the use of it with *poieō* [ᵀᴳ4160, ᶻᴳ4472] (make) and its employment as the virtual equivalent of *sunōmosia* [ᵀᴳ4945, ᶻᴳ5350] means it should be understood as a gathering for secret plotting, a component of its range of meaning (Barrett 1998: 1072; Witherington 1998:694; cf. Polybius *History* 4.34.6; Herodotus *Persian Wars* 7.9).

23:16 *Paul's nephew . . . told Paul.* A number of scholars explain the nephew's ready access to Paul by appealing to the Roman practice of allowing Christian prisoners to receive family, friends, and support (Kee 1997:267; Talbert 1997:204). Another points to Paul's particular circumstances, which required only light custody (Witherington 1998:695). He was a Roman citizen who had not yet been charged and was being kept not in prison but in the Roman barracks. Rapske (1994b:148) sees Paul, after several life-threatening encounters with the Jews, being held in protective custody with little access to visitors. It is the nephew's age and the consequent judgment by the authorities that he was a harmless youth that made his visit possible.

23:17-18, 22 *young man.* The nephew is described as *neanias* [TG3494, ZG3733] and *neaniskos* [TG3495, ZG3734] (diminutive of the former). A *neanias* is between 20 and 40 years old and a *neaniskos* is at the lower end of that range—between 22 and 28 (Pythagoras in Diogenes Laertes *Lives of the Eminent Philosophers* 8.10; Philo *Creation* 105, following Hippocrates). Keeping in mind that the commander took him by "the hand" (23:19) and Rapske's view that it is more likely that a harmless youth would be allowed to visit Paul (1994b:148), the nephew was probably at the lower end of the range.

23:21 *don't do it!* This renders *mē peisthēs* [TG3361/3982A, ZG3590/4275], which may be understood as "Don't believe them" or "Don't be persuaded by them" (Johnson 1992:404) or, as the NLT, "Don't do it!" i.e., acting on such belief or persuasion.

COMMENTARY

Paul would not have to wait long to act on the Lord's vision. The very next morning, more than forty Jews joined together in a scheme to do away with him. In a strong show of determination, they placed themselves under a curse, calling on God to send them to perdition if they did not fulfill their intent to kill Paul (23:12). They sealed their determination with a fast from food or drink until the deed was done. (*m. Nedarim* 3:1, 3 has provisions for release from a vow where circumstances prevent its conditions being met.)

The vow may have been an extension of a commitment to remove the curse of God from a defiled Temple by seeing to it that the perpetrator would experience "death at the hands of heaven" (see notes and commentary on 21:28-32). It appears that in Jewish thinking, zealous people would take on themselves that curse if God's offended holiness was not avenged.

The enemies of the gospel, in the end, had only the self-destructive power of self-imposed curses to try to realize their plans. What a feeble hope in comparison to the providential, saving power of God! And how ironic—those who placed themselves under a curse in order to remove a curse assumed that they were doing the will of God when, in reality, they were enemies of Jesus. These dedicated plotters were also deceptive plotters. In order to maneuver Paul into a situation where they could get at him, they asked the commander to bring Paul down again to the Sanhedrin. Presumably he would again be temporally released and therefore be under lightened security (cf. 22:30). The pretense was stated as a desire to more thoroughly explore his case so as to make a legal determination. But before Paul drew near to the Sanhedrin chamber, the plotters planned to kill him as they had vowed. There is more detail here about the machinations of the enemies of God's mission than we have previously met (contrast the description of the plot against Jesus in more general terms, Luke 22:1-6). The detail, in part, is necessitated by the narrative plot, for it provides the necessary corroborative background to the nephew's report to the commander (23:20-21). At the same time, the threefold repetition of the plot (23:12-13, 14, 21) and the twofold relating of the Sanhedrin's involvement (23:15, 20) serves to communicate the seriousness of the danger for Paul.

Providentially, Paul's nephew, a young man probably in his early twenties (see note on 23:17), heard of their plan to ambush Paul. He reported it to Paul, who then sent him with his message up the chain of command through a centurion ("officer," NLT) to the tribune ("commander," NLT; 23:17-18).

Paul, a Roman citizen in protective custody in the senior officers' quarters of the Antonia fortress, had the relative freedom and standing that the changes in the narrative require. He could deal in private with his nephew. With officers who had orders to accommodate him and grant his reasonable requests, he could summon a centurion and tell him to take the nephew to the tribune, and his request would be honored.

As the centurion reported to the commander, he unconsciously gave Paul a title that would become for the apostle a mark of persecution and a badge of honor. From now on, Paul was known as "Paul, the prisoner" (23:18; 25:14, 27). For freedom-loving ancients, to identify with someone in prison, deprived of liberty because of alleged or proven wrongdoing, could be a matter of shame (2 Tim 1:8). But for Paul that shame turned to honor when he lengthened the title to say "Paul, the prisoner of Christ Jesus" or "prisoner for the sake of Christ Jesus" (Eph 3:1; 4:1; Phlm 1:1, 9).

In a kind and discreet way, the commander interrogated the nephew (23:19-21). Evidently, the Sanhedrin had already lodged its request, for the young man urged the tribune, "Don't do it!" (23:21). The commander took the plot seriously, asking the young man to depart and not tell anyone that he had reported this (23:22).

With the emphasis through repetition on the murderous plot being hatched by this gang of forty against God's messenger, a destructive momentum developed that appeared unstoppable. If the Sanhedrin cooperated, surely the commander would be duped. But God's providence intervened in the form of a young relative whom God used to foil the plot. Thus, the uncovering of the murderous plot against Paul shows that God's providential ruling and overruling in the affairs of humankind is more than enough to thwart dedicated and deceptive conspiracy, especially when courageous and discerning humans do their part.

◆ L. Paul Is Sent to Caesarea (23:23-35)

23Then the commander called two of his officers and ordered, "Get 200 soldiers ready to leave for Caesarea at nine o'clock tonight. Also take 200 spearmen and 70 mounted troops. 24Provide horses for Paul to ride, and get him safely to Governor Felix." 25Then he wrote this letter to the governor:

26"From Claudius Lysias, to his Excellency, Governor Felix: Greetings!

27"This man was seized by some Jews, and they were about to kill him when I arrived with the troops. When I learned that he was a Roman citizen, I removed him to safety. 28Then I took him to their high council to try to learn the basis of the accusations against him. 29I soon discovered the charge was something regarding their religious law—certainly nothing worthy of imprisonment or death. 30But when I was informed of a plot to kill him, I immediately sent him on to you. I have told his accusers to bring their charges before you."

31So that night, as ordered, the soldiers took Paul as far as Antipatris. 32They returned to the fortress the next morning, while the mounted troops took him on to Caesarea. 33When they arrived in Caesarea, they presented Paul and the letter to Governor Felix. 34He read it and then asked Paul what province he was from. "Cilicia," Paul answered. [35]"I will hear your case myself when

23:35 Greek *Herod's Praetorium.*

your accusers arrive," the governor told him. Then the governor ordered him kept in the prison at Herod's headquarters.*

NOTES

23:23 *200 soldiers . . . 200 spearmen . . . 70 mounted troops.* Sending 470 troops does not "stretch credulity" (contra Spencer 1997:216; Fitzmyer 1998b:726) but was reasonable security, given the nature of the terrain, the anticipated ambush attack, and the general unrest in Judea at that time (Rapske 1994b:154; Witherington 1998:696). The garrison cohort of 1000 would temporarily be reduced by one third to one half, so they would have to return quickly (Keener 1993:393; cf. 23:32).

spearmen. The exact translation of *dexiolabous* [TG1187, ZG1287] (etymologically, "taking by the right [hand]") cannot be recovered because of lack of other occurrences in ancient literature. One suggestion that explains the term and ameliorates the "large number of troops" difficulty is the translation "led horses," which provides mounts for the 200 troops (Lake and Cadbury 1979:293; this also solves the supposed problem of a 35-mile overnight forced march on foot, Longenecker 1981:535-537). Another suggested translation is "light armed local police auxiliary," which would not be part of Roman garrison cohort (Kilpatrick 1963; Witherington [1998:696] doubts such existed).

23:25 *this letter.* The Gr. reads, *epistolēn echousan ton tupon touton* ("a letter having this pattern"). While some see this qualifier as claiming that Luke reproduced only the general purport or gist of the correspondence (Barrett 1998:1082; 3 Macc 3:30), others see it as a verbatim report of what became part of the court records for Paul's case (Judge in Horsley 1981:77-78). Witherington (1998:698) probably correctly sees the phrase as describing a "type of letter," an *elogium*—an official report explaining a legal matter.

23:29 *their religious law.* This rendering of *tou nomou* [TG3551, ZG3795] *autōn* ("their law") provides additional explanation, as does the Western text (614 2147 syr[h(mg)]), which after *autōn* [TG846, ZG899] adds *Mōuseōs kai Iēsou tinos* [TG3475/2424, ZG3707/2652], resulting in "the law of Moses and a certain Jesus."

23:31-32 *the soldiers took Paul as far as Antipatris.* Pointing to the terrain and ancient military practice, Bruce (1988:435) and Witherington (1998:697) believe the 35-mile overnight forced march was possible (contra Haenchen 1971:648; Barrett 1998:1086). Marshall (1980:372) suggests that the infantry did not go the whole way to Antipatris, while the cavalry did.

23:34 *province . . . "Cilicia."* At this time, Cilicia was not an independent province (it became one in AD 72) but instead was a part of Syria (Keener 1993:394). Since Judea, like Cilicia, was a part of Syria, for Felix to send the case on to the legate in Syria, citing the home origin of the accused, would probably have been viewed as an "annoying avoidance tactic" (Rapske 1994b:155; cf. Keener 1993:394). Further, such extradition would have created a great inconvenience for the Jewish leaders, whose goodwill Felix needed.

23:35 *the prison at Herod's headquarters.* Lit., Felix ordered Paul "guarded in the praetorium of Herod." The palace of Herod the Great at Caesarea had been taken over as the administrative headquarters and residence of the Roman governor. Probably in one of the rooms of this palace, not necessarily a prison, Paul experienced routine incarceration. As Rapske (1994b:157-158) characterizes it, "In contrast to the lightened military custody of Acts 24:23, Paul was closely watched, virtually immobile, in complete isolation from friends and associates."

COMMENTARY

Acting on the news of the plot (23:20-21), the commander called two of his centurions and instructed them to prepare for Paul's transfer in protective custody to Caesarea. The large number of troops, moving out under the cover of darkness ("nine o'clock tonight," 23:23—lit., the "third hour of night"; nighttime in Roman reckoning was calculated from sundown), shows the seriousness of the threat (see note on 23:23). The commander provided ample means of transport for Paul: "horses" (actually "mounts," or any domesticated animal used for riding, 23:24) may have been used as relays, or for baggage, or for personnel, either Paul's guards or traveling companions (Williams 1985:390). The orders were to set Paul on the mount and to convey him safely to Caesarea. Because he lacked the legal authority to hear Paul's case, the tribune may have already decided to transfer him to Felix. The news of the plot probably, then, only accelerated the process.

The governor in question was Felix. He had served under Cumanus, administering Samaria (AD 48–52), and he succeeded him as governor until his own recall in AD 59. Originally a slave, he was emancipated either by Antonia Minor, daughter of Mark Antony and mother of Emperor Claudius, or by Claudius himself, depending on whether Antonius (Tacitus *Histories* 5.9) or Claudius (Josephus *Antiquities* 20.137) is his correct *gentilicum* ("clan name"). Felix's tenure was marked by ongoing disturbances among the people, whether from the old-style terrorist-hoodlums (*lēstēs* [TG3027, ZG3334]), messianic impostors and false prophets (cf. 21:38), or the new threat—*sicarii* (*sikariōn* [TG4607, ZG4974]; cf. 21:38), assassins with their "short dagger" terror (Josephus *Antiquities* 20.160-61; *War* 2.252-253). The brutal measures he took to deal with these only turned the Jews more against him and stirred up more unrest. Tacitus said Felix "practiced every kind of cruelty and lust, wielding the power of king with all the instincts of a slave" (*Histories* 5.9).

Luke related the contents of a letter that accompanied Paul (23:26-30). It opens in the conventional way with the tribune, who identifies himself as Claudius Lysias (see note on 22:28), sending greetings to Governor Felix, who was addressed with the honorific title "his Excellency" (23:26; this was appropriate to this office, though Felix was not a member of the equestrian class). The commander then rehearsed his conduct with the prisoner and his assessment of the charges against him (23:27-29). Placing his conduct in the best possible light by stretching the truth, the commander said he "removed [Paul] to safety" because he knew he was a Roman citizen (23:27; in fact, Claudius only learned this later, after he had both bound Paul and was about to scourge him—facts he conveniently omitted). The commander's assessment was that Paul's offense concerned disputes regarding their religious law. This shows Paul's reorienting of his case before the Sanhedrin had been effective (see note on 23:6). As Gallio beforehand and Festus afterward, the commander understood the charges as theological and irrelevant to a Roman court. For this reason, he declared Paul innocent of all crimes before Roman law (23:29; cf. 18:17; 25:19). The commander concluded with his motivation for transferring Paul to Felix's custody—the "plot to kill" Paul. The object of such vigilante justice, which had even embroiled the

Sanhedrin as willing coconspirators, was such a potential source of continuing civil unrest that, in the tribune's judgment, the most judicious way for him to keep public order was to send this Roman citizen off to the coast and the governor's praetorium (23:30). He had decided to defuse the situation further by instructing Paul's accusers to settle their score with him by bringing their charges before Felix.

The 35-mile nighttime leg of Paul's transfer went without incident. Traversing the Judean hill country, either through Bethel or via the more southerly route to Lydda and then ten miles north, the military contingent came to Antipatris (modern Kulat Ras el Ain; 23:31). A military station at a trade route crossroads on the border of Samaria and Judea—just at the foot of the Judean hill country—it signaled safety to the troops, both geographically and ethnically. The topography and populace most amenable to Jewish ambush was behind them at this point. Ahead was a flat coastal plain inhabited predominantly by Gentiles. The infantry and spearmen returned home, while the cavalry took Paul the remaining 25 miles to Caesarea (23:32). There the officers "presented Paul and the letter to Governor Felix" (23:33).

Paul was now a step closer to Rome both geographically and judicially. Providentially, Paul was so secure in Gentile hands that the Jews' plot was completely thwarted. God had now set in motion Paul's centrifugal "mission in chains" from Jerusalem to Rome (23:11; cf. 1:8). This was also the final move of Paul's gospel witness away from Jerusalem. Though he would continue to witness "to the Jew first" (cf. 28:17-27), Jerusalem's refusal to receive the gospel message and constant intent to destroy its messengers sealed its judgment from God (Luke 13:34-35; 21:20, 24; Acts 22:18, 22; 25:3).

A Roman judge had a choice whether to try a defendant in his home province, the province where he was apprehended, or where the alleged crime occurred (*Digest* 48.3.7, 11). Felix thus tried to avoid this potentially troublesome case by inquiring after Paul's home province (23:34). Felix might have wanted to show a courtesy to the monarch of a client kingdom. Paul's reply, however, boxed Felix in (see note on 23:34). Politically sensitive both to the legate of Syria, Ummidus Quadratus, to whom he was responsible, and to the Jewish aristocracy who would be inconvenienced by any change of venue, Felix decided to take the case himself and assigned Paul to regular incarceration in "Herod's headquarters" (Herod's praetorium; see note on 23:35). Pilate was unable to transfer jurisdiction over Jesus to Herod Antipas. As a result, Jesus' prophetic declaration that he would suffer in Jerusalem was fulfilled (Luke 23:6-7). So here, God had so worked through a Roman official's sensibilities that Paul was kept on the most direct path for fulfillment of his mission to Rome (23:34-35; cf. 19:21; 23:11).

In the transfer of Paul to Felix's custody, God used a combination of Roman vigilance for public order, regard for legal proceedings, and sensitivity to political realities to accomplish the very opposite of the Jewish plot. As a result, Paul was kept alive and secure in the hands of the Romans. In the process, God placed him a step closer judicially and geographically to the fulfillment of his promise that Paul would bear witness in Rome (23:11).

◆   M. Paul Appears before Felix (24:1-27)

Five days later Ananias, the high priest, arrived with some of the Jewish elders and the lawyer* Tertullus, to present their case against Paul to the governor. ²When Paul was called in, Tertullus presented the charges against Paul in the following address to the governor:

"Your Excellency, you have provided a long period of peace for us Jews and with foresight have enacted reforms for us. ³For all of this we are very grateful to you. ⁴But I don't want to bore you, so please give me your attention for only a moment. ⁵We have found this man to be a troublemaker who is constantly stirring up riots among the Jews all over the world. He is a ringleader of the cult known as the Nazarenes. ⁶Furthermore, he was trying to desecrate the Temple when we arrested him.* ⁸You can find out the truth of our accusations by examining him yourself." ⁹Then the other Jews chimed in, declaring that everything Tertullus said was true.

¹⁰The governor then motioned for Paul to speak. Paul said, "I know, sir, that you have been a judge of Jewish affairs for many years, so I gladly present my defense before you. ¹¹You can quickly discover that I arrived in Jerusalem no more than twelve days ago to worship at the Temple. ¹²My accusers never found me arguing with anyone in the Temple, nor stirring up a riot in any synagogue or on the streets of the city. ¹³These men cannot prove the things they accuse me of doing.

¹⁴"But I admit that I follow the Way, which they call a cult. I worship the God of our ancestors, and I firmly believe the Jewish law and everything written in the prophets. ¹⁵I have the same hope in God that these men have, that he will raise both the righteous and the unrighteous.

¹⁶Because of this, I always try to maintain a clear conscience before God and all people.

¹⁷"After several years away, I returned to Jerusalem with money to aid my people and to offer sacrifices to God. ¹⁸My accusers saw me in the Temple as I was completing a purification ceremony. There was no crowd around me and no rioting. ¹⁹But some Jews from the province of Asia were there—and they ought to be here to bring charges if they have anything against me! ²⁰Ask these men here what crime the Jewish high council* found me guilty of, ²¹except for the one time I shouted out, 'I am on trial before you today because I believe in the resurrection of the dead!' "

²²At that point Felix, who was quite familiar with the Way, adjourned the hearing and said, "Wait until Lysias, the garrison commander, arrives. Then I will decide the case." ²³He ordered an officer* to keep Paul in custody but to give him some freedom and allow his friends to visit him and take care of his needs.

²⁴A few days later Felix came back with his wife, Drusilla, who was Jewish. Sending for Paul, they listened as he told them about faith in Christ Jesus. ²⁵As he reasoned with them about righteousness and self-control and the coming day of judgment, Felix became frightened. "Go away for now," he replied. "When it is more convenient, I'll call for you again." ²⁶He also hoped that Paul would bribe him, so he sent for him quite often and talked with him.

²⁷After two years went by in this way, Felix was succeeded by Porcius Festus. And because Felix wanted to gain favor with the Jewish people, he left Paul in prison.

24:1 Greek *some elders and an orator.*   24:6 Some manuscripts add an expanded conclusion to verse 6, all of verse 7, and an additional phrase in verse 8: *We would have judged him by our law, ⁷but Lysias, the commander of the garrison, came and violently took him away from us, ⁸commanding his accusers to come before you.*   24:20 Greek *Sanhedrin.*   24:23 Greek *a centurion.*

NOTES

24:1-27 Johnson's (1992:415) and Brown's (1996) evaluations of this passage's historicity are negative. Others think the speeches are Lukan compositions (Dunn 1996:311; Barrett 1998:1091). Winter (1991; 1993:305-336), Rapske (1994b:158-172), and Sherwin-White (1963:48-70), however, make a strong case for the course of the proceedings, the rhetorical moves of the forensic speeches, and Felix's handling of the matter as accurately reflecting first-century Roman legal proceedings within the *extra ordinem* system available to provincial governors. The fact that such proceedings, including the content of speeches, were written down makes it likely that Luke could write up this scene with the aid of written sources.

24:1 *elders and the lawyer.* The reading in the NLT mg, *some elders and an orator,* correctly gives the literal meaning of the phrase *presbuterōn* [TG4245/A, ZG4565] *tinōn kai rhētoros.* It should be noted that a common function of a *rhētōr* [TG4489, ZG4842] was to serve as a lawyer (P. Oxyrhynchus 1.37, col 1.4ff, [AD 49]; P. Oxyrhynchus 2.237, col. 7.25, [AD 186]).

24:2-3 *Tertullus presented the charges against Paul.* It is commonplace among commentators to label Tertullus's exordium, particularly his description of conditions during Felix's tenure, as "blatantly false flattery" (Keener 1993:394). Winter (1991:515), however, demonstrates that Tertullus is telling the truth, when "peace" is understood not as tranquility but as pacification (the restoration of law and order in an extremely volatile situation) and "reforms" refer to his skill as a jurist.

24:4 *bore.* The word *enkoptō* [TG1465, ZG1601] is better understood as "hinder" as applied to time; hence, "detain." The idea of keeping things short is a common sentiment in the *exordia* (meaning "introduction") of speeches (cf. Lucian *Two Indictments* 16: "But not to prolong my introduction when the water [in the water clock] has been running freely this long time, I will begin my complaint").

24:6-7 The NLT rightly relegates to a footnote a longer reading found in later mss, primarily Western (E 044 𝔐 33 614 1739 it^gig syr^(p)). This reading came into English versions and their numbering systems via the Textus Receptus. Johnson (1992:414) finds the content, though not original, psychologically plausible, but Witherington (1998:708) disagrees. He sees the negative comments about the Romans as unlikely. Evidently the abrupt ending of the shorter reading's relative clause with *ekratēsamen* [TG2902, ZG3195] (we arrested) led copyists to supply the sequel of the longer ending (Metzger 1994:434).

24:10 *for many years.* This is not simply rhetorical exaggeration (contra Fitzmyer 1998b:734) but a basically true statement (Witherington 1998:709) if one combines Felix's tenure as administrator of Samaria under Cumanus (AD 48-52; Tacitus, *Annals* 12.54) with his time as governor of Judea (AD 52-57; Josephus *War* 2.247; *Antiquities* 20.137; Winter 1991:523).

24:11 *no more than twelve days ago.* This is not merely a literary addition of the "seven days" in 21:27 and the "five days" in 24:1 (contra Fitzmyer [1998b:735] who says the number does not square with the narrative's time referents and may involve this simple math). Rather, it encompasses the time of Paul's activity in Jerusalem: day 1—arrival (21:17); day 2—negotiations with James (21:18); days 3-9—purification (21:27); day 10—before the council (22:30); day 11—discovery of plot (23:16-21); day 12—transfer to Caesarea (23:32; after 6 p.m., according to Jewish reckoning; see Haenchen 1971:654).

24:15 *I have the same hope in God that these men have, that he will raise both the righteous and the unrighteous.* Here is an exaggeration if the accusers, the Sadducean high priest and elders, only are meant. At the most only some would be of the Pharisaic persuasion (Dunn 1996:313). Paul, addressing a Gentile, was probably thinking of them qualitatively as Jews, the majority of whom (with some of their leaders) did have a resurrection hope (Witherington 1998:711).

24:17 *After several years away.* Lit., "after many years." This is, again, not necessarily an exaggeration if Paul was referring either to the time of his official break with Judaism at his conversion in the mid-30s (Barrett 1998:1107) or to the Jerusalem council, his last lengthy visit (AD 49; cf. his last visit five years ago, 18:22).

with money to aid my people. As the record of the church delegation in 20:4 hints, and Paul in his letters explicitly relates (Rom 15:26; 1 Cor 16:1; 2 Cor 8:4; 9:1, 13), this monetary aid probably refers to the collection that Paul made among the Gentile churches for the poor in the Jerusalem church (Barrett 1998:1108). It is less likely that it points simply to an act of Jewish piety (contra Talbert 1997:207).

to offer sacrifices to God. Although "sacrifices" in the Gr. syntax looks like an afterthought and may thus point to the sacrifices Paul agreed to pay for the poor Jewish Christians under a Nazirite vow, or as part of his own purification (21:24; Johnson 1992:413; Witherington 1998:712), it could well indicate a thanksgiving offering for the safe delivery of the collection (Williams 1985:400).

24:18 *as I was completing a purification ceremony.* The perfect passive participle that this clause represents (*hēgnismenon* [TG48, ZG49]) refers to being in a state of ritual purity, "having been and continuing to be purified" (Barrett 1998:1108; Dunn 1996:314), not completing rites (contra NLT; Fitzmyer 1998b:736-737). It was part of Paul's defense against the charge of "trying to desecrate the Temple" (24:6).

24:22 *quite familiar with the Way.* Lit., "knowing more accurately the things concerning the Way." This description indicates that Felix understood the Christian movement better than Paul's accusers, at least better than they thought he did (Barrett 1998:1111-1112; Witherington 1998:713; the elative sense is possible but less likely, contra NLT; Fitzmyer 1998b:739). He was better informed about the beliefs and practices of Christianity and hence knew some of the charges were bogus (Winter 1991:165-166).

24:23 *custody.* This is not *custodia libera*, confinement without chains (contra Barrett 1998:1113) but, on the analogy of Agrippa I's detention in Rome (Josephus *Antiquities* 18.235), a lightened military custody in which Paul was still in chains (26:29), held in a room in Herod's praetorium with a soldier (a centurion) assigned to him, though not dependent on his keepers to sanction his every activity.

24:27 *Felix was succeeded by Porcius Festus.* Though Eusebius placed the change of governors from Felix to Festus at AD 55–56, Bruce (1990:484) and Witherington (1998:716) correctly argue—from the impression Josephus gives of a brief tenure and the change of coinage in Palestine—that Festus probably commenced his tenure in AD 59 (Josephus *Antiquities* 20.182-197; *War* 2.271).

COMMENTARY

With a sense of urgency, only "five days later," the presiding officer, Ananias the high priest, and a representative number of the Sanhedrin, arrived with their lawyer Tertullus in Caesarea (24:1). Following standard judicial procedure, Luke reports they didn't simply intend to press charges but actually "present their case" before Felix.

The trial began as Paul was called in and Tertullus made the case for the Jews. In this forensic speech's exordium (24:2-4), we find a *captatio benevolentiae*, which skillfully achieves ancient rhetoric's goal of obtaining the judge's good will, attention, and readiness to learn (Quintillian *Institutio oratoria* 4.1.50). Tertullus noted benefits of Felix's tenure ("peace" and "reforms") with which he would contrast the charges he made against Paul (24:2). The "peace" admittedly was more a pacification of a territory through an ongoing series of search-and-destroy missions against hoodlum terrorists, including that Egyptian messianic pretender with whom Lysias had confused Paul (21:38; Josephus *War* 2.253, 261-265; *Antiquities* 20.160-161). Felix had also enacted law reforms through his "foresight" (*pronoias* [TG4307, ZG4630]; 24:2). Possibly these followed through on Emperor Claudius's edicts concerning maintaining peace in Jewish communities (18:2; *Greek Papyri in the British Museum [P. Lond.]* 1912, lines 96-100). Tertullus, in another standard rhetorical move, declared his intent to move to the charges directly and deal with them briefly. This quality of reasonableness, patience, and mercy, by which one may move beyond the strict bounds of legality in hearing a case, may be a hint that even the Jewish accusers knew they did not have much of a case (Johnson 1992:410; Witherington 1998:707).

As Tertullus laid out the charges against Paul in his *narratio* (the narration of the facts of the case, 24:5), he moved from the general to the more specific. Paul was a "troublemaker" (lit., a "plague"; *loimos* [TG3061/A, ZG3369]); he stirred up insurrection among all the Jews throughout the world; he was "a ringleader of the cult known as the Nazarenes" (24:5). Given the disposition of Claudius and the situation in Palestine, these were the most serious of criminal charges (cf. 17:6-7; Luke 23:2) and were framed in a most provocative way. Emperor Claudius's letter to the Alexandrines (November 10, AD 41) uses similar language. He warned the Jews that if they persisted in suspicious activities, he would "by all means take vengeance on them as fomenters of what is a general plague infecting the whole world" (*Greek Papyri in the British Museum [P. Lond.]* 1912, line 99). The way Paul fomented such insurrection was as a "cult" ringleader, the leader of an unauthorized minority movement within Judaism. Tertullus used a contemptuous nickname for Christians, "Nazarenes," derived from Nazareth, the hometown of their leader Jesus. The contempt grew out of the town's obscurity or its illegitimacy as the Messiah's hometown (John 1:46; 7:41-42). Felix had to constantly deal with theologically motivated civil uprisings from such movements (Josephus *War* 2.253-165).

Tertullus's proof that these facts were true was Paul's attempt to defile the Temple and the Jewish leaders' response in arresting him, committed as they were to aiding Rome in maintaining public order (24:6). During this period, Rome had taken responsibility as protector of the Temple as a holy site (Josephus *War* 6.128). The lawyer's persuasive conclusion became an invitation to the judge to examine Paul for himself. As the enemies of the righteous one surrounded him to attack (Ps 3:7 LXX), so the Jews there "chimed in, declaring that everything Tertullus said was true" (24:9).

With the defense's turn next, Felix motioned for Paul to speak. The apostle's *captatio benevolentiae* was more brief, but no less ingratiating (24:10). Because of Felix's competence in judging "Jewish affairs" (lit., "this nation"; 24:10), gained through a long tenure (see note on 24:10), Paul had confidence to make his defense. Whereas Tertullus's introduction with its references to peace and reforms prepared the way for criminal charges of insurrection (24:2-3), Paul framed his case in terms of internal Jewish matters, and theological ones at that, thereby focusing Felix's attention on his role as judge over the Jewish nation.

After a very brief *narratio* (24:11), Paul engaged in his proof by picking up the charges one after another and showing each to be groundless. In his statement of the facts of the case, he narrowed the environment of the alleged crime from his activities "all over the world" to Jerusalem. This matched the extent of Felix's jurisdiction. He said Felix could "quickly discover" that the apostle had neither opportunity nor motive for such insurrectionist or blasphemous activity. There was too little time, since he had arrived in Jerusalem "no more than twelve days ago" (see note on 24:11), and his whole purpose was "to worship at the Temple."

Paul then took up the first charge: being a troublemaker who incited the Jews to riots and rebellions against the Roman government (24:12-13; cf. 24:5a). He insisted that he was not arguing in the Temple. That is, he had confined himself to the Christian community (21:17-26) and was not engaged in any activity of persuasive witness among unbelieving Jews (cf. 17:2, 17; 18:4; 19:8-9) that would seek to attract them to a movement his accusers labeled seditious. Further, neither in synagogues nor in the city at large did he incite a riot. Paul closed this defense with the blanket claim that his accusers could not prove their accusations (24:13). This was certainly true for any charges of empire-wide incitement of Jewish rebellion against the state. The Jerusalem leaders would have no firsthand knowledge of it. They could not prove any seditious activity at the Temple, as the weakness of the wording of their proof showed: "trying to desecrate the Temple" (24:6).

Then he answered the second charge, that he was a "ringleader of the cult known as the Nazarenes" (24:5b). Paul so redefined the sect, which he called "the Way," that no basis was left for claiming that it was a theologically-motivated seditious nationalist movement (24:14-16). Paul did confess that he lived his life as a service of worship to God according to "the Way" (24:14). While Luke can use *latreuō* [TG3000, ZG3302] (to offer service in worship) to refer to the carrying out of specifically religious duties (Luke 2:37; Acts 7:7; 26:7), he and Paul also employed it, as here, to characterize the whole of one's life as a Christian (Luke 1:74; Acts 27:23; Rom 1:9; 12:1; Phil 3:3). Similarly, Christianity, or the lifestyle it commended, became known as "the Way" (9:2; 19:9, 23; 22:4, 22; cf. 1QS 9:16-21). Both the Dead Sea Scroll community and the New Testament church via John the Baptist's ministry had used as their mandate Isaiah 40:3: "Prepare the way for the LORD's coming!" (Luke 3:3-6; 1QS 8:13-16). The Dead Sea Scroll community prepared the way for the Lord through the study of the law, but Jesus' teaching set his followers on a more eschatologically imminent, ethically radical, profoundly personal, and dynamically evangelistic "way" (Luke 14:25-33; Acts 1:8; John 14:6; Pathrapankal 1979:533-539).

Paul also emphasized the Christian's continuity with Old Testament Jewish faith. He worshiped the same God, "the God of our ancestors" (24:14; cf. 3:13; 5:30; 7:32). He appealed to the same authority—believing all that is written in the law and the prophets—whether for his gospel message (Luke 24:25-27, 44; Acts 13:29, 33; 26:22, 27) or his ethic (23:5). The particular belief he declared in common with his Jewish compatriots was "a hope" (24:15), the event that triggers the final fulfillment of salvation blessings: the resurrection of the righteous and unrighteous (see note on

24:15). Indeed, Israel's stance concerning its individual and national destiny was to wait in hope for the salvation of God (Ps 119:166; Isa 25:6-8; 66:9; Joel 3:15-16; Mal 4:5-6). The content of that hope was the Resurrection (Isa 26:19; Dan 12:2; *1 Enoch* 51:1-2). According to Paul's argument, since this salvation blessing is beyond this life and is all God's doing, Paul's life, lived according to the Way, could hardly be the impetus for inciting insurrectionist activity among the Jews. In fact, Paul concluded his defense against this second charge with the assertion that such a belief, including a coming judgment at the final resurrection, actually enabled him "to maintain a clear conscience before God and all people" (24:16; cf. 23:1).

Paul then answered the third charge—that he had attempted to desecrate the Temple (24:6; 17-18a). The purpose and propriety of his visit excluded such sacrilege. His was the purpose of a pious pilgrim: almsgiving and sacrifices (see note on 24:17). When found in the Temple, he was engaged in ritual purification (cf. 21:26). Before his persuasive conclusion, Paul returned once more to the other charges and denied them: neither a crowd nor rioting surrounded him (24:18b).

Paul's persuasive conclusion (24:19-21) revolved around the absence of eyewitness accusers and what he considered his one chargeable offense. A time-honored Roman judicial principle was that before any verdict, accusers must face the accused in person, and there must be opportunity for a defense (25:16; Appian *Roman History: Civil Wars* 3.54). For the alleged offense of Temple defilement, let alone the accusation of empire-wide incitement of insurrection, Jews from the province of Asia should be present to accuse him, but they were not (24:19). The only "crime" Ananias and the elders witnessed was the shouted confession in the high council (Sanhedrin): "I am on trial before you today because I believe in the resurrection of the dead!" (24:21; cf. 23:6). This was no crime before the state, only a matter of intramural theological debate among the Jews (cf. 23:29).

To end on the idea of resurrection was not only good legal defense strategy but also good evangelism. As we will see in the follow-up witness with Felix, to speak of the final accounting before God and the eternal destiny that flows from it was to point to one of the certainties of human existence. Many may run from it, following alternate paths of personal eschatology—reincarnation or immediate annihilation—but all will have to face it. The resurrection and the promise of eternal salvation must be at the heart of all gospel preaching (Luke 24:46-47; Acts 17:30-31; 26:23).

The facts of the case were not yet clear to Felix. The two *narratiae* diverged at key points. Was Paul seditious or not, especially since he had to be rescued from the midst of a riotous crowd? Did Paul try to defile the Temple or not, especially since key eyewitnesses were absent? Felix, being "quite familiar with the Way" (see note on 24:22), knew that by reputation this sect of the Nazarenes were not insurrectionists. Still he wanted to get the independent witness of Lysias Claudius. So to avoid an action unpopular with the Jewish leaders, who could cause trouble for him if they so chose, and to leave open the possibility of a bribe from Paul (cf. 24:17, 26), Felix declared, "*Amplius*" (Papyrus Tebtunis 1.22.9)—an adjournment to a fuller hearing in which he could make a decision based on the testimony of Lysias Claudius.

Felix consigned Paul to a lightened military custody with his friends (lit., "his own"; cf. 4:23), who relieved the prison system by attending to his physical needs for daily food and clothing. After several days, Felix and his Jewish wife Drusilla came to the section of the palace where Paul was being kept and sent for him. Drusilla, one of the three daughters of Agrippa I (12:1-23), was born in AD 38. When she was fourteen, Drusilla's brother Agrippa II (25:13-26:32) gave her in marriage to Azizus, King of Emesa, a small kingdom on the Orontes. Then she was encountered by Felix, whom Tacitus said indulged in "every kind of barbarity and lust" (*Histories* 5.9). Captivated by Drusilla's beauty, Felix wooed her away from Azizus with the aid of a Cyprian Jew named Atomus, who pretended to be a magician. Drusilla married Felix as much to escape the enmity of her sister Bernice, who abused her because of her beauty, as in response to his amorous spell (Josephus *Antiquities* 20.139-144). Felix was thrice married (Suetonius *Claudius* 28). This Drusilla replaced another Drusilla, the granddaughter of Antony and Cleopatra. Felix and Drusilla would have been known to some in Luke's Roman audience, since they went to Rome after Felix was removed from his procuratorship in AD 59.

To such a dissolute couple, Paul preached "faith in Christ [Messiah] Jesus" (3:20; 5:42; 17:3; 18:5; 20:21). Jesus, "the Righteous One," is the one to whom Paul was to bear witness and on whom he and everyone must depend for salvation blessings (22:14-16, 18). Those salvation blessings include, above all, the forgiveness of sins, which must be embraced in a repentant turning from sin and turning to God, and Paul knew that if he was to help Drusilla and Felix understand how urgent it was for them to embrace the Good News, he had to first declare the bad news of the "coming day of judgment" for all who do not meet the standards of "righteousness" and "self-control" (24:25). Such cardinal virtues would have been familiar (Plutarch *Moralia* 97E), but not the "coming day of judgment." Felix, a Roman freedman, probably knew it only in a different form, being "vaguely persuaded that souls went down from the tomb to some deep places where they received rewards and punishments" (Cumont 1959:86).

As Jesus promised (John 16:8-11), the Spirit so worked through Paul's preaching that terror gripped Felix, but it did not lead to humble faith. Felix used procrastination to stay in control of his own destiny, temporally speaking. He would determine when and to what extent he would consider these matters in the future (24:25). And following common provincial administrative practice, he wanted money from Paul in exchange for his release (24:26; Josephus *Antiquities* 20.215; *War* 2.273). He was evidently willing to trade the hope of eternal life later for the hope of money now (24:15, 26). Jesus warned of the unevenness of such a trade (Luke 9:25; cf. Luke 8:14).

Felix eventually left office under a cloud. A Jewish delegation's complaint to the emperor about his ruthless suppression of a dispute between Jews and Gentiles in Caesarea led to his removal (Josephus *Antiquities* 20.182; *Wars* 2.266-270). He sought to do the Jews a favor by leaving Paul in prison (24:27). Paul's plight was clearly a miscarriage of justice and unworthy of a Roman citizen, but it continued to provide the protection from the hostile Jewish opposition that was needed if Paul was ever to get to Rome.

In conclusion, Paul defended himself before Felix and took opportunities to witness with a message that brought out the distinctive character of God on mission. The message dealt with each person's eternal destiny. Since it was a call to embrace the hope of a divine resurrection of the righteous (24:15), the final fulfillment of salvation blessings would be beyond this life, removing the charge of revolution from the Christian movement."

◆ N. Paul Appears before Festus (25:1-22)

Three days after Festus arrived in Caesarea to take over his new responsibilities, he left for Jerusalem, ²where the leading priests and other Jewish leaders met with him and made their accusations against Paul. ³They asked Festus as a favor to transfer Paul to Jerusalem (planning to ambush and kill him on the way). ⁴But Festus replied that Paul was at Caesarea and he himself would be returning there soon. ⁵So he said, "Those of you in authority can return with me. If Paul has done anything wrong, you can make your accusations."

⁶About eight or ten days later Festus returned to Caesarea, and on the following day he took his seat in court and ordered that Paul be brought in. ⁷When Paul arrived, the Jewish leaders from Jerusalem gathered around and made many serious accusations they couldn't prove.

⁸Paul denied the charges. "I am not guilty of any crime against the Jewish laws or the Temple or the Roman government," he said.

⁹Then Festus, wanting to please the Jews, asked him, "Are you willing to go to Jerusalem and stand trial before me there?"

¹⁰But Paul replied, "No! This is the official Roman court, so I ought to be tried right here. You know very well I am not guilty of harming the Jews. ¹¹If I have done something worthy of death, I don't refuse to die. But if I am innocent, no one has a right to turn me over to these men to kill me. I appeal to Caesar!"

¹²Festus conferred with his advisers and then replied, "Very well! You have appealed to Caesar, and to Caesar you will go!"

¹³A few days later King Agrippa arrived with his sister, Bernice,* to pay their respects to Festus. ¹⁴During their stay of several days, Festus discussed Paul's case with the king. "There is a prisoner here," he told him, "whose case was left for me by Felix. ¹⁵When I was in Jerusalem, the leading priests and Jewish elders pressed charges against him and asked me to condemn him. ¹⁶I pointed out to them that Roman law does not convict people without a trial. They must be given an opportunity to confront their accusers and defend themselves.

¹⁷"When his accusers came here for the trial, I didn't delay. I called the case the very next day and ordered Paul brought in. ¹⁸But the accusations made against him weren't any of the crimes I expected. ¹⁹Instead, it was something about their religion and a dead man named Jesus, who Paul insists is alive. ²⁰I was at a loss to know how to investigate these things, so I asked him whether he would be willing to stand trial on these charges in Jerusalem. ²¹But Paul appealed to have his case decided by the emperor. So I ordered that he be held in custody until I could arrange to send him to Caesar."

²²"I'd like to hear the man myself," Agrippa said.

And Festus replied, "You will—tomorrow!"

25:13 Greek Agrippa the king and Bernice arrived.

NOTES

25:8 *crime against . . . the Roman government.* Johnson (1992:421) asks whether this defense indicates the Jews had shifted their accusations against Paul from a focus on disturbances "among the Jews" to inciting Jewish insurrection against the Romans. Spencer (1997:223), however, rightly sees this as a direct rebuttal of Tertullus's charges in 24:5. Barrett (1998:1126) points back to Claudius Lysias's misidentification of him with the revolutionary Egyptian (21:38).

25:9 *Are you willing to go to Jerusalem and stand trial before me there?* Paul's interpretive response and appeal (25:10-11) finds Festus's offer problematic and introduces ambiguity into what, on the surface, seems to be a straightforward proposal for a change of venue but was actually grounded in the governor's desire "to please the Jews." Most commentators, following Roman law and Festus's promise not to change jurisdictions, say Paul wanted to avoid going to Jerusalem either because he feared death from ambush along the way (cf. 25:3) or the undue negative influence of the Jerusalem venue on Festus, whose pro-Jewish proposal indicated his judicial impartiality was already compromised (Barrett 1998:1127). In Jerusalem, Festus would probably choose the Sanhedrin or Sanhedrin sympathizers as his advisory council and would be subject to the pressure of a public hostile to Paul (Rapske 1994b:186; Fitzmyer 1998b:744). The threat, however, may have been even more serious. Festus may have been trying to deceive Paul by proposing a change in venue, which would have become a de facto, if not de jure, change in jurisdiction (Krodel 1986:446; see note on 25:11).

25:11 *no one has a right to turn me over to these men to kill me.* Lit., "no one is able to make a gift of me to them." Paul's figurative language plays on the governor's desire to please the Jews ("to grant them a favor," *charin katathesthai* [TG5485/2698, ZG5921/2960]; 25:9; cf. 24:27) and manifests what he was convinced would be the result: a verdict according to the Jews' wishes, hence "making a gift" of him to them. Indeed, Festus interpreted the Jews' initial request of asking a favor against Paul as violating Roman law since it would, without trial, convict him. Paul rightly perceived that if Festus was intent on pleasing Jews who had such aims, the legal process in Jerusalem could only result in a miscarriage of justice—a death-penalty verdict against him.

I appeal to Caesar. Because Paul appealed before the verdict was rendered, scholars have debated whether or not he was actually invoking *provocatio*, the Roman citizen's right to appeal against the verdict of a magistrate in criminal cases calling for capital, corporeal, or economic punishment (Rapske 1994b:186-188). Though some do not appear to see the irregularity (Barrett 1998:1130; Witherington 1998:723), most of those who do conclude it is an unusual or less common employment of the right (Keener 1993:397; Sherwin-White 1963:57-68).

25:12 *Festus conferred with his advisers.* Scholars debate whether Festus was compelled to grant the appeal (Fitzmyer 1998b:746). Johnson (1992:422) says that since Paul's case dealt in *extra ordinem* matters—i.e., matters beyond established Roman law—the appeal could be ignored. Rapske (1994b:188) says its unusual circumstances (see note above on 25:11, "I appeal to Caesar") makes it doubtful that Festus was compelled to grant it. Sherwin-White (1963:65) and Barrett (1998:1131), however, strongly contend that *provocatio*'s effect was automatic, stopping the judicial process until it was taken up by the higher court. Festus's purpose in consulting his advisers would then not be to determine whether to grant the appeal but to determine if this were the type of case in which it applied (Witherington 1998:723).

25:13-22 Though not denying the historical possibility of a meeting of Festus and Agrippa and Bernice, many commentators routinely judge that Luke's reports of these private conversations were his own composition, since it is unlikely he had an eyewitness source

(Dunn 1996:317-318; Barrett 1998:1134; Fitzmyer 1998b:748). Some say the content may have been deduced from statements in the public hearing (23:23-27; Longenecker 1981:547). Given Festus's self-exoneration, which does not necessarily contribute to a Lukan theme of upright Roman officials but does explain the depth of Paul's dilemma, it is plausible to suppose Luke had access to informants for this private scene (Williams 1985:411).

25:13 *Bernice.* Most commentators simply report the widespread rumors of Bernice's incestuous relationship with her brother Agrippa II (Josephus *Antiquities* 20.145-146; *War* 2.217; *Juvenal Satires* 5.156-160; Spencer 1997:225; Barrett 1998:1135; Fitzmyer 1998b:749; Witherington 1998:728). Talbert (1997:20) and Fernando (1998:593) treat them as fact, while Keener (1993:398) and Dunn (1996:321) doubt their veracity. Though Bernice may have simply served as consort for her unmarried brother, the strength of the rumors and the fact that Bernice married Polemo, king of Cilicia, in order to quash them, probably means they had some basis in reality (note Josephus's wording at *War* 2.217).

to pay their respects. The NLT takes the aorist participle *aspasamenoi* [TG782, ZG832] (greet, pay respects) as showing purpose. While unusual (one would expect a future participle), it is so understood by Johnson (1992:425) and Fitzmyer (1998b:749). Barrett's (1998:1135) suggestion of coincident action "arriving and greeting" makes good sense in the immediate context and is congruent with normal participial usage.

25:18 *expected.* The term *hupenooun* [TG5282, ZG5706] may mean "suppose, suspect, under-stand, take cognizance of." "Suspect" would be a harsher meaning, indicating that the Jews had presented a poor case (Rapske 1994b:184), and "take cognizance of" would, it seems, reflect legal phrasing—*de quibus cognoscere volebam*, meaning, "of which I could take cogni-zance," referring to the taking up of a case. "Supposed" or "expected" (NLT), though, is preferred because it points to the contrast between the kind of case Festus would have expected (one involving charges according to Roman law) and the kind of case that was actually presented to him (one involving the points of a theological intramural debate; Barrett 1998:1138).

25:19 *their religion.* Some see this as just a neutral use of *deisidaimonias* [TG1175, ZG1272] ("religion, superstition"; Dunn 1996:321; Fitzmyer 1998b:750). Since, however, Festus was treating Agrippa II as an outsider to Judaism (it is *"their* religion," not his) and was making remarks that were fairly disparaging, it is better to take the reference as pejorative, accord-ing to the normal use of the word (Witherington 1998:730).

COMMENTARY

Festus's tenure as procurator began with the competent efficiency that would mark his brief administration (AD 59–61; Josephus *Antiquities* 20.182-197; *War* 2.271). A mere three days after his arrival in the province, he was on his way to Jerusalem to meet the Jewish national leadership (25:1-2). Within the environ-ment of revolutionary-inspired civil unrest, "the leading priests and other Jewish leaders" wasted no time in laying out their case against Paul, an alleged inciter of insurrection (25:2). They persistently "implored" Festus (*parekaloun* [TG3870, ZG4151], imperfect tense) for a favor "against" Paul (*kata* [TG2596, ZG2848], 25:3; not rendered in NLT). They wanted a change of venue for Paul's trial, a seemingly innocent request, which masked a more sinister intent: to ambush and kill Paul (cf. 23:16, 21). They would use treachery to be rid of Paul, as their predecessors had with his Lord (Luke 22:2-6; Acts 2:23). Given how the newly appointed high

priest Ishmael b. Phiabi and the priestly elite conducted themselves, the perpetra-
tion of such a plot was entirely possible (Josephus *Antiquities* 20.178-181, 194-196).

Festus asserted his authority as procurator and, for his own convenience, denied
their request; however, he invited them to accompany him back to Caesarea, where
the prisoner was incarcerated, and to make their case against him there (25:4-5). No
matter the Roman official's motive, whether duty to maintain public order (21:32-
36; 23:23-35), self-interest to curry favor with Jewish leaders (24:27), or personal
convenience, God's hand was most apparent in orchestrating human affairs so that
Rome would continue to protect God's messenger. Here is another small reminder
that God's providence indeed protects until the mission is complete (cf. 20:23-24).

In less than two weeks, Festus made good on his promise. Festus sat down on the
"judgment seat" (*bēma* [TG968, ZG1037], the elevated platform and rostrum from which
a magistrate would hear cases and deliver judgments) and "ordered that Paul be
brought in" (25:6). Paul, humanly speaking, was indeed powerless before the human state. He faced a seemingly overwhelming assault from his accusers, who
hurled many serious accusations, none of which could be proved (25:7).

Neither the prosecution nor the defense portions of this trial are given in much
detail (Luke implicitly asks us to rely on the appearance before Felix, as well as the
preceding narrative for details). Luke does, however, give in crisp terms Paul's defense about three matters: "I am not guilty of any crime against the Jewish laws or
the Temple or the Roman government [lit., "Caesar"]" (25:8). The Jews had indeed
consistently charged Paul—both before their own people and Roman authorities—
with teaching and action against the law (21:28; cf. 24:5) and the Temple (21:28).
Before the Roman authorities, they introduced the charge of inciting insurrection
against the Roman government (24:5). Paul had stoutly defended himself in each
of these areas (law—22:3; 24:14-16; Temple—22:17; 24:17-18; Roman government—24:11-13). This capsule summary of Paul's defense in 25:8 manifests the
truth about first-century Christianity's two defining relationships. As to Judaism, it
had not betrayed its religious roots. It stood in direct continuity with the Old Testament faith in its theology, ethics, and worship. As to the state, Christianity was no
revolutionary disrupter of the civil order, though in its own way it would produce a
radical transformation of society, one heart at a time.

With unsubstantiated charges (25:7) and a ringing defense (25:8), we expect Festus to find Paul "not guilty as charged" and to release him. But justice had been compromised by favoritism. In order to do the accusers a favor, Festus decided to
prolong the trial by proposing a change of venue (see note on 25:9). At the very least,
Festus was placing himself in a position to be strongly influenced by the Jerusalem
Jews who had been persistently hostile to Christianity. At the worst, he intended to
pursue a change of jurisdiction, de facto if not de jure, by making the Sanhedrin his
advisory council in determining the case. He, knowingly or unknowingly, placed
Paul in mortal danger of murderous ambush on his journey to Jerusalem.

Paul's shrewd and courageous response shows he was fully cognizant of the
future dangers. In reverse parallelism, which climaxes in his appeal to Caesar, he

declared his understanding of his present judicial standing before both Roman and Jew, and its future consequences. In 25:10-11 he placed at the center a confession of his own integrity and his willingness to submit to the outcomes of the judicial process:

> A. "This is the official Roman court, so I ought to be tried right here."
>> B. "You know very well I am not guilty of harming the Jews" (lit., "I have wronged the Jews in no way as you also know very well").
>>> C. "If I [have done wrong or] have done something worthy of death, I don't refuse to die."
>> B. "But if I am innocent, no one has a right to turn me over to these men to kill me."
> A. "I appeal to Caesar!"

Paul maintained his complete innocence with regard to the Jewish accusations and insisted that, in the light of such status, Festus had no right to make a gift of him to the Jews (see note on 25:11). It was not right for the proposed change of venue to become a de facto change of jurisdiction. So, being tried before a Roman court, he invoked his status as a Roman citizen. Employing a right of every Roman citizen, he appealed for a trial before the imperial court, which, if recognized as in order, would immediately halt the proceedings before Festus and transfer them to Rome.

In this one deft move, Paul accomplished three things. He avoided almost certain death by ambush (25:3); to a great extent he neutralized the Jewish compromise of the Roman judicial system (25:9); and he assured his witness in Rome and in that way retained the initiative of the divine control of his personal destiny (23:11; cf. 9:15).

Hearing Paul's request, Festus "conferred with his advisers" (25:12). It was customary for provincial administrators to have a council of advisers—higher-ranking military officers, younger civil servants in training, and dignitaries from the local population—to help evaluate court cases (4 Macc 17:17; Josephus *Against Apion* 2.177). Assured that the charges against Paul were a case that could be appealed, Festus granted Paul's declaration. "Very well! You have appealed to Caesar, and to Caesar you will go!" (25:12).

While we might expect Luke to move us swiftly to Rome, his interest in making sure we have a firm grasp on the Jews' animosity, Christianity's innocence before the state, and the Christian gospel itself, causes him to build to the climax by slowing his narrative down. In Festus's private and public reviews of Paul's case with Agrippa, we meet an interesting use of "functional redundancy" which, though more and more abbreviated, still gives us insights into these themes.

King Agrippa and his sister Bernice arrived to pay their respects to Festus (the NLT mg indicates that the sibling relationship is not explicit in the Greek text). King Agrippa was Marcus Julius Agrippa II (AD 27–100), son of Agrippa I (12:1-25) and great-grandson of Herod the Great (Matt 2:1-23). Brought up in Rome in the court of Claudius, he was a favorite of the emperor, though too young to immediately succeed his father at his death in AD 44. In AD 50, following the death of his uncle (Herod of Chalcis, AD 48), Agrippa was granted the petty kingdom of Chalcis, northeast of Judea. He later exchanged it for the tetrarchy of Philip, Abilene (or Abila), Trachonitis, and Acra (the tetrarchy of Varus) in AD 53. In AD 56, Nero added to Agrippa's kingdom the Galilean cities of Tarichea and Tiberias with their surrounding lands and the Perean city of Julias (or Betharamphta) with fourteen villages belonging to it (cf. Josephus *War* 2.220-223, 247, 252; *Antiquities* 20.104, 138, 159). Agrippa had supreme power in Jewish religious life, for the Romans gave him the right to appoint the high priest and custodianship of the Temple treasure and the high priest's vestments (Josephus *Antiquities* 20.213, 222). He was the last of the Herodian line.

Accompanying him was his sister Bernice, a year younger than he. She had been engaged to Marcus, a nephew of the philosopher Philo of Alexandria. Then she married her uncle Herod, King of Chalcis. At his death she returned to live with her brother Agrippa II, and it was widely rumored that she was engaged in an incestuous relationship with him (see note on 25:13).

As Festus laid out Paul's case to Agrippa in private (25:13-22), we learn the depths of Paul's Jewish opponents' animosity. When they first broached the subject to Festus in Jerusalem, they did not simply lay out a case against Paul; they actually asked for a guilty verdict and sentence (25:15). Possibly the Jewish leaders had explained to Festus about crimes that merited "death at the hands of heaven" and how the Romans had accommodated the Jews' concerns about Temple defilement offenses (see comment at 21:30; cf. Josephus *War* 6.124-126). Festus's reliance on a basic principle of Roman justice provided Paul's initial protection (25:16). "Our law, Senators, requires that the accused shall himself hear the charge preferred against him and shall be judged after he has made his own defense" (Appian *Roman History: Civil Wars* 3.54).

As Festus reported Paul's trial at Caesarea (25:17-21), we learn of another defect in the Jews' case. Not only were their charges unproven (25:7), they were not about crimes against the state as Festus was expecting (25:18). The governor evidently agreed with Paul that he had committed no crime against the Roman government (25:8). Rather, as Claudius Lysias had concluded before Festus (23:29; cf. Gallio's assessment, 18:15), the charges were simply something about their own religion. Festus added the specific issue: Jesus' Resurrection, expressed from an unbelieving Roman's perspective—"it was something about . . . a dead man named Jesus" (*tethnēkotos* [TG2348, ZG2569], perfect tense, having the inference that he was still dead), "who Paul insists is alive" (25:19). Though more general references to "resurrection of the dead" had peppered Paul's defense (23:6; 24:15, 21), we now know that Jesus' Resurrection was the central point of contention. Paul certainly made that clear in his speech before the Temple mob (22:7-10, 14-15, 17-21). In early Christian witness, it had become the defining moment for the eternal destiny for all humans. For the Jews, it was the key warrant for Jesus' messiahship. God's salvation was indeed accomplished in him. Just as importantly, it was the essential foundation for any supernatural working of "salvation applied," making possible a saving encounter with the Savior for all who would believe.

Festus hid from Agrippa any indication that his judicial impartiality has been compromised by "wanting to please the Jews" (25:20; cf. 25:9). He simply said that he was at a loss as to how to try this case. Furthermore, Paul had appealed to Caesar—literally, "he appealed to be kept for his Majesty's decision," which indicates he was not only asking for removal from a Roman provincial tribunal to the imperial court but was also explicitly claiming Roman protection during the process (25:21). Agrippa had some curiosity about this prisoner who was hated by the Jewish leadership but innocent as far as Festus was concerned, and who, at his own request, appealed to Caesar. So Agrippa said he would like to hear Paul for himself (25:22). With customary efficiency (25:6, 17), Festus promised a hearing on the next day.

In the end, we realize that Paul's appeal to Caesar reveals that a witness for "God on mission" must shrewdly and courageously seize every opportunity to avoid situations that would prevent him from achieving his divinely ordained goal.

◆ O. Paul Speaks to Agrippa (25:23–26:32)

23So the next day Agrippa and Bernice arrived at the auditorium with great pomp, accompanied by military officers and prominent men of the city. Festus ordered that Paul be brought in. 24Then Festus said, "King Agrippa and all who are here, this is the man whose death is demanded by all the Jews, both here and in Jerusalem. 25But in my opinion he has done nothing deserving death. However, since he appealed his case to the emperor, I have decided to send him to Rome.

26"But what shall I write the emperor? For there is no clear charge against him. So I have brought him before all of you, and especially you, King Agrippa, so that after we examine him, I might have something to write. 27For it makes no sense to send a prisoner to the emperor without specifying the charges against him!"

CHAPTER 26

Then Agrippa said to Paul, "You may speak in your defense."

So Paul, gesturing with his hand, started his defense: 2"I am fortunate, King Agrippa, that you are the one hearing my defense today against all these accusations made by the Jewish leaders, 3for I know you are an expert on all Jewish customs and controversies. Now please listen to me patiently!

4"As the Jewish leaders are well aware, I was given a thorough Jewish training from my earliest childhood among my own people and in Jerusalem. 5If they would admit it, they know that I have been a member of the Pharisees, the strictest sect of our religion. 6Now I am on trial because of my hope in the fulfillment of God's promise made to our ancestors. 7In fact, that is why the twelve tribes of Israel zealously worship God night and day, and they share the same hope I have. Yet, Your Majesty, they accuse me for having this hope! 8Why does it seem incredible to any of you that God can raise the dead?

9"I used to believe that I ought to do everything I could to oppose the very name of Jesus the Nazarene.* 10Indeed, I did just that in Jerusalem. Authorized by the leading priests, I caused many believers* there to be sent to prison. And I cast my vote against them when they were condemned to death. [11]Many times I had them punished in the synagogues to get them to curse Jesus.* I was so violently opposed to them that I even chased them down in foreign cities.

[12]"One day I was on such a mission to Damascus, armed with the authority and commission of the leading priests. [13]About noon, Your Majesty, as I was on the road, a light from heaven brighter than the sun shone down on me and my companions. [14]We all fell down, and I heard a voice saying to me in Aramaic,* 'Saul, Saul, why are you persecuting me? It is useless for you to fight against my will.*'

[15]"'Who are you, lord?' I asked.

"And the Lord replied, 'I am Jesus, the one you are persecuting. [16]Now get to your feet! For I have appeared to you to appoint you as my servant and witness. You are to tell the world what you have seen and what I will show you in the future. [17]And I will rescue you from both your own people and the Gentiles. Yes, I am sending you to the Gentiles [18]to open their eyes, so they may turn from darkness to light and from the power of Satan to God. Then they will receive forgiveness for their sins and be given a place among God's people, who are set apart by faith in me.'

[19]"And so, King Agrippa, I obeyed that vision from heaven. [20]I preached first to those in Damascus, then in Jerusalem and throughout all Judea, and also to the Gentiles, that all must repent of their sins and turn to God—and prove they have changed by the good things they do.

[21]Some Jews arrested me in the Temple for preaching this, and they tried to kill me. [22]But God has protected me right up to this present time so I can testify to everyone, from the least to the greatest. I teach nothing except what the prophets and Moses said would happen—[23]that the Messiah would suffer and be the first to rise from the dead, and in this way announce God's light to Jews and Gentiles alike."

[24]Suddenly, Festus shouted, "Paul, you are insane. Too much study has made you crazy!"

[25]But Paul replied, "I am not insane, Most Excellent Festus. What I am saying is the sober truth. [26]And King Agrippa knows about these things. I speak boldly, for I am sure these events are all familiar to him, for they were not done in a corner! [27]King Agrippa, do you believe the prophets? I know you do—"

[28]Agrippa interrupted him. "Do you think you can persuade me to become a Christian so quickly?"*

[29]Paul replied, "Whether quickly or not, I pray to God that both you and everyone here in this audience might become the same as I am, except for these chains."

[30]Then the king, the governor, Bernice, and all the others stood and left. [31]As they went out, they talked it over and agreed, "This man hasn't done anything to deserve death or imprisonment."

[32]And Agrippa said to Festus, "He could have been set free if he hadn't appealed to Caesar."

26:9 Or *Jesus of Nazareth.* 26:10 Greek *many of God's holy people.* 26:11 Greek *to blaspheme.* 26:14a Or *Hebrew.* 26:14b Greek *It is hard for you to kick against the oxgoads.* 26:28 Or "*A little more, and your arguments would make me a Christian.*"

NOTES

25:24 *the man whose death is demanded by all the Jews.* Some see the phrase "all the Jews" here simply as quantitative hyperbole (Dunn 1996:322; Fitzmyer 1998b:752) However, given Luke's other descriptions (cf. 4:32; 5:14; 15:12; 21:26; 23:7; cf. the parallel, Luke 23:1) and the fact that Festus wanted to stress the seriousness of the opposition to Paul, others take the phrase in an official political sense—"the assembly" (Johnson 1992: 427; Barrett 1998:1146; Witherington 1998:732). In this case, it is the Sanhedrin as legal representatives of the nation.

25:26 *the emperor.* This translates *tō kuriō* [TG2962, ZG3261] (the sovereign Lord), which was given a divine connotation when addressed to Roman emperors by subjects in the eastern provinces, though it is unlikely that a Roman would use it this way (Keener 1993:398). There was a remarkable rise in the frequency of such usage under Nero and his successors (Deissmann 1978:353).

26:2-3 *I am fortunate, King Agrippa, that you are the one hearing my defense today.* Paul's *captatio benevolentiae*, again, is not flattery (contra Johnson [1992:432], who detects some). But Paul, as he also did through his *narratio* (26:4-21), was seeking to situate the case as a Jewish intramural theological debate (Marguerat 1995:141). His use of *makarios* [TG3107, ZG3421] (blessed), then, is probably sacred (Witherington 1998:739), not secular (contra Johnson 1992:431 and NLT's "fortunate").

26:4 *my own people.* Congruent with 22:3, *tō ethnei* [TG1484, ZG1620] *mou* refers not to Cilicia but to the Jewish nation, with Jerusalem being the further geographical specification (Williams 1985:416).

26:6 *because of my hope in the fulfillment of God's promise made to our ancestors.* Many see this hope as the messianic hope brought to fulfillment in Jesus' Resurrection (Haenchen 1971:683; Tannehill 1992:266; Johnson 1992:432). Some see this hope as the Jewish hope for a future resurrection of the dead (cf. 23:6; 24:15, 21; Spencer 1997:226; Fernando 1998:594; Fitzmyer 1998b:756). There is no explicit statement in the immediate context about Jesus' Resurrection.

26:8 *any of you.* Given the Roman Festus's perplexity over "resurrection" (25:19) and the Jewish aristocracy's Sadducean disdain for it (23:8), this proposition was being properly addressed to this audience, not to Jews of Luke's own day (contra Fitzmyer 1998b:757; cf. Johnson 1992:327).

26:9 *oppose the very name of Jesus the Nazarene.* Though some say "name" refers to Christ's power and presence among his people (Polhill 1992:500) or to the message about Jesus (esp. his Resurrection; O'Toole 1978:49), others say it refers to members of the Christian movement, who have called upon, been baptized into, and were known by that name (Witherington 1998:741; cf. 2:38; 9:14; 11:26; 26:14).

26:10 *I cast my vote against them when they were condemned to death.* Since Paul may have been too young to have participated as a voting member of the Sanhedrin, this affirmation should be understood figuratively. He had sided with the Sanhedrin against Christians (Fitzmyer 1998b:758). Though multiple executions of Christians would have been illegal (under Roman rule the Sanhedrin normally did not exact the death penalty), they are historically plausible, given the circumstances in Judea in the wake of Stephen's death (Keener 1993:399; Williams 1985:417).

26:11 *to curse Jesus.* This translation of *blasphēmein* [TG987, ZG1059] (the NLT supplies the object, "Jesus") rightly understands this is neither a blaspheming of God the Father nor a confession of Jesus as Messiah, Lord, and Savior, which pre-Christian Paul would have considered blasphemy (contra Dunn 1996:327). Rather, from the Christian point of view, this refers to a denial of Christ (Barrett 1998:1156; Witherington 1998:742). The Christian perspective is present elsewhere in the immediate context when Paul labels Christians as "believers" (lit. "saints").

26:14 *It is useless for you to fight against my will.* The NLT mg supplies the literal rendering: "It is hard for you to kick against the oxgoads." This proverb is absent from the other accounts (9:4; 22:7) but was commonplace in Gr. literature (for examples, see Barrett 1998:1158); it did not originate with Luke or Paul as an explanatory embellishment appropriate to the Gentile audience in the room at Caesarea. A more direct background, apropos for use by the risen Lord with the Pharisee Saul, is the "goads" figure in Eccl 12:11 (cf. Rabbinic use of the Eccl 12:11 figure, Strack and Billerbeck 1978:2.770).

The divine will, which Paul finds it hard to fight against, was not God's pushing Paul to become a Christian (contra Johnson 1992:735) or to enter upon his lifelong mission (contra Fitzmyer 1998b:758; Witherington 1998:743; Spencer 1997:227). Instead, as the Lord's prior question indicated, Paul's persecution program was a hard fight against the Lord's saving purposes in the spread of the gospel and the growth of the church (cf. Marguerat 1995:152).

26:16-18 *I have appeared to you to appoint you as my servant and witness . . . Yes, I am sending you to the Gentiles.* This Damascus road commission (not present in chs 9 and 22) is not a literary move to keep interest (contra Barrett 1998:1158) nor a telescoping of commissions originally given by Ananias and the risen Lord in the Temple (contra Marshall 1980:396). A better explanation is that Luke, for maximum dramatic effect, has delayed relaying this fact of Paul's conversion until this last recounting of Paul's Damascus road experience (Hedrick 1981:427). A close look at Ananias's role reveals that he never gave Paul a commission; his role was confirmation through healing and baptizing (9:17-18; 22:16). In fact, Ananias's own words contain an allusion to the risen Lord's commission on the Damascus road (22:14-15). As his letters contend, Paul did receive his commission directly from Jesus (Gal 1:1, 15-16), and we learn here that this occurred on the road to Damascus.

26:18 *to open their eyes, so they may turn. . . . Then they will receive forgiveness.* The syntax contains three parallel purposes according to Fitzmyer (1998b:760): an "opening," a "turning," and a "receiving." Barrett (1998:1162) and the NLT appropriately subordinate each succeeding purpose. Even though there is no connective placing them in parallel, the parallel purpose infinitive form of the "turning" and "receiving" could point, however, to taking them in tandem as dual purposes for "opening" the eyes.

by faith in me. This may not only go with "set apart" (as Fitzmyer 1998b:760) but also with all the preceding descriptions of regeneration (Barrett 1998:1162).

26:20 *and throughout all Judea.* This rendering of *pasan te tēn chōran tēs Ioudaias* [TG2449, ZG2677] supplies a preposition ("throughout") to smooth out the syntax, just as the Byzantine text (E H L P and apparently many minuscules) has the addition *eis* [TG1519, ZG1650] before this phrase (Metzger 1994:438). Taking the prepositionless original as an accusative of extent overcomes grammatical awkwardness and harmonizes historically with Gal 1:22-23. Barrett (1998:1163) and Johnson (1992:437) point out the problem, while Fitzmyer (1998b:760) calls the statement in Acts hyperbole. Rather, understood as an accusative of extent, it refers to all Paul's subsequent witness activity in Judea after his limited contacts noted in Galatians (Williams 1985:423).

26:21 *for preaching this.* The Gr. *heneka toutōn* [TG1752/3778, ZG1915/4047] refers more generally to Paul's mission to the Gentiles where they embrace salvation blessings on the same basis as Jews (Dunn 1996:330; Barrett 1998:1164), instead of referring more specifically to his message (contra NLT) or to the charges brought against him (21:28; contra Johnson 1992:438).

26:23 *the first to rise from the dead, and in this way announce God's light to Jews and Gentiles alike.* Paul was claiming that the universal mission is a post-Resurrection activity of Christ (Marguerat 1995:153; cf. 3:26; 5:31).

26:24-25 *Too much study has made you crazy!* Given the cause Festus identifies, the NLT has correctly understood *mainomai* [TG3105, ZG3419] as a derogatory declaration of insanity, not a complimentary affirmation of being inspired by the gods (Barrett 1998:1167; contrast Bruce 1990:505). Still, Paul's use of *apophthengomai* [TG669, ZG710] (I am saying) in his response points to inspired speech, a counter to the charge of madness (cf. 2:4, 14-15). It may be indicating the character of the divine inspiration with which he spoke "sober truth" (Keener 1993:400; contra Barrett 1998:1168).

26:28 *Do you think you can persuade me to become a Christian so quickly?* The NLT mg gives an alternative rendering: "A little more, and your arguments would make me a Christian." To get at the best understanding of the text here, several questions must be asked: Does *en oligō* [TG1722/3641E, ZG1877/3900] mean "in a short time" (Fitzmyer 1998b:764; the NLT text); "with few arguments" (Witherington 1998:751; the NLT mg); or "with little effort" (Barrett 1998:1170)? Was it the process Agrippa was describing—"you are 'persuading' me to be a Christian" (*peitheis* [TG3982, ZG4275]; assumed but not expressed in the NLT mg note)—or Paul's supposition—"you believe, are 'persuaded' (*peithē*; present middle passive indicative) that you can make me a Christian" (codex Alexandrinus and the NLT text)? Is the original wording the more difficult *poiēsai* [TG4160, ZG4472] ("to make" or, as a technical theatrical term, "to act, play"), or is it *genesthai* [TG1096, ZG1181] (to become)? If it is the former, is Paul (as the NLT) or Agrippa the subject? What is the tone of the remark? Is it a dismissive or disdainful retort, "a trivial jest, a bitter sarcasm, a grave irony, a burst of anger," in each case indicating Paul's points have struck a nerve (Talbert 1997:214; Stott 1990:376; Spencer 1997:229; Fitzmyer 1998b:764)? Or, is it "an expression of sincere conviction" (Keener 1993:400)? Paul's response seems to require the following rendering: "Are you *persuading* me that in such a short *time* you have *made* me a Christian?" The tone is one of sophisticated avoidance by a slightly embarrassed king.

COMMENTARY

Paul's speech before Festus and Agrippa not only climaxes his ministry in Jerusalem (21:17–26:32), it forms a fitting inclusio to the main body of Paul's missionary work (9:1–26:32). This speech is the most clearly articulated summary of the Good News of salvation in Acts—the very message of Luke–Acts. At the heart of Paul's proclamation, we see the risen Christ actively on mission, giving salvation blessings to Jews and the nations (26:22-23).

Underscoring the importance of this address, we find a king and his consort assembling "with great pomp, accompanied by military officers and prominent men of the city" (25:23). In stark contrast, Paul was brought in at Festus's orders, powerless and in humiliating chains.

Festus's introduction (25:24-27), the third account of his dealings with Paul, highlights the nature of the Jewish opposition, as well as the Romans' dilemma about how to process this innocent prisoner. Festus invited those present to look at this spectacle, enough to cause at once disdain and wonder. Here was a prisoner who had ignited such hostility among the whole Jewish community that their demands were delivered in bloodthirsty shouts: "He must not live any longer" (25:24, literal translation).

In spite of such opposition, Festus's assessment, given for the first time, declared that according to Roman law, "he has done nothing deserving death" (25:25). Like his Lord, Paul would be declared innocent three times, a full exoneration in a judicial system where the accused was given three opportunities to defend himself (23:29; 25:25; 26:31; cf. Luke 23:4, 15, 22). Festus passed over the political pressure, which had compromised his judicial impartiality, and his perplexity about the case, both of which led to his offer of a change of venue and Paul's subsequent appeal to Caesar (25:9-11, 20-21). Rather, he moved directly to mention that appeal and his dilemma. Festus needed to find charges that would accompany the prisoner to Rome. Since Festus had nothing definite to write to the emperor, he thought an informal hearing before Agrippa would help (25:26). The king was well acquainted with Judaism. Stressing again Paul's innocence, Festus asserted that it "makes no sense to send a prisoner onto the emperor without specifying the charges against him" (25:27).

Agrippa gave Paul permission to make his defense (26:1). Though Paul proceeded to represent this as a defense, Agrippa spoke more generally of fact-finding concerning Paul's beliefs and behavior. The apostle began his defense "gesturing with his hand," stretching it out as would an orator (Quintillian *Institutio oratoria* 11.3.84ff). With a *captatio benevolentiae* to begin his exordium, which was at once courteous and accurate, Paul set all he was about to say within a religio-theological framework (26:2-3; see notes). He declared it a "blessing" (not "fortunate" as the NLT; see note on 26:2) that he was about to give a defense against the Jews' charges before one so well informed about their customs and controversies (cf. the Romans' similar assessment of Paul's case, 23:29; 25:19). With the same intent as Tertullus, but with a contrasting expression, he begged the king's patience in listening to him (26:3; cf. 24:4).

Since this was a fact-finding hearing, the bulk of Paul's "defense" was taken up with a *narratio,* an account of the events of the case as he understood them (26:4-21). He did not rehearse the immediate events of his final visit to Jerusalem. The specific charges relating to those events had not been proven, and Festus had set those charges aside (25:18-19). Rather, Paul described his upbringing, conversion, commission, and ministry to explain why he stood on the Christian side of the controversy concerning the reality of the risen Christ, who was extending salvation without distinction to all peoples. In the process, Paul presented a variety of proofs that should have assured his hearers that his assertions were true (Neyrey 1984:216, 221). In doing so, he seamlessly moved from defense to witness, fulfilling his divine commission, this time before a king (9:15).

Paul introduced himself with statements about his upbringing (26:4-5) and the controverted issue (26:6-7). Both revealed that he was in continuity with the practices and beliefs of faithful Israel. His "thorough Jewish training" (better, "manner of life") had been lived out according to the Old Testament and the Jewish ideal of piety from "earliest childhood" (26:4; see Luke 18:21). Not only was this public knowledge to the Jews, especially those of Jerusalem, but they could also testify, if they were willing, to Paul's membership among the Pharisees (see 23:1, 6; 24:16, 19), a sect he called "the strictest sect of our religion" (in terms of ritual practice; 26:5). Josephus says of the Pharisees, "There was a group of Jews priding itself on its adherence to ancestral custom and claiming to observe the laws of which the Deity approves" (*Antiquities* 17.41).

In a reverse parallelism (26:6-7), the apostle asserted that the charge against him— the controverted issue, namely the divine promise to the fathers of a messianic end-time salvation—was what all the devout of Israel hoped for (cf. 12:5; Luke 22:44). In fact, Paul said that they consistently served God in corporate worship, hoping to attain to that goal (cf. Phil 3:11-14). Paul was certainly on solid ground when he claimed that he stood in continuity with the Old Testament saints and intertestamental Jews who had hope for messianic end-time deliverance (Isa 25:6-12 LXX; 51:5 LXX; 2 Macc 2:18; *1 Enoch* 40:9; *Testament of Benjamin* 10:11; *2 Baruch* 30:1).

Why then the controversy? Why did the Jews say it was wrong for Paul to have this hope? We do not learn why until the speech's *probatio,* the statement of the proposition to be proven (26:21-22). Our reading of Paul's consistent missionary message, especially as expounded at Pisidian Antioch (13:23, 32), leaves us in no doubt that Paul stood accused because he had proclaimed that the salvation promises had been fulfilled and the hope was now a present reality in the risen Lord Jesus. What Paul did at this point in his speech was to raise the question that was at the heart of the issue: "Why does it seem incredible to any of you that God can raise the dead?" (26:8; cf. 1 Cor 15:13, 16). To Agrippa, if he was under the influence of aristocratic Sadducean thought, God's raising the dead was unbelievable (23:9). Festus had already declared himself on this subject (25:19). Paul, by dealing in probabilities and framing the resurrection in terms of God's work, laid the groundwork for removing a wrong presupposition that was preventing some of his hearers from embracing Jesus and his Resurrection.

Paul immediately identified with his audience by saying he too thought that it was his moral duty "to oppose the very name of Jesus the Nazarene" (26:9). Though we earlier learned that the imprisonment and death of Christians occurred in the wake of his persecutions (9:1; 22:4), we now see clearly that the authority of the Sanhedrin was behind all this police action (26:10). Paul's initial tactic in stamping out this movement was corporal punishment in order to exact a blasphemous denial of Christ (26:11; cf. Matt 10:17; 23:34; Pliny the Younger *Letters* 10.96.5). The strength of his persecution could be seen in its intensity, for it was powered by an exceedingly furious rage (NLT "violently opposed"). Paul even "chased them down in foreign cities" (26:11).

However, on one of those forays, again with the leading priests' "authority and commission" (26:12), Paul had a life-changing encounter with the risen Lord Jesus (26:12-18; this is Paul's second telling and Luke's third account of the experience; cf. 9:1-9; 22:5-11). This retelling, in its own way, emphasizes that the encounter was personal: he had seen the light, the risen Lord in his glory, and he had heard him in his own native tongue, Aramaic (26:13-16). The encounter was awesome; the light shone around both Paul and his companions. The encounter was supernatural; the light came from heaven and was "brighter than the sun"—it was so overpowering that Paul said that they all fell down (26:13-14). The light is a suitable metaphor for the revelation and salvation the Lord brings (Luke 2:32; Isa 42:6; 49:6).

Then the Lord's voice came: "Saul, Saul, why are you persecuting me? It is useless for you to fight against my will" (see note on 26:14). This haunting question unmasked Paul's true guilt as he pursued a life of self-righteous zeal in Christian persecution. And it did so by revealing his true opponent: the risen and exalted Lord and Savior Jesus. What he had just chronicled of the believers' stubborn courage—their willingness to endure prison and death, refusing to "blaspheme" their Lord, even under the whip, and continuing to spread their message even as they were scattered by persecution so that Paul had to pursue them to foreign cities (26:10-11)—should have been large clues that he was fighting not against men but against God (cf. 5:39; 8:3-4). He had been "kicking against the oxgoads" of God's will.

Paul responded with curiosity, if not humble submission: "Who are you, lord?" (26:15). The Greek term *kurie* [TG2962, ZG3261] can also be rendered "Lord." From a Christian perspective, Paul tells us "the Lord replied, 'I am Jesus, the one you are persecuting'" (26:15). Such words spoken from heaven brought their own revelatory light. Jesus is indeed risen from the dead and at the Father's right hand! Christians are so peculiarly his people that to persecute them is to persecute him—and this was what Paul had been doing.

As was hinted at in the previous accounts, Paul now explicitly speaks of his conversion as also involving his personal commission by the risen Lord to a lifework of gospel witness (26:18-20). As with the Old Testament prophets, Jesus immediately placed Paul in a role of servant before his master, commanding him, "Now get to your feet!" (26:16; cf. Jer 1:7-8, 17-19; Ezek 2:1-2). He marked out his mission, his audience, and its outcomes (26:16-18). He appointed Paul a "servant" (*hupēretēs* [TG5257, ZG5677], meaning "assistant") and a "witness" (this second term further specifies the first; 26:16). With the term for "servant," Jesus stressed that Paul was to do exactly his master's bidding (cf. 13:5; Luke 1:2; 4:20), and he may have been implying that the master himself would be there with him in the mission (cf. 14:3, 27; 15:12), though admittedly the Lord went on to say that he was "sending" Paul on mission to the people and the Gentiles. Paul was specifically to bear witness to that of which he had direct personal knowledge: "Tell the world what you have seen and what I will show you in the future" (26:16; cf. 22:17-21; 23:11; 26:22). This mission would not be without its opposition (cf. 9:16), for Jesus promised to "rescue" Paul from the two groups in his immediate audience: the Jews ("your own people") and "the Gentiles" (26:17).

As he described his mission's purpose in terms of outcomes (26:18), Paul was actually fulfilling part of Jesus' commission. He winsomely laid before his audience the salvation blessings that could be theirs if they too would but trust this risen Savior. With a healing metaphor, Jesus told Paul he was "to open their eyes" (26:18). Consistent with using the metaphor of "closed eyes" for a sinful condition (28:27; Isa 6:10; cf. Luke 19:42) and "seeing eyes" for those blessed to witness God's saving purposes (Luke 2:30; 10:23; cf. Isa 42:7), "to open their eyes" indicates the spiritual health gained by turning to Christ.

Further expanding on this spiritual health, Paul pointed to its twofold purpose in terms of the transformation and the final blessing it entails. Those who receive Paul's witness would experience a double turning—"from darkness to light and from the power of Satan to God" (26:18). They could leave the gloom, ignorance, and evil and enter the light of hope, revelation, and goodness found in the living presence of the Risen One (Luke 2:32; Acts 13:47; Isa 49:6). They could exchange the bondage of Satan's power for the gracious sovereignty of God, who is greater (Luke 4:36; 5:24; Acts 8:19).

This spiritual health would yield two blessings: "forgiveness for their sins" (26:18; cf. Luke 24:47; Acts 13:38) and a new eternal destiny grounded in a new identity. Those who believe have "a place" (*klēros* [TG2819, ZG3102], a lot or portion of an inheritance; Ps 77 [78]:55 LXX) "among God's people, who are set apart by faith" in Jesus (26:18; cf. 16:31; 20:21, 32; 24:24). Indeed, "faith in me [Jesus]" is the way all the salvation described is to be appropriated.

The whole course of Paul's life, down to and including the very words he was speaking (26:19-22a), was simply obeying the commission that came to him by a "heavenly appearance" (*ouraniō optasia* [TG3770/3701, ZG4039/3965], not "vision from heaven" [NLT], which is less immediate; 29:19; cf. 12:9). He had faithfully fulfilled the mission's scope, especially ethnically, to Jews in Damascus, Jerusalem, throughout all Judea, and also to the Gentiles (29:20; cf. 9:19-22, 26-30; 13:46; 14:27; 18:6; 19:10). He had proclaimed those human responsibilities that mark salvific transformation: the need for repentance and conversion and a life worthy of that change (26:20; cf. 26:18). Such a proclamation proved that although Paul did not insist on ritual purity for Gentiles to claim inheritance among God's people, the apostle was concerned that ethical purity characterize all members of this restored people of God, those who are set apart by faith in Jesus.

On account of his mission to present this salvation on the same basis to Jew and Gentile, the Jews arrested Paul in the Temple and tried to kill him (21:30-32). But God had been faithful to his promise, rescuing Paul from Jew and Gentile (26:17), so that Paul could testify, even on that very day, that he had borne witness "to everyone, from the least to the greatest" (26:22; cf. 9:15; 22:15).

Having brought his audience up to the present moment, Paul now laid out his *probatio* (the issues to be proven)—in this case, the gospel message (26:22b-23). The warrant for his proposition is Moses and the prophets. His proclamation was in continuity with Old Testament Judaism, for he preached nothing other than what they said was about to happen (26:22b; cf. 1 Cor 15:3-4). Understanding that this message was disputed among the Jews, he introduced its content with *ei* [TG1487, ZG1623] (NLT, "that"; 26:23), a rhetorical device for indicating a proposition that must be argued for (cf. 17:3). The Messiah would suffer; the Messiah would be the first to rise from the dead; the Messiah would proclaim light to the people (NLT, "Jews") and the Gentiles. Though he would not have opportunity to do so, Paul could have proven each of these points from Old Testament Scripture (Luke 22:37 from Isa 53:12; Acts 13:34-35 from Isa 55:3 and Ps 16:10; Acts 13:47 from Isa 49:6). Jesus' saving death, Resurrection, exaltation, and present witness with and through his messengers to the availability of salvation blessings to those who repent and believe in him, are the hermeneutical keys to the full understanding of the Old Testament, especially its messianic Resurrection hope. Paul would gladly plead guilty to being a witness to the reality of this message and its resurrection hope (23:6; 24:21; cf. 25:19).

Interrupting Paul in an emotional outburst, Festus called him "insane" and "crazy" (26:24). To speak of resurrection or of a resurrected one on a mission was to have taken leave of one's senses under the burden of "too much study" (26:24). As far as Festus was concerned, Jesus was dead (25:19, *tethnēkotos* [TG2348, ZG2569] perfect tense, completed action with continuing effects); rational discussion could not take place on any other basis.

Paul's *refutatio* not only denied Festus's evaluation but affirmed that he was speaking sober truth (see note on 26:25). His statements corresponded to reality. Paul pointed out that he could speak frankly about this matter, since the fulfillment of the salvation message concerned public events that had not happened "in a corner" and were surely already known to Agrippa (26:26). Paul modeled the truth that the Christian message, grounded as it is in objective historical fact, never fears a judicious assessment of the facts. Gospel witnesses are confident that such an evaluation will point to, if not necessitate, the Scripture's interpretation of those facts.

At this point Paul turned to Agrippa and laid the groundwork for the reception of such a divine interpretation of these recent events by asking him about his belief in the Old Testament prophets (26:27). In this *peroratio*, or persuasive conclusion, he identified with Agrippa by affirming that he knew that Agrippa did believe the Old Testament prophets and their promises of the messianic hope. Agrippa knew that the events, which Paul claimed were their fulfillment, had occurred. All that was left for Agrippa to do was to embrace the Christian message, affirm Jesus as the risen Messiah, call on his name for salvation, and become his follower.

Agrippa, under conviction from Paul's Spirit-filled preaching, was well aware of the path the apostle had led him down, though he would not follow. Slightly embarrassed and in sophisticated, dismissive avoidance, he broke in with the question, "Do you think you can persuade me to become a Christian so quickly?" (see note on 26:28). Agrippa thought only in terms of human persuasion. Paul knew that any conversion is God's work, so he said he would pray to God for such an outcome. So important was this message to the eternal destiny of Agrippa and all who heard Paul that the length of time it would take for them to be persuaded was irrelevant. What was important was that they should become the same as Paul—a Christian. Then, with a touch of pathos, Paul added, "except for these chains" (26:29).

When the hearing was over, the dignitaries exited and in private discussion agreed on Paul's innocence: "This man hasn't done anything to deserve death or imprisonment" (26:31; the third declaration of innocence, cf. 23:19; 25:25). As if to explain the anomaly of an innocent Roman citizen in chains, Agrippa added, "He could have been set free if he hadn't appealed to Caesar" (26:32). These declarations of innocence make it clear that Paul and Christianity could not be charged with sedition against the state. Nothing in the conduct of the messengers called the truthfulness, value, and benefit of the message into question.

◆ P. Paul Sails for Rome (27:1-12)

When the time came, we set sail for Italy. Paul and several other prisoners were placed in the custody of a Roman officer* named Julius, a captain of the Imperial Regiment. ²Aristarchus, a Macedonian from Thessalonica, was also with us. We left on a ship whose home port was Adramyttium on the northwest coast of the province of Asia;* it was scheduled to make several stops at ports along the coast of the province.

³The next day when we docked at Sidon, Julius was very kind to Paul and let him go ashore to visit with friends so they could provide for his needs. ⁴Putting out to sea from there, we encountered strong headwinds that made it difficult to keep the ship on course, so we sailed north of Cyprus between the island and the mainland. ⁵Keeping to the open sea, we passed along the coast of Cilicia and Pamphylia, landing at Myra, in the province of Lycia. ⁶There the commanding officer found an Egyptian ship from Alexandria that was bound for Italy, and he put us on board.

⁷We had several days of slow sailing, and after great difficulty we finally neared Cnidus. But the wind was against us, so we sailed across to Crete and along the sheltered coast of the island, past the cape of Salmone. ⁸We struggled along the coast with great difficulty and finally arrived at Fair Havens, near the town of Lasea. ⁹We had lost a lot of time. The weather was becoming dangerous for sea travel because it was so late in the fall,* and Paul spoke to the ship's officers about it.

¹⁰"Men," he said, "I believe there is trouble ahead if we go on—shipwreck, loss of cargo, and danger to our lives as well." ¹¹But the officer in charge of the prisoners listened more to the ship's captain and the owner than to Paul. ¹²And since Fair Havens was an exposed harbor—a poor place to spend the winter—most of the crew wanted to go on to Phoenix, farther up the coast of Crete, and spend the winter there. Phoenix was a good harbor with only a southwest and northwest exposure.

27:1 Greek *centurion;* similarly in 27:6, 11, 31, 43. 27:2 *Asia* was a Roman province in what is now western Turkey. 27:9 Greek *because the fast was now already gone by.* This fast was associated with the Day of Atonement (*Yom Kippur*), which occurred in late September or early October.

NOTES

27:1 *When the time came.* To smooth the abruptness of the transition from 26:32, the NLT turns *hōs de ekrithē* [TG2919, ZG3212], "when it was decided," into a more generalized statement.

27:9 *so late in the fall.* The NLT mg is helpful: "Greek *because the fast was now already gone by.* This fast was associated with the Day of Atonement (*Yom Kippur*), which occurred in late September or early October." Observed on the tenth day of Tishri, in AD 59 this would have been October 5 (Marshall 1980:406). Using Jewish feast days for time reckoning does not necessarily mean Paul observed the feast (contra Dunn 1996:338; cf. Barrett 1998:1188).

Paul spoke to the ship's officers. This is not a historically unlikely speaking out of turn (contra Johnson 1992:447). It was customary for a cautious pilot to seek advice of anyone on board with maritime knowledge (Seneca *Ad Lucilium* 14.8; Rapske 1991:11). Paul's offer of advice was in character (Dunn 1996:338), in line with his social status (Barrett 1998:1179) and his nautical experience (2 Cor 11:25; Witherington 1998:763).

27:10 *I believe.* This rendering of *theōrō* [TG2334, ZG2555] (I can see, I perceive) indicates this was Paul's human opinion based on his knowledge of sea travel, not a prophecy (contra Keener 1993:401) or a combination of the two (contra Krodel 1986:474).

27:11 *the officer . . . listened . . . to the ship's captain and the owner.* Many commentators assert that the Roman officer was in charge of a ship either commandeered for his purposes or already in the imperial service (e.g., Dunn 1996:338; Johnson 1992:447; Keener 1993:402) and that "the ship's captain and the owner" had to persuade him to proceed with the voyage. Rapske (1991:10-12), however, convincingly shows that the centurion was simply a passenger, persuaded by the chief navigational and commercial officer not to disembark but stay on board and proceed with them even during this dangerous time.

The *kubernētēs* [TG2942, ZG3237] ("pilot," NLT—"ship's captain") clearly designates a steersman, the chief of which could be designated "captain," since he had the final responsibility for the navigational aspects of the voyage (Ulpian *Digest* 19.2.13.2; Rapske 1991:11). The ship's "owner" is designated in Gr. as the *naukléros?*[TG3490, ZG3729] and was most likely the *exercitor*, the "ship entrepreneur or manager," one to whom revenues from the voyage would come; he may have also been the *magister nauis*, "director of the expedition," and even the *dominus nauis*, the actual "ship owner."

27:12 *exposed harbor.* Given the contrast with Phoenix and its protected harbor, this may be the most likely reason (NLT; Fitzmyer 1998b:775), though not the only reason why Fair Havens was *aneuthetou* [TG428, ZG460] (inconvenient). Barrett (1998:1191) suggests insecure anchorage and lack of social amenities for passengers and crew during the winter.

Phoenix. See Finegan (1981:196) for the location and description of the site.

COMMENTARY

As Paul sails for Rome, Luke reminds us of his prisoner status. He and other prisoners had been "placed in the custody" of a centurion who determined the timing and means of transport for his movements (27:1). Julius was in the "Imperial Regiment," an auxiliary cohort stationed in Palestine that had received the honorary title *Sebastē* [cf. TG4575, ZG4935], "Augustus's, imperial." Paul's traveling companions included at least Luke and a Macedonian Christian named Aristarchus (27:2; cf. 19:29; 20:4; Col 4:10; Phlm 1:24). Julius chose a homeward-bound coasting vessel that was about to call at ports on the "coast of the province of Asia" until it came to its homeport, Adramyttium, located on the province's western coast south of Troas, east of Assos and facing the island of Lesbos.

Borne along by the Syrian coastal current—the Nile water that runs north—the ship, probably moving at a speed of about three knots, would have covered the 69 nautical miles to Sidon in 23 hours (27:3). Sidon, the mother city of the Phoenicians, with its double harbor, figures prominently in Luke's Gospel as a model of repentant Gentile receptivity to the teaching of Jesus (Luke 6:17; 10:13-14; cf. 4:26). It was probably evangelized during the Hellenistic Jewish Christian dispersion after Stephen's martyrdom, and Paul may have visited the church there a number of times earlier in his ministry (11:19, 30; 12:25; 15:3). Displaying what the ancients viewed as one of the highest qualities of civilized kindness (Plutarch *Moralia* 402A; Philo *Special Laws* 2.141), the centurion permitted Paul to visit with friends (27:3). These Christians probably met Paul's needs both materially and physically (Luke 10:34).

When they sailed, they did not proceed by a direct route west toward Crete or Rhodes, passing along south of Cyprus. Their square rigged vessel could not readily tack into the prevailing west or northwest winds of that season so as to make headway in a zigzag fashion on the open seas. Rather, sailing "north of Cyprus," they used the island as a shield against the wind (27:4). They were also able to take advantage of the westward two-mile-per-hour current along the southern coast of Asia Minor, as well as the land breezes that flow down the valleys perpendicular to the sea at night (cf. Heliodorus *Aethiopica* 4.16.10). Beyond Cyprus, they headed into open sea, south of the provinces of Cilicia and Pamphylia until they landed at "Myra, in the province of Lycia" (27:5). Myra, on the western third of Asia Minor's south coast, was a chief port of the imperial grain service, a regular port of call for grain vessels taking the northerly route from Alexandria to Rome. Archaeological remains of the grain storage facilities attest to its importance.

At Myra, the centurion found an Alexandrian ship "bound for Italy" and put his company on board (27:6). Possibly part of the imperial grain fleet, its presence at Myra in the early fall probably indicates it was on a second run. Evidently, the owners were trying to squeeze this one in before the winter. Of considerable capacity, this vessel was large enough to accommodate passengers and crew numbering 276 (27:37; cf. Josephus's report of one such ship carrying 600 persons, *Life* 15). Lucian (*The Ship* 5) describes a ship 180 feet long, well over 45 feet wide, and 44 feet deep.

The west winds continued to impede their progress so that after "several days" they scarcely arrived at Cnidus, a port at the western end of a long promontory of southwest Asia Minor which stretches out into the Aegean between Cos and Rhodes (27:7). Moving beyond Cnidus, the wind was so strong in preventing their westward progress that they dropped under the leeward side of Crete, sailing past Salmone, a cape on Crete's east coast (27:7). Again, the navigator hoped to use the island as a shield. Even so, keeping close to the coast, they made westward progress with difficulty, finally arriving at Fair Havens, a harbor at the midpoint of Crete's south coast, twelve miles east of Cape Matala and five miles from Lasea (27:8).

The ancients divided the navigational year on the Mediterranean into four periods (Hesiod, *Works and Days* 663-668; cf. *Genesis Rabbah* 6:5b, "The crossing of the Great Sea too: Thus saith the Lord, who giveth a way in the sea [Isa 43:16]—from Pentecost until the Festival [Tabernacles]"—mid-May to mid-October). Optimum sea travel could be expected during the summer months, May 15 to September 15. Dangerous times for sailing were September 16 to November 10 and March 11 to May 14. Sea travel on the Mediterranean ceased between November 11 and March 10.

As the ship was in port at Fair Havens, it was already the dangerous period for any voyages. Vegetius described the dangers of "winter sailing" as scant daylight, long nights, dense cloud cover, poor visibility, and double raging of winds, showers, and snows (*Military Institutions of the Romans* 4.39).

Paul, with wisdom born of much sea travel, including travel involving a shipwreck and being lost at sea (2 Cor 11:25), gave his advice to the ship's officers. He warned that if they continued the voyage, it would be accompanied by much loss of cargo, the ship, and lives (27:10). Paul's was so totally committed to his mission that he had a reputation for risking his life for it (15:26). Indeed, he could declare that his life had no value to him except in the mission's accomplishment (20:24).

Still, if he knew that the mission was to include a particular future event—witness before Caesar in Rome—he should be proactive in seeking to preserve his life so that he could participate in what God had promised him (23:11).

The centurion listened to the ship's captain and its financial manager rather than Paul (see note on 27:11). The centurion had his party stay on board, as the majority (*hoi pleiones* [cf. TG4119A, ZG4498])—whether ship officers, crew, or all on board— made a plan to risk a 40-mile journey out in open sea around Cape Matala, if somehow they might be able to arrive at Phoenix and winter there. Fair Havens's situation was "inconvenient" for winter anchorage (see note on 27:12). Phoenix, at the west of the promontory Cape Mouros, was more suitable. The present Phoinika Bay fits the description, for it has an inlet that faces southwest, and there are traces of an inlet, now marred by silting and an earthquake, that faced northwest.

◆   Q. The Storm at Sea (27:13-26)

¹³When a light wind began blowing from the south, the sailors thought they could make it. So they pulled up anchor and sailed close to the shore of Crete. ¹⁴But the weather changed abruptly, and a wind of typhoon strength (called a "north-easter") burst across the island and blew us out to sea. ¹⁵The sailors couldn't turn the ship into the wind, so they gave up and let it run before the gale.

¹⁶We sailed along the sheltered side of a small island named Cauda,* where with great difficulty we hoisted aboard the lifeboat being towed behind us. ¹⁷Then the sailors bound ropes around the hull of the ship to strengthen it. They were afraid of being driven across to the sandbars of Syrtis off the African coast, so they lowered the sea anchor to slow the ship and were driven before the wind.

¹⁸The next day, as gale-force winds continued to batter the ship, the crew began throwing the cargo overboard. ¹⁹The following day they even took some of the ship's gear and threw it overboard. ²⁰The terrible storm raged for many days, blotting out the sun and the stars, until at last all hope was gone.

²¹No one had eaten for a long time. Finally, Paul called the crew together and said, "Men, you should have listened to me in the first place and not left Crete. You would have avoided all this damage and loss. ²²But take courage! None of you will lose your lives, even though the ship will go down. ²³For last night an angel of the God to whom I belong and whom I serve stood beside me, ²⁴and he said, 'Don't be afraid, Paul, for you will surely stand trial before Caesar! What's more, God in his goodness has granted safety to everyone sailing with you.' ²⁵So take courage! For I believe God. It will be just as he said. ²⁶But we will be shipwrecked on an island."

27:16 Some manuscripts read *Clauda*.

NOTES

27:14 *a "northeaster."* Not occurring elsewhere in Gr. literature, *Eurakulōn* [TG2148A, ZG2350] (𝔓74 ℵ A B* syrᵖᵃˡ copᵇᵒ, ˢᵃ), a Greek-Latin combination of *Euros* (east or southeast wind) and *Aquilia* (north wind), evidently caused some copyists difficulty. The more common *Eurokludōn* [TG2148, ZG2352], "a southeast wind which stirs up waves," is a later, widespread reading (B² 044 𝔐 syr) picked up by the Textus Receptus and NKJV— "Euroclydon" (Metzger 1994:440; Barrett 1998:1194). Hemer (1975:103) has found

Eurakulōn in a Latin inscription, a twelve-point wind-rose incised in a pavement at Thugga in proconsular Africa. For a description of the Mediterranean winter weather configurations see Finegan 1981:197.

27:16 *Cauda*. This name (*Kauda* [TG2802A, ZG3007]) is found in 𝔓74 ℵ² B (044) syr^p. Some mss (ℵ* A^vid 33 1739 𝔐 syr^h) read *Clauda* (so NLT mg). Metzger (1994:440) reports, without comment, scholars' view that *Kaudos* or *Gaudos* is the "true form" of the word but that it was frequently spelled with a lambda, hence *Klauda* appears in some mss.

27:17 *bound ropes around the hull of the ship*. Haenchen (1971:703) notes four methods of frapping: vertically in the hold or underneath the hull, horizontally on deck or around the hull (he opts for the last method). Casson (1971:91) says that vertical frapping was customary for merchant ships and horizontal for warships. Some recent commentators (Johnson 1992:448; Fitzmyer 1998b:776) are uncertain what method was used, and the NLT does not specify. Barrett (1998:1196) says the ropes were run at right angles to the ship's axis.

***sea anchor*.** Luke used a general term, *skeuos* [TG4632, ZG5007] (gear), to refer to what was lowered. Does this refer to the main yard carrying the main sail (Williams 1985:435), the sails (Witherington 1998:766), the sea anchor (Dunn 1996:339; Fernando 1998:612; Fitzmyer 1998b:776), or all the equipment on which the ship's course and speed depended—the rudder, tackle, and anchor (Marshall 1980:409)? Given the expressed danger of drifting to the "sandbars of Syrtis," the action that would most impede progress— lowering of the sea anchor—is most likely (so NLT).

27:19 *ship's gear*. Keener (1993:402) understands this gear as the main yard spar, as long as the deck, which would take most of the manpower on deck to lower. Clark (1975:145) proposes that the *skeuos* [TG4632, ZG5007] of 27:17 and 27:19 are the same and that the crew failed in its first attempt to throw it overboard. Others see the gear as miscellaneous spare gear and tackle (cf. Barrett 1998:1198; Fitzmyer 1998b:777; Dunn 1996:339).

27:21 *Men, you should have listened to me in the first place*. Paul was not giving in to the human temptation of saying "I told you so" (contra Dunn 1996:339); rather, he was establishing a warrant for why they should listen to him in the present crisis (Witherington 1998:767).

COMMENTARY

According to an ancient literary pattern he was familiar with, Luke presents the storm in terms of natural causes but with a divine outcome, according to the angel's word (cf. Lucian *The Ship* 7-9; Aelius Aristides *Sacred Tales* 2.12-14; Josephus *Life* 13-16). This pattern emphasizes not only Paul's innocence (God does not send the storm to judge him) but also the unstoppable nature of the divine mission to carry the gospel to Rome by means of this innocent one. The key for comprehending such divine purposes is faith (27:25).

When "a light wind began blowing from the south," the ship's officers and crew thought they could make it, so they weighed anchor and sailed along close to the shore (27:13). The greed powering their plan (27:12) blinded them to the truly unusual, and therefore potentially transient, nature of these favorable circumstances. As they rounded Cape Matala, three or four miles away, a "typhoon strength" wind from the northeast blew down from 8,056-foot Mount Ida (27:14). The strong cold wind that normally blows across the Mediterranean in the winter from a general northeasterly direction is caused by a depression over Libya that induces a strong flow of air from Greece.

So totally was the ship in the wind's control that after it "caught" the vessel (27:14), the crew was not able to maneuver to face the wind so as to keep the waves from striking it broadside. Rather, they had to surrender to the wind's power and let the craft be driven by it (27:15). Mercifully, they were driven under the protection of the lee of "a small island named Cauda," 23 miles west of Cape Matala (27:16). Then the crew took three steps to prevent "damage" to the ship (cf. 27:10). To prevent the rough seas from smashing it against the ship's stern, they hoisted and secured on deck the dinghy they were towing (27:16). To strengthen the hull against the continual battering of the waves, they banded the ship, undergirding it with ropes running vertically under its center hull, four or five turns (see note on 27:17). To slow the ship down in its southwestward trajectory toward the damaging sandbars of the Syrtis, they "lowered the sea anchor" (27:17). This was a broad piece of wood held vertical by a weight below and an empty barrel on top. One hundred miles off the Libyan coast and 300 miles in circumference, Syrtis has deep waters with shallows; "the result is, at the ebb and the flow of the tides, that sailors sometimes fall into the shallows and stick there, and that safe escape of a boat is rare" (Strabo *Geography* 17.3.20).

On the second and third days, the crew began to deal with "loss" (27:18-19; cf. 27:10). To avoid the loss of the ship and the lives of those on board, "as gale-force winds continued to batter the ship," the crew lightened it by throwing the precious cargo overboard (27:18). The next day, still faced with the immediate prospect of going down, they heaved miscellaneous spare gear and tackle over the side (27:19). Even with these heroic efforts to keep the ship sound and afloat, all on board were still at the mercy of the elements as this terrible winter storm pressed in on them. The unrelenting stormy weather disoriented them, for it hid the sun and stars from them for many days, and these were their only means of navigation. Finally, all hope of being saved was gone (27:20). Indeed, "no one had eaten for a long time" (27:21; *asitia* [TG826, ZG826], "lack of food/appetite," indicates it was voluntary). Was it anxiety, seasickness, or the inedibility of the foodstuffs (i.e., the storm spoiled the food or made cooking impossible)? Or did the natural desire for self-preservation peter out as death appeared more likely?

Paul stood in their midst and gave a word of encouragement. In an elegant turn of phrase echoing his warning, he established his authority by reminding the crew that if they had obeyed him, they would have avoided the damage and loss (27:21; cf. 27:10). Then he gave further advice—in the form of a command, with a prophecy for its rationale (cf. 27:10): "Take courage! None of you will lose your lives, even though the ship will go down" (27:22). The cargo was lost; the ship would be lost; but not one human life would perish.

This prophecy's basis was divine revelation. The previous night an angel of God had come and stood beside Paul (27:23). Such an appearance was silent testimony of God's sovereign superiority over this force of nature. Humans were at its mercy, but it was no obstacle for the dispatch of an angel to deliver God's message. Paul testified that this God owned him (27:23; cf. 9:15; 26:16), and he owned this God as his God in worship (cf. Luke 1:74; 2:37; Acts 24:14).

The angel delivered a message of encouragement, which reaffirmed a divine promise and announced a gracious gift (27:24). As the Lord did at Corinth, the angel urged Paul to stop being afraid (cf. 18:9). He repeated that it was necessary for Paul to stand trial before Caesar (23:11). God in his grace had decided not only to preserve Paul so that he could finish his mission in witness before Caesar but also to preserve all those who traveled with him as a gift to him. Paul then predicted that the means of preservation would be via God's ordinary providence: a shipwreck on an island (27:26).

◆   R. The Shipwreck (27:27-44)

27About midnight on the fourteenth night of the storm, as we were being driven across the Sea of Adria,* the sailors sensed land was near. 28They dropped a weighted line and found that the water was 120 feet deep. But a little later they measured again and found it was only 90 feet deep.* 29At this rate they were afraid we would soon be driven against the rocks along the shore, so they threw out four anchors from the back of the ship and prayed for daylight.

30Then the sailors tried to abandon the ship; they lowered the lifeboat as though they were going to put out anchors from the front of the ship. 31But Paul said to the commanding officer and the soldiers, "You will all die unless the sailors stay aboard." 32So the soldiers cut the ropes to the lifeboat and let it drift away.

33Just as day was dawning, Paul urged everyone to eat. "You have been so worried that you haven't touched food for two weeks," he said. 34"Please eat something now for your own good. For not a hair of your heads will perish." 35Then he took some bread, gave thanks to God before them all, and broke off a piece and ate it. 36Then everyone was encouraged and began to eat—37all 276 of us who were on board. 38After eating, the crew lightened the ship further by throwing the cargo of wheat overboard.

39When morning dawned, they didn't recognize the coastline, but they saw a bay with a beach and wondered if they could get to shore by running the ship aground. 40So they cut off the anchors and left them in the sea. Then they lowered the rudders, raised the foresail, and headed toward shore. 41But they hit a shoal and ran the ship aground too soon. The bow of the ship stuck fast, while the stern was repeatedly smashed by the force of the waves and began to break apart.

42The soldiers wanted to kill the prisoners to make sure they didn't swim ashore and escape. 43But the commanding officer wanted to spare Paul, so he didn't let them carry out their plan. Then he ordered all who could swim to jump overboard first and make for land. 44The others held onto planks or debris from the broken ship.* So everyone escaped safely to shore.

27:27 The *Sea of Adria* includes the central portion of the Mediterranean.   27:28 Greek *20 fathoms . . . 15 fathoms* [37 meters . . . 27 meters].   27:44 Or *or were helped by members of the ship's crew.*

NOTES

27:27 *on the fourteenth night . . . we were being driven across the Sea of Adria.* "Being driven across" is better understood as "being tossed up and down" (Philo *Migration* 148; Barrett 1998:1202). If the ship, being tossed up and down, still moves westward from Cauda at the rate of one and a half knots, in two weeks (324 hours) it will have covered 482 nautical miles. On a course of a very shallow curve, the ship would be at Malta, 471 nautical miles from Crete (Smith 1978:124-128). Witherington (1998:770-771) is still positive on these calculations, while Gilchrist (1996:41) labels the attempt to establish precise figures based on rough estimates and certain assumptions about consistent wind speed and direction and the speed of a grain ship as "statistical legerdemain." Heeding Gilchrist's caution, we may still believe that an arrival at Malta after two weeks of travel under such storm conditions was possible.

27:28 *120 feet deep . . . 90 feet.* Or, as the NLT mg reads, "*20 fathoms . . . 15 fathoms* [37 meters . . . 27 meters]." The sailors threw a lead line over board. The "lead had a hollow on the underside which, filled with tallow or grease, brought up samples of the bottom" (Casson 1971:246; cf. Herodotus *History* 2.5). A "fathom" was the distance between fingertips with the arms extended—approximately six feet (Harrison 1986:420).

27:30 *the sailors . . . lowered the lifeboat as though they were going to put out anchors.* While some see the sailors' motives as a legitimate and praiseworthy attempt to fix the ship's position by anchoring the bow that was misunderstood by Luke and Paul (Dunn 1996:340; Barrett 1998:1205), most see it as an act of desperation for self-preservation— they were preparing to abandon ship (Witherington 1998:771; Fitzmyer 1998b:778; Johnson 1992:454).

27:35 *he took some bread, gave thanks, . . . and broke off a piece and ate it.* Given the occasion, with the presence of unbelieving soldiers, crew, and passengers, and the absence of references to the cup or explicit references to the Lord's Supper, many scholars assert that Luke is portraying only an ordinary traditional Jewish meal (Keener 1993:403; Marshall 1980:414; Kistemaker 1990:936) with either a simple witness to the God of Israel (Dunn 1996:341) or a gesture of pastoral care, as Paul encourages all to take sustenance (Johnson 1992:455). Still, the cluster of terms distinctive to the words of institution suggest that the meal, though itself not a Eucharist, does allude to the Lord's Supper (Barrett 1998:1209). Bruce's (1988:492) proposed nuanced understanding probably runs beyond the evidence: "To the majority it was an ordinary meal, while those who ate with eucharistic intention (Paul and his fellow-Christians) it was a valid eucharist." Yet, it should be kept in mind that, at this point in early church history, the Eucharist was probably still taken as a part of ordinary meals.

27:40 *lowered the rudders.* Following Liddell and Scott, Barrett (1998:1212) understands the loosening of the rudders as the dismantling of the "crossbar/yoke," the steering apparatus of the rudders. As such, the crew gave up on driving the ship. Most, however, see the crew loosening the rudders from their lashed position on deck during the storm and placing them in the water for steering as they aimed the boat to shore (Johnson 1992:456; Fitzmyer 1998b:780; Witherington 1998:774).

27:41 *But they hit a shoal and ran the ship aground too soon.* The identity of the maritime feature and the subject of the action in this sentence are disputed. Lit. it reads, "coming upon a place of two seas they beached/ran the ship aground" (*peripesontes de eis topon dithalasson epekeilan* [TG2027A, ZG2131]). The term *dithalasson* [TG1337, ZG1458] (meaning "composed of or possessing two seas") has been understood as a channel connecting two bodies of water (Keener 1993:403). But this is an incorrect reading of Strabo (*Geography* 2.5.22; 12.3.10), according to Gilchrist (1996:43-44). Many see it as a "sandbar" or "shoal" which divides the sea and creates two bodies of water (Johnson 1992:456; Dunn 1996:342; Kee 1997:291). Barrett (1998:1213) recognizes that the term does not normally indicate such a feature (according to Gilchrist [1996:43] the Greek words used for "sandbar" or "shoal" are *this* and *tainia,* and for "reef" it is *herma*), but he concludes that events in the immediate context: the ship's break up and the swimming to shore, demand that *dithalasson* be understood as denoting some such feature here. A better understanding of the passage overall is to take *dithalasson* [TG1337, ZG1458] as a patch of rough seas created by the crosscurrents and crosswinds of two seas coming together (Dio Chrysostom *Orations* 5.8-9; Lucan *Civil War* 8.563-566; Gilchrist 1996:46; Fitzmyer 1998b:780). In Gilchrist's (1996:50) reconstruction, the ship traversed St. Paul's Bay and went into the channel between the mainland and The Saint Paul's Islands, where it encountered the cross-seas as it emerged from the channel and ran aground.

the force of the waves. It is difficult to decide whether "of the waves" (*tōn kumatōn* [TG2949, ZG3246]) is original (supported by 𝔓74 ℵ² C 33 1739 𝔐 syr) or was a later explanatory addition. Given their penchant for brevity, the Alexandrian copyists (ℵ* A B) may have deleted it (Metzger 1994:442). It does correctly note the source of "the force" (Dunn 1996:342), which was the waves, not the impact of running aground which relates only to the ship's bow (Barrett 1998:1213; contra Gilchrist 1996:47).

27:44 onto . . . debris. "Debris" renders *epi tinōn* [TG5100, ZG5516] ("some things" or "some persons"), taking it as neuter (Fitzmyer 1998b:780). Barrett (1998:1215) convincingly argues that it refers to persons—swimmers taking non-swimmers on their backs to safety.

COMMENTARY

Over a two-week period, completely at the mercy of the storm, the ship had been tossed up and down while moving across the central Mediterranean (see note on 27:1). In New Testament times, "the Sea of Adria" (27:27) included a portion of the Mediterranean stretching between Crete and Malta (Pausanias *Description of Greece* 5.25.3; Ptolemy *Geography* 3.4.1, 15). In the middle of the night, still navigationally blind—the storm hid the stars and the darkness kept them from seeing land on the horizon—the sailors "sensed land was near" (27:27). Perhaps they sensed this from the waves' change of motion into a running swell or from the sound of surf crashing on the shore.

The sailors immediately assessed the situation by casting a lead line overboard to take depth soundings (see note on 27:28). After a short interval, their second sounding uncovered the sea floor thirty feet closer. Continuing to lack the wherewithal to navigate the ship, as the crew had feared while foundering on the sandbars of the Syrtis (27:17), they now feared imminent shipwreck on a rocky shore (27:29). The crew sprang into action and hurled four anchors from the ship's stern, probably by casting a cable with two anchors attached from each side of the stern. This would not only halt the ship's progress but, if properly placed, also position its bow facing the shore to prevent the waves from making damaging broadside blows. Even with this move, the sailors were still powerless. So, they prayed for daylight, when they might at least see the shore.

The sailors' pagan "faith," however, did not allay their fears. Under the pretext of using the lifeboat, or "dinghy" (*skaphē* [TG4627, ZG5002]) for positioning anchors from the bow, they tried to abandon the ship (27:30). Paul courageously told the centurion and sailors, "You cannot be saved unless they stay aboard" (27:31, literal translation). Luke consistently uses "salvation" vocabulary throughout this account (27:20, 31, 34, 44), but for rescue from mortal and physical rather than spiritual dangers. Indeed, the divine rescue would take place by ordinary providence, not miraculous intervention. What was miraculous was God's comforting reassurance by the angel's word to Paul: "God in his goodness has granted safety to everyone sailing with you" (27:24). On this warrant, Paul warned his custodian, the centurion, who, in response, heeded Paul (27:31). Impulsively or wisely, the soldiers cut the ropes, so that the lifeboat fell away (27:32). The passengers' and crew's fate would now be the same.

"Just as day was dawning," Paul tried to prepare all on board for the final push to land (27:33). He begged them all to take food (27:33-34). The sentiment "you haven't touched food for two weeks" (27:33) deals as much with the voyagers' state of mind as with their physical condition. Literally, Paul said, "Today is day fourteen you have continued in anxious expectation, voluntarily without food, eating nothing." As a result of these circumstances, the apostle encouraged them to take a meal with the reason that it is "for your own good." (27:34). If they didn't, they would be in no condition to successfully participate in God's providential rescue of them. The reason they should eat and prepare to participate is the certainty of that rescue which Paul put in the form of a proverbial saying about its completeness: "not a hair of your heads will perish" (27:34; note the use in OT and Jesus' teaching: 1 Sam 14:45; 2 Sam 14:11; 1 Kgs 1:52; Luke 21:18). So complete would be this physical rescue under divine providence that not even a hair—the most easily detachable part of the human body—would be lost in the process.

Paul then led by example. "He took . . . bread, gave thanks to God before them all, and broke [it]. . . and ate it" (27:35). Originally the Eucharist was part of the everyday meals of believers (2:42, 46; 20:7, 11). The words of institution probably bracketed everyday meals of the believers, so the sanctifying giving of thanks and inaugural breaking of bread took on a kerygmatic significance in combination with Jesus' words, "This is my body given for you" (Luke 22:15-20). Some allusion to the Lord's Supper may be in the background here (see note on 27:35). What is in the foreground, however, is Paul following a common Jewish meal pattern (b. Berakhot 16a, 17a; 1 Tim 4:4), though with strong affinities to Jesus' feeding of the five thousand (Luke 9:16-17). In both situations, the issue is basic sustenance, whether on the high seas or in the wilderness. Luke particularly brings out Paul's offering of a blessing over the food as a witness, when he says he did it "before them all" (27:35). Although the passengers and crew, for a fortnight at the mercy of life-threatening elements, had been bereft of any indication of God's providential goodness, the same God who permitted this severe rain also brought the rains and fruitful seasons that made possible the bread that was before him. Paul ate before them as an act of faith. He believed that there would be a rescue (27:24-26), and he must recover his strength to be in a position to benefit from it.

The daylight the crew had prayed for (27:29) came, and though they did not recognize the coastline, they could make out friendly features—a bay with a beach (27:39). They decided to beach the ship (see note 27:39). Three preparatory steps enabled the crew to set the ship on course to head for shore (27:40). After cutting loose the anchors and leaving them in the sea, they untied the ropes that held the rudders (see note on 27:40). These two large paddles, secured during the storm, were lowered into place on each side of the ship at the stern to provide steerage. Finally, they "raised the foresail" to the wind. This sail sloped forward almost like a bowsprit and also provided steerage. When the ship hit a shoal and ran aground, the crew was forced to beach the ship (27:41; cf. Homer *Odyssey* 9.148). The prophecy of the ship's destruction (27:22) came true, for with the bow stuck fast, the ship would eventually break up, as the surf constantly pounded the stern (27:41).

One last threat at sea faced Paul—the plan of the soldiers to kill the prisoners so that they would not swim away and escape (27:42). The centurion, though, wanting to spare Paul, thwarted it (27:43). Again, the Roman authorities protected Paul (21:33-36; 23:10, 23; 25:1-12). This time, however, that protection also meant preserving the lives of others. The other prisoners knew that God had indeed granted the lives of all who traveled with Paul to him (27:24).

The centurion ordered the swimmers overboard first and then those who needed to use planks from the ship as floats and those who would swim on the backs of others (see note on 27:44). "So everyone escaped safely to shore" (27:44). The comforting prophetic word had been fulfilled to the last letter (27:22, 34). The strongest of natural forces threatening Paul's existence had been unable to thwart God's purposes for him. For Paul's part, courageous faith kept him aligned with God's plan.

◆   S. Paul on the Island of Malta (28:1-10)

Once we were safe on shore, we learned that we were on the island of Malta. ²The people of the island were very kind to us. It was cold and rainy, so they built a fire on the shore to welcome us.

³As Paul gathered an armful of sticks and was laying them on the fire, a poisonous snake, driven out by the heat, bit him on the hand. ⁴The people of the island saw it hanging from his hand and said to each other, "A murderer, no doubt! Though he escaped the sea, justice will not permit him to live." ⁵But Paul shook off the snake into the fire and was unharmed. ⁶The people waited for him to swell up or suddenly drop dead. But when they had waited a long time and saw that he wasn't harmed, they changed their minds and decided he was a god.

⁷Near the shore where we landed was an estate belonging to Publius, the chief official of the island. He welcomed us and treated us kindly for three days. ⁸As it happened, Publius's father was ill with fever and dysentery. Paul went in and prayed for him, and laying his hands on him, he healed him. ⁹Then all the other sick people on the island came and were healed. ¹⁰As a result we were showered with honors, and when the time came to sail, people supplied us with everything we would need for the trip.

NOTES

28:1 *Malta.* This is an island 58 miles south of Sicily and 180 miles north of Cape Bon in Tunisia. The proposal that Acts actually references the island of Mljet, off Dubrovnik in the Adriatic (Meinardus 1976), has been effectively answered by Keener (1993:404) and Witherington (1998:775). Warnecke's (1987) more recent suggestion of the western Greek island of Kephallenia, 311 miles south of Mljet, has been thoroughly critiqued by Wehnert (1990).

28:3 *poisonous snake*. This literal rendering of *echidna* [^{TG}2191, ^{ZG}2399] highlights the potential historical difficulty, since currently no poisonous snakes are found on Malta. The effects of human habitation of the island over the centuries readily accounts for their disappearance (Hemer 1989a:153).

28:4 *justice*. Luke is not translating some Punic god into the "idiom of the Greek poets" (contra Keener 1993:404). Rather, these islanders, Phoenician/Punic in language and culture (Strabo *Geography* 17.3.15-16), had their own deity, named *Suduk*, meaning "Justice" (Philo of Byblos *Phoenician History*, as reported in Eusebius *Preparation for the Gospel* 1.10).

28:6 *they . . . decided he was a god*. The lack of rebuke to the islanders' exclamation is not because Luke contradicts himself and here presents Paul as a "divine man" (contrast 14:14-15; contra Conzelmann 1987:223). The preceding and following contexts provide explicit correctives, as Paul declared and acted out his dependence on God (cf. 27:24, 25, 35; and 28:8). Any positive use of the exclamation as a declaration of Paul's innocence must always be seen from the angle of Paul operating with the delegated authority of Jesus (Spencer 1997:235; cf. Luke 10:19).

28:7 *chief official of the island*. With the aid of inscriptional evidence (*Corpus inscriptionum greacarum* 14.601, *prōtos Melitaiōn kai patrōn*), most agree this *prōtō* [^{TG}4413, ^{ZG}4755] *tēs nēsou* is the chief local magistrate of Malta (Barrett 1998:1224; Fitzmyer 1998b:783). Witherington (1998:780), however, leaves open the possibility that Publius could simply be a notable citizen, a benefactor (cf. 13:50; 17:4).

28:8 *ill with fever and dysentery*. "Malta fever" (*Micrococcus melitensis*) in the nineteenth century was traced to the milk of Malta goats, and a vaccine was developed for it in 1887. Untreated, it lasted an average of four months, but in some cases up to two or three years (Longenecker 1981:565; Keener 1993:405).

28:10 *honors*. "Honors" is the preferred rendering here (Barrett 1998:1226). The clear usage of this idiom elsewhere to indicate "honors" (Josephus *Antiquities* 20.68), the lack of any clear indication that an ongoing medical ministry through Dr. Luke was occurring (as distinct from the initial healing ministry of 28:8-9), and the distinction between the "honors" and the supplies placed on board, point to the fact that these were neither monetary gifts as traveling funds (contra Witherington 1998:780; cf. Acts 4:32; 7:16; 19:19) nor fees paid for professional medical services (Bruce 1988:500 raises this as a possibility; cf. 1 Tim 5:17).

COMMENTARY

The crew and passengers learned that they were on the island of Malta once they were safely on shore (28:1; contrast 27:39). For the first time in fourteen days, they knew where they were—at least in relation to the rest of the Mediterranean world. They had been rescued from the disorientation that had led to anxiety, fear, even despair (27:17, 20, 29, 33). The island of Malta, strategically located in the narrows of the Mediterranean, had been settled from Phoenician Carthage in the sixth century BC (Strabo *Geography* 17.3.15-16). Rome had captured it from Carthage in 216 BC. Later, Augustus had settled veterans and their families there.

God, in his providence, continued the rescue, for far from facing slavery or even death at the hands of ethnically different, hostile islanders, these "people of the island" (*barbaroi* [^{TG}915A, ^{ZG}975], "non-Greek speakers" of a Punic [Carthaginian] dialect) were "very kind" to the survivors (28:2; cf. 27:3). They further rescued the voyagers from the deleterious effects of the weather by building a fire and gathering and welcoming the shipwrecked passengers and crew around it. Though the temperature may have been as warm as 50 degrees Fahrenheit, it was "rainy" (28:2). The rigors of the journey and the swim to shore undoubtedly had soaked the travelers to the bone. As Paul gathered sticks to lay on the fire, a poisonous snake, driven out by the heat, fastened itself on his arm (28:3).

The islanders, steeped in an animistic worldview, thought of the gods as using the forces of nature, especially storm and sea, for retributive justice (28:4). The Greeks viewed Justice as a virgin daughter of Zeus who kept watch for any injustice done on earth and reported it to her father, who then dispensed retributive justice to make it right, including destroying ships at sea (Hesiod *Works and Days* 239, 256; Plutarch *Moralia* 161F). These Maltese with Punic/Phoenician background saw their deity, *Suduk* ("Justice"), pursuing Paul, a murderer (see note on 28:4). They thought Paul had outwitted the deity in escaping the storm and shipwreck and that now "Justice" was counterattacking through the snake (28:4; cf. Pliny *Natural History* 8.85-86). In a Greek epigram, Statyllius Flaccus tells of a mariner who escaped the whirlwind and fury of the deadly sea, only to be slain by a viper on the Libyan sand (*Greek Anthology* 7.290).

Unceremoniously, Paul "shook off the snake into the fire and was unharmed" (28:5). Paul was not immune to all harm, for the Lord promised him in his commission that Paul would suffer for him (9:16). Yet, he also promised that Paul would not suffer any debilitating, let alone death-dealing harm—the kind that would prevent him from fulfilling his mission for his Lord. The islanders kept expecting Paul to become inflamed (either to "swell up" or burn with fever) or "suddenly drop dead" (28:6)—as the poison would act to destroy blood corpuscles and vessels. Although they closely observed Paul for a long time, their expectations went unfulfilled. All they saw was that no harm came to him physically, which was also a sign that he was not morally harmful, and certainly no murderer (cf. 25:5; Luke 23:41). They changed their minds and began to say, or repeatedly said, "He is a god!" (See note on 28:6.)

After this, Paul was shown hospitality by Publius, the chief official, or prominent citizen, on the island (see note on 28:7). Luke says he welcomed "us" (whether the entire group of survivors or just Paul and his companions is unclear, as also 28:10) to his estate and showed kind hospitality for three days (28:7). If it was Paul and his companions (i.e., Christians), there may be a hint that the gospel had been preached and believed. In Acts, hospitality, the sharing of possessions with fellow Christians, is often a mark of conversion (cf. 2:42, 46; 10:6, 48; 16:15, 34; 21:16).

As Jesus was, with Peter's mother-in-law (Luke 4:38-41), Paul was alerted to a physical need in the older generation. Publius's father was "ill" (lit., "lying in bed seized") with "fever and dysentery" (see note on 28:8). Through Paul, a healing took place in such a way that the islanders clearly knew that its source was not Paul, "a god," but God. While Jesus rebuked the fever of Peter's mother-in-law, Paul prayed and laid hands on the sick one (28:8; cf. Luke 4:39). Nonetheless, the aftermath was the same—crowds of sick "came and were healed," (28:9; lit., "were approaching one after another and were being healed." *prosērchonto* and *ether-apeuonto* are imperfect verbs denoting continuous action or action at intervals; cf. Luke 4:40-41). Again, such a response and such a ministry makes best sense in the context of the preaching of the gospel, as a demonstration that salvation is for the whole person (cf. 8:4-8; 14:3, 9-10, 15). Indeed, as in Jesus' inaugural ministry and in the gospel's advance into Samaria and central Asia Minor, the initial thrusts of God's mission into new geographical and ethnic territories involved very concrete signs of salvation blessings.

As a further token that Paul and Luke had shared in spiritual things with the Maltese, the islanders responded by giving them physical things (cf. Paul's articulation of the dynamic, 1 Cor 9:11; cf. Rom 15:27). With many honors (see note on 28:10) and all sorts of things they would need for the trip, they put Paul and his companions on board a different ship.

◆ ## T. Paul Arrives at Rome (28:11-16)

¹¹It was three months after the shipwreck that we set sail on another ship that had wintered at the island—an Alexandrian ship with the twin gods* as its figurehead. ¹²Our first stop was Syracuse,* where we stayed three days. ¹³From there we sailed across to Rhegium.* A day later a south wind began blowing, so the following day we sailed up the coast to Puteoli. ¹⁴There we found some believers,* who invited us to spend a week with them. And so we came to Rome.

¹⁵The brothers and sisters* in Rome had heard we were coming, and they came to meet us at the Forum* on the Appian Way. Others joined us at The Three Taverns.* When Paul saw them, he was encouraged and thanked God.

¹⁶When we arrived in Rome, Paul was permitted to have his own private lodging, though he was guarded by a soldier.

28:11 The *twin gods* were the Roman gods Castor and Pollux. 28:12 *Syracuse* was on the island of Sicily.
28:13 *Rhegium* was on the southern tip of Italy. 28:14 Greek *brothers.* 28:15a Greek *brothers.*
28:15b *The Forum* was about 43 miles (70 kilometers) from Rome. 28:15c *The Three Taverns* was about 35 miles (57 kilometers) from Rome.

NOTES

28:14 *And so we came to Rome.* The double reference to the arrival at Rome (cf. 28:16) neither betrays Luke's eagerness to bring the account to its climax (contra Fernando 1998:614) nor points to the larger geographical area, the "administrative district of Rome" (contra Fitzmyer 1998b:787). Most see the first reference as introductory ("in this way we came to Rome"), pointing out the manner in which Paul arrived at Rome, i.e., welcomed and escorted by the Roman Christians (Witherington 1998:787).

28:16 The Western text (614 𝔐 it^gig syr^h** cop^sa) has an expansion that passed over into the Byzantine text (many minuscules and some lectionaries), which is the basis for the KJV and NKJV translations. After "Rome" it adds, "the centurion delivered the prisoners to the captain of the guard." The precise identity of this "captain of the guard" is disputed (Fitzmyer 1998b:789). Consensus seems to be building around the chief administrative officer of the Praetorian Guard, whose prefect was entrusted with all the prisoners of the provinces (Rapske 1994b:176; Sherwin-White 1963:108-110; cf. Pliny *Letters* 10.57.2).

COMMENTARY

"Three months after the shipwreck" (28:11) was at the earliest the end of January or the beginning of February. Pliny (*Natural History* 2.47) says that sea travel resumed after February 7; Vegetius (*Military Institutions of the Romans* 4.39) says after March 10 (cf. Josephus *War* 2.203). At one of Malta's large harbors, Paul and the rest of the passengers and crew found "an Alexandrian ship with the twin gods (*Dioskouroi* [ᵀᴳ1359, ᶻᴳ1483]) as its figurehead" (28:11). The gods Castor and Pollux were twin sons of Tyndareus, king of Sparta. They had been immortalized as gods from the union of Leda, queen of Sparta, and Zeus. Seeing their constellation (Gemini) while on the high seas was thought to be a sign of good fortune. They were the patron deities of sailors and protectors of innocent seafarers, and their cult had devotees in Egypt as well as Italy (Epictetus *Discourses* 2.18.29). Euripides presents them as rescuers of those who cherish divine law and justice and as punishers of perjurers (*Electra* 1342-1355).

For Paul to book passage on the *Castor and Pollux*, which had wintered at Malta, was ironic. An implied criticism of the gods and their actual ability to save may be present, as Paul, whose God saved him in the midst of a winter storm, now traveled on a ship which, although named for the protectors of seafarers, had to seek the safety of harbor for the winter. At the same time, the ship's figurehead was a silent witness to Paul's innocence.

After a 60-mile voyage north, the ship stopped at Syracuse on the southeast coast of Sicily, the triangular island at the tip of the boot of the Italian peninsula (28:12). They stayed for three days at this provincial capital city, famed for fishing, shipbuilding, and bronze work.

The 70-mile passage to Rhegium was uneventful (see note on 28:13). This Italian port is six or seven miles from Messina, across the strait that separates Sicily from Italy. The next day, on the strength of a "south wind," the ship moved northward and in two days covered the 175 nautical miles (overall speed, five knots) to Puteoli.

Puteoli, because of its location in the Bay of Naples and its man-made jetties, was at this time, in Strabo's word, "a very great emporium"—Rome's main port of entry from the east (Strabo *Geography* 5.4.6). Since Josephus mentions a Jewish colony there (*War* 2.104), it is not surprising that Paul and his Christian companions "found some believers" there (28:14). Their invitation to spend a week with them, of course, presupposed a request to the centurion and his consent (cf. 27:3). Paul's experience of instant but genuine intimacy and full-orbed mutual commitment in the company of believers at Puteoli is a refreshing picture of what the gospel brings.

"And so we came to Rome" (28:14). While looking back and climactically marking the precise fulfillment of God's promise to Paul (23:11; 27:24), this note also points forward, telling the reader to look at the way Paul and his party came to Rome—in the company of Roman Christians who came to give him the kind of welcome reserved for dignitaries (28:15). Paul made his way 20 miles up the *Via Compana* to its intersection with the *Via Appia*, the Appian Way (28:15). Satius called this Roman road "the worn and well-known track of Appia, queen of the long roads"

(*Silvae* 2.2.12). The 130-mile trek to Rome probably took five days. Moving through hill country and returning to the coast only three times, this road passed through the Pontine Marshes, in which a canal had been constructed in an attempt at draining them. At the northern end of the marsh, 43 miles from Rome, was "the Forum on the Appian Way" (28:15)—"crammed with boatmen and stingy tavern-keepers" (Horace *Satires* 1.5.3-6). Eight miles farther was *Three Taverns* (Cicero *Letters to Atticus* 2.10). At both of these "halting stations," Christian believers from Rome who had heard that Paul and the others were coming greeted him and provided for this imperial prisoner a reception and escort to Rome fit for an emperor (28:15).

"When Paul saw them, he was encouraged and thanked God" (28:15). He was thankful to God for the realization of a long-standing desire—to bear witness in Rome (cf. 19:21; Rom 1:10-12; 15:22-24, 30-32). Without divine guidance, reassurance, and providential aid through many obstacles, Paul never would have made it. Paul took courage, especially at the sight of the Roman Christians (28:15). Because the Judaizing opposition either followed Paul to Rome or was already there (cf. Phil 1:15, 19), this show of support was surely most significant to him.

As Paul and his companions "arrived in Rome" (28:16), they were no doubt struck with, as Horace says, "the smoke, the riches, and the din of wealthy Rome" (*Odes* 3.29.12)—the ancient world's largest city, capital, and hub of the Empire. Here Paul experienced a very light form of military custody in his own lodgings, where he remained chained at the wrist to a soldier of the Praetorian Guard (28:16). Each guard would have served a four-hour shift (Phil 1:13; Josephus *Antiquities* 18.169).

◆   ## U. Paul Preaches at Rome under Guard (28:17-31)

[17]Three days after Paul's arrival, he called together the local Jewish leaders. He said to them, "Brothers, I was arrested in Jerusalem and handed over to the Roman government, even though I had done nothing against our people or the customs of our ancestors. [18]The Romans tried me and wanted to release me, because they found no cause for the death sentence. [19]But when the Jewish leaders protested the decision, I felt it necessary to appeal to Caesar, even though I had no desire to press charges against my own people. [20]I asked you to come here today so we could get acquainted and so I could explain to you that I am bound with this chain because I believe that the hope of Israel—the Messiah—has already come."

[21]They replied, "We have had no letters from Judea or reports against you from anyone who has come here. [22]But we want to hear what you believe, for the only thing we know about this movement is that it is denounced everywhere."

[23]So a time was set, and on that day a large number of people came to Paul's lodging. He explained and testified about the Kingdom of God and tried to persuade them about Jesus from the Scriptures. Using the law of Moses and the books of the prophets, he spoke to them from morning until evening. [24]Some were persuaded by the things he said, but others did not believe. [25]And after they had argued back and forth among themselves, they left with this final word from Paul: "The Holy Spirit was right when he said to your ancestors through Isaiah the prophet,

²⁶'Go and say to this people:
When you hear what I say,
    you will not understand.
When you see what I do,
    you will not comprehend.
²⁷For the hearts of these people are
    hardened,
and their ears cannot hear,
and they have closed their eyes—
so their eyes cannot see,
    and their ears cannot hear,
    and their hearts cannot understand,

and they cannot turn to me
    and let me heal them.'*

²⁸So I want you to know that this salvation from God has also been offered to the Gentiles, and they will accept it."*

³⁰For the next two years, Paul lived in Rome at his own expense.* He welcomed all who visited him, ³¹boldly proclaiming the Kingdom of God and teaching about the Lord Jesus Christ. And no one tried to stop him.

28:26-27 Isa 6:9-10 (Greek version).   28:28 Some manuscripts add verse 29, *And when he had said these words, the Jews departed, greatly disagreeing with each other.*   28:30 Or *in his own rented quarters.*

NOTES

28:17 *local Jewish leaders.* Williams (1994:130) rightly concludes that *tōn Ioudaiōn prōtous* [TG4413, ZG4755] is "far too imprecise" for identifying the particular office holders (contrast Barrett [1998:1237], who labels them heads of synagogues). They might have been simply prominent members of the community and not even office holders at all.

28:21-22 Barrett (1998:1241) contends it is historically improbable that the Jewish community would be ignorant of Paul's case, either by verbal report or correspondence from Jerusalem Jews, and that they seemingly would have no firsthand knowledge of Christianity. Fernando (1998:625) and Witherington (1998:799) give plausible explanations of the Jewish ignorance of Paul's case in terms of Paul's recent arrival in Rome and his ship's arrival ahead of any correspondence about Paul from Jerusalem. Alternatively, lack of communication from Jerusalem may indicate the Jewish authorities there decided not to go to the expense and effort of pursuing their admittedly weak case in Roman imperial court. Barrett (1998:1242), following Sherwin-White (1963:112-119) and Hemer (1989a:157), insists this possibility is not strong, given the Roman preference for enforcing prosecution. There was an understandable isolation of Jewish leaders from the predominantly Gentile Christian community there since their return after the expulsion under Claudius (18:2). This explains their lack of firsthand knowledge of Christianity.

28:26-27 The NT text form follows the LXX of Isa 6:9-10 except for placing the phrase "to this people" (*ton laon* [TG2992, ZG3295] *touton*) after the first verb. The NLT follows the MT word order. The shift in Hebrew vowel pointing from imperatives to finite causative verbs (the latter underlie the LXX) in the description of the dullness of heart, hardness of hearing, and closed eyes, probably reflects the Sopherim's theological preference for emphasizing Judah's willful disobedience over against God's judicial blinding through the prophet's message (Archer and Chirichigno 1983:93).

28:28 *this salvation from God has also been offered to the Gentiles, and they will accept it.* Does Paul's quote and statement indicate that Luke believes the rejection of the Jews is final and therefore there is no continuing mission to the Jews? Some answer the question "yes" on both counts. Either they see a failure of the Jewish mission and a "replacement" of it by the Gentile mission (Tyson 1988:137; cf. Haenchen 1971:128-129), or they declare the mission a success according to God's purposes and view the church of the Jewish remnant and Gentiles according to a "restoration-exclusion" model (Jervell 1972a). Others respond with a qualified "yes" to these questions. They distinguish between an official or corporate Jewish rejection, which is final, and that of individual Jews who, as part of the believing remnant, do accept the gospel (Polhill 1992:544-545; Marguerat 1993b:85). They conclude that the Jewish mission may be over but not the obligation to witness to individual Jews.

A growing number of scholars, however, see in these verses neither a final rejection nor an end to the Jewish mission. They see in the immediate, larger Lukan and, indeed, OT context, God's saving mission from the beginning, comprehending both Jew and Gentile (Van de Sandt 1994:343; Dunn 1996:355; Seccombe 1998:369). They see (esp. in the OT prophets) the offer of a final hope to Israel, even though a majority reject it now (Brawley 1998:274, 296; Witherington 1998:802). Fusco (1996:10) asserts that Luke does not give that future hope here because he has already given it in Jesus' teaching (Luke 13:31-35; 19:41-44; 21:24b). These scholars contend that the Isa 6 quote functions not as a statement of final judgment of the Jews but as both an interpretation of the mixed Jewish response to the gospel and a warning about the tremendous responsibility involved in hearing the message (Johnson 1992:473; Seccombe 1998:369).

28:28-29 As the NLT mg notes, "Some manuscripts add verse 29, *And when he had said these words, the Jews departed, greatly disagreeing with each other.*" (These mss are 𝔐 it syr^h**; so TR). Since this longer reading lies behind the KJV and NKJV, it came over into English Bible versification (Metzger 1994:444). Hence, the NLT accounts for it in a footnote.

28:30 *at his own expense.* This is the best rendering of *en idiō misthōmati* [TG3410, ZG3637], which normally means "at one's own expense" (*Sylloge inscriptionum graecarum* 831; cf. 615). The NLT mg also offers the rendering "in his own rented quarters"; although there are no other occurrences for *misthōma* as a rented house, Demosthenes 28.1 does show the use of a cognate verb for hiring a house.

28:31 The ending of Acts is not simply a result of Luke writing as far as he knew the events of Paul's life (Johnson 1992:473; contra Fernando 1998:625). Nor is it only a matter of theology—that Luke desired to end on a positive, triumphant note in line with his overall purpose to show the unstoppable advance of the gospel (contra Dunn 1996:343; Fitzmyer 1998b:791; Barrett 1998:1250). Rather, using the "rhetoric of silence," Luke drew his readers in, recruiting them to finish a suspended narrative plot line begun at 1:8 (Marguerat 1993b; Rosner 1998:230; Witherington 1998:816). With Paul in chains, it is now upon Luke's readers to become the witnesses to the ends of the earth.

COMMENTARY

Soon after his arrival in Rome, Paul called together local Jewish leaders (28:17). Perhaps he wanted to find out what they knew about his case and thereby seek to head off their intervention on behalf of the Jerusalem Jews (cf. Josephus *Antiquities* 17.300; *War* 2.80-92). More likely, as ever, he was pursuing his practice of taking the gospel to the Jews first (13:5, 14; 14:1; 16:13; 17:2, 10, 17; 18:4; 19:8). The Jewish community in Rome during the mid-first century was large (40,000–50,000) and influential, inhabiting "the great section of Rome on the other side of the Tiber" (Philo *Embassy* 155).

Here, for the first time in Acts, Paul interprets his legal circumstances outside a law court setting (28:17-20). He described his basic condition as a prisoner in the custody of the Romans from the time he was arrested in Jerusalem, even though he had committed no chargeable offense against either his own people or their customs (28:17; cf. the charges made 21:28; 24:6; 25:7; and their unsustainability, 25:7, 10, 18, 25; 26:31).

Paul then reviewed his appearance before Festus, and for the first time we learn some key details that explain why the appeal to Caesar was so necessary (28:18-19). Although prior repetitions of the hearing (original scene, 25:6-12; repetitions, 25:14-21, 24-27) reveal both Festus's conclusion that Paul was innocent (25:18, 25) and the Jews' strong opposition (25:15, 24), we learn that the Romans had actually "wanted" to (or better, "were planning to," *eboulonto* [TG1014, ZG1089]) release Paul (28:18; cf. 26:32) and that the Jews strongly protested (28:19). This probably occurred between Paul's defense and Festus's asking Paul whether he would agree to a change of venue (25:8-9). The Jews' protest, then, may be what motivated Festus to want to do them a favor. Festus's decision to release Paul may explain why the change of venue issue was in the form of a question and why Paul in his response could so boldly say, "You know very well I am not guilty" (25:10).

Further Paul wanted to assure these leaders in Rome that he was in no way motivated to appeal to Caesar in order "to press charges against" his own people (28:19)—that is, bring a countersuit for malicious prosecution (*Digest* 48.1.5; 48.16.1-3). Such, indeed, was the case with the Jews, given the weakness of their case (25:7, 10-11, 18) and their hostile initiatives against Paul (25:15, 24). In fact, in order to give the Jewish leaders in Rome this reassurance, Paul wanted to become acquainted with them and speak to them (28:20). The NLT rendering also brings out the fact that the subsequent statement about why he was a prisoner could also have motivated Paul to request this meeting. Speaking of the "hope of Israel" as the cause of his prisoner status gave a positive reason for his circumstances (28:20), but more than that, it also gave an opportunity for his persecution "to turn out for a witness" (Luke 21:13). He stated the point of controversy, which had led to his arrest and imprisonment, in the briefest and most palatable of terms—"the hope of Israel"—the long awaited messianic salvation (cf. 23:6; 24:15; 26:6-8; cf. the NLT expansion, "the Messiah—has already come," which brings in the distinctive Christian understanding of Jewish messianic Christology and eschatology).

The Jewish leaders responded that they had heard nothing by letter or verbal report from Judea "against" Paul (28:21; lit., "anything evil concerning you"; cf. 18:14; 25:18). Acts 9:2 and 28:21 and Justin Martyr (*Dialogue* 17) give the only evidence that central supervision from Jerusalem via envoys extended into the Diaspora during the first century. As far as these Roman Jews were concerned, Christianity was just another Jewish sect, and one held in ill-repute everywhere (28:22; cf. 25:5, 14). They, however, wanted to hear Paul's opinion (*phroneis* [TG5426, ZG5858], "thoughts") on the matter.

On the appointed day, a large number of Jews (cf. 13:44) came to "Paul's lodging," his rented housing (28:23; cf. 28:16, 30). From morning until evening Paul explained to them the Kingdom of God, giving them additional and different information about the Christian faith (28:23). Though it was Luke's shorthand way of referring to the gospel message (1:3; 8:12; 19:8; 20:25; 28:31), "the Kingdom of God" was actually the eschatological highway into the heart of the pious Jew (Luke 13:28-29; 14:15; 19:11; 23:42, 51; Acts 1:6). And the Good News was that God's reign, "the hope of Israel," was already in their midst in a salvation accomplished by the crucified, risen, and exalted Messiah, Jesus, and now applied by the outpouring of salvation blessings.

But the Jews would only embrace this Good News if they could be convinced that Jesus was the Messiah and that, though now unseen at the Father's right hand, his Kingdom reign had already begun. Paul therefore tried to persuade them about Jesus from the Old Testament Scriptures (cf. Luke 24:25-27, 44-48; Acts 13:23-29; 17:3-4; 26:22, 27-28;). The response to Paul's witness was mixed: "Some were persuaded by the things he said, but others did not believe" (28:24). In stark contrast to the unity of the true people of God (2:43; 4:32; 5:12), this mixed response led the Jewish crowd to argue back and forth among themselves and depart divided (28:25).

Lest the Jews take this mixed reaction as an opportunity to dismiss the Christian message of the Kingdom as just a sectarian opinion attracting some and not others, and lest they conclude that Jesus is not the true Messiah, Paul used Isaiah 6:9-10 to interpret to them their reaction, thereby showing that a mixed reaction to God's message is both within God's plan and has devastating eternal consequences for those who respond negatively (28:26-27).

In his introductory formula, Paul affirmed the divine origin of Scripture: "The Holy Spirit . . . said . . . through Isaiah the prophet" (28:25). He also pointed to their ancestors (using the accusatory "your ancestors") so that they would realize that what was true of the fathers was also now true of the sons (cf. 7:51-52). Paul placed himself in the grand prophetic tradition by reporting Isaiah's commission to a task that would produce the same results as the apostle had just experienced. There was a hearing and seeing of saving truth without its appropriation (Isa 6:9). Though there may still be a hint of the idea of divine judicial hardening in the use of the passive—"the hearts . . . are hardened" (28:27; lit., "have been made fat," i.e., insensitive to the truth)—the reason for this lack of responsiveness is clearly portrayed in terms of the human listeners' responsibility—"their ears cannot hear, and they have closed their eyes" (28:27). This sinful condition has a negative purpose that the prophet gives in chiastic order: not seeing with the eyes, hearing with the ears, or understanding with the heart. It also involves a failure to "turn" to God (28:27), which leaves them in their lost condition (cf. 3:19; 26:18, 20). Though this is a strong warning not to persist in unbelief, it is not necessarily the final word on his hearers' eternal destiny. The last phrase gives hope, for God speaks of his intent to heal those who do turn.

With the word "so" (oun, 28:28), Paul drew an inference from the quote, showing that God would not be thwarted in his mission. Paul let his hearers know that divine revelation (cf. similar introductory formulas in 2:14; 13:38) bore witness that the scope of God's saving mission includes the Gentiles (Ps 67:2; cf. Ezek 3:4-7; 2:3-5), just as it does the Jews (Acts 13:26). And it will be successful: "They will accept it" (28:28). The verb is akousontai [TG191A, ZG201]: "They will hear" (cf. Luke 8:8, 18; Acts 4:4; 10:44; 18:8; 19:10).

Although this is the third and final time Paul spoke of Jewish rejection and

Gentile reception (13:46; 18:6), it is carefully nuanced. Luke was not saying that the Jews' rejection was final or that the mission to the Jews was over (see note on 28:28). Of the three statements, this is the only one in which Paul did not explicitly say he was turning from the Jews to the Gentiles. Further, his statement about salvation being sent to the Gentiles is in the past tense. What is contrasted is not the two missions but the different audiences' responses to the one mission. Indeed, Paul continued to welcome "all who visited him," presumably both Jew and Gentile (28:30).

In a final summary statement (28:30-31), Acts achieves what Luke had set out to prove: God is on mission with and through his bold witnesses, unstoppably giving salvation blessings to all nations (Luke 24:47; Acts 1:8). Acts ends with a simple yet open-ended picture of Paul's life in Rome. "For the next two years, Paul lived in Rome at his own expense" (28:30). During this period, Paul "welcomed all who visited" him, to whom he proclaimed the Good News and the arrival of God's reign in the saving work of the Lord Jesus Christ (28:23). How did Paul bear witness? With complete freedom. Inwardly, he knew no pressure of fear to conceal or obscure or hesitate about the truth. Rather, "boldly" and by the power of the Spirit—candidly, clearly, and confidently—he was preaching and teaching (2:29; 4:13, 29-31; 9:27; 13:46; 14:3; 19:8; 26:26; cf. Eph 6:19-20; Phil 1:15-20).

The outward freedom Paul knew is framed by the very last word of Acts: *akōlutōs* [TG209, ZG219], "unhindered" (NLT, "And no one tried to stop him"). This shows the Roman government's attitude toward Christianity: christianity did not pose such a threat to either the civil order or the Roman way of life that one of its advocates would have to be muzzled during house arrest. But more than government tolerance, this term indicates that God's mission—the gospel preached in Jesus' name to all nations—will not be thwarted. In the very last word of Acts, Luke converts the reader into an active participant. By the power of the Spirit, the reader must also add his or her own chapter of bold, unhindered witness to God's unstoppable mission.

BIBLIOGRAPHY

Aland, Barbara
1985 Entstehung, Charakter und Herkunft des sog. westliches Textes untersucht an der Apostelsgeschichte.
    Pp. 5-65 in *Ephemerides Theologicae Lovanienses* 62.

Alexander, Loveday C. A.
1993 *The Preface to Luke's Gospel: Literary Convention and Social Context in Luke 1:1-4 and Acts 1:1.*
    Cambridge: Cambridge University Press.

Anderson, James N.D.
1970 *Christianity and Comparative Religion.* London: Tyndale.

Archer, Gleason L.
1964 *A Survey of Old Testament Introduction.* Chicago: Moody.

Archer, Gleason L. and G. C. Chirichigno
1983 *Old Testament Quotations in the New Testament.* Chicago: Moody.

Arnold, Clinton E.
1989 *Ephesians, Power and Magic: The Concept of Power in Ephesians in the Light of Its Historical Setting.*
    Cambridge: Cambridge University Press.

Ascough, Richard S.
1998 Civic Pride at Philippi: The Text-critical Problem of Acts 16.12. *New Testament Studies* 44:93-103.

Atkinson, William
1995 Pentecostal Responses to Dunn's Baptism in the Holy Spirit: Luke–Acts. *Journal of Pentecostal Theology* 6:87-131.

Aune, David
1987 *The New Testament in Its Literary Environment.* Philadelphia: Westminster.

Baird, William
1980 Ascension and Resurrection: An Intersection of Luke and Paul. Pp. 3-18 in *Texts and Testaments: Critical Essays on the Bible and Early Church Fathers.* Editor, W. Eugene March. San Antonio: Trinity University Press.

Balch, David L.
1990a The Areopagus Speech: An Appeal to Stoic Historian Posidonius against Later Stoics and Epicureans.
    Pp. 52-79 in *Greeks, Romans and Christians: Essays in Honor of Abraham J. Malherbe.* Editors, David L. Balch, Everett Ferguson, Wayne A. Meeks. Minneapolis: Fortress.

1990b The Genre of Luke–Acts: Individual Biography, Adventure Novel, or Political History? *Southwestern Journal of Theology* 33:5-19.

Barnes, Colin
1997 Paul and Johanan ben Zakkai. *Expository Times* 108:366-367.

Barrett, C. K.
1982 Salvation Proclaimed: XII. Acts 4:8-12. *Expository Times* 94:68-70.

1994 *A Critical and Exegetical Commentary on the Acts of the Apostles,* vol. 1 (chs 1-14). International Critical Commentary. Edinburgh: T & T Clark.

1998 *A Critical and Exegetical Commentary on the Acts of the Apostles,* vol. 2 (chs 15-28). International Critical Commentary. Edinburgh: T & T Clark.

Bartchy, S. Scott
1991 Community of Goods in Acts as an Idealization or Social Reality. Pp. 309-318 in *The Future of Early Christianity: Essays in Honor of Helmut Koester.* Editor, Birger A. Pearson. Minneapolis: Fortress.

Bassler, Jouette M.
1985 Luke and Paul on Impartiality. *Biblica* 66:546-552.

Bauckham, Richard
1995 James and the Jerusalem Church. Pp. 415-80 in *The Book of Acts in its Palestinian Setting.* Editor, Richard Bauckham. The Book of Acts in Its First Century Setting, vol 4. Grand Rapids: Eerdmans.

1996 James and the Gentiles (Acts 15:13-21). Pp. 154-184 in *History, Literature, and Society in the Book of Acts.* Editor, Ben Witherington III. Cambridge: Cambridge University Press.

Bayer, Hans F.

1998 The Preaching of Peter in Acts. Pp. 257-276 in *Witness to the Gospel: The Theology of Acts*. Editors, I. Howard Marshall and David Peterson. Grand Rapids: Eerdmans.

Berger, Klaus

1995 *Theologiegeschichte des Urchristentums: Theologie des Neuen Testaments*. 2nd rev. and enlarged ed. Tübingen: Francke.

Black, C. Clifton

1998 John Mark in the Acts of the Apostles. Pp. 102-120 in *Literary Studies in Luke–Acts: Essays in Honor of Joseph B. Tyson*. Editors, Richard P. Thompson and Thomas A. Phillips. Macon, GA: Mercer University Press.

Blomberg, Craig

1998 The Christian and the Law of Moses. Pp. 397-416 in *Witness to the Gospel: The Theology of Acts*. Editors, I. Howard Marshall and David Peterson. Grand Rapids: Eerdmans.

Blue, Brad

1998 The Influence of Jewish Worship on Luke's Presentation of the Early Church. Pp. 473- 498 in *Witness to the Gospel: The Theology of Acts*. Editors, I. Howard Marshall and David Peterson. Grand Rapids: Eerdmans.

Bock, Darrell

1998 Scripture and the Realization of God's Promises. Pp. 41-62 in *Witness to the Gospel: The Theology of Acts*. Editors, I. Howard Marshall and David Peterson. Grand Rapids: Eerdmans.

Bockmuehl, Markus

1995 The Noachide Commandments and the New Testament Ethics with Special Reference to Acts 15 and Pauline Halakhah. *Révue Biblique* 102:72-101.

Bolt, Peter

1998 Mission and Witness. Pp. 191-214 in *Witness to the Gospel: The Theology of Acts*. Editors, I. Howard Marshall and David Peterson. Grand Rapids: Eerdmans.

Borgen, Peder

1988 Catalogues of Vices, the Apostolic Decree and the Jerusalem Meeting. Pp. 126-141 in *The Social World of Formative Christianity and Judaism: Essays in Tribute to Howard Clark Kee*. Editors, Jacob Neusner et al. Philadelphia: Fortress.

Bosch, David J.

1991 *Transforming Mission: Paradigm Shifts in Theology of Mission*. Maryknoll, NY: Orbis Books.

Botha, Pieter J. J.

1995 Community and Conviction in Luke–Acts. *Neotestamentica* 29:145-165.

Braun, Michael A.

1977 James' Use of Amos at the Jerusalem Council: Steps toward a Possible Solution of the Textual and Theological Problems. *Journal of the Evangelical Theological Society* 20:113-121.

Brawley, Robert L.

1988 Paul in Acts: Aspects of Structure and Characterization. Pp. 90-105 in *Society of Biblical Literature 1988 Seminar Papers*. Editor David J. Lull. Atlanta: Scholars Press.

1998 The God of Promises and the Jews in Luke–Acts. Pp. 279-296 in *Literary Studies in Luke–Acts: Essays in Honor of Joseph B. Tyson*. Editors, Richard P. Thompson and Thomas E. Phillips. Macon, GA: Mercer University Press.

Brehm, H. Allan

1997 Vindicating the Rejected One: Stephen's Speech as a Critique of the Jewish Leaders. Pp. 266-299 in *Early Christian Interpretation of the Scripture of Israel*. Editors, Craig A. Evans and James A. Sanders. Sheffield: Sheffield Academic.

Breytenbach, Cilliers

1993 Zeus und der lebendige Gott: Anmerkungen zu Apg 14.11-17. *New Testament Studies* 39:396-413.

Brock, Sebastian P.

1974 Barnabas: huios parakleseos. *Journal of Theological Studies* 25:93-98.

Brown, H. Stephen

1996 Paul's Hearing at Caesarea: A Preliminary Comparison with Legal Literature of the Roman Period. Pp. 319-332 in *SBL 1996 Seminar Papers*. Editor, Eugene H. Lovering, Jr. Atlanta: Scholars Press.

Bruce, F. F.

1974 The Speeches in Acts—Thirty Years After. Pp. 53-68 in *Reconciliation and Hope.* Editor, Robert Banks. Grand Rapids: Eerdmans.

1976 Is the Paul of Acts the Real Paul? *Bulletin of the John Rylands Library* 58:282-305.

1987 Paul's Use of the Old Testament in Acts. Pp. 71-79 in *Tradition and Interpretation in the New Testament: Essays in Honor of E. Earle Ellis on His 60th Birthday.* Editors, Gerald F. Hawthorne with Otto Betz. Grand Rapids: Eerdmans.

1988 *The Book of Acts.* Rev. ed. Grand Rapids: Eerdmans.

1990 *The Acts of the Apostles: The Greek Text with Introduction and Commentary.* 3rd rev. ed. Grand Rapids: Eerdmans.

Buckwalter, H. Douglas

1998 The Divine Saviour. Pp. 107-124 in *Witness to the Gospel: The Theology of Acts.* Editors, I. Howard Marshall and David Peterson. Grand Rapids: Eerdmans.

Bullock, John D.

1994 Was Saint Paul Struck Blind and Converted by Lightning? *Survey of Opthamlology* 39:151-160.

Burchard, Christoph

1985 A Note on *Rhema* in Jos As 17:1f; Luke 2:15, 17; Acts 10:37. *Novum Testamentum* 27:281-295.

Callan, Terrance

1993 The Background of the Apostolic Decree (Acts 15:20, 29; 21:25). *Catholic Biblical Quarterly* 55:284-297.

Calvin, John

1965 *The Acts of the Apostles 1-13.* Calvin's Commentaries. Editors, David W. Torrance and Thomas F. Torrance. Grand Rapids: Eerdmans.

Capper, Brian

1995 The Palestinian Cultural Context of Earliest Christian Community of Goods. Pp. 323-356 in *The Book of Acts in its Palestinian Setting.* Editor, Richard Bauckham. The Book of Acts in Its First Century Setting, vol. 4. Grand Rapids: Eerdmans.

Carson, D. A., Douglas J. Moo, and Leon Morris

1992 *An Introduction to the New Testament.* Grand Rapids: Zondervan.

Casson, Lionel

1971 *Ships and Seamanship in the Ancient World.* Princeton: Princeton University Press.

Charles, J. Daryl

1995 Engaging the (Neo-) Pagan Mind: Paul's Encounter with Athenian Culture as a Model for Cultural Apologetics (Acts 17:16-34). *Trinity Journal* 16:47-62.

Chilton, Bruce D.

1992 Judaism. Pp. 398-405 in *Dictionary of Jesus and the Gospels.* Editors, Joel B. Green and Scot McKnight. Downers Grove: InterVarsity.

Clark, David J.

1975 What Went Overboard First? *Bible Translator* 26:144-146.

Cohen, Shaye J. D.

1979 *Josephus in Galilee and Rome: His Vita and Development as a Historian.* Leiden: Brill.

1986 Was Timothy Jewish (Acts 16:1-2)? Patristic Exegesis, Rabbinic Law, and Matrilineal Descent. *Journal of Biblical Literature* 105:251-268 .

1989 Crossing the Boundary and Becoming a Jew. Pp. 13-33 in *Harvard Theological Review* 80.

Comfort, Philip W.

1992 *The Quest for the Original Text of the New Testament.* Grand Rapids: Baker.

2007 *New Testament Text and Translation Commentary.* Carol Stream: Tyndale.

Conzelmann, Hans

1987 *Acts of the Apostles: A Commentary.* Philadelphia: Fortress.

Cowton, Christopher

1996 The Alms Trade: A Note on Identifying the Beautiful Gate. *New Testament Studies* 42:475-476.

Cross, F. L. and E. A. Livingstone, editors

1997 *Oxford Dictionary of the Christian Church.* 3rd ed. Oxford: Oxford University Press.

Croy, N. Clayton
1997 Hellenistic Philosophers and the Preaching of the Resurrection. *Novum Testamentum* 39:21-39.

Culy, Martin M. and Mikeal C. Parsons
2003 *Acts: A Handbook on the Greek Text.* Waco: Baylor University Press.

Cumont, Franz V. M.
1959 *Afterlife in Roman Paganism.* Reprint, New York: Dover Publications.

Darr, John A.
1998 Irenic or Ironic? Another Look at Gamaliel before the Sanhedrin (Acts 5:33-42). Pp. 121-140 in *Literary Studies in Luke–Acts: Essays in Honor of Joseph B. Tyson.* Editors, Richard P. Thompson and Thomas A. Phillips. Macon, GA: Mercer University Press.

Das, A. Andrew
1993 Acts 8: Water Baptism and the Spirit. *Concordia Journal* 19:108-134.

Daube, David
1990 On Acts 23: Sadducees and Angels. *Journal of Biblical Literature* 109:493-497.

deBoer, Martinus C.
1995 God-Fearers in Luke–Acts. Pp. 50-71 in *Luke's Literary Achievement: Collected Essays.* Editor, Christopher M. Tuckett. Sheffield: Sheffield Academic Press.

Deissmann, Adolph.
1978 *Light from the Ancient East: The New Testament Illustrated by Recently Discovered Texts of the Graeco-Roman World.* Grand Rapids: Baker.

Derrett, J. Duncan M.
1977 Ananias, Sapphira, and the Right of Property. Pp. 193-200 in *Glimpses of the Legal and Social Presuppositions of the Authors.* Studies in the New Testament, vol. 1. Leiden: Brill.
1995 Akeldama (Acts 1:19). *Bijdragen* 56:122-132.

DeSilva, David A.
1994 Paul's Sermon in Antioch of Pisidia. *Bibliotheca Sacra* 151:32-49.

DeWaard, Jan
1971 The Quotation from Deuteronomy in Acts 3, 22.23 and the Palestinian Text: Additional Arguments. *Biblica* 52:537-540.

von Dobbeler, Axel
1996 Mission und Konflikt: Beobachtungen zu prosexein in Acts 8,4-13. *Biblische Notizen* 84:16-22.

Domeris, William R.
1993 Cellars, Wages and Garden: Luke's Accommodation for Middle Class Christians. *Hervormde Teologiese Studies* 49:85-100.

Downing, Gerald
1995 Theophilus' First Reading of Luke–Acts. Pp. 91-109 in *Luke's Literary Achievement: Collected Essays.* Editor, Christopher M. Tuckett. Sheffield: Sheffield Academic.

Dunn, James D. G.
1970 *Baptism in the Holy Spirit: A Re-examination of the New Testament Teaching on the Gift of the Spirit in Relation to Pentecostalism Today.* London: SCM.
1996 *The Acts of the Apostles.* Narrative Commentaries. Valley Forge: Trinity Press International.

Dupont, Jacques
1964 *The Sources of Acts: The Present Position.* London: Darton, Longman & Todd.

Edgar, Thomas
1988 The Cessation of the Sign Gifts. *Bibliotheca Sacra* 145:371-386.

Elliott, John H.
1991 Household and Meals versus Temple Purity: Replication Patterns in Luke–Acts. Pp. 102-108 in *Biblical Theology Bulletin* 21.

Ellis, E. Earle
1970 The Role of the Christian Prophet in Acts. Pp. 55-67 in *Apostolic History and the Gospel: Biblical and Historical Essays Presented to F. F. Bruce on His Sixtieth Birthday.* Editors, W. Ward Gasque and Ralph P. Martin. Grand Rapids: Eerdmans.
1991 To the End of the Earth (Acts 1:8). *Bulletin for Biblical Research* 1:123-132.

Epp, Eldon J.

1966 *The Theological Tendency of Codex Bezae Cantabrigiensis in Acts.* Cambridge: Cambridge University Press.

Erickson, Richard J.

1993 The Jailing of John and the Baptism of Jesus. *Journal of the Evangelical Theological Society* 36:455-466.

Esler, Philip F.

1987 *Community and Gospel in Luke–Acts.* Cambridge: Cambridge University Press.

1992 Glossolalia and the Admission of the Gentiles into the Early Christian Community. *Biblical Theology Bulletin* 22:136-142.

Everts, Jenny

1994 Tongues or Languages? Contextual Consistency in the Translation of Acts 2. *Journal of Pentecostal Theology* 4:71-80.

Fernando, Ajith

1998 *Acts.* NIV Application Commentary. Grand Rapids: Zondervan.

Fiensy, David A.

1995 The Composition of the Jerusalem Church. Pp. 213-236 in *The Book of Acts in Its Palestinian Setting.* Editor, Richard Bauckham. The Book of Acts in Its First Century Setting, vol. 4. Grand Rapids: Eerdmans.

Finegan, Jack

1981 *The Archaeology of the New Testament: The Mediterranean World of the Early Christian Apostles.* Boulder: Westview.

Fitzmyer, Joseph A.

1998a "A Certain Sceva, a Jew, a Chief Priest" according to Acts 19:14. Pp. 232-38 in *To Advance the Gospel: New Testament Studies.* 2nd ed. Grand Rapids: Eerdmans.

1998b *The Acts of the Apostles.* Anchor Bible, vol. 31. New York: Doubleday.

Frankfurter, David

1994 The Magic of Writing and the Writing of Magic: The Power of the Word in Egyptian and Greek Traditions. *Helios* 21:189-221.

French, David

1994 Acts and the Roman Roads of Asia Minor. Pp. 49-58 in *The Book of Acts in its Graeco-Roman Setting.* Editors, David W. J. Gill and Conrad Gempf. The Book of Acts in Its First Century Setting, vol. 2. Grand Rapids: Eerdmans.

Friesen, Steven J.

1993 *Twice Neokoros: Ephesus, Asia, and the Cult of the Flavian Imperial Family.* Leiden: Brill.

Fusco, Vittorio L.

1996 Luke–Acts and the Future of Israel. *Novum Testamentum* 38:1-17.

Gaffin, Richard B., Jr.

1996 A Cessationist View. Pp. 23-64 in *Are Miraculous Gifts for Today? Four Views.* Editor, Wayne A. Grudem. Grand Rapids: Zondervan.

Gage, Warren A. and John R. Beck

1994 The Gospel, Zion's Barren Woman and the Ethiopian Eunuch. *Crux* 3/2:35-43.

Gasque, W. Ward

1978 The Book of Acts and History. Pp. 54-72 in *Unity and Diversity in New Testament Theology.* Editor, Robert A. Guelich. Grand Rapids: Eerdmans.

Gaventa, Beverly Roberts

1982 "You Will Be My Witnesses": Aspects of Mission in Acts of the Apostles. *Missiology* 10:413-425.

2003 *The Acts of the Apostles.* Nashville: Abingdon.

Gempf, Conrad

1993a Athens, Paul at. Pp. 51-54 in *Dictionary of Paul and His Letters.* Editors, Gerald F. Hawthorne, Ralph P. Martin, and Daniel G. Reid. Downers Grove: InterVarsity.

1993b Public Speaking and Published Accounts. Pp. 259-304 in *The Book of Acts in Its Ancient Literary Setting.* Editors, Bruce Winter and Andrew D. Clarke. The Book of Acts in Its First Century Setting, vol. 1. Grand Rapids: Eerdmans.

Gilchrist, J. M.

1996 The Historicity of Paul's Shipwreck. *Journal for the Study of the New Testament* 61:29-51.

Giles, Kevin N.

1985 Luke's Use of the Term *ekklēsia* with Special Reference to Acts 20.28 and 9.31. *New Testament Studies* 30:135-142.

1997a Church Order, Government. Pp. 219-226 in *Dictionary of the Later New Testament and Its Developments.* Editors, Ralph P. Martin and Peter H. Davids. Downers Grove: InterVarsity.

1997b Prophecy, Prophets, False Prophets. Pp. 970-977 in *Dictionary of the Later New Testament and Its Developments.* Editors, Ralph P. Martin and Peter H. Davids. Downers Grove: InterVarsity.

Gill, David W. J.

1994a Achaia. Pp. 433-454 in *The Book of Acts in its Graeco-Roman Setting.* Editors, David W. J. Gill and Conrad Gempf. The Book of Acts in Its First Century Setting, vol. 2. Grand Rapids: Eerdmans.

1994b Acts and Roman Religion: Religion in a Local Setting. Pp. 79-92 in *The Book of Acts in its Graeco-Roman Setting.* Editors, David W. J. Gill and Conrad Gempf. The Book of Acts in Its First Century Setting, vol. 2. Grand Rapids: Eerdmans.

1995 Paul's Travels through Cyprus (Acts 13:4-12). *Tyndale Bulletin* 46:219-228.

Gooding, D. W.

1980 Demythologizing Old and New and Luke's Description of the Ascension: A Layman's Appraisal. *Irish Biblical Studies* 2:95-119.

Gordon, Alasdair B.

1971 The Fate of Judas according to Acts 1:18. *Evangelical Quarterly* 43:97-100.

Gowler, David B.

1991 *Host, Guest, Enemy, and Friend: Portraits of Pharisees in Luke and in Acts.* New York: Peter Lang.

Green, Joel B.

1997 Acts of the Apostles. Pp. 7-24 in *Dictionary of the Later New Testament and Its Developments.* Editors, Ralph P. Martin and Peter H. Davids. Downers Grove: InterVarsity.

1998 Salvation to the End of the Earth: God as the Saviour in the Acts of the Apostles. Pp. 83-106 in *Witness to the Gospel: The Theology of Acts.* Edited by I. Howard Marshall and David Peterson. Grand Rapids: Eerdmans.

Grudem, Wayne

1982 *The Gift of Prophecy in 1 Corinthians.* Washington, DC: University Press of America.

Guthrie, Donald

1990 *New Testament Introduction.* Rev. ed. Downers Grove: InterVarsity.

Haenchen, Ernst

1971 *The Acts of the Apostles: A Commentary.* Philadelphia: Westminster.

Hamblin, Robert L.

1974 Miracles in the Book of Acts. *Southwestern Journal of Theology* 17:3-17.

Hamm, Dennis

1984 Acts 3:12-26: Peter's Speech and the Healing of the Man Born Lame. *Perspectives in Religious Studies* 11:199-217.

Hansen, G. Walter

1994 Galatia. Pp. 377-396 in *The Book of Acts in its Graeco-Roman Setting.* Editors, David W. J. Gill and Conrad Gempf. The Book of Acts in Its First Century Setting, vol. 2. Grand Rapids: Eerdmans.

Harris, Murray J.

1983 *Raised Immortal: Resurrection and Immortality in the New Testament.* Grand Rapids: Eerdmans.

Harrison, Everett F.

1986 *Interpreting Acts: The Expanding Church.* Grand Rapids: Zondervan.

Havelaar, Henriette

1997 Hellenistic Parallel to Acts 5.1-11 and the Problem of Conflicting Interpretations. *Journal for the Study of the New Testament* 67:63-82.

Hedrick, Charles W.

1981 Paul's Conversion Call: A Comparative Analysis of Three Reports in Acts. *Journal of Biblical Literature* 100:415-432.

Heimerdinger, Jenny
1995 Unintentional Sins in Peter's Speech: Acts 3:12-26. *Revista Catalana de Teologia* 20:269-276.

Hemer, Colin J.
1975 Euraquilo and Melita. *Journal of Theological Studies* 26:100-111.

1976 The Adjective Phrygia. *Journal of Theological Studies* 27:122-125.

1977a Acts and Galatians Reconsidered. *Themelios* 2:81-88.

1977b Luke the Historian. *Bulletin of the John Rylands Library* 60:28-51.

1977c Phrygia. A Further Note. *Journal of Theological Studies* 28:99-100.

1989a *The Book of Acts in the Setting of Hellenistic History.* Tübingen: J. C. B. Mohr.

1989b The Speeches of Acts, Part 1: The Ephesian Elders at Miletus. *Tyndale Bulletin* 40:239-259.

Hennecke, Edward
1963 *New Testament Apocrypha.* 2 vols. Philadelphia: Westminster.

Hill, Craig C.
1992 *Hellenists and Hebrews: Reappraising Division within the Earliest Church.* Minneapolis: Fortress.

1997 Hellenists, Hellenistic and Hellenistic-Jewish Christianity. Pp. 462-468 in *Dictionary of the Later New Testament and Its Developments.* Editors, Ralph P. Martin and Peter H. Davids. Downers Grove: InterVarsity.

Horn, Friedrich W.
1997 Paulus, das Nasirat, und die Nasirer. *Novum Testamentum* 39:117-137.

1998 Die Gütergemeinschaft der Urgemeinde. *Evangelische Theologie* 58:370-383.

Horsley, G. H. R.
1981 *New Documents Illustrating Early Christianity.* A Review of Greek Inscriptions and Papyri Published in 1976, vol. 1. Sydney: Macquarie University Press.

1983 *New Documents Illustrating Early Christianity.* A Review of Greek Inscriptions and Papyri Published in 1978, vol. 3. Sydney: Macquarie University Press.

1994 The Politarchs. Pp. 419-432 in *The Book of Acts in its Graeco-Roman Setting.* Editors, David W. J. Gill and Conrad Gempf. The Book of Acts in Its First Century Setting, vol. 2. Grand Rapids: Eerdmans.

van der Horst, Pieter W.
1992 A New Altar of a Godfearer? *Journal of Jewish Studies* 43:32-37.

1994 The Altar of the "Unknown God" in Athens (Acts 17.23) and the Cults of "Unknown Gods" in the Graeco-Roman World. Pp. 165-202 in *Hellenism-Judaism-Christianity.* Editor, Pieter W. van der Horst. Kampen: Kok Pharos.

Humphrey, Edith M.
1995 Collision of Modes?—Vision and Determining Argument in Acts 10:1-11:18. *Semeia* 71:65-84.

Hurtado, L. W.
1997 Christology. Pp. 170-184 in *Dictionary of the Later New Testament and Its Developments.* Editors, Ralph P. Martin and Peter H. Davids. Downers Grove: InterVarsity.

Jervell, Jacob
1972a The Divided People of God: The Restoration of Israel and Salvation for the Gentiles. Pp. 41-74 in *Luke and the People of God: A New Look at Luke–Acts.* Minneapolis: Augsburg.

1972b The Law in Luke-Acts. Pp. 133-152 in *Luke and the People of God: A New Look at Luke–Acts.* Minneapolis: Augsburg.

1984 The Signs of an Apostle: Paul's Miracles. Pp. 77-95 in *The Unknown Paul. Essays on Luke–Acts and Early Christian History.* Minneapolis: Augsburg.

Jewett, Robert
1997 Mapping the Route of Paul's Second Missionary Journey from Dorylaeum to Troas. *Tyndale Bulletin* 48:1-22.

Johnson, Dennis E.
1990 Jesus Against the Idols: The Use of the Isaianic Servant Songs in the Missiology of Acts. Pp. 343-353 in *Westminster Theological Journal* 52.

Johnson, Luke T.
1992 *The Acts of the Apostles.* Sacra Pagina. Collegeville, MN: Liturgical Press.

Johnston, George
1981 Christ as *Archēgos*. *New Testament Studies* 27:381-384.

Karris, Robert J.
1979 Missionary Communities: A New Paradigm for the Study of Luke–Acts. *Catholic Biblical Quarterly* 14:80-91.

Kearsley, R. A.
1994 The Asiarchs. Pp. 363-76 in *The Book of Acts in its Graeco-Roman Setting*. Editors, David W. J. Gill and Conrad Gempf. The Book of Acts in Its First Century Setting, vol. 2. Grand Rapids: Eerdmans.

Kee, Howard Clark
1997 *To Every Nation under Heaven: The Acts of the Apostles*. The New Testament in Context. Editors, Howard Clark Kee and J. Andrew Overman. Harrisburg: Trinity Press International.

Keener, Craig S.
1993 *The IVP Bible Background Commentary: New Testament*. Downers Grove: InterVarsity.

Kemmler, Dieter Werner
1975 *Faith and Human Reason: A Study in Paul's Method of Preaching as Illustrated by 1–2 Thessalonians and Acts 17:2-4*. Leiden: Brill.

Kilgallen, John J.
1990 Did Peter Actually Fail to Get a Word in? (Acts 11,15). *Biblica* 71:405-410.

1993 Acts 20:35 and Thucydides 2.97.4. *Journal of Biblical Literature* 112:312-314.

1994 Paul's Speech to the Ephesian Elders: Its Structure. *Ephemerides Theologicae Lovanienses* 70:112-121.

1997 Acts 13:4-12: The Role of the *Magos*. *Estudios Bíblicos* 55:223-237.

1998a Clean, Acceptable, Saved: Acts 10. *Expository Times* 109:301-302.

1998b Your Servant Jesus Whom You Anointed (Acts 4,27). *Révue Biblique* 105:185-201.

Kilpatrick, George D.
1963 Acts 23, 23: *dexiolaboi* [= 'spearmen from the local police']. *Journal of Theological Studies* 14:393.

Kistemaker, Simon J.
1990 *New Testament Commentary: Exposition of the Acts of the Apostles*. Grand Rapids: Baker.

Klauck, H. J.
1994 With Paul in Paphos and Lystra: Magic and Paganism in Luke–Acts. *Neotestamentica* 28:93-108.

Kodell, Jerome
1974 The Word of God Grew. The Ecclesial Tendency of *Logos* in Acts 6,7; 12,24; 19:20. *Biblica* 55:505-519.

Koester, Helmut
1982 *Introduction to the New Testament*. 2 vols. Philadelphia: Fortress.

1995 Ephesos in Early Christian Literature. Pp. 119-40 in *Ephesos: Metropolis of Asia; An Interdisciplinary Approach to Its Archaeology, Religion, and Culture*. Editor, Helmut Koester. Valley Forge: Trinity Press International.

Krodel, Gerhard
1986 *Acts*. Augsburg Commentary on the New Testament. Minneapolis: Augsburg.

Külling, Heinz
1993 *Geoffenbartes Geheimnis: Eine Auslegung von Apostelsgeschichte 17, 16-34*. Zürich: Theologischer Verlag.

Kurz, William S.
1990a *Farewell Addresses in the New Testament*. Collegeville, MN: Liturgical Press.

1990b Narrative Models for Imitation in Luke–Acts. Pp.171-89. in *Greeks, Romans, and Christians*. Editors, David L. Balch, Everett Ferguson, and Wayne A. Meeks. Minneapolis: Fortress.

1997 The Effects of Various Narrators in Acts 10-11. *New Testament Studies* 43:570-586.

Lake, Kirsopp
1979 Note XV: The Conversion of Paul and the Events Immediately Following It. Pp. 188-195 in *Additional Notes to the Commentary. The Beginnings of Christianity, Part I: The Acts of the Apostles*, vol. 5. Editors, F. J. Foakes-Jackson and Kirsopp Lake. Grand Rapids: Baker.

Lake, Kirsopp and Henry J. Cadbury
1979 *English Translation and Commentary. The Beginnings of Christianity, Part I: The Acts of the Apostles*, vol 4. Editors, F. J. Foakes-Jackson and Krisopp Lake. Grand Rapids: Baker.

Lampe, G. W. H.
1965 Miracles in the Acts of the Apostles. Pp. 165-178 in *Miracles: Cambridge Studies in Their Philosophy and History.* Editor, C. F. D. Moule. London: Mowbray.

Larkin, William J., Jr.
1977 Luke's Use of the Old Testament as a Key to His Soteriology. *Journal of the Evangelical Theological Society* 20:325-335.

1995 *Acts.* IVP New Testament Commentary Series. Downers Grove: InterVarsity.

Larsson, Edvin
1993 Temple Criticism and Jewish Heritage: Some Reflections on Acts 6-7. *New Testament Studies* 39:379-395.

Légasse, Simon
1990 Encore ΕΣΤΩΤΑ En Acts 7,55-56. *Filología Neotestamentaria* 3:63-66.

Legrand, Lucien
1989 The Angel Gabriel and Politics: Messianism and Christology. *Indian Theological Studies* 26:1-21.

1990 *Unity and Plurality: Mission in the Bible.* Maryknoll, NY: Orbis Books.

LeRoux, L. V.
1991 Style and Text of Acts 4:25(a). *Neotestamentica* 25:29-32.

Levinskaya, Irina A.
1990 The Inscription from Aphrodisias and the Problem of God Fearers. *Tyndale Bulletin* 41:312-318.

1996 *The Book of Acts in Its Diaspora Setting.* The Book of Acts in Its First Century Setting, vol. 5. Grand Rapids: Eerdmans.

LiDonnici, Lynn R.
1992 The Image of Artemis Ephesia and Greco-Roman Worship: A Reconsideration. *Harvard Theological Review* 85:389-415.

Liefeld, Walter L.
1995 *Interpreting the Book of Acts.* Grand Rapids: Baker.

Lin, Szu-Chuan
1998 *Wundertaten und Mission: Dramatische Episoden in Apg 13-14.* Frankfurt: Peter Lang.

Lindemann, Andreas
1995 Die Christuspredigt des Paulus in Athen (Act 17,16-33). Pp. 245-256 in *Texts and Contexts: Biblical Texts in Their Textual and Situational Contexts—Essays in Honor of Lars Hartman.* Editors, Tord Fornberg and David Hellholm. Oslo: Scandinavian University Press.

Linton, Olof
1974 The List of Nations in Acts 2. Pp. 44-53 in *New Testament Christianity for Africa and the World.* Editors, Mark E. Glasswell and Edward W. Fasole-Luke. London: SPCK.

Litke, Wayne
1996 Acts 7:3 and Samaritan Chronology. *New Testament Studies* 42:156-160.

Lohfink, Gerhard
1976 *The Conversion of Saint Paul: Narrative and History in Acts.* Chicago: Franciscan Herald.

Longenecker, Richard N.
1981 Acts in *John and Acts.* Expositor's Bible Commentary, vol. 9. Editors, Merrill C. Tenney and Richard Longenecker. Grand Rapids: Zondervan.

Lönnqvist, Kenneth A.
1992-93 New Vistas on the Countermarked Coins of the Roman Prefects of Judaea. *Israel Numismatics Journal* 12:56-70.

Lüdemann, Gerd
1987 The Acts of the Apostles and the Beginnings of Simonian Gnosis. *New Testament Studies* 33:420-426.

1989 *Early Christianity According to the Traditions in Acts.* Minneapolis: Fortress.

Luter, A. Boyd
1995 Women Disciples and the Great Commission. *Trinity Journal* 16:171-185.

Lyons, William J.
1997 The Words of Gamaliel (Acts 5.38-39) and the Irony of Indeterminacy. *Journal for the Study of the New Testament* 68:23-49.

Malherbe, Abraham J.
1983 *Social Aspects of Early Christianity.* Philadelphia: Fortress.

Maloney, Linda M.
1991 *All That God Had Done with Them. The Narration of the Works of God in the Early Christian Community as Described in the Acts of the Apostles.* New York: Lang.

Marguerat, David
1993a La Mort d'Ananias et Saphira (Ac 5.1-11) dans la stratégie narrative de Luc. *New Testament Studies* 39:209-226.

1993b The End of Acts and the Rhetoric of Silence. Pp. 74-89 in *Rhetoric and the New Testament.* Editors, S. E. Porter and T. H. Olbricht. Sheffield: Journal for the Study of the Old Testament.

1995 Saul's Conversion and the Multiplication of Narrative in Acts. Pp. 127-155 in *Luke's Literary Achievement: Collected Essays.* Editor, C. M. Tuckett. Sheffield: Sheffield Academic.

Marshall, I. Howard
1980 *The Acts of the Apostles: An Introduction and Commentary.* Grand Rapids: Eerdmans.
1989 The Present State of Lucan Studies. Pp. 52-57 in *Themelios* 14.

Marshall, I. Howard and David Peterson
1998 *Witness to the Gospel: The Theology of Acts.* Grand Rapids: Eerdmans.

Martin-Asensio, Gustavo
2001 *Transitivity-Based Foregrounding in the Acts of the Apostles: Function-Grammatical Approach to the Lukan Perspective.* Sheffield: Sheffield Academic Press.

Martin, Luther H.
1995 Gods or Ambassadors of God? *New Testament Studies* 41:152-156.

Marx, Werner G.
1980 Luke, the Physician, Re-examined. *Expository Times* 91:168-171.

Mason, Steve
1992 *Josephus and the New Testament.* Peabody, MA: Hendrickson.

Maurizio, L.
1995 Anthropology and Spirit Possession: A Reconstruction of the Pythia's Role at Delphi. *Journal of Hellenic Studies* 115:69-86.

Maynard-Reid, Pedrito U.
1997 Samaria. Pp. 1075-1077 in *Dictionary of the Later New Testament and Its Developments.* Editors, Ralph P. Martin and Peter H. Davids. Downers Grove: InterVarsity.

McComiskey, Thomas Edward
1985 *Amos, Micah.* Pp. 269-331, 395-445 in *Expositor's Bible Commentary,* vol. 7. Grand Rapids: Zondervan.

McCready, Wayne O.
1992 Sadducees and Ancient Sectarianism. *Religious Studies and Theology* 12:79-97.

McLean, John A.
1994 Did Jesus Correct the Disciples' View of the Kingdom? *Bibliotheca Sacra* 151:215-227.

McRay, K. L.
1994 Foreign Gods Identified in Acts 17:18? *Tyndale Bulletin* 45:411-412.

Meers, Alan
1993 Who Went Where and How? A Consideration of Acts 17:14. *Bible Translator* 44:201-206.

Mehat, André
1992 Les écrits de Luc et les événements de 70: Problémes de datation. *Revue de l'histoire des religions* 209: 149-180.

Meinardus, Otto F. A.
1976 St. Paul Shipwrecked in Dalmatia. *Biblical Archaeologist* 39:145-147.
1981 The Site of the Apostle Paul's Conversion at Kaukab. *Biblical Archeologist* 44:57-59.

Metzger, Bruce M.
1994 *A Textual Commentary on the Greek New Testament.* 2nd ed. Stuttgart: German Bible Society.

Mitchell, Alan C.
1992 The Social Function of Friendship in Acts 2:44-47 and 4:32-37. *Journal of Biblical Literature* 111:255-272.

Moberly, R. B.
1993 When was Acts Planned and Shaped? *Evangelical Quarterly* 65:5-26.

Morgado, Joe, Jr.
1994 Paul in Jerusalem: A Comparison of His Visits in Acts and Galatians. *Journal of the Evangelical Theological Society* 37:55-68.

Morray-Jones, C. R. A.
1993 Paradise Revisited (2 Cor. 12:1-12): The Jewish Mystical Background of Paul's Apostolate. Part 2: Paul's Heavenly Ascent and Its Significance. *Harvard Theological Review* 86:265-292.

Moule, Charles F. D.
1977 *An Idiom Book of New Testament Greek.* Cambridge: Cambridge University Press.

1982 The Ascension according to Acts 1:9. Pp. 54-63 in *Essays in New Testament Interpretation.* Cambridge: Cambridge University Press.

Moulton, James H.
1908 *Prolegomena.* 3rd ed. *A Grammar of New Testament Greek,* vol. 1. Edinburgh: T & T Clark.

1963 *Syntax.* By Nigel Turner. *A Grammar of New Testament Greek,* vol. 3. Edinburgh: T & T Clark.

Moxnes, Halvor
1994 The Social Context of Luke's Community. *Interpretation* 48:379-389.

Murphy-O'Connor, Jerome
1993 Paul and Gallio. *Journal of Biblical Literature* 112:315-317.

Neudorfer, Heinz-Werner
1998 The Speech of Stephen. Pp. 275-294 in *Witness to the Gospel: The Theology of Acts.* Editors, I. Howard Marshall and David Peterson. Grand Rapids: Eerdmans.

Neyrey, Jerome H.
1984 The Forensic Defense Speech and Paul's Trial Speeches in Acts 22–26: Form and Function. Pp. 210-24 in *Luke–Acts: New Perspectives from the Society of Biblical Literature Seminar.* Editor, Charles H. Talbert. New York: Crossroad.

Nobbs, Alanna
1994 Cyprus. Pp. 279-290 in *The Book of Acts in its Graeco-Roman Setting.* Editors, David W. J. Gill and Conrad Gempf. The Book of Acts in Its First Century Setting, vol. 2. Grand Rapids: Eerdmans.

Nolland, John L.
1980 A Fresh Look at Acts 15:10. *New Testament Studies* 27:105-114.

O'Toole, Robert F.
1978 *Acts 26: The Christological Climax of Paul's Defense (Ac 22:1–26:32).* Rome: Biblical Institute Press.

1994 What Role does Jesus' Saying in Acts 20,35 Play in Paul's Address to the Ephesian Elders? *Biblica* 75:329-349.

1995 You Did Not Lie to Us (Human Beings) but to God (Acts 5.4c). *Biblica* 76:182-209.

Parker, David C.
1992 *Codex Bezae: An Early Christian Manuscript and Its Text.* Cambridge: Cambridge University Press.

Parsons, Mikeal C.
1998 Isaiah 53 and Acts 8. Pp. 104-119 in *Jesus and the Suffering Servant: Isaiah 53 and Christian Origins.* Editors, W. H. Bellinger and W. R. Farmer. Harrisburg, PA: Trinity Press International.

Pathrapankal, Joseph
1979 Christianity as a "Way" according to the Acts of the Apostles. Pp. 533-539 in *Les Actes des Apôtres: Traditions, rédaction, théologie.* Editor, J. Kremer. Leuven: Leuven University Press.

Pearce, Sarah J. K.
1995 Flavius Josephus as Interpreter of Biblical Law: The Council of the Seven and the Levitical Servants in *Antiquities* 4.214. *Heythrop Journal* 36:477-491.

Penner, Todd C.
1996 Narrative as Persuasion: Epideictic Rhetoric and Scribal Amplification in the Stephen Episode in Acts. Pp. 352-367 in *SBL 1996 Seminar Papers.* Editor, Eugene H. Lovering, Jr. Atlanta: Scholars Press.

2004 Madness in the Method? The Acts of the Apostles in Current Study. *Currents in Biblical Research* 2:223-293.

Pervo, Richard I.
1987 *Profit with Delight: The Literary Genre of the Acts of the Apostles.* Philadelphia: Fortress.

Pillai, C. A. Joachim
1979 *Early Missionary Preaching: A Study of Luke's Report in Acts 13.* Hicksville, NY: Exposition Press.

Pinnock, Clark H.
1990 Toward an Evangelical Theology of Religions. *Journal of the Evangelical Theological Society* 33:359-367.

1991 Acts 4:12—No Other Name Under Heaven. Pp. 107-116 in *Through No Fault of Their Own: The Fate of Those Who Have Never Heard.* Editors, William V. Crockett and James G. Sigountis. Grand Rapids: Baker.

Plevnik, Joseph
1991 Son of Man Seated at the Right Hand of God: Luke 22:69 in Lucan Christology. *Biblica* 72:331-347.

Plümacher, Eckard
1992 Eine Thukydidesreminiscenz in der Apostelgeschichte (Act 20,33-35-Thuk. II 97,3f). *Zeitschrift für die neutestamentliche Wissenschaft und die Kunde der Älteren Kirche* 83:270-275.

Plymale, Stephen
1991 *The Prayer Texts of Luke–Acts.* New York: Lang.

Polhill, John B.
1992 *Acts.* New American Commentary. Nashville: Broadman.

Praeder, Susan M.
1987 The Problem of First Person Narration in Acts. *Novum Testamentum* 29:193-218.

Rapske, Brian
1991 The Importance of Helpers to the Imprisoned Paul in the Book of Acts. *Tyndale Bulletin* 42:3-30.

1994a Acts, Travel and Shipwreck. Pp. 1-48 in *The Book of Acts in its Graeco-Roman Setting.* Editors, David W. J. Gill and Conrad Gempf. The Book of Acts in Its First Century Setting, vol. 2. Grand Rapids: Eerdmans.

1994b *The Book of Acts and Paul in Roman Custody.* The Book of Acts in Its First Century Setting, vol. 3. Grand Rapids: Eerdmans.

1998 Opposition to the Plan of God and Persecution. Pp. 235-256 in *Witness to the Gospel: The Theology of Acts.* Editors, I. Howard Marshall and David Peterson. Grand Rapids: Eerdmans.

Rapuano, Yehudah
1990 Did Philip Baptize the Eunuch at Ein Yael? *Biblical Archeology Review* 16/6:44-49.

Reeder, Ellen D.
1987 The Mother of the Gods and a Hellenistic Bronze Matrix. *American Journal of Archeology* 91:423-440.

Reinbold, Wolfgang
1998 Die "Hellenisten." Kritische Anmerkungen zu einem Fachbegriff der neutestamentlichen Wissenschaft. *Biblische Zeitschrift* 42:96-102.

Reinhardt, Wolfgang
1995 The Population Size of Jerusalem and the Numerical Growth of the Jerusalem Church. Pp. 237-266 in *The Book of Acts in Its Palestinian Setting.* Editor, Richard Bauckham. The Book of Acts in its First Century Setting, vol. 4. Grand Rapids: Eerdmans.

Richard, Earl
1978 *Acts 6:1–8:4. The Author's Method of Composition.* Missoula: Scholars Press.

1982 The Creative Use of Amos by the Author of Acts. *Novum Testamentum* 24:37-53.

Richardson, Don
1981 *Eternity in Their Hearts.* Ventura, CA: Regal.

Riesner, Rainer
1995 Synagogues in Jerusalem. Pp. 179-212 in *The Book of Acts in its Palestinian Setting.* Editor, Richard Bauckham. The Book of Acts in Its First Century Setting, vol. 4. Grand Rapids: Eerdmans.

Robertson, A. T.
1934 *A Grammar of the Greek New Testament in the Light of Historical Research.* Nashville: Broadman.

Roloff, J.
1981 *Die Apostelgeschichte.* Das Neue Testament Deutsch 5. Göttingen: Vandenhoeck

Ropes, James H.
1979 *The Text of Acts. Beginnings of Christianity, Part I: The Acts of the Apostles,* vol. 3. Editors, F. J. Foakes Jackson and Kirsopp Lake. Grand Rapids: Baker.

Rosner, Brian
1998 The Progress of the Word. Pp. 215-234 in *Witness to the Gospel: The Theology of Acts.* Editors,
     I. Howard Marshall and David Peterson. Grand Rapids: Eerdmans.

Ross, J. M.
1992 The Extra Words in Acts 18:21. *Novum Testamentum* 34:247-249.

Safrai, Samuel
1974 Relations between the Diaspora and the Land of Israel. Pp. 184-215 in *The Jewish People in the First
     Century: Historical Geography, Political History, Social, Cultural and Religious Life and Institutions,*
     vol. 1. Editors, Samuel Safrai and Menahem Stern. Philadelphia: Fortress.

1976 Home and Family. Pp. 728-792 in *The Jewish People in the First Century: Historical Geography,
     Political History, Social, Cultural and Religious Life and Institutions,* vol. 2. Editors, S. Safrai and
     M. Stern. Philadelphia: Fortress.

Sanders, John E.
1988 Is Belief in Christ Necessary for Salvation? *Evangelical Quarterly* 60:241-259.

1992 No Other Name: An Investigation in the Destiny of the Unevangelized. Grand Rapids: Eerdmans.

Sandnes, Karl O.
1993 Paul and Socrates: The Aim of Paul's Areopagus Speech. *Journal for the Study of the New Testament*
     50:13-26.

1998 Beyond "Love Language": A Critical Examination of Krister Stendahl's Exegesis of Acts 4:12. *Studia
     Theologia* 52:43-56.

van de Sandt, Huub
1990 The Fate of the Gentiles in Joel and Acts 2. An Intertextual Study. *Ephemerides Theologicae
     Lovanienses* 66:56-77.

1992 An Explanation of Acts 15:16-21 in the Light of Deuteronomy 4:29-35 (LXX). *Journal for the Study
     of the New Testament* 46:73-97.

1994 Acts 28:28: No Salvation for the People of Israel? An Answer in the Perspective of the LXX.
     Ephemerides Theologicae Lovanienses 70:341-358.

Schürer, Emil
1973 *The History of the Jewish People in the Age of Jesus Christ (175 BC–AD 135),* vol. 1. Rev. ed. Editors,
     Geza Vermes, Fergus Millar, and Matthew Black. Edinburgh: T & T Clark.

1986 *The History of the Jewish People in the Age of Jesus Christ (175 BC–AD 135),* vol. 2. Rev. ed. Editors,
     Geza Vermes, Fergus Millar, and Matthew Black. Edinburgh: T & T Clark.

Schwartz, Daniel R.
1983 Non-Joining Sympathizers (Acts 5, 13-14). Pp. 550-555 in *Biblica* 64.

Scott, J. Julius
1991 The Cornelius Incident in the Light of Its Jewish Setting. *Journal of the Evangelical Theological Society*
     34:475-484.

Seccombe, David
1998 The New People of God. Pp. 349-372 in *Witness to the Gospel: The Theology of Acts.* Editors,
     I. Howard Marshall and David Peterson. Grand Rapids: Eerdmans.

Segal, Peretz
1989 The Penalty of the Warning Inscription for the Temple of Jerusalem. *Israel Exploration Journal* 39,
     nos. 1/2:79-84.

Sherwin-White, Adrian Nicholas
1963 *Roman Society and Roman Law in the New Testament: The Sarum lectures, 1960-61.* Oxford:
     Clarendon Press.

Slingerland, Dixon
1991 Acts 18:1-18, the Gallio Inscription, and Absolute Pauline Chronology. *Journal of Biblical Literature*
     110:439-449.

1992 Suetonius' *Claudius* 25.4 and Acts 18, and Paulus Orosius' *Historiarum adver. paganos libri VII:*
     Dating the Claudian Expulsions of Roman Jews. *Jewish Quarterly Review* 83:127-144.

Sloan, Robert B.
1991 Signs and Wonders as a Rhetorical Clue to the Pentecost Discourse. *Evangelical Quarterly*
     63:225-240.

Smith, David
1996 What Hope after Babel? Diversity and Community in Gen. 11:1-9; Ex. 1:1-14; Zeph. 3:1- 13 and Acts 2:1-13. _Horizons in Biblical Theology_ 18:169-191.

Smith, James
1978 _The Voyage and Shipwreck of Saint Paul._ Minneapolis: James Family Christian Publishing.

Soards, Marion L.
1990 The Historical and Cultural Setting of Luke–Acts. Pp. 33-47 in _New Views on Luke and Acts._ Editor, Earl Richard. Collegeville, MN: Liturgical Press.

Spencer, F. Scott
1992 The Ethiopian Eunuch and His Bible: A Social-Science Analysis. _Biblical Theology Bulletin_ 22:155-165.
1997 _Acts._ Readings: A New Biblical Commentary. Sheffield: Sheffield Academic.

Stendahl, Krister
1981 Notes for Three Bible Studies. Pp. 7-18 in _Christ's Lordship and Religious Pluralism._ Editors, Gerald H. Anderson and Thomas F. Stransky. Maryknoll: Orbis.

Stott, John
1990 _The Spirit, the Church and the World: The Message of Acts._ Downers Grove: InterVarsity.

Strack, Hermann L. and Paul Billerbeck
1978 _Kommentar zum Neuen Testament aus Talmud and Midrasch._ 7th ed. 4 vols. Munich: C H Beck.

Strange, W. A.
1992 _The Problem of the Text of Acts._ Cambridge: Cambridge University Press.

Stronstad, Roger
1984 _The Charismatic Theology of St. Luke._ Peabody, MA: Hendrickson.

Sylva, Dennis D.
1987 The Meaning and Function of Acts 7:46-50. _Journal of Biblical Literature_ 106:261-275.

Szesnat, H.
1993 What did the _skēnopoios_ Paul produce? _Neotestamentica_ 27:391-402.

Talbert, Charles H.
1974 _Literary Patterns, Theological Themes and the Genre of Luke–Acts._ Missoula: Scholars Press.
1997 Reading Acts: A Literary and Theological Commentary on the Acts of the Apostles. New York: Crossroad.

Tannehill, Robert C.
1986 _The Narrative Unity of Luke–Acts: A Literary Interpretation,_ vol. 1. Philadelphia: Fortress.
1990 _The Narrative Unity of Luke–Acts: A Literary Interpretation,_ vol. 2. Philadelphia: Fortress.
1992 The Narrative Strategy in the Scenes of Paul's Defense: Acts 21:27–26:32. _Forum_ 8:255-269.

Tanton, Lanny T.
1990 The Gospel and Water Baptism: A Study of Acts 2:38. _Journal of the Grace Evangelical Society_ 3:27-52.
1991 The Gospel and Water Baptism: A Study of Acts 22:16. _Journal of the Grace Evangelical Society_ 4:23-40.

Taylor, Justin
1994 Why Were the Disciples First Called "Christians" at Antioch? (Acts 11,26). _Révue Biblique_ 101:75-94.

Thiessen, Gerd
1996 Hellenisten und Hebräer (Apg. 6,1ff). Gab es eine Spaltung der Urgemeinde? Pp. 323-346 in _Geschichte, Tradition, Reflexion: festschrift für Martin Hengel 70. Geburtstag. Fruhes Christentum,_ vol. 3. Editor, Hermann Lichtenberger. Tübingen: Mohr Siebeck.

Treier, Daniel J.
1997 The Fulfillment of Joel 2:28-32: A Multiple Lens Approach. _Journal of the Evangelical Theological Society_ 40:13-26.

Tomes, Roger
1995 Why Did Paul Get His Hair Cut? (Acts 18.18; 21.23-24). Pp. 188-197 in _Luke's Literary Achievement: Collected Essays._ Editor, Christopher M. Tuckett. Sheffield: Sheffield Academic Press.

Trebilco, Paul R.
1989 Paul and Silas—"Servants of the Most High God" (Acts 16.16-18). _Journal for the Study of the New Testament_ 36:51-73.

1994 Asia. Pp. 291-362 in *The Book of Acts in its Graeco-Roman Setting*. Edited by David W. J. Gill and Conrad Gempf. The Book of Acts in Its First Century Setting, vol. 2. Grand Rapids: Eerdmans.

Turner, Max M. B.
1981 Spirit Endowment in Luke/Acts: Some Linguistic Considerations. *Vox Evangelica* 12:45-63.

1998 The "Spirit of Prophecy" as the Power of Israel's Restoration and Witness. Pp. 327-348 in *Witness to the Gospel: The Theology of Acts*. Editors, I. Howard Marshall and David Peterson. Grand Rapids: Eerdmans.

Tyson, Joseph B.
1985 Acts of the Apostles, The. Pp. 10-11 in *Harper Bible Dictionary*. Editor, Paul J. Achtemeier. San Francisco: Harper & Row.

1988 The Problem of Jewish Rejection in Acts. Pp. 124-137 in *Luke–Acts and the Jewish People: Eight Critical Perspectives*. Editor, Joseph B. Tyson. Minneapolis: Augsburg.

Vielhauer, Phillip
1966 On the "Paulinism" of Acts. Pp. 33-50 in *Studies in Luke–Acts*. Editors, Leander E. Keck and J. Louis Martyn. Nashville: Abingdon.

de Villiers, Pieter G. R.
1990 The Medium is the Message: Luke and the Language of the New Testament against a Graeco-Roman Background. *Neotestamentica* 24:247-256.

Viviano, Benedict and Justin Taylor
1992 Sadducees, Angels, and Resurrection (Acts 23:8-9). *Journal of Biblical Literature* 111:496-498.

Wagner, C. Peter
1995 *Lighting the World*. The Acts of the Holy Spirit Series 2. Ventura, CA: Regal Books

von Wahlde, Urban C.
1995 The Problems of Acts 4:25a: A New Proposal. *Zeitschrift für die neutestamentliche Wissenschaft und die Kunde der Älteren Kirche* 86:265-267.

1996 Acts 4,24-31: The Prayer of the Apostles in Response to the Persecution of Peter and John—and its Consequences. *Biblica* 77:237-244.

Wall, Robert W.
1991 Successors to the Twelve according to Acts 12:1-17. *Catholic Biblical Quarterly* 53:628-643.

1998 Israel and the Gentile Mission in Acts and Paul: A Canonical Approach. Pp. 437-58 in *Witness to the Gospel: The Theology of Acts*. Editors, I. Howard Marshall and David Peterson. Grand Rapids: Eerdmans.

2003 *The Acts of the Apostles*. New Interpreter's Bible, vol. 10. Editors, Robert W. Wall, J. Paul Sampley, N. T. Wright. Nashville: Abingdon.

Wallace, Daniel B.
1996 *Greek Grammar Beyond the Basics: An Exegetical Syntax of the New Testament*. Grand Rapids: Zondervan.

Warnecke, Heinz
1987 *Die Tatsächliche Romfahrt des Apostels Paulus*. Stuttgart: Katholisches Bibelwerk.

Watson, Duane F.
1991 Paul's Speech to the Ephesian Elders (Acts 20.17-38): Epideictic Rhetoric of Farewell. Pp. 184-208 in *Persuasive Artistry: Studies in New Testament Rhetoric in Honor of George A. Kennedy*. Editor, Duane F. Watson. Sheffield: Sheffield Academic Press.

Wedderburn, A. J. M.
1993 The Apostolic Decree: Tradition and Redaction. *Novum Testamentum* 35:362-389.

Wehnert, Jürgen
1990 Gestrandet: Zu einer neuen These über den Schiffbruch des Apostels Paulus auf dem Wege nach Rom (Apg 27—28). *Zeitschrift für Theologie und Kirche* 87:67-99.

Wenham, Gordon J.
1981 The Theology of Unclean Food. *Evangelical Quarterly* 53:6-15.

Wenham, J. W.
1972 Did Peter go to Rome in AD 42? *Tyndale Bulletin* 23:94-102.

1991 The Identification of Luke. *Evangelical Quarterly* 63:3-44.

White, L. Michael
1995 Urban Development and Social Change in Imperial Ephesos. Pp. 27-81 in *Ephesos: Metropolis of Asia; An Interdisciplinary Approach to Its Archaeology, Religion, and Culture*. Editor, Helmut Koester. Valley Forge, PA: Trinity Press International.

Williams, David John
1985 *Acts: A Good News Commentary.* San Francisco: Harper & Row.

Williams, Margaret H.
1994 The Structure of Roman Jewry Reconsidered—Were the Synagogues of Ancient Rome Homogenous? *Zeitschrift für Papyrologie und Epigraphik* 104:129-142.

Wilson, Robert
1979 Simon and Gnostic Origins. Pp. 485-491 in *Les Actes des Apôtres: Traditions, rédaction, théologie.* Editor, J. Kremer. Leuven: Leuven University Press.

Wilson, Stephen G.
1973 *The Gentiles and the Gentile Mission in Luke–Acts.* Cambridge: Cambridge University Press.

1983 *Luke and the Law.* Cambridge: Cambridge University Press.

Winter, Bruce W.
1991 The Importance of the *Captatio Benevolentiae* in the Speeches of Tertullus and Paul in Acts 24:1-21. *Journal of Theological Studies* 42:505-531.

1993 Official Proceedings and the Forensic Speeches in Acts 24–26. Pp. 305-336 in *The Book of Acts in Its Ancient Literary Setting.* Editors, Bruce Winter and Andrew D. Clarke. The Book of Acts in Its First Century Setting, vol. 1. Grand Rapids: Eerdmans.

1996 On Introducing Gods to Athens: An Alternative Reading of Acts 17:18-20. *Tyndale Bulletin* 47:71-90.

1999 Gallio's Ruling on the Legal Status of Early Christianity. *Tyndale Bulletin* 50:213-224.

Winter, Bruce W. and Andrew D. Clarke, editors.
1993 *The Book of Acts in Its Ancient Literary Setting.* The Book of Acts in Its First Century Setting, vol. 1. Grand Rapids: Eerdmans.

Witherington, Ben, III
1996a Editing the Good News: Some Synoptic Lessons for the Study of Acts. Pp. 324-347 in *History, Literature, and Society in the Book of Acts.* Editor, Ben Witherington III. Cambridge: Cambridge University Press.

1996b *History, Literature, and Society in the Book of Acts.* Editor, Ben Witherington III. Cambridge: Cambridge University Press.

1998 The Acts of the Apostles: A Socio-Rhetorical Commentary. Grand Rapids: Eerdmans.

Witherup, Ronald D.
1992 Functional Redundancy in the Acts of the Apostles: A Case Study. *Journal for the Study of the New Testament* 48:67-96.

1993 Cornelius Over and Over and Over Again: Functional Redundancy in the Acts of the Apostles. *Journal for the Study of the New Testament* 49:45-66.

Wycherley, R. E.
1968 St. Paul at Athens. *Journal of Theological Studies* 19:619-621.

Zerhusen, Bob
1995 An Overlooked Judean Diglossia in Acts 2? *Biblical Theology Bulletin* 25:118-130.